DICTIONARY OF THE
NAPOLEONIC WARS

DICTIONARY OF THE
NAPOLEONIC WARS

Stephen Pope

Facts On File, Inc.

Dictionary of the Napoleonic Wars

First published in the UK by
Cassell
Wellington House, 125 Strand
London WC2R 0BB
www.cassell.co.uk

Facts On File, Inc.
11 Penn Plaza
New York NY 10001

Cataloging-in-Publication information is available from Facts On File.

ISBN: 0-8160-4243-8

Facts On File books are available at special discounts when purchased in bulk quantities for
businesses, associations, institutions or sales promotions. Please call our Special Sales Department in
New York at 212/967-8800 or 800/322-8755.

You can find Facts On File on the World Wide Web at
http://www.factsonfile.com

Design by Gwyn Lewis
Jacket design by Cathy Rincon

Printed in Finland

10 9 8 7 6 5 4 3 2 1

This book is printed on acid-free paper.

CONTENTS

NOTES ON USAGE

This dictionary has been designed and written with breadth and interconnection in mind. Its structure and cross-referencing system should enable any reader, informed or otherwise, to interpret its details with the benefit of overview, and vice versa.

The widest-ranging entries – generics covering theatres, home fronts or distinct wars – provide narrative and contextual information on a broad scale, combining to form a coherent overall picture of the wars fought between 1792 and 1815. These are cross-referenced with a second stratum of relatively broad entries offering briefings on particular offensives, armed forces, tactics, weapons types, etc. This second level also includes succinct overview entries concerned to place the wars in a global context, examining their impact on developing societies outside Europe.

Every non-specific entry contains cross-references highlighting the descriptions of events, actions, leaders, weapons and miscellaneous details that form the third layer of entries. These in turn signal connections with relevant areas of the wider picture, so that readers can navigate a coherent path through the whole dictionary from any entrance point.

Though fitting broadly into this simple pyramidal structure, and always concerned with context, each entry is written to stand alone as a simple reference tool. The only exceptions are those headings that function simply as cross-references, included to cover complications of nomenclature and to provide the maximum number of logical access points for the non-expert user.

Readers familiar with the author's dictionaries covering more recent world wars will be struck by the relative shortage of statistical data surrounding weapons, casualties, etc. This reflects the standards of an age short on precision instrumentation and far less committed than our own to accuracy for its own sake. Official figures surrounding military operations are generally imprecise and, because most authorities treated them purely as an extension of propaganda, as unreliable as they are diverse. Generally speaking, consensus approximations have been used when available, and alternatives presented otherwise.

The maps at the end of the book are, apart from those indicating the shape of particular battles, primarily intended to help the reader navigate around those places discussed in the entries, and are therefore most concerned with naming and marking locations.

INTRODUCTION

Anybody looking at the world of the late twentieth century and wondering just how it got here, or for any reason needing to understand its dynamics, must look to its sociopolitical roots. This is one of the fundamental reasons for studying history and, more particularly, for investigating major wars as hothouses of accelerated development and destruction.

Most of us recognize the enormous impact on modern technologies, geopolitical tensions and social systems exerted by the Second World War, but that relatively recent and spectacularly well-documented conflict has so completely dominated our historical perspective that anything before it has been all but lost to popular culture.

This is true of the First World War. A massive and momentous bloodbath that broke Europe's monopolistic control over the technological age, and brought down the curtain on a world run by emperors, it has been reduced to a few unconnected sepia clichés on the margins of modern popular culture. It is even more true of the Napoleonic Wars. More than two decades of all-out global conflict that marked the birth of the world as we know it, they no longer form part of our basic historical language, at least not in Britain.

The great names from those days that still echo through our halls of fame – Wellington, Nelson, Waterloo, Trafalgar, Austerlitz perhaps, and Napoleon himself – have lost their visible connections to the real world we inhabit. Part of an unrivalled pantheon of epoch-making movers and shakers that dominated those twenty years, they have become one-dimensional caricatures from a time of swashbuckling fantasy.

This book is an attempt to provide access to that age for anybody interested in its course and wider ramifications. Primarily concerned to lay out the basic shape and structure of the wars, using dictionary format and rigorous cross-referencing to enable a balance between overview and detail, it also seeks to provide a sense of historical location, highlighting the many links between that particularly exciting slice of the past and our present. Its first task is therefore to offer a short narrative of the events in question, and to place them in broad historical context.

Eighteenth-Century Warfare – Dynasts at Work

The outbreak of the first major war between the established monarchies of Europe and the revolutionary French republic, in spring 1792, came at the end of a century that had seen warfare's widespread acceptance as a standard extension of international diplomacy. Around a continent ruled by accomplished and committed dynasts, skill in the art of war was viewed as a sine qua non of national (that is, family) progress, but it was an art form refined far beyond the clumsy carnage of the Middle Ages.

In tune with the enquiring spirit and pursuit of the rational that characterized the times, the practice of war grew increasingly formalized and scientific as the eighteenth century progressed. Armies became smaller, better-disciplined and less wantonly destructive, while the object of war was not to annihilate an enemy, but to achieve a position of negotiating strength in pursuit of a profitable peace. Wars of **siege** and manoeuvre, with few decisive battles, tended to produce inconclusive results that left both sides relatively undamaged and encouraged more wars.

Before 1792, the last general conflagration between the **great powers** had been the Seven Years War (1756–63), which was the eleventh major European war of the century. It was followed by a Russo-Turkish war of 1768–74, the American War of Independence (1778–83), a war for the Bavarian succession between **Austria** and **Prussia** (1778–9), an Austro-Russian war against the **Ottoman Empire** in the Balkans (1787–92), and the Russo-Swedish war of 1788–90.

Clear winners and losers had emerged from these conflicts by the

1780s. The empires of **Russia**, **Great Britain** and Austria, along with the flourishing kingdom of Prussia, had all grown larger and stronger at the expense of the Ottoman Empire, **France** and **Sweden**, while the eastern European empires of **Poland** and Lithuania had virtually disappeared. The winners were all states able to rely on relatively stable internal conditions; the losers had suffered the self- sustaining effects of socio-economic strife, which contributed to military failure and in turn to further internal discord. Of the losers only France remained a genuine great power, but its military and economic strength were being eroded by chronic insolvency and social unrest long before the outbreak of revolution in summer 1789.

The French Revolution prompted loud expressions of outrage from the established political classes within Europe's monarchies, becoming more strident with the humiliations subsequently heaped on King **Louis XVI** and his family. It generated equally high-profile demonstrations of support by radical elements in every corner of the continent, but beyond the small states on its southern and eastern frontiers the political cataclysm engulfing France did not exert an overwhelmingly dominant influence on international affairs before 1792.

The Russian regime of **Catherine** the Great was far more interested in expanding its trade and territories westward. Apart from frequent border wars with Sweden, Poland and the Ottoman Empire, this strategy entailed direct rivalries with Prussia (over Poland and the Baltic) and Austria (over Poland and the northern Balkans). Though Russia's deeply conservative ruling élites were genuinely appalled by revolutionary ideas, France was hardly a direct threat to their ambitions, with only mutual interests in the eastern **Mediterranean** threatening to disturb long-term friendly relations. Catherine gave shelter, money and ostentatious vocal support to French royalists, but her principal motive for stirring up trouble in the west was to distract Austria and Prussia from interests closer to home.

Though the Revolution and the prospect of its spread excited passionate responses, both for and against, at all levels of society in Britain, a government aware of England's own revolutionary tradition maintained a position of strict non-involvement in French internal affairs. British strategic ambitions, dominated by the sea-borne commerce that was an essential stimulus to its great wealth, did not require European territorial gains, and its view of the continent was largely defensive. Britain would fight European great powers for its colonies and trade routes, as evidenced by the regular imperial wars of the previous century, but only the emergence of a single, dominant continental power, or a threat to its security across the English Channel, would persuade it into a war inside Europe. Meanwhile Britain relied on diplomacy and the threat behind its massive naval strength to ensure a stable balance between the competing interests of other great powers.

With no overseas possessions and few trading interests, the emerging kingdom of Prussia had been Britain's strongest continental ally until the 1780s, when its naked territorial ambitions had triggered London's instinctive opposition to destabilizing tendencies. National and dynastic aggrandizement was the dominant obsession of King **Frederick William II** and his advisers, focused on the three-way struggle for parts of Poland with Austria and Russia, on the future of the **Netherlands** and northern Germany (including **George III**'s homeland, **Hanover**), and above all on the contest with Austria for ultimate control over the splintered, anachronistic **Holy Roman Empire**.

Though never remotely impressed by revolutionary ideas, the Prussian court was not given to crusades on other people's behalf, and its support for exiled French royalists was little more than lip service. Its gathering interest in military action to restore the royal French regime reflected confidence that, in the style of the earlier eighteenth century, easy military pickings in France could be translated into north German territorial gains at the conference table. Needing an ally willing to exchange northern conquests for southern, and unable to count on any British support for aggressive action, Frederick William's restlessness dictated a change of attitude towards his traditional worst enemy, Austria.

Habsburg Austria's complicated and uncertain diplomatic position helped transform international self-interest and ideological apathy into concerted action against revolutionary France. Austria's aggressive designs on Poland and the Balkans entailed involvement in the eastern power struggle with the Ottoman Empire, Russia and Prussia, but the empire was also engaged in a perennial and earnest contest with the latter to establish itself in control of Germany as a whole. The situation in Germany was complicated by the emperor's leadership of the Holy Roman Empire, which not only dragged him into an endless round of acrimonious petty disputes and minor territorial exchanges, but forced him to play a role in the politics of the French eastern frontier.

The other driving force behind Habsburg strategy was fear of the empire's internal collapse. The emperor's sprawling, multiracial dominions, administered by a ponderous centralized bureaucracy, were fertile ground for nationalist aspirations, as emphasized by a rebellion in the Austrian Netherlands of 1789–90, which coincided with threats of secession from Hungary and Galicia. In this respect, Austria had more to fear than most from French revolutionary ideology, particularly since Habsburg possessions in the Netherlands and northern Italy were so close to its source.

Austria was a long-term ally of France, reflecting shared suspicion of Prussia in the mid-eighteenth century. The alliance had offered few tangible advantages to either side, beyond protection against diplomatic isolation or war along the eastern French frontier, and it was effectively killed off by the Revolution, but however much new emperor Leopold II deplored the constraints placed upon King Louis, and upon his sister Marie-Antoinette, he had no real desire to risk the empire's interests elsewhere by a costly war against France.

A conscientious dynast, Leopold was willing to do whatever he could to help his sister and to hasten the downfall of a revolutionary regime widely assumed to be both deeply unpopular and on the point of collapse. The latter assumption, fed by the optimism of royalist exiles, matured into a certainty that the disorganized French would not dare risk the displeasure of emperors, and guided Leopold's diplomacy through 1791.

Rapprochement with Prussia in August 1791, the provocative Declaration of **Pillnitz** that followed, and subsequent threats in support of the French monarchy were viewed as gestures in Vienna, where they were expected to subdue the revolutionaries. In fact, the gestures brought France to the brink of war, and the moderating influence behind them disappeared with Leopold's death on 1 March 1792. The solemn young **Francis II**, faced with a French government apparently bent on war, was ready to teach it a lesson and form an aggressive alliance with an enthusiastic Prussia.

Europe's lesser powers played a relatively marginal role in shaping the overall diplomatic picture. The fading military power of Sweden, governed by a mad king, threw genuine support behind the royalist cause, but could achieve little on its own. The naval and commercial power of the independent Netherlands was primarily directed towards internal and colonial matters, while the Ottoman Empire, preoccupied with its basic survival, remained aloof from infidel disputes while hoping to profit from their fall-out. The enfeebled, poverty-stricken empire of **Spain**, though strongly moti- vated by medieval emotional and family attachments to the Bourbon monarchy, could barely maintain its internal cohesion and worldwide imperial communications, let alone bring any sig- nificant influence to bear on the great powers to its east.

The swarms of French **émigrés** who flocked in ever-increasing numbers to the courts of Europe, both great and small, exercised more diplomatic influence than they realized or deserved during the immediate prewar period. Tolerated and publicly encouraged to seek restitution by most of the great powers, but never given the full military support they wanted, they enjoyed more success with Europe's more modest rulers, most notably the Electors of Mainz and Trier, just across the French frontier.

Though an irrelevance in international terms, the small émigré armies built up at these frontier sanctuaries fuelled chaos and para- noia inside France, expressed as increasing hostility towards their presumed protectors in Vienna. More importantly, and even less deliberately, émigrés acted as a vital source of disinformation mud- dying the waters of European policy towards France. Often the only voices claiming current information about conditions inside France, their innately optimistic visions of imminent and popular counter-revolution helped convince the major German powers that the French regime would either concede or crumble at the slightest blow.

All the strategic imperatives exercising the rest of Europe had meanwhile ceased to matter in France. In the hysterical atmosphere that pervaded Parisian politics, every step on the road to regicide was accompanied by very real fear of retribution among political groups riding uneasily on a tide of mob radicalism. Caught between the mob below, royalist insurrection on every side and vengeful foreign monarchs on high, they responded with rising defiance. Based on an understandable faith in the universal rhetoric of revo- lutionary ideology, which had become the main hard currency of French politics, this crystallized into righteous aggression with the rise of the Brissotin party, whose brief dominance of the National

Assembly was enough to channel apparently uncontrollable national energies into foreign war.

Increasingly convinced that Marie-Antoinette, numberless crypto-royalists, an émigré army and the Austrian government were all part of a gigantic plot to bring down the Revolution, the population in Paris moved more solidly behind the war party with every attempt to bluff it into submission. Encouraged in its own faith by that of radicals abroad, the Assembly eventually demanded that Leopold II remove émigré forces from Mainz and Trier in late 1791. Vienna's sincere attempt to bully the Electors into doing so made no difference in Paris, and on 20 April 1792 the revolutionary government, still nominally represented by Louis XVI, declared war against Francis in his capacity as King of Hungary, a device rather optimistically intended to free Prussia from alliance obligations towards Austria.

The Revolutionary Wars

The wars fought by the French Republic against two coalitions of European powers between 1792 and 1801 are often known as the **Revolutionary Wars**, as distinct from the twelve years of conflict that followed **Napoleon**'s ascent to supreme power in **France**. The opening conflict, later called the War of the **First Coalition**, began in spring 1792 with a shambolic French invasion of the Austrian Netherlands and ended with the Austro-French Peace of **Campo Formio** in 1797.

Like most of the long wars in modern history, the war of 1792 was expected to be over in a matter of weeks. Once the people of **Belgium** had failed to rise up in decisive support of a chaotic **French Army**, and Prussia had formally allied with Austria (on 24 July) for an invasion across the Rhine, few in Europe expected the ramshackle units defending Paris to last for long against superbly drilled and fully equipped German armies.

Against all odds, French forces more than held their own in 1792. Allied reliance on the tactics (and many of the generals) that had served for the wars of the mid-eighteenth century proved fatal, and the first major French attempt at resistance brought the Duke of **Brunswick**'s invasion army to a halt at **Valmy** in September. As shocked allied forces drew back to regroup, the French flung themselves into Belgium once more, winning a genuine victory at **Jemappes** to bring them up to the Dutch border by the end of the year.

The momentous year of 1793 was a time of illusions on all sides. In Paris, an increasingly radical government drew boldness from the belief that its revolutionary fervour was ripe for export, and prepared invasions of the independent Netherlands and Spain. In London, a British government appalled by the prospect of Dutch Channel ports in French hands joined the Coalition before the spring season, along with the Dutch, **Naples** and Spain, but the French Assembly managed to pre-empt them all with its own declarations of war.

As allied forces prepared to attack along the **Rhine**, in **Flanders**, on the **Pyrenean** frontier and along the Genoan coast towards the newly conquered French province of **Nice**, the mighty **Royal Navy** took to the seas in search of French commerce and warships. Once more it seemed as if the French Revolution, now embarking on the bloody purges of the 'Terror', was about to be swamped by overwhelming force.

French dreams of immediate universal revolution collapsed at the first hurdle. The army in Flanders suffered a serious defeat at **Neerwinden** in March, lost its commander, **Dumouriez**, to defection, and tumbled all the way back to the French frontier. As internal chaos matured into rebellion in the **Vendée** and the south, and Coalition forces took control of **Toulon**, French armies on other fronts could do no more than cling on against superior numbers.

Allied assumptions proved equally false. On the Rhine and in Flanders, numbers, training and equipment again proved irrelevant without a coherent inter-allied strategy or a more mobile approach to offensive warfare. The impoverished Spanish could meanwhile do little to capitalize on their advantage in the Pyrenees, and no allied power was prepared to commit large-scale ground forces to enlargement of the Toulon bridgehead.

Stalemate at Toulon emphasized perhaps the most disappointing of all the allied failures during the early war years – the inability of the combined Coalition navies to make sea power a decisive factor in European land warfare. The Spanish court, among others, had gone to war in the comforting belief that British **blockade** strategy would reduce France to surrender in a matter of weeks, but the

Royal Navy lacked the operational sharpness or strategic coherence to fulfil its many roles efficiently. **Naval warfare** would remain an essentially separate contest, primarily concerned with the future of global imperialism, for much of the next two decades.

In short, the allies let France off the hook in 1793, and by 1794 it was already too late for a rapidly splintering Coalition to impose its will on a resurgent republic. The Terror may have sharpened intellectual opposition to the French Revolution elsewhere, but it had a salutary effect on French national unity and preparedness for war. The effective suppression of rebellion in the provinces, crowned by the recapture of Toulon from an inert allied force in December, and the wholesale military reforms of war minister Lazare **Carnot**, had enabled a significant strengthening of French forces on the frontiers by the spring.

At the same time allied cohesion was evaporating, with Prussia and to a lesser extent Austria distracted by the prospect of a **Polish rebellion**, and arguments aplenty surrounding joint policy on the Rhine and in Flanders. The ambitious spring offensives planned for those two fronts never fully materialized, and though an advance was attempted in Flanders, it again fell foul of old-fashioned **cordon** tactics before being halted by a revitalized French army. In June, French general **Jourdan's** victory at **Fleurus** turned the tide in the theatre, precipitating the withdrawal of Austrian, British, German and Dutch forces by the end of the year, and by January 1795 republican forces had conquered the Netherlands.

Elsewhere, allied arguments prevented much activity on the Rhine, the **Spanish Army** ran out of steam in the Pyrenees, and a French army (fortified by the influential presence of Napoleon as its artillery commander) consolidated its positions west of Genoa. In the wider world, the British pursued a policy of **colonial** aggrandizement, picking up territorial gains in the **West Indies**, but remained largely powerless to do more than finance their partners in a European land war that was beginning to appear unwinnable.

British money could do little to prevent the virtual collapse of the Coalition in 1795. As the Netherlands (and most of the **Dutch Navy**) fell under long-term French control, Prussia's enthusiasm for war in the west waned to the point of neutrality. Anxious to focus attention to the east, where Russia was making the most of a relatively free hand in Poland, Berlin made peace with France at **Basle** in the spring. Negotiations in the same Swiss town took an exhausted Spain out of the war in July, leaving Britain and Austria as the major partners in a much reduced alliance.

Though French forces were unable to capitalize on allied inactivity in 1795, and the frontier theatres remained largely stagnant, the year saw the establishment of the relatively stable **Directory** regime in Paris. While the Austrians held their ground at the Rhine and in northern Italy, and the British concerned themselves with acquiring former Spanish or Dutch colonies, Carnot continued the process of expanding and reorganizing the army in an atmosphere of relative sociopolitical calm.

By 1796 the numerical advantage in the field had swung to the French side, and Carnot's reforms combined with inspired generalship to bring a succession of important victories against depleted enemies. From the Rhine, Jourdan and **Moreau** briefly threatened the Danube before the Austrians found an efficient commander in Archduke **Charles**, who had restored the position by autumn. On the **Italian** front, where the outspoken General Bonaparte was given his first independent command in March, a small French army swept all before it in a year of brilliant campaigning. By early 1797 Napoleon had knocked **Piedmont** out of the war, driven Austrian forces from northern Italy, suppressed anti-French activity throughout central Italy and repulsed three successive Austrian counter-invasions from the Tyrol. In the spring he drove Austrian forces back towards Vienna, and the Habsburg Empire finally sued for peace at **Leoben** in April 1797.

A binding treaty was delayed while the Austrians contemplated British inducements to fight on, but was signed at **Campo Formio** in October. Dictated to a hapless Habsburg court by a confident Bonaparte, it was sufficiently harsh virtually to guarantee war in the future, but for the time being it brought the First Coalition to an end and left Britain as the only major power fighting a victorious, expanded France.

Though the only nation able to afford the escalating cost of contemporary warfare without suffering severe economic disruption, and still able to offer huge cash or material **subsidies** to prospective allies, Britain found itself isolated and under threat of invasion by 1797. British armies had proved no less tactically inflexible and no more effective against innovative French **infantry tactics** than those of their allies, and the much-vaunted power of the Royal Navy had so far failed to deliver so much as a glimpse of victory in Europe.

Not only were French **convoys** still able to reach home ports in spite of costly and exhausting naval blockades, but French warships could still escape from their Atlantic and Mediterranean bases to disrupt British merchant trade. Colonial victories, though useful boosts to British popular morale and imperial wealth, had begun to seem less important than security at home, particularly once the conclusion of French peace with Austria freed the Directory to prepare a full-scale invasion of **England** across the Channel.

By way of a rehearsal, and in the hope of exploiting popular nationalism in Britain's oldest colony, French forces had attempted an invasion of **Ireland** at **Bantry Bay** in the last days of 1796. It failed, thanks to poor planning and worse weather, but the ease with which French ships slipped past the Royal Navy's Channel Fleet encouraged a heightened sense of vulnerability in Britain. To make matters worse, the Royal Navy erupted into mass mutiny at **Spithead** and the **Nore** during the summer of 1797, and fear of invasion began seriously to undermine Britain's hitherto cast-iron **war finances**. None the less the **Pitt** government, reluctant to embark on European conflict in 1793, was by now determined to fight the spectre of a single dominant continental power, and the year proved to be a watershed in British conduct of the wars.

Even before the mutinies, signs of the navy's revival had been confirmed by the Mediterranean Fleet's crushing victory over the Spanish at Cape **St Vincent**, and the settlement of seamen's grievances over the summer promoted a significant long-term improvement in service efficiency. In October the North Sea Fleet inflicted an equally comprehensive defeat on the Dutch at **Camperdown**, completing its restoration of confidence and putting any danger from a combination of hostile navies into perspective.

Meanwhile the French government was finding peace abroad no easier to maintain than calm at home. Wily politicians such as **Barras** and **Talleyrand** had replaced the bloodthirsty ideologues of **Robespierre**'s Terror, but could only maintain power through a succession of coups against opponents to the left and right. With the Directory becoming ever more dependent on direct support from the army, this was the time of the generals in Paris.

Established commanders such as Moreau, Jourdan and **Bernadotte** became darlings of Parisian politics, along with particularly dashing figures such as **Hoche** and **Joubert** (both of whom died before fulfilling their political potential). As guarantors of at least some military support, they were all potential figureheads for the many groups engaged in a constant tangle of conspiracies against a manifestly unpopular regime.

The most dashing and successful general in France was Napoleon Bonaparte, conqueror of Italy. Given command of the Army of England in early 1798, he rapidly concluded that the enterprise was doomed, and set about finding other avenues to glory. Supported by Talleyrand, he secured government approval for an ambitious and risky invasion of the Ottoman **Middle East**. Gambling that the operation would reap a fortune in booty and interfere with British domination in India, but also that it would not provoke war in Europe, Napoleon, his small army and the French Mediterranean Fleet sailed from Toulon in May 1798.

By that time the Directory's unwillingness to halt the process of revolutionary expansion had already brought France close to a new war with its continental rivals. French interference in the affairs of **Switzerland** and central Italy encouraged a powerful war party in Vienna, outraged the Pope and Naples, and alarmed new Russian tsar **Paul I**, whose own Mediterranean ambitions were also threatened by French occupation of the **Ionian Islands**.

Napoleon's evasion of British naval patrols, his capture of **Malta** and his successful landing in **Egypt** smoothed the path of that diplomatic rarity, a Russo-Turkish alliance, and **Nelson's** destruction of the French fleet at the **Nile** on 1 August gave European governments in general the push they needed to come together in a **Second Coalition** against France. The Nile disaster incidentally cut Napoleon off from Europe, and though he won a number of more or less irrelevant battle victories in reaching the limit of his army's endurance at **Acre** in 1799, he took no part in the opening campaigns of the European war.

The Second Coalition, sponsored as ever by British money and promoted by Pitt's determined diplomacy, came together only slowly. Prussia refused to join, and French prospects seemed bright for a while, as the excitable Neapolitans, egged on by Nelson in an unofficial capacity, launched a unilateral invasion of the **Papal States** in November 1798. Naples received only token support from Russia, limited naval aid from Britain, and no help at all from Austria beyond the loan of General **Mack** as C-in-C, so that the **Neapolitan** campaign ended with French forces in control of mainland Naples by February 1799. Encouraged by the ease of the victory, the Directory finalized ambitious plans for pre-emptive offensives on the **Rhine** and in northern Italy.

French confidence was short-lived. A Russo-Turkish naval expedition had embarked on a leisurely conquest of the Ionian Islands in October, but more powerful Russian forces were on their way west, and though Austria had been reluctant to honour an agreement with the tsar for a joint spring offensive, the **Austrian Army** was ready when the French attacks came.

French armies were not the well-motivated forces they had been in 1796. Jourdan's reckless advance from the Rhine met defeat at **Stockach** in March 1799, and his retreat forced **Masséna to** fall back into Switzerland, while General **Schérer's** offensive on the Italian front failed to take **Verona** even before the arrival of Russian reinforcements under **Suvorov** in mid-April. As Archduke Charles moved from the Rhine to threaten the **Swiss** front, Suvorov drove Moreau (Schérer's replacement) west towards Genoa and routed **Macdonald's** army up from Naples at the **Trebbia**. A major French counter-offensive in Italy failed at **Novi** in August and, with Masséna by now holding the last line of defence around Zurich, the total defeat of France appeared certain by the autumn.

Coalition chaos came to the republic's rescue. Alarmed by Russian success in Italy, Austrian chief minister **Thugut** suddenly switched strategies in the summer, effectively forcing Suvarov to redeploy in Switzerland while Archduke Charles moved north to new positions on the Rhine. This reduced the principal threat to French security, along the Genoan coast into Provence, and gave Masséna the chance to exploit the changeover in Switzerland. This he did brilliantly, driving poorly led Austro-Russian forces back from **Zurich** to the Rhine by late autumn.

Meanwhile grandiose Coalition plans to undermine French security with attacks elsewhere bore little fruit. British Mediterranean forces were too stretched by multiple defensive commitments in the theatre to strike at the rear of French positions in Italy, and a delayed Anglo-Russian invasion of French **North Holland** was both too late and too feeble to achieve any serious impact.

Despite its autumn recovery, and the defection of mad Tsar Paul from the Coalition in December, a war-weary France remained in serious peril as the winter approached. Powerful Austrian armies were still massed on its Italian and German frontiers, and the Directory government's authority had declined to the point at which its downfall appeared certain. The return to France of Napoleon Bonaparte had meanwhile added a uniquely potent element to the brew of conspirators and would-be rulers in Paris.

Napoleon's characteristically well-orchestrated **propaganda** campaign had contrived to present his Egyptian failures as a succession of glittering triumphs against dangerous enemies. After administering a final thrashing to a Turkish force at **Aboukir** in July 1799, following which he was informed of the dire military situation in Europe, he escaped from Egypt with a few companions and, leaving his army to fend for itself under **Kléber**, reached the French southern coast in October.

Proceeding to Paris in triumph, Napoleon accepted an offer from Director **Sieyès** to play the role of military figurehead in a proposed coup d'état, though he was only approached after Moreau had turned down the chance. Supremely ambitious and self-confident, the thirty-year-old Bonaparte turned the tables on his civilian co-conspirators in the aftermath of the **Brumaire** coup that ousted the Directory on 9–10 November 1799, and a new constitution established him as the head of a new **Consulate**.

Though he was popular with the French masses, and accepted as the price of strong government by a broad spectrum of political opinion in Paris, Napoleon's ability to hold on to supreme power depended on bringing the ongoing war to a swift and successful conclusion. Unable to persuade Moreau to launch an unconventional and bold offensive on the Rhine, he made plans to strike at the Austrian position in northern Italy.

Despite the departure of Russian forces, Austrian commander **Melas** was expected to mount an invasion of Provence in spring 1800, but only after the remaining French enclave around Genoa had been mopped up. While French troops, now led by the reliable Masséna, held out in **Genoa**, Napoleon marched a newly assembled Reserve Army from France into positions behind the Austrian armies, and then defeated them as they turned to meet the threat at **Marengo** (14 June). Though a close-run thing, the new First Consul's brilliant campaign of manoeuvre succeeded in driving the Austrians out of Italy once more and cemented his own political position for the foreseeable future.

Vienna refused to make peace at once, but the renewal of hostilities on the Rhine and Moreau's victory over Archduke **John** at **Hohenlinden** brought an end to resistance in December. A new

Austro-French treaty, even more harsh than the last, was signed at **Lunéville** in February 1801, putting the Second Coalition out of its misery and leaving Britain to fight on with only the militarily irrelevant Portuguese and Turks as allies.

While Napoleon basked in his success, beginning an intensive period of internal reform that established his regime on relatively stable dictatorial foundations, Britain faced the consequences of failure. Irish controversies, along with his own depression, had brought seventeen years of government by Pitt to an end, and the new **Addington** administration took control amid generalized acceptance that peace with France was inevitable, if only as a matter of good business.

In truth, the Anglo-French war had almost died a natural death by early 1801. French domination of mainland Europe and the Royal Navy's power over the sea lanes cancelled each other out, and direct conflict between the two powers had been reduced to a sideshow in Egypt, where **Abercromby**'s British army completed the expulsion of French troops after a spring success at **Alexandria**. At the same time, Tsar Paul's sudden anti-British enthusiasm had brought an **Armed Neutrality** league of northern powers to the brink of a new war against Britain.

Nelson nipped Armed Neutrality in the bud with another major battle victory, this time over the Danes at **Copenhagen** in early April 1801, and Paul's assassination eased Anglo-Russian tensions, but the French held a clear tactical advantage in the lengthy negotiations that produced the preliminary Anglo-French Treaty of **Amiens** in October 1801. Though not formalized until the following February, the peace was effective immediately. As the British government hastened to demobilize, and ordinary serving men all over the world prepared for the scrapheap, wealthy Britons flocked to Paris, where the Revolution, declared complete by the incoming Consulate, had become an instant tourist attraction.

Ten years of warfare between European great powers had already touched every known corner of the globe, entangling even the pacifist **United States** in its colonial and commercial ramifications. The wars had left Austria exhausted, Prussia unmoved, Russia apparently cured of western European adventure and Spain reduced to a feeble, dependent alliance with France. They had brought economic crisis and territorial loss to every major belligerent except Britain, which continued to reap wealth from an expanding trade empire on a scale undreamed of by its rivals, and France, now in control of its 'natural' frontiers at the Rhine, the Alps and the Pyrenees. Both were secure for the time being – Britain protected by its navy, France by a network of buffer states in the Low Countries, Germany and Italy – but any hope that the late eighteenth 0century's two superpowers might settle into a period of peaceful coexistence was fleeting.

The Napoleonic Wars

Britain and France were again at war from May 1803, and remained locked in uninterrupted conflict until April 1814. In the years before 1812, thanks in part to the free-spending coalition diplomacy of successive British governments, France also faced military challenges from Austria (in 1805 and 1809), Prussia (1806–7) and Russia (1805–7). All were defeated, and by 1810 Napoleon's writ had been extended to include all of Italy, much of the Balkans, eastern Spain, most of Germany, Poland and all the states along the expanded French frontiers.

Following Napoleon's decision to risk all by invading Russia in 1812, and his costly failure, more and more states turned against France, until by 1814 Paris was menaced by an alliance of almost every sovereign power in Europe. Inevitable French defeat brought peace and the removal of Napoleon, but he returned to Paris in spring 1815 and reclaimed control after the restored royal family had fled, triggering a final spasm of armed conflict in Flanders that ended with his ultimate defeat in June.

These conflicts are known collectively as the Napoleonic Wars, a name that reflects the extent to which Bonaparte's personal ambitions and talents were responsible for their outbreak and course.

After his triumphs against the Second Coalition, Napoleon had stamped his particular brand of ruthless diplomacy on the peace that followed. Austria was shown no mercy, and negotiations with Britain were distinguished by his blunt refusal to make genuine concessions. The result was a smouldering resentment in Vienna, bound to flare into aggression once the Habsburg economy and army had recovered, and a clear sense of a bad bargain in London.

Convinced that French security demanded the ultimate defeat of

Britain, and of his ability to deliver just that, Napoleon had already embarked on a self-perpetuating spiral of aggression and limitless ambition in the name of national defence. British negotiators at Amiens had been trying to establish a genuine peace, while Napoleon sought only a truce in order to build up strength for a renewed confrontation. Though he was able to bully the British into giving up almost all of their wartime colonial conquests, and accepting no more than his promises of non-aggression in return, he was not able to keep his restless expansionism in check for long enough to give the treaty any real credibility.

While the British contented themselves with sneering at Addington, delaying their agreed evacuation of Malta and generally adopting a wait-and-see attitude, the First Consul wasted no time in demonstrating his contempt for treaty agreements. Switzerland, central Italy and the Netherlands were annexed, and a major expedition was sent to the West Indies, where it temporarily restored French control in **Santo Domingo**. The British soon accepted that peace had been a mirage and, encouraged by new tsar **Alexander I**, a discredited government finally dug in its heels and went to war rather than quit Malta.

Royal Navy blockades were resumed, and colonial forces began reclaiming their pre-Amiens prizes, but the British strategic situation remained essentially as it had been in 1801. Still unable to strike any direct blow against French mainland hegemony, British forces could only tread water and hope that diplomacy would again provide powerful continental allies.

Napoleon, though absorbed in the business of elevating himself to First Consul for life (1802) and then head of a new French Empire (1804), began the new war determined to succeed where the Directory had failed, and to carry out the cross-Channel invasion of England. As long as peace lasted on other fronts, he could devote the great majority of French military resources to the task, and a formidable army was assembled at bases along the Channel coast during 1803–4.

Though the new Army of England, and the construction of hundreds of transport vessels, spread fresh alarm in Britain, and hastened the return of Pitt to power as an established war leader, Napoleon quickly recognized that the invasion was unlikely to succeed in the face of large-scale Royal Navy interference. Displaying a blindness to the technical realities of naval warfare, he responded by orchestrating a highly ambitious decoy campaign. French and allied Spanish warships were ordered to break out from their Mediterranean and Atlantic bases, speed to the West Indies, and then return to the English Channel while British fleets were still pursuing the bait.

Set in motion in spring 1805, the plan called for levels of efficiency far beyond the capacity of either the French or the Spanish sea services, and fell apart almost at once. A combined Franco-Spanish fleet under Admiral **Villeneuve** did, however, escape from the Mediterranean, and sailed to Martinique with a three-week head start over Nelson's British Mediterranean Fleet, but by the time it had completed its return journey to Europe the invasion of England had been effectively abandoned. Anyway unable to get past British forces still patrolling the Channel approaches, Villeneuve fled with his fleet into Cadiz.

Already with serious doubts about its feasibility, Napoleon had abandoned the invasion once it became certain that he faced a new war in mainland Europe. He had never doubted that another war would come, and though France was manifestly in need of a longer period of relatively peaceful reconstruction, he had made little effort to postpone its arrival. The sequence of affronts to diplomatic nicety that had outraged all Europe in 1802–3 was continued with the kidnap and judicial murder of royalist exile the Duc d'**Enghein** in 1804, an act that shocked informed opinion worldwide but particularly appalled the tsar, who responded warmly to the Pitt government's proposal of an alliance at the end of the year.

The **Third Coalition** was born on 11 April 1805, when Britain, Russia, Sweden and the Neapolitan government on **Sicily** signed an offensive alliance at St Petersburg. Austrian emperor Francis, not for the last time dominated by an overconfident war party at court, had agreed a defensive alliance with Russia in November 1804, and formally joined the Coalition on 9 August. Though Prussia again held back, reinforcing its international reputation for unscrupulous opportunism, the new allies concocted a spectacularly ambitious offensive scheme to achieve their stated aim of restoring Europe's 1789 boundaries.

Largely funded by Britain – which otherwise confined its contribution to naval operations and slow preparations for secondary attacks in the Baltic and Naples – the plan envisaged Austrian offensives in Italy and **Bavaria**, the latter with large-scale support from the **Russian Army**. Austro-Russian mobilization was under way by the late summer, and Napoleon ordered the newly retitled **Grande Armée** to redeploy from the Channel coast to Bavaria on 26 August.

The brief campaign that followed encapsulated all the drama, optimism and ultimate frustration of the war years in three explosive months. Another campaign of illusions, apparently destined to produce final victory for one side or the other, it turned out to be no more than a staging post in the prolonged determination of Europe's geopolitical future.

Even before the war got fully under way, the illusion that sheer weight of numbers virtually guaranteed victory had infected Coalition attitudes, despite an attack plan that lacked even the rudiments of coordination. The most outlandish fantasies were entertained in Vienna, where Habsburg leaders (Archduke Charles aside) assumed not only that Napoleon would march his army from the Channel to meet the threat to Italy, but that a marginally reformed Austrian Army was powerful enough to attack in Bavaria without waiting for Russian support. Bolstered by the further illusion that Russian troops would be in place by mid-October, General Mack and Archduke **Ferdinand** led the advance in September, only for their army to be spectacularly outmanoeuvred and forced to surrender en masse at **Ulm**.

The Grande Armée – superbly trained, highly motivated and brilliantly led by Napoleon in person – now set off in pursuit of the one Russian column that had reached Germany, and captured **Vienna** in the process, but was thwarted by General **Kutuzov**'s resolute retreat on approaching reinforcements. Napoleon now found that the victory at Ulm had propelled him into serious danger. Unable to prevent Kutuzov and an Austrian remnant from meeting up with the main Russian army around Olmütz, he was aware that Archduke Charles and the secondary Austrian force were attempting to cut off his rear from Italy. The open secret of Prussia's belated adherence to the Coalition multiplied that threat, and with news of financial chaos in Paris his need for a quick, decisive victory became urgent.

As Europe anticipated the final demise of the 'Corsican ogre', or at least a French retreat that would irreparably damage his enormous military reputation, Napoleon enticed Austro-Russian forces into a full-scale battle on ground of his own choosing. On 3 December 1805 he won his most famous and technically impressive victory at **Austerlitz**, routing significantly superior numbers, forcing Austria into immediate peace and sending a shocked Alexander scurrying back to Russia ahead of his surviving troops.

Austerlitz wiped out the Third Coalition at a stroke. Subsidiary allied operations were abandoned forthwith, and the subsequent Treaty of **Pressburg** left a shrunken Habsburg Empire incapable of further military adventure for several years. Prussia was punished too. Though Berlin had not quite got round actually to declaring war on France before Austerlitz, the eternally vapid King **Frederick William III** had been forced to swallow all semblance of national pride and, on pain of invasion, had accepted the savage Convention of **Vienna**. Like most of Napoleon's diplomacy, both agreements stored up trouble for later.

But as Napoleon basked in the illusion of total victory, ignoring Talleyrand's wise advice to make a friend of Austria, the British were celebrating a victory of their own. The emperor had ordered Villeneuve's fleet in Cadiz to transport its thousands of accompanying troops to the Italian theatre, and to abandon time-honoured tactics of evasion by accepting battle in the event of interference from the British. Like most French naval officers, Villeneuve was aware of the Royal Navy's overwhelming technical and tactical combat superiority, and sailed with a heavy heart. His Combined Fleet was duly annihilated by Nelson at **Trafalgar** on 19 October.

News of the defeat reached Napoleon in the aftermath of Ulm. Although it appeared of marginal significance compared with his achievement on land, and had cost Britain its greatest naval leader, it had effectively closed the world's sea lanes to the French Empire for the foreseeable future. The long stalemate between France and Britain, apparently shattered a few weeks later at Austerlitz, was in fact cemented at Trafalgar.

One pillar of European opposition to France had been decisively broken. Pitt died at the start of 1806, and **Grenville**'s new British government reacted to its loss of allies by opening peace talks. Treated with open contempt by Napoleon, British feelers were withdrawn when their prime mover, **Fox**, died a few months later, by which time another continental war was in preparation.

The War of the **Fourth Coalition** was begun by Prussia, although Napoleon's diplomatic insensitivity played its usual part. Prussia's ruling élite, the epitome of patriotic pride, had been horrified by the indignities of Vienna, and been helpless spectators as Napoleon used his secure dominance of western Germany to dismantle the Holy Roman Empire, replacing it with his own political creation, the Confederation of the **Rhine**. A crass demonstration of Napoleon's authority as the new arbiter of German affairs – the arrest of nationalist publisher Johann **Palm** – pushed an increasingly fevered Prussian court over the edge, and in August 1806, barely six months after ratification of the Vienna convention, King Frederick William authorized war against France.

Though surprised and dismayed by the need to fight another costly foreign war so soon, Napoleon had kept the Grande Armée fully mobilized and was far better prepared for a new campaign than his adversaries. Berlin's assumption that the **Prussian Army** was still the first-class force it had been in the 1780s was belied by a slow mobilization process that was never completed, and by an almost farcical failure of strategic planning. Like the Austrians in 1805, but with even less justification, C-in-C Brunswick and his quarrelsome subordinates gambled on Russian forces reaching the scene before Napoleon. With no definite attack plan in mind, they simply advanced across the Elbe into **Saxony**, which had been bullied into joining the fight, and waited to be attacked by the French.

Napoleon soon obliged. Marching the Grande Armée up from the south, he took advantage of poor Prussian dispositions to rout his opponents at the twin battles of **Jena** and **Auerstädt** in mid-October. The victory, which owed something to luck and a great deal to the combat prowess of French marshal **Davout**, wrecked the Prussian war effort, and all but the far east of the country was under French occupation by early November. But though it enabled Napoleon to enter Berlin in triumph, and confirmed his army as the military wonder of the age, the campaign did not end the war. Instead Frederick William and the court fled to the eastern outpost of Königsberg, to be met by an allied Russian army. Though French economic and political stability demanded his presence in Paris, Napoleon was forced to march further east in search of another victory that would secure his latest conquests.

The campaigns in Poland of winter 1806–7 and the following spring were messy affairs, hidebound by appalling weather conditions and even more miserable for participants than the usual run of contemporary warfare. After occupying **Warsaw**, Napoleon was frustrated through the winter by Russian evasion and freezing conditions. Mud and snow contributed to his failure to achieve more than an inconclusive draw at **Eylau** in early 1807, but he got his decisive victory in the end, finally bringing a weary tsar to the peace table after a brutal slugging match at **Friedland** in June.

On other fronts, the British had been capable of inflicting no more than pinpricks since 1805. A local victory at **Maida** in support of Neapolitan royalists was the **British Army**'s only notable achievement of the period, and the Royal Navy had run out of fleets to demolish. Most of Britain's naval forces were thus condemned to the drudgery of patrolling trade routes or enforcing coastal blockades, but although the rude health of the nation's economy testified to improving efficiency, their efforts did not seem likely to win the war in the near future.

On the other hand, the Royal Navy's routine 'stop and search' procedures – by which it policed the world's trade routes for whatever was deemed contraband – were provoking mounting international outrage, and combined with Napoleon's continued military success to promote Britain's diplomatic isolation. French propaganda's portrayal of Britain as the 'tyrant of the seas', encouraging war as a means of growing ever richer, had begun to ring true since 1805. It seemed to be confirmed by a pre-emptive **amphibious** assault on **Copenhagen** in early 1807, which killed about 2,000 civilians and kept the **Danish Navy** out of French hands, but outraged even British public opinion and pushed **Denmark** itself into an alliance with Napoleon that lasted until 1814.

The arrangement of an apparently very amicable peace between Russia and France at Tilsit in July 1807 left Britain in the role of Europe's outcast, as Napoleon and Alexander carved mainland Europe into agreed spheres of influence, and a subsidiary treaty reduced Prussia to a second-class power under close French supervision. The treaties confirmed Russia's acceptance of all Napoleon's conquests and political creations, including Jérôme **Bonaparte**'s new German Kingdom of **Westphalia**, and established a French protectorate over part of Poland. It also made provision for future deposition of the Spanish and Portuguese monarchies, gave Russia carte blanche to expand into **Finland**, made vague mutual promises about the future of Turkey and committed the tsar to taking part in economic sanctions against Britain.

For a moment in the aftermath of Tilsit it appeared as if Napoleon had ensured a long and triumphant peace, but he had already sown the seeds of future instability. Certain as ever that 'perfide Albion' was the malign source of all Europe's troubles, but unable to harm it with his armies, the emperor had embarked on an ambitious and ultimately self-destructive attempt to defeat Britain by economic warfare. Imperial decrees issued at **Milan** and **Berlin** in 1806 established the basic principles of an international counter-blockade, later known as the **Continental System**, that sought to close all mainland Europe's coasts to British trade.

The system never came close to achieving its desired effect, despite subsequent modifications, and proved impossible to enforce with any efficiency. It also disrupted the internal economy of the French Empire far more than it slowed the growth of British prosperity, which suffered no more than a brief blip, yet it remained central to Napoleon's imperial strategy over the next few years. His determination that it should succeed was an important factor in the subsequent breakdown of relations with Portugal, Spain and Russia, and ultimately soured relations between France and all its client states.

Apart from its economic imbalances, and its dependence on Napoleon's personal survival, several other factors undermined the French Empire's apparent stability after 1807. The key alliance with Russia left a number of potential disputes unresolved – especially over the futures of Constantinople and Poland – and as such depended heavily on the goodwill of both leaders. Tsar Alexander may have been dazzled by Napoleon at Tilsit, but his admiration was soon tempered by the economic cost of hostility to Britain and by deep-seated anti-French sentiments at court. Meanwhile the French emperor regarded Tilsit, like all his major treaties, as little more than a pause in the pursuit of ever-expanding ambitions.

The inflation of Napoleon's personal horizons to encompass the prospect of a universal European monarchy was perhaps the most fundamentally disabling element at work in France after 1807. Restless and supremely convinced of his own destiny, he proved incapable of halting the spiral of conquest and war that had propelled him to glory. The very extent of his successes admittedly made it unlikely that rival powers would let him rest for long, but he showed little inclination to soothe their attitudes with compromise or appeasement.

This failure encouraged a perceptible erosion of faith among the Parisian political establishment. Napoleon still commanded mass popular support in France, retained a powerful grip over the mechanisms of state control and had created a new nobility of his own to provide political armour, but Talleyrand in particular had already concluded that obsessive expansionism would lead to national disaster. He took it upon himself to act as the tsar's secret informer at Tilsit, and the **Talleyrand–Fouché** plot of 1808 was his attempt to devolve the imperial succession on the uncomplicated **Murat**. Reduced to a marginal role in the imperial administration after the plot's discovery, he spent the next six years cultivating contacts with exiled royalists and foreign diplomats, seeking a lasting peace that would stabilize post-revolutionary France and Europe.

Napoleon could see long-term peace only in the elimination of all hostile forces, and of any allies that pursued imperial strategies with insufficient enthusiasm or efficiency. With Italy, Germany and Poland under fairly secure control, and the attempted conquest of **Illyria** slowly extending the empire's Balkan frontiers, his eye for rational improvement fell on the Iberian peninsula. Within a few weeks of Tilsit, a French army under **Junot** was sent into **Portugal**, an inveterate (if militarily irrelevant) British ally and trading partner. It had conquered the virtually undefended country by the end of the year, forcing the Portuguese royal family to take up residence in its Brazilian colony.

Once Portugal had been brought into the Continental System, it was the turn of Spain. Nominally a French ally, and heavily implicated in the attack on Portugal, Spain had been reduced to political paralysis by a combination of national poverty and rampant factionalism, revolving around the unending feud between King **Charles VI**, chief minister Prince **Godoy** and Crown Prince **Ferdinand**. Convinced that the country and its people were ripe for assimilation into the empire, Napoleon sent French troops across the frontier in spring 1808, triggering a six-year **Peninsular War** that would eventually play a major part in his downfall.

French forces experienced little difficulty in reaching and occupying Madrid, and Napoleon deposed the Bourbon royal family at **Bayonne** in early May, but his belief that the campaign was as good as won proved entirely false. In a surge of conservative loyalty to the old regime that was genuinely beyond his understanding, the Spanish people rose up in almost universal revolt against their conquerors, after a short-lived but passionate uprising in **Madrid** on the first two days of May had triggered civil disobedience and the formation of rebel **juntas** all over the country. The rebellion proved impossible to suppress by short-term military action and its leaders were quick to appeal to London for aid, a move that finally offered the British an arena of direct confrontation with French land forces.

The Peninsular War is often described as a running sore, slowly poisoning the Napoleonic empire, and the analogy is a good one. Napoleon ordered French forces into a limited Spanish offensive during the summer of 1808, but he had severely underestimated the depth of the rebellion. His armies not only failed to achieve their basic aims of capturing a few major rebel strongholds, but suffered the first of many embarrassing defeats – by Spanish forces at **Bailén** in July. The setback persuaded new Spanish king Joseph **Bonaparte** to quit Madrid for new positions behind the Ebro, and convinced Napoleon to lead the full Grande Armée through the Pyrenees that autumn.

Another defeat, by a small British army at **Vimeiro** in August, compelled French forces to evacuate Portugal, and introduced the enterprising General **Wellesley** to the theatre, but the opening phases of the autumn campaign at the Ebro seemed to justify Napoleon's confidence. Sweeping past ill-coordinated **Spanish Army** elements, the emperor reoccupied Madrid in November and prepared to move into the south and west of the country.

He was prevented from doing so by the new British commander in **Portugal**, General **Moore**, whose failed attempt to join forces with the Spanish left 35,000 British troops isolated north of Madrid. Once Moore's initial contacts with French forces had alerted Napoleon to his presence, the emperor led a desperate pursuit as the outnumbered British expedition fled for the coast. Though Moore himself was killed during the final confrontation at **Corunna** in mid-January 1809, most of his army escaped, and its performance fatally undermined Napoleon's wider strategy in Spain.

Imperial business had taken the emperor back to Paris before the chase was over, and he never returned to the theatre. The postponement of his offensive into western Spain had given the rebellion time to recover its strength before campaigning began in 1809, and though an army under **Soult** occupied northern Portugal from March, the British had been given a chance to re-establish their position in the rest of the country.

Without Napoleon's personal leadership, a conflict that always kept at least 200,000 imperial troops occupied spiralled out of French control. The emperor's consistent underestimates of the difficulties faced by his commanders were partly to blame, as were their collective failure to follow a coherent strategy in his absence, and the dedicated resistance of Spanish regular or **guerrilla** forces, but the vital element that turned Spain into a serious threat to French security was a highly effective British land campaign. Gathering momentum as London's confidence in its ground forces increased, and given crucial support from a Royal Navy at last able to use its control of sea lanes to direct strategic effect, it was brilliantly orchestrated and led by Wellesley, who won fame as Lord **Wellington** through a sequence of supremely well-organized and disciplined successes over the next five years.

More than a match for the best of Napoleon's military subordinates, Wellington was a superb strategist, tactician and organizer, but his small army was fortunate in never having to face either the emperor himself or the full might of French arms throughout the Peninsular campaigns. This was partly because Napoleon clung to the belief that only incompetence stood between France and victory in Spain, but also reflected the extent to which the French Empire had been forced on to the defensive by the weight of its own rapid expansion.

All Napoleon's wars after 1807 were fought against a backdrop of manpower shortages, and the Grande Armée's attack on Spain in autumn 1808 had left only about 150,000 troops available to police and defend his sprawling frontiers. This temporarily increased his dependence on alliance with Russia, particularly since Austria was rumoured to be preparing a new challenge, and forced him back to the conference table with an increasingly disillusioned tsar at **Erfurt** in October 1808. Although Napoleon received the guarantees of benevolent neutrality he needed to guard his back during the Spanish invasion, a distinctly cool Alexander would give no definite undertakings of military assistance in the event of a French war on two fronts.

Along with news of the Talleyrand–Fouché conspiracy, it was evidence of Austrian preparations for war that brought Napoleon back from Spain before his work there was done. Emperor Francis had made the best of his utter humiliation at Pressburg in 1806, meekly retitling himself Francis I of Austria after the demise of the Holy Roman Empire and giving Archduke Charles the opportunity to commence long-term military reforms, but he was incapable of resisting the influence of a hawkish majority at court for very long.

Fed a rose-tinted view of both the Austrian Army's prospects and the willingness of other German states to rise up against the tyranny from across the Rhine, and persuaded that the extension of French resources into the Peninsula was too good an opportunity to miss, Francis declared a 'war of German liberation' against France in early 1809.

Slow to mobilize or come up with any settled plan of campaign, the Austrians massed around the Danube expecting to outnumber the French, but Napoleon recruited troops from all over the empire with his usual relentless energy, and was able to put a large, if inexperienced army in the field by April. The campaign that followed nevertheless began promisingly for what, with the British planning a supporting invasion of the Netherlands, was technically the **Fifth Coalition** against France.

Unable to leave a politically volatile Paris until the campaign was under way, Napoleon was forced to rescue his army from the confusion it seemed to suffer whenever he left a subordinate (in this case staff supremo **Berthier**) in command. Aided by the pessimistic caution of Archduke Charles, in command of the Austrian force but convinced it was not ready for war, Napoleon was able to separate the wings of the Austrian force and march on Vienna, but his first attempt to win a decisive victory ended in failure after a drawn battle at nearby **Aspern–Essling** in May. Better preparation, and the defensive mentality of his opponent, eventually brought Napoleon a conclusive victory on almost the same ground at **Wagram** in July, and induced Vienna to accept yet another punitive peace. Delayed while the belated British support operation came to an undistinguished end at **Walcheren**, the treaty was signed at **Schönbrunn** that autumn.

The broad brush-strokes of modern history leave plenty of room for tantalizing 'ifs', and the question of what might have been had Napoleon chosen to consolidate his empire is a perennial favourite. What if the emperor had reacted to signs of overextension by offering Austria generous terms and making real concessions to Russian territorial ambition? What if he had either pulled out of Spain altogether or concentrated overwhelming force against Wellington? Could he have secured peace with Britain? Would an end to the cycle of recruitment and economic extortion have prevented the puppet states to the south and east from eventually turning against French hegemony?

The answer to those questions is probably no. It was too late for the architect of Campo Formio to make a friend of Austria without giving up Italy, and long-term friendship with Russia was probably conditional on withdrawal from Poland and the Balkans. It is unlikely that military action on any scale could have completely quashed the Spanish rebellion, and by 1809 any retreat from Spain was likely to be interpreted in London as an invitation to advance. Any real hope of a negotiated peace with Britain had passed with the end of the Grenville administration in 1807, and the need to reduce French power in Europe had since become both political and commercial orthodoxy in London, sustained by clear signs that both the Continental System and Napoleon's Russian alliance were breaking down. As for the integrity of the French Empire, it had only ever been maintained by conquest, and even the most benevolent regional administrations were unable to inspire more than token loyalty from local populations.

In any case it had been a willingness to gamble for the highest possible stakes, rather than measured caution, that had propelled Napoleon to the heights he reached by 1809, and he was self-consciously sanguine about the risks attached to his modus operandi. Like a medieval warlord, he focused his long-term ambitions on dynastic rather than personal glory, and was thus freed to react with unbridled aggression to opportunity and danger alike.

Napoleon's dynastic ambitions, hitherto focused on the elevation of his relatives to various vacant thrones, were concentrated on the twin grails of marriage into one of Europe's established ruling families and production of a male heir. He was already married, but the notoriously libidinous Empress **Joséphine** was both ageing and infertile. Having confirmed his own procreative capacity by impregnating his Polish lover, **Maria Walewska**, Napoleon began negotiations with both the Russian and Austrian courts in 1810.

Napoleon divorced Joséphine in late 1809, and married Austrian princess **Marie-Louise** the following March. The union not only produced the coveted heir a year later, but outraged the Russian court and indicated the direction in which Napoleon's ambitions were moving. Certain that French and Russian expansionism must eventually clash, he had always intended to force the tsar into a less balanced alliance at some stage, and though he was careful to appease Russia by the gift of Bessarabia at Schönbrunn, the process of preparation for a new war was under way by late 1810.

For some time immediately after the consecutive campaigns in Spain and Germany, an exhausted French Empire was incapable of aggression on such a large scale. Along with Napoleon's ongoing refusal to recognize the need for another all-out effort west of the Pyrenees, this relative weakness helped Anglo-Iberian forces gradually to take the initiative in Spain during 1809–11.

Returning to the theatre after Moore's death, Wellesley had cleared Soult from **Oporto** and the rest of Portugal by the summer of 1809, and won a defensive victory across the frontier at **Talavera** in July before retiring in good order to await the inevitable French counter-offensive. It came in 1810, when Masséna led a force into the Portuguese heartlands around Lisbon, only to discover that the newly titled Lord Wellington's prepared defences at **Torres Vedras** were virtually impregnable. Masséna ended the year slinking back towards the frontier with his starving troops, and neither Napoleon's subsequent wrath nor regular beatings handed out to scattered Spanish forces could prevent Wellington from taking the offensive in 1811.

Wellington was seldom a reckless general. His 1811 campaign on the Portuguese frontier against the larger frontline forces of Soult and Masséna (who was soon replaced by **Marmont**, another of the original **Marshalate**) was a model of realistic restraint. Determined not to repeat the errors of Moore, he spent the year avoiding defeat while trying to seize control of **fortresses** at **Badajoz** and **Ciudad Rodrigo** that would secure the rear of any further advance. Certain that he could not be dislodged from Portugal, he retreated across the border at the end of the year, prepared to wait for more favourable circumstances in 1812.

By the start of that earthshaking year, Napoleon had bigger things on his mind than a frontier skirmish in the far west. Oblivious to the doubts of some of his most trusted advisers, he was almost ready for war against Russia. Since August 1811, when the emperor's furious denunciation of Alexander during a speech in Paris had made the breakdown of their friendship both public and final, French imperial propaganda, diplomacy, requisition and recruitment had been geared towards the stupendous enterprise of invading western Russia from Poland.

While fending off the threat of assassination that faced any tsar with an unsuccessful foreign policy, Alexander had done his best to maintain peace with Napoleon, whose armies were after all supposed to be invincible. By spring 1812 he had given up hope, and was clearing his lines for military action by negotiating peace on his other frontiers. Expansionist **Russo-Turkish** and **Russo-Swedish** wars, in progress since 1806 and 1809 respectively, were quickly brought to negotiated ends, and talks opened with Britain that were the seed of a new **Sixth Coalition** against France.

During the night of 23 June 1812, the first of more than half a million invading troops crossed the Vistula from Poland into Russia. Napoleon had deployed his unwieldy, multinational force – which included contingents from every French satellite and ally – in three vast columns. They faced two frontline Russian armies, under **Barclay de Tolly** and **Bagration**, and Napoleon planned to bring one or the other to decisive battle at the first opportunity. Widely separated at first, the Russian armies retreated east on converging paths, and Napoleon followed. Unable to coordinate the sort of pincer manoeuvre that had triumphed so often with smaller armies in Italy and Germany, he repeatedly failed to trap the Russians through July and August, but kept on upping the stakes by leading his army deeper into the barren wilderness towards Moscow.

At the other end of Europe, French armies were also marching east by the summer of 1812, but in retreat from western Spain. Wellington had begun the year with a surprise winter attack to take Ciudad Rodrigo, and then moved south to secure Badajoz in the spring, before thrusting into central Spain. His victory over Marmont at **Salamanca** in July, the most impressive allied success in the peninsula to date, prompted French withdrawal from **Cadiz** and south-western Spain, and triggered King Joseph's second flight from Madrid.

Both Wellington and Napoleon had advanced into trouble, albeit on different scales and for different reasons. Wellington had no difficulty bringing French forces to a fight. Once he had made his only serious mistake of the campaign, and advanced to the vital road junction at **Burgos** without the strength to take it quickly, his opponents concentrated powerfully enough to force a long and arduous retreat to the frontier. The autumn withdrawal cost Wellington's small Anglo-Portuguese army several thousand losses, but it survived as a coherent force and was quickly replenished to resume the offensive in 1813.

The catastrophe that befell Napoleon's invasion of **Russia** was altogether more terminal. By early September he had pursued his quarry within range of Moscow, and seized the important city of **Smolensk**, but was becoming desperate for the battle that would force Alexander into peace. He got his confrontation when, after passing under the command of the veteran Kutuzov, the combined Russian armies eventually turned to fight at **Borodino**, but the ghastly, tactically barren battle of attrition that followed achieved little for either side. The Russians were forced to quit the battlefield and resumed their retreat, but the tsar still refused to countenance peace talks, and Napoleon's subsequent advance to **Moscow** offered little succour to about 100,000 French troops in desperate need of food and shelter.

The departing citizens of Moscow destroyed three-quarters of its buildings with fires, and left precious little behind by way of supplies. As Napoleon waited in vain for the tsar to see sense, his army slowly starved in a wasteland that was becoming more dangerous as winter snows approached. When he finally ordered its withdrawal west on 19 October, hastened by a surprise **Cossack** strike against his forward units at **Vinkovo**, it was an acknowledgment of total failure. He was aware that the long journey back to Poland meant death and despair to most of his men – and to the sprawling, booty-laden **baggage train** that accompanied them – but he also knew that getting home as quickly as possible represented his only chance of political survival.

The war years were littered with epic withdrawals in appalling conditions, but the horrors of the British trek across the ice to escape Flanders in 1795, Suvorov's odyssey through the Swiss Alps in 1799 or Moore's last march to Corunna pale beside the Grande Armée's suffering during its well-documented retreat from Moscow. Most of its number died of exposure, although a few were claimed by half-hearted Russian pursuers, and fewer than 30,000 effectives reached safety west of the **Beresina** in late November. Though flank forces fared rather better, Napoleon's military position and reputation were in tatters by the time he left the front for Paris in early December.

The turmoil that greeted the emperor in his capital, where rumours of his death had already generated a bizarre attempt by **Malet** to overthrow the regime, mirrored seismic reactions all over Europe to the Grande Armée's demise. Suddenly no longer the invincible warlord, his few troops frantically regrouping in Germany while Russian reinforcements pushed west of the Niemen, Napoleon threw himself into the task of recruiting yet another army as the diplomatic structure of his empire began crumbling away.

To nobody's surprise, Prussia was the first French ally to change sides. Despite their reluctant commitment of troops to Napoleon's invasion force in 1812, Prussia's ruling élites still seethed at the humiliations of 1805–7. Its army had been reformed to promote and exploit a burgeoning nationalism born of loathing for French control, and took the lead in throwing it off at the end of 1812, when General **Yorck**'s corps with the Grande Armée negotiated a separate neutrality agreement with Russian forces at **Tauroggen**. Yorck's action ignited a powder keg of anti-French feeling all over Germany, and only Frederick William's ingrained fear of Napoleon kept Prussia out of the Sixth Coalition until mid-February, by which time Russian forces were nearing Berlin. Prussian forces then joined their allies in an advance against new French positions west of the Elbe, and the rest of Europe got ready to back the winners.

That he was able to put a large army in the field for the campaign in **Germany** of 1813 testifies to Napoleon's extraordinary administrative talents. That he came close to winning it with a force of young conscripts, many of them in their mid-teens, is a measure of his command skills and strength of personality. Though all but shorn of experienced officers and NCOs, his troops inflicted tactical defeats on smaller allied forces at **Lützen** and **Bautzen** during the spring, and for a time the Sixth Coalition looked like going the way of its predecessors.

But though these early setbacks exposed the pessimism still affecting Coalition field commanders, and sparked furious strategic arguments among allied leaders, French armies were simply too weak to exploit their successes. They tried, but simultaneous drives north towards Berlin and east to the **Katzbach** soon became bogged down, so that both sides were grateful for a temporary **armistice** agreed in early June.

Recuperation did the Coalition more good than Napoleon. When fighting resumed in mid-August, the allies had been joined by Sweden and Austria, giving them a greatly increased numerical advantage, and were armed with the **Trachenberg Plan**, an agreement to direct offensive efforts only against Napoleon's detached subordinates in Germany. Meanwhile French armies had been replenished by more fresh recruits, but remained weak at the top, Russia having claimed many of the best commanders and reduced others, such as **Ney**, to shadows of their former selves.

Faced by multinational armies menacing his positions in Saxony from the north, east and south-east, Napoleon won another impressive victory to thwart Austrian commander **Schwarzenberg**'s attack on **Dresden** in late August, but it was rendered cosmetic by the failures of subordinates. Sticking to their plan, allied armies won vital victories over outlying French forces under **Oudinot**, Ney, **Vandamme** and Macdonald, compelling Napoleon to pull all his remaining strength together for a last stand at **Leipzig** in mid-October. Defeat over three days at Leipzig, in what became known as the 'Battle of the Nations', left him with no option but to fall back west of the Rhine, though garrison forces still occupied **Hamburg**, Dresden and a number of other important fortresses.

Leipzig put an end to French control in Germany. Bavaria, one of the main beneficiaries of alliance with Napoleon, had changed sides before the battle, and was joined in its aftermath by **Baden**, **Württemburg** and a host of smaller German states. By November only Saxony remained loyal, and only because French forces still occupied its capital.

By the end of the year French control in Italy was also under imminent threat. Murat, given the occupied kingdom of Naples when Joseph Bonaparte had moved to Spain in 1808, was steeling himself to betray his brother-in-law and march to support an Austrian invasion of northern Italy. French north Italian possessions, unified as the Kingdom of **Italy** since 1805, were among the more stable imperial outposts, largely thanks to the benign governance of Napoleon's viceroy and stepson, Eugène de **Beauharnais**. Beauharnais had managed to raise a fresh Italian army since the Russian campaign, and chose to mount a defence from strong positions in Italy rather than retreat into southern France.

French troops in Spain had little choice but to seek sanctuary inside the frontier. Wellington's renewed offensive from the Portuguese frontier in spring 1813 had been an unalloyed triumph, outflanking French forces before defeating King Joseph and Marshal Jourdan at **Vitoria** in June, a success that had effectively liberated Spain. After holding off a counter-offensive by new C-in-C Soult at **Sorauren**, Wellington had carried the fight into the Pyrenees during the autumn, and by the end of the year he was across the border.

With hindsight, the total defeat of Napoleon in 1814 seems inevitable. Overwhelmingly powerful armies were threatening every frontier, his political supporters in Paris were openly defecting in droves, and the French economy lay in ruins after a final spasm of patriotic endeavour had raised a small army for national defence. Yet contemporary Europe was conditioned to expect miracles from Napoleon, and the acrimonious collapse of coalitions against him. Every coalition from 1791 to 1809 had fallen apart as much through its own internal tensions as French force of arms, and there seemed a good chance that the strategically diverse sixth version would do the same in 1814.

Fundamental differences of aim and approach informed the main Coalition allies: Alexander was bent on occupying Paris by way of revenge, yet wary of wasting Russian lives in pursuit of German strategic aims; Austrian emperor Francis had a daughter in the French court, was desperate not to lose another war, and generally leaned towards a negotiated peace in return for Italy; Prussian king Frederick William, who accompanied the two allied emperors on campaign through 1813–14, did whatever Alexander did, but with an eye on the future of northern Germany and a characteristic lack of fire (in contrast to his C-in-C, **Blücher**).

The cement that held the three monarchies together through countless strategic and personal disputes during 1813–14 was provided by Britain. More interested in restoring the profits of lasting peace than in any territorial ambitions, and barely distracted by half-hearted involvement in an **Anglo-American War** triggered by its blockade policies, the British government sought unity above all. Foreign minister **Castlereagh**'s judicious use of diplomacy and subsidy through a series of critical allied summits deserves much of the credit for the Coalition's relatively firm grasp of its own destiny during 1814.

Though in the grip of rapid physical deterioration and mental instability, the latter characterized by extremes of pessimistic lethargy and optimistic fantasy, Napoleon managed to run rings round the multi-pronged allied invasion of western **France** for several weeks. Rushing his compact little army along internal lines, he struck lightning blows at Schwarzenberg and Blücher in turn, performing very much like his old self during a whirlwind '**Six Days Campaign**' in February that temporarily halted the allied advance. But the odds against him were lengthening and pressure for royal restoration was mounting in Paris, so that the single major defeat he suffered, at **Laon** in March, was enough to shatter his army's fragile resistance.

Caught out of position during a bold sortie towards the eastern frontier, he was unable to prevent the two main allied armies from converging on Paris, and after a last defence by the few troops holding the suburbs at **Montmartre** the city fell at the end of March. Napoleon still had some 60,000 troops at his disposal outside the capital, and was planning to fight on to the end, but Ney led surviving marshals in persuading him into **abdication** in early April.

News of his resignation, and the imminent royal restoration in Paris, ended fighting on other European fronts. In a brief **Italian** campaign, Beauharnais had checked an Austrian advance, and Murat had gone to great lengths to avoid any actual fighting, so that the viceroy was able to negotiate a settlement at **Schiarino-Rizzino** that offered him a chance, illusory as it turned out, of retaining his offices in peacetime.

By now thoroughly established as Britain's greatest living soldier, the ever-circumspect Wellington had sent home most of his vengeful Spanish Army allies before advancing into south-western France in the new year. By early April Soult's dwindling army had been driven into its final enclaves at **Toulouse** and **Bayonne**. Soult, destined for a long and honoured career in the service of successive post-Napoleonic governments, surrendered gracefully enough on confirmation of his master's downfall, but the besieged garrison at Bayonne ended the War of the Sixth Coalition with a last, futile sortie against surprised British forces some days later.

With peace throughout Europe secured for the first time in more than a decade, the Coalition allies remained in the French capital to supervise the restoration of King **Louis XVIII** and formalize the return of France to its 1792 frontiers by the Treaty of **Paris**. As the heads of Europe's great powers moved on to the Congress of **Vienna**, there to unmake the world created since the French Revolution, an exhausted continent settled down to reconstruction on the assumption that it had seen the last of the great Corsican adventurer.

It was a view held with less certainty inside France. The greed and blind reaction of the king's returning entourage, coupled with inevitable economic problems, made the restoration's mass popularity a fleeting thing. Napoleon's exile on the nearby island of **Elba** was punctuated by frequent calls from politicians and soldiers, who kept him in touch with mounting nostalgia for his regime throughout France. Even Talleyrand, who had personally welcomed allied armies into Paris, became convinced that a restrained emperor was more likely to rebuild France than the inert King Louis.

And so, while Castlereagh, Wellington, **Metternich** and a host of other advisers to kings and emperors discussed indemnities and the future of Poland, Napoleon and his small personal guard slipped back into France in March 1815. It was touch and go at first, but once the emperor had been welcomed into Grenoble his passage to Paris was a triumphant procession, and his approach brought old comrades flocking to the cause. Ney's emotional betrayal of the crown helped induce the king's flight to Belgium, and the support of troops disgruntled by months of reduced status and unemployment ensured Napoleon's return to power on arrival in the capital.

Napoleon in 1815 was not the all-powerful dictator of 1804. A significant number of his former lieutenants had remained loyal to the king, while his acceptance by the Paris Assembly and Senate was distinctly lukewarm, and conditional on his success in maintaining stability. The need to appease political opinion in Paris partly inspired his immediate attempts to make peace with the former Coalition allies, but the man who had contemptuously refused various relatively generous offers of terms in early 1814 does not seem to have doubted the need to fight in 1815, and his overtures were also a means of gaining time for mobilization.

Either way, the grandees at Vienna were having none of it. By late March they had formed themselves into a powerful **Seventh Coalition**, and were putting together a fresh set of joint invasion plans. Their aggression freed Napoleon from the stigma of having started the war, and French mobilization caught the allies in the familiar position of having only one of their invasion forces in the field at the start of a campaign. Two armies – a multinational force under Wellington, and a Prussian contingent under Blücher – were formed up in Flanders by the early summer, and though they outnumbered Napoleon's new army in combination, he planned to advance between them and defeat them in detail.

The campaign that ended the **Hundred Days** of Napoleon's return opened with all the hallmarks of one of his classic victories. Advancing across the Sambre into Belgium, the French army caught the two allied forces in a state of scattered confusion, and defeated

Blücher's typically rash advance at **Ligny**. Although Ney's French left wing was unable to seize the vital junction linking allied forces at **Quatre Bras**, Wellington's subsequent withdrawal from the position seemed to complete their separation. If Napoleon could confront and beat Wellington, the war would be won.

There the resemblance to 1805–6 ended. The French Army of 1815 was a fragile thing, commanded by an emperor deep in decline. Fatigued, lethargic and overconfident to the point of laziness, he left ill-chosen subordinates to take critical decisions without clear orders, and above all underestimated his opponents. In Wellington he faced an expert in the arts of defensive warfare, who withdrew to well-chosen positions and was a match for Napoleon's sledge-hammer tactics when the French attack came. Prussian commander Blücher was a man so dedicated to offensive warfare that defeat at Ligny sent him, not into retreat as Napoleon assumed, but hastening to Wellington's side at **Waterloo**, where the French army was comprehensively defeated after a hard day's fight on 18 June.

The crowning victory did not destroy French military capability – more than 100,000 men could still be raised to defend Paris – but it broke the emperor's political hold in the capital, and seems to have quenched his spirit. Fittingly enough, it was the arch-plotter **Fouché** who led calls for Napoleon's second abdication four days after the battle, and it was the same man who offered the ex-emperor a ship at Rochefort, where he hastened in the hope of flight to America. It was a false hope. Royal Navy forces had already occupied the port, and Napoleon could only give himself up, after which he was kept on board warships until his final dispatch to St Helena a few weeks later.

The wars were now emphatically ended. King 'Louis the Inevitable' came home once more, and royalist reaction had its day in France. Coalition delegates resumed their debates in Vienna, and restored most of the Italian and larger German monarchies to something approaching their prewar condition, although they fudged the perennially insoluble problem of defining Poland and inflicted undue punishment on Saxony's unfortunate king. Russia, Austria and Prussia returned to the business of extending their land empires, armed against radical mass politics by a loose **Holy Alliance** of like-minded autocrats, and Britain resumed its conglomeration of wealth, trade and colonies. Inspired by Castlereagh and Metternich to work self-consciously towards a lasting peace, the delegates at Vienna quickly found that stability was impossible without a revived France to anchor the future of western Europe, and Talleyrand's skilful insinuations between the lines dividing other states quickly re-established French rights to a voice among the great powers.

The dynastic creations of the Napoleonic era were largely erased. Westphalia, the Kingdom of Italy and all the other republics or monarchies established since 1789 disappeared, and most were returned to more or less liberalized versions of their former regimes. Most of the Bonapartist monarchs were quietly pensioned off with money and small estates, but Murat met his death at the hands of vengeful Calabrians after the failure of his farcical 'War of **Italian Independence**' in 1815. Of Napoleon's two empresses, Joséphine had died in 1814, and Marie-Louise returned to Austria. Napoleon himself died of stomach cancer on St Helena in 1821, after years spent distorting the past for the ears of the few who were listening. The depth of the peace that settled over the great powers after 1815 was such that the event caused barely a ripple in Europe.

Europe was to remain untroubled by major wars until the 1850s. The stability created by the Vienna congress – and its four successors to 1823 – enabled a golden age of prosperity for the great powers, which developed a cultural, political and economic grip over the wider world that was to shape twentieth-century history. The same decades could hardly, however, be called years of peace. Mass politics, civil rights, nationalism and revolution had arrived to stay, heralding an age of wars within states that no concert of governments could prevent.

Within a few years of 1815, radical liberal or nationalist movements were engaged in armed struggles for political liberties against restored regimes in Spain, Italy, the Habsburg Empire and across the Ottoman world. In Russia and a gradually unifying Germany, the lessons of the 1790s were absorbed by new generations as weapons against resurgent autocracy. In France, the Bourbon restoration lasted only fifteen years before the regime was overthrown by a more populist monarchy. Even in Britain, where freedom from tyranny was taken for granted by much of the population, only the government's dazzling wealth enabled it to soothe the world's most advanced workforce before unrest turned to full-scale revolt.

The ruling élites of the nineteenth century found no means to suppress or absorb these new forces at work in the post-Napoleonic world, and went to their destruction in the early twentieth still struggling to keep the lid on an upsurge of popular aspirations. In this sense, as a blueprint for future social change, the work of the French Revolution, republic and empire defied all Europe's attempts at deconstruction.

Perspectives

A short, essentially military, narrative inevitably tells a somewhat one-dimensional story. More than just an elaborate shake-up and redefinition of Europe's great power structure, the wars of 1792–1815 were also the first genuinely national struggles in modern history and the first truly global wars.

Like the wars of the present, and in stark contrast to the mannered family squabbles of the dynastic Middle Ages, the Revolutionary and Napoleonic Wars were fought by entire peoples. Their sheer scale forced major belligerents to bring a degree of rationalization and centralization to the conduct of warfare that warped cultural, political and economic development at an unprecedented pace.

Armed forces of ever-increasing size could not have been maintained or equipped for long on the slender yields from ancient feudal obligations. Following from the cataclysmic example of the French Revolution, the wars saw the introduction of new legal and governmental systems that provided the individual incentives necessary to promote increased state output, and gave the splintered, supply-inefficient world of feudal Europe a determined shove into oblivion.

Many of these were by-products of French conquest. Successive republican constitutions of the 1791–1804 period spawned a bumper crop of imitations, and the French Empire imposed variations on its constitution (and the legal **Code Napoléon**) wherever its writ ran. Though many of the new systems introduced in Switzerland, Italy, Germany, Poland, the Netherlands, Illyria, the Ionian Islands and parts of Spain were short-lived, and German constitutions in particular often left great swathes of feudal privilege intact, postwar reaction would never succeed in squeezing the genie of civil rights back into the bottle.

Wartime opposition to French expansion or control also wrought permanent social change. It was a powerful stimulus to national self-awareness in Italy and Germany, which would both complete the process of unification within a few decades of 1815, and triggered a resurgence of militant patriotism in Prussia that would have momentous consequences for the twentieth century. In backward and conservative Spain, the long rebellion against French occupation gave emerging liberal politics a chance to find a national voice, and fostered energetic opposition to a reactionary postwar monarchy.

Although the ruthless centralism of postwar chancellor Metternich was to keep the multi-ethnic Habsburg Empire together in some style through the nineteenth century, its almost constant need for money and troops to fight France after 1792, along with regular defeats and loss of territory, made it particularly vulnerable to the new ideologies of self-determination. Wartime Vienna faced separatist stirrings among its ethnic Poles, Czechs and other Slavs, while the feudal élites that held local power in the Kingdom of Hungary demanded an increased share in imperial decision-making as the price of providing wartime resources, and would maintain an unstinting campaign of self-interest disguised as nationalist ideology into the twentieth century.

Even those nations apparently immune to rapid change were subject to subtle but significant wartime social shifts. In Russia, where a massive manpower reservoir made socio-economic reorganization almost unnecessary, the wars completed the nation's entry into the mainstream of European affairs. We cannot know whether the western contagion of radical politics was responsible for a dramatic upsurge in provincial rebellion during the 1790s, but it did take root among a dissatisfied intelligentsia, spawning a revolutionary tradition that would eventually lay low the Romanov dynasty.

In mainland Britain, so rich that everyday life seemed almost untouched by the wars, the stealthy acceleration of land enclosure and industrialization had greatly enlarged the landless urban underclass by 1815, and peace abroad heralded decades of internal strife.

Neither Britain's wealth nor its wartime political calm extended to its oldest, nearest and most oppressed colony. Riven by religious, economic and political divisions, Ireland was considered ripe for rebellion or civil war even before radical ideology and potential French invasion were added to the brew. The failed **Irish Rebellion** of 1798 was the climax to years of mounting turmoil, and the Act of **Union** that absorbed Ireland into Great Britain from 1800 was in part a product of the French wars.

The wars of 1792–1815 were world wars in all but name, and their direct effects loom large in the background of modern global geopolitics. They formed an important stage in the centuries-old struggle to define stable frontiers between Islam and Christendom, establishing an Anglo-French presence in Egypt and the eastern Mediterranean that was still causing trouble in the 1950s. The strain of fighting European invasion also reduced the multiracial Ottoman Empire's capacity to fight a rising tide of separatism in its distant provinces, and it spent the remaining hundred years of its existence on the brink of internal collapse, kept in being largely because predatory European empires were too mutually paranoid to let it die.

Further afield, the young republic of the United States was forced to make new choices as its dedication to trade came into conflict with its ideological refusal to indulge in international warfare. Though the federal government banned all overseas commerce for a time, trade won the argument, bringing formation of the **US Navy** in 1794, naval wars with France and the **Barbary** pirates at the turn of the century, and ultimately a full-scale naval and frontier conflict with British Empire in 1812. Almost meaningless in military terms, and eventually abandoned as a draw at the end of 1814, the Anglo-American War confirmed US willingness to fight for the right to commercial expansion, and that the nation's pioneers would travel in ships as well as covered wagons.

An eye for trading opportunities characterized the contemporary US, and none was more spectacular than Napoleon's offer, accepted with alacrity, to sell the vast former Spanish territory of **Louisiana** in 1803. The purchase more than doubled the size of the United States at a stroke, and was perhaps the most significant territorial exchange of the era, ensuring that the expanding republic, rather than France, Spain or Britain, would become the most important land power in North America.

Its energetic search for new markets also encouraged US support for national independence movements in **South America**, which burst into life after Napoleon had overthrown the monarchs of Spain and Portugal. The continent's economic development had long been rigidly geared to the provision of cheap commodities for

Europe, but its colonial administration was by now in the hands of men whose connections with imperial headquarters were little more than nominal. The presence of the Portuguese royal family after 1807 delayed Brazil's breakaway for a time, but former Spanish colonies from Mexico to Peru erupted into wars of independence that immortalized Simón **Bolívar** and created many of the region's modern states. Within a few years of 1815, Washington would stake claim to its own special interests in the region, the first step towards establishing US economic dominance in place of European.

The wars saw the British establish themselves as the dominant power in the Caribbean, completing a process of island accumulation begun during the Seven Years War, but not even the Royal Navy possessed the resources, or indeed the inclination, to take control of all the many French, Spanish and Dutch colonies in the West Indies. On one major island, the divided Franco-Spanish colony of Santo Domingo/Hispaniola, the vacuum left by European distraction was filled by the first glimpse of a distant, post-imperial future. Apprised of their love for civil liberty by his French masters in the 1790s, native leader Toussaint **L'Ouverture** and his successors eventually fought off all-comers to enter the nineteenth century as the independent republic of Haiti.

Much of Africa remained unexplored, but the French revolutionary government's absolute rejection of slavery was an important staging post on the way to its formal abolition in other European states, which eventually forced colonial administrations to find other uses for coastal West Africa. In the south, the British opened a long and tragic chapter in regional history by seizing the Cape Colony from the Dutch, and the wartime efforts of both French and British forces to pacify turbulent tribal elements south of Egypt opened the way for future colonial penetration of sub-Saharan East Africa.

East of what would one day be the Suez Canal (a project first mooted by Napoleon's invading army of scholars and engineers in 1798), the British did an even more thorough job of excluding their European rivals from the spoils of trade and colonialism. The Dutch held a considerable lead in the Far East before the wars, but their often draconian hold over the Pacific and Indian Ocean spice islands had been all but eliminated by 1810. French and Dutch strategists also entertained realistic hopes of securing a major share in the increasing flow of wealth from India, until the colonial campaigns of the early Revolutionary Wars greatly reduced their territorial interests along its southern coasts. By 1805, a series of campaigns against native opponents by British viceroy **Wellesley** (Wellington's brother) had transformed the East India Company's sprawling leaseholds into the local superpower that would become the Raj.

From a purely economic perspective, the wars had only one winner. Apart from extending and securing its empire, Britain achieved an almost monopolistic control over contemporary means of global communication. The Royal Navy can be said to have failed in its vaunted role as a war-winning weapon, and its defeat of all possible rivals only gradually assisted the overthrow of Napoleon's continental empire, but by 1815 it had become clear that an unchallenged right to make use of the sea lanes was going to prove more valuable than any number of territorial acquisitions. Supremely equipped to exploit its priceless prize, industrial Britain enjoyed a massive economic lead over the rest of the world by the end of the wars, and used the decades of peace to extend its wealth and power, assuming the role of world arbiter and policeman.

All history is interconnected, and without context most of it is fable. The Napoleonic Wars are by no means the only past events implicated in the formation of modern geopolitical landscapes, but they were an important crucible, consigning many redundant structures to rapid meltdown, and giving solid, permanent form to new concepts. In that respect they display clear links with the present, but any reader evaluating the achievements and failures of the Napoleonic Wars by the standards of 1914–18, let alone those of 1939–45, is missing a point of context central to understanding both their scale and the behaviour of participants.

Our experience of modern life, or received images of Flanders and Okinawa, offer little insight into just how difficult it was to wage world war during the Enlightenment. The horse and the wind were the main providers of locomotive power, medicine was barely emerging from dependence on superstition and leeches, and long-range communication had just discovered the benefits of **semaphore**, though it could still take months for messages to travel overseas.

The business of raising and equipping armies of half a million men, or sending fleets of battleships on tropical missions, involved an enormous amount of painstaking hard work at a time when most government bureaucracies were either too small or too inefficient to manage a modern hospital. All the effort and expense was then likely to be undermined by any number of natural phenomena that were still beyond humanity's power to dominate: more wartime naval vessels were wrecked by the elements than by any kind of hostile action; and the vast majority of casualties on land or sea fell victim to the twin terrors of disease and exposure.

If most ordinary people were likely to find only discomfort and death in the practice of warfare, and their leaders knew that the best-planned strategic initiative amounted to a hugely expensive lottery ticket, what motives kept the business of state aggression afloat? The only convincing answer lies in the differences between human expectations now and then.

Life for most people in eighteenth-century Europe was nasty, brutish and short by modern standards. Even those at the most comfortable social levels were liable to be struck down at any time by death in any one of myriad, often mysterious, guises. Saving oneself for a comfortable retirement was not therefore the sensible option it may appear today, and people tended to pin any hopes for the future on their successors. Broadly speaking, since death was likely with or without glory, they flung themselves at any opportunity, however remote, to win renown or betterment for their children.

This apparently reckless immediacy was applied as much to financial as to military speculation, providing stimulus for the full flowering of entrepreneurial capitalism, and was also reflected in contemporary standards of personal behaviour. To modern minds, the Enlightenment appears an age of bawdy indiscipline, and we can only marvel that military and civil societies equipped with so few mechanisms for exerting restraint managed any kind of deliberate strategic activity. There were a few famous exceptions, like Pitt, whose public conduct looked forward to the austere self-righteousness of the Victorians, but on the whole the wars were waged with a passion and concern for personal gratification that were far removed from modern martial images of dutiful self-sacrifice.

On the most practical and basic level, it was extremely difficult to control large groups of people, be they civilians bent on affray or soldiers determined to desert, loot or pillage. Except in a few élite units, and to some extent in the better-run naval services, military rank and file were not spoiled for alternative career choices, and Wellington's celebrated assessment of them as the 'scum of the earth' was hardly controversial. Army commanders on all sides and of all temperaments routinely abandoned any pretence at preventing troops from ravaging captured towns, and in many forces they risked murder in attempting to halt unauthorized retreats. Even the Royal Navy – easily the most disciplined and efficient naval force in the world – suffered more than a thousand recorded mutinies during the war years.

Not that élite status guaranteed superior demeanour. At the very top, the war years were a vintage period for mad or bad monarchs. A case can be made for portraying Napoleon as a dangerous megalomaniac, and all contemporary Bourbons as intellectually retarded, while Paul I was only the most obviously certifiable among a series of eccentric Romanovs, and the hereditary rulers of the Scandinavian kingdoms were apparently doomed to madness. The British throne passed from a senile madman to an obese, self-obsessed Prince Regent, and though Prussian king Frederick William III was essentially normal, he was one of history's most patently spineless figures. The long reign of Habsburg emperor Francis, a masterpiece of mediocrity, was ultimately made to look rather successful by the shambling misfits in power elsewhere.

The senior servants of kings and emperors operated on a level of decorum, or lack of it, that would shock even the most assiduous modern tabloid reader. Everyday business in the British House of Commons was lubricated by copious quantities of champagne, and was conducted by a wealthy coterie of part-time politicians, most of them full-time playboys and laughable dandies by modern standards. The war years encompassed the assassination of prime minister Perceval in the lobby of the Commons, a notorious duel between foreign minister Castlereagh and war minister Canning, along with several examples of ministers hardly ever seen at their posts, yet British political debate was relatively sober. All over Europe, and in the United States, national and regional government was characterized by behaviour that was often petty, violent, licentious, corrupt, incompetent or just plain lazy.

The military picture was much the same. Most of the allied generals being briefed on the eve of the Battle of Austerlitz were too drunk to speak, and alcohol abuse was a serious problem at the highest level in every armed force. Looting, fraud or corruption on the part of commanding generals was viewed as normal, and only merited exposure if either passion or political necessity called for an officer's downfall. Some French generals, Masséna and Vandamme for example, earned reputations as spectacularly successful looters, and the downside of the French Army opening up its highest offices to talented men from all backgrounds was the frequency with which its senior figures betrayed their humble roots in public.

Even the most heated arguments between modern leaders, whether civil or military, usually amount to no more than verbal exchanges, but rows between Enlightenment leaders were rather more exciting. Napoleon's subordinates frequently came to blows or drawn swords in the middle of vital campaigns, and the Marshalate positively bristled with lifelong personal vendettas. Prussian field marshal Blücher had once been cashiered from the army as violent and dangerous, while Nelson may have been the greatest fighting seaman that ever lived, but was also petulant, prone to tears and one of the most vainglorious heroes of an egomaniac era. As in the political field there were exceptions, and Wellington stands out, along with one or two staff officers in most major armies, as belonging to a more professional future.

The more one looks at the age of Revolutionary and Napoleonic warfare, whether in detail or overview, the more one is struck by its histrionic nature. It is as if Europeans were self-consciously living through the destruction of an old, familiar world. Casting off the shrouds of superstition and adjusting their horizons to encompass the whole planet, they seem dead set on extracting every drop of melodrama from the plunge into what might be an abyss or a golden future. We know what became of their last hurrah. It turned their world into ours. History cannot say whether Pitt, Metternich or Talleyrand would have approved.

THE DICTIONARY

A

Abdication of Napoleon (1814)

French emperor **Napoleon** Bonaparte's voluntary withdrawal from power, signed on 6 April 1814 after the campaign for **France** had destroyed the last remnants of his armies and administration. En route for the capital on 31 March, when news reached him of **Marmont's** surrender at **Montmartre**, Napoleon refused to accept total defeat. Returning south to Fontainebleau, and naming Orléans as his new centre of government, he called up every French unit for a resumption of hostilities.

By 3 April Napoleon had mustered 60,000 troops in the area, and planned to march on Paris, but **Ney** led senior commanders in refusing to fight on. News that Marmont had deserted to the allies finally convinced him that he could no longer remain in power. On 4 April he sent Ney, **Macdonald** and **Caulaincourt** to Paris with an offer of abdication, conditional on the establishment of a regency for his son, but with French resistance melting away on all fronts, allied leaders demanded unconditional abdication.

Napoleon drafted a document renouncing all claims to power for himself and his heirs on 6 April. While negotiations proceeded towards a formal agreement, he became increasingly depressed at Fontainebleau, and used a bag of poison worn around his neck to attempt suicide on 12 April. The poison had weakened with age, and he survived to become Emperor of **Elba** by the Treaty of **Fontainebleau** on 16 April.

Abensberg, Battle of

French attack against Austrian forces in the Danube sector during the opening phase of the War of the **Fifth Coalition**. Launched on 20 April 1809, it was an attempt to wrest the initiative in the theatre from the Austrian army of Archduke **Charles**. A minor French victory at **Tengen** on 18 April had convinced local commanders that the whole of the Austrian northern wing was in flight, and on the strength of their reports **Napoleon** reorganized his strike forces for an attack to cut off its retreat.

Two of **Davout's** divisions were seconded to a new provisional corps led by **Lannes**, just arrived from Spain, that would operate on the left of a general advance east on Abensberg. Lefebvre's three **Bavarian** divisions, reinforced by **Vandamme's** 12,000 **Württemberg** troops, would form the centre of the advance, and **Oudinot** would lead two divisions on the right. Once the Austrian centre had been pierced, Davout and **Masséna** would lead pincers cutting the flanks to the north and south respectively.

The attack began well on 20 April, crashing through the thin Austrian cordon around Abensberg during the morning, and inflicting heavy losses on **Hiller's** corps further south. By late afternoon Napoleon was convinced that the final destruction of Austrian forces had become a formality, but though the Austrian armies lost about 10,000 men and 30 guns during the day, his optimism was the product of a series of illusions. The true strength of forces facing Davout in the north, and the significance of French failures on the flanks at **Ratisbon** and **Landshut**, gradually became clear to Napoleon over the next 24 hours. Realizing that most of the Austrian army was still advancing on Davout, he ordered a mass flank attack around **Eckmühl** for 22 April. *See* **Map 12**.

Abercromby, Ralph (1734–1801)

Veteran **British Army** officer, recalled from early retirement and promoted major-general in 1793, whose cautious, methodical approach to field command enjoyed mixed results in a number of important actions. After fighting in **Flanders** during 1794, he was given command of the 1796 expedition to the **West Indies** that captured **St Lucia**, Demerara and **Trinidad**, after which he held home commands until 1799. Put in charge of the opening phase of that autumn's Anglo-Russian expedition to **North Holland**, he displayed an unwillingness to take risks that helped doom the enterprise to frustration, but was nevertheless appointed **Mediterranean** C-in-C from June 1800. Reaching his command at **Minorca** too late to intervene in that year's **Italian campaign**, he withdrew from an attempt to storm **Cadiz** before following instructions to expel French forces from **Egypt**. He was killed on 21 March 1801 at **Alexandria**, a victory on which his subsequent good reputation has largely rested.

Aboukir, Battle of

The last battle fought by **Napoleon** in the **Middle East**, a crushing victory over numerically superior **Turkish Army** forces at the Egyptian coastal fortress of Aboukir in summer 1799 (*see* **Map 7**). Escorted from its base in Rhodes by the **Royal Navy**, the Turkish force had reached Egyptian waters in early June, while Napoleon was still bringing his depleted army back into **Egypt** from the abortive siege of **Acre**.

Spurning an opportunity to march on Cairo and exploit the unpopularity of French administration, Turkish commander Mustafa Pasha dallied off the coast until 15 July, when his forces occupied the peninsular fortress of Aboukir and dug in to await attack. Dividing his 20,000 troops into three groups, he deployed two lines of trenches in front of the fortress and left a smaller force inside the walls, while both shores of the peninsula were patrolled by **gunboats**.

Even given time to prepare, Napoleon could muster only 7,700 troops and 17 field guns, but does not seem to have doubted the wisdom of an offensive with such a small force. It attacked the first Turkish line at dawn on 25 July, sending divisions under **Lannes** and Destaing against fortified hills on either flank, and launching **Murat's cavalry** through the gap created in the centre. Defenders soon fled to the short second line, which held against infantry attack but was undermined by Napoleon's concentration of **artillery** against its western end. Cavalry could then 'roll up' the line, driving defenders into the sea, and Mustafa's army was effectively destroyed by the end of the day.

The fortress garrison surrendered on 2 August, by which time Ottoman losses totalled 13,000 dead (11,000 of them drowned), 2,000 missing and 5,000 prisoners, including Mustafa. During negotiations for the evacuation of prisoners with British naval commander **Smith**, Napoleon learned of the **Second Coalition's** initial successes against France, prompting his immediate departure for home and the transfer of command in Egypt to General **Kléber**. Subject to the gloss of Napoleonic **propaganda**, the victory at Aboukir was heralded in France as proof of Bonaparte's enduring genius, and was a catalyst for popular adulation on his return.

Aboukir, Second Battle of *See* Battle of **Alexandria**

Aboukir Bay, Battle of See **Nile**, Battle of the

Acre, Siege of

The climax to the French invasion of the **Middle East**, an attempt by **Napoleon's** small army to take the powerful **fortress** of Acre, almost 500km beyond the Syrian border with **Egypt** (*see* **Map 7**). Bonaparte had marched into Syria in February 1799 without a fixed plan of campaign beyond forcing the **Ottoman Empire** into a rapid peace. Suffering from fatigue, ammunition shortages and a gathering plague epidemic, some 11,000 French troops reached Acre on 17 March. Perhaps underestimating the determination of its garrison, commanded by French **émigré** Colonel **Phélypeaux**, Napoleon immediately set his forces for a **siege**.

The army's heavy **artillery**, sent from Egypt by

sea, had been captured by a **Royal Navy** squadron under Commodore **Smith**, and light guns were unable to dent the thick stone walls of the fortress. Napoleon was reduced to mounting frontal infantry assaults, all of which failed under fire from 250 fortress guns and Smith's offshore **gunboats**. An attempt to relieve Acre by Achmed Bey's Ottoman Army of Damascus was met and repulsed on 17 April (Battle of Mount Tabor), but this minor success cost perhaps 300 French casualties. In mid-May news reached Napoleon that British warships were escorting an Ottoman army from Rhodes to Egypt, and he broke off the siege on 20 May. Abandoning operations in Syria, he pulled his remaining 7,000 troops back into Egypt.

Addington, Henry (1757–1844)

Speaker of the British House of Commons from 1789, Addington became prime minister of **Great Britain** on **Pitt's** resignation in 1801. One of Pitt's less prominent supporters, his principal qualification for the post was **George III's** favour, guaranteed by his rigid opposition to all things liberal and to **Catholic emancipation**. Lacking the prestige or force of personality to impose his will over the cabinet, Addington never had a high popular reputation, and though his government was expected to deliver peace with France, it was discredited by the rapid breakdown of the **Amiens** agreement. Manifestly not a war leader, Addington gave way to Pitt after opposition factions united against him in May 1804. Created Viscount Sidmouth in 1805, he held minor offices until 1812, when he was appointed Home Secretary in the **Liverpool** government. His decade in office was distinguished by savage repression of Luddite rioters and the Peterloo Massacre of reformist protesters in 1819.

Afrancesados

Spanish term, literally 'pro-French', used originally to describe admirers of French culture or revolutionary ideology, but applied to supporters of the occupying French regime in **Spain** after 1808. Also known as Joséfinos, after King Joseph **Bonaparte**, their numbers tended to grow in proportion to French military success in the **Peninsular War** but always included representatives of the liberal intellectual classes. More than 12,000 Spanish families followed Joseph back to France in 1813, and collaborators who remained in postwar Spain faced brutal retribution if identified.

Alba des Tormes, Battle of

The third major battle fought between **Spanish Army** forces and invading French formations in late autumn 1809. Following a costly defeat at **Ocaña** on 19 November, Spanish forces defending the bridge over the River Tormes at Alba, just south-east of Salamanca, were overwhelmed by elements of **Soult's** army, reinforced since its expulsion from **Portugal** earlier in the year. The attackers suffered about 300 casualties, and inflicted 3,000 casualties on the Spanish, helping convince British commander **Wellington** to withdraw his increasingly exposed army into Portugal for the winter (*see* **Peninsular War**; **Map 22**).

The bridge at Alba was also the scene of an important postscript to the Battle of **Salamanca** in July 1812, when Spanish general d'España's unauthorized withdrawal from positions guarding the river allowed **Marmont's** defeated forces to escape probable entrapment.

Albeck, Battle of

Small but significant prelude to the fall of **Ulm**, fought on 11 October 1805 near the village of Albeck on the north bank of the Danube (*see* **Map 12**). As French forces prepared to move west along either side of the Danube against Austrian forces around Ulm, frontline commander **Murat** anticipated **Napoleon's** orders. On 11 October he sent two of **Ney's** three divisions to join the drive south of the river, overriding the latter's protests and leaving General **Dupont's** 4,000 men isolated on the north bank. Dupont promptly ran into 25,000 Austrians, including 10,000 **cavalry**, under General Wrebeck, who had been sent to probe for weaknesses in the French position.

Denied the option of retreat by the enemy's cavalry superiority, Dupont launched an apparently hopeless attack near the village of Albeck. At the end of a hard day's fighting against enormous odds, some 1,500 French infantry were able to withdraw in good order, while the Austrians retired on the nearby camp at Michelsburg to prepare for a second attack at **Elchingen**. The affair poisoned the relations between Ney and Murat, who attracted Napoleon's fury for the original error, and the two marshals remained bitter enemies for life.

Albuera, Battle of

Messy engagement fought on 16 May 1811 between **Beresford**'s allied forces besieging **Badajoz** and **Soult**'s French Army of the South marching up from **Cadiz** to its relief (*see* **Map 22**). Beresford had been investing Badajoz since late April, but received the news that Soult's 25,000 men were approaching from the south-east on 12 May. Moving to a low ridge running through the village of Albuera, facing Soult's anticipated line of approach from the east (a position recommended by C-in-C **Wellington**), he was joined by 14,000 Spanish reinforcements under **Cuesta** and **Blake** on 15 May, bringing his strength up to 37,000 men and 50 guns.

Blake's 12,000 Spaniards were still taking up positions on the allied right when Soult attacked early on 16 May. Unaware of Spanish reinforcements, Soult opened operations with a feint attack against the allied centre before surprising Blake with a flank attack. Beresford ordered the whole Spanish contingent to turn south and face the attack, but Blake committed only part of his force in the belief that the main attack would still come from the east. An unsupported counterattack by a single British brigade across the French flank was broken up by 3,500 **Polish** cavalry before close-quarters infantry combat erupted on the allied right.

Soult's slight numerical advantage on the field was nullified by a well-drilled defensive performance until **Cole** threw his reserves into the battle on his own initiative, after which British line deployment gradually wore down French forces attacking in columns (*see* **Infantry Tactics**). Forced back to his starting positions after the failure of an attack by **Wrede**'s reserve, Soult withdrew south towards Cadiz on 18 May.

The battle cost almost 6,000 allied and an estimated 7,000 French casualties, and Beresford's clumsy victory had given defenders time to wreck his siege works at Badajoz. Criticized for failure either to guard his flanks with sufficient **skir-**mishers or to exercise effective control over subordinates, Beresford was returned to administrative duties with the **Portuguese Army** shortly afterwards. *See also* **Peninsular War**.

Alexander I, Tsar (1777–1825)

Ruler of **Russia** from 24 March 1801, the day he almost certainly participated in the murder of **Paul I**, Alexander reflected the uneasy mixture of autocratic tradition and Enlightenment ideas that had characterized his education at the court of **Catherine** the Great. Though his sanity was never in serious doubt until his last years, and his enthusiasms were tempered with innate caution, he remained an essentially unpredictable figure throughout his reign.

Initially determined on internal reform, Alexander worked with a small group of liberal nobles (the 'unofficial committee') to modify the regime's educational, administrative and serf labour systems during the first three years of his reign, but lost interest as the prospect of European war loomed after 1803. He supported the reforming ideas of **Speranski** during a second spell of peace between 1809 and 1812, but was never prepared to risk alienating court interests by forcing through substantial changes.

Quick to end Paul's ill-fated **Armed Neutrality** initiative, he executed subsequent foreign policy changes gradually, with a wary eye on potentially lethal court opposition. His youthful fascination with **Napoleon** faded after the Duc d'Enghein's murder in 1804, and he joined the **Third Coalition** in April 1805. He was steadfastly hostile to France until the defeat of the **Fourth Coalition** in 1807, but his admiration for a triumphant Napoleon was rekindled at **Tilsit**. Though he was disillusioned by the time the two emperors met again at **Erfurt** in autumn 1808, Alexander was careful to avoid an open breach until war appeared inevitable in early 1812.

From the time of the French invasion until 1815, he was the most obdurate of Napoleon's royal opponents. His determination to exact revenge for the occupation of **Moscow** and his influence over Prussian king **Frederick William III** were major factors in maintaining the **Sixth Coalition**'s offensive impetus in 1813–14, and he took an active part in the campaigns for

Germany and France. He played a leading role at the Congress of Vienna in 1814–15, working to establish hegemony over Poland, and was the prime architect of the largely notional but much reviled Holy Alliance of Christian rulers. He subsequently retreated into otherworldly personal isolation, influenced by his relationship with Latvian mystic Madame de Krüdener, and his popularity slumped during a decade of postwar repression under chief minister Arakcheyev.

Alexandria, Battle of

First and decisive confrontation, sometimes known as the Second Battle of Aboukir, between French forces occupying Egypt and General Abercromby's invading British expeditionary force. Abercromby's 15,000 troops (without cavalry support) had been dispatched to the Middle East in spring 1801, but promised support from the Turkish Army had not materialized by the time they reached Aboukir Bay on 2 March, escorted by Admiral Keith's Mediterranean Fleet.

Heavy winds delayed a landing until 8 March, when the force got ashore under fire from garrison forces in Aboukir Castle, and advanced troops under General Moore overwhelmed forward French positions. Having suffered some 600 casualties, Abercromby spent the next three days landing supplies and artillery before leaving two regiments to invest the castle and marching east along the narrow isthmus towards Alexandria.

Overall French commander Menou could call on a total of about 24,000 troops scattered around the colony, but his 10,000-strong field force was still en route to Alexandria when Aboukir Castle fell on 18 March, by which time Abercromby's slow progress had brought his main army (already shorn of some 3,000 sick) into positions about 5km short of the city. Menou reached Alexandria on 19 March, and attacked the British during the night of 20–21 March.

The attack began with a feint against the British left, before two columns struck at the right and centre-right of Abercromby's position. Moore, in command until Abercromby arrived, spotted the feint and threw reserves against the main attacks. The engagement degenerated into confused carnage through the remaining hours of darkness, but hard-pressed British units held

their ground, and inflicted heavy casualties before the French withdrew shortly after daylight, having suffered some 3,000 casualties. British losses were lighter, about 1,400 killed and wounded, but they included Abercromby, who died of a thigh wound sustained just before dawn.

Though a quicker advance would have made it unnecessary, Abercromby's victory against a well-supplied French force of at least equal strength went some way to repairing the British Army's battered reputation, and was fatal to French morale. Utterly confident of success before the battle, Menou could only retreat on Cairo, aware that the British could starve his army out of Egypt, and that capitulation was only a matter of time. See 'Ganteaume's Cruise'; Map 7.

Algeciras, Battle of

Naval action fought in summer 1801 after the Royal Navy's Gibraltar squadron under Saumarez intercepted a French force trying to escape the Mediterranean. Two French ships-of-the-line and six smaller craft under Admiral Linois had left Toulon in mid-June, bound for a rendezvous with Spanish Navy forces and a joint attack on the West Indies, but fled to Algeciras when faced with five British battleships. The British squadron attacked the port on 21 June and caused enough damage to delay Linois, though the 74-gun *Hannibal* ran aground under the guns of Spanish shore batteries. A relief squadron of four Spanish battleships and one French was sent from Cadiz to escort Linois to Ferrol, but contrary winds gave Saumarez time to repair his own ships and attack the entire Franco-Spanish force at sea on the night of 13–14 July. In the confusion of a night action, two 112-gun Spanish three-deckers attacked each other, both exploding with the loss of some 2,000 lives, and a French 74-gunner (*Antoine*) was captured by a five-strong British force that lost no ships. The defeat ended any immediate prospect of active Franco-Spanish naval cooperation up to the Peace of Amiens. See Map 8.

Almeida, Siege of See Battle of Fuentes de Oñoro

Alten, Karl von (1764–1840)

Alten served as an infantry officer in his native Hanoverian Army from 1781, fighting under the Duke of **York** in **Flanders** from 1793 to 1795. He entered British service after **Hanover** fell under French control in 1803, commanding two brigades of light infantry during the **Copenhagen** operation of 1807. After serving under **Moore** in **Sweden** (1808) and during the **Corunna** campaign (1808–9), he was transferred north to take part in the 1809 **Walcheren** expedition, but returned to the **Peninsular** theatre as a major-general in autumn 1810. He fought at **Albuera** in spring 1811, took over the 4th Division in October, and eventually replaced **Craufurd** in command of the Light Brigade in May 1812. Less dashing but more reliable than his predecessor, he retained the post until the end of the war, playing an important part in **Wellington's** 1813–14 campaigns. Alten led a British division in 1815 at **Quatre Bras** and **Waterloo**, where he was seriously wounded, and commanded Hanoverian forces in occupied France until 1818, when he became foreign minister of Hanover.

Altenkirchen, First Battle of

The first major action on the **Rhine** front in 1796, an attack in June by French forces against the northern wing of Austro-German positions east of the river. Despite the **First Coalition's** virtual collapse in 1795, Austrian C-in-C Archduke **Charles** deployed about 145,000 troops on the Rhine by mid-1796. About 50,000 were watching **Moreau's** southernmost French force on a line from Strasbourg to the Swiss frontier, and 70,000 were gathered east of Mainz, facing most of **Jourdan's** 70,000-strong northern army. Jourdan's northern wing, some 22,000 men under **Kléber**, crossed the Rhine north of Düsseldorf, turned south against the 24,000 troops of the Duke of Württemberg's allied left, and approached its outposts from 1 June. On 4 June Kléber attacked the main Austrian positions at Altenkirchen, about 50km north of the Lahn, where **Lefebvre** in the centre, flanked by regiments under **Soult** and **Ney**, swept the Austrians into a retreat on Freylingen, capturing 1,500 prisoners and 12 guns. Rapid pursuit, and the crossing of French reinforcements at Neuwied and Bonn, drove Württemberg back to the positions across the Lahn by 9 June. *See* Battle of **Ukerath**; **Map 3**.

Altenkirchen, Second Battle of

One of two major engagements fought on the **Rhine** front in April 1797 (the other was at **Diersheim**). French northern sector commander **Hoche** was aware that an armistice was imminent when he eventually launched his 70,000 well-equipped troops against General Werneck's 40,000 Austrians from 17 April. As **Championnet's** French left wing moved south-east from its bridgehead at Düsseldorf, Werneck began pulling in his scattered **cordon** around Altenkirchen, leaving just a scratch force at Neuwied, where Hoche crossed in strength from the small hours of 18 April. Werneck's concentration was still in progress when he was attacked from both north and west during the afternoon, losing 5,000 men and 27 guns in the process of falling back to the Lahn. Austrian forces had been pursued to the gates of Frankfurt by 23 April, when both commanders agreed to a truce on the news of the preliminary peace at **Leoben**. *See* **Map 3**.

Alvintzi, Josef d' (1735–1810)

Transylvanian-born soldier, in Habsburg service since the 1750s, who was promoted general in the late 1770s and held various staff positions before taking part in the war of 1789–90 against the **Ottoman Empire**. He commanded a division in **Flanders** during the **First Coalition's** opening campaigns, fighting at **Neerwinden** in 1793, and led a corps on the **Sambre** the following year. Recalled to Vienna in 1795, he replaced **Würmser** as a member of the **Aulic Council**, and followed him to the **Italian** front in 1796, first as local commander in the Tyrol, and then as regional C-in-C. He fared no better against **Napoleon** than his predecessor, suffering defeats at **Arcola** and **Rivoli**, after which he was promoted field marshal and withdrawn from frontline service. Imperial governor in Hungary from 1798, he retained an influential voice in the **Austrian Army's** tortuous reform process until his death.

Amberg, Battle of

French defeat that ended **Jourdan's** second invasion across the **Rhine** in summer 1796. Victory at **Forcheim** on 7 August had taken his army up the River Naab, but he faced a major counter-offensive after Austrian C-in-C Archduke **Charles** arrived with strong reinforcements. Jourdan elected to withdraw from the Naab to Amberg on the night of 23 August, pulling in his outlying forces to take up strong positions behind the town.

Wartensleben's Austrian column attacked next day, while **Kray**'s division moved east to cut the only line of retreat on Sulzbach, and Charles endeavoured to outflank the entire French army to the west. Overwhelmed by superior numbers after heavy fighting, the French managed to escape along the road to Sulzbach thanks to **Ney**'s success in keeping Kray's **cavalry** at bay. Both sides lost an estimated 4,000 men during the day.

Charles resumed his advance around the French right wing over the next few days, and Jourdan withdrew further north-west, picking up **Bernadotte**'s isolated unit on 28 August and continuing to Bamberg. After considering a stand there, he took the open road to Schweinfurt on the Main, with Austrian vanguards hot on his heels, but he was cut off to the west after Charles took possession of **Würzburg** from 1 September. *See* **Map 3**.

Amiens, Peace of

The treaty, signed in preliminary form on 1 October 1801 and finalized the following March, that ended eight years of war between **Great Britain** and **France**. Never regarded as more than a truce by **Napoleon**, and viewed at best as necessary but inordinately expensive by most informed British opinion, the peace survived for little more than a year.

Both powers had good reasons to seek peace in 1801. France needed time to recover from the economic chaos brought on by years of continuous warfare and an increasingly efficient British **blockade**, as well as a breathing space in which to organize the conquests confirmed by its victory over the **Second Coalition**. Napoleon had promised peace to a people desperate for reconstruction on coming to power in 1799, and was well aware of his need to secure popular loyalty by fulfilling the pledge.

Britain had been fighting without major allies since **Austria**'s acceptance of French terms at **Lunéville**, and its leaders recognized that **naval** supremacy alone would not bring outright victory. War weariness was affecting every section

of British society from the throne down, and the resignation of **Pitt**'s government in February 1801 removed the principal barrier to a negotiated settlement.

Fundamental incompatibility of British and French strategic ambitions lay behind the failure to translate such compelling arguments for a ceasefire into a lasting peace. The conciliatory attitude of the new **Addington** administration represented Britain's earnest desire for long-term peace in the name of greater national wealth, which it was generally assumed would follow from a period of unfettered global trade domination. Napoleon's main priority was a secure platform for the future Anglo-French war that he regarded as inevitable, and he was willing to risk the breakdown of negotiations to secure every possible strategic advantage.

The future Lord **Liverpool**, Addington's foreign minister, opened preliminary negotiations in London during September 1801. Exploiting evident British determination that agreement should be reached, and following Napoleon's precise instructions, French envoy Otto won serial concessions and gave little ground before the 'Preliminaries of Amiens' were signed on 1 October.

Britain accepted French control over the **Netherlands**, German states on the west bank of the Rhine, Savoy, **Piedmont** and Nice, as well as agreeing to return most recent **colonial** conquests, retaining only Dutch **Ceylon** (Sri Lanka) and Spanish **Trinidad**. Unaware that French forces there had surrendered, a fact already known to Napoleon, the British also agreed to evacuate **Egypt**. France was to guarantee the independence of **Switzerland**, restore the **Papal States** to the Vatican and quit **Naples**, while Napoleon made very vague commitments to restore (eventually) the Dutch and Piedmontese ruling houses. No agreement was reached on the restoration of Anglo-French trade relations or over payments for the upkeep of **prisoners of war**.

Greeted with delight in France, the Preliminaries caused mounting consternation in Britain once initial euphoria had died down. Talks towards a formal treaty opened in Paris on 20 November, and subsequent meetings were held in the north-eastern city of Amiens, but British chief negotiator Lord Cornwallis, an old soldier with little diplomatic experience, failed to win any major concessions in talks with a French delegation headed by Joseph **Bonaparte**. Apart from an agreement to guarantee mutually the independence of **Malta**, the final agreement signed on 25 March 1802 was substantially no different from the preliminaries.

Cornwallis signed the treaty without reference to his government's mounting fears that Napoleon intended to resume his expansionist policies sooner rather than later. French troops had already been sent to **Santo Domingo**, a puppet Batavian Republic had been set up in the Netherlands and Napoleon had become president of a new **Italian Republic**, all in defiance of the agreement's spirit. Subsequent French interference with the **Holy Roman Empire**, Switzerland and Italy, and evidence of Napoleon's expansion plans in the eastern **Mediterranean**, prompted Addington's ministry (with Russian encouragement) to take a stand over the agreed evacuation of Malta in early 1803.

By refusing to quit the island unless Napoleon reversed his encroachments since October 1801, British ministers accepted responsibility for breaking the letter of the treaty. Their willingness to resume the war was emphasized in subsequent Anglo-French talks, during which **Talleyrand** made strenuous efforts to keep the peace, but which ended with a British ultimatum on 10 May. Though Napoleon's reply was couched in peaceful terms, it failed to provide the requisite guarantees of future Dutch independence, and **George III** announced a state of war in a speech from the throne on 18 May.

Amphibious Warfare

In theory one of the great strategic advantages offered by contemporary sea power, the coordination of military and naval forces to mount an attack on a hostile shore was in practice restricted to a peripheral role throughout the period. Swedish and Russian forces were specialists in combined army and navy operations among the archipelagos of the shallow Baltic, and fought several actions around amphibious landings during the **Russo-Swedish War** of 1808–9. French forces were prepared on several occasions for an amphibious invasion of **England** across the Channel, and undertook landings with mixed success in the **Middle East** and **Ireland**. Otherwise the field was dominated by the British, seeking ways to translate growing dominance of **naval** theatres into strategic impact on land.

No methods or guidelines existed for combined operations by British forces in 1793, an oversight punished with a series of amphibious failures against well-defended coastal targets, notably at **Ostende**, **Ferrol** and **Cadiz**. Though direct assaults were more effective in the reduced circumstances of **colonial** warfare, operations closer to home succeeded only when defenders performed badly (as at **North Holland** and **Alexandria**) or when troops were landed well away from hostile forces and marched into action across unfamiliar terrain, as at **Maida**, **Copenhagen** or **Barrosa**. No serious attempt was made to land troops in the fighting sectors of the main European fronts.

British failures owed much to the technical difficulty of landing troops under fire in uncertain weather conditions, and of keeping sailing ships offshore to enable their supply or withdrawal. They also reflected government unwillingness to commit sufficient troops to operations, reluctance among detached British generals to risk heavy losses to an undermanned army, a generalized failure to appreciate the importance of reconnaissance, and enduringly poor relations between the **Royal Navy** and the **British Army**.

Amstetten, Battle of

The first serious combat between French and Russian forces during the War of the **Third Coalition**, fought on 5 November 1805 around Amstetten, on the River Ils (*see* **Map 12**). Marshal **Murat's** French vanguard had been leading the pursuit of **Kutuzov's** retreating Russian army since late October, and launched an immediate attack when contact was made. Murat hoped the Russians would turn and accept a major battle before they were reinforced, but Kutuzov would not be drawn, and deployed Prince **Bagration's** rearguard to hold off the attack while the rest of his army made for the Danube. By the end of the day Bagration had suffered some 8,000 casualties but had held his ground, and was able to extricate survivors during the night. Left with little idea of Kutuzov's exact whereabouts, Murat then abandoned the pursuit and directed his attention to the capture of **Vienna**.

Ancients, Council of

The upper legislative body created by the French Constitution of Year III in 1795. Comprising 250 notables aged 40 or over, with 80 seats subject to review every year, the council was a purely consultative body, empowered to deliberate on, accept or reject legislation proposed by the lower Council of **Five Hundred**. The council's first meeting took place in October 1795, and its last was on 9 November 1799, when it voted its own abolition in accepting the authority of a provisional **Consulate** during the **Brumaire** coup. *See also* **France**.

Ancona, Siege of

The main undertaking of a joint Russo-Turkish naval expedition to the **Italian** theatre that left the **Ionian Islands** in May 1799. The eastern Italian port of Ancona was garrisoned by some 3,000 French and Italian troops under General Monnier, and protected by three old (and otherwise useless) Venetian **ships-of-the-line** blocking the harbour entrance. The allied squadron fired off a few ineffective long-range broadsides before settling down to an inefficient close **blockade** of the port, and an Austrian division under General Frölich began a siege on 17 October. The siege was slowed by two successful French sorties, but Monnier acknowledged the hopelessness of his overall position by agreeing terms on 13 November. Furious that they were not consulted over the terms, the Russians and Turks returned to the eastern Mediterranean. *See* **Map 9**.

Anglo-American War (1812–15)

Sprawling and incoherent conflict between the **United States** and **Great Britain**, fought around the former's frontiers and eastern coastlines, that was triggered by the British **Royal Navy**'s application of **blockade** tactics to neutral shipping. European interference with what Americans considered legitimate trade, in the name of wars they considered immoral and irrelevant to their interests, had caused US friction with **France** and Britain since the early 1790s, and had contributed to the decision to form a **US Navy** in 1794. American attention was increasingly concentrated on British behaviour after 1805, by which time no other naval power was capable of seriously disrupting neutral trade.

London's reaction to French adoption of the **Continental System** against British shipping was an extension of its own blockade by the **Orders in Council** of November 1807. An attack on the USS *Chesapeake* by the British *Leopardstown* (27 June 1807) had recently brought outraged protests from Congress, and the Orders were now employed to authorize the stopping and searching of US merchantmen, the seizure of ships and contraband cargoes, and the forced transfer of British-born American crews into Royal Navy service.

Congress responded with a series of Embargo Acts forbidding all overseas trade, designed to redirect US economic effort towards internal expansion, and to end a wartime boom in the European carrying trade. They proved impossible to enforce in the face of determined evasion by powerful east coast merchants, and were replaced in March 1809 by a Non-Intercourse Act that made resumption of trade with Britain and France conditional on repeal of their blockade laws. An attempt by the British ambassador in Washington, David Erskine, to broker a mutual exemption agreement was rejected by British foreign minister **Canning** in August, and the Act remained in effect until May 1810, when it was repealed.

The repeal should have improved Anglo-American relations, but was accompanied by a threat to resume prohibition if either Britain or France failed to rescind its blockade laws within three months of the other doing so. A promise by **Napoleon** that the Continental System would no longer apply to US shipping, though never kept, triggered an ultimatum by Congress to Britain on 2 November, and restrictions were reapplied to British shipping from 2 March 1811.

Mutual tension mounted through the year, encouraged by the slow pace of transatlantic communications, by the clash between the USS *President* and a British warship in May, and by a growing minority in Washington who believed a war might drive the British out of Canada. The British government's confirmation that it would not rescind the Orders in Council reached the US in April 1812. News that the **Percival** government had changed its mind might have averted further conflict, but the British premier's assassination in May delayed any announcement, and the US declared war on 19 June.

The war was contested by very small forces on both sides, often supported by unreliable militia units or paid native tribesmen. The British built up a successful naval blockade of the US coast, but fighting was initially restricted to small actions at sea (and on the Great Lakes), where US commerce raiders enjoyed considerable success against British merchant traffic, and along the Canadian frontier, where both sides began operations with minor invasions.

The opening move in the land war, by 2,500 US militia under General William Hull, was held just inside the Canadian border by an even smaller British garrison in July, and Hull withdrew to Detroit. A British and native force then crossed into the US, capturing Fort Dearborn (now Chicago) on 15 August, and capturing Hull's forces in Detroit the next day. A second US invasion of Canada collapsed on the Niagara River at **Queenston** in mid-October, and an expedition north of Lake Champlain under General Dearborn withdrew in November before meeting any resistance.

Though a British fleet sacked Hampton in early 1813 after failing to take the port of Norfolk, Virginia, the pattern of indecisive sorties further north dominated the war through the year. Some 1,600 US troops under General Pike captured and burned York (Toronto) on 24 April, and an amphibious attack took Fort George in late May, before Pike's force was scattered by the British at **Stony Creek** on 6 June.

Despite raids against American training camps by regional British commander General Proctor early in the year, General Harrison had assembled some 7,000 US troops for an autumn offensive by the time US Navy forces routed the British naval flotilla on Lake **Erie** on 10 September. Harrison's men crossed the lake to drive Proctor out of Detroit on 29 September, and caught up with him at **Thames River** on 5 October. A British amphibious attack on the Lake Ontario port of **Sackett's Harbor**, led by governor-general Prevost of Upper Canada, had failed

in May, encouraging an ambitious, two-pronged American offensive under General Wilkinson against **Montreal**, where some 15,000 British troops were in the process of concentration. Attacks via the St Lawrence and Lake Champlain failed, and the last honours of the year went to the British, who captured Fort Niagara (18 December), burned the town of Buffalo and wrecked the US Navy's dockyards at Black Rock.

By this time the effect of the war on US economic and political life was beginning to bite. The Royal Navy's coastal blockade, established in the Delaware and Chesapeake Bays from November 1812, had been extended to cover the whole coastline from Norfolk to New York the following May, and pushed further north to include Long Island Sound in November.

The serious economic disruption suffered by the developed north-eastern states fuelled their strong opposition to the war, which became entwined with their ongoing disputes over federal policies towards continental expansion and slavery. Massachusetts had at first refused to take any part in the war, while Connecticut had rejected federal demands for militia forces. Though both states eventually succumbed to pressure in Congress, radical demands for secession from the union (never far from the surface of US political life in the first decades of independence) reflected mounting determination to restore trading links with Europe.

British efforts had so far been conducted without the help of resources from Europe, but by early 1814 it became clear to US leaders that the defeat of Napoleon was imminent. President Madison accepted British foreign minister **Castlereagh**'s offer of peace negotiations in January 1814, and they eventually began in Ghent on 8 August. In the meantime another US expedition towards Niagara, led by Wilkinson's replacement General Brown, took Fort Erie and defeated British forces at **Chippewa** on 5 July, but was forced back and besieged in the fort after a fierce struggle with General Drummond's reinforced British defenders at **Lundy's Lane** on 25 July.

Although the Canadian frontier struggle remained evenly poised, the arrival of substantial reinforcements from Europe enabled the

British to extend the war's scope during the late summer. The naval blockade was pushed north as far as Boston from 25 April, and a British division under General Ross landed in Chesapeake Bay before defeating American garrison forces at Bladensburg on 24 August. It took nearby **Washington** next day, and fired the city's major public buildings, but the invasion stalled after another landing failed to capture Baltimore (12–14 September). Meanwhile a major offensive down Lake Champlain by Prevost and 14,000 **Peninsular War** veterans was thwarted at **Plattsburg** on 11 September.

Because of the scattered nature of administrative authority and settlements in the predominantly untamed North American continent, capture of important US cities or forts was never the decisive act it could be in countries with a well-developed central government. The loss of Washington had relatively little direct impact on people accustomed to thinking of their state as their country, and peace talks were primarily driven by war-weariness on the British side and a desire to end internal bickering in the US.

A convention of north-eastern states was already meeting in **Hartford** to propose far-reaching restrictions on federal power when the last major attack of the war began with the landing of 14,000 British troops near New Orleans on 13 December. Though the Treaty of **Ghent** ended the war on 24 December, this information did not reach the US until February 1815, and British commander **Pakenham** meanwhile launched an attack against General **Jackson**'s relatively tiny army. Though it need not have been fought, the Battle of **New Orleans** (8 January 1815) was the greatest American victory of the war, inflicting heavy losses in the process of driving the British down the Mississippi to the Gulf of Mexico, where survivors sailed for home.

Though it produced no significant territorial gains for either side, and can be viewed as one of the era's more pointless conflicts, the war has been credited with profound effects on US society, helping to establish a sense of national identity among American citizens and boosting political confidence in the nation's potential for expansion. On the British side, the war's impact was largely restricted to the Royal Navy, which

had been worsted in a number of ship-to-ship actions by US **frigates**, and reacted to the shock by reassessing its own requirements for small warships. *See* **Map 27**.

Arakcheyev, Alexei Andreievich (1769–1834)

Russian soldier and politician who began his career as an **artillery** officer, but impressed the future Tsar **Paul I** with his ideas for military reform, and was briefly inspector-general of the **Russian Army** on the latter's accession to the throne in 1796. Dismissed at the behest of conservative factions at court, he was restored to favour by **Alexander I** in 1803, when he became inspector-general of artillery, and was war minister for a time in 1808. A member of Russia's first Council of State in 1810, but dismissed along with **Speranski** in 1812, he is primarily associated with the period of repression after 1815, known as the Arakcheyevshchina, when he served as the reclusive tsar's chief minister and dominated internal affairs. He retired on Alexander's death in 1825.

Arcis-sur-Aube, Battle of

Austrian C-in-C **Schwarzenberg**'s most aggressive action during the 1814 campaign for **France**, an ambush of French forces as they advanced east across the River Aube in late March 1814. After winning a surprise victory at **Reims** on 13 March, and narrowly failing to exploit consequent allied confusion, **Napoleon** marched 23,000 troops towards St Dizier and Joinville on the upper Marne, where he could cut the supply lines of allied armies approaching Paris and move close to much-needed troops stranded in frontier garrisons.

To keep the allies off balance, Napoleon planned to attack **Wrede**'s garrison en route at Arcis-sur-Aube, but first reports of French movements convinced Schwarzenberg that he was heading for Troyes. Reacting with unaccustomed vigour, Schwarzenberg reversed his retreat from the Seine and advanced between Troyes and Arcis.

French forces approached Arcis down both banks of the Aube on 20 March, reaching and taking the abandoned town unopposed. Accepting reports that the area was clear, Napoleon was just east of Arcis with **Ney** when Wrede's cavalry launched a full-scale attack just after two. **Sebastiani**'s outnumbered cavalry were quickly forced back, and only the arrival of General Friant's division at the Aube bridge prevented a rout. Napoleon rallied troops in person, at one point riding his horse over a smouldering howitzer shell and emerging unscathed when it exploded. Attacks had ceased by nightfall, and the arrival of 2,000 more cavalry under **Lefebvre-Desnouëttes** enabled Sebastiani to close the day with a successful night charge.

While French forces assumed they had beaten off a strong rearguard attack, Schwarzenberg spent the night positioning 80,000 troops in a wide arc behind ridges south and east of Arcis. Reinforcements meanwhile brought French strength in the area up to about 28,000 men, but Schwarzenberg believed it to be far greater and delayed any attack next morning. He remained inactive when the truth became clear to Napoleon, who immediately ordered a full-scale withdrawal.

Aided by **pontoon** equipment that had at last arrived from Paris, and by Schwarzenberg's fully restored caution, much of Napoleon's army was across the Aube before the first allied attack opened in mid-afternoon, and Napoleon was able to extract the remainder towards Sompius with only about 3,000 losses. Allied forces, shorn of about 4,000 casualties, made no attempt at pursuit, and Napoleon returned to his planned move on St Dizier. *See* **Map 26**.

Arcola, Battle of

Crucial French victory on the **Italian** front in 1796, won around Arcola, on the River Alpone in northern Italy, from 15 to 17 November (*see* **Map 6**). Generally accepted as one of **Napoleon**'s most brilliant tactical performances, the battle saved French forces in the theatre from almost certain defeat by a larger Austrian army.

In an attempt to regain control of the strategically vital **Quadrilateral** region, two invading Austrian forces under **Alvintzi** had thrown Napoleon on to the defensive by the second week of November. Outnumbered in the field, and reluctant to draw reinforcements from the siege of **Mantua**, Napoleon left some 13,000 troops under **Vaubois** to cope with the northern Austrian column, led by General Davidovich, and gathered

his main strength around Verona. After his attempt to halt Alvintzi's advance on the city failed at **Caldiero** on 12 November, he faced encirclement unless a second attack succeeded quickly.

Napoleon planned a characteristic sweep around the Austrian flank, aiming to force Alvintzi's retreat by cutting his rear communications at Villa Nova, and then confront it across the narrow, marshy strip separating the Adige from the Alpone, where numerical superiority would count for little. Success depended on speed and secrecy to prevent Alvintzi retreating too soon or advancing on Verona.

Alvintzi was approaching Verona by 14 November, and Napoleon recalled 3,000 men to its defence from Vaubois before leading 18,000 troops across the Adige at Ronco, some 30km to the south-east, next morning. Alvintzi knew nothing of French plans at this stage, but detachments guarding the Adige and the Alpone rivers slowed flank marches up their banks by **Masséna** and **Augereau**. Though Masséna quickly secured the western flank, Augereau was stopped by 2,000 well-placed Croatian troops guarding the bridge over the Alpone at Arcola.

While Napoleon sent 3,000 men to cross the Adige further south at Albaredo, Austrian reinforcements reached both the garrison at Arcola and Masséna's front. By the time the Albaredo detachment took the town from the east that evening, Alvintzi had withdrawn to occupy Villa Nova in strength. Worried by reports of renewed movements against Vaubois, Napoleon withdrew his entire force across the Adige that night, ready to move north if needed.

Receiving no word from Vaubois, Napoleon repeated the operation next day, once more sending his army across the Adige at Ronco, and attacking re-established Austrian positions around Belfiore and Arcola. After a day of costly frontal attacks, Belfiore was recaptured but Arcola remained in Austrian hands, while a detachment from the town thwarted an attempt to bridge the Alpone further south. Napoleon again retired all but a small advanced guard west of the Adige, ready to meet crisis elsewhere.

Heavy casualties had brought Alvintzi close to retreat, and his increasingly ragged force had split into two. Some 6,000 troops were in the marshes west of Villa Nova, and Alvintzi controlled about twice as many east of the Alpone, between Villa Nova and Arcola. Napoleon meanwhile received 3,000 reinforcements from Mantua during the night, and returned to the attack next morning.

Napoleon struck at Alvintzi's larger force, detailing Masséna to hold the marshlands while Augereau repeated the first day's move through Albaredo. Masséna met strong resistance at the Ronco crossing, but his 8,000 men forced their way across before tricking the garrison at Arcola into an ambush. Augereau sent part of his force to cross the Adige still further south at Legnano, and eventually overcame strong opposition at Albaredo, but could not break through Austrian defences east of the river.

A trick turned the battle. Napoleon sent a small party of **Guides** across the river unobserved, and their noisy demonstration in the rear of an Austrian division triggered a hasty withdrawal north, opening the way for Augereau to link up with Masséna around Arcola. By the end of the day their combined approach had prompted a full-scale Austrian retreat towards Vicenza, and the French army returned to Verona next day, having inflicted at least 7,000 casualties at a cost of some 4,500. With Verona secure, Napoleon turned his attentions north to General Davidovich and his 18,000 men, who soon retreated from the danger of encirclement.

Argentina *See* **South America**

Armed Neutrality Agreement (1800)

Mutual declaration by **Russia**, **Prussia**, **Denmark** and **Sweden** that each would cooperate to prevent ships of the British **Royal Navy** from searching or confiscating their trading vessels at sea. The impetus to common action was an invitation to other northern powers by Tsar **Paul I** of Russia, issued on 27 August 1799, and the Armed Neutrality pact was formally inaugurated in conventions signed by Denmark and Sweden on 16 December 1800. Prussia joined two days later.

The declaration was ostensibly a mutual protest at **Great Britain**'s high-handed treatment of neutral shipping as part of its **blockade** policy, but Russia's few Baltic traders were hardly affected by British actions, and Paul's invitation

was generally recognized as an expression of hostile intent towards Britain. His motives for switching to an anti-British policy are obscured by his erratic nature, but most modern commentators regard the move as either a reaction against the failure of the **Second Coalition**, an attempt to replace it with a league of northern powers headed by Russia, or the first step towards alliance with a victorious **France**. Paul in fact proposed cooperation with Armed Neutrality to **Napoleon** in January 1800, at which time it appeared to present a serious threat to British Baltic trade.

The motives binding other powers to Armed Neutrality offered little hope of cohesion. Denmark had come close to a trade war with Britain in summer 1800, and sought the protection of its northern neighbours. Sweden joined primarily to avoid isolation between Russia and Denmark, and made promises of continued friendship to London. The Prussian monarchy was interested in the acquisition of **Hanover** from King **George III** and in the reversal of British trade inroads into northern Germany. Only Denmark made any discernible maritime contribution, and all three Baltic powers retained an essentially opportunistic attitude, alert to the economic consequences of failure against the British.

After months of increasingly hostile diplomatic exchanges with Britain, Danish troops occupied Hamburg in late March, and Prussian forces entered Hanover. The British responded by sending a powerful Royal Navy force into **Copenhagen** harbour, where it pulverized the Danish fleet to destruction. This, and news of Paul's assassination (23 March), prompted the withdrawal of Danish and Prussian land forces. New tsar **Alexander I**'s lack of enthusiasm for Armed Neutrality effectively ended its active life, though the agreement was not formally terminated until June 1801.

Armistice of 1813

The pause in the campaign for **Germany** agreed by allied and French leaders on 4 June 1813, shortly after the Battle of **Bautzen**. The idea of an armistice had been floated just before the battle, and dismissed by Tsar **Alexander**, but a

36-hour suspension of hostilities was arranged on 2 June. A conference at Plaswitz two days later agreed to open peace negotiations and declared an armistice until 20 July, bringing fighting in Germany to a halt.

In accepting a temporary peace and withdrawing to Dresden, **Napoleon** acknowledged that his exhausted army, short of ammunition and shorn of almost 115,000 men since April, could not achieve more without large-scale **cavalry** reinforcement. He also bought time to address the growing threat from **Austria**, expected to turn against France at any moment.

Allied numbers were also shrinking, and morale had been damaged by two major defeats. Russian and Prussian commanders regarded a victory as essential to bring Austria into the conflict, and were prepared to fight another battle at Schweidnitz, but were in the process of being outflanked when the armistice took effect and could feel satisfied that it was to their benefit (*see* **Map 25**).

Neither side seems to have seriously expected a lasting peace, and both spent the ensuing weeks preparing to resume hostilities, while the allies achieved a series of diplomatic successes. **Russia** and **Prussia** each received £2 million **subsidies** from **Great Britain** on 15 June, and Austria was offered £500,000 to enter the war. **Sweden** formalized its support for the allies on 7 July, and Austria signed the secret **Reichenbach** Convention on 19 July, agreeing to join the coalition if Napoleon refused its terms as mediator.

As laid out by **Metternich**, Austrian terms demanded the effective removal of French power east of the Rhine and were inevitably rejected, but Napoleon accepted an allied request to extend the armistice to 16 August. Supposedly a last chance for negotiated settlement, the extension enabled both sides to finalize battle plans and complete reinforcement. Austria declared war on France on 12 August, and **Blücher's** Prussians advanced from Breslau next day, bringing the armistice to an end three days early.

Armour

Although heavy **cavalry** forces in all the major contemporary armies wore iron (or occasionally leather) body armour at the start of the Revo-lutionary **Wars**, and **cuirassiers** in continental armies still wore the immensely heavy breastplates (*cuirasses*) for which they were named, the practice was already anachronistic. Armour offered no protection against massed volleys of **musket** fire at close range, or against **artillery**, and was only really valuable during close combat with mounted opponents, when its immense weight created as many problems as it solved. Armoured troopers needed the strongest mounts, suffered from restricted mobility in combat, and could often hardly move at all if unhorsed, drawbacks that led some forces to experiment with reduced protection, such as the half-cuirasse tried by Russian, Austrian and other German cavalry. Though lighter because it dispensed with the rear half of the rider's protection, this offered French heavy troopers (who retained their full armour throughout the war period) an obvious target area in close combat, and merely resulted in increased casualties.

Arndt, Ernst Moritz (1769–1860)

Important German nationalist writer and spokesman, born on the Baltic island of Rügel (then part of **Sweden**), who worked in **Prussia** from 1800. He wrote several widely read tracts criticizing the French Napoleonic regime and promoting the idea of pan-German national identity before he was forced into exile by the French conquest of northern Germany in 1806. After spending three years in Stockholm, he returned to Germany in disguise, writing a series of popular nationalist songs and becoming private secretary to reforming Prussian administrator **Stein** in 1812. An inveterate agitator for liberal reform, he was dismissed from government service in 1818, but remained an icon of nationalist groups in Germany until his death.

Artillery (Land)

Land-based artillery of the period fell into two broad categories: long-barrelled cannon, which projected a ball at high velocity along a flat trajectory to achieve distance, and were primarily designed for smashing whatever was in their path; and howitzers, which shot a projectile at a high angle from a short, wide barrel, and were designed to fire over an obstacle, such as a fortification, at personnel or other 'soft' targets beyond.

Cannon were usually described according to the weight of their projectile, and howitzers categorized according to their barrel calibre. All barrels were smooth-bored tubes made of iron, which tended to split after a time, or of 'gunmetal', a bronze alloy that often warped when it became hot.

Cannon ranged in size and weight according to their intended use: the lightest 3- and 4-pounders were mobile field weapons, used to support fast-moving light infantry and **cavalry** forces, or for difficult terrain; larger field cannon, between 6- and 12-pounders, were used to support armies in static positions, and to provide bombardment during set-piece engagements; the biggest mobile cannon, 18- or 24-pounders, were primarily deployed with **siege trains**, and also performed a static role as **fortress** or coastal defence weapons, along with giant 32-pounders and mortars. Small **carronades**, an important feature of **naval warfare**, were also used as a form of short-range garrison defence.

Mobile weapons were all mounted on two large wheels, with a 'trail' at the back; for transport purposes, this was attached to a two-wheeled ammunition carriage ('limber'), which was in turn hooked up to a team of horses. The process of 'limbering up' was time-consuming, and guns were often hauled manually, using ropes attached to the carriage, for rapid transport over short distances.

Aiming and firing of cannon were not particularly sophisticated. Directing the gun was achieved by 'traversing', which meant dragging the trail to the required position and manoeuvring the barrel in its wake. The barrel could be raised or depressed a few degrees by using wooden blocks ('quoins') or a simple screw mechanism, but this did not provide sufficient elevation to enable complex targeting (over the heads of friendly troops, for example). Range could be more than doubled by an elevation of two or three degrees, but accuracy quickly fell away.

A cannon's range and destructive power depended principally on the type and weight of ammunition in use. Simple **round shot** fired from a 24-pounder at ideal elevation could travel for about 1.5km before hitting the ground, and cause serious damage while ricocheting to a halt

over a considerable distance, but a 3-pounder could not expect to travel much more than half the distance, and the heaviest **canister** shot had a maximum range of about 600m.

Most wide-mouthed howitzers were short-barrelled, but the **Russian Army** introduced long-barrelled howitzers, known as 'unicorns', from 1805. Howitzers usually fired explosive '**common shell**', though the **British Army** made increasing use of **shrapnel** as howitzer ammunition, and **incendiary shells** were occasionally employed on land, primarily for siege operations.

The rate of fire achieved by contemporary field gunners was generally dictated by the time taken to make even minute changes of aim. Though unaimed shots could be loosed off at more than 12 rounds per minute, this was generally regarded as a waste of precious ammunition, which presented serious resupply problems, and one to three shots per minute under fire was considered standard.

The invention of **Congreve rockets** provided the British and Austrian artillery arms (which were the only forces to use them) with an alternative means of incendiary attack, but they were wildly inaccurate weapons, disliked by many commanders, and primarily useful for either firing wooden towns or frightening opponents with their capacity for random damage.

The technical and tactical development of artillery during the war decades was dominated by the **French Army**. Its artillery arm inherited a virtually intact corps of well-trained officers in 1792, and was already using the pioneering **Gribeauval system** of standardization and deployment, subsequently copied by its opponents. Wartime French developments copied elsewhere included a steady increase in the number of light 'horse batteries' attached to **cavalry** units and the employment of soldiers, rather than civilians, to drive gun carriages and **caissons** into action.

French fighting tactics, similarly influential, were ultimately dominated by **Napoleon**, who had demonstrated his faith in massed batteries for field operations during the 1794–7 **Italian campaigns**, and sponsored a considerable increase in the army's firepower after he took over government in 1799. From a total strength of about 1,100 guns in the mid-1790s, the artillery arm expanded by 1810 to deploy more than 2,000 guns with the field army and another 500 in a central reserve, along with countless fortress defence weapons.

The massing of artillery to inflict a devastating bombardment on a single location entailed removal of close support for infantry, and Napoleon was forced to reinstate regimental allocations of light 4-pounders once the quality of French infantry troops declined after 1809. Similar considerations inhibited other armies from fully adopting what was a highly successful shock tactic on the battlefield.

Of the other major European land forces, the **Austrian Army** of the 1790s used myriad cannon and howitzer types, mostly adaptations of 40-year-old patterns, and their manifest inadequacy prompted partial introduction of new designs along Gribeauval lines. The relatively cumbersome 6-pounders attached to cavalry units were eventually replaced by more mobile horse batteries, but the Austrians devoted the majority of their guns to infantry support before Archduke **Charles's** reforms of 1806–9, after which batteries were deployed at brigade level and a large artillery reserve concentrated for massed attacks.

The **Prussian Army** reorganized its artillery arm for massed operations after its defeats of 1806, and tried to imitate the Gribeauval system, but **Prussia's** manufacturing sector was never able to meet the demand for new weapons, and many units were still using mixed batteries of non-standard cannon in 1815. Frontline batteries were again dissipated into an infantry support role from 1813, though heavier guns were grouped with corps or army reserves.

Technically inferior before 1805, **Russian Army** artillery underwent a revolution during subsequent military reforms. A few standard and much-improved designs were adopted, restricting field equipment to new 6-pounder and 12-pounder cannon, along with the range of long-barrelled howitzers. Most factories in **Russia** existed to provide arms for the state, and the tsar's artillery was always well supplied, though chronically short of educated officers and often poorly handled. The army could deploy about 1,500 frontline guns by 1812, and new tactical instructions stressed the need to emulate French massed attacks. Though this was seldom achieved in practice, sheer weight of numbers made the Russian artillery a force to be reckoned with in 1813–14.

The **British Army's** establishment of land guns was relatively small, and remained inadequate for any kind of major continental operation until about 1810, when the **Peninsular War** began to stimulate growth. Some technical reforms along French lines were attempted during the 1790s, including formation of horse artillery units from 1793, and a military corps replaced civilian supply drivers in 1794, but the inferior quality of British cannon compared to their French counterparts was only addressed after substantial forces had been committed to the Peninsular campaign. A new 9-pounder did not fully replace the old 6-pounder until 1815, but new light howitzers were introduced more quickly and provided British forces with superior mobile weapons. Limited resources were reorganized into 60-gun battalions from 1802, reflecting recognition that the dispersal of guns for infantry support had become outdated, and field artillery was almost exclusively devoted to massed operations after 1808. *See also* **Siege Warfare; Artillery (Naval).**

Artillery (Naval)

Artillery aboard warships was categorized according to the weight of **roundshot** fired, ranging from the biggest long-range 32-pounders down to 6-pounders, although armed merchantmen and **gunboats** often used smaller weapons. A 32-pounder shot could tear through the entire length of a target ship from anything under about 100m, and much closer ranges were commonplace in **naval** combat. The largest guns were only mounted by **ships-of-the-line**, and most **frigates** carried 18-pounders as their main armament, still enabling them to smash several feet of solid hardwood from standard range. Large warships in some navies also also carried light **carronades** as secondary armament for close-quarters action, and specialist 'bombs' were fitted with **mortars**.

A large warship's main guns were located on

one, two or three gun decks, running the entire length of the ship on both sides and necessitating the clearance of cabin structures, personal effects, mess rooms and other living areas when they were run out for action. Secondary guns were grouped at the rear of the ship, high around the quarterdeck, giving the clearest possible line for anti-personnel fire on to an enemy ships' decks. One or two heavy guns were usually located at the front and back of a big man-of-war as 'bow chasers' and 'stern chasers'.

The key to the deployment of heavy guns in combat was the broadside. Manoeuvring apart, the vital prerequisite to a successful broadside was simultaneous fire. The combined effect of up to 50 heavy rounds striking any warship at close quarters was usually devastating, and often put it out of action almost at once, but synchronization in battle required a high level of discipline and training, especially if the combat involved repeated broadsides. The British enjoyed a clear technical advantage throughout the wars in this respect, and it was fundamental to their almost unbroken run of combat victories.

Roundshot remained by far the most common ammunition in naval use, but **grapeshot** was standard issue for anti-personnel work and incendiaries were useful for actually destroying (rather than defeating) a target. Explosive **common shell** was occasionally used against land targets, but was generally considered too dangerous for deployment in a sea fight. Warships left harbour carrying all the ammunition they expected to need, and it accounted for a large proportion of their load, but shortages of powder or shot could become critical on long voyages, and it was not unknown for desperate captains to retrieve spent balls from the shallows in the aftermath of a battle. *See also* **Artillery (Land)**.

Artois, Charles Philippe de Bourbon, Comte d' (1757–1836)

The youngest brother of French King **Louis XVI**, his violent opposition to any kind of liberal reform prompted his departure from France in 1789, and he remained abroad as a focus for extreme royalist **émigrés** until 1814. His reactionary fervour following the restoration, when he was a moving force behind the **White Terror**

against former republicans, contributed to rapid popular disenchantment with the regime of **Louis XVIII**, and his own reign as Charles X (from 1824) ended in revolution, abdication and resumed exile in 1830.

Aspern–Essling, Battle of

Major confrontation of 21–22 May 1809 between French and Austrian armies on the north bank of the Danube a few kilometres east of Vienna. French forces had controlled Vienna since 13 May, but found its bridges over the Danube destroyed and strong Austrian forces on the north bank preventing their repair. **Napoleon** needed to cross the river if he was to have any chance of inflicting a decisive defeat on the army of Archduke **Charles** before it was reinforced by Archduke **John**'s army from Italy (*see* War of the **Fifth Coalition**).

By 17 May Napoleon could call on about 82,000 troops around Vienna, with another 35,000 under **Davout** a few days' march away. He was not aware that Charles had reabsorbed **Hiller's** detached corps to bring his local strength up to 115,000 men, or that they were in good positions around the plain just north of the river.

While Charles delayed any attacking moves in the hope that help would materialize from Italy, Napoleon sought out alternative crossing points. He settled on a location about 6km east of the city, where a relatively slow and shallow bend in the river was almost filled by the island of Lobau, some 15km square and only about 100m from the north bank.

Advanced French units forded the river to occupy Lobau on 19 May, and the first troops were across a hastily constructed bridge on to the island at about noon next day. A short trestle structure over the second half of the river was complete that evening, and **Masséna**'s men (with part of **Bessières**'s cavalry) established themselves in the northern villages of Aspern and Essling. Meanwhile the southern bridge had been broken by an Austrian hulk, floated downstream on a fast current, and no more French troops reached Lobau before morning.

Charles was excellently placed to pounce on the French bridgehead. He could call on 77,000 more men in four corps (under Hiller, **Bellegarde**,

Hohenzollern and Rosenburg) within easy striking distance, and another 28,000 were within close support range. Well informed of French movements by a detachment overlooking Lobau, he ordered an attack to drive the French back over the river for 21 May.

Because high waters and a procession of heavy or burning objects sent downriver had again broken the French bridge, only 16,000 infantry and 7,000 **cavalry** were north of the river when first contact was made with advancing Austrian units just after one. The main attack, by three Austrian corps against the left of the French position around Aspern, was held off until early evening, when General Molitor's defending division fell back. French reinforcements then crossed the reopened bridge to launch repeated counter-attacks, and Aspern changed hands six times before nightfall found each side holding part of the village.

An advance by 25,000 Austrian troops had developed much more slowly against the French right at Essling, where General Boudet's division (temporarily led by **Lannes**) beat off a series of attacks during the evening and retained full control of the village. In the centre, French and Austrian cavalry fought out the afternoon, but although Bessières received reinforcements late in the day neither side approached a decisive breakthrough.

The day ended in stalemate, but Charles had achieved his limited aim of halting any French advance and prepared to resume the attack next day. Napoleon meanwhile sent for reinforcements from Davout and spent the night pouring men into the bridgehead. By the time a renewed attack opened at dawn on 22 May French strength in the sector had more than doubled, but some 62,000 defenders and 144 guns still faced at least 100,000 Austrians and 240 guns.

Charles again focused his attacks against the French flanks. Masséna held off an assault on Aspern for two hours before counter-attacking to recapture the village, and a smaller attack against Essling made no significant progress before Napoleon seized the initiative by sending Lannes's three central divisions forward just after seven. Suffering and inflicting heavy casualties, they slowly forced Prince Hohenzollern's corps

back, but were running low on ammunition when Charles led a counter-attack that halted their advance. Aware that a third break in the Lobau bridge had postponed the arrival of Davout's corps, Napoleon pulled his men back to the Aspern–Essling line.

Austrian forces had resumed their attacks on the two villages by ten, and were threatening to push back the French centre. Essling fell, and although it was retaken by the **Young Guard**, the French situation was becoming desperate. The southern bridge had hardly reopened when it was smashed for a fourth time, and French forces barely held off the last Austrian attack before they were ordered back on to Lobau at two. Their fighting withdrawal was eventually completed in the small hours of 23 May, and the bridge to the north bank was destroyed soon afterwards.

The battle remains a source of controversy, with some authorities treating it as a victory for Charles and others regarding it as a draw. In tactical terms, Charles achieved his very limited aims while Napoleon's plans were clearly thwarted, but both sides suffered heavily, the Austrians losing almost 23,500 men killed or wounded, against perhaps 22,000 French losses. French dead included **St Hilaire** and Lannes, the latter the first of the **Marshalate** to be killed in action.

French **propaganda**, which put losses at only 4,100, could not disguise a serious blow to Napoleon's prestige. With several French-controlled German states threatening nationalist rebellion, he needed a decisive victory more than ever, and set about preparing a second crossing of the Danube. *See* Battle of **Wagram**; **Map 12**.

Auerstädt, Battle of

One of two battles fought between French and Prussian forces on 14 October 1806 that decided the opening phase of the War of the **Fourth Coalition**. While French emperor **Napoleon** was preparing to attack **Hohenlohe**'s 38,000 Prussian troops at **Jena**, the Duke of **Brunswick**'s main Prussian army was retreating towards the Elbe and a collision with Marshal **Davout**'s much smaller French corps 13km to the north at Auerstädt. All the relevant commanders were confused: Napoleon thought he was attacking the Prussian main body, and Hohenlohe believed he faced a French flank detachment; Brunswick was expecting a major French concentration to his north-east, and Davout was marching south-west to support Napoleon with a flank attack (*see* **Jena–Auerstädt Campaign**).

News that Davout's corps was to his north at Naumburg on 13 October, threatening Prussian lines of communication with Leipzig and Berlin, had triggered Brunswick's retreat. Davout's 27,000-strong III Corps was in fact one of two northern flank detachments (the other was **Bernadotte**'s I Corps), and his orders for 14 October were to march west on Apolda, supported by Bernadotte unless the latter had already carried out his previous day's instructions to move south on Dornburg. This manoeuvre put Davout directly in the path of the Prussian retreat, while Bernadotte chose to ignore the latest order and marched for Dornburg that day. Perhaps an expression of personal pique at receiving instructions via Davout, Bernadotte's extraordinary decision kept him out of the ensuing battle.

While the battle at Jena was opening, Davout accompanied General Gudin's leading division through dense early morning fog towards what appeared to be substantial Prussian forces camped around Auerstädt. By eight that morning Gudin's division had pushed through light Prussian advance guards to reach the River Lissbach beyond the village of Pöppel, but Davout's other two divisions (led by Generals Friant and Morand) were still some distance behind.

Brunswick, commanding 63,000 men and 230 guns, was by now aware of French forward positions and still assumed they were part of the main army. Although he sought above all to avoid a major battle, he gathered a division and 12 squadrons of **cavalry** opposite Gudin at the Lissbach, but an initial attack went badly wrong when **Blücher** led the cavalry into a series of premature and unproductive charges. A more coordinated attack was launched after a second Prussian division (Wartensleben) arrived, but failed as Friant's division and the corps artillery reached the front to bolster the French position, though it overran an isolated regiment further

south to threaten Davout's left flank.

With Morand still 5km away and no sign of Bernadotte, Davout threw every available reserve into a stand at the village of Hassenhausen, and the Prussians launched a series of unsuccessful frontal assaults on an obstacle they could have outflanked. Brunswick was killed in action at about this stage, but King **Frederick William III** failed either to take personal control or to appoint a new field commander, and Prussian cohesion began to break down.

Sufficient Prussian cavalry had gathered for an attack on Hassenhausen by about eleven, but it was not given artillery support and Morand's newly arrived division was able to repel the charge. A third Prussian division (Prince of **Orange**) joined the battle at about the same time, but was forced back when Morand counterattacked and overran Wartensleben's forces. Frederick William refused to commit his substantial reserves to the sector, apparently believing that Napoleon was present and conjuring some unbeatable masterstroke, and Davout drove his three divisions forward to take the villages of Pöppel and Rehausen on the Prussian flanks.

Threatened with envelopment, Frederick William was compelled to withdraw his whole line, hoping to fall back on the covering force at Jena, but rapid deployment of French artillery had turned retreat into rout by twelve thirty. Davout's corps set off in pursuit of the fleeing Prussians, but was too exhausted to inflict further serious damage after brushing aside a last stand by Blücher's division, and operations were halted before dark.

Against overwhelming odds, Davout had inflicted 13,000 losses (including 3,000 prisoners) and captured 115 guns, losing some 7,000 men in the process. When Napoleon first heard reports of the battle, in the aftermath of what he still thought was his own defeat of Brunswick at Jena, he refused to believe the news, but for once gave his subordinate full credit when the truth emerged. Davout eventually became Duke of Auerstädt; Bernadotte, who had ignored repeated calls for help, narrowly escaped court martial proceedings. *See* **Map 16**.

Augereau, Pierre-François-Charles
(1757–1816)

French soldier, a fruiterer's son, who earned a reputation as a reliable and doughty divisional commander on the **Pyrenean** front, on the **Rhine** and during the **Italian campaigns** of 1796–7, receiving **Napoleon's** public praise for his performance at **Castiglione** in 1796. One of the original **Marshalate** created in 1804, he commanded the camp at Brest during preparations for the invasion of **England** and headed the **Grande Armée's** VII Corps through the Wars of the **Third** and **Fourth Coalitions**. Though he missed the Battles of **Ulm** and **Austerlitz**, Augereau was at **Jena** in October 1806 and suffered a very bad day at **Eylau** the following February, when he was wounded and his corps decimated.

Created Duke of Castiglione in March 1808, Augereau fought in the **Peninsular War** from June 1809 until transferred to Germany the following year. Napoleon's oldest active marshal, he was spared participation in the 1812 **Russian campaign**, but returned to the front line to lead IX Corps at **Leipzig** in 1813. Given command of the Army of the East (or the Rhône) for the defence of **France**, he spent early 1814 raising an army at Lyon to threaten the rear of the allied advance on Paris, but showed little enthusiasm for the task. His army eventually moved north from the city in early March, but retreated at the first sign of allied opposition and disintegrated after a desultory action at Saint-Georges on 18 March. Entering royal service in April, he did not return to Napoleon's side during the **Hundred Days** of 1815, but was retired in disgrace when he refused to take part in **Ney's** treason trial.

Aulic Council

The advisory committee to Emperor **Francis II** that was the principal forum for military and strategic planning in **Austria**. An appointed body, presided over by the war minister, the council's influence had varied since its foundation in 1501, but it had been central to Austrian military administration since the reign of Empress Maria Theresa, and was a complex, unwieldy body by the 1790s. A European by-word for administrative inefficiency, tactical inflexibility, factionalism and strategic incoherence, the mixed military–civilian council was usually a force for political conservatism and military optimism, but lost influence in the later war years as **Metternich** accrued power in the new office of chancellor.

Austerlitz, Battle of

Epic confrontation between the French **Grande Armée** and allied Austro-Russian forces massed in south-eastern Germany, fought on 2 December 1805 in the area between Brno and Olmütz (*see* **Map 13**). The battle ended as a crushing French victory that brought the War of the **Third Coalition** to a sudden conclusion, and is widely regarded as **Napoleon's** most brilliant tactical triumph.

Despite his success at **Ulm** in October 1805, and the subsequent occupation of **Vienna**, Napoleon's campaign against the Third Coalition faced potential disaster by late November. Though the **Austrian Army** in Germany was reduced to a remnant, his forces had failed to catch **Kutuzov's** retreating Russian column before it could withdraw on strong reinforcements around Olmütz. While Tsar **Alexander** and Emperor **Francis** prepared to reclaim the initiative in the theatre, their combined strength raised to 89,000 men (and 278 guns) by the arrival of the **Russian Imperial Guard** on 24 November, Napoleon's forward units drew up around Brno, some 20km to the west.

Far from home, and facing imminent bankruptcy of the government in Paris, Napoleon was fast running out of options. With two Austrian armies still at large to his rear, and the **Prussian Army** mobilizing against him, any withdrawal was bound to be interpreted as a defeat, and pursuit of any further allied retreat would be asking for encirclement. Only a quick and decisive battle victory, bringing peace on his own terms, would restore the situation in his favour.

To achieve this, Napoleon needed to persuade the allies to fight a battle on ground of his own choosing, where he would be able to negate their numerical advantage. During the last days of November, he selected a restricted area just west of Austerlitz as his preferred battlefield, and set in motion an elaborate deception designed to provoke an allied attack.

Opening negotiations with allied envoys through General **Savary**, he gave every impression of being anxious to avoid battle and agree peace. Keeping his reinforcements at a distance, so that allied estimates put his strength at only about 40,000 men, he withdrew his troops from the dominant Pratzen Heights west of Austerlitz, and left his right flank weak, inviting attack.

The French front line looked suitably weak. On the left, **Lannes** and 20,000 men held positions running south from the heavily fortified hillock known as the Santon; **Soult**'s 17,000 troops were stretched across the centre, holding villages along the shallow valley of the Bosenitz and Goldbach brooks; and **Davout**'s fast-moving corps was summoned from around Vienna to bolster the threatened right wing. Napoleon also called up **Bernadotte** from Iglau to join **Oudinot**, the **Imperial Guard** and most of his **cavalry** in the reserve, which was hidden from allied view behind the Zurlan Heights on the French centre-left, and brought total French strength up to more than 73,000 men and 139 guns.

The plan was risky in the extreme, depending on allied commanders swallowing the bait in its entirety, and on the ability of his own right wing to withstand attack by superior numbers. Fortunately for Napoleon, the allied high command fell for his deception in a manner so haphazard that its attack plans were drawn up in haste and confusion.

Allied counsels were hopelessly divided from the moment an attack on the French became a realistic possibility. Emperor Francis, inclined to caution, preferred a further withdrawal that would enable reinforcements to reach the theatre, a view supported by some Austrian commanders and Kutuzov. Tsar Alexander, whose troops made up all but 15,000 of the allied field army, was impatient for a victory that would justify his commitment of force so far from home, and eventually came down on the side of his more hawkish advisers, who shared the popular European view that Napoleon was cornered and ripe for a beating.

After allied forces had occupied the Pratzen Heights, commanders considered a welter of battle plans before finally agreeing a course of action on the night of 1–2 December. Presented by Austrian chief of staff Weyrother, and adopted at a nocturnal meeting during which most senior officers were either drunk or asleep, it envisaged a massed manoeuvre south against the French right by 60,000 men under **Buxhowden**, leaving **Bagration**'s 17,500 to pin the French left, and some 9,000 men of the Imperial Russian Guard behind the Pratzen Heights in the centre. Commentators have since regarded Weyrother's plan as basically workable, but hampered by insufficient logistic preparation and fatally flawed in its assumption that Napoleon was intent on a defensive battle.

The first of Buxhowden's strike force had begun moving south along the Pratzen Heights by midnight, convincing Napoleon that the allies had fallen for his ruse, but also that his far right needed reinforcement. He ordered Soult's corps to focus its planned advance a little further south, and transferred 3,000 of its troops to positions around Tilnitz. These early movements masked growing confusion among allied commanders, many of whom had still not received their official orders by morning.

Morale among the rank and file on both sides was high – with the French army in particular fired up for the battle that might mean the end of its long, exhausting campaign – as a cold winter's dawn rose shrouded in a thick mist. By seven the highest ground in the battle zone was just becoming visible to commanders watching from heights behind the lines, and Buxhowden's advance against the French right was already running an hour late, delayed as units became lost or entangled in the fog. Fighting began in the extreme south shortly afterwards. An Austrian division under General Kienmayer formed the vanguard attacking towards Tilnitz, followed by corps under **Doctorov** and Langeron, a Polish division, and finally 23,000 men under Generals Kollowrath and Miloradovich.

Doctorov's corps reached the front line at about eight, after which the thin French screen around Tilnitz crumbled, defenders retreating behind the Goldbach. Just to the north, west of the Goldbach around Sokolnitz, Langeron's corps and the Poles were only prevented from breaking through the French line by their own delays in crossing the stream, which enabled General Friant's division to plug the gap. The respite was temporary. As two French units fired on each other in the continuing mist, Langeron brought up artillery to burst through and take Sokolnitz by nine, while the Polish division got across the Goldbach to seize Sokolnitz Castle.

Though the allies were poised to sweep across his lines of retreat, the fog had lifted from the Pratzen Heights shortly after eight to show Napoleon the last of the allied troops departing. At about eight thirty he ordered Soult, whose troops were still hidden by mist at the foot of the slopes, to occupy the Heights. Soult's corps swept forward in two divisions, under **Vandamme** and **St Hilaire**, overwhelming surprised and out-numbered defenders to occupy the summit within an hour.

A dispirited Kutuzov attempted to call back the rear of Miloradovich's corps, but few units could be turned around in time to face the attack, and allied troops fell back in confusion towards Austerlitz. Commentators have since blamed Kutuzov for not pulling Buxhowden's entire force back to the Heights, and his perfor-mance throughout the battle has been criticized as passive, but a confused allied command structure did not give him clear authority, and the ponderous advance against the French right could not anyway have been reversed in time to prevent Soult from cutting the allied army in half.

Anticipating a counter-attack, Napoleon ordered Soult to secure his new positions, and sent Bernadotte's corps forward in support on the left. Bernadotte advanced to take the village of Blasowitz, but was quickly driven back by part of the Russian Imperial Guard. The Russian Guards had been sent in by Bagration, in command of allied forces to the north of the front and still without clear instructions. Their capture of Blasowitz prompted Lannes, whose primary function was to prevent Bagration from joining the battle in the centre, to advance his forces.

Supported by **Murat**'s heavy horse, and abet-ted by the piecemeal deployment of Russian cav-alry against it, Lannes's corps was eventually halted by Bagration's massed **artillery**, and at ten thirty a strong allied counter-attack was launched against the Santon. After advancing a few hundred metres and capturing Bosenitz, the attack was repulsed by **Suchet**'s outnumbered division guarding the hillock, and Lannes advanced his right to retake Blasowitz at about the same time.

French advance beyond Blasowitz was con-tested by Lichtenstein's Russian cavalry, but Murat led his heavy troops into a charge that overwhelmed superior numbers after a few min-utes' heavy fighting. Once Lichtenstein's troop-ers fled, the Russian force abandoned any attempt to join the battle in the centre. Fighting on the sector had abated somewhat by about noon, Bagration having suffered about 8,000 losses (half of them as prisoners), but still in command of an essentially coherent force.

Meanwhile French forces in the far south were fighting a desperate battle for survival. Though Davout had arrived to take personal command by nine, and most of Buxhowden's massed re-serves remained trapped in bottlenecks across the Goldbach, fewer than 11,000 French troops were barely holding 35,000 attackers when Napoleon ordered Oudinot's division to their aid shortly before ten.

By that time news of Soult's new position on Pratzen Heights was diluting the allied southern thrust, as Langeron began redeploying to sup-port counter-attacks in the centre. Kutuzov had rallied enough of Buxhowden's rearmost infantry by ten thirty to attack St Hilaire's division from three sides, with fighting fiercest at the southern end of the Heights, beyond the village of Pratzen. Desperate defence by the brigade holding the position, culminating in a **bayonet** charge, gave Soult just enough time to bring up the six can-non that constituted his reserve artillery, and their brilliant deployment forced Langeron – in practical command of the sector because Bux-howden was drunk – to withdraw on Sokolnitz and summon reinforcements from the south.

Though apparently a scene of almost static, half-frozen chaos, the battle had taken decisive shape by noon: the allied attack in the south had been halted and was abating; French forces were established on the Pratzen Heights to its rear; and Bagration had been cut off to the north. Napoleon, who had moved his headquarters on to the Heights, now ordered his forces into the next stage of his plan. While Davout was instructed to take the offensive, and Lannes left to his own devices, Soult's corps was ordered to wheel right and attack the flank of Buxhowden's forces, with Bernadotte called up to the Heights in its place.

The manoeuvre was in progress, but Bernadotte had not yet arrived in support, when Grand Duke Constantine's Russian Guard cavalry launched an attack against Vandamme's division that caught its exposed flank. Napoleon ordered **Bessières**, in command of the French Imperial Guard cavalry, to the rescue of Vandamme's infantry, and after a murderous confrontation the Russian horse broke and fled, leaving hundreds of dead on the field. The cavalry engagement ended the allied centre's resistance, and shortly after one thirty Napoleon was able to open the final phase of his attack plan, sending 25,000 troops from the Heights to annihilate the remnants of Buxhowden's wing.

As Davout advanced beyond Telnitz and Sokolnitz, Vandamme and Oudinot moved to cut off any northern and eastern escape routes, taking Augezd within an hour. Inside the trap, Buxhowden had lost any semblance of control over the mingled units of Langeron, Doctorov and the Pole Prszebyszewski. By the time a belated order to withdraw arrived from Kutuzov, the only possible escape lay in finding a route east through the frozen ponds at their backs.

Elements of Kienmayer's Austrian corps had already found a way out by that route, and Doctorov drew up his remaining 5,000 troops in front of the ponds, launching a last-ditch counter-attack to give **Cossack** reconnaissance forces time to find an escape path. Before this had been accomplished, superior French numbers had routed the counter-attack, and allied survivors began fleeing in disarray across the frozen ponds. The accumulated weight of the guns, horses and men piling on to the ponds, along with red-hot shot directed into them by French artillery, turned the flight into a massacre as the ice crumbled. The exact number drowned in the freezing water remains in doubt, with Napoleon subsequently claiming that the ponds took 20,000 lives and Habsburg sources admit-

ting to only two deaths in the water, but modern historians generally accept a figure of about 2,000. All accept that the Russian right had disintegrated by the time French guns stopped firing, and that only a few disorganized stragglers escaped the trap.

By mid-afternoon, Bagration in the north commanded the last coherent allied force. Lannes and Murat, who had remained static for several hours in the absence of any direct orders from Napoleon, were under pressure around the Santon until about three, when Bagration (also still without clear orders of any kind) began a measured withdrawal down the road to Olmütz. As French forces on their right thrust forward to take Krzenowitz, Murat and Lannes made no attempt to sweep round Bagration's flank and prevent him from protecting the main body's bedraggled retreat.

While his marshals bemoaned their lack of orders, Napoleon was raging at their inactivity, a breakdown in communications that denied him the total triumph he would later claim. With Bagration's corps continuing to present a formidable obstacle to limited French attacks in the north, a significant portion of the allied force, including a bewildered Tsar Alexander, was able to stagger away as darkness fell.

By five in the evening the battle had ended. Though no two sources agree on casualty figures, the Grande Armée had lost fewer than 2,000 dead, about 7,000 wounded and some 570 prisoners, out of perhaps 45,000 troops actually engaged in the fighting (several units, like the Imperial Guard infantry, had not fired a shot during the battle). Allied forces, all of which were actively engaged in the fight, had lost perhaps 15,000 dead or wounded (11,000 of them Russians), and another 12,000 prisoners, along with most of their guns and equipment. They also suffered thousands more casualties in the aftermath, as typhus ripped through Russian forces on the march home.

Austerlitz brought the Third Coalition to an almost immediate end. Alexander returned to Russia at once, reaching St Petersburg in ten days, and was followed by the remaining 25,000 men of his battered army. Emperor Francis sued for peace on 3 December, and met

Napoleon in person next day, quickly agreeing an armistice that set up the Peace of **Pressburg**, signed near Vienna towards the end of the month.

Though aided by the errors of his opponents, Napoleon's victory remains one of the great tactical performances in the annals of European warfare. Facing superior numbers, he had controlled the actions of allied leaders, set up the tactical position he required, and then split the allied army in two, before annihilating its elements in detail. Successful during his earlier **Italian campaigns**, this offensive incarnation of Napoleon's **grand tactics** was to confound opponents whenever it was applied until the campaign for **Germany** in 1813, by which time his enemies would finally have learned ways of bringing superior strength efficiently to bear.

Austria

Usually called Austria by contemporaries, the sprawling collection of kingdoms, principalities and duchies ruled by the Habsburg dynasty suffered from an inevitable lack of internal coherence compared with the larger nation states of western Europe. The empire in 1792 was centred on the Habsburg family's hereditary 'homelands' (*Erblande*) of Upper and Lower Austria, the Tyrol, Vorarlberg, Styria, Carinthia, Carniola, Bohemia and the Austrian Adriatic coastal strip. The family also controlled the lands of the Hungarian crown, Transylvania, part of Galicia, the **Austrian Netherlands** (Belgium), large parts of Italy and pockets of territory along the upper Rhine (*see* **Map 1**).

The head of the Habsburg family ruled Austria and its possessions as emperor, but was King of Hungary and its attached territories, giving rise to the title 'Imperial and Royal' (Kaiserlich und Königliche) applied to the **Austrian Army** and other imperial institutions. The Habsburg offices usually included leadership of the **Holy Roman Empire**, but this ancient and essentially separate jurisdiction was dependent on the cooperation of German princes, and was redundant in terms of political control by the late eighteenth century.

The emperor exercised personal rule over the Austrian Empire itself through ministers serving on an appointed state council, but Hungary, the Netherlands, his Italian possessions and the Tyrol were all administered by regional diets. Imperial policy was conducted through the ear of the monarch, with factions around the Viennese court vying for favour, and most senior military or administrative posts were in practice reserved for the nobility, many of whom retained feudal privileges throughout the period.

A total population of about 27 million in 1800 included some 8 million Germans, along with about 5 million Hungarians, 4 million Czechs, large numbers of Walloons, Flemings, Italians, Poles, Serbs and Croats, and many smaller ethnic groups. Only about one in 20 citizens lived in towns containing more than 20,000 people, and about a third of the population was engaged in basic agricultural activity. Farming methods in the Austrian heartlands and parts of Bohemia were modern by contemporary standards, but Alpine regions were agriculturally backward and some outlying eastern provinces had barely progressed beyond tribal culture. The empire's largest city, Vienna, housed almost 250,000 people in 1800, and the only other cities of any size were Prague (about 75,000 people) and Budapest (55,000).

The empire had appeared close to collapse in the early eighteenth century, but although the long reign of Emperor Joseph II saw a reduction of Austrian influence in Germany, it also witnessed substantial territorial gains at the expense of **Poland** and the **Ottoman Empire**. Joseph died in 1790, and his last years were marred by an upsurge in ethnic separatism. Though their powers were severely limited, regional diets could obstruct the transfer of goods, taxes and soldiers to Viennese control, and functioned as vociferous mouthpieces for local interests. The Belgian Vonckist uprising of 1789–90 coincided with threats of secession from Hungary and Galicia, reinforcing Vienna's defensive determination to hold on to its provinces on the grounds that voluntary concessions could presage imperial disintegration.

The aggressive side of Habsburg policy was a commitment to essentially medieval dynastic expansionism. This entailed semi-permanent states of mutual suspicion and conflict with the

Ottoman Empire in the south, with **Prussia** in Germany and Poland, and with **Russia** in Poland and the Balkans. Despite long-term alliance in the decades before 1789, potential conflict with **France** arose out of their mutual frontiers around the upper Rhine and in the Netherlands, but Austria was in many ways a natural ally of **Great Britain**, if only because the one area of potential dispute, the Netherlands' Channel ports, was virtually irrelevant to Vienna's other strategic priorities.

Austria's role in the diplomatic breakdown that triggered the War of the **First Coalition** was less aggressive than that of Prussia or France, but misguided provocation of delicate republican sensibilities in 1791–2 by Joseph's successor, Leopold II, helped plunge Austria into two decades of military and economic disaster. Leopold died in 1792, and was succeeded by **Francis II**, who remained in power throughout the decades of European war.

The **Revolutionary Wars** were immensely costly in territorial terms. By the peace treaties of **Campo Formio** (1797) and **Lunéville** (1801), the empire lost control of most of its Italian territories, parts of southern Germany and the Netherlands, practically guaranteeing pressure on the monarchy to undertake a further war against France at the first viable opportunity. A broad consensus in favour of the war policies of the 1790s among the emperor's advisers, headed by **Thugut**, now gave way to divisive factionalism.

Francis at first put his trust in enlightened conservatives, led by Archduke **Charles** (his younger brother) and foreign minister **Cobenzl**, who sought a long period of peace in which to complete a programme of social and military reforms. Their basic aim was to promote growth of the 'national spirit' and **élan**, perceived as the secret of French military success, but the empire was not by nature 'national', and most feudal or educational reform was focused on its German-speaking subjects. Some important political changes were nevertheless introduced. Cabinet government was adopted in 1801, with ministers having responsibility for particular departments for the first time, and a new codification of the criminal law was issued in 1803.

A war party itching to reclaim lost territories had also gathered in Vienna, headed by General **Mack** and the emperor's long-standing confidant **Colleredo**. Never a particularly consistent or strong-minded monarch, but inclined to bursts of wilful self-determination, Francis was gradually swayed by the hawks. Overruling warnings from Charles that the army was unprepared for war, he took Austria into the **Third Coalition** against France on 9 August 1805.

The catastrophic defeats at **Ulm** and **Austerlitz** in 1805 brought a rapid end to the war, effectively ended the careers of the non-royals most closely involved and once more cost the empire dear. The Treaty of **Pressburg** demanded payment of huge indemnities and forced Austria to give up its remaining possessions in Italy, the Vorarlberg, southern Germany and the Tyrol. To complete the empire's humiliation, **Bavaria** and **Württemberg** were freed from all obligations to the Holy Roman Empire, presaging its abolition by **Napoleon** in July 1806. His armies and finances shattered, the emperor could only accept his loss of international influence and become 'Francis I, Emperor of Austria', having transformed that title from elective to hereditary in 1804.

Charles resumed control over military development in 1806, but the extent of Austria's failure soon brought renewed calls for revenge, now led by foreign minister **Stadion** and the Empress Ludovica (who married Francis in January 1808, nine months after the death of his first wife, Maria Theresa). Too weak to risk military reprisals by joining the **Fourth Coalition** in 1806, Francis eventually came round to Stadion's argument that intensive reorganization had rendered the army capable of defeating the French, and that reforms to the educational and recruitment systems had created the basis for a more genuinely national war effort.

Charles remained adamant that more time was needed, but the abolition of the cabinet system in June 1808 effectively silenced argument. Seduced by Napoleon's apparent weakness, and a belief that Germans everywhere were ready to rise up against French domination, Francis made a secret commitment to war on 8 February 1809. Austria's fourth attempt to beat France since

1792 ended in another defeat at **Wagram** in July 1809, and another comprehensive humiliation under the terms of the **Schönbrunn** Treaty, stripping the empire of about a fifth of its remaining population. A war indemnity of about 85 million francs and restriction of the army to a maximum of 150,000 men completed the empire's reduction to second-class international status for as long as Napoleon was in a position to police the agreement.

Habsburg economic policy was based on the desire for internal self-sufficiency, and the empire's common customs frontier was used to exact punitive tolls on foreign imports. Some internal customs barriers still existed through the war period, but their ill effects on imperial finances were trivial compared with the cost of successive struggles against France. Austrian **war finance** lurched into terminal crisis after 1809, with rampant inflation and reduced income obstructing attempts at social, educational and military reform.

Stadion was replaced after the defeat by the infinitely more cautious Count **Metternich**, and the army was restored to about 250,000 men (including **Landwehr** militia) during the rapprochement with France that followed Napoleon's marriage to the emperor's eldest daughter, **Marie-Louise**, in early 1810. A full military alliance with France followed in March 1812, requiring the army to provide troops for the **Russian campaign**, and although a number of officers resigned in protest, Metternich was unwilling to risk any dispute with Napoleon before he judged the time right.

Metternich was responsible for keeping Austria out of the **Sixth Coalition** until the **armistice** of summer 1813, thus ensuring that preparations for war were completed well in advance. Once the defeat of France had been achieved in 1814, Metternich represented Francis at the Congress of **Vienna**, securing restoration of the empire's pre-1792 boundaries, along with additional territories in Dalmatia, Carniola, Salzburg and the new northern Italian kingdom of Lombardy-Venetia. He also worked with British foreign minister **Castlereagh** to establish the basis for a lasting peace, and sought to lessen friction with Prussia and Russia by attaching Austria to the **Holy Alliance** of conservative monarchs.

Internal dissent had not been soothed by two decades of war, and had centred on the ever-querulous Hungarian diet. Always jealous of its separate rights and privileges, the diet had forced concessions over the use of the Hungarian language in return for providing troops in 1805, and regional agitation (much of it French-sponsored) continued through the 1809 war. A confrontation with Vienna over introduction of new paper money culminated in the diet's dissolution on 30 May 1812, and Francis ruled Hungary by personal decree for the next 13 years.

Hungary's fate was symptomatic of the reactionary postwar policies supervised by Metternich. Committed to maintenance and gradual southerly expansion of the empire, he worked to strengthen its central authority at the expense of ethnic or liberal interests. Aided by Stadion, who returned to office as finance minister from 1814, and by a formidable police service under Count Sedlnitzky, he was able to survive the repercussions of widespread famine in the immediate postwar years to restore the empire's financial position, and to maintain its territorial integrity through the next three decades. *See* **Map 30**.

Austrian Army

The army of the Habsburg emperor, as opposed to the forces he usually commanded as head of the **Holy Roman Empire**, had been created in its contemporary form as the Imperial and Royal Army (Kaiserlich und Königliche Armee) in 1745. Supreme command was vested in the person of the emperor, who appointed all officers above the rank of major and was generally very active in military affairs.

Coming to the throne on the eve of war with France, **Francis II** inherited an army unreplenished since war with Turkey and far below its nominal strength. Francis was no soldier, sometimes taking nominal field command but not attempting direct control of formations, and he generally preferred civilian advisers to military strategists.

Strategic planning emerged from a variety of overlapping sources. The emperor's personal entourage exercised varying degrees of influence at different times, and his advisory **Aulic Council** functioned as a faction-ridden forum for strategic debate. It spawned a military committee with an ill-defined role in 1792, and much practical planning work devolved on the Grand War Council (Hofkriegsrat), a mixed civilian–military institution that was always overwhelmed by its ramshackle responsibility for a welter of administrative detail.

Operational efficiency was undermined by the army's anachronistic organization along regimental lines, and a shortage of officers competent to lead large, mixed formations. An officer corps dominated by high-born amateurs was unreceptive to tactical innovation, and few mechanisms existed for nurturing military talent from outside the aristocracy. Field regulations required every army commander to consult with the leaders of its various components before undertaking any major manoeuvre, stifling initiative and further slowing the operations of forces already desperately short of **field trains**.

With no hope of appealing to any kind of patriotic emotion in a multi-ethnic, multilingual empire, the army relied for manpower on a combination of volunteer enlistment and partial **conscription**, the latter riddled with exemptions at every social level except the lowest, and applied only in the Austrian 'imperial homelands'. Hungary provided imperial troops by a form of conscription, local authorities imposing quotas on individual districts, but they seldom matched nominal strength in practice. The only part of the empire under universal conscription was the Military Border area (*Grenz*) on the **Ottoman** frontier, where the active male population as a whole formed a partly trained militia.

Border zone militia provided the Imperial Army with 17 light infantry regiments in 1792, although they were widely regarded as unsuitable for frontline operations. The regular army comprised 57 infantry, 37 **cavalry** and three field **artillery** regiments. Along with garrison, **fortress**, technical and depot troops, its paper strength was some 360,000 men, but only about 230,000 troops were actually mobilized.

The army's performance during five years as the military mainstay of the **First Coalition** included a few inconclusive victories on the **Rhine** in 1796 that made the reputation of the emperor's younger brother, Archduke **Charles**, but were otherwise fruitless, revealing the weakness of the army's rigid insistence on orthodox eighteenth-century **infantry tactics**, and the vulnerability of its **cordon** approach to higher tactics.

The brief period of peace before the War of the **Second Coalition** (1799–1801) afforded little opportunity for reform, apart from a few cosmetic changes inspired by chief minister **Thugut**. The army had grown to a nominal strength of 400,000, but it actually numbered about 300,000. Let down by the government's strategic inconsistencies, and ultimately outfought by **Napoleon** and **Moreau**, its resounding defeat provoked a much more serious attempt at reform after 1801.

The task was given to Charles, the only senior commander to have emerged with much credit from the **Revolutionary Wars**, but he planned for an extended period of peaceful reconstruction, and his long-term measures had achieved little more than trivial administrative changes by 1805. As the prospect of another European coalition loomed, the emperor abandoned Charles, his peace policy and his realistically gloomy view of the army's prospects in favour of the rose-tinted plans of a war party guided by General **Mack**.

The Austrian Army that fought the War of the **Third Coalition** was understrength, mustering 80,000 men fewer after mobilization than in 1799, and again saddled with a fundamentally flawed strategy. Although some measures had been taken to halt the artillery arm's deterioration, the number of cavalry regiments had been reduced to 35 and the overall quality of the officer corps had fallen still further. A series of hasty reforms pushed through by Mack from April 1805, including complex but superficial alterations to infantry tactics, only added to the army's confusions.

The disasters of **Ulm** and **Austerlitz**, followed by a purge of those held responsible, left Charles once more in position to rehabilitate the army. Some progress was made in modernizing infantry tactics, and a version of the **infantry** square was introduced in 1807, but the importance of properly trained **skirmishers** was not fully appreciated. The cavalry arm's infantry support role was stressed over its more traditional strike role, and belated steps were taken to rationalize the artillery arm for concentrated deployment. The problem of incompetence at the highest level was barely addressed, and the army still employed 422 generals (with an average age of 63) in 1807. The Austrian Army lost only 49 generals killed in action between 1792 and 1815, compared with 219 in the **French Army**, an attrition rate that provided few promotion opportunities for ambitious young officers.

It was recognized that improved conditions for enlisted men would improve their fighting enthusiasm, and service periods were shortened to encourage volunteers, but the government was deeply suspicious of anything bearing the revolutionary taint of a people in arms. The work of Spanish **guerrillas** in the **Peninsular War** eventually prompted expansion of the territorial army (**Landwehr**), but it was seldom trusted with frontline duties.

The 1806–9 reforms were far from complete, and Charles retained many of the tactical orthodoxies that had already failed three times, but a majority of the army command and the emperor's civilian advisers had persuaded Francis into renewed war preparations by early 1809. The army's field strength had recovered to almost 285,000 men – including some 181,000 line infantry, about 50,000 part-trained levies and Grenze, 22,000 reinforcements and about 32,000 cavalry – but while most of the trained troops fought well in the 1809 campaign, they were again disadvantaged by chaotic central planning.

Defeat at **Wagram** brought forth the usual calls for military reform, and Charles retired permanently from command. Francis entrusted reconstruction of the army to the relatively junior General **Radetsky**, who faced a combination of reduced population and shrinking budgets but managed to establish a basis for future expansion. Treaty obligations to France required disbandment of the militia and reduction of the standing army to no more than 150,000 men, but the militia were soon reinstated and regular

army strength stood just above 250,000 by 1811, as Napoleon sought to sustain Austrian friendship by relaxing the rules.

An Austrian corps of some 24,000 infantry and 6,000 cavalry, led by **Schwarzenberg**, fought under Napoleon's direct command during the **Russian campaign**, losing 7,000 men in battle and 4,000 to exposure before negotiating a local neutrality convention with the Russians in January 1813. For the next few months, while Austria remained cautiously aloof from the **Sixth Coalition**, the army was quietly expanded and mobilized.

When war was declared on France in August, the army fielded almost 200,000 men in Bohemia, along with 37,000 guarding the heartlands and another 39,000 on the Danube. By the end of the month almost 480,000 troops were under arms, and 568,000 men had been mobilized by spring 1814, with frontline strength kept at around 200,000 in the main theatres throughout. Supply was unable to match manpower increases, and the Austrian Army was the worst-equipped major force fighting in **France**, a situation worsened by the late arrival of material **subsidies** from **Great Britain**.

The Austrian Army of 1814 was still sprawling, top-heavy and burdened with an inefficient medieval bureaucracy. Deep-seated internal divisions along ethnic or factional lines, and the entrenched conservatism of an autocratic leadership, remained major obstacles to reform. It had nevertheless displayed a steady improvement in operational efficiency after 1805, and its solid if unspectacular performance during the campaigns of 1813–14 confirmed its emergence as a genuinely effective, if limited, instrument of imperial policy.

Austrian Navy

The Habsburg Empire had little experience of **naval warfare** by the late eighteenth century. Its only coastline opened on to the northern and eastern Adriatic, and was easily cut off from the **Mediterranean** or the wider oceans. Small-scale experiments with a naval squadron based on Trieste were all but abandoned in 1790, and most of its **gunboats** transferred to the flotilla patrolling the Danube frontiers. By early 1793, increased budgets had restored five small warships and seven gunboats to the 'Trieste Navy', and they won a minor victory on 26 March 1797, when they helped a **Venetian Navy** 64-gunner drive off French attacks on the harbour at Quieto. Four old **frigates** and two dozen small craft were taken from **Venice** in 1798, forming an 'Austro-Venetian Navy'. It remained virtually inactive until defeat at **Wagram** in 1809 deprived Austria of any Adriatic interests, at which point it was disbanded along with the Danube flotilla. Reconstituted in April 1814 with four former French **ships-of-the-line**, two frigates and two **corvettes**, the navy was again allowed to decay, and **Austria** made no serious effort to develop as a naval power until the late nineteenth century.

Austrian Netherlands

Contemporary name for the predominantly Catholic southern provinces of the Netherlands that were under Habsburg control until 1789, and periodically thereafter until their annexation by **France** in 1795. United with Holland under the Dutch crown from 1815, they achieved independence as the sovereign kingdom of Belgium in 1831. *See* The **Netherlands**.

Ayvaille, Battle of

French victory on 18 September 1794 over Austrian forces retreating from **Flanders** that precipitated a further Austrian withdrawl to the Rhine. Austrian commander **Clairfait** had positioned his forces on a line east of the Meuse between Stocken and Ayvaille in late August, with General **Kray** holding a bridgehead across the river at Maastricht and a strong central position at La Chartreuse, opposite Liège (*see* **Map 2**). French theatre commander **Jourdan** launched **Schérer's** right wing towards Ayvaille on 18 September, while **Kléber's** left launched a secondary assault around Maastricht. Schérer's well-organized attacks drove 25,000 Austrians north-east towards Verviers, and the garrison at La Chartreuse could only follow. As further French attacks disrupted efforts to re-form his left wing on 20 September, Clairfait pulled his whole army back to a line centred on Aix-la-Chapelle, leaving Maastricht's isolated garrison under **siege**. Rapid French pursuit took Aix on 22 September, and Jourdan ignored **Carnot's** orders make Maastricht his priority, concentrating for an attack on the new allied line in front of the River **Roer**.

B

Badajoz

Western Spanish fortress town that guarded the southern of the two main roads into **Portugal**, and was central to the **Peninsular War** campaigns of 1811 and 1812 (*see* **Map 22**). Once French failure at the **Torres Vedras** lines in autumn 1810 had secured Portugal against invasion, British commander **Wellington** sought control of Badajoz and **Ciudad Rodrigo**, its counterpart on the northern road, to cover the rear of any offensive into Spain. Meanwhile hunger and disease forced **Masséna's** French army out of Portugal altogether, and **Soult** marched a force north from the siege of **Cadiz** to invest the Spanish garrison at Badajoz from 26 January 1811.

Faced by solid resistance, Soult had made little progress when French defeat further south at **Barrosa** on 5 March, and Masséna's withdrawal north on the same day, forced him to prepare a withdrawal. Resorting to deception, he used the garrison commander's death as a pretext for opening negotiations and bluffed Spanish forces into surrender on 9 March.

Wellington ordered **Beresford** and 20,000 troops to recapture Badajoz in late April. Though lacking sufficient **artillery**, Beresford opened a siege on 7 May, but withdrew five days later to meet Soult's returning army at **Albuera**. French raids destroyed Beresford's **siege** works while he was away, but they had been restored by 24 May, and Badajoz was eventually surrounded by 14,000 allied troops under Wellington's command. Handicapped by continued equipment shortages, they withdrew on the approach of 58,000 troops, and the garrison was relieved on 20 June.

After his seizure of Ciudad Rodrigo in January 1812, Wellington left detachments under **Hill** and **Graham** to guard against French incursions from the north and south, and led his remaining 27,000 troops (with heavy artillery) to open a third siege of Badajoz on 16 March. General Phillipon's 5,000-strong garrison was very well supplied, and attacking operations were hindered by spring floods and regular French sorties from strengthened fortifications. Signs that **Marmont** (Masséna's replacement) and Soult were preparing relief operations eventually prompted an all-out assault on the virtually intact defences on the evening of 6 April.

An ill-coordinated attack got under way more than two hours late, and costly infantry assaults achieved nothing for more than an hour. Wellington was close to abandoning the operation when a frontal attack by **Picton's** division managed to capture part of the castle and **Leith's** division successfully stormed the north-western ramparts. The combined pressure broke the defence soon after midnight, and Phillipon retired across the Guadiana River into the San Cristobal fort before surrendering on terms next day. French forces had suffered 1,350 casualties but the attack cost Wellington 3,350 men, bringing his overall losses for the siege close to 5,000. As he planned an offensive towards **Salamanca**, survivors pillaged the town for three days.

Badajoz, Treaty of *See* War of the **Oranges**

Baden

South-west German principality formed in 1771 by the union of Baden-Baden and Baden-Durlach under the rule of Margrave Charles Frederick. Charles Frederick gave loyal support to **Austria** through the **Revolutionary Wars**, committing his army's two infantry regiments and three **cavalry** companies to the allied cause. Baden suffered widespread devastation as a battleground, and was forced to pay a large indemnity as the price of peace when French forces swept west of the **Rhine** in 1796.

Baden's size was considerably increased by the reorganization of the **Holy Roman Empire** in February 1803, by which time relations with France had greatly improved, largely through the work of ambassador von Reitzen in Paris. They reached a new low in March 1804, when the Duc d'**Enghein** was abducted from the Baden town of Ettenheim. Powerless to translate protest into active resistance, Baden signed an alliance with France on 1 October 1805, and profited by **Napoleon**'s subsequent victory over the **Third Coalition**, gaining considerable territory by the Treaties of **Brno** and **Pressburg** in December.

The ageing Charles Frederick, titled Elector since 1803, became a grand duke in August 1806 as a reward for joining the Confederation of the **Rhine**, and later that year his heir, Charles Ludwig Frederick, married Napoleon's step-daughter, Stéphanie de Beauharnais. The army was subsequently enlarged for French imperial service, providing four infantry and two cavalry regiments (one of them absorbed from the **Bavarian Army** to reflect frontier changes) for the campaigns of 1806–7 and 1809, the **Peninsular War** and the 1812 **Russian campaign**, when most of the 9,000 Baden troops were killed.

Charles Ludwig Frederick became grand duke on his grandfather's death in June 1811, by which time territorial acquisitions from **Württemberg** had quadrupled Baden's size in less than a decade. With Reitzen as chief minister from 1809 to 1810, and again from 1813 to 1818, he enacted a series of constitutional and social reforms on the French model, and eventually introduced a parliamentary constitution in 1818. Loyal to France through the campaign for **Germany** in 1813, he was eventually persuaded to join the **Sixth Coalition** on 24 November, and was allowed to keep his territorial acquisitions by the Congress of **Vienna**. *See* **Maps 1, 30**.

Baggavout, Karl Federovich (1761–1812)

Estonian-born officer who saw service with the **Russian Army** in **Poland** and against the **Ottoman Empire** before 1792, and who commanded a division during the War of the **Third Coalition** against France in 1805. He fought in the **Russo-Swedish War** during 1808, and was given command of II Corps, part of **Barclay de Tolly**'s first Army of the West, for the 1812 campaign. Present at **Borodino** in early September, he was killed in action during October.

Bagration, Peter, Prince (1765–1812)

Highly regarded Russian commander, from a noble Georgian background, who joined the tsar's army in 1782 and held minor commands under **Suvorov** during his **Italian** and **Swiss** campaigns in 1799. Commanding the rearguard of **Kutuzov**'s advanced army in Germany in November 1805, he held off much more numerous French forces at **Hollabrünn**, and performed better than most during the subsequent allied defeat at **Austerlitz**.

Bagration led formations at **Eylau**, **Heilsberg** and **Friedland** in 1806–7, and took part in both the **Russo-Turkish** and **Russo-Swedish** Wars during the years of peace with France. Popular both inside and outside the army, he was given command of the Second Army of the West for the **Russian campaign** of 1812. After taking part in the defence of **Smolensk**, and arguing with **Barclay de Tolly**, he led the left wing of reorganized Russian forces at **Borodino** in September, but was wounded during the battle and died of an infection later that month.

Bailén, Battle of

The first major Spanish success of the **Peninsular War**, won by Andalusian forces over a French army under General **Dupont** on 20 July 1808. Dupont had entered southern Spain with 13,000 troops in June, under orders to take Córdoba and Seville as part of a wider attempt to snuff out the nascent Spanish rebellion. Forced by local insurgents to evacuate Córdoba, he had retreated to the plains around Andújar when the arrival of General Vedel's division in mid-July brought his strength up to 23,000 men, seemingly enough to assure control of the region.

Dupont's troops were mostly raw recruits, suffering under sweltering conditions, and peasant support had helped swell the Andalusian army of General **Castaños** to 30,000 men. Unwilling to admit failure by retreating to the relative safety of the Sierra Moreno, and too weak to storm Córdoba, Dupont lingered at Andújar while Castaños mobilized. When he eventually decided to withdraw, Dupont sent Vedel ahead with 10,000 men to clear the road while the rest of his army moved slowly behind, laden with 1,200 invalids and 500 wagons of loot from Córdoba. By 18 July a 50km gap separated the two.

General **Redding**'s 17,000 Spanish troops occupied the town of Bailén on 19 July, confronting Dupont's advance while Castaños led another 13,000 from Andújar against its rear. Realizing he was cut off from Vedel, Dupont launched five attacks against Bailén, but all failed for lack of frontline coordination. He opened surrender negotiations later the same day, partly because his troops were close to mutiny (one Swiss brigade had already defected to the Spanish side).

Talks were briefly suspended when Vedel's advance units arrived to disperse Spanish rearguards, but Vedel merely withdrew before returning to take part in negotiations. Dupont surrendered his army on 21 July, including Vedel's troops still at large, and 18,000 men marched into captivity two days later. Senior officers received **parole**, but promises of repatriation for troops were broken.

A massive boost to rebel morale, Bailén persuaded Joseph **Bonaparte** to quit Madrid for the line of the Ebro, and was followed by French setbacks at **Saragossa** and **Vimeiro**. It also damaged the **French Army**'s reputation for invincibility, emboldened Pope **Pius VII** openly to denounce **Napoleon**, and added weight to the arguments of a war party in **Austria**. Napoleon reacted by imprisoning Dupont for the rest of the war, and held long-term grudges against most of the senior officers involved, but he also recognized the need to transfer large-scale reinforcements to Spain from eastern Europe. *See* **Map 22**.

Baird, David (1757–1829)

British soldier, promoted major-general and posted to **India** in 1798, who took part in the 1799 **Seringapatam campaign**, and led the Indian force that arrived just too late to take part in the expulsion of French forces from **Egypt** in 1801. A brief spell as governor of the **Cape Colony** from 1806 ended in dismissal after the failure of the **Buenos Aires** expedition the following year, but Baird returned to England in time to command a division at **Copenhagen** and led reinforcements to join **Moore**'s army in Spain before **Corunna**. Though not given another active command, he was appointed C-in-C for Ireland in 1820.

Balloons

The first manned flight by balloon had been carried out by the brothers Montgolfier as recently as 1783, but the magnitude of the subsequent popular craze for ballooning in **France** encouraged early, if small-scale, attempts to make military use of air power as a reconnaissance and **artillery** observation aid. At the instigation of French scientist Nicolas Conté, a few balloons were used for these purposes during 1793–4, and enjoyed some success at the Battle of **Fleurus**, stimulating the formation of an experimental balloon company. Basic technical and organizational problems had barely been addressed, so that the company achieved little before it was disbanded by First Consul **Napoleon**, and military use of balloons was not revived until the colonial wars of the mid-nineteenth century.

Bank Crisis, British

The British **Pitt** government's early **war finance** policies entailed maintenance of a substantial national debt, which in turn depended on a well-developed banking system's credit with the nation's investors. The success and viability of the system aroused controversy throughout Europe during the **Revolutionary Wars**, and a considerable school of economic thought, strongest in **France** but with adherents everywhere, held that **Great Britain** was only a crisis of popular confidence away from economic collapse.

By early 1797 the prediction seemed likely to come true. Five years of war had shrivelled

British bullion reserves, and French plans to invade **England** on the back of victories everywhere else had eroded popular confidence. The French **Bantry Bay expedition** of late 1796 started a trickle of hard currency withdrawals from banks in northern Britain, and this suddenly accelerated to a flood in late February 1797 on news of a French landing in **Pembrokeshire**. Panic had set in by the time the invasion scare was over on 25 February (a Friday), forcing the government to suspend payments in hard currency the next day.

The Bank of England began issuing paper money on the same day, and doubts about its general acceptance at face value were quelled by a statement on 27 February that the bank possessed £10 million in bullion reserves. The crisis disappeared almost overnight, completing a permanent transition that secured the British war effort against future psychological sabotage.

Bantry Bay Expedition

Unsuccessful French attempt to invade **Ireland**, launched in December 1796. Encouraged by Irish nationalist leader Wolfe **Tone**'s claims that the Irish were ready to rebel, and by the enthusiasm of General **Hoche**, French war minister **Carnot** prepared a force of 15,000 troops and a strong naval escort at the Atlantic port of Brest during autumn 1796. The British government was alert to the danger by mid-November, and had anyway been preparing coastal defences against a possible invasion of **England**, but most of the force on **blockade** duty was in winter quarters when 17 French **ships-of-the-line**, 26 other warships and troop transports left Brest on 15 December.

Military commander Hoche and naval commander de Galles were not aware that three clearly visible **frigates** were the only British ships on station. Hoche ordered the fleet to steer south on 16 December to avoid the presumed blockade, but a gathering storm prompted de Galles to signal a course change that afternoon. In gloomy conditions, the signal was missed by many of his ships, which split into two groups. Confusion mounted during the night as **Pellew**'s frigate *Indefatigable* got among the French in the dark, and by morning three French ships were wrecked

and the rest were dispersed in three groups. The frigate *Fraternité*, with Hoche and de Galles aboard, was missing.

Pellew alerted British authorities to the escape on 20 December, and Channel Fleet C-in-C Bridport (Alexander **Hood**) received the news in Portsmouth next day, by which time most of the French fleet had regrouped off the south-west coast of Ireland. The fleet attempted to sail up Bantry Bay from 22 December, but head winds and poor seamanship prevented significant progress before Christmas Day, when acting commander Admiral Bouvet called off the invasion.

French ships departed in widely separated squadrons, the last finally leaving the bay on 3 January, but Bridport's fleet failed to intercept any of them. Pellew's destruction of the *Droits de l'Homme* provided small consolation, but most of the French force, including the commanders' lost frigate, got safely back to Brest by 14 January, and the episode contributed to general dissatisfaction with the **Royal Navy**'s performance at a difficult time in the **naval** war.

Bar-sur-Aube Conference

Important meeting of allied leaders held at the eastern French town of Bar-sur-Aube on 25 February 1814, at a time when the campaign for **France** was going badly for the forces of the **Sixth Coalition**. The meeting was attended by Tsar **Alexander**, Austrian emperor **Francis**, Prussian king **Frederick William**, Swedish crown prince **Bernadotte** and British Foreign Secretary **Castlereagh**. Allied C-in-C **Schwarzenberg**'s cautious behaviour occasioned much criticism, but he was given permission to continue the withdrawal of his southern army to the Plain of Langres. All parties supported a decision to send 35,000 troops south to guard against any threat from **Augereau**, who was slowly building a new French army at Lyon, but Russian and Prussian aggression was reflected in the proviso that Schwarzenberg must resume his advance if French forces moved north against **Blücher**'s army. Despite Bernadotte's protests, the forces of **Bülow** and **Winzingerode** in the far north were placed under the aggressive Prussian's independent command, a decision soon vindicated at **Laon**.

Barbary War

Sporadic naval conflict of 1801–5 between the **United States** and the Pasha of Tripoli, most important of the Barbary States along the **Mediterranean** coast of North Africa (*see* **Map 8**). Nominally subject to **Ottoman Empire** authority, Tripoli was the main base for pirates who menaced all Mediterranean merchant shipping, and the US government paid the pasha an annual financial 'tribute' to provide protection against attacks.

American refusal to increase the tribute brought a declaration of war from Tripoli on 14 May 1801, forcing the **US Navy** to provide escort warships for Mediterranean merchantmen, and the war escalated when the USS *Philadelphia* and its crew were captured after running aground off Tripoli on 31 October 1803. A US squadron scuttled the *Philadelphia* during a raid against Tripoli harbour on 16 February 1804, and the city was bombarded by American vessels during August and September.

The war came to an end after US **marines** were landed on the Barbary coast in 1805. They captured the port of Derna on 26 April, and were threatening Tripoli itself when the pasha came to terms, agreeing to release prisoners for a ransom of $60,000 and to waive future tributes from the United States. Barbary pirates remained a threat to US and other shipping in the western Mediterranean, and their activities prompted a brief resumption of hostilities between March and June in 1815, which took the form of punitive raids on the Algerian coast by a squadron of **frigates** and smaller craft.

Barclay de Tolly, Mikhail Andreas (1761–1818)

A third-generation Russian with Scottish ancestry, born in the Baltic province of Livonia (modern Latvia), Barclay de Tolly entered Russian service in 1776, and his administrative talents earned steady promotion from the ranks through campaigns against the **Ottoman Empire**, **Sweden** and **Poland**. A major-general by 1806, he commanded the Russian right wing at **Pultusk** and was seriously wounded at **Eylau** the following spring, after a performance that earned promotion to lieutenant-general and

the admiration of Tsar **Alexander I**.

He took part in the **Russo-Swedish War** of 1809, and was appointed war minister the following year. Armed with the tsar's support, but opposed by a conservative faction among senior officers, he instigated widespread reforms of the **Russian Army** over the next two years. Along with improvements to internal communications, standing defences and weaponry, a thoroughgoing administrative overhaul produced a larger, more rationally organized army by 1812.

Barclay led the First Army of the West, the largest force opposing the French invasion in 1812, but proved an unadventurous field commander and attracted growing criticism for his policy of permanent retreat during the first phase of the **Russian campaign**. As an atmosphere of rising patriotic hysteria inside Russia demanded a more aggressive strategy, popular demands for Barclay's replacement were backed by false rumours of his treachery, based solely on the French appearance of his name. After evacuating the important city of **Smolensk**, he was superseded in command by **Kutuzov** on 29 August, and resigned after leading the Russian right wing at **Borodino** in September.

Still much admired by Alexander, he returned to corps command in **Germany** during 1813, reaching the theatre in time to fight at **Bautzen**, and accompanied the tsar throughout the campaign. As senior Russian commander among the allied armies, he directed the attack on the southern perimeters at **Leipzig** in October, and was officially appointed Russian C-in-C in **France** for the 1814 campaign. Promoted field marshal and granted a princedom after Napoleon's defeat, he led Russian forces heading for France during the **Hundred Days** of 1815, but saw no action.

Bard, Fort, Defence of

The tiny fort at Bard stood in a narrow valley on the Dora Baltea River, north-west of Ivrea, and blocked the path of the French Reserve Army in May 1800, as it advanced through the **Great St Bernard Pass** to attack Austrian forces on the **Italian** front (*see* **Map 9**). Garrisoned by only 400 men and 26 cannon of assorted vintage, the fort resisted initial attacks by advanced French units from 20 May, inducing advance guard commander **Lannes** to send his infantry on through the hills around the fort. He was also able to send six guns and their **caissons** past the fort during the nights of 24 and 25 May. The rest of **Napoleon**'s infantry circumnavigated the obstacle as it arrived, but **artillery** and **cavalry** were unable to proceed further until the eventual capitulation of fort commandant Colonel Bernkopf on 5 June, which gave them just time to join the battle at **Marengo**.

Barras, Paul Jean François Nicolas, Comte de (1755–1829)

French aristocrat and former soldier whose life as a Parisian rake was transformed by the **French Revolution**. Embracing radical ideals with ferocious intensity, Barras was an original member of the **Jacobin** club and served as a deputy for his native Var region. He won national fame as a political representative during the recapture of **Toulon** in 1793, along with notoriety for his brutal reprisals against royalists, and was a central figure in the 1794 **Thermidor** coup that overthrew **Robespierre**.

The most important member of the **Directory** government that followed, he supervised the end of the **Terror** and developed an aptitude for the retention of power, organizing alternate political coups against royalist and radical elements in Paris. At the same time his personal greed and the regime's ill-concealed corruption made Barras extremely unpopular. Viewed as the personification of a manifestly unsustainable regime, his days were numbered after the resignation of his chief political ally, **Talleyrand**, in February 1799.

His relationship with **Napoleon**, begun at Toulon and extended after the latter's part in the **Vendémiaire** coup, was never close but had been mutually beneficial. A former lover of **Joséphine** de Beauharnais, Barras possessed the political acumen to recognize both the value and the danger of Napoleon's strengths. He was responsible for giving the young Corsican his first independent command in Italy, but gave his support to the **Brumaire** coup of November 1799 too late to have any hope of office under the **Consulate**. He spent the rest of his life in retirement, enjoying a considerable fortune amassed during the 1790s.

Barrosa, Battle of

Victory by an allied expeditionary force over French forces near **Cadiz** on 5 March 1811. Some 25,000 French troops had been besieging Cadiz since February 1810, facing a garrison of similar strength, but local commander **Victor** was required to detach 8,000 of his best troops to aid **Soult**'s attack on **Badajoz** in early 1811. This coincided with an allied plan to land a force from Cadiz some 80km south at Tarifa, and then to attack the besieging force from the rear with the support of a strong sortie from the city (*see* Map 22).

Commanded by Spanish general La Peña, whose 8,000 **Spanish Army** regulars were joined by **Graham**'s 5,000 British and Portuguese troops, the expedition set sail on 21 February, but suffered a series of delays. Bad weather forced Graham's contingent to land further down the coast at Algeciras, and the two elements were not reunited until 27 February. The operation was two days behind schedule by 3 March, and unable to support the attack from Cadiz, which had only limited effect.

When allied forces moving west along the coast did make contact with French troops on 5 March, around heights just north of the landmark tower at Barrosa, La Peña's troops fled and Graham was forced to retire in their wake. Rallying his men, Graham charged his two brigades back up the slope to scatter General Laval's 7,000 troops and march on Cadiz. Graham suffered 1,200 casualties, and the Cadiz siege was not seriously disturbed, but the victory was a major **propaganda** success and confirmed a growing belief that British troops could defeat the French on equal terms. *See also* **Peninsular War**.

Basle, Treaties of (1795)

The treaties that ended Prussian and Spanish involvement in the **First Coalition** were both signed in the neutral Swiss town of Basle during 1795. The defection of **Prussia**, more interested in the ongoing crisis in **Poland** and only kept in the war by British **subsidies**, had been expected for months before King **Frederick William II** finally signed an agreement with France on 5 April. Prussia recognized French control of the north German lands west of the Rhine until the end of the war, after which France agreed to help secure compensation for Berlin elsewhere in Germany. The naked venality of these terms, which entailed the first official recognition of the French republic by a major Christian monarchy, damaged Prussia's already poor reputation in European diplomatic circles.

Prussian defection triggered a rush to make peace among the Coalition's weaker nations, and **Spain** was facing invasion across the **Pyrenean** frontier when it signed a treaty with France on 12 July 1795. Negotiated on the Spanish monarchy's behalf by chief minister **Godoy** (henceforth known as the 'Prince of Peace'), it returned French-held Pyrenean passes to Spain in exchange for the cession of Hispaniola, the Spanish colony then engaged in a frontier war with French **Santo Domingo**. Its principal strategic side effects were confined to **colonial** and **naval** warfare.

Basque Roads, Attack on the

Partially successful British attempt to destroy a **French Navy** fleet that escaped from the **blockade** of Brest in spring 1809. French admiral Willaumez had slipped past Admiral Gambier's **Royal Navy** squadron on 2 February with eight **ships-of-the-line** and four smaller warships, aiming to link up with ships from Lorient and Rochefort for a raid on the **West Indies**. Manoeuvring in the channels off the western French coast, Willaumez picked up three ships-of-the-line from Rochefort and by 26 February his ships were anchored in the Basque Roads, an offshore approach channel covered by **artillery** batteries on the Ile d'Aix (*see* **Map 18**).

Hemmed in by shallows, the French fleet was bottled up by Gambier's 11 battleships, eight frigates and 18 smaller ships, which were all in position by mid-March. Unable to approach a position the French fleet (now commanded by Admiral Allemand) considered impregnable, Gambier got permission from London to attack with **fireships**.

The highly rated Captain Cochrane arrived with a frigate, nine fireships and a supply of **Congreve rockets** on 26 March, and attacked on the evening of 11 April, sending two small ships packed with gunpowder to blow up the French boom cable blocking the Roads. Several fireships drifted through the gap created, forcing the entire French fleet to drift away from the danger. All but two battleships and a frigate ran aground on the shallows in the darkness.

Gambier delayed authorizing any attack next day, allowing most of the French to escape to Rochefort at high tide, though two battleships surrendered when British ships eventually moved in, and another two (along with a frigate) were scuttled. The action confirmed Cochrane's high reputation as a fighting commander, and most of the senior French officers involved were arrested, but Gambier was criticized for his caution and not given another important command.

Bassano, Battle of

Set-piece engagement, fought on 8 September 1796, that ended the second Austrian invasion of Lombardy during that year's **Italian campaign**. Driven back into the Tyrol after defeat at **Castiglione** in early August, Austrian C-in-C **Würmser** responded to **Napoleon**'s subsequent advance up the Adige by leading 20,000 troops down the Brenta valley further east, planning to sweep west across French lines of retreat and relieve **Mantua**.

After a victory at **Roveredo** cleared the road up the Adige to Trent, Napoleon turned the tables on Würmser, rushing 22,000 troops down the Brenta valley to strike at the Austrian rear. Leaving Trent on 6 September, French forces burst through Austrian rearguards at Primolano, and had covered some 50km to approach Bassano by nightfall on 7 September. Würmser, hitherto confident of a French withdrawal down the Adige, had turned to block the Brenta valley with two divisions at Bassano, and Napoleon attacked them early next morning.

After advances by **Augereau** and **Masséna** against the Austrian flanks, an élite reserve under Colonel **Lannes** smashed through the centre. Austrian troops scattered, leaving behind about 4,000 prisoners, 35 guns and two invaluable **pontoon** trains. Some 3,500 survivors of one Austrian division fled for the Adriatic coast, but Würmser resumed his westward march towards the Adige, eventually gathering some 16,000 troops by the time he reached the isolated sanctuary of Mantua a week later. *See* **Map 9**.

Bataillon Carré

The flexible, innovative and efficient refinement of the **corps system** developed by **Napoleon** and first employed by the **French Army** during the early stages of the **Jena–Auerstädt** campaign in 1806. Army corps in a given theatre manoeuvred in a square formation, so that vanguard, flank and rear positions were determined by the army's direction, which could thus be altered at maximum speed. Though deployed far enough apart to make use of separate supply and forage facilities, the components were in position to concentrate in attack or defence as occasion demanded, and to reinforce any threatened corps before it could be isolated. The system's tactical advantages were obvious, and its flexibility served Napoleon well when it worked, but the logistic and communications challenge involved was beyond any other contemporary European army, and a decline in the overall quality of French troops made it impossible to implement from 1812, as Napoleon discovered at **Smolensk**.

Batavian Republic

The client state established under French auspices in 1795 by Dutch opponents of the **Orange** dynasty in the independent Netherlands. Never economically or politically secure, the republic was replaced in 1806 by a puppet Kingdom of Holland under Louis **Bonaparte**. *See also* The **Netherlands**.

Battleships *See* **Ships-of-the-line**

Bautzen, Battle of

The second major engagement between allied and French forces during the 1813 campaign for **Germany**, fought on 20–21 May at Bautzen, about 50km east of the River Elbe (*see* **Map 25**). General **Wittgenstein's** allied army had taken up fortified positions around Bautzen after its defeat at **Lützen** in early May. **Napoleon** had followed the retreat as far as Dresden by 9 May, but lack of reconnaissance **cavalry** forced him to delay a full-scale attack, and send **Macdonald's** three corps ahead to gather the necessary intelligence.

After Macdonald reported the allies massed around Bautzen on 16 May, Napoleon ordered **Oudinot's** corps round their southern flank, and told **Ney** to move some of his detachment from Torgau towards the northern flank. Ney misun-

derstood the order, and another on 18 May telling him to swing east towards Orsha and the allied rear, so that two days later he was still not in position.

About 96,000 allied troops were drawn up along ridges either side of and behind Bautzen when Napoleon reached the scene early on 19 May. He spent the rest of the day drawing up his own 150,000 men, while a strong allied reconnaissance was driven off to the north of the line. Ney was the key to Napoleon's battle plan, expected to sweep behind the allied right flank while its centre was pinned down by Macdonald and **Marmont**, but he was still some 30km north at Maukendorf, and out of touch with the situation at Bautzen. Tsar **Alexander**, committed to a defensive battle, had meanwhile decided that the main French attack would come against his left, and had concentrated accordingly.

To give Ney time to reach his position, Napoleon delayed the frontal attack until noon on 20 May, when an artillery bombardment opened on the allied positions. The first infantry attacks were launched about three hours later, and had crossed the River Spree to take the forward position of Bautzen itself by six in the evening. An attack by Oudinot's corps in the south was sufficiently ferocious to convince allied commanders that the main effort was under way there, and reserves were dispatched to the sector. Ney's corps was still being ignored at nightfall.

Satisfied with the first day of fighting, but aware that Ney was still short of his designated position, Napoleon ordered him to attack the Russian right on the morning of 21 May, and entrusted **Lauriston's** corps with the task of advancing into the allied rear. The three corps in the centre were expected to resume their attacks, and **Soult** (on temporary secondment from the **Peninsular** theatre) was to supervise a clinching assault by the reserve.

Still mistaken for the main French thrust, Oudinot's attack on 21 May met strong resistance, and his corps lost some ground after Napoleon refused to send in reinforcements, but Marmont and Macdonald made better progress in the centre. Assuming that Ney was drawing reserves to the allied right, Napoleon launched

Soult's 20,000 infantry and 1,000 cavalry against **Blücher's** central fortifications at two in the afternoon.

Soult's corps took the pivotal fort of Kreschwitz within an hour, but could not bring up artillery support and stalled at the plateau beyond, suffering heavy casualties. Meanwhile the three central corps, backed by all the artillery Napoleon could muster, were slowly battering the allied centre-left into submission, and the tsar ordered a limited withdrawal in front of Oudinot at about four. Allied resistance was beginning to fade all along the line when Napoleon finally sent the **Imperial Guard** against the sector around Bauschütz. Its charge forced Blücher to fall back, and triggered a general allied retreat.

Ney had finally reached his objective, the village of Preititz, too late to encircle Blücher, and then wasted time in repeated frontal attacks on the village. Though reinforced by **Reynier's** corps, he was entangled until evening, enabling allied forces to complete an orderly withdrawal towards Weissenberg and Löbau. French attempts at immediate pursuit were ended by a storm during the night, by which time each side had suffered some 20,000 casualties. Though another clear French victory, the battle had not crushed the allied armies, and mutual exhaustion encouraged moves towards an **armistice** over the following days.

Bavaria

The south German state of Bavaria, ruled by the Wittelsbach family since the twelfth century, was an electorate in 1792, comprising the fragmented territories of Bavaria, the Rhineland Palatinate, Upper Palatinate and Zweibrücken, along with the Duchies of Berg and Jülich. Though one of the larger German states, it still harboured several independent statelets and bishoprics within its borders, and remained a relative minnow in international terms.

As a member of the **Holy Roman Empire**, Bavaria was obliged to furnish troops for the fight against revolutionary **France** in summer 1792, but declared its neutrality in October, and provided only token contingents to the **Revolutionary Wars**. Munich was threatened by

French forces advancing from the **Rhine** in 1796, reinforcing Elector **Maximilian Joseph's** policy of neutrality and subjecting the country to the ravages of occupying armies, a process repeated during the latter stages of the War of the **Second Coalition**.

The imperial reorganization of March 1803 enabled Bavaria to rationalize its internal frontiers, but the key to rapid growth from the turn of the century was alliance with France from 1801. Maximilian Joseph's refusal to abandon the alliance under pressure from Vienna to join the **Third Coalition** in autumn 1805 brought an Austrian invasion of Bavaria in early September. Some 25,000 **Bavarian** troops fought with French forces in the campaign that climaxed at **Austerlitz**, and the subsequent peace transformed Bavaria's size and status. The loss of Würzburg was more than compensated for by the acquisition of Vorarlberg, Brixen, Trent and the Tyrol from **Austria**, and Maximilian Joseph became a king.

Maximilian Joseph allowed the French emperor to detach **Berg** and Jülich in 1806, but gained the cities of Augsburg and Nürnberg in return, and secured his daughter Augusta's marriage to Napoleon's stepson, Eugène de **Beauharnais**. Bavaria became a founder member of the Confederation of the **Rhine** in July, and quit the defunct Holy Roman Empire in August.

Still locked into French alliance, Bavaria was again a theatre of war during the opening phases of the War of the **Fifth Coalition** in 1809, but Napoleon's eventual triumph was not an unmixed blessing. The war triggered Andreas **Hofer's** prolonged revolt against Bavarian rule in the Tyrol, and the peace terms accepted by Austria in October brought only the annexation of Salzburg and the Inn-Viertel provinces in exchange for the loss of Trent.

Bavarian troops joined the **Russian campaign** of 1812, but Maximilian Joseph abandoned Napoleon by the Treaty of **Ried**, signed just before the battle of **Leipzig** in October 1813, switching allegiance early enough to share in the successful **Sixth Coalition's** spoils. The postwar Congress of **Vienna** required Bavaria to return the Tyrol and Salzburg to Austria, but it gained Würzburg and most of Frankfurt in exchange, confirming it as the largest state separating the Habsburg Empire from **Prussia**.

Bavarian Army

The armed forces of **Bavaria** comprised a total mobilized strength of about 27,000 infantry in 1792, organized into ad hoc brigades for operational purposes. Eight regiments of **cavalry** totalled some 5,750 troops, but horses were available for only a quarter of these. About 1,200 men served in the **artillery** arm, but it never operated as a distinct tactical unit, its guns being distributed in groups of four to each infantry regiment.

Five Bavarian infantry regiments and one of cavalry fought on the **Rhine** front against France from 1793 with the army of the **Holy Roman Empire**, taking part in the siege of **Mainz**, where the majority served as neutral garrison troops after 1795. A slightly scaled-down army provided a division (some 9,200 men) for the latter stages of the **Second Coalition**'s campaign on the Rhine, joining **Austrian Army** forces in defeat at **Hohenlinden** in December 1800 before Elector **Maximilian Joseph**'s alliance with France.

Almost the whole army took part in **Napoleon**'s lightning triumph over the **Third Coalition** in 1805, and two divisions fought alongside French forces against **Prussia** in 1806, principally involved in **siege** operations against second-line **fortresses**. Three Bavarian divisions formed **Lefebvre**'s VIII Corps with the **Grande Armée** in 1809, and subsequently moved west to put down **Hofer**'s Tyrolean rebellion. Two divisions formed **Gouvion St Cyr**'s VI Corps for the 1812 campaign, a total strength of 30,000 infantry, 2,000 cavalry and 60 guns. The cavalry was virtually wiped out at **Borodino**, and the infantry ended the retreat from **Moscow** with a fighting strength of 68 men.

The army was rebuilt for the 1813 campaign, and formed a corps under the Bavarian **Wrede** in its opening phases, but changed sides and fought against France at **Leipzig** and **Hanau**. Bavarian troops saw plenty of action during the campaign in **France** of 1814, taking part in the Battles of **Brienne** and **Arcis-sur-Aube**, but almost none during the **Hundred Days** campaign of 1815, when they joined Austrian troops in an uneventful invasion of east-central France.

Bayonets

All contemporary armies used bayonets attached to the end of **muskets** or **rifles** as a cutting weapon for close-combat purposes, and most resembled knives rather than swords, although a few rifles were equipped with longer blades. A gun could be fired with the bayonet in place, but removal was simple and it could be stored in an attached scabbard, though **Russian** and **Prussian Army** commanders tended to deploy infantry with bayonets permanently fixed.

Small-scale bayonet fights took place regularly between **skirmishers** or infantry contesting small strongpoints, but advances in **infantry tactics** during the eighteenth century had rendered the carnage of massed bayonet charges obsolete. Those that did take place, like a successful charge by a British company against French positions at **Roncesvalles** in July 1813, tended to attract heavy **propaganda** coverage, reflecting the bayonet's honoured place in contemporary military culture.

Bayonne Conference

Summit meeting begun at the French border town of Bayonne in April 1808 between **Napoleon**, members of the Bonaparte dynasty and the Bourbon rulers of Spain. The conference was originally called by Napoleon as a means of imposing strategic unity on his unruly family, with the future of **Spain** as a secondary issue, but was in fact dominated by Spanish affairs after a crisis gave the French emperor an opportunity to intervene in the bitter dispute between King **Charles IV** and his son **Ferdinand**.

Delegates gathered at Bayonne between 16 and 30 April. The Spanish party, including Charles, Ferdinand, the queen and chief minister **Godoy**, faced a combination of high pageant and hard bargaining as Napoleon put into effect a scheme to depose the Bourbons. Charles was quickly induced to abdicate for a second time (he had retracted his hasty abdication of 17 March), and signed a document consigning the succession to Napoleon's discretion. A week of threats and psychological pressure eventually persuaded Ferdinand to renounce his own claim to the throne on 6 May, at which point he was shown his father's abdication and the royal family departed for gracious imprisonment in France.

On the same day the vacant crown was reluctantly accepted by Joseph **Bonaparte**, hitherto King of **Naples**, but only after Louis **Bonaparte** and Lucien **Bonaparte** had turned it down. Napoleon remained at Bayonne until 20 July, by which time the Neapolitan crown had been transferred to **Murat**. *See also* **Madrid Uprising**; **Peninsular War**.

Bayonne, Siege of

The south-western French city of Bayonne, just inside the Pyrenean border with Spain, was surrounded by allied forces from 26 February 1814, after Marshal **Soult**'s main army had been driven east towards **Orthez**. Besieged by General **Hope**'s two British divisions, General Thouvenot's 14,000 garrison troops were still holding positions east of the city, along both banks of the River Adour, when word reached the area on 13 April of **Napoleon**'s fall and a general ceasefire. In an atmosphere of relaxed allied vigilance, Thouvenot launched a surprise attack on allied outposts around the village of St Etienne, just north of Bayonne, at three in the morning on 14 April. Though warned of the raid by French deserters, local allied commanders had been given outdated information about its timing, and the attack quickly broke through British lines. Although a counter-attack forced the French back into the city by dawn, the sortie caused immense confusion behind allied lines (during which Hope was twice wounded and temporarily captured) and a total of 1,743 unnecessary casualties, 905 of them French. Thouvenot eventually surrendered Bayonne on 26 April, finally accepting Napoleon's **abdication** 20 days after the event.

Beauharnais, Eugène Rose de (1781–1824)

The son of the empress **Joséphine** by her marriage to General Alexandre de Beauharnais, who was executed for his failure to defend **Mainz** in 1793, Eugène became one of **Napoleon**'s most trusted and capable lieutenants. Though not at first in favour of the marriage, he served as an aide to Napoleon during the **Italian campaigns** (1796–7) and in the **Middle East** (1798–9), where he was wounded at **Acre**. Always well treated by

his stepfather, he was promoted general in 1804, becoming a Prince of the Empire and colonel-general of the **Imperial Guard** light cavalry in 1805. Formally adopted by the emperor in 1806, he married Auguste Amélie, the daughter of Bavarian king **Maximilian Joseph**, an arranged union that proved happy and lasting.

As Napoleon's viceroy in the new Kingdom of **Italy** from 1805, Beauharnais combined important political and military roles with considerable success. A temperate and conscientious administrator, he carried through constitutional reforms with conspicuous fairness and became genuinely popular in Italy. He commanded the theatre's defence against Austrian invasion during the War of the **Fifth Coalition** in 1809, and won an impressive victory at **Raab** before joining the emperor at **Wagram**.

His undoubted military abilities were rewarded with command of the **Grande Armée**'s northern wing during the 1812 **Russian** invasion, and he was one of few French commanders to emerge from the campaign with an enhanced reputation, notably for his actions at **Borodino** and **Maloyaroslavets**. When **Murat** returned to **Naples** late in the year, Beauharnais took overall command of the army's rump during the opening stages of the campaign for **Germany**, overseeing its withdrawal to defensible positions behind the Elbe. After fighting at **Lützen**, he left to organize the defence of his kingdom, where he led a final Italian campaign before agreeing the Peace of **Schiarino-Rizzino** with the allies in 1814.

His hopes of retaining the kingdom with allied approval were disappointed, but he was compensated with a pension and titles (Prince of Eichstadt and Duke of Leuchtenberg). He did not attempt to rejoin Napoleon in 1815, keeping a promise to his father-in-law that he would avoid involvement in French affairs, and lived the rest of his life in Munich, performing charitable work for former imperial servants in distress.

Beauharnais, Joséphine *See* **Joséphine, Empress**

Beaulieu, Johann Peter (1725–1819)

Born in the Netherlands, Beaulieu commanded a division against the opening French offensive at

Valenciennes in April 1792, and subsequently fought in **Flanders** and on the **Rhine** before his appointment as Austrian C-in-C on the **Italian** front in early 1796. Up against **Napoleon's** first independent command, he suffered serial defeats before the collapse of his positions on the Mincio at **Borghetto** drove his army out of Italy altogether in June, after which he was retired.

Belgium, Conquest of (1792)

The first successful offensive carried out by French forces on the eastern frontiers during the War of the **First Coalition**. After victories at **Valmy** and **Lille** had secured the frontiers, French C-in-C **Dumouriez** took advantage of allied distractions in **Poland** to mount an autumn invasion of Belgium, and defeated Austrian forces at **Jemappes** on 6 November. His army followed an Austrian retreat deep into Belgium from 13 November, winning a hard-fought engagement against rearguards at Anderlecht that day and entering Brussels to an enthusiastic welcome the next.

Before the fall of Brussels prompted his resignation, Austrian commander the Duke of Saxe-Teschen divided his defensive forces, sending **Clairfait** to protect Antwerp while **Beaulieu** guarded the road to Namur. Both cities were abandoned in late November as Austrian forces united for the defence of Liège, and then withdrew east to La Chartreuse, enabling Dumouriez to mop up the rest of Belgium. Liège opened its gates on 28 November, an increasingly radical Walloon garrison at Antwerp surrendered on 30 November after a **siege** lasting only two days, and Namur capitulated on 2 December. A final thrust on 6 December sent Clairfait reeling back far beyond the Meuse, before French northern forces went into winter quarters, and Dumouriez began preparing a spring invasion of the independent **Netherlands**. See **Austrian Netherlands**; **Map 2**.

Bellegarde, Heinrich von (1756–1845)

German soldier whose father was war minister in his native **Saxony**, but who joined the **Austrian Army** in 1778. Bellegarde served against Turkey in 1788–9, and fought against **France** in the War of the **First Coalition**, becoming chief of staff to Archduke **Charles** on the **Rhine** in 1796. A corps commander on the **Swiss** and **Italian** fronts in

1799, he suffered a minor defeat at **San Giuliano**.

Governor of Galicia from 1806 to 1808, he commanded a corps for the campaign of 1809, fighting at **Aspern–Essling** and **Wagram**. When Austria returned to war in 1813, Bellegarde led Austrian forces through the **Italian campaign** against **Beauharnais** until the local peace of **Schiarino-Rizzino** in 1814, and defeated **Murat's** 'independence' movement at **Tolentino** in May 1815. He returned to a political career in Vienna from 1816 until 1825, when blindness forced his retirement.

Belleisle Raid

Failed attempt by small **British Army** force under General Maitland to take the French islands of Belleisle and Houédic, just off the coast of Brittany, in late spring 1800. Faced with demands for troops in the **Mediterranean**, where General **Stuart** proposed to attack French forces around **Genoa** from **Minorca**, the government chose to establish a support base for a royalist **Chouan** rebellion in western France. Unaware that the rebels had already been crushed, 6,000 troops put to sea in May, found Belleisle too strongly defended to risk an attack, and remained off the coast for five weeks pending further orders. They were eventually transferred to take part in equally quixotic attempts on **Spanish Navy** bases at **Ferrol** and **Cadiz**.

Benavente, Battle of

Small but important clash on 29 December 1808 between British rearguards and forward French cavalry units during General **Moore's** rapid retreat from **Sahagún** to **Corunna** (see **Peninsular War**). After more than a week of fruitless pursuit through foul weather, elements of the French **Imperial Guard** cavalry met and engaged what appeared to be a small British covering force near Benavente, on the River Esla. Attacking across the river, they were surprised by **Paget's** much larger force of British cavalry, which had been concealed within the town, and thrown back with the loss of 55 casualties and 73 prisoners, including commanding officer **Lefebvre-Desnouëttes**. The setback signalled the failure of **Napoleon's** attempt to encircle Moore before he could reach the town of Astorga, which was occupied by leading British units later the same day. See **Map 22**.

Bennigsen, Levin August (1735–1826)

German-born **Russian Army** officer who entered **Catherine** the Great's service in 1773, and was promoted to command an army wing during the **Russo-Polish War** of 1792. One of the conspirators involved in the murder of Tsar **Paul I** in 1801, he led the third Russian force committed to the campaign of 1805, and was **Kamenskoi's** deputy in Poland during late 1806, demonstrating an adventurous tendency at **Pultusk** in December. In command of Russian forces facing Napoleon after Kamenskoi was killed in January 1807, he escaped French attempts to cut off his army at **Ionkovo** and **Eylau** in February, and at **Heilsberg** in June, but suffered a decisive defeat at **Friedland**. He led the Russian left wing at **Borodino** in 1812, but disputes with C-in-C **Kutuzov** prompted his temporary retirement late in the year. He returned to command at the head of the Reserve Army after Kutuzov's death in 1813, and was ennobled by Tsar **Alexander I** immediately after his success at **Leipzig** in October.

Beresford, William (1768–1854)

The illegitimate son of an Irish nobleman, Beresford was commissioned into the **British Army** in 1785, and served as an infantry captain at **Toulon** and **Corsica** in 1793–4. He commanded a regiment in **India** from 1799, leading it to **Egypt** in 1801, and helped recapture the **Cape Colony** as a brigadier-general in 1806. Later that year he led land forces with the ill-fated **Buenos Aires** expedition, and was a Spanish prisoner for six months in its aftermath. He escaped to England in 1807, and was promoted major-general in April 1808, serving with **Moore** at **Corunna** before accepting the task of reorganizing the **Portuguese Army** the following spring. Beresford's success as a Portuguese marshal is viewed as his most important contribution to the **Peninsular War**. He returned to British field command to lead the allied detachment sent to **Badajoz** in April 1811, but was replaced shortly after a poor performance at **Albuera** in May, and was present at subsequent actions as titular head of Portuguese forces. Occasionally given control of large formations during the war's last stages, he led two divisions in support of the 1814 Bordeaux rising. He was created a baron in 1814 and remained in Portugal until 1822, when he returned to a political career in Britain, serving in **Wellington's** first cabinet in 1828.

Beresina, Battles of the

A series of actions fought around the small town of Studienka, on the River Beresina near Borisov, between 25 and 29 November 1812 (*see* **Map 23**). The climax to that year's **Russian campaign**, they enabled the French **Grande Armée** to escape complete destruction at the end of its disastrous retreat from **Moscow**.

By 21 November **Napoleon's** dwindling central army, down to perhaps 25,000 effectives, was limping west from Smolensk towards the Beresina, pursued by **Kutuzov's** 50,000-strong main Russian army to the north. Victory at **Polotsk** on 14 November had only temporarily halted the advance of another 30,000 Russian troops to the north under General **Wittgenstein**, and a third Russian army in the south (34,000 men under Admiral **Tshitshagov**) had captured the vital supply centre of Minsk before seizing the Beresina bridges at Borisov.

News that the last feasible river crossing had fallen reached Napoleon next day at Bobr, and he rushed every available man forward to join forces with **Oudinot**, whose local victory at **Loshnitsa** on 23 November at least returned the town of Borisov to French control. The juncture brought Napoleon's effective strength up to about 50,000 men, but the Beresina bridges had been destroyed and Tshitshagov remained in possession of the west bank. With Russian armies approaching from the east and north, the near-freezing river appeared an insuperable barrier.

Napoleon was considering a desperate attempt to swing north past Wittgenstein and make contact with **Wrede's** isolated corps before marching on Vilna, but General **Corbineau's** brigade discovered a ford across the Beresina at Studienka, about 13km north of Borizov, on 24 November. The west bank of the crossing area was occupied by Tshitshagov's northern units, and lack of **pontoon** equipment (destroyed earlier in an attempt to streamline the retreat) made any crossing extremely hazardous, but an attempt was begun next day.

Diversionary operations took place along the river during 25 November, and Oudinot's demonstration south of Borisov convinced Tshitshagov to withdraw forces opposite Studienka. The west bank at the ford was quickly secured by 400 French cavalry, and covered by a 44-gun artillery battery set up on the east side. After working all night, and destroying much of Studienka for wood, General Eblé's engineers had opened a flimsy bridge across the river by the early afternoon of 26 November, and a larger bridge was in operation two hours later.

Oudinot's corps and the **Imperial Guard** were quickly across the bridges and secured the causeway leading from the river to the road, left intact by Tshitshagov's forces. Victor and **Davout**, charged with covering the crossings, were hardly disturbed on the first day, partly because Kutuzov considered a battle unnecessary and had delayed his army's advance. The greatest obstacle to French efficiency was the army's attached mass of perhaps 40,000 civilians, stragglers and refugees, gathered around the bridges but not included in the formal crossing schedule.

Tshitshagov had become aware of French positions late on 26 November, and next morning attacked Oudinot's corps, guarding the west bank at Stachov. The French were forced to withdraw several kilometres during a full day's fighting, but the new line held. On the east side, Wittgenstein's forward units drove Victor's corps back towards Borisov, but failed to upset the cohesion of its withdrawal towards Studienka. With Kutuzov's forces still out of range the French crossing continued unhindered throughout 27 November.

The collapse of the larger bridge at Studienka during the afternoon triggered several hours of mass panic as troops and non-combatants scrambled for the one remaining bridge, resulting in hundreds of deaths before the broken bridge was reopened in the evening, but by nightfall around 25,000 French troops were over the river. Only Victor's 13,000-strong corps remained on the east side, along with the great majority of non-combatants.

On the west bank, Tshitshagov again attacked Oudinot in strength early on 28 November, and almost succeeded in breaking through the French line before it rallied. Oudinot was wounded leading a counter-attack, and **Ney** took command of the sector, launching a cavalry charge that inflicted about 2,000 casualties and drove the Russians back to Stachov for the rest of the day.

Non-combatants had resumed chaotic attempts to crowd across the bridges when Victor's corps, occupying a ridge just south-east of Studienka, was attacked by Wittgenstein at about eight the same morning. Though weakened by the loss of a division that had blundered into captivity during the night, Victor held off the Russians with the help of a **Baden** brigade sent back across the river, but Wittgenstein got round his extended left flank by noon and artillery started attacking the Studienka bridges.

Thousands more civilians were crushed to death or killed by the near-freezing water as mass panic erupted, multiplying when the larger bridge again collapsed. By siting an artillery battery on the west bank, Napoleon was able to relieve the pressure on Victor's left, and most of his corps was safely across the river an hour after midnight. Once the last troops were on the west bank, and after a delay while refugees were exhorted to take their last chance for safety, General Eblé carried out instructions to fire the Beresina bridges at nine next morning, triggering one more disastrous panic.

The French army could now proceed to Vilna, but the cost of its escape had been high. Estimates suggest that Napoleon lost 20–30,000 combatants during the four days, against about 10,000 Russian casualties. The number of non-combatants killed can only be guessed, but is thought to be in the region of 30,000. The river remained clogged with their frozen bodies for several weeks.

Berg

An independent German duchy on the east bank of the Rhine, Berg had been owned by the ruling house of **Bavaria** since 1742, but was ceded along with neighbouring Jülich to the French Empire in 1806 (*see* **Map 1**). Napoleon united Berg with Cleves (some of which had been taken by France in 1795, and the rest in 1805) to found a Grand Duchy for **Murat**, and it became part of the Confederation of the **Rhine** later that year. Napoleon became Grand Duke in July 1808, when Murat moved to **Naples**, and acted as regent for his nephew, Louis Bonaparte, from March 1809. Three regiments of Berg infantry and one of cavalry served with French imperial forces, but were virtually wiped out during the 1812 **Russian campaign**. A volunteer light infantry unit and a regiment of **hussars** were formed to fight with the allies from December 1813, and served **Prussia** after it was given both Berg and Cleves by the postwar Congress of **Vienna**.

Bergen, Battle of

The main attack by Anglo-Russian forces invading **North Holland** in 1799, an unsuccessful attempt on 19 September to break through General **Brune**'s defensive positions blocking the route south from Helder to Amsterdam. British forces had reached the North Holland peninsula in late August, and taken the Dutch naval base at Helder. No further aggression was attempted before the arrival of overall C-in-C the Duke of **York** and General Hermann's allied Russians brought allied strength above 40,000 men, by which time Franco-Dutch forces had recovered from their initial confusion, and taken up positions along a line some 10km south of the River Waal between Bergen and Oude-Karspel.

A three-pronged allied advance, planned by committee, was eventually launched on 19 September. **Abercromby** led a wide manoeuvre to outflank the French right wing, while a frontal attack against the line itself was spearheaded by Russian forces, and a coastal thrust under **Dundas** struck at French positions in the south-west of the peninsula around Alkmaar. The operation collapsed after Hermann's Russians attacked early, and Abercromby's force made little effort to intervene in the centre after slowly making its way round the French flank to Hoorn. Although Brune's command lost 4,000 men, half of them as prisoners, allied forces had retired to their original positions all along the line by the end of the day, having lost 900 British and an estimated 2–3,000 Russian troops. *See* **Map 2**.

Berlin Decrees

The declaration of sanctions against British trade, made by **Napoleon** in newly occupied Berlin on 21 November 1806, that formed the basis of the French emperor's **Continental System** of economic warfare against **Great Britain**. Coming in the midst of the War of the **Fourth Coalition**, and a clear indication that Napoleon had not lost sight of his most consistent enemy, the decrees closed all ports under French control to British goods, outlawed 'all commerce and all correspondence' with Great Britain, and authorized confiscation of British property (along with internment of British nationals) in French-held areas. None of these measures was in itself new, but their combination and the effort subsequently devoted to their enforcement marked the first coherent attempt to use economic warfare as a strategic weapon against Britain.

Bernadotte, Jean-Baptiste-Jules (1763–1844)

The son of a lawyer from Pau, Bernadotte was an NCO in the pre-revolutionary **French Army** and commissioned in late 1791. He fought the **First Coalition** on the **Rhine** and in **Flanders**, leading a brigade at **Fleurus** and becoming a divisional general in October 1794, before taking part in the **Italian campaigns** of 1796–7. He remained in Italy until 1798, when he was ambassador to Vienna for a few days before the breakdown of diplomatic relations with **Austria**.

An ostentatiously passionate republican, and trusted by the **Directory** government, he began the War of the **Second Coalition** commanding 48,000 troops on the northern sector of the Rhine around Mannheim, but was forced to retreat after **Jourdan**'s failure at **Stockach** and quit his command for Paris shortly afterwards. Given the job of war minister from July 1799, he was dismissed in September but remained an influential political figure in Paris when the November **Brumaire** coup brought **Napoleon** to power.

Bernadotte became a state councillor and received an army command in 1800, rewards for not actually opposing the coup, and was appointed governor of **Hanover** in 1804. In May that year he was one of the original **Marshalate**, and commanded I Corps on the northern wing of the **Grande Armée**'s advance into Bavaria against the **Third Coalition** in 1805.

An impressively tall and handsome figure, apparently much given to boasting, Bernadotte was one of Napoleon's least aggressive commanders. His corps was at **Ulm** and **Austerlitz** in 1805, but he was threatened with court martial the next year when it failed to join the Battle of **Auerstädt**. He survived Napoleon's anger, perhaps because he was married to the emperor's former lover Désirée Clary, and led the subsequent French pursuit operation, making important new friends by his lenient treatment of Swedish prisoners of war at **Lübeck**.

After commanding occupying forces in northern Germany, Bernadotte was returned to frontline command in 1809, leading **Saxon** forces (as IX Corps) against the **Fifth Coalition**, but he was dismissed on the spot during an inept performance at **Wagram** and again relegated to secondary duties. Sent to command forces facing the British **Walcheren expedition**, he was sacked for the last time in September after an ill-judged outburst of boasting was reported to Napoleon.

Anxious to cultivate French friendship, and misreading his current status, the Swedish States-General elected Bernadotte as heir to the childless King **Charles XIII** in August 1810. The new Crown Prince of **Sweden** abandoned France for his adopted country, taking effective control over affairs of state and initiating alliance with **Russia** by the **St Petersburg** treaty of 1812. The following year he committed Sweden to the **Sixth Coalition** and led his army in **Germany**, inflicting a major defeat on **Ney's** corps at **Dennewitz** in September 1813 but displaying his usual slow caution in arriving late at the crucial Battle of **Leipzig** in October. The campaign embraced the almost incidental invasion of Danish Holstein, helping Sweden's acquisition of **Norway** from the Danes by the Treaty of **Kiel** in January 1814.

Bernadotte's Swedes played a relatively minor role in the 1814 campaign for **France**, concentrating on mopping-up operations in northern Germany and the Low Countries. Satisfaction of Swedish territorial ambitions, along with his rather improbable belief that he might succeed Napoleon, influenced his reluctance to fight on

French soil, and he kept Sweden out of the **Seventh Coalition** in 1815.

Though his military failings owed something to Napoleon's discouragement of tactical initiative, it is generally agreed that Bernadotte was a better monarch than soldier. His reign as king of Sweden (1818–44) was characterized by liberal reform and harmonious relations with parliament, and his dynasty outlasted any of Napoleon's royal creations, remaining on the throne at the end of the twentieth century.

Bernstorff, Christian Günter, Count von (1769–1835)

The most important Danish politician of the Napoleonic period, Bernstorff began his career as a diplomat in 1787, and replaced his father as foreign minister on the latter's death in 1797. He was chief minister from 1800 until 1810, struggling with the impossible task of balancing British domination of **Denmark's** vital sea trade against the threat of land invasion from **Napoleon's** armies. After supervising many of the social and economic reforms undertaken during the latter stages of King **Frederick VI's** regency, he returned to diplomatic duties in 1811, representing his country at the Congress of **Vienna**. In 1817, while serving as Danish ambassador to Berlin, he transferred to his allegiance to **Prussia** at the suggestion of chancellor **Hardenberg**, becoming foreign minister the next year and remaining a prominent political force until his retirement in 1832.

Berthier, Louis-Alexandre (1753–1815)

Napoleon's chief of staff from 1796 until 1814, Berthier was an officer in the pre-revolutionary French Army, and served under **Lafayette** during the early campaigns against the **First Coalition**. Promoted brigadier-general in March 1795, and to divisional command three months later, he was serving as chief of staff to the Army of the Alps before his transfer to head Napoleon's staff in Italy on 2 March 1796.

After the **Italian campaigns** of 1796–7, he took command of the Army of Italy when Napoleon returned to Paris, and presided over the invasion of the **Papal States** in early 1798. He spent a brief period with forces preparing to invade **England** before accompanying Napoleon to the **Middle East**, and was among the officers chosen to return to France with him in autumn 1799. At his chief's side during the **Brumaire** coup, and minister of war for a few months in its aftermath, Berthier was nominal C-in-C of the Reserve Army for the **Italian campaign** of 1800 (but in practice chief of staff to a First Consul forbidden military command by the constitution), and was wounded at **Marengo**.

Again minister of war from October 1800, he was created marshal in 1804 and was appointed chief of staff to the **Grande Armée** for the 1805 campaign against the **Third Coalition**, a role he fulfilled in all its subsequent campaigns to 1814. Though some authorities regard him as little more than a glorified secretary, pointing to his poor performance as temporary C-in-C during the opening manoeuvres against the **Fifth Coalition** in 1809, Berthier's staff work is generally viewed as vital to Napoleon's military successes. As the pivotal figure rationalizing the administrative work of the **Grand Quartier-Général** and Napoleon's household, he displayed energy, imagination and a fine-tuned ability to interpret his master's commands, earning his popular nickname 'the Emperor's wife'.

Berthier's efforts won Napoleon's absolute trust and were rewarded with regular grants of titles and estates. Though he gave up the war ministry in 1807 to devote himself to military work, he was already Prince of Neuchâtel (1806) and became Prince of Wagram in 1809. With the Grande Armée throughout the gruelling campaigns of 1812–14, he was exhausted by the time of Napoleon's **abdication**, and subsequently accepted semi-retirement as captain of the Royal Guard. He refused to rejoin **Napoleon** in 1815, carrying out his duties by escorting the royal family to Ghent at the start of the **Hundred Days** and then retiring to Bamberg, where he died after falling from a window in mysterious circumstances on 1 June.

Bertrand, Henri-Gatien (1773–1844)

French engineering officer, commissioned in 1793, who fought during the **Italian** campaign of 1797 and with the **Middle East** expedition before his promotion to brigadier-general in

1800. An aide to **Napoleon** during the campaigns against the **Third** and **Fourth Coalitions**, he achieved divisional rank in May 1807, and was responsible for construction of the Danube bridges used at the Battles of **Aspern–Essling** and **Wagram** in 1809.

After serving for three years as governor of **Illyria**, Bertrand returned to field service as a corps commander during the 1813 campaign for **Germany** before replacing **Caulaincourt** as controller of Napoleon's household administration in November. One of the emperor's most devoted servants, he returned to action for the campaign for **France** in 1814, and subsequently accompanied Napoleon through his exile in **Elba**, the **Hundred Days** of 1815 and his final confinement on St Helena. Bertrand returned to French service on Napoleon's death, and came out of retirement to escort the former emperor's body back to Paris in 1840.

Bessières, Jean-Baptiste (1768–1813)

French cavalryman, the son of a surgeon, who fought in the ranks on the **Pyrenean** front before receiving his commission (for the second time) in 1793. As a member of the **Guides**, he fought under **Napoleon** during the 1796 **Italian campaign**, earning praise for his performance at **Rivoli**, and went to the **Middle East** as a major in 1798. He was with the Consular Guard **cavalry** during the **Marengo** campaign in 1800, and was promoted brigadier-general that year, becoming a divisional commander in 1802. One of the original **Marshalate** in May 1804, he subsequently led the mounted arm of the élite **Imperial Guard** at **Austerlitz**, **Jena**, **Eylau** and **Friedland**.

He commanded a corps in the **Peninsular** theatre from March 1808, but enjoyed less success in managing larger and more complex formations. He fought at **Medina del Río Seco** and **Somosierra**, but was recalled to Paris in March 1809 to lead the **Grande Armée**'s cavalry reserve against the **Fifth Coalition**. Ennobled as the Duke of Istria in May 1809, Bessières replaced the disgraced **Bernadotte** in command of the Army of the North in September, and was governor of Paris for two months before moving to Strasbourg from March 1810.

He returned to the Army of the North the following January, and spent a second spell in Spain before leading the Imperial Guard cavalry through the **Russian campaign** of 1812 and the early stages of the 1813 struggle for **Germany**. Bessières was killed by a cannonball on 1 May 1813, shortly after his appointment as overall commander of the Imperial Guard and just before the Battle of **Lützen**.

Bianchi, Victor Friedrich, Baron (1768–1855)

Viennese-born **Austrian Army** officer, commissioned in 1787 and promoted brigadier-general in 1807, who commanded the left wing of the allied army at **Dresden** in 1813 and led a corps at Leipzig. Bianchi operated in southern **France** during the campaign of 1814, and earned the title Duke of Casalanza for leading the force that restored **Naples** to Bourbon rule in 1815.

Biberach, Battle of

Large-scale rearguard action, fought on 2 October 1796, that helped **Moreau's** French army escape Austrian pursuit of its retreat to the **Rhine**. Moreau had pulled back from the Danube on news of **Jourdan's** defeat at **Amberg** further north, but Austrian sector commander Latour was slow to pursue a stronger enemy, and French forces were beyond the River Riss at Biberach by the time they came under serious pressure in late September. With Austrian detachments approaching both his flanks, Moreau paused to attack Latour's central positions east of Biberach on the morning of 2 October. Latour's 23,000 men were no match for Moreau's 40,000, and **Desaix** overwhelmed a weak right wing to penetrate Biberach itself, taking about 4,000 prisoners. Latour extricated the rest of his force by evening, and pulled back from the Riss overnight, but Moreau was still in some danger, with 20,000 men edging round his northern flank along the Danube and Archduke **Charles** marching down the Rhine towards his rear. *See* Battle of **Emmendlingen**; Map 4.

Bidassoa River

River flowing inland from the Bay of Biscay at the Franco-Spanish frontier that was the focus of operations on the **Pyrenean** front in 1793–4, and during the **Peninsular War** campaigns of late summer and autumn 1813. The battles fought at **Vera** and **San Marcial** on 31 August 1813 are sometimes known collectively as the Battle of the Bidassoa, and the battles that opened the allied invasion of south-western France on 7 October, fought at **Irun** and **Vera**, are sometimes grouped as the Bidassoa Crossing. *See* **Map 5**.

Bingen, Battle of

Attack across the **Rhine** east of Mainz by **First Coalition** forces on 28 March 1793 that halted French incursions into north-western Germany. While the French invasion of the **Netherlands** was foundering at **Neerwinden**, General Custine's 45,000 French troops on the Rhine had been waiting to meet an offensive from **Brunswick's** 55,000 Prussians and 25,000 assorted Germans. News from Neerwinden encouraged an allied advance from 27 March, and an attack by two divisions on the French left wing around Bingen established a bridgehead across the Rhine that day. Lured away from Mainz in support, Custine was attacked by **Hohenlohe's** Prussians as they crossed the river on 28 March, and he retreated along the west bank towards Worms. Brunswick settled down to besiege 6,000 garrison troops cut off in **Mainz**, but sent **Würmser** south to cross the Rhine near Spire. The threat to his rear compelled Custine to retreat another 80km to the Lauter, guarding north-eastern routes into Alsace. *See* **Map 3**.

Black Legion

The most celebrated of several wartime units known as the Black Legion was a small force of exiles from **Brunswick** that joined the allies after their homeland was incorporated into **Westphalia** in 1806. Formed by the deposed Duke Frederick William, it wore black and sported a suitably vengeful death's head insignia. Taken into Austrian service, it comprised three infantry battalions, a small cavalry regiment and four light cannon by 1809, and led an anti-French rising in southern Germany during the War of the **Fifth Coalition**. The legion captured Dresden on 8 June and Leipzig ten days later, before retiring into Brunswick itself, but was compelled to retreat after Austria's defeat at **Wagram** in July. Frederick William led his force on an epic march to the mouth of the River Weser, where it met a

Royal Navy squadron and was taken into British service. Though increasingly diluted by foreign troops, the legion joined British forces in the **Peninsular War** from 1810, and cavalry detachments later served in **Sicily**. It was recalled to Germany in 1813 to form the basis of the restored duke's national army. *See also* **Pembrokeshire Raid**.

Black Mountain, Battle of the *See* Battles of Figueras,

Blake, Joachim (1759–1827)

One of the most effective Spanish generals of the **Peninsular War**, Blake came into his own leading small regular units and **guerrilla** bands after suffering defeats in 1808 as captain-general of the Galician army at **Medina del Río Seco** and **Espinosa**. Admired for his personal bravery, Blake was taken prisoner in 1812, returning to postwar **Spain** to become an active political opponent of reactionary king **Ferdinand VII**.

Blockade (Naval)

In the narrowest sense, a naval blockade could involve guarding a single harbour entrance to regulate maritime arrivals and departures. In its widest sense, as applied by the British government throughout the war period, strategic blockade involved using naval forces in an attempt to cut off all contact between an enemy state and the sea lanes.

The only force capable of mounting strategic blockade operations was the British **Royal Navy**, and it began a campaign to strangle the economy of **France** into surrender as soon as sufficient warships were available in 1793. For the next few years most British fleets attempted to seal off coasts using the 'open blockade' system, keeping their larger warships far out to sea in the hope of intercepting slow merchant **convoys**, and of tempting hostile fleets out of port to be ambushed.

The system had the advantage of allowing warships to make frequent trips home for rest and repair, but needed luck and operational vigour to succeed. Under the gentlemanly command of admirals such as **Howe** and **Hotham**, French convoys were able to slip into port with lifesaving regularity, and French fleets could escape from Brest and Toulon to inflict serious losses on British merchant traffic. When the trap did close on French battlefleets, they were usually let off lightly.

The British **Mediterranean** Fleet under **Jervis** had instituted the much more effective, if more arduous, practice of 'close blockade' by 1798. By deploying fast **frigates** within sight of blockaded harbours, and keeping a number of **ships-of-the-line** posted constantly just over the horizon, Jervis was ready to pounce on anything entering or leaving, and if for some reason his battleships were called away, the frigate patrols would remain, daring hostile shipping to risk an escape.

The maintenance of close blockade imposed an enormous strain on ships, and on crews required to spend months on station, often in conditions of extreme tedium and discomfort. The overall drain on British naval resources was equally telling, as the 1798–1814 period saw close blockades established all over Europe and along the east coast of the **United States**.

Established as British naval orthodoxy once Jervis became First Lord of the Admiralty (navy minister) in 1801, the system was a success, despite its not infrequent breakdowns and the limitations it imposed on the Royal Navy's more direct offensive potential. It is doubtful if blockade alone could have defeated **Napoleon**, but it did provoke severe economic disruption, some regional hardship and the emperor's obsessive streak. Napoleon's determination to succeed with his own economic counter-offensive, the ultimately fruitless **Continental System**, warped French imperial strategy from its inception in 1806, and was a major factor contributing to the empire's breakdown.

Britain's blockade policy entailed severe diplomatic difficulties with neutrals. From 1793, the Royal Navy exercised a self-appointed right to stop and search any neutral vessel suspected of trading with an enemy, and to confiscate ships and cargoes deemed to be breaking contraband rules of its own devising. This outraged neutrals going about what they considered legitimate business, and the introduction of more stringent regulations by **Orders in Council** from 1807 deepened international mistrust of British motives. Imposed on neutral shipping wherever it was encountered, British search and confiscation procedures provided a unifying cause for the nations of the **Armed Neutrality** League in 1800–1, and were directly responsible for the outbreak of subsequent wars against **Denmark** and the United States.

Blücher, Gebhardt Leberecht von (1742–1819)

The most successful and famous **Prussian Army** field commander of the period, Blücher was perhaps the most single-mindedly aggressive general employed by any belligerent. An uncomplicated, energetic and outspoken leader, oblivious to personal danger, he has a place in German popular culture comparable with that of **Wellington** in Britain.

Born near Rostock, Blücher was the son of a retired army captain, and entered military service with the Swedish **cavalry** in 1757. He fought against Prussian forces in the Seven Years War until 1760, when he was captured and changed sides, becoming a junior officer of Prussian **hussars**. He remained in Prussian service until 1770, when he was dismissed for repeated insubordination and excessive debauchery. He retired to become a farmer, only returning to military service after the death of Frederick the Great.

Recommissioned as a major in 1787, he was a colonel of hussars during the early campaigns on the **Rhine** in 1793–4. Promoted brigadier-general in March 1794, and major-general in June, he distinguished himself during the actions in the **Vosges** that autumn, but was denied further active service in the **Revolutionary Wars** by Prussian neutrality after 1795.

A strident voice for a return to war whenever the opportunity arose, though somewhat discredited by a number of further brushes with higher authority, Blücher commanded a cavalry corps under **Brunswick** when Prussia fought France in 1806. His impetuous opening attack at **Auerstädt** set the pattern for a disastrous defeat, but he redeemed himself with a characteristically stubborn last stand to aid **Hohenlohe**'s subsequent retreat, and led a secondary force of survivors to **Lübeck**, where his was the last major Prussian formation to surrender in early November.

Paying the price for his growing reputation and very public hatred of the French, Blücher was specifically forbidden from holding senior command by the terms of the 1807 **Tilsit** peace. Incapacitated by illness through most of 1808, he served as governor of Pomerania and Colberg, but was forced to abandon the latter command when French forces moved east in 1812. He remained in contact with **Scharnhorst, Gneisenau** and other senior officers working towards a genuinely national army after 1809, and was appointed full general in command of Prussian field forces when **Frederick William III** joined the **Sixth Coalition** in early 1813.

Blücher's forces played a central role in allied defeats at **Lützen** and **Bautzen**, after which he formed a highly successful partnership with chief of staff Gneisenau, who provided cerebral detachment to balance his chief's inevitable insistence on attack. Blücher commanded the allied Army of Silesia in the east of the theatre during the second phase of the campaign for **Germany**, defeating **Macdonald** at the **Katzbach** and sweeping north to join the decisive convergence on **Leipzig**.

Quarrelling incessantly with allied commanders, Blücher led his army into **France** as a field marshal in early 1814, pushing towards Paris from the east. By now imbued with a deep personal detestation of **Napoleon**, he made increasingly furious efforts to persuade the assembled monarchs into an immediate drive on the French capital, but was ordered to follow a more cautious strategy. Able to advance virtually unimpeded after the vital victory at **Laon**, he entered Paris with his army in late March.

Blücher subsequently fell ill and returned to Prussia a hero, visiting Britain en route. He was about to retire when Napoleon's return from **Elba** brought him back into the field for the **Hundred Days** campaign. He disappeared, presumed killed, during the latter stages of an initial defeat at **Ligny** that was partly the product of his usual eagerness to give battle, but returned to reverse his army's subsequent retreat in time to intervene decisively at **Waterloo**.

Created Prince of Wahlstadt, Blücher spent his last years in retirement on his Silesian estates. He was known in Prussia as 'Alte Vorwärts' (Old

Forward), and accused by Napoleon of a 'hussar complex'. His best qualities were inspirational rather than technical or tactical, and he was closer in style to the Russian **Suvorov** than to Wellington, with whom he is more usually compared.

Bolívar, Simón (1783–1830)

Known as the Liberator of **South America**, Bolívar was from a wealthy Venezuelan family, and travelled to Madrid in his youth to study law. He was in Paris in 1789, and strongly influenced by the ideological atmosphere of the **French Revolution**. He returned to South America to take part in the failed Venezuelan rebellion of 1811–12, fighting under **Miranda**, before crossing into New Granada (Colombia) and recapturing Caracas from royalist forces in 1813. Expelled into exile in Jamaica in 1814, he returned with British help in 1817 to wage a long and ultimately successful campaign of liberation that had created a large republic of Colombia under his dictatorship by 1825, but his plans for a federalist empire met strong separatist opposition, and the splinter republics of Venezuela, Ecuador, Peru and Bolivia had been established against his will before his death.

Bombs

Contemporary British term for the missiles thrown by **mortars**, and for small mortar-armed warships. Naval bombs were shallow-draught vessels, strengthened to carry one or (more usually) two heavy mortars and withstand their recoil. Inevitably cumbersome, they were easy targets for hostile gunners and not equipped to defend themselves against other warships. Bombs were usually employed in support of major warships attacking coastal **fortresses** or other static defence positions. On at least one wartime occasion, at the **Basque Roads** in 1809, the **Royal Navy** made use of 'bombships', hulks packed with gunpowder and exploded near a target.

Bonaparte, Caroline (1782–1839)

The youngest sister of **Napoleon**, and the most venal of his immediate family, Caroline was born Maria Annunziata but renamed at her brother's insistence. Married to **Murat** in 1800, she demonstrated a voracious appetite for honours and titles, regularly badgering Napoleon on her husband's behalf. After Murat became King of

Naples in 1808 she displayed a similar addiction to political intrigue. Almost immediately involved in the abortive **Talleyrand–Fouché** conspiracy, she proved willing to plot against both Napoleon and Murat to preserve her throne. She was in contact with the allies from late 1812, but lost Naples in 1814 and lived the rest of her life in Florence, granted a pension and the title Countess of Lipona (an anagram of Napoli) by the French government.

Bonaparte, Eliza (1777-1820)

Napoleon's eldest sister left her Corsican husband soon after his elevation as Prince of Piombino in 1805, and aided Napoleon's ambitions for the unification of Italy under his control by becoming Grand Duchess of **Tuscany** in 1809. Exiled in 1814, she spent her last years in Trieste.

Bonaparte, Jérôme (1784-1860)

The youngest and most dashing of **Napoleon**'s brothers, Jérôme began his career with a brief spell of service in the **Consular Guard** before transferring to the **French Navy** in 1800. Originally best known for his playboy tendencies, he took unauthorized leave to visit the **United States** in 1803, and married an American woman, Elizabeth Patterson, by whom he fathered a son. He was recalled to France and returned to naval duties by Napoleon, who regarded the marriage as interfering with his dynastic plans.

Jérôme was promoted rear-admiral in 1806, after he brought six merchant prizes back to France in another unauthorized operation. He then joined the **Jena–Auerstädt campaign** against **Prussia**, commanding a division of the **Bavarian Army** until 1807. Reluctantly accepting Napoleon's insistence that he divorce his wife and marry Princess Catherine of **Württemberg**, he was named King of **Westphalia** by the Treaty of **Tilsit** that July.

Bombarded with advice from Paris, and saddled with enormous commitments to the French Empire, Jérôme was always likely to be removed from power at his brother's whim, but proved a reasonably popular and effective ruler. Governing whenever possible through native ministers, and selling crown properties to meet most of his imperial obligations, he made the **Westphalian Army** one of Napoleon's most effective foreign units, and led it during the campaign of 1809.

Jérôme was given command of the **Grande Armée's** southern wing for the **Russian campaign** of 1812, fuelling rumours that he was about to become king of a restored **Poland**. His performance and subsequent resignation remain controversial. Some authorities regard his lethargy around **Minsk** as a major factor in early French failures, but others suggest that Napoleon had always planned to leave him in Poland, and accordingly chose to believe **Davout's** version of events.

Jérôme returned to Westphalia in mid-July, and set about raising more forces for Napoleon's 1813 campaign in **Germany**, but was eventually driven from his kingdom by the approach of allied armies in October 1813. He remained in Paris until the eve of its fall in 1814, when he escorted the Empress **Marie-Louise** out of France. Returning the following May to command a division during the **Hundred Days** campaign, he played an important but unfortunate role at **Waterloo**, and remained in postwar exile until 1847, when he returned to an honoured place among the dignitaries of Napoleon III's regime.

Bonaparte, Joseph (1768–1844)

French emperor **Napoleon's** older brother was trained as a lawyer, and was active in Corsican politics until exiled with the rest of his family in 1793, when he settled in Toulon and married Julie Clary. Although already well connected among liberal politicians in Paris, he was quick to build a diplomatic career on the back of Napoleon's successes, securing election to the Council of **Five Hundred** in 1797, before serving as ambassador to **Parma** and the **Papal States**.

A moderately capable diplomat and administrator, well intentioned and gracious, his career scaled heights beyond his expectations or talents. He helped negotiate the Treaties of **Lunéville** and **Amiens**, and was left in administrative control of Paris when Napoleon was away fighting the **Third Coalition** in 1805. The following year he was given command of the force that occupied **Naples**, and became King Joseph

of Naples on 30 March 1806. A liberal reformer at heart, he tried to protect his Neapolitan subjects from imperial exploitation, and dismantled the state's feudal constitution, but frequent disagreements with his brother seldom amounted to independent action, and he was bullied into leaving Naples and becoming King of **Spain** in 1808.

Joseph's reign in Spain began on 6 June 1808, but his liberal intentions were swamped by the escalation of the **Peninsular War**, his own inability to dominate French military commanders in the theatre and the unshakeable hostility of most Spaniards (*see* **Alfrancescados**). Joseph returned to Paris after defeat at **Vitoria** in 1813, and never returned to Spain. He was entrusted with the vital task of governing Paris during the campaign for **France** in early 1814, but proved unable to marshal military resources or political support in a crisis-riven capital. After Napoleon's final defeat in 1815, Joseph spent most of his life in the United States, but returned to Europe to spend his last years in Florence.

Bonaparte, Louis (1778–1846)

The fourth of the Bonaparte brothers, Louis received military training and served as an aide with **Napoleon** during the 1796 **Italian campaign**. Apparently a strong-willed and hearty figure at this stage, he lapsed into a lifelong battle with ill-health after his passionate love for **Joséphine's** niece Emilie was forbidden by Napoleon and he was taken on the **Middle East** expedition. Transferring to the cavalry in 1799, he was promoted brigadier-general in 1803 and achieved divisional rank next year. From September 1805 he led French forces in the **Netherlands**, and he was crowned head of the puppet Kingdom of **Holland** in May 1806.

He took his new role seriously, and soon fell into serious dispute with his brother by refusing to subordinate the rights of his subjects to French imperial requirements. He gained no credit for the allied failure at **Walcheren** in 1809, and the breach with Napoleon was widened by the breakdown of his marriage to Hortense de **Beauharnais**, but it was his unwillingness to enforce the **Continental System** against British trade that sealed his fate. Still a sickly man, Louis was bullied by Napoleon into abdicating his throne on 1 July 1810, after which the kingdom was incorporated into the French Empire. He never returned to public life, devoting himself to literary pursuits until his death in Italy.

Bonaparte, Lucien (1775–1840)

The black sheep of the Bonaparte family, **Napoleon**'s second brother took part in post-revolutionary politics, and helped the **Brumaire** coup to succeed in 1799 as a member of the Council of **Five Hundred**, but retired from public life in 1804 after spells as interior minister and ambassador to **Spain** during the **Consulate**. Refusing all offers of imperial dignity, he lived the rest of his life privately in Italy, apart from a brief, unhappy stay in the **United States**.

Bonaparte, Napoleon (1769–1821)

The defining figure of the age, and one of the most extraordinary talents to grace any epoch of European history, Napoleon rose from a relatively humble background to win fame as a successful general in the 1790s and to seize supreme power in France from late 1799, ruling the French as emperor from 1804 until his abdication in 1814. Though he was restored to power for a few months in 1815, military defeat forced his second abdication, and he spent the rest of his life in exile.

He was born Napoleone Buonaparte at the port of Ajaccio, Corsica, on 15 August 1769. The second of eight children, he spoke native Italian but was a French citizen, Corsica having been annexed by France the previous year. His father was a lawyer and minor aristocrat, with political ambitions but very little money, and the family relied on social connections to provide opportunities for the children. These secured Napoleon and his older brother Joseph places at a mainland school in Autun from 1778, and he completed his basic education at Brienne, in Champagne, where he displayed an early flair for mathematics.

Transferred to the Paris Ecole Militaire from 1784, Napoleon was commissioned second lieutenant in the royal French **artillery** a year later. His father died in 1785, and over the next few years he divided his time between garrison duties and prolonged visits to his family, becoming increasingly embroiled in Corsican politics as a supporter of nationalist leader Pascal Paoli. Meanwhile he was an assiduous student of his craft, subsequently giving credit as mentor to Baron du Teil, his commandant during a posting to Autun in 1786.

A committed supporter of the **French Revolution**'s egalitarian ideals, Napoleon was in Paris when the monarchy collapsed in summer 1792. He returned to Corsica to find the island in political turmoil, and was forced to settle in southern France with his family after a bitter break with Paoli. By now a captain, but with little combat experience, he was given a first chance to shine in late 1793, when he was appointed artillery adviser to the siege of rebel **Toulon**. He devised the attack plan that recaptured the port in December, earning a high reputation in army circles and immediate promotion to brigadier-general.

After recovering from a thigh wound received at Toulon – the only serious injury of his career – he was appointed artillery commander with General **Dumerbion**'s Army of Italy for its spring offensive in 1794, receiving much of the credit from an unambitious C-in-C for its limited successes round **Saorgio**. Plans for another offensive were thwarted by a cautious government, and Napoleon was arrested as a **Jacobin** sympathizer after the **Thermidor** coup of July 1794. Released after three weeks, he returned to Italy in time to orchestrate another limited success around **Dego** in September, but was at first unable to secure a command under the **Directory** regime.

He spent much of 1795 in Paris, badgering the government to adopt his plans for a major Italian offensive and occasionally working for war minister **Carnot**'s nascent staff organization, the **Bureau Topographique**. A period of personal frustration, during which he resigned his commission, was ended by the **Vendémiaire** coup of 1795, when his characteristically ruthless use of **grapeshot** to halt civilian insurgents helped save the government. The incident established Bonaparte among the soldier-politicians close to the heart of republican affairs, and he received the appointment he craved in early 1796, replacing **Schérer** as C-in-C to the Army of Italy from March, shortly after marrying **Joséphine** de Beauharnais in Paris.

The **Italian campaigns** of 1796–7 cleared the theatre of hostile forces, knocked Austria out of the war and effectively ended the **First Coalition**. They also established Napoleon as a popular military hero, and introduced many of the operational trademarks that would bring him unprecedented martial success over the next decade. Along with a preference for organization of his army into three advanced columns with a strong force in reserve, the campaigns demonstrated his ability to plan and execute rapid manoeuvre on a large scale. His boldness, his instinctive appreciation of an enemy's physical and psychological weak spots, and his ability to identify and concentrate against a single vital point inspired some of his best-known victories at **Montenotte**, **Lodi**, **Castiglione**, **Arcola** and **Rivoli**.

At the same time he began his career as a statesman, founding the **Cisalpine** and **Cispadene** Republics along the Po valley, and forcing both the **Papal States** and **Tuscany** into peace with France. He negotiated the preliminary Peace of **Leoben** with Vienna in April 1797 (and its confirmation at **Campo Formio** in October) without reference to his government, imposing a harsh peace that made future Austro-French war almost inevitable.

Napoleon's obvious ambition encouraged an insecure Directory to keep him out of Paris, hence his appointment to command the army preparing to invade **England** in October 1797. His thirst for action sharpened by Joséphine's well-documented infidelities, and his sense of destiny confirmed by his Italian achievements, he quickly decided that an invasion was likely to fail, and began planning an expedition to the **Middle East**. The scheme received strong support from a growing network of political contacts, by now including foreign minister **Talleyrand**, and was authorized by the government in spring 1798.

Like many contemporaries, Napoleon believed that conquest of **Egypt** would bring fabulous wealth and strike a blow against British security in **India** at very little risk of provoking war in Europe. He was wrong. After capturing **Malta** en route, he defeated Arab forces at the **Pyramids**, occupied **Cairo** and established a colony in Egypt, but **Nelson**'s destruction of French **Mediterranean** sea power at the **Nile** cut the expedition off from France. Napoleon marched into Syria in spring 1799, intent on seizing Constantinople and somehow threatening British India, but was unable to advance beyond **Acre**.

Nelson's success had helped cement a **Second Coalition** of European powers against France, and the new war was going badly by the time Napoleon marched his plague-ridden army back from Syria to defeat a Turkish invasion at **Aboukir** in July 1799. His response to news of the peril facing France was typically resolute and pragmatic. Abandoning his army, and accompanied by only a few close associates, he slipped out of Egypt aboard a fast **frigate** in August, and evaded British patrols to land in France, at Fréjus, on 9 October.

Napoleon's conduct in the Middle East had attracted criticism from **Kléber** and other senior subordinates, but no breath of dissent had reached France, where views were shaped by the C-in-C's carefully orchestrated **propaganda** campaign. Arriving in Paris with his popular reputation undiminished, he hesitated only briefly before accepting an offer from **Sieyès** to take part in the **Brumaire** coup that dispatched a tottering Directory government on 9–10 November.

Expected to function as a figurehead leader, Napoleon turned the tables on his co-conspirators after Brumaire. Given crucial support by Talleyrand and **Fouché**, he forced through a new constitution that effectively gave him supreme power in the **Consulate**. With a war-weary France still in a state of advanced political volatility, and Coalition armies menacing its frontiers, the new First Consul's immediate priority was to secure that power by delivering a victorious peace.

His second **Italian campaign**, an audacious attack across the Alps against the rear of Austrian forces menacing Provence, ended with a narrow but decisive victory at **Marengo** (14 June 1800), and **Moreau**'s success on the **Rhine** at **Hohenlinden** finally brought Vienna to terms at **Lunéville** in February 1802. By that time a preliminary peace with Britain had been signed at **Amiens** and the First Consul was politically unassailable at home.

Napoleon's absence on campaign had signalled

an upsurge in opposition to his personal rule in Paris, but it was stifled by a wave of arrests, executions and deportations in the immediate aftermath of Marengo. Already exercising autocratic powers, ruling by decree or through his appointed Council of State, he used the years of relative peace that followed to establish a stable and effective personal dictatorship.

Sure that war was bound to come again soon, Napoleon focused his domestic policies on establishing broad support for his regime, and on marshalling resources for military expansion. The rationalization of French legal life by the **Code Civil**, reconciliation with the Catholic Church through the **Concordat**, and a series of amnesties intended to attract **émigrés** back into France were all designed to encourage national consensus. Sweeping fiscal, political, judicial and socio-economic reforms streamlined and centralized every aspect of government activity, stabilizing the currency and stimulating economic revival, which was further encouraged by government intervention in the nation's industrial, agricultural, educational and welfare systems.

An inexhaustible propagandist, Napoleon spared no expense in promoting the new regime's triumphalist image. He began restoring his dilapidated capital with a series of ambitious public works, including the Louvre, the Quai d'Orsay, the Arc de Triomphe, a welter of commemorative parks, plans for a regulated water supply and the restoration of many churches wrecked during the Revolution.

Even before a grateful Senate and nation were persuaded to make him First Consul for life in August 1802, Napoleon had begun assuming the trappings of monarchy, instituting a new nobility under his patronage with formation of the Légion d'Honneur. This process was extended with the creation of princes, arch-officials, counts and barons after his elevation as hereditary head of a new French Empire in May 1804.

By that time many of the personnel and methods that would sustain Napoleon through the next decade were in place. Although he found it expedient to give important roles to some of the more amenable 'political generals' of the Directory era, such as **Bernadotte**, most of his chief military subordinates had risen to prominence in his wake. Men such as **Murat**, **Berthier**, **Ney**, **Davout**, **Soult** and **Lannes** had fought through most of his campaigns, and formed the backbone of the **Marshalate** after 1804, but were seldom given opportunities for independent action, a weakness that would prove expensive once military commitments outgrew the emperor's capacity for direct personal management.

As he cemented his grip over state patronage, Napoleon's supporters included personal followers, led by his family and army elements, and those politicians who shared Talleyrand's view that France needed a period of reconstruction under a single strong leader. The same basic belief, allied to understandable faith in his military prowess, lay behind the genuine mass popularity that acted as a buffer against political disenchantment at the centre.

Gradually dispensing with the paraphernalia of representative government, Napoleon governed his empire through his retinue. Whether formally attached to the personal household, or to the army's **Grand Quartier-Général** staff organization, loyal bureaucrats like Berthier, **Caulaincourt** and **Cambacérès** functioned as his executive in all matters of state. Through them, he imposed his extraordinary personality and unique political insights on every aspect of public affairs, displaying phenomenal energy and application punctuated by occasional bouts of lethargy, which became more serious and frequent in his later years. A lightning analyst, blessed with the gift of certainty, he nevertheless remained above all a warlord, and his restless pursuit of territorial expansion in the name of security dominated the empire's policies and development after 1804.

Napoleon made little effort to preserve the peace secured in 1802. His moves to tighten French control over **Switzerland**, central Italy and the **Netherlands** helped push an exasperated British government into a new war from May 1803, prompting resurrection of French plans for a cross-Channel invasion of England. Though he recognized that the enterprise was extremely hazardous, Napoleon was sufficiently ignorant about the realities of **naval warfare** to send the combined French and Spanish fleets on an almost suicidal decoy mission, a major strategic error that culminated in their annihilation at **Trafalgar** in October 1805.

Trafalgar banished the French Empire from the world's sea lanes for the duration, but Napoleon regarded overseas possessions as little more than imperial bargaining chips, and by the end of 1805 it hardly seemed to matter. His cavalier diplomacy, especially his execution of the Duc d'**Enghien** in 1804, had smoothed the formation of a powerful **Third Coalition** against France, but its grandiose offensive plans came to rapid grief in autumn 1805, and it collapsed after calamitous defeats at **Ulm** and **Austerlitz**. Brilliantly conceived and conducted by Napoleon, the campaign confirmed French domination of Italy and the Low Countries, creating the welcome illusion of total victory.

The illusion was short-lived. Punitive treaties imposed at **Pressburg** and **Vienna** had left both Austria and Prussia thirsting for revenge, as was Russian tsar **Alexander I**, and Napoleon's execution of German nationalist publisher Johann **Palm** in April 1806 helped push the relatively untried Prussians into a new conflict that summer. Napoleon won another crushing victory at **Jena–Auerstädt** in October, but Prussian king **Frederick William III** fought on from his eastern frontier, forcing the emperor to march into **Poland**.

Compelled to spend the winter in **Warsaw**, Napoleon was welcomed by Polish leaders as the potential liberator of their unhappy country. He treated their hopes with the pragmatic cynicism that was his response to all ideologies, dangling the possibility of national restoration as a means of securing recruits for his armies and long-term support from leading nationalists. He also acquired a new lover, forming a lasting liaison with Polish noblewoman Maria **Walewska**, who replaced the inconstant (if fundamentally loyal) Empress Joséphine at the centre of his affections.

A narrow victory over Russian and Prussian forces at **Friedland** finally broke the **Fourth Coalition** the following spring. A new alliance with Alexander at **Tilsit** in July 1807, accompanied by another savage settlement with a prostrate Prussia, seemed to secure imperial frontiers to the east, and to provide protection against fur-

ther aggression from Austria or a new British-led coalition. Napoleon returned to Paris in late July as the undisputed master of central and western Europe, but was unable, or unwilling, to halt the spiral of European warfare.

In many ways a supremely rational and calculating man, justly credited with sweeping away the debris of European feudalism, Bonaparte was also the continent's last great dynast. In his shameless promotion of family glory, self-conscious imitation of imperial Roman forms and frequent lapses into behaviour that appears immature by modern standards, he was a quintessentially medieval figure. As such he demolished his enemies as a matter of personal honour, as much for satisfaction as from necessity, and this is nowhere more clear than in his obsessive hatred of **Great Britain**.

Britain was beyond conquest, but Napoleon was never prepared to seek a lasting peace with the nation he blamed for all the wars fought by France since 1792. His fleeting efforts at détente – in 1801–2, and when the pacifist **Fox** dominated the London cabinet in 1806 – were never backed by genuine concessions, and his strenuous attempts to break the economic grip of British naval **blockade** by imposing the **Continental System** of universal trade sanctions warped imperial policy after 1806. Napoleon never fully understood the System's economic implications, but its manifest lack of success (and the enforcement problems it created) strained relations with client rulers, drove him to assume more direct control over their economies and encouraged his restless urge to conquer.

Desire to enforce the System prompted French conquest of **Portugal** in late 1807, and encouraged an invasion of **Spain** the following March. By late spring Napoleon had deposed the Spanish royal family at **Bayonne**, installing his brother Joseph **Bonaparte** as king, but nationwide rebellion forced the emperor to assume personal command of a renewed invasion in the autumn. Recapturing Madrid with ease, he was distracted by pursuit of a small British army to **Corunna**, leaving much of Spain in rebel hands and the British still holding part of Portugal when he returned to Paris in January 1809.

His departure from Spain, prompted by

Austrian preparations for a new war and news of the **Talleyrand–Fouché** conspiracy, reflected an ill-informed overconfidence that marred his conduct of the **Peninsular War** as a whole. Dictatorial but distant, he subsequently ran the conflict by remote control, never appreciating the difficulties of campaigning in Spain, the fundamental strength of **Wellington**'s position in the west or the depth of Spanish popular commitment to rebellion.

The attacks on Spain left only 150,000 troops to defend the empire's other frontiers, emphasizing the gap between Napoleon's ambitions – by now fixed upon establishment of a single European ruling dynasty – and the reality of his military and political positions. Concentration of forces in Spain forced him to appease a disenchanted tsar at **Erfurt** in autumn 1808, and encouraged vengeful hawks in Vienna to believe that a 'German war of liberation' could defeat an overstretched **Grande Armée** in 1809.

At the same time Napoleon faced new troubles at the heart of his imperial organization. Talleyrand was operating as the tsar's agent by the time of Erfurt, and subsequently led a clandestine movement to reach an accommodation with Britain. Bonaparte family relations were also deteriorating fast, as imperial demands brought repeated conflicts with Murat in Naples, Louis **Bonaparte** in Holland, Joseph in Spain, Eugène de **Beauharnais** in the Kingdom of **Italy** and even the inventively loyal Jérôme **Bonaparte** in **Westphalia**.

Vienna's declaration of war in early 1809, along with the continuation of hostilities in Spain (where British forces again cleared Portugal of French troops) ensured that France remained on a war footing, and that Napoleon was not long in Paris that spring, reaching the front at the Danube in late April. Though his armies were packed with raw recruits, and no match for the forces of 1805–7, he still managed to force an Austrian surrender after victory on the Danube at **Wagram** in July. Failure of a British invasion of Holland at **Walcheren** confirmed defeat of the **Fifth Coalition**, and the subsequent Treaty of **Schönbrunn** added further Balkan territories to Napoleon's empire (*see* **Map 21**).

At the height of its extent and apparent stability, the empire was not cured of its fundamental weaknesses, and its opulence could not mask the fact that Napoleon, known outside France as the 'Corsican ogre', was the most hated man in Europe. He was fully accepted as legitimate leader by the majority of French people, but his family were always branded upstart usurpers by Europe's more established royal houses, although after 1809 he was able to contemplate marriage into one of them.

Though Joséphine was a popular and hardworking empress, her inability to provide an heir combined with Napoleon's dynastic ambitions to render the marriage redundant by late 1809, when he obtained a divorce and opened negotiations in St Petersburg and Vienna. His wedding in March 1810 to **Marie-Louise** of Austria, teenage daughter of Habsburg emperor **Francis**, finally brought the Bonaparte family into the college of old European monarchies. It was also an emotional success, prompting bursts of well-publicized sexual bragging by Napoleon, and producing a son in 1811. Meanwhile Walewska, the mother of Napoleon's illegitimate child, left Paris for Poland, and Joséphine retired to her estate at Malmaison.

By mid-1811 Napoleon was planning to resolve mounting tensions with Russia by further aggression. Though the Peninsular War remained far from won, he went out of his way to provoke conflict with the tsar, and built up a vast army in Poland to back threats with action if Alexander failed to make improbable concessions. The **Russian campaign** that followed in 1812 shattered the myth of French military invincibility, triggered rapid break-up of the empire and was a catastrophe for which Napoleon was largely to blame.

He embarked on the invasion against all logic and advice, alienating informed opinion in Paris, and his preparations were marked by rampant overconfidence. He seems to have ignored the lessons learned in Poland during 1806–7, and supplied his armies on the assumption that the war would be brief and victorious. Once the campaign was under way, he tried to assert the kind of personal control that had succeeded with smaller armies, so that French forces were clumsily directed and his subordinates often left without clear instructions. Above all, he failed to alter a strategy that was manifestly flawed, gambling again and again on further, potentially fatal, eastern advances when Russian forces evaded his attempts to force battle.

Unable to extract a decisive victory from the campaign's one great confrontation, at **Borodino** in September, and forced to pull back from **Moscow** in October, he knew his gamble had failed, yet remained convinced that a renewed military effort could recover the situation. Once retreating French forces had crossed the **Beresina**, his first priority was to reassert control in a panic-stricken Paris, where rumours of his death had prompted the bizarre **Malet** conspiracy and state finances were close to collapse. Quitting the remnant of his army on 5 December, he reached Paris thirteen days later, after an arduous journey involving a day's travel by sledge.

Enduring personal charisma enabled him to restore order in the capital, and to scrape together a substantial army for the campaigns of 1813, but failure in Russia had coincided with Wellington's breakthrough offensive in Spain, and his system of alliances was crumbling. Prussia joined the **Sixth Coalition** in February 1813, and Napoleon suffered diplomatic reverses after every military setback during the subsequent campaign for **Germany**. Though far from his decisive best, and guilty of poor judgment in selection and instruction of subordinates, Napoleon won tactical victories at **Lützen**, **Bautzen** and **Dresden** in 1813, but increasingly efficient allied evasion tactics, his own uncertainties and the failures of subordinates eventually forced him into a desperate defensive battle against Coalition armies converging on **Leipzig** in October.

Defeat at Leipzig signalled the end of French control in Germany. The Confederation of the **Rhine** collapsed and all the main German states joined the Coalition. As Austrian and Neapolitan forces prepared to invade Italy, and Wellington approached the Pyrenean frontier, Napoleon rejected offers of peace along the 'natural frontiers' and fought on, raising another army of conscripts to join with surviving veterans in the defence of **France** from late January 1814.

Popular support for the regime was at last crumbling under the strains of defeat, and the emperor was never able to call on more than about 120,000 men in 1814. Conducting a highly mobile and imaginative campaign, which included a series of four victories during the celebrated **Six Days Campaign** in February, he reprised his greatest martial glories when his back was against the wall, but could only delay the advance of much larger allied armies on Paris.

Though some commentators date his mental decline from 1805–6, Napoleon was displaying clear signs of instability by early 1814. Prey to alternate bouts of blind optimism and fatalistic pessimism, he retreated into long periods of inactive contemplation at vital times, and treated increasingly depressed subordinates to frequent bursts of irrational fury. He also misjudged the diplomatic mood of his enemies, refusing offers of terms until it was much too late, and placing unjustified faith in the dynastic benevolence of his Habsburg father-in-law.

Defeat at **Laon** in March 1814, and failure of a final thrust behind Coalition lines, left Paris at the allies' mercy by the end of the month, and political support for the regime had collapsed by the time their armies entered the capital on 31 March. Though he wanted to fight on from the provinces, and briefly held out for recognition of his son's titles, Napoleon agreed to an unconditional **abdication** on 6 April. Even in defeat, he was able to inspire the devotion in the common soldier that characterized his entire career. He still commanded 60,000 loyal troops when his marshals persuaded him to step down, and was swamped by volunteers when selecting the 600 **Imperial Guard** veterans he was permitted to take into exile on **Elba**.

Napoleon spent the next few months organizing his tiny new kingdom along imperial lines, but retained considerable interest and influence in French affairs. As the restored royal government blundered into almost immediate unpopularity, he was kept in close touch with events by a stream of visiting notables. They included the ever-loyal Maria Walewska and her infant son, but Empress **Marie-Louise** returned to Austria, and he never saw his legitimate heir again.

Napoleon had no doubts about the wisdom of

his return to France on 1 March 1815, and his belief that the French people would welcome him back was soon confirmed. Landing with only about a thousand troops, he won over a unit sent to stop him at **Laffrey** and then proceeded to Paris in triumph, entering the capital on 20 March after the royal family had fled to Belgium. In control of the army but unable to rely on political support in Paris, he styled himself 'Protector of the Revolution' and altered the imperial constitution to include democratic institutions. Doubts about his sincerity were probably well justified, but were put on hold pending conclusion of a new war with the other great powers, now formed into a **Seventh Coalition**.

Napoleon had sought peaceful relations with the allies, but he expected war, and was as usual prepared to gamble everything on victory. The **Hundred Days** campaign that followed demonstrated that he was still a military force to be reckoned with, but also that his talents had greatly diminished since 1805, or even 1814. He threw away the advantages of surprise and an initial victory over **Blücher**'s Prussians at **Ligny** by relying almost lazily on ill-chosen subordinates, and allowed himself to be drawn into battle on ground of Wellington's choosing at **Waterloo**, where slapdash overconfidence contributed to French defeat on 18 June 1815.

Napoleon still commanded a substantial army, but defeat turned the Chamber of Deputies and the senate against him. Arriving back in the capital on 20 June, he abdicated again next day after Fouché had led overnight calls for his removal, and departed to the west coast port of Rochefort (via Malmaison) in the hope of securing passage to the **United States**. He arrived on 3 July to find the **Royal Navy** already there, and boarded a British frigate to give himself up five days later. Taken to the Ile d'Aix, where he was transferred to HMS *Bellerophon*, he spent three weeks confined on board in Plymouth harbour before moving to HMS *Northumberland* and beginning his journey into lifetime exile on the remote island of St Helena.

Napoleon remained on St Helena, under the terse supervision of British general **Lowe**, from 17 October 1815 until his death from stomach cancer on 5 May 1821, dictating a series of highly coloured memoirs that presented his career as a quest for lasting peace, and found scapegoats for every failure. Though his death caused a brief stir in Europe, it was by then a political irrelevance in a continent anxious to forget the upheavals of the war years. The liberal revolution in Paris of 1830 paved the way for his rehabilitation as a French national icon, and his body was returned to Paris for ceremonial burial in 1840.

Napoleon remains a very controversial figure. He has been viewed as the godfather of modern dictatorship and as the last medieval warlord, as visionary and madman, as tyrant and liberator, as revolutionary and reactionary, as Europe's greatest soldier and (occasionally) as a lucky general blessed with incompetent opponents.

He was without doubt the most effective military tactician, strategist and organizer of his day, rivalled only by the far less ambitious Wellington. Though the quality of his armies owed much to Carnot and other earlier reformers, the scale of his conquests and the brilliance of his greatest victories place him among the finest commanders of any age. If his military achievements were short-lived, his reputation as a legislator rests on the foundation of systems that are still in existence. Though he again borrowed and adapted from the work of predecessors, his clarity of purpose and willingness to address the most universal issues provided a blueprint for post-feudal societies all over Europe.

Napoleon was only 51 years old when he died. For almost twenty years from 1796 he had dominated world affairs more completely than any single individual before the twentieth century, when technological progress had made global politics a less fantastic concept. Though faith in personal destiny ultimately overcame his reason, the combination of *realpolitik* and audacity that propelled him to glory mark him as a uniquely dynamic individual force, a one-man valve through which the medieval world flowed into the modern. *See also* **France**; **Grand Tactics**; **Strategy**.

Bordeaux

The main port in south-western **France**, and an important centre for trade with the Atlantic colonies, Bordeaux was a potential royalist stronghold throughout the revolutionary and Napoleonic periods. Linked but not directly associated with the **Vendée** rebellion in the mid-1790s, the city suffered mounting economic depression as **colonial** and **naval** successes enabled the British to stifle overseas commerce, and its situation became critical after the introduction of the **Continental System** intensified the trade war in 1806. By early 1814 the city and surrounding countryside were in open revolt against **Napoleon**, and **Wellington** detached a force under **Beresford** from his **Peninsular** army to bring the territory under allied control by March. Declaring itself a royal province, Bordeaux welcomed the Duc d'Angoulême, nephew of the exiled King **Louis XVIII**, ashore on 12 March, and became the main allied supply base during the last stages of Wellington's campaign in south-west France.

Borghetto, Battle of

Successful French attack on 30 May 1796 against Austrian positions on the River Mincio at Borghetto (*see* **Map 9**). After a series of victories during the first six weeks of his 1796 **Italian campaign**, Napoleon still sought to secure his gains against a reinforced counter-attack with a decisive battle against Austrian forces. Two-thirds of Austrian commander **Beaulieu's** 28,000 troops were deployed along the east bank of the Mincio, strung out along a front from Lake Garda to Mantua without the benefit of a tactical reserve. After a brief diversion to put down popular uprisings in Milan and Pavia, Napoleon moved east in late May to join his own 28,000 men around Brescia for an attack on the Austrian centre around Borghetto.

Using tactics that had worked at **Lodi**, an élite French formation suffered only minimal losses in seizing the bridge at Borghetto, and the French army poured across in its wake to threaten Beaulieu's rear. Unable to concentrate his scattered forces quickly, Beaulieu could only retire beyond the Adige. Most of his army was pursued north up the banks of Lake Garda into the Tyrol, but 4,500 isolated troops further south were driven back into **Mantua**. Napoleon was almost captured while with a forward outpost on 1 June

(an incident that prompted his formation of the **Guides**), but had taken effective control of the vital **Quadrilateral** region within a week, though Beaulieu's flight robbed him of a decisive victory and heralded a period of defensive consolidation.

Borgö Decree

A statement issued by Tsar **Alexander I** on 27 March 1809, following Russian seizure of **Finland** at the start of the **Russo-Swedish War**, that guaranteed respect for the religious, legal and constitutional rights of its people. Finland became an autonomous grand duchy within the Russian Empire, with the tsar as grand duke, and was thus spared the cultural and political russification usually inflicted on newly conquered territories.

Borodino, Battle of

The only full-scale confrontation between French and Russian armies during the **Russian campaign** of 1812, fought on 7 September around the village of Borodino, some 120km west of Moscow (*see* **Map 23**).

After a major attempt to trap retreating Russian armies had failed at **Smolensk** in August, **Napoleon** pursued defenders towards Moscow from 25 August, and his forces approached the small village of Borodino on 5 September. Russian tsar **Alexander** had meanwhile abandoned his policy of permanent retreat, partly in response to crusading popular support for national defence, and new C-in-C **Kutuzov** had chosen to meet the invader at Borodino.

Russian forces occupied strong defensive positions overlooking a stretch of broken terrain, protected by earthwork fortifications around forward strongpoints. A fight for one such strongpoint, the redoubt at Schivardino, took up the afternoon and much of the evening of 5 September, but it fell with the arrival of **Poniatowski's** flank corps. Both sides then spent most of 6 September planning the forthcoming battle.

Kutuzov commanded a total of about 72,000 infantry and 17,000 regular **cavalry**, along with 7,000 **Cossack** horsemen and perhaps 10,000 volunteer **Opelchenie**, supported by 640 guns. The reorganized French strike force had left Smolensk with 124,000 infantry and 32,000 cavalry, supported by 587 guns, but the rigours of marching had reduced the total number of troops available to Napoleon to fewer than 135,000, all in poor fighting condition.

Kutuzov had spread his forces along an 8km front winding south from the junction of the Kalatsha and Moskva rivers. Though the majority of French troops were approaching across easier terrain on his left (south-western) flank, Kutuzov's main strength was on his right, where **Barclay de Tolly** commanded the First Army. The **Imperial Russian Guard** was stationed near the village in the centre, and **Bagration's** smaller Second Army occupied the whole sector from the 'Great Redoubt' (a major earthwork south of Borodino) to the village of Utitsa. Russian reserve formations were also dangerously close to the front line, and Kutuzov was relying heavily on the durability of his hastily constructed fortifications.

Napoleon decided against attempting anything subtle with his weakened army, and ordered a frontal assault on Bagration's positions for the next morning, including a full-scale attack on the Great Redoubt and backed by diversionary operations against the Russian wings. The attack opened at six in the morning on 7 September.

On the French left, **Beauharnais** stormed and took Borodino, while **Davout** made hard-won gains against a group of arrow-shaped hill fortifications (or *flèches*) in the centre and Poniatowski's corps took Utitsa. All three advances hit trouble shortly after seven: Beauharnais rushed his leading division beyond Borodino, to be thrown back on the village with heavy losses by a Russian counter-attack; Davout's struggle in the sector degenerated into a long battle of attrition; and Poniatowski found his advance beyond Utitsa blocked by artillery and concealed infantry.

Beauharnais moved two of his divisions out of Borodino and across the Kalatsha shortly afterwards, for the planned attack on the Great Redoubt, while Kutuzov transferred unemployed troops south from the far right of the line. Napoleon meanwhile committed **Ney** and **Junot** to support Davout in the centre, leaving only the **Imperial Guard** in reserve, but the Russian

positions held. **Montbrun** was among several generals killed in the fighting.

The battle degenerated into inconclusive carnage over the next two hours. The attempt to storm the Great Redoubt was thrown back after a hand-to-hand struggle, and Poniatowski lost ground after making minor gains beyond Utitsa, forcing Napoleon to commit part of **Mortier's** reserve **Young Guard** to his aid. The three corps in the centre, with 250 guns at their backs, were gathered for a massed assault shortly after ten, but the terrain forced them to advance in tightly packed, massed formations, and they were easy targets for Bagration's 300 guns. The death of Bagration, one of thousands killed on both sides during the attack, eventually turned the action, but the Russians withdrew in good order to new positions behind a nearby ravine, where repeated French attacks were thrown back.

By noon the Russian line had bulged but not broken. Napoleon refused to commit the rest of the Guard against its centre, which was soon bolstered by the arrival of **Ostermann-Tolstoi's** corps from the quiet northern sector, and instead concentrated for a mass attack against the Great Redoubt. Delayed for almost an hour while Beauharnais led a division to repel a cavalry attack on Borodino, the attack on the Redoubt began shortly after two. Beauharnais led a frontal assault with three divisions, covered by a bombardment from 400 guns and supported by a cavalry attack against its rear. The four Russian regiments holding the Redoubt were literally wiped out, and it fell within an hour.

Beauharnais massed all available cavalry to exploit the central breakthrough, and complete French victory appeared close, but the arrival of Barclay de Tolly's two fresh cavalry corps held the line after a limited withdrawal. Napoleon was still unwilling to employ the Guard, but did commit an additional 80 guns from his reserve artillery to halt a counter-attack by **Doctorov's** corps and part of Grand Duke Constantine's reserve.

By late afternoon, mutual exhaustion had reduced the intensity of fighting around the Russian centre, and a last attempt by Poniatowski to break through the Russian left was foiled by its planned withdrawal in line with the army's new positions. Firing had died away all along the front by six, and Kutuzov began a planned withdrawal at dawn on 8 September. Quite incapable of pursuit, the French army settled on possession of the battlefield.

Though casualty estimates vary considerably, Borodino was unquestionably the bloodiest battle of the 1792–1815 period, costing the Russian Army perhaps 40,000 casualties and inflicting 30–50,000 losses on Napoleon. Kutuzov could justifiably claim to have avoided a conclusive defeat, and could eventually expect reinforcements, but the French army could ill afford the men and ammunition expended during the day. Marked by command incompetence on both sides (although Napoleon had the excuse of a heavy cold), the battle left the French with a clear road to Moscow, but no immediate prospect of overall victory. *See* **Map 24.**

Boxtel, Action at

Minor engagement at the start of French offensive operations into the **Netherlands** during autumn 1794, distinguished as the first combat experience of British lieutenant-colonel Wesley, the future Duke of **Wellington**. Elements of General **Pichegru**'s Army of the North seized the Duke of **York**'s outpost at Boxtel, some 30km east of Breda, from Hessian troops on 14 September (*see* **Map 2**). Four British regiments under General **Abercromby** were sent to mount a counter-attack in the night, but failed against overwhelming French numerical superiority, though they were able to fight their way out and join a general allied withdrawal to the Meuse (*see* **Flanders Campaigns**).

Brienne, Battle of

The second in a series of French attacks on relatively isolated allied formations during the opening phase of the campaign for **France** in 1814. As soon as he took direct command of hopelessly outnumbered French forces on 26 January, **Napoleon** went on to the offensive against allied columns moving towards Paris from the south-east and east. He narrowly missed General **Blücher**'s 25,000-strong force on the Marne at **St Dizier** (27 January), and followed its continued advance to Brienne on the River Aube (*see* **Map 26**).

Leading about 30,000 troops, most of them untried recruits, Napoleon hoped to take advantage of allied overconfidence and surprise Blücher from the rear as he marched north-west from Brienne. His orders were intercepted, and **Sacken**'s corps had moved back to reinforce Olssufiev's Russians holding the town by the time the first French troops arrived on the morning of 29 January.

Napoleon launched **Grouchy**'s cavalry against Brienne as soon as contact was established, but a major attack was delayed until mid-afternoon, when infantry under **Ney** and **Victor** reached the front. Ney's two divisions attacked the town, and part of Victor's corps stormed the nearby château, while the rest of his troops tried to advance south of Blücher's positions, towards Bar-sur-Aube. As Ney's inexperienced troops fought off allied **cavalry** attacks, Victor's main body was pushed back some distance by the allied right wing, but the deadlock was broken when the French forces took the château during the evening. Fighting died down after an allied counter-attack had failed, and Blücher pulled out of Brienne during the night, moving south towards **Schwarzenberg**'s much larger allied army.

Although a boost to shaky French morale, Brienne was a very limited victory. It cost Blücher's army about 4,000 casualties, against 3,000 French losses, but had alerted the allies to the danger from Napoleon's 'hit and run' attacks without seriously disrupting their plans for concentration against Paris. Both commanders were almost captured during the battle: Blücher barely escaped from the château; and Napoleon's command point was briefly surrounded by **Cossacks** before they were driven off by **Corbineau**'s cavalry.

British Army

Very much the second service of a country that relied almost entirely on the enormous **Royal Navy** to enforce its strategic interests, the British Army's main roles were **colonial** policing and internal security, and its total strength amounted to only about 45,000 troops in 1793, two-thirds of them stationed abroad. Peacetime economies had reduced home regiments to far below their paper strengths, and though an extra 17,000 troops were voted by parliament in December 1792, such a force could not exert a serious influence on major continental wars.

Though its troops were the best (and most regularly paid) in Europe, the army attracted far fewer volunteers than the navy, partly because soldiers and **marines** were less well cared for, but also because they attracted none of the popular respect enjoyed by sailors. Without the benefit of **press gangs** or **conscription**, regiments could only recruit from the very poorest sections of society, frequently resorting to sweeps of prisons and other illegal expedients.

Most officers came from the land-owning classes, purchased their commissions, and were generally left to their own devices once rich enough to command a regiment in peacetime. Competent officers found colonial experience no substitute for money, influence or seniority once they came home, and regular abuses of the purchase system also encouraged corruption throughout the chains of supply, transport, equipment and manpower allocation.

Shortages of volunteers in the 1790s revived the traditional practice of incorporating foreign regiments into the British Army. Almost 80 such regiments were raised before 1802 by private citizens, German princes or **émigrés** from all over Europe. Their quality defied generalization, ranging from excellent units of exiled officers to thinly disguised bands of **deserters**.

In operational terms, the army of the **Revolutionary Wars** was backward. Though all expeditions abroad involved cooperation with the navy, no system for joint operations or established chain of command existed before 1801, and **amphibious** operations were characterized by unproductive inter-service bickering. No staff or officer training organization existed until the foundation of a military college at Sandhurst in 1799, and there was no permanent system for organizing regiments into higher formations.

British **infantry tactics** in 1793 were borrowed from the **Prussian Army** of Frederick the Great. Despite the limited reforms of **Dundas**, and the tendency of regimental commanders to drill their men how they pleased, most troops were trained to attack in rigid line formation. Infantry were originally armed with the 42-inch 'Brown Bess'

musket, but ease of production encouraged adoption of the inferior East India Company 39-inch design, which was more likely to split on firing.

Outdated Prussian orthodoxy also influenced **cavalry** tactics, though the British made no technical distinction between light and heavy horse. Designation depended on the size and weight of individuals, so that all cavalrymen were expected to carry out both light duties and heavy shock operations. British **artillery** and **engineers** lay outside the mainstream of army administration. Run by the government's Ordnance Office, they were not subject to the vagaries of purchase and influence in the selection of senior officers. The Royal Engineers were an all-officer organization, and the Royal Artillery comprised eight troops of horse artillery and six foot battalions by 1800.

The army was strategically subordinate to the navy before 1803, and its wartime strength was dispersed around the world in line with the **Pitt** government's global approach to offensive operations. While home defence was largely entrusted to established volunteer and **militia** forces, which underwent an enormous if somewhat random wartime expansion, regular troops were committed to the defence of **Ireland** and other colonial garrisons, as well as a wide selection of more or less poorly prepared attacks against marginal targets.

Repeated reinforcement of the **West Indies** alone cost the army 100,000 deaths or invalid discharges by 1799, drastically curbing its offensive potential elsewhere, and an army sent to aid the **First Coalition** in **Flanders** from 1793 to 1795 achieved nothing of lasting value. Despite rapid recruitment in the mid-1790s, Britain still only possessed 32,000 regular troops in home bases by early 1798, and though some 80,000 troops were available for European operations by summer 1799, they were frittered away in half-hearted expeditions to **North Holland**, **Ferrol** and **Cadiz**. The army's only unalloyed successes anywhere before the **Amiens** peace were **Abercromby**'s sideshow victory at **Alexandria** in 1801 and the **Seringapatam campaign** in **India**, neither of them particularly useful in a European context.

Signs of reform were evident by the turn of the

century. As effective army C-in-C from February 1795, the Duke of **York** was a far better administrator than field commander. Some attempt was made to address the army's complete lack of light infantry, and merit was introduced as a factor in command selection. A few reforming senior officers, led by **Moore**, were meanwhile implementing new training methods, designed to foster initiative and promote flexible tactics. Perhaps the most important change to take place before 1803 was in the government's attitude to ground forces. Pitt's last budget before his resignation made provision for a regular army of 220,000 men, and this massive expansion was well under way by the time hostilities ended.

The British Army that returned to war in 1803 was still burdened with a top-heavy command chain and lacked strategic focus, so that an improved combat record did more for service morale than for the war effort as a whole. General **Stuart**'s isolated victory on the Neapolitan coast at **Maida** in 1806 provided evidence that British troops could face French veterans on equal terms, but was the only offensive action in a **Mediterranean** theatre that occupied 22,000 men by 1809. The most impressive success was won by **Wellesley** (who had influence as well as ability) on the Portuguese coast at **Vimeiro** in August 1808, but Moore's subsequent advance into **Spain** ended in a desperate escape from **Corunna**, and the **Walcheren expedition** of 1809 was a fiasco in the tradition of the 1790s.

Failure at Walcheren confirmed Napoleon's effective control of the Baltic, Channel and Mediterranean coasts, and without allies elsewhere the British government's mounting support for Spanish rebels in the **Peninsular War** was not cluttered by alternative options. Beginning at **Oporto** and **Talavera** in 1809, the army's long series of victories in Spain owed something to its improved fighting efficiency, and to the efforts of allied **Portuguese** and **Spanish** forces, including **guerrillas**. The emergence of Wellesley (ennobled as Lord **Wellington** from autumn 1809) as a formidable commander was another vital element, as were French command failings, but the belated focus of British military and economic potential on a single strategic aim was equally important.

Only Britain possessed the wealth to keep large armies overseas properly supplied for long periods, and its navy was the only force able to guarantee the security of maritime supply routes. Wellington's superb organizational performance, and his highly developed awareness of logistic priorities, made these advantages count against French armies required to live off an increasingly inhospitable land.

Wellington was always careful never to deploy more men than he could supply, and never possessed more than 50,000 British troops in his allied army. A total of 747,670 men served with the army between 1793 and 1815, a far smaller proportion of the population than that recruited by contemporary France, but wastage, breadth of responsibility and logistic restrictions meant that no army stronger than 50,000 men ever took the field.

Only about one-seventh of the 210,000 allied troops deployed in Flanders during the 1815 **Hundred Days** campaign were British. The disproportionate credit they received for the success at **Waterloo** masked continuing weaknesses, especially in senior command structure, but completed the British Army's wartime transformation into a fighting force respected both at home and abroad.

Brno, Treaty of

Agreement signed between **France**, **Baden** and **Württemberg** on 12 December 1805, following French defeat of the **Third Coalition** at **Austerlitz**. The two German states each received territory from the **Holy Roman Empire** as reward for allying with **Napoleon** before the campaign, and were further expanded when **Austria** was forced to sign the punitive Treaty of **Pressburg** two weeks later.

Brueys d'Aigailliers, François Paul (1753–98)

One of the most experienced commanders in the post-revolutionary **French Navy**, Brueys had begun his career with the royal service in 1766. A captain from 1792, he was dismissed as a suspected royalist the following year and remained unemployed until his reinstatement in 1795, after which a growing lack of competent officers around him encouraged rapid promotion. He became a rear-admiral in 1796, and was promoted vice-admiral to take command of naval forces accompanying the **Middle East** expedition in May 1798. Indecision and flawed defensive dispositions contributed to his fleet's virtual annihilation on 1 August at the Battle of the **Nile**, where he was killed aboard his flagship, *L'Orient*.

Bruix, Eustache (1759–1805)

A junior officer in the royal **French Navy**, Bruix received captain's rank in 1793 and (after a brief period in disgrace for political incorrectness) worked as a staff officer at Brest until late 1796, when he took part in the **Bantry Bay** expedition. Promoted rear-admiral in 1797, he was widely regarded as one of the post-revolutionary navy's few rising stars, a reputation reinforced by an energetic performance as minister of marine from 1798 to 1799. Sent back to Brest as a vice-admiral in March 1799 to lead a major Franco-Spanish sortie into the British-held **Mediterranean** (subsequently known as **'Bruix's Cruise'**), his lack of initiative contributed to its ultimate failure and undermined his professional credibility. Transferred to command potential invasion forces at Boulogne in 1803, and made Inspector of the Ocean Coasts in 1804, he died in Paris the following winter.

'Bruix's Cruise'

Name given to a sortie of early summer 1799 by Admiral **Bruix**'s French fleet from Brest, with the half-hearted support of a Spanish fleet from Cadiz. The operation briefly threatened British domination of the **Mediterranean**, where **Nelson**'s victory at the **Nile** in August 1798 had left the few surviving **French Navy** warships scattered and powerless.

By 1799 the only major French battlefleet was at the Atlantic port of Brest, where it was watched by Alexander **Hood**'s British fleet, while allied **Spanish Navy** units were under **blockade** in Cadiz, Ferrol and Carthagena. A combined breakout was planned by the **Directory** government in December 1798, and the highly regarded Bruix was appointed to Brest to carry it out in March 1799. The difficult tasks of preparing rotting ships and securing Spanish cooperation were successfully carried out without

alerting the British, who expected a renewed attempt to invade **Ireland**, and Bruix exploited blockade laxity to slip away unnoticed with 25 **ships-of-the-line** and ten **frigates** on the evening of 25 April.

British authorities rushed all available units to the defence of home waters once they were aware of Bruix's escape on 27 April, and the French were safely off Cadiz on 4 May. Bruix decided against attacking **Keith**'s 16-strong blockading force, partly because many of his ill-managed vessels were already storm-damaged, and dashed for the Straits of Gibraltar. Keith followed, but Spanish admiral Mazarredo waited until 12 May before venturing out of Cadiz with 17 barely seaworthy ships-of-the-line.

Bruix had caught British Mediterranean forces dangerously scattered, and was temporarily in a position to attack much smaller **Royal Navy** detachments at **Malta**, **Sicily**, **Minorca** or **Naples**. Ambiguous orders and understandable pessimism about his fleet's prospects, as well as a collision between three of his ships just beyond Gibraltar, instead persuaded Bruix to run for Toulon, which was reached on 14 May. Mazarredo's fleet ran into a storm two days later, and limped into Carthagena with 11 damaged ships on 20 May.

Bruix remained based at Toulon, delivering much-needed supplies to the **Italian** front, while British forces concentrated against him, but British Mediterranean C-in-C **Jervis** fell ill in early June, and command passed temporarily to Keith, who adopted a defensive posture. Bruix was able to leave Toulon on 8 June and slip into Carthagena to join Spanish forces, before their combined 42 battleships sailed for Cadiz on 29 June. Reinforced from Britain, Keith took up belated pursuit with 29 ships-of-the-line from 7 July, and the threat of his approach was enough to persuade Mazarredo to join a further dash north to Brest, where the cruise ended on 8 August. A major scare for the Royal Navy, triggering an important re-evaluation of blockade techniques, its main achievement from a French point of view was the absorption of Mazarredo's fleet. *See* **Map 18**.

Brumaire Coup

The coup d'état in Paris of 9–10 November 1799 that established the **Consulate** as the government of **France**, with **Napoleon** at its head. Military failure against the **Second Coalition**, combined with economic chaos and war weariness, had rendered the **Directory** government's position manifestly untenable by the time Napoleon reached Paris from **Egypt** on 16 October. A number of other important generals, including **Jourdan** and **Bernadotte**, were already in the capital, and the coup planned by the relatively moderate Director **Sieyès** was by no means the only conspiracy in progress.

While the extreme **Jacobin** parties proceeded with caution, Sieyès cast around for a military figurehead. His first choice, **Joubert**, had been killed in August, and he sought out Napoleon after both **Moreau** and **Macdonald** had turned him down. Though Napoleon detested Sieyès, he accepted the role on the advice of his brother Lucien **Bonaparte** (president of the Council of **Five Hundred**) and ex-Director **Talleyrand**.

In the days leading up to the coup, strenuous efforts were made to win the support of influential military and political figures, but the attitude of the Council of Five Hundred remained in doubt to the last. Sieyès and co-conspirator Roger-Ducos came to an arrangement with Director **Barras** on 9 November, placing their colleagues Gohier and Moulin under house arrest, while Moreau, **Murat** and **Sérurier** led detachments in securing the city streets, and **Lefebvre** added his support to the cause. The upper Council of **Ancients** quickly passed legislation naming Napoleon as 'executor' of a provisional new constitution, with Sieyès and Roger-Ducos as the other 'provisional consuls'.

Napoleon's visit to the Council of Five Hundred next day was delayed long enough for Jacobins to pack the chamber, and he was ejected when he demanded their support. Instead of sending for help from loyal army units, the delegates debated the matter until driven out by Napoleon at the head of a company of troops. A rump council led by Lucien Bonaparte then rushed through legislation confirming the Consular government in office.

With the crisis overcome, Napoleon quickly made himself de facto leader of the Consulate. Sieyès and Roger-Ducos were persuaded into virtual retirement within a few weeks, and were replaced by **Camabacérès** and **Lebrun**, while Napoleon's leading supporters took up positions of power. Talleyrand returned to the foreign office, **Fouché** took over the police, and sympathetic army officers received promotions or high commands. On 13 December, the results of a plebiscite produced an overwhelming vote of support for the new constitution, which came into effect next day. When the Provisional Consulate came to an end on 25 December, its reaffirmation named Napoleon as First Consul, officially inaugurating the era of his personal control over France.

Brune, Guillaume-Marie-Anne (1763–1815)

A journalist who seems to have entered military service with the Paris **National Guard** in 1789, Brune commanded French forces occupying **Switzerland** in 1798, led a division against **Second Coalition** forces invading **North Holland** in 1799, and commanded French forces on the **Italian** front after **Napoleon's** departure in summer 1800. One of the most ardent republicans among French senior commanders, he played a peripheral part in Napoleon's subsequent campaigns and was the only member of the **Marshalate** never ennobled.

Ambassador to Turkey in 1804, he was left behind to command the base at Boulogne when the **Grande Armée** marched on **Ulm** in 1805, and became governor-general of the German **Hanseatic** cities in December 1806. He received his biggest command in spring 1807, when he was put in charge of the 60,000-strong army of occupation in central Germany, but was dismissed for agreeing terms with Swedish forces at **Stralsund**. Still unemployed in 1814, he took service with the restored monarchy, but rejoined **Napoleon** during the **Hundred Days**, guarding south-western France against incursion or rebellion. He was murdered by a mob of extreme royalists at Avignon while returning to Paris after **Waterloo**.

Brunswick

North German duchy that maintained close political and military connections with **Prussia** (*see* **Map 1**). Charles, Duke of **Brunswick**, commanded **First Coalition** forces invading eastern France from 1792 to 1794, and was killed leading the Prussian army at **Auerstädt** in 1806, after which the state was absorbed into the Kingdom of **Westphalia**. The disinherited Duke Frederick William raised a small force for allied service, and his **Black Legion** formed the basis of a new national army when Brunswick was restored to his rule in late 1813. The Brunswick Corps, including some 5,000 infantry and a regiment of **hussars**, was with **Wellington's** army in 1815 at **Quatre Bras**, where the duke was killed, and at **Waterloo**.

Brunswick, Charles William Ferdinand, Duke of (1735–1806)

Ruler of the Duchy of **Brunswick** since his father's death in 1780, and a distinguished senior commander with the **Prussian Army** since the Seven Years War, Charles was widely regarded as Europe's finest general in the late 1780s. A scholarly man and relatively enlightened autocrat, he was married to the sister of British king **George III** and was a considerable force for Anglo-Prussian friendship. After he had turned down an offer to take command of the **French Army** in early 1792, he was a natural choice to lead the **First Coalition's** opening invasion of France.

Steeped in the military practices of the mid-eighteenth century, he launched his invasion in the mannered style of that era, issuing a pious mission statement (the **Brunswick Manifesto**) before embarking on a painstaking reduction of French frontier strongpoints. French refusal to keep to the rules at **Valmy** prompted his bewildered retirement into Germany, and his second invasion attempt in spring 1793 stalled at **Mainz**. Plagued by disputes with Austrian commander **Würmser** and the persistent interference of Prussian king **Frederick William II**, he resigned and went home in early 1794. He returned to senior command in 1806 at the request of Prussian queen **Louise**, but stumbled to almost immediate disaster against **Napoleon's** very modern methods, and died of wounds received at **Auerstädt** in October.

'Brunswick Manifesto'

The statement of intent issued under the name of allied commander the Duke of **Brunswick** on 1 August 1792, prior to the **First Coalition's** opening invasion of France. Written by a French royalist **émigré**, it threatened righteous vengeance on any Frenchman who harmed the Bourbon royal family. As a **propaganda** exercise the manifesto was a spectacular own goal, provoking a storm of popular indignation in revolutionary **France**, triggering formal abolition of the monarchy and contributing to a mood of defiant national self-defence.

Bucharest, Peace of (1812)

The agreement that ended the six-year **Russo-Turkish War**. Brokered by British diplomat Stratford Canning, it was signed by local Russian commander **Tshitshagov** and **Ottoman** emissary Khaled Effendi on 28 May 1812. The lingering war in the Balkans, conducted on a fairly desultory basis since 1806, was effectively ended by Russian willingness to make concessions, above all by withdrawing from the Ottoman provinces of Moldavia and Wallachia (modern Romania). The sultan in Constantinople, anxious to address endemic internal strife, was glad to accept only the loss of Bessarabia, and Tsar **Alexander's** suspension of Russian expansion into the Balkans was prompted by the imminent threat of invasion by **France** (*see* **Russian Campaign**, 1812).

Buenos Aires Expedition, 1806–7

Slapdash British attempt to establish a **colonial** foothold in Spanish **South America**, conducted without serious planning or preparation after Commodore **Popham's** fleet had aided recapture of the **Cape Colony** from the Dutch in early 1806. News reached Popham in April that the South American colonies of Montevideo and Buenos Aires were ready to abandon allegiance to **Spain** and he sailed part of his fleet to **South America** on his own initiative. British forces took control of Buenos Aires on 9 July 1806, before moving on to Montevideo, but the garrison was soon compelled to surrender by native forces under Spanish commanders. British occupation of Montevideo was never secure. Though reinforcements under Admiral Sterling reached the port in early 1807, sickness, supply shortages and the attacks of colonial forces (one of which captured a British 12-gun schooner) prompted abandonment of the adventure in the autumn, and Popham returned home to censure by a subsequent court martial. *See* **Map 19**.

Bülow, Friedrich Wilhelm von (1755–1816)

Noble Prussian officer who achieved divisional command in 1813 and, along with **Blücher** and **Yorck**, did much to restore the reputation of the **Prussian Army**'s senior command during the campaign for **Germany**. Quickly promoted to corps command as Prussian numbers mounted, he won battles against **Napoleon**'s subordinates at **Gross-Beeren** and **Dennewitz** (for which he was created Count Dennewitz), and fought at **Leipzig** in October. On the northern flank of the allied advance into eastern **France**, he played an important part at **Laon** in March 1814, and his corps made a vital contribution to the final victory at **Waterloo**.

Bureau Topographique

The department used as an office of central military planning by French war supremo **Carnot** from 1793. The Bureau became the basis for a general staff organization, supervising the logistic, strategic and sometimes tactical operations of forces in the field, and as such gave the **French Army** a considerable administrative edge over its opponents during the **Revolutionary Wars**. Organized on a regional basis, with an office dedicated to each of the army's designated fronts, the Bureau was largely manned by officers selected for their education, many of them **engineers**. **Napoleon** was seconded to the **Italian** desk for a time in 1795, and subsequently included the bureau in his much larger **Grand Quartier-Général** organization.

Burgos, Siege of (1812)

The Spanish **fortress** city of Burgos, on the only good road from Madrid to France, was a vital communications centre throughout the first five years of the **Peninsular War**. Following his victory at **Salamanca** in summer 1812, **Wellington** marched north on Burgos with 35,000 troops in September, and the bulk of French forces in the region withdrew on news of his approach. Even with a garrison of only 2,000 men, Burgos was a formidable obstacle. The city's strengthened defences were dominated by its castle, lying immediately to the north of the old town, and by a strong fortification, known as the Hornwork, on heights north-east of the castle.

Allied forces had invested the city by 19 September, and Wellington's preliminary attack took the Hornwork that night, but subsequent progress was hindered by shortages of **siege** equipment. Attempts to storm the castle failed on 23 and 29 September, and another foundered with the loss of 250 casualties on 1 October. A final assault was launched on 18 October, when 600 infantry charged the walls in the wake of a **mine** explosion, but again ended in failure and cost another 200 men. By that time French forces were gathering both to relieve Burgos and to attack **Hill**'s contingent holding Madrid, forcing Wellington to lift the siege during the night of 21–22 October.

Short of supplies and pursued by 50,000 troops under **Suchet** (who enjoyed a three to one advantage in **cavalry**), the retreating army fought a rearguard action at Venta del Pozo, some 40km south of Burgos, on 23 October, and reached Valladolid two days later. Wellington's plan to make a stand there was disrupted when French advanced guards established a bridgehead over the Douro, and Madrid was abandoned in the face of **Soult**'s 60,000 men on 31 October, Hill's 28,000 troops joining the increasingly battered army's retirement towards Portugal.

French pursuit was halted on 6 November, and the allied army reached Salamanca three days later, but Wellington ordered a further withdrawal to winter quarters at the border fortress of Ciudad Rodrigo. A combination of appalling weather and supply failures killed 2,000 allied troops before survivors reached the fortress on 18 November, and General Edward **Paget** was among another 1,000 taken prisoner en route, bringing allied losses to about 6,000 men since the end of August. *See* **Map 22**.

Busaco, Battle of

The major action of General **Wellesley**'s tactical withdrawal through **Portugal** during the summer of 1810. Having conducted his planned retreat west along the Coa and Mondego rivers, Wellesley turned to face **Masséna's** invading French army on ground of his own choosing at Busaco, north-east of Lisbon (*see* **Map 22**). Though Masséna's slow progress through **Spain** had cost him a quarter of his fighting strength – mostly to disease, **desertion** and the needs of garrisons – his 60,000 troops still outnumbered Wellesley's 25,000 British and 25,000 Portuguese, but well-trained defenders were well positioned on hillsides and capable of maintaining discipline under fire. Masséna launched simple frontal assaults throughout 27 September, and made no impression at all before retiring at the end of the day. Having inflicted damage on his enemy at little cost to his own strength, Wellesley resumed his retirement towards prepared defences in the **Torres Vedras** hills. *See also* **Peninsular War**.

Buxhowden, Friedrich Wilhelm (1750–1811)

One of many east Germans in **Russian Army** service, Buxhowden commanded an infantry corps under **Suvorov** during the occupation and partition of **Poland** in 1794–5, and was subsequently governor of the Russian provinces. He led the second of three Russian armies sent to aid the **Third Coalition** in 1805, taking command of the allied left wing at **Austerlitz**, and his corps fought for the **Fourth Coalition** at **Golymin** in December 1806. After taking part in the **Russo-Swedish War** of 1808–9, he spent the rest of his active career as governor of **Finland**.

C

Cadiz Raid

A failed raid on the south-western Spanish naval base at Cadiz of October 1800 that was a low point in the contemporary history of British **amphibious** operations. An attempt on the Spanish base at **Ferrol** had failed dismally in August, but the **Pitt** government's determination to force an exhausted and disillusioned **Spain** into peace prompted immediate preparations for a similar assault on Cadiz. **Abercromby**'s Gibraltar command was reinforced to 21,000 men by the troops from Ferrol, and sailed with **Mediterranean** naval forces on 3 October (*see* **Map 8**). An argument at sea between the two commanders, centred on Admiral **Keith**'s unwillingness to guarantee that he would provide offshore support regardless of weather conditions, ended with Abercromby calling off the attack at the last moment on 6 October. A violent storm blew the returning ships out into the Atlantic next day, and the expedition had become an international laughing stock by the time it finally regained Gibraltar on 24 October.

Cadiz, Siege of

The great Andalusian port and naval base of Cadiz became the capital of independent **Spain** after the Supreme **Junta** fled to the city on the fall of Seville in late 1809 (*see* **Map 22**). Though its geographical location on a small peninsula made long-term defence viable, it was held by a garrison of only some 2,400 local volunteers in early 1810, but French moves on the city were delayed while **Soult**'s Army of the South con-

solidated its position in Seville. Some 13,000 reinforcements had reached the city by the time French troops under **Victor** sealed off land approaches on 5 February 1810, and General **Graham**'s Anglo-Portuguese brigade arrived by sea later that month.

French besieging forces were never able to stop the **Royal Navy** from supplying Cadiz, or to breach manmade landward defences protected by marshlands, but allied attempts to raise the **siege** were similarly unsuccessful, though failure of an Anglo-Spanish expedition in spring 1811 was masked by Graham's subsidiary victory at **Barrosa** on 5 March. Cadiz remained under siege until summer 1812, an operation eventually involving some 60,000 French troops and subject to a constant trickle of casualties from sickness, **guerrilla** raids and allied sorties. Soult eventually withdrew his forces from 24 August 1812, after defeat at **Salamanca** had prompted French abandonment of Andalusia.

Cadoudal, Georges (1771-1804)

French royalist agitator, a leader of anti-revolutionary uprisings in the **Vendée** during the immediate post-revolutionary period, and of the **Chouans** in Brittany from 1794. In exile after their defeat at **Quiberon** in 1795, he attempted to revive the Chouan movement in 1799–1800, and subsequently refused to suspend royalist activities despite **Napoleon**'s promise of senior army rank. Appointed a lieutenant-general by exiled royalist leader **Artois**, he organized a failed attempt on Napoleon's life in December

1800 and then fled to England, where he received financial support for a return to France. Landing in Normandy on 21 August 1803, he travelled to Paris to initiate what became known as the Cadoudal Plot against the **Consulate**, conspiring with **Pichegru** in a failed attempt to abduct Napoleon on 14 January 1804. Arrested in March, Cadoudal was executed in June, and the main consequence of his last conspiracy was a thorough purge of the regime's leading political opponents by police chief **Fouché**.

Cairo Uprising (1798)

Before their invasion of the **Middle East** in 1798, French planners had assumed that **Egypt**, riven by chronic social instability and almost universal hatred of the governing **Mameluke** caste, was ripe for colonial rule. Though the people of Cairo accepted French occupation passively enough in July 1798, British naval victory at the **Nile** in August and the **Ottoman** sultan's announcement of **jihad** in October combined to ignite a disorganized but intense popular revolt. Though quickly and comprehensively put down, it forced French commander **Napoléon** to devote time to the city's pacification, and to establishing effective martial law. Despite the conscientious efforts of social planners and scientists to bring the fruits of Enlightenment culture and institutions to Egypt, an increasingly repressive French regime could never again hope to govern with popular assent.

Caisson

Contemporary term for an ammunition wagon.

Caldiero, Battle of (1796)

Unsuccessful French attack on 12 November 1796 against Austrian army positions around Caldiero, just east of the River Adige in northern Italy (*see* **Map 9**). The outnumbered French Army of Italy, commanded by **Napoleon**, had been forced back to the line of the Adige by a two-pronged Austrian invasion from the north in early November. On its eastern wing, Austrian C-in-C **Alvintzi** had forced **Masséna's** covering French division back from the Brenta valley before leading 17,000 men towards a rendezvous with 18,000 troops under Davidovich around Verona.

After a brush with French rearguards on 11

November, Alvintzi deployed some 8,000 advanced troops around Caldiero. Though heavily outnumbered overall, Napoleon concentrated 12,000 men under Masséna for an attack on the town. Poor weather delayed the operation until the morning of 12 November, by which time Alvintzi had brought up the rest of his strike force, and Masséna's leading division was driven back with 2,000 casualties. The defeat forced Masséna back to the west bank of the Adige, and left Napoleon with only some 21,000 troops to block two Austrian armies converging on Verona. Reluctant to draw reserves from **Mantua**, he opted for a desperate last strike at Alvintzi around **Arcola**. *See also* **Italian Campaigns**, 1792–7.

Caldiero, Battle of (1805)

The only major engagement fought on the Italian front during the War of the **Third Coalition** in 1805. Archduke **Charles**, commanding some 80,000 Austrian troops in the theatre, had abandoned plans for a major offensive by late September 1805, pending news of the main Bavarian campaign. Marshal **Masséna's** French Army of Italy had also been ordered on to the defensive, and an armistice between the two sides held along the line of the River Adige until 11 October, when the French commander gave the stipulated six days' notice that he was planning to open hostilities.

A French attack on Austrian positions at the Adige was duly launched on the night of 17–18 October, intended only as a diversion to prevent Charles from a rapid withdrawal into **Bavaria**. Although it established a bridgehead over the river, the attack merely hastened a planned Austrian retirement to new positions further east around Caldiero (*see* **Map 9**).

Receiving news of the French victory at **Ulm**, both commanders prepared attacks, Charles intending to disrupt pursuit of his retreat into Bavaria, and Masséna seeking to pin the Austrians to the spot. Some 39,000 French infantry and 4,000 **cavalry** attacked Charles's positions, defended by about 42,000 infantry and 6,000 cavalry, on 29 October. Unable to penetrate beyond forward defences on the first day, Masséna resumed his attacks on 30 October, leading the main infantry charge against the Austrian centre in person, and forcing Charles to commit his last reserves. The Austrians held on until nightfall, and managed to repel a series of strong assaults against their left wing all through the next day.

Masséna withdrew during the evening of 31 October, having lost about 7,000 men and inflicted an estimated 5,700 casualties. Both sides claimed a victory, each with some justification. Charles had held his ground and damaged his attackers, but Masséna had delayed an Austrian retreat on Vienna that was not fully under way until 11 November, too late to influence the Bavarian campaign.

Cambacérès, Jean-Jacques Régis de (1753–1824)

French politician, a minor noble born in Languedoc and trained in law, who was elected to the **National Convention** in 1792 and survived the ensuing **Terror** by devoting his energies to legal reform. Conscientious and well versed in the law, he was a member of the Council of **Five Hundred** and briefly minister of justice in 1799 before his support for **Napoleon** during the coup of **Brumaire** earned him the post of Second Consul a few weeks later. Cambacérès remained Napoleon's most trusted legal consultant and administrator throughout the **Consulate** and empire, though his advice against key decisions (including the abduction of the Duc d'Enghein, the invasion of **Spain** and the **Russian campaign**) was tolerated rather than followed. Created imperial Arch-Chancellor (1804) and Duke of **Parma** (1808), he generally chaired Senate and Council of State meetings in the emperor's absence, and made a major contribution to the **Code Napoléon**, for which his *Projet de Code Civil* formed the basis. He entered royal service after the restoration of 1814, but rejoined Napoleon during the **Hundred Days** and was exiled in the aftermath, returning to France and retirement in 1818.

Camp Followers

Large numbers of civilians travelled with all contemporary field armies, some with official sanction, others on a private basis. Those in army employment usually included auxiliary supply personnel, particularly mule or wagon drivers, and many forces also used civilians to drive **artillery** vehicles. Many officers supplemented the services of a soldier as batman with privately employed servants, and a regulated number of wives and children were permitted to accompany their husbands on campaign. Private suppliers of food, alcohol and tobacco also proliferated in the wake of any large field force, as did unofficially attached women, who were tolerated and even encouraged by many army commands, partly because they performed valuable domestic functions. Advancing French forces were often accompanied by female *cantinières* selling tots from their brandy casks.

None of these people, or the gaggles of refugees and fugitives that swelled their ranks, was part of an army's official calculations, and they could pose enormous logistic problems for a force on the move. As well as the difficulties caused by an inevitable proportion of criminals, camp followers blocked roads, complicated river crossings and added a dimension of confusion to any withdrawal. They also faced most of the dangers and discomforts of field operations without protection. Vulnerable to attack by hostile raiding parties or exposure in the event of their army's flight, camp followers suffered and died in large (though usually uncounted) numbers during any long or difficult campaign, and thousands were killed during the French retreat across the **Beresina** in 1812.

Camperdown, Battle of

Important naval action fought between British and Dutch fleets off the west coast of **North Holland**, near Camperdown, on 11 October 1797 (*see* **Map 18**). The French-controlled **Netherlands** had been at war with **Great Britain** since 1795, forcing the **Royal Navy** to **blockade** the 16 Dutch **ships-of-the-line** across the English Channel at Texel. Rendered more urgent in the light of French plans for the invasion of **England** in 1797, and made much more difficult by the serious **Spithead** and **Nore** naval mutinies, the blockade had succeeded largely because the **Dutch Navy's** poor condition was matched by its morale.

Dutch commander de **Winter** abandoned plans to aid the French invasion project in

August, prompting a temporary relaxation of the British blockade to allow **Duncan's** fleet a refit. Only four British ships-of-the-line were on station off Texel when de Winter's 16 slipped out of harbour on 6 October. Ordered to attack targets of opportunity, de Winter sailed south-west until informed that Duncan was in pursuit from the British base at Yarmouth, when he turned for home.

Duncan had already reached Texel by the time the Dutch ships returned on 11 October, and had taken up positions just off the coast. Anxious to force battle before de Winter could reach shallow water, Duncan manoeuvred to get the wind behind his ships and sped towards the Dutch fleet as soon as it was sighted. By eleven that morning his leading ships were approaching a well-formed Dutch defensive line, and he ordered an immediate 'free-for-all' attack as the coast loomed.

Largely by accident, Duncan's 16 ships split into two divisions, striking at the rear and vanguard of de Winter's fleet while leaving the central six or seven ships unattended. Four ships at the rear of the Dutch line were outgunned by nine British warships, and had all surrendered within two hours. At the head of the line Duncan's flagship, the 74-gun *Venerable*, and the 64-gun *Ardent* were almost overwhelmed by superior numbers before a Dutch ship caught fire and drifted out of control, forcing a temporary pause. Other British ships came up in support, and four more Dutch ships-of-the-line had surrendered by the time de Winter was compelled to give up his shattered flagship. His surviving vessels fled for the coast and the battle ended shortly after three.

Duncan's ships attempted no pursuit and casualties on both sides were heavy, about 1,150 Dutch against 825 British, but the loss of nine major warships and two frigates (none of which proved fit for British service) ended any practical threat to British security from the Dutch Navy. The action also reversed any ill-effects of Britain's mutinies (it was largely fought by former mutineers), and reinforced a growing recognition that aggression and discipline were more valuable to **naval warfare** than careful maintenance of formation.

Campo Formio, Treaty of

The peace settlement that ended five years of war between **Austria** and **France**, signed at Passeriano, near Campo Formio in northern Italy, on 17 October 1797. Based on the preliminary agreement negotiated by **Napoleon** at **Leoben** in April, the final treaty required Vienna to cede the **Austrian Netherlands** to France, accept French occupation of the **Ionian Islands**, abandon pretensions to control over Lombardy, recognize the **Cisalpine** and **Ligurian** republics, and agree (in secret) to France occupying the west bank of the Rhine. France agreed to compensate minor rulers dispossessed in the Rhineland, and Austria was left in control of Dalmatia, the Frioul and the lands east of the Adige formerly owned by **Venice**, concessions that effectively guaranteed the future revival of Habsburg **Italian** ambitions.

Canister

A type of **artillery** ammunition consisting of a hollow tin projectile filled with **musket** balls, which scattered among enemy troops when fired. Canister was used by all the main armies of the period, as were the very similar case-shot and short-range **grapeshot**. All were proven technology by the 1790s and far more widely employed than air-bursting **shrapnel**, an invention of the Napoleonic period.

Canning, George (1770–1827)

London-born politician, a fine orator who abandoned his early Whig affiliations to support **Pitt's** coalition from 1794. He held a number of relatively minor posts up to 1806, and was a ferocious critic of the **Grenville** government's desultory conduct of the war during a brief spell in opposition after Pitt's death. Rewarded with elevation to foreign minister in the **Portland** government of 1807–9, his aggressive stance was matched by punitive action against **Copenhagen** in 1807, intervention in the **Peninsular War** and refusal to exempt the **United States** from British **blockade** regulations. Canning was strongly opposed to the 1809 **Walcheren expedition**, and his subsequent attacks on **Castlereagh** provoked a duel between them in its aftermath. His inevitable resignation heralded the government's fall, and he held no further high office until 1822.

Cannonade

Contemporary term for an **artillery** bombardment.

Cape Colony, Seizure of

A vital staging post for European seaborne trade with **India** and the Far East, the Dutch Cape Colony became a target for British attack after France conquered the **Netherlands** in early 1795. A **Royal Navy** squadron of five **ships-of-the-line** and two **sloops** under Admiral Elphinstone, with 800 troops on board, reached the colony in August. After the Dutch governor had refused a surrender demand, General Craig's troops and about 1,000 sailors were landed to drive a mixed force of Dutch and Hottentot militia from their camp near Cape Town on 7 August. A Dutch counter-attack failed on 3 September, and the arrival of British reinforcements from India persuaded the colony to capitulate on 14 September. A **Dutch Navy** squadron reached the Cape the following August, but surrendered peacefully when faced with the eight battleships of Elphinstone's enlarged fleet. The colony was returned to the Dutch by the terms of the Peace of Amiens in 1802, but was recaptured against minimal opposition by troops under General **Baird** in 1806. *See* **Map 19**.

Capri, Capture of (1809)

Island off the coast of **Naples**, occupied by the British in 1799 and within sight of the capital itself, that was selected by **Murat** as the target of his first overseas military action on becoming king. Forbidden from attacking **Sicily** by **Napoleon**, Murat needed a quick success to establish his new reign, and 2,000 picked French troops under General Lamarque attacked Capri on 4 October 1809. Scaling the high cliffs at either end of the island, and surprising garrison forces deployed to defend the central lowlands, Lamarque's men forced British commander Colonel **Lowe** to withdraw his 1,000 troops into the lowland town of Capri, where they were besieged. After storms prevented a **Royal Navy** relief force from reaching the island, Lowe surrendered on 18 October. Still expecting British warships at any moment, Lamarque opted for a quick settlement, allowing defenders to leave for Sicily on one year's **parole**. The operation attracted only criticism from Napoleon, reflecting his growing mistrust of Murat since the **Talleyrand–Fouché** conspiracy of late 1808. *See* **Map 8**.

Carabinier

A French heavy cavalryman, or élite light infantryman.

Carbines

Short-barrelled **muskets** (or in a very few cases **rifles**), designed to be light and compact enough for use by **cavalry**. Carbines could be fired while the user was mounted or on foot, and were primarily employed by troopers acting as **skirmishers**. With a very short effective range, and even less accuracy than standard muskets, they were otherwise largely restricted to companies deployed on the flanks of an army and liable to sudden attack by infantry. The **French Army** was an exception, making widespread use of a far more effective long carbine, and issuing its **dragoons** with an even longer 'dragoon musket'. Both comprehensively outranged the firearms used by allied cavalry, giving French mounted forces a distinct advantage during skirmishes.

Carbonari

An Italian secret society, along Masonic lines, that took its name from the similar French **Charbonnerie** (charcoal-burners') society and became synonymous with the spread of underground anti-French agitation and **guerrilla** activity during the later Napoleonic period. Apparently inspired by contact with occupying French soldiers, Carbonari groups first appeared in the southern Italian kingdoms of **Naples** and **Sicily** during the early 1800s, but their political character, though broadly radical, was defined by regional circumstances. By 1814 Carbonari lodges had spread throughout Italy, and most had identified French imperialism as their prime enemy, while a significant number endorsed arguments for a united, independent Italy. Carbonari activity declined in the north after 1815, but the societies continued to exert a strong destabilizing influence on the oppressive Bourbon regime that ruled Sicily and Naples.

Carnot, Lazare (1753–1823)

French officer of engineers, a middle-class Burgundian who was commissioned in 1773 and whose political career began with his election as deputy for Pas de Calais in 1791. A leading military adviser with the **National Convention** in 1792, and a committed republican, he played a central role in raising the **French Army**'s *levée en masse* and took part in the Battle of **Wattignies** before his appointment as head of the Committee of **Public Safety**'s War Section in August 1793, charged with rescuing the war effort from post-revolutionary chaos. An astonishingly productive worker in the Napoleonic mould, Carnot was responsible for the widespread reforms that are generally credited with making possible the army's successes in the 1790s, and which lay behind its imperial triumphs.

Technically only a brigadier-general, he used the appointment of political representatives with field armies to impose some discipline on their hordes of untrained **fédérés**. He supervised the *Amalgame* in 1794, substituting an incoherent mass of volunteer formations with numbered demi-brigades, and greatly increased the stress on mobility within the artillery arm. Aware of the need for good communications in a multi-front war, he extended the army's **semaphore** system and pioneered the development of **balloons** for reconnaissance purposes. Instituting the **corps system** as army doctrine, and rationalizing its overall deployment into 13 field armies, he pioneered the attachment of staff sections to independent commands, and turned the **Bureau Topographique** into an embryonic general staff.

Backed by the committee's dictatorial powers, Carnot worked tirelessly to establish arms and matériel factories all over France, and somehow produced equipment for most of the army by 1796. He managed to keep **war finances** afloat by raising or forcing loans, and requisitioned resources where necessary, but his guiding principle (adopted by most French forces until 1815) was that war should be able to pay for itself by a combination of forage, looting and conquest.

He broke with **Robespierre** in time to survive **Thermidor** as the **Directory**'s war minister, and was its president for a time in 1796. He fled France after the **Fructidor** coup of September 1797, but returned after the **Brumaire** coup of late 1799, and was appointed war minister for the **Consulate** in 1800. His republican views sat uncomfortably with **Napoleon**'s dictatorship,

and he lost his ministry in December 1800, serving as a member of the **Tribunate** until 1807 but becoming increasingly marginalized after he opposed establishment of the empire in 1804.

Virtually ignored by Napoleon until January 1814, when he was promoted divisional general and given command of the Antwerp garrison, he nevertheless retained considerable prestige as the original 'architect of victory', and his willingness to support Napoleon's return to power in 1815 (in return for a noble title and the interior ministry) was an important factor enabling the formation of a government during the **Hundred Days**. Exiled from July 1815, he spent his last years in Magdeburg.

Carra St Cyr, Claude (1760–1834)

Commissioned into the royal French infantry in 1774, and a veteran of American campaigns under **Lafayette**, Carra St Cyr retired briefly in 1792, but re-enlisted as a volunteer on the outbreak of war. Promoted brigadier-general in 1795, he was a military adviser and envoy to the **Ottoman Empire** until 1798, when he returned to France to take up an active field command. He fought during the **Italian campaigns** of 1799–1800, first with **Masséna**'s Army of Italy and then with **Napoleon**'s Reserve Army, taking part in the Battle of **Marengo**. Though he also fought at **Aspern–Essling** in 1809, Carra St Cyr was primarily employed as a garrison commandant over the next decade, serving at **Magdeburg** from 1806, Dresden from 1809 and Hamburg from 1810. Dismissed from the latter post in March 1813, after losing a minor engagement during the early stages of the campaign for **Germany**, he fought with **Vandamme**'s corps later that year, and was governor of French Guiana from 1814 to 1819.

Carronade

A small, short-range **artillery** weapon, with a wide barrel, that was developed in Scotland by the Carron iron foundry and subsequently used by British and other armed forces as an adjunct to larger weapons. Used by land armies only to provide close-range defence for **fortresses** and other static positions, carronades proved a very effective 'skirmishing' weapon in the context of **naval warfare**. Employed in numbers by the

Royal Navy, and to a lesser extent in most other contemporary navies, they functioned as supplementary bow or stern weapons aboard **ships-of-the-line**, and as secondary armament aboard smaller warships, although one experimental British **frigate**, HMS *Glatton*, was equipped only with 56 carronades.

Case-Shot *See* **Canister**

Cassano, Battle of

Russian marshal **Suvorov**'s first success during the **Italian** campaign of 1799, an attack on 26 April against numerically inferior French forces strung out along the River Adda. Suvorov had taken command of **Second Coalition** forces at the Mincio from 15 April. Leaving **Kray**'s 20,000 troops besieging Peschiera and Mantua, he led 50,000 troops west through mud-drenched conditions on 17 April, taking Brescia before reaching French forward positions around Cremona on 20 April. Some 28,000 French troops, commanded by **Moreau** since **Schérer**'s resignation in mid-April, were holding a 120km front along the Adda. They held off a preliminary Austrian attack at Lecco on 25 April, but Suvorov got a division across the river during the night and launched a full-scale attack next morning. **Bagration**'s Russian division renewed the assault on Lecco without success, but a bridgehead was established at Trezzo, and four divisions under **Melas** smashed past the division holding the bridge at Cassano. Delays at Lecco prevented the whole allied army from getting across the river until 27 April, and it met strong resistance west of Cassano before Moreau ordered a general retreat behind the River Ticino, but **Sérurier**'s division pulling back from Lecco was surrounded and forced to surrender on 29 April. *See* **Map 6**.

Castaños, Francisco Xavier (1756–1852)

Perhaps the most militarily competent of the **Spanish Army**'s older generation of commanders during the **Peninsular War**, Castaños was born in the Biscay area and studied military theory in Germany. As captain-general of the Army of Andalusia in 1808, he won a stunning victory at **Bailén** in July, for which he was ennobled as the Duke of Bailén, but his long-term support for former chief minister **Godoy** was not forgotten by the Regency Junta in Madrid, and he was dismissed after suffering defeat at **Tudela** in November. Reinstated in 1810, he later fought under **Wellington** at **Albuera**, **Salamanca** and **Vitoria**, and joined the Spanish Council of State in 1825, enjoying a long retirement as a distinguished courtier.

Castiglione, Battle of

Pivotal engagement during the **Italian campaign** of 1796, fought south of Lake Garda on 5 August. As **Würmser**'s 25,000 Austrians advanced south to take Verona, threatening either to relieve **Mantua** or to join up with another 18,000 troops (Quasdanovich) approaching down the opposite bank of Lake Garda, French commander **Napoleon** ordered his two forward divisions (**Masséna** and **Augereau**) to concentrate west of the River Mincio, and called up **Sérurier**'s division from Mantua. Würmser halted his advance at Valeggio for three days from 30 July to await news from Mantua, giving French forces time to manoeuvre into position between the two Austrian formations. Outnumbered more than two-to-one, Augereau prevented any advance by Würmser while Masséna defeated Quasdanovich at **Lonato** on 3 August.

Turning on Würmser, Napoleon concentrated 21,000 men north-west of his strong positions on the heights south-east of Castiglione during 4 August, calling up another 9,500 reinforcements from Brescia and Mantua to assure local manpower superiority. He planned a frontal attack all along the Austrian line to mask a flank attack on its right, which would in turn distract defenders from a final massed assault against its weakened left.

Opened early on 5 August, the operation around Castiglione began exactly according to Napoleon's plan, but went awry with the slightly premature launch of General Fiorella's flank attack and Würmser's decision to hold back reserves from the frontal battle, which enabled the Austrians to form an L-shaped line and hold their left wing. Würmser clung tenaciously to his positions until late morning, when the last 2,500 of Napoleon's reinforcements arrived to strike at the Austrian right, seizing the adjoining heights and triggering a general withdrawal. Würmser moved north towards Peschiera, where 5,000 fresh troops were waiting to cover the retreat, and escaped a brief pursuit with the loss of 3,000 men and 20 cannon. Combined with Masséna's second victory at Lonato, Castiglione ended the Austrian offensive, enabling Napoleon to resume the interrupted siege at Mantua. *See* **Map 6**.

Castlereagh, Robert Stewart, Viscount (1769–1822)

Ulster-born politician and diplomat who entered the Irish parliament as a Whig in 1790, becoming an important voice for Anglo-Irish union before joining the Tory Party in 1795 to support **Pitt**'s unionist policy. As Pitt's Secretary for Ireland from 1798, he oversaw ruthless suppression of the **Irish Rebellion** and application of the Act of **Union**, but resigned from government in protest at **George III**'s repudiation of **Catholic emancipation**.

Recalled to office as minister for Indian affairs by the **Addington** government, Castlereagh took the important job of minister for war and the colonies when Pitt returned to the premiership in 1804, was briefly in opposition during the **Grenville** ministry, but returned to the post under **Portland** in 1807. An aloof and apparently arrogant personality, with an incoherent public speaking style, he was made the popular and political scapegoat for the failure of the **Walcheren expedition** in 1809, and reacted to the injustice by fighting a celebrated duel with **Canning** that left both men temporarily exiled from office.

Castlereagh returned to government as foreign minister under **Liverpool** from 1812, and held the office until his death. His conciliatory attitude to the ambitions of the allies, along with shrewd distribution of **subsidies**, were vital factors knitting together the **Sixth Coalition** in 1813–14, and he shared with **Metternich** the credit for engineering a sustainable balance between the European **great powers** at the post-war Congress of **Vienna**.

His unpopularity in Britain grew more pronounced after 1815, and he was unfairly regarded as instigator of the Liverpool administration's repressive social policies. Marquis of Londonderry after his father's death in 1821, he committed suicide in August 1822. His funeral procession was jeered through the streets of London.

Cathcart, William Schaw, Earl (1755–1843)

Scottish nobleman who abandoned legal studies for the army, and was a divisional commander with **York**'s expeditionary force to **Flanders** in 1793–5. He was C-in-C of **British Army** forces in **Ireland** from 1803 to 1805, and commanded the military element of the 1807 **Copenhagen** expedition before turning to a diplomatic career that culminated in a role as envoy to **Alexander I** during the 1813–14 campaigns in **Germany** and **France**. His son Charles fought at **Maida**, **Walcheren** and in the **Peninsular War**, and was a staff general at **Waterloo**.

Catherine II ('The Great'), Empress (1729–96)

Empress of Russia from 1762, an indomitable and ruthless ruler whose reputation for greatness derived largely from the massive expansion of **Russia** that took place during her reign. Engaged in a war of expansion with **Turkey** when the **Revolutionary Wars** broke out in 1792, she played an opportunist diplomatic role in mobilizing European monarchies against **France**, and reaped territorial reward by annexing part of **Poland** and the Baltic province of Courland. The unfortunate and powerful impact of her fearsome personality on the development of her son, **Paul I**, and her grandson, **Alexander I**, helped shape their eccentric adult personalities.

Catholic Emancipation (British)

Roman Catholics (and Nonconformist Protestants) had been effectively barred from public office in **Great Britain** since the Test Act of 1673, which required all officials to embrace Anglican doctrine. Prime minister **Pitt** had all but promised Irish leaders that exemption from the Test Act, or 'emancipation', would be granted once the Act of **Union** between Protestant Britain and Catholic **Ireland** had been accepted. The bitter controversy surrounding the issue was resolved in the short term by King **George III**, who refused emancipation in 1801 on the grounds that it would infringe his coronation oath, prompting the resignation of Pitt and most of his leading supporters, including **Grenville** and Castlereagh. The issue remained central to political dispute in Britain until repeal of the

Test Act in 1828, and the passage of a Catholic emancipation bill the following year.

Caulaincourt, Armand-Augustin-Louis (1773–1827)

After a relatively undistinguished military career that began with the royal army in 1787, and continued through the **Revolutionary Wars**, Caulaincourt was chosen by **Talleyrand** to undertake a Franco-Russian friendship mission to St Petersburg in 1801, and subsequently became one of **Napoleon**'s most loyal and trusted lieutenants. Trusted with organizing the Duc d'**Enghein**'s abduction in 1804, and explaining it to the **Baden** government, he became imperial ambassador to St Petersburg after the Peace of **Tilsit**, holding the post until 1811, and was created Duke of Vicenza in 1808. As official controller of the imperial household (*see* **Grand Quartier-Général**), he advised against the **Russian** invasion but nevertheless travelled with the army in 1812, and was the emperor's chosen companion for his return to Paris at the end of the campaign. Appointed foreign minister in 1813, he led peace negotiations with the allies during the campaigns for **Germany** and **France**, and remained loyal to Napoleon after the first **abdication**, refusing Talleyrand's offer of a post in the provisional government. A reluctant foreign minister during the **Hundred Days** of 1815, he retired after the second restoration.

Cavalry

Contemporary cavalry fell broadly into heavy, light and medium categories. Heavy cavalry, including **cuirassiers**, **carabiniers** and heavy **dragoons**, was primarily used for offensive operations on the battlefield, ideally delivering a decisive charge to clinch final victory in any major engagement. Sometimes wearing cumbersome body **armour**, they were armed with **sabre**, **carbine** and one or two **pistols**, and were mounted on the most powerful horses available.

Light cavalry – including light dragoons, **Uhlans** (or lancers), élite **hussars** and **Cossacks** – was used offensively on the battlefield for skirmishing, infantry support or mounting localized attacks on enemy infantry, and was employed at other times for reconnaissance work and raiding,

as a screen against hostile scouting, or as an army's first line of outpost defence. Armed with smaller sabres than heavy troopers, regular light horsemen carried similar firearms, but Cossacks and irregular horsemen serving with **Ottoman** or **guerrilla** forces carried a wide variety of traditional, improvised or stolen weaponry.

The term 'medium cavalry' referred to any mounted troops that did not fit either of the other categories, and though most were described as dragoons their equipment and functions varied in different armies. Though seldom assigned their original role, as a rapid mobile reserve intended to fight on foot in support of infantry, dragoons were capable of performing the full spectrum of mounted duties, and were the mainstays of most European cavalry arms.

For much of the eighteenth century, cavalry was regarded as the principal means of waging offensive warfare, and other arms were deployed primarily to prepare opponents for attack by massed horsemen, but the dramatic effectiveness of new **infantry tactics** employed during the **Revolutionary Wars** persuaded many European military planners to treat cavalry as little more than a supporting arm. Though **Napoleon** bucked the trend by concentrating his heavy cavalry for mass charges during major actions (at **Eylau**, for example), contemporary cavalry was more often deployed in small formations attached to infantry units than grouped together as a major offensive weapon.

The principal offensive manoeuvre undertaken by all forms of cavalry was the charge, an operation calling for discipline and the observance of basic rules. Attacking cavalry formations could advance in linear or column formation, the former being far more common, although advance in column was less taxing in terms of horsemanship and made a comeback as armies grew and training standards declined. Advance in line originally comprised three broad ranks of troopers, but by 1800 all the major armies had abandoned the third rank as a hindrance to rapid turning manoeuvres. Attacking cavalry would advance slowly at first, ensuring that horses remained fresh at the moment of contact, and accelerate gradually to reach a fast gallop over the last 50m. Defending cavalry would advance to meet an oncoming charge, aiming to minimize the attackers' momentum advantage. The second attacking line would hold back from first contact, ready to give the charge 'second wind'.

If and when charging horsemen broke through their opponents, they were required to reorganize, turn and repeat the attack from the rear, but this part of the operation frequently proved beyond the discipline of troopers. All the major armies, particularly the British, suffered instances of over-excitement spoiling successful charges, as exhilarated horsemen careered beyond enemy lines to launch reckless attacks far into the rear. At the other extreme, lack of attacking enthusiasm by some of Europe's less successful cavalry arms, notably those of the **Spanish** and **Neapolitan** armies, often led them to abandon an advance at the first sign of opposition from highly rated **French** or **Polish** forces.

Firearms were too clumsy, inaccurate and unreliable to be used by cavalrymen during battles, and their pistols were little more than ornaments, but **carbines** were used in most light cavalry roles. All except the French models remained distinctly inferior to infantry muskets, but in every other respect the mounted trooper enjoyed enormous advantages over the infantryman in direct combat.

At the most fundamental level, the mounted soldier was a terror weapon. The sheer size and speed of a few horsemen could overwhelm small numbers of men caught in open country. A cavalry unit of any size could expect to rout foot soldiers unless their victims were properly organized into **infantry squares**, use of which stimulated a generalized expansion of mobile 'horse artillery' for rapid support of cavalry attacks.

Every branch of cavalry warfare was dependent on supplies of good horses. Both the French and the British armies faced perennial shortages of home-produced horses, and the quality of French mounts was regarded as particularly poor. The eastern powers enjoyed plentiful supplies of high-quality animals, and Napoleon was able to secure large numbers of highly prized German horses by conquering most of them, but British problems were only solved after the reconquest of **Germany** in 1813 had reopened supply lines across the English Channel.

Cavalry was regarded as the élite arm of every army. Except in the post-revolutionary French cavalry, which had lost almost all its aristocratic officers by 1793, officers were generally drawn from the highest social classes, but regardless of social rank they enjoyed a reputation for dash and glamour reflected in the personal fame achieved by many cavalry commanders. The overbearing and often reckless **Murat** in many ways epitomized the age, but **Grouchy**, **Craufurd**, **Cotton** and the Cossack **Platov** were among many other cavalry leaders to achieve legendary status during the period.

Ceva, Battle of

The first French attempt, on 16–17 April 1796, to follow up victory on the **Italian** front at **Montenotte** with a decisive strike against Piedmontese forces further west. Isolated from Austrian forces to the east by **Napoleon's** advance, General Colli's 13,000 Piedmontese retired west on Ceva, pursued by 24,000 French troops. Delayed by stout resistance from 900 garrison troops at the ruined fortress of Cosseria, and a two-day battle to secure rear lines at **Dego**, **Augereau's** division led a failed French attack against the Ceva positions on 16 April, and Colli held off assaults by both Augereau and **Sérurier** next day. Napoleon was prevented from a third attempt by Colli's overnight retirement to stronger positions, centred on the village of St Michele, where Sérurier's frontal assault on 18 April failed after Augereau's flank manoeuvre became bogged down at the Tanaro. Another attack next day collapsed after Sérurier's hungry troops treated an initial breakthrough as an invitation to forage, persuading Napoleon to pause and reorganize his faltering forces. *See* Battle of **Mondovi**; **Map 6**.

Ceylon, Capture of

Dutch settlements in southern **India** were seized by regional British forces in 1795, once they were aware that the **Netherlands** had quit the **First Coalition**, but final reduction of the major Dutch possession, Ceylon (Sri Lanka), was undertaken by a combined force from the newly acquired **Cape Colony** the following spring. A regiment of **British Army** regulars, escorted by a **frigate** and three **sloops,** anchored off Ngombo on 5

February and landed troops for a march on the capital, Colombo. After a prolonged skirmish with local Dutch forces on 12 February, British troops surrounded Colombo on 14 February, and the island capitulated two days later. Ceylon was one of the few British **colonial** gains retained under the terms of the 1802 **Amiens** treaty. *See* **Map 19**.

Champagny, Jean-Baptiste de
(1756–1834)

French politician, a nobleman who specialized in naval affairs as an aristocratic delegate to the pre-revolutionary States-General. He retired from politics in 1791, but returned in 1799 as navy minister under the **Consulate** and was subsequently appointed ambassador to Vienna. He became the empire's minister of the interior in 1804, holding the post until he replaced **Talleyrand** as foreign minister in 1807, supervising relations with the puppet and client states established since 1805. Dismissed in 1811, Champagny took royal service in 1814 but rejoined **Napoleon** during the **Hundred Days**. Stripped of his imperial honours in the aftermath, he was allowed to live the rest of his life in Paris.

Champaubert, Battle of

The first in a rapid sequence of French victories, known collectively as the **Six Days Campaign**, over allied forces invading **France** in 1814. Two allied armies had been converging on Paris since their victory at **La Rothière** on 1 February, but **Schwarzenberg**'s slow advance from the south gave **Napoleon** a chance to attack **Blücher**'s army on the Marne in isolation. Once he was aware of Blücher's line of advance, early on 9 February, Napoleon led 30,000 troops to intercept it around the village of Champaubert, about 100km west of Paris.

Confident that the French were effectively beaten, Blücher had allowed his forces to become spread out, partly in response to Schwarzenberg's worries about a possible French concentration in the area between the two armies, and his dispositions left General Olssufiev's 5,000 men virtually isolated around Champaubert. They were quickly overrun by **Marmont**'s corps, with **Ney** in support, when Napoleon reached the town on the morning of 10 February.

Olssufiev was taken prisoner, and only about 1,000 of his troops managed to escape. French forces suffered about 200 casualties in reaching a position between the two wings of Blücher's advance, a situation exploited by Napoleon at **Montmirail** next day. *See* **Map 26**.

Championnet, Jean-Etienne
(1762–1800)

The illegitimate son of a servant, Championnet worked as a cook in Barcelona and Lyon before joining the **National Guard** of his native Valence in 1789. Commissioned in 1790, he joined a **fédéré** battalion in 1792 and was elected its commanding colonel that August. He was provisionally promoted brigadier-general in September 1793, after his relatively peaceful suppression of royalist elements at Besançon, and subsequently fought on the **Rhine** under **Hoche**. A full brigadier-general from February 1794 and a divisional commander in June, he was with **Jourdan**'s army at **Fleurus**, and remained on the **Rhine** through the offensives of 1796, fighting at **Amberg** and **Würzburg** before taking temporary command of the northern sector for a time in early 1797.

After spells commanding the right wing of the army preparing to invade **England**, and with Rhine forces around Mainz, Championnet was transferred to Italy as C-in-C of the 'Army of Rome' in October 1798. He led French forces to success in the **Neapolitan campaign**, occupying **Naples** in January 1799 and organizing the formation of the short-lived Parthenopean Republic before his criticisms of the **Directory** government prompted a recall in February. Arrested en route for France, he was charged with corruption and failure to obey orders, but was acquitted and returned to action in command of French forces in northern Italy. After failing to defeat Austrian forces at **Genola** in November, he fell victim to the fever sweeping through his army and resigned at the end of the year, dying at Antibes on 9 January.

Chaptal, Jean-Antoine (1756–1832)

French chemist, spared retribution for his role in anti-**Jacobin** activities in Montpellier during the mid-1790s so that his scientific and administrative skills could be employed to improve ammunition output for the revolutionary **French Army**. Appointed to the Council of State by the **Consulate**, he was interior minister from 1800, supervising large-scale reforms of government administration, working to improve the country's standards of technical education and establishing a string of public works programmes. Chaptal retired to his factories in 1804, but continued to function as an unofficial adviser to both the empire and the restored monarchy.

Charbonnerie

Originally a society of Parisian charcoal-burners, the Charbonnerie became a semi-secret forum for radical political debate and conspiracy after soldiers began joining during the **French Revolution**. Mutating into a kind of soldiers' freemasonry, the society was vociferously loyal to **Napoleon**, and was subsequently suspected of conspiring to overthrow **Louis XVIII**'s restored regime. *See also* **Carbonari**.

Charleroi, Siege of *See* Battles of **Sambre**; Battles of **Fleurus**,

Charles IV, King (1748–1819)

King of **Spain** and its colonies since 1788, Charles was dominated by his wife, Marie Louise of Parma, and government policy passed into the supremely self-serving hands of her lover, Prince **Godoy**. Charles was a passive bystander as Godoy committed Spain to alliance with **France** in 1795, and his subsequent contributions to Spanish affairs were negative. A long-running feud with his son **Ferdinand** paralysed the monarchy at vital times and offered opportunities for French intervention in Spanish affairs, while his readiness to abdicate (twice) under pressure in 1808 was an important factor enabling the deposition of the Bourbon dynasty at the **Bayonne** Conference in May. An honoured prisoner at Valençay in France from 1808 to 1814, he moved to Marseilles when Ferdinand reclaimed the Spanish throne, and died in Rome a forgotten man.

Charles XIII, King (1748–1818)

The brother of Swedish king Gustavus III, and a former admiral in the **Swedish Navy**, Charles served as regent to **Gustavus IV** from 1792 to 1796, but left the running of affairs to a cabal of nobles led by Baron Reuterholm. He played little part in public life during the reign of Gustavus, and was no more than an elderly figurehead when he resumed the regency after the coup of March 1809. Elected king in June, he again left the government of **Sweden** largely to others, relying on Danish crown prince Christian Augustus until his sudden death in May 1810, and conceding power to **Bernadotte** on his arrival as the new crown prince in October. He became King of Norway by the Treaty of **Kiel** in January 1814.

Charles, Archduke (1771–1847)

The younger brother of Habsburg emperor **Francis** (and the older brother of Archduke **John**), Charles was the most respected **Austrian Army** commander of the war period, and displayed a consistent ability to run **Napoleon** a good second. During the first decade of the nineteenth century he was also an important military reformer, and a political influence for moderation among the bellicose court factions of Vienna, but his relatively brief career was hampered by physical frailty, enigmatic temperament, and the emperor's failure to give him consistent support.

Brought up in the Duke of Saxe-Teschen's household, Charles entered the Austrian Army in 1792 and saw his first action at **Jemappes** in the autumn. Given a corps command for **Saxe-Coburg**'s 1793–4 campaign in **Flanders**, he fought at **Maastricht** in February 1793 and played a vital role in the victory at **Neerwinden** in March. Charles led his corps at **Landrecies** the following spring, and emerged with more credit than most from the defeat at **Fleurus**.

Already displaying characteristic organizational qualities, attention to detail and tactical awareness, as well as the compulsive caution that often restricted his successes, Charles retired at the end of 1794 to devote his time to military writings, but replaced **Clairfait** in overall command of Austrian forces at the **Rhine** in early 1796. Though forced back to the Danube by French attacks in the summer, he made his name with an autumn counter-offensive, winning victories over **Jourdan** at **Amberg** and **Würzburg** before narrowly missing a chance to trap **Moreau** at **Schliengen** in October.

Charles took 30,000 troops to Italy in early February 1797, and encountered Napoleon for the first time during the **Frioul** campaign a few weeks later. His escape with an almost intact army confirmed his status as the one senior Austrian general to emerge from the War of the **First Coalition** with credit. He accepted command of Austrian field forces in February 1798, but his position was undermined by exclusion from **Alvintzi**'s royal commission for army reform, and his opposition to participation in the **Second Coalition** was overruled by a court war party centred on the empress.

Though he considered his army unready for war, Charles halted a French offensive across the **Rhine** at **Ostrach** and **Stockach** in spring 1799, before transferring his main strength south to drive **Masséna** back beyond **Zurich** on the **Swiss** front. Unable to break through Masséna's mountain positions during the summer, he returned to the Rhine for the autumn in line with Vienna's altered strategic priorities, but remained static while Austrian positions collapsed elsewhere. Pleading ill-health, he resigned his command to **Kray** in March 1800, escaping the odium of subsequent Austrian defeats.

His reputation intact, Charles was appointed war minister in early 1801 and given wide-ranging powers of reform. Committed to the basically defensive military orthodoxies of his predecessors, and guided by administrative protégé **Fassbender**, Charles set in motion long-term organizational changes that achieved little of tangible value before 1805, but left the army's outdated tactical methods alone. Gloomily aware of its continuing combat weakness, he made vain efforts to dissuade Francis from joining the **Third Coalition** in 1805, and was relegated to the secondary command in Italy, where he won a minor victory at **Caldiero**.

With most of his rivals discredited, Charles was given another chance to reform the army from 1806. Though restricted by his own innate conservatism, factionalism at the centre and bureaucratic inefficiency everywhere, he improved the army's field organization and operational methods, but his reforms remained incomplete by the time Francis again fell prey to optimism in 1809.

Given overall strategic control of the Austrian Army for the first time during a campaign he regarded as premature, Charles revealed his strengths and weaknesses in 1809. Indecisive in the planning stage, and pessimistically concerned to preserve his army throughout, he displayed a tactical nimbleness that reduced the impact of defeats at **Abensberg** and **Eckmühl**, and almost beat Napoleon at **Aspern–Essling** in May.

Apparently on the verge of ending Napoleon's career, Charles was transformed from hero to scapegoat by his defeat at **Wagram** in July, and his subsequent surrender at **Znaim**. He resigned his command a few days later, and never again held an important military command. Shunned by the emperor and most senior officers, he was ignored throughout the campaigns of 1813–15, apart from a brief spell as commandant at Mainz during the **Hundred Days**. He spent the rest of his life in retirement, refusing a military appointment even after the death of Francis in 1835, and restoration of his reputation began only during the 1860s.

Chassé, David Henri (1775–1849)

An officer with the Dutch Army until 1792, when he joined the revolutionary **French Army**, Chassé returned to the French-controlled **Netherlands** in 1795 and subsequently commanded Dutch troops in French imperial service. A Dutch major-general in the **Peninsular War** from 1808, he fought at **Talavera** before rejoining the French Army lists, becoming a brigadier-general in late 1810 and a baron of the empire the following year. He remained in French service until March 1814, when he was wounded at **Arcis-sur-Aube**, but fought for the allies during the 1815 campaign, leading a division under the Prince of **Orange** at **Waterloo**.

Chasseurs

Contemporary French term, used in many continental European armies to denote either light **cavalry** (*chasseurs-à-cheval*) used primarily for skirmishing operations, or members of light infantry units (*chasseurs-à-pieds*). Specialist mountain troops were also sometimes known as *chasseurs*.

Château-Thierry, Battle of

The third action of the **Six Days Campaign** that temporarily halted the **Sixth Coalition**'s invasion of eastern **France** in February 1814. Following up rapid strikes against elements of **Blücher**'s army at **Champaubert** (10 February) and **Montmirail** (11 February), **Napoleon** led 20,000 troops in pursuit of **Yorck** and **Sacken** as they retreated north towards the Marne. He ordered **Macdonald**'s corps, defending the road to Paris, forward to occupy the Marne crossing at Château-Thierry, but its failure to respond enabled most allied troops to get across the river before Napoleon caught up with Yorck's rearguard at Château-Thierry on 12 February. An immediate attack by **Ney**'s corps captured 1,500 Russians on the right of the allied line, and its retreating rearguard suffered another 1,200 casualties, while the French lost only 600 men in the process of occupying the town by nightfall, but the escaping allies destroyed the town bridge. Lack of **pontoon** equipment forced Napoleon to wait at Château-Thierry while it was repaired, by which time Yorck and Sacken had escaped beyond the Ourcq, and a renewed allied offensive on the Seine had forced him to turn south. *See* Battle of **Vauchamps**; **Map 26**.

Chatham, Earl of (1756–1835)

The older brother of prime minister William **Pitt**, he inherited his celebrated father's title in 1778 and began a military career in the same year. Like many senior officers in the **British Army**, he was more involved in political than military affairs, and only marginally interested in either. He was First Lord of the Admiralty from 1788, but his notorious neglect of the office encouraged his replacement by Earl Spencer in the coalition of 1794. He held honorific cabinet posts for the remainder of Pitt's years in office, and played an equally inert role in the **Addington** administration. A lieutenant-general in command of Army Ordnance from 1801 to 1806, he was passed over for command of the **Peninsular** campaign in 1808, but was given overall charge of the **Walcheren expedition** in 1809. Appointed primarily because many generals would only serve under a figure of his seniority, he was roundly condemned by a subsequent enquiry into the

expedition's failure. Though promoted full general in 1812, he held no further field command or important political position, eventually serving as governor of Gibraltar from 1820 to 1835.

Châtillon-sur-Seine

French town that was the scene of occasional and unproductive peace talks between allied envoys and French ambassador **Caulaincourt** during February 1814. *See also* Campaign for **France**.

Chaumont, Treaty of

The agreement between allied leaders of the **Sixth Coalition**, signed on 9 March 1814, that bound them to the final destruction of **Napoleon** and ended months of unproductive dispute about the ultimate aims of their campaign in **France**. Coalition plans worked out during an emergency summit at **Bar-sur-Aube** on 25 February had been rendered obsolete by **Blücher**'s advance to **Meaux** and his subsequent move north of the Aisne, and a second conference opened at Chaumont, on the upper Marne, on 1 March (*see* **Map 26**). It was attended by Russian tsar **Alexander**, Austrian Emperor **Francis**, Prussian king **Frederick William** and British Foreign Secretary **Castlereagh**, who distributed £5 million in **subsidies** and is generally credited as the architect of the agreement. The allies offered Napoleon peace on the basis of the 1791 French frontiers. In the (inevitable) event of the terms not being accepted by 11 March, each promised not to conclude a separate peace until the war was won, even if it should take 20 years. Buoyed by recent victories, Napoleon rejected the terms out of hand, and the allies made no further peace offers.

Cherasco, Peace of

The agreement between **France** and **Piedmont** that ended the latter's participation in the War of the **First Coalition** from 28 April 1796. Piedmontese Army commander General Colli had asked for an armistice on 23 April, immediately after his forces had been driven out of **Mondovi** by **Napoleon**'s Army of Italy. The French commander ignored the suggestion until his forward units had captured Cherasco and Alba on 25 April, ensuring that no aid could reach Piedmont from Austrian forces further east. He then agreed to halt his advance on Turin in return for the right to garrison Piedmontese **fortresses** and passage through Piedmont for French troops. Perforce accepted by King Victor Amadeus in Turin, the terms were carried to Paris by Colonel **Murat** and duly ratified by the **Directory** government. *See* **Italian Campaigns**, 1792–7; **Map 6**.

Chippewa, Battle of

The opening engagement of the **US Army**'s final attack on Canada during the **Anglo-American War** of 1812–15, fought just south of Niagara Falls at the junction of the Niagara and Chippewa rivers on 5 July 1814. After the failure of a major autumn offensive against **Montreal**, US forces near the fiercely disputed Niagara frontier had been rebuilt and given rudimentary training under the command of General Brown, the hero of **Sackett's Harbor**. Brown led 3,500 troops across the southern end of the Niagara to take Fort Erie at the start of July before marching north along the Canadian side of the frontier, and was met at Chippewa by half as many British regulars under General Riall. Although Brown's troops scattered the British and continued their northward march towards Lake Ontario, reinforcements were already reaching the theatre from Europe, and the Americans' slow advance was halted at **Lundy's Lane** later that month. *See* **Map 27**.

Chouans

The Breton word for 'screech owls' and the name adopted by royalist rebels in post-revolutionary Brittany, after the nickname of early insurgent leader Jean Cottereau. Most Chouans were peasants, led by royalist local dignitaries, and though the movement gained widespread mass support as part of the rebellion in La **Vendée** during 1794, it was suppressed by the army in 1796 and only occasionally threatened a revival during the next five years.

Christian VII, King (1749–1808)

King of **Denmark** from 1766 until his death, and married to a sister of British king **George III** (his cousin), Kristian was mentally unstable from an early age. Dominated by his wife and her favourites, he was declared insane in 1784 and the country was subsequently ruled by his son, **Frederick VI**, as regent.

Cintra, Convention of

Ceasefire agreement signed by British and French commanders in **Portugal** on 22 August 1808, the day after General **Wellesley**'s victory at **Vimeiro**. Negotiations were handled on the British side by Generals Bullard and **Dalrymple**, who had just arrived to overrule Wellesley's plans for an attack on **Junot**'s 26,000 troops in Lisbon. Though French forces were isolated, battered and short of supplies, their negotiators (led by the younger **Kellermann**) secured excellent terms in return for quitting Portugal. Laden with weapons and loot, Junot's army was subsequently transported back to France by the **Royal Navy**. News of the agreement sparked political outrage in **Great Britain**, and all three generals were recalled to face an enquiry, leaving **Moore** in command at Lisbon. Wellesley, though eventually exonerated, did not return to Portugal until the following year, and neither Bullard nor Dalrymple received another active command.

Cisalpine Republic

Encompassing Lombard territories north and south of the River Po, and including the great commercial centre of Milan, the Cisalpine was the largest of the puppet republics established after the French conquest of northern Italy in October 1796. Largely the creation of **Napoleon**, its government was modelled on the French **Directory** and carefully vetted to exclude extreme **Jacobin** elements. Originally named the Transpadane Republic, it was formally established from 9 July 1797 and expanded under the Treaty of **Campo Formio** in October to include the **Cispadine Republic** and former Venetian territories west of the Adige. The Swiss province of Valtelline was added in November, and the republic was formally recognized by **Austria** in 1801. The region's armed forces operated as a semi-autonomous element of the **French Army** (first as the Lombard Legion and then as the Cisalpine Army), reinforced by a number of **Polish** émigré units. The state was renamed the Italian Republic in 1802, Napoleon taking the title of President, and ceased to exist in 1805, when it became the main component of the new Kingdom of **Italy**. *See* **Maps 1, 6**.

139

Cispadine Republic

Short-lived puppet state set up in northern Italy under French republican auspices during **Napoleon**'s triumphant **Italian** campaign in 1796. Centred on the former Duchy of Modena, it was formally established in October 1796, when a 'national assembly' at Modena declared universal male suffrage and abolished surviving feudal forms. The deposed Duke Hercules II of Modena chose exile rather than compensation, and died in 1803. The republic was absorbed by the **Cisalpine** Republic by the terms of the 1797 **Campo Formio** treaty, and returned to its pre-revolutionary status under Duke Francis IV from 1814. *See* **Map 1**.

Ciudad Rodrigo, Seizure of

The western Spanish fortress of Ciudad Rodrigo was the most important **fortress** on the northern of two roads into **Portugal** (*see* **Map 22**). Along with its southern counterpart, **Badajoz**, it was the primary short-term objective of **Wellington**'s Anglo-Portuguese forces in the **Peninsular** theatre during 1811.

Wellington's capture of Almeida in May 1811 was intended as a preamble to a move on Ciudad Rodrigo, but **Beresford**'s failure to take Badajoz forced a delay, and the appearance of **Marmont**'s French relief force at **El Bodón** in September ended any hopes of further advance that year. Aware that only a surprise attack would prevent numerically superior French forces from concentrating to defend the fortress, Wellington launched a thrust at Ciudad Rodrigo from his winter quarters on the Coa River in the new year. Marching through snow, his army arrived at Ciudad Rodrigo on 7 January and stormed the walls 12 nights later, suffering only 500 casualties (including General **Craufurd**). The speed of Wellington's success enabled a further march on Badajoz before French armies scattered around Spain could move to its defence. *See* **Peninsular War**.

Clairfait de Croix, Charles Joseph, Count (1736–1798)

Born in the **Austrian Netherlands**, Clairfait fought against the **Ottoman Empire** from 1788, and was one of the more successful Austrian commanders during the War of the **First Coalition**.

He commanded a division during the **Valmy** campaign in 1792, fighting at **Jemappes** and **Neerwinden** before taking command of a corps on the **Flanders** front in 1794. He succeeded **Saxe-Coburg** in command of allied forces in the theatre later that year, and led his army in retreat from the **Roer** to the **Rhine**, where he cooperated with **Würmser**'s forces to oppose French attacks around **Mannheim** during autumn 1795. Though a generally efficient commander, Clairfait shared the stifling faith in **cordon** warfare common to senior **Austrian Army** officers, and retired when the relatively unorthodox Archduke **Charles** was elevated to the army's highest command in early 1796.

Clarke, Henri-Jacques-Guillaume (1765–1818)

Of Irish descent, Clarke was commissioned into the French Royal Army in 1781 and served for a time in the London embassy before 1789. Briefly dismissed as politically unreliable in 1792, he was promoted brigadier-general in 1793 and achieved divisional command two years later, serving with the **Bureau Topographique** until posted to **Napoleon**'s Army of Italy in 1796. He became an enthusiastic supporter of Bonaparte, backing the **Brumaire** coup in 1799 and becoming an important member of the consular household. He was governor of occupied Vienna from late 1805, and of Berlin in 1806, before his appointment as war minister in 1807. A competent administrator, but inevitably denied responsibility for policy, Clarke held the post until 1814, when he rallied to the restored monarchy. Loyal to the king through the **Hundred Days**, he was again war minister from 1815 to 1817.

Clausel, Bertrand (1772-1842)

French soldier who joined the **National Guard** in 1789, becoming a brigadier-general a decade later. He served during the 1799–1800 **Italian campaign** (fighting at **Novi**) and in the **West Indies** before his promotion to divisional command in 1802. After holding commands in the **Netherlands**, Italy and **Illyria**, he joined the Army of Portugal from 1810, and made his reputation at the Battle of **Salamanca** in 1812, when he took control of the army after **Marmont** was injured. Though unable to reinforce

Jourdan's central army at **Vitoria** in 1813, he led a corps under **Soult** for the rest of the **Peninsular War**, taking part in all the main engagements of its latter stages. Clausel led Napoleonic forces fighting royalists around **Bordeaux** in 1815, and was exiled in the US after the second Bourbon restoration, returning to France and a political career in 1820.

Clausewitz, Karl von (1780–1831)

Prussian officer who fought in the **Revolutionary Wars** and was a French prisoner for three years after his capture at **Auerstädt** in 1806. A member of reforming war minister **Scharnhorst**'s staff, he defected from the Prussian contingent that took part in the 1812 **Russian campaign**, and fought for the tsar until 1814, taking part in the siege of **Riga** and helping negotiate the **Tauroggen** agreement in December 1812. Back with the **Prussian Army** in 1815, he was **Thielmann**'s chief of staff during the **Hundred Days** campaign, and was a major-general in command of the Berlin military academy from 1818 until his retirement in 1830. Published posthumously in 1833, his celebrated study of contemporary warfare, *Vom Krieg* (On War), enshrined the concepts and tactics of Napoleonic warfare as European military orthodoxy.

Cleves *See* Berg

Coalitions

The series of multinational military alliances formed against **France** between 1792 and 1815 were known as coalitions. Although seven distinct coalitions are usually identified, the history of anti-French diplomacy in the period is far less well defined than this suggests, partly because the relatively slow pace of international communications meant that multiple alliances could take many months to arrange. Most of Europe's dynastic rulers, particularly those in smaller states, entertained a highly expedient view of alliances in general, and membership of some coalitions fluctuated wildly, though **Great Britain** and its subsidies were part of every combination against France from 1793 to 1815. *See* **First**, **Second**, **Third**, **Fourth**, **Fifth**, **Sixth** and **Seventh Coalitions**.

Cobenzl, Ludwig von (1753–1809)

From a family that had served the Habsburgs as diplomats for 300 years, Cobenzl took part in negotiations for the partition of **Poland** in 1795, and the Treaty of **Campo Formio** in 1797, before replacing **Thugut** as imperial foreign minister in late 1800. Because the Emperor **Francis** took an active interest in foreign affairs, and generally preferred the advice of conservative courtiers like **Colloredo**, Cobenzl was never able to carry through a policy of his own. Something of an outsider in court circles, he lacked the personal support to protect himself from dismissal as a scapegoat after **Austerlitz**, and retired in December 1805.

Cockades

Rosettes in the national colour or colours worn for identification purposes on the headgear of regular soldiers in all the major contemporary European armies.

Code Civil

Perhaps the most significant and lasting of **Napoleon**'s achievements, the Code Civil was a comprehensive reformation of the French system of civil law. Defining and cataloguing French civil law in the light of changes made by successive revolutionary regimes since 1789, it was primarily designed to enable efficiency and order in state administration, but has survived in part to form the basis of the modern French legal system.

The legal system of the royal regime had been riddled with anomalies and regional distinctions. Many of these had been swept away by some 14,000 separate pieces of revolutionary legislation, and five attempts had been made at codification under the **National Convention** and **Directory** regimes, but the law remained in a state of confusion when Napoleon came to power as First Consul in late 1799.

With France on the verge of peace, the enormous task of codifying and drafting was carried out during the second half of 1801. The details of the code's 2,281 articles were hammered out by an expert commission, including **Portalis**, and Napoleon played a prominent part in the process, heading the commission and attending in person 36 of the 87 Council of State sessions devoted to the task. A draft code was complete by the end of 1801, but negotiations with potential opponents delayed its publication until 21 March 1804.

Published in three sections, dealing with personal rights, property rights and the transfer of property, the code contained little that was completely new, but maintained revolutionary principles of equality before the law, freedom of conscience and freedom from an established Church. It also confirmed the abolition of feudal privileges and the right of free enterprise, along with legal titles to land and property taken from the Church or émigrés since the Revolution, and it established variations to the traditional system of primogeniture.

In other respects the code reflected Napoleon's taste for conservative paternalism. Women were declared legally subordinate to men in the context of the family, which was confirmed as the basis of society, and prohibition of workers' organizations (a measure inherited from the Convention) contributed to the legal superiority of employers in industrial disputes.

Administered in **France** by departmental prefects, and renamed the Code Napoléon in 1807, the new legal system was eventually implemented throughout the French Empire, although the extent to which it was modified varied considerably according to local conditions and the attitudes of regional authorities. Those French-controlled provinces actually assimilated into imperial France, along with those states closest to its frontiers, tended to be most completely and enduringly subject to the code. In more distant imperial outposts, notably in **Poland** and other eastern European satellites, attempts to cooperate with established feudal landlords produced hybrid dilutions of the code that withered under postwar repression by the empires of the **Holy Alliance**.

Five more codes, similarly combining liberal and conservative elements, were produced during the imperial period: a Code of Civil Procedure was published in April 1806; a Commercial Code, regulating and streamlining both industrial and agricultural trade, appeared in August 1807; a Criminal Code organized the principles and procedures of state justice from October 1808, backed by a Penal Code from February 1810. The immensely complicated task of producing a Rural Code was also completed, but arguments over the final version prevented its adoption before Napoleon's fall. The Code Napoléon was substantially retained by the restored monarchy after 1814, though it was again named the Code Civil from 1818.

Code Napoléon

Name officially applied from 1807 to the **Code Civil**, the comprehensive new civil law formulated by the Napoleonic regime in 1804.

Codogno, Battle of

Relatively minor skirmish, fought during the night of 8–9 May 1796, that completed a series of manoeuvres bringing **Napoleon**'s French Army of Italy into Austrian territory north of the River Po. After defeating **Piedmont** in late April, Napoleon's immediate target was **Beaulieu**'s Austrian army on his right. The Austrian commander was quick to pull north-east from Acqui, and mutiny by starving troops slowed General La Harpe's pursuing division. Beaulieu was north of the Po by 30 April, and deployed his 40,000 men on the Agogno to threaten any French pursuit at Valenza or south of Pavia.

Napoleon chose instead to cross the Po far to the east at Piacenza, hoping to surprise Beaulieu and block any further Austrian escape. While **Masséna** and **Sérurier** mounted diversionary operations around Valenza, **Dallemagne** led a force of 3,600 élite infantry and 2,500 **cavalry** to reach Piacenza on the morning of 7 May. Beaulieu had responded to French preparations by sending General Liptay's division to guard Pavia and points east on 4 May, and moving his whole line east to the Ticino two days later. On news of the first French crossings, he ordered Liptay to block any advance and got his entire army on the road to Piacenza by late on 7 May.

Despite lack of **pontoon** equipment, Dallemagne and La Harpe's supporting division were over the river by mid-afternoon, driving Liptay's forward units back on the village of Fombio. While **Augereau** crossed further west and the rest of Napoleon's army abandoned diversions to march east, La Harpe and Dallemagne stormed

Fombio next morning, and swept on to make contact with Beaulieu's advanced guards around Codogno. The ensuing night action fluctuated, and La Harpe was killed by friendly fire, but the Austrians eventually withdrew.

The action cost only a few dozen casualties on each side, but Beaulieu wasted his temporary numerical advantage north of Piacenza by ordering a general withdrawal east beyond the Adda. Able to complete his own concentration unhindered on 9 May, Napoleon rushed his army to the Adda crossing at **Lodi**, convinced that only a decisive victory would prevent Austrian reinforcement and ultimate French defeat. *See* **Italian Campaigns, 1792–7; Map 9**.

Cole, Galbraith Lowry (1772–1842)

Irish nobleman commissioned into the British **cavalry** in 1787, who served in the **West Indies** in 1794 and fought at **Alexandria** in 1801. He commanded a regiment for the first time in **Malta** from 1805, serving as **Stuart's** second-in-command at **Maida** the following year, and was promoted major-general in 1808. He joined the **Peninsular campaign** in 1809, playing a small part in the Battle of **Busaco** in autumn 1810 and saving the day at **Albuera** the following May. Cole returned to Britain for a time in late 1811, primarily in order to take up a parliamentary seat, but was back at **Salamanca** in 1812. He led his division through the campaigns of 1813–14, but his one experience of independent command, at **Roncesvalles** in July 1813, was not a success. He missed the **Hundred Days** campaign in 1815 because he was on his honeymoon, but served with allied forces occupying France until 1818, and was governor of the Cape Colony from 1828 to 1833.

Collingwood, Cuthbert (1750–1810)

Born in Newcastle, Collingwood entered the **Royal Navy** aged 11 and saw early service in North America and the **West Indies**, establishing a close and enduring friendship with **Nelson** from 1778. Collingwood captained a **ship-of-the-line** at the Battle of the **First of June** in 1794, and won national acclaim for his prominent part at **St Vincent** in 1797. One of a generation of exceptional British naval officers, many of them brought together in the **Mediterranean**

Fleet under **Jervis**, he was outshone only by Nelson, and enjoyed a reputation for imperturbable cool under pressure.

Collingwood was Nelson's second-in-command with the Mediterranean Fleet from 1803, leading one of the two British battle lines at **Trafalgar** in 1805 and earning great credit for bringing the battered fleet safely to port in the subsequent storms. As Nelson's replacement (and a vice-admiral), he excelled at the complex task of patrolling the vast Mediterranean theatre, husbanding inadequate resources to maintain **blockades** of hostile ports and support allied forces in the **Peninsular War**. Generally recognized as Britain's finest active naval commander after 1805, Collingwood enjoyed the complete trust of his political masters, and frequently anticipated their strategic requirements (as at the **Dardanelles** in 1807). An established national hero, rewarded with a peerage, he died at sea in 1810, his health broken by the hardships of permanent blockade duty.

Colloredo, Franz, Count von (1731–1807)

Deeply conservative Austrian nobleman who was tutor to the future Emperor **Francis** and an important adviser after his accession in 1792. Colloredo's hostility to any kind of liberal reform covered military affairs, as well as constitutional and religious matters, and he was one of the most obdurate opponents of the 'pacifist' party of army reformers headed by Archduke **Charles**. As such he was deeply associated with conduct of the 1805 campaign in Bavaria, and was dismissed into retirement in November, before the allied defeat at **Austerlitz**.

Colonial Warfare

The expansion of European maritime commerce during the seventeenth and eighteenth centuries had encouraged the establishment of colonies, trading posts and coastal waystations all over the world. Though its wealth and the power of its **Royal Navy** had made **Great Britain** the world's leading colonial power by 1792, **France**, **Spain**, **Portugal** and the independent **Netherlands** all boasted substantial overseas possessions.

Apart from Portugal, which had no major interests outside Brazil, the Netherlands was the weakest of these, with only a few possessions in the Caribbean to complement its primary interest in trade with the Far East. Spain, though in steep national decline and thought unlikely to keep its empire indefinitely, still controlled almost the whole of **South America**, and owned much more of North America than the infant **United States**. Spain also contested dominance of the north-west and west African coastlines with France, and retained a Pacific outpost in the Philippines, but its influence in the spectacularly lucrative Caribbean was being eroded by France and Britain.

France had suffered badly in its colonial contests with Britain earlier in the century. Its interest in North America had been reduced to token offshore possessions, and its attempts to penetrate the Far East rebuffed, but it still owned several important Caribbean islands, as well as outposts in Africa and the Indian Ocean island of Mauritius, and was actively seeking to carve out its own area of colonial dominance in the eastern **Mediterranean**. French colonial strategists considered the Middle East their natural area of expansion, but quite apart from the nascent threat of Russian expansionism in the region, they found themselves, like everyone else, blocked by the British.

British sea power was intrinsically linked with what had been a period of impressive imperial proliferation, despite the loss of the USA in the 1780s. In the east, colonial growth had followed trade, so that an expanding viceregal regime was in the process of consolidating a firm hold over the vast subcontinent of **India**, while British merchants were spreading their interests further east. In the west, the British crown still owned the fertile wilderness and fisheries of Canada, was a major power in the Caribbean and sought to expand its hitherto minor role in South America. Otherwise the maintenance of commercial traffic called for the occupation and development of naval bases and trading posts all over the world. The British government kept a jealous eye on any rival that might interfere with its commercial network, especially on the main sea and overland highways to the east, around the Dutch **Cape Colony** and across the **Ottoman** provinces in the eastern Mediterranean.

The adherence of Britain, Spain and the Netherlands to the **First Coalition** against republican France in early 1793 signalled the beginning of a worldwide colonial war that continued until 1814, though its character changed after the turn of the century, once **Napoleon** began treating French overseas possessions as expendable bargaining chips in his drive to establish a pan-European monarchy.

By contrast, British strategists of the 1790s tended to regard European continental struggles as distractions from the important business of worldwide expansion, and a significant proportion of the country's active military contribution to the **Revolutionary Wars** involved grabbing the colonies of its enemies. British forces were dispatched to seize French, Spanish and Dutch possessions in the **West Indies** on a regular basis up to 1801, though they suffered occasional setbacks against well-coordinated French forces in the region. The Cape Colony, **Ceylon** and most other Dutch possessions in the **Indian Ocean** had fallen with little fuss by 1796. Almost incidentally, Viceroy **Wellesley** completed the suppression of anti-British elements in southern India, crushing **Tipu Sahib** of Mysore at **Seringapatam** in May 1799.

By the terms of the Anglo-French **Amiens** peace in 1801, Britain agreed to return all the colonies taken from European powers except Ceylon and the Spanish Caribbean island of **Trinidad**, and began the process of recapturing them as soon as war resumed in 1803. By 1807, British forces had retaken most of the smaller West Indian islands, and reduced Dutch possessions in the east to Batavia (Dutch Java), Ambiona and Ternate in the Moluccas, one of the Celes islands and Borneo. With slender resources in the theatre, and French commerce raiders to keep them busy, the British had taken Ambiona, Java and French Mauritius by 1811, but made no effort to exploit the colonies before 1814.

Britain's colonial record was less impressive on the American mainland. An expedition to Spanish South America suffered embarrassing defeats at **Buenos Aires** and Montevideo in 1806–7, and trade disputes with the United States escalated into an **Anglo-American War**

(1812–15) that ended as an undistinguished draw after a ramshackle campaign along the Canadian frontier. The British Empire none the less made substantial gains from two decades of war, and retained control over its French and Spanish conquests, along with Ceylon and the Cape Colony, at the Congress of **Vienna**.

Other colonial powers took relatively few positive steps to secure or increase their empires. France launched a major bid to conquer the **Middle East** in 1798, and had established a colonial administration in **Egypt** before its forces were ejected by the British in 1801. Several French expeditions were also sent to the West Indies, culminating in **Napoleon**'s dispatch of a large army to **Santo Domingo** in 1802, which failed so completely that no further attempt was made. The other important piece of colonial business conducted by France was the acquisition of **Louisiana** from Spain by the Treaty of **San Idelfonso** in 1800, and its sale to Washington three years later, a transaction that more than doubled the size of the United States.

Spain was never in a military or economic position to conduct offensive colonial operations, and most of its energies were concentrated on the **Peninsular War** by the time the South American colonies rose in revolt under **Bolívar** and **Miranda**. What began with the formation of **juntas** in imitation of homeland rebels became an anti-royalist war of liberation that had established independent states all over Central and South America by the immediate postwar period. A powerless Portuguese government would probably have lost control over Brazil at the same time, but the royal family's ten-year residence in the colony after 1807 delayed moves towards independence. Dutch colonial operations were restricted to an abortive attempt to retake the Cape Colony in 1796, and the defence of Java from 1807 by a force under General Daendels.

European governments and forces conducting colonial warfare laboured under enormous difficulties, particularly in distant tropical theatres. The limitations of contemporary long-range communication meant that colonial campaigns were often won or lost without reference to home authorities, and that accurate strategic planning at the centre was impossible. The other great regulator of tropical campaigns was disease. Contemporary **medicine** could not diagnose, treat or prevent the spread of tropical diseases, and they took an enormous toll of Europeans sent to colonial outposts. Thousands of soldiers, sailors and administrators died in the East and West Indies, and duty in the tropics was regarded with justified dread by most ordinary servicemen. Most tropical disease victims died, although those who survived one campaign were more likely to stay healthy on subsequent visits.

The poor condition of most European armies on colonial duty meant that native personnel were the most useful troops in many theatres. Generally immune to disease, and familiar with often treacherous terrain, they were a key element of campaigns fought in India, Canada, South America and the West Indies, where Toussaint **L'Ouverture** and his successors achieved a rare reversal of colonial trends, defeating French, Spanish and British forces on Santo Domingo to create the independent state of Haiti in 1804. *See* **Map 19**.

Common Shell

Contemporary British term for explosive **artillery** ammunition. Consisting of a ball of explosive material with an attached fuse, which was ignited in the act of firing the gun, common shell was capable of inflicting far more damage than ordinary **roundshot**. It was the ammunition most usually used with howitzers and **mortars**, although the **British Army** made increasing use of its own invention, **shrapnel**, during the last decade of the wars. Explosive shells were seldom used by **naval** forces because they presented too great a risk of on-board fire, but were standard ammunition for 'bombs', specialist warships armed with mortars.

Concordat

Agreement of July 1801 between the consular government of **France** and the Roman Catholic Church that reinstated the latter as an officially recognized and sponsored religious organization, but that fell far short of restoring its former position of power in French society.

After the **French Revolution**'s nationalization and sale of Church properties, French clergymen theoretically owed their posts to election by franchised citizens, and depended on the state for their upkeep. This arrangement was never formalized, and the **Directory**'s law of 21 February 1795 – permitting equality and tolerance, but no public funding, for all religions – created financial problems for clerics that were still fomenting at the start of the **Consulate** in late 1799. The tolerance expressed by the law encouraged a Catholic revival in France, especially among women, giving rise to arguments that the Concordat merely recognized the rebirth of the Church in France after the fact.

Napoleon had little interest in religion, but recognized it as a force for social order, and sought reconciliation with a hostile papacy from a position of strength after his victory at **Marengo** in 1800. After months of secret negotiations with papal envoy **Consalvi**, accompanied by repeated threats of military action against the **Papal States**, an agreement was signed with **Pius VII** on 15 July 1801. By the time it was published on 18 April 1802 (an Easter Sunday), Napoleon had greatly increased the state's power to control Church activities by adding the **Organic Articles** without consulting Rome.

As published, the Concordat re-established a Church structure in France and conferred the legitimacy of papal blessing on the Napoleonic regime. Pius formally recognized the French government, accepted the need for all French bishops to take an oath of allegiance to the state (though many French clerics refused to do so), and renounced all claims to Church property confiscated since the Revolution.

Napoleon meanwhile stopped short of endorsing Catholicism as the state religion, recognizing it only as the 'religion of the vast majority of French citizens'. He accepted Pius as head of the Church, agreed to consult the papacy on all clerical appointments, and undertook to pay the clergy, thus increasing their dependence on the regime.

Essentially an attempt to create a Church of state servants obedient to the head of government, the Concordat encouraged French popular approval for the Consulate and empire, aiding pacification of the **Vendée** and other royalist enclaves. It also gave Napoleon freedom to make agreements with other religious groups, so that Protestant and Jewish bodies were put under state auspices during the empire. Its great flaw from Napoleon's point of view was the necessary inclusion of papal sanction, which offered an alternative supreme authority to which dissenting French clerics would appeal time and again.

French relations with the papacy remained stormy after 1802, and broke down completely from 1808. The imperial government's excommunication in 1809 triggered the imprisonment of Pius VII, and he was forced to sign a revised Concordat, essentially agreeing to support whatever the French government did. This remained technically in force until 1905, and the papacy agreed a series of concordats with other European states after 1815, but many of its privileges were restored on the fall of the empire.

Congreve Rockets

Invented at the British Royal Laboratory by Sir William Congreve, rockets saw limited subsequent service with the **British Army** as relatively mobile **artillery**. Congreve rockets resembled giant fireworks, comprising a shell (either **canister**, '**common shell**', **shrapnel** or **incendiary**) attached to a long stick, which was fitted into a small tripod for firing. A medium rocket with a 12-pounder shell was that most commonly used in field operations, but the largest field rockets carried 32-pounder shells and weighed several hundred kilograms, while rockets intended for static bombardment were larger and heavier.

Two mounted companies of rocket troops were eventually raised for British service, taking part in the bombardment of **Copenhagen** in 1807, and seeing limited action during the **Peninsular War**. One company also served during the 1813 campaign for **Germany**, and were the only British troops at the Battle of **Leipzig**. Rockets were likely to career wildly off course at any time after firing, and were capable of spectacular U-turns that could threaten friendly troops. Although this sometimes helped unnerve opponents, as during operations before the Battle of **Orthez** in early 1814, and did not prevent their use in **siege** operations, many allied commanders (**Wellington** included) regarded them as an irritating novelty and their deployment as a waste of perennially precious horses. A few rockets were also supplied to the **Austrian Army** during the final war years.

Consalvi, Ercole (1757–1824)

Influential Catholic churchman, born in Rome, who was accused by the French government of complicity in the death of General Duphot during a riot in the city of December 1797, an incident that provoked French invasion of the **Papal States** and his own temporary imprisonment. He was secretary of the conclave in Venice that elected **Pius VII**, and became secretary of state to the new papal administration, subsequently negotiating the **Concordat** with **Napoleon**. The moderation of his anti-French views cost him influence over the next five years, but his growing mistrust of Napoleon was expressed in personal rivalry with the emperor's uncle, Cardinal Fesch. After refusing to attend Napoleon's second marriage in 1811, he was exiled to Reims and imprisoned at Béziers in 1813–14. He was chief papal delegate to the Congress of **Vienna**, where he secured full restoration of the Papal States. A committed patron of the liberal arts and sciences, Consalvi pursued a postwar policy of internal reform, ending a wide variety of feudal privileges, but lost office on the death of Pius VII in 1823.

Conscription

Forced recruitment of some troops, usually on a local basis, had taken place throughout Europe for centuries, but organized mass conscription of a large national population was a post-revolutionary French innovation. Faced with the approach of hostile armies across its virtually undefended eastern frontiers, the French Convention passed a 'Réquisition' law in 1793, rendering all able-bodied men aged 17–35 liable for military service. Another manpower crisis in 1798 persuaded the **Directory** regime to take up General **Jourdan**'s long-standing proposals for a conscription law, the first time the word was used in that context.

For the next 16 years, male French civilians were classified each year according to age and marital status. The conscripts required each year (their number decided by **Napoleon** after he took power) were drafted in class order and selected within their class by ballot. Although

the system in theory provided **France** with a vast reservoir of manpower, many conscripts avoided service by going into hiding. The problem became acute after 1812, so that only about one eighth of almost a million men called up in 1813–14 actually saw service, many of them teenage '**Marie-Louises**'.

Of the other major powers, both **Austria** and **Prussia** conscripted an increasing number of troops for national service in **Landwehr** reserve units, while the **Ottoman Empire** recruited troops on the basis of local medieval customs and obligations. The **Russian Army** maintained prodigious manpower levels by means of a royal levy, declared whenever an imperial emergency threatened, that conscripted a stated number of men per hundred from the empire's tax census. Though inefficient and rotten with corruption, the levy system benefited from the sheer size of **Russia**'s population, and could be declared as often as the tsar liked (five times in 1813 alone).

The only form of conscription employed in **Great Britain**, which otherwise relied on volunteers or mercenaries for its land forces, was local balloting of men for service in the home defence **militia**, and anyone selected was entitled to pay for a substitute. The **Royal Navy** employed quasi-official conscription in the form of **press gangs**, which were a vital adjunct to the flow of volunteer and 'bounty' recruits (men given relatively large ex-gratia payments in return for enlistment). Other naval powers used similar tactics to top up warship complements, and impressed a greater proportion of convicts than the British, but their manpower needs were never on a comparable scale.

Constellation, USS

One of the original four **frigates** built for the infant **US Navy** in 1794, the 36-gun *Constellation* was the first vessel in US history to win a victory over a European warship. After the **United States** declared war on **France** in 1798, its 15 frigates were primarily engaged in preventing French commercial expansion in the **West Indies**. On 9 February 1799 the *Constellation*, commanded by Commodore Thomas Truxton, ran across the French 26-gunner *L'Insurgente* off the island of Nevis. Apparently unaware that he was at war with the US (and suffering from acute crew shortages), French captain Barreault allowed the American frigate to draw alongside and launch a full broadside before battle was joined. After more than an hour of fighting, during which *L'Insurgente* lost its mainmast and suffered 73 casualties (against one American killed and two wounded), Barreault surrendered his ship as a prize.

Consular Guard *See* **Imperial Guard (French)**

Consulate

The government system introduced to **France** after the **Brumaire** coup of November 1799. A proclamation forced through the Councils of **Ancients** and **Five Hundred** on 10 November, under the eyes of **Napoleon's** troops, established Bonaparte, **Sieyès** and Ducos as 'Provisional Consuls' in executive control of the republic. The latter conspirators were soon replaced by the more pliable **Cambacérès** and **Lebrun**, and a plebiscite confirmed the consuls in office before the system was formalized under the Constitution of Year VIII on 14 December. Napoleon held the office of First Consul and effective political control, though it was not secure until his victory at **Marengo** in June 1800. The collapse of the **Second Coalition**, consequent territorial gains and the achievement of peace with **Great Britain** cemented his dictatorial position, and he became Consul for Life in May 1802, an appointment confirmed by a massive majority in a subsequent referendum. A constitutional amendment of August 1802 gave Napoleon the right to nominate a successor, and the logical step to absolute monarchy was taken on 18 May 1804, when the Consulate was abolished and Napoleon became Emperor of the French.

Continental System

Emperor **Napoleon's** ambitious attempt to cripple the trade and war effort of **Great Britain** by imposing a continent-wide ban on the import or transit of British-owned or -manufactured goods. The idea of defeating Britain by a universal boycott of its trade, widely recognized as the source British wealth, had been discussed in post-revolutionary **France**, but Napoleon's **Berlin Decrees** of 1 November 1806 were the first serious step towards putting the theory into practice. The full expression of what came to be known as the Continental System, or Continental Blockade, was contained in Napoleon's first and second **Milan Decrees** (23 November and 17 December 1807), which supplied a detailed agenda of prohibition, signalled the first strenuous attempts at enforcement, and extended the ban to the open seas.

The Milan Decrees may have been part of a coherent economic strategy aimed at bringing Britain to its knees, or a reaction to British **Orders in Council**, but once their enforcement proved impossible the system was modified to take into account a massive smuggling boom. The Trianon **Decree** (5 August 1810) permitted entry of British colonial goods into Europe at extremely high tariffs, but failed to damage Britain's credit or undermine the public confidence that sustained its national debt. British gold reserves rose steadily after 1810, and the balance of trade with continental Europe was restored in its favour.

The system inflicted far more damage on the internal economy of Europe as a whole. Blockade of British goods tended to promote growth in France as the largest alternative supplier, and a plethora of inland tariffs and regulations placed French allies at a severe economic disadvantage. Some commentators have viewed the Trianon Decree not as a direct attack on Britain, but as Napoleon's bid for a major share in Britain's trade domination at the expense of all third parties.

The system remained in force until 1814, and Napoleon took it very seriously, demanding full cooperation from allies and dependencies, but they proved unable (and sometimes unwilling) to make it work, and the replacement of recalcitrant satellite rulers like Louis **Bonaparte** made little difference. Despite a French **propaganda** campaign presenting it as a common attack on maritime tyranny, and the depth of British unpopularity after the **Copenhagen** incident of 1807, the system's clear failure and the economic hardship it caused promoted a steady reversal of Britain's diplomatic isolation.

Convoys

The standard contemporary means of protecting merchant shipping from attack at sea. Convoys were regulated by **naval** forces, which announced the times that they would provide escorting warships along specified routes, and invited ships to gather at the port of departure. Often consisting of 100–200 ships, convoys might be escorted by only two or three frigates for much of their journey. These were generally enough to deal with pirates, **privateers** or other armed raiders, and battlefleets were often called out to shepherd convoys through dangerous final approaches. Unpopular with naval authorities because they were difficult to manage without mishap, they were disliked by merchant skippers because they were very slow, but high insurance premiums deterred most from taking their chances as solo 'runners'. The biggest, richest and most frequent convoys ran between Europe and the West Indies, a journey that usually took about nine weeks. They travelled between October and June to avoid the late summer hurricane season. *See also* Battle of the **First of June**; Action off Cape **St Vincent**.

Copenhagen, Bombardment of

Pre-emptive strike by British land and naval forces against the capital of neutral **Denmark** in September 1807. Anglo-Danish relations had improved for a time after the British attack of 1801, but intermittent **Royal Navy** harassment of Danish merchantmen had maintained an undercurrent of mutual antagonism and suspicion. French victories in eastern Europe left Denmark under pressure from France to ally or risk incursions across its southern borders, and from Britain to ally or risk the collapse of its maritime economy.

Danish crown prince **Frederick** wavered, and British foreign minister **Canning** chose to interpret uncertainty as a prelude to hostility, issuing a request for guarantees from Denmark on 18 July, along with a demand that its entire fleet be handed over. A powerful Royal Navy fleet of 25 **ships-of-the-line** was sent to Copenhagen, ostensibly to take possession of the Danish fleet but accompanied by 29,000 troops under Lord **Cathcart** (including Major-General **Wellesley**). Trapped into war, the Danish government refused to hand over its ships, prompting troop landings to invest the city and a ferocious

bombardment of the port itself (*see* Battle of **Roskilde**). The town was attacked on three successive nights (2–5 September), **Congreve rockets** proving particularly effective incendiaries against its wooden buildings. Almost 2,000 civilians died in the fires that followed, and the cathedral was among major buildings destroyed. Forced into surrender, the Danish government handed over its 17 ships-of-the-line, along with stores and equipment worth an estimated £2 million, and the British withdrew with their booty.

Though it achieved its immediate military aims, the attack prompted ostentatious shock and outrage in European and American diplomatic circles, and was regarded with dismay by many critics in Britain. In confirming the widespread view that Britain was at least as dangerous to the free development of nations as **France**, it signalled a period of British diplomatic isolation, and encouraged initial acceptance of Napoleon's **Continental System**. *See also* **Gunboat War**.

Copenhagen Raid (1801)

Punitive action by the **Royal Navy** against the Danish capital in spring 1801, and **Great Britain**'s principal response to the threat posed by the **Armed Neutrality** League of northern nations. As Armed Neutrality came into force during the opening months of 1801, the British government launched a diplomatic offensive against the relatively weak Danes and Swedes, and backed it with Admiral Hyde-Parker's 26 **ships-of-the-line** (supported by seven **frigates** and 23 other craft). Hyde-Parker was ordered to protect Denmark or Sweden from Russian hostility if negotiations with either were successful, but to begin operations by disabling the **Danish Navy** if they were not. The elderly and cautious Hyde-Parker was chosen for seniority, but navy chief **Jervis** attached the aggressive **Nelson** as second-in-command.

After delaying sailing to await the outcome of negotiations, Hyde-Parker reached the approaches to Copenhagen on 19 March, by which time British diplomats had been expelled from Denmark. He was gradually won over by Nelson's bold plan for attacking the Danish fleet at its anchorages in Copenhagen, and sailed through an ineffective coastal barrage to anchor some 12km north-east of the Danish capital on 30 May.

Heavy shipping could approach Copenhagen harbour only along channels from the north or from the south-east. The city was protected by its castle at the western harbour entrance, shore batteries along the sea wall to the east, and the 70-gun Trekroner, or Crown Battery, perched at the junction of the two channels. The Danish fleet was predominantly grouped along the inner edge of the south-eastern channel, where 14 ships-of-the-line were supported by floating batteries. Six battleships were stationed west of Trekroner in the final approaches to the harbour, but were under separate field command.

Despite Hyde-Parker's fear of Swedish or Russian intervention, Nelson's two-pronged attack plan got under way on 1 April. While Hyde-Parker and 14 battleships (including the three-deckers most threatened by grounding in the shallows) approached the western Danish squadron from the north, Nelson led the main attack against the eastern Danish line with 12 ships-of-the-line and all the support vessels. Nelson took his ships cautiously through uncharted shallows to approach his chosen attack position south-east of the Danish line, and was ready to sweep towards its southernmost point on the morning of 2 April.

Three of Nelson's battleships ran aground in the process of coming alongside the Danish line, though two were able to attack and seriously damage the rearmost Danish ships with the help of supporting frigates. Nelson's other frigates moved ahead to distract the northern end of the line and the Trekroner, and seven British battleships (centred on Nelson's flagship *Elephant*) engaged in a series of static close gunnery duels with the ten central Danish ships and four floating batteries.

Superior gunnery, and the close-quarters value of British **carronades**, was gradually overwhelming Danish defences by early afternoon, but the northern supporting division had made little progress against difficult winds and currents. In the belief that Nelson was losing, Hyde-Parker called off the battle at about the same time. His signal was ignored by Nelson (making the theatrical gesture of reading it through his blind eye) and by Graves, commanding the rear of the line. The Danish flagship, *Dannebroge*, caught fire shortly afterwards and drifted out of control, and the majority of defending ships had ceased firing within another hour, though boarding parties met continued resistance until Crown Prince **Frederick** accepted a truce that evening.

The battle had cost 1,035 Danish killed or wounded, against 944 British. With Copenhagen now under threat from an unopposed bombardment, the Danes agreed to break with the Armed Neutrality League and suspend maritime operations until mid-July. The British fleet resupplied at Copenhagen until 5 May, eventually sailing east after Nelson had replaced Hyde-Parker in overall command. It was turned back from the Russian base at Revel by news of Tsar **Paul's** assassination, which ended Armed Neutrality without further conflict.

Corbineau, Jean-Baptiste Juvenal (1776–1848)

French soldier, a **cavalry** officer since 1789, who served in **Flanders**, on the **Rhine** and in **Switzerland** during the **Revolutionary Wars**. Promoted brigadier-general in 1811, after fighting against the **Fourth Coalition** and in the **Peninsular War**, he was with **Oudinot's** corps during the 1812 **Russian campaign**, and played a vital reconnaissance role during battles of the **Beresina** in November. As a divisional commander on **Napoleon's** personal staff in 1813–14, he helped save the emperor from capture at the Battle of **Brienne**, but subsequently took royal service and eventually retired just before his death.

Cordon System

The cautious military orthodoxy that dominated European warfare before 1792. A product of the mannered 'wars of position' fought during the mid-eighteenth century, and particularly associated with the successes of the **Prussian Army**, the cordon system applied to both offensive and defensive operations. An advancing army would spread available forces across a very wide front to halt an attack wherever it came, clearing all potential enemy strongholds from the flanks or rear before moving forward. If defending, an army would seek to cover all potential lines of attack, and threatened detachments were expected to hold on until neighbours arrived. This worked well in an age of relatively small armies, tending to focus wars on individual strongpoints, usually **fortresses**, and on the prolonged **sieges** required to break them down. It proved less effective against the massed manpower of the post-revolutionary **French Army**, which devised offensive **infantry tactics** aimed at rapid breakthrough of the cordon's weak point, and insisted on seeking out field engagements when on the defensive. The **First Coalition**'s rigid adherence to cordon tactics brought repeated failure on all the main European fronts, and faith in the system was a feature of **Austrian** and Prussian Army operations deep into the Napoleonic era.

Corps System

The practice of grouping units within campaigning armies into large, militarily and administratively self-contained formations on a permanent basis. The largest standing formation in most peacetime armies was the regiment, comprising two or more battalions. Regimental battalions might or might not fight together on campaign, when orthodox eighteenth-century armies deployed their forces by brigades, containing battalions equivalent to two or more regiments and a full strength of anything from 2,000 to 5,000 men. Grouping of brigades into divisions under independent commanders, and of divisions into corps, was instituted on an occasional and temporary basis whenever circumstances called for a substantial independent detachment.

The permanent use of divisions and corps was pioneered in French armies of the 1760s, and reintroduced to the revolutionary **French Army** by **Carnot** in 1794. It had not become standard practice in French forces (or elsewhere) by the time **Napoleon** came to power at the turn of the century, after which the corps system was employed wherever French forces operated in army strength until 1815.

As spectacularly demonstrated by Napoleon's **Grande Armée**, the system offered important operational advantages in terms of manoeuvre and supply. Each corps was a complete army in miniature (as was a division in microcosm), usually but not always commanded by a member of the **Marshalate**. It included infantry, **cavalry**, **artillery**, specialist, supply and administrative components, and was expected to be capable of fighting alone, even against superior numbers, until reinforcements arrived. Manoeuvring as an independent unit, but ideally within supporting distance of other corps, it also enjoyed the benefits of independent supply lines and forage resources, important considerations in a French Army that travelled very light.

Its movements pre-planned in detail by Napoleon, and facilitated by his **Grand Quartier-Général** staff organization, the corps system reached a peak of refinement in the **Bataillon Carré** formation first employed during the 1806 **Jena–Auerstädt campaign**. Though its potential failings were demonstrated during the **Peninsular War**, when the absence of Napoleon's controlling influence allowed field commanders to operate almost without mutual reference, the system's obvious tactical advantages in an age of mass armies had encouraged its universal imitation by 1815.

Corsica, Occupation of (1794–6)

The north **Mediterranean** island of Corsica, where **Napoleon** was born and spent his youth, had been an offshore possession of **Genoa** for more than three centuries before it was sold to **France** in 1768, and had been in a state of almost constant rebellion against French rule ever since. Rebel leader Paoli (a formative influence on the young Bonaparte) eventually accepted French sovereignty in 1789, but harmony was short-lived and revolt erupted again in spring 1793.

Paoli's appeals for overseas help fell on deaf ears until early 1794, when British Mediterranean Fleet C-in-C **Hood** selected Corsica as a **Royal Navy** base. Some 1,400 troops were escorted to Corsica in February, but **Dundas** refused to attack 3,500 French regulars at Bastia and Calvi with such a small force, and Hood ordered Captain **Nelson** and the crew of the battleship *Agamemnon* to besiege Bastia themselves. Nelson lost an eye during the ensuing campaign, which ended with the garrison's surrender on 10 August, after **British Army** reinforcements under **Stuart** had taken over the operation.

In the aftermath of the takeover, and at the request of local representatives, the British appointed a viceroy to administer the island, but Corsica's 650km of coastline and proximity to the French coast made it a defensive liability after **Napoleon**'s 1796 victories on the **Italian** front. New Mediterranean C-in-C **Jervis** received orders to quit the theatre altogether in late September, and evacuated his forces from Corsica through October. The last British personnel were leaving the island on 2 November when the first troops landed from **Tuscany** to re-establish French control for the rest of the period. *See* **Martello Towers; Map 8.**

Corunna, Battle of

Successful defence of the north-west Spanish port by British forces under General **Moore** in January 1809, enabling their safe evacuation under the noses of **Soult**'s pursuing French corps. The British retreat towards Corunna, begun at **Sahagún** on 23 December 1808, had occupied most of the French Army of Spain until 29 December, when a minor action at **Bena-vente** rendered Moore's complete encirclement improbable. Napoleon then left the chase to Soult's expanded corps (36,000 men, including 6,000 cavalry), with **Ney**'s 16,000 men as support, while the rest of the army was redeployed and the emperor himself prepared to leave the **Peninsular** theatre.

Moore had intended to rest at Astorga, and perhaps make a stand, but decided to continue his dash to Corunna and moved his men quietly back on to the road on 31 December. Bad weather, disease and problems with discipline were more of a threat than Soult's strung-out corps, which was in no position to provide major opposition when Moore turned to offer battle at Lugo on 6 January. The British retreat was resumed without engagement three days later, and Moore's first three divisions reached Corunna on 11 January, **Paget**'s fourth arriving next day.

No transport shipping was waiting for them, but Soult delayed any attack to concentrate his forces, giving Moore two days to resupply and destroy anything he could not use (including 4,000 barrels of gunpowder). British transports reached Corunna on 14 January, and by evening Moore was evacuating the first troops. By the next day he had only 15,000 infantry still in Corunna, while French strength around the town had grown to 15,000 infantry and 4,500 cavalry.

Soult attacked on the afternoon of 16 January, striking hardest at Moore's left in an attempt to isolate **Baird**'s division by taking the height of Monte Moro, but failing to make significant progress against solid British defence. By the time the French retired in the evening they had lost some 1,500 men, but Moore was among about 800 British dead and injured. The British evacuation was not again seriously disturbed, and the last troops left Corunna on 18 January. A brigade that marched to Vigo Bay meanwhile escaped unmolested.

Moore had lost a total of 5,000 men during the retreat, and was heavily criticized in Britain, but has since been credited with saving the army and distracting Napoleon from more strategically important operations in western Spain and Portugal, enabling the resumption of British operations in the theatre under **Wellesley** later in 1809. *See* **Map 22.**

Corvettes

Small, fast, flush-decked warships, with a single gun deck and no more than about 20 cannon. Much smaller than **frigates**, corvettes were essentially a type of **sloop**, and the term was originally used only by the **French Navy**.

Cossacks

Large communities of warrior peasants within imperial **Russia**, owing wartime military service to the tsar in lieu of peacetime serfdom. Subdivided into several geographical groups, of which the Don Cossacks was the largest, they were excellent horsemen renowned for fierceness rather than discipline. Providing all their own equipment, except for a **musket** supplied by the regular **Russian Army**, they fought as light **cavalry**, performing reconnaissance and harassment duties. As such Cossacks were fearsome enemies, but a tendency to ignore strategic requirements in favour of impetuous charges limited their value in set-piece engagements. *See also* **Platov**, Matvei Ivanovich.

Cotton, Stapleton (1773–1865)

Colourful British **cavalry** officer, a captain of **dragoons** when he fought in **Flanders** under **York**, who met **Wellington** while serving in **India** during the late 1790s, and made his reputation commanding an under-strength mounted arm during the **Peninsular War**. Promoted major-general in 1805, Cotton led a brigade at **Oporto** and **Talavera**, and became overall commander of Wellington's cavalry, covering the slow retreat to the **Torres Vedras** lines and playing an important role at **Salamanca**, where he was wounded. He returned to action just after **Vitoria** in 1813, and led British cavalry for the rest of the Peninsular campaign. Ennobled as Baron Combermere in 1814, but passed over in favour of **Paget** as commander of British cavalry during the **Hundred Days**, he was a successful postwar colonial administrator, and embarked on a long parliamentary career in 1835.

Courtrai, Battle of

The second of three attempts by **First Coalition** forces to halt the French offensive in northwestern **Flanders** during May 1794. After his defeat at **Moescroen**, Austrian general **Clairfait** was ordered to advance on Courtrai as soon as **York**'s supporting allied corps reached nearby Tournai. He moved forward from 8 May, pushing **Vandamme**'s advanced brigade back to the outskirts of Courtrai, where he paused until attacked by 20,000 French troops under **Souham** on 11 May. Though unable to make serious inroads on Austrian positions, the attacks persuaded a pessimistic Clairfait to retreat all the way to Thielt, abandoning Menin. The move left the allies strung out along a 100km front in the sector, and French forces separating the Austrians from York, who had repelled attacks near Tournai on 10 May. The allies made a last attempt to recover some offensive momentum a few days later, launching a complex drive on **Tourcoing**. *See* **Map 2**.

Craonne, Battle of

Inconclusive confrontation during the 1814 campaign for **France**, fought on 7 March between **Blücher**'s allied army east of Paris and **Napoleon**'s much smaller French force. Blücher had retired across the Aisne in early March, and joined corps under **Bülow** and **Winzingerode**

around Laon to bring his strength up to about 100,000 men. Napoleon, in pursuit with a strike force of perhaps 44,000 troops, faced a mounting crisis on his secondary front south of Paris, so that both commanders were anxious to force a confrontation.

French forces seized the bridge over the Aisne at Berry-au-Bac on 6 March and moved northwest towards Laon, but ran into a trap half set by Blücher, who planned to lure Napoleon into a frontal attack against 30,000 men drawn up on the plateau behind Craonne, some 18km short of Laon, and then launch Winzingerode and 11,000 **cavalry** against the French right.

Sacken's corps had not reached Craonne by 6 March, but Napoleon attacked **Voronzov**'s troops in the position that evening, and **Ney** had gained a foothold on the plateau by nightfall. Sure he was facing only a rearguard, Napoleon planned an enveloping operation for the next day, employing pincer attacks to the north and south of a frontal assault. Blücher was able to get Sacken into position and set his trap properly.

Both plans went badly wrong on 7 March: Ney launched Napoleon's northern pincer attack before **artillery** had been brought forward and was beaten off with heavy losses; Winzingerode's flank operation collapsed amid marshy terrain. Fighting ended inconclusively when Blücher ordered his forces back to Laon late in the day. Napoleon lost 5,400 men at Craonne, against about 5,000 allied losses, and hastened his forces forward in the belief that he was pursuing the rearguard of a retreat, a misreading of Blücher's mood that soon proved costly at **Laon**. *See* **Map 26**.

Craufurd, Robert (1764–1812)

Commissioned into the **British Army** as an infantry officer in 1779, Craufurd served in India from 1787, and fought as a captain in the first war against **Tipu Sahib** of Mysore. He resigned his commission in 1793, serving with two foreign regiments in British pay before becoming an official attaché to the **Austrian Army** during the **Italian campaign** of 1797. A staff officer during operations against the 1798 **Irish Rebellion**, and in **North Holland** the following year, he was still a colonel in 1807, when he commanded light infantry during the abortive expedition to **Buenos Aires**. Though taken prisoner, he was one of the few officers to emerge from the fiasco with credit, and became a brigadier-general in command of **Moore**'s specially trained Light Brigade in late 1808.

Craufurd's brigade took part in the retreat to **Corunna**, and returned to the **Peninsular** theatre immediately after the Battle of **Talavera** in July 1809. Over the next two years, the Light Brigade was expanded to divisional strength by the addition of two **Portuguese Army** battalions, and Craufurd earned a reputation as an exceptionally talented but occasionally rash light infantry leader. His screening of the allied northern flank during preparations for the defence of Portugal in 1810 was generally exemplary, and subsequent performances at **Busaco** and **Fuentes de Oñoro** demonstrated considerable battlefield skills. Promoted major-general in June 1811, he died of wounds received during the capture of **Ciudad Rodrigo** in January 1812.

Cuesta, Gregorio García de la (1740–1812)

Spanish nobleman and soldier, born in Old Castille, who fought under **Vivas** in the **Pyrenean campaign** of 1793–5, and was president of the Castille Council from 1798. Dismissed by **Godoy** in 1801, he was appointed captain-general of Old Castille by Crown Prince **Ferdinand** when France invaded in 1808. Dismissed again by the Regency Junta in Madrid after failing to commit his troops in support of **Blake**'s Galicians at **Medina del Río Seco** in July, he fought as captain-general of the Army of Estramadura for the 1809 campaigns in western Spain, suffering another defeat at **Medellín** in March, and his attempts to cooperate with **Wellesley**'s British force were characterized by mutual exasperation. An old-regime dignitary, with little sympathy for **junta** politics, allied needs or strategic reality, he played a final, undistinguished role in the summer victory at **Talavera** before a stroke ended his participation in the **Peninsular War**.

Cuirassiers

Name originally given to **cavalry** troops wearing leather or plate upper body **armour** (cuirass), but applied to contemporary heavy cavalry with or without such protection.

Czartoryski, Adam Jerzy, Prince (1770–1861)

Polish nobleman who fought against his country's partition in 1792 and 1794 but entered Russian service after losing his estates in the latter struggle. A close personal friend of the future Tsar **Alexander**, he became imperial foreign minister in 1801 and led negotiations for Russian participation in the War of the **Third Coalition**. Though he lost his ministerial post after **Russia**'s military defeat in 1807, Czartoryski retained the tsar's personal confidence, and accompanied him to the Congress of **Vienna** in 1814. A senator in postwar **Poland**, he was the country's president during the failed 1830 revolution and spent the rest of his life as an exile in Paris.

D

Dalberg, Karl Theodor von (1744–1817)
German churchman and politician, a relatively liberal nationalist who held senior administrative posts, both secular and clerical, with several city states within the **Holy Roman Empire** before becoming Archbishop-Elector of Mainz in 1802. Mainz was the only diocesan city to retain its independence after the imperial reorganization of 1803, but after his attempts to revive the empire as a political force had failed, Dalberg turned to **Napoleon** as the likely creator of a unified Germany, and took part in the imperial coronation of 1804. In 1806 he was given a specially created post as Prince-Primate to the Confederation of the **Rhine**, but his efforts to federalize its component states met with universal hostility from their ruling princes. Created Grand Duke of Frankfurt in 1810, he fled to exile in Zurich in late 1813, where he spent his last years justifying his career in pan-German terms.

Dalhousie, George Ramsey, Earl of (1770–1838)
Scottish aristocrat who led a regiment in the **West Indies** during the 1790s, and became one of the less successful among **Wellington**'s senior commanders during the latter stages of the **Peninsular War**. Dalhousie's 7th Division performed poorly during the retreat from **Burgos** in autumn 1812, and failed to reach the battlefield on time at **Vitoria** the following July. His mistakes before the Battle of **Roncesvalles** in August all attracted serious criticism from Wellington, but aristocratic influence within the **British** Army remained strong enough to render an earl virtually immune from dismissal. After 1815 he served as governor of Canada and C-in-C in **India**.

Dallemagne, Claude (1754–1813)
An NCO with the royal French infantry until commissioned in 1791, Dallemagne was at **Toulon** in 1793, and was a brigadier-general in Italy from 1794. With **Masséna**'s division at the start of the 1796 **Italian campaign**, he led the French advance guard across the Po in early May, playing important roles at **Lodi** and **Lonato**. After taking part in the siege of **Mantua**, he was promoted to divisional command in August 1796, but abandoned active service for a political career in 1799 and retired from the army altogether in 1802. He returned to the colours in 1807, commanding a division with occupying forces in Pomerania and helping thwart the allied **Walcheren expedition** in 1809, finally retiring shortly before his death.

Dalrymple, Sir Hew Whitefoord (1750–1830)
An example of the command weakness that plagued the **British Army** before its long **Peninsular War** campaign imposed reform on an officer corps dominated by social influence, wealth and seniority. A moderately competent soldier, able to purchase his regimental command at 40, Dalrymple's wealth ensured steady subsequent promotion, while the army's relative idleness kept him out of dangerous field commands until 1808, when he was sent to take overall control of allied forces in **Portugal** after

Wellesley's victory at **Vimeiro**. Happy to endorse the policy of inaction imposed by his predecessor, the slightly less elderly General Burrard, he was recalled after signing the controversial Convention of **Cintra**. Never again entrusted with an important command, he was promoted full general in 1812 and ennobled in 1815.

Danish Army

By the time **Denmark** went to war in 1807, its infantry forces comprised one élite guard and 14 line regiments, each of two battalions, although their strength was doubled when volunteer territorials (Landevaern) were incorporated into line units to face the British at **Roskilde**. By 1813 its total infantry strength was just over 50,000 troops, including about 5,000 **jägers** armed with **rifles**, and Danish **cavalry** mustered a nominal strength of about 7,200 men, although full establishment was seldom approached. Apart from performing observation and occupation duties along the frontiers and in northern Germany, and briefly opposing the British in 1807, the army fought a campaign against **Sweden** in 1808 and operated in support of retreating French forces during the 1813 campaign for **Germany**.

Danish Navy

The Danish Navy of the 1790s was a small but competent and confident force, built up to protect **Denmark**'s vital seaborne trade. It included 38 **ships-of-the-line** (the largest of them 90-gunners) and 20 **frigates**, along with many coastal craft, but though Denmark's geographical position enabled the navy to bottle up the Baltic almost at will, its global military value was restricted by the proximity of Britain's much larger **Royal Navy**. This was graphically illustrated in 1801, when the fleet was attacked and defeated by **Nelson**, in **Copenhagen**, losing 18 ships-of-the-line and three frigates.

The setback altered Danish naval priorities, and ship construction was subsequently concentrated on light craft for operations in strategically important home waters. The second British bombardment of Copenhagen in 1807 effectively ended the navy's interest in fleet operations, costing 19 major warships, 16 smaller ones, ten sloops and 25 **gunboats**. The last Danish ship-of-the-line, the *Prince Christian Frederick*, was sunk by the British in 1808, but the navy proved highly adept at harassing British shipping with light craft during the six-year **Gunboat War** that followed, reflecting the high quality and morale of its personnel.

Danton, Georges Jacques (1759–94)

Born into a peasant family at Arcis-sur-Aube, and a lawyer in Paris by 1789, Danton emerged as a leading political figure during the early years of the **French Revolution**. Famed for his thunderous oratory and uncompromising **Jacobin** views, he was exiled briefly in 1791 but returned to become the new republic's justice minister in autumn 1792, playing an important part in rallying the French population to resist **Brunswick**'s invading army. President of the Jacobin Club, he was effective head of the **National Convention** government in early 1793, sponsoring the king's execution, masterminding the defeat of moderate 'Girondin' elements and becoming an original member of the Committee of **Public Safety**. Danton quit the Committee in July after it was expanded to include **Robespierre** and his allies, retiring to his home town with his young second wife, but 'Dantonism' remained a threat to Robespierre's position in the Convention. He returned to Paris in the late autumn to campaign for an end to the **Terror** and peace with the **First Coalition**, but was arrested for treason in March 1794. He was guillotined on 5 April after a typically flamboyant performance in his own defence had threatened to ignite popular opposition to the government.

Danzig, Siege of (1807)

One of the most important trading centres among the **Hanseatic** towns, the Baltic **fortress** of Danzig was besieged by French forces between 18 March and 27 May 1807 (*see* **Map 17**). A siege planned for January was postponed while French forces concentrated on fighting the Russians at **Ionkovo** and **Eylau**, but Napoleon issued orders on 18 February for **Lefebvre**'s newly formed corps to invest Danzig. Both a bulging supply base and a potential landing place for reinforcements, Danzig was garrisoned by 16,000 Prussian troops under Kalkreuth, renowned for his defence of **Mainz** in 1793. The landward approaches to its strong fortifications were littered with streams and marshes, and the city was well provisioned for a long **siege**.

Lefebvre's 20,000-strong force, largely composed of **Polish**, **Saxon** and **Italian** units, surrounded Danzig on 18 March, and was close to the main defences by the middle of April. Before a full-scale assault could be mounted, British and Russian warships landed 8,000 Russian reinforcements (under the younger Kamenskoi) at the mouth of the Vistula on 10 May. They wasted several days establishing coastal defences before advancing on Danzig from 15 May, when 15,000 fresh French reserves (under **Lannes** and **Oudinot**) drove them back with 1,500 casualties.

Though Kamenskoi made no further attempt to relieve the city, garrison troops launched a successful raid on 20 May, but the arrival of another 11,500 French troops (**Mortier**) rendered their position hopeless. Kalkreuth opened negotiations for surrender on 22 May, surrendering on good terms five days later.

Dardanelles Operation

The **Royal Navy**'s unsuccessful attempt in February 1807 to impose British strategic priorities on the **Ottoman Empire**, and keep it out of a potential alliance with **France**. French envoy **Sebastiani**'s agitation for the renewal of Turkey's long-standing disputes with **Russia** had met a positive response in Constantinople, and sultan Selim III's formal deposition of viceroys in the Danube provinces triggered Russian intervention from October 1806. Embroiled in preparations to fight France further north, Tsar **Alexander** asked the British to stop Turkey from going to war.

The British **Grenville** administration, in theory still the sultan's ally, hesitated before acting. Partly to forestall any threat to overland communications with **India**, but primarily to divert pressure from Russia, British ambassador Arbuthnot was eventually instructed on 14 November to demand Sebastiani's removal from Constantinople on pain of attack by the Royal Navy.

The move had been anticipated by British Mediterranean C-in-C **Collingwood**, who had ordered three **ships-of-the-line**, a **frigate** and a

sloop to the Dardanelles in early November, followed by another five battleships and supporting smaller craft. Overall command of the expedition was given to Admiral **Duckworth**, whose instructions were to bombard Constantinople or seize the **Turkish Navy**'s battlefleet only if the sultan remained bent on war with Russia. Four Russian battleships under Admiral Siniavin at Corfu meanwhile prepared to join them.

The presence of the advance British squadron at the mouth of the Dardanelles Straits from early December, and of the 80-gun *Canopus* off Constantinople itself, did not prevent the sultan's formal declaration of a **Russo-Turkish War** on 27 December. A frigate evacuated British citizens from the city on 29 January, and Duckworth's ships were concentrated at the mouth of the straits by 10 February. News of Duckworth's approach had meanwhile put the Turkish government's attitude in doubt, and Sebastiani began preparing his own evacuation while overseeing improvements to shore batteries covering the straits.

Nine days of contrary winds, and accidental loss of the *Ajax* to fire on 14 February, eroded Duckworth's initial confidence in safe passage through the straits, but he was committed to action by Arbuthnot's aggressive diplomacy. Exploiting the first fair wind, he entered the straits on the morning of 19 February, leaving two battleships on guard at the mouth. Turkish shore batteries opened fire, effectively placing the Ottoman Empire at war with Britain, but the absence of many defending troops celebrating the end of Ramadan helped the British force reach the Sea of Marmora virtually undamaged.

Though Sebastiani had worked hard to improve defences in the straits, no attempt had been made to fortify Constantinople, but foul weather prevented Duckworth's ships closing on the city in force, and on 20 February they were compelled to take shelter off an island some 12km to the south. Light winds made any move impossible next day, by which time Turkish ministers had recovered from their initial panic, and delayed British action with negotiations while defences were prepared.

Duckworth found himself becalmed until the evening of 28 February, by which time Sebastiani and a small corps of French engineering officers had transformed the city's defences and further reinforced the straits' defences. Against the advice of some subordinates, notably **Smith**, Duckworth elected to withdraw with the wind. After cruising within sight of Constantinople on 1 March, in the vain hope of provoking a fight, the British departed overnight, suffering extensive damage (and about 120 casualties) before regaining the Mediterranean on 3 March.

Though reinforced by four Russian battleships, Duckworth refused to undertake a second attempt unless ground forces could be provided to tackle the shore batteries, a condition never likely to be satisfied. Criticized as timid by British contemporaries, Duckworth's failure was a blow to British prestige in the eastern Mediterranean, and hastened the collapse of Anglo-Russian relations, but is now generally regarded as a strategically justified concentration on the Royal Navy's wider **Mediterranean** responsibilities. *See* Battle of **Lemnos**; **Map 18**.

David, Jacques-Louis (1748–1825)

Celebrated French neoclassical painter, who voted for the execution of King **Louis XVI** as a member of the **National Convention**, and whose **Jacobin** enthusiasms twice brought imprisonment after the **Thermidor** coup of 1794. A friend of **Napoleon** from 1797, he was appointed imperial court painter in 1804, and subsequently devoted much of his artistic energy to **propaganda** in the form of grandiose canvases depicting imperial triumphs. Exiled as a regicide in 1816, he spent the rest of his life in Brussels.

Davout, Louis Nicholas (1770–1823)

Arguably the finest corps commander among **Napoleon's** marshals, Davout was born in Burgundy to a minor noble family, and followed his father into the royal **cavalry** in 1788. Though a supporter of the **French Revolution**, he was dismissed from the regular army in 1791, but immediately elected colonel in command of a volunteer battalion. He fought at **Neerwinden** in March 1793, and first came to public notice just afterwards, when he refused orders from **Dumouriez** to march on Paris. Though rewarded with promotion to brigadier-general in July, he was retired along with other former nobles in August.

Reinstated from October 1794, Davout commanded cavalry on the **Rhine** front, fighting around **Mannheim** in 1795, at **Kehl** and **Haslach** in 1796, and at **Diersheim** in spring 1797. His capture of correspondence between **Pichegru** and royalist **émigrés** helped trigger the **Fructidor** coup later that year, and his close relations with immediate superior **Desaix** brought an introduction to Napoleon, culminating in a staff appointment with the **Middle East** expedition in 1798. Still under Desaix, he fought at the **Pyramids** and **Aboukir**, but was captured by the British on his way home in 1800.

Promoted divisional general on his return to service in July 1800, he fought in the latter stages of the **Italian campaign** against the **Second Coalition**, and was one of the original **Marshalate** in 1804. He led III Corps with great success against the **Third Coalition** in 1805, playing an important role at **Austerlitz** and demonstrating organizational abilities which made his command the most efficient in the **Grande Armée**. These qualities were fully tested in October 1806, when his outnumbered detachment won a crucial victory at **Auerstädt** to seal **Prussia's** rapid defeat.

After fighting through the war against the **Fourth Coalition**, and leading Napoleon's right wing at **Eylau**, Davout was governor-general of **Warsaw** from summer 1807, and became Duke of Auerstädt next year. He returned to the head of III Corps for the campaigns of 1809, performing vital service at both **Eckmühl** and **Wagram**, after which he held a number of senior commands (as Prince of Eckmühl) in Germany.

Davout led I Corps through the 1812 **Russian campaign**, performing with his usual vigour during the opening advances, and replacing Jérôme **Bonaparte** in command of the Grande Armée's southern wing in July. He won a minor victory at **Mohilev** and fought at **Smolensk**, but his corps was replaced as rearguard to the retreat from **Moscow** after a crushing defeat at **Fiodoroivskoy** in November. In command at Dresden during the early stages of the campaign for **Germany**, he was transferred to hold **Hamburg** from May 1813, eventually surrendering a year later and suffering royal banishment from Paris.

He rejoined Napoleon during the **Hundred Days** of 1815 but was not given a field command. Never particularly popular, but untainted by sycophancy or personal ambition, he was instead war minister and military governor of Paris. He held the capital until 3 July, when he evacuated garrison troops to western France by agreement with the allies. He turned his forces over to royal control on 14 July, and remained under house arrest until his partial reinstatement in 1817. His titles were fully restored in 1819.

Dego, Battle of

The climax of **Dumerbion**'s second offensive on the **Italian** front in 1794, a relatively minor action fought on 21 September in the Alpine foothills north-west of Genoa. Plans drafted by artillery commander **Napoleon** for an attack into **Piedmont** had been interrupted by political turmoil inside **France** during the summer, giving Austrian forces under General Wallis time to concentrate for a counter-attack through the mountains towards Savona, supported by a secondary attack from the sea with **Royal Navy** assistance. Once Napoleon had returned in late August from a brief spell under arrest, Dumerbion followed his plan for a pre-emptive attack in defiance of government orders to remain on the defensive.

French troops moved swiftly up either bank of the Bormida's western branch from 19 September, threatening the flank of any advance on Savona and separating the Austrians from their Piedmontese allies. Surprised Austrian forces fell back to protect their lines of retreat at the village of Dego, where they lost 42 guns in a rearguard action on 21 September, before abandoning their offensive and retreating towards Acqui overnight. The immediate threat past, Dumerbion overruled Napoleon's objections and halted operations from 24 September, withdrawing to a defensive line running inland from Vado to Ormea. *See* **Map 6**.

Dego, Second Battle of

The more celebrated of two battles at Dego took place on 14–15 April 1796, during the opening phase of **Napoleon**'s first offensive as **Italian** theatre C-in-C. After defeating an Austrian detachment at **Montenotte** on 12 April, Napoleon marched west to attack Colli's isolated Piedmontese forces, leaving **Masséna**'s 8,500 troops around Dego to guard against interference from the rest of **Beaulieu**'s Austrian army. Masséna found the village occupied by perhaps 5,000 Austrians, but was forbidden from attacking on 13 April while the main French force was struggling to overcome a small Piedmontese garrison at Cosseria.

Though Cosseria held out overnight, Masséna was authorized to attack Dego next morning, and his men stormed the town at about noon, taking some 4,000 prisoners before dispersing in search of forage. French forces were still scattered when General Wukassovich and 5,000 Austrian reinforcements reached Dego during the night, overwhelming the village and capturing all Masséna's **artillery**. Napoleon rushed east with General La Harpe's 8,000-strong division to launch a fresh attack on Dego later on 15 April, losing another 1,000 men but driving Wukassovich into full retreat before resuming his drive against the Piedmontese at **Ceva**. *See* **Map 6**.

Denmark

With a small population and limited resources for agricultural or industrial development, the Scandinavian kingdom of Denmark was economically dependent on seaborne trade, and its large merchant fleet was **Great Britain**'s main competitor in northern European waters. Foreign policy was otherwise dominated by regional issues, principally a long-term territorial dispute with **Sweden** over control of Norway, a Danish province in 1792.

A palace coup in 1784 had replaced the idiot king **Christian VII** with his son Frederick as regent. Guided by foreign minister **Bernstorff**, Frederick sought to avoid entanglement in **great power** conflicts. Denmark remained neutral during the **Revolutionary Wars**, but the government's attempt to protect trade by introducing a **convoy** system almost brought war with Britain in 1800, bringing a British naval squadron to Copenhagen in August to ensure that escort warships remained in port.

Denmark joined other northern states in the League of **Armed Neutrality** against Britain from December 1800, but a punitive expedition virtually destroyed the **Danish Navy** at **Copenhagen** in early April, and Anglo-Danish relations were strained until the Battle of **Trafalgar** confirmed Britain's naval supremacy in 1805. By September 1806, when Denmark exploited dissolution of the **Holy Roman Empire** to occupy the northern German state of Holstein, Danish ports were once more doing thriving business with British shipping.

Napoleon's subsequent occupation of **Prussia** introduced the dangerous possibility of French expansion into Denmark. Not calmed by Danish deployment of troops in Holstein as a precautionary measure in July, Britain's fear of a Franco-Danish alliance brought pre-emptive action in August. British troops landed in Denmark on 16 August, fighting off a Danish force at **Roskilde** on 29 August, and a second naval bombardment of **Copenhagen** killed at least 2,000 citizens in early September. Driven into war against Britain, Denmark signed an alliance with **France** in October.

The war's impact was felt most keenly in Norway, which was economically dependent on British trade and suffered serious food shortages under the ensuing **blockade**. The Royal Navy also cut sea communications between Oslo and Copenhagen, forcing the government to maintain administrative control through a special commission (Regjeringskommission), headed by Prince Christian Augustus as *Stattholder*.

In March 1808, shortly after the death of King Christian and his son's accession as **Frederick VI**, the dispute with Sweden over Norway escalated into armed conflict. With support from **Bernadotte**'s French army in northern Europe, the Danes held off a Swedish invasion of Norway and forced an armistice in December. Christian Augustus sought to extend his powers by demanding independent control of Norwegian foreign policy, but the final Treaty of Jönköping (signed on 10 December 1809) was negotiated by Copenhagen and involved no territorial changes. Rumours that the death of Christian Augustus in May 1810 was caused by poisoning provoked separatist unrest in Norway, and the autocratic Frederick abolished the Regjeringskommission late in the year.

Denmark was an active ally to France, but its relatively vigorous prosecution of a seven-year **Gunboat War** along Baltic trade routes brought economic ruin and few compensatory gains. The country was declared bankrupt in January 1813, and its diplomatic position became hopeless once Sweden joined the **Sixth Coalition** in July, prompting voluntary cession of Norway by the Treaty of **Kiel** in early 1814 (*see* Convention of **Moss**). Postwar economic recovery was slow, and Denmark suffered basic shortages well into the 1820s, but King Frederick had revived cabinet government in 1814 and remained sufficiently popular to stay in power until his death in 1839. *See* **Maps 1, 30**.

Dennewitz, Battle of

Successful attack by **Bernadotte**'s Prusso-Swedish force on **Ney**'s French army advancing towards Berlin during the 1813 campaign for **Germany**. Seeking to exploit his incomplete victory at **Dresden** in late August, Napoleon had appointed Ney to lead 80,000 men against the Prussian capital. Deprived of 25,000 troops by the need to reinforce **Macdonald** on the eastern sector, Ney attacked confidently when he found part of Bernadotte's 80,000-strong army drawn up near Dennewitz, some 65km south-west of Berlin, on 6 September. As they approached, French columns were ambushed from the flank by **Bülow**'s 10,000 Prussians, and Ney divided his forces to meet the threat rather than concentrating against the weaker allied flank. At the end of a confused fight the French withdrew south, having suffered about 10,000 casualties against some 7,000 allied losses. Ney retreated to Torgau on the Elbe, followed cautiously by Bernadotte, and pressure elsewhere prevented Napoleon sending reinforcements before all French forces were pulled behind the Elbe on 24 September. *See* **Map 25**.

Desaix, Louis Charles (1768–1800)

One of the most consistently successful French generals of the **Revolutionary Wars**, Desaix renounced his noble background to fight on the **Rhine** front from 1792. Promoted brigadier-general in September 1793, he fought under **Pichegru** at the **Geisberg**, and was a divisional commander in the **Vosges** the following summer. He made his reputation during **Moreau**'s invasion across the Rhine in the second half of 1796, taking part in all the major battles that followed the French crossing at **Kehl** in June. A senior commander with **Napoleon**'s 1798 expedition to the **Middle East**, he led the seizure of **Malta** and fought at the **Pyramids**, but was captured by the British (along with his protégé, **Davout**) en route for France in 1800. One of Napoleon's favourite generals, he returned to action on the **Italian** front in time for the Battle of **Marengo**, where he was killed leading the decisive French attack.

Desertion

By the standards of the late twentieth century, the armies and navies of the **Revolutionary** and Napoleonic Wars suffered enormous and constant losses to desertion. Although occasionally politically inspired – like that of French general **Dumouriez** in 1794, or entire German units during the Battle of **Leipzig** in 1813 – the overwhelming majority of desertions were motivated by personal considerations, and carried out unhindered by virtually helpless authorities.

When armies were in heavily populated areas, or warships in busy ports, commanders could do little, short of keeping their men permanently under guard, to prevent deserters from slipping away into crowded streets, and even less to recapture them. Armies operating far from home in inhospitable terrain generally suffered less desertion, largely because would-be absconders had nowhere pleasant to go, but banditry was a popular option in more comfortable southern European theatres, attracting men from both sides during the **Peninsular War**.

The practice of employing foreign mercenary or **émigré** units within the national armies of **great powers**, as well as **conscription** and **press gangs**, all encouraged desertion, but its prime catalyst was always defeat. Those armies with the least successful fighting records – the **Spanish**, **Neapolitan** and **Turkish** armies, for instance – regularly lost a majority of surviving personnel to desertion after major defeats (as well as significant numbers before or during battles), and a long retreat was likely to take a heavy toll from even the best-motivated forces.

Given the dangers, discomforts and abuses faced by an ordinary soldier or sailor in the course of duty, it is hardly surprising that large numbers of men chose to abscond. A significant proportion of those eventually caught were nevertheless taken after re-enlisting, having deserted one unit in order to claim a volunteer's 'bounty' payment from another.

Diersheim, Battle of

French victory over Austrian forces along the southern sector of the **Rhine** front in April 1797, the last major action in the theatre during the War of the **First Coalition**. French commanders on the Rhine had been ordered to attack across the river in support of **Napoleon**'s successes on the **Italian** front, but both **Hoche** in the north and **Moreau** in the south delayed any operation until victory in Italy was almost secure. Moreau's advanced divisions under **Vandamme** and **Davout** crossed the river in boats around Diersheim in the night of 19–20 April, defeating 4,000 Austrians to establish themselves east of the river by early afternoon. Sufficient reinforcements were across a **pontoon** bridge by morning to hold off an attack by Sztarray's 17,000 Austrian troops on forward positions at Diersheim and Hanau, and the arrival of Lecourbe's division with strong **cavalry** support turned the battle. Moreau launched an immediate counter-attack on the main Austrian positions between Litzenheim and Freystätt, driving his surprised and disorganized opponents into a chaotic retreat by evening. Both sides suffered about 3,000 casualties during the fighting, but the French took as many prisoners and captured the fortress at Kehl late in the day. Moreau's half-hearted pursuit was halted by news of the Preliminaries of **Leoben**, as was an Austrian move against the French flank from Mannheim. *See* Second Battle of **Altenkirchen; Map 3.**

Diez, Juan Martín (1775–1825)

One of the most celebrated Spanish **guerrilla** leaders of the **Peninsular War**, known as El Empecinado (from *pecina*, 'slime') and reputedly more humane than many of his peers. Diez, who may have fought against France on the **Pyrenean** front in 1793–5, led partisan attacks on French communications from summer 1808. Based in Guadalajara, he is believed to have commanded some 5,000 guerrillas by 1810, and survived the war to become a vociferous critic of King **Ferdinand VII**, eventually suffering execution for his part in the rebellion of 1820.

Directory

The executive ruling body in **France** from 1795 to 1799, established by the Constitution of Year III and dissolved by the **Brumaire** coup that brought **Napoleon** to power. Brought into being during the last weeks of the **National Convention** government, and in office from 27 October 1795, the Directory of Five was elected by the Councils of **Ancients** and **Five Hundred**. Pursuing a moderate course between reviving **Jacobin** and royalist extremes, it found its popularity evaporating after the peace of 1797, and the next two years were distinguished by a procession of coups and counter-coups, most notably government-inspired 'popular' purges of right- and left-wing opponents by the coups of **Fructidor** (1797) and **Floréal** (1798). The Directory had already lurched into deep economic crisis when its disastrous start to the War of the **Second Coalition** made its replacement, and that of the constitution, a matter of timing.

Doctorov, Dmitri Sergeivich (1750–1862)

Russian infantry commander whose career is generally obscure, but who played a prominent role in several of the period's most important battles. He commanded a division during **Buxhowden**'s ill-fated advance at **Austerlitz** in 1805, helped hold off superior French numbers at **Golymin** late the following year, and led the central infantry reserve that bore much of the hardest fighting at **Eylau** in February 1807. During the French invasion of 1812, Doctorov took part in the defence of **Smolensk**, commanded a corps at **Borodino** in September, and led Russian forces at the Battle of **Maloyaroslavets** in October.

Dombrowski, Jan Henryk (1755–1818)

Polish soldier, born in Upper Silesia, who served with the Army of **Saxony** before joining the forces of his native land in 1791. Forced into exile after the Third Partition of **Poland** in 1795, he formed a Polish legion in France and fought under **Napoleon** during the **Italian campaigns** of 1796–7 and 1799–1800. Promoted divisional general in 1800, he returned to Poland with Napoleon in 1806, raising a division at Posen

(Poznan) that subsequently fought at **Danzig** and **Friedland**. He commanded a division under **Poniatowski** in Galicia during the campaign against the **Fifth Coalition** in 1809, and took part in the 1812 **Russian campaign**, where he was wounded at the **Beresina** in November. Dombrowski took command of VII (Polish) Corps after Poniatowski's death at **Leipzig** in 1813, but went home on Napoleon's fall in 1814. Reinstated in the Polish Army by Tsar **Alexander I**, he sat in the postwar Polish senate until his retirement in 1816.

Donzelot, François Xavier (1764–1843)

French soldier in royal service from 1783, he received a **cavalry** commission in 1792 and served on the **Rhine** from 1793 to 1797. With the **Middle East** expedition from 1798, he achieved brigade command in March 1801, signing the surrender of Cairo to British forces in late June. A divisional general from December 1807, he commanded occupation forces in the **Ionian Islands** until they came under British control in 1814. Donzelot led a division during the **Hundred Days** campaign in 1815, fighting at **Waterloo**, and was suspended for several years before returning to royal service and becoming governor of Martinique (1827–8).

Doppet, François Amédée (1753–99)

A former cavalryman and medical student by the time he joined the French **National Guard** in 1790, Doppet was elected battalion commander in 1792 and achieved divisional rank in September 1793, when he replaced the elder **Kellermann** in command of the Army of the Alps. After completing the capture of **Lyon** in October, he commanded French forces on the eastern sector of the **Pyrenean** front, but retired sick after manpower shortages had undermined his winter campaign east of Perpignan. He returned to the Pyrenees as a divisional commander in 1794, but was removed from front-line responsibilities in 1795 and retired two years later, subsequently failing in a bid to join the Council of **Five Hundred**.

Dörnberg Conspiracy

An attempt in April 1809 to overthrow the regime of King Jérôme **Bonaparte** in **Westphalia**, one of several threats to Napoleonic domination in western Germany following an Austrian declaration of war against France couched in terms of a German nationalist crusade. Colonel von Dörnberg, a 41-year-old native of **Hesse-Cassel** employed in the **Westphalian Army**, had been planning rebellion since 1806. An influential group of former Hessian officers and nobles at his Homberg headquarters, united only in mutual hatred of French occupation, maintained secret communications with Prussian authorities until the war of spring 1809 provided an opportunity for action. Dörnberg travelled to Cassel to arrest the king in late April, relying on support from peasants, disaffected troops and **Schill**'s Prussian rebels to the north. When peasant agitation alerted authorities in Cassel, and local **Westphalian Army** units refused to join the uprising, Dörnberg fled the city, but returned at the head of 5,000 virtually unarmed peasants on 23 April. Jérôme had only 1,500 troops in Cassel, but refused flight and was proved right later that day, when 200 regular infantry, 25 cavalry and two guns confronted and overwhelmed the peasant force a few kilometres short of the city. *See* **Map 21**.

Dragoons

Regular, non-specialist **cavalry** troops, intended to fight mounted or on foot. A dragoon was originally a seventeenth-century **carbine**, so called because it breathed fire like a dragon, and dragoons were originally any mounted troops so armed.

Dresden, Battle of

The successful French defence of Dresden, a vital supply base straddling the River Elbe in **Saxony**, against a major attack by allied forces of the **Sixth Coalition** on 26–27 August 1813. Both sides opened major offensives as the **armistice** on the front ended in mid-August, but **Napoleon** quickly abandoned his own drive on Breslau when news reached him on 22 August of an allied attack towards his main base at Dresden, guarded by a single corps under **Gouvion St Cyr**. Allied commanders had intended to launch their biggest field army, **Schwarzenberg**'s 230,000 men, at Leipzig, but had limited their ambitions when French forces briefly threatened the army's flank at Zittau on 20 August.

Faced by the approach of 150,000 allied troops

from the south-east, St Cyr's advance guards were driven back into the city during 22 August, and **Wittgenstein**'s leading allied corps reached the suburbs next day. Napoleon decided against the direct relief of St Cyr on 23 August, and began gathering for an attack across the Elbe further east, aiming to cut Schwarzenberg's rear lines at Königstein and Pirna. The plan relied on St Cyr holding out at Dresden, but also on **Oudinot** and **Macdonald** keeping other allied armies busy to the far north and north-east respectively.

Word of Oudinot's defeat at **Gross-Beeren**, and his subsequent retreat from the Berlin region, reached Napoleon on 25 August, and news that Dresden might fall at any time prompted another change of plan. Reducing the force attacking Pirna to a single corps (**Vandamme**), he marched the **Imperial Guard**, the reserve **cavalry** and two line corps to rescue St Cyr.

St Cyr had improvised improvements to defences south and west of the city, and his first line of defence was a series of outposts in outlying villages and buildings, the strongest of them behind the walls of the Gross Garten park. Driven back from the city by St Cyr's counterattack on 25 August, and unsure of the garrison's strength, the allies delayed a major attack on Dresden itself until next day, and moves towards the outposts got slowly under way at dawn. The attack had driven back forward French positions soon after nine, but Napoleon and the Guard reached Dresden at about the same time.

Allied preparations for a new attack were complete by eleven, with 150,000 men drawn up south of the city and 70,000 French troops in position behind earthwork defences, but Napoleon's presence triggered an argument between the three monarchs with Schwarzenberg's force. Tsar **Alexander** wanted to break off the action at once in accordance with the **Trachenberg Plan**, but Prussian king **Frederick William** was in favour of continuing the attack and Austrian emperor **Francis** was undecided. An order postponing any action pending a decision failed to reach Schwarzenberg in time, and the allied attack opened at around noon without royal permission.

Allied assaults on Dresden's southern defences continued through the afternoon, but St Cyr's troops held their lines and French artillery on the north bank inflicted heavy casualties, particularly on Wittgenstein's right wing. Napoleon launched a counter-attack with four Guard divisions just after five thirty, **Mortier** leading the recapture of Gross Garten on the allied right, and **Ney** forcing Schwarzenberg to commit reserves in the allied centre. By nightfall French forces had regained their original outposts, at which point **Victor** and **Marmont** arrived to bring Napoleon's strength up to 120,000 men. Vandamme's successful attack on **Pirna** restricted the reinforcements available to Schwarzenberg, and only another 12,000 allied troops reached Dresden overnight, while heavy rain turned the small River Weisseritz into a considerable barrier between the two armies.

Both sides planned renewed attacks next morning. Allied commanders grouped 100,000 men for a central assault and left about 25,000 on each flank. Hopes that General **Klenau** and 21,000 more troops would arrive in time to help **Bianchi**'s left wing proved unfounded. Napoleon planned a characteristic double pincer movement, holding the centre with 50,000 troops, backed by the Guard as reserve, while **Murat** led 35,000 men round the French right and 35,000 more (under Ney and Mortier) advanced on the left, where Vandamme was ordered to push deeper into the allied rear.

The French attack opened first, and enjoyed immediate success on both flanks, particularly the allied left. By occupying the vital bridge over the Weisseritz at Plenau, French forces prevented the mass of allied troops in the centre from crossing to rescue Bianchi's wing, which was pinned against the river and had been completely destroyed by mid-afternoon, some 13,000 survivors becoming prisoners. Heavily outnumbered French forces in the centre were able only to hold their positions.

Fighting died down in the early evening, and allied commanders planned another attack for 28 August, but continued rain was reducing the battle zone to a morass, and news of Vandamme's movements in the rear prompted a withdrawal overnight. Napoleon sent his subordinates in pursuit next morning, while he remained in Dresden to absorb news of Macdonald's heavy defeat at the **Katzbach** on 26 August.

Though a crushing French victory, inflicting about 38,000 casualties on the allies at a cost of 10,000 losses, the success at Dresden was undermined by the failures of Macdonald and Oudinot, and by Vandamme's inability to close the trap on Schwarzenberg's retreating army. The rapid but ill-coordinated French advance from Dresden left his corps isolated, and he suffered a severe reverse at **Kulm** on 30 August, enabling the allied army to escape and renewing the optimism of its leaders. *See* **Map 25**.

Dresden, Treaty of *See* **Poland**

Droits de l'Homme, Destruction of the

One of the most celebrated naval actions of the wars, fought off the north-west French coast on the night of 13 January 1797 between two British **frigates** and the French 74-gun **ship-of-the-line** *Droits de l'Homme*. In heavy weather, its decks crammed with troops, *Droits de l'Homme* was among the last French ships to return from the **Bantry Bay** expedition, and was sighted by Captain **Pellew**'s frigate *Indefatigable* as it approached its home port of Brest. A southwesterly gale snapped two of the French ship's topmasts almost immediately afterwards and Pellew, recognizing that the high seas would make use of the battleship's lower guns difficult, took the normally unacceptable risk of launching an attack. Helped by the extreme difficulty of hitting a low target at close range from a battleship's upper guns, *Indefatigable* and *Amazon*, a second frigate that joined the fight about an hour later, chased the French ship downwind, launching alternate attacks before dodging away. They had inflicted some 250 casualties when the group came upon the rocks of Audierne Bay, south of Brest. Most of the crew aboard *Amazon* escaped when it was wrecked on the rocks, and *Indefatigable* steered clear, but *Droits de l'Homme* hit the shore side-on and foundered with the loss of an estimated 1,000 lives. Their unprecedented feat cost the two frigates 37 killed and wounded.

Drouet, Jean-Baptiste (1765–1844)

One of many senior French officers who owed rapid advancement to the social upheavals in **France** during the **Revolutionary Wars**, Drouet enlisted in the royal army at 16 and was a brigadier-general by 1799, fighting at **Zurich** that September and **Hohenlinden** the following year. Promoted to divisional command in 1803, he fought at **Austerlitz** in 1805, and took part in the eastern campaigns of 1806, 1807 and 1809. Often known by his imperial title, the Comte d'Erlon, he served in the **Peninsular War** from 1810 to 1814, taking part in the Battles of **Fuentes de Oñoro**, **Vitoria** and **Toulouse**, and was quick to rejoin **Napoleon** in 1815 after a brief period in royal service. Given command of I Corps in Flanders, he was blamed for missing the Battles of **Ligny** and **Quatre Bras** on 16 June, but was a victim of poor staff work and confusion among his superiors. A vigorous performance at **Waterloo** restored his reputation, but he spent the next decade in exile under a death sentence until pardoned and restored to the army lists.

Drouot, Antoine (1774–1847)

French artillery and staff officer, commissioned in 1793, who fought in **Flanders** during the **Revolutionary Wars**, and was among the soldiers present at **Trafalgar** in 1805. Wounded at **Wagram** in 1809, he was a colonel at **Borodino** three years later, and was promoted brigadier-general in January 1813. Under **Napoleon's** direct command throughout the campaign for **Germany**, he commanded the 50-gun battery that helped win the battle at **Hanau**. Drouot performed a similar role through the 1814 campaign in **France**, and accompanied Napoleon to **Elba** after his **abdication** in April, becoming the island's governor. In command of the **Imperial Guard** at **Waterloo** in 1815, he was acquitted of treason in its aftermath and retired in 1825.

Düben, Battle of

Unsuccessful attack by 150,000 French troops on **Blücher's** allied army in **Germany** as it advanced south beyond the River Elbe towards Leipzig in mid-October 1813. Blücher's 60,000 men, along with Crown Prince **Bernadotte's** 80,000 Prussians and Swedes, formed the northern wing of a two-pronged allied advance, and **Napoleon** led his strike force north from Leipzig on 7 October, planning to destroy each component in turn. Though poorly informed of allied dispositions

by his weak **cavalry** arm, Napoleon guessed that Blücher's force was concentrated around Düben, about 35km north-west of Leipzig, but his infantry advanced too slowly to take the Prussian commander by surprise. Blücher had already begun a withdrawal by the time Napoleon moved against Düben on 9 October, and the attack caught only a single rearguard division. Assuming he had at least forced a Prussian retreat, Napoleon advanced cautiously towards Bernadotte, but Blücher ignored the presence of a large French army in his rear, and moved west to the River Saale before turning south for Leipzig. *See* **Map 25**.

Duckworth, John Thomas (1748–1817)

Controversial **Royal Navy** commander who was a captain at the Battle of the **First of June** in 1794, and served in the **Mediterranean** Fleet under **Jervis**, leading naval elements during the capture of **Minorca** in 1798 and subsequently commanding a battleship squadron on the island. He went to the **West Indies** to lead forces occupying Scandinavian possessions in 1801, and returned to the Mediterranean as **Collingwood's** second-in-command, and a vice-admiral, from 1805. His hitherto excellent reputation was ruined by failure to attack Constantinople after forcing the **Dardanelles** in spring 1807, and he was not given another important combat post, although he ended his career in command of the lucrative Jamaica station.

Dugommier, Jacques (1738–94)

A veteran of the Seven Years War, Dugommier was a French colonial administrator in 1789, but returned to **France** in 1791 and rejoined the army. Promoted divisional general and given command of the **Toulon** siege in November 1793, he led the port's recapture in December, before transferring to command French forces on the eastern sector of the **Pyrenean** front. His victories at **Le Boulon** and **St Laurent** had driven Spanish forces back across the frontier by autumn, but he was killed by **mortar** fire around **Figueras** on 17 November.

Duhesme, Philibert Guillaume (1766–1815)

An officer in the French **National Guard** from 1789, Duhesme was a brigadier-general at

Fleurus in 1794, and served on the **Rhine** front before taking part in the **Italian campaigns** against the **Second Coalition**. He remained in Italy until 1808, when he was transferred to the **Peninsular** theatre, where he used subterfuge to seize the fortress of Barcelona during the initial French invasion of **Spain**. He was governor of the city until 1810, when he was recalled to France to face corruption charges, which effectively suspended his career until 1813, when he became governor of Kehl. Duhesme was recalled to field command during the 1814 campaign for **France**, when he led a division of **Victor's** corps at **Brienne** and **La Rothière**. He had risen to command two divisions of the **Young Guard** by 1815, when he fought with **Napoleon** at **Ligny** and at **Waterloo**, where he was fatally wounded.

Dumas, Mathieu (1753–1837)

Minor French noble, commissioned into the pre-revolutionary French Army in 1773, who ultimately became **Napoleon's** leading military supply specialist. He fought the **First Coalition** on the **Rhine**, but was exiled from 1793 to 1794 and from 1797 to 1799. Recalled by Napoleon and given a brigade command under **Macdonald** in Switzerland, he was entrusted with the formation of Napoleon's Reserve Army for the **Italian campaign** in 1800, and was the **Grande Armée's** quartermaster-general during the 1805 campaign against the **Third Coalition**.

Dumas was Joseph **Bonaparte's** war minister in **Naples** from 1806, and followed him to the **Peninsular** theatre in 1808. As **Victor's** chief of staff, he triggered the pursuit of **Moore's** British force to **Corunna** by redeploying I Corps on his own initiative (*see* **Peninsular War**). Returned to administrative duties with the Grande Armée from 1809, Dumas proved equal to his greatest challenge in 1812, when he organized the provision of equipment, supplies and long-range supply systems for some 600,000 men during the **Russian campaign**. Captured at **Leipzig** in 1813, he was released in 1814 and rejoined Napoleon as commander of the **National Guard** during the **Hundred Days** of 1815. Retired from military command after **Waterloo**, he pursued a political career in Paris until his retirement in 1832.

Dumerbion, Pierre Jadart (1737–97)

Veteran French officer who spent much of his career in the American colonies before appointment to divisional command in May 1793. Appointed C-in-C with the Army of Italy the following January, he handled the poisoned chalice with great caution, following the recommendations of government-appointed political advisers whenever possible. They in turn relied for strategic advice on **Napoleon**, the army's **artillery** commander, whose direction of the year's **Italian** operations enabled Dumerbion to hand over command to **Kellermann** with his reputation intact in November. Quick to give Napoleon credit for his success, the old general retired immediately.

Dumouriez, Charles François (1739–1823)

The most successful French general at the start of the **Revolutionary Wars**, Dumouriez had joined the royal **cavalry** in 1758 and became a major-general in 1788. As governor of the naval base at Cherbourg, he joined the local **National Guard** in 1789 and was subsequently elected to the **National Convention**, becoming foreign minister in the Girondist government of 1792.

Anxious to halt the **French Revolution's** rapid radicalization, Dumouriez helped persuade **Louis XVI** to take responsibility for the Convention's declaration of war on **Francis II** in April, before taking command of field forces on the north-eastern frontier. Ambitious and energetic, he led French armies to victory at **Valmy** in September, and masterminded the conquest of **Belgium** before the end of the year. His political influence at its peak, he proposed and organized an invasion of the **Netherlands** for early 1793, and returned to Paris to work against the king's execution.

Failure made him a marked man among the increasingly powerful **Jacobin** radicals, and he was ordered back to the front in February 1793. He faced arrest and probable execution after his invasion of Holland collapsed at **Neerwinden**, and made an unsuccessful bid to rally his army for a march on Paris before fleeing to Austrian lines on 5 April. He never returned to **France**. Shunned as a traitor by the continental monarchs, he eventually settled in Britain from 1800, but his only active contribution to the allied war effort was as an occasional adviser to **Peninsular War** commanders.

Duncan, Adam (1731–1804)

British admiral, a Scot born in Dundee, who had seen many minor actions but no major fleet engagements during a long career before his recall from half-pay to command the **Royal Navy**'s new North Sea Fleet in 1795. Charged with maintaining a **blockade** against the newly hostile **Dutch Navy**, he earned national renown for patrolling the Dutch coast with only two ships during the **Nore** mutiny of 1797, and for inflicting a comprehensive defeat on de **Winter**'s fleet off **Camperdown** that October. Ennobled by a grateful monarch, Duncan retired from his command in 1801.

Dundas, David (1735–1820)

British artillery officer, a major-general from 1790, who was responsible for such tactical reform as had been undertaken by the **British Army** at the start of the **Revolutionary Wars**. His books of drill instructions, the first produced in 1788, were standard army issue and insisted on the use of line formation for attacking purposes. Though they introduced a broader line of only two ranks' depth, they were otherwise a tribute to anachronistic **Prussian Army** methods, and were to be superseded by the more flexible, pragmatic approach to **infantry tactics** associated with **Moore**, **Craufurd** and **Wellington**. After seeing action at **Corsica** and during the **Flanders campaign** in 1794, he was promoted lieutenant-general in 1797, took part in the **North Holland** campaign of 1799 and became a full general in 1802. He held the largely honorary command of English home forces from 1809 until his retirement in 1811.

Dundas, Henry (1742–1811)

Scots lawyer who was an abidingly powerful member of the **Pitt** government in **Great Britain**, first as Home Secretary (1791–4) and then as war minister (1794–1801). In the latter capacity he maintained a notoriously effective network of spies and informants, but was the principal promoter of an unfocused imperial strategy that frittered away British resources on a variety of small-scale **colonial** or marginal European adventures. Dundas was ennobled as Viscount Melville in 1802, while in opposition with Pitt, but returned to government as First Lord of the Admiralty (naval minister) in 1804. His tenure ended in 1806 when he was charged with corruption, but he was acquitted of major charges (though found guilty of negligence) and resumed his long-held place on the royal advisory Privy Council from 1807.

Dunkirk, Siege of

Attack on the French Channel port of Dunkirk in autumn 1793 by the Duke of **York**'s British, **Hanoverian** and Dutch army in **Flanders**. After a dispute over strategic priorities, the allied offensive into north-eastern France of August 1793 was split into two. **Saxe-Coburg**'s Austrian troops remained on the French frontier, besieging **Quesnoy**, while York's 50,000 men marched north to invest Dunkirk, a very British strategic priority. After a series of hard-won victories against outpost defences in late August, the **siege** got properly under way once **Royal Navy** support arrived at the end of the month. Siege guns were in position from 3 September, but French communications remained open to the southwest, enabling reinforcements and a new command team (**Souham** and **Hoche**) to reach the garrison. After the portion of his army guarding communications had been defeated at **Hondschoote** on 8 September, York abandoned the siege and retired to defensive positions in Flanders. *See* **Map 2**.

Dupont, Pierre (1765–1840)

French soldier, originally commissioned into the Dutch Army in 1784. He joined the **French Army** in 1791, achieved divisional command in 1797, and was **Berthier**'s chief of staff during the **Italian campaign** of 1800, fighting at **Marengo**, before leading the French reoccupation of **Tuscany**. Dupont played an important part in the campaign against the **Third Coalition** of 1805, leading his division at **Albeck** and saving **Gazan**'s division at **Dürrenstein**. He fought at **Halle** in 1806, and at **Friedland** in 1807, before taking part in the invasion of **Portugal**, and was ennobled as the Comte de l'Etang in 1808. His career collapsed with defeat by Spanish rebel forces at **Bailén** in July, and he was imprisoned until the **abdication** of 1814. Briefly minister of war, he fled into exile during the **Hundred Days** of 1815, but returned to pursue a long and active political career.

Dürrenstein, Battle of

The only independent attack undertaken by General **Kutuzov's** Russian army during the War of the **Third Coalition**. French forward units, led by **Murat** and **Lannes**, had been in pursuit of Kutuzov's 40,000 men since late October, when Austrian capitulation at **Ulm** had left the Russians in an exposed position south of the Danube. Murat and Lannes caught the Russians at **Amstetten** on 5 November, but were unable to force a major engagement, and then ignored standing orders in pursuit of the militarily irrelevant prize of **Vienna**. That left **Mortier's** recently formed VIII Corps isolated north of the Danube, with its four divisions stretched along a broad front and the whole Russian army in close proximity.

Kutuzov was determined to avoid a major battle until he had made contact with General **Buxhowden's** 30,000 reinforcements, advancing slowly from the Russian frontier, but turned and struck General **Gazan's** isolated division near Dürrenstein on the morning of 11 November. Gazan's 5,000 men (with Mortier in personal command) were outnumbered eight to one, supported by only ten cannon and trapped with their backs to the river, but they held off Russian attacks until dusk, suffering 3,000 casualties and inflicting 4,000. As annihilation loomed, the arrival of General **Dupont's** division persuaded Kutuzov to break off the engagement and continue his withdrawal, but the impulsive Murat found himself the object of **Napoleon's** fury for the second time in a month (*see* Battle of **Albeck**). *See* **Map 12**.

Dutch Navy

Though small, the Dutch Navy had been responsible for elevating the independent **Netherlands** to world-power status in the seventeenth and early eighteenth centuries, and still enjoyed a very high reputation at the start of the **Revolutionary Wars**. Its 44 **ships-of-the-line**, 43

frigates and 100 smaller ships were well-maintained, crewed and commanded, and performed with a confidence built on a long tradition of fighting the British **Royal Navy** on equal terms.

Allied to the British from 1793, Dutch warships played little active role in the War of the **First Coalition** before the French conquest of the Netherlands in early 1795, when the icebound main fleet was captured at **Texel**. A total of 31 battleships, 18 frigates, 16 **corvettes**, 33 armed brigs and 72 **gunboats** came under French control, along with about 25,000 crewmen and two regiments of **marines** (subsequently transferred to army service).

Dutch naval personnel were generally antirepublican, and their commanders were regarded with increasing suspicion by French authorities as ships and morale degenerated through inactivity. Locked in port by a British **blockade**, while plans to aid French forces in the invasion of **England** came to nothing and occasional **colonial** losses dampened spirits still further, the main fleet ventured out of Texel only as a means of maintaining operational readiness.

The comprehensive defeat of Admiral de **Winter's** sortie off **Camperdown** in October 1797 ended any prospect of a major Dutch fleet action against the Royal Navy, and the capture of another seven battleships, 18 frigates, many small craft and 6,000 sailors during the allied **North Holland** expedition in August 1799 sealed the navy's decline.

Dutch vessels on colonial service enjoyed little success. A major attempt to rescue the **Cape Colony** ended disastrously on 17 August 1796, when three battleships, two frigates and four sloops were forced to surrender to a larger British force. Dutch naval forces in the **Indian Ocean** suffered steady attrition at the hands of the British, culminating in the fall of Java in 1811.

Surviving European warships functioned primarily as a coastal defence force from 1800, and were harnessed to enforcement of the **Continental System** until their absorption by French imperial forces in 1810. Reconstituted as an independent force in early 1814, the navy's confidence had been permanently undermined, and it never again aspired to global influence.

E

Eagles *See* **Standards** (Military)

Eastern Question

Contemporary euphemism for the problems and potential surrounding the presumed imminent collapse of the **Ottoman Empire**, which in fact survived until 1918.

Ebelsberg, **Battle of** *See* Battle of **Ebersberg**.

Ebersberg, Battle of

The town of Ebersberg (or Ebelsberg) stands just south of the Danube at its junction with the River Traun, about halfway between **Ratisbon** and Vienna (*see* **Map 12**). On 3 May 1809, in the aftermath of French victories at **Abensberg** and **Eckmühl**, it was the scene of a major rearguard action by retreating Austrian forces under General **Hiller**, who was trying to delay the French army's advance on Vienna.

Hiller's closest pursuers were **Masséna's** 21,000 troops, but by the time the Austrians turned to face them at the Traun, drawing up 40,000 men and 70 guns on the east bank, a temporary French formation led by **Lannes** was racing for a river crossing just north of Ebersberg and an attack on the Austrian rear. After a preliminary action at Wels on 2 May, Masséna launched a full-scale frontal assault across the Ebersberg bridge next morning. The bridge was stormed at ten, and the leading French divisions eventually won control of Ebersberg at a cost of almost 3,000 casualties, killing perhaps 2,000 defenders and capturing another 4,000. Hiller made no attempt to commit his main body, deployed on a ridge just beyond the town, and later withdrew

safely towards Vienna. Masséna's clumsily executed victory robbed Lannes of a potentially much greater triumph, but he knew nothing of Lannes's plans and might not have been given another chance to bring Hiller to battle.

Eckmühl, Battle of

The climax to the War of the **Fifth Coalition's** confused opening phase, fought on 22 April 1809 around the north Bavarian town of Eckmühl. **Napoleon's** arrival at the front on 17 April had restored coherence to French manoeuvres, but three days later the French emperor mistakenly assumed that Austrian forces under Archduke **Charles** had been decisively beaten at **Abensberg**. In fact Charles was still at the head of some 80,000 troops, and advancing on Marshal **Davout's** reduced III Corps to the north of the main French army around Landshut.

Davout's 20,000 men held off Austrian attacks throughout 21 April, receiving only minor reinforcements while the rest of the army waited to pounce on Charles's anticipated retreat. Napoleon eventually recognized the threat to Davout in the small hours of 22 April, and issued immediate orders directing all available forces towards Eckmühl for an attack on the Austrian flank.

Charles began redeploying his forces that morning, intending to leave 40,000 men facing Davout while the remainder moved west to Abbach, hoping to block the path of French reinforcements. Before these manoeuvres were properly under way, Napoleon and the main French army appeared from the south at about one thirty in the afternoon. Pinned down by an immediate frontal attack from the whole of Davout's command, which made impressive progress despite its numerical inferiority, Charles could do little to protect his southern flank, which was attacked later in the afternoon by **Lannes** and some 30,000 troops. With support from **Lefebvre** on the opposite flank, Lannes took the town of Eckmühl by nightfall. Charles was compelled to withdraw his army, shorn of some 12,000 men, towards the Danube overnight, but French forces were incapable of serious pursuit before the following morning, when most of the army was set on the road to **Ratisbon**. *See* **Map 12**.

'Egalité', Louis-Philippe (1773–1850)

The future King Louis-Philippe of the French was the eldest son of the Duc d'Orléans, the most politically radical member of the French royal family during the early years of the **French Revolution**. Like his father, he renounced his noble titles and adopted the nickname 'Egalité', although hostile royalists and **Jacobins** tended to call him the Duc de Chartres. He fought in the opening campaigns of the **Revolutionary Wars** as a divisional commander under **Dumouriez**, but his background inevitably aroused the suspicions of an increasingly radical government, and under threat of arrest he fled to the Austrian lines with his chief. After spells living in Switzerland, the USA and England, he married the daughter of Neapolitan king **Ferdinand** in 1809, and was restored to his estates after 1815, weathering royal displeasure to live in Paris until the revolution of 1830 that brought him to power.

Egypt

A province of the **Ottoman Empire** since 1517, Egypt was a semi-autonomous cauldron of political turmoil throughout the period. The regionally dominant **Mameluke** caste, led by **Ibrahim Bey** and **Murad Bey**, had declared independence and been overthrown by a Turkish invasion in 1786, but returned to power as Ottoman subjects when a plague killed the imperial governor in 1791.

Ibrahim and Murad cooperated with Turkish forces against **Napoleon**'s invasion of the **Middle East** from 1798, forming temporary alliances with various tribal groups, but their power struggle was resumed after French withdrawal in 1801. As the Mamelukes (sometimes with British support) sought to regain control of the country, an Albanian force sent to Egypt by the sultan eventually came under the command of Mehmet Ali, who formed an alliance with Ibrahim's faction to defeat three successive Ottoman expeditions.

The return of prominent Mameluke exile Mahommed Bey al-Alfi from Britain in February 1804 triggered factional war. Mehmet Ali seized power in the name of the Egyptian people, forming a temporary alliance with Ottoman forces to drive al-Alfi and Ibrahim out of the country. The alliance broke down after a Kurdish army was landed to assist it, and provoked popular revolt by its excesses against civilians. Mehmet Ali was proclaimed governor, and organized a massacre of Mameluke leaders that seemed to secure his hold on power, despite British pressure in favour of al-Alfi, whose death in 1806 defeated the purpose of a British expeditionary force that reached Egypt in 1807.

Once the British had withdrawn in September 1807, Mehmet was able to impose his rule on Egypt without serious interruption. Another massacre of their leaders in 1811 persuaded surviving Mamelukes to settle in the south of the country, signalling a permanent decline in their power, and though almost constantly at war with someone, Mehmet ruled until his death in 1849. *See* **Map 7**.

El Arish, Convention of

Preliminary treaty signed between the **Ottoman Empire** and French C-in-C **Kléber** on 21 January 1800 that allowed for the peaceful evacuation of French forces from the **Middle East**. The treaty was largely the work of **Royal Navy** captain Sidney **Smith**, whose squadron had been supporting Turkish operations in the theatre, but who possessed no authority to make diplomatic agreements on such a scale. A British government with no intention of escorting French troops back to Europe refused to ratify the agreement, and hostilities were resumed at **Heliopolis** when the news got back to Cairo in late March.

El Bodón, Battle of

Minor **Peninsular War** engagement, fought on 25 September 1811, as allied and French forces competed for control of **Ciudad Rodrigo**, a vital **fortress** on the road into **Spain** from **Portugal**. Allied commander **Wellington** had been delayed by failure to take the other important stronghold at **Badajoz**, and **Picton's** Anglo-Portuguese detachment watching the Ciudad Rodrigo area was surprised by the arrival of **Marmont's** 50,000 troops around El Bodón. Attacked in scattered positions by **Montbrun's** 2,500 French **cavalry**, Picton's troops managed to escape with only minor losses after a skilled rearguard action, but the presence of Marmont's army ended any prospect of further allied advances that year.

Elan

French word, literally 'ardour' or 'dash', that became an internationally recognized contemporary term describing the attacking vigour of French land forces during their two decades of success up to 1812. Often considered a side effect of the patriotism unleashed by the **French Revolution**, French military *élan* of the period was much admired and imitated, but seldom equalled.

Elba

Small **Mediterranean** island, between the coasts of **Tuscany** and **Corsica**, that was a British naval base during the War of the **First Coalition**, but fell under French control from late 1796 (*see* **Map 8**). Neapolitan king **Ferdinand** formally ceded Elba to France by the 1801 **Florence** treaty, and annexation was completed in August 1802. Elba became a nominally independent state by the terms of **Napoleon's** first **abdication** in 1814, coming under his personal rule, though his government of the island's population (about 100,000 in 1800) was subject to supervision by the European **great powers**. Napoleon arrived on Elba under **Royal Navy** escort on 4 May, along with 600 members of the **Imperial Guard**, and immediately began planning its administrative system, but the island was near enough to France for him to keep in close touch with Parisian affairs. He received regular visits from soldiers, politicians, family members, and even his former lover Maria **Walewska**, so that he

was able to time his escape from Elba in late February 1815 to coincide with a resurgence in his popularity.

Elchingen, Battle of

Small but famous French victory over Austrian forces near **Ulm**, won on 14 October 1805 (*see* **Map 12**). The French advance west along either side of the Danube had suffered a setback at **Albeck** on 11 October, when frontline commanders **Murat** and **Ney** allowed General **Dupont's** division to become isolated north of the river. They were ordered to its relief when the advance was renewed on 14 October, and Ney tried to cross the Danube at Elchingen that morning, but found the bridge partly destroyed and 9,000 Austrian troops defending the north bank. Leading his men in person, Ney oversaw reconstruction of the bridge under heavy fire, marched troops across it and stormed the town, capturing two Austrian regiments and opening the way for Murat to relieve Dupont. Austrian forces were not given another opportunity to force a gap in the French cordon around Ulm, and Ney was later created Duke of Elchingen for his personal bravery during the action.

Embabeh, Battle of *See* Battle of the **Pyramids**

Emigrés

Those French citizens who fled the country for political reasons during and after the **French Revolution**. Though people of various classes and political persuasions quit **France** in numbers during the period, the term is usually associated with royalist exiles. Banned from France as a body on pain of imprisonment, or in particular cases death, they included most of the French nobility along with a significant number of administrators, military officers and experts from the middle ranks of royal service.

The Comte d'**Artois** and three other royal princes took self-imposed exile just after the fall of the Bastille in July 1789, triggering a first wave of noble departures, and the pattern was repeated after each of the revolution's dramatic upheavals. Although émigré agitation for a counter-revolutionary invasion enjoyed support from the minor Rhineland princes who were most directly threatened by French radicalism, it had little impact on the policies of European great powers, which had more selfish motives for forming the **First Coalition** against France.

Relentless émigré optimism nevertheless encouraged **Prussia** and **Austria** to misjudge the mood in Paris, and exiles helped draft the controversial Declaration of **Pillnitz** in 1791. They also formed themselves into small armies on the Rhine, and conducted a campaign to destabilize France from their headquarters at Koblenz, heightening French fears of an international conspiracy against the Revolution. Their international influence declined steadily after 1792, but they fought in independent units on the **Rhine** front from 1793 to 1797, made strenuous efforts to rouse popular support by infiltrating regional communities, and were involved in a number of abortive invasion attempts, usually with British aid and typified by the failure at **Quiberon** in 1795.

Emigré numbers mounted through the last years of the nineteenth century, as successive French regimes sought to purge themselves of potential enemies, but **Napoleon**'s determination to place his regime above factionalism prompted efforts at reconciliation under the **Consulate** and empire. Beginning with a series of amnesties issued between March 1800 and April 1802, Napoleon reduced the list of those banished to counter-revolutionary leaders and clergymen who refused to accept the **Concordat**. By offering restitution of property not already sold off, or first options to repurchase, he attracted the majority of exiles (perhaps 40,000 people) back to France over the next ten years.

A minority of royalists at large, mostly nobles in senior Bourbon service, continued to plot for restoration throughout the Napoleonic period, and any hope of diehards accepting amnesty evaporated in 1804 after the **Cadoudal** conspiracy of 14 January and the Duc d'**Enghein**'s execution. Emigrés eventually returned to France as a group on the restoration of King **Louis XVIII** in 1814. They formed a class of reactionary office-holders and courtiers whose predatory reclamation of privileges encouraged Napoleon's return in 1815, and who were sponsors of a **White Terror** against former republicans after the second restoration.

Emmendlingen, Battle of

The only defeat suffered by **Moreau**'s French army from the **Rhine** during its offensive into southern Germany in autumn 1796. After checking General Latour's pursuit from the east at **Biberach** in early October, Moreau got his retreating army through the Black Forest and back to Freiburg by 13 October, outpacing an attempt by Archduke **Charles** to get behind him from the north. Joining forces north of Freiburg, Charles and Latour launched attacks against Moreau's march beyond the River Elz towards Strasbourg on 19 October. Struggling through heavy rain and marshy ground, the Austrian right wing made no progress against **Desaix**, but French troops were forced out of Emmendlingen in the centre, and a counter-attack by **Gouvion St Cyr** only temporarily delayed the right's collapse around Waldkirch. Moreau withdrew across the Elz that evening, and divided his army after its right wing was further penetrated next day, sending Desaix west across the Rhine and moving his remaining divisions some 40km south to **Schliengen** by 22 October. *See* **Map 4**.

Enghein, Louis Antoine Henri de Bourbon Condé, Duc d' (1772–1804)

French nobleman, a distant relation of the royal family, who quit France with his parents in 1792 and subsequently fought with **émigré** forces on the **Rhine**. He retired to the town of Ettenheim in **Baden** when the royalist army was disbanded after the Peace of **Lunéville** in 1801. In early 1804, after exposure of the **Cadoudal** and **Pichegru** conspiracies, **Napoleon** chose to accept flimsy evidence of Enghein's implication in the plots. He was abducted from Ettenheim by French troops on the night of 14–15 March, taken to France and tried by a military court in Vincennes. Denied a defence lawyer, he was found guilty of treason and shot on 21 March. Intended to discourage royalist sedition, and carried out despite opposition from many of his closest advisers, Napoleon's illegal abduction and judicial murder of Enghein backfired. A diplomatic disaster that outraged international opinion and contributed to the formation of the **Third Coalition** against France, it also undermined Napoleon's subsequent efforts to lure influential émigrés back into imperial service.

Engineers

Specialist forces, often known as 'sappers', employed by contemporary armies for a wide variety of highly important tasks. These included the design, construction and supervision of **siege** works or static defences (of which **Wellington's** lines at **Torres Vedras** were perhaps the prime example), along with the building of bridges, roads and military facilities in general.

Engineering officers were technicians, trained in both the scientific and the military principles of their trade, and engineering troops in most armies received specialist training, with **miners** forming an essentially separate cadre within engineering corps. The particularly vital job of throwing **pontoon** or improvised bridges across rivers during frontline operations was generally entrusted to expert 'pontooneers' (*pontonniers*). Many of the manual duties associated with engineering work were carried out by less skilled 'pioneer' units, virtually labour battalions that often contained ill-trained conscripts, militia forces or **prisoners of war**.

Among Europe's major land forces, the **French Army** possessed the largest, best-equipped and most skilled engineering arm in Europe. It separated its engineers (but not its *pontonniers*) from the artillery arm in 1793, and subsequently maintained a single organization for sappers, miners and officers. French engineering troops were distributed at corps level in companies, with a substantial force kept back as a central reserve. The army deployed about 10,000 engineers at its peak in 1812, supported by a specialist engineering train for field work, an artisan company and a number of labour battalions.

The **Austrian Army's** engineering forces comprised a separate corps of officers controlling mining and sapper battalions, responsible for siege and field work respectively. These were augmented by pioneer units in wartime, usually drawn from militia, along with both regular and militia pontoon corps. **Russian Army** engineers were not organized as a separate regiment until 1812, although a pioneer regiment (including companies of miners) existed during the 1790s and there were two after 1806. The Engineer Corps of the **Prussian Army** consisted only of officers and sergeants, who controlled a Pioneer Corps that had expanded to include eight siege and ten field companies by 1815. The **British Army's** Royal Engineers was a very small but well-trained cadre of officers. The only troops directly at their disposal were ten companies of 'Artificers', craftsmen primarily concerned with the maintenance of fortifications, so that most engineering work in the field was carried out by unskilled infantry under officer supervision.

England, Invasion of

Fear of invasion across the English Channel was one of the principal motives behind **Great Britain's** enormous investment in the **Royal Navy**, and preventing any hostile power from controlling its southern ports was basic to British foreign policy. Failure to prevent French conquest of **Flanders** and the **Netherlands** by late 1795 placed Britain in a state of preliminary readiness for invasion, and an increasingly confident French **Directory** government began making concrete plans to mount one after the Peace of **Campo Formio** in October 1797.

An Army of England was called into being under rising star **Napoleon**, while Generals **Joubert** and Truguet were sent to encourage naval preparations in the Netherlands and **Spain** respectively. A fleet of specialized, flat-bottomed transport ships was put under construction at boatyards all along the southern Channel coast, but French authorities did not necessarily expect to need them, trusting in native republicanism or bankruptcy to implode Britain's war effort.

The threat of invasion at **Bantry Bay**, **Pembrokeshire** and **Killala Bay** in 1796–8 had the opposite effect, helping ignite patriotic defiance, and British responses to a **bank crisis** in February 1797 reduced the threat of sudden bankruptcy. Forced to think in strictly military terms, the republican government tested the viability of a seaborne invasion in spring 1798, when a dress rehearsal failed to take the lightly defended **Saint Marcoufe** islands, and the plan was effectively scrapped with the Directory's decision in April to support Napoleon's expedition to the **Middle East**.

The danger of invasion remained largely a figment of British **propaganda** until the **Amiens** peace collapsed in May 1803, when Napoleon began forming a new Army of England in camps at Boulogne and elsewhere on the Channel coast. French propaganda maintained an unceasingly confident line, but the enterprise faced the same practical difficulties of transporting such a big army across the sea and avoiding Royal Navy intervention.

More than 2,000 men were drowned when Napoleon ignored a gale to insist on a practical test of the landing craft in July 1804, and so the invasion was called off for that year. British defence preparations on land assumed crisis proportions, with mass training and recruitment of **militia** along the south coast supported by a chain of new **Martello towers**, but naval commanders remained confident that no fleet – let alone the clumsy, shallow craft being constructed in French-controlled Channel ports – could get past their swarms of patrolling warships.

Although he had assembled 177,000 men and 2,000 flat boats for the task by the end of 1804, Napoleon had also recognized that invasion was impossible as things stood. Far-fetched schemes for a Channel tunnel aside, his solution was a sophisticated decoy mission to lure the Royal Navy into giving up local superiority in the Channel for a few vital days. Launched by imperial decree on 22 March 1805, the campaign had misfired weeks before **Villeneuve**'s apocalyptic defeat at **Trafalgar** in October, and from late August Napoleon abandoned invasion plans and marched his army to fight the **Third Coalition**.

Britain remained self-consciously on the alert against attack until France lost control over the Low Countries in 1813–14, and the French regime never publicly admitted that invasion was impossible, but Napoleon's reliance on the **Continental System** to produce an economic victory reflected his recognition of the fact after 1805.

Erfurt, Congress of

Summit meeting between **Napoleon** and Russian tsar **Alexander I** that opened in late September 1808 at the German city of Erfurt (*see* **Map 16**), and sought to address a deterioration in Franco-Russian relations since their alliance at **Tilsit** in July 1807.

By mid-1808, anti-French feeling in St Petersburg had been revived by the damaging economic effects of adherence to the **Continental System**, along with growing doubts about Napoleon's intentions towards **Turkey** and **Poland**. Napoleon was meanwhile determined to keep Russia out of Turkey and in the Continental System, but needed Alexander's continued friendship as he prepared to strip imperial defences for the invasion of **Spain**.

Both monarchs reached Erfurt on 27 September, and two weeks of high pageant and hard bargaining followed. Alexander was not overawed as he had been at Tilsit, and matched Napoleon's obduracy on major issues. With the help of insider information supplied in secret by **Talleyrand**, who hoped to undermine what he considered Napoleon's expansionist folly, the tsar got the better of the uneasy compromise that emerged as the Convention of Erfurt, signed on 12 October.

Alexander approved Napoleon's forthcoming Spanish intervention, and made vague promises of support in the event of Austrian aggression. Napoleon accepted Russian expansion into Wallachia and Moldavia (modern Romania), and went some way towards satisfying Alexander's demands for a reduction in outstanding Prussian war indemnities. The central issue of Constantinople was pointedly ignored, and an appeal to British king **George III** for a general peace was a mere formality. They parted as allies on 14 October, never to meet again, but though Alexander's promise to police Austria seemed to give Napoleon the security he sought, Vienna's aggressive behaviour in 1809 met no resistance from Russia.

Erlon, Comte d' *See* **Drouet**, Jean-Baptiste

Escadrille Sacrée (Sacred Squadron)

Name given by **Napoleon** to a formation of 500 officers grouped as a **cavalry** unit during the desperate latter stages of the 1812 **Russian campaign**. Formed on 22 November 1812, shortly before the **Beresina** crossing, it was drawn from those officers who still had horses, and its troop commanders were all generals.

Espinosa, Battle of

The principal action of **Napoleon**'s 1808 **Peninsular War** offensive, fought on 10 November along the line of the River Ebro in Navarre (*see* **Map 22**). French plans to draw attacking

Spanish flank forces far from their bases before punching through the centre and encircling them had been upset by **Lefebvre's** unauthorized attacks on **Blake's** 30,000-strong army of Galicians and Asturians on the north-western wing. Blake's advance on Bilbao had been halted by a French attack at Pancorbo on 31 October, but he had interrupted his retreat to inflict a defeat on pursuing French forces at **Valmaseda** on 5 November. Four days later Blake halted at Espinosa, deployed his army in strong defensive positions, and prepared to face his pursuers again.

Victor's 21,000 men reached Espinosa on 10 November. Blake's troops (and six guns) held off attacks throughout the day and still occupied the town at nightfall, but a more carefully coordinated operation routed the Spaniards next morning. Blake suffered perhaps 3,000 casualties and lost another 8,000 men to **desertion**, but was able to escape to Reynosa and ultimately evaded three pursuing French corps to bring 10,000 survivors across the mountains to relative safety in León. Espinosa and the simultaneous triumph further east at **Gamonal** left Napoleon free to concentrate strength against the Spanish right pincer at **Tudela**.

Espionage

Spies of one sort or another were central to the intelligence-gathering operations of armies in the field and belligerent governments. Most overseas envoys were given government funds with which to pay networks of informers and bribe local officials, but though spies were able to transmit strategically important information to governments, the time taken for messages to travel long distances meant that espionage was generally most useful to army commanders operating close to hostile lines. Armies would send individual officers into hostile country on particular missions to report on geographical features or troop movements, while clandestine operatives would maintain written contacts with any friendly sources inside enemy territory. Disguised agents and native fifth columnists, closer to the professional spy of the twentieth century, were also employed by all sides, penetrating opposition high commands, fostering popular and political discontent or simply reporting on detailed dispositions in ports or armed camps.

Espoz y Mina, Don Francisco (1781–1836)

Spanish **guerrilla** commander, who fought with regular Aragonese forces for a time in 1808 before joining his nephew's partisan band, taking command in March 1810. Recognized as colonel-in-chief of partisans in Navarre by the **juntas** of Aragon and Castile in September, Espoz controlled an estimated 13,500 troops when his forces were absorbed by the regular **Spanish Army** in 1813. Forced into postwar French exile by the reactionary government of **Ferdinand VII**, he returned to Spain in 1833.

Ettlingen, Battle of

The climax of **Moreau's** offensive from the **Rhine** in summer 1796, a French attack on 9 July against Austro-German positions north of **Rastatt**. Austrian C-in-C Archduke **Charles** had joined General Latour's retreating corps on a line between Mühlberg and Ettlingen, bringing their combined strength to about 40,000 troops (almost half of them **cavalry**). Moreau's pursuing army, 65,000 strong with the arrival of **Gouvion St Cyr's** division, attacked the positions on 9 July. St Cyr pushed the allied left back from the Alb River north of Gernsbach, but a central attack by **Desaix** degenerated into a prolonged and bloody struggle for the village of Malsch, which changed hands several times but was held by Austrians at nightfall. Though hardly defeated, Charles gave orders on 12 July for his entire army's retirement to the Danube, leaving detachments guarding Mannheim, Philipsbourg and Stuttgart. As Charles marched to put himself between the French and Vienna, and rendezvous with the remnants of southern frontier forces beaten at **Haslach** on 14 July, Moreau took time to secure his lines of retreat before following. *See* Battle of **Neresheim**; **Map 3**.

Etruria *See* **Tuscany**

Eugen, Frederick Charles Paul Louis, Duke of Württemberg (1788–1857)

Though his father (the Prince of Württemberg) was a **Prussian Army** commander, who led reserve troops during the **Jena–Auerstädt campaign** of 1806, Eugen became a staff officer with the **Russian Army** in its aftermath. After serving on **Bennigsen's** staff, he was promoted to corps command after the Russian retreat from **Smolensk** in 1812, fighting at **Borodino**, **Krasnoe**, **Lützen** and **Bautzen**, after which he led the rearguard during the allied retreat. He commanded troops guarding the allied army's flank during its attack on **Dresden** in August 1813, suffering defeat at **Pirna** but taking part in the victory at **Kulm**, and was at **Leipzig** in October. Prominent during the invasion of France in 1814, particularly at **Arcis-sur-Aube**, he retired to write his memoirs after **Napoleon**'s abdication in April.

Eylau, Battle of

Major engagement between French and Prussian forces on 7–8 February 1807, fought around the East Prussian town of Preussiches Eylau (*see* **Map 17**). Anxious to bring the War of the **Fourth Coalition** to a speedy conclusion, **Napoleon** pursued Russian forces north towards Königsberg through bitter winter conditions after failing to surprise them at **Ionkovo** on 3 February. French vanguards brushed with Russian troops on 6 February at Hoff, where both sides lost more than 2,000 men, and commander **Bennigsen** opted to make a stand when the Russian retreat reached Eylau that evening.

Though glad to accept battle, Napoleon could muster only 30,000 men (under **Soult** and **Murat**) against Bennigsen's 67,000 when fighting began on the afternoon of 7 February, as a minor skirmish escalated to become a more general conflict around the town graveyard. It changed hands several times before Bennigsen withdrew his forward units to the ridge beyond Eylau, giving the French possession of the town for the remainder of the night. By the time fighting died down both sides had lost about 4,000 men.

Apart from those French troops billeted in town buildings, both sides passed the night in bitter cold. Winter conditions had also stranded French supply trains far from the front, while Russian logistics were anyway in chaos, so that both armies were desperately short of food. Another 15,000 French troops had arrived that evening, while **Davout**'s 15,000 men were due next day and **Ney**'s corps just to the north-west was busy preventing General Lestoq's 9,000 Prussians from linking up with Bennigsen.

Largely because blizzard conditions made overview impossible, eye-witness accounts of the battle fought on 8 February differ widely, and controversy surrounds many aspects of the engagement. It is generally assumed that Davout and Ney brought most or all of their troops into the battle during the course of the day, and that Bennigsen was eventually joined by Lestoq's Prussians, bringing each side up to a total strength of about 75,000 men. Napoleon was definitely outnumbered during the first part of the day, and the Russians always held a considerable advantage in **artillery**, with 460 guns against about 200.

Able to make out the Russian formations occupying a ridge some 1,200m away, Napoleon concentrated his available forces on heights just north of the town to face a frontal attack, relying on Ney and Davout to arrive on his flanks. Bennigsen launched an artillery barrage from eight a.m., but his massed batteries proved relatively easy targets for French counter-fire, and Soult's corps on the French left was able to undertake a preliminary attack. It was driven back when Russian infantry charged to the assault at about nine, and Davout's leading division (Friant) was met by a strong cavalry attack from the Russian left wing at about the same time.

To relieve pressure on both his flanks, Napoleon ordered the 9,000 men of **Augereau**'s VII Corps to attack the centre through the blizzard. Marching blind, they veered slightly off course, losing contact with **St Hilaire**'s supporting division and advancing directly into massed Russian artillery fire. Augereau himself was wounded as VII Corps lost at least 5,000 men in an hour (many to French gunners firing into the gloom) before reeling back into Eylau, pursued by **Doctorov**'s Russian infantry reserve.

Fighting had again focused on the graveyard when Napoleon, down to his last attacking option, committed Murat's cavalry reserve to a charge against the Russian centre. Murat's 10,500 horsemen swept forward in two columns at eleven thirty, smashing through forward Russian infantry and overwhelming the largest (70-gun) artillery battery before turning and charging back through the shattered ranks.

One of the most celebrated cavalry charges in European history, it cost 1,500 casualties but enabled Napoleon to stabilize his position at a vital time.

By early afternoon Davout's corps was advancing on the Russian left, forcing Bennigsen to bend his line at right angles and opening a period of heavy generalized fighting. Increasing French numbers gradually told, but Lestoq's Prussians joined the fight more than two hours before the first of Ney's troops reached the battlefield, and the Russians had conceded only a few hundred metres when fighting died down at around eleven that night.

Bennigsen withdrew his army overnight, providing technical justification for French claims to a victory at Eylau, but posterity has treated the battle as a ghastly draw. Though the **Grande Armée** inflicted an estimated 15,000 casualties over the two days, it lost at least as many troops (perhaps even 25,000) and was far too exhausted to mount any sort of pursuit. Severely damaged, both armies returned to winter quarters to prepare for a decisive confrontation in the spring (*see* Battle of **Friedland**).

F

Fassbender, Mathias von (1764–1840)
Austrian civil servant, a minor Rhineland noble who became an official with the **Holy Roman Empire's** war department after French forces occupied his home town of Trier. He organized intelligence operations for Archduke **Charles** during the **Rhine campaign** of 1796, and was appointed the archduke's personal adviser in 1799. When Charles took control of the **Austrian Army** in 1801 Fassbender was given wide-ranging powers of administrative reform. Seen by some contemporaries and historians as the guiding influence behind the archduke's policies up to 1805, he was an efficient bureaucrat but made a predictably large collection of enemies among an army establishment always suspicious of civilian interference. He was forced to resign in March 1805, a victim of the emperor's decision to support **Mack's** war party, and never regained imperial favour.

Fédérés

Contemporary name given to the volunteer recruits who flocked to serve the **French Army** at the start of the War of the **First Coalition**. Directed by the government simply to present themselves at the frontier and save the nation from allied invasion, they generally had little training or equipment when called upon to fight, and at first displayed understandable instability in the face of hostile fire. The fédérés held their ground under attack for the first time at **Valmy** in September 1792, when their ranks were stiffened by the elder **Kellermann's** deployment of regular units in their midst, an expedient that quickly became standard practice. *See also* **Infantry Tactics**.

Ferdinand IV, King (1751–1825)

The Bourbon King of **Naples** and **Sicily** (as Ferdinand III) since 1759, when his father became King Charles III of Spain, Ferdinand was primarily interested in hunting and farming, and known to his subjects as *il lazzaroni* ('the yokel'). Guided after their marriage in 1768 by his Habsburg wife Maria Carolina, he allowed her to steer Neapolitan foreign policy away from **Spain** and towards **Austria**. He shared his wife's extreme distaste for liberal ideas, and their attempts to suppress mounting popular radicalism contributed to his enforced exile in 1798–9 and again from 1806 until 1815. On both occasions he took refuge in Sicily, where his government style was tempered by reliance on military support from the liberally inclined British. Amid rising internal violence, he handed power to his eldest son as regent from 1809, agreed to a liberal constitution on his return to the throne in 1812 and accepted the queen's exile in 1813. She died in September 1814, and Ferdinand married his mistress before returning to power over the 'Two Sicilies' following **Murat's** fall in 1815. His subsequent reversion to repression undid most of the liberal reform undertaken in both kingdoms during the war years, and they were plagued by bitter civil unrest throughout the next decade.

Ferdinand VII, King (1784–1833)

The eldest son of King **Charles IV** of **Spain**. Ferdinand's young adult life was dominated by almost permanent conflict with his father. Their feud culminated in an unsuccessful conspiracy against chief minister **Godoy** in 1807 that ended with Ferdinand's arrest for treason. Despite a temporary reconciliation, the court soon reverted to an atmosphere of malevolent intrigue, father and son expecting assassination by the other's agents. The political chaos developing around their feud, and their appeals to **Napoleon** for mediation, paved the way for French invasion in 1808.

Ferdinand claimed the throne for a short period after Charles's abdication in March 1808, but was deposed at the **Bayonne** Conference in May, and news of his replacement by Joseph **Bonaparte** sparked Spanish rebellion against French occupation. He cut an unappealing figure – unintelligent, unattractive, reactionary and more inclined to petulance than firmness – but his consistent opposition to Godoy ensured mass support among a disaffected but staunchly royalist population throughout the **Peninsular War**.

From May 1808 Ferdinand endured virtual imprisonment at **Talleyrand**'s French estate in Valençay, France, but was restored to the throne in 1814. Rejecting the liberal Constitution of Cadiz granted by Napoleon in 1812, his reign was characterized by diehard conservative repression, interrupted only by a brief period of constitutional government following a popular rebellion in 1820. His death, without a male heir, plunged Spain into a six-year war of succession.

Ferrol Raid

Abortive attempt by 13,000 British troops, with **Royal Navy** support, to seize the north-western Spanish naval base of Ferrol in August 1800 (*see* **Map 8**). Intended as a blow that would knock the wavering Spanish government out of its unpopular alliance with France, and originally proposed by naval authorities, the operation was carried out without any foreknowledge of the terrain, garrison strengths or the port's extremely strong fortifications. Landing on the coast near Ferrol on 18 August, C-in-C General Pulteney quickly recognized that his force was too small for the task, and re-embarked after a few skirmishes with Spanish outpost troops and arguments with naval officers bent on **prize money**. The force was then directed south to **Cadiz**.

Fichte, Johann Gottlieb (1762–1814)

German philosopher, born in **Saxony**, who was a disciple of Emmanuel Kant in his youth, and elaborated on his mentor's work to identify the metaphysical (and morally decisive) concept of ego with that of a united German nation. Forced from his post at the University of Jena by accusations of atheism in 1799, he spent the rest of his life in Berlin, apart from a brief period of exile during the French occupation of 1806–7. He delivered a celebrated and influential series of 'Addresses to the German Nation' in 1807–8, calling for pan-German unity in opposition to French imperialism, and in 1810 became rector of the new Berlin University, which emerged as a focal point for patriotic and anti-French opinion in **Prussia**.

Field Train

Contemporary term for a field army's mobile support services, responsible for delivering weapons, ammunition, horses, engineering equipment and supplies to fighting formations. Most continental European armies maintained a permanent field train in peacetime, usually equipped with sufficient men, wagons and horses to meet a sudden emergency, though financial constraints meant they were often cut back beyond usefulness. The **French Army**'s commitment to securing military supplies, as well as provisions, from wherever it was operating reduced the importance of slow-moving, undermanned field trains before 1812 and contributed to its superior operational mobility.

Fifth Coalition, War of the

The fifth combination of European powers against post-revolutionary **France** was formed in April 1809, when **Austria** formally joined **Great Britain** at war against **Napoleon**, and ended by the Treaty of **Schönbrunn** in October, when the French emperor dictated terms to the defeated Austrians.

Austria's decision to resume its struggle against France was not unexpected. The punitive Peace of **Pressburg** in 1805 had guaranteed future ill-feeling in Vienna, and three years of intensive reform under Archduke **Charles** had since improved the **Austrian Army**. Charles himself remained adamant that it was not ready to take on the French, but from late 1808 the court was dominated by an increasingly confident war party.

The opening stages of the **Peninsular War** had spread French military resources dangerously thin, and Napoleon was thought unlikely to raise more than 200,000 men for a campaign in Germany. Meanwhile defeats at **Bailén** and **Vimeiro** had severely weakened the **French Army**'s aura of invincibility, and the French people were reported (by **Talleyrand** to **Metternich**) as deeply war-weary. There were also signs of popular, nationalist support for war among the Habsburg Empire's German speakers, and there were hopes that the subject peoples of western Germany were ready to rebel against French rule. Most importantly, a New Year meeting with Tsar **Alexander I** confirmed that he would remain neutral, despite the **Erfurt** agreement of autumn 1808. Thus fortified, Emperor **Francis** and the **Aulic Council** made a secret commitment to war on 8 February 1809.

Napoleon had been anticipating trouble from Vienna since 1806, and news of Austrian preparations brought him back to Paris from **Spain** in January 1809. Mass **conscription** had brought a total 270,000 men under arms in the previous four months, and he set about expanding **Davout**'s Army of the Rhine with conscripts and veterans from Spain.

A scratch occupation force of some 100,000 men in January, Davout's command had become a strike force of about 175,000 troops concentrated in southern and central Germany by early April. Reorganized into four corps (under Davout, **Masséna**, **Lefebvre** and **Oudinot**), it was commanded by **Berthier** pending Napoleon's arrival at the front. Napoleon could also call on 16,000 men in northern Germany under **Bernadotte**, **Poniatowski**'s 18,000 Polish troops in the east, more than 10,000 men in **Illyria** under **Marmont** and 68,000 occupying Italy.

Against French expectations that Austrian forces would be divided about equally between the German and Italian fronts, only 50,000 regular troops and 50,000 **Landwehr** had been sent to Italy under Archduke **John**. Archduke **Ferdinand** commanded another 40,000 guarding the emperor's Polish interests, but Charles could call on some 200,000 men for an attack in Germany. Fortunately for Napoleon, it was delayed by frequent changes of campaign strategy during March 1809.

The first plan agreed by the Aulic Council envisioned an attack by all eight of Charles's corps on Davout's Rhine army, but the centre of operations was moved to the Danube once it became clear that **Prussia** would not join the war to protect the northern flank. After prolonged arguments, the high command eventually ordered two corps (about 58,000 men) to attack from north of the Danube, with the river crossing at Ratisbon as their primary target, sent three more (66,000 troops) against the town from the south, and deployed another three (60,000 troops) for a drive on Landshut further south.

Napoleon expected to be attacked in the Upper Danube region on or around 15 April, though he had little precise knowledge of Austrian plans or positions. He intended to remain on the defensive in Italy while his German army absorbed and then reversed an offensive on the Danube. On 30 March, still in Paris to avoid triggering Austrian action too soon, he ordered Berthier to deploy around the Upper Danube region, with a centre of operations at Ratisbon, in a version of the **Bataillon Carré** formation first employed during the 1806 **Jena–Auerstädt campaign**.

Poor weather, interfering with **semaphore** operations, caused the emperor's orders to reach the front out of sequence, and Berthier, whose lack of aptitude for field command belied his administrative qualities, became confused. When the Austrian attack came earlier than expected, on 9 April, French commanders were in process of carrying out a series of conflicting instructions that left Davout and Lefebvre dangerously isolated to the north around Ratisbon and Landshut.

The attack was launched without a formal declaration of war, and a message of Austrian intentions was delivered to the French envoy in Munich only on 11 April, by which time Charles's main advance south of the Danube was across the

River Inn and approaching the River Isar. Despite Napoleon's instructions to concentrate at the Lech in the event of a surprise attack, Berthier fanned his army out to meet all approaches.

Only the slow pace of Austrian advance saved the French from being caught scattered all over the region. The Austrian centre finally came within skirmishing range of Lefebvre's forward positions at the Isar on 16 April, and crossed the river that evening. Hastened by appeals from Berthier, Napoleon reached the battle zone next day, just as the Austrians were poised to drive a wedge between Davout and Lefebvre to the north and the rest of the army further south.

Napoleon's first instinct was to order a rapid concentration of his army behind the River Ilm, about halfway between Ratisbon and the Lech, but he had underestimated the size of the threat facing Davout's 47,000 men. Once Davout's preparations for a move south had been noted by an increasingly confident Archduke Charles, all five Austrian corps north and south of the Danube, at least 80,000 men, were ordered to converge on Ratisbon. Lefebvre's 20,000 **Bavarian** troops could not hope to screen a withdrawal against such odds.

In the hope of persuading Charles to turn west, Napoleon ordered a general concentration around Ingolstadt on 18 April. Davout was ordered south, and delayed by a clash with Charles at **Tengen**, but was able to rendezvous with Lefebvre late next day. Both commanders then reported to Napoleon that the northern Austrian wing was in full retreat, and he chose to believe them, concentrating on cutting off an imagined escape and reorganizing for an attack on the Austrian centre around **Abensberg** on 20 April.

The attack went well, but Napoleon erred in assuming that total victory was virtually assured. Tengen had merely damaged Charles's advance guard, and the French garrison at **Ratisbon** had surrendered without destroying its vital bridge across the Danube. Meanwhile Masséna's failure to reach **Landshut** allowed **Hiller's** Austrian southern wing to withdraw safely.

Even when Napoleon realized the extent of his miscalculations, he expected Charles to retreat once faced by a properly concentrated French army. Lefebvre and Davout were ordered to press forward and encourage Austrian withdrawal, but by late on 21 April it was clear that they were barely holding off a continued Austrian advance. Finally, in the small hours of 22 April Napoleon resolved to concentrate all his available forces around **Eckmühl** for an attack on the Austrian flank. It succeeded, forcing Charles to retreat over the Danube and bringing his total losses for the campaign to 30,000, but exhaustion rendered immediate French pursuit impractical, and it was abandoned in the face of resistance by Austrian rearguards at Ratisbon next day.

Rather than drive on into Bohemia, Napoleon chose to turn his armies back to Vienna in the hope of attracting both Charles and John, who had opened operations in Italy by defeating **Beauharnais** at **Sacile** on 16 April, to the capital's defence. Davout was sent north of the Danube to harass Charles, and Lefebvre's remaining Bavarians guarded the right flank against John's forces in the Tyrol. The rest of the army, soon reinforced by Bernadotte from the north and the **Imperial Guard** from Spain, marched east along the south bank of the river, in pursuit of Hiller's ongoing retreat.

Hiller fought rearguard actions at Wels on 2 May, and at **Ebersberg** next day, seeking to buy time for the capital's defence, but an attempt by Charles to march round the Bohemian mountains and get between the French and Vienna was easily outpaced by Napoleon's columns. French forces were near the capital by 10 May, and the threat of bombardment brought its surrender three days later.

Apart from providing much-needed supplies, occupation of Vienna solved few of Napoleon's immediate problems. As in 1805, Emperor Francis was not induced to seek peace by the loss, and on this occasion Austrian troops destroyed all four Danube bridges before occupying the suburbs north of the river to prevent their repair. Napoleon needed to cross the river, at its fastest and deepest in the late spring, if he was to have any chance of inflicting a decisive defeat on Charles. Even if the French army could get over the Danube, Charles might double back on Vienna or John's 30,000 men might reach Austria ahead of Beauharnais's slightly larger force.

By 17 May Napoleon had some 82,000 troops around Vienna, while Charles had brought his army close to the capital north of the Danube, linking up with Hiller to bring his strength up to about 115,000 men. Apart from an attempted river crossing by a detachment to the west at Linz, which was held off by Bernadotte's Saxons on 17 May, Charles made no offensive move. He deployed his forces around the broad plain separating the Danube from the hills north of Vienna, and made defensive preparations while waiting for his brother's arrival.

The first French attempt to cross the Danube in strength, using the island of Lobau to the east of Vienna as a staging post, was hastily planned and executed, suffering an expensive rebuff at **Aspern–Essling** on 21–22 May. The damage inflicted on Napoleon's reputation by what was at best a drawn battle gained added significance at a time when several French-controlled German regions appeared ripe for rebellion, a factor that intensified his need for a rapid and decisive success.

Joined by reinforcements from Illyria and Beauharnais, who had kept John's army at bay with an important victory at **Raab** (14 June), Napoleon launched a second attempt to cross the river at **Wagram** in early July. His narrow but decisive victory swung the balance of political power away from the Habsburg war party. Charles extricated most of his army from the Danube, but was eventually caught by Marmont and Masséna on 10 July at **Znaim**, where he signed an armistice two days later, beginning the negotiating process that culminated in the Treaty of Schönbrunn on 14 October.

Apart from its ongoing **naval** and Peninsular campaigns, Britain gave little military assistance to Austria until it was too late. As in 1793, 1798 and 1805, Britain's limited available land forces were committed to an expeditionary campaign in northern Europe. As usual, the attempt was ill-conceived, delayed beyond strategic usefulness and poorly executed. An allied expeditionary force of some 40,000 troops under Lord **Chatham** landed on the Dutch coast at **Walcheren** in mid-August, but dithered indecisively after capturing Flushing on 13 August and eventually re-embarked on 30 September, having achieved nothing more than a pause in the Austro-French peace process. *See* **Map 12**.

Figueras, Battles of

The principal action on the western sector of the **Pyrenean** front during autumn 1794, a series of French attacks north-east of Figueras in November that shifted the focus of fighting decisively into Spanish territory (*see* **Map 5**). French commander **Dugommier** opened his offensive against 50,000 troops holding the Spanish line on the morning of 17 November, and though his left wing's secondary attack failed, **Augereau** drove the Spanish back from St Laurent on their left. Resumed attacks next day produced a similar result, with French efforts achieving little near the coast while Augereau eventually routed the Spanish left, which reconvened near Figueras shorn of most of its equipment. Dugommier was killed during the morning of what is sometimes called the Battle of the Black Mountain.

Though his centre was exposed to a possible counter-attack towards Bellegarde, **Pérignon** took over French forces and pressed on with the offensive, strengthening his right for a third attack on 20 November. The Spanish left wing collapsed again after General de la Union was killed leading up reinforcements from Figueras, and General Sauret's attacks against the Spanish right finally carried his troops beyond Estrella. Having lost an estimated 10,000 casualties, Spanish forces (now under General Amarillas) abandoned Figueras to a French **siege** and tumbled back on Gerona, leaving the roads into central Spain unguarded. French losses were probably above the 700 claimed by Pérignon. Some 9,000 exhausted Spanish survivors left at the powerful **fortress** of Figueras were penned in the citadel after republican citizens let French troops into the town, and they surrendered on 26 November.

Finland

A province of **Sweden** since the twelfth century, the Scandinavian territory north-west of St Petersburg was a prime target for an expanding **Russia** in the eighteenth century. Eventually conquered during the **Russo-Swedish War** of 1808–9, the province secured a guarantee of autonomous status by the **Borgö** Decree of March 1809, although Finnish troops, formerly grouped in their own regiments within the **Swedish Army**, were absorbed into the **Russian Army**. Finland remained under Russian control until the revolutions of 1917, and its autonomy was not subject to serious pressure until the late nineteenth century.

Fiodoroivskoy, Battle of

Attack by Field Marshal **Kutuzov**'s main Russian army on the sprawling French retreat from **Moscow** during the **Russian campaign** of 1812. Shortly after **Napoleon** reached Shakovo at the head of his army on 3 November, Russian advance guard commander Miloradovich struck at the French rearguard near Fiodoroivskoy, some 40km further east. Led by 20,000 **cavalry**, with perhaps 10,000 infantry in support, the attack cut off and surrounded **Davout**'s rearmost I Corps, which was only able to escape when **Beauharnais**, leading IV Corps just ahead of Davout, sent back two divisions to open up a channel through the Russians. Though the two corps were able to join forces, they suffered very heavy losses and remained in considerable danger until a division from **Ney**'s corps arrived from Viasma, where a secondary Russian attack had been beaten off with heavy loss. By nightfall the French column was reunited, though Davout's formation never recovered its former discipline and rearguard duties were subsequently performed by Ney's corps. *See* **Map 23**.

Fireships

One of the best-known but most dangerous **naval warfare** tactics, the use of old ships set aflame to spread conflagration and confusion among hostile fleets was rare by the late eighteenth century. Because all warships were wooden, and fireships could not be navigated, a change of wind could prove disastrous for the attacking side, and commanders never risked deliberately letting fire loose in crowded battle conditions. Generally only employed against static targets that could not be approached by conventional means, such as ships in harbour under the protection of coastal **artillery**, fireships enjoyed their only significant wartime success when used by the **Royal Navy** at the **Basque Roads** in April 1809.

First Coalition, War of the

The prolonged confrontation between **France** and a fluctuating combination of European states that opened with a French declaration of war against the Habsburg emperor **Francis II** on 20 April 1792. It ended in autumn 1797, when Austro-French settlement left **Great Britain** as the only major power still at war against France.

The traditional view of the war as a clash between volatile republican and outraged royalist ideologies contains some truth, but its outbreak and course were primarily determined by pragmatic dynasts and politicians accustomed to treating war as a normal extension of diplomacy. The **French Revolution** prompted displays of horror from conservative élites elsewhere, and generated high-profile support among radical elements from St Petersburg to Lisbon, but the political future of France was not a prime strategic concern for Europe's other **great powers** before 1792.

The **Russia** of **Catherine** the Great was above all interested in westward territorial and commercial expansion, and Catherine's principal motive for stirring up trouble in the west was to distract other powers from her drive into **Poland** and the **Ottoman Empire**. Britain was similarly aloof from any direct interest in an attack on France, and only the emergence of a dominant continental power, or a threat to security across the English Channel, would persuade it to fight a European land war.

The diplomacy of **Prussia** was dominated by territorial ambitions in north-west Germany, the **Netherlands** and Poland. Though support for exiled French royalists was little more than lip service, a gathering interest in military action to restore the French regime reflected confidence that, in the eighteenth-century style, easy victories could be translated into north German territorial gains at the conference table. Needing an ally willing to exchange northern conquests for southern, and unable to count on any British support for aggressive action, King **Frederick William II** turned to his traditional Austrian enemies.

The foreign policy of **Austria** was a hybrid of dynastic expansionism and defence of the Habsburg Empire's fragile integrity. Aggressive designs on Poland, the Balkans and southern Germany entailed friction with the Ottoman Empire, Russia and Prussia. The situation in Germany was complicated by the emperor's nominal leadership of the **Holy Roman Empire**, which embroiled Vienna in a tangled web of minor German conflicts, and compelled involvement in the politics of the French eastern frontier.

Austria's multi-ethnic empire was clearly a potential breeding ground for radical ideology, and Emperor Leopold II (the brother of French queen Marie-Antoinette) was willing to demand restoration of royal liberties from a revolutionary regime widely assumed to be on the point of collapse. Encouraged by the optimism of royalist exiles, Leopold viewed rapprochement with Prussia in August 1791, and the provocative Declaration of **Pillnitz** that followed, as gestures that would chasten rather than inflame the revolutionaries. The moderating influence behind the gestures disappeared with Leopold's death on 1 March 1792, and the accession of the solemn young Francis. Faced with the intolerable demands of a French government apparently bent on war, Francis was ready to teach it a lesson and form an aggressive alliance with an enthusiastic Prussia.

The strategic imperatives exercising the rest of Europe had ceased to matter in France. Increasingly convinced of a conspiracy linking Marie-Antoinette, counter-revolutionary insurrection, **émigré** invasion and the Austrian court, the government and population in Paris moved more solidly behind the **Brissotin** war party with every attempt to bluff it into submission. Encouraged by its own faith in the spread of revolution abroad, a fervent **Legislative Assembly** demanded that Leopold remove émigré forces from Mainz and Trier in mid-December 1791. Vienna's sincere attempt to do so made no difference to the Brissotin bandwagon, and on 20 April 1792 France (still nominally represented by King Louis) declared war against Francis in his capacity as King of Hungary, a device that technically freed other powers from any defensive obligation to Austria.

French troops occupied positions along the eastern and southern frontiers. Armies of about 50,000 men under Rochambeau and **Lafayette** guarded the northern stretch from the coast to the Ardennes, and Lückner commanded a slightly smaller force on the Rhine to the south. The south-coast frontier with **Piedmont** was covered by Montesquieu's 50,000 troops. Masterpieces of ill-discipline and disorganization, all four forces were well below their paper strength, even before deductions were made for garrison forces.

Hostilities opened with a French invasion of the **Austrian Netherlands**, which collapsed in a single spring day around **Valenciennes**, before the focus of fighting moved south to the **Rhine**, where Austrian and Prussian armies were gathering for an offensive. With invasion apparently imminent, the French Assembly lurched further to the left during the summer, calling on every citizen to defend the frontiers and encouraging demands for the deposition of the king. Meanwhile Frederick William, Emperor Francis and a host of less illustrious German rulers agreed alliance terms at Mainz, and Prussia formally declared war against France on 24 July.

The allied **Brunswick Manifesto** was a mission statement designed to frighten the French people into submission and protect the Bourbon monarchy, but its effects were very different. Its arrival in Paris on 3 August triggered the imprisonment and effective deposition of King Louis amid rampant civil unrest, and its threats of retribution fuelled a growing will to fight within a rapidly swelling frontier army of volunteer **fédérés**.

The Duke of **Brunswick's** allied army at the Rhine appeared to face little opposition on the road to Paris, but its slow advance was blocked, to universal amazement, at **Valmy** in late September. While Brunswick retreated back across the Rhine, French reinforcements further north broke a partial **siege** of **Lille** in early October, and the army in the far south took possession of the Ligurian coast after capturing **Nice** on 28 September.

French C-in-C **Dumouriez** used a further respite granted by Austro-Prussian distractions in Poland to follow up the relief of Lille with a much stronger invasion of **Belgium**. His victory over Austrian forces at **Jemappes**, near Mons, on 6 November marked the debut of a transformed

French Army, boasting new **infantry tactics** and an emerging **élan**, or offensive spirit, that was to sweep all before it when properly deployed over the next few years. Though stalemate had already set in on the Rhine, French armies were at the independent Dutch frontier when fighting ended for the winter.

Before hostilities could be resumed in 1793, the coalition was massively strengthened by Britain's adherence. The French government had declared the waters of the Scheldt Estuary open to all shipping from 16 November, and Britain's position as guarantor of international agreements restricting it to Dutch traffic provided an excuse to begin war preparations. They were enough to postpone, but not cancel, Dumouriez's planned invasion of the independent Netherlands.

French preparations recommenced from 10 January, in line with the bellicose mood of an increasingly anti-British national assembly, and British envoys began making military arrangements with Prussian and Austrian authorities the day before King Louis's execution on 21 January provided a convenient good cause. After announcing the annexation of Belgium on 31 January, the French Assembly hastened the inevitable by declaring war on Britain and the Netherlands the following day. The diplomatic repercussions of this rash gesture appeared likely to crush France, as Britain wielded its influence and **subsidies** to gain the active support of **Naples**, **Portugal** and **Spain** as coalition members (although France again pre-empted the fact by declaring war against the latter on 7 March), and assured the benevolence of **Sweden** and Russia.

As the campaigning season approached, France faced a Spanish invasion across the Pyrenees, a combination of Austrian and Italian forces gathering east of Nice, a British-led allied army arriving to aid Austria in the Low Countries, and 120,000 allied troops on the Rhine. Almost 350,000 hostile troops aside, an economically crippled republic could expect the **Royal Navy** to stifle its fleets, attack its colonies and throttle its overseas commerce. Meanwhile France was struggling to keep its armies in the field at all. Their paper strength amounted to some 270,000 men, but internal unrest, industrial chaos

and infrastructural breakdown disrupted their pay, morale and supplies, leaving them lurking near the frontiers in a state of unpredictable volatility.

While allied offensive plans matured slowly, Dumouriez opened his invasion of the Netherlands in mid-February, but **Miranda's** defeat at **Maastricht** and his own failure at **Neerwinden** (18 March) brought it to a rapid end. Like most French generals, Dumouriez was deeply embroiled in the volatile politics of the centre, and escaped the wrath of his increasingly powerful **Jacobin** enemies by joining a growing list of defectors to the allies on 5 April.

As the **Terror** gripped France, an unstable French regime was forced to commit stretched resources to the **Pyrenean** front, and to deal with royalist rebellion in La **Vendée**, **Lyon** and **Toulon**. Demoralized troops and commanders on the eastern frontiers were in no state to prevent an allied invasion, but coalition leaders already hidebound by strategic disputes made no effort to mount a serious spring offensive. What was to be a long and largely pointless allied campaign in **Flanders** was inaugurated by a slow advance to the French frontier, before armies there and on the Rhine settled down to establishing a **cordon** of absolute security along a wide front, besieging Valenciennes, Condé and **Mainz** through the summer.

While the appointment of **Carnot** as French war minister began a reform process that would transform the republic's military capabilities, the allies finally opened a new Flanders offensive in August. It not only split into factions – the British driving for **Dunkirk**, the Austrians besieging **Quesnoy** – but found French forces larger, better motivated and guided by the inspired authority of Carnot. French counter-attacks at **Hondschoote** and **Wattignies** had cleared northeastern France of invaders, isolated garrisons apart, by the late autumn.

French fortunes improved on every front that season. Allied Rhine armies retreated east of the river after a minor defeat at the **Geisberg**, and allied capture of Toulon was reversed by the first military success attributed to **Napoleon**, then an artillery major with the republican force besieging the city. A Piedmontese invasion of French

Savoy was herded back across the frontier by the elder **Kellermann** in October. Even in the Pyrenees, where a defeat at **Truillas** had put French forces on the defensive, Spanish enthusiasm was manifestly fading, partly reflecting the failure of Britain's much-vaunted **blockade** to win the war quickly.

The revolution in military tactics and organization effected by Carnot had borne fruit by the beginning of 1794. Mass **conscription** had put 1.5 million men under arms during the previous year, and the war minister now controlled 15 armies with a total field strength of almost 800,000 men. Some 280,000 were in the northeast with the armies of the Ardennes and the North; in the east, another 200,000 were with the armies of the Moselle and the Rhine; about 120,000 guarded the Pyrenean and Italian fronts, and 85,000 were with the Army of the Interior. Carnot's doctrine insisted that these troops should feed themselves off the land they occupied, and the French government was understandably anxious to send them abroad.

By contrast, allied cohesion and relative strength were waning fast. Able to put no more than 430,000 men into the field on all fronts, their 180,000 troops in Flanders and 145,000 on the Rhine were outnumbered for the first time. Renewed civil war (and Russian meddling) in Poland mattered more to both Vienna and Berlin than the western campaigns, and radical pressure within many of the Coalition's smaller members was combining with military disappointment to undermine their allegiance to the alliance. British subsidies nevertheless bought Prussian agreement (never honoured) to keep 62,000 men in the field for the spring campaign, and Austrian cooperation (arranged by General **Mack** in London) for a joint spring offensive in Flanders.

The new year opened with Brunswick's resignation from the allied Rhine command (6 January), and the capture of his last forward outpost west of the river on 19 January. As both sides on the Rhine adopted defensive postures, the quiet was broken only by the dismissal of **Hoche** for complaining about it, and the main actions of the spring took place in Flanders and Italy.

An allied offensive in Flanders again stalled at the first garrisoned stronghold, but new French northern commander **Pichegru** launched his own offensive all along the front from 26 April, winning victories at **Courtrai** (11 May) and **Tourcoing** (18 May) that drove the Austrian contingent east, and left **York**'s isolated corps exposed around **Tournai**. A combination of French armies under **Jourdan** then moved against the allied left wing at the **Sambre**, and won a pivotal victory at **Fleurus** in June. Aware that his government planned to abandon the Low Countries, Austrian commander **Saxe-Coburg** withdrew towards the Dutch frontier, dragging York back with him, while Pichegru and Jourdan converged in their wake.

Meanwhile **Dumerbion**'s French forces on the Italian frontier, following an offensive scheme devised by Brigadier-General Bonaparte, had taken **Saorgio** and reopened trade links with Genoa by early May, and defeat at **Le Boulon** had forced Spanish troops to fall back behind the east Pyrenean frontier. On the Rhine, French armies returned to the offensive in the **Vosges** Mountains in July, and increasingly dissonant Austro-Prussian forces once more retreated east of the river.

In an imperial and **colonial** context, a British expedition to the **West Indies** threatened to sweep French authorities out of the Caribbean until checked in the summer by tropical disease and French reinforcements. Commercial and **naval** warfare meanwhile settled into a pattern of essentially Anglo-French conflict that would endure though the 1790s, with the Royal Navy taking combat honours at the Battle of the **First of June**, but unable to enforce the blockade efficiently or find a means of significantly influencing the European land struggle.

The summer saw a change of regime in France, **Robespierre** losing his influence and his life after late July's **Fructidor** coup, but Carnot remained in office and French field armies continued to grow in size and vigour while morale and motivation drained from their opponents.

The autumn campaigns of 1794 ended all immediate danger to French national security. In the north, Jourdan drove **Clairfait**'s Austrians back from the Meuse and the **Roer** to the Rhine by August, and Pichegru pushed York's isolated corps beyond **Nijmegen**. His army had conquered the Netherlands (and captured the Dutch fleet at **Texel**) by late January, opening up the prospect of a cross-Channel invasion of **England** that was to form part of French strategic thinking for the next decade.

Though the Rhine remained quiet through the autumn, French forces were poised to invade Spain across the Pyrenees after breaking through on either end of the front at **San Marcial** and **Figueras**. In north-western Italy, Napoleon's temporary imprisonment after Fructidor almost gave the allies time to mount an attack, but he returned to plan a small victory at **Dego** that at least secured French communications for the winter.

By the following spring, repeated failure had finally broken the coalition's superficial unity. **Tuscany** made peace with France in anticipation of Prussia's defection (confirmed by the Treaty of **Basle** on 5 April), and the French government concluded treaties with the new Dutch Batavian Republic in May, with **Luxembourg** and Sweden in June, and with Spain in July. The latter agreement (also made at Basle) ended fighting in the Pyrenees, and a fierce autumn campaign around **Mannheim** between Austrian and French armies on the Rhine achieved only a mutually exhausted truce at the end of the year. In northern Italy, where allied armies were still threatening offensive action, **Schérer's** late autumn offensive pushed the Austro-Piedmontese back from **Loano**.

The French **Directory** government made command changes for the new year's campaigns, replacing Pichegru with **Moreau** on the Rhine, and divesting itself of a troublesome rising star by appointing Napoleon to command in Italy. Originally forbidden offensive operations pending a major attack on the Rhine, Napoleon got his orders changed and led his army to victories at **Montenotte**, **Dego** and **Mondovi** that put Piedmont out of the war. Victories at **Codogno**, **Lodi** and **Borghetto** had driven Austrian forces out of Lombardy altogether by the end of May, leaving only a besieged garrison at **Mantua**, which underwent two separate sieges before finally capitulating to French forces later in the year.

Napoleon's triumphant army then set about securing its astonishing successes, putting down a series of local rebellions and bringing the **Papal States** and Tuscany under effective French control. Meanwhile Austrian reinforcements from the Rhine enabled a succession of attempts to recover northern Italy, but Napoleon defeated all three – at **Lonato** and **Castiglione** in August, at **Bassano** in September, and finally (against heavy odds) at **Arcola** in November.

After a quiet spring on the Rhine, both French armies on the front launched offensives in June. New Austrian C-in-C Archduke **Charles** halted Jourdan in the north, but was surprised by Moreau's sudden sweep across his rear from **Kehl** in late June. Forced to retreat behind the Danube, a move that triggered defection from the coalition of **Württemberg**, **Baden** and a number of small Rhineland states, Charles concentrated to drive back Jourdan's second offensive at **Amberg** and **Würzburg**, but could not prevent Moreau's successful withdrawal from potential encirclement, and a French defensive victory at **Schliengen** in October left the front in its usual impasse at the end of the year.

Austro-French peace negotiations, triggered by the near-exhaustion of French resources, continued through the winter, but were undermined by Vienna's confidence in a renewed offensive into northern Italy. Its decisive defeat at **Rivoli** in January 1797, along with the fall of Mantua and Napoleon's subsequent invasion of the **Frioul**, finally broke Vienna's will to fight in the spring, and the coalition came to an effective end when Francis II accepted the peace terms dictated by Napoleon (without any authority) at **Leoben** on 17 April.

With few illusions about the coalition's future, Britain had made peace overtures to France in late 1796, but talks foundered on French demands that Britain return all its wartime colonial gains. Though fortified by another major naval victory at Cape **St Vincent** in February, a simultaneous **bank crisis** reflected mounting economic pressure on an unpopular **Pitt** government to make peace, and negotiations reopened at Lille in July 1797.

Though the Directory was almost equally anxious for peace, colonial disputes again prevented progress, and British envoy Lord Malmesbury eventually left Lille on 18 September. The Leoben terms were confirmed at **Campo Formio** in October, leaving Britain (and an inert Portugal) alone at war with France. Anglo-French conflict continued through 1797–8 in a largely naval and colonial context, against a background of ongoing French plans to invade England or **Ireland**, and Pitt's unceasing efforts to form a **Second Coalition**. *See* **Maps 1–6**.

First of June, Battle of the

The first major naval engagement of the **Revolutionary Wars**, and the **Royal Navy's** first important victory, fought on 1 June 1794 in the North Atlantic, some 650km off the coast of Brittany (*see* **Map 19**). The weakened condition of the post-revolutionary **French Navy** had been masked by inactivity and the inefficiency of British **blockade** tactics during the first 18 months of the wars, but **Villaret's** Brest Fleet was ordered to sea in spring 1794 to guarantee safe passage of a vital food **convoy** – some 120 ships en route from the **United States** – at a time of near-famine in **France**.

Villaret sailed with 26 **ships-of-the-line** on 16 May, while **Howe's** long-range British blockading force was far out in the Atlantic searching for the convoy. Howe found Brest empty after returning with 25 ships-of-the-line on 19 May, and set off in pursuit. After destroying two French **corvettes** on 25 May, Howe sighted and chased the French fleet on 28 May, but Villaret succeeded in evading attack, keeping his ships together and drawing the British away from the convoy.

Howe was able to launch a partial attack next day, briefly isolating and damaging the rear of a well-formed French battle line, but fog prevented further action by either force over the next two days, and Villaret was reinforced to replace four vessels already damaged in action. Aware that the convoy would be within Howe's range for several more days, Villaret accepted battle on 1 June.

In line with British naval practice, Howe's priority was destruction of the French battlefleet, and he regarded the convoy as a secondary target. His policy of long-range blockade was designed to tempt the French into sailing, and

he was confident of victory. Ignoring contemporary naval orthodoxy, he ordered his captains to approach the French battle line on a diagonal course from the windward side, pass through it and attack from the leeward side, preventing the enemy from escaping with the wind (*see* **Naval Warfare**).

Howe sighted the French fleet early on 1 June, and gave signals at eight thirty to execute the manoeuvre, but only five battleships (apart from his own flagship, *Queen Charlotte*) carried out his instructions to the letter. Others held back to arrive in position late, or simply attacked from the windward side, and some were unable to pierce the line without coming under fire from British ships. Though imperfectly delivered, Howe's attack was devastatingly effective, throwing Villaret's battle line into rapid confusion and developing into separate mêlées around isolated French ships. Villaret's flagship, *Montagne*, led those ships not directly attacked to form a new line some 5km downwind, but French battleships caught between British broadsides were overwhelmed. By the time firing stopped at around eleven thirty, nine French ships-of-the-line had been totally dismasted (against two British) and two more had surrendered. A twelfth, *Vengeur du Peuple*, sank a few hours later.

A period of reorganization followed, as Howe gathered his fleet together and sought to prevent his most damaged ships from drifting towards Villaret's new line. Five French prizes escaped to rejoin Villaret in heavy winds, giving the French fleet an appearance of cohesion that persuaded Captain Curtis, given temporary command by an exhausted Howe, to call off pursuit by undamaged British ships. The British fleet then concentrated on securing its six remaining prizes, and Villaret was allowed to take his battered force home without interference next day.

Howe then sailed for England, ignoring the French convoy and turning tactical victory into a strategic setback, a fact that enabled French **propaganda** to present the engagement as a triumph for Villaret. Howe's tactics had nevertheless claimed six prizes and 3,500 French casualties, at a cost of about 1,100 British casualties and no ships, as well as demonstrating the means by which hostile fleets could be brought to battle in future. Immediately dubbed the 'Glorious First of June' in Britain, the battle also raised popular morale in a country starved of victories.

Fismes, Battle of *See* Campaign for **France**,

Five Hundred, Council of

The lower house of the Legislative Assembly during the **Directory** period in **France**. Brought into being by the 1795 Constitution of Year III, its personnel represented the republicanism of the middle classes and reflected the regime's narrow electoral franchise. Members were required to be over 30, and were elected for three years. Their duties included the drafting and passage of legislation, which was then presented to the upper house (Council of **Ancients**) for acceptance or rejection. The chamber also had the authority to declare or end wars, and to select the members of the Directory itself, but exercise of these powers required the presence of at least 200 members, and Council policy could usually be manipulated by a few well-motivated men in high places (*see* **Brumaire**). About 200 Council of Five Hundred members reappeared in the first legislative assembly of the **Consulate**, which was elected on an even narrower franchise.

Flanders Campaigns (1792–5)

The war between **France** and the powers of the **First Coalition** for control of the **Netherlands** and the north-eastern French frontier. It began with the first major military operation of the war years, an abortive French attack around **Valenciennes** in April 1792, and a second unsuccessful attempt in June. A more concerted French invasion conquered **Belgium** in the autumn, winning a pivotal victory at **Jemappes** on 6 November, but the campaigns got fully under way with the commitment of large allied forces to the theatre from spring 1793.

Despite the Coalition's expansion during the winter, a defiant French government opened the campaigning season with an invasion of the independent Netherlands. **Dumouriez** commanded some 30,000 French troops on the Dutch frontier, and another 70,000 were threatening Maastricht just west of the Meuse. About 70,000 Austrians were ranged against them, but were about to be reinforced for an offensive by 38,000 British, German and Dutch troops. While allied offensive plans stagnated, Dumouriez launched four divisions across the Dutch border to attack Breda on 17 February, and took the town eight days later.

The first of the Duke of **York's** British contingent landed at Helvoetsluys on 5 March, its escorting **gunboats** helping relieve the French siege of nearby Williamstadt, and the faltering French advance ground to a halt after 10 March, when Dumouriez left for the Meuse on news of **Miranda's** reverse at **Maastricht**. Though Dumouriez rallied Miranda's dispirited army, his defeat by the advancing Austrians at **Neerwinden** on 18 March brought the French invasion to an effective end. Forced back to Louvain, and aware that **Jacobin** leaders were after his head, Dumouriez made a vain attempt to rouse his disgruntled **fédérés** for a march on Paris before fleeing to the Austrian lines on 5 April.

French confusion, exacerbated by an allied victory on the **Rhine** at **Bingen**, was not exploited by allied commanders in the Low Countries. Distracted by the pitfalls of coalition diplomacy and logistics, they spent April gradually building up troops along the Franco-Belgian frontier, advancing only in response to ill-conceived French attacks around **St Amand** in early May, before halting to establish absolute security along a wide front.

While a crumbling French administration faced Rhine and **Pyrenean** invasions, along with internal revolt in La **Vendée**, allied armies on the eastern frontiers were immobilized by **sieges** of Condé and Valenciennes (and that at **Mainz**) until late July. When 100,000 allied troops in Flanders eventually resumed their advance in early August, against perhaps 40,000 ragged French recruits, their strategic unity collapsed almost at once. York's 50,000 troops marched north on 10 August to invest **Dunkirk**, a prize with particular appeal in London, while **Saxe-Coburg's** 45,000 Austrians stuck to their rigid **cordon** system and halted to besiege **Quesnoy**.

Though Quesnoy fell on 11 September, the respite granted to hard-pressed republican forces gave both the **Terror** inside France and **Carnot's** reforms of **French Army** organization time to take significant effect. Under Carnot's supervision, new French theatre C-in-C Houchard broke the Dunkirk siege with a victory at **Hondschoote** on 8 September. A subsequent retreat to Lille cost Houchard his head, and command passed to **Jourdan**, whose victory at **Wattignies** (15–16 October) forced the Austrians back from Mauberge and into winter quarters.

Coburg returned to the field in response to a French offensive all along the front from 21 October. French attacks drove allied outposts back on Menin and Tournai, and made rapid progress in the far north, where **Vandamme** drove émigré forces into Nieuport on the first day. The arrival of British naval and military reinforcements relieved the port on 30 October, and allied counter-attacks elsewhere restored the front to stalemate for the winter. The French government ordered another attack in early November, but it broke down in foul weather and its most tangible result was Jourdan's replacement by **Pichegru**.

Both sides prepared major offensives in Flanders for spring 1794. Carnot's mass **conscription** drive had raised strength in the theatre to about 250,000 men, and allied troops on the front faced superior numbers for the first time. Saxe-Coburg gathered together 160,000 men south-west of Le Cateau, under the nominal command of Emperor **Francis II**, and advanced from 17 April towards the main French positions between Guise and Cambrai. After forcing advanced French units back, Coburg halted on 20 April to besiege **Landrecies**.

Pichegru launched his counter-offensive against the whole allied position in Flanders during late April. While the Army of the Moselle moved north towards the allied southern flank at the **Sambre**, Pichegru massed about 45,000 men for a strike at the allied centre around Landrecies. Though his assaults failed on 26 April, **Souham** and **Moreau** had already begun preliminary attacks against allied coastal positions. Their victories at **Moescroen** (29 April), **Courtrai** (11 May) and **Tourcoing** (18 May) drove Austrian forces east and left York to defend an exposed salient around **Tournai** against French attacks on 23 May.

Austrian withdrawal reflected Vienna's waning interest in the defence of the Netherlands and the mounting threat from French forces on the Sambre. Carnot had responded to Austrian reinforcement of the Sambre positions by risking Prussian aggression and ordering Jourdan's 40,000 men north from the Rhine to join French forces south-west of Charleroi. After a series of inconclusive battles along the Sambre, Jourdan arrived to take command of the new, enlarged Army of the Sambre and Meuse on 4 June, and held off an attempt to relieve Charleroi by Saxe-Coburg's entire army at **Fleurus** on 26 June.

With his government about to pull out of the Netherlands altogether, Coburg turned a drawn battle into a major French victory by retiring his army towards Brussels, forcing York's isolated northern corps to retreat in its wake. As the whole allied army withdrew behind the River Dyle, Pichegru and Jourdan advanced to meet at Brussels on 11 July.

The combined French force of perhaps 170,000 men moved up to the Dyle next day, and minor attacks drove the allied armies further apart, Coburg's 80,000 Austrians across the Meuse and York's 35,000 men north-east towards the coast, with 15,000 Dutch troops forming a bridge between them. Government orders prevented a French advance into Holland until allied fortresses in Flanders had been reduced, at task eventually completed by **Schérer** at Condé on 30 August.

New French attacks on Dutch outposts began on 26 August, and Moreau's detachment had moved along the coast to the mouth of the Scheldt by 28 August. Jourdan began a cautious advance all along the front on 4 September, again spearheaded by Pichegru's northern wing, which thrust into the large gap between passive allied armies (taking York's outpost at **Boxtel** on 14 September). New Austrian commander **Clairfait** retreated from the Meuse after defeat by Jourdan's larger army at **Ayvaille**, and drew back across the Rhine when pursuing French forces attacked at the **Roer** on 2 October. While a detachment doubled back to complete the reduction of Maastricht, French forces swept forward to occupy Cologne (9 October) and Koblenz (25 October), putting them in touch with the French Rhine armies at Trier.

As Anglo-Dutch forces fell back on the defence

of Holland, Pichegru moved against their outposts from 23 September. Though flooding slowed French advances, news of Clairfait's withdrawal prompted York to fall back behind the Waal from 4 October. He withdrew again after his extended line was attacked in the centre by Souham's 12,000 troops on 19 October, taking up positions facing east between the Waal and the Lech, with the Dutch army on his left at Gorcum. Pichegru concentrated on reducing isolated positions still in allied hands, taking Venloo on 26 October and **Nijmegen** on 8 November, a defeat that prompted York's further retreat north across the Rhine.

York left the Netherlands on 2 December, General Walmoden taking overall control of an allied force riven with typhus and desperately short of supplies. Mud and rain had turned to bitter frost, and French forces used floating ice to get across the Waal at Tuil on 28 December. Despite a British counter-attack under **Dundas**, the Dutch-held fortress at Gorcum fell on 2 January, and Walmoden moved back across the Lech on 6–7 January. After another French attack had severed communications with Austrian forces, about 18,000 British and Hanoverian troops finally parted from the Dutch army, abandoning Arnheim to march north for the Ysel. Their crossing of freezing, open wastelands to Munster was hardly pursued, but had killed about 6,000 men by the time it ended on 17 January.

The Prince of Orange resigned his offices on the same day, before quitting his virtually undefended and largely pro-republican country, and Pichegru entered the open city of Amsterdam on 20 January, effectively completing the conquest of the Netherlands. The freezing winter, by far the coldest in contemporary living memory, played one more trick on allied defensive plans, when the **Dutch Navy**'s battlefleet, locked in the ice at **Texel**, became the first in history to be captured by a **cavalry** charge on 30 January.

A muted spring campaign opened with French advances against Walmoden from 24 February. Though severely restricted by flooding, they sent British survivors back to Lingen and Emden, where they were relieved on 8 March by Prussian forces. The British decamped to Bremen, sailing

away on 25 March, and the effective end of fighting in the theatre was confirmed by Prussia's withdrawal from the Coalition by the Treaty of **Basle** in July. *See* **Map 2**.

Fleurus, Battle of

Vital French victory over the **First Coalition** on 26 June 1794, when **Jourdan**'s Army of the Sambre and Meuse fought off an allied attempt to recapture Charleroi, on the Sambre in southwest Belgium (*see* **Map 2**). Concentration of about 90,000 French troops against Charleroi had forced a smaller Austrian army to withdraw up the **Sambre** during April and May, and persuaded Austrian C-in-C **Saxe-Coburg** to concentrate for a relief operation. Charleroi surrendered on 25 June, leaving Jourdan just time to adapt his army's **siege** positions before the allied attack went in next morning.

Coburg attacked the French ring round Charleroi from all sides, ignoring an opportunity to concentrate overwhelming strength against one part of Jourdan's stretched line, but the bulk of his forces advanced from the north and west in three columns. On the right, the Prince of **Orange** and some 15,000 troops were halted by **Kléber** and **Bernadotte**, and withdrew on news of Charleroi's surrender. On the left, **Beaulieu**'s 17,000 Austrians pushed French defenders very slowly back to the Sambre.

The central allied attack, by about 20,000 men under Kaunitz and Archduke **Charles**, struck French positions from the north-west around Fleurus, some 15km north of Charleroi. Charles stormed and took the town itself, but three attacks failed to dislodge defenders from fortified positions beyond. Just to the east, Kaunitz was halted when Jourdan sent part of **Lefebvre**'s division to support **Championnet**'s well-positioned forces. Pouring reserves into the sector, Jourdan had forced Kaunitz to retreat before confirmation of Charleroi's fall prompted Coburg to abandon the offensive in mid-afternoon.

Though effectively a drawn battle, costing both sides about 5,000 casualties, Fleurus was a turning point in the struggle for control of **Flanders** and the **Netherlands**. Under instructions from his government not to waste resources, and abandoning Mons without a fight, Coburg retired his army towards Brussels and occupied the future field of **Waterloo**, presaging a complete Austrian withdrawal from the theatre in July and compelling **York**'s isolated northern corps to retreat in its wake.

Flintlock

Another name for a **musket**.

Floréal Coup

Political act of exclusion engineered by the **Directory** government on 19 May 1798 (22 Floréal by the **Republican Calendar**) that was the corollary to the previous year's **Fructidor** manoeuvre against royalists. The radical **Jacobin** left, in abeyance since the fall of **Robespierre**, had gained ground at the elections of May 1798, and the Directors packed the assembly to vote a ban on the presence of 106 left-wing representatives. Securely back in control of parliament, they attempted to address the hyperinflation and supply crises that had wrecked their popularity, but had made only limited progress before a new continental war intervened. *See also* **France**

Florence, Treaty of

The agreement that forced **Naples** to form an alliance with **France**, signed by Neapolitan king **Ferdinand IV** on 28 March 1801. Bound to come to an arrangement after **Austria** had quit the **Second Coalition** at **Lunéville** in February, Ferdinand agreed to cede **Elba** and the port of Taranto to France, the latter to be manned by a 15,000-strong French garrison at Neapolitan expense. His agreement to close Neapolitan ports to British shipping and goods was even more damaging to the state's fragile economy, and the treaty was a source of constant friction with France during the four years of its duration.

Floridablanca, Don José Moñino y Redondo, Count of (1728–1808)

Spanish statesman who served King Charles III as chief minister and retained the post when **Charles IV** came to the throne in 1788. Also foreign minister, he presided over a deterioration of relations with **France**, the traditional ally of Bourbon **Spain**, in the aftermath of the **French Revolution**. Although he issued a series of strong protests against the treatment of King **Louis XVI**, and French failure to support Spain in colonial disputes with **Great Britain**, Floridablanca was aware of Spain's military and economic weakness and sought neutrality. None the less too bellicose for the queen's liking, he was replaced by the even older Count Aranda in February 1792, and subsequently imprisoned by the **Godoy** regime. He was appointed first president of the central rebel **junta** in 1808, but died at Seville a few weeks later.

Flushing, Capture of *See* **Walcheren Expedition**

Fluvia, Battles of the

General **Schérer**'s opening offensive on the eastern sector of the **Pyrenean** front, launched on 25 April 1795 against Spanish positions along the River Fluvia (*see* **Map 5**). While a French column under General Charlet swung towards Camprodón to strike the Spanish left flank, Schérer led the main body of his army in a two-pronged frontal attack at the Fluvia. The advance ran into two Spanish divisions engaged in a strong reconnaissance operation north of the Fluvia, and forced them back, but could not get across the river that night. Attacks resumed next day, and cleared both banks of the river during the morning, but counter-attacks by Spanish **cavalry** and General O'Farrill's division held up Sauret's French left wing, while reserves under Vives and La **Romana** stopped **Augereau** on the right, forcing Schérer to retire on his new base at Rosas in the evening. A second French attempt on Spanish lines failed in late May, after which both sides paused to await the outcome of peace talks at **Basle**.

Fombio, Battle of *See* Battle of **Codogno**.

Fontainebleau, Treaty of (1807)

Franco-Spanish agreement, signed on 27 October 1807, that secured formal Spanish cooperation with **Junot**'s French invasion of **Portugal**, and permission to station troops along his lines of retreat. The agreement also made provision for the future partition of Portugal. Spanish chief minister **Godoy** was promised control over conquered territories south of Tagus, and the north of the country, including Lisbon, was under the nominal control of **Tuscany**'s ruling family, whose Italian territories had recently been given to Elisa **Bonaparte**. *See also* Invasion of **Spain**.

Fontainebleau, Treaty of (1814)

The formal agreement between the victorious allies of the **Sixth Coalition** and **Napoleon**, signed on 16 April 1814, that finalized the latter's **abdication** of 6 April. Napoleon himself played no part in negotiations towards the treaty, which were completed on 11 April by **Caulaincourt**, **Ney** and **Macdonald**, but was granted absolute rule over the Mediterranean island of **Elba**. Empress **Marie-Louise** became Duchess of **Parma**, with succession passing to her son, the short-lived Napoleon II. Other members of Napoleon's family lost their titles and territorial possessions but were granted pensions. Napoleon left Fontainebleau for the coast at St Raphael on 20 April, after bidding an emotional farewell to his remaining troops and selecting the 600 **Imperial Guard** veterans that he was permitted to take to Elba.

Forcheim, Battle of

The principal action of **Jourdan's** second offensive across the **Rhine** in summer 1796. His first attack on the northern sector had been thwarted after initial success at **Altenkirchen** in early June, but Austrian withdrawals to meet **Moreau's** offensive further south gave him the opportunity for a second attempt. He crossed the Rhine at Düsseldorf, Neuwied and Cologne during the first days of July, approaching the northern flank of Wartensleben's 70,000 Austrians scattered along the east bank north of Mainz.

Heavily outnumbered, Wartensleben fell back from the Lahn to Rosbach by 10 July, when an attempted counter-attack collapsed, and had retreated beyond the Main by 12 July. French forces took Frankfurt four days later, and Wartensleben kept moving east, crossing the loops of the Main before turning south and marching on Forcheim, where pursuing French forces (led by **Kléber** after Jourdan fell ill at the end of July) attacked his positions on 7 August.

Kléber sent **Lefebvre** against the Austrian right, **Championnet** and **Bernadotte** against the left, and Collaud against Forcheim in the centre, where **Ney's** regiment took the town (an action that won him promotion to brigadier-general). Forced to withdraw his centre, Wartensleben retreated his entire force to Amberg and Sulzbach,

but French pursuit attacks persuaded him to retire again, and his army finally halted to await reinforcements beyond the River Naab on 20 August. *See also* Battle of **Amberg**; **Map 3**.

Fortresses

Powerful static defence points, armed with the heaviest **artillery**, were a basic feature of contemporary warfare. Guarding frontiers, important communications points, towns or coasts, they could maintain a sufficiently strong garrison to threaten the rear of any attacking force that passed them by. Eighteenth-century military orthodoxy therefore insisted on reduction and capture of all strongpoints en route during any advance into hostile territory, and attacking forces usually moved ahead of a **cordon** of mutually supporting fortresses, sacrificing any hope of speed or surprise in favour of secure supply depots and flank protection. In defensive terms, chains of closely linked fortresses could house sufficient resources for a longer campaign, and for counter-attacks along secure internal lines.

Fortress design, and the **siege warfare** techniques used against it, had evolved to a high level of sophistication by 1792, and though many fortresses were based on medieval structures, adaptations of old castles and modern designs shared a number of common features. The basic unit of a fortress was the 'bastion'. Open at the rear, its four walls formed points that covered frontal and flank approaches, and stood behind a deep ditch protecting them from infantry attack. One or more rings of bastions, connected by walls or earthworks, comprised the main defences of a fortress proper, and a clutch of bastions inside the ring formed a 'citadel', the heart of the defence. Citadels in old-established fortresses could take a number of other forms, such as a stone castle on high ground within city walls.

Obvious avenues of approach for attacking forces could be covered by heavy artillery concentration and by forward strongpoints ('outworks') often based on farmhouses or other existing buildings. The more sophisticated permanent fortifications featured a man-made slope ('glacis') leading up to the ditch, covered ways and communications passages cut into bastion walls, pocket strongpoints inside bastions ('redoubts'), specially protected gun sites ('casements'), raised gun platforms and back-up fortifications ('retrenchments') inside a defensive ring's most vulnerable points. Stone walls were often clad with earth, to absorb artillery fire and reduce the danger to defenders from flying splinters, but many temporary or outer fortifications were simply earthworks, equally absorbent but less durable.

Though fortresses were important (and ubiquitous) throughout the period, remaining the focus of innumerable sieges as well as a magnet for troops and supplies, their ability to shape a campaign was severely restricted by the ascendancy of mobile land warfare on the main European fronts. Away from northern and central Europe, armies were smaller, supplies more scarce and roads rarer, so that fortresses like those at **Acre**, **Badajoz** or **Corsica** could still determine the length and outcome of a campaign. Coastal fortresses also remained a formidable deterrent to attack by warships (*see* **Naval Warfare**).

Fouché, Joseph (1759–1820)

French politician, one of the most enduring and resourceful figures to emerge from the revolutionary period. Born in Nantes, and sent to study for the priesthood, he abandoned work as a religious teacher for revolutionary politics, and was a **Jacobin** deputy in the **National Convention** from 1791. A commited supporter of **Robespierre** in 1793, and strongly associated with the **Terror**, he was one of the commissioners notorious for exacting brutal revenge on the populace after the rebellion in **Lyon**.

Fouché's extreme sensitivity to political change enabled him to escape retribution after the 1794 **Thermidor** coup, and he performed administrative work for the **Directory** government, but was aware of the **Brumaire** conspiracy before it took place and gave it his support. Rewarded with the post of **Napoleon**'s chief of police, he became a feared man, operating a network of secret police and informers that purged opposition of all political persuasions inside **France**. Retaining the post until 1802, and again from 1804 to 1810, he was responsible for exposing the **Cadoudal** plot of 1804 (and many less tangible conspiracies), and followed up with a

characteristically wide-ranging attack on current opponents, but he was a realist rather than a zealot, and opposed the **Enghein** abduction as a political error.

Named Duke of Otranto in 1806, he was hardworking, shrewd and resourceful, but not remotely loyal. Napoleon's discovery of the **Talleyrand–Fouché** plot to warp the imperial succession in late 1808 brought no immediate punishment, such was his importance to internal stability in time of war, but he was removed from office in 1810 on suspect evidence of conspiring with exiled royalists.

Subsequently employed on minor missions away from Paris, he maintained political links with the capital and returned to make his peace with the restored king in 1814. In contact with Napoleon on **Elba** at the same time, he became chief of police again during the **Hundred Days** of 1815, but managed to save himself in the aftermath of **Waterloo**, leading the movement for a second abdication in the Chamber of Deputies. Briefly employed by **Louis XVIII**, but sent on a diplomatic mission to **Saxony** in the wake of court outrage at his retention, he was exiled in his absence and lived his last years in Trieste.

Fourth Coalition, War of the

The war of 1806–7 fought between **France** and an alliance of European powers, headed by **Prussia**, **Russia** and **Great Britain**. Forced into existence by Prussia's unilateral declaration of war in late summer 1806, the Coalition was never able to present a coherent threat to French national security, suffering a series of military disasters before Russia and Prussia were compelled to acknowledge Napoleon's mastery of central Europe by the Peace of **Tilsit** in July 1807.

Prussia had joined the **Third Coalition** too late to take part in any fighting, but was punished by **Napoleon** anyway. The humiliating Convention of **Vienna**, ratified in February 1806, stirred outrage among some elements of the Prussian middle classes, nobility and officer corps, reinforcing the hawkish attitudes of a powerful court faction gathering around Queen **Louise**. The kidnap and execution of German nationalist publisher Johann **Palm** in April, and Napoleon's sudden offer to return **Hanover** to **George III** in June, further eroded the peaceful intentions of King **Frederick William III**, who restored former chief minister **Hardenberg** to favour before secretly agreeing to war on 7 August.

The decision was hardly well timed. Only a reluctant **Saxony** and a half-hearted **Sweden** could be expected to provide rapid military support, and much depended on help arriving from Russia before Napoleon could force a confrontation. No clear plan of campaign existed, and the anachronistic **Prussian Army** had barely embarked on its first real reforms in half a century.

From Napoleon's point of view another war was undesirable. Popular French exultation after **Austerlitz** had owed much to war-weariness, and by summer 1806 the emperor was fully absorbed in the urgent business of economic recovery. Not aware of Prussian war plans until early September, but secure in the knowledge that he had some 160,000 troops already mobilized east of the **Rhine**, he delayed any response in the hope that Prussia would pull back from the brink. He eventually left Paris on 24 September, after reports indicated Prussian troop concentrations in Saxony.

Prussian mobilization was slow and inefficient, so that only about half of its 200,000 troops ever reached Saxony, and those in position by early October were straddled along a 100km front west of the Elbe. Napoleon meanwhile gathered his forces from their stations all over Germany with characteristic purposefulness. Unable to guess at Prussian strategy (because none existed), he sought to get between his immediate opponents and their slowly advancing allies, as he had done in Bavaria the previous year. Leaving only about 30,000 men under Louis **Bonaparte** to guard against any Prussian move towards the Rhine, he began moving the rest of his army, some 150,000 strong, north through the Thuringian forests on 8 October.

Deployed in a sophisticated **Bataillon Carré** formation, the **Grande Armée** marched towards the left flank of Prussian forces, hidden by the forests until the last moment. It defeated isolated Prussian forward units at **Saalfeld** on 10 October, and this minor setback persuaded Prussian C-in-C **Brunswick** to retreat from an exposed position his army should never have occupied. Though

Napoleon misread Prussian moves, directing his largest force against the rearguard while **Davout** found himself in the path of the main body marching for the Elbe, French forces destroyed Brunswick's army with simultaneous victories at **Jena** and **Auerstädt** on 14 October. Sweeping into Prussia, the Grande Armée rounded up the last coherent Prussian field force at **Lübeck** in early November, by which time Napoleon had already occupied Berlin (27 October).

The lightning **Jena–Auerstädt campaign** effectively knocked Prussia out of the war, persuaded Saxony to become a French ally (11 December), and enabled Napoleon to occupy the Prussian client states of **Brunswick** and **Hesse-Cassel**. The Prussian Army had lost 25,000 casualties, 140,000 prisoners and 2,000 guns, yet Frederick William maintained a belligerent posture from the relative security of Königsberg, refusing peace terms and waiting for 140,000 Russian troops promised by the tsar (and paid for by British **subsidies**).

Despite fears of Austrian aggression in the south, and clear indications that Paris wanted peace, Prussian obduracy forced Napoleon to advance further east to secure his latest victories. After issuing the **Berlin Decrees** on 21 November, inaugurating the ill-fated **Continental System** of economic warfare against Britain, Napoleon moved into the Prussian sector of partitioned **Poland**, heading for a reported concentration of Russian troops in the Warsaw area.

The Grande Armée's march from Berlin to **Warsaw** in late 1806 was a gruelling introduction to east European winter conditions, and **Bennigsen**'s Russians had withdrawn east across the Vistula by the time the first of Murat's cavalry reached the city on 28 November. Further pursuit was thwarted by mud and poor roads, and the French retired on Warsaw for reorganization and recuperation after inconclusive engagements at **Pultusk** and **Golymin** on 26 December.

Napoleon remained in the city until late January, when Bennigsen suddenly attacked Ney and Soult on the French left wing, driving them westward. Making a characteristic attempt to get behind the advancing Russians, Napoleon marched his main force north towards Königsberg, but his plans were captured by Bennigsen, and deep snow reduced French columns to a crawl. When attacked, the Russians were ready, first at the indecisive Battle of **Ionkovo** (3 February) and then over two days of confused fighting in appalling conditions at **Eylau** (7–8 February), where the Grande Armée suffered more casualties than its opponents for the first time. Badly in need of resupply and reinforcement, Napoleon had no choice but to withdraw to winter quarters.

During the early spring, when operations were restricted to a renewed **siege** of **Danzig**, Napoleon rebuilt frontline forces. By calling up French conscripts a year early, draining rear areas of trained troops and filling the gaps with increasing numbers of allied troops, including two new **Polish** divisions, he raised his strength east of the Rhine to about 300,000 men by the end of April 1807, including 100,000 occupying Germany under General **Brune**. Armies in Italy, detachments guarding the Channel coast and garrison troops brought total **French Army** strength up to around 600,000 troops.

Prussia and Russia, encouraged by another injection of British money, reaffirmed their determination to drive Napoleon out of Germany by signing the Convention of Bartenstein in April. Bennigsen's army, reinforced to 115,000 troops, threatened to relieve Danzig in May, but precautionary French deployment along the Alle and Narev rivers dealt with the few uncoordinated attacks that actually took place. Danzig fell in May, releasing 20,000 troops for operations elsewhere, and the main French force advanced up the Alle after Bennigsen exposed his lines of retreat with another westward move in early June.

Its first attack, at **Heilsberg** on 10–11 June, proved indecisive and the Russians escaped northwards, but Napoleon sent Murat and Soult racing for Königsberg, forcing Bennigsen to turn and defend the city in strength at **Friedland** on 14 June. An overwhelming French victory, Friedland was the last major action of the war. By 19 June French troops had advanced to reach the River Niemen near Tilsit, where peace treaties were signed by both Russia (7 July) and Prussia (9 July), leaving Britain alone at war with France.

No serious land fighting had taken place on other fronts, but Britain had launched a preemptive attack on neutral **Copenhagen** in April 1807, provoking widespread outrage elsewhere and exacerbating the country's almost complete diplomatic isolation in the years immediately after Tilsit. *See* Sieges of **Magdeburg** and **Stralsund; Dardanelles Operation; Maps 16, 17.**

Fox, Charles James (1749–1806)

Contemporary **Great Britain**'s foremost advocate of liberal reform, a spellbinding (if somewhat histrionic) parliamentary debater, whose rivalry with perennial prime minister William **Pitt** formed the central axis of British political life after 1784. Foreign minister in **Portland**'s 1783 government, Fox spent the next 22 years in opposition, using his enormous parliamentary influence as a counter-weight to Pitt's increasingly bellicose position, and proving a formidable and persistent critic of war against **France**. Always a popular figure, especially among Britain's wealth of political cartoonists, his stormy temperament and fondness for high living left him in poor health by the time Pitt's death brought him back to office in January 1806. As Foreign Secretary in **Grenville**'s 'Ministry of All the Talents', he was on the point of opening peace negotiations with France and of abolishing slavery when he died in October, signalling the government's fall and the end of a British political era.

Foy, Maximilien Sebastien (1775–1825)

French artillery officer, commissioned in 1792, whose early career was held back by his independent political views. Temporarily removed from the army by **Robespierre**, but reinstated after the 1794 **Thermidor** coup, he fought on the **Rhine** and **Swiss** fronts during the **Revolutionary Wars**, but outspoken opposition to the creation of the empire in 1804 delayed his promotion to brigadier-general until 1808. Sent to **Spain**, he fought at **Corunna**, **Oporto** and **Busaco** before his promotion to divisional command in late 1810. He played an important role at **Salamanca** in 1812, and remained in the **Peninsular** theatre until wounded at **Orthez** in February 1814. Retained by the restored royal government, he joined **Napoleon**'s march to Paris the following March, and led a division of **Reille**'s corps during the **Hundred Days** campaign in June, fighting at **Quatre Bras** and being wounded at **Waterloo**, after which he was temporarily retired.

France

The oldest unified monarchy in Europe, France was the best established of the **great powers** that acted as arbiters of eighteenth-century continental affairs. Before 1789 it was governed as an absolute monarchy by the Bourbon family, branches of which also held the thrones of **Spain** and **Naples**. The monarchy sat atop an anachronistic, basically feudal, socio-economic system that supported a sprawling, often unproductive nobility and allowed only token political representation for other classes.

Though it was mainland Europe's largest in the 1780s, the French economy lagged far behind that of **Great Britain** in terms of both size and industrialization. Parts of the country, particularly the north-east, were among the continent's most developed regions, but the south and west remained splintered and primarily agrarian, while economic activity as a whole was hidebound by innumerable internal customs barriers.

Most towns were still walled, medieval market centres, and Paris remained by far the largest city. With about 600,000 inhabitants in 1790 (out of a national population of some 27 million), the capital was the overwhelmingly dominant heart of French political, fiscal, commercial and cultural activity. It was also near to the headquarters of royal government at Versailles, and centralization was an important factor enabling power to change hands with increasing frequency after the regime's collapse in 1789.

Royal French foreign policy revolved around its global rivalry with Britain, but was also heavily involved in continental dynastic or territorial disputes. As a maritime and **colonial** power, France had endured a series of disappointments during the wars of the decades before 1789, most notably the loss of Canada to Britain during the calamitous Seven Years War (1756–63), but it retained important possessions in the **West Indies**, the **Indian Ocean** and along the southern coasts of **India** itself. Strategists of the 1780s (both royal and mercantile) aimed to expand French Indian interests at British expense, and to establish deep commercial penetration of the eastern **Mediterranean**, which was already a vital source of raw materials for the cottage manufacturing industries of Provence, in southern France.

Hopes of dominating Aegean and Levantine trade encouraged a fairly close relationship with the **Ottoman** government in Constantinople, but this was no barrier to friendship with **Austria** (a long-term ally) or **Russia**. Both the eastern empires were viewed in Paris as important counterweights to the westward expansionism of **Prussia**, which was also mistrusted as Britain's principal continental ally. Similar concerns kept France on friendly (if generally apathetic) terms with the Scandinavian kingdoms, while family connections effectively guaranteed the benevolence of Spain and Naples.

The breadth of its foreign policy commitments meant that the royal government needed a great deal more money than its antiquated economic infrastructure could provide. Forced to pay for unsuccessful wars with expensive loans, the monarchy had spiralled into irrevocable debt long before the 1780s, and financial failure was the principal catalyst for the regime's political collapse.

Peasant unrest in a poverty-stricken countryside, most of it focused against village-level feudal privileges, had been a major problem since the mid-1770s, exacerbated by anachronistic agricultural methods and mounting inflation. In urban centres, and above all in Paris, poverty and rising prices encouraged popular anger, and violent demonstration was commonplace in the capital after 1787. Meanwhile the more prosperous non-aristocratic classes, politically marginalized and economically frustrated, drank deep of the Enlightenment's new liberal doctrines, and were well versed in the ideologies of Rousseau and the American Revolution by 1788.

At the top of French society King **Louis XVI**, on the throne since 1774, faced mounting crisis with characteristic lack of resolution. Aware that fiscal reform was unavoidable, but reluctant to strike at the traditional bases of his absolute rule, he failed to back a succession of reforming ministers against entrenched noble conservatism. Some 200,000 aristocrats, many of them barely subsisting on meagre yields from feudal estates, were represented at the centre by the consultative Paris *parlement*, and led by a powerful court party gathered around the Comte d'**Artois** and Queen Marie-Antoinette.

Noble pressure eventually forced the king to summon the medieval States-General in August 1788, and the crown responded by appealing for popular support for reform through lists of grievances from every parish, but both moves backfired on their instigators. By identifying attacks on noble privilege with the king's name, the call for petitions encouraged rural unrest; and the meeting of the States-General at Versailles in May 1789 provided a forum for the Third Estate, representing the interests of commoners, to demand full political representation.

The Third Estate unilaterally declared itself a National Assembly in June 1789, an act generally accepted as the opening shot of the Revolution. The next two years saw the uneasy establishment of a constitutional monarchy in France, as the largely middle-class Assembly struggled to impose a moderate liberal constitution against the threats of counter-revolution from above and extreme **Jacobin** rebellion from the streets of Paris, where wage labourers and the unemployed (collectively known as *sans-culottes*) had joined with small businessmen, artisans and radical politicians to become a powerful political force.

Amid mounting anarchy in the provinces and a confused power struggle at the centre, the Assembly framed a new constitution. Largely the work of centre-left groups – with Barnave, Dupont, the Lameth brothers and **Sieyès** among their leaders – the Civil Constitution was adopted by the Assembly in November 1790, and accepted by the king in September 1791. It was framed with cooperation from **Lafayette**, Mounier and other figures to the right of the Assembly, but a left-wing Jacobin minority remained aloof in the name of greater democracy (*see* **French Revolution**).

Distinctly middle class in outlook, the new constitution was quickly undermined by opposition from all sides. Its acceptance by the king was pure lip service, while the queen and those royal princes who had not emigrated were actively plotting the Assembly's overthrow. A minority of former aristocrats, headed by the actively radical Duc d'Orléans, were enthusiastic supporters of the middle-class revolution, and several thousand nobles had emigrated since 1789, but most remained in France to provide a

focus for counter-revolutionary activity in both Paris and the provinces. A divided priesthood also became an important agency of provincial counter-revolution, particularly in the more backward, devout southern and western regions.

Broadly speaking, the peasantry reacted to a lack of tangible gains since 1789 by maintaining pressure at local level for land and voting rights. More focused campaigns to ease voting restrictions emerged in provincial towns and cities, led by shopkeepers, artisans and labourers whose tax contributions were insufficient to qualify them as voters. In Paris, the political appetites of these classes had been whetted by their essential role in the events of 1789, and cultivation of their support by factions battling for power in the Assembly helped turn political divisions into revolutionary confrontations.

After a period of relative calm during 1790, when food prices in particular had stabilized, popular agitation revived in early 1791. Radical middle-class members of the influential, extra-parliamentary Cordeliers Club began supporting the demands of unemployed and disenfranchised citizens, but the spark that ignited renewed revolution was the royal family's failed attempt to escape from Paris in June, which severely undermined popular faith in both crown and constitution. Encouraged by Cordeliers and Jacobin Club radicals, crowds invaded the streets to demand the foundation of a republic.

The Assembly's attempts to cover up Louis's treachery calmed fears for the royal family abroad, and the threat of armed conflict with vengeful European monarchies appeared to recede, but pressure for war was building inside France itself. The queen and her cohorts were promoting conflict with Austria as a means of destroying the Revolution, and the new Legislative Assembly (which convened in October 1791) quickly fell under the sway of a vociferous, left-wing war party. Led by Jacques-Henri Brissot, and including several deputies from the south-western Gironde region, it sought and gained mass support among the Paris boroughs ('sections') for an armed revolutionary crusade across Europe.

The Brissotin party was never more than a loose association of like-minded deputies, and was not supported by the most extreme left-wingers, but Brissot's impassioned oratory helped carry the vast majority, inside and outside the Assembly, towards war. While Austria and land-greedy Prussia dithered on the brink of armed intervention to restore the monarchy's former status, every diplomatic step they took was represented in Paris as part of a reactionary conspiracy with roots deep in French political society. An atmosphere of paranoid hysteria had overtaken the capital by the time the Assembly (in the name of the king) declared war against Habsburg emperor **Francis II** on 20 April 1792.

Jacobin leader **Robespierre** had argued almost alone against war on the grounds that it would demand strong central government and open the way for dictatorship rather than democracy. Ultimately he was right, and the Brissotins were not long able to control the democratic forces they had unleashed. The approach of war forced the king to dismiss Narbonne and other reactionary advisers, and its outbreak brought a number of Brissot's supporters into key positions (most notably General **Dumouriez** as the government's military adviser), but early defeats by **First Coalition** forces wrecked hopes of instant universal revolution and triggered renewed socio-economic chaos.

With **Brunswick**'s Prussians poised to attack towards Paris, and most of the capital's troops already at the frontiers, the *assignat* (a government bond issued as currency since 1790) tumbled to less than two-thirds of its face value. Renewed food shortages and Marie-Antoinette's blatant intrigues brought riots in Paris, but the Brissotins disassociated themselves from mob calls for the king's deposition, allowing Jacobin radicals to assume leadership of a mass movement towards a republic. After the provocative **Brunswick Manifesto** of 1 August had further inflamed passions, a combination of angry citizens, **National Guard** troops, visiting provincial militia and Jacobin politicians stormed the king's residence at the Tuileries on 10 August, forcing the royal family to take refuge in the Assembly chamber.

While elections were called for a new National Convention, Prussian forces were moving west from Verdun, and a sense of impending disaster may have fuelled a series of bizarre, apparently unplanned attacks on the city gaols by armed mobs in early September. Notorious as the 'September Massacres', they killed perhaps 1,500 prisoners, political and otherwise, and though apparently encouraged by some politicians, they were subsequently disclaimed by all parties.

The new Convention, chosen by universal male suffrage but with a complicated system of primaries that limited the direct influence of poorer provincial classes, met for the first time on 20 September. Its first act, responding to by now overwhelming popular pressure, was to depose the king and declare a republic, governed by an executive council of ministers selected from, but not sitting in, the Assembly.

Drawn from the same predominantly middle-class social strata as its predecessor, the Convention was composed of three main political groupings. A majority of unattached independent deputies, known as the 'Plain', was courted by two opposing left-wing parties. The Brissotins, by now usually called Girondins, were the larger group, providing most of the government ministers, while the more extreme Jacobin left of Robespierre, Marat and **Danton** was known as the 'Mountain' because of the high seats it occupied in the chamber.

All the groups adhered to many of the liberal principles enshrined in the 1791 constitution, but the Mountain consisted largely of Parisian deputies, willing to adapt their policies and identify themselves with insurrection in the capital. The Girondins dominated the Parisian press, but were mostly provincials who inevitably tended to promote national interests above those of Paris, and were likely to be held responsible for any setbacks in prosecution of the war.

As long as French armies enjoyed success, as they did for the rest of 1792 after their surprise defeat of Brunswick's invasion at **Valmy** on 20 September, Brissot and the Girondins could count on majority support from the Plain, and afford to ignore popular demands for central controls over food prices – but the tide of war turned in early 1793. After popular pressure had been instrumental in the Assembly's decision to execute the king on 23 January, a move that drove many moderates into permanent opposition, the First Coalition expanded to include Britain, the **Netherlands** and Spain. On the main battle-front in **Flanders**, French forces tumbled back to the frontier after defeat at **Neerwinden** in March, and their commander, the Girondin Dumouriez, defected to the Austrians.

Girondin attempts to recover popular credibility by blaming the defection on Danton, who had been sent to the front as mediator, merely promoted Jacobin solidarity, and an increasingly desperate government responded by strengthening its powers. The basis of future dictatorship lay in its creation of a Revolutionary Tribunal and a Committee of **Public Safety** as watchdogs over political opponents, along with 'revolutionary committees' to perform the same function in the Paris sections. Central authority was further fortified by the appointment of central government plenipotentiaries ('representatives on mission') to the military fronts and the provinces, but their often draconian approach to local administration sharpened regional opposition as well as bureaucratic efficiency.

These, initially temporary, measures were not enough to maintain control over a nation spiralling into economic chaos and civil war. The *assignat* had lost half its face value by spring 1793, and provincial demands for greater local autonomy had become entwined with support for a restored constitutional monarchy. In Paris a new wave of food riots erupted in the spring and the city's Commune, an assembly by now functioning as an important link between radical politicians and the streets, imposed a maximum price on bread in the capital in March. Popular calls for the Assembly to follow suit were backed by left-wing journals and the radical clubs.

An attempt by an extreme group known as the 'Enragés' to purge the Assembly of Girondins by popular revolt failed on 10 March, frustrated by the Mountain's unwillingness to let power pass into the hands of other radicals or the *sans-culottes*, but Robespierre's party was only awaiting a more favourable opportunity to seize control itself. On 5 April the Jacobins issued a public invitation to the Paris sections to gather at the Assembly and evict its Girondin leaders. Most of the sections had promised support within a few days, and the Commune soon gave its backing.

Unmoved by the government's belated introduction of a Maximum Law fixing bread prices in May, Jacobin leaders formed a Central Revolutionary Committee, which raised armed bands from the sections and took control of an enlarged National Guard before mobilizing to surround the Assembly at the end of the month. After the deputies had failed in an escape bid, they surrendered to popular demands on 2 June, when 29 Girondin members were arrested, along with two government ministers, giving the Mountain both a majority and a popular mandate to form a new administration.

The new Jacobin regime secured its position by passing a new constitution through the Assembly and local councils before the end of June. The Constitution of 1793 (Year II by the **Republican Calendar**) was far more genuinely democratic than its predecessors, with all male citizens given the vote and considerable direct influence over their representatives, but it made little effort to satisfy popular demand for guaranteed food supplies and prices, and was never applied in practice as the country as a whole slid towards anarchy.

Moderates and royalists retained considerable influence in Paris itself, and a revolt was growing in the south of the country that would see **Lyon**, Nantes, **Bordeaux**, Marseilles and **Toulon** fall into hostile hands during the summer. A royalist, Catholic uprising had broken out in the western **Vendée** region during March, followed by a **Chouan** rebellion further north in Brittany, and the need to divert troops against internal targets weakened efforts to hold the Flanders, **Rhine** and **Pyrenean** fronts against invasion forces. Meanwhile inflation was out of control, with the *assignat* down to 36 per cent of face value in June and 22 per cent in August.

Despite the Maximum Law, bread shortages again brought Paris to boiling point during the summer. Popular calls for stricter central price controls and reprisals against speculators reached a peak in August and September, before the Jacobin Convention took steps to satisfy both the small traders who dominated the Commune and their *sans-culotte* allies. Emergency measures enacted on 5 September included the establishment of relief pay for the Parisian unemployed and formal adoption of the **Terror**, by which coercion and summary punishment became government policy wherever they were deemed necessary to the Revolution's survival. On 29 September, the Assembly passed a general Maximum Law that placed relatively low ceilings on the price of bread and most other basic commodities, as well as pegging wages to a fixed point above 1790 levels.

The Terror was viewed by its creators as the only way to ensure the Revolution's survival, and represented the high point of partnership between Jacobin leaders and the Parisian *sans-culottes*, who were organized into *armées révolutionaires* and sent to extract supplies from the provinces. Representatives on mission were now officially required to hunt down counter-revolutionaries, speculators and other perceived enemies of the people, and the often conflicting activities of 'terrorist' elements, National Guard militia and local political committees spread violent confusion across France.

Under the circumstances, the Paris Convention endorsed creation of a strong central authority, and the months following the Jacobin takeover saw the Committee of Public Safety emerge as a national executive armed with dictatorial powers. In July 1793 Robespierre and his chief lieutenants (St Just and Couthon) replaced a significant minority of 'Dantonists', who were concerned to represent the views of the provinces and sought a negotiated settlement with the Coalition. Under Robespierre's direction, the committee began applying its powers in the widest sense, taking sole responsibility for direction of the Terror and the wars on the frontiers.

The new dictatorship was formalized during the autumn. On 10 October the Mountain pushed through a decree declaring the Terror permanent until the Revolution's completion, and a law giving full executive authority to the Convention's two principal committees came into force on 4 December. The Committee of General Security was responsible for the police and internal security, including the flow of Revolutionary Tribunal victims to an increasingly busy guillotine, and the Committee of Public Safety controlled all other aspects of government. Representatives on mission were brought under stricter central control, while the powers of local authorities, the National Guard and the Paris sections were curbed.

These measures, forced on Robespierre and his allies by pressure of events, completed the transition of the Terror from near-anarchy to centralized control, and effectively saved the French republic. Ruthless commandeering of resources and execution of political opponents improved both the material condition and the morale of French armed forces, and temporarily calmed the population of Paris. Firm central direction, especially the inspired organizational and reforming work of war minister **Carnot**, channelled these improvements into effective military action both inside France and abroad.

Strong forces were sent to put down the rebellions in the south and west, culminating in the ejection of allied naval forces from Toulon in December 1793, and local populations were subject to savage reprisals. The armies on the frontiers were remodelled, expanded and concentrated for offensives that gained ground on the **Italian** and Pyrenean fronts in spring 1794. They also halted a major allied invasion attempt from Flanders, and eventually drove Coalition forces into full retreat from the Netherlands after a conclusive victory at **Fleurus** in June.

Successes against the First Coalition could not bring long-term stability to the capital. Nor could they save the Jacobin regime from the fruits of its own terrorism, as Robespierre's belief that only the direction of a 'single will' could save the Revolution promoted savage purges against opposition from both the right and the left.

The left-wing leaders of the Commune and sections, especially the popular demagogue Hébert, were threatening to ignite full-scale civil war. Popular hostility aroused in the provinces by the ruthless behaviour of 'Hébertist' terrorists, like the particularly savage **Fouché**, was sharpened by their violent 'dechristianization' campaign, which combined belief in the 'goddess of Reason' with attacks on even those "jurist" priests who had embraced the regime. The closure of all the Paris churches by the commune in November 1793 finally brought condemnation of the left from Robespierre, and encouraged Danton to return to Paris from rural exile. Danton's relatively moderate group of 'Indulgents', which included the journalist Camille Desmoulins, won strong support in the Convention for a series of stinging attacks on the committee.

After purging the section assemblies of extremists, the committees found an excuse to arrest Hébertist leaders when they attempted to raise an insurrection against the Dantonists in spring 1794. Hébert and his Cordeliers Club associates were guillotined on 25 March, and the consequent threat of a right-wing revival was met by the arrest of the Dantonists, most of whom were executed on 5 April.

Meanwhile the Jacobin alliance with the Paris *sans-culottes* had been breaking down under economic pressure. The Terror only temporarily boosted supply levels from the provinces, so that the Maximum Laws soon collapsed and a thriving black market fed renewed inflation. Food protesters again took to the streets from early 1794, but the government responded to pressure from the Plain by introducing a less stringent version of the general Maximum in March. This move back towards a free market incensed small consumers and brought financial speculators back into the open, sending a recovering *assignat* into free fall. The (now Jacobin) Commune made a belated attempt to reduce wages in Paris to something like the levels required by the Maximum in July, a move that cemented popular disenchantment.

By that time Robespierre's party had lost its grip on the Assembly. Widely (and probably falsely) suspected of ambitions for long-term dictatorship, Robespierre became a focus for fear and resentment after a law of 10 June streamlining the Revolutionary Tribunal's work was passed without consulting the Committee of General Security. Determined to reassert its authority, the committee embarked on the 'Great Terror', executing almost half of the Paris guillotine's 2,600 victims over the next few weeks. Widespread revulsion, especially after Fleurus had removed the apparent need for continued bloodletting, was nevertheless focused against the better-known Committee of Public Safety.

Apparently ignorant of his weakening position, and increasingly isolated even on the committee, Robespierre was overthrown by the parliamentary coup of **Thermidor** in late July.

He was executed two days later, along with Saint-Just and 20 other supporters. Another 71 members of the Paris Commune were guillotined on 28 July, bringing the Great Terror to a final climax.

Thermidor brought the moderate, propertied men of the Plain to power in the Convention, led by hard-bitten politicians such as **Talleyrand** and Sieyès, along with former 'terrorists' such as **Barras**. To their right, a group of 75 surviving Girondins and a few constitutional monarchists returned to their seats, while the Mountain formed a dwindling and largely uninvolved left-wing rump. A new council of ministers quickly brought the Terror to an end, diluting the powers of the two main committees by spreading their work across another sixteen, and providing for frequent re-election of members. Regional committees were similarly curbed, while the Paris Commune was abolished and the sections purged of Jacobins.

The government of autumn 1794 faced all the same problems that had beset its predecessors. Violence still blighted the provinces, where the government could do nothing to stop revenge attacks against former terrorists and 'dechristianizers'. Government dedication to the free market brought softening of the Maximum Laws in October, and their abolition in late December, encouraging inflation that pushed the *assignat* down to a fifth of its face value. By the following May the *assignat* was at 7.5 per cent of its face value and, with wages quite unable to match rising costs, 1795 saw near-famine in the countryside and another upsurge of extra-parliamentary agitation in Paris.

The Paris sections were loosely divided into Jacobin, Hébertist and moderate camps, and independent bands of middle-class young men (*jeunesse dorée*, or 'gilded youth') had appeared on the streets to fight extremists in the Convention's name. Once the bread ration, still being sold at fixed prices alongside the free-market trade, began to fail in late March, the Hébertists were able to rouse the mass of *sans-culottes* for direct attacks on the convention in April (**Germinal**) and May (**Prairial**). Both failed, the latter after four days, and the savage reprisals that followed finally broke the hold of the *sans-culottes* over Parisian politics.

The 'Thermidorians' made no attempt to significantly alter Jacobin military policy. Carnot retained the war ministry, and his methods continued to enjoy spectacular success. In Flanders, Jourdan and **Pichegru** had advanced beyond the **Roer** in autumn 1794, and completed the capture of the independent Netherlands (along with most of the **Dutch Navy**) the following January. Spanish forces were in full retreat on the Pyrenean front by spring 1795, and soon joined Prussia in withdrawing from the Coalition altogether. The strategic insights of **Napoleon** Bonaparte, a young artillery general who had made his name at Toulon, helped French forces consolidate limited gains on the **Italian** front, and the revolt still dividing the Vendée crumbled after **Hoche** had routed a British-sponsored royalist invasion at **Quiberon Bay** in July 1795.

Though Britain and Austria still remained firmly committed to war, France had begun to gain from the experience in territorial terms. The southern territories of **Nice** and **Savoy** had been annexed early in the war, and they were joined by the Austrian Netherlands as a whole in 1795, along with several Dutch frontier provinces. Though the British had seized a few small French colonies in the West Indies, the acquisition of **Santo Domingo** as part of the Peace of **Basle** with Spain seemed adequate compensation. A war of republican defence was becoming a lucrative exercise in national expansion.

By autumn the government was ready to introduce its new Constitution of Year III, which returned to a restricted franchise and indirect elections, but was more democratic than the 1791 version. Local assemblies were given very limited autonomy, and the new Legislative Assembly was to be divided into two houses, the Councils of **Five Hundred** and **Ancients**, with executive power vested in a five-man **Directory**. Part of the Assembly, and one Directorship, were to be re-elected every year, but the danger of an electoral swing to the left or right was answered by a law insisting that two-thirds of the new legislature be drawn from members of the current Convention.

The latter provision caused political and popular uproar in Paris, outraging even the moderate bourgeois who now controlled most of the sections. When the government drafted troops into the capital to prevent trouble, almost every section responded by rejecting the constitution and massing for direct action, a situation skilfully exploited by moderate royalists, encouraged back into Parisian politics by the end of the Terror. Their bid to seize power by the coup of **Vendémiaire** (5 October) was only foiled after Director Barras called in Napoleon and several other young republican generals, who used artillery to disperse a popular march on Assembly.

His part in saving the new constitution propelled Napoleon into a position of real political influence for the first time, and appeared to establish the Directory in power, but the regime was never able to rise above reaction in the face of opposition from left and right. Defeat of the royalists prompted a brief Jacobin revival but, as political clubs and radical newspapers began to reappear, the *assignat* was disappearing, to be replaced as worthless in February 1796. The new government bond, the *mandat territorial*, collapsed the following summer, feeding hyperinflation that inflicted extreme poverty on all but the wealthiest social classes. Mounting criticism from the left culminated in an abortive Jacobin coup in early 1797, and a fresh purge of radicals, presenting royalists with an opportunity to re-establish their influence.

As in 1794, the success of French arms abroad conspired to put the sitting government in jeopardy. Carnot remained at the war ministry as a Director, and his work bore triumphant fruit in the campaigns of 1796–7. French armies gained the initiative on the Rhine and, under Napoleon's brilliant guidance, drove Austrian forces from northern Italy. Napoleon secured peace with Austria at **Leoben** in spring 1797, ending the First Coalition, and the harsh terms imposed entirely on his own initiative reflected the **French Army's** political strength. It increased still further after the elections of April 1797 gave constitutional monarchists majorities in both legislative houses.

Unable to count on support from the increasingly right-wing Carnot or new, royalist Director Barthélemy, Barras called in troops under

Augereau and Hoche to purge the Assembly of 214 royalists by the coup of **Fructidor** on 1 September 1797. Hundreds of deportations followed, many of them royalist priests or returned **émigrés**, with Barthélémy and Council of Five Hundred chairman Pichegru among those imprisoned.

In the brief political lull that followed, the Directory made efforts to come to an arrangement with Britain, but though its threatened invasion of **England** was called off, the decision to allow the overtly ambitious Napoleon to lead an expedition to the **Middle East** in spring 1798 ended all hope of peace. Napoleon's attack on **Egypt**, and loss of the French Mediterranean Fleet at the **Nile** (1 August), multiplied the damage inflicted on French industrial development and overseas trade by the British naval **blockade**, and hindered the government's simultaneous attempts at economic reform.

After a Jacobin revival in the elections of spring 1798 had been nipped in the bud by another parliamentary coup (of **Floréal**), limited tax and currency reforms were introduced, but even a series of good harvests could not long sustain **war finances** still dominated by costly loans. With rebellion again brewing in the west of France, a Directory unwilling to sponsor a return to the Terror sought economic salvation in territorial expansion. Moves to extend French influence in **Switzerland**, central Italy and Germany gave the British government an opportunity to build a **Second Coalition** against the republic, and from autumn 1798 the Directory was again conducting a major war.

Though Carnot had fled France after Fructidor, the introduction of national **conscription** in September 1798 enabled the Directory to plan ambitious offensives at the **Rhine**, on the **Swiss** front and in the **Italian** theatre. All came to grief in spring 1799, and the annual elections made clear the extent to which its record had discredited the Directory. Most of the government's candidates were defeated, and the Jacobin revival repeated in greater strength. Sieyès joined the Directory, and promptly organized the parliamentary removal of its right-wing members.

With allied armies poised to invade France through Switzerland and Provence by the summer, and already in **North Holland**, a mild version of the Terror was introduced as a means of maintaining the regime's security and meeting the emergency. Stern measures were taken against draft dodgers, and the families of absent royalists were arrested as hostages, while immediate financial needs were met by forced loans.

The military situation eased in the autumn, as **Masséna** drove the allies from Switzerland, Russian forces were removed from the southern frontier and the Duke of **York** withdrew from North Holland. Neither the Directory nor its constitution retained much support by that time, but Jacobins encouraged towards a coup by the popular mood and royalists outraged by the Directory's assumption of emergency powers were both pre-empted by Sieyès. After **Moreau** had turned him down, and the popular General **Joubert** had been killed, Sieyès secured the support of Napoleon, back in Paris after leaving his army in Egypt, to provide military backing for the successful coup of **Brumaire** on 9–10 November 1799.

Surrounded by regular troops, the Assembly was forced to accept a provisional dictatorship, and spent the next few weeks wrangling over the details of a new constitution. Sieyès planned an elaborate system that re-established universal male suffrage, but only for the indirect election of a 'national list' from which the executive appointed a Senate. This in turn selected a Tribunate to frame laws, a Legislature to pass them, and a Grand Elector as executive head of government. The elector, a role intended for Napoleon, chose his two co-executive consuls, one for foreign and one for home affairs, but could be dismissed at any time by the Senate.

With help from Talleyrand, Fouché and supporters in the Assembly, Napoleon outmanoeuvred Sieyès, securing an apparent compromise that replaced the Grand Elector with a First Consul. In office for ten years, the First Consul was empowered to make all state appointments, and to select a Council of State that overrode the Tribunate as the source of new laws. Law could be initiated by the First Consul himself using decrees, or *senatus-consulta*. The **Consulate** came into being in February 1800 after a national plebiscite had approved the new constitution by

3 million votes to 1,500, and it quickly became clear that Napoleon planned to use the *senatus-consulta* and Council of State to impose a personal dictatorship.

At this stage, with France still facing the immediate threat of invasion from the Rhine and northern Italy, Napoleon's power base remained shaky. His departure on campaign in May 1800 was the signal for a renewed upsurge of intrigue against the regime in Paris and a revival of royalist activity in the provinces. Napoleon's narrow but decisive victory over the Austrians at **Marengo** in June, which again cleared Italy of hostile forces, sent popular confidence in the new government soaring, and Moreau's success at **Hohenlinden** in December knocked Vienna out of the war. With the Second Coalition dead, and Britain his only active enemy abroad, Napoleon took steps to stifle opposition and place his regime on more secure foundations.

During 1801 the First Consul embarked on a round of arrests, deportations and executions that removed most of his opponents from the Tribunate. He stripped the senate of power to nominate tribunes, purged Paris of Jacobin elements and expelled intellectual opponents such as salon hostess Madame de **Staël**. A plot to overthrow the regime among senior army officers was broken up at an early stage by a combination of threats and inducements, cementing his mistrust of Moreau and mending fences with the influential **Bernadotte**.

During the period of relative peace between 1801 and the resumption of general European war in 1805, Napoleon inaugurated an enormous programme of social and economic reforms. Much of his work, and that of the Council of State, was primarily concerned to secure and strengthen power at the centre, but its overall effect was to provide France with a workable system of government for the first time in decades.

Financial reform was urgently needed to meet the government's postwar cash crisis. Along with the sale of remaining state lands and the use of war booty to defray routine expenses, the assessment and collection of existing taxes was streamlined (more than doubling yields), and non-military government expenditure was monitored more strictly than ever before. In peacetime these expedients enabled the Consulate to avoid the imposition of new taxes, maintain strict limits on grain exports and hold grain prices at artificially low levels, though they were not enough to finance major wars after 1805.

Napoleon's wider economic policy aimed at stability as a means of enhancing the state's military capabilities. The creation of the Bank of France in 1800 laid the foundations for greater economic coherence, unifying control over the national debt and the issue of paper money. Gold and silver coin began to reappear in circulation, and inflation was brought under control. Long-term industrial and agricultural stagnation was addressed by central government intervention, with agencies monitoring every aspect of production and sponsoring a plethora of reward schemes. Output and employment levels rose appreciably in some sectors, notably the northern French wool industry, and subsequent military success opened up new international markets for French goods in Europe, but overseas trade remained severely restricted by British naval supremacy.

Napoleon's active interest in social welfare programmes reflected an abiding concern to maintain the regime's mass popularity by satisfying basic peasant needs, but was never allowed to interfere with political or military priorities. Widespread modernization of workhouses and experiments with basic workers' insurance were balanced by ruthless suppression of trades unions (damned as intrinsically 'Jacobin'), strict monitoring of craft guild activities and a law compelling workers to carry an official permit at all times.

New laws aimed at broadening the country's educational base required each commune to establish a primary school, and each *département* at least one secondary school, with the *lycée* system introduced as a bridge between school and university. Simultaneous state interference in curriculum design, while promoting a valuable concentration on mathematics and the sciences, reduced teaching of the arts to a bare functional minimum and, in the manner of twentieth-century totalitarian states, replaced all teaching of modern history with a course extolling the virtues of Charlemagne. Teachers themselves, a majority of them clerics, were subject to close and frequent state scrutiny.

The growth and widespread use of a sophisticated network of secret police and informers was the key to maintaining political supremacy at the centre, but general maintenance of law and order was entrusted to the first French national police force, established in 1802 and represented in every local commune. Fouché was given control of an expanded police ministry, a role for which he proved exceptionally well qualified, providing Napoleon with daily bulletins on the positions and ambitions of political opponents.

Police were backed by a corps of centrally appointed circuit judges, sent out into the country from 1803, and by the creation of special tribunals to deal with treasonable activities. Every *département* was governed by an appointed prefect, every district by a sub-prefect and every commune by a mayor, all appointed from the centre and assisted by councils – essentially the system employed by the royal autocracy before 1789.

The most enduring monument to Bonaparte's administrative energy remains the legal system still known as the **Code Napoléon**. Two expert commissions, later merged, worked from 1801 under **Cambacérès** (but with considerable input from Napoleon himself) to complete a new Civil Code in 1804, followed by a Commercial Code (1807), Criminal Code (1808) and Penal Code (1810). Promoting tolerance, equity before the law, the sanctity of personal property and the domestic dominance of the male, the Civil Code is still operative in parts of western and central Europe.

Napoleon's creation of the Légion d'Honneur was the first step towards founding a new nobility and flew in the face of the most cherished revolutionary principles. Opponents recognized that a class of 'notables' dependent on his personal patronage would serve to strengthen further the leader's position, but despite fierce criticism, even in the tame Council of State, the Légion was established in May 1802.

The emergence of a new nobility was echoed by a growing cult surrounding Napoleon himself. Everyday life under the Consulate was more comfortable and secure than at any time in recent memory, and state **propaganda** was careful to nurture a sense of plenty's dependence on the person of the First Consul. Genuine popular admiration for Napoleon, above all in the lower ranks of the army, provided both a valuable defence against conspiracy and fuel for his campaign to establish himself as hereditary ruler.

Failed assassination plots in 1802 and 1803 were a godsend in this respect, sparking popular fears for the regime's security, but it was the conclusion of peace with Britain at **Amiens** in 1802, an achievement greeted with rejoicing all over France, that gave Napoleon the opportunity to alter the constitution. On 8 May 1802, two days after the treaty had been publicly proclaimed, the Senate formally proposed his elevation to First Consul for life, with increased powers over the Senate and the right to nominate his own successor. Another plebiscite voted overwhelmingly in favour of the idea, though some sections of the army expressed opposition, and the Life Consulate was confirmed in August.

Now a monarch in all but name, and surrounded by a court at the Tuileries that aped the manners and dress of its royal counterparts, Napoleon used the public outcry generated by the revelation of the royalist **Cadoudal** conspiracy (and the alleged involvement of the Duc d'**Enghein**) to pressurize the Senate into proposing his elevation as Emperor of the French on 18 May 1804. Another plebiscite followed on 6 November, displaying signs of official tampering but producing a majority of 2.5 million in favour of the proposal to 8,000 against. Napoleon was crowned in sumptuous splendour on 2 December, bringing the French Revolution full circle from royal autocracy to imperial dictatorship.

The coronation at Notre Dame cathedral was attended by the new Pope, **Pius VII**, demonstrating that Napoleon had, at least temporarily, solved one of the most intractable problems facing his republican predecessors. The **Concordat** agreed with the Catholic Church in 1801 ended a decade of schism with Rome, interrupted the rich growth of cults and sects that had characterized French religious life since the early 1790s, and enabled millions of citizens to accept the political status quo with a clear conscience. He soon sacrificed good relations with the Vatican by adding the **Organic Articles** to the agreement, but they were deemed necessary to ensure direct government control over the clergy.

Religious tolerance, extended to Protestants, Jews, Muslims and other minority faiths, reflected Napoleon's anxiety to draw as many people as possible into partnership with the regime, as did a series of laws encouraging the return of all but the most obdurate royalist 'ultras' back into France from exile. As long as he enjoyed a reputation as an international peacemaker, and his government was engaged in a high-profile programme of generally applauded reforms, this policy was very successful, but both peace and the pace of reform collapsed after 1803.

The establishment of the French Empire in 1804 brought few important constitutional changes. Police powers were further extended, the functions of the court were formalized and a new nobility was openly promoted. Headed by Joseph **Bonaparte** and Napoleon's other brothers as Princes of the Empire, the imperial aristocracy included the new **Marshalate** and six Imperial Arch-bureaucrats, along with dozens of barons and counts.

After 1804 government policy was dominated by the business of waging wars, as expansionism promoted international conflict and vice versa. Even before the breakdown of relations with Britain in May 1803, Napoleon had demonstrated his contempt for treaty arrangements by annexing **Piedmont**, establishing a new puppet republic in northern Italy, forcing a new constitution on Switzerland, failing to evacuate Holland and interfering in the affairs of the crumbling **Holy Roman Empire**.

These and subsequent diplomatic outrages had helped Britain to form a **Third Coalition** against France from late 1804. It was crushed at **Austerlitz** in December 1805, but British naval superiority had already been decisively confirmed at **Trafalgar** and Napoleon's imposition of punitive peace treaties helped bring about a **Fourth Coalition** from summer 1806. That eventually collapsed after Russian defeat at **Friedland** in June 1807, enabling Napoleon to make what appeared a lasting peace with the tsar at **Tilsit** in July, but the pace of French expansion hardly slowed in the aftermath.

Attacks on **Portugal** in 1807, and on **Spain** the following spring, failed to secure French rule, triggering a Spanish popular rebellion and a six-year **Peninsular War** against Anglo-Iberian ground forces, but victory over the Austrians in 1809 ended a short-lived **Fifth Coalition**. The subsequent **Schönbrunn** Treaty brought the empire close to the limits of its expansion, which were reached during the relatively peaceful years of 1810–11. By early 1812, excluding nominally independent satellites, the Grand Empire of France comprised 130 *départements*, with a total population of some 44 million people (*see* **Map 21**).

To the south, the **Ligurian** and **Cisalpine** Republics had disappeared in 1805, the Genoese coastline joining the empire and the remainder passing under indirect French control as the Kingdom of **Italy**, where **Beauharnais** ruled as Napoleon's viceroy until 1814, his territories eventually extending east into modern Slovenia. Mainland Naples became a puppet kingdom from 1806, under first Joseph Bonaparte and later **Murat**, and by 1809 France had annexed Parma, **Tuscany** and the **Papal States**.

Across the Adriatic, the **Ionian Islands** had been French since the 1790s, and the Dalmatian coast came under imperial control as the province of **Illyria** in 1809. Further north, Switzerland was no more than nominally independent, and had donated the cantons of Valois and Geneva to France by 1810. The former Austrian Netherlands had been part of France since 1793, but the frontier was pushed east in 1810, when Louis **Bonaparte's** client kingdom of Holland was annexed.

To the east, victory at **Jena–Auerstädt** in 1806 paved the way for the replacement of the Holy Roman Empire by a French-sponsored, and largely obedient, Confederation of the **Rhine**, including **Bavaria**, Baden, **Württemberg**, **Saxony** and surviving smaller independent German states, along with the French-controlled Duchy of **Berg** and a new client Kingdom of **Westphalia** (ruled by Jérôme **Bonaparte**). By 1811 the **Hanseatic** ports of Bremen, Lübeck and Hamburg had been annexed, along with parts of southern **Denmark**, bringing the French north-eastern frontier up to the Baltic coast. Even further east, the establishment of the puppet Grand Duchy of **Warsaw** in what had been **Poland** provided a buffer against future Russian aggression.

As sources of manpower and economic support, both the empire and its satellites were vital to Napoleon's pursuit of apparently insatiable dynastic ambitions. These were dominated by his desire to establish a universal European monarchy, and intensified by the birth of a son and heir to his Habsburg second wife **Marie-Louise** in 1811, but were focused after 1806 on an attempt to defeat Britain by a continent-wide trade embargo, known as the **Continental System**. Never fully enforced or effective, the system did boost the trading performance of French industry, providing protectionist tariffs and a greater share of the European market – but it drained client and satellite economies, straining diplomatic relations on both sides, and determination to make it work helped push Napoleon into military adventures his empire could not sustain.

Constitutional changes after 1804 were overwhelmingly concerned with strengthening central controls over an expanding empire. Inside imperial France, the emperor governed through the personal organizations of his household (La Maison) and military staff (Grand Quartier-Général), effectively dispensing with other political institutions. The Legislature and Council of State were rarely consulted on policy matters after 1805, and the Tribunate was abolished altogether in 1807, changes affirmed by a new constitution of the Grand Empire in 1808.

Across the wider empire, the appearance of liberal reform was maintained in relations with independent satellite states, but not for long. Popular support was courted by programmes of public works, widespread abolition of feudal institutions, and the summoning of democratically elected assemblies to rubber-stamp new constitutions, but approval soon came to matter less than efficient economic and military exploitation. From 1805 elected assemblies began to be replaced by nominated legislatures, and executive authority concentrated in the hands of politically reliable imperial appointees with strong military support.

As wars followed wars, imperial administration of annexed and satellite territories became identified with the imposition of taxation and conscription, promoting widespread hostility to French rule. In France itself, the agricultural and industrial reforms of the Consulate, combined with preferential tax rates and tariffs, ensured relative prosperity up to and beyond 1812, which in turn bolstered popular support for Napoleon. Though conspiracies against the government were an everyday fact of life in Paris and in the provinces, where brooding cells of committed royalist agitators were a constant nuisance, they could never expect mass backing, and were anyway subject to strict press censorship.

Like its policies, the internal stability of imperial France was heavily dependent on the patronage and personal charisma of the emperor. Fear of anarchy in the event of his death prompted the **Talleyrand–Fouché** conspiracy of 1808, aimed at conferring the succession on Murat as a figurehead for its organizers, and uncertainty beneath the façade of imperial grandeur was startlingly revealed when rumours of Napoleon's demise on campaign sparked the **Malet** conspiracy in 1812.

By that time Napoleon had lost some of his most important political allies in Paris. Fouché's plotting brought his eventual dismissal in 1810, and Talleyrand was actively conspiring with the empire's enemies from 1808, but they could do little to effect change. The emperor's presence, reinforced by the loyalty of household staff, most military officers and the majority of new nobles, was always enough to maintain order in the capital, even after the catastrophe of 1812.

Napoleon's decision to invade Russia in 1812, controversial at the time even among his aides, is acknowledged as his greatest strategic error. Hugely expensive in terms of resources, and an unmitigated military disaster, the **Russian campaign** destroyed a **Grande Armée** of more than half a million men, triggering rapid disintegration of Napoleon's diplomatic position. He might have made peace with an expanding **Sixth Coalition** at the end of 1812, albeit only by agreeing to shrink France back to its 'natural frontiers', but instead raised a new army to contest control of **Germany** in 1813.

Defeat in Germany, sealed by the Battle of

Leipzig in October 1813, left France itself facing invasion for the first time since 1799, and Napoleon's popular support at last began to crumble. Scenting victory, royalist agents and agitators were pouring into the provinces from abroad, and old hostilities in the south and west were revived, with Bordeaux surrendering unilaterally to the allies in early 1814.

Still refusing to consider allied peace terms, Napoleon resorted to the tactics of his revolutionary predecessors, issuing emergency decrees that sent troops into the provinces to enforce requisitions and conscription, but response was muted or hostile in many areas. The Legislature, recalled to endorse national defence measures in early 1814, was dissolved by the emperor after ten days of unproductive wrangling, while lack of enthusiasm for the continued struggle extended to imperial administrators and senior army officers.

At the end of January 1814, with Coalition armies already invading eastern **France**, Napoleon left Paris to fight a desperate campaign of manoeuvre against numerically overwhelming forces. Joseph Bonaparte, forced to flee his kingdom in Spain by the success of **Wellington's** offensives in the peninsula, was left in Paris to govern in Napoleon's stead, but proved quite incapable of containing rampant opposition, orchestrated by Talleyrand. As even imperial authorities began making open preparations for royal restoration, Napoleon was denied troops and vital equipment from Paris, and his calls for large-scale popular resistance were less effective in inciting **guerrilla** activity than the behaviour of advanced **Cossack** units.

Napoleon was eventually outmanoeuvred in March 1814, and the allies occupied the capital at the end of the month. The Legislature promptly declared the emperor deposed, proclaiming the restoration of the exiled King **Louis XVIII**, pretender to the throne since the death of his nephew in 1795. The **abdication** of Napoleon followed on 6 April, after his marshals had refused to fight on, and Louis reached Calais from Britain on 14 April. The Treaty of **Paris** between France and the allies brought the war to a formal close at the end of the month, and a separate agreement signed at **Fontainebleau**

consigned Napoleon to exile on **Elba**.

On his return to Paris the king issued a royal charter promising to uphold the liberal reforms of the Revolution, and accepted many imperial officials and commanders into royal service. With France returned to its 1792 frontiers by the Paris treaty, but spared indemnities and given representation at the postwar Congress of **Vienna** (a role performed by Talleyrand as foreign minister), the broad support of a war-weary population seemed to promise a long period of peaceful reconstruction.

The new government's popularity was fleeting. In the wake of the king's return, a rush of loyal émigrés, many of them extreme counter-revolutionary 'ultras', had to be rewarded with offices and estates. Their predatory demands, only part-satisfied by the transfer of property from discredited imperial servants, encouraged fears among the middle classes and rural peasantry that Church and secular lands were about to revert to their former owners. Meanwhile a much-reduced royal army sent large numbers of rank-and-file troops home to disgruntled unemployment, and retired successful veteran officers on half-pay to accommodate former exiles.

Growing disenchantment with the new order was communicated to Napoleon through numerous political and military contacts, Talleyrand inevitably prominent among them, and the former emperor slipped back into France from Elba on 1 March 1815. Though initial popular and political reactions to his arrival were uncertain, he gathered support as he approached Paris, winning over a succession of military units sent to stop him, including the forces of royal cavalry commander **Ney** on 14 March. The royal family fled across the frontier into Belgium on 19 March, and Napoleon re-entered the capital next day.

Though welcomed as a saviour by the populace, and in de facto control of the army, Napoleon could not hope to reclaim the autocratic powers he had enjoyed before 1814. Styling himself 'Protector of the Revolution', he issued an amendment to the imperial constitution that sought to satisfy a broad spectrum of liberal opinion by restoring manhood suffrage and guaranteeing the new aristocracy's property rights. It was uneasily accepted by the Senate, but few were convinced of its sincerity, and Napoleon's leadership in 1815 was always conditional on a rapid success over the other great powers, which formed a **Seventh Coalition** on 25 March.

The brief period of Napoleon's restoration, known as the **Hundred Days**, was dominated by preparations for the campaign that ended in defeat at **Waterloo** on 18 June. At least part of the capital's population retained its faith in Napoleon after the battle, but it did break his fragile hold over the Parisian political establishment. The indestructible Fouché led calls for his abdication in the Senate within days of Waterloo, and the emperor obliged on 22 June, subsequently giving himself up to British naval authorities in Rochefort. Ignoring the claims of the infant Napoleon II, the Chamber announced a provisional government, and declared for the king when he returned to Paris under Prussian escort on 8 July.

A second Treaty of **Paris**, signed that November, reduced France to its 1790 frontiers, imposed indemnities and left the country under military occupation for the next three years. With Napoleon safely out of the way on distant St Helena, Louis was able to establish a partnership with the new aristocracy of France, its wealth and power based on post-feudal economic methods and systems, while keeping constant pressure from reactionaries among the old nobility at bay.

Though he soon dispensed with Talleyrand and other high-profile imperial relics, and executed Ney for treason, Louis respected most of the property arrangements inherited in 1814, left the revolutionary Church settlement and the Concordat intact, and restored many of Napoleon's surviving generals to senior office. Louis's death in 1824 brought the deeply conservative Charles IX to the throne, and he was overthrown by a liberal revolution in 1830, power passing to a more tightly controlled constitutional monarchy under King Louis-Philippe, son of the radical Duc d'Orléans and (under the name 'Egalité') a former revolutionary general.

France, Campaign for (1813–14)

The invasion of France by the allies of the **Sixth Coalition** during late 1813 and the first quarter of 1814. In the wake of allied victory in **Germany**, operations centred on eastern France, where fewer than 100,000 French troops faced more than three times their number approaching the **Rhine** in late 1813. At the same time, allied forces under **Bellegarde** opened a final **Italian campaign** against viceroy **Beauharnais**'s small defending army, and **Wellington**'s offensive in the **Peninsular** theatre maintained its drive into south-western France. Military pressure on France was compounded by mounting political instability, aggravated by war-weariness and ongoing British **blockade**.

The most immediate problem facing **Napoleon** was manpower shortage. The loss of almost a million troops in 1812–13 could not easily be made good, particularly now that satellite territories to the east had changed sides. Gambling on the allied Rhine armies needing several months to rest and reorganize, he explored every conceivable source of conscripted manpower from late 1813, and made simultaneous diplomatic efforts to reduce the danger to his other frontiers. Pope **Pius VII** was restored to Rome as a sop to popular opinion in Italy, and the Treaty of **Valençay** was agreed with **Ferdinand VII** of Spain. Napoleon never came close to achieving his target of 900,000 fresh troops, but was given time to try by allied delays and divisions.

Austrian emperor **Francis**, supported by his cautious C-in-C **Schwarzenberg**, was anxious to recover control of northern Italy but not to destroy France completely, where his daughter **Marie-Louise** was empress. Swedish crown prince **Bernadotte** was similarly reluctant to attack France, apparently in the hope that the French people would turn to him as Napoleon's successor, and **Great Britain**'s innate commitment to European balance of power inclined its government to seek a negotiated peace. On the other hand, Russian tsar **Alexander** was determined to avenge the invasion of 1812, and Prussian king **Frederick William** was committed to supporting his Russian ally, though he was less aggressive than **Blücher** and other Prussian commanders.

After a fractious summit meeting at Frankfurt, allied leaders agreed on 16 November to offer Napoleon negotiations on the basis of the 1799 'natural frontiers', and the three armies gathered along the Rhine suspended offensive preparations. Napoleon played for time, calling for an international congress before provisionally accepting the terms on 30 November, but by then the allied position had shifted. Unable to trust Napoleon's intentions, the allies insisted on restoration of the 1792 frontiers. Once these deliberately unacceptable terms had been rejected, the pause in operations ended with a three-pronged allied offensive into eastern France from late December.

After an Austrian division had moved into undefended Switzerland, Bavarian general **Wrede** crossed the Rhine on 22 December to invest Hunigen. In the north, **Bülow's** Prussians and **Graham's** British expeditionary force moved to occupy Holland and threaten Antwerp prior to a sweep through Belgium into France. In the centre, Blücher's 100,000 men crossed the Rhine between Coblenz and Mannheim from 29 December, aiming to hold Napoleon's attention with a frontal offensive. Further south, Schwartzenberg's army of 200,000 men (and several monarchs) began moving towards the upper Rhine around Colmar on 1 January, preparing to swing against the French right flank and make contact with allied forces coming up from Italy and Spain. Bernadotte's substantial Russo-Swedish force was left in Germany to isolate **Davout's** French corps still at **Hamburg**, and to maintain pressure on other isolated French eastern garrisons.

At this stage Napoleon had about 67,000 men scattered along the whole eastern frontier from Switzerland to the north coast, with only a reduced **Imperial Guard** and about 30,000 half-trained militia in reserve. Recruitment efforts were failing, and the army was desperately short of equipment and NCOs. On the diplomatic front, the Spanish government refused to ratify the Valençay agreement, **Murat** brought **Naples** into the coalition against France on 11 January, and **Denmark** ended smouldering hostilities with the allies three days later. In Paris, senior imperial officials were openly anticipating a restored monarchy, and **Talleyrand** was already in contact with the exiled king.

Political considerations kept Napoleon in Paris while his hopelessly outnumbered eastern forces retreated from the approaching allies. **Victor's** 10,000 men guarding the southern sector of the frontier gave up Strasbourg and Nancy without a fight, and **Marmont's** 16,000 troops were back in Metz by 13 January. Both corps had retired behind the Meuse by 17 January, pulling **Ney's** incomplete **Young Guard** corps with them. Napoleon committed **Mortier** and the Guard to support the southern flank, but Blücher met little concerted resistance as his army swept over the Meuse on 22 January.

By the time Blücher's advance guard crossed the Marne next day, Schwarzenberg's army was approaching Bar-sur-Aube, only 40km to the south-west, despite a six-day pause on the Plain of Langres to await the outcome of new peace overtures. Given time to block the resumed advance, Mortier's Guards (and part of **Gérard's** corps) fought a determined rearguard action at Bar-sur-Aube on 24 January, but were then forced to retire west on Troyes. Meanwhile in the far north, Bülow and Graham were driving **Macdonald's** 15,000 men back towards the Meuse from their original positions around Liège.

Excluding northern forces, some 200,000 allied troops were now approaching Paris, and French recruitment efforts had placed only about 85,000 men in their path. Though aware that its defences were in poor condition, and likely to be undermined by treachery from within, Napoleon was determined to hold his capital at all costs, but knew by late January that his presence was needed at the front. Appointing Joseph **Bonaparte** as effective regent in his absence (a post for which his elder brother proved quite unsuitable), the emperor left Paris on 25 January to assume direct command of his forces.

On arrival at the front next day, Napoleon embarked on a whirlwind campaign in the area south-east of Paris. Though fairly flat and open, it was crossed and bordered by a number of large rivers – including the Meuse, Aisne, Aube, Marne, Seine and Yonne – that formed the keys to the campaign, along with the bridges across them and the main roads leading to Paris.

Recognizing that a major battle, win or lose, would overstretch his forces, Napoleon relied on rapid movement along internal lines of communication, unencumbered by the need for **field trains**, to inflict hit-and-run defeats on isolated allied units.

His first target was Blücher's army, advancing in two widely separated columns, but he missed it at **St Dizier** on 27 January and inflicted only minor damage at **Brienne**, on the Aube, two days later. Pursuing Blücher's orderly retreat south, the small French army was surprised by a counter-attack at **La Rothière** on 1 February, suffering a defeat that shook military and popular morale.

Napoleon's only hope of survival appeared to lie in a negotiated peace, and this remained a viable possibility. First suggested in mid-January, and proposed by the allies on 29 January, a peace conference at Châtillon-sur-Seine opened on 3 February, with **Caulaincourt** acting as Napoleon's envoy. French troops meanwhile took up defensive positions on the Seine around Troyes, while Marmont's corps was ordered to attempt the recapture of Arcis-sur-Aube.

Although Schwarzenberg and Blücher followed up La Rothière with drives towards Paris up the Seine and the Marne, a series of minor setbacks during the next few days emphasized their different attitudes to the campaign. Marmont took Arcis-sur-Aube on 3 February, and **Grouchy's** cavalry held off Russian attacks on the road linking Arcis to general headquarters at Troyes. Further north, **Yorck** was blocked by French resistance at Vitry, and a **Cossack** attack failed at Sens, on the Yonne. Schwarzenberg responded by slowing down, worried by word of a new French force gathering at Lyon (under **Augereau**), but Blücher raced up the Marne towards the capital, once more reducing resistance to isolated components.

After planning an attack on Schwarzenberg, Napoleon belatedly realized the extent of Blücher's ambition on 5 February, and that Macdonald's slim corps was the only obstacle in his way. He rushed all available forces towards Nogent, leaving Mortier to undertake a brief sortie from Troyes along Schwarzenberg's right flank next day, which sent the Austrian commander scurrying back to Bar-sur-Aube. Mortier's return to Nogent on 7 February brought French strength there up to about 70,000 men.

Mass panic in Paris was reported to Napoleon at Nogent on 6 February, along with the news that Brussels had fallen to Bülow's army, that Murat's defection was confirmed, and that allied envoys at Châtillon-sur-Seine were insisting on the 1792 frontiers as the sole basis for negotiation. After a day absorbing these shocks in private, the emperor emerged late on 7 February to reject allied terms and find Blücher.

Blücher was eventually reported concentrating 25km to the east around Montmirail on the morning of 9 February. Leaving Macdonald to deal with Yorck's 18,000 troops north of the Marne around Epernay, and detailing 34,000 men (Victor and **Oudinot**) to guard the Seine bridges against Schwarzenberg, Napoleon led about 30,000 troops east as far as Champaubert.

Schwarzenberg had resumed his advance as far as Troyes by 9 February, but allied plans for a concerted drive up the Marne by Blücher, Yorck and **Kleist's** newly arrived reinforcements soon fell apart. Facing communications difficulties now that snow had turned to pouring rain, Blücher spread his 50,000 troops for a wide enveloping movement towards Sézanne, setting up a sequence of French victories, known as the **Six Days Campaign**, that is generally regarded as one of Napoleon's finest military achievements.

In particular, Blücher's dispositions left Russian general Olssufiev and 5,000 men virtually isolated around **Champaubert**, where they were overrun by Napoleon's 30,000 men on 10 February. Blücher's attempts to regroup came too late to prevent the defeat of **Sacken's** corps at **Montmirail** next day, and though French success at **Château-Thierry** on 12 February was diluted by Macdonald's failure to block the Marne crossing, Blücher's attempted counter-attack was repulsed at **Vauchamps** on 14 February. The whirlwind campaign inflicted 20,000 allied casualties in five days, and helped French morale, but its practical effects were nullified by the arrival of **Winzingerode's** 30,000 Russians from Bülow's northern command, who joined up with Blücher at Châlons.

Meanwhile Schwarzenberg's southern advance

had driven the combined forces of Oudinot, Victor and Macdonald as far west as Guignes and Chalmes on the River Yerre, a mere 30km from Paris. Briefly soothed by the victories of the previous week, panic was once more rife in the capital by 15 February, when Schwarzenberg halted to evaluate possible threats to his flanks. Before his planned withdrawal could get under way, Napoleon routed his advance guard at **Valjouan** on 17 February, and won another victory at **Montereau** next day.

Montereau reinforced Schwarzenberg's caution, and inflated Napoleon's confidence. Despite suspension of the Châtillon talks on allied initiative, Napoleon was once more demanding restoration of the 'natural' French frontiers as a precondition of peace. He changed his mind after pursuit of Schwarzenberg to Troyes was thwarted by the lack of intact bridges across the Seine. On 21 February, as the main allied armies were reunited at Méry-sur-Seine, Napoleon offered the Austria peace on the basis of the 1792 frontiers, but Tsar Alexander and British foreign minister **Castlereagh** had already convinced Francis to fight on.

Schwarzenberg won permission to resume his retreat at an allied summit meeting on 22 February, and an infuriated Blücher was ordered to pull back on his right flank. The withdrawal cheated Napoleon, approaching Troyes with about 74,000 men (after another influx of conscripts), of the major battle he was still seeking. Another allied meeting at **Bar-sur-Aube** on 25 February allowed Schwarzenberg to retreat back to the Plain of Langres, with the proviso that he must advance if Napoleon turned north against Blücher.

Blücher had anyway resumed his drive on Paris from 24 February. Though he invited attack from the rear with a series of futile attacks against Marmont and Mortier around **Meaux**, Blücher moved north of the Marne from 1 March. Lack of **pontoon** equipment prevented French pursuit before Blücher took most of his men across the Aisne near Soissons to link up with Winzingerode and Bülow, bringing his strength above 100,000 men.

With Napoleon busy elsewhere, Schwarzenberg resumed his southern advance towards Bar-sur-Aube from 26 February, forcing temporary front commander Macdonald back to Nogent by 5 March. Meanwhile a vital meeting at **Chaumont** finally cemented allied unity, ending all prospect of Austria making a separate peace.

Both Blücher and Napoleon were now anxious for battle. Summoning Marmont from Meaux, Napoleon hurried across the Aisne at Berry-au-Bac on 6 March and moved towards Laon, some 30km to the north-west. French forces ran into a trap set by Blücher near **Craonne** that evening, and though allied troops were withdrawn after a messy engagement next day, Napoleon's outnumbered forces were fortunate to escape decisive defeat at **Laon** on 9–10 March.

By that time, **Soult** and **Suchet** were being pushed into south-west France by Wellington, and Beauharnais was under severe pressure in Italy. Maison's force on the north-east frontier had pulled back to Lille, and garrison forces scattered around the eastern frontiers were hopelessly isolated. Inside France, Augereau's tentative advance from Lyon had been reversed at the first sign of opposition on 9 March, and **Bordeaux** was in revolt, declaring for the allies on 12 March. Paris seemed likely to repudiate Napoleon at any time, and only about 75,000 bedraggled conscripts were left to keep the allied armies at bay.

Still claiming that he could achieve peace on his own terms, Napoleon promptly swept east to inflict a stunning defeat on a detached Prussian corps at **Reims** (13 March). Both Blücher and Schwarzenberg were startled into halting their advances, but Napoleon could only march his tired troops to the aid of Macdonald, who had been forced west as far as Provins.

Another manoeuvre against Schwarzenberg's rear opened on 17 March, but was frustrated by another withdrawal, and Blücher advanced on the same day to defeat Marmont's covering force at Fismes. After a last attempt to reopen peace talks had been ignored, Napoleon planned a move against the extreme rear of the allied positions, marching east towards St Dizier and Joinville on the upper Marne, where he could block the reinforcement lines of both armies and get close to French garrisons at Metz and Verdun.

To keep the allies off balance, he planned to repeat his coup at Reims by attacking Wrede's garrison at **Arcis-sur-Aube**, but was surprised on 20 March by Schwarzenberg's uncharacteristic advance, and was fortunate to escape with only 3,000 losses after a two-day battle. Resuming his move on the Marne, Napoleon brushed aside 8,000 cavalry sent to block his path to reach St Dizier on 23 March.

Captured documents had already revealed his plans to the allies. Encouraged by news that Augereau had abandoned Lyon, they opted for a bold response at the **Sommagices** summit on 24 March. While Winzingerode led 10,000 men towards St Dizier to disguise their intentions, both allied armies were sent directly towards Paris, Schwarzenberg overrunning Mortier and Marmont en route at **La-Fère-Champenoise** (25 March).

Napoleon spent four days at St Dizier, expecting reinforcements and word of an allied retreat. On 26 March his forces chased off Winzingerode's approach, but news of La-Fère-Champenoise convinced him that his manoeuvre had failed. Dissuaded by his senior commanders from continuing the war on the frontiers, he marched for Paris on 28 March. Schwarzenberg and Blücher joined forces at Meaux, 40km short of Paris, on the same day.

The Empress Marie-Louise and Napoleon's young son left Paris next day, followed on 30 March by Joseph Bonaparte and those government officers not already preparing to welcome the allies. Napoleon left his flagging troops at Troyes on the same day, and rushed ahead accompanied by a small staff, but the combined allied armies were almost at the capital, and French forces surrendered at **Montmartre** that night.

As 145,000 troops occupied the capital, and Talleyrand proclaimed the empire's dissolution, Napoleon refused at first to admit defeat. Returning south to Fontainebleau, he gathered troops for a resumption of hostilities, but the refusal of his marshals to fight and Marmont's defection to the allies prompted a conditional offer to abdicate on 4 April, followed by unconditional **abdication** on 6 April. Plans for Napoleon's future were formalized in the Treaty of **Fontainebleau** ten days later, and he sailed aboard a British warship on 28 April to become ruler of **Elba**. The restored government of exiled

King **Louis** XVIII signed the Treaty of **Paris** on 30 April, ending the War of the Sixth Coalition and returning France to its 1792 frontiers. *See* **Map 26**.

Francis II, Emperor (1768–1835)

Serious-minded and reserved, but impressionable and occasionally reckless, Francis became head of the Habsburg and **Holy Roman Empires** on the death of Emperor Leopold II in 1792. More sincerely committed to anti-revolutionary causes than his father, he took **Austria** into the disastrous **First Coalition** with **Prussia**, leading his forces in person for part of the 1793–4 campaign in **Flanders** and narrowly escaping capture at **Tourcoing**.

Never able to formulate a consistent foreign policy over the next 15 years, he was alternately swayed by the cautious appeasement strategy of a group eventually centred on Archduke **Charles**, and the belligerent optimism of a more prominent court war party. Gathered around his wives (Empress Maria Theresa until her death in 1807, Empress Ludovica from early 1808), and led by chief ministers **Thugut** and **Stadion**, the hawks usually won. Francis suffered further disasters after joining the **Second** and **Third Coalitions**, culminating in the 1805 defeat at **Austerlitz** (when he was again in personal command of Austrian forces). Retitled 'Francis I, Emperor of Austria' when **Napoleon** dissolved the Holy Roman Empire in 1806, he was persuaded into another failed attack on France in 1809.

After the 1809 defeat at **Wagram**, Francis relied increasingly on new chief minister **Metternich**, accepting the need for peaceful reform of his administration and the **Austrian Army**, and appeasing France to the extent of marrying his daughter **Marie-Louise** to Napoleon. This encouraged him to favour a negotiated settlement after he had joined the **Sixth Coalition** in August 1813, though he again accompanied his armies through subsequent campaigns in **Germany** and **France**. Metternich guided his policy of moderation at the postwar **Vienna** congress, arranged membership of the conservative **Holy Alliance**, and supervised reconstruction and maintenance of the empire throughout the last two decades of his reign.

Frauenfeld, Battle of

Unsuccessful French attempt to halt the steady advance of Austrian forces from the east during the **Swiss campaign** of 1799. Launched by C-in-C **Masséna** on 26 May, the French attack struck at each of the two separated Austrian corps as they drove west of the River Thur. Archduke **Charles** found his advance guard thrown back across the river beyond Andelfingen, but destruction of the town's bridge prevented pursuit. The attack against Hötze's advanced units holding a bridge over the Thur at Frauenfeld enjoyed initial success, **Oudinot** getting his division across the river downstream from the village, but Austrian general Petrasch could not be dislodged from the crossing until **Soult's** reserve arrived late in the day. The combined French forces took the bridge and 1,500 prisoners, but retired when Hötze arrived with substantial reinforcements early on 27 May. Charles launched a counter-attack against **Ney** and the French centre on the same day, forcing Masséna to withdraw his headquarters to **Zurich**, where he began concentrating his scattered units for a full-scale defensive campaign. *See* **Map 4**.

Frederick VI, King (1768–1839)

The son and heir of Danish king **Christian VII**, Frederick orchestrated the palace coup that deposed his father in 1784 and subsequently ruled as regent. Willing in his youth to accept the advice and liberal tendencies of experienced ministers, he presided over the abolition of feudal serfdom, prohibition of slave trading and reform of **Denmark's** criminal laws. In maturity he became increasingly concerned to restore royal authority, and abolished cabinet government altogether after his accession to the throne in 1808.

Already embroiled in an alliance with **France** and war against **Great Britain**, Frederick persisted with reactionary internal policies during the first years of his reign, taking steps in 1810 to curtail the semi-autonomous commission that governed Norway, but reacted to the economic and diplomatic disasters accompanying **Napoleon's** downfall by restoring ministerial powers in 1814. Enduringly popular with ordinary Danes, and back in alliance with the élite classes, he was able to guide the monarchy safely through the slow, painful process of postwar reconstruction, and granted Denmark's first parliamentary constitution in 1834.

Frederick Augustus I, King (1750–1827)

Elector of **Saxony** since 1763, Frederick Augustus was a conscientious and popular ruler, primarily concerned to promote economic and social stability. He reluctantly committed **Saxon** troops to the **Revolutionary Wars** in line with his obligations to the **Holy Roman Empire**, and was bullied into commitment to the Prussian cause in autumn 1806, but made a lasting peace with **Napoleon** at **Posen** in December, joining the Confederation of the **Rhine** and assuming the title of King. He accepted nominal sovereignty over the new Grand Duchy of **Warsaw** in 1807, and remained a French ally through the campaigns of 1809 and 1812. Restrained from desertion to the **Sixth Coalition** after April 1813 by the presence of a French army on Saxon soil, Frederick Augustus was Napoleon's only German ally by mid-November, when Dresden fell to Russian forces. Restored to a much-reduced kingdom by the Congress of **Vienna**, he was welcomed back by a generally royalist population and devoted his postwar energies to economic reconstruction.

Frederick William II, King (1744–97)

Nephew and successor to Frederick the Great as King of **Prussia**, he took the throne in 1786 and courted initial popularity by repealing some of his uncle's harsher tax laws. Soon revealed as a weak-willed man, prone to over-reliance on unqualified advisers, he lost public favour by curtailing press and religious freedoms in 1788, and followed an incoherent but expensive expansion programme before 1792. His naked opportunism helped provoke the War of the **First Coalition**, and his most significant contribution before pulling out in 1795 was the constant interference in army operations that drove C-in-C **Brunswick** to resignation in late 1793.

Frederick William III, King (1770–1827)

Son and heir of Prussian king **Frederick William II**, he received a military education and held active commands during the War of the **First Coalition** from 1792 to 1794. King of **Prussia** on his father's death in 1797, he rescinded some of the monarchy's more repressive legislation, and was less inclined to reactionary intolerance than his predecessor, but earned a reputation for indecision and dependence on the formidable Queen **Louise**.

Her ardent faith in Prussia's international destiny led the king into a disastrous entanglement with the **Third Coalition** in 1805, and the folly of a unilateral declaration of war against a victorious France in 1806. He was forced into virtual exile in the East Prussian port of Königsberg after the rout of his armies at **Jena–Auerstädt** in autumn 1806, and his subsequent role in international affairs reflected his military weakness.

Allowed back to Berlin by **Napoleon** in late 1809, he was still a reluctant French ally in 1812, and wavered in the face of overwhelming popular and political opposition to the alliance, even after the **Russian campaign**. The prospect of Russian troops reaching Berlin eventually outweighed his fear of Napoleon, and he accompanied his armies through the campaigns of 1813–14, but he remained an uncertain figure, dominated by the strategic dictates of Tsar **Alexander I** and the unbridled aggression of his field commanders. Ruler of a much enlarged kingdom after 1815, he followed Alexander's lead in joining the **Holy Alliance** of conservative monarchs, seeking to reinforce royal autocracy and to secure economic hegemony over northern Germany.

Freikorps

Independent military units formed in **Prussia**, **Austria** and elsewhere in Germany just before and during the 1813 campaign of 'national liberation'. Generally raised by local aristocrats in the name of liberty from the French yoke, and often comprising the self-equipped sons of nobles or the increasingly nationalist middle classes, they were most prevalent in Prussia, operating against French imperial communications and inciting insurrection against garrison forces. Many Freikorps units, including the officially sponsored corps under Adolf **Lützow**, were absorbed by the expanding **Prussian Army** from the time of its commitment to the **Sixth Coalition** in March 1813.

Freire de Andrade, Gomez (1752–1817)

Much travelled son of a Portuguese diplomat, born in Vienna, who fought with **Portuguese** forces supporting **Spain** on the **Pyrenean** front in 1793–5, but entered French service in 1808, taking part in the siege of **Saragossa**. A divisional commander with the **Grande Armée** during the 1812 **Russian campaign**, for much of which he occupied an administrative post in Lithuania, he succeeded **Davout** as governor of **Dresden** in August 1813 and became an allied prisoner there in November. He returned to **Portugal** in 1814, and was shot as an anti-royalist conspirator three years later. His namesake, General Bernardo Freire de Andrade, also fought in the Pyrenees, but subsequently fought against the French in the **Peninsular War**, commanding a brigade at **Vimeiro** before his murder by mutinous troops in 1809.

French Army

The French Royal Army had declined in quality during decades of economic breakdown before 1789. Apart from the ill effects of pay and supply shortages on enlisted troops, the officer corps had become a bloated burden on the treasury, with only a third of those commissioned in active service. Promotion above captain was restricted to nobles, except in the more technical **artillery** and **engineers**, and enlisted men almost never became officers, encouraging solid support for the **French Revolution**'s radical reforms among junior officers and NCOs.

Senior officers emigrated in droves after 1789, and the army's predominantly aristocratic **cavalry** arm virtually disintegrated, but many infantry regiments remained in service under officers elected by troops. Regular forces were principally concerned with internal security during the 1789–92 period, but were concentrated close to the eastern frontiers as war approached, and were augmented by the volunteer (and politically volatile) **National Guard**, as well as essentially useless local militia forces in provincial communities.

As the threat of foreign interference mounted, local militia were disbanded and reconstituted as part of an enlarged National Guard, some of which was pressed into frontline service from

March 1791. Appeals were also issued for volunteers, known as **fédérés**, and the first 169 battalions were formed late in the year. These contained a large number of former royal troops returning to service, but a second batch raised in early 1792 included a large proportion of untrained men effectively forced into service.

These measures produced a paper army of only about 150,000 frontline troops on the outbreak of war, but popular attitudes to service were transformed during the summer. As hostile armies gathered on the eastern frontiers, and the government's rallying call of *la patrie en danger* ('the homeland in danger') became manifestly urgent, large numbers of enthusiastic volunteers streamed to the front in defence of the Revolution.

French forces that fought the **First Coalition** during the autumn were a shambles in organizational terms, but were numerically strong and relatively well motivated, though hopelessly ill-equipped, and incapable of manoeuvre beyond frenzied charge or flight. Their pivotal victory at **Valmy** in September 1792 was hardly a battle, but the new army's first genuine triumph, at **Jemappes** in November, introduced **infantry tactics** that emphasized its strengths.

Regular French infantry were trained according to 1791 regulations, which required advance into battle in column, and a manoeuvre into line abreast at the last moment. Volunteer armies were incapable of anything so sophisticated, encouraging the use of better-trained regulars in large numbers as **skirmishers** before the mass of raw recruits was hurled against a chosen point.

Highly effective against orthodox European forces employing thin **cordon** defence systems, new tactics were undermined through most of 1793 by internal chaos that disrupted pay, morale and supplies, so that field formations were neither reliable nor at anything like their paper strength. The artillery arm remained a relatively formidable force, still able to benefit from the innovations of the pre-revolutionary **Gribeauval system**, but attempts to rebuild the cavalry were thwarted by lack of horses or time to train new troopers. Infantry forces remained critically short of everything except an acute awareness of their political rights. Commanders always faced the possibility that troops would go home, refuse to fight, demand a change of leadership or execute them as traitors, a fate that befell several generals after defeats during the early frontier campaigns.

The army's high command was equally volatile. Even more than their counterparts in other European armies, French generals of the **Revolutionary Wars** were political figures, their military competence often a secondary consideration. Early republican commanders frequently quit the front for factional battles in Paris, and an increasingly paranoid government soon began burdening them with political observers, creating a dangerous division of operational authority and adding to command insecurity.

Once the **Terror** got under way in 1793, failed commanders could expect imprisonment or execution, and the government's radicalization provoked a steady stream of resignations or defections. Both **Lafayette** and **Dumouriez**, the most prominent defectors of the 1792–3 period, fled almost certain execution, and even official heroes such as the elder **Kellermann** could plummet from grace. Many generals (such as **Dumerbion** in northern Italy) preferred to protect themselves by simply obeying the dictates of political attachés.

On the other hand, rapid command turnover provided opportunities for talented junior officers such as **Moreau**, **Pichegru**, **Jourdan**, **Masséna** or **Napoleon** (who fought as a general for the first time on the Italian front in spring 1794) to reach the top quickly. Their emergence played a part in the army's dramatic transformation into a war-winning weapon during 1794, but the man principally responsible was Lazare **Carnot**, military adviser and war minister to successive revolutionary governments.

As new head of the Committee of **Public Safety**'s war section, Carnot supervised the introduction of mass **conscription** in August 1793, issuing a *levée en masse* that made all males of 18–25 liable for military service, and put 1.5 million Frenchmen under arms by the end of the year. His celebrated *Amalgame* of 1794 reorganized the army's confused jumble of three-battalion regiments into 213 numbered infantry and cavalry demi-brigades, each containing one regular and two volunteer battalions. Though unpopular with troops, the new system was well suited to the adoption of more formal infantry tactics, and the development of a flexible approach combining line and column (*ordre mixte*) was backed by an increase in light, mobile artillery for direct infantry support. Carnot adopted the **corps system** for deployment of large formations, and had organized the mass of new conscripts into 13 field armies by 1795, each with a nominal strength of 100,000 men and linked to the capital by a radically expanded **semaphore** system.

Army pay, supplies and equipment remained a serious problem, despite efforts to raise loans and open new factories, and Carnot made a virtue of necessity by establishing the principle that war should pay for itself by a combination of forage, looting and conquest. This policy of living off the land they occupied, which remained standard practice to 1815, gave French forces a vital operational edge over orthodox armies unable to move faster than their slow supply wagons. It also encouraged a strategy of waging war on foreign soil, and Carnot was deeply involved in planning a series of ambitious offensives from 1794. In the process, he introduced method to the business of strategic control, turning the **Bureau Topographique** into an embryonic general staff.

Carnot's reforms, applied to vastly increased manpower and abetted by allied sluggishness, reversed the course of the war during 1794–5, bringing victories on the **Flanders**, **Pyrenean** and **Italian** fronts. Eighteen months of relative internal stability under the **Directory** government had improved the army's supply and equipment situation by early 1796, and Napoleon's continued success in Italy soon brought **Austria** to the peace table.

Still needing the army's political support, and even more anxious to feed it on foreign soil once internal rebellion had been quashed, the Directory planned an invasion of **England**, sponsored Napoleon's expedition to the **Middle East** in 1798 and opened the war against the **Second Coalition** with a highly ambitious set of offensives in early 1799. Bereft of Carnot since the 1797 **Fructidor** coup, and able to field fewer

than 280,000 men now that the fervour of national defence had passed, the army lacked the basic resources to carry them through, and only allied strategic incoherence saved France from complete disaster by autumn.

Napoleon's return from **Egypt** and accession to power after the **Brumaire** coup in November 1799 brought a rapid, if partial, reconstruction of the army. The corps system, hitherto not fully applied, was instituted throughout, and promises of imminent peace encouraged improved recruitment levels. Most immediately, Napoleon created a central reserve force that turned the tide of war in Italy, and its victory at **Marengo** brought the republican army its first extended period of peacetime reconstruction.

Having delivered victorious peace, Napoleon became the sole guiding force behind army organization, strategy and tactics. Much of its subsequent success derived from his appreciation that efficient operational control was essential to victory in any campaign of manoeuvre, and much of its character derived from the personal nature of that control. Napoleon led his armies in the field through many of their most important campaigns, and exercised tight, detailed supervision over others. Many of his most important military reforms, practices and innovations were designed to facilitate efficient strategic and tactical control.

After three years' training at Channel camps for another crack at England, French field forces after 1805 were far better equipped and prepared than their predecessors. Demi-brigades were turned back into numbered line regiments from 1803, but infantry tactics were still based on *ordre mixte*, although an army containing a large proportion of veterans was deemed to need less direct artillery support (until after 1812), and Napoleon increasingly chose to group his guns in large batteries for massed shock bombardments at tactically important moments. Otherwise the Gribeauval system remained basic to artillery operations, and attempts to update it never fully matured. Given time to train recruits, and fresh supplies of horses from conquered or allied territories, French cavalry completed a transformation begun against the Second Coalition. Acknowledged as the world's most formidable mounted force after 1805, it was a first-class reconnaissance or pursuit force, and won a fearsome battle reputation under **Murat**.

In organizational terms, the corps remained the army's basic unit for major operations, but Napoleon refined the system so that by late 1806 he could manoeuvre massed forces as a **Bataillon Carré**, its corps always in position for defensive or offensive concentration within a day. Carnot's tiny central planning organization was magnified out of all recognition, the **Grand Quartier-Général** becoming a complex bureaucracy, but the emperor's parallel household staff (La Maison) was the principal recipient of his direct orders, and certain staff personnel, notably **Berthier** and **Caulaincourt**, performed key executive roles.

The personal nature of Napoleon's government and army command was emphasized by his deliberate severance of the link between military command and political power. Napoleon promoted only in recognition of competence and loyalty. Successful generals could expect titles, administrative posts scattered around the expanding empire, or even the (largely irrelevant) war ministry, but were kept carefully away from any real political power in Paris.

Napoleon's monopoly of authority was perhaps the greatest weakness of a senior command that could boast an extraordinary number of competent field generals, and a pantheon of exceptional battlefield leaders, including Murat, **Lannes**, **Soult**, **Ney**, **Davout** and **Masséna**. In 1804 the cream of the army's field generals (and a few semi-retired dignitaries) became the first members of the imperial **Marshalate**, which eventually included 29 officers, but the title had no operational significance, and Napoleon's military subordinates were unaccustomed to exercising strategic initiative, proving less successful when required to act independently.

Beginning with the rout of **Third Coalition** forces at **Ulm** and **Austerlitz** in late 1805 – a logistic, strategic and tactical tour de force that is generally regarded as the most impressive campaign fought by any army of the period – French ground troops made Napoleon master of continental Europe in four years. The peace settlement that followed **Wagram** in 1809 left the army to police an enlarged continental empire,

but territorial expansion provided large numbers of troops and horses, along with supplies rendered scarce by Britain's naval **blockade**.

Manpower contributions were compulsory from Napoleon's clients and puppets, who were expected to pay the upkeep of native forces attached to French armies and of occupying imperial troops. Some allied and satellite forces were scattered around the army in small groups, like unreliable **Neapolitan** troops or **Polish** units suspected of nationalist ambition, but most of the larger contingents, such as the allied **Bavarian** and **Saxon** armies or the **Italian** and **Westphalian** satellite armies, functioned as army corps in their own right, usually under a French commander. Non-French personnel made up a growing proportion of imperial strength, and accounted for more than half of the **Grande Armée** in 1812.

The army's aura of invincibility was barely dented during the first decade of the nineteenth century. The few fringe setbacks it suffered – such as those at **Maida**, **Bailén** or **Vimeiro** – caused excitement elsewhere out of all proportion to their strategic significance, and drawn battles such as **Eylau** and **Aspern–Essling** were the nearest it came to a major defeat before 1812. Napoleon's élite **Imperial Guard** was the most feared land force in Europe, and the veteran **Old Guard** was undefeated anywhere until **Waterloo** in 1815.

The cost and wastage of almost constant campaigning, along with a steady extension of military responsibilities and the tightening grip of blockade, eventually wore down the empire's military and economic resources. The **Peninsular War** kept 200–300,000 men occupied at all times, and Napoleon only raised the 270,000 troops deployed against Austria in 1809 by extending conscription and leaving other imperial defences dangerously thin. High casualty rates in Spain were compounded by **Wellington**'s repeated successes, which demonstrated that French battle tactics were vulnerable to well-trained opponents under the right conditions, and that dependence on local resources could be dangerous.

Partly because of its sheer size, the army that fought the **Russian campaign** of 1812 was in many respects inferior to the highly professional forces of 1805 and 1806–7. Its cavalry remained matchless in the charge, though less proficient in the fields of routine reconnaissance and horse care, and the artillery arm had been expanded to field a total of 1,422 guns, but the infantry's effectiveness had been reduced by doubts about the loyalty or quality of some allied troops, inexperience among French conscripts and a shortage of seasoned NCOs and junior officers. The army's overall efficiency was further compromised by Napoleon's attempt to direct an army of 650,000 men single-handedly in such a vast operational theatre.

The army's supply system was revised to meet the challenge of Russian conditions, reverting to pre-revolutionary reliance on supply-trains and utilizing 25,000 transport vehicles (drawn by 90,000 horses) along with 200 supply boats for use on the River Niemen. These and a welter of other supply and logistic arrangements were the responsibility of Intendant-General **Dumas**, but their effectiveness varied from corps to corps, and overall failures to provide adequate **medical** facilities or supplies of warm clothing were to prove very costly.

The 1812 campaign destroyed Napoleon's military machine, and although he was able to produce new armies for the campaigns of 1813–15, they were never of the same calibre as the forces that had conquered Europe. The army that fought in **Germany** was largely composed of raw conscripts, many of them teenage 'Marie-Louises', often led by equally inexperienced junior officers, a situation made worse by the concentration of most veteran troops in the Imperial Guard and the loss of imperial recruiting grounds. Many veteran senior commanders had either been killed or, like **Junot** and Ney, been diminished by the Russian experience, though Napoleon's inspirational leadership and tactical brilliance remained potent forces.

Unwilling or unable to recognize the depth of his weakness, Napoleon set about creating another new army from late 1813. More than 900,000 conscripts were called up from every possible source, including much of the National Guard, **French Navy** personnel, government officials of every type, and ordinary citizens either too old or young for military service.

Recruitment was backed by a major **propaganda** campaign, and new taxes were announced to finance the army, but mass evasion reflected the exhaustion of a French people that supplied a total of 2,015,000 men to Napoleon's armies between 1799 and 1814. Napoleon could never call on more than about 85,000 frontline troops during his 1814 campaign in **France**, and morale had collapsed before his eventual **abdication** in early April.

Many surviving senior commanders joined returning **émigrés** in royal service, but the majority returned to Napoleon's side in 1815. Apart from the personal guard that accompanied him from **Elba**, the army that fought in the **Hundred Days** was based around some 180,000 royal troops (mostly conscripts retained from the 1813–14 campaigns), and about 90,000 generally more experienced volunteers, along with personnel culled from every other source of trained men. Most were retained by the monarchy after Napoleon's second abdication, but the officers who had deserted royal service in 1815 were dismissed, exiled or, in the case of Ney, executed. Most had been pardoned before the general amnesty of 1821, and several former Napoleonic officers enjoyed successful postwar careers.

French Navy

Though **France** possessed the world's second-largest navy in the late eighteenth century, and could at least hold its own against most other sea powers, its fleets were no match for the British **Royal Navy**. Under the royal regime, French sea power had seldom been harnessed to the national interest in the manner accomplished by **Great Britain**, and this remained true after the **French Revolution**, which also effectively destroyed service discipline and a largely royalist officer corps.

The navy possessed 81 **ships-of-the-line**, 69 **frigates** and 141 **sloops** or other smaller warships in 1790, but many were in poor condition and desperately short of skilled seamen. Large French ships were longer, more slender, easier to manoeuvre and often more heavily armed than their British counterparts, but inferior seamanship and gunnery more than compensated for any advantage in direct combat. Although the carronade had been in limited use since 1783, the navy had otherwise paid little attention to the many minor innovations, especially in gunnery practice, that had improved British efficiency since the Seven Years War.

Conditions for crews were bad enough to discourage volunteers, and a steadily worsening manpower crisis was exacerbated by the heavy priority given to **French Army** recruitment throughout the war period. French naval officers, drawn mostly from the aristocracy and the merchant fleets before the Revolution, were generally well educated in naval theory, but many had become **émigrés** or purge victims by 1793. Naval officers were subject to occasional anti-royalist purges throughout the **Revolutionary Wars** period, and were always accompanied by government-appointed political officers, who interfered with command decisions and were a threat to any admiral's personal security.

In strategic terms, both before and after the Revolution, the French Navy was primarily designed to protect the nation's colonies and trade, particularly the merchant traffic flowing from the **West Indies** and across the **Mediterranean**. Its main Mediterranean base at Toulon was well placed to enable operations all over the theatre, and the French Atlantic coast contained major naval bases at Brest and Rochefort/Lorient (*see* **Maps 8, 18**). In addition, given a history of war against Britain, many of the navy's smaller craft were deployed along the English Channel coast, ready to challenge invaders and make what impact they could on trade traffic.

France faced no hostile fleets until Britain, the **Netherlands** and **Spain** joined the **First Coalition** in early 1793. Only Britain was likely to undertake aggressive action on any scale, but though the British spent most of the year mobilizing, French weakness was emphasized by a mutiny in Admiral de Galles's Brest fleet, which had to be recalled from its **blockade** of the rebellious **Vendée** region.

The equally rebellious condition of southern France gave the Royal Navy an opportunity to inflict a mortal wound on the republic in August 1793, when **Hood's** Mediterranean Fleet captured **Toulon**, but the army's well-planned counter-attack retook the port, and the depart-

ing allies left 27 ships-of-the-line, 13 frigates and 14 sloops in French hands, though most were in various states of disrepair.

While British forces strove to enforce long-range blockades in the Mediterranean and the Atlantic, the navy took advantage of its luck to find a useful and successful strategic role. Able to slip out of port almost at will, and adept at avoiding battle if discovered, French fleets concentrated on escorting vital imports to starving home ports, and on inflicting maximum possible disruption to the trading patterns of enemies. Successful **convoy** raiders such as Captain **Perrée** became the toast of the service.

Intelligent strategy could not alter the fundamental tactical inferiority of French ships and crews, as displayed at the Battle of the **First of June** off Ushant in 1794, but combat defeats might not matter in strategic terms. Admiral **Villaret** was feted as a hero after the First of June defeat, because a vital grain convoy got through to Brest while the battle was taking place. Furthermore the British regularly missed other opportunities to defeat French fleets, most notably off **Leghorn** and the Ile de **Groix** in 1795.

Though efficiency and morale were still falling, and a series of colonial defeats diminished its strength overseas, land victories and diplomatic shifts transformed the navy's strategic situation in 1795–6. Alliances with Spain and the Netherlands stretched British resources; **Hotham's** slack blockade allowed the Toulon fleet to strike effective blows against convoys off **St Vincent** and elsewhere; and **Napoleon's** successful **Italian campaigns** ultimately drove the British out of the Mediterranean altogether.

This was the high point of French naval success during the war period. Mediterranean commander de **Brueys** was able take over the **Venetian Navy** and the British base on **Corsica** at leisure, while a squadron was sent to harass British trade in the **Indian Ocean**, but the illusion of ascendancy was short-lived. While the **Directory** government planned a series of naval offensives, most field commanders remained deeply pessimistic about their chances of success, and their caution contributed to the long run of operational failures that followed.

As naval resources focused on the possible

invasion of **England**, the navy suffered embarrassment and losses during an abortive attempt to land on the Irish coast at **Bantry Bay** at the end of 1796. All hope of an immediate invasion was ended by British defeats of the Spanish at Cape **St Vincent** and the Dutch at **Camperdown** in 1797, and the offensive focus switched to the Mediterranean in 1798, when the Toulon fleet escorted Napoleon's expedition to the **Middle East**. Its defeat at the **Nile** (1 August) shattered French pretensions to Mediterranean supremacy and triggered a rush to join the **Second Coalition**.

Once more reduced to a defensive role wherever it operated, the navy returned to its policy of trade warfare, but found a revitalized Royal Navy capable of enforcing efficient blockades. With small squadrons penned in Alexandria, **Malta**, the **Ionian Islands** and Venice, no fleet left at Toulon, and the Atlantic fleets equally well policed, French forces achieved little in European waters before 1802. Two sorties from the Atlantic into the Mediterranean – **'Bruix's Cruise'** and **'Ganteaume's Cruise'** – fell victim to command timidity, and the main action involving French warships before the Peace of **Amiens** was a minor defeat off **Algeciras** in July 1801.

Napoleon's personal control over all French military affairs dominated naval operations from 1801. He had little understanding of (or interest in) the technical difficulties of **naval warfare**, and deployed fleets primarily as a means of supporting his continental ambitions, and was even more inclined to overrule the practical objections of professionals than his predecessors. His career as a naval strategist began with renewed plans to invade England, and the assembly of a new fleet of transports and **gunboats** (along with crews) for the purpose.

After wasting valuable crews on the ill-conceived **Santo Domingo** expedition in 1802, he returned to the problem of conquering England in 1803, ordering into effect the over-elaborate decoy operation that ended in disaster at **Trafalgar** in October, when **Nelson** wiped out both **Villeneuve's** Mediterranean fleet and its Spanish equivalent. French battlefleets were never again more than a notional threat to allied maritime security, and the navy found its energies consumed by Napoleon's determination to enforce the **Continental System** against the British, with surviving fleet units generally employed for coastguard, customs and harbour defence duties, or as long-range commerce raiders.

Eleven ships-of-the-line under Admiral Willaumez broke out of Brest in December 1805, and split into two raiding groups, but five were destroyed at the Battle of **Santo Domingo** by British forces in February 1806, and four more were subsequently damaged in the Caribbean. The only survivors were Jérôme **Bonaparte's** ship, which brought home six merchant prizes without authorization in 1806, and the flagship, which eventually brought Willaumez back to France in February 1807.

Apart from one other attempt to send a sizeable squadron to the West Indies, thwarted at the **Basque Roads** in April 1809, the rest of the war years were a story of decay and failure. Quite unable to hinder British coastal operations in the **Peninsular** theatre or the colonies, the navy had no major role to play in the great land campaigns further east. Increasingly starved of men and resources as Napoleon strove to keep massed armies in the field, it was a moribund and strategically aimless force by 1814, playing almost no part in the 1815 campaign.

By the end of the **Hundred Days**, the wartime French Navy had lost a total of 94 ships-of-the-line (50-gunners and above), 187 frigates (of 26 to 44 guns) and about 220 smaller warships bearing ten guns or more. It had been overtaken by the **Russian Navy** in terms of strength and fighting efficiency, and despite a steady revival under the restored royal regime, it was never again able to offer a convincing challenge to the British as a global naval power.

French Revolution

The series of uprisings that deposed the autocratic French monarchy. Though generally taken as opening in summer 1789, the Revolution was the product of long-term financial, political and social weaknesses in the essentially feudal system that had supported the royal regime, and was sparked by the monarchy's attempts to reform the state's fiscal systems in the face of entrenched noble opposition.

Noble pressure eventually forced the king to

summon the States-General, a medieval gathering of the nation's representatives, in August 1788. Expecting the Estates to defend noble privileges, the crown attempted to marshal popular support for reform by calling for lists of grievances from every parish in January 1789, but by the time the States-General convened at Versailles in May it had been hijacked as an instrument of revolution by the middle classes.

The States-General comprised three houses that had always deliberated and voted separately, enabling the noble First Estate and the clerical Second (dominated by its minority of senior churchmen) to ignore the views of the commoners' Third Estate. Mostly drawn from the literate, propertied classes, the Third Estate demanded double representation at Versailles, and that the three houses sit as one. Inspired by Mirabeau and other renegade nobles, and with support from a significant number of minor clergy, it declared itself a National Assembly in June, a revolutionary act legitimized by a reluctant monarch later that month.

The National Assembly became the 'Constituent Assembly' in July, and began preparing a new constitution. Meanwhile its radicalization was hastened by the political situation in Paris, where the spread of literacy, a thriving independent press, food shortages and rising bread prices helped focus popular anger against the old regime. In mid-July 1789, when the dismissal of reforming finance minister Necker raised the spectre of royal reaction against the Assembly, the capital erupted into full-blown mass insurrection.

The violent seizure of the virtually empty Bastille prison on 14 July signalled the Parisian citizenry's arrival as a major political force, and compelled the king to compromise with the Assembly, but it also persuaded the Constituents to protect the new regime against mob rule and associated **Jacobin** extremists. The Paris **National Guard** was established on 17 July, with **Lafayette** as its first commander, becoming part of an uneasy trio of military authorities, alongside bands of armed citizens and the loyal units of regular **French Army** troops being steadily summoned to the capital by the monarchy.

Threatened by counter-revolution from above

and extremist pressure from below, the Constituents formally abolished feudalism in August, and began formulating the Revolution's most famous statement of principle, the Declaration of the Rights of Man. Adopted by the Assembly in late August, and published as a preamble to the new constitution in 1791, the Declaration asserted the sanctity of individual rights to property, security, equality before the law and resistance against oppression. Though never taken as a literal blueprint for government by future revolutionary regimes, it was one of the most important influences on popular political thinking throughout Europe over the next century.

Outside Paris, most urban communities reacted to the news of revolution by imitating it. Though little in eighteenth-century France was consistent across the nation, and local regimes that took power were remarkable for their social diversity, most large towns and cities became the centres for regional assemblies, recruited their own National Guard units and fell under the control of more or less middle-class politicians. In rural France, what was already a slow-burning peasant uprising erupted into widespread attacks on the property, feudal records and persons of local aristocracy, often carried out in the name of a king believed to be on the side of reform.

Poor communications, a general increase in the number of vagrants throughout France, and rumours that the first noble émigrés had hired bands of brigands to exact revenge on law breakers fuelled an outbreak of mass panic in almost every rural French region during late July and August 1789. Known as the 'Great Fear' (*Grande Peur*), the panic stimulated formation of armed bands all over the countryside, presaging years of confusion and violent uncertainty across much of southern and western France.

The ongoing food crisis, and ostentatious royalist demonstrations by regular army forces, were the triggers for an extension of mob rule in Paris by the autumn. The Constituents could only climb aboard the radical bandwagon when thousands of citizens marched to Versailles in October, backed by 20,000 National Guardsmen and a reluctant Lafayette, to demand the removal of king and Assembly to the capital. The settlement of revolutionary government inside Paris, and the royal family's virtual house arrest at the palace of the Tuileries, appeared to satisfy immediate demands of the citizen mobs, known as *sans-culottes* (literally 'trouserless'), but the Assembly's prompt imposition of martial law was unable to stabilize an endemically volatile political situation.

Against a background of brooding popular extremism and gathering royalist counter-revolution, the Assembly declared a new Civil Constitution in force from November 1790. It was reluctantly accepted by the king in September 1791, after his political position had been severely undermined by an attempt to escape to the frontier in June.

The 1791 constitution recognized Louis as hereditary King of the French, but abolished all other aristocratic rights and titles. Executive authority lay with a new Legislative Assembly. A single chamber required to hold new elections every two years, it represented a far broader constituency than any contemporary British parliament, although franchise restrictions excluded millions of poorer 'passive' citizens from the electoral process.

The king's political powers were restricted to the appointment of advisers, ambassadors and military commanders, along with the 'suspensive veto', by which he could delay any non-financial legislation for four years. He could not dissolve the Assembly, and his decisions on matters of war and peace were subject to its approval. Military forces, already largely purged of nobles and royalists (often at the instigation of rank-and-file radicals), were required to take an oath to the 'nation' as well as to the king, and National Guard militia remained under the control of local administrations.

The country as a whole was divided into 83 administrative *départements*, which still form the basis of French provincial organization, and subdivided into cantons, districts and, at the lowest level, 44,000 newly designated communes, each governed by a mayor and council. The municipality of Paris, divided into 60 electoral districts since 1789, was reorganized into 48 'sections'. Locally elected committees formed the basis of regional government at every level.

The constitution created two national courts, the Court of Appeals and the High Court, the latter dealing with crimes against the state. At local level, elected tribunals and juries replaced the feudal judiciary, and an assessed land tax on all properties was introduced in place of the central government's feudal revenues, along with duties on movable goods, incomes and business profits. These proved insufficient to meet current expenditure, let alone outstanding debts, and were anyway impossible to collect, prompting the decision to nationalize Church property and put it up for sale. Immediate financial requirements were meanwhile met by issuing interest-bearing government bonds, or *assignats*, which were quickly accepted as currency but began to depreciate alarmingly after 1790.

More positive economic steps taken by the constitution included the abolition of internal customs barriers and the establishment of a national weights and measures system. No ideological scruples were allowed to get in the way of maintaining competitive tariffs with foreign countries, and the Constituents dealt with their fear of labour uprising by passing the notorious Le Chapelier Law of June 1791, by which all combinations of workers were prohibited, a position that had not changed by 1814.

The Assembly's attempt to reform the Church sparked both controversy and violence. The majority of poor churchmen supported nationalization of Church property, and few objected to the dissolution of unproductive monasteries in February 1790, but a Civil Constitution for the Church was adopted in July 1790 without consulting a general synod. Schism between those 'jurist' or 'refractory' churchmen who took the required oath to the constitution and those who refused was sharpened when Pope **Pius VI** condemned the jurists in 1791 (once he had failed to secure control of the papal enclave at Avignon), and suspended the only two jurist bishops, one of whom was **Talleyrand**. From that point, large numbers of non-jurist clergy and their flocks were forced into long-term opposition to the Revolution.

Formal adoption of the 1791 constitution was accompanied by claims that the Revolution was complete, but it was destined to go through several more stages during the next decade.

Constitutional monarchy collapsed with the proclamation of a republic in September 1792, and the liberal 'Brissotin' government that replaced it was overthrown in summer 1793 by Jacobin extremists. Led by **Robespierre**, they introduced a democratic constitution but administered the **Terror** as a dictatorship through the Committee of **Public Safety**, until overthrown by moderates during the coup of **Thermidor** in July 1794.

The 'Thermidorians' produced another constitution, introducing the **Directory** regime in 1795, and maintained a fragile hold on power by conducting successive coups against both Jacobins and constitutional monarchists. Bereft of political credibility, and blamed for military failures against the **Second Coalition**, the Directory finally toppled in November 1799, when the **Brumaire** coup brought **Napoleon** to power as head of a new **Consulate**, at which point all authorities agree that the French Revolution was over. *See also* **France**.

Friedberg, Battle of

A victory that marked the high point of **Moreau's** 1796 offensive from the **Rhine** into southern Germany. Success at **Neresheim** had brought Moreau's Army of the Rhine and Moselle up to the River Schmutter, about halfway between Ulm and Munich, by 21 August (*see* **Map 4**). Aware that Austrian C-in-C Archduke **Charles** had taken most of his army north against **Jourdan**, but ignorant of its fate, Moreau launched a supporting offensive against General Latour's depleted cordon between the Danube and Switzerland on 24 August. Successful flank attacks exposed Latour's central positions either side of Friedberg, and they were pulled back to the Iser just in time to prevent **Desaix** from cutting lines of retreat. Having lost 1,800 men and 17 guns during the day, Latour marched north to the Danube, where he made contact with his extreme right wing and 10,000 reinforcements left behind by Charles. Moreau made little effort to advance beyond the Iser, apart from an unsuccessful attempt to capture the bridge at Munich, while he sought to confirm rumours of Jourdan's defeat at **Amberg**. Once it had been provided by German newspapers on 10 September, he abandoned further offensive action and withdrew towards the Rhine (*see* Battle of **Biberach**).

Friedland, Battle of

The comprehensive French victory over Russian forces in East Prussia on 14 June 1807 that ended the War of the **Fourth Coalition**. French forces under **Napoleon** had been seeking a decisive confrontation since the previous autumn, but their latest attempt to get between Russian commander **Bennigsen** and his base at Königsberg had failed at **Heilsberg** on 10–11 June.

Immediately after the Heilsberg battle, Napoleon dispatched **Murat's** cavalry and **Soult's** corps on forced marches to Königsberg, hoping to force Bennigsen to defend the city, and accompanied his army's main strike force towards Domnau, where he expected the Russians to fight. He also detached **Davout** to the west as a supporting link with Murat, and **Lannes** northeast to prevent Bennigsen from escaping into Russia via the river crossing at Friedland. Bennigsen in fact directed his army towards Friedland, aiming to strike at Lannes's 12,000 men before they could be supported, and fierce skirmishes were in progress by the time Napoleon realized this during the evening of 13 June.

Russian attacks on Lannes became heavier from dawn on 14 June, but were carried out with little urgency, and a period of increasing numerical superiority was wasted. Bolstered by **Grouchy's** cavalry command, some 17,000 French troops faced odds of almost three to one, but the arrival of **Mortier's** corps had brought French strength up to 35,000 men by nine thirty, and the front was stable when Napoleon reached Friedland at noon.

Recognizing that Bennigsen was deploying his forces in a vulnerable position, with their backs against two tight bends in the Alle, Napoleon elected to attack without waiting for his more distant corps to reach the field. By late afternoon the numerical odds had anyway been reversed, with the arrival of the **Imperial Guard** and **Victor** bringing local French strength up to about 80,000 against Bennigsen's 60,000. Both sides fielded about 120 guns.

The French attack got under way at five thirty, spearheaded by **Ney** on the right, and caught the Russian left wing (led by **Bagration** and Kologribov) in the process of withdrawing across the Alle for the night. After conceding forward positions it staged an impressive fightback, and the French were saved only by Napoleon's deployment of support from part of Victor's reserve corps.

Led by **Dupont's** division, Victor's troops drove back the Russian cavalry and rushed his artillery forward, wreaking havoc on massed infantry at close range. While Lannes and Mortier held off a Russian counter-attack to his left, Ney and Dupont turned north to advance on Friedland itself, sweeping attempted counter-attacks into the river. As the first French troops entered the burning town, Bennigsen sent in the **Russian Imperial Guard**, but they were unable to do more than delay what became a rout, and Ney was in control of Friedland by mid-evening.

His success was not matched on the French left, where Napoleon's unwillingness to commit more reserves and Grouchy's reluctance to attack a numerically inferior Russian cavalry force allowed Bennigsen to extricate his remaining troops, using the only surviving bridge over the Alle and a ford north of the town. Their escape marked the effective end of the battle, and fighting had died down by eleven.

The battle cost the **Grande Armée** no more than 10,000 casualties, against at least 20,000 Russian losses, and finished Bennigsen's army as an independent fighting force. Made possible primarily by Bennigsen's almost suicidal dispositions and Lannes's holding action during the morning, but owing something to the enterprise of Victor and Ney, Napoleon's victory was enough to bring Russian tsar **Alexander** to terms, and peace was signed at **Tilsit** in July. *See* **Map 17**.

Frigates

Perhaps the most valuable class of contemporary warship, frigates were smaller and faster than **ships-of-the-line**, generally carrying between 26 and 44 guns, and were immensely versatile weapons. They functioned as the 'eyes' of a battlefleet on manoeuvres, and as 'cruisers' patrolling trade routes or watching over harbours under **blockade**. They could operate as fast commerce raiders in distant waters, and were powerful enough in their own right to defeat anything less than a battleship. Heavy armament also meant frigates could operate as strategic weapons, able to dominate coastal areas in lieu of larger craft that were more difficult to maintain in distant **colonial** outposts.

No major navy could possess too many frigates, but the **Royal Navy's** need was particularly critical in view of its uniquely varied global role, and successive British **Mediterranean** commanders in particular suffered from a generalized shortage of the class. Despite the highly successful record of British frigates in action, it was the infant **US Navy** that demonstrated their value most conclusively, mounting a very effective campaign against British trade with its large, imaginatively handled ships during the **Anglo-American War**.

Frioul, Invasion of (1797)

The final phase of Napoleon's **Italian campaigns** against the **First Coalition**, intended to secure the regional control won at **Rivoli** and **Mantua** earlier in 1797. A new Austrian army of 50,000 men soon began gathering in the Frioul and Tyrol regions, under the relatively dynamic command of Archduke **Charles**. Napoleon was too weak to mount an immediate attack, moving south with 9,000 men to force peace terms on the **Papal States**, but reinforcements reached the front in his absence, and by late February he could call on 60,000 troops for a major offensive.

Napoleon's basic aim was to drive through the Frioul towards Vienna, but he took precautions against any threat from Austrian forces further west, sending some 17,000 troops under **Joubert** up the Aviso into the Tyrol. His own four divisions, about 43,000 troops, opened operations with a preliminary crossing of the Brenta and a feint towards Trent, taking the Austrian forward outpost at Primolano on 1 March. Charles's incomplete forces in the Frioul were concentrated between San Vito and Spilimbergo along the west bank of the Tagliamento, guarding the southwestern approaches to Austria proper and offering a good line of rapid withdrawal into mountain terrain. Delayed by snow, the main French advance against them got under way on 10 March.

Napoleon moved east to Sacile, which was occupied after a skirmish on 15 March. **Bernadotte** and Guieu got their divisions across the Tagliamento at Valvasone next day, prompting a general withdrawal to Udine, but Napoleon's rapid pursuit quickly forced Charles back to the line of the Isonzo, where **Masséna**'s northern wing destroyed three Austrian divisions at **Tarvis** on 17 March. With Joubert making good progress in the Tyrol, Napoleon swept towards Vienna, reaching Klagenfurt on 29 March.

A further advance took Napoleon to Leoben on 7 April, but he was still 120km from Vienna when the Austrians accepted his offer of an armistice next day. Napoleon had stretched his army to the limit, and was happy to promote peace as a way of buying **Moreau** time to open a **Rhine** offensive, producing formal peace proposals (without waiting for government authority) on 16 April. Signed next day by Emperor **Francis** as the Preliminaries of **Leoben**, they ended the Austro-French conflict in Italy and formed the basis for the final Peace of **Campo Formio**. *See* **Map 6**.

Fructidor Coup

Large-scale purge of suspected royalists and other political opponents carried out by the **Directory** government of **France** in September 1797. The regime's unpopularity in the country was increasingly mirrored by political weakness at the centre during 1797, and by the summer a substantial minority of the Assembly, including Council of **Five Hundred** president **Pichegru**, was openly in favour of a royal restoration. The Directors summoned **Hoche** and his Army of the Sambre and Meuse to the capital in August, and **Augereau**'s troops stormed the Assembly's meeting place at the Tuileries on the night of 3–4 September (18–19 Fructidor by the **Republican Calendar**), arresting Pichegru and any other suspects on the premises. Subsequent arrests and flights, including that of war minister **Carnot** to Geneva, temporarily secured the government against pressure from the right, but its position remained precarious, and it soon resorted to similar tactics against radicals (*see* **Floréal Coup**).

Fuentes de Oñoro, Battle of

An attempt in May 1811 by **Masséna**'s French Army to break **Wellington**'s siege of Almeida, one of the key Spanish fortresses on the northern road from **Portugal**. Masséna's invasion army had been driven out of Portugal in March, and Wellington had detached a force to **Badajoz** before marching 37,000 men to Almeida. Masséna returned with 47,000 men at the start of May, finding Anglo-Portuguese forces in defensive positions along a high ridge north-east of Almeida. Preliminary actions took place all along the line throughout 3 and 4 May, while Masséna concentrated his forces, and a full-scale frontal assault against the British right wing followed on 5 May.

Repeated French **cavalry** charges were unable to disperse British **infantry squares**, but drove outnumbered British cavalry from the field, forcing Wellington to shorten his lines. The reduced line held until the end of the day, and Masséna withdrew his battered army overnight, a move interpreted by some commentators as evidence of his half-hearted commitment to the fight. Anglo-Portuguese units had also been severely mauled, and part of the Almeida garrison was allowed to escape unmolested after the town's surrender on 6 May. Though hardly a tactical victory, the action achieved Wellington's basic aim of enabling an advance towards the more formidable fortress of **Ciudad Rodrigo**. *See also* **Peninsular War**.

Fusil

Contemporary English term for a light **musket**, modelled on weapons used by bird-hunters, that saw limited use with British forces of the period, equipping a few light infantry units. Fusils were also issued to particularly youthful or diminutive members of British home defence volunteer units.

Fusilier

A widely used term with different meanings for various contemporary armies. In German armies, light infantry were designated as fusiliers, but the fusiliers of a French infantry battalion were the non-élite troops occupying the centre of the line. All British infantry armed with **muskets** or **rifles** were originally known as fusiliers, but by the late eighteenth century there were only three Fusiliers infantry regiments (7th, 21st and 23rd).

G

Gaeta, Siege of

The only significant attempt by **Neapolitan Army** forces to defend the kingdom against French conquest in 1806. Violently anti-republican commander Hesse-Philippstahl, a minor north German prince, defied 10,000 troops of Joseph **Bonaparte**'s occupying French army at the small **fortress** of Gaeta, on the Calabrian south-west coast, through the early summer, and its survival encouraged British intervention from **Sicily** in late June. British commander **Stuart** planned to relieve Gaeta after his victory at **Maida** on 6 July, but Hesse-Philippstahl was invalided out of the fortress after being wounded by falling masonry on 10 July, and it fell a few days later, leaving Neapolitan resistance to bandits and **carbonari**. *See* **Map 9**.

Galleys

Single-decked warships, powered primarily by oars but often also equipped with a single sail, that were obsolete in terms of late eighteenth-century **naval warfare**, but were still used in large numbers by several navies. Most useful in the shallow waters of the Baltic, the Black Sea and the **Mediterranean**, they remained in service with the **Russian**, **Swedish**, **Turkish**, **Neapolitan**, **Venetian** and **Austrian** forces, although they saw little action and less success.

Gamonal, Battle of

French victory near Burgos on 10 November 1808 that helped wreck Spanish offensive plans along the line of the River Ebro, leaving powerful French forces in control of the road to Madrid. A divided Spanish command had concentrated most of its strength on the flanks of the front, planning to launch pincer attacks against French supply lines. While the Spanish flank attacks failed at **Espinola** in the north and **Tudela** in the south, **Napoleon**'s counter-strategy called for a mass attack through Burgos in the centre, protected only by General Galuzzo's 10,000 Asturians (*see* **Peninsular War**).

Bessières began moving towards Burgos on 6 November, but progress was slow until **Soult** took over command three days later. Facing 67,000 French troops, Spanish commander Count Belvedere (standing in while Galuzzo faced treason charges in Madrid) took the surprising decision to move his 10,000 men out of Burgos and meet them at the nearby village of Gamonal. Poorly armed, trained, led and positioned, Spanish units quickly disintegrated under French **cavalry** attacks on 10 November. Perhaps 6,000 Spanish troops escaped towards Lerma, and Napoleon set up his headquarters at Burgos that night. *See* **Map 22**.

Ganteaume, Honoré Joseph Antoine (1755–1818)

After joining the royal service as an ordinary seaman, Ganteaume was a captain in the post-revolutionary **French Navy** from early 1794, and was wounded at that year's Battle of the **First of June**. As First Captain (chief of staff) to C-in-C **Brueys** with the **Middle East** expedition in 1798, he survived the explosion that destroyed the flagship *L'Orient* during the Battle of the **Nile**, and remained in **Egypt** until August 1799, when he skippered the vessel that brought **Napoleon** back to France. He was a rear-admiral with the navy's principal battlefleet in Brest from 1800, but his freedom of action was severely limited by British **blockade** and the poor condition of his ships. He led the unsuccessful sortie to Alexandria known as 'Ganteaume's Cruise' in 1801, displaying a caution and pessimism common to French **naval** commanders, and took part in the 1802 **Santo Domingo** expedition. Back in Brest as a vice-admiral from May 1804, he took command in the **Mediterranean** after **Trafalgar**, a post he held until 1814, though his forces saw little action beyond the occasional supply of French garrisons. He resumed royal service on the restoration in 1814, remaining loyal to the crown until his death.

'Ganteaume's Cruise'

Failed French attempt to relieve the isolated garrison of **Egypt**, mounted in summer 1801 by a naval squadron under Admiral **Ganteaume**. Undaunted by the failure of 'Bruix's Cruise' in 1799, **Napoleon** began planning for an expedition to save his **Middle East** forces soon after the **Brumaire** coup brought him to power. As the depth of **French Navy** weakness became clear, he settled for a limited operation in April 1800, ordering Brest commander Ganteaume to break into the Mediterranean with a small, fast squadron.

Ganteaume's seven **ships-of-the-line**, two **frigates** and 2,500 troops put to sea on 9 January 1801, taking advantage of a lucky wind change to dash south past the British **blockade** on 15 January. His ramshackle ships had already suffered serious storm damage and an outbreak of typhus when they successfully ran the Straits of Gibraltar, and false intelligence from the captain of a captured British **sloop** convinced him to dash for Toulon.

Reaching the French base on 18 February, he was ordered to leave port on 9 March, but more damage in high winds forced him back into Toulon from 5 to 25 April. Six battleships and three frigates eventually sailed for Egypt, but scout vessels found **Keith**'s Mediterranean Fleet already there to support **Abercromby**'s invasion force. Ganteaume returned to Toulon on 22 July,

having captured the detached battleship *Swiftsure* en route, and remained there until the Peace of **Amiens**. *See* **Map 8**.

Gaudin, Martin Michel Charles (1756–1841)

A tax official for the pre-revolutionary French regime, and a treasury official under the **Directory**, Gaudin was appointed minister of finance when the **Consulate** achieved power in 1799, holding the post until 1814. A competent and honest administrator, he founded the Bank of France and introduced a number of new, indirect taxes. Although most direct taxes were retained from the Revolutionary period, methods of collection were centralized and streamlined to great effect, particularly by the establishment of a national tax register (*cadastre*). Gaudin's part in rescuing **France** from the brink of post-revolutionary financial collapse was rewarded with elevation to the imperial peerage, as Duke of Gaeta, in 1809, and he was reappointed to his ministry during the **Hundred Days** of 1815, before accepting royal service and ending his career as governor of the Bank of France from 1820.

Gazan, Honoré Theodore Maxime (1765–1845)

Gazan's long and arduous career in French military service began with the royal army's **artillery** arm in the early 1880s, and he was a member of the royal bodyguard from 1786 to 1791. He fought against the **First Coalition** on the **Rhine** and **Italian** fronts as a **National Guard** officer, and was a brigadier-general from April 1799. Promoted divisional general on the battlefield at **Zurich** in September, he was in besieged **Genoa** the following spring and remained in Italy until the end of the campaign against the **Second Coalition**. His division took part in **Villeneuve**'s ill-fated naval expedition of 1805, but was transferred to Germany after **Trafalgar**, fighting under **Lannes** at **Dürrenstein** in November 1805 and through the War of the **Fourth Coalition**. In the **Peninsular** theatre from 1808 to 1814, he fought under **Marmont**, **Soult** and **Jourdan** before becoming chief of staff to the army as a whole when Soult took overall command after **Vitoria**. Retired at his own request in January 1815, he was slow to join **Napoleon** during the **Hundred**

Days, eventually organizing militia forces in Picardy, but returned to royal service on the second restoration and finally retired in 1832.

Geisberg, Battle of the

The action that ended the **First Coalition's** offensive across the **Rhine** of autumn 1793, fought on 26 December in the area south of Weissenburg (*see* **Map 3**). After pursuing a French retreat south towards Strasbourg, **Brunswick's** Austro-Prussian army settled down for the winter in November, but faced unexpected threats from two directions. The French Army of the Moselle advanced east from the Sarre (Saar) under **Hoche** in late November, but was unable to take Kaiserslautern on the far allied right, and **Pichegru's** Army of the Rhine drove Prussian forces menacing Strasbourg back from Bitche during mid-December.

Prussian withdrawal obliged **Würmser's** nearby Austrian contingent to pull back, and Pichegru concentrated 35,000 men for an attack on its new positions around Weissenburg on 26 December. Supported by two divisions under **Desaix** on the right, and by three divisions from Hoche in the Vosges, the French advance was met at the Geisberg River by 4,000 Austrian troops on a reconnaissance sortie. Their comprehensive defeat triggered the last of many arguments between Brunswick and Würmser, who withdrew his Austrians that evening and retreated across the Rhine at Philippsburg on 30 December. Prussian forces followed, and crossed around Mainz on the same day, leaving an isolated garrison at Fort Vauban as the only allied presence west of the river.

Genoa, Republic of *See* **Ligurian Republic**

Genoa, Siege of

The investment of north-west Italy's major port by **Second Coalition** forces between 20 April and 4 June 1800. Austrian plans for a spring offensive on the **Italian** front hinged on taking the city, an important supply base and a threat to any invasion of southern France (*see* **Map 6**). Austrian C-in-C **Melas** opened operations at the head of 90,000 troops on 5 April, and advanced west through the mountains to Nice. Supported by the British **Royal Navy**, the attack achieved surprise and initial success, isolating **Suchet's**

eastern wing from the rest of **Masséna's** French army and driving some 18,000 men of the main body into Genoa. Leaving 20,000 men to guard the Alpine passes, Melas sent General Ott's 24,000 men, supported by warships on **blockade** stations, to put the city under **siege** by 20 April.

New French leader **Napoleon** was already forming a Reserve Army inside France, aiming to sweep through the Alps and encircle Austrian forces, but Masséna's survival in Genoa was vital to the plan. Seriously short of military supplies and with low food stocks when the siege began, Masséna received orders to hold out at all costs, and fought an imaginative delaying campaign. Mounting incessant sorties (one of which cost the services of **Soult**, captured on 11 May), and suppressing the protests of the starving city population, he was eventually forced to request terms on 2 June.

Coming just as Melas ordered the siege abandoned, French agreement to surrender on 4 June delayed the Austrian concentration against Napoleon by several days. Masséna's convincing threat to fight his way out also won his army the right to depart fully armed, and with no **parole** agreement preventing it from joining Napoleon.

Genola, Battle of

The only important action in northern Italy during the autumn of 1799, fought on 4–5 November some 60km south of Turin. The departure of Russian forces from the **Italian campaign** in September had left both sides with about 45,000 men in the theatre. As limited operations focused on the besieged French garrison at Coni, and French commander **Championnet** led an advance on the town, Austrian C-in-C **Melas** concentrated some 35,000 troops for an attack on the French left wing. Expecting Melas to retreat, Championnet pushed forward until his left collided with Austrian advanced divisions on the morning of 4 November. Grenier's French division was driven into full retreat by the early afternoon, and **Victor's** barely held its positions around the village of Genola until ordered back by Championnet. By mid-afternoon both were in full flight, and Melas drove them out of their overnight positions next day. Championnet lost some 6,500 men during the two days, against about 2,000 Austrian casualties, but was able to reorganize and hold a line at Mondovi for the winter, though Coni fell on 4 December. *See* **Map 6**.

Gentz, Friedrich von (1764–1832)

German statesman who entered the administrative service of his native **Prussia** in 1785 and, although sympathetic to the early liberal ideals of the **French Revolution**, became increasingly pro-British after 1794. His anti-revolutionary writings established him as a valued polemicist in Prussia and **Austria**, where he lived and worked from 1802, and his anti-French attitude matured into extreme conservatism in the years before his employment as an adviser to **Metternich** in 1812. As such he was appointed secretary-general to the Congress of **Vienna** in 1814, and fulfilled the role at subsequent European **great power** conferences into the 1820s.

George III, King (1738–1820)

Constitutional ruler of **Great Britain** from 1760 until 1811, George was also the hereditary Elector of **Hanover**. He was popular in Britain during the early years of his reign, but his image as a threat to parliamentary rights gradually eroded his standing, and his occasional bouts of madness, now believed to have been caused by the disease porphyria, encouraged ridicule among the literate classes. His uneasy alliance with **Pitt** after 1783 ushered in a long period of political stability, though the young prime minister gained most of the popular credit at first.

An avid agriculturalist, in line with the fashion of the day among educated north Europeans, George was still lampooned as the stubborn but eccentric 'Farmer George' in 1793, but an upsurge in popular patriotism fuelled his metamorphosis into a genuinely popular icon by the end of the century. A shrewd and serious man, deeply opposed to any form of liberal experimentation, he played a major role in his transformation by fostering an image of wartime political unity, giving public support to Pitt's governments and stressing the ideological aspect of war against France. He also portrayed himself as a paragon of conservative family values, though his family was normal only by contemporary royal standards. Relations with **George, Prince of Wales**,

had been poisoned by his son's scandalous debaucheries, and Queen Charlotte (of **Mecklenburg-Strelitz**, his wife since 1861) was afraid to be alone with her husband.

George forced Pitt's resignation in 1801 over the issue of **Catholic emancipation**, characteristically refusing to break his coronation oath as defender of the Protestant faith. Generally applauded, his stand initiated a period of renewed parliamentary instability, and his popularity flourished as ministries came and went over the next decade. After the illness of his favourite daughter triggered a final lapse into madness in late 1810, and establishment of a regency the following January, George remained the subject of ostentatious popular affection until his death. He is principally remembered worldwide as the man who drove the **United States** to independence, though his generally high reputation in Britain rests on the relatively stable cultural and commercial prosperity of his reign.

George, Prince of Wales (1762–1830)

The eldest son of British king **George III**, he regularly disgraced himself during an extended youth of financial and hedonistic excess, living in virtual estrangement from his father for most of the war years. Occasionally called upon to act as regent during the king's bouts of madness, he took power permanently as Prince Regent in 1811, by which time an early flirtation with reformist politicians had been cured. He remained a reactionary figure until his death, becoming King George IV in 1820, but seldom intervened in the routine business of government, partly because **Liverpool's** Tory administration (1812–27) generally avoided any social policy that might be interpreted as liberal. Though an intelligent observer, and alert to any erosion of his political rights, George was lazy, impressionable, frivolous and inclined to public eccentricity, while his corpulence and dandyism combined to produce an unfavourable physical impression. 'Prinny' was thus a poor substitute for his father as a national symbol during the later war years but, though he was subject to widespread ridicule, 'king and country' patriotism in **Great Britain** was already too well established to be undermined by his failings.

Gérard, Maurice Etienne (1773–1852)

French soldier, commissioned in 1792, who saw action on the **Rhine**, in **Italy**, in **Switzerland** and in **Bavaria** (where he was wounded at **Austerlitz**) before he was promoted brigadier-general in November 1806. He fought at **Eylau** in 1807, before becoming **Bernadotte's** chief of staff in northern Germany, and was at **Wagram** in 1809. He fought at **Fuentes de Oñoro** in the **Peninsular** theatre, and took part the 1812 **Russian campaign**, becoming a divisional general after **Borodino** and enduring the subsequent retreat as part of **Beauharnais's** command. With **Macdonald's** corps during the first phase of the 1813 struggle for **Germany**, he led XI Corps at **Leipzig**, and emerged as one of Napoleon's more important commanders during the campaign for **France**, fighting at **Brienne** and **La Rothière** before taking command of II Corps. Rejoining the emperor from royal service in 1815, he fought at **Ligny** and **Wavre**, subsequently living in exile until 1817, when he returned to Paris and a successful politico-military career.

Germany, Campaign for (1813)

The War of the **Sixth Coalition's** central phase, a multifaceted and busy campaign that followed from the **Russian campaign** of 1812, and ended with the retreat of French forces across the **Rhine** in late 1813.

After retreating into **Poland** and East Prussia at end of 1812, the remnant of the French **Grande Armée** was under **Murat's** temporary command. Comprising only some 40,000 troops, many of them in very bad condition, it was clearly incapable of fulfilling **Napoleon's** original orders to defend the line of the Vistula, given as he left the front in early December.

Field Marshal **Kutuzov's** Russian armies had been forced to pause at the Vistula frontier for rest, supply and reinforcement, but recommenced their westward advance from 16 January, moving to occupy Warsaw on 7 February. Murat withdrew on Posen, leaving General **Rapp** with 30,000 men at the port of Danzig and smaller garrisons at Thorn and Modlin. Murat then returned to his kingdom of **Naples**, handing command to Eugène de **Beauharnais**.

Beauharnais could not hope to defend Posen.

His army was in no condition to fight, the local population was increasingly hostile and the Russians were coming, virtually unhindered by the region's frozen rivers. In line with new orders to hold the River Oder, he retired further west to Frankfurt, where he was joined by **Gouvion St Cyr's** corps (bringing frontline strength up to 30,000 men), but reports that the Russians had crossed the river further north prompted a further westward move, first towards Berlin and then to Wittenburg on the Elbe, which was reached on 6 March. Despite Napoleon's optimistic instructions, the line of the Elbe was too long to hold, and Hamburg was abandoned six days later.

These sensible manoeuvres did not please Napoleon, who overestimated the fighting capacity of Eugène's army, and virtually ignored the growth of popular and political opposition to France in Germany. The loyalty of his German allies had always depended on French military strength, and its decline fuelled an intellectual and emotional nationalist movement that had been growing throughout Germany for several years, but was most clearly defined in **Prussia**.

Acute military weakness and King **Frederick William III's** timidity had ensured Prussia's grudging loyalty to an unpopular alliance before 1812, but the highly publicized Convention of **Tauroggen** unleashed a torrent of support for renewed war among the Prussian élite and middle classes. Emboldened by the prospect of Russian troops reaching Berlin, the king signed the Convention of **Kalisch** in late February, promising to join the Coalition in the near future, and an open declaration of war against France followed on 13 March. News of the long-anticipated defection reached Paris two weeks later.

Prussia's involvement multiplied the immediate threat to French security in Germany. In the north, General **Wittgenstein's** column was advancing west from Marienwerder along a wide front, and Prussians under **Yorck** and **Bülow** soon brought his strength up to 40,000 men. An ailing Kutuzov was lingering near Kalisch with perhaps 30,000 men, but General **Winzingerode's** 13,000-strong advance guard was already well into Saxony, where it linked up with **Blücher's** 25,000 Prussians to march on Dresden, which was occupied on 27 March. Meanwhile Crown Prince **Bernadotte** of **Sweden** was assembling an army of 28,000 men in Pomerania, and an Anglo-German force of about 9,000 troops was operating around Stralsund (*see* **Map 21**).

The first significant action of the campaign took place on 3 April, when Beauharnais attacked Wittgenstein around **Möckern**, but he could not be stopped from marching to join Blücher around Dresden. Allied concentration convinced Beauharnais to abandon the upper Elbe, and he executed another general withdrawal to the River Saale, a position strong enough to buy time for Napoleon's urgent recruitment drive to bear fruit.

Napoleon had been working hard to rebuild his army. Extended **conscription**, transfers from the **Peninsular** theatre and drafts of **National Guard** militia into the regular army had brought his strength in Germany up to about 200,000 men by early April, and measures were in hand to provide at least some of the 450,000 more he wanted. About 121,000 men (four line corps and the **Imperial Guard**) were deployed at the River Main, another 58,000 troops were with Beauharnais at the Saale, **Davout** commanded 20,000 men west of Hamburg, and **Sebastiani**'s 14,000 cavalry were operating around the lower Elbe. The army as a whole was dangerously short of **cavalry**, but enjoyed considerable numerical superiority over about 110,000 allied troops in the theatre.

Though his strength remained well below the 300,000 men he felt were needed (partly because **Bavaria** and **Saxony** had not yet provided troops), and he doubted his conscripts' capacity for complex manoeuvres, Napoleon planned to exploit his advantage with an offensive towards Berlin and the besieged garrisons of Danzig, Thorn and Modlin. The development of a major allied offensive from Dresden towards the Saale forced the plan's postponement, but its regular revival was a feature of the campaign as a whole.

Reasonably sure that Napoleon was about to go on to the offensive, Blücher and Wittgenstein had been advancing their armies cautiously west beyond the Elbe, and forward patrols were in the vicinity of Saalfeld by 9 April. Aware of their probable numerical inferiority, but confident of

operational superiority, they intended to destroy part of Napoleon's army before it could concentrate. Operations were speeded up from mid-April once this policy was endorsed by Tsar **Alexander** and Frederick William, who accompanied reinforcements to the front, bringing the number of allied troops approaching the Saale by 24 April up to 73,000, including 25,000 cavalry and supported by more than 500 guns.

Though starved of reconnaissance forces, Napoleon reacted to the Russian advance by ordering his main army up to the Saale on Eugène's right, and preparing a counter-offensive towards Dresden, intended to sever Blücher's communications with Silesia and Berlin. The French armies began moving east over the Saale towards Leipzig on 1 May.

While Beauharnais pushed towards Schladelbach, Napoleon's troops drove in two columns towards Naumberg (**Bertrand** and **Oudinot**) and Lützen (**Ney** and **Marmont**). News of the advance cut short allied command disputes surrounding Kutuzov's replacement by the relatively junior Wittgenstein, and concentration was ordered for an attack on the French right flank around Lützen. French forces met strong opposition on the first day, particularly around **Poserna**, and Ney's corps was attacked in strength by Wittgenstein next morning at **Lützen**, where Napoleon won a victory that could not be exploited for lack of cavalry.

Though in no way decisive, Lützen restored Napoleon's military reputation and persuaded the allies to retreat east. Characteristically determined to seek a conclusive victory, Napoleon split the main body of his own army in two from 4 May. He led the larger force towards Dresden, reported destination of at least some of Wittgenstein's army, and sent the rest north-east under Ney to hold the Elbe crossings at Wittenberg and **Torgau** (with orders to incorporate the **Saxon Army** once its government had agreed to cooperate).

Renewed arguments among allied commanders centred on Prussian anxiety for Berlin. This was heightened by Ney's northward move, but a compromise was reached. Bülow's thus far unemployed corps covered the Prussian capital while the main body withdrew beyond the Elbe to make a stand at **Bautzen**. The withdrawal, harassed by Beauharnais at Colditz on 5 May, was marred by failure to destroy the Dresden bridges on 8 May, enabling Napoleon to occupy the suburbs that day and establish protective bridgeheads across the Elbe on 9 May.

Once Napoleon had ascertained that the allies were massing at Bautzen, he recalled Ney's northern detachment and attacked the position on 20 and 21 May, but was again deprived of a decisive triumph by shortage of pursuit strength (along with Ney's failure to cut lines of retreat). The defeat provoked another bout of allied squabbling – during which **Barclay de Tolly** replaced Wittgenstein in command of Russian forces – and a retreat towards the Silesian town of Schweidnitz, in position to exploit any Austrian declaration of war on France or move to the defence of Prussia.

Napoleon meanwhile moved his main army east towards the Katzbach and sent Oudinot towards Berlin, while Davout was ordered to push forward from the lower Elbe. Ravaged by sickness and frequent **Cossack** raids, Napoleon's inexperienced troops were unable to force an end to the campaign. Davout occupied Hamburg on 28 May, but Oudinot's corps was defeated by Bülow's Prussians around Luckau on the same day, and the main army made only very slow progress east against heavy allied rearguard resistance, eventually reaching Breslau on 1 June.

Fighting came to a sudden halt next day, when a 36-hour ceasefire was agreed, and was suspended from 4 June by an **armistice**, after which Napoleon withdrew to Dresden. Eventually extended to 16 August, the armistice suited both sides in early June, giving them a chance to rebuild shattered forces, but the allies gained most from the pause. By mid-August, Napoleon had mustered about 440,000 men for his main armies in Germany, and another 250,000 troops were scattered elsewhere (including General **Wrede**'s Bavarian contingent at the River Inn), while the allies could call on about half a million men at the main front, maintained a vast superiority in cavalry, and were assembling another 350,000 reserves. At the same time the allies made diplomatic gains: Sweden joined the Coalition on 7 July, and **Austria** agreed to join at **Reichenbach** 12 days later.

The armistice was brought to a premature end by Austria's formal declaration of war on 12 August and Blücher's advance from Breslau next day. Coalition forces were grouped into four main armies: Bernadotte's Army of the North (110,000 Prussians and Swedes) at Berlin; Blücher's Army of Silesia (95,000 men) south of Breslau; **Bennigsen**'s 60,000-strong Army of Poland was being formed in the rear; and the largest force, **Schwarzenberg**'s Army of Bohemia (230,000 men), was organizing near the upper Elbe. After more arguments, which also produced the **Trachenberg Plan** to avoid battle with Napoleon himself and seek limited victories against his subordinates, allied commanders decided on 17 August to mount a three-pronged attack towards Leipzig.

News of **Wellington**'s successes in Spain boosted allied morale and seems to have depressed Napoleon, who took the unusual step of consulting (but ignoring) subordinates before again dividing his army in two. Some 250,000 men were massed under his command in a defensive position along the Elbe either side of Dresden, and Oudinot was given charge of 120,000 troops around Luckau for another attempt on Berlin. Division of his strength and pursuit of a secondary success is generally considered one of Napoleon's major errors, and the next few days revealed the extent to which he had lost the initiative. After massing for an easterly attack on Blücher, he switched south towards Zittau to menace Schwarzenberg's rear lines on 18 August, but changed his mind again two days later and resumed the drive against Blücher, who retreated in line with the Trachenberg Plan, about which Napoleon knew nothing.

Next day an appeal for help arrived from Gouvion St Cyr at Dresden, which had replaced Leipzig as the cautious Schwarzenberg's main target. Leaving **Macdonald** in charge of holding operations against Blücher, Napoleon marched back towards Dresden, but on 23 August he decided against the direct relief of St Cyr, and began preparing an attack across Schwarzenberg's rear at Königstein and Pirna. News of Oudinot's defeat at **Gross-Beeren** (23 August) arrived two days later, along with word that

Dresden could only hold out for another day. Changing his plans for the last time, Napoleon left a single corps to attack Pirna and marched to rescue St Cyr.

Delayed by St Cyr's counter-attacks, a major allied assault on **Dresden** was repelled on 26 August by Napoleon and 70,000 French troops. Another 50,000 French troops arrived overnight, while **Vandamme's** successful attack on **Pirna** kept allied reserves busy and helped Napoleon win a major victory next day. The success was undermined by Macdonald's simultaneous defeat at the **Katzbach**, by Oudinot's retreat in the wake of Gross-Beeren, and by Vandamme's severe reverse at **Kulm** on 30 August, which allowed Schwarzenberg's retreating army to escape.

While allied armies still threatened on three fronts, lack of cavalry, constant raids on communications and the inexperience of his army robbed Napoleon of the power to find or concentrate against opponents, and allied strategy forced constant shifts of priorities as his subordinates were menaced in turn. Napoleon's personal decline into bouts of lethargy and indecision was another factor in his failure to retain the initiative in a campaign increasingly shaped by allied strength in depth.

While Schwarzenberg retreated over the Bohemian mountains, Napoleon ordered another drive towards Berlin on 2 September, this time led by Ney, but Blücher's continuing advance on Macdonald's front forced him to reduce the operation's scale next day. Napoleon marched east from Dresden to rally Macdonald's shaken troops, but Blücher withdrew from their advance east of Bautzen.

Before Napoleon could resume preparations to take Berlin, Schwarzenberg's army recrossed the Elbe and sent a force under Barclay de Tolly towards Dresden. Forced to react, Napoleon marched his main army for Kulm, in the rear of Barclay's advance, but the whole of Schwarzenberg's army quickly pulled back across the Elbe. Napoleon halted pursuit by his flagging conscripts on 10 September, by which time news had reached him from the northern sector of Ney's retreat from **Dennewitz**.

The next two weeks brought a succession of crises that kept Napoleon fatally off balance. Before Ney could be helped, he was forced to respond to Schwarzenberg's renewed feint towards Dresden, news that Bernadotte and 80,000 troops were approaching the Elbe from the north, and Blücher's resumed attacks on Macdonald's enfeebled corps.

As French armies careered from sector to sector, crumbling in the face of critical supply shortages and the loss of 200,000 effective troops since mid-August, Napoleon eventually began withdrawing all his forces to positions west of the Elbe on 24 September, abandoning hope of directly relieving garrison forces further east.

At the same time Bernadotte's army to the north established its first bridgeheads across the Elbe, and Blücher began marching to its aid next day, freed by the arrival of Bennigsen's army. Their combined 140,000 troops, along with 180,000 men under Schwarzenberg and Bennigsen, were now directed towards Leipzig, the vital link in Napoleon's communications with the Rhine and home. After a week of skirmishes as allied forces manoeuvred into position, Blücher and 60,000 troops reached the Elbe at Wartenberg on 3 October, defeating Bertrand's under-strength corps before crossing the river next day and advancing alongside Bernadotte to Delitsch, only 30km north of Leipzig.

Now based around Leipzig, Napoleon could still deploy almost 250,000 men, and was well placed to outnumber either of the allied armies approaching the city. Leaving Murat in command of 43,000 men to ward off the southern attack, and two corps (**Mouton** and St Cyr) to guard Dresden, he led 150,000 men north on 7 October, but an attack at **Düben** failed to surprise Blücher, who executed a difficult withdrawal west to the Saale. Without sufficient cavalry to track allied positions, Napoleon could only order a cautious advance north towards Bernadotte's positions around Dessau while awaiting developments on the southern front.

Schwarzenberg's snail-like advance on Leipzig, now with an army of 240,000 men, was slowed even further by Murat's delaying action at Borna on 10 October, and Ney prevented part of Bernadotte's army from crossing the River Mulde near Dessau on 12 October, but allied forces were now close enough together to plan a combined attack on Leipzig. Tsar Alexander sent Wittgenstein's column forward from the south on 13 October to reconnoitre French positions, and Napoleon, realizing that the allied northern pincer had not been stopped, gave orders on 14 October for his armies to concentrate on the city.

Preceded by a large-scale but indecisive cavalry engagement at **Liebertwolkwitz** on 14 October, the confrontation at **Leipzig** (16–19 October) was the second largest battle of the age (after **Borodino**), and allied victory was decisive). What was left of French political influence in Germany crumbled in its wake: Bavaria had joined the allies before the battle, **Württemberg** abandoned Napoleon at its height, and Saxony fell under allied occupation (though Dresden's French garrison held out until 11 November). The rest of the Confederation of the **Rhine** evaporated as Napoleon retreated west along his supply lines towards Frankfurt and Mainz.

The French retreat was shadowed by the allies but not seriously troubled before reaching Erfurt on 23 October. An attempt to block its withdrawal by General Wrede's Bavarians at **Hanau** was defeated in late October, and about 70,000 troops (along with perhaps 40,000 stragglers) reached the virtual safety of Frankfurt, only 30km from the Rhine, on 2 November. About 100,000 French troops still in Germany – with Davout's corps at the lower Elbe, or numerous garrisons and occupation forces – were now hopelessly isolated. All except Davout's garrison at **Hamburg** were compelled to surrender over the next few weeks, most unconditionally after allied commanders refused to ratify negotiated terms. Their capture brought total French losses during the campaign to about 400,000 men, along with all German territory east of the Rhine. Increasingly pressed by allied advances through Spain to the west, a gravely weakened France could only prepare to defend its national frontiers in 1814 (*see* Campaign for **France**). *See* **Map 25**.

Germinal, Insurrection of

The first attempt at mass revolution in **France** after the coup of **Thermidor** in 1794 had brought a moderate parliamentarian regime to power. The catalyst for rebellion was the control exercised by left-wing 'Hébertist' politicians over a significant minority of Parisian electoral districts, and it was triggered by a cut in the bread ration imposed after the 'Thermidorians' had removed overall price restrictions. The Paris Assembly was occupied on 1 April 1795 by protesters demanding bread and a return to the democratic constitution of 1793, but they lacked leadership or a coherent programme, and eventually submitted peacefully to eviction by loyal **National Guard** units. The government then took steps to suppress popular agitation. Paris was placed under martial law, with General **Pichegru** as military commander, and several left-wing deputies were deported to the tropics, but no attempt was made at significant economic intervention and food shortages continued to stir up trouble all over France. *See also* Insurrection of **Prairial**.

Ghent, Treaty of

The agreement between **Great Britain** and the **United States**, signed on 24 December 1814 after more than four months of negotiation, that ended the **Anglo-American War**. The treaty involved no territorial changes, apart from acknowledging British possession of a few small islands off the coast of Maine, and failed to address long-standing disputes over fishing and navigational rights in American waters, but both governments agreed to recognize the integrity of extant North American frontiers. Diplomatic agreement did not end the war immediately, primarily because the northern European city of Ghent lay 4,000 miles from the battle zone, and fighting continued until the following spring, when news of the treaty finally filtered through to field commanders.

Gneisenau, Augustus Wilhelm (1760–1831)

One of the period's most celebrated staff officers, Gneisenau was born in **Saxony** and served with several German armies before entering the **Prussian Army** in 1786. He took part in the campaign in **Poland** of 1794, and commanded the Colberg garrison during the War of the **Fourth Coalition** in 1806, but his most important work was carried out under War Department director

Scharnhorst from 1808 to 1810, when he helped reorganize **conscription** and officer training, and made an important contribution to development of a functioning general staff.

Gneisenau was appointed chief of staff to **Blücher's** army in **Germany** after Scharnhorst was killed at **Lützen** in May 1813. His cautious, calculating approach to field operations proved an effective foil to his elderly chief's almost pathological attacking tendency, and the partnership remained in position through the following year's struggle for **France**. Like his French counterpart, **Berthier**, Gneisenau's temperament proved less suited to overall field command, and his cautious performance at **Laon** in March 1814 allowed **Napoleon** to escape a major defeat.

He was inclined to play safe at a crucial stage during the **Hundred Days** campaign of 1815, when he was again Blücher's principal lieutenant. Intending to withdraw away from **Wellington's** allied army after the defeat at **Ligny**, he was overruled when Blücher returned to his post, and organized rapid transfer of three corps to the battle at **Waterloo**. A postwar governor of Berlin, he died of cholera leading Prussian troops in Poland.

Godoy, Manuel de (1767–1851)

The central political figure in **Spain** between his accession to the presidency of the State Council in 1792 and the Bourbon dynasty's temporary deposition in 1808, Godoy owed his rise from the ranks of the Royal Guard to the patronage of his lover, Queen Marie-Louise. Though no republican, he tried and failed to keep Spain out of the War of the **First Coalition** in 1793, and negotiated the unilateral Treaty of **Basle** with France in 1795, for which he was granted the title 'Prince of Peace'. Though removed from office after a French smear campaign in 1798, he returned to power in 1800 and subsequently tightened his hold over court affairs.

Godoy led Spanish forces against **Portugal** during the brief War of the **Oranges** in 1801, and took Spain into the War of the **Third Coalition** as a French ally in 1805, but lost any influence with **Napoleon** when he was caught conspiring with Prussian authorities during the early stages of the **Jena–Auerstädt campaign** in 1806.

Acutely aware of French military superiority, he could hardly oppose the Treaty of **Fontainebleau** in October 1807, and secured a share in the proposed partition of Portugal in return for French use of Spanish facilities, but it proved a poor bargain, providing Napoleon with a springboard for intervention in Spanish affairs.

Greedy, self-serving and a born intriguer, Godoy became by far the most unpopular man in a disaffected Spain, blamed for wartime economic hardships and suppression of Crown Prince **Ferdinand's** imagined liberal tendencies. He was no more admired abroad, and nobody complained when Napoleon forced him into exile with the royal family after the **Bayonne** Conference in May 1808. He spent the rest of the war years in comfortable but impotent confinement as a French pensioner at Compiègnes, and never returned to Spain.

Goethe, Johann Wolfgang (1749–1832)

The great German poet, playwright and scientist was born in Frankfurt, and trained as a lawyer before becoming a journalist in 1771. A court official with the Duke of Weimar in 1785, he was no admirer of French radical ideology during the 1790s, and was an observer with **Brunswick's** allied army at the Battle of **Valmy** in 1792. His prescient assessment of its import – 'from this day and this hour dates a new epoch in the history of the world' – contributed to his lionization by German **Jacobins** and nationalists, as did the individualist tone of his later novels, but Goethe was never comfortable with their support. He eventually became convinced that **Napoleon** represented the way forward for European society, particularly after the emperor made a point of meeting him at **Erfurt** in 1808, and remained aloof from the chorus of bellicose patriotism, centred on **Prussia**, that accompanied the campaign for **Germany** in 1813.

Golymin, Battle of

Engagement between French and Russian forces near the Polish town of Golymin, some 65km north of Warsaw, one of two actions fought in the theatre on 26 December 1806 (*see* **Map 17**). The action was precipitated by **Napoleon's** orders of 24 December, sending two corps (**Augereau** and **Davout**) and **Murat's** cavalry north from the

Ukra River in search of Marshal **Kamenskoi's** retreating Russians. A total of about 38,000 men met the advance guard of **Buxhowden's** Russian corps (18,000 men, with little **cavalry** support, under Generals Gallitzin and **Doctorov**) 20km to the north-west at Golymin. The two Russian divisions held good defensive positions, but French weight of numbers drove them back once Davout's troops became involved in the fight, and forced their withdrawal into a wood north of the town. Although General **Morand's** division eventually cleared the woods, an attempt to cut the Russian line of retreat towards Makov failed with heavy casualties. Fighting ended at nightfall with Gallitzin virtually surrounded, but still in control of the road and able to escape before morning. Both sides are believed to have lost about 800 men in the action, which was instrumental in persuading Napoleon to abandon operations for the winter. *See also* Battle of Pultusk.

Gouvion St Cyr, Laurent (1764–1830)

A painter who joined the French revolutionary army as a volunteer in 1792, St Cyr served on the **Rhine** front during the War of the **First Coalition**, and was promoted divisional general in 1794. After service in both the German and **Italian campaigns** against the **Second Coalition**, he was ambassador to Madrid (1801–3) and took command of the army sent to pacify **Naples** during the War of the **Third Coalition** in 1805, moving into northern Italy in October to help **Masséna** pin Austrian forces south of the Alps.

St Cyr was promoted to corps command from December 1806, and remained in Italy until 1808, but his reputation suffered during a spell of duty in the **Peninsular War**. Charged with gaining full control of Catalonia from 1808, he quit his post in 1809 before a replacement arrived and was left without an important command until restored to first-line duty for the **Russian campaign** of 1812. Promoted marshal after winning the first Battle of **Polotsk** in August, he resigned after being wounded at the second battle in November. An enigmatic, relatively withdrawn character, he made a brief return to frontline service in early 1813, but fell ill again, resurfacing as a corps commander at **Dresden** in August and commanding the city's defence until his surrender in November. Returned to France and royal service in June 1814, he lay low during the **Hundred Days** after his royalist army deserted to Napoleon, and retired in September 1815 after a brief spell as war minister.

Goya y Lucientes, Francisco José de (1746–1828)

Spanish painter, chief artist at the court of King **Charles IV** from 1799, whose canvases depicting the **Madrid Uprising** against the French invasion of 1808 – *Dos de Mayo* (Second of May) and *Tres de Mayo* (Third of May) – were celebrated indictments of Napoleonic tyranny. Admired then and now for the sombre realism of his work, he produced a series of etchings between 1810 and 1814 examining the savage **guerrilla** fighting that formed a subtext to the **Peninsular War**, but their anti-French **propaganda** value and Goya's patriotic credentials were undermined by employment at the court of Joseph **Bonaparte**. An opponent of the reactionary King **Ferdinand VII**, he left Spain in 1824 and spent his last years in Bordeaux.

Graham, Thomas (1748–1843)

The son of a Scottish laird, Graham lived the life of a conventional gentleman farmer until 1792, when his wife died in southern France. Her coffin's subsequent search by French customs officers looking for contraband persuaded Graham to fight the revolutionaries, and after acting as an unofficial aide with British forces at **Toulon** in 1793, he returned home to raise an infantry regiment (the 90th Foot) at his own expense. Commissioned as a temporary lieutenant-colonel in 1794, he led his regiment at **Quiberon Bay** and was an official British observer with Austrian forces during the **Italian campaigns** of 1796, taking part in (and escaping from) the siege of **Mantua**.

Graham served on various **Mediterranean** stations before 1802, and spent several years as a civilian before joining **Moore's** expeditions to **Sweden** and Spain in 1808. He was with Moore at **Corunna** in January 1809, and was promoted major-general later in the year, leading a brigade at **Walcheren** but being invalided home at an early stage. He returned to the **Peninsular** theatre as lieutenant-general in command of the **Cadiz** garrison in 1810, and sealed his reputation by victory at **Barrosa** in March 1811 before joining **Wellington**'s main army in June. Soon placed at the head of a three-division corps, he played a subsidiary role at **Badajoz** in early 1812 but was invalided home in July because of an eye infection.

He was back in action in time to play an important part in the victory at **Vitoria** in 1813, and led the siege of **San Sebastian**, which fell before eye trouble again forced him home. After leading a British contingent with forces on the northern flank of allied operations in **Germany** and **France** from late 1813, he retired and was ennobled as Baron Lynedoch in May 1814.

Grand Quartier-Général

The **French Army**'s central headquarters, developed under **Napoleon** to become the first modern military staff organization. Institutionally fluid and increasingly complex, it eventually administered departments controlling every aspect of army life, including **prisoners of war**, legal affairs, pay, records, security, headquarters administration, supply and maps, as well as staffs for specialist arms, the **Imperial Guard** and other individual formations.

Though it ultimately employed more than 10,000 personnel, the GQG was not a particularly efficient or rational organization, and Napoleon's parallel household staff (La Maison) was in practice responsible for most of his planning and logistic successes. The household was essentially a means of executing Napoleon's often very detailed orders, and overlapped with the headquarters staff, most notably in the person of Marshal **Berthier**, who headed both and was vital to the system's practical coherence. Berthier also accompanied Napoleon on campaign, when orders were transmitted and intelligence received through a travelling staff organization (Petit Quartier-Général). Other vital staff members included the enterprising henchman **Caulaincourt**, commissary chief of staff Daru and Colonel (later General) Bacler d'Aube, Napoleon's indispensable master of the map table.

Grand Tactics

All planned deployment of troops, on any scale, can be described as tactical, but grand tactics are the theory and practice of military operations using large forces. In the context of a lengthy campaign, or when simultaneous conflicts are taking place within an army's sphere of operations, grand tactics often overlap with the purely military application of **strategy**.

The **cordon** system of campaign strategy perfected by Frederick the Great had reduced grand tactics to virtual redundancy by the late eighteenth century, largely because it was dominated by **siege** operations and involved very few large battles. The post-revolutionary **French Army**, as reorganized by **Carnot**, developed simple massed **infantry tactics** to break through allied cordons, but it was **Napoleon's Italian campaign** of 1796 that ushered in a new era of sophisticated offensive battle tactics.

Although he was often forced to improvise when his deployments or intelligence went awry, Napoleon's battle tactics were generally variations on a single theme. A frontal attack by his advanced units would be used to pin the attention of hostile forces while a substantial portion of his army advanced round either flank in the greatest possible secrecy. Frontal attackers, usually heavily outnumbered at first, would be steadily reinforced to ensure that the main battle appeared to be maturing on their front, but a substantial reserve would be kept back. Once convinced that most enemy reserves had been committed to the frontal battle, Napoleon would order in the attack on their flank, wait until it had distracted forces from the centre, and then hurl his reserve into a climactic frontal onslaught.

Other European armies attempted to imitate Napoleon's methods, but were generally unable to achieve the combination of speed, surprise and battlefield flexibility that made them work. Familiarity also brought diminishing returns for French forces, and **Wellington**'s more pedestrian approach to battles succeeded by anticipating aggression. His insistence on giving battle at a location of his own choosing, and ability to render a good defensive position almost impregnable, were less susceptible to organizational mishap than Napoleon's bold thrusts, and lured

French attackers to destruction time and again. His final counter-attack at **Waterloo**, which routed an army exhausted by repeated failed assaults on his positions, demonstrated the offensive potential of a system founded primarily on well-organized defence.

Grande Armée

The term, first used by **Napoleon** in an order of 29 April 1805, that was generally taken to describe the imperial **French Army** when gathered as a body for a major campaign.

Grapeshot

Ammunition used by **artillery** for close-range anti-personnel operations. Like **canister** and case-shot, grapeshot scattered musket balls across a wide area, but because the balls were contained in a canvas bag (rather than a metal container), they exploded straight out of the barrel and tended to maim rather than kill outright. Grapeshot's potential as a crowd control weapon was nicely demonstrated by **Napoleon**, whose infamous delivery of a 'whiff of grapeshot' to the Paris mob quickly restored order during the **Vendémiaire** coup of October 1795.

Great Britain

The island monarchy of Great Britain comprised the united kingdoms of England and Scotland, and the principality of Wales, a total of about 9 million people in 1792. Its constitutional monarch, **George III**, governed in largely informal partnership with an élite class of landowners, bureaucrats and lawyers that dominated parliament. The monarchy's role was not precisely defined, and George III's assertions of royal prerogative triggered occasional political crises throughout his long reign, but both sides were broadly content with a status quo that maintained the ruling class in unchallenged power, and neither sought a major confrontation.

The country was administered by a cabinet drawn from both houses of parliament, most ministers coming from the noble House of Lords. They were appointed by the king, but his choice was effectively restricted to groups capable of carrying a majority in the lower House of Commons. Ministers functioned separately most of the time, cabinets rarely meeting in full, but collective government became more usual during the war years, especially after 1806.

Political opposition centred on practical issues rather than ideology, and the Whig and Tory groupings in parliament were fluid factions within a single social group rather than parties in the modern sense. Most leading figures belonged to a flourishing class of dynasts, farmers, merchants or industrialists that displayed little hunger for political power. Senior politicians often refused the premiership, and some ministers (such as Lord **Chatham**) were notoriously hard to find at work.

The British electoral system, though held up by apologists as a model for constitutional government, entitled only about 400,000 men to vote, and many parliamentary constituencies were 'rotten' or 'pocket' boroughs in the gift of vested interests. An elaborate network of patronage guaranteed success to any ministry that called an election, and factional rather than popular support was the key to retaining office. The king provoked a crisis when he engineered the fall of the Shelborne administration in 1783, but royal support and assiduous parliamentary management enabled his successor, William **Pitt**, to remain in office for 17 years.

Most British people, though effectively disenfranchised and economically exploited, accepted the status quo with barely a murmur by European standards. Constitutional reform groups existed among the middle classes, and rapid urbanization was throwing up a sprinkling of more seditious dissidents, but broad approval of the political system was discernible at all levels of society.

Relative political stability was encouraged by national prosperity, evident everywhere but the remote fringes of Wales and the Scottish Highlands. Britain was by far the richest nation on earth in the late eighteenth century, and was getting richer all the time. Spared the institutionalized penury of continental feudal systems, British governments, landowners and employers could afford to exercise moderation or buy support whenever social upheaval threatened. Geographical position and national characteristics aside, their wealth was a product of empire, trade and industrial revolution, linked and protected by the military might of the **Royal Navy**.

240

The British Empire began in **Ireland**, subject to centuries of maltreatment and hardly better off after Dublin was granted its own parliament in the 1780s. The poverty-stricken, politically oppressed condition of Ireland, and the possible emancipation of a Catholic majority hitherto excluded from office-holding, were controversial issues in Britain before and during the war period. Attempts at reform by the Pitt ministries of the 1790s met a wall of opposition, led by a reactionary Anglo-Irish administration and George (sworn enemy of Catholicism by his coronation oath), and the period's most dramatic cabinet upheavals followed the Act of **Union** that made Ireland part of the new United Kingdom in 1800.

Hunger for trading opportunities had been the dynamic force behind decades of rapid imperial expansion further afield. Defeat of the French in Canada and achievement of dominion over **India** in the 1750s had been balanced by loss of the **United States** in the 1780s, but global growth was still in full swing at the outbreak of the **Revolutionary Wars**. The first settlements had just been established in Australia, expansion in India was proceeding under recently established crown control, and Britain controlled a growing list of small but valuable outposts all over the world. Settlements in the **West Indies** were seen as the most commercially important possessions, but India was catching up fast.

Britain was the world's leading trading nation in 1792, and its merchant fleet of more than 10,000 ships dwarfed all rivals. Fuelled by booming public demand for tea, coffee, sugar and other colonial goods, the value of imports had rocketed from £6 million in 1720 to £37 million in 1789, enriching private shareholders and a government committed to high tariffs. Contemporary economic orthodoxy viewed international trade as the key to national wealth, so that protection of Baltic, Atlantic, Far Eastern and Mediterranean sea lanes was basic to British imperial strategy.

The unprecedented vitality of Britain's production and manufacturing sectors underpinned both territorial and commercial expansion. Agriculture was still the dominant activity in most of a naturally fertile country. Led from the top by the king ('Farmer George'), British landowners took the science of farming more seriously than many of their continental counterparts, and their methods were acknowledged as the most advanced in Europe. Wartime governments would face food shortages brought about by a combination of bad harvests and closed continental markets, and could do little to alleviate them beyond offering bounties for grain imports, but Britain was less threatened by famine than any major rival.

The mass appropriation of common pastures and old feudal smallholdings by major landowners, accomplished through a series of eighteenth century Enclosure Acts, helped multiply overall production, and the rural poverty it created among the newly landless was hardly evident in 1792. Despite a growing population, and endemic unemployment, landless labour was still more of a resource than a problem, providing unskilled urban workforces to drive an industrial revolution that was fully under way only in Britain.

London was the largest and busiest city in Europe, with a population surging beyond 800,000 in the early war years, and further north new cities like Liverpool, Manchester and Birmingham were springing up to accommodate the first flush of mass industrialization. New technology and cheap colonial raw materials, along with plentiful labour, capital and coal, were spawning vast new manufacturing industries, above all the Lancashire cotton industry, that employed Britain's merchantmen to export their mass-produced wares at unbeatable prices.

Despite the confident hopes of its proponents, the ideological challenge of the **French Revolution** met little response from the British people, and aroused less excitement than expected in Ireland. A long history of mutual antagonism had accustomed mass opinion to opposing anything French, and high-profile radical support from groups like the London Corresponding Society represented a tiny minority of educated opinion, increasingly marginalized as the excesses of post-revolutionary **France** became known. At the political centre, the Pitt government's position fell somewhere between the warm welcome given to revolutionary ideals by the **Fox** Whigs and the emotive abhorrence expressed by Burke. Though generally disapproving, it felt no need to interfere with French internal affairs as long as they did not threaten imperial interests.

Britain had no direct interest in continental shifts of power or territory beyond the king's personal possession of **Hanover**, which was not part of the British Empire. Colonial competition, and concern to prevent the rise of any dominant rival on mainland Europe, nevertheless involved London in the alliances and antagonisms of prewar continental diplomacy.

Few areas of direct conflict existed with **Austria**, which had little interest in exploiting its trade outlets in the **Netherlands**, but traditionally good relations with **Prussia** had been soured by British attempts to block its expansion into north-west Germany and **Poland**. Britain's stand over Poland in 1791 chilled relations with **Russia**, which was both expansionist and a growing trade rival, and a subsequent thaw reflected London's mistrust of the less remote Baltic powers, **Sweden** and **Denmark**. Long-term friendship with **Portugal**, along with colonial rivalry and possession of Gibraltar, were the main causes of friction with **Spain**, and Britain's interest in the **Ottoman Empire** sprang from a desire to prevent any rival controlling overland routes to India.

Britain's chief rival and most likely invader was France, an enemy in every war since the Middle Ages. Though none of Britain's strategic priorities demanded membership of the **First Coalition** in spring 1792, conquest of **Belgium** during the autumn put French forces in control of the navigable Scheldt and poised to seize the Dutch Channel ports. The prospect roused Britain to open war preparations during the winter, though little attempt was made at practical cooperation with an alarmed Dutch government. Few in Britain expected a bellicose French regime to pull back from the Scheldt, and war was regarded as certain even before the execution of **Louis XVI** in January 1793. Pitt and foreign minister **Grenville** still hesitated to initiate hostilities, reflecting lack of enthusiasm for anything so disruptive, but were saved the trouble by a French declaration of war on 20 February.

Apart from the brief truce of 1801–3, Britain remained at war until spring 1814, fighting France throughout and almost every other European state at some time, as well as the US and the princes of southern India. During the first eight years of the struggle, Britain mobilized its obvious strengths against France, using the Royal Navy as its principal offensive weapon, and subsidies to allies as compensation for the small, poorly organized **British Army**'s inability to make a significant contribution to the land war.

This expedient strategy, in line with Pitt's view of the war as a blip in Britain's business development, was undermined by French success (alternatively viewed as a failure of will by the continental allies), but also by its own lack of focus. Despite relatively easy **colonial** successes, and an unbroken series of combat victories – most notably at the Battles of the **First of June** (1794), **St Vincent** (1797), **Camperdown** (1797), the **Nile** (1798) and **Copenhagen** (1801) – sheer breadth of responsibility kept British naval resources at full stretch. Early failures to impose effective **blockades** had been remedied by 1798, but any chance of the navy heavily influencing the main land theatres was squandered on irrelevant small-scale **amphibious** adventures (a speciality of war minister **Dundas**).

Available land forces were also wasted on sideshows. An expeditionary force floundered pointlessly in **Flanders** until its ignominious withdrawal in early 1795, and thousands died during an expedition to the West Indies in 1794. Manpower shortage and fear of invasion delayed further major operations on the European mainland until 1799, when an Anglo-Russian force invaded **North Holland** but achieved little before retiring. Remaining spare troops were then dispatched piecemeal against French and Spanish coastal targets, while the few stationed in the **Mediterranean** were unable to intervene in the **Italian campaign**. Aside from the defeat of **Tipu Sahib** in India, British troops made their first strategically useful contribution to the war effort in 1801, when a force took **Alexandria** and completed the expulsion of French forces from **Egypt**.

The success came too late to affect Anglo-French peace negotiations, typifying a very bad war for British diplomacy. Provision of **subsidies** provided no guarantee that allies would actually fight, and could not prevent Prussia or Spain from abandoning alliances in 1795. French conquest of the Netherlands, most of Italy and the west bank of the **Rhine** left Britain on the defensive by late 1796, driven from the Mediterranean and defending the southern coasts of **England** from the overt threat of invasion. Pitt's determination, further subsidies and French aggression enabled the formation of a **Second Coalition** in 1798–9, but its failure left Britain diplomatically isolated and even less popular than France.

From a European point of view, Britain had spent the war years expanding its empire and paying others to sustain a conflict that worked in its favour. Accusations of national selfishness were justified, if hypocritical. As long as the Baltic remained open, providing entry into Europe through the **Hanseatic** ports, the closure of other European coasts harmed Britain less than its rivals. After a short initial dip, wartime trade figures recovered from 1798, so that by 1800 exports had risen by half and imports had doubled. International jealousy was reinforced by the navy's constant interference with neutral trade, which inspired the anti-British **Armed Neutrality** League of Baltic powers in 1800–1, and aroused diplomatic hostility everywhere, ultimately triggering the **Anglo-American War**.

Pitt's initial expectation of a short conflict encouraged him to float expensive private loans as the mainstay of **war finance**, supported by rises in import duties and the 'assessed' taxes (on property and servants) that struck at the relatively wealthy. Having doubled the national debt within a few years, and after a **bank crisis** had exposed the limitations of credit, Pitt resorted to innovation, floating the first publicly subscribed loan in 1797 and introducing direct **income tax** in 1798.

Parliament's pragmatic acceptance of the unpopular income tax reflected increased overall prosperity, but masked a sharp decline in the status of the poorer masses. Wages had not kept pace with a steady inflation that had seen prices rise by roughly 500 per cent in 50 years, unemployment was still high and a number of bad harvests triggered local famine and bread riots. Discontent found no outlet in republicanism,

and virulent anti-French **propaganda** preached to the converted.

Rising mass patriotism played a part in the king's transformation from a figure of fun before the wars into a genuine national icon by 1800. The prospect of invasion (and government bounties) brought a flood of recruitment to home defence **militia** and volunteer forces from 1794, spreading administrative chaos and igniting a popular sense of national crisis for the first time. Emergency measures, including the construction of **Martello towers**, and a series of false alarms – the **Bantry Bay** expedition, the **Spithead** and **Nore** mutinies of 1797, the **Pembrokeshire Raid** and the **Irish Rebellion** of 1798 – fuelled a mood of popular defiance that found a logical symbol in George.

By late 1800 Pitt was exhausted and depressed. His leadership abilities were widely acknowledged, and absorption of the **Portland** Whigs into a coalition from 1794 had secured his control over parliament, but he had suffered heavy criticism for his strategic conduct of the war, and relations with the king had cooled. He and most of his supporters resigned in February 1801 over the king's refusal to accept **Catholic emancipation** as the price of annexing Ireland.

The new **Addington** cabinet was trusted by the king and welcomed as likely to hasten a peace that seemed necessary once the Treaty of **Lunéville** had deprived Britain of its last major ally. The **Amiens** treaty, by which Britain returned most of its colonial conquests in return for very little from **Napoleon**, was generally received with resigned dismay, but its rapid collapse discredited Addington's immediate military cutbacks. His government's failure to achieve any significant success during the first months of war mobilized a union of factions against him, bringing Pitt back to power in 1804.

Britain's new war opened in May 1803 and began as a rehearsal of the old. Increasingly dominant British naval forces set about reclaiming colonial conquests, and re-establishing blockades, but no rapid strategic victory appeared likely. French forces were meanwhile massing on the Channel coast for another invasion bid, and Pitt again looked for allies to break the deadlock, knitting together a **Third Coalition** in spring 1805.

For a moment in the autumn, **Nelson's** success at **Trafalgar** and Napoleon's isolation in **Bavaria** seemed to presage total victory, but the Austro-Russian catastrophe at **Austerlitz** had dispelled the illusion by the end of the year, leaving France even more firmly established as the dominant power on the continent. Trafalgar was still important, setting long-term limits on French expansion and economic potential, but only deepened the strategic stalemate.

Pitt died in 1806, leaving a vacuum at the centre of British politics that his successors failed to fill. Guided by the consistently pacifist Fox, Grenville's coalition 'Ministry of All the Talents' made peace overtures to France, but met uncompromising refusal to contemplate concessions. The death of Fox, and the king's continued refusal to accept Catholic emancipation, drove Grenville and most of Pitt's old following from office in spring 1807. They made little effort to regain power, which fell into the hands of an undistinguished cabinet under the elderly Portland. Weak in parliament, and careful to avoid upsetting the king, it survived largely because no credible alternative emerged.

Political inertia was matched by continued strategic drift. Britain was a helpless spectator as **Jena–Auerstädt** and **Friedland** made Napoleon master of Europe from the Pyrenees to the Vistula by 1807. His **Continental System** closed most of Europe to British commerce, and his 1808 invasion of **Spain** threatened to shut one of the last open doors. Austria challenged French dominion again in 1809, but Napoleon's triumph at **Wagram** enlarged his domain still further.

Britain could only maintain its standard strategy of economic offensive and military diversion. The navy fought no great battles after Trafalgar, and its bid to make a strategic impact at the **Dardanelles** failed in 1807. The army's only contributions to the land wars of 1805–7 were a pinprick success on the Neapolitan coast at **Maida**, and the dispatch of a force into the Baltic that ended up in allied Sweden. A combined attack on neutral **Copenhagen** in spring 1807 kept the **Danish Navy** out of French hands, but pushed Britain's diplomatic reputation to a wartime low and triggered a seven-year war against Denmark.

The one clear land success, **Wellesley's** victory at **Vimeiro** in August 1808, was ruined by lenient terms given to French forces at **Cintra**, and an advance from Lisbon to aid Spanish rebels ended in a narrow escape at **Corunna**. An invasion of French Holland at **Walcheren**, a belated effort to aid Austria in 1809, was utterly unproductive.

Portland died shortly after his most influential ministers, **Canning** and **Castlereagh**, fought a duel over responsibility for Walcheren and resigned, but the rump of the cabinet struggled on under **Perceval**. Absorbed in the business of maintaining credit, tax revenues and parliamentary approval, it did nothing to alleviate rising social problems as mass pauperization gathered pace, but presided over the first signs of a break in the strategic pattern.

Wellesley returned to Portugal in spring 1809. His victories at **Oporto** and **Talavera** cleared the country of French forces and earned ennoblement as Lord **Wellington**. Facing the inevitable prospect of a French counter-attack, the government stuck with its involvement in the **Peninsular War**. By 1812 its continued support for Wellington, in the face of considerable criticism, had helped open up an opportunity to strike directly at the French Empire, although improved army training methods, the Duke of **York's** administrative reforms, naval control of the Iberian coastline and brilliant field command also played their part.

Before Napoleon's retreat from **Moscow** put Britain's Peninsular efforts into perspective, Perceval was dead, shot by a deranged bankrupt in the House of Commons. Political and strategic continuity was maintained by the new administration, led by the veteran Lord **Liverpool**, which tightened the essentially reactionary social policies of the previous two cabinets, suspending the Habeus Corpus Act and earning a popular reputation for repression.

After several rehearsals, the king lapsed into madness for the last time in 1810, and **George**, Prince of Wales, assumed royal duties as regent. He was cured of his liberal flirtations, but still a frivolous and malleable figure. However the Prince Regent's unfortunate public image did no immediate harm to the monarchy's popular position. Almost 20 years of war had bred popular resignation rather than opposition by 1812, and a decade's dedicated bestialization of Napoleon by politicians, press and cartoonists had helped solidify support for the British system.

Britain's business was still booming. The Continental System proved a diplomatic and practical disaster for Napoleon, enabling the tightening of blockade regulations by new **Orders in Council** and ultimately improving Britain's global trade position. Rising tax incomes were only partly offset by a steady increase in evasion, and the smooth transition to paper money after 1797 kept government credit reasonably buoyant.

As Napoleon's empire began to atrophy in the wake of his **Russian campaign**, Britain was in the familiar position of financing the **Sixth Coalition** and striving to reconcile its various strategic priorities. Foreign minister Castlereagh played an important and energetic role in maintaining Coalition unity, making judicious use of subsidies to ensure allied commitment to Napoleon's total defeat in 1814.

Britain emerged as far and away the main beneficiary of the wars. All its rivals had been weakened, and its grip on global trade had been turned into a virtual monopoly, exercised by an imperial merchant fleet of almost 25,000 ships. Its wealth and empire had grown, while industrial and infrastructural development had accelerated. Napoleon's sudden reappearance in 1815, and his defeat at **Waterloo**, interrupted halfhearted attempts to win the Anglo-American War (of which the British public was barely conscious) but strengthened Britain's diplomatic position, confirming its emergence as a continental land power.

Castlereagh and Wellington, the hero of the hour and an experienced politician, made strength count at the postwar Congress of **Vienna**. Able to remain aloof from the continental conflicts that divided other Coalition powers, they secured retention of most colonial gains, and Castlereagh worked to establish a peaceful balance of power in Europe that lasted for almost 40 years.

Those decades saw Britain cement its status as the world's only global superpower, but were a period of intense social strain. The long-term effect of enclosures was a rural pattern of wealth concentrated at the top, above a mass of poor landless labourers, and this was increasingly mirrored in urban industrial areas. The Liverpool government's faith in repression, confirmed by the Peterloo Massacre in 1819, contributed to a steady escalation of unrest, which eventually focused on the popular Chartist movement for electoral reform and was ultimately soothed by the 1838 Reform Act.

Great Powers

Contemporary term describing those European nations and empires that were held capable of exerting military and economic influence over the continent as a whole. Four states – **France**, **Great Britain**, **Austria** and **Russia** – were undisputed great powers in the late eighteenth century, and **Prussia** had emerged to join them since its victories in the Seven Years War (1756–63). The **Ottoman Empire's** appalling military record was in the process of rendering its international influence marginal, and several other European nations, including **Spain**, **Sweden**, **Poland**, **Venice** and **Naples**, had lost their pretensions to great power status during a century of dynastic wars. The dominance exercised by the five leading powers over the Congress of **Vienna** ushered in a long period of geopolitical stability, with only the **United States** (and arguably a unified Italy) emerging to challenge the established order by the early twentieth century.

Great St Bernard Pass

Alpine link between Switzerland and northern Italy, used by most of the French Reserve Army in late May 1800 en route for its campaign against Austrian forces poised to invade southern France. The need to reach Italy before the fall of **Genoa**, as well as **Moreau's** failure to send promised reinforcements to the alternative St Gotthard Pass, influenced **Napoleon's** decision to pour most of the 60,000 strong Reserve Army through the Great St Bernard, the shortest route to Italy but also the most difficult for **artillery** transport. Though hindered by cold, heavy snow and the danger of avalanche, and often presented as an epic of endurance, the crossing was primarily a triumph of planning and organization.

The French advance guard, some 8,000 men under **Lannes**, set off up the pass in the small hours of 15 May, and brushed past Austrian outposts until they ran into determined resistance from the tiny garrison at Fort **Bard** on 19 May. The action at Fort Bard prevented large-scale French artillery and **cavalry** transfer for two weeks, but by 24 May about 40,000 French infantry, and six guns, were concentrated on the Lombard plain around Ivrea, with another 26,000 on the way through other passes. With **Masséna** still holding out in Genoa, and Austrian C-in-C **Melas** showing no signs of reacting to his presence, Napoleon was free to move on Milan (occupied on 2 June) and then to reconcentrate his army across Austrian lines of retreat at Stradella. *See* **Italian Campaigns**, 1799–1800; **Map 6**.

Grenades

Despite continued widespread use of the term **grenadier**, the hand grenade was virtually obsolete by the late eighteenth century. Essentially a small version of the **common shell**, ignited with a match and then thrown or fired at the enemy, it was sometimes used as a **naval** weapon during close-quarters actions, fired either from a small **artillery** piece or from a cup attached to the muzzle of a specially adapted **musket**.

Grenadiers

Originally those infantrymen selected to carry **grenades**, and the company in which they were grouped, grenadiers were simply the élite company within a battalion by the late eighteenth century. The term was also applied to élites within élites, such as the British Grenadier Guards or the Horse Grenadiers of the Napoleonic **Imperial Guard**.

Grenville, William Wyndham, Baron (1759–1834)

Born into the heart of the British political establishment – his father had been prime minister in the 1760s, and he was related to **Pitt** – Grenville served in a variety of government offices before his appointment as Home Secretary in 1790. Ennobled that year, and promoted to Foreign Secretary in 1791, he played an important part in **Great Britain**'s decision to go to war with France in 1793, and guided British diplomacy through

the **Revolutionary Wars**. A strong supporter of **Catholic emancipation**, he resigned alongside **Pitt** when it was refused by the king in 1801, but he returned as Foreign Secretary in 1805 and became prime minister after Pitt's death in 1806. Grenville's short-lived 'Ministry of All the Talents' opened fruitless peace talks with **Napoleon**, but did not long survive the death of **Fox**, its dominant figure. Grenville slipped from the centre of affairs after its fall in 1807, content to remain in listless opposition through an era of broad parliamentary consensus.

Gribeauval System

The all-embracing and highly effective system of organizing, arming and deploying an army's **artillery** arm developed by French nobleman the Comte de Gribeauval (1715–89) during the 1760s. Gribeauval introduced standardization of cannon design, equipping the army with regulation 4-, 8- and 12-pounder field guns, as well as a 6-inch howitzer, and designating anything heavier as **siege** or **fortress** artillery. Gun carriages and spare parts were also standardized, and the overall weight of cannon was greatly reduced to improve mobility. More detailed reforms – including the introduction of metal axles, superior gunsights and prepackaged ammunition – were backed by rigorous training of gunners and their officers, who were taught the mathematical principles of their profession and remained the most technically proficient branch of the **French Army** in 1792. Overall organization was also rationalized, each regiment comprising a regulation 20 companies along with its own depot and training facilities.

In place by the mid-1770s, and modified by his successors, Gribeauval's methods formed the basis of French Army artillery operations throughout the war years, giving it a clear advantage over less mobile, reliable or accurate opponents. Though **Napoleon** appointed a committee headed by **Marmont** to produce a revised system, which replaced 4-pounders with 6-pounders and increased the proportion of 12-pounders, it was introduced very slowly after its acceptance in 1803 (partly because the new 6-pounder proved of inferior design), and the old system was restored by the royal army from 1818.

Groix, Ile de, Battle of the

Minor British naval victory off the coast of Brittany on 23 June 1795, when the **Royal Navy**'s Channel Fleet under Admiral Alexander Hood (Lord Bridport) prevented **Villaret**'s Brest Fleet from interfering with the landing of French royalist forces at **Quiberon** Bay. News that Villaret's fleet was out of Brest and threatening Admiral Warren's expeditionary squadron brought Bridport to sea, and he was in sight of the French force on 22 June. Taking up positions between Villaret and Warren, Bridport shadowed the French fleet along the coast as far as Ile de Groix, moving into the attack the following afternoon once it was clear that they were making for shelter in nearby L'Orient. Close combat lasted until early evening, by which time three French **ships-of-the-line** had surrendered, and the rest of Villaret's fleet had held the wind to reach L'Orient. *See* Map 18.

Gross-Beeren, Battle of

Allied victory over French forces in **Germany** on 23 August 1813, the first of several defeats suffered by **Napoleon**'s subordinates during the campaign's second phase. While Napoleon led the main French army in operations around **Dresden**, a northern attack towards Berlin had been entrusted to **Oudinot** and about 120,000 troops, including 30,000 moving east from Hamburg under **Davout**. The advance forced Prussian and Swedish forces back until **Bertrand**'s corps ran into General Tauenzien's 13,000 Prussians as it approached Blankenfelde (*see* **Map 25**). While the two forces were engaged, **Reynier**'s 27,000-strong corps marched against the Prussian flank at Gross-Beeren, capturing both the village and the heights beyond by late afternoon. **Bülow**'s 38,000 Prussians reached the scene soon afterwards, breaking through **Saxon** forces on Reynier's relatively weak right to retake the village, and the French withdrew after a counterattack failed. The French lost 3,000 men and inflicted 1,000 casualties in what was a minor defeat, but it persuaded Oudinot to order a general retirement to Wittenberg, pulling Davout back to Hamburg in his wake.

Grouchy, Emmanuel (1766–1847)

A hereditary marquis who joined the royal **French Army** in 1780, and led cavalry on the eastern frontiers during the opening campaigns against the **First Coalition**. Dismissed for his noble birth in 1793, he was reinstated and promoted divisional general in 1794, helping **Hoche** put down the **Vendée** rebellion the following year. He was again under Hoche during the ill-fated **Bantry Bay** expedition, and fought under **Moreau** on the **Italian** front in 1799. After a spell as a **prisoner of war**, he was exchanged and resumed frontline command at the **Rhine**, fighting at **Hohenlinden** in late 1800.

Grouchy was one of several brilliant officers who helped make French **cavalry** the most feared in Europe during the Napoleonic era. He led divisions of the **Grande Armée** during all its successful campaigns, and his battle record included **Ulm**, **Ionkovo**, **Eylau**, **Friedland**, **Wagram** and **Borodino**, where he was wounded. Between eastern campaigns, he took part in the invasion of **Spain** in 1808, putting down the **Madrid Uprising** as city governor, and served under **Beauharnais** in Italy.

After commanding a cavalry corps under Beauharnais during the **Russian** invasion of 1812, and leading the **Escadrille Sacrée** formed by **Napoleon** before the **Beresina** crossing, he was too ill to play a major part in the struggle for **Germany** but was one of Napoleon's most useful commanders during the 1814 defence of **France**. Appointed inspector-general of cavalry under the restored monarchy, he defected on Napoleon's return and became the last appointment to the imperial **Marshalate**, receiving his baton on 15 April 1815.

Grouchy had little experience of infantry warfare, but was given command of the French right wing for the **Hundred Days** campaign. His clumsy manoeuvring slowed the French attack at **Quatre Bras**, and his misguided assumption of a Prussian retirement opened the way for **Blücher**'s intervention at **Waterloo**. He executed a successful fighting retreat in the aftermath, but was later given most of the blame for the French defeat by Napoleon on St Helena. Exiled by the returning monarchy, he lived in the **United States** until the general amnesty of 1821.

Guadeloupe Campaign (1794)

Struggle for control of the French Windward Island possession that was a turning point in the hitherto successful British invasion of the **West Indies** in 1794. British forces under Sir Charles Grey, escorted by a **Royal Navy** fleet under Admiral **Jervis**, had reached the Caribbean in March, capturing Martinique and **St Lucia** before moving on to attack Guadeloupe from 11 April. The French garrison held out until 20 April, after which the island was left in the hands of some 300 troops (most of them local French royalists) under **Dundas**. As yellow fever struck the garrison, reinforcements from France landed on 6 June. Led by Victor Hughes, and able to enlist local support by denouncing slavery, they eventually forced about 40 British survivors to escape on boats. Dundas was picked up by Jervis, and they returned to Guadeloupe with Grey on 19 June, but retired after a few indecisive skirmishes, leaving **Graham**'s regiment to hold out. Hughes was reinforced first and began operations in the early autumn, forcing Graham's disease-ridden force to surrender on 6 October. *See* **Map 20**.

Guerrillas

Contemporary name introduced to describe irregular Spanish troops fighting French forces in the **Peninsular War**. Guerrilla means 'little war' in Spanish, and the irregular armies began as small, spontaneously formed bands of ex-soldiers, outlaws and peasants, who escaped French control by taking to the countryside and fought the invaders by whatever means possible.

Guerrilla bands sprang up all over occupied **Spain** amid the intense patriotism that followed the **Madrid Uprising** in summer 1808, and the rebel Central **Junta** ordered their organization into *partidas* of 100 foot (or 50 mounted) fighters in December. Central control over guerrilla activities proved impossible in practice, and the size of units varied according to local conditions, some remaining tiny and isolated while others became small armies under the control of ambitious local warlords. Estimates of overall guerrilla numbers vary wildly, but at least 7,000 were with officially recognized *partidas* at the start of 1812 – including deserters from all the combatant armies, clerics and a prominent minority of women – and rapid expansion in the wake of subsequent allied victories may have brought another 30,000 into the movement by the end of the year.

Guerrillas were an important factor in the ultimate defeat of French forces in Spain. Most prevalent in the north-east of the country (though a waning influence under **Suchet**'s benign governorship in Catalonia), they specialized in surprise hit-and-run attacks on outposts and lines of communication, but the larger bands sometimes seized small towns or even established administrative control over isolated regions. Guerrilla bands provided occasional operational support for Anglo-Iberian regular forces from 1812, and some units were absorbed into the **Spanish Army** during the war's latter stages, but they generally came and went at their own convenience, often dispersing for long periods to enjoy their loot.

Though French losses to guerrilla raids in manpower and matériel can only be estimated, some authorities put casualties as high as 50,000 men, and the damage caused to imperial morale and military efficiency is well documented. Unable to eradicate guerrilla forces, which were usually based in inaccessible mountain areas and enjoyed the support of local populations, French armies were required to maintain strong garrison forces deep inside the occupied zones. Supply trains, couriers, senior officers in transit and other potential rebel targets always needed mounted escorts, sometimes 2–300 strong, while **desertion** was greatly encouraged by the inescapable threat of sudden ambush or small-scale terrorist action.

Though honoured as a crucible of Spanish patriotism, the guerrilla war was characterized by brutality, atrocities and mutual unwillingness to take prisoners. Guerrilla bands frequently fought among themselves, many refused to accept instructions from anybody, and some were simply bandits. Leaders like **Espoz y Mina** or **Diez** were politically motivated figures who made an important contribution to the war effort, but others maintained their positions by sheer terror, and savage attacks against collaborators (**Alfrancesados**) encouraged establishment support for King **Ferdinand**'s postwar crackdown on semi-autonomous guerrilla bands.

Routinely exaggerated by contemporary allied **propaganda**, the successes of Spanish guerrillas have influenced resistance movements ever since, but they were not unique. Italian **carbonari** societies were employing similar tactics against French rule in **Naples** as early as 1806, and thousands of displaced soldiers and civilians fought a guerrilla war behind French lines during the **Russian campaign** of 1812. A few French citizens in the areas south-east of Paris responded to allied invasion by forming guerrilla bands in 1814, but the campaign for **France** ended before popular resistance developed significant momentum.

Guides

Originally the personal escorts of **French Army** generals during the **Revolutionary Wars**, the Guides were established as a standing element in his armies by **Napoleon** in 1796. Individually selected for intelligence and versatility, they performed a variety of administrative tasks, mounted or on foot, and were often used as light cavalry for escort duties. They eventually formed a cadre within the **Imperial Guard**.

Gunboat War, The (1807–14)

Name often given to the prolonged naval conflict between **Great Britain** and **Denmark** that followed from the British bombardment of **Copenhagen** in 1807. Though local commander Peymann had signed a treaty with the departing British after the attack, Danish crown prince **Frederick** refused to ratify the agreement, and the two countries remained at war. The **Danish Navy** had effectively ceased to exist as a battle force, and naval authorities opted to concentrate rebuilding on small craft for attacks on British trade entering or leaving the Baltic (*see* **Map 18**). Supported by coastal **artillery** batteries, purpose-designed Danish **gunboats** (powered by a combination of oars and sail) took a steady toll of British and allied merchant traffic over the next few years. They were aided by unlicensed pirates, who took several hundred merchant ships before 1814, and opposed by a fleet of British small warships, which themselves captured almost 400 vessels. Apart from occasional clashes between British and Danish **frigates**, the war remained the province of 'mosquito' fleets until an Anglo-Danish peace was signed in January 1814.

Gunboats

Contemporary gunboats were usually little more than armed rowing boats, carrying between one and three cannon (normally 6-pounders) on reinforced mountings. Used by all navies, they were invaluable as harbour or coastal patrol craft, capable of enforcing their will on unarmed merchant ships or lightly armed privateers, but were also used in lines to block narrow waterways. Gunboats could seldom be deployed successfully against warships except in large numbers or against a crippled foe. A single hit from a large cannon was enough to smash them to pieces, while the inordinate weight of their armament made them difficult to manoeuvre and ensured that they sank almost instantly. *See also* **Naval Warfare**.

Gusinoe, Crossing at

Successful crossing of the River Dnieper that was the key to an extraordinary escape by the remnants of Marshal **Ney's** rearguard III Corps during the latter stages of the 1812 **Russian campaign**. Originally detailed to join the French retreat east from Smolensk on 17 November, Ney had never received instructions ordering him to leave a day earlier. Out of touch with **Davout's** corps up ahead, his 6,000 infantry and 12 guns had marched for **Krasnoe** through heavy snow and along appalling roads, but arrived on 18 November to find the road west blocked by the whole Russian advance guard. Russian commander Miloradovich sent Ney a surrender demand, delivered while Russian guns were still firing and not strictly speaking under a flag of truce, but Ney took the messenger prisoner. Ney managed to escape with his troops to the north under cover of darkness, deceiving lookouts by lighting campfires before they left, but **Platov's** fast-moving **Cossacks** were in pursuit next morning. Although many of Ney's troops fell victim to their incessant raids, a remnant had crossed the Dnieper at Gusinoe by the morning of 20 November. About 900 survivors rejoined **Napoleon** at Orsha on the evening of 21 November, a feat for which Ney earned the sobriquet 'bravest of the brave'. *See* **Map 23**.

Gustavus IV, King (1778–1837)

The son of King Gustavus III of **Sweden**, but subject to a regency government for four years after his father's assassination in 1792, Gustavus was an autocratic, introspective figure. Primarily interested in economic development, he avoided foreign entanglements and introduced enclosure laws in 1803 that greatly increased the country's agricultural output. An innate loathing of all things liberal (and his presence in **Baden** when the Duc d'**Enghein** was kidnapped) eventually prompted abandonment of Swedish neutrality, and he joined the **Third Coalition** in 1805. The rest of his reign was dominated by the consequences of his action, which included the loss of Pomerania to France, Russian conquest of **Finland** and defeat by Franco-Danish forces in Norway. Deposed by a military coup on 11 March 1809, he was imprisoned and replaced by **Charles XIII**, his former regent. Exiled with his family from December 1809, he lived under assumed names in Germany, divorced his wife in 1812, and ended his days in Switzerland.

Gyulai, Ignatius (1763–1831)

Austrian soldier, a divisional commander at **Hohenlinden** in 1800, who led the defeated army's rearguard during the retreat from **Wagram** in 1809 and commanded a corps during the campaign for **Germany** in 1813. Best known for his dogged efforts against the strongpoint of Lindenau during the three-day Battle of **Leipzig** in October, he was promoted field marshal in 1814 and was governor of Bohemia from 1823.

H

Habsburg Empire *See* **Austria**

Haiti *See* **Santo Domingo**

Halle, Battle of

Action fought around the north German town of Halle on 17 October 1806, and the most significant of several setbacks suffered by Prussian forces attempting to regroup after the battles of **Jena** and **Auerstädt**. Marshal **Bernadotte's** 20,000-strong I Corps, which had missed both victories, led the subsequent pursuit operation. Its vanguard division (**Dupont**) met the only major Prussian force so far untouched by the fighting – the Duke of Württemberg's 13,500 infantry, 1,700 cavalry and 38 field guns – after racing to Halle through 17 October. Württemberg could have withdrawn to the Elbe, where **Hohenlohe** was attempting to organize other surviving units for a defence of Berlin, but he opted to stand and fight. Outnumbered and faced by veterans with something to prove, Württemberg's disheartened troops were quickly overrun, fleeing the battlefield in disarray and suffering 5,000 losses. Bernadotte, who admitted to only 800 casualties at Halle, resumed operations towards **Prenzlau** and **Lübeck**. *See* **Map 16**.

Hamburg, Defence of (1813–14)

The city of Hamburg was one of the most powerful **fortresses** east of the Rhine (*see* **Map 25**), and was occupied by Marshal **Davout's** French XIII Corps on 28 May 1813, at the height of the campaign for **Germany**. Ordered to hold the city at all costs, Davout launched a characteristically energetic campaign against a similar number of Prussian troops in the area, winning a number of minor engagements. Despite steadily shrinking manpower, food and ammunition supplies, his forces displayed no signs of abandoning Hamburg after French armies withdrew east at the end of the year, and the allies deployed a large portion of **Bernadotte's** Russo-Swedish army to watch the city during the 1814 campaign for **France**. Davout was still in control of Hamburg when the War of the **Sixth Coalition** ended in April, and eventually surrendered to the allies on 27 May 1814, obeying orders delivered by General **Gérard** from King **Louis XVIII**.

Hamilton, Emma, Lady (*c*.1767–1815)

Infamous as the mistress of British admiral **Nelson**, Emma Hamilton (*née* Ryan) was born in the north-west English county of Cheshire. She pursued a turbulent romantic career in London, bearing two children and indulging in several high-profile affairs before moving to **Naples** in 1786, where she married British diplomat Sir William Hamilton five years later. The couple were intimate friends of King **Ferdinand** and Queen Maria Carolina, and Lady Hamilton first met Nelson at court in 1793. They became lovers when Nelson returned to Naples after the Battle of the **Nile** in 1798, and the British admiral's infatuation extended to an almost obsessive determination to restore the Neapolitan monarchy after the French occupation of January 1799. She gave birth to Nelson's daughter, Horatia, in 1801, and the couple lived together for a time before the resumption of Anglo-French war in

1803, but she was viewed by popular and naval opinion as a bad influence on a national hero, and shunned by British high society. She inherited Nelson's considerable fortune on his death in 1805, but squandered her wealth and died in poverty.

Hanau, Battle of

The last major action of the campaign for **Germany**, fought on 30 October 1813 as an Austro-Bavarian army under General **Wrede** attempted to block the retreat of French forces from **Leipzig** to Frankfurt and the Rhine. As **Napoleon** led about 100,000 survivors along the line of the River Main, Wrede rushed 43,000 troops (including most of the **Bavarian Army**) from the Danube to Hanau, at the junction of the Main and Kinzig rivers just east of Frankfurt. Believing that Napoleon was retiring further north, and that he faced only a flank guard, Wrede took up hasty positions just north-east of the town on both sides of the Kinzig.

Napoleon ordered **Macdonald**'s infantry and **Sebastiani**'s cavalry, some 17,000 troops, against the allied left when he reached Hanau on 30 October. Backed by General **Drouot**'s 50 guns, and supported by **Victor**'s arriving corps, the attack pushed Wrede's left wing into the Kinzig by mid-afternoon, while his right became uselessly entangled in crossing the only linking bridge. Wrede lost about 9,000 men at Hanau and eventually regrouped survivors on a line running east of the town to the bridge, allowing French rearguard detachments to occupy the town and prevent interference with the open road to Frankfurt. *See* **Map 25**.

Hanover

North-west German state that was a natural target for Prussian expansionism in the eighteenth century, except that its Elector was also ruler of **Great Britain**. British king **George III** governed his German inheritance from a distance, appointing a viceroy (*Statthalter*), who wielded executive authority through an assembly of notables, theoretically elected but in practice appointed from among Hanover's leading families.

The **Hanoverian Army** served as part of the **Holy Roman Empire**'s forces in **Flanders** from 1794, remaining in the field until **Prussia**'s withdrawal from the **First Coalition** in 1795 forced Hanover's neutrality, and Prussia's refusal to join kept Hanover out of the **Second Coalition**. The state was briefly occupied (with French consent) by Prussian forces in the war's last weeks, but gained the bishopric of Osnabrück by the peace agreed at **Lunéville** in 1801, reflecting **Napoleon**'s desire for an accommodation with Britain.

Hanover was occupied by French forces after the collapse of the Anglo-French **Amiens** peace in 1803, and was a pawn in Napoleon's wider diplomatic schemes for the next decade. He offered Hanover as a sweetener to Prussia during preparations for the War of the **Third Coalition**, but proposed its return to George III in a bid to come to terms with Britain in June 1806. After the defeat of Prussia that autumn, he incorporated Hanover's southern half into the puppet Kingdom of **Westphalia**. The northern rump remained under occupation until 1810, when it was attached to **Oldenburg** and annexed by France.

Hanover recovered its independence in spring 1813, when the opening phase of the campaign for **Germany** drove French forces further south. The army was re-formed to fight in **France** the following year, and took part in the 1815 **Hundred Days** campaign. A new 85-member assembly was convened as the basis for viceregal restoration in 1814, and the Congress of **Vienna** subsequently elevated Hanover to the status of kingdom. Limited parliamentary democracy was introduced with a new constitution in 1819, and dynastic ties with Britain were eventually loosened in 1837, when an old law forbidding female succession prevented Queen Victoria from taking the throne.

Hanoverian Army

Though its uniforms and equipment resembled **British Army** issue, and the two forces frequently cooperated in the field, the Hanoverian Army of 1793–1803 maintained its own administration and command structure. The infantry in 1794 comprised 13 line regiments, one light infantry regiment and the élite Foot Guards, a total of some 18,000 men. The army's greatest strength was the excellence of its 6,500 **cavalry** troops, which benefited from the high quality of

Hanoverian horses, and its single **artillery** regiment deployed 38 guns in 1794. Hanoverian forces fought under the Duke of **York** in the **Flanders campaign**, but remained neutral from 1795 until the army was disbanded under French control in 1803. Some Hanoverians subsequently fought with **Westphalian** and **Prussian** forces, but many exiles took service with the British Army's élite King's German Legion (KGL). An independent Hanoverian Army, ultimately about 10,000 strong, was raised under British aegis when French occupation ended in 1813. By the end of the year 27 **Landwehr** battalions had been raised, and these were merged with line units to form the ten regular Hanoverian regiments that took part in the **Hundred Days** campaign of 1815.

Hanseatic League

A confederation of northern European merchant cities formed in the twelfth century, that included more than 150 towns and monopolized Baltic trade during its heyday in the fourteenth century. Though the league ceased to exist as an administrative entity in the mid-seventeenth century, its name was preserved in everyday usage into the late eighteenth, when many of its most important north German cities – **Hamburg**, **Lübeck**, Bremen and **Danzig**, for example – were recognized as independent states. Their independence was lost when the French Empire took control of northern Germany during the War of the **Fourth Coalition**, and most were annexed by France from late 1806. As such their small armed forces, hitherto retained only for local security, were absorbed into the imperial army as the Hanseatic Legion. All the Hanseatic cities were restored to their pre-1806 status by the Congress of **Vienna**.

Hardenberg, Karl August von (1750–1822)

German statesman and diplomat, who began his administrative career in his native **Hanover** and worked in **Brunswick**, Ansbach and Bayreuth before the latter's assimilation by **Prussia** in 1791 brought him into the service of Berlin. He helped **Haugwitz** negotiate the Treaty of **Basle** with France in 1795, and was elevated to the Prussian cabinet on **Frederick William III's** accession in 1797. One of the king's most trusted advisers, taking the foreign ministry in 1804, he sought to moderate the warlike tendencies of Queen **Louise** and her entourage, but was dismissed on **Napoleon's** insistence after the defeats of 1806–7. He was recalled from exile at Riga to replace **Stein** as chief minister in 1810, and continued his predecessor's reforms of the Prussian military, civil service, local government, and education and taxation systems. He helped persuade the king to join the **Sixth Coalition** in spring 1813, and was made a prince in recognition of his services in 1814, subsequently representing Prussia at the Congress of **Vienna**. His broadly liberal views ran contrary to those of **Metternich** and **Alexander I**, and his postwar career was overshadowed by Prussia's drift to reaction as part of the **Holy Alliance**.

Hartford Convention

An assembly of delegates from New England that met in Hartford, Connecticut, from 15 December 1814 until 5 January 1815 to discuss their several grievances concerning **United States** government policy, particularly their long-standing disapproval of the **Anglo-American War**. Connecticut, Massachusetts, Rhode Island, Vermont and New Hampshire sent representatives to the meeting, which was primarily determined to reopen trade links with Europe but also raised fears that the **Louisiana Purchase** (1803) would create an unbreakable slave-owner majority in Congress. Though a minority of delegates demanded secession from the US, the Convention instead agreed to petition Washington for constitutional amendments, but news of the **Ghent** peace and the victory at **New Orleans** rendered its demands irrelevant.

Haslach, Battle of

French victory at the southern end of the **Rhine** front on 14 July 1796, won by General Ferino's corps guarding the rear of **Moreau's** advance north-east on **Ettlingen**. After Moreau's victory at the **Kinzig** in late June, Ferino had advanced south-east towards General Frölich's largely German army between the Kinzig and the Elz. His attack on the centre of the allied position around Haslach drove Frölich back into the Black Forest, forcing allied flank columns to retreat in turn. Frölich was then ordered all the way back to the Danube by C-in-C Archduke **Charles**, but the withdrawal of **Württemberg** and **Baden** from the **First Coalition** deprived him of most of his German troops. *See* **Map 4**.

Haugwitz, Christian August Heinrich Kurt, Count von (1752–1832)

Prussian statesman, born in Silesia, who became foreign minister in 1792, negotiated the Second Partition of **Poland** in 1793 and was the principal architect of the Treaty of **Basle** with France in 1795. His attitude to republican France, equivocal in the early 1790s, had hardened by 1798, when he tried to bring King **Frederick William III** into the **Second Coalition**, but after his replacement by **Hardenberg** in 1804 he sought to establish friendlier relations with **Napoleon**. Still a figure of great influence, Haugwitz was the unfortunate diplomat chosen to deliver an ultimatum to the French emperor prior to **Prussia** joining the **Third Coalition** in autumn 1805. Interviewed after **Austerlitz** and bullied into agreeing the humiliating Convention of **Vienna**, he was reduced to something of an international laughing stock and retired on the treaty's formal signature in February 1806.

Hawkesbury, Viscount *See* **Liverpool**, Earl of

Heilsberg, Battle of

The action that opened the War of the **Fourth Coalition**'s concluding phase, fought in East Prussia on 10 June 1807. Both sides in the theatre had been reinforced since the carnage at **Eylau** in February, but **Napoleon** was able to field some 220,000 men against about 115,000 Russians by the beginning of May. Russian commander **Bennigsen** nevertheless attacked first in early June, launching a series of hit-and-run strikes against forward French positions on the River Passarge, including an action at Spanden (5 June) that forced a wounded **Bernadotte** to relinquish his command to **Victor**.

Napoleon responded with a second attempt to cut Bennigsen's retreat on Königsberg by an advance up the River Alle. Although he was careful to avoid a repeat of the security leak that upset his plans before the February battle at **Ionkovo**, he again found the Russians concentrated ahead of him.

Bennigsen had originally planned to fight on the Alle at Güttstadt, but decided instead to offer battle around the well-fortified supply centre of Heilsberg, where he had massed 90,000 troops by the morning of 10 June (*see* **Map 17**). Still determined to cut Bennigsen off from Königsberg, Napoleon ordered 50,000 men (under **Murat**, **Soult**, **Ney** and **Lannes**) into a direct attack on Heilsberg that morning, backed by **Davout** and **Mortier** on the Russian right flank.

The day's fighting achieved nothing. Murat's advanced **cavalry** was pinned down by well-positioned Russian **artillery** 3km short of Heilsberg until Soult arrived in mid-afternoon. The advance was again halted when Murat was attacked by Russian cavalry under **Bagration**, and resumed after the timely arrival of reinforcements under **Savary**. Russian counter-attacks, backed by massed artillery, then drove the French back, but Lannes reached the battlefield in the evening and insisted on launching a night attack. This gained little but suffered heavily, bringing French losses to 10,600 troops against perhaps 8,000 Russian casualties.

The anticipated resumption of fighting next day never really materialized. Napoleon again sent Davout and Mortier against the Russians' flank, aiming to force them out of strong positions in the riverside hills, but Bennigsen responded by withdrawing towards Bartenstein that night. The French sealed an expensive token victory by taking Heilsberg in the small hours of 12 June, along with a haul of abandoned Russian supplies. *See also* Battle of **Friedland**.

Helder, Capture of *See* Invasion of **North Holland**

Heliopolis, Battle of

Victory by French forces over Turkish troops outside Cairo on 20 March 1800, the first action in the **Middle East** theatre after the breakdown of peace negotiations between French commander **Kléber** and **Ottoman** authorities. Kléber had been seeking a way to extract his shrinking and depressed army from its unsustainable occupation of **Egypt**, and negotiations with the sultan's representatives had begun in the autumn. The Convention of **El Arish** had made provision for peaceful French evacuation, but was rejected by the British government, Turkey's ally in the **Second Coalition**. By the time this news reached Kléber in Cairo, on 18 March, **Ibrahim Bey's** Turkish army had advanced from El Arish to take possession of the city.

Facing 40,000 potentially hostile troops, handily placed to add momentum to gathering civil unrest, and with only 10,000 troops at his disposal, Kléber launched a surprise dawn attack on the main Turkish camp at Heliopolis on 20 March. Taken completely by surprise, the Turkish army put up only limited resistance before fleeing north. French forces were in pursuit of a beaten army by nightfall, and had driven the Turkish force out of Egypt altogether by 27 March, but civil uprisings in Cairo were not finally suppressed until late April, by which time **Abercromby's** British expedition was en route for Alexandria.

Helvetic Republic *See* **Switzerland**

Hesse-Cassel

Small north German state that was a traditional source of mercenary troops for British service. Ruling landgrave William IX committed the Hessian Army (ten regiments) to the War of the **First Coalition** as a member of the **Holy Roman Empire**, but joined **Prussia** in making peace at Basle in 1795. Neutral through the War of the **Second Coalition**, William accepted French territory around Mainz in return for his possessions west of the Rhine in its aftermath. He agreed a neutrality treaty with **Napoleon** just before the 1806 **Jena–Auerstädt campaign**, but Hesse-Cassel was invaded anyway, becoming part of the new Kingdom of **Westphalia**. William fled to **Austria**, where he raised a small unit of about 1,000 men for service in the 1809 campaign, but returned after French forces had withdrawn from **Germany** in November 1813, when the Hessian Army was re-created for service with the allies. His titles and privileges were formally restored by the Congress of **Vienna**, and he proceeded to reverse the reforms of the Napoleonic era. *See* Map 1.

Hesse-Darmstadt

West German state, ruled throughout the period by Landgrave Louis X (1753–1830), that had a tradition of loyalty to **Austria**. Hesse-Darmstadt troops fought with the **First Coalition** against France, but Louis remained neutral through the War of the **Second Coalition**, and subsequently ceded his territories west of the Rhine to France in return for parts of **Westphalia**. Hesse-Darmstadt joined the Confederation of the **Rhine** in 1806, Louis taking the title Grand Duke, and contributed troops to all the major French campaigns until its defection after **Leipzig** in October 1813. Two regiments of re-formed infantry (along with a volunteer **Jäger** unit) subsequently fought with the allies. Louis was permitted to retain his elevated title by the Congress of **Vienna**, but was required to cede land to **Prussia**, **Bavaria** and the newly independent state of Hesse-Homburg. *See* **Map 1**.

Hill, Rowland (1772–1842)

Perhaps the most consistently successful British general serving under **Wellington** in the **Peninsular War**, Hill was a junior aide with British forces at **Toulon** in 1793, and took the rank of major in **Graham's** privately raised regiment the following year. He took practical command of the regiment as lieutenant-colonel in May 1794, and led it at **Alexandria** in 1801. Hill began a long association with the Peninsular theatre commanding a brigade at **Vimeiro** in 1808. He was at **Corunna** in early 1809, at **Oporto** in May, and led a division at **Talavera** in July, before malaria forced his replacement by **Beresford**. He returned to Spain in May 1811, leading a two-division corps on the southern flank of Wellington's operations against **Badajoz** in 1811–12, and performing a similar covering role to great effect during the subsequent drives to **Salamanca** and **Burgos**. A corps commander throughout the offensives of 1813–14, he confirmed a reputation for careful planning, reliable execution and thoughtful man-management. Ennobled in 1814, he commanded a multinational allied corps during the **Hundred Days** campaign, and was prominent at **Waterloo** in June 1815. He retired from active service after three years with the allied army of occupation in Paris, but was promoted full general in 1825, and returned to become **British Army** C-in-C from 1828 to 1842.

Hiller, Johann (1754–1819)

Born in Brody, Hiller entered the **Austrian Army** as an artillery officer in 1770 and fought throughout the **Revolutionary Wars**. Influential in court circles after the turn of the century, he consistently opposed the cautious reforming policies of Archduke **Charles**, and the two men became bitter personal enemies. Hiller was among the foremost proponents of war in 1809, when Charles counselled an extended period of peaceful military reform, and served with some misgivings as a corps commander under the archduke during the subsequent campaign. He led the southern wing of the force defeated at **Abensberg** in April, and fought at **Aspern–Essling**, but cited ill-health when relinquishing his command in late May and returned only in July, when he led the Austrian right wing at **Wagram**. His last wartime post was in command of the Austrian southern wing during the 1813–14 **Italian campaign**.

Hispaniola *See* **Santo Domingo**

Hoche, Louis Lazare (1768–97)

A **fusilier** with the royal **French Army** in his youth, Hoche was a **National Guard** sergeant in Paris after 1789, and received a commission on the outbreak of the **Revolutionary Wars** in 1792. Serving with **fortress** garrisons on the **Rhine** frontier, he enjoyed extremely rapid promotion, becoming a brigadier-general in September 1793 and achieving divisional rank the following month, along with command of the Army of the Moselle. A popular hero for his part in that December's victory at the **Geisberg**, his meteoric rise was temporarily halted by arrest and imprisonment in March 1794, but he was released in July and rebuilt his reputation by crushing the **Vendée** uprising at **Quiberon** in July 1795.

Influential enough to convince war minister **Carnot** that an invasion of **Ireland** was feasible, he commanded the **Bantry Bay** expedition in December 1796, and avoided blame for its failure because he spent the whole operation searching for his army at sea. He returned to the Rhine in early 1797, winning a minor victory at **Altenkirchen**, and led his Army of the Sambre and Meuse to the gates of Paris in support of the **Fructidor** coup in September. Still regarded as one of the most energetic and enterprising revolutionary generals, he died a few weeks after returning to his frontier command.

Höchstädt, Battle of

French attack east of the **Rhine** during the latter stages of the War of the **Second Coalition**, launched on 19 June 1800, after **Moreau**'s reorganized Army of the Rhine and Switzerland had pushed **Kray**'s tentative Austrian offensive back on the supply town of Ulm. Moreau swung his army round Kray's flank to attack Austrian positions some 60km down the Danube at Höchstädt. Initial French assaults took defenders by surprise, and though Kray was able to bring up reserves and hold the position throughout a day's heavy fighting, Moreau took the town and secured both banks of the river during the night. Having lost an estimated 5,000 of his 70,000 troops, most of them as prisoners, Kray withdrew to the River Inn before morning, and had been pursued beyond Munich before a truce at Parsdorf ended fighting in the theatre on 28 July. *See* **Map 4**.

Hofer, Andreas (1767–1810)

Tyrolean rebel leader, a former innkeeper who fought for the **Austrian Army** from 1796 until 1805, when **Austria** ceded the Tyrol to **Bavaria** by the Treaty of **Pressburg**. A prominent agitator against Bavarian (and by extension French) control, Hofer was recruited by the Austrian government in 1808, and given support to lead a popular rebellion in 1809. Triggered by the limited Austrian success at **Aspern–Essling** in May, the rising defeated **Bavarian Army** forces at the Battle of Iusel Berg, and drove back a French invasion force sent in the wake of Austrian defeat at **Wagram**. Hofer was in control of Innsbruck and effective ruler of the Tyrol by the time the Emperor **Francis** broke a promise to the rebels by agreeing peace with France at **Schönbrunn** in October. Freed from the Danube, a combined French–Bavarian force under **Lefebvre** retook Innsbruck on 20 November, and Hofer was captured after he fled into the mountains. Taken to Mantua, he was executed on 20 February 1810.

Hohenlinden, Battle of

The engagement between French and Austrian forces in Bavaria that ended the War of the

Second Coalition, fought on 3 December 1800 after the breakdown of prolonged peace talks had triggered a resumption of hostilities on the Rhine front. Austrian forces had ended the spring campaign in disarray after defeat at Höchstädt, and though they were reinforced to a total strength of about 120,000 men over the summer, poor morale was not helped by the appointment of the inexperienced Archduke John to command in place of Kray (after all the older archdukes had turned down the post). French theatre C-in-C Moreau had meanwhile amassed 180,000 men, and was preparing to advance south from Munich in the event of the summer truce breaking down.

Austrian emperor Francis, committed to continuing the war by new British subsidies and influenced by the hawks of Thugut's court faction, ended the truce on 13 November, but a planned advance from the River Inn was delayed until 29 November by bureaucratic inefficiency and bad weather. By the time John began a sweeping manoeuvre around Moreau's northern flank, French forces were advancing against his own left, towards Vienna, and John turned east to advance on Munich in response to the threat against the capital. On 2 December he met Moreau's central forces, also delayed by bad weather, about 30km east of Munich in the Hohenlinden Forest.

French light infantry had taken up good defensive positions either side of the only good road to the city, and repelled initial Austrian breakthrough attempts before both armies attacked next day. While Ney held off strong frontal assaults from the Austrian centre, a flank attack launched on his own initiative by General Richepanse surprised and defeated John's left wing, which suffered heavy casualties as it fell back over broken ground. John was compelled to withdraw his whole force, and retreat turned to rout as it fled towards Vienna, losing 18,000 men before trying and failing to make a stand around Salzburg.

Moreau's pursuing army, which had lost about 7,000 men, was poised to march on Vienna by the time Archduke Charles took command of Austrian forces on 17 December. Unable to muster coherent formations for continued resistance, and anyway in favour of immediate peace, Charles was given authority to negotiate an armistice on Christmas Day at Steyr, bringing the Austro-French war to an end. See Map 3.

Hohenlohe, Friedrich Ludwig von, Prince (1746–1818)

A member of the Württemberg nobility who entered Prussian military service in 1768 and fought in the Rhine theatre during the War of the First Coalition, commanding a division at the successful defence of Kaiserlautern against Hoche in November 1793. At 60, he was one of the Prussian Army's more youthful commanders at the start of the War of the Fourth Coalition in 1806. He led the left wing of Brunswick's army in Saxony, but his rash deployments were punished at Jena in October. After rallying defeated elements for the subsequent retreat, he was taken prisoner by pursuing French forces at Prenzlau on 28 October, and was eventually released into retirement in 1808.

Hollabrünn, Battle of

Relatively minor engagement during the War of the Third Coalition that helped Kutuzov's Russian army in Bavaria complete its escape from pursuing French forces in autumn 1805. The impetuous seizure of Vienna by Marshals Murat and Lannes had deprived Napoleon of one opportunity to cut off the Russians before they could join up with reinforcements to the northeast. Urged on by a furious emperor, Murat returned to the pursuit and caught up with the Russian army around Hollabrünn, some 40km north-west of Vienna, on 15 November.

Prince Bagration, commanding the Russian rearguard, met Murat at nearby Schöngraben that morning, and convinced him that an armistice had been agreed. Murat finally attacked Bagration's 6,000 troops in strength during the evening of 16 November, after receiving angry orders to that effect from Napoleon, but Kutuzov had already led most of his troops away. Outnumbered five to one during the night fight that ensued, Bagration's corps eventually withdrew after suffering 2,400 casualties and inflicting some 1,200 losses on Murat. Kutuzov's main body joined Buxhowden's reinforcements at Olmütz two days later. See Map 12.

Holland, Kingdom of *See* **Netherlands**, The

Holy Alliance

Largely meaningless agreement to govern on principles of 'justice, Christian charity and peace' signed by the rulers of **Russia**, **Austria** and **Prussia** on 26 September 1815, and subsequently by all of Europe's Christian sovereigns except the King of **Great Britain** (on constitutional grounds) and Pope **Pius VII**, who would not associate with Protestants. Drawn up by Russian tsar **Alexander I**, and a reflection of his increasingly mystical view of monarchy, the alliance became a popular by-word for reactionary autocracy over the next three decades, but its vague idealism (dismissed as verbiage by **Castlereagh** and **Metternich**) had little actual influence on the policies followed by signatories.

Holy Roman Empire

The title originally taken by the empire of Charlemagne at the start of the ninth century, and subsequently used to describe the authority supervening the Catholic principalities and kingdoms of Germany. With only occasional interruptions, the Holy Roman Emperor had been a member of the Habsburg family since the thirteenth century, and usually the King of Austria. By the end of the eighteenth century the title was largely honorific, and although Emperor **Francis II** could in theory demand troops and taxes from other German rulers by declaring an imperial emergency, all but the smallest states had developed independent foreign and domestic policies.

The empire began to disintegrate with French conquests east of the **Rhine** during the **Revolutionary Wars**, and it was fundamentally reorganized in 1802, primarily in order to compensate those more important states – like **Bavaria**, Saxony and **Württemberg** – that had suffered territorial losses. Dozens of small west German states disappeared with the reorganization, and many more lost their independence after **Napoleon**'s victory over the **Third Coalition** effectively ended Austrian influence over the empire. Napoleon announced the empire's abolition on 12 July 1806, establishing the Confederation of the **Rhine** (25 July) as an alternative authority under French control. Francis accepted his change

of status in August and adopted the title Francis I, Emperor of Austria, a style used by his successors until the Habsburg family's eclipse in 1918.

Hondschoote, Battle of

The highlight of a French counter-offensive in **Flanders** against allied forces besieging **Dunkirk** in early September 1793. The port had been threatened since late August by about 30,000 of the Duke of **York**'s troops, while another 18,000 were guarding approaches from the south around the village of Hondschoote, on the River Yser some 10km south of Dunkirk (*see* **Map 2**).

French war minister **Carnot** had meanwhile reinforced General Houchard, the new French commander in Flanders, and planned his counter-attack. Covered by a sortie from Dunkirk, **Jourdan** led two divisions against **Hanoverian** general Freytag's covering force on the evening of 6 September, but neither attack achieved lasting gains. After reinforcing Dunkirk with a fresh division, Houchard repeated the operation on 8 September. A frontal attack by Jourdan and **Vandamme**, supported by a militia division on the flank, forced defenders at Hondschoote to retreat towards Dixmunde, while any interference by York was prevented by **Hoche**'s strong raid from Dunkirk. Though York lost no ground at Dunkirk, the prospect of encirclement persuaded him to withdraw that night.

The actions of 6 and 8 September cost both sides some 3,000 men, and Houchard's attacks on Dutch forces stranded at Menin inflicted perhaps another 2,000 casualties. Though part of York's force combined with **Beaulieu**'s Austrian division from **Quesnoy** to drive Houchard back to Lille (and execution for his failure) on 15 September, the battle had edged allied forces on to the defensive in Flanders.

Hood, Alexander (1727–1814)

Veteran British naval commander, younger brother of the more energetic Samuel **Hood**, who had seen more than half a century of service on the outbreak of the **Revolutionary Wars**. He was with **Howe**'s Channel and **Mediterranean** fleets during the War of the **First Coalition**, taking part in the Battle of the **First of June** in 1794, for which he was ennobled as Lord Bridport. He took command of the Channel Fleet in 1795, and defeated **Villaret** off **Groix** later that year, but was not otherwise a conspicuous success in the post, earning widespread criticism for his lax response to the French **Bantry Bay** expedition at the end of 1796. He retired after his replacement by Admiral **Jervis** in 1801.

Hood, Samuel (1724–1816)

The future Viscount Hood entered the **Royal Navy** in 1741 (as did his younger brother Alexander **Hood**), becoming a **frigate** captain in 1756 and serving as a rear-admiral in the American War of Independence. He defeated **Fox** for the parliamentary seat of Westminster in the 1784 election, and was a vice-admiral from 1787. Given command of the Mediterranean Fleet in 1793, he captured **Toulon** that autumn and took **Corsica** the following August. One of several senior commanders who recognized and encouraged the unorthodox brilliance of **Nelson**, Hood was recalled later in 1794 after quarrelling with new navy minister Spencer. Promoted full admiral, and ennobled as Lord Hood two years later, he ended his career as commander of the British naval academy at Greenwich. His name was perpetuated in the **Mediterranean** by his nephew, also Samuel Hood, who was one of Nelson's most trusted commanders in the theatre and was a vice-admiral on his death in 1814.

Hope, John (1765–1823)

The younger brother of the Scottish Earl of Hopetoun, and a member of the British House of Commons from 1790, Hope served as adjutant-general under **Abercromby** in the **West Indies** (1796), in **North Holland** (1800) and at **Alexandria**, where he was wounded. A lieutenant-general from 1808, he was **Moore's** second-in-command during that year's expeditions to **Sweden** and Spain, taking part in the retreat to **Corunna**, and led a division at **Walcheren** in 1809 before returning to the **Peninsular War**. He replaced **Graham** as commander of **Wellington's** 1st Division in autumn 1813, leading it through the subsequent battles at the **Nivelle** and the **Nive**, but twice allowing himself to be surprised by French counter-attacks during the latter operation. Hope commanded allied forces besieging **Bayonne** in 1814, suffering two wounds and the indignity of capture during the French attack

on the city on 14 April. He inherited the family earldom in 1819, thus ending confusion with the **British Army**'s other General John Hope, who had been adjutant-general at **Copenhagen** in 1807 and commanded a brigade at **Salamanca** in 1812.

Hotham, William (1736–1813)

An example of much that was wrong with the **Royal Navy**'s high command at the start of the **Revolutionary Wars**, Hotham succeeded **Hood** in command of the Mediterranean Fleet in early 1794. Close to retirement age, and nobody's idea of an aggressive commander, he demonstrated a characteristic unwillingness to take risks during the action off **Leghorn** later that spring, and his reluctance to risk damage to his ships by maintaining a close **blockade** of hostile ports allowed regular raids by French warships on British merchant **convoys**. Hotham's supine approach exasperated a number of subordinates, including **Nelson**, before his replacement by **Jervis** in 1795, after which he was not again trusted with a combat command.

Howe, Richard, Earl (1726–99)

Veteran British naval officer who was First Lord of the Admiralty (navy minister) for five years until 1788, when he was ennobled and returned to active command. A fine naval technician, responsible for important innovations in signalling and battle tactics, he was regarded as the senior **Royal Navy** officer most in sympathy with the welfare of ordinary sailors. When he was in command of the Channel Fleet, charged with stifling French maritime activity in the north Atlantic, his narrow view of **naval warfare** contributed to the early inefficiency of British **blockade** strategy, and he won a spectacular but strategically empty victory at the Battle of the **First of June** in 1794. Elderly and crippled by gout, Howe was promoted full admiral in 1796, and remained in command of the Channel Fleet until his retirement in March 1797, after which he received and ignored a series of sailors' petitions that presaged the **Spithead** mutiny. Something of a father figure to the navy as a whole, he performed one last service later that year, touring ships to calm sailors' fears of official betrayal during a second wave of mutinies.

Howitzers *See* **Artillery** (Land)

Humboldt, Karl Wilhelm von
(1767–1835)

Prussian politician, diplomat and linguist, born in Potsdam, whose younger brother was the celebrated naturalist Alexander von Humboldt. Karl Humboldt received his first official appointment as Prussian envoy to Rome in 1801, but his most important work was as Prussia's first minister of education. Though he only occupied the post from February 1809 until June 1810, when pressure from France forced a change of administration on King **Frederick William III**, he was responsible for widespread reforms and the creation of what is now the Humboldt University of Berlin. He returned to diplomacy in 1810, becoming ambassador to Vienna and playing a major role in bringing **Austria** into the **Sixth Coalition**. Ambassador to London from 1817, he was one of many liberals to abandon the reactionary atmosphere of postwar **Prussia**, retiring in 1819 to work on a pioneering study of the Basque language.

Hundred Days, The (1815)

The name generally given to **Napoleon's** brief return to power from exile on **Elba** in 1815. The restored monarchy was generally welcomed by a war-weary population after Napoleon's **abdication** in April 1814, but the honeymoon was brief. Despite granting a relatively liberal constitution (the 'Bourbon Charter'), and making genuine attempts at economic reconstruction, royal government under an inert **Louis XVIII** was soon identified with the predatory, reactionary activities of returning noble **émigrés** and royal officials.

Napoleon's reputation meanwhile reaped the fruits of revolutionary nostalgia, particularly among the mass of peasantry most likely to suffer from any reclamation of aristocratic landholdings. French soldiers formed another class adjusting to reduced prospects, and many senior officers kept in touch with Elba, as did various French politicians, including **Talleyrand** and **Fouché**. Well informed about affairs in France, and hardly content in his new domain, Napoleon was ready by early 1815 to gamble on a return as 'protector' of the Revolution.

He sailed from Elba on 26 February, and reached the southern French port of Cannes on 1 March, accompanied by a personal guard of about 1,000 men, four guns and three generals (**Bertrand**, **Drouot** and Cambronne). The news reached a surprised government in Paris four days later, and was not known in London until 10 March. Immediate popular response to the return was cautious, and official reactions were sluggish, as Napoleon avoided royalist Marseilles by moving north through the Alps towards Grenoble. After winning over an infantry regiment blocking his route at **Laffrey**, Napoleon reached Grenoble on the evening of 7 March, and was welcomed as a returning hero. It was a defining moment, and Napoleon enjoyed overwhelming popular support, fuelled by demagogue oratory, throughout his subsequent journey north.

News of Napoleon's approach triggered an upsurge of **Jacobin** agitation and popular rioting in Paris. Troops sent south to stop Napoleon by a nervous government invariably repeated the drama of Laffrey and joined his cause, most notably royal cavalry C-in-C **Ney** and his men at Auxerre on 14 March. In an atmosphere of mounting hysteria, the court fled for exile in Ghent on 19 March, and Napoleon entered the capital to take over the government next day.

Though returned to power on a wave of mass sympathy, Napoleon was not the absolute monarch of 1804, and de facto control of the army was his strongest guarantee of support from a lukewarm Chamber of Deputies. The new government was dressed in populist, revolutionary colours, including appropriate figureheads like **Carnot**, but **propaganda** alone could not rouse enthusiasm for a return to war, and Napoleon was required to adopt a conciliatory attitude to the allies.

Never more than a gesture to public opinion, his peace overtures received the expected response from the **Vienna** delegates, and the **Seventh Coalition** against France came into being on 25 March. All negotiations with Napoleon were promptly halted and an Anglo-Prussian force of 150,000 troops put into the field at once. Now able to brand the allies as aggressors, Napoleon ordered French mobilization on 8 April.

In preparing for the campaign that followed, shortages of weapons, ammunition, horses and supplies were addressed by a last, broadly successful, call for sacrifice in the name of national defence, but patriotic appeals and returning old soldiers were not enough to overcome the army's critical manpower shortage. The acid test of **conscription** was applied to public support at the end of April, and Napoleon was able to deploy 280,000 men for defence of the frontiers by June, with another 150,000 conscripts expected to join them over the next six months.

The allies were meanwhile planning to commit more than 650,000 troops to a five-pronged offensive into eastern France, and hoped to field a million men within six months. In the north, **Wellington** and 110,000 allied troops were to advance from Brussels, supported by **Blücher** and 117,000 Prussians moving west from Namur; **Schwarzenberg**'s 210,000 Austrian troops were to move on the upper Rhine, followed by **Barclay de Tolly**'s 150,000 Russians, and an Austro-Italian force of 75,000 men was to attack Provence from northern Italy. Intended to grind down French resistance from all directions, the strategy had as its main weakness the fact that only Wellington and Blücher were in the field by early May.

Napoleon faced two basic options. He could either repeat his 1814 mobile defence of **France**, using internal lines to check allied attacks from all directions, or he could launch an immediate offensive against the two forces in the Netherlands, hoping that a quick victory would shake Coalition unity. Recognition that Wellington and Blücher were commanding essentially separate armies, communications diverging towards their respective homelands, persuaded Napoleon that a bold strike might drive them apart, leaving them open to destruction in detail. The decision to seek immediate victory was made sometime in early May, and war minister **Davout** was sent instructions to prepare supplies and equipment on 13 May.

Allied forces gathering in the Low Countries were widely dispersed. Blücher's 105,000 infantry, 12,000 cavalry and 296 guns were divided between **Zeiten** around Charleroi and Fleurus, **Thielmann** based on Ciney, **Bülow** near Liège and Blücher's central forces around Namur. Further south, **Kleist**'s 26,000 Prussians were watching the Moselle. Wellington's 79,000 infantry, 14,000 cavalry and 196 guns were even more scattered. He was based on Brussels, commanding a reserve of 25,000 men, and corps were stationed around Braine-le-Comte (under the Prince of **Orange**) and Ath (**Hill**), but some 17,000 men were deployed in garrisons, and **Paget**'s heavy **cavalry** was concentrated around Grammont and Ninove. Only about a third of his troops were British.

Well informed of allied dispositions by numerous French sympathizers in Belgium, Napoleon calculated that it would take three days for the two main armies to come together as a single force. He planned to occupy the road linking them before they could do so, forcing them further apart by a campaign of rapid manoeuvre against each in turn. Speed was important, but so was surprise, and a complete ban on land or sea traffic out of northern France accompanied concentration of French troops from 6 June.

Little or no warning of a major offensive reached Prussian headquarters until 14 June, when Napoleon reached his forward headquarters at Beaumont. The secret assembly of 122,000 troops (including 22,000 cavalry) and 366 guns on the Belgian frontier was a brilliant organizational achievement, and gave Napoleon an edge at the start of the campaign, but his army suffered from crucial basic failings.

The **French Army**'s most glaring weakness in 1815 was at senior command level. Napoleon's accelerating physical decline had eroded his energies, and the fighting qualities of **Soult** were no substitute for the absent **Berthier**'s gifts as chief of staff. One of the frontline army's two wings was entrusted to Ney, no strategist and a spent force since 1812, and the other to **Grouchy**, a cavalryman with little experience of commanding infantry. Meanwhile Davout remained in Paris as governor, **Suchet** (the best available staff officer) commanded a secondary front at Lyon, and the services of **Murat** were rejected, despite his quixotic War of **Italian Independence** against Austrian forces in the spring.

Refusal to employ Murat's talents was an emotional reaction to past treachery, and the psychological condition of Napoleon's army as a whole has been seen as a factor undermining its fighting capabilities. Some personnel at all levels had been unswerving supporters of Napoleon, others had changed sides twice in a year, but all lived under a shadow of treason that could only be banished by total victory, encouraging reckless operational bravado and irrational responses to pressure.

Fired-up but fragile, Napoleon's strike forces converged on the Sambre in three main columns from the early hours of 15 June. The central column of **Mouton**'s corps and the **Imperial Guard** (under **Drouot**) was flanked on the left by corps under **Reille** and **Drouet**, and on the right by **Vandamme** and **Gérard**. Four corps of reserve cavalry formed the vanguard. Though initial development was delayed by a combination of bad luck and staff ineptitude, the advance took allied leaders completely by surprise.

Blücher had only been informed of the French build-up around Beaumont the previous day, and his typical reaction to news of the advance was to order a general concentration in its path around Sambreffe. Wellington knew nothing of French activities until late on 14 June, and reacted to concrete information the following afternoon by assuming that Napoleon was aiming for Mons, Ath and his own Channel communications. On the afternoon of 15 June, and again in the evening, he issued orders deploying his forces to protect their western flank, widening the gap between the two allied armies.

During the afternoon of 15 June, once most of his army was across the Sambre, Napoleon set about completing their separation. Ney and the left wing pushed towards the vital road junction of **Quatre Bras**, astride the principal link between the two allied armies, and Grouchy's right was sent towards Fleurus to harass Blücher's presumed retreat. Largely through command incompetence, Grouchy became bogged down in the suburbs of Fleurus for the night, and Ney halted short of Quatre Bras.

Their failures appeared relatively insignificant to Napoleon next morning. Convinced that both allied armies were retreating, he planned to focus his strength against Wellington at Quatre Bras, but after reports of a Prussian build-up in front of St Amand he joined his right wing to win a hard-fought victory at **Ligny** that afternoon. Its impact was diluted by Ney's failure to attack the Prussian flank from Quatre Bras, where he was involved in a battle of his own that day, but French forces were left in an apparently strong position. A severely exhausted Napoleon failed either to confirm his belief that Ney had taken Quatre Bras or to send a major reconnaissance force to watch Blücher's movements, and planned to concentrate against Wellington's presumed retreat on Brussels next day.

Blücher himself was missing in action after the Ligny battle, and control of his army's retreat passed temporarily to chief of staff **Gneisenau**, who selected the town of Wavre as the first concentration point of a full-scale retreat. Blücher returned to headquarters in the small hours of 17 June, shaken but determined to come to Wellington's aid, and the Prussian army was redirected to prepare an advance from Wavre towards Wellington's left flank around Mont-St-Jean.

Inaccurate reconnaissance reports from **Pajol**'s advanced cavalry reinforced Napoleon's view that Blücher was retreating next day, and it was not until late morning that he reacted to news of Wellington's continued presence at Quatre Bras. Having wasted five hours of daylight, evidence of an increasing tendency to lethargy, Napoleon sent Grouchy with 33,000 troops to prevent any intervention from Blücher, ordered Ney to launch an immediate frontal attack at Quatre Bras, and led his reserve towards Wellington's eastern flank.

News of Blücher's defeat had already prompted Wellington's gradual withdrawal from Quatre Bras towards Mont-St-Jean, where he intended to join forces with a Prussian contingent and offer battle. The withdrawal proceeded unmolested by Ney's apparently hypnotized forces until Napoleon reached Marbais in the early afternoon and galvanized them into an advance. Disrupted by a storm, French pursuit came too late to catch Wellington, and the allied army reached positions on a ridge at Mont-St-Jean by nightfall. The two armies met next day in what became known as the Battle of **Waterloo**, when the arrival of Prussian forces at a vital time sealed Napoleon's final and most conclusive defeat.

Despite losing 25,000 men, and another 16,000 to capture or **desertion** over the next two days, French military power was not broken at

Waterloo. Grouchy was able to extricate 25,000 troops from a subsidiary action at **Wavre** and 55,000 men had regrouped on the frontier town of Philippeville within a few days. By the end of the month 117,000 troops were available for the defence of Paris, along with substantial forces in frontier garrisons and another 170,000 conscripts in training. Reduced by the need to cover French frontier **fortresses**, the combined armies of Blücher and Wellington totalled only 118,000 men by late June, while Austro-Italian advances in the south had been repelled by Suchet's forces, and Schwarzenberg's opening moves across the Rhine had been halted by **Rapp**'s small force.

Waterloo left Napoleon on much weaker political ground. After handing command of the army to Soult at Philippeville on 20 June, he reached Paris next day. He remained popular with the masses, but retained little support in either the Chamber of Deputies or the Senate. Fouché led the Chamber of Deputies in declaring itself immune to dissolution and issuing abdication demands, and Napoleon obliged next day, renouncing his titles in favour of his son and retiring to his palace at Malmaison.

While Fouché opened negotiations with the allies, Blücher and Wellington drove Grouchy back on Paris, but were halted outside the city by Davout's 117,000 men on 30 June. By that time allied communications had become severely stretched, but the provisional government turned down Napoleon's offer to repeat his 1814 campaign as a serving general, and the former emperor's future became the focus of attention as military operations subsided.

Offered a ship by Fouché, Napoleon travelled to the port of Rochefort, hoping to sail for exile in the United States, but arrived on 3 July to find a **Royal Navy** squadron blocking any escape. He eventually volunteered to go aboard HMS *Bellerophon* on 15 July, preferring capture by the British government to arrest by local authorities. Hopes of being permitted to settle in Britain or America were quickly disappointed, and he remained on board until the ship sailed, transferring to another vessel for the long journey to the South Atlantic island of St Helena, from which he never returned. The reconstruction of Europe resumed in his wake, and the restored monarchy signed a second Treaty of **Paris** on 20 November 1815, inaugurating four decades of peace between the major powers. *See* **Map 30**.

Hungary *See* **Austria**

Hussar

English term for light **cavalry**, often the élite units in a given army, derived from the Hungarian word for light horseman and in general European use by the late eighteenth century, as in the French *hussard* or the German *Husar*.

Hyères Islands, Action off the

One of several opportunities to inflict a major defeat on **French Navy** fleets missed by **Royal Navy** commanders in the mid-1790s (*see* **Naval Warfare**). British **Mediterranean** commander **Hotham** failed to catch Admiral **Martin**'s Toulon fleet off **Leghorn** (Livorno) in March 1795, but was given another chance on 13 July, when his 23 **ships-of-the-line** caught Martin's 17 off the Hyères Islands, near the French coast just east of Toulon. After a brief general combat, the 74-gun *Alcide* caught fire and surrendered, but Hotham made little effort to pursue Martin's subsequent flight, and his single prize blew up shortly afterwards.

I

Ibrahim Bey (1735–1817)

A Slav from the **Ottoman Empire's** Danube provinces, sold into **Mameluke** service as a child, Ibrahim was governor of Cairo before assuming joint control over **Egypt** with **Murad Bey**. Able to maintain virtual autonomy from a feeble central government, they were driven from power by **Napoleon** in 1798, and Ibrahim withdrew into Syria after the Battle of the **Pyramids**. He returned to reoccupy Cairo under the terms of the 1800 **El Arish** agreement, but withdrew again after it broke down and he was attacked at **Heliopolis**. Unable to dominate the scramble for power that followed French evacuation, he escaped the Mameluke massacres of 1811 but never again occupied a central position in Egyptian politics.

Illyria

Contemporary term for the largely rural region bordering the north-eastern Adriatic coast, comprising parts of modern Slovenia, Croatia, Bosnia-Herzegovina and Montenegro. The so-called Illyrian Provinces were the enlarged area, including the Tyrol to the north and Belgrade to the east, that was incorporated into the French puppet Kingdom of **Italy** after the Peace of **Schönbrunn** in 1809, and remained under French control until 1814. *See* **Map 9**.

Imperial Guard (French)

The élite formation of the imperial **French Army** between 1804 and 1815, originally formed by **Napoleon** in 1799 as the Consular Guard. Drawn from units of the small guard corps employed by the **Directory** regime and Napoleon's own **Guides**, the Consular Guard was employed as a shock reserve during Napoleon's **Italian campaign** of 1800, most notably at **Marengo**.

Some 3,000 strong in 1800, it had grown to include about 8,000 infantry and 3,000 **cavalry** (with **artillery** support) by 1804, when it became the Imperial Guard in accordance with Napoleon's change of status. By 1812 it had become an army of more than 56,000 men, subdivided into 'Old Guard' units with at least five years' service and two campaigns behind them and a '**Young Guard**' chosen from the best of each year's conscripts, with other units designated the 'Middle Guard'. The Guard also included individual élite gendarme, **marine** and **Mameluke** formations.

Though the Guard cavalry was used as a shock or pursuit weapon during the campaigns of 1805–9, and the Young Guard was used as a battle reserve in 1809, notably at **Aspern–Essling**, the Guard infantry was hardly used in battles after 1805, when it delivered the final knockout blow at **Austerlitz**. Held back as a last-resort weapon, it eventually came into its own during and after the **Russian campaign**. Though not committed at **Borodino**, it was the only French unit in good fighting condition by the time of the second **Krasnoe** battle in mid-November, and reinforced its international reputation for invincibility through the campaigns of 1813–14.

Though the Guard as a whole became a bloated force of more than 112,000 men during the 1814 campaign for **France**, the Old Guard at least retained its mystique and absolute loyalty to the end. Six hundred of its survivors were selected to accompany Napoleon into exile on **Elba**, and formed the nucleus of his escort during his return to power in 1815, when a reduced Imperial Guard of 22,000 veterans took part in the **Hundred Days** campaign. The shocking sight of its failure against **Wellington's** lines triggered the final French collapse at **Waterloo**.

Imperial Russian Guard

The élite force of the **Russian Army**, also known as the Tsar's Lifeguard, and renowned as one of the finest fighting units in contemporary Europe. The Russian Guard was known for its superb appearance, physical strength, discipline and manoeuvring skill, though its officers were generally no better than others drawn from the nobility. Steadily expanded through the war years, the Guard was reorganized in 1811 to comprise an infantry division of three brigades and two **cavalry** divisions (five regiments). Guard infantry was split into two divisions from 1813, and two more cavalry regiments had been added by 1814.

Incendiary Shells

Standard issue with most contemporary land and naval **artillery** forces, incendiary shells (commonly called 'carcasses') were similar to the explosive **common shell** but contained a number of holes for different fuses and were packed with highly flammable material. Particularly valuable in the context of **naval warfare**, in that fire was the most effective means of actually sinking a warship, incendiaries were also employed by land armies as ammunition for howitzers, **mortars** and **Congreve rockets**, but their use was normally restricted to **siege** or other static operations against wooden targets. Similar shells fitted with shorter fuses were timed to explode in mid-air for use as flares.

Income Tax

The novel means of **war finance** adopted in **Great Britain** from early 1799. Prime minister **Pitt** proposed a direct tax on the incomes of the wealthy for the first time in his budget of December 1798. The measure aroused predictable opposition from the propertied classes, but passed comfortably through both houses of parliament, reflecting recognition at the political centre that Britain's policy of floating loans on the European money markets was undermining national credit (*see* **Bank Crisis**). The original tax took a proportion of every income above £60 per annum, rising to 10 per cent of annual incomes over £200 (some 75,000 people), and revenues had risen to £13 million by 1813, twice the annual expenditure of **Prussia** but no more than a useful contribution to British government expenditure of about £200 million per year.

India

The Asian subcontinent had been opened up to European merchants during the maritime expansionist drive of the sixteenth and seventeenth centuries, and the southern part of the peninsula had been a literal battleground between native rulers and competing trading companies, principally from **France**, the **Netherlands** and **Great Britain**.

The richest and most militarily powerful of these was the British East India Company. Spreading out from its great trading posts at Calcutta and Madras, it controlled much of southern India by the time the British government introduced the India Act in 1784. The Act subordinated East India Company administrators to a crown-appointed Board of Control, and crown predominance was stressed in the trial of former company governor Warren Hastings on corruption charges, which lasted seven years and ended with his acquittal in 1795.

Trade with Europe had expanded rapidly through the eighteenth century to become a factor in British **colonial** planning second only in importance to the **West Indies**, but India remained an anarchic patchwork of squabbling principalities and regional empires in the 1780s. British control was strengthened under royal governor-general Lord Cornwallis (1786–93), but Richard **Wellesley's** term as viceroy from 1793 was a watershed in the establishment of firm British control over the subcontinent as a whole.

Wellesley implemented a concerted offensive policy against opposition from native rulers, negotiating military alliances with friendly princes that secured their tenure as imperial clients and their support in a series of local wars. The most serious of his wars, the **Seringapatam campaign** of 1799, broke **Tipu Sahib**'s expansionist Mysore empire. He increased the British military establishment around Calcutta and along the important south-western trading coasts, and gave full support to colonial campaigns against French and Dutch possessions round southern India in the early years of the European war.

By the time Wellesley returned to Britain in 1805, to be succeeded by Lord Minto, he had helped the East India Company extend its control as far as Afghanistan and Burma, while the success of his diplomatic network in bringing peace and relative prosperity to a splintered region helped make British rule enduringly popular with India's traditional ruling élites. By 1820 the nineteenth-century Raj was essentially in place, and British culture was beginning to overlay élite traditions amid a mounting trade bonanza.

Although other European interests were effectively expelled from India during the first years of the war, French authorities made numerous attempts to destabilize the British regime. These focused on support for Tipu in the 1790s, and generally emanated from the French island colony of Mauritius, although **Napoleon** hoped to reach India from the **Middle East** in 1798–9. French efforts after 1800 were largely restricted to conspiracies with disaffected minor princes, which could never be completely ignored but had negligible wider effect. *See* **Map 19**.

Indian Ocean

The Indian Ocean was an active if sparsely populated **naval** theatre for much of the war period. The major sea power in the region was the **Royal Navy**, which maintained several old **ships-of-the-line** and a number of fast **frigates** at bases in **India**, and used former Dutch colonies after their seizure in 1795–6. A squadron of frigates under Admiral Sercey was sent to the Indian Ocean from France in March 1796. Initially charged with transporting reinforcements to French island settlements, it subsequently sailed to the Coromandel coast of India, where it took a heavy toll of British Indian merchant shipping.

Moving east in response to British misinformation about rich pickings on the Straits of Malacca, Sercey's force fought an inconclusive action against two British 74-gunners in late September, before resuming its commerce-raiding career. Operating singly, Sercey's frigates were a constant menace to British shipping throughout the Far East during 1797–8, but were hunted down by Rear-Admiral Rainier's reinforced British squadron in 1799.

French reinforcements under Admiral Linois reached the theatre in July 1803, and Admiral **Pellew** took command of British forces the following year, but though the French sank some merchant shipping, no major actions took place before December 1810, when Admiral Bertie led a successful British raid on the important French colony of Mauritius. Six French frigates and a number of smaller warships were captured in the process of taking the island, bringing the **French Navy**'s eastern campaign to an end. *See* **Colonial Warfare**; **Map 19**.

Infantry Squares

Infantry squares (or more usually rectangles) were the accepted means of defence against **cavalry** attack in all armies, and were highly effective if properly formed by disciplined troops. By manoeuvring a body of troops into a square – with **musket** fire pouring out from all directions, and **bayonets** (or sometimes **pikes**) preventing close contact with its edges – infantry could hold out almost indefinitely against unsupported attacking horsemen, and inflict heavy casualties in the process. Defensive firepower was multiplied by positioning field **artillery** at the corners of squares, out of the defenders' line of fire, but the development of horse artillery for the rapid support of attacking cavalry presented a real threat, because squares presented such easy targets for gunners. *See also* **Infantry Tactics**.

Infantry Tactics

Infantry forces formed the basis of every contemporary army, and the vast majority of military personnel were common foot soldiers. The fighting techniques applied to them by the late eighteenth century were largely dictated by the performance limitations of increasingly large bodies of men, often given only rudimentary training and armed with an imprecise basic weapon in the **musket**.

Ordinary infantry soldiers fell into one of three broad categories for fighting purposes. Most troops belonged to 'line' companies, meaning that they took their places in the heart of any battle formation, but every battalion contained a number of élite companies, usually termed **grenadiers**, that operated on the flanks, and contemporary armies also made increasing use of 'light infantry'. Deployed as **skirmishers** or shock troops in anything up to divisional strength, or as individual companies within battalions, light infantry were picked for mobility and encumbered with less equipment than their line counterparts.

In operations involving large numbers of infantry, commanders could only hope to maintain control by manoeuvring them en masse. Musket fire was also most effective in massed volleys, and although dense groups of men provided ideal targets for hostile **artillery**, they enabled defence against **cavalry** attack by the formation of **infantry squares**. Contemporary battle tactics, and the training behind them, were therefore devised with tightly packed formations of several hundred, or even several thousand, troops in mind.

A conventional infantry attack of the period would be preceded by the forays of skirmishers, detailed to soften up opposing outposts and launch localized attacks on important positions. At the start of the **Revolutionary Wars**, the **French Army** began using skirmishers on a much grander scale than ever before, partly to ease the path of virtually untrained volunteers with line units, and the practice was adopted as orthodoxy by other armies over the next two decades. The result was a generalized increase in the use of light infantry, though the **Austrian Army** for one never fully came to terms with the art of skirmishing.

The tactics used by the main body of line infantry, following up the skirmishers, were also transformed in the French revolutionary armies. Military orthodoxy before 1792 adhered to attack in 'linear' formation, that is in a broad line three or four men deep per battalion. Given that troops were well drilled, line attack offered

maximum weight of volley and allowed the rapid performance of simple manoeuvres, but French **fédéré** infantry was an untrained rabble. Its commanders could only attempt line operations with veteran battalions, and advance the majority of troops behind the skirmishers in 'column', on a much narrower front, relying on the momentum of a massed charge at a particular spot to break through hostile lines.

The success of French column tactics, which often ignited panic in otherwise disciplined defenders, inspired their imitation by other armies, particularly as they put larger, less completely trained forces into the field. The discovery that column attack had disadvantages, most notably the dense and inviting targets it offered enemy artillery, nevertheless brought a return to at least occasional use of linear tactics by the later Napoleonic period.

The French Army modified its own column tactics into the more sophisticated *ordre mixte* system after **Carnot**'s administration had reinstated proper training. A combination of line and column approach, *ordre mixte* could be applied to a formation of any size, but at demi-brigade (i.e. regimental) level it involved forming the central battalion in line three deep and drawing up flanking battalions in column with a two-company (80-man) frontage. One company from each battalion was used for skirmishing to protect the front of the line. Flexibility was the system's great advantage: the centre battalion could easily form into column, and wing battalions equally easily into line, depending on requirements; if the formation came under cavalry attack, it was also easy to form an infantry square.

Though in general hugely successful, French infantry tactics were ultimately matched by those of the **British Army**, which was the only major force to rival the French development of light infantry as strike troops, and remained committed to linear deployment in action. British emphasis on musket proficiency, on concealment of troops until the last possible moment, and on careful choice of defensive positions reduced the effectiveness of French skirmishers, and enabled defenders to maintain cohesion until hostile columns were almost upon them. A column or *ordre mixte* attack against an intact, battalion-width line at close range faced an overwhelming firepower disadvantage and risked being outflanked.

First conclusively demonstrated at **Maida** in 1806, the potential superiority of British line formation over *ordre mixte* or column attack was confirmed by **Wellington** during the **Peninsular War**, but some modification proved necessary to protect the vulnerable edges of a line, which were particularly vulnerable to cavalry attack. The problem was solved by deployment of flank battalions left and right of the main advance, often in column, which provided defence against surprise attack and aided rapid formation of infantry squares. *See also* **Elan**; **Corps System**; **Grand Tactics**.

Inkovo, Battle of

Minor action fought between Russian and French **cavalry** detachments on 8 August 1812. The battle was the most significant manifestation of an abortive Russian counter-offensive launched two days earlier from around Smolensk. Operating well in advance of slow-moving infantry columns, about 7,000 **Cossacks** under General **Platov** attacked 3,000 French cavalry near the town of Inkovo, some 40km west of Smolensk (*see* **Map 23**). The French were driven off, having suffered several hundred casualties. The action alerted **Napoleon** to the Russian offensive, prompting an immediate order to concentrate around Lyosno in expectation of the battle he had been seeking, but also persuaded Russian commander **Barclay de Tolly** to suspend operations as a precaution against a retaliatory attack. By 10 August Napoleon had resumed his movements towards **Smolensk**, and when Barclay de Tolly again began a cautious, limited advance from 13 August, he received no cooperation from Second Army commander **Bagration** and the offensive soon petered out completely. *See also* **Russian campaign**.

Ionian Islands

The seven small islands off the Greek Adriatic coast, of which Corfu is the largest and most important, were owned by **Venice** until transferred to French control by the 1797 **Campo Formio** treaty. They were considered an important base for naval expansion into the eastern

Mediterranean, and 2,000 French troops had occupied Corfu by 28 June (before the treaty had been finalized).

French administration was initially welcomed by a population glad to be rid of Venetian rule, but economic exploitation brought local uprisings before the islands were organized into three French *départements*. A **French Navy** squadron was stationed at Corfu, and French occupation was accepted by the **Ottoman** government, but French security was compromised by the formation of the **Second Coalition**.

While Ali Pasha, the hitherto friendly Ottoman governor of Albania, occupied French-controlled mainland enclaves, Russian admiral Ushakov's combined Russo-Turkish fleet – a total of 16 **ships-of-the-line** and six **frigates** – reached the island of Hydra on 27 September 1798. Slowly picking off minor garrisons, the combined force reached Corfu on 4 November, and had the town under **siege** and a ragged naval **blockade** by 20 November. Defenders held out until 3 March, when the massacre of an outpost garrison by Turkish troops persuaded General Chabot to accept peace terms.

Turkish forces retained provisional control until 1801, when an Ionian (or Septinsular) Republic was formed under Turkish sovereignty and Russian administration. Russo-Turkish relations subsequently worsened, and a Russian takeover appeared imminent when the islands were returned to France under the terms of the 1807 **Tilsit** treaty.

Russian departure from the theatre left **Great Britain** as the only power capable of challenging French control over the islands, and a force of about 1,900 men sailed from **Sicily** in autumn 1809, reaching the Islands on 1 October. Supported by the **Royal Navy** squadron watching the Adriatic, they took the lightly defended outposts on Zante, Cephalonia, Ithaca and Cerigo, capturing about 150 **Italian** troops in the process. The British stormed Santa Maura in early 1810, but no attempt was made to take Paxos or Corfu, which became the last outpost of the Napoleonic Empire to capitulate in 1814. *See* **Map 8**.

Ionkovo, Battle of

The inconclusive engagement that opened the War of the **Fourth Coalition** in 1807, fought on 3 February around Ionkovo on the River Alle (*see* **Map 17**). Marshal **Bennigsen**, the new commander of Russian forces in **Poland**, launched 75,000 troops on a westward drive from Königsberg in mid-January, aiming to push widely stretched French forces back from the River Vistula before the spring campaigning season. Their manoeuvres persuaded **Bernadotte's** northern French corps to give ground and **Napoleon** issued orders for a counter-offensive on 27 January. Bernadotte was instructed to maintain his retreat, drawing Bennigsen further west, while three French corps, the cavalry reserve and the **Imperial Guard** were rushed north from Warsaw to cut Russian lines of retreat.

Napoleon's orders fell into Russian hands en route for Bernadotte, and were known to Bennigsen by the time they became active on 1 February. Realizing the danger, he pulled his army back to block the French advance. Certain by 3 February that the Russians were informed of his plans, Napoleon expected them to fight a rearguard action around Allenstein, but reached the town to find 40,000 men drawn up 10km to the north-west around Ionkovo (Jenkendorf).

Though he could only call on five divisions, plus elements of the Guard and **Murat's** cavalry, Napoleon launched an immediate attack along familiar lines. Murat led three divisions in a frontal assault, while Soult commanded the other two in a flanking manoeuvre intended to cut escape routes north and then fall on the Russian rear. Soult's advance began well, taking Güttstadt, but became bogged down trying to reach the main battlefield and had only just managed to get across the Alle at Bergfriede when darkness halted operations. The French frontal attack was not ready to start until mid-afternoon, and had achieved only its initial objectives by nightfall.

Reinforced overnight, Napoleon expected a victory next day, but Bennigsen had withdrawn his army and was out of reach on the way to Landsberg by morning. French pursuit began at once, forcing a brief encounter at Hoff on 6 February before Bennigsen turned to face the French at **Eylau**.

Ireland

A colony of **Great Britain** in 1792, Ireland had endured centuries of political and economic oppression by the London government in tandem with a self-interested and narrow Protestant élite ruling from Dublin, where it exercised a complete hold over the viceregal parliament. Most of the country was rural, underpopulated, Catholic and poor, but the Protestant province of Ulster to the north was more prosperous and socially developed. While the south had periodically been driven to rebel by famine, demagogues and priests, the northern Irish were unlikely to start a peasant revolt but more susceptible to radical ideology.

Politicians in England were well aware of Ireland's problems and injustices, but the attempts of **Pitt**, and **Portland** Whig members of his coalition, to introduce reform in 1794–5 were blocked by **George III** and Dublin vested interests. Irish hopes of **Catholic emancipation** (freedom to hold office) were raised and then dashed, contributing to the popularity of small but growing radical groups such as the United Irishmen.

The representations of exiled United Irishmen leader Wolfe **Tone** helped persuade the French government that the time was ripe for republican rebellion, but an attempt to provoke it with an invasion failed at **Bantry Bay** at Christmas 1796. Mounting tension in Ulster through 1797, and crass political mismanagement by the Anglo-Irish regime, triggered a full-scale Irish rebellion in 1798, but it had been put down by British troops before minimal French aid reached **Killala Bay** in the autumn.

The Pitt government finally addressed the gathering danger of civil war in the colony by effectively purchasing the support of Dublin politicians for an Act of **Union** annexing Ireland to Britain, and won popular Catholic assent by promising emancipation in the aftermath. The king's refusal to keep Pitt's promise after the legislation had been passed in early 1801 brought down the government and provoked political upheaval in London until Catholic rights were finally granted in the 1820s. Though Ireland became part of a new United Kingdom, and the occasional threat of renewed French intervention was never realized, the provinces remained in a condition of chronic turbulence, and a significant portion of **British Army** strength was devoted to their policing throughout the war period.

Irish Rebellion (1798)

Major uprising against British rule in **Ireland** that was the climax of prolonged intrigues between Irish nationalist rebels and the French **Directory** government. After the French **Bantry Bay** expedition's failure in late 1796, leaders of the nationalist United Irishmen party organized themselves as a military committee and began preparations for a full-scale rebellion. While their chief representatives in France, Dr McNevin and Wolfe **Tone**, resumed efforts to gain substantial military support, the Bantry Bay fiasco had prompted an increase in the **British Army**'s Irish establishment.

Rebel plans to seize Dublin Castle were aborted after betrayal in March, but the delayed insurrection went ahead in late May. Attacks on 24 May against British detachments south-west of Dublin, and around the capital itself, were repulsed with hundreds of casualties by garrison forces under **Dundas**, but operations against isolated British outposts enjoyed greater success. Some 15,000 lightly armed rebels under Bagnal Harvey defeated troops guarding the south-western port of Wexford next day, before marching inland to New Ross, where they were routed by a British division on 5 June. British C-in-C Lake defeated Harvey's reorganized rebels on 21 June, and his subsequent victory over some 5,000 Protestant rebels in the north at Ballinahinch, south of Belfast, had effectively suppressed the uprising by the time tangible French support arrived.

Two French expeditions were mounted to aid the rebellion. The first landed at **Killala Bay** on the north-west coast on 22 August, but surrendered on 8 September. A second expedition was intercepted by a **Royal Navy** squadron en route for **Lough Swilly**, in the far north, on 12 October and virtually destroyed. Its failure ended any immediate danger to British rule in Ireland, and closed a rebellion that, as widespread as it was disorganized, had claimed an estimated 30,000 lives in five months.

Irun, Battle of

One of two **Peninsular War** engagements fought on 7 October 1813, at the start of the allied offensive across the Bidassoa River into southwestern France. After the defeats at **San Marcial** and the first Battle of **Vera** on 31 August, French commander **Soult** fell back across the Bidassoa frontier to defend a 25km front from Vera to the Biscay coast (*see* **Map 5**).

Expecting an allied offensive but unsure of its exact direction, Soult divided 47,000 troops into frontline units led by **Drouet** in the south, **Clausel** in the centre and **Reille** in the north, keeping 8,000 men in reserve. The Bidassoa Estuary was considered impassable, and only 10,000 troops were allocated to Reille's sector, but allied C-in-C **Wellington** discovered that the estuary could be crossed at low tide, and planned his main attack there.

The next low tide was on 7 October, and Wellington led four divisions across the estuary from seven thirty that morning. Allied divisions at Maya and Roncesvalles meanwhile undertook demonstration manoeuvres along Drouet's front, and **Alten**'s Light Division, supported by two Spanish divisions, launched a secondary attack on a hill just north-east of Vera.

The main British attacks, at Irun and just to the south at Behobie, achieved complete surprise and were quickly successful, driving Reille's forces out of their coastal defences within 90 minutes and advancing to take the village of Hendaye by eleven thirty. Reille had little choice but to withdraw, and Soult could only follow suit once he realized his flank had been turned. Although casualties were fairly light, Wellington losing 400 men to Reille's 450, the French left behind all their **artillery** and most of their baggage train. *See* Second Battle of **Vera**.

Italian Army

The ground forces of the Kingdom of **Italy** were among the most reliable and loyal of **Napoleon**'s satellite armies. The army's development from the inefficient army of the **Cisalpine Republic**, which comprised some 23,000 peasant conscripts and a **Polish** legion when the kingdom was founded in 1805, was largely the work of viceroy **Beauharnais**. An active military reformer and a competent field commander, Beauharnais improved the army's training processes, founded new military academies and introduced an organizational structure on the **French Army** model. Its total strength up to about 45,000 men by 1809, the army performed well at **Sacile**, **Raab** and **Wagram** during the 1809 campaign against **Austria**, and some 30,000 Italian troops took part in the **Peninsular War** from 1808 to 1814, suffering 21,000 losses. Only 7,000 of the 27,000 troops committed survived the 1812 **Russian campaign**, but the army's association with nascent Italian nationalism helped Beauharnais rebuild it in 1813, and a division fought in **Germany**. Its national quality contributed to Beauharnais's decision to fight the defensive **Italian campaign** of 1814, and it was holding its own against invading Austrian forces when the war ended.

Italian Campaigns (1792–7)

The fluctuating five-year struggle between France and the allies of the **First Coalition** for control of Italy, centred on the north of the country but embracing conflict further south in **Tuscany**, the **Papal States** and **Naples**. Peripheral operations opened during the autumn of 1792, when 30,000 French troops annexed **Nice**. Withdrawal of French forces to deal with internal revolt at **Lyon** prompted a Piedmontese invasion of French Savoy in August 1793, but 18,000 troops were driven back across the frontier when the elder **Kellermann** returned with 12,000 men to win engagements at Argentines (11 September) and St Maurice (4 October).

Meanwhile **Austrian** and **Neapolitan** Army forces were being assembled to drive the French back from Nice into Provence. By spring 1794 about 45,000 allied troops, including Piedmontese forces, were holding strong positions in the mountains to the north, and the **Royal Navy** was strangling the French supply lines through Genoa. An allied attack was pre-empted by the French Army of Italy, now commanded by **Dumerbion**, who accepted artillery commander **Napoleon**'s plan for a two-pronged offensive that took **Saorgio** in mid-April and secured mountain passes into **Piedmont** by early May.

The opening phase of Napoleon's second offensive plan, a coordinated move by the armies of Italy and the Alps into an area known as 'the Barricades', just north of the Col de l'Argentières, was carried out without serious difficulty in June. War minister **Carnot** then vetoed further offensive operations, partly to keep troops close to counter-revolutionary hotspots in southern France, and an appeal against the decision had not been answered when Bonaparte was arrested as a supporter of the fallen **Robespierre** on 6 August.

Napoleon was returned to the front two weeks later, but the pause in French operations gave quarrelsome allied commanders time to prepare a two-pronged attack on Savona. The Army of Italy's command team ignored government orders to remain on the defensive and adopted Napoleon's plan for a pre-emptive attack to secure lines to Genoa. Once this was achieved with a victory at **Dego** in September, Dumerbion withdrew to defensive positions protecting Savona.

The front saw no more serious fighting until summer 1795, by which time Napoleon had resigned from the army and Dumerbion's command had passed to the elder Kellermann. An Austrian offensive opened on 29 June, forcing the Army of Italy's 30,000 troops to fall back beyond Loano, where Kellermann announced plans to retreat into France unless reinforced.

Carnot's response was to coopt Napoleon into the **Bureau Topographique** staff organization, and to adopt his plans for attacks towards Vado and Ceva. **Schérer** took over from Kellermann with orders and reinforcements to carry out the attack, which surprised the Austrians at **Loano** in late November before both sides went into winter quarters. Napoleon's winter-long political campaign, directed through the war ministry, to force Schérer into more ambitious action culminated in the latter's resignation, and the **Directory** appointed Bonaparte in his place on 2 March 1796, imagining that he was being dispatched to relative obscurity.

With the main spring attack planned for **Moreau** and **Jourdan** on the **Rhine**, Napoleon's initial orders envisaged a secondary invasion into Piedmont. The strategy's ultimate aim of trapping Austrian forces in the Alps by a gigantic pincer movement was more optimistic than practicable, and Bonaparte won permission to open operations with a more ambitious advance on Acqui and Ceva.

Napoleon reached the Army of Italy on 27 March 1796. Strung out between headquarters in Nice and forward areas around Savona, vulnerable to British warships off the coast and bandits in the mountains, his forces were desperately short of food and supplies. Mutiny, **desertion** and royalist conspiracy were rife after months without pay, and only some 37,000 troops and 60 guns were left. Bonaparte was more fortunate in having **Berthier** as his chief of staff, and three capable divisional commanders in **Sérurier**, **Augereau** and **Masséna**.

Allied commander **Beaulieu's** three armies were widely scattered and virtually incapable of mutual support along poor lateral roads. His 30,000 Austrians held a line centred on Acqui, while Colli's 20,000 (mostly Piedmontese) troops were to the north between Cuneo and Cosseria, and General Corrigan's 20,000 men were west of Turin, watching Kellermann's 20,000 troops in the Alps.

To reach the fertile plains of Lombardy, the French army needed control of six mountain passes, from the Col di Tendé in the west to the eastern Bochetta Pass. Once into the plains, it would face the choice of advancing either north or south of the River Po. The relatively small streams crossing the southern sector, between the river and the Appennines, were much less daunting obstacles than the series of broad rivers that formed excellent defensive positions between the Po and the Alps, but the northern route provided direct access to the area (known as the **Quadrilateral**) that controlled passes north into Austria (*see* **Map 6**).

Aware that only peace with Piedmont would secure his back for operations further east, Napoleon moved his headquarters forward to Savona on 9 April, but his planned thrust against the link between Beaulieu and Colli at Carcare was pre-empted by an Austrian offensive on 10 April. Aimed at the far French right on the coast around Voltri, it was thwarted by an expert retreat and the delay of Argenteau's simultaneous drive towards Savona.

Napoleon responded by moving on Carcare next day, and catching Argenteau in a pincer at **Montenotte** on 12 April before turning against Colli's 13,000 frontline troops. Delayed by the appearance of strong Austrian detachments at **Dego** on 14 and 15 April, reduced French forces failed against Piedmontese positions at **Ceva** but swept into Piedmont after a decisive victory at **Mondovi** on 21 April. His supplies replenished, Napoleon advanced towards Turin on 23 April before dictating peace terms to the terrified Piedmontese king at **Cherasco** on 28 April. Fraught with potential dangers, the French April offensive had cost some 6,000 French casualties, but had taken 15,000 allied prisoners and inflicted an estimated 10,000 casualties.

Napoleon used a brief pause for reorganization to prepare an attack against Beaulieu's army to the west, calling up detachments guarding the Alpine passes and demanding reinforcements from his government. The Austrian commander, intent on a rapid retreat towards potential reinforcements, meanwhile retired to the east bank of the Agogno around Valeggio, well placed to strike at any French crossing of the Po around Valenza or Pavia.

Napoleon concentrated his army, now 40,000 strong, south of the Po in positions close to both crossings, but surprised the Austrians by moving across the river far to the east at Piacenza from 7 May. A minor defeat at **Codogno** during the night of 8–9 May was enough to persuade Beaulieu into a full-scale retreat east of the Adda. Still determined to bring the Austrians to battle, Napoleon won a famous victory on the Adda at **Lodi** (10 May), before abandoning further pursuit and sending Masséna to occupy unprotected Milan on 13 May.

Though by no means annihilated, Beaulieu's army had been driven from north-western Italy, and Lodi confirmed Napoleon's rising status in France. Able to impose his own strategy on the Directory, and to extract 10,000 reinforcements from Kellermann's Army of the Alps, he prepared a renewed attack on Austrian forces, now gathered around Mantua.

The warm welcome that greeted Napoleon's triumphant arrival in Milan on 15 May soon cooled as his army fell to looting, led by generals with an eye for fine art, and he extracted indemnities to provide its pay. His fears for the army's rear lines were banished by confirmation from Paris of the Cherasco agreement on 21 May, and he led 30,000 men out of Milan next day in search of battle with Beaulieu, leaving 5,000 troops to besiege a small Austrian garrison holding out in the citadel.

Beaulieu's thin cordon along the east bank of the Mincio collapsed after French forces broke through at **Borghetto** on 30 May, and the bulk of his army was chased out of Lombardy altogether over the following week, regrouping in the Tyrol at Trent. Some 4,500 troops further south were driven back into Mantua, joining 7,500 men of the city garrison to hold off immediate French attacks.

In effective control of the Quadrilateral, but again deprived of a decisive battle victory, Napoleon was forced to think in defensive terms. Uprisings during early June in Tortona, Pozzolo and Arquarta were put down with exemplary brutality, and Napoleon led a division south to bring the Papal States and Tuscany under French control. A formal **siege** of the imposing **fortress** at **Mantua** meanwhile made little progress, and was abandoned on 31 July after General **Würmser's** reinforced Austrian army was reported advancing from Trent.

With French armies inactive on the Rhine, 25,000 reinforcements had been added to the Austrian army at Trent from 18 June. Charged with relieving Mantua and then reconquering northern Italy, Würmser led 50,000 men south in three columns from early July. Napoleon rushed some 20,000 troops into positions between the two main Austrian columns, and kept them apart with rearguards while he struck them in turn at **Lonato** and **Castiglione** (3–5 August), driving Würmser back into the Alps.

Despite Mantua's continued resistance, and his own doubts about overextending tired French forces, Napoleon made an effort to follow Directory instructions for a new offensive from late August, moving 33,000 men up the Adige towards Trent in support of an offensive at last under way on the Rhine. Würmser, who had suffered almost 17,000 losses since July, was meanwhile reinforced for a second attempt to relieve

Mantua. Aware of French intentions, he left 25,000 men under General Davidovich to defend Trent and led another 20,000 down the Brenta to get behind Napoleon's advance.

The French advance overwhelmed Austrian forces at **Roveredo** on 4 September, and Trent fell next day, when Napoleon received definite word of Würmser's move. Instead of retreating, as Würmser expected, he set off down the Brenta after Würmser on 6 September. A bewildered Würmser failed to halt the menace at his back on 8 September at **Bassano**, and then surprised Napoleon by marching his 12,000 survivors towards the Adige. Urgent French pursuit could not stop him reaching Mantua on 12 September, and only Masséna's arriving vanguard foiled a strong breakout attempt on 15 September.

French invasion forces on the Rhine front were back at the frontier by the end of October, freeing Austrian leaders to divert resources to Italy. By that time Napoleon's army numbered almost 42,000 men, but a third were sick and another 9,000 were at Mantua. Against a background of simmering anti-French conspiracy among the independent states, Napoleon sought to impose greater stability by founding the **Cisalpine** and **Cispadine** Republics, but was again forced to adopt a defensive military posture.

A new Austrian offensive from the north, led by **Alvintzi**, was ready by the start of November. Recognizing that French forces were divided, the Austrian plan again involved two main advances, Alvintzi leading 28,000 troops down the Brenta towards Bassano and Davidovich moving on Trent with another 18,000. Convinced by Austrian disinformation that Alvintzi's force was acting alone, Napoleon ordered **Vaubois** to attack what he believed was a small force north of Trent, and began concentrating at Verona for an attack on Alvintzi.

Vaubois's defeat north of Trent by Davidovich on 4 November threw Napoleon's attacking plans into disarray, and attempts by Masséna to halt the eastern Austrian advance failed on 6 November. Napoleon was compelled to pull his divisions back to the line of the Adige, while Davidovich elected to pause pending assistance from his chief. Alvintzi was on his way with 17,000 troops, and held off an attack on his positions at **Caldiero** on 12 November, forcing a French withdrawal on Verona. Both sides were quickly reinforced, but Napoleon was still outnumbered. He saved his army with the three-day victory at **Arcola** (15–17 November), driving Alvintzi's army into retreat on Vicenza and freeing him to concentrate against Davidovich, who had resumed his slow advance but quickly retreated to avoid encirclement.

The Directory government was anxious for peace with Vienna by late November 1796, but talks broke down over Austrian demands to resupply the garrison at Mantua. Meanwhile both sides in the theatre were reinforced before Alvintzi's final offensive was launched in the new year. It was decisively halted at **Rivoli** on 14–15 January, suffering 14,000 losses, and though **Provera's** subsidiary column approached Mantua, its subsequent encirclement triggered the city's final surrender on 2 February, completing the eviction of Austrian forces from northern Italy.

Mantua's fall did not induce Vienna to sue for peace, and Napoleon was obliged to launch a spring invasion of the **Frioul**, driving back yet another Austrian army under Archduke **Charles**, before an obdurate Habsburg administration signed a provisional peace at **Leoben** on 17 April. As formalized at **Campo Formio** in October, it ended hostilities between France and Austria in Italy.

Italian Campaigns (1799–1800)

The campaign fought between French forces and those of the **Second Coalition** for control of northern Italy. With war against **Austria**, **Russia** and **Great Britain** either declared or imminent, French forces in Italy were severely stretched during the early spring of 1799. French C-in-C **Schérer** commanded a nominal 60,000 troops, but the **Neapolitan campaign** had distracted almost half of them south by the new year, while other detachments were securing Florence and Lucca.

Given no instructions to concentrate his forces by the **Directory** government, and facing 60,000 Austrian troops across the Adige under **Melas**, Schérer opted to pre-empt the expected arrival of 50,000 Russians in Italy by launching an attack at the first opportunity. The offensive opened on 26 March, suffering defeats by temporary Austrian commander **Kray** at **Verona** (30 March) and **Magnano** (5 April) before Schérer retired west beyond the River Adda, leaving about 8,000 troops garrisoning **fortresses** in the **Quadrilateral** region.

Melas was slow to follow up, and had barely crossed the Mincio when he was superseded in overall command by Marshal **Suvorov**, arriving at the head of Russian reinforcements on 15 April. While Kray reduced the fortresses, Suvorov smashed through outnumbered French defences at **Cassano** on 26 April, and new French C-in-C **Moreau** abandoned Lombardy to retire behind the River Ticino.

Lumbering Austro-Russian pursuit reached Milan on 29 April, and Suvorov moved his headquarters up to Pavia on 1 May, leaving a detachment to besiege 1,500 French troops in the Milan citadel. Moreau meanwhile split his remaining strength in two, covering the road to Turin at Valenza while **Victor** led half the army south to Alessandria as support for **Macdonald's** army coming up from **Naples**. Suvorov sent two divisions to obstruct Macdonald's approach, and advanced his main body west, but halted after an initial attack across the Po around Valenza failed on 11 May.

Moreau by now had only about 9,000 troops under his direct command, and quit Valenza after his limited counter-attack around Marengo had been repulsed by **Bagration** on the night of 15–16 May. Initially aiming for Turin, Moreau chose instead to avoid Suvorov by turning south and retiring on Mondovi. Suvorov was welcomed into Turin by the populace on 27 May, and halted his advance, sending detachments to guard the mountain passes. While in Turin, he proclaimed **Piedmont's** restoration to its king, and an alarmed Austrian chief minister **Thugut** began demanding his transfer to the **Swiss** front.

Despite the need to reinforce their northern flank against a minor attack from **Masséna's** French army in Switzerland, Austro-Russian forces had overcome French garrisons at the Milan citadel, Ferrara, Ravenna and Rimini by the end of the month. Macdonald meanwhile pulled out of a rebellious Naples on Directory orders, and marched north to take Piacenza on 16 June, but suffered a crushing defeat by Suvorov's concentrated army at the **Trebbia** on 18–19 June. Macdonald escaped brief pursuit to bring a remnant of his force to Genoa on 17 July, where he joined Moreau, who had retired to the coast after a brush with Suvorov's rearguard at **San Giuliano**.

Suvorov's advance guard reached Novi by 27 June, but the Austrian **Aulic Council** halted allied offensives pending the fall of French-held Mantua, Alessandria and Tortona. Alessandria fell four days later after a three-week allied siege, and Mantua's 12,000-strong garrison surrendered on 27 July. Meanwhile Moreau was transferred to the **Rhine**, and **Joubert** reached Genoa to take command in Italy on 18 July.

During intense summer heat, both sides built up their forces for autumn offensives, and 38,000 French troops marched north-west from the Genoese coast on 9 August. Surprised by the arrival of allied reinforcements from Mantua, Joubert was killed as his offensive collapsed at **Novi** in 15 August. Moreau, still awaiting transfer to the **Rhine**, led survivors back to organize the defence of Genoa.

While **Championnet**'s Army of the Alps conducted a few strategically irrelevant pinprick raids against Suvorov's northern Piedmontese outposts, attention focused on the isolated French outpost at Tortona, under siege since late June. Moreau sent a detachment to relieve the town on 8 September, and succeeded easily, largely because Suvorov began transferring his army to the **Swiss** front on the same day. He turned and retook the town on 11 September, but then followed orders from Vienna and took his Russians out of Italy.

The switch of allied emphasis to Switzerland in late summer 1799 was a turning point in the war, granting hard-pressed French forces in Italy a vital respite and wasting a clear opportunity to invade southern France. Melas was ordered to resume the offensive into France at the first opportunity, but needed time to build up the necessary strength without Russian support, and apart from a limited French offensive that failed at **Genola** (4–5 November), the theatre remained relatively quiet until spring 1800.

Russia had withdrawn from the Coalition by the spring, but Melas could call on about 100,000 men in northern Italy, against Masséna's 50,000 French troops scattered around the theatre. Melas had been ordered to take Genoa before attacking west into Provence, while Kray led a secondary advance on the Rhine. The plan offered the advantages of British naval assistance, but was unlikely to bring a quick overall victory and ignored any danger from a French Reserve Army, then being organized at Dijon by **Napoleon**, now First Consul of France.

Melas advanced cautiously from Nice from early April, and 24,000 Austrian troops were besieging **Genoa** by 20 April, supported by a British naval **blockade**. Ordered to hold out at all costs, Masséna was still defying food shortages in late May, when Napoleon led the Reserve Army across the Alps. Most of Napoleon's troops passed through the difficult **Great St Bernard Pass**, reaching the Lombard plain after circumventing outpost resistance at **Fort Bard**. The Reserve Army occupied Milan on 2 June and Piacenza five days later, before some 40,000 troops (though very little **artillery**) concentrated at the village of Stradella, blocking land communications between Melas and Austria.

Napoleon hoped to catch Melas in a panic retreat, and then to trap the Austrians between his own army and Masséna's, but Genoa's eventual surrender on 4 June forced him to go in search of a battle before the Austrians could concentrate their scattered detachments. Melas meanwhile responded to the threat to his rear by moving his main force north towards Turin, and then turning east to seek a confrontation. The armies clashed for the first time at **Montebello** on 9 June, and Melas attacked the French at **Marengo** on 14 June. His ultimately convincing defeat prompted an armistice at Alessandria next day, and Austrian forces abandoned all of northern Italy pending the outcome of new peace talks, allowing French forces to return to positions along the Adige.

Along with Moreau's defeat of Kray's secondary offensive on the Rhine, Marengo effectively forced the Austrians to the peace table. Hostilities spluttered to a halt in Italy and elsewhere while peace negotiations took place at Leoben through the summer and autumn, but were resumed from late November after British subsidies persuaded Austria to resume the fight. French forces in northern Italy, now commanded by General **Brune**, advanced across the Adige during early December, but little serious fighting took place before Austrian defeat at **Hohenlinden** brought the war to a final conclusion. *See* **Map 9**.

Italian Campaign (1805) *See* Second Battle of **Caldiero**; War of the **Third Coalition**

Italian Campaign (1813–14)

The subsidiary struggle for control of northern Italy during the latter stages of the War of the **Sixth Coalition**. French defeat at **Leipzig** in October 1813, and **Napoleon's** subsequent retreat west of the Rhine, triggered Austrian plans for an invasion of northern Italy across the Alps. Eugène de **Beauharnais**, French viceroy in the Kingdom of **Italy**, also faced possible invasion from the south, where the King of **Naples**, Joachim **Murat**, was playing a complex game of survival.

While cultivating **carbonari** and other Italian nationalist groups, Murat had already approached the Coalition as a potential ally, and ostentatiously abandoned the **Continental System** in November 1813. He had also written to Napoleon offering to command a combined Italian and Neapolitan army against the Austrians. By the time Napoleon was persuaded into accepting the proposal by foreign minister **Caulaincourt**, Murat had received an offer of alliance with **Austria** (31 December). Assuming British approval, he agreed to fight the French in return for vague promises of Austrian support in the aftermath, and moved forward to join the **Neapolitan Army**, which had reached Bologna without serious difficulty by mid-January.

Against Napoleon's (albeit unclear) orders, Beauharnais opted to defend northern Italy from potential twin-pronged attack rather than risk taking his Italian troops to fight on French soil. With **Bellegarde's** Austrians approaching from the north-east, and Murat from the south, he pulled his army back from the Adige to the Mincio on 3–4 February, hinging his two-front defence on the **Quadrilateral** fortresses of Mantua and Peschiera. His response to offers of kingship for joining the allies was a successful counter-attack across the Mincio on 8 February, which slowed Bellegarde and ended all talk of abandoning Italy, but left his own force disorganized and much reduced. The success was further diluted by the simultaneous advance of General Nugent's Austrian forces round his southern flank, which took Parma and threatened Piacenza.

Evading Austrian demands for offensive action, Murat agreed to attack French forces when he heard of Napoleon's defeat in **France** at **La Rothière**, but halted preparations on news of his victories during the **Six Days Campaign**. His inaction forced Nugent to fall back on Parma, but Beauharnais was sufficiently alarmed to switch the focus of his defence south, sending 20,000 men across the Po at Piacenza to take Parma and Reggio (2–4 March).

After his prevention of an Austro-Neapolitan attack on Reggio had further enraged Austrian commanders, Murat's problems mounted with the arrival of a small Anglo-Sicilian force at Leghorn (Livorno) on 14 March, and British ambassador Bentinck's immediate demand that he evacuate independent **Tuscany**. Subsequently offered shaky deals by Napoleon, Bellegarde and a less abrasive British mission, Murat finally came off the fence in late March when news arrived that the allies were approaching Paris, attacking Franco-Italian forces at Piacenza from 14 April.

The attack was still in progress when news arrived of Napoleon's **abdication** and the **Schiarino-Rizzino** truce between Beauharnais and Bellegarde (16 April). As fighting ended, Murat abandoned hope of extending his dominions to the Po and withdrew south in early May to deal with mounting internal troubles. Beauharnais, his troops still garrisoning Italian fortresses in accordance with the truce agreement, returned to Milan and made vain efforts to retain his kingdom in peacetime, while Bellegarde paused to await their outcome. *See* **Map 9**.

'Italian Independence', War of (1815)

The characteristically cavalier attempt by **Murat**, the French King of **Naples**, to conquer southern and central Italy at the head of a crusade for Italian national liberation in spring 1815. Murat's diplomatic position was worsening as the Congress of **Vienna** edged closer to the restoration of Bourbon king **Ferdinand**, and an attempt to bully France into recognizing his regime met with threats from Austrian chancellor **Metternich**, his only formal ally. Murat reacted to this, and news of **Napoleon**'s escape from **Elba**, by deciding to fight someone. Ignoring his wife and senior ministers, who wanted him to fight Napoleon, Murat decided to attack the Austrians in northern Italy, declaring war on 15 March.

Murat's army, on paper 95,000 men, actually amounted to 35,000 infantry and 5,000 cavalry. Most were already in the **Papal States**, preparing to march north, and they advanced up both coasts from 19 March. Murat's proclamations of Italian independence en route were greeted with indifference by local populations, and failed to attract former Franco-Italian officers to his cause. The crusade even failed to please Napoleon, who still hoped to restore his position without a war.

Still sure that a quick victory would light the flame of national liberation, Murat took Bologna without a fight on 2 April, won a minor victory over a small Austrian force at Padano, and occupied Modena. Short of pay, food and equipment, his army was already showing signs of disintegration. It got across the Po at Ochiobello on 8 April, but fell apart against Austrian commander Frimont's first small attacks on Ochiobello (10 April) and Modena. As Neapolitan forces melted away, Murat had little choice but to order a general retreat.

As Austrian columns concentrated in pursuit down both coasts, **Bianchi**'s corps marched around the flank of Murat's larger force via Florence, getting behind the retreat and routing it at **Tolentino** on 2–3 May. Murat and a few guard units reached Naples on 18 May, but **Royal Navy** forces had already arrived, and forced Queen Caroline to renounce any opposition to Austrian occupation. Such support as Murat enjoyed quickly evaporated on news of Tolentino, and he fled Naples for France with a few followers on 19 March. Caroline gave herself up to the British two days later, ending the Napoleonic era in Naples.

Italian Republic *See* **Cisalpine Republic**

Italy, Kingdom of

A French imperial creation, formed in 1805 by merging the puppet **Ligurian** and **Cisalpine Republics** into a single northern Italian state. Its establishment contravened the terms of the Austro-French Treaty of **Lunéville** (1801), and was one of several diplomatic affronts that influenced **Austria**'s decision to join the **Third Coalition**. Joseph **Bonaparte** refused an offer of the crown, and **Napoleon** was crowned in Milan cathedral on 26 May 1805, but practical administration of the kingdom was given to viceroy Eugène de **Beauharnais** from early June.

The kingdom's experience of Napoleonic rule was in many ways archetypical. It underwent rapid and considerable expansion, acquiring Austrian Adriatic territories under the **Pressburg** Treaty (December 1805) and a share in the partition of the **Papal States** in 1808. Its people benefited from a constitution modelled on the **Code Civil**, and many of its elements are still part of Italian law, but suffered the economic burdens of almost continuous warfare on Napoleon's behalf, along with a disastrous requirement to join the **Continental System**.

The **Italian Army** formed a major component of French forces in all campaigns from 1805, ultimately providing 50,000 men (mostly under Beauharnais's command) for the **Russian campaign** in 1812. The allies of the **Sixth Coalition** invaded in 1814, and Eugène's **Italian campaign** ended with an armistice at **Schiarino-Rizzino** on 16 April.

Sending delegates to the allies in Paris, Eugène attempted to secure his status by civilian election, but pro-Austrian and Italian nationalist opponents united to defeat **Melzi**'s bid for control of the senate. Amid scenes of (partly staged) anti-Bonapartist mob violence, Eugène departed for exile with his father-in-law, the King of **Bavaria**, on 26 April. Italian troops restored order until **Bellegarde**'s Austrians arrived to prepare the way for wholesale restoration of prewar authorities by the Congress of **Vienna**. *See* **Map 21**.

J

Jackson, Andrew (1767–1845)

American soldier and politician, born in Carolina, who saw of brief service in the American War of Independence, when he was taken prisoner. A lawyer in Tennessee from 1788, he helped to write the state constitution, served as a Congressman in 1796, was a Senator in 1797–8 and a Supreme Court judge from 1798 to 1804. He retired from public life in 1806 after a series of duels with political opponents, but led 2,500 Tennessee militia troops as their major-general on the outbreak of the **Anglo-American War** in 1812. Despite federal orders to disband forces considered irrelevant to a war on the Canadian border, he marched them to Nashville, which formed the base for a successful campaign against rebellious Creek Indians between September 1813 and March 1814.

Appointed a regular **US Army** major-general in May, and given overall command of the southern United States, Jackson invaded Spanish Florida and took Pensacola before marching to the defence of **New Orleans** in early 1815. A popular national hero after the victory at New Orleans, and the only US general to emerge from the war with particular distinction, he was briefly Florida's first governor after its annexation by the US in 1819, and returned to the Senate in 1823. Narrowly defeated in the 1824 presidential election, he became the seventh president of the United States four years later.

Jacobins

Contemporary term used to describe the most radical French revolutionary grouping of the 1790–4 period, which was dominated by members of the Jacobin Club. Properly called the Society of Friends of the Constitution, the club was founded in Paris by moderate liberals in 1789, and met in a former Dominican monastery on the Rue St Honoré. In recognition of their devotion to St Jacques the monks were known as Jacobins, a nickname applied to members after the club was infiltrated and taken over by extreme left-wing elements during 1790. Bitterly opposed to more moderate political factions, and increasingly dominated by **Robespierre** and his supporters, the Jacobins came to dominate Parisian politics by mid-1793. Jacobin clubs sprang up all over **France**, and were prime instruments of the **Terror** in Paris and other French cities, but were systematically broken up after the **Thermidor** coup of 1794. The Paris club finally closed on 12 November, but its name survived as a generic for radical republicans.

Jäger

German term, literally 'rifleman', used to describe light infantry or light cavalry. A 'Jäger' scheme introduced to the **Prussian Army** during February 1813 gave the term a slightly different connotation, in that it enabled individuals with enough wealth to buy their own uniforms and weapons to form volunteer units in advance of **conscription**.

Janissaries

Warrior class that formed the regular backbone of the **Turkish Army**. Established in the four-teenth century, and governed by a strict, reli-giously inspired code of practice, the Janissaries were drawn from the **Ottoman Empire's** Christ-ian provinces, usually in the Balkans. They fought with a combination of modern firearms (a matter of individual acquisition) and tradi-tional weaponry, regulated by tactics and train-ing that owed much to personal honour and ceremonial. Dedicated and fierce fighters, capa-ble of rapid small-scale manoeuvres, they were ill-suited to large-scale coordination and could usually be overcome by the rehearsed **infantry tactics** of regular European forces.

United by oaths of loyalty to officers and class, the Janissaries held an important place in the Ottoman political process. Mostly housed in gar-risons throughout the empire, with at least 10,000 troops based in Constantinople most of the time, they were a powerful force for conser-vatism, able to force traditionalist policies on a succession of sultans. Regional garrisons tended to specialize in brutal official brigandage, and Janissaries were the most hated and feared ele-ment of Ottoman society long before Selim III came to power in 1789 and began the process of curbing their influence. *See also* **Mamelukes.**

Jellacic vom Buzim, Franz, Baron von (1746–1810)

A divisional commander with the **Austrian Army** during its war against the **Ottoman Empire** from 1789 to 1792, Jellacic fought on the **Rhine** front during the War of the **First Coalition**. He was on the **Italian** front against the **Second Coalition** until spring 1799, when he moved to a divisional command under Archduke **Charles** on the **Swiss** front. He was in command of a corps under **Mack** in **Bavaria** during the War of the **Third Coalition**, and his career ended with the army's surrender at **Ulm**.

Jemappes, Battle of

The **French Army's** second major victory against **First Coalition** forces, a successful attack on 6 November 1792 around the village of Jemappes, near Mons in the Austrian **Netherlands** (*see* **Map 2**). French success at **Valmy** in September had been followed up by minor triumphs along the **Rhine** and at **Nice**. After an Austrian army on the Belgian frontier failed to take **Lille** in early October, C-in-C **Dumouriez** exploited a new popular enthusiasm for voluntary enlistment to assemble an army of perhaps 100,000 men for an invasion.

Austrian commander Duke Albert of Saxe-Teschen deployed his much smaller army all along the frontier to meet the expected advance, relying on **Clairfait's** reinforcements from the Rhine to cover his south-eastern wing around Charleroi. Clairfait had not arrived when Du-mouriez opened a complex operation against the Austrian line on 3 November. Covered by sec-ondary advances on Tournai and against Clairfait's approach, as well as a diversion against the Austrian advance guard around Ath, Dumouriez and 40,000 troops reached Saxe-Teschen's 14,000 men guarding Mons on 5 November.

Saxe-Teschen's troops had occupied fortified positions on high ground running from the village of Jemappes to Cuesmes on their left. Dumouriez opened a bombardment of the posi-tions at eight next morning, and followed up with attacks against both the Austrian flanks. **Beaulieu's** division stopped the French right, and the other flank movement became bogged down in muddy conditions, before Dumouriez ordered it to abandon **artillery** and launch a frontal infantry assault on Jemappes at about eleven.

Timed to coincide with a full-scale charge against the Austrian centre and **Egalité's** advance against the inner flank of the Jemappes position, the attack suffered heavy losses and captured only a section of the Austrian right. Egalité organized a second infantry charge that took another portion of the line around Jemappes, and Saxe-Teschen ordered an evacuation towards Mons as his line began to crumble during the afternoon.

French pursuit brought Austrian losses for the day up to an estimated 5,000 men. French casu-alties are a matter of guesswork, but Dumouriez was forced to halt his exhausted army's advance into Belgium from 8 November, by which time it had taken Mons and Tournai. *See also* Conquest of **Belgium.**

Jena, Battle of

One the two major battles fought between French and Prussian forces in **Saxony** on 14 October 1806. The climax of a characteristic campaign of manoeuvre, **Napoleon**'s victory at Jena, along with **Davout**'s triumph against long odds at **Auerstädt**, effectively eliminated Prussia from the War of the **Fourth Coalition**.

The **Prussian Army**'s slow mobilization and strategic uncertainty had left it dithering in allied Saxony, west of the Elbe, by early October, but the approach of French forces through the Thuringian Forest (and a minor defeat at **Saalfeld**) had prompted a hasty withdrawal on Leipzig. While 63,000 troops under King **Frederick William III** and C-in-C **Brunswick** moved north-east via Auerstädt from the night of 13 October, Prince **Hohenlohe**'s 38,000 men (and 120 guns) were instructed to hold at Jena as protection for the main body's withdrawal.

By the afternoon of 13 October, Napoleon was convinced most of the Prussian army was at Jena, and he was preparing an attack from positions around Landgrafenberg, the commanding height overlooking the town. By the small hours of 14 October, 25,000 French troops and 42 guns had been packed on to the highest peak. Another 25,000 men and 30 guns were within tactical range by morning, and a further 40,000 troops (under **Ney**, **Soult** and **Murat**) would reach the area over the next few hours.

While Brunswick was moving towards Davout's corps on the road north, the French attack at Jena began at dawn on 14 October, catching the Prussians spread out over a relatively wide area and still in the grip of command confusion. Lannes's central corps was temporarily thrown back by Prussian counter-attacks, but **Augereau** on the left and Soult on the right made better progress. Within four hours a small French bridgehead over the Saale had been enlarged sufficiently to make room for reinforcements.

Napoleon ordered a pause to organize new deployments, but Soult's forward division on the right (led by **St Hilaire**) faced an immediate counter-attack by General Holtzendorff's division sweeping down from the north around Dornburg. The attack was thrown back towards Apolda, but pursuit was halted when a major Prussian concentration materialized in front of Lannes in the centre. Belatedly recognizing that he faced more than the expected flanking force, Hohenlohe had sent for support from Rüchel before gathering together almost all his available infantry and sending them against the Landgrafenberg position.

Some 20,000 Prussian troops were lined up ready for the attack by eleven, when Ney's advance guard launched an unauthorized attack away to the left towards Vierzehnheiligen, charging beyond support range before being surrounded by Prussian **cavalry**. Napoleon sent Lannes forward to relieve them, but Lannes was repulsed after a fierce fight and Ney was forced to pull back his beleaguered **infantry squares**.

Hohenlohe failed to exploit the opportunity, ordering his infantry to halt and await Rüchel's reinforcements. A second attack by Lannes was stopped, thanks to the last-minute appearance of a Saxon division, but French detachments did penetrate between the Prussian centre and right, forcing Hohenlohe to plug the gap with his last reserves.

Hohenlohe was running short on manpower, but Napoleon's strength was reaching its peak. He had a reserve of some 42,000 troops by early afternoon, and launched a renewed massed attack shortly before one. Augereau and St Hilaire resumed their earlier advances on the flanks, and sheer weight of numbers cut through the Prussians in the the centre, persuading Hohenlohe to order a general retreat.

Orderly at first, the Prussian withdrawal degenerated once Murat's reserve cavalry got at it, and only General Tauenzien's northern wing managed a disciplined withdrawal. Rüchel's corps, belatedly marching up from Weimar, met fleeing survivors of the Prussian centre on the road at Kappellendorf and only briefly attempted to make a stand east of the River Sulbach, losing 4,000 prisoners in the process.

Against about 5,000 French casualties, Hohenlohe lost some 25,000 men at Jena (including 15,000 prisoners), and only nightfall saved the remainder. Napoleon thought he had defeated the whole Prussian army, and expected his northern wing to round up many more prisoners next day, only to discover that Davout had spent the day fighting off Brunswick's main body at Auerstädt. *See* **Jena–Auerstädt Campaign; Map 16.**

Jena–Auerstädt Campaign

The rapid defeat of **Prussia** by the French **Grande Armée** that opened the War of the **Fourth Coalition** in autumn 1806. Prussia's decision to start the war, taken secretly in August 1806, had been followed by a lengthy and confused period of preparation. **Prussian Army** mobilization was slow and inefficient, so that only about half of its projected 200,000 troops were concentrated west of the Elbe, in allied **Saxony**, when **Napoleon** began concentrating 150,000 men for a response in mid-September.

The Prussian high command in Saxony, led by the aged Duke of **Brunswick** but with King **Frederick William III** in attendance, was unable to agree on a plan of campaign. Two plans for attacking south-west towards France were set in motion and abandoned, before news of Napoleon's advance towards the southern Saxon frontier prompted a decision to wait for the French. A withdrawal towards an allied Russian army being assembled on Prussia's eastern frontier was probably a wiser course, but no Prussian leader seems to have advocated such a move.

Home affairs kept Napoleon in Paris until 24 September. Though he could not be certain of enemy plans, he had decided to drive his army between the allies and force the Prussians to accept battle in defence of Berlin. Leaving only 30,000 men to protect the French frontiers, he had ordered his army to concentrate at Bamberg, poised for a march through the Thuringian Forest.

Napoleon expected Brunswick to turn east and protect his army's communications once French positions became obvious, and was delighted when the Prussians remained strung across a broad front in their forward positions. Untroubled by receipt (via Paris) of Berlin's belated war ultimatum on 7 October, he launched his forces along the three roads through the forest and into Saxon territory next day. Still uncertain of exact Prussian positions, he deployed the whole army in a precise, mutually supporting formation that he named the **Bataillon Carré.**

First contact between the forces took place on the opening day, when the central of three French columns, headed by **Murat** and **Bernadotte**, met and overran the 9,000 men (6,000 Prussian and 3,000 Saxon) of General Tauenzien's isolated detachment at Schleiz, driving them back towards Auma. This relative skirmish convinced **Hohenlohe**, commanding some 38,000 troops of Brunswick's left wing, to group his forces west of the River Saale preparatory to crossing and relieving Tauenzien. Not only was the crossing forbidden by Brunswick, waiting passively around Erfurt some 50km to the west, but Hohenlohe's unclear orders left an advanced guard (8,300 men under Prince Louis Frederick) exposed around **Saalfeld**, where it was overrun by **Lannes**'s corps (at the head of the western French column) on 10 October.

Saalfeld had a powerful effect on Prussian morale, prompting the high command to abandon offensive plans and look to its rear lines. Anticipating a French drive towards Leipzig, Hohenlohe drew back to Jena while Brunswick concentrated his main force of some 63,000 men on Weimar. Meanwhile Napoleon revised his initial supposition that Brunswick was retiring north-east towards the Elbe and came to expect a general confrontation around Erfurt.

On 12 October Napoleon ordered his army to perform a gigantic left wheel, so that it faced west towards the Saale. Lannes and **Augereau**, now forming the vanguard, were instructed to push towards Jena and Kahla respectively, while the new northern wing of **Davout** and Bernadotte was expected to sweep down on Brunswick's flank once the anticipated battle was under way.

The appearance of Davout in the north at Naumburg on 13 October convinced Prussian commanders to avoid a major battle. The main bulk of the army was now committed to a full retreat on Leipzig, via Auerstädt, and Hohenlohe was required to perform a purely defensive function around Jena, covering the retreat with the support of 15,000 men brought up to Weimar under General Rüchel. These orders reached Hohenlohe just in time to prevent him launching an attack on a French bridgehead across the Saale. Instead he entered Jena and occupied the heights of Landgrafenberg.

Napoleon was in fact concentrating the Grande Armée around Landgrafenberg, believing he faced the main Prussian mass, and was vulnerable to attack overnight, but by morning he had mustered 50,000 men in the Jena area and was expecting another 40,000 before the end of the day. They would face a total of 38,000 Prussians and 120 guns, scattered across a much wider area than the Grande Armée and led with considerably less certainty.

Though the battle around **Jena** on 14 October ended in a complete French victory, it was a hard fight, and the weight of French numbers proved the decisive factor. Some 13km north at **Auerstädt**, Davout's 27,000-strong III Corps followed orders to march towards Apolda on 14 October, but ran into Brunswick's 63,000 men. Its remarkable victory was achieved without the help of Bernadotte, who took his 20,000 troops south to Dornburg and played no part in the battle, a possibly deliberate misinterpretation of orders that almost earned him a court martial.

French pursuit of total victory began in earnest on 15 October. While Murat and **Ney** mopped up the remnants of Frederick William's armies, corps under **Soult** and Bernadotte drove north-east into central Prussia, and Napoleon led the rest of the Grande Armée on Berlin. Only General **Blücher's** fighting retreat to the port of **Lübeck** gave the French much trouble, but he was forced to surrender after Murat stormed the town on 5 November. After pausing at Potsdam and personally looting the tomb of Frederick the Great, Napoleon entered Berlin on 27 October, capturing 4,000 guns and 100,000 **muskets**.

The lightning campaign of autumn 1806 did not end the war. Frederick William refused peace terms, and waited in distant Königsberg for 140,000 Russian troops promised by the tsar, so that Napoleon was forced to advance further east in search of final victory. *See* Occupation of Warsaw; Map 16.

Jérôme I, King *See* **Bonaparte**, Jérôme

Jervis, John (1735–1823)

Perhaps the most important naval commander of the age, and the most celebrated after **Nelson**, Jervis rose to high command in the British **Royal Navy** without the benefit of wealth or influence,

becoming a lieutenant in 1755 and reaching the rank of rear-admiral 32 years later. A strict disciplinarian, who demanded and got the highest standards of training and technical proficiency from his captains, he was promoted vice-admiral in 1793, and commanded the expedition to the **West Indies** before taking over the British Mediterranean Fleet in 1795.

During his four-year tenure in the **Mediterranean** Jervis turned his fleet into the most efficient naval fighting unit in the world, and gave full rein to talented subordinates such as Nelson, **Collingwood**, **Troubridge** and **Saumarez**. Always short of resources at a time when Britain appeared threatened by invasion, he defeated a much larger Spanish fleet at **St Vincent** in 1797 (for which he was ennobled as Earl St Vincent), and masterminded the re-establishment of British dominance in the theatre during 1798–9.

Ill health forced him to resign his command in summer 1799, but he returned to command the Channel Fleet for a time before serving as First Lord of the Admiralty (navy minister) in the **Addington** government from 1801. Responsible for cutbacks in the aftermath of the **Amiens** treaty, he remained at the Admiralty until 1806, when he returned to command the Channel Fleet. Illness forced his final resignation from active service the following year, but he was promoted Admiral of the Fleet in 1821.

Jihad

The Muslim concept of jihad ('holy war') reflected the religious basis on which the Sultan of Turkey ruled the **Ottoman Empire**, and was his traditional response to attack by infidels. Occasionally invoked against all the European **great powers** during the two centuries before the empire's collapse in 1918, jihad proved a particularly useful weapon against French occupation of **Egypt** from 1798 to 1801. The sultan's declaration of holy war on 9 September 1798 triggered a full-scale uprising in **Cairo**, in which an estimated 3,000 people died, and provided a stimulus for anti-French agitation throughout the colonial period.

John, Archduke (1782–1859)

The younger brother of Habsburg emperor **Francis II** and Archduke **Charles**, John received only rudimentary military training before being given command of the army defeated at **Hohenlinden** in 1800. Generally inclined to support the policies of Charles, but never a major political figure, he commanded an army covering the Tyrolean Alps during the War of the **Third Coalition** in 1805, and displayed a capacity for adequate if unadventurous leadership. Again given command of a secondary force in 1809, this time in Italy, he was defeated by **Beauharnais** at **Raab** in June and retired from military command at the end of the campaign.

John, Prince of Braganza (1767–1826)

Effective ruler of **Portugal** since 1792, and married to the daughter of Spanish king **Charles IV**, John viewed the expansion of republican France with understandable unease and maintained a generally positive attitude to his alliance with **Great Britain**. French invasion forced his flight, after some hesitation and under **Royal Navy** protection, to Portuguese Brazil in late 1807, and he was still in **South America** when he became King John VI on the death of his mother in 1816. He eventually returned to Portugal in 1821 and established a limited form of constitutional government.

Jomini, Antoine Henri (1779–1869)

Swiss-born soldier, military theorist and historian who began his career as a bank clerk in Paris but joined the French army during the 1798 revolution in **Switzerland**. On returning to Paris in 1804 he wrote a study of military tactics that made his reputation as a theorist, and he was appointed to **Ney's** staff during the War of the **Third Coalition** in 1805. Transferred to **Napoleon's** headquarters staff for the campaigns of 1806–7, he returned to Ney's side as chief of staff and acknowledged strategic guru after **Eylau**.

Created a baron of the empire in 1808, and promoted brigadier-general in 1810, Jomini fought with Ney in the **Peninsular War** but also undertook several diplomatic missions to St Petersburg. His close personal relationship with Tsar **Alexander** prompted Jomini's refusal of a frontline role for the 1812 **Russian campaign**, but he served as governor of Vilna and Smolensk before rejoining Ney for the 1813 campaign in **Germany**. After fighting at **Lützen** and **Bautzen**,

he was arrested on the orders of **Berthier**, long a bitter personal rival, and responded by defecting to the allies on 15 August 1813. Much of Ney's usefulness as an independent field commander departed with him.

Appointed to the tsar's personal staff as a lieutenant-general in the **Russian Army**, Jomini was a senior adviser to allied leaders through the 1814 campaign, and took part in the Congress of **Vienna**. He remained in Russian service until his retirement in 1848, producing a number of works that established him as a military scholar to rival **Clausewitz**.

Joseph I, King *See* **Bonaparte**, Joseph

Joséphine, Empress (1763–1814)

A West Indian Creole, and a celebrated beauty in her youth, Marie Rose Joséphine Tascher de la Pagerie married French aristocrat and future republican general Alexandre de Beauharnais in 1779. She bore him two children and became a well-known Paris socialite, taking a string of important politicians as lovers after her husband's execution for his failure at **Mainz** in 1793. She met **Napoleon** while seeking the return of her late husband's sword in 1795, and they married on 9 March 1796. Probably less enamoured than her younger husband, Joséphine indulged in several fairly public romantic liaisons while Napoleon was on campaign, and the marriage was close to breakdown in 1799, a situation encouraged by steady hostility from the Bonaparte family. By contrast Napoleon had already developed a flourishing relationship with Joséphine's two children, and received loyal service in return from her son, Eugène de **Beauharnais**. Often volatile, the marriage lasted until 1809, and Joséphine performed a valuable public role as empress, proving enduringly popular with ordinary French people even after she was divorced in favour of the younger, better-connected and more fertile **Marie-Louise** of **Austria**. Her health already failing, she retired to her estate at Malmaison after the divorce, and her death in May 1814 was greeted with widespread dismay in France.

Joubert, Barthèlemy-Catherine (1769–1799)

French soldier, a sergeant in the Dijon **National Guard** from 1789, who was commissioned into the regular army while fighting on the lower **Rhine** in 1792. A brigadier-general in 1795, the year after his transfer to the Army of Italy, he played a prominent part in the **Italian campaigns** of the next three years, fighting at **Montenotte**, **Mondovi**, **Lodi**, **Castiglioni** and **Rivoli**. Promoted divisional general in December 1796, he was transferred to the **Netherlands** from late 1797, but returned to command the armies of Italy and Rome the following year. He left Italy again in early 1799, but was back in August to replace **Moreau** at the head of French forces defending the frontier zone against the **Second Coalition**. His death in battle against Russian forces at **Novi** on 15 August 1799 deprived France of one of its most charismatic and popular military heroes, and forced conspirators against the **Directory** government in Paris to seek an alternative military figurehead for their planned coup (*see* **Brumaire Coup**).

Jourdan, Jean-Baptiste (1762–1833)

The son of a Limoges surgeon, Jourdan was one of the most important military figures in **France** during the **Revolutionary Wars**. An elected lieutenant-colonel in his local **National Guard** from October 1791, he fought at **Jemappes** and **Neerwinden** before promotion to brigadier-general in May 1793. He rose to divisional command two months later, was wounded at **Honschoote** in September, and returned to **Flanders** to lead the Army of the North at **Wattignies**. Temporarily out of favour during the winter, he went to the **Rhine** front as commander of the Army of the Moselle in April 1794, followed **Carnot's** instructions to take part of his army north to the **Sambre**, and won a vital victory at **Fleurus** in June.

Returned to the Rhine for the campaigns of 1795, he was retired after suffering defeat by Archduke **Charles** at **Würzburg** in September. Among the more politically radical French generals, he became a member of the Council of **Five Hundred** in Paris, and his prestige won him its presidency. He gave his name to the law establishing **conscription** in France in September 1798, before returning to the field against the **Second Coalition**. Again facing Archduke Charles on the Rhine, he was dismissed once more after his invasion army blundered to defeat at **Stockach** in March 1799.

By then known as 'the Anvil', because he had survived so many beatings, Jourdan returned to the Council, and was almost exiled for opposing the **Brumaire coup** in November, but **Napoleon** preferred to employ him as an administrator in the **Cisalpine** Republic and occupied **Piedmont**. He was appointed to command the Army of Italy, and to the **Marshalate**, in May 1804.

As Joseph **Bonaparte's** chief of staff, he spent two years in **Naples** before transferring to **Spain**, where he shared the failures of other senior French commanders during the **Peninsular War**, taking the blame for the climactic French disaster at **Vitoria** in June 1813, after which he was retired. Jourdan took royal service in 1814, but rejoined Napoleon during the **Hundred Days** of 1815, briefly commanding on the Rhine for the last time in June. Re-employed by the monarchy after Napoleon's second abdication, he presided over the court that condemned **Ney** for treason, and ended his days as an honoured elder statesman.

Junot, Andoche (1771–1813)

Junot joined the **French Army** in 1792 and was a sergeant when he first served **Napoleon** as an aide at **Toulon** in 1793. He remained by Napoleon's side through the **Italian campaigns** of 1794–7, and was an adjutant major with the **Middle East** expedition in 1798. Taken prisoner trying to escape back to France, he was soon exchanged and confirmed in his acting rank of brigadier-general, becoming a divisional general in 1801. Ambassador to Lisbon in 1805, but recalled for a frontline command against the **Third Coalition**, he was governor of **Parma** in 1806 and was civil governor of Paris from October of that year.

Junot commanded the invasion of **Portugal** in 1807, and became its governor as the Duc d'Abrantès after a rapid conquest, but defeat by **Wellesley** at **Vimeiro** in 1808 spoiled his military reputation. He commanded formations against the **Fifth Coalition** and during the 1812

Russian campaign, when he was blamed for failure to cut off Russian forces at **Smolensk**. Already prone to bouts of mental instability, he was removed from the front line in January 1813, and broke down completely while governor of Venice in July. Returned to Paris, he committed suicide by throwing himself from a window.

Junta

The Spanish word for 'assembly' or 'meeting'. Regional juntas all over **Spain** coordinated early opposition to the French invasion of 1808, and the ongoing rebellion was directed by a Supreme (or Central) Junta from September of that year until its successful conclusion in 1814. The organization never rose above factional disputes to provide coherent strategic leadership during the **Peninsular War**, and was never trusted by the established ruling classes in Spain. The juntas established in **South America** during 1811, ostensibly in support of the deposed King **Ferdinand**, were in fact expressions of regional autonomy, and formed the bases for new independent governments in the immediate postwar period.

K

Kalisch, Convention of

Secret agreement between Tsar **Alexander I** of **Russia** and Prussian king **Frederick William III**, ratified on 28 February 1813, by which **Prussia** agreed to join the **Sixth Coalition** against France in the immediate future. In return for Prussian commitment of 80,000 troops against **Napoleon**, Alexander promised 150,000 men of his own and formally recognized Prussia's pre-1806 frontiers. Both parties agreed not to make a separate peace with **France**. Frederick William had bowed to almost unanimous political pressure in signing the Convention, and delayed any open declaration of hostilities until 13 March, by which time French troops had been withdrawn west of Berlin to the line of the Elbe (*see* Campaign for Germany).

Kamenskoi, Alexander, Count (1731–1807)

Veteran Russian commander, whose distinguished career culminated in appointment as C-in-C of forces in Poland and East Prussia during the War of the **Fourth Coalition**. Kamenskoi was far too old to control the operations of a major army, and left most of the work and decision-making to his immediate subordinates, **Bennigsen** and **Buxhowden**. The experience of winter warfare north of Warsaw during the last days of 1806 persuaded him to retire, but formalities were pre-empted when he was assassinated by an aggrieved peasant on 9 January 1807.

Kamlach, Battle of

Small but quintessential encounter between French republican and **émigré** forces during the allied retreat from the **Rhine** to the Danube in summer 1796. The Prince of Condé's small royalist division, part of General Frölich's outnumbered allied force on the upper Rhine, launched a reckless counter-attack against General Abattucci's pursuing brigade on the River Kinzig at Kamlach on 13 August (*see* **Map 3**). An infantry charge, led by the Duc d'**Enghein**, took part of the village before reinforcements brushed the royalists aside, inflicting 500 casualties in the course of an action inspired by old-regime emotion rather than any tactical or strategic intent.

Kara Djordje Petrović (*c.*1752–1817)

Serbian nationalist hero, popularly known as 'Black George', and founder of one of that country's two ruling dynasties (the Karadjordjevic line). Kara was a pig-trader from Topola who became a leader of Serbian rebels fighting for independence from **Ottoman** rule. Elected to lead the national rebellion in February 1804, he overthrew regional Ottoman governor (and noted bandit) Pasvan Oglu and occupied Belgrade, where a Serbian National Council elected him hereditary king in December. Helped by the outbreak of the **Russo-Turkish War** in late 1806, Kara was able to hold off relatively feeble imperial attempts to restore control, and was effective ruler of an independent Serbia until 1813, when peace with Russia freed Constantinople to send a sizeable army against Belgrade. Kara was forced to flee Serbia for Austria in September 1813, and moved to Russia the following year. He remained in exile until 1817, when he attempted to return to Serbia and was murdered by Milos Obrenovich, leader of a new national rebellion. Obrenovich was subsequently elected hereditary prince of a semi-independent Serbia under nominal Ottoman control, a title disputed by Kara's son Alexander and at the root of a conflict between the two dynasties that undermined Serbian political stability into the twentieth century.

Katzbach, Battle of the

The second of three defeats suffered by **Napoleon**'s subordinates in **Germany** during late August 1813. Along with setbacks at **Gross-Beeren** and **Kulm**, the failure of **Macdonald**'s eastern Army of the Bobr at the River Katzbach on 26 August rendered Napoleon's simultaneous triumph at **Dresden** almost meaningless.

Napoleon had been leading his main strike force east to meet **Blücher**'s allied Army of Silesia, which withdrew on its approach, but departed for Dresden on 22 August, leaving Macdonald in command of about 100,000 men at the River Bobr. Ordered only to prevent any allied advance, Macdonald chose to follow what he assumed was a retreat, but Blücher quickly returned his marginally larger force to the offensive in line with the allied **Trachenberg Plan** to target Napoleon's lieutenants.

Both sides were surprised when they met around the Katzbach on 26 August. In heavy rain that precluded use of **artillery**, Macdonald launched more than two-thirds of his army against the allied right wing near the town of Jauer, but its columns became separated and were forced into a fight for survival while **Lauriston**'s lone corps bore the brunt of allied attacks in the centre. Unable to reconcentrate, French forces were driven back in disarray, losing perhaps 15,000 casualties and most of their guns. Blücher's army suffered an estimated 5,000 losses, and continued an advance towards **Bautzen** that was only halted when Napoleon returned to the sector in September. *See* **Map 25**.

Kehl, Manoeuvre on

General **Moreau**'s surprise attack on the southern sector of the **Rhine** front in summer 1796, a river crossing around Kehl, near Strasbourg, that placed his Army of the Rhine and Moselle in the rear of Austro-German forces massed around Mannheim (*see* **Map 3**).

Allied C-in-C Archduke **Charles** had left the southern half of his front relatively exposed by marching reserves north in response to **Jourdan**'s victory at **Altenkirchen**, and sector commander Latour withdrew west of the Rhine from 8 June, concentrating 50,000 troops behind a bridgehead around Mannheim. Moreau's 40,000 men, and another 52,000 French troops from the Vosges and the Saar (under **Desaix** and **Gouvion St Cyr**) concentrated to attack the bridgehead on 14 June.

After preliminary attacks against Latour's outposts, Moreau changed his mind on news of Jourdan's retreat in the north. Switching his point of attack south, he launched a demonstration around Mannheim on 22 June to cover a Rhine crossing at Gambsheim and Kehl. His advance guard was east of the river in the small hours of 24 June, Desaix surprising scattered allied forces and capturing the Kehl fortress with ease. By 26 June Moreau, whose reputation was made by the success, had amassed 34,000 troops east of the river to oppose half as many Austrians on the **Kinzig**.

Keith, George (1746–1823)

Scottish **Royal Navy** officer, one of **Hood**'s captains at **Toulon** in 1793 and rear-admiral in command of the force that captured the **Cape Colony** from the Dutch in 1795, an operation that made his fortune in **prize money**. Naval commander during the seizure of **Ceylon** (Sri Lanka) in 1796, he became second-in-command to **Jervis** in the **Mediterranean**, and took over on the latter's resignation in 1800. The appointment upset **Nelson**, who subsequently kept up a remorseless smear campaign that helped undermine Keith's reputation in Britain. Though he failed to intercept '**Bruix's Cruise**' while in temporary command in summer 1799, and was blamed for the failure of the **Cadiz Raid** in 1800, he generally handled his complex command with cautious competence. Promoted full admiral after his fleet assisted at **Alexandria** in 1801, he held various commands in home waters from 1803 to 1815, and was ennobled as Viscount Elphinstone in 1814, acting as liaison officer between the British government and **Napoleon** during the 1815 negotiations for the former emperor's exile on St Helena.

Kellermann, François Etienne Christophe ('the Elder') (1735–1820)

Commissioned in 1753, Kellermann was an experienced field commander when appointed to lead the French Army of the Centre defending the eastern frontier in August 1792. His prominent role at **Valmy** assured his fame (especially after the defection of **Dumouriez**), but his career never again reached such heights. Transferred from the **Rhine** to the Army of the Alps in 1793, after quarrelling with General Custine and narrowly escaping trial, he led the capture of **Nice** and defeated an invasion from **Piedmont**, but was dismissed in the autumn for failing to besiege rebel **Lyon** with sufficient vigour. Restored to favour in January 1795, he again commanded in the Alps, but played a secondary role to **Napoleon** during the **Italian campaigns** of 1796, and retired from active service in September 1797. A Senate member from 1799, he was an honorary appointee to the **Marshalate** in 1804, and performed valuable administrative work organizing **National Guard** and reserve forces. In royal service from 1814, he played no part in the **Hundred Days** of 1815.

Kellermann, François Etienne ('the Younger') (1770–1835)

Commissioned as a cavalryman in 1775, Kellermann returned from the **United States** at the start of the **Revolutionary Wars** to serve under his father, the hero of **Valmy** and commander of French forces in the Alps. He made his mark under **Napoleon** during the **Italian campaigns** of 1796–7. Promoted brigadier-general in 1797, he fought under **Macdonald** during the **Neapolitan campaign** of 1798–9, and won divisional command after playing a vital part in Napoleon's victory at **Marengo** in 1800. Wounded at **Austerlitz**, he began a long spell of **Peninsular** service as cavalry commander with

the 1807 invasion of **Portugal**, where he negotiated the controversial Convention of **Cintra** in 1808. Recalled from Spain in May 1811, he missed the 1812 **Russian campaign** through illness and retired in early 1813. Weeks later he was back in action commanding **Ney's** cavalry in **Germany**, fighting at **Lützen** and **Bautzen**, and he remained on active service through the 1814 campaigns. Briefly reconciled with the monarchy, he was retired from the army after rejoining Napoleon at **Quatre Bras** and **Waterloo**, but was allowed to inherit his father's title in 1820, and held a number of administrative offices over the next decade.

Kiel, Treaty of

The agreement signed by **Great Britain**, **Sweden** and **Denmark** on 14 January 1814 that ended the latter's alliance with **France**. In no position to dictate terms, Denmark was forced to cede Norway to Sweden and Heligoland to Britain, receiving only a relatively tiny parcel of land in northern Germany as compensation. *See* **Map 30**.

Killala Bay Raid

The first of two French expeditions mounted to aid the 1798 **Irish Rebellion**. Four French **ships-of-the-line** from Rochefort reached Killala Bay on the north-west Irish coast on 22 August, landing General Humbert's 1,150 troops, along with four guns and arms for 3,000 rebels, before departing at the first opportunity. Humbert swept aside local **militia** forces and advanced inland, picking up a few local rebels en route, before attacking and defeating British C-in-C Lake's interception force of 2–3,000 British regulars at Castle Bar on 27 August. The little French army then turned north-east towards Belfast, and new viceroy Lord Cornwallis responded by leading 20,000 British troops to meet it at Carrick, on the River Shannon, where the French were surrounded and surrendered on 8 September. *See* **Lough Swilly Expedition**; **Map 18**.

Kinzig, Battle of the

The first major engagement on the southern sector of the **Rhine** front after **Moreau's** surprise crossing of the river at **Kehl** in late June 1796. News of the crossing reached Austrian sector commander Latour late on 24 June, but he waited to flush out any feint before sending General Sztarray's 17,000 troops south from Mannheim to block Moreau at the River Kinzig. Moreau had assembled 34,000 troops east of the Rhine by the time Sztarray was in position on 26 June, and advanced up both banks of the Kinzig next day to attack 12,000 **Württemberg** and **Baden** troops in the allied centre. Although part of the attacking force got lost, **Desaix** outflanked the left wing of the allied position near Willstett on 28 June, and Sztarray retired north-east beyond the Rench to **Rastatt**, leaving 1,800 casualties behind. *See* **Map 3**.

Kjöge, **Battle of** *See* Battle of **Roskilde**

Kléber, Jean-Baptiste (1753–1800)

Born in Strasbourg, Kléber joined the **Bavarian Army** in 1777 and was a lieutenant when he returned to civilian life in France eight years later. A volunteer in 1789, he led a **National Guard** battalion at the **Rhine** during the opening campaigns of the **Revolutionary Wars**, and was promoted brigadier-general in August 1793. Successful operations against rebels in La **Vendée** earned him promotion to divisional command the following April, and he fought under **Jourdan** at **Fleurus** in June.

One of the most politically active French generals, Kléber withdrew from active command after 1794 to concentrate on the **Jacobin** cause, and his acceptance of **Napoleon**'s invitation to join the expedition to the **Middle East** in 1798 was something of a relief to the **Directory** government. Wounded during the initial attack on Alexandria, and prominent at the siege of **Acre**, Kléber suddenly found himself in command of the expedition when Napoleon left for France in August 1799. Stranded with little hope of resupply or reinforcement, he arranged a peaceful evacuation by the Convention of **El Arish** in January 1800, and after it was repudiated he defeated a large Turkish army at **Heliopolis**. He was managing to maintain a perilous hold on Cairo when he was assassinated by a member of its hostile population on 14 June 1800.

Kleist, Friedrich Heinrich Ferdinand Emil, Graf von Nollendorf (1762–1823)

One of the younger and more consistently successful **Prussian Army** commanders, Kleist fought in the **Revolutionary Wars**, and commanded the garrison at **Magdeburg** through its brief siege during the War of the **Fourth Coalition**, suffering French captivity for a time after its surrender. Kleist led a corps under **Blücher** during Prussia's next conflict with France, fighting at **Kulm** and **Leipzig** in 1813, and performed particularly well at **Laon** the following spring, but his corps along the Moselle played only a marginal role in the **Hundred Days** campaign of 1815.

Korsakov, Alexander Mikhailovic (1753–1840)

Russian general, one of the younger commanders in the Tsar's service when he led a corps of reinforcements to the **Swiss** front in summer 1799. His failure to cooperate efficiently with Austrian forces in the theatre contributed to a heavy defeat by **Masséna** at the Second Battle of **Zurich**, and he had retreated to the Rhine by the time his forces were recalled in the winter. None the less promoted general in 1801, he was appointed governor of Lithuania, a post he held for almost three decades.

Krasnoe, First Battle of

Unsuccessful attack by Marshal **Murat**'s **cavalry** corps on an outlying Russian division around Krasnoe, on the River Dnieper some 50km from Smolensk, on the afternoon of 14 August 1812. Murat's forces were in the vanguard of Napoleon's sweeping manoeuvre against **Smolensk**, and reached Krasnoe at about three in the afternoon. Russian commander **Barclay de Tolly** had left General Neveroski's division (some 8,000 infantry and 1,500 **cavalry**) to guard the Dnieper's southern bank around Krasnoe, and Murat attacked at once, forcing the heavily outnumbered Russians to form a single **infantry square**. Murat seems to have lost his temper when the square failed to collapse, refusing to allow **Ney**'s supporting infantry to move up and launching a total of 40 cavalry charges. They all failed without **artillery** support, which was bogged down in transport bottlenecks, and Neveroski withdrew survivors towards Smolensk overnight. The action gave Barclay de Tolly warning of the approaching attack on the city, and influenced Napoleon's decision to halt for regrouping throughout 15 August. *See* **Russian Campaign**; **Map 23**.

Krasnoe, Second Battle of

Minor attack on pursuing Russian forces launched by **Napoleon** on 17 November 1812, during the latter stages of the **Grande Armée's** retreat from **Moscow**. Forced back on supplies at Vitebsk and Minsk, Napoleon left Smolensk at the head of an estimated 41,500 men on 12 November. Anxious to gain time for his scattered forces to close up before Russian commander **Kutuzov** cut the road behind him, he launched a counter-attack by the 16,000-strong **Imperial Guard**, the one French formation still in fighting condition. Their assault drove 35,000 surprised Russians into a rapid retreat south, enabling most of the French army to catch up with the emperor during the day. News that General Tormazov's southern Russian army was approaching the Dnieper crossings to the west at Orsha meant that Napoleon could not wait for Ney's rearguard, which was given up as lost. *See* **Russian Campaign**; **Gusinoe**; **Map 23**.

Kray, Paul, Baron (1735–1804)

Hungarian-born **Austrian Army** commander, promoted major-general in 1790 after successes against the **Ottoman Empire**, who fought under **Clairfait** in **Flanders**, where he was forced to surrender Maastricht after defeat at **Ayvaille** in September 1794. As one of Archduke **Charles's** senior divisional commanders on the **Rhine**, he took part in victories at **Ukerath**, **Amberg** and **Würzburg** during 1796, and began the War of the **Second Coalition** as second-in-command to **Melas** on the **Italian** front. In temporary charge of the theatre when Melas fell ill, he won victories at **Verona** and **Magnano** before handing over supreme command to **Suvorov**. Kray was promoted field marshal and replaced Archduke Charles on the Rhine in March 1800, but his tactically unadventurous spring offensive collapsed with defeat at **Höchstädt**, and he was retired during the summer.

Kulm, Battle of

Engagement south-east of **Dresden**, fought on 30 August 1813, that enabled the retreating army of Prince **Schwarzenberg** to escape probable encirclement. To coincide with his massed defence of Dresden, **Napoleon** had detached 32,000 men under General **Vandamme** for an attack over the Elbe east of the city, intended to cut across allied lines of retreat. After his victory at **Pirna** on 26 August and Napoleon's success the next day at Dresden, Vandamme was ordered to penetrate deeper into the allied rear, but poor coordination between advancing French formations left his forces isolated when they ran into General **Ostermann's** 44,000-strong flank guard around Priesten, about 35km south-east of Dresden. The two armies engaged in an inconclusive frontal battle until General **Kleist**, withdrawing from Dresden with 10,000 Prussian troops, stumbled on the rear of French positions around Kulm. Trapped French forces fought hard, and inflicted 11,000 casualties during the day's fighting, but lost more than 15,000 men (including Vandamme, taken prisoner). The defeat ended French hopes of exploiting the victory at Dresden, and repaired much of the damage it had caused to allied morale. *See* Campaign for **Germany**; **Map 25**.

Kutuzov, Prince Mikhail Golenischev (1745–1813)

The son of a military engineer, Kutuzov was a veteran of campaigns in **Poland** and against the **Ottoman Empire**, and had served as ambassador to Constantinople, before he took command of the first wave of Russian troops sent to aid the **Third Coalition** in 1805. After reaching **Bavaria** too late to save the Austrian army at **Ulm**, and executing a skilful retreat to Olmütz, his (apparently drunken) objections to allied attack plans at **Austerlitz** were overruled, but he subsequently marshalled defeated Russians and led them safely into Poland.

Temporarily retired after the 1805 campaign, Kutuzov was recalled to serve in the **Russo-Turkish War**, commanding forces on the Danube in 1811–12, before replacing **Barclay de Tolly** as overall field commander at the height of the **Russian campaign**. Taking his post on 29 August, he confronted **Napoleon** at **Borodino** in early September, but seems to have exercised little personal control over the battle. By now he was approaching 70, and his pursuit of Napoleon's retreat to the Polish frontier was more dogged than dashing, earning severe criticism from colleagues. Made Prince of Smolensk by a grateful tsar at the end of the Russian campaign, he was replaced in command of the western front by **Wittgenstein** in April 1813. Already severely ill, he died in Silesia a few weeks later. Despite his undoubted strategic and tactical limitations, Kutuzov was an effective leader of troops, and is generally recognized as one of Napoleon's most determined opponents.

L

La Rothière, Battle of

Allied attack on 1 February 1814 against the small French army defending approaches to Paris during the campaign for **France**. Since coming under **Napoleon**'s personal command on 25 January, French forces had been pursuing **Blücher**'s relatively isolated Prussian column across the region between the upper Seine and the Marne. After a minor victory at **Brienne** on 29 January, Napoleon followed Blücher as far as La Rothière, where he paused to take stock of allied positions next day (*see* **Map 26**).

In heavy snow that made reconnaissance difficult, both sides planned major operations for 1 February. Blücher had made limited contact with **Schwarzenberg**'s large allied army to the south-west, and was given command of 53,000 men for a direct assault around La Rothière. Napoleon decided that allied activity was a ruse, and ordered his forces to join the **Imperial Guard** on the Seine at Troyes. French movements were well under way when reports of Blücher's activities brought them to a halt pending developments, and some 40,000 French troops were drawn up about 5km south of Brienne, along a line running east from the Aube, when Blücher's attack opened just after one.

On the French right, at the Aube, **Sacken**'s corps failed to dislodge **Gérard**'s outnumbered divisions from Dienville, and **Victor**'s corps in the centre withstood heavy artillery attacks to hold part of La Rothière itself. On the French left, **Wrede**'s repeated assaults had pushed **Marmont** back up the eastern road to Brienne by

about four, when the first allied reserves under **Barclay de Tolly** entered the fight. Napoleon threw his tactical reserve, **Ney**'s two **Young Guard** divisions, into the centre, and they retook La Rothière, but Marmont's wing was lucky to escape with an orderly withdrawal, made possible because allied **Württemberg** cavalry attacked their **Bavarian** counterparts by mistake.

Amid continuing snowfalls, Napoleon extricated his forces during the evening, and they retreated north towards Troyes. Both sides had suffered about 6,000 casualties, but La Rothière was unmistakably an allied victory. A boost to the confidence of allied commanders south of Paris, it inflicted disproportionate damage on fragile French morale, and Napoleon lost 4,000 men through **desertion** in the next two days.

La Vendée *See* **Vendée**, La

Lafayette, Marie Joseph Paul de Motier, Marquis de (1757–1834)

French nobleman and soldier whose youthful contribution to the American War of Independence had won international fame. A liberal in favour of political reform, he was a leading member of the Assembly of Notables from 1787, and was a vice-president of the revolutionary National Assembly in 1789. He formed the **National Guard** in July 1789, but his genuine enthusiasm for reform never matched the pace of radicalization in Paris, and he trod an increasingly dangerous path between populism and a desire to reconcile the monarchy with the new order.

He left the capital to command the Army of the Centre on the eastern frontier in the abortive **Valenciennes** offensive of April 1792, before returning to Paris to raise moderate support against **Jacobin** leaders. Sent back to the frontier under protest in July, he was dismissed from command after arresting government representatives at his Sedan headquarters, and responded to recall orders by giving himself up to the Austrians on 19 August. Expecting the usual hero's welcome, he was imprisoned, and remained in captivity until the peace of 1797, when he settled in western Germany.

Though offered the US embassy by the **Consulate**, Lafayette refused all contact with **Napoleon**'s regime, and returned to France on the restoration in 1814. He remained in Paris during the **Hundred Days**, and was elected to Napoleon's last Chamber of Deputies, but was one of the first to demand a second abdication after **Waterloo**. A long and turbulent postwar career reached its final climax during and after the revolution in France of 1830, when he was again a key figure and resumed command of the National Guard.

La-Fère-Champenoise, Battle of

The last major action of the 1814 campaign for **France**, fought on 25 March between **Schwarzenberg**'s allied army advancing on Paris and French forces under **Mortier** and **Marmont** en route to join **Napoleon**'s planned manoeuvre against the allied rear around St Dizier (*see* **Map 26**).

Napoleon had been waiting for his reinforcements since 23 March, but Mortier and Marmont were still some 60km west of St Dizier when they met leading elements of Schwarzenberg's 90,000-strong army at La-Fère-Champenoise. Forced back by vastly superior numbers, they left two divisions of conscripts (4,000 men) to hold the town against the 20,000 troops of Schwarzenberg's leading corps. Only 500 of the rearguard escaped to join 20,000 survivors reeling back towards Paris, and Schwarzenberg hurried on to Meaux, where he joined forces with **Blücher**'s army on 28 March.

News of the defeat informed Napoleon that the allies had not retreated in response to his eastern manoeuvre, and he left St Dizier for Paris on the same day. He was still 30km from the city, at Essonnes, when he received news of its surrender on 31 March. *See also* **Montmartre**, Battle of.

Laffrey, Confrontation at

Highly dramatic meeting on 7 March 1815 between the returning Emperor **Napoleon**, at the head of about 1,000 troops of his personal guard, and a regiment of the royal French Army. Napoleon's tiny force was making for Grenoble, avoiding **Masséna**'s garrison at royalist Marseilles, but was blocked by the regular 5th Regiment at Laffrey, about 25km south of the city. Addressing the regulars personally, Napoleon made an emotive appeal to past comradeship, and followed up with a fictional account of his official summons to Paris, winning them over almost immediately. The success was the turning point enabling Napoleon's **Hundred Days** in power. His arrival in France had been greeted with popular and official uncertainty, but the ecstatic welcome accorded his enlarged 'army' when it reached Grenoble on the evening of 7 March was the first of many on the road to Paris.

Lake Erie, Battle of

Victory by **US Navy** forces over British light naval vessels on Lake Erie in September 1813 that typified the success of small American warships during the **Anglo-American War**. American hopes of annexing Canada's most fertile regions had received an early setback with the fall of Detroit to the British in August 1812, and any attempt to recover the town depended on control of Lake Erie (*see* **Map 27**). A British flotilla of six small warships enjoyed unopposed domination of Erie until mid-1813, when a hastily assembled fleet of nine converted American craft, manned by crews from the east coast states, began patrolling the lake. The two flotillas met on 10 September, and Commodore **Perry**'s American forces proved stronger ship for ship in the confrontation that followed, largely thanks to accurate **rifle** fire from regular **US Army** troops employed as **marines**. Once the British flotilla had been scattered, Perry's ships were used to carry 7,000 troops under General Harrison to Detroit, which fell on 29 September (*see* Battle of **Thames River**).

Lances

Generally viewed as an outdated weapon by the early eighteenth century, but never abandoned as a light **cavalry** weapon by **Polish forces**, the lance made something of a comeback during the war period. This reflected the dispersal around Europe of Polish lancers, who served with the **French**, **Austrian** and **Russian** armies, all of which subsequently reintroduced native lancer units (as did the **Prussian Army**).

Long and cumbersome, the lance called for skill and careful training. Though effective against infantry, and useful in skirmishing or reconnaissance roles, it was of limited value against other mounted troops. Although lancers (known as **Uhlans** throughout central and eastern Europe) sometimes held off conventionally armed horsemen by maintaining formation with their weapons outstretched, they were generally at a serious disadvantage against troops armed with **sabres**. The lance was also favoured by irregular mounted forces, notably **guerrillas** in **Spain**, and was standard (often self-made) equipment for many **Cossack** units.

Landrecies, Battle of

The opening gambit of **Pichegru's** French offensive against **First Coalition** forces in **Flanders** during spring 1794, a bid to relieve the besieged garrison of Landrecies, where the centre of **Saxe-Coburg's** allied drive towards the French frontier had ground to a halt on 20 April (*see* **Map 2**). Some 45,000 French troops moved on Landrecies from 26 April. A frontal assault by 25,000 men under General Chappuis was counter-attacked by **York's** Anglo-German corps after poor manoeuvring slowed its advance, and Austrian **cavalry** under **Schwarzenberg** sent its left wing fleeing back to Cambrai. Meanwhile General Ferrand swung round to attack the town from the east with about 10,000 troops, but was turned back by Austrians under Archduke **Charles**, who took command after **Alvintzi** was wounded. Chappuis was captured during the ensuing withdrawal (carrying Pichegru's orders for an attack against allied positions further north) and his corps suffered some 4,000 losses, against perhaps 2,000 allied casualties. Landrecies surrendered to the allies on 30 April,

freeing Coburg to bolster his threatened flanks (*see* Battles of **Tourcoing**, **Fleurus**).

Landshut, Battle of

The capture of the Bavarian town of Landshut, and its important bridge across the River Isar, by French forces on 21 April 1809. **Napoleon** had recovered the initiative on the Danube front the previous day, attacking the Austrian centre at **Abensberg** and splitting the army of Archduke **Charles** in two. Mistakenly believing that the Austrian southern wing, some 35,000 troops under General **Hiller**, was the larger Austrian force, he sent most of his army in pursuit along the east bank of the Isar late on 20 April.

Napoleon also thought **Masséna** had carried out instructions to get behind the Austrian retreat at Landshut, but Hiller had in fact already occupied the town, and **Lannes** was the first French commander on the scene. He was in the suburbs with Napoleon's advance guard by the late evening of 21 April, but his attack failed to dislodge the Austrians from the bridge or the town beyond. Napoleon arrived a few hours later, and ordered a single detachment of grenadiers under General **Mouton** to charge the bridge. Their attack succeeded, but Hiller had already evacuated the town, and most of his corps escaped towards Neumarkt. While 20,000 French troops under **Bessières** maintained the pursuit, the rest of Napoleon's army turned north towards **Eckmühl** on news that Charles was still at large further north. *See* **Map 12**.

Landwehr

The term used to describe conscript reserve units introduced to the wartime **Prussian** and **Austrian** armies, and to many smaller German forces. Prussian Landwehr, formed for the 1813 campaign in **Germany**, were conscripts aged 17–24, given full training and sent into battle alongside regular units, whose efficiency and fighting value they rivalled. Landwehr expansion was encouraged by governments in most of Germany as a stimulus to growing ethnic self-awareness, but the government of **Austria** was deeply suspicious of raising regionally based forces for the same reason. Austrian **Poland** was excluded from Landwehr conscription, while the Hungarian diet refused to take part until Vienna agreed concessions to its regional autonomy. Largely drawn from Croatia and other imperial fringe territories, Austrian Landwehr were first employed in 1805 and had reached a nominal field strength of some 250,000 men by 1809, but were generally restricted to second-line duties.

Lannes, Jean (1769–1809)

A former apprentice dyer, who was elected junior officer on volunteering for the **French Army** in 1792, Lannes became one of **Napoleon's** most potent battlefield commanders. Though sometimes unable to distinguish between dash and recklessness (like fellow Gascons **Murat** and **Ney**), he was an excellent advance guard commander, free from political ambition, and arguably the best man in contemporary Europe to lead desperate charges against strong defences.

Lannes collected the first of many wounds during the **Pyrenean campaign** of 1793–4, and was a battalion commander on the **Italian** front from 1795, earning Napoleon's praise and promotion to brigadier-general for his actions at **Montenotte**. He was among the first across **Lodi** Bridge in May, and took part in the suppression of Italian uprisings later that month. Wounded at **Mantua** in September, and at **Arcola** in November, he was with **Augereau's** detachment during the **Rivoli** campaign in the new year, and subsequently commanded Napoleon's advance guard pacifying **Tuscany** and the **Papal States**.

Already one of Bonaparte's most trusted companions, Lannes travelled with the **Middle East** expedition of 1798, and had been given command of a division when severely wounded at **Acre** in April 1799. He recovered to fight at **Aboukir** in July, picking up another wound, and accompanied Napoleon to France in August, taking command of the Consular headquarters staff after the **Brumaire coup**.

As commander of Napoleon's advance guard during the **Marengo** campaign of 1800, he won important preliminary actions at the **St Bernard Pass**, **Fort Bard** and **Montebello** in May. Partly in line with **propaganda** requirements, he received little immediate credit for the latter success, but became Duke of Montebello in 1808.

After spells on diplomatic service in **Portugal**, and with forces massing against **England**, he was appointed to the **Marshalate** in 1804, and led the **Grande Armée's** V Corps during the campaigns of 1805–6. He played important roles at **Ulm** and **Austerlitz** in 1805, shared the blame with **Murat** for allowing Russian forces to escape after **Dürrenstein**, but also won acclaim for their inventive seizure of **Vienna**. He was at **Saalfeld**, **Jena** and **Pultusk** before illness (and a wound) forced him out of action until spring 1807, after which he led a reserve corps at **Danzig** and commanded the French centre at both **Heilsberg** and **Friedland**.

Again a corps commander with Napoleon's 1808 invasion of **Spain**, he won the Battle of **Tudela** and commanded the latter stages of the **Saragossa** siege in early 1809. Transferred to Germany, he fought in most of the actions on the Danube against the **Fifth Coalition**, but died on 31 May 1809 of wounds sustained at **Aspern–Essling**.

Laon, Battle of

The most important action of the 1814 campaign for **France**, fought just south of Laon on 9–10 March, as **Blücher's** army threatening Paris from the east was pursued by **Napoleon's** smaller French force (*see* **Map 26**). After narrowly failing to draw Napoleon into a trap at **Craonne** on 7 March, Blücher deployed 85,000 troops and 150 guns in good positions facing south in front of Laon, with **Winzingerode** leading his right, **Bülow** in the centre and two corps (**Kleist** and **Yorck**) along a ridge on the left wing. Anxious to chase Blücher away before turning south to face another allied army on the Seine, and convinced he was pursuing the rearguard of a retiring army, Napoleon ordered **Ney** and **Mortier** to seize Laon from the south early on 9 March. As the thick morning fog lifted, it became apparent that they were facing an entire army.

Without waiting for **Marmont's** 10,000 reinforcements, delayed en route from **Meaux**, Napoleon committed the rest of his 37,000 troops to the battle. Too weak to mount a full-scale offensive, he launched a series of limited frontal attacks against the allied centre through the afternoon. Blücher held back any major counterattack in the belief that 90,000 French troops were in the area and a flank attack was imminent.

Marmont did arrive to attempt a flanking manoeuvre against the extreme allied left during the afternoon, but had only captured the outlying village of Athies before he halted for the night, and failed to secure the narrow defile on which his retreat depended. Yorck and Kleist attacked Marmont at seven that evening, with two reserve corps in support, and his surprised corps barely escaped complete destruction.

Though he heard of Marmont's disaster before dawn, Napoleon elected to stay and fight a limited frontal action on 10 March, giving Marmont breathing space to reorganize his remaining 6,500 troops north of Berry-le-Duc. Blücher meanwhile ordered Yorck and Kleist to pursue Marmont beyond Festieux, and prepared his reserve corps (Langeron and **Sacken**) to move against Napoleon's right flank.

Blücher was ill that morning and command passed to chief of staff **Gneisenau**, who was taken in by Napoleon's demonstrations in the centre. He called off the flank operation, and no major allied attack developed before Napoleon began withdrawing during the evening. Gneisenau sent Winzingerode's corps against the French left next morning, but it was comfortably held off by Ney's rearguard around Clacy, enabling Napoleon and Marmont to escape towards Soissons.

The French had been fortunate to lose only 6,000 troops (against about 4,000 allied losses) when annihilation seemed probable, but the battle had been a serious setback for Napoleon, who by now faced military and political collapse throughout his empire. Able to call on only 75,000 dispirited and inexperienced troops to stop two 100,000-strong allied armies bent on his destruction, he sought to snatch the initiative with a rapid strike against allied forces at **Reims**.

Larrey, Dominique Jean (1766–1842)

French surgeon, appointed as senior doctor with the Army of the Rhine in 1792, whose ceaseless campaigns to improve basic **medical** conditions in the **French Army** bore fruit after he accompanied **Napoleon** to the **Middle East** in 1798. Subsequently attached to all **Grande Armée** operations as surgeon-general, he established a measure of respect for sanitation in French field armies, and supervised many innovations in both the management and the equipment of field hospitals. His most renowned work nevertheless remained strictly practical, and he became famous throughout Europe for his feats of medical organization in the midst of carnage. Ennobled for his efforts at **Aspern–Essling** and **Wagram**, he worked through the **Russian campaign** of 1812, and was always loyal to Napoleon. Wounded at **Waterloo** in 1815, he was a leading medical authority in postwar France.

Lauriston, Jacques Alexandre Bernard Law (1768–1828)

Indian-born **French Army** artillery officer, commissioned in 1785, who saw service on the **Rhine** front against the **First Coalition** but was retired when the war ended. Returning to the army in 1800 as an aide to **Napoleon**, he fought at **Marengo** in June and was a negotiator during the **Amiens** peace talks with **Great Britain**. Promoted brigadier-general in 1802, he achieved divisional rank before sailing with **Villeneuve** for the 1805 **Trafalgar** campaign. He was governor of Venice from late 1807, and commander of the **Imperial Guard** artillery during the invasion of **Spain**, rejoining Napoleon's staff for the Danube campaign in 1809, when his massed artillery played a vital role at **Wagram**. In 1810 he escorted new empress **Marie-Louise** to Paris, and he was ambassador to St Petersburg from February 1811. He joined invading French forces at **Smolensk** in August 1812, leading peace envoys sent to Tsar **Alexander** from **Moscow**, and was a corps commander in **Germany**. Captured at **Leipzig**, he was imprisoned until Napoleon's **abdication**, when he entered royal service. Loyal to the monarchy during the **Hundred Days**, he was created a Marshal of France in 1823.

Le Boulon, Battle of

French attack in late April 1794 against prepared Spanish positions on the **Pyrenean** front at Le Boulon, about 30km south of Perpignan. **Dugommier**'s 35,000 French troops opened offensive operations against a slightly smaller Spanish army from 27 March, advancing to the heavily fortified mountain position at Le

Boulon, where they halted to make careful attack preparations. General de la Union took charge of Spanish forces in late April and began moving troops back to Ceret for an attack against the French flank. His redeployment was caught by preliminary French attacks against unprotected heights to his left on the night of 29–30 April, and he was unable to prevent French capture of two forts overlooking the Boulon position. He decided to abandon his own attacking plans and withdraw beyond the Pyrenees, but **Pérignon** and **Augereau** scattered the retreat by attacking the Spanish left on the morning of 1 May, and a new line between Collioure and St Laurent was only established on 4 May. After initial attacks on the line had failed, exhausted French forces settled down to besiege frontline garrisons through the summer. *See* **Map 5**.

Lebrun, Charles François (1739–1824)

Conscientious French administrator, trained as a lawyer, who played a leading role in attempts to reform the monarchy's finances during the 1770s. He was recalled from retirement to serve as a deputy in the States-General of 1789; his moderate views earned imprisonment during the **Terror** of 1793–4, but he was released by the **Directory** government and elected to the Council of **Ancients** in 1795. He was appointed Third Consul shortly after the 1799 **Brumaire coup**, involving himself in legal and administrative as well as financial reform. On **Napoleon's** establishment as Emperor in 1804, Lebrun became one of 12 imperial 'Grand Dignitaries', taking the title Arch-Treasurer and concentrating on **war finances** until 1805, when he was transferred south to supervise French annexation of the **Ligurian Republic** as its governor-general. Created Duke of Piacenza in 1808, he was again entrusted with a provincial governorship from 1810, taking administrative control of the **Netherlands** after Louis **Bonaparte's** abdication. Restored to royal service in 1814, he was exiled after joining the regime of the **Hundred Days**, but allowed home in 1819.

Leclerc, Victor Emmanuel (1772–1802)

French soldier whose career accelerated when he married Pauline Bonaparte, **Napoleon's** favourite sister, in 1797. Promoted brigadier-general shortly afterwards, and given divisional command in August 1799, he fought under **Moreau** on the **Rhine** in 1799–1800, and led a detachment that arrived too late to aid **Spain** in the 1801 War of the **Oranges**. His most prominent command came at the end of the year, when he led 20,000 men to overthrow the regime of Toussaint **L'Ouverture** at **Santo Domingo**, where he died of yellow fever on 2 November 1802.

Lefebvre, François Joseph (1755–1820)

Born in Alsace, and a sergeant of the Royal Guard in 1789, Lefebvre joined the revolutionary **French Army** in 1792. He spent most of the next five years on the **Rhine** front, becoming a brigadier-general in December 1793, but moved north to lead a division under **Jourdan** at **Fleurus** and the **Roer**. He took part in Jourdan's 1796 Rhine offensive at **Altenkirchen**, **Forcheim** and **Würzburg**, and fought at **Ostrach** under the same commander in early 1799. Wounded and returned to Paris, he failed to secure membership of the **Directory** before becoming the capital's military commander, aiding the **Brumaire coup** by using troops against the Council of **Five Hundred**.

An uncomplicated man, steadily loyal to **Napoleon**, Lefebvre was an original member of the **Marshalate** in 1804, but was left in a **National Guard** command during the 1805 campaign against the **Third Coalition**. Back in the field from September 1806 as **Mortier's** replacement in command of V Corps, he fought at **Jena** and led the **siege** of **Danzig**. A brief **Peninsular** career brought a victory at **Valmaseda** in 1808, and in March 1809 he moved east to the Danube, where his **Bavarian** corps fought at **Abensberg** and **Eckmühl**, but was transferred in May to put down Hofer's Tyrolean rebellion.

Lefebvre led the **Imperial Guard** infantry through the 1812 **Russian campaign**, the struggle for **Germany** in 1813 and the following year's defence of **France**, and rejoined Napoleon for the 1815 **Hundred Days** campaign after briefly serving the restored monarchy. Though he did not return to military service after Napoleon's final fall, he was officially forgiven by the royal government in 1819 and restored to his titles as a peer of France.

Lefebvre-Desnouëttes, Charles (1773–1822)

One of **Napoleon**'s favourite soldiers, Lefebvre-Desnouëttes joined the **National Guard** cavalry of his native Paris in 1789, but left the army two years later, reappearing as a junior officer with the Army of the Alps in 1793. Posted to various frontier armies during the War of the **First Coalition**, and subsequently transferred to northern Italy, he was appointed as one of First Consul **Napoleon**'s aides in February 1800, and was at **Marengo** later that year.

He fought at **Austerlitz** on Napoleon's staff in 1805, and was a brgadier-general under Jérôme **Bonaparte** for the campaign of 1806. He remained with Jérôme through 1807, as a divisional commander with the **Westphalian Army**, but was recalled to French colours and **Peninsular** service in 1808. Wounded at **Saragossa** in June, he returned to Spain with a division of the **Imperial Guard** light cavalry, fighting at **Somosierra** but suffering capture by the British at **Benavente** in December. He eventually escaped in 1812, joining the **Russian** invasion and accompanying Napoleon to Paris during the latter stages of the retreat.

After fighting through the campaign for **Germany**, he was given command of the **Young Guard** cavalry for the defence of **France**, and was among the first senior officers to rejoin Napoleon after his return from **Elba** in 1815. Lefebvre-Desnouëttes led a light cavalry division with **Ney**'s left wing during the **Hundred Days** campaign, and fled a death sentence to live as an exile in the US, Albania and the Netherlands, eventually drowning in a shipwreck off Ireland.

Leghorn, Naval Action off (1795)

Minor brush between British and French fleets in the **Mediterranean** that illustrated the early difficulties surrounding the **Royal Navy**'s practical enforcement of its **blockade** policy. Ordered to transport 5,000 troops against rebels on **Corsica**, French admiral **Martin** led 15 **ships-of-the-line** and three **frigates** out of **Toulon** on 3 March 1795. Missed by British Mediterranean C-in-C **Hotham**'s lax long-range blockade, the French fleet captured a storm-damaged 74-gun battleship (HMS *Berwick*) on 7 March. Hotham

eventually put to sea with 13 battleships from his Tuscan base at Leghorn (Livorno) on 9 March, and made contact with Martin's ships two days later, but foul weather prevented any general engagement over the next 48 hours. On the night of 12 March, the 80-gun French battleship *Ça Ira* collided with the *Censeur* and dropped out of line. It was attacked and severely damaged by a lone British 64-gunner, **Nelson**'s *Agamemnon*, but Hotham let the French depart after a brief exchange of fire on 14 March. Both *Ça Ira* and *Censeur* were captured, but the rest of Martin's force regained Toulon on 24 March, and the British *Illustrious* was lost to bad weather on the way back to Leghorn. The action prompted abandonment of French plans for Corsica, but Hotham's gentlemanly performance attracted criticism from Nelson and other subordinates. *See* **Naval Warfare**; **Map 8**.

Leipzig, Battle of

The climax of the campaign for **Germany** in 1813, a decisive struggle for the vital communications centre of Leipzig fought from 16 to 19 October between French armies east of the Rhine and the combined allied forces of the **Sixth Coalition**. Also known as the Battle of the Nations, it followed from **Napoleon**'s failure to exploit his tactical victory at **Dresden** in late August, and subsequent inability to halt the slow advance on Leipzig of allied armies to its southeast and north.

Tsar **Alexander**, travelling with **Schwarzenberg**'s allied southern wing, sent **Wittgenstein**'s column forward on 13 October to reconnoitre French positions at Leipzig. Napoleon gave orders on 14 October for his armies to concentrate on the city and arrived there around noon, by which time Wittgenstein's reconnaissance force was involved in a fierce but indecisive battle with **Murat**'s cavalry at **Liebertwolkwitz**. By nightfall some 177,000 French troops were around Leipzig, facing more than 200,000 allied troops to the south, and another 54,000 with **Blücher**. **Bernadotte** was some distance further north with another 80,000 Prussians and Swedes.

The easiest approaches to Leipzig were from the south-east and east, where open terrain was dotted with ridges and hamlets. Rivers, woods and marshes provided some natural defence in other directions. The city's man-made defences were in poor condition, but French forces had fortified the suburbs and constructed a strong redoubt at Lindenau, which dominated the marshy approaches to the west. Contingency plans for withdrawal were focused on the roads north, where lack of cavalry meant that Blücher's exact positions were not known.

Napoleon spent 15 September planning an attack east from the city by 120,000 troops, adopting his standard tactic of a frontal attack masking a pincer movement, followed by a final thrust to break the allied centre. **Barclay de Tolly**, technically the overall allied commander, planned secondary attacks from the north, north-west and west, and a main assault by 77,500 troops under Wittgenstein on the French southern positions linking the outlying villages of Markkleeberg, Wachau and Liebertwolkwitz.

The battle to the south of the city opened just after eight thirty on 16 October in wet and misty weather, and the main allied attacks were fully under way within the hour. **Kleist**, **Eugen** and Russian general Gortschakov attacked the village line held by **Victor**, **Mortier** and **Lauriston**, while Meerveldt's Austrians moved up towards **Poniatowski's** western French flank, but General Klenau's intended attack on **Macdonald's** opposite flank failed to materialize. Napoleon meanwhile held back his own attacks while Macdonald and **Sebastiani** struggled through foul weather to reach their positions.

An indecisive frontal battle raged across the southern sector for much of the morning. Meerveldt made limited progress across the marshes, capturing the village of Dolwitz before being halted; Kleist took Markkleeberg but was pinned there by French artillery; Eugen captured, but then lost, Wachau; and Gortschakov was thrown back from Liebertwolkwitz. Allied attacks finally lost impetus at around eleven, after Napoleon broke with his usual practice by bringing up his reserves, including the **Imperial Guard**, at an early stage.

Napoleon had also recalled **Marmont's** corps from its position watching the northern Halle road to join Macdonald's attack, but Blücher

attacked from the north-west at about ten. Sector commander **Ney** ordered Bertrand's corps south instead, but it was switched to repel **Gyulai's** attack on the causeway to Lindenau, and only a reduced corps under **Souham** joined Macdonald's offensive.

Allied attempts to maintain the initiative were halted by French counter-attacks from about midday. **Augereau** and Mortier brought their reserve corps into the southern line and slowly drove the allies back to their original positions, while Macdonald swept Klenau from the heights of the Kolm Berg. Sebastiani's cavalry became tangled in a fight near Klein Possna and Souham's corps failed to arrive on time, so that Macdonald's flank attack had achieved little by two, when Napoleon ordered a massed advance in the centre, led by Murat's 10,000 cavalry.

The allies fell back, but Murat's failure to bring up infantry support enabled Russian cavalry to protect a limited withdrawal. Allied reinforcements under General **Bianchi** arrived to counterattack the French left just after four, driving Augereau and Victor back beyond Markkleeberg. Meerveldt also made progress on the far left, but part of the French Guard and a single, hastily redirected division of Souham's corps restored French gains by the end of the day. Napoleon missed the latter stages of what is sometimes called the Battle of Wachau because he was with Marmont's corps at **Möckern**, where Blücher forced French lines back a few kilometres after a hard fight.

The first day's fighting cost about 25,000 French casualties and about 30,000 allied. In territorial terms it ended as a draw, but the allies were expecting almost 150,000 more troops (under Bernadotte and **Bennigsen**), while Napoleon awaited only **Reynier's** 14,000 reinforcements. Facing mounting odds, Napoleon considered ordering a withdrawal, and made plans to secure his army's passage west, but eventually decided to wait an extra day. His offer of armistice, sent through returned captive General Meerveldt, merely stiffened allied resolution.

Neither side attempted any major advance on 17 October. By the end of the day allied reinforcements were in place, and allied commanders were finalizing plans for a six-pronged attack, when Napoleon decided on a preliminary withdrawal. During the small hours of 18 October, in torrential rain, French forces south of Leipzig pulled back from their outer positions, and work was belatedly begun on bridges across the rivers around Lindenau.

Austrian attacks from the west and south-west were held off while field trains and part of the cavalry began their withdrawal during the morning. During the afternoon neither Barclay de Tolly's attacks on the southern front nor renewed efforts to the south-west made much progress, but in the east Bennigsen slowly drove Macdonald back on the city, and Bernadotte eventually pushed forward in the north. French forces in the latter sectors were forced back into the suburbs by nightfall, their line broken by the defection of two **Saxon Army** divisions.

Napoleon made the final decision to evacuate Leipzig that evening, and the full withdrawal began at about two in the morning. It suffered no interference from the allies for the first five hours, and suggestions of an armistice gained the French a little more time, so that fighting in the suburbs was only really under way by about ten. Allied attacks were then held off by **Oudinot**'s 30,000 rearguard troops, but the retreat was ruined by the premature destruction of the last bridge west to Lindenau, mistakenly blown up when still crowded with French troops and needed to evacuate the rearguard. Some of the rearguard managed to swim the river, but Poniatowski (promoted marshal the previous day) was drowned in the attempt, and survivors taken prisoner included Reynier and Lauriston.

Casualties around Leipzig between 16 and 19 October can only be estimated at perhaps 55,000 allied losses and 38,000 French troops killed or wounded, but another 30,000 of Napoleon's troops were captured on the final day and 5,000 defected to the allies during the battle. French forces also lost more than 300 guns, along with virtually all their wagons and stores. The defeat was a major political disaster for Napoleon, signalling collapse of the **Rhine** Confederation and of French influence in Germany. *See* **Map 25.**

Leith, James (1763–1816)

Scottish soldier who achieved brigade command with the **British Army** in 1804, and fought at **Corunna** with **Moore**'s expedition to **Spain** in 1808–9. He was back in the **Peninsular War** from 1810, commanding a division under **Wellington** until 1812 and playing a major role in the capture of **Badajoz**, after which he returned home to a knighthood and promotion. Lieutenant-general in command of British forces in the **West Indies** from 1814, he died at his Barbados headquarters.

Lemnos, Battle of

Major engagement fought on 19 June 1807 between **Russian** and **Turkish** fleets in the eastern **Mediterranean**. Russian admiral Seniavin's eight **ships-of-the-line** from the **Ionian Islands** had arrived too late to support British operations at the **Dardanelles**, but took the island of Tenedos as a base from which to **blockade** the Turkish fleet. Admiral Pustochkine's Black Sea fleet blocked the entrance to the Bosphorus at the same time, leaving Constantinople short of supplies and contributing to the overthrow of **Ottoman** sultan Selim III.

Using Tenedos as bait, Seniavin sailed his fleet west on 7 May, and doubled back when Turkish commander Said Ali Pasha brought eight battleships and six **frigates** out of the straits to attack the island. Contrary winds slowed Seniavin's return, and though the Russians destroyed three ships run aground just off the Dardanelles coast on 10 May, the rest of the Turkish fleet escaped under the guns of coastal **fortresses**. Turkish forces escaped again when they fell for a similar ruse on 5 June, but were trapped the third time on 10 June, when nine battleships, five frigates and 70 **galleys** were driven to the nearby island of Imbros. Winds allowed Seniavin to send his ships round the island to strike from the rear on 14 June, but the Turks broke away to attack Tenedos and land a force of **Janissaries**. Arriving off Tenedos on 17 June, Seniavin at last had the Turkish fleet cut off from the Dardanelles and followed its flight west to the island of Lemnos.

Seniavin had served on British ships, and emulated **Royal Navy** tactics when he attacked the Turkish battle line off Lemnos at dawn on 19

June. Dividing his force into two columns, he massed his strongest ships to isolate and out-number the centre of the Turkish line. Several Russian ships were damaged during the approach, and the battle developed into a virtually static artillery duel. The Turkish vanguard escaped Admiral Grieg's smaller column, but superior Russian gunnery and Grieg's return to the centre forced the 84-gun *Sedd-ul-Bakir* to surrender before a sudden calm ended fighting by late morning.

Seniavin was able to overtake a Turkish withdrawal towards the Dardanelles next morning, destroying two more ships-of-the-line and three frigates, and then returned to Tenedos to take the surrender of besieging forces. While he took his fleet back to the Adriatic, three Turkish captains were publicly strangled for their poor performance during the action.

Leoben, Preliminaries of

The peace agreement signed on 17 April 1797 by Austrian emperor **Francis II** at Leoben, about 150km south-west of Vienna, that removed **Austria** from the **First Coalition**, and ended fighting on the **Italian** and **Rhine** fronts (*see* **Map 6**). Inspired and concluded by **Napoleon**, in his capacity as Italian front C-in-C and without authority from the **Directory** government, the Preliminaries formed the basis of the final Peace of **Campo Formio**, signed in October.

Liebertwolkwitz, Battle of

Large-scale **cavalry** action around the village of Liebertwolkwitz, some 7km south-east of Leipzig, on 14 October 1813. As the armies of the **Sixth Coalition** drove towards **Leipzig** from the south-east and north, **Napoleon** had concentrated almost 250,000 men between them by early October. While he marched to deal with the threat from the north, **Murat** was left in command of about 42,000 troops (including almost 10,000 cavalry) and 156 guns to protect Leipzig's southern approaches. Napoleon's failure at **Düben** on 9 October encouraged Tsar **Alexander** to test the Leipzig defences with a strong reconnaissance force under **Wittgenstein**. Moving north-west from 13 October, it was met by Murat next day, and the two cavalry forces were engaged for several hours before the French began a steady withdrawal, leaving Liebert-

wolkwitz in allied hands by early afternoon. Though technically defeated, Murat had done his job well enough. Napoleon had reached Leipzig with strong reinforcements around noon, and the village was retaken when Wittgenstein retired that night. *See* **Map 25**.

Ligny, Battle of

One of two simultaneous engagements that opened the **Hundred Days** campaign in 1815 (the other was at **Quatre Bras**), fought on 16 June between French and Prussian forces around the Belgian villages of St Amand and Ligny. A French army of 122,000 men had crossed north of the Sambre on 15 June, taking the two allied armies in the theatre (a total of about 210,000 troops) by surprise, and was on the threshold of positions separating them by the end of the day.

Immediate allied reactions played directly into **Napoleon's** hands by increasing the distance between their forces. To the west of the French position, **Wellington's** composite allied army was ordered to protect its communications with the Channel coast, turning it away from **Blücher's** Prussian army further east. Wellington realized his error early on 16 June, and led his reserve from Brussels to hold the vital road junction linking the allied armies at Quatre Bras, but Blücher meanwhile marched forward to concentrate in the path of the French advance south-west of Sambreffe.

Napoleon expected Blücher to retreat, and planned to strike first at Wellington, but changed his mind after right wing commander **Grouchy** reported the presence of **Zeiten's** 32,000 troops around Ligny. Delighted by Blücher's apparent determination to offer battle, he began concentrating for an attack, but it proved a slow process, and several hours were spent bringing up his reserve (**Gérard's** corps and the **Imperial Guard**). On the Prussian side, corps under Pirch and **Thielmann** reinforced Zeiten during the day, so that by mid-afternoon some 84,000 allied troops and 224 guns faced almost 80,000 men and 210 guns.

Prussian forces were stretched along a 12km defensive line running along the stream through Ligny, its three or four obvious crossing points guarded by one of ten villages or hamlets fortified as strongpoints. Visited briefly by Wellington during preparations, Blücher ignored advice to position most of his infantry on reverse slopes as bad for morale, and French **artillery** opened attacks at about two thirty by wreaking havoc on Prussian reserves crowding forward slopes behind the stream. **Vandamme** and Gérard followed up with frontal charges, while Grouchy led most of the **cavalry** to pin down Blücher's left wing, but French attacks made only gradual gains amid heavy fighting.

Ney had been instructed to send troops from Quatre Bras for an attack on the rear of the Prussian right flank, and Napoleon sent orders hurrying the attack once Blücher had been forced to commit the bulk of his reserves against the frontal assault. When news arrived that a battle was in progress at Quatre Bras, Napoleon called up **Mouton**'s corps from Charleroi, where it had inexplicably been left without orders, and sent new instructions to Ney, intended to move **Drouet**'s corps against the Prussian right.

Perhaps because Napoleon's handwriting was illegible, Drouet's corps became very confused, marching north and then east before eventually appearing alongside Vandamme's corps at about five thirty. An hour before it was expected, and in the wrong place, Drouet's arrival was reported as a Prussian advance, temporarily halting Vandamme's operations and delaying an attack by the 10,000 fresh troops of the Imperial Guard. By the time Drouet had been identified and redirected against the Prussian right, all but one of his divisions had marched back towards Quatre Bras under conflicting orders from Ney.

French frontal attacks had meanwhile suffered heavy losses, but morale remained high and they had forced Blücher to commit most of his reserves to sustain the faltering Prussian line. Blücher had been hoping for support that day from Wellington, or from **Bülow**'s approaching corps, but was forced to think in terms of holding out until nightfall. He used the respite granted by French confusion to lead a counter-attack on Vandamme at about six thirty, but it was turned back when part of the **Young Guard** intervened. An hour later, in gathering darkness and heavy rain, the élite veterans of the Imperial Guard finally charged at Ligny, and quickly broke through to capture the village. The Prussian centre finally disintegrated after a cavalry counter-attack was driven off by the Guard's **infantry squares**, and Blücher himself narrowly escaped death or capture when his horse was killed.

Blücher lost 16,000 men at Ligny, inflicting perhaps 12,000 casualties on Napoleon's army, but French victory was incomplete. Darkness helped the relatively intact Prussian right and left wings to retire in good order, and Napoleon's personal exhaustion may have influenced his decision to limit pursuit. French forces subsequently lost contact with the Prussian main body, forcing Napoleon to make assumptions about its condition and behaviour that would prove fatally inaccurate two days later at **Waterloo**. *See* **Map 28**.

Ligurian Republic

One of several puppet states established around the borders of **France** after the War of the **First Coalition**, the Ligurian Republic was founded in June 1797 to replace the independent north-west Italian republic of Genoa, which had been under virtual French control since the **Nice** campaign of 1792. The new republic was given a constitution on the French model, and was the focus of heavy fighting during the War of the **Second Coalition**. It was dissolved under **Lebrun**'s supervision in June 1805, part joining the new Kingdom of **Italy** and the remainder being absorbed into the French Empire prior to becoming part of a newly created transalpine French province in 1809. Encouraged by British promises to re-establish the republic of Genoa, a successful rebellion detached the region from French rule in 1814, but it was given to the restored Kingdom of **Sardinia** by the Congress of **Vienna** and never regained its independence. *See* **Maps 1, 9**.

Lille, Siege of (1792)

The climax to an allied invasion of north-eastern France in autumn 1792 that was launched in support of **Brunswick**'s ill-fated march on Paris via **Valmy**. French C-in-C **Dumouriez** had rushed men south to meet Brunswick's advance, leaving about 14,000 troops to defend the north-eastern frontier. Local Austrian commander Saxe-Teschen could call on about 20,000 troops for frontline duties, with reserves scattered in garrisons, and attacked French forces between 2 and 5 September, driving them inside Lille's powerful **fortress**. About 15,000 Austrian troops and 50 guns moved up to Lille from 25 September, but could not completely surround the city or prevent the arrival of French reinforcements freed by Brunswick's withdrawal, and faced 25,000 defenders by early October. With his ammunition running low, and news arriving of Brunswick's retreat, Saxe-Teschen abandoned bombardments on 6 October, and withdrew over the next two days. The relief of Lille fuelled gathering popular optimism in France, stimulating voluntary enlistment in the **French Army** and encouraging Dumouriez to mount an autumn invasion of **Belgium**. *See* **Map 2**.

Lindenau *See* **Leipzig**, Battle of

Line-of-battle Ships *See* **Ships-of-the-line**

Liverpool, Robert Banks Jenkinson, Earl of (1770–1828)

Durable English politician who entered parliament as a Tory in 1791 and, apart from a 14-month spell in opposition during 1806–7, held government office for 34 years from 1793. Created Lord Hawkesbury in 1803, he succeeded his father as Earl of Liverpool in 1808. As foreign minister under **Addington** (1801–4) he negotiated the **Amiens** peace with **France**, and he was Home Secretary in **Pitt's** second administration, turning down an offer of the premiership in 1806 and returning to the Home Office under **Portland** in 1807. Widely perceived as the most powerful man in the **Perceval** cabinet of 1809–12, in which he held the important post of minister for war and the colonies, he accepted a second invitation to form a government on Perceval's assassination, and held office as prime minister until his retirement after a stroke in 1827.

Though lacking the important gift of public oratory, Liverpool was Regency **Great Britain's** supreme political manager, and brought unity to the Tory Party after years of internecine squabbling. He was a committed free-trader, and his government's economic policies were generally liberal in nature, but its repressive approach to popular dissent and harsh imposition of corn taxes (unfairly blamed on foreign minister **Castlereagh**) earned a reputation for reactionary conservatism on social issues.

Loano, Battle of

The climax to General **Schérer's** offensive on the **Italian** front in late 1795, a winter attack on Austro-Piedmontese forces pinning the French Army of Italy against the coast east of Nice. Schérer took command in Italy from early October with orders from war minister **Carnot** to undertake an offensive devised by **Napoleon**, then a staff adviser in Paris. Some 16,000 French troops were moved to Nice from the **Rhine** and **Pyrenean** fronts, bringing Schérer's strength up to about 42,000 men, but were not in position until mid-November.

Some 40,000 allied troops north and east of French positions had advanced along the coast to Loano during the summer, but further attacks had been delayed by disputes between Piedmontese general Colli and Austrian commander De Wins. De Wins had just been replaced by General Wallis when the French offensive opened (after heavy snow caused a final week's delay) on 23 November.

Following instructions from Paris, Schérer divided his army into three columns, with **Augereau** and **Masséna** leading attacks along the coast and inland towards Ceva respectively, while **Sérurier** commanded the left wing against Colli's Piedmontese in the mountains. Unprepared for action so late in the year, Wallis abandoned Loano to Augereau in mid-afternoon, and withdrew to Finale after hearing that Masséna had driven D'Argenteau's centre north to the Bormida.

Masséna advanced through the mountains to trap a Piedmontese division next day, and Sérurier's initial difficulties against Colli were eased by the transfer of 5,000 reinforcements from the coast on 25 November. Colli withdrew on Ceva three days later, and Wallis pulled his army back to Acqui on 29 November, abandoning a wealth of supplies at Savona. Having brought **Piedmont** to the point of peace negotiations, the French advance halted in worsening weather. *See* **Map 6**.

Lobau, Count of *See* **Mouton**, Georges

Lodi, Battle of

Relatively minor but celebrated French victory on the **Italian** front in 1796, an attack on Austrian forces holding the bridge across the River Adda at Lodi on 10 May. French C-in-C **Napoleon**'s surprise crossing of the Po at Piacenza, and a trivial setback at **Codogno**, had driven **Beaulieu**'s 35,000 Austrians east across the Adda by 9 May. A rearguard of 10,000 men under General Sebottendorf was left to hold the bridge at Lodi, and though pursuing French vanguards occupied the town itself on 10 May, they could make no progress against 1,000 troops and 12 guns on the eastern side of the bridge.

An élite force of 3,500 French **grenadiers**, assembled specifically for the Po crossing, eventually charged the bridge in dramatic style, capturing it at the second attempt. Sebottendorf's almost immediate counter-attack was halted by the arrival of French divisions under **Masséna** and **Augereau**, and he retreated after a French **cavalry** detachment forded the river upstream to threaten his flank. Having suffered only a few hundred casualties, and inflicted almost 2,000, Napoleon occupied unprotected Milan, where he defied **Directory** orders to share Italian command with **Kellermann** and began planning a new offensive. *See* **Map 6**.

Lonato, Battle of

One of two prolonged and essentially simultaneous engagements fought on the **Italian** front, just south-east of Lake Garda, that saved **Napoleon**'s French Army of Italy from probable defeat by **Würmser**'s larger Austrian force in early August 1796. Napoleon's whirlwind spring offensive had seized northern Italy in less than two months, but failure to force a decisive battle or take **Mantua** left French control vulnerable to a counter-offensive from the Tyrolean Alps. This duly materialized in late July, columns under Würmser and General Quasdanovich advancing down the east and west banks of Lake Garda respectively.

Würmser's eastern column brushed aside **Masséna**'s forward units on 29 July, compelling French abandonment of Verona, and Quasdanovich took Salo before being held by **Augereau**'s division at Brescia on 1 August. As he rushed

troops north from the Mantua, Napoleon was fortunate that Würmser failed to coordinate the rapid junction of his two forces south of Lake Garda. Unsure if Mantua needed immediate relief, Würmser halted at Valeggio on 30 July to await news, and Napoleon's army was barring the way by the time he moved towards the slower Quasdanovich three days later.

While Augereau's outnumbered troops held Würmser at bay, Masséna was sent against Quasdanovich, whose 18,000 men were prevented from advancing beyond Lonato and forced into a temporary retreat after a hard day's fighting on 3 August. Napoleon turned the bulk of his army against Würmser around **Castiglione** on 5 August, while Masséna fought off a renewed challenge from Quasdanovich, sometimes called the Second Battle of Lonato, and forced 10,000 Austrian survivors into a full-scale withdrawal. *See* **Map 6**.

London Naval Agreement (1794)

Accord reached between the British government and **United States** envoy John Jay on 17 November 1794 that defused a potential crisis over **Great Britain**'s 'stop and search' policy towards neutral merchant shipping. Since Britain had joined the **First Coalition**, its maritime **blockade** had entailed the search of neutral vessels and the seizure of those deemed to be carrying contraband. The **Royal Navy** had seized a number of US trading vessels in the **West Indies**, and the London agreement exempted American shipping from interference in the Caribbean. Regarded as a betrayal in **France**, where the government enjoyed very friendly relations with George Washington's administration, the arrangement altered the emphasis of French **naval** and **privateer** activities in the West Indies, which eventually provoked a local Franco-American war in 1798.

Loshnitsa, Battle of

French counter-attack against Russian forces threatening the **Grande Armée**'s retreat across the **Beresina** in late 1812, launched on 23 November around the Plain of Loshnitsa, near the vital river crossing at Borisov (*see* **Map 23**). Once French forces had lost control of the depot city of Minsk in early November, the city's garrison retreated to Borisov, pursued by Admiral

Tshitshagov's Russian corps. Attacked by three Russian divisions, General **Dombrowski's** vastly outnumbered force abandoned Borisov after a ten-hour struggle on 21 November, leaving **Napoleon's** approaching army without access to a bridge over the Beresina. **Oudinot's** corps had been preparing an advance for 24 November, but counter-attacked across the plain a day early and captured 1,000 prisoners along with a considerable quantity of stores. The Russians withdrew to the far bank of the river, abandoning the town of Borisov and destroying bridges behind them. *See also* **Russian Campaign**.

Lough Swilly Expedition

A second French attempt to aid the 1798 **Irish Rebellion**, intercepted by British naval forces on 12 October (*see* **Killala Raid**). Commodore Bompart's 74-gun **ship-of-the-line** *Hoche* and eight **frigates**, along with 3,000 troops and field artillery, left Brest to aid the rebels in mid-September, but their departure was immediately spotted by **Royal Navy** forces on **blockade** duty. After a feint west, Bompart turned for his true destination, Lough Swilly in the far north of Ireland, but was intercepted by Commodore Warren's three British battleships, three frigates and two **sloops** on 11 October. Storm damage had already rendered the *Hoche* virtually unmanageable, and it surrendered within two hours of Warren's attack next morning. Three French frigates also surrendered on the spot, and three of the five that escaped were later captured by pursuing British frigates. The victory calmed British fears of French intervention in **Ireland**, and ended the career of Irish rebel leader Wolfe Tone, captured aboard the *Hoche*.

Louis XVI, King (1754–93)

King of **France** from 1774, Louis was a well-intentioned but essentially feeble ruler, never capable of dominating the volcanic social and economic forces that ultimately destroyed his regime. Deep-seated popular respect for royal authority was eroded by his failure to adopt a consistent line either for or against constitutional reform during the first months of the **French Revolution**, and all hope of identifying the crown with social reform vanished after his attempted flight to the Netherlands was intercepted at Varennes on 21 June 1791. Though he took an oath to the constitution of the **Legislative Assembly** in September, and accepted nominal responsibility for declaring war on **Austria** in April 1792, Louis never regained the trust of the Revolution's political leaders and became the target of mob abuse once the forces of the **First Coalition** began advancing into France in August. Forced to seek shelter with his immediate family in the Temple building from 10 August, he was declared deposed by the new **National Convention** and brought to trial by the new republic in December. Refusing to answer charges of treason, Louis was guillotined on 21 January 1793.

Louis XVIII, King (1755–1824)

Brother of the deposed French king **Louis XVI**, he fled to Brussels in 1791 and proclaimed himself regent to the imprisoned boy-king, Louis XVII, in 1793. French military success forced his undistinguished government-in-exile to migrate steadily eastwards – to **Brunswick** and then to Warsaw – before it decamped to **Great Britain** in 1807. As pretender to the throne after Louis XVII's death in 1795, he lived quietly in southern England until **Napoleon's** fall seemed imminent in 1814.

Already in contact with **Talleyrand**, and proclaimed king in pro-British **Bordeaux** on 12 March 1814, Louis landed at Calais to claim his throne on 14 April. Though prematurely aged, very fat and unable to walk unsupported because of severe gout, he was greeted everywhere as a saviour, but the stresses of postwar reconstruction and the reactionary behaviour of returning émigrés soon brought popular disillusion.

He fled to Ghent with his family during the **Hundred Days** of 1815, until recalled to France (by **Davout**) on Napoleon's second abdication. Chastened by the experience, and now known as 'Louis the Inevitable', he pursued an essentially moderate course over the next decade. Though he soon dispensed with the services of Talleyrand, **Fouché** and other imperial throwbacks, and was unable to prevent the reactionary **White Terror** massacres of 1815, he achieved longer-term restraint of a powerful ultra-royalist faction led by his younger brother, the Comte **d'Artois**.

Louise, Queen (1776–1810)

The daughter of the Duke of **Mecklenburg-Strelitz**, she married the future Prussian king **Frederick William III** in 1793, and was the dominant figure at the Prussian court from his accession in 1797. Universally recognized as a strong-willed champion of Prussian national interests, she was far more popular than her husband, attracting a powerful circle of political supporters behind a programme of internal reform to secure the monarchy's autocratic status and an aggressive foreign policy aimed at territorial expansion. After **Prussia**'s defeats by France in 1806–7, she accompanied her husband to **Tilsit**, attempting to flatter and cajole **Napoleon** into granting a merciful peace, but the French emperor was not moved to make significant concessions, and Louise remained his bitter enemy until her death.

Louisiana Purchase

The sale of Louisiana, a vast colonial territory owned by **France**, to the **United States** in 1803. Some six times the size of the modern US state, Louisiana had been a Spanish colony until 1800, when it was ceded to France by the Treaty of **San Idelfonso**. French authorities had left the sitting Spanish governor in office, and his decision in October 1802 to bar American river traffic from New Orleans, a vital trading post for developing territories inland, triggered negotiations between Washington and Paris for sale of the city.

Special envoy James Monroe reached France on 12 April 1803, a day after French foreign minister **Talleyrand** had informed US ambassador Livingstone that the whole of Louisiana was for sale. The American diplomats signed a treaty and two conventions agreeing the sale for $15 million on 2 May, an arrangement ratified by the US senate on 20 October. Louisiana was occupied in two separate ceremonies, the north in December 1803 and the south the following March, and eventually became the eighteenth state of the Union on 4 June 1812.

Though it fuelled internal friction between American political forces promoting overseas trade and those committed to inland expansion, the purchase is generally recognized as one of history's great bargains, more than doubling the size of the United States at a stroke. That the French Empire was prepared to part with such a potentially valuable possession reflected both **Napoleon**'s chronic need for cash and the extent to which his ambitions were focused on continental Europe.

L'Ouverture, Toussaint (1743–1803)

The first independent ruler of Haiti, L'Ouverture fought against black rebels for the Spanish authorities of Hispaniola in the early 1790s, but joined forces with the French governor of **Santo Domingo** to help defeat a Spanish invasion in summer 1794. His ideological support for a French government committed to the abolition of slavery, and a practical talent for massacring Europeans, were rewarded with the rank of brigadier-general in 1794, and he was promoted divisional general next year. L'Ouverture's troops, far superior to European forces in local conditions, had cleared most Spanish and British contingents from the island by mid-1898, but his ambitions for Haiti's independence had by then brought him into conflict with France. French forces were compelled to quit the island late in the year, but it took L'Ouverture until 1801 to bring a united Haiti under his full control, and to impose a degree of political stability. His regime was toppled by General **Leclerc**'s powerful invasion force in February 1802, and L'Ouverture was deported to France, where the environmental trauma of prison life soon killed him.

Lowe, Hudson (1769–1844)

Irish soldier who saw service at **Toulon**, **Minorca** and **Alexandria** during the **Revolutionary Wars**, but spent much of the period 1805–14 as a liaison officer with anti-French forces in Italy, and was in command of the garrison on **Capri** when it was captured by **Murat** in 1808. Promoted major-general in 1814, he was appointed governor-general of St Helena late in 1815, and was the officer responsible for overseeing **Napoleon**'s captivity on the island for the next six years. Lowe treated his charge with ill-disguised contempt and made little effort at communication, behaviour criticized by contemporary Europeans and reciprocated by the former emperor. Knighted and transferred to Antigua in 1821, he spent the rest of his career in colonial service.

Lübeck, Fall of (1806)

The last act of the **Prussian Army**'s disintegration in the aftermath of the 1806 **Jena–Auerstädt campaign**. By the end of October, General **Hohenlohe**'s surrender at **Prenzlau** and the collapse of garrison defences at Stettin had left General **Blücher** in command of the last coherent Prussian force in the field. While Hohenlohe had been making for the Oder, Blücher had marched north-west from the Elbe, planning to open operations against the rear of the main French advance. With **Bernadotte**'s corps in close pursuit and **Soult**'s only a day behind, Blücher soon modified his aggression, withdrawing towards the **Hanseatic** port of Lübeck, where he hoped to join with reinforcements promised by **Sweden**, thus far an inactive member of the **Fourth Coalition**.

After picking up a detachment under the Duke of Weimar, to bring his overall strength up to about 22,000 men, Blücher passed up the chance to turn and attack Bernadotte's 12,000 troops and marched his entire army into Lübeck on 5 November. The first French troops entered Lübeck at almost the same time, and Bernadotte had forced 10,000 men under **Scharnhorst** into surrender before nightfall. Blücher fled the city at the head of 10,000 survivors, but accepted the hopelessness of his position next day and surrendered to overall commander **Murat** from the nearby town of Ratkau (*see* **Map 16**).

French capture of Lübeck also trapped a Swedish division that had just arrived to support the Prussians. While French troops looted the city, Swedish officers and troops were treated with exemplary courtesy by their chief captor, behaviour that contributed directly to Bernadotte's election as Crown Prince of Sweden in 1810.

Lundy's Lane, Battle of

The last major engagement of the campaign for control of the Great Lakes and surrounding territory during the **Anglo-American War** of 1812–15, a clash on 25 July 1814 between British and US forces contesting the Niagara River frontier. An American invasion force under General Brown had crossed the Niagara and defeated General Riall's British regulars at **Chippewa** (5 July), but Brown had halted his 2,600 troops around Niagara Falls on hearing of strong British reinforcements arriving to the north via Lake Ontario. Assuming that Brown was in retreat, Riall sent a detachment in pursuit from Fort St George, but it halted in the presence of superior forces just north of the falls at Lundy's Lane.

Generals Riall and Drummond rushed forward reinforcements, and some 1,700 British troops were in the area when Brown moved north late in the afternoon of 25 July. Brown's aim was to draw British forces away from his supply depots to the south, but General Scott's brigade ran into Riall's troops almost at once. Scott launched an immediate frontal attack on British defensive positions and broke through on his right (capturing Riall in the process), but the rest of Drummond's line held into the evening. By nightfall both sides had received reinforcements, and fierce fighting went on until Brown and Scott had been wounded, after which US third-in-command General Ripley ordered a withdrawal.

The battle cost the British almost 800 casualties, including 94 dead, and Brown's army lost 172 killed, 572 wounded and 110 missing. The American force retreated to Fort Erie, where it was besieged by Drummond until 17 September, when its successful breakout was the last significant action of the Canadian frontier war.

Lunéville, Peace of

The agreement between **France** and **Austria**, signed on 8 February 1801, that ended the latter's involvement in the War of the **Second Coalition**, leaving **Great Britain** as the only major power still at war with the French republic. Negotiations had opened after the Austrian defeat at **Hohenlinden** in December 1800, and the treaty was essentially a reprise of the 1797 **Campo Formio** agreement. French possession of the **Austrian Netherlands** was reaffirmed, and France agreed to compensate Rhineland princes whose lands had been seized during the war. The **Cisalpine Republic** was extended to include **Parma**, and the latter's duke was given control over **Tuscany** in return, while the King of **Naples** was restored and the Pope confirmed as ruler of the **Papal States**. Though Austria hardly lost any territory relative to 1797, the terms represented the complete failure of Habsburg attempts at recovery, and did little to improve the prospects for long-term friendship between Paris and Vienna.

Lützen, Battle of

The first major confrontation between French and allied armies during the 1813 campaign for **Germany**, fought on 2 May near the Saxon city of Lützen (*see* **Map 25**). The beginning of May found both armies in the process of offensive operations east of the River Saale. French armies began moving towards Leipzig on 1 May, aiming to occupy the Elbe crossing behind General **Wittgenstein's** Russian army advancing slowly from the south-east. Warned of French movements by their dominant **cavalry** forces, allied commanders concentrated between Leipzig and Altenburg for an attack on **Napoleon's** right flank around Lützen.

French forces met heavy resistance along most of their front during the first day, with the most serious fighting taking place around **Poserna**, but **Ney's** advanced corps had occupied Lützen by nightfall and was ordered to protect the eastern flank of the next day's advance on Leipzig. Instructed to hold his position in the unlikely event of a major allied attack, Ney failed to carry out a precautionary reconnaissance or deploy sufficient forces in the villages beyond the city.

Russian reconnaissance had missed the fact that three of Ney's divisions were at Lützen, so that Wittgenstein opted for an attack on Ney's apparently fragile outlying forces around Kaja. With Prussian general **Kleist** occupying Leipzig on its right, and general **Miloradovich** guarding its left at Zeitz, **Blücher's** main Prussian strike force advanced towards Kaja from eleven a.m. on 2 May.

Already running four hours late, the Russian attack hit immediate difficulties. Blücher's cavalry was thrown back after blundering into both of Ney's forward divisions, giving the surprised French time to occupy the villages of Gross Görschen and Starsiedl. When the next allied attack came just before noon, strong Russian **artillery** almost forced a breakthrough at Gross Görschen, but Ney arrived with his three fresh divisions to restore the position with a counter-attack.

Napoleon was en route for Leipzig, as planned,

when he became aware of the threat facing Ney. Leaving a single division to deal with Leipzig, where Kleist was already preparing evacuation, he ordered the rest of his army to the battle zone. Two corps (**Macdonald** and **Lauriston**) were recalled from **Beauharnais's** northern wing to attack the Russian right, with **Marmont** and **Bertrand** on the left, and the **Imperial Guard** forming a central reserve around Kaja.

Finding Ney and Marmont under heavy pressure when he took personal command at about two thirty, Napoleon sent in counter-attacks all along the line, but refused to commit the Guard to the fight, preferring to wait for Bertrand, whose advance had been distracted by the Russian contingent around Zeitz.

Allied attacks were meanwhile faltering. Blücher had been wounded, and **Yorck** took over his tiring frontline troops, but could not be reinforced while General Tormasov's reserves were held back by the tsar, who had no idea of the threat developing against the Russian flanks. Wittgenstein was worried about the flanks, but was unable to commit substantial reserves until four, when he launched an immediate attack against the village line in the centre.

The attack drove the French back towards Kaja, but was eventually halted when part of **Mortier's** reserve **Young Guard** joined the defence. The French line held out until about six, when Macdonald and Bertrand swept against the Russian flanks. Napoleon then unleashed a 70-gun artillery battery, massed at very close range, against the Russian centre, and followed its bombardment with a full charge by the Imperial Guard. This well-orchestrated coup sent Wittgenstein's army reeling back in confusion, but nightfall and cavalry shortages hampered French exploitation efforts, and pursuing infantry were soon halted by Prussian cavalry.

An undoubted if indecisive French victory, Lützen shook the confidence of the allied army, which suffered up to 20,000 casualties (estimates vary, but Prussian dead included chief of staff **Scharnhorst**). Napoleon, who had lost at least 20,000 men, dared not allow the allies time to recover, and followed their eastward retreat in search of a decisive success. *See* Battle of **Bautzen**.

Lützow, Adolf (1782–1834)

Prussian soldier, born in Berlin and present at the Battle of **Auerstädt** in 1806, who was authorized to form a volunteer **Freikorps** by army chief of staff **Scharnhorst** at the start of the campaign for **Germany** in 1813. The Lützow-Korps, or Black Jägers, became the most famous of many independent units conducting operations against French rear areas during the campaign, and its commander was subsequently revered as an early German nationalist hero. Lützow led his troops as part of the **Prussian Army** during the campaigns of 1814–15, and commanded a regiment of **Uhlans** at the Battle of **Ligny**.

Luxembourg

One of many small independent principalities on the prewar eastern French frontier, the Grand Duchy of Luxembourg formed part of the front line during the campaigns along the **Rhine** of 1793–5, with the town of Trier a focus for repeated confrontation at the northern end of the theatre. **Prussia's** withdrawal from the **First Coalition** in spring 1795 left the capital exposed to overwhelming French force, and its 12,500 troops surrendered to General Hatry on 7 June. Luxembourg was then annexed by France, and remained in French hands until 1815, when its independence was formally restored by the Congress of **Vienna**.

Lyon, Siege of (1793)

Encouraged by rebellion in La **Vendée**, the three most important cities in the strongly royalist south of **France** – Lyon, Marseilles and **Toulon** – were in the hands of anti-republican popular leaders by July 1793, forcing the elder General **Kellermann** to deploy his otherwise largely inactive Army of the Alps against them. Leaving 12,000 troops to guard the Swiss frontier, Kellermann sent detachments to Marseilles and Toulon, and led some 8,000 men to Lyon in late July. Facing about 20,000 citizens organized for the city's defence, Kellermann delayed any attack in the hope of reaching a negotiated agreement, while poor organization, and interception of reinforcements en route from Marseilles, prevented royalists from attacking in superior numbers. Harassed by a government determined to make an example of the rebels, and sent 5,000 reinforcements, Kellermann mounted a desultory **siege** through August and September, and the failure of a major sortie on 8 October enabled his replacement, **Doppet**, to seize the badly damaged city two days later.

M

Maastricht, Battle of

The first major setback for French forces invading the independent **Netherlands** in spring 1793. General **Miranda** had advanced his Meuse army north along the river towards Venloo from 11 February, guarding the right flank of the main invasion force under C-in-C **Dumouriez**. He pulled back on the approach of **Saxe-Coburg's** imperial forces from the east, and settled down to besiege Maastricht with 20,000 troops on 20 February. Saxe-Coburg sent 35,000 men (under **Clairfait**, the Prince of Württemberg and Archduke **Charles**) against French positions running east of the Meuse from Maastricht on 2 March, driving General Lanoue's disorganized division back from Aix-la-Chapelle and forcing the whole French right to retreat across the Meuse towards Liège. The rest of Miranda's command was scattered as it joined a retreat that finally halted at Louvain (Leuven), where he scraped together some 13,000 survivors and was joined by Dumouriez. Archduke Charles, in operational command of the Austrian force, halted the chase at the Meuse, but eventually moved south-west to confront Dumouriez at **Neerwinden** on 18 March. *See* Battle of the **Roer**; Map 2.

Macdonald, Jacques Etienne Joseph Alexandre (1765–1840)

The son of an exiled Scot, commissioned into the royal **French Army** in 1784, Macdonald was a staff officer with **Dumouriez** and **Pichegru** during the early campaigns against the **First Coalition**. A brigadier-general from August 1793, he fought in **Flanders** at **Hondeschoote**, **Tourcoing** and **Tournai** before promotion to divisional command in November 1794. He went to Italy as governor of Rome in 1798, played a major role in the **Neapolitan campaign** from November, and replaced **Championnet** in command of the Army of Naples from February 1799. Prone to overconfidence, he suffered a disastrous defeat at the **Trebbia** in June that damaged his reputation and almost handed the **Italian campaign** to the allies.

Transferred to the **Rhine** in late 1799, he was **Moreau's** second-in-command until 1801, when he undertook a diplomatic mission to **Denmark**. He risked disgrace to support Moreau against treason charges in 1804, and was left without a command for the next three years, returning to active service in 1807 with Joseph **Bonaparte's** reorganized **Neapolitan Army**. His troops fought under **Beauharnais** in Italy against the **Fifth Coalition** in 1809, and marched north to play an important part in the victory at **Wagram**. Promoted marshal in the field on 12 July, he became the Duke of Tarentum in December.

After holding a **Peninsular** command in Catalonia, he led X Corps on the northern wing of the **Grande Armée** for the 1812 **Russian campaign**, spending most of the year in a fruitless siege of **Riga**. He commanded the French right wing during the first phase of the campaign for **Germany** in 1813, fighting at **Lützen** and **Bautzen**, but suffered another major defeat at the **Katzbach** in August. Almost captured at **Leipzig**, but successful at **Hanau** in late October, he fought a somewhat fatigued campaign in **France**, failing to motivate his troops into action at **Château-Thierry** and urging Napoleon to quit his throne after the fall of Paris.

Macdonald accompanied **Ney** and **Caulaincourt** in delivering the emperor's **abdication** offer to allied leaders on 4 April. Entering royal service, he escorted the king into exile at the start of the 1815 **Hundred Days**, and played no part in the subsequent campaign, enjoying a long and honoured postwar retirement.

Maciejowice, Battle of

The defeat that effectively ended the nationalist uprising in **Poland** of 1794. Facing a combined Russian and Prussian invasion during the autumn, Polish rebels under General Kosciusko were concentrated in fortified positions protecting Warsaw. They had already halted attacks by Prussian forces in July, and an attempt to bring up **siege trains** from Danzig and Thorn had been thwarted by peasant bands in the countryside, but Kosciusko's position was undermined by the advance from the east of 14,000 Russians under **Suvorov**.

Suvorov defeated General Sirakowski's rebel column at Korschin on 19 September, and moved to join General Fersen's 12,000 Russians in front of Warsaw, forcing Kosciusko to abandon his defensive security in the hope of preventing the juncture. Without waiting for reserves to arrive, Kosciusko's 10,000 men met Fersen's Russians near Maciejowice on 4 October. Unaware that Suvorov was already across the Vistula and in contact, Kosciusko accepted battle next day. Quickly outflanked by Russian **cavalry** on their left, the Poles broke and fled, leaving their wounded commander to be taken prisoner. Suvorov and Fersen then united for a march on Warsaw (*see* Battle of **Praga**).

Mack, Karl Leiberich von, Baron (1752–1828)

Austrian officer, in service since 1770, who was a commoner by birth but ennobled for bravery at the siege of Belgrade in 1789. A staff colonel at the start of the **Revolutionary Wars**, he resigned after the Battle of **Neerwinden** in 1793, but was promoted major-general later that year and led delegates in London planning the **First Coali-**tion's spring offensive in January 1794. On the **Rhine** front from April, he resigned again in 1795, but was recalled in 1797 and promoted to divisional command, taking detached duty as C-in-C of the **Neapolitan Army** in October 1798. Forced to flee into French captivity for his own safety after his **Neapolitan campaign** failed in early 1799, he broke **parole** to escape from Paris in 1800, and spent the next few years in semi-retirement on his Bohemian estate.

Mack had built a considerable reputation as a military theorist, developing a self-consciously 'scientific' approach to tactics and manoeuvres that never worked in practice but found considerable favour at the Viennese court. A dedicated self-promoter with a highly optimistic view of the **Austrian Army**'s capabilities, he returned to favour in 1805 and was given effective control over planning for the forthcoming War of the **Third Coalition**. Responsible for the ill-advised policy of sending Austria's main army into an unsupported advanced position, and for its abject surrender at **Ulm** in October 1805, his relatively humble background sealed his fate as the disaster's prime scapegoat. Dismissed and court-martialled, he was sentenced to death, commuted to 20 years' imprisonment. The sentence was lifted in 1808, and he was pardoned in 1819.

Madrid Uprising (1808)

Bloody but short-lived popular revolt against French occupation of the Spanish capital that broke out on 2 May 1808. It erupted in protest at **Napoleon**'s effective deposition of the Spanish royal family, and heralded a nationwide rebellion for the restoration of 'king and church' in **Spain**.

Popular enthusiasm had greeted the arrival of French troops in Madrid on 24 March, but C-in-C **Murat**'s refusal to recognize Prince **Ferdinand** as king and the strain of supporting an occupying army had sparked riots in the city on 1 April. Pacified without much difficulty by military governor **Grouchy**, Madrid remained in a state of uneasy calm until 2 May, when news of French orders to arrest those members of the royal family not already at **Bayonne** brought rioters on to the streets in far greater numbers.

While stray Frenchmen were being murdered

by lynch mobs, French **cavalry** and a detachment of **Mamelukes** were called in from outside the city, but met determined resistance and only restored a semblance of order after three hours of street fighting had left 150 Frenchmen and perhaps 500 Spaniards dead. Murat immediately imposed martial law, deployed **artillery** inside the city to deal with any repetition and began a savage reprisal programme.

The events of 2 May ended any hope of popular cooperation with French rule in Madrid, but this was not recognized by Napoleon, who believed that Joseph **Bonaparte's** arrival as Spain's new king would be welcomed as a guarantee of stability. Instead news of Ferdinand's deposition sparked separate anti-French risings all over Spain during the last ten days of May, and by 10 June every regional **junta** had taken up arms against the invader. Though Joseph was recognized by the tame Regency Junta in Madrid, he faced a hostile reception on his arrival in the summer, and fled the capital almost immediately on news of the French defeat at **Bailén**. *See also* **Peninsular War**.

Magdeburg, Siege of

The key Prussian **fortress** of Magdeburg, guarding the natural frontier of the Elbe, stood in the path of French forces pursuing the defeated Prussian Army after the Battles of **Jena** and **Auerstädt** in October 1806 (*see* War of the **Fourth Coalition**). The remnants of General **Hohenlohe's** routed army took shelter in the fortress just before **Murat's** French **cavalry** arrived outside the walls on 20 October. Hohenlohe refused Murat's surrender demand and escaped from Magdeburg the next day, leaving 25,000 troops under General **Kleist** to face investment by some 40,000 French troops under **Soult** and Ney.

The brief **siege** that followed was a desultory affair, conducted by only 18,000 French troops once Soult's corps had been returned to front-line duties, and enlivened only by a few skirmishes. A failed Prussian sortie on 4 November was followed by a French threat of artillery bombardment, and Kleist opened surrender negotiations on 7 November, marching his troops out of the fortress as prisoners of war four days later.

Though hardly of epic proportions, the defence was one of very few serious attempts to stem the French advance on Berlin. *See* **Map 16**.

Magnano, Battle of

The second defeat suffered by French forces on the River Adige at the start of the 1799 **Italian campaign**. After his enforced retreat from **Verona** on 30 March, French C-in-C **Schérer** abandoned plans to cross the Adige near Lake Garda and prepared to meet an Austrian attack on his main positions around Magnano. It opened at around midday on 5 April, and the central Austrian advance on Magnano took the undefended town, but it was counter-attacked just beyond and driven back with about 1,000 losses. The most serious early fighting took place on the southern flank, where 14,000 men under **Victor** and Grenier drove 7,000 Austrians back towards Tomba, but temporary Austrian commander **Kray** (deputizing for **Melas**) sent in 10,000 reserves to drive the French back to the River Tartaro in disarray. Kray then switched his reserves against **Moreau's** central French advance, which was making good progress on the southern approach to Verona, and which held its ground against counter-attacks until ordered to join a general French withdrawal that evening. Schérer took his battered army, shorn of at least 5,000 casualties, west across the Mincio next day, and retired beyond the Adda on 12 April. Snail-like Austrian pursuit halted on 15 April, when Russian commander **Suvorov** arrived to supersede Melas, signalling a general pause for reorganization in the theatre. *See* **Map 6**.

Maida, Battle of

Limited British victory against French forces occupying southern Italy in July 1806. French invasion of **Naples** had installed Joseph **Bonaparte** as king in February, but the maintenance of small-scale resistance in the south-west, particularly at **Gaeta**, encouraged the dispatch of General **Stuart's** 5,200 British troops from **Sicily** to aid a supposed anti-French rebellion. Not given **cavalry** support, the expedition reached the Calabrian coast on 30 June, finding no sign of active popular royalism.

Local French commander **Reynier** marched to meet the British with some 6,400 troops of his own, including about 1,000 cavalry, and launched an immediate attack when he came up on the British line around the village of Maida on 6 July. French troops advanced across open country in columns, and Stuart's men held their fire behind a ridge until the last moment, before advancing to launch repeated close-range **musket** volleys and a **bayonet** charge. Stuart lost only 330 men in the action, inflicting 1,700 casualties and taking 1,000 prisoners as the French fled. He made no attempt to pursue Reynier, proceeding down the coast towards Gaeta and re-embarking for Sicily on news of its fall. Though strategically irrelevant, Stuart's victory was welcome to a **British Army** bereft of recent triumphs, and offered a glimpse of **infantry tactics** that would later succeed in the **Peninsular** theatre. *See* **Map 9.**

Mainz, Siege of (1793)

The focus of operations on the **Rhine** front during the summer of 1793, the **fortress** city of Mainz was besieged by **First Coalition** forces after their victory at **Bingen** in late March had driven French forces south beyond Worms (*see* **Map 3**). Prussian forces under Kalkreuth opened siegeworks on 6 April, and allied C-in-C **Brunswick** followed orthodox eighteenth-century **cordon** tactics in halting his entire army to protect their flanks. Garrisoned by some 22,000 French troops, Mainz was under full **siege** by 14 April, but tactical indecision and occasional French sorties delayed attacks on outpost positions until mid-June. Unable to feed such a large defending force, the city eventually surrendered on 22 July.

The French government had meanwhile assembled 90,000 troops under Generals Houchard and Beauharnais (husband of the future Empress **Joséphine**) for an offensive from Alsace to relieve Mainz, but they were not ready to advance until 18 July and halted on news of the surrender. Beauharnais retreated when threatened by **Würmser's** Austrian corps a few days later, and was guillotined for his failure, but the garrison at Mainz (and those at fortresses in **Flanders**) had given the government a vital breathing space by distracting invasion forces, and their **parole** terms permitted immediate redeployment against rebels in La **Vendée**.

Maison, Nicolas Joseph (1771–1840)

A volunteer with the French **National Guard** in 1789, Maison fought in **Flanders** at the start of the War of the **First Coalition**, but was dismissed from the army in 1793. Provisionally recommissioned as a captain in 1794, he was fully reinstated from 1796, fighting on the **Rhine** and **Italian** fronts before 1801, and under **Bernadotte** against the **Third Coalition** in 1805. He was at **Austerlitz**, and commanded a brigade against the **Fourth Coalition**, becoming **Victor's** chief of staff in 1807. Created a baron of the empire in 1808, he fought in the **Peninsular** campaign of that year and in Germany against the **Fifth Coalition** in 1809. With **Oudinot's** corps during the 1812 **Russian campaign**, he was given divisional rank after the first Battle of **Polotsk** in August, surviving to fight in **Germany** during 1813 and on the north-eastern frontier during the 1814 defence of **France**. Pledged to royal service after **Napoleon's** abdication, he took no part in the **Hundred Days** campaign of 1815, and enjoyed a successful postwar political career, culminating in spells as foreign minister and war minister.

Malet Conspiracy

Attempted coup in Paris that almost succeeded in overthrowing the Napoleonic regime in October 1812. Brigadier-General Claude-François Malet (1754–1812), a republican soldier who had been an inveterate opponent of **Napoleon's** personal government, was imprisoned for conspiracy in 1808 but transferred to a mental institution in Paris two years later. He escaped on 23 October 1812 and announced Napoleon's death, along with the formation of a new republic. Amid uncertainty surrounding the **Russian campaign** the claim was believed by a number of senior officials, but the bluff broke down when the capital's military governor challenged Malet, who shot him dead. Arrested on the spot, Malet was tried and executed on 29 October, along with 16 republican conspirators.

Maloyaroslavets, Battle of

Indecisive but significant engagement fought between the vanguards of French and Russian forces on 24 October 1812, during the early stages of the **Grande Armée's** retreat from **Moscow**.

Napoleon had opted for a south-westerly retreat that would lead his army through fertile areas en route for Smolensk, but into the path of **Kutuzov**'s Russian army around Kaluga. Increasingly miserable French troops set out on 19 October for the important road junction of Maloyaroslavets, on the River Lusha about 110km south-west of Moscow. Weighed down by loot, and slowed by heavy rain over the first two days, the Grande Armée was not a difficult target, and Russian **cavalry** kept Kutuzov well informed of its positions, but no attempt was made to prevent French progress until 22 October, when General **Doctorov**'s corps eventually left Tarutino for Maloyaroslavets.

The first division of **Beauharnais**'s leading French corps reached the bridge over the Lusha north of Maloyaroslavets on the evening of 23 October, and drove off a small **Cossack** detachment to occupy the town, but a strong Russian counter-attack during the night forced it back over the river. Doctorov's **artillery** drove off an attack on the bridge at dawn next morning, but the arrival of French guns turned the next attempt, and the town changed hands several times during the morning's fierce fighting that followed.

Kutuzov had moved the rest of his army into positions some 30km south of the town during the day, and the first reinforcements reached Maloyaroslavets to sustain flagging Russian resistance during the late morning, but Doctorov decided to abandon the town when Beauharnais committed his last reserves shortly after noon. Beauharnais's corps suffered about 4,000 casualties during the day.

The Russians did not go far, occupying a ridge just to the south, and their artillery fire dissuaded Napoleon from attempting a major river crossing. Russian forces withdrew towards Kutuzov's main position in mid-afternoon, but though the battle was claimed as a French victory, Napoleon's subsequent actions turned it into a tactical defeat. He would not risk exposing his troops to a renewed attack that day, and dropped plans to use the roads to Smolensk from Maloyaroslavets, turning the army towards Oshogivo, Mojaisk and a route home that condemned it to starvation. *See also* **Russian Campaign**.

Malta, Seizure of

The central **Mediterranean** island of Malta had been governed by the Order of the Knights of St John since the sixteenth century. Well positioned as a naval base, it was vulnerable to conquest after losing the protection of the French monarchy, but the knights secured a defensive alliance with Tsar **Paul I** in November 1797, ceding Russian control over their Polish branch in return.

French forces en route for the **Middle East** in 1798 had orders to seize Malta, and Admiral **Brueys**'s escort fleet arrived off the island on 9 June. Troops under d'Hilliers and **Desaix** were landed next day and occupied Valetta on 12 June, having lost only three dead to small-scale resistance. Over the next five days **Napoleon** restructured the island's administration and deported all but a few French knights who chose to join his army. Most migrated to St Petersburg, where Grand Master Hompesch was deposed in favour of the tsar on 7 November 1798.

Napoleon left 4,000 men under **Vaubois** to garrison the island, and **Nelson** opened British efforts to dislodge them in late October, when troops were landed ashore to support local rebels against French rule. Five warships were left on permanent station at the harbour approaches, but supply difficulties forced the British to loosen their blockade in summer 1799, enabling Vaubois to gather supplies from the surrounding countryside and maintain resistance at Valetta. After a series of attacks by 2,300 British and **Neapolitan** troops, supported by some 4,000 native militia, in June 1800, and the arrival of another 1,500 British reinforcements, food shortages finally forced French surrender on 5 September.

The British government agreed to surrender Malta to the Knights of St John, and thus to **Russia**, by the terms of the **Amiens** peace in 1802. With Russian agreement, they held on to the base through early 1803 pending Napoleon's fulfilment of treaty obligations, and it became a source of mounting Anglo-French tension before the resumption of war in 1803. Still a **Royal Navy** base in 1815, it became a British imperial possession after the Congress of **Vienna**. *See* **Map 8**.

Mamelukes

Elite mounted troops in the service of the **Ottoman Empire**, originally recruited in the thirteenth century from European (mostly Balkan) child slaves sold at Middle Eastern markets. Renowned as fierce warriors and superb horsemen, Mamelukes were the dominant ruling caste in the semi-autonomous Ottoman province of **Egypt** in the late eighteenth-century, ruling by a combination of brute force and arrangement with Constantinople. The regime's unpopularity and instability encouraged French assumptions that Egypt was ripe for invasion in 1798, and the three-year campaign in the **Middle East** triggered a descent into factionalism from which Mameluke influence never recovered.

Mamelukes were tactically naïve by contemporary European standards, possessing only a few ancient firearms (seldom used) to back up their standard weaponry of scimitar, ball-and-chain, mace and dagger. They suffered regular defeats against French forces, but their fierceness and formidable close-combat performance impressed European observers, and **Napoleon** recruited a number for service in his personal guard. They later fought with the Consular and **Imperial Guard**, but remained dangerously difficult to discipline and were never deployed in groups of more than 100 men. Napoleon's personal Mameluke, the giant Roustan, became an international figure of some notoriety, lurking menacingly at his master's side during all public appearances.

Mannheim Campaign (1795)

A series of major operations on the **Rhine** front in autumn 1795 that left both sides in the theatre almost exactly where they started. The withdrawal of **Prussia** from the **First Coalition** in the spring left about 170,000 Habsburg troops in the theatre, under **Clairfait** to the north and **Würmser** to the south. They faced about 145,000 French troops under **Pichegru** and **Jourdan**, who were ordered to combine for an offensive across the Rhine in the early autumn.

Jourdan's forces crossed the river at the northern end of the allied line on 6–7 September, taking Düsseldorf with ease, and moved south down the east bank from 8 September. The Austrian corps in their path retreated from Neuwied, allowing three more French divisions to cross the Rhine there, and by 20 July Jourdan had collected 60,000 men along the north bank of the Lahn between Nassau and Wetzlar. French troops marching south from positions west of Mainz took Mannheim on the same day, and news of this threat to his rear sent Clairfait even further south, so that he was across the Main by 23 July.

Pichegru was slow to advance from Mannheim into the ground between the Austrian armies, halting after a failed attack towards Heidelberg (led by brigades under **Davout** and **Bertrand**) on 24 September. While Jourdan detached **Kléber** to besiege Austrian forces in Mainz, and Pichegru remained inactive, Clairfait had time to collect 25,000 reinforcements from Würmser and return to the Main for an attack of his own from Frankfurt on the night of 10–11 October. Threatening to outflank Jourdan's left wing, it drove French forces back over the Rhine at Düsseldorf, Bonn and Neuwied from 16 October, though Kléber had to fight off Austrian **cavalry** for a day because the Neuwied bridge was blown early by French **engineers**.

Clairfait would not be drawn north again, concentrating on the Main while Würmser drove Pichegru back into Mannheim with attacks on 18 and 29 October. The second attack coincided with a successful Austrian sortie against 30,000 French troops west of Mainz, but Clairfait followed up the success very slowly, eventually attacking Pichegru at the Pfrin on 10 November and driving him back beyond Mannheim to the Queich by 16 November. Mannheim's 6,000 garrison troops surrendered on 22 November, and further attacks by both sides achieved nothing in increasingly bad weather before Clairfait proposed an armistice for the winter on 19 December. The exhausted armies on the Rhine ceased fire along agreed demarcation lines from 1 January. *See* **Map 3**.

Mannheim Offensive (1799)

Abortive French attack across the **Rhine** in late summer 1799, undertaken in an attempt to take pressure from the **Italian** front, where **Joubert's** French army was defeated at **Novi** in mid-August.

Temporary French commander General Muller was holding the length of the frontier with only about 52,000 troops, but led about 22,000 men across the river at Mannheim on 26 August. They were pursuing General Sztarray's retreating Austrian corps west towards Heidelberg when it was joined on 11 September by Archduke **Charles** with 25,000 reinforcements from the **Swiss** front. Frightened into retreating back across the Rhine, Muller left only a brigade under Laroche to defend Mannheim. Attacked from two directions, and defending walls partly demolished during the French advance, Laroche was forced to surrender on 18 September. *See* Map 3.

Mantua, Sieges of (1796)

The imposing **fortress** city of Mantua, at the confluence of the Mincio and Po rivers in northern Italy, was the linchpin of Austrian imperial control over Lombardy and one of the pillars of its **Quadrilateral** defence system (*see* **Map 6**). Isolated from **Beaulieu's** retreating army after defeat at **Borghetto** in late May 1796, 4,500 Austrian troops fell back on Mantua, bringing garrison strength up to 12,000 men and 316 guns. French C-in-C **Napoleon's** initial attempt to storm the defences failed on 31 May, and he began planning a major attack immediately afterwards.

Guarded on its northern and eastern sides by three lakes, and by marshlands to the south and west, Mantua was a tough target. Its sophisticated fortifications were further protected by a series of outer strongpoints, including the citadel. The Fort St Georges outpost fell to a French attack on 3 June, but Napoleon marched **Augereau's** division south next day, leaving **Sérurier** and 9,000 troops to conduct a formal **siege**.

Napoleon's success in pacifying the **Papal States** and **Tuscany** yielded enough heavy **artillery** to form a **siege train**. Taken first to Milan, where the citadel garrison was forced to capitulate on 29 June, it was at Mantua to support a failed assault on 17 July. With no sign of the garrison faltering, artillery was deployed to undertake the city's painstaking reduction, but the approach of **Würmser's** reinforced Austrian

army from the Tyrol forced Napoleon to abandon the siege on 31 July, leaving behind 179 guns.

A second siege of Mantua was established from 24 August 1796, and formed a backdrop to **Italian** operations for the next six months. After his defeat at **Bassano**, Würmser led survivors into Mantua on 13 September, raising the garrison's strength to 23,000 men but multiplying pressure on food supplies. Würmser led a major breakout attempt two days later, but lost 4,000 men and 28 guns when **Masséna's** division arrived to support besieging forces.

Despite losses to disease, Mantua was running dangerously short of rations by the time **Alvintzi's** renewed Austrian invasion retreated from **Arcola** in late November. A subsidiary column of some 7,000 troops under **Provera** managed to approach Mantua during the Battle of **Rivoli**, but was halted by Sérurier's troops on 15 January. Würmser's final breakout attempt failed to penetrate the cordon next morning, and Napoleon's main army arrived that afternoon, compelling Provera to surrender at La Favorita and prompting the capitulation of 16,000 effective garrison troops on 2 February.

Marengo, Battle of

The major confrontation between French and Austrian forces on the **Italian** front in 1800, fought on 14 June at the Plain of Marengo, a few kilometres east of Alessandria (*see* **Map 9**). Austrian C-in-C **Melas** had launched his opening offensive of the year in April, but had waited for **Genoa** to fall before beginning a planned invasion of France. This gave **Napoleon** time to bring the French Reserve Army across the **Great St Bernard Pass** and concentrate it around Stradella, placing 40,000 troops directly across the Austrian line of retreat.

Genoa's fall on 4 June deprived Napoleon of the initiative, giving Melas an alternative supply route, and French units were sent forward to seek out a confrontation before the Austrians, then dispersed around north-east Italy, could concentrate their superior numbers. Melas meanwhile called Ott's 18,000 men up from Genoa, and marched towards Alessandria in search of the French. As they converged, neither commander knew much of the other's intentions. Napoleon remained convinced Melas was trying to retire on Genoa, and sent a division under **Desaix** to cut off all potential escape routes, while Melas believed that only a quick victory would prevent Napoleon receiving large-scale reinforcements.

After a preliminary engagement at **Montebello** on 9 June had revealed the whereabouts of the two armies, Melas concentrated his forces around Alessandria for an attack on French positions across the Plain of Marengo. Launched early on 14 June, in bright and clear conditions, it was slowed by inadequate **pontoons** over the Bormida River, but still took Napoleon by surprise. Two divisions under **Victor** held off the brunt of the attack for an hour before Napoleon committed reinforcements, bringing his total strength on the battlefield up to about 15,000 men, with only 600 cavalry and 15 guns, against some 30,000 Austrians with 5,000 cavalry and 100 guns.

By mid-morning Napoleon had realized he was facing more than a rearguard, and issued orders recalling Desaix (and another detached division under Lapoype), but with pressure building against his outnumbered troops in the centre, and a flank attack threatening to sweep round his rear from the north, his position remained desperate. Although a counter-attack against the northern flank delayed the collapse of its central position, the entire French army, now totalling about 23,000 men, was driven into full-scale retreat by mid-afternoon.

At this stage Melas, slightly wounded and considering the battle won, left conduct of pursuit operations to his chief of staff, General Zach. Zach's heavy-handed manoeuvring gave Napoleon time to reorganize his forces around San Giuliano, and allowed Desaix to join the battle, almost two hours earlier than expected. In the early evening Napoleon launched a well planned and executed counter-attack, preceded by a concentrated bombardment from his few available guns, that caught the approaching Austrians strung out in columns. An opportunist flank charge by **Kellermann's** 400 cavalrymen turned the retreat of their forward units into a rout, and vigorous French pursuit had driven the Austrians from the field by nine, with only Ott's troops on the northern wing retiring in good order.

Napoleon's uncharacteristic division of forces on the eve of the battle had almost proved fatal, and the victory cost around 7,000 French casualties, with Desaix among the dead. The Austrians lost about 6,000 dead and 8,000 prisoners, along with 40 guns, and the defeat broke Melas. He asked for an armistice next day and the same evening signed the Convention of Alessandria, agreeing to withdraw all Austrian forces (including garrison troops) from northern Italy, and to suspend all military operations in the theatre pending Vienna's response to a new French peace offer. Though the Austrian government delayed a peace settlement until after its defeat on the **Rhine** in December, Napoleon's victory at Marengo ended the War of the **Second Coalition** in Italy. *See* **Map 10**.

Maret, Hughes-Bernard (1763–1839)

French lawyer who developed his political career as publisher of the *Bulletin de l'Assemblée* (subsequently merged with the *Moniteur* to become the official government organ), and served as a diplomat from 1792 to 1799. A supporter of the **Brumaire coup**, he became secretary-general to the **Consulate** and then head of **Napoleon's** personal office. Maret functioned as a conduit between the dictator and his ministers, all of whom (except **Talleyrand**) were required to submit their reports through his office. Trusted to select and reproduce ministerial news for publication in the *Moniteur*, he also fulfilled a vital **propaganda** role. He was created Duke of Bassano in 1809, and was imperial foreign minister from 1811 until his replacement by **Caulaincourt** in 1813. Remaining loyal to Napoleon after the **abdication**, he was exiled for five years after the **Hundred Days**.

Marie-Louise, Empress (1791–1847)

The daughter of Austrian emperor **Francis**, Marie-Louise became **Napoleon's** second wife in 1810, after negotiations for a Franco-Russian marriage had broken down. The young princess was married by proxy on 11 March, and a religious ceremony was held after her arrival in Paris the following month. A much-admired beauty, and popular with her new subjects, she developed a strong emotional and sexual attachment to Napoleon, and fulfilled her principal

317

obligation to him when she gave birth to their son on 20 March 1811. Marie-Louise returned to Vienna with her son when Napoleon abdicated in 1814, and remained there during the **Hundred Days** of 1815. Created Duchess of **Parma**, Piacenza and Guastalla in 1816, she remarried twice and was a benevolent if unimaginative ruler. Expelled from her realm by a revolution in 1831, she died in Vienna.

Marie-Louises

Contemporary nickname, after the Empress Marie-Louise, given to young conscripts called up by the **French Army** to compensate for the enormous losses of 1812–13. Often in their mid-teens, they formed the backbone of forces under Napoleon's command in 1813 and 1814, but inevitably lacked the savoir-faire or stamina of more experienced troops.

Marines

Troops carried on board warships, armed as infantry and utilized by all contemporary European navies. Primarily intended to disembark for land operations or take part in boarding actions, they were also used as **snipers** during **naval** engagements, and as military police. Marines formed a distinct service, and were usually drawn from regular line units. Some marines, like the **Russian Navy** troops caught up in the 1812 campaign, were transferred to permanent land duty, and **Napoleon** regularly turned ordinary naval crews into ground troops. Most navies regarded trained seamen as too precious to be wasted on land, while both naval and land army authorities tended to regard marines as second-class soldiers, in contrast to the high reputation enjoyed by modern **amphibious** troops.

Marmont, Auguste Frédéric Louis Viesse de (1774–1852)

Born in Châtillon-sur-Seine, Marmont followed his father into the **French Army** as an **artillery** officer in 1792. He took part in the successful recapture of **Toulon** in late 1793, and won minor celebrity as a company commander under **Pichegru** during actions around **Mannheim** in autumn 1795. With **Napoleon** as an aide on the **Italian** front in 1796, he took part in the pacification of the **Papal States** as a temporary brigadier-general in February 1797.

Marmont served under **Desaix** in the **Middle East**, taking part in the capture of **Malta** and the Battle of the **Pyramids**. He accompanied Napoleon back to France in autumn 1799 and became a state council member after the **Brumaire** coup in November. His work during the **Italian campaign** of 1800 was rewarded with promotion to divisional general after the victory at **Marengo**, and he was in command of artillery preparing for the invasion of **England** from 1803 to 1805.

Marmont was a corps commander against the **Third Coalition** in 1805, helping take **Ulm** before moving to the **Italian** theatre, and found himself embroiled in Balkan politics as military governor of Dalmatia from 1806. He remained on the Adriatic coast until 1809, fighting off incursions by Russian **Mediterranean** forces (for which he was ennobled in 1808 as the Duke of Ragusa), pressing into **Illyria** and attempting to spread French influence into the north-western **Ottoman** provinces. Recalled to the Danube in 1809, his corps was in reserve at **Wagram** and won the final engagement against the **Fifth Coalition** at **Znaim** in July, for which he was promoted marshal a few days later.

Returned to command in what now became French Illyria, he was eventually transferred to the **Peninsular War** in April 1811, taking over the Army of Portugal shortly after his arrival. He thwarted **Wellington**'s attempts to take **Badajoz** and **Ciudad Rodrigo** that autumn, winning an important minor victory at **El Bodón**, but was roundly defeated and severely wounded at **Salamanca** in July 1812. He was out of action for the rest of the year, returning to lead his corps through all the major battles of the 1813 campaign for **Germany**.

Marmont was one of Napoleon's most important commanders during the defence of **France** in 1814. He played a part in minor victories at **St Dizier**, **Champaubert**, **Vauchamps**, **Meaux** and **Reims**, but suffered vital defeats against heavy odds at **Laon** and **La-Fère-Campenoise** in March. His surrender to the allies after being thrown back on **Montmartre** by overwhelming numbers was a major factor influencing Napoleon's acceptance of allied **abdication** terms, and was never forgiven by the emperor's apologists. He shared the royal family's exile during the **Hundred Days**, and was a loyal servant of the postwar monarchy, but quit France after the 1830 revolution and spent the rest of his life repairing a reputation warped by Napoleon's accusations of treachery.

Marseillaise, La

The modern French national anthem was composed in 1792 as a response to imminent invasion by the **First Coalition**, and its origins had nothing to do with Marseilles. Rouget de Lisle, a minor composer with the **French Army**'s Strasbourg garrison, wrote the tune as a marching song, and members of the city mayor's household added lyrics that drew heavily on contemporary recruitment posters. Performed in Strasbourg for the first time on 19 April, the 'Chant de Guerre de l'Armée du Rhin' ('Battle Song of the Rhine Army') gained fame and a new name when passing **fédéré** detachments brought it to Marseilles, where it was hijacked by local **Jacobins** as the anthem of a few hundred volunteers marching on Paris. It fulfilled its original role as an aid to national defence throughout the **Revolutionary Wars**, contributing to the morale and **élan** of French forces in battle, and remained popular throughout the **Consulate** and empire despite **Napoleon**'s attempts to have it banned as a relic of radicalism.

Marshalate

The title Marshal of France was created by **Napoleon** on becoming emperor in May 1804. Though it conferred no specific military responsibilities beyond those of a divisional general, the rank was usually accompanied by grants of property and money that ensured the recipient's long-term wealth, and was much coveted. The original Marshalate comprised 18 officers, three of them honorary awards to men in retirement, and another eight were created between 1807 and 1815. One more general, **St Hilaire**, was killed before he could receive his baton of office.

Martello Towers

Simple stone defensive fortifications, thick-walled circular towers constructed in numbers on the south coast of **Great Britain** during the invasion scare of 1804 and subsequent national emergencies. They were modelled on and imprecisely named after the tower at Mortella Point,

Corsica, that was captured by the **Royal Navy** in 1794. *See also* Invasion of **England**.

Martin, Pierre (1752–1820)

French-Canadian seaman, an experienced maritime quartermaster by the time he was commissioned into the **French Navy** in 1788. Promoted lieutenant in 1792, he profited from the mass desertion of royalist officers to reach the rank of rear-admiral by the end of the following year. With the **Mediterranean** Fleet under **Villaret** from early 1794, he escaped British admiral **Hotham** and potential disaster off **Leghorn** in March, and led several subsequent raids on allied merchant shipping and trading posts, becoming vice-admiral in command of Toulon from March 1796. He was replaced by Admiral **Brueys** in October 1797, and held shore commands until his enforced retirement in 1814, returning to service only briefly during the **Hundred Days**.

Masséna, André (1758–1817)

Recognized as one of **Napoleon**'s most effective military subordinates, Masséna was born in the autonomous province of Nice, became a ship's boy in 1771 and enlisted in the royal army four years later, rising to the rank of sergeant-major by the time he left the service in 1789. Subsequently a trader, and possibly a smuggler, at the small southern port of Antibes, he joined the **National Guard** in 1791, and was an elected lieutenant-colonel on the **Italian** front in 1792.

Promoted brigadier-general in August 1793, he was given a divisional command for his part in the recapture of **Toulon**. His division spearheaded **Dumerbion**'s Italian offensive at **Saorgio** in spring 1794, but illness kept him from the front during the autumn and winter. He was back for **Schérer**'s late autumn offensive of 1795, doing well at **Loano** in November, and played a vital part in **Napoleon**'s successful campaigns of 1796–7.

Masséna helped win victories at **Montenotte**, **Dego**, **Mondovi**, **Codogno** and **Lodi** during spring 1796, leading the first French troops into Milan on 13 May. He led strike forces through the major actions surrounding Austrian attempts to relieve **Mantua** in the autumn, suffering defeat only at **Caldiero** in November, and was Napoleon's most effective general at

Rivoli and in the **Frioul** during early 1797.

Rewarded with an independent command on the **Swiss** front from early 1799, he held a line west of **Zurich** through a spring and summer of allied success elsewhere, and eventually counterattacked in the autumn to drive Austro-Russian forces back beyond the Rhine. Transferred to lead the Army of Italy in early 1800, he was caught with his force scattered by an Austrian spring offensive and driven into **Genoa**, but his prolonged resistance to the subsequent **siege** gave Napoleon time to get behind the Austrians at **Marengo**. Though removed from peacetime command for corruption, he was an original member of the **Marshalate** in 1804, and returned to the Italian theatre against the **Third Coalition** in 1805, preventing Archduke **Charles** from joining allied forces in Germany before **Austerlitz**.

Masséna spent most of his time in Italy, living up to his reputation as a world-class looter, until called up to lead the **Grande Armée**'s V Corps against the **Fourth Coalition** in January 1807. He returned to Italy after **Tilsit**, but was again given a corps when war resumed against Austria in 1809, taking a leading role in all the campaign's major actions, including **Aspern–Essling**, where he covered the army's withdrawal with celebrated composure, and **Wagram**.

Duke of Rivoli since 1808, he was created Prince of Essling in early 1810, and entered the **Peninsular War** in April as the reluctant commander of forces charged with driving **Wellington** out of **Portugal**. Defeat at **Busaco** in September was followed by failure to breach the **Torres Vedras** defences, and he was recalled after another reverse at **Fuentes de Oñoro** in May 1811, serving in home commands until 1814. Always comfortable with hedonism, Masséna only rejoined Napoleon under pressure during the **Hundred Days** of 1815, taking command of the Paris National Guard, and he retired to his pleasures after **Waterloo**.

Mauberge, **Siege of** *See* **Wattignies**, Battle of

Maximilian Joseph I, King (1756–1825)

Elector of **Bavaria** from 1795, Maximilian Joseph maintained the Wittelsbach family's tradition of friendship with France during the early years of his reign. Bavaria had already declared its neutrality in the War of the **First Coalition**, but obligations to the **Holy Roman Empire** required him to provide a contingent of troops against France, and he was forced to cede the Upper Palatinate (on the west bank of the Rhine) to **Napoleon** after the **Second Coalition**'s defeat in 1801. He signed a French alliance in 1801, and presided over the country's subsequent expansion under French protection, taking the title of King in early 1806. Careful to hedge the family's dynastic bets by marrying his daughter Auguste to Eugène de **Beauharnais**, he abandoned the faltering French cause in time to ensure a share of the **Sixth Coalition**'s victory spoils, and Greater Bavaria was one the few products of Napoleonic hegemony to survive the wars. An enthusiastic promoter of modernization in the **Bavarian Army**, he was sufficiently enlightened to grant Bavaria a constitution in 1817.

Maya Pass, Battle of the

One of two battles fought on 25 July 1813 (the other was at **Roncesvalles Pass** to the south-east) that opened the last major French offensive of the **Peninsular War**. French C-in-C **Soult**'s two-pronged attack on **Wellington**'s army in the northern Pyrenees was aimed at the besieged city of **Pamplona**, where he planned to resupply before sweeping behind allied forces concentrated near the northern coast.

Wellington's 60,000 troops were stretched by **sieges** at Pamplona and **San Sebastian**, and by the need to block the three main passes through the Pyrenees. The Maya was held by only 6,000 men when it was attacked at ten thirty on the morning of 25 July by **Drouet**'s 20,000 French troops. The defence was led by the inexperienced Brigadier-General Pringle, who left his main strength too far back to protect a forward outpost, which was rapidly overrun, and then engaged his other battalions one at a time as they reached the front. His chief, General Stewart, returned from headquarters to take control during the afternoon, and a reserve brigade from **Dalhousie**'s division helped hold Drouet in the pass until corps commander **Hill** arrived during the evening and ordered a withdrawal to Irurita.

Drouet did not pursue, anticipating a trap, and

Stewart's division was able to take up new positions around **Sorauren**. The battle had cost 2,000 French casualties, against 1,500 British, and the four guns lost by Stewart were the only **artillery** lost by Wellington during his Peninsular campaigns. *See* **Map 5**.

McGrigor, James (1771–1858)

In an age when most military **medicine** was practised by untrained orderlies or otherwise unemployable doctors, the **British Army's** James McGrigor was an efficient, innovative exception. After training in his native Scotland, he saw service in **Flanders**, the **West Indies**, **India** and **Egypt** before becoming inspector-general of British military hospitals in 1809. Two years later he joined **Wellington's** staff in the **Peninsular War**, and helped make his allied army perhaps the healthiest in Europe. Comparable with French medical chief **Larrey**, both as an organizer and as a firm advocate of improved sanitation, he was knighted in 1814 and was head of the army's medical services for 36 years after 1815.

Meaux, Battle of

A series of attacks on 27–28 February 1814 by **Blücher's** allied army against French forces guarding the Marne at Meaux, some 40km west of Paris (*see* **Map 26**). While **Napoleon's** small French strike force pursued **Schwarzenberg's** southern allied army beyond Troyes, Blücher led 53,000 men west over the Aube on 24 February, and then turned north against **Marmont's** 6,000 troops around Sézanne. Marmont retired north while Napoleon prepared to attack Blücher's rear.

By 27 February it was clear that Blücher was driving for Paris. While **Macdonald** was left in command around Troyes, **Mortier's** corps joined Marmont to block the allied advance at Meaux, and Napoleon marched towards Sommeous to cut Blücher's communications. Blücher launched three costly and unsuccessful attacks against Marmont around Meaux before deciding on 1 March, as a precautionary measure, to move all his forces north of Marne and burn its bridges. By the time Napoleon reached the river the Prussians were moving north towards Laon and reinforcements. Still without **pontoon** equipment, long overdue from Paris, Napoleon was unable to follow in time to prevent the allied forces from linking up north of the Aisne on 5 March. *See also* Campaign for **France**.

Mecklenburg-Schwerin

The larger of the two Mecklenburg duchies on the Baltic coast of Germany, Mecklenburg-Schwerin played no part in the **Revolutionary Wars**, but was occupied by French forces after the **Jena–Auerstädt campaign** of 1806. Duke Frederick Francis I agreed to join the Confederation of the **Rhine** in April 1808, but was the first German ruler to abandon French alliance in March 1813. Not subject to postwar territorial changes, Mecklenburg-Schwerin became a Grand Duchy in 1815. *See* **Map 1**.

Mecklenburg-Strelitz

Tiny independent duchy on the Baltic German coast, birthplace of Prussian queen **Louise**, that had been separated from the larger territory of **Mecklenburg-Schwerin** since 1701. Though not occupied by French forces in Germany after 1806, largely thanks to the intercession of Bavarian king **Maximilian-Joseph**, Mecklenburg-Strelitz joined the Confederation of the **Rhine** in February 1808. Ruling duke Charles followed other small German states in abandoning **Napoleon** after **Leipzig** in 1813, and the state underwent no immediate postwar changes beyond elevation to the status of Grand Duchy. *See* **Map 1**.

Medellín, Battle of

Failed attack by General La **Cuesta's** Army of Estremadura on **Victor's** French corps south of Medellín, near the River Guadiana in central western **Spain**, on 28 March 1809. Cuesta's 24,000 troops, weak in both **cavalry** and **artillery**, mounted a simple frontal attack on strong French positions, and it was halted almost at once by Victor's 18,000 men. French cavalry overran Spanish horsemen on Victor's left, and Cuesta's infantry collapsed after a charge by French **dragoons**. Spanish forces fled in disarray but the disaster, like earlier defeats in New Castille at Uclés (22 January) and Ciudad Real (27 March), did not diminish popular enthusiasm for the fight against French invasion. Cuesta had suffered an estimated 10,000 losses, but was able to rebuild his army with volunteers, and to take part in **Wellesley's** Spanish campaign later that year. *See* **Peninsular War; Map 22.**

Medicine

In a military context, European medicine of the Napoleonic period was called upon to deal with large numbers of battle casualties, health problems associated with mass encampment in insanitary conditions, and the ill effects of both in alien, sometimes tropical, environments. In an age before the discoveries of bacteria or effective anaesthetic, contemporary medical services were in no way equipped to deal efficiently with any of these things, and their work was given very low priority by governments and military authorities.

The best-equipped land forces might deploy one surgeon per battalion, sometimes aided by orderlies with basic medical training, but more often by unskilled soldiers or walking wounded. In armies with particularly severe personnel shortages, like the **Austrian** and (above all) the **Russian** forces, surgeons were available only at regimental level, if at all, and their duties were frequently carried out by semi-trained undersurgeons. A surgeon and at least one mate were part of the crew of major warships in British, French or Dutch service, but were rarer in the navies of less sophisticated societies.

The best doctors tended to avoid military employment, primarily because life in the army or aboard ship was about the least attractive career open to a medical man, and if the testimony of countless field commanders is to be believed, large numbers of the surgeons in military service were incompetent drunks. Few soldiers accepted treatment voluntarily from any surgeon if survival appeared possible without it, reflecting the considerable risk of fatal infection, most probably from gangrene, septicaemia or some other form of blood poisoning, or of death through shock while in surgery.

Treatment of battle wounds did not require advanced medical skills. The surgeon might find and remove a bullet manually from an uncomplicated flesh wound, but might also leave it to work free of the body in time. Serious bullet or sabre wounds to the limbs were treated by amputation, the one operation at which a significant

number of surgeons excelled. Examples of surgeons performing dozens of successful amputations during the course of a day, with sufficient speed to reduce shock-related deaths, were fairly commonplace, and the process saved more lives than any other military medical practice.

The role of field hospital was filled by the surgeon's cramped quarters aboard ships and by emergency casualty tents to the rear of land battles. No organized systems existed for evacuating wounded to the latter, and battle casualties might lie on a battlefield for days before being picked up by details from the winning side. Those who survived initial treatment would be transported (sometimes in special ambulance convoys, but usually in whatever wagons were available) to a rudimentary hospital established in the nearest town, but officers were usually spared these 'palaces of disease', convalescing as guests in private houses.

As demonstrated by a few outstanding medical officers – most notably imperial French Surgeon-General **Larrey** and James **McGrigor**, head of Anglo-Portuguese medical services during the **Peninsular War** – it was possible to save a large proportion of wounded troops given careful organization, determined improvisation and strict adherence to the best available codes of practice. It was not possible for contemporary surgeons to save men from the rampant effects of disease in alien environments, and sickness was responsible for many more military casualties than battle wounds.

European **colonial** armies serving in tropical conditions were routinely decimated by disease, and sickness rates in Europe's many damp, cold, hot or otherwise unhealthy war zones were also appalling. At a time when the dangers of stagnant water were not fully understood – and when the best non-surgical treatments included bleeding with leeches and a bottle of boiled wine – malaria, cholera and any number of unidentified 'fevers' (often named, like **Walcheren** fever, after the location they affected) killed thousands of land troops and forced many thousands more to be invalided home.

Warships were obvious breeding grounds for disease, and though British and American ships were well on the way to defeating scurvy with fresh food, little could be done to protect sailors ashore. Disease aboard ship was at least a containable threat, and naval vessels with plague or other contagion on board were required by most services to remain at sea in isolation for several weeks, flying a quarantine flag, before being allowed ashore.

Medina del Río Seco, Battle of

The first major battle of the **Peninsular War**, fought on 14 July 1808 between elements of **Bessières's** French army occupying Galicia and the combined rebel forces of Generals **Blake** and **Cuesta**. As rebellion erupted all over Spain in the aftermath of the **Madrid Uprising**, Bessières was charged with the vital task of guarding the sole road between France and Madrid through Galicia.

On 14 July two French divisions, fewer than 12,000 men under Generals **Mouton** and Merle, met about 24,000 Galician and Castilian troops at Medina del Río Seco, some 40km north-west of Valladolid (*see* **Map 22**). Outnumbered French forces stormed entrenched Spanish positions atop a shallow ridge, an impressive display of **élan** that put Blake's Galicians to flight after Cuesta refused to commit his 6,500 Castilians at the critical time. The victory should have freed French reinforcements for advanced forces in southern Spain, but the Andalusian army's shock surrender at **Bailén** (23 July) was the first of several blows that drove French armies on to the defensive.

Mediterranean Theatre

The shallow Mediterranean had been a cockpit for competing national and imperial interests since ancient times, and remained central to European international relations in the late eighteenth century. A more or less vital trade and communications artery for all those regional states with extended coastlines, many of which contained few or no roads, it was also an economic highway for European **great powers**, linking the Atlantic with the Black and Red Seas to open up markets in and beyond the **Ottoman Empire**.

The eastern Mediterranean was a magnet for expanding European empires in the late eighteenth century. Warships at Toulon not only protected maritime trade into southern **France**, but stood ready to press long-standing **colonial** and commercial claims in Ottoman Greece, Syria and **Egypt**. Expansion into the Aegean via Constantinople was basic to **Russia's** foreign policy, and **Great Britain** was unwilling to stand aside while anybody else took control over land routes to **India**. The set of predators around the sultan's creaking regime was completed by **Austria**, committed to pushing Ottoman frontiers back beyond the Balkans and Greece.

Elsewhere in the Mediterranean, opportunities for great power expansion were more limited. West of Egypt, the inhospitable Barbary coast was under only nominal Ottoman control, housing nests of pirates who preyed on European and American trading vessels, particularly after war to the north encouraged merchantmen to hug the African shores. European colonial authorities supervised trade from north-west Africa to Europe, particularly to **Spain**, which had regarded the western Mediterranean as its private domain for centuries.

Spain's naval decline was reflected in British possession (and slow military development) of Gibraltar at the gateway to the Atlantic, last challenged in the early 1780s, but long-term strategic control of the French and Spanish coastlines further east was not open to dispute. The collapse of **Venice** and **Naples** as regional sea powers made the Italian and Balkan coasts vulnerable to takeover, along with their offshore islands, and it was in this region that the priorities of Mediterranean and European land warfare were most closely linked.

Few contemporary states were capable of exploiting all the Mediterranean's strategic opportunities. Spain's American interests and the **Spanish Navy's** poverty precluded ambitions to the east, the **Russian Navy** needed permission to enter the Mediterranean at all, and even if the **Austrian Navy** grew into a strategically useful force it would be penned inside the Adriatic. Only the large, centrally located **French Navy** and the immense British **Royal Navy** were capable of influencing, and competing for, all corners of the theatre.

Apart from minor French operations around **Nice**, war reached the Mediterranean when

Britain joined the **First Coalition** in early 1793, followed by Spain. Once it had mobilized, the Royal Navy struck the first blow, when **Hood's** Mediterranean Fleet induced starving **Toulon's** surrender to Coalition forces on 27 August. Hood seemed to have placed the theatre at the centre of European conflict, but the failure of allied governments to provide sufficient supporting troops and Toulon's recapture in December set a pattern of British inability to turn Mediterranean tactical success into mainland strategic impact.

Troop shortages and the difficulties of long-range communication aside, the immediate problem facing British authorities after the fall of Toulon was a lack of secure bases east of Gibraltar. Hood addressed the matter by authorizing an attack in support of anti-French rebels on **Corsica**, which occupied most available **British Army** forces from February to August 1794. Otherwise, allied warships sought to keep the weakened French fleet bottled up in Toulon, and to aid land campaigns on the **Italian** and **Pyrenean** fronts, but all navies devoted most of their Mediterranean energies to trade warfare through the mid-1790s.

The French held their own, avoiding battles with superior British forces and taking advantage of lax British **blockade** tactics to slip out of Toulon for coastal raids or attacks on **convoys**, notably off Cape **St Vincent** in October 1795. Their success was abetted by the performance of Hood's successor from early 1794, the unambitious **Hotham**, who missed battle opportunities off **Leghorn** in March 1795 and the **Hyères Islands** in June.

Smaller craft were meanwhile engaged in permanent offensives against enemy trade and each other. Merchant ships along the coastal and local sea lanes were under constant threat from hostile **sloops**, **gunboats** and other small warships, along with nests of **privateers**, as they crawled along the northern coasts. Expensive to both sides but decisive for neither (and a **prize money** bonanza for successful naval officers), light naval warfare remained a constant feature of Mediterranean conflict until 1814.

The First Coalition's collapse radically altered the balance of naval power in the Mediterranean. Spain left the Coalition in 1795, and

French conquest of the **Netherlands** forced the British to return warships to the North Sea. By late 1796, Spain was a French ally and **Napoleon's** successes had given the republic control over almost the whole Italian coastline. New British Mediterranean C-in-C **Jervis**, with only 14 **ships-of-the-line**, found himself facing a combined Franco-Spanish fleet of 42 battleships. French troop landings forced him to abandon Corsica in November, and on 16 November he sailed out of the Mediterranean altogether, leaving only an observation squadron of **frigates** under **Nelson** as he fell back on Gibraltar and friendly Lisbon.

The Franco-Spanish alliance achieved little during its brief time in control of the theatre. Toulon C-in-C de **Brueys** took over the **Venetian Navy's** ancient warships, and his fleet assisted in the occupation of Corsica, but it proved impossible to organize a major combined offensive with Spanish forces unwilling to leave the western Mediterranean. Jervis meanwhile transformed the exiled but reinforced British fleet into a formidable fighting and patrol force. Though Nelson's sortie against **Tenerife** in July 1797 ended in farce, Jervis had caught and routed the Spanish fleet off **St Vincent** (just outside the Mediterranean) in February.

The establishment of peace in mainland Europe at **Campo Formio** (October 1797) encouraged the **Directory** government to risk Mediterranean adventures without support. The Toulon fleet accompanied an army to the **Middle East** in spring 1798, but Napoleon's conquests of **Malta** and **Egypt** were overshadowed by its loss to Nelson's pursuing detachment at the **Nile** on 1 August. Nelson's victory sealed the formation of a **Second Coalition** in Europe, and restored the Royal Navy's Mediterranean pre-eminence at a stroke, but also radically extended its responsibilities.

An unlikely alliance of the Russian and **Turkish** navies entered the theatre to capture the French-held **Ionian Islands**, and Napoleon's army fought its way up the eastern Mediterranean coast as far as **Acre**, where **Smith's** British naval squadron helped Ottoman ground forces halt its advance. British warships found themselves called upon to blockade Alexandria and

Malta (with small-scale assistance from the **Portuguese Navy**), as well as the Spanish and French coasts, while assisting in the **Neapolitan campaign** on the Italian mainland. The capture of **Minorca** in autumn 1798 provided them with a good western Mediterranean base, but added to defensive responsibilities that severely restricted offensive potential.

During the opening phases of the **Italian campaign** in 1799, allied armies almost drove the French from Italy, but received little support from Mediterranean naval forces. Ushakov's Russian fleet eventually launched a few ineffectual attacks on French-held Adriatic targets, and the Royal Navy mounted a blockade of besieged **Genoa**, but British plans to land an army in north-west Italy came to nothing. The small British land force available for offensive Mediterranean operations was wasted in an ill-conceived **amphibious** attack on **Cadiz**, and Napoleon's victory at **Marengo** (June 1800) ended hopes of intervention in Italy.

The theatre slipped into strategic impasse after Marengo. French armies had conquered Naples in early 1799, forcing the royal family's evacuation to **Sicily**, where they ruled under British protection until 1814. Though an important base, Sicily needed constant protection from attack, and occupation reduced rather than increased British offensive potential. Neutral Russian forces were restricted to occupation of Corfu after 1799, and Franco-Spanish naval operations reduced to occasional timid sorties from the Atlantic (*see* '**Bruix's Cruise**'; '**Ganteaume's Cruise**'). Malta fell to the British in September 1800, but the Austro-French Peace of **Lunéville** the following February left Britain fighting alone.

A successful British attack on **Alexandria**, finally putting troops to constructive use and expelling French forces from Egypt, was the last major action in the theatre before the **Amiens** agreement of October 1801 brought temporary peace, punctuated only by the **US Navy**'s occasional campaign against the **Barbary** pirates (1801–5). Britain renounced all its wartime conquests in the Mediterranean as part of the peace, but London's mistrust of Napoleon's intentions (encouraged by Russia) delayed evacuation of Malta. A source of increasing Anglo-French tension through 1802, the island was still a British base when war resumed in May 1803.

The second decade of war saw the British Mediterranean Fleet establish unchallenged control of the theatre's sea lanes, and C-in-C Nelson's annihilation of the French and Spanish fleets at **Trafalgar** in October 1805 ended any direct threat from either. Nelson's successor, **Collingwood**, still faced a complex array of defensive duties with inadequate numbers of warships, and chronic shortage of allied troops in the theatre still precluded decisive intervention in the mainland struggle for Europe.

British forces from Sicily won a small success at **Maida** in 1806, but were unable to prevent French reconquest of Naples, and spent the rest of the war on the defensive, losing their outpost on **Capri** in 1808 but holding off an attack by **Murat** from the mainland in 1810. From 1806, a small British fleet patrolled the Adriatic, where **Marmont**'s army was attempting to extend French control down the Balkan coast, but could do nothing about victories on the Danube that added **Illyria** to the French Empire in 1809. A larger British fleet made futile efforts to prevent the Ottoman Empire from allying with France by forcing the **Dardanelles** to reach Constantinople in February 1807, but achieved nothing and withdrew.

Russian warships, and a few troops, had remained in the theatre since 1798. They fought a relatively successful campaign along the Balkan Adriatic coast from their Corfu base, and played an undistinguished role in the 1805–6 defence of southern Italy, but consistently ignored British suggestions for a major combined operation. Russian forces responded to appeals too late to join the Dardanelles operation, but C-in-C Seniavin remained in the Aegean to inflict a serious defeat on the Turkish fleet at **Lemnos** in June 1807 before his operations were curtailed by the Franco-Russian **Tilsit** peace. By then at war with the Ottoman Empire, the Russians sailed out of the theatre via Gibraltar at the end of the year (with Collingwood's cooperation) and did not come back.

Alongside the ceaseless business of patrol, blockade, search and seizure, the **Peninsular War** became the main focus for Mediterranean naval operations after 1808. Restored to Minorca by the rebel Spanish **junta**, British Mediterranean warships made their most valuable contribution to the European land war in support of **Wellington**'s long campaign, and cooperated effectively with Spanish rebels from **Cadiz** to Catalonia until 1814.

Barely affected by the brief resumption of European hostilities in 1815, the Mediterranean entered the postwar era under effective supervision by the British, who secured retention of Malta and a protectorate over the Ionian Islands at the Congress of **Vienna**. The victors otherwise left most of the region's underlying strategic disputes unresolved, restoring most prewar political boundaries around the Mediterranean rim, and British commitment to peaceful status quo in the name of commerce remained the principal guarantee of general peace. *See* **Map 8**.

Melas, Michael Friedrich Benoit (1729–1806)

Transylvanian-born **Austrian Army** officer, whose command of forces on the **Italian** front in 1799–1800 was the pinnacle of an unremarkable career spanning more than half a century. Absent for the victories at **Verona** and **Magnano**, and then superseded by **Suvorov**, he was in full control of the spring offensive in 1800 that stalled at **Genoa** and was crushed at **Marengo** in June. His subsequent capitulation to **Napoleon** ended his active career, and he formally retired in 1803.

Melzi d'Eril, Francesco (1753–1816)

From a powerful and wealthy aristocratic Milanese family, related to Spanish rebel leaders the **Palafox** brothers, Melzi was a leading Habsburg bureaucrat during the early 1790s, serving on the city's administrative council. He threw his full support behind **Napoleon** in the wake of the 1796 **Italian campaign**, playing a leading role in the rigged consultation process that preceded formation of the **Cisalpine Republic**. He retired in 1798, but was appointed vice-president (under Napoleon) of the puppet Italian Republic from 1802. Strongly anti-clerical, he outraged **Pius VII** by imposing state regulation of Church affairs, attacked feudal economic privileges, sought to radicalize universities and attempted to reorganize the **Italian Army**. He also annoyed Napoleon

by persistent efforts to secure greater Italian autonomy, and quarrelled with military governor **Murat**. Opposed in principle to the republic's transformation into the Kingdom of **Italy** in 1806, he gradually lost his executive powers under viceroy **Beauharnais**, but received properties and titles in compensation, becoming Duke of Lodi in 1808. He was briefly back at the centre of affairs in 1814, when he led the 'French party' in Milan, attempting to secure the kingdom's survival after Napoleon's fall.

Menou, Jacques-François de Boussay, Baron de (1750–1810)

A member of the French noble First Estate in 1789, Menou was a **cavalry** colonel on the **Rhine** front from 1792. Promoted divisional general in 1793, he retired for two years after being wounded, returning to service as a staff officer in 1795. Given command of the tiny Army of the Interior, he was temporarily arrested for support of the royalist **Vendémiaire** uprising in July, and was not given another field post until 1798, when he took part in **Napoleon**'s expedition to the **Middle East**. After fighting at **Aboukir** in August 1799, he was left in **Egypt** as **Kléber**'s second-in-command when Napoleon returned to France, and took over on his chief's assassination in June 1800. A Muslim convert, married to a native woman, he was not the man to rouse a dispirited army. Defeated by the British at **Alexandria** in March 1801, he had little choice but to surrender in August, and held no further combat commands after his repatriation.

Metternich, Clemens Lothar Wenzel, Count (1773–1859)

The great Habsburg statesman of the nineteenth century, Metternich was born in Koblenz and followed his Austrian father into a diplomatic career, serving in the **Netherlands** before becoming envoy to **Saxony** in 1800. Promoted to the Berlin embassy in 1802, he moved to Paris after **Austerlitz** and remained there until December 1808, when he returned to Vienna convinced that France was ripe for military defeat. After helping persuade Emperor **Francis** to prepare for war in 1809, he replaced **Stadion** as foreign minister and chief imperial adviser after the defeat at **Wagram** in July, and negotiated the **Schönbrunn** alliance. Though no ally of Archduke **Charles**, he made efforts to lay the basis for future **Austrian Army** expansion beyond treaty restrictions, and sought rapprochement with **Napoleon** until **Austria** recovered its strength.

Metternich helped arrange Napoleon's marriage to the emperor's daughter, **Marie-Louise**, and agreed to a formal alliance committing Austrian Army forces to the 1812 **Russian campaign**, but was careful to hedge his bets, informing Tsar **Alexander** that Austria's contribution was no more than a token gesture. Always determined to fight the tide of ethnic separatism that threatened the empire's integrity, he refused to encourage the sort of patriotic nationalism that inspired **Prussia**'s renewed war effort in 1813, and kept Austria out of the campaign for **Germany** until the late summer.

Created a prince for overseeing Austria's eventual alliance with the **Sixth Coalition**, Metternich began working to maintain **France** as a counterweight to Prussia and **Russia** as soon as Napoleon had been driven west of the Rhine, and preservation of the international status quo through the balance of power became his diplomatic trademark. He led calls for a negotiated settlement with Napoleon until March 1814, and is generally regarded, along with British foreign minister **Castlereagh**, as the architect of the lasting peace agreement that emerged from the Congress of **Vienna** in 1814–15. He helped force compromises over the future of **Poland** and Saxony, but also committed Francis to the **Holy Alliance** with Russia and Prussia, laying the foundations for the conservative, anti-constitutional policy he was to follow as Austrian chancellor until 1848.

Middle East Campaign (1798–1801)

The ill-fated French attempt, promoted and initially led by **Napoleon**, to found a **colonial** empire in **Egypt** and Syria, both provinces of the **Ottoman Empire**. Launched in spring 1798, the expedition achieved little in geopolitical or military terms before its final abandonment in August 1801, but Napoleon used **propaganda** to turn its early successes into a springboard for his assumption of political control in **France**.

The French expedition's primary objective was annexation of Egypt, an idea that was nothing new. In practice a self-governing fiefdom with little direct responsibility to the Ottoman Sultan, Egypt remained an exotic mystery to most Europeans, exciting visions of wealth by conquest and of a gateway to imagined African riches. More tangibly, Egypt was a potential axis for overland trade with **India**, where French strategists sought to challenge **Great Britain**'s commercial dominance.

Napoleon's personal interest in the Middle East stemmed partly from determination to build on the fame won during his **Italian campaigns** of 1796–7, and partly from the enthusiastic promptings of **Talleyrand**, who saw colonial wealth as the key to French economic growth. Napoleon began organizing an expeditionary force at Toulon as early as March 1797, while Talleyrand worked to secure **Directory** approval. The government in Paris was slow to give its blessing, but doubts about the expedition's intrinsic value were eventually outweighed by a desire to keep the hero of Italy at a safe distance. On 12 April 1798 Napoleon received orders to capture Egypt and secure 'free and exclusive possession of the Red Sea' for France.

The Army of Egypt sailed from Toulon on 19 May aboard some 400 transports, escorted by four **frigates** and 13 **ships-of-the-line** under Admiral de **Brueys**. Napoleon commanded 35,000 reasonably well-equipped troops, and could call on **Berthier** as chief of staff, but the army was otherwise short of experienced senior officers and travelled with only 1,350 horses. The party was accompanied by a battalion of scholars, writers, artists and scientists, whose functions included investigation of a possible canal linking the Red Sea and the **Mediterranean**.

France was at war with Britain in 1798, but not with the Ottoman Empire. The sultan had recognized the French republic three years earlier, and French military advisers were part of a sluggish trend towards imperial modernization, encouraging hopes in Paris (as expressed by Talleyrand) that the Ottoman government would not risk war for a distant province. Continued peace with Turkey would bar the **Russian Navy** from the Mediterranean, and reduce the likelihood of any major European reaction to French aggression, but was only likely to hold if Napoleon appeared to be winning.

The greatest active threat to French success was the British **Royal Navy**, which might have intercepted the Army of Egypt at any time during its crossing. Napoleon's apparently spontaneous decision to seize the island of **Malta** (held since the Crusades by the superficially military Knights of St John) greatly increased this risk, and provided an obvious excuse for intervention by other powers. He was lucky. The island was taken after only token resistance, other European powers made no protest and French delay at Malta added significantly to gathering British confusion.

Though reliable intelligence informed British war secretary **Dundas** of Napoleon's destination, a divided government had split Royal Navy forces to protect **Naples** (as first priority), **Spain**, **Portugal** and Egypt. Mediterranean commander **Jervis** had sent **Nelson** with 14 ships-of-the-line and seven frigates to cover Egypt, but he reached Alexandria in mid-June to find no sign of the French, and had sailed to **Sicily** for resupply by the time Napoleon's army landed at nearby Marabout on 1 July.

Napoleon immediately dispatched 5,000 men to bombard and take Alexandria, and split his remaining forces in two, leading 15,000 troops overland to the Nile settlement of El Rahmaniya, and sending the rest by river under General **Desaix**. The two formations were reunited on 12 July, and next day defeated local forces under co-governors **Murad Bey** and **Ibrahim Bey** at **Shubra Khit**, just north of El Rahmaniya. Marching for Cairo, the French overcame the ill-coordinated attacks of some 60,000 men blocking their path at the Battle of the **Pyramids** on 21 July.

Napoleon duly took Cairo on 22 July, but was barely established before news reached him of Nelson's crushing naval victory over Brueys at the Battle of the **Nile** on 1 August. Though Bonaparte's propaganda department had sent home exaggerated reports of sweeping victories over exotic foes, and the establishment of a French colony could begin in earnest with the fall of Cairo, Nelson's victory left the Army of Egypt trapped in the Middle East, without secure supply lines from Europe or protection against

British coastal attack. It also hardened European diplomatic responses to French aggression, stimulating the formation of a **Second Coalition** against France.

Aware that his personal reputation depended on continued success, and in the hope of a forcing a favourable peace on the Ottoman Empire, Bonaparte planned a pre-emptive attack on the sultan's forces gathering in Syria, but was delayed by the unexpected outbreak of revolt in **Cairo**. By the time Napoleon eventually marched for Syria on 10 February 1799 the need to garrison Egypt (along with continued wastage of troops) had reduced his attacking force to only 13,000 men and 52 field guns.

Lack of strength or definite purpose did not stop Napoleon presenting the invasion of Syria in sweeping geopolitical terms. It was preceded by a well-publicized ultimatum denouncing the Ottoman governor of Syria, Ahmed Pasha Djezzar, and by a message to **Tipu Sahib** of Mysore (whose fight against British control of southern India was on the point of defeat by General **Harris**), assuring him that an 'invincible' French army was marching to his aid.

The real invasion was a more mundane affair. Napoleon marched north-east from Cairo to Qatiya, and then east along the coast, occupying the border town of El Arish on 19 February and taking Gaza, well inside Syria, 11 days later. Advancing north, the French met serious opposition for the first time at Jaffa, where the Turkish garrison fought for three days before surrendering on 7 March.

Almost half of the 2,500 Turkish prisoners taken at Jaffa proved to have been **paroled** after earlier actions in Egypt, and Ottoman disregard for European conventions of war presumably triggered Napoleon's decision to have them all shot. Often cited by contemporary (and some modern) British commentators as evidence of Napoleon's brutality, the mass execution is more generally viewed as a reflection of his pragmatism, given that his undersupplied, plague-ravaged army was incapable of maintaining prisoners. French prisoners in Turkish hands were regularly tortured and killed.

Leaving a garrison behind to guard hundreds of sick troops, Napoleon marched his shrinking army to **Acre**, almost 250km to the north, where it laid siege to the ancient fortress city from 17 March until mid-May, defeating a Turkish relief effort at Mount Tabor in April. News that the Royal Navy was escorting a Turkish army from Rhodes to Egypt forced Napoleon to break off the siege in mid-May, by which time his army was down to about 7,000 effectives, and retreat to protect Cairo.

About 20,000 Turkish troops under Mustafa Pasha were already off the Egyptian coast by the time Napoleon reached Cairo in early June, but they made no attempt to march on the city. Instead Mustafa occupied the coastal **fortress** of **Aboukir** on 15 July and dug his troops in for a defensive battle. Given time to organize a small force, Napoleon attacked the fortress on 25 July, and had destroyed Mustafa's army by the time it fell on 2 August.

Turkish prisoners were released to local British naval commander **Smith**, and in the course of gentlemanly negotiations Napoleon was shown newspapers describing the Second Coalition's initial victories. He opted to quit Egypt almost at once, and sailed for France aboard a fast **frigate** on 24 August, accompanied by selected key officers, including Berthier, **Lannes** and **Murat**. Slipping past British warships, Napoleon reached the French coast at Fréjus on 9 October, just in time to reap popular adulation for a much-exaggerated victory at Aboukir.

General **Kléber** was left in command of the French remnant in Egypt, and despite orders to the contrary had little choice but to seek an honourable means of escape. By the Convention of **El Arish** (21 January 1800) the Ottoman Empire agreed to allow a peaceful French evacuation, but Smith had brokered the agreement without permission from the British government, which refused ratification. Forced to seek a stronger bargaining position by taking the offensive, Kléber attacked and defeated Ottoman forces at **Heliopolis** on 20 March, enabling him to hold Cairo.

Kléber was assassinated on 14 June, and command passed to General **Menou**, a converted Muslim who seems to have believed (mistakenly) that his administration would be allowed to stay in Egypt once the British recognized its 'civilizing' influence. This possibility was also explored by Napoleon, but his diplomacy made no impression on the British government's determination to clear Egypt. With Anglo-French peace apparently imminent, some 15,000 British troops under General **Abercromby** were eventually sent to put an end to French colonial pretensions in spring 1801.

Menou's fatigued forces suffered a decisive defeat on 21 March at **Alexandria** (where Abercromby was killed), and final French capitulation followed on 31 August, before British reinforcements arriving on the Red Sea coast from India were needed. Surviving French personnel were transported home by the British, but in their ignominious return made far less impact in Napoleonic France than had the imagined glories of their early adventures. *See* **Map 7**.

Milan Decrees

Announcements made in Milan on 23 November and 17 December 1807 that revised and strengthened the **Continental System** of economic warfare against **Great Britain**, as inaugurated by the **Berlin Decrees** of 1806. The decrees signalled the first strenuous attempts to enforce the system and placed the burden of proving that goods were not contraband on neutral captains. They also extended the ban on intercourse with Britain to the open seas by declaring that all vessels submitting to British **blockade** regulations, as tightened earlier in November by new **Orders in Council**, were committing an act of war against the French Empire.

Militia (British)

The home defence reserve force of **Great Britain**, recruited on a territorial basis using a ballot system that made provision for purchased exemptions. Called into being at times of national emergency, the militia provided a steady trickle of trained reserves for the regular **British Army** on a volunteer basis. Although not required to serve overseas, militia units did take part in foreign expeditions as volunteers, notably during the abortive invasion of **North Holland** in 1801. During the period when **England** was menaced by French invasion, militia forces were backed up by companies of volunteers. Originally made up of men wealthy enough to provide their own equipment, volunteer forces were broadened from 1803 to include almost half a million men. Their level of training was defined by individual commanders, and their area of service strictly localized, but some volunteers were placed in control of coastal **artillery** batteries or **Martello towers**.

Mines

A feature of the elaborate **siege** operations that characterized eighteenth-century warfare, mines were tunnels dug by attacking troops that led towards target fortifications. Once the tunnel was underneath a defensive position, it would be filled with as much gunpowder as possible and exploded. Unlikely to surprise defenders, who would usually mount raids to disrupt tunnelling work, they were principally intended to destroy fortifications and encourage surrender according to the martial etiquette of the pre-revolutionary era. Slow, uncertain and occupying specialist troops, mines were seldom important during mobile campaigns dependent on weight of numbers at the point of crisis, and their wartime employment was largely restricted to attacks on particularly obdurate second-line **fortresses**.

Minorca

A **Spanish Navy** base at the beginning of the period, the Balearic island of Minorca was primarily distinguished by its excellent harbour at Port Mahon. It was a British target once **Spain** became a French ally in 1795, at which time the **Royal Navy** lacked adequate **Mediterranean** facilities east of Gibraltar. A particular enthusiasm of British war minister **Dundas**, an invasion of Minorca was planned during 1798 and took place that autumn.

An Anglo-Portuguese force of some 3,000 troops under **Stuart** reached the island on 7 November, escorted by **Duckworth**'s naval squadron. Deprived of all field **artillery** by an administrative blunder, Stuart sent Colonel **Graham** with a detachment to cut communications between Minorca's two main settlements, at Port Mahon and Ciudadella, and proceeded to bluff their garrisons into surrender. The last 3,600 Spanish troops capitulated on 19 November, and Stuart completed the conquest without a single casualty.

Close to hostile coasts and difficult to defend, Minorca tied down 6,000 British troops and four **ships-of-the-line**, inhibiting British offensive operations in the theatre until its return to Spain under the terms of the **Amiens** peace. Various proposals for reconquest came to nothing before 1808, when Spanish garrison troops were sent to fight in the **Peninsular War** and the rebel **junta** opened the island to British shipping. Port Mahon functioned as a British naval base for the rest of the wars, but troops could never be spared for its defence, which became a particular cause for anxiety after French **prisoners of war** were moved from besieged **Cadiz** to Minorca in April 1809. *See* **Map 8**.

Minsk, Manoeuvre on

The second attempt by **Napoleon** to force a major battle during the **Russian campaign** of 1812. The rapid retreat of **Barclay de Tolly**'s First Army had frustrated both Napoleon's original plan to drive a wedge between the two main Russian forces and his subsequent attempt to intercept the withdrawal at **Vilna** (28 June). Uncertain of the exact whereabouts of either Russian army, Napoleon sent a large detachment under **Murat** in pursuit of Barclay de Tolly, while **Davout** led the remainder in search of **Bagration**'s smaller Second Army and a small reserve was kept at Vilna.

Virtually paralysed by heavy rain, food shortages and growing exhaustion, French manoeuvres had hardly got under way by 1 July, when Bagration was reported moving towards Vilna from the south-west, en route for the First Army's latest position at Sventsiani. Napoleon immediately ordered Davout to march against Bagration, and brought his strength up to 50,000 men after **Beauharnais**'s delayed flank force had finally reached Vilna on 4 July. With 30,000 troops at Vilna to prevent Bagration's escape to the north, and Jérôme **Bonaparte**'s 55,000 men ordered to advance across his southern flank, Napoleon was confident of trapping the 45,000-strong Second Army.

Napoleon was let down by subordinates. Jérôme made little effort to advance beyond Ochmiana before 6 July, enabling Bagration to double back unhindered on news of Davout's approach. Davout sped towards Minsk, but by the time he reached the city (8 July) the Second Army was on its way south-west to Bobriusk. Jérôme's reluctance to advance his **Westphalian** forces is generally blamed for the missed opportunity, but Davout's failure to keep him informed of the situation may also have been important. The two men actively hated each other, and Napoleon's subsequent decision to put Jérôme under Davout's command was probably a calculated insult. Jérôme left the **Grande Armée** for **Westphalia** on 14 July. *See* **Map 23**.

Miranda, Francisco de (1756–1816)

Born in Caracas, Venezuela, Miranda fought in the American War of Independence before moving to Europe and commanding French revolutionary troops against the **First Coalition**. With **Dumouriez** for the invasion of the **Netherlands** in 1793, he was defeated at **Maastricht** in March, and defected to the allies in 1794. He interested British war minister **Dundas** in a variety of schemes for the overthrow of Spanish rule in **South America**, none of which bore fruit, and returned to Venezuela from London when it declared its independence in 1811. Given command of the army, and made dictator the following year, he made peace with royalist forces in July 1812, earning the contempt of **Bolívar** and other nationalist leaders. They made no attempt to intervene when he was arrested in contravention of peace terms, and he died a prisoner in Spain.

Mockern, Battle of

Subsidiary action fought during the first day of the Battle of **Leipzig**, 16 October 1813, as allied forces under **Blücher** approached the city from the north. Blücher had made careful preparations before attacking improvised French lines around Mockern just after two in the afternoon. A heavily outnumbered **Polish** division from **Souham**'s corps was slowly forced back on the French right, but Prussian general Langeron missed the chance to inflict a heavy defeat on General Delmas's stray French division returning from the north, mistaking it for a corps and temporarily retiring. General **Yorck**'s corps struck at **Marmont**'s central forces around the village of Mockern, but his leading division was driven off late in the afternoon. The refusal of **Württem-**

berg cavalry to follow up the success (a prelude to the state's defection to the allies on 18 October), and Yorck's commitment of his entire **cavalry** strength against subsequent infantry attacks, enabled the Prussians to reverse the situation and sweep Marmont's men out of Mockern, but the French had stabilized their lines a few kilometres behind the village by nightfall. The day's fighting in the sector had cost Yorck 24,000 men, a third of his strength, and Marmont about 10,000 casualties. *See* **Map 25**.

Möckern, Battle of

The first major action of the campaign for **Germany** in 1813, an attack on 3 April by 30,000 troops under Eugène de **Beauharnais** on General **Wittgenstein**'s 50,000 Russian and Prussian troops around Möckern, some 25km east of Magdeburg (*see* **Map 25**). Intended to prevent Wittgenstein from crossing the Elbe further south around Rosslau and effecting a junction with **Blücher**'s army near Dresden, the hastily organized French attack surprised a portion of his command and continued over two days of confused fighting. It had not provoked a general retreat by the time false reports that the Rosslau crossing was already taking place triggered a French withdrawal. Able to claim a victory, but dissuaded from his earlier intention of attacking the rear of French positions, Wittgenstein then took his troops across the river and marched to join Blücher.

Moescroen, Battle of

The first allied response to the French offensive in north-western **Flanders** of spring 1794. In support of French commander **Pichegru**'s ill-fated central attack on **Landrecies**, preliminary movements by **Souham**'s left wing had begun against allied coastal positions on 25 April, and some 50,000 troops moved north-west from Lille next day. As Souham led his right towards Courtrai, and **Moreau**'s left moved on Menin, allied sector commander **Clairfait** was hurrying north with 18,000 troops from Tournai, where he had moved in response to French feints. Souham overwhelmed a **Hanoverian** brigade at Moescroen on 28 April. and went on to take Courtrai by the time Clairfait recaptured the village at the end of the day, placing allied forces between the French armies and Lille. Souham and Moreau doubled back during the night to attack the Austrian position from two sides early next morning, and four hours of heavy fighting eventually drove the outnumbered allies into a withdrawal that degenerated into rout. French capture of 1,200 prisoners was offset by the surrender of 6,000 troops at Landrecies on 30 April, freeing York's allied corps to join Clairfait for an attack on Courtrai. *See* Map 23.

Mohilev, Battle of

One of the few clear French victories of the 1812 **Russian campaign**, a subsidiary action on 23 July between Prince **Bagration**'s Second Russian Army and Marshal **Davout**'s shadowing French force. After avoiding a French trap around **Minsk** in early July, Bagration marched his 45,000 troops south-east before crossing the Beresina River and resuming his attempt to join **Barclay de Tolly**'s First Army to the north. Though the main French effort had been redirected against the First Army at the Dvina, Davout and 50,000 men were charged with blocking Bagration's approach. Moving north along the west bank of the Dnieper, Bagration found his route blocked by Davout at Mohilev, and his attack against French positions was driven back with several thousand losses on 23 July. Unwilling to prolong the engagement, Bagration was forced to turn east once more, and was unable to keep a planned rendezvous with the First Army at **Vitebsk**. *See* Map 23.

Moncey, Bon Adrien Jannot de (1754–1842)

A lawyer's son, Moncey joined the royal **French Army** at 15 and, though out of uniform for long periods in between, was commissioned in 1779. A captain from 1791, he fought on the **Pyrenean** front during the War of the **First Coalition**, taking part in the victory at **San Marcial** in August 1794, after which he replaced General Muller as C-in-C of the north-western sector. He had advanced beyond Pamplona by the time the **Basle** treaty ended the Franco-Spanish War in summer 1795.

Suspended as a suspected royalist for two years after the 1797 **Fructidor coup**, he returned to action against the **Second Coalition**, serving on

the **Swiss** and **Italian** fronts, but spent much of his subsequent career in administrative posts. Inspector-General of Gendarmerie when he was appointed to the **Marshalate** in 1804, he led a corps during the invasion of **Spain** in 1808, fighting at **Tudela** and **Saragossa**, but spent the next five years in France.

Moncey led **National Guard** troops fighting around **Montmartre** in the last hours of the 1814 campaign for **France**, but supported **Napoleon** in a non-combat role during the **Hundred Days** campaign. Imprisoned briefly for refusing to take part in **Ney**'s postwar trial, he was restored to royal favour in 1816 and resumed active campaigning in Spain during the 'police action' of 1823.

Mondovi, Battle of

Strategically important French victory on 21 April 1796 that was a turning point in that year's **Italian campaign**. After French victories at **Montenotte** and **Dego** had cut them off from **Beaulieu**'s allied Austrian army, General Colli's Piedmontese forces had thwarted **Napoleon**'s attacks at **Ceva** and St Michele before tired and hungry French troops were rested on 19 April. Napoleon altered his line of communications to lessen any threat from Beaulieu, and called up **Masséna**'s division to join a renewed attack on 21 April, but Colli withdrew at the last moment, fighting off French **cavalry** pursuit to regroup around Mondovi. An act of uncharacteristic boldness by **Sérurier**, who led an immediate charge of Colli's defences before they were fully manned, swept the Piedmontese out of the well-stocked town the same day, and gave the starving French army access to the fertile Lombard plains. Napoleon advanced on Turin from 23 April, forcing **Piedmont**'s withdrawal from the **First Coalition** at **Cherasco** on 28 April. *See* Map 6.

Montalivet, Jean-Pierre Bachasson (1766–1823)

French lawyer, a moderate liberal during the revolutionary period, who became a government administrator during the **Consulate**, and was appointed national Director of Bridges and Highways in 1806. He succeeded Crétet as interior minister in 1809, and held the post until

Napoleon's defeat in 1814. Montalivet presided over his department's ongoing expansion to regulate almost every function of national life in **France**. His interior ministry eventually controlled more than 220 separate departments, its responsibilities including national and local government administration, agriculture, food supply, trade, mines, roads, bridges, ministerial accounts, prisons, public welfare, education, censorship, the arts and sciences, local government finances, archives and statistics.

Montbrun, Louis-Pierre (1770–1812)

French cavalry officer who joined the army in 1789 and was commissioned five years later, seeing service on the **Rhine** during the **Revolutionary Wars**. Promoted brigadier-general shortly after taking part in the Battle of **Austerlitz**, and given a divisional command for the 1809 campaign against the **Fifth Coalition**, he fought in the **Peninsular War** in 1810–11 and during the 1812 **Russian campaign**. He was killed on 7 September 1812, leading an attack on a Russian strongpoint at **Borodino**.

Montebello, Battle of

Subsidiary engagement on the **Italian** front between French and Austrian detachments around the Lombard town of Montebello on 9 June 1800 (*see* **Map 9**). Napoleon's surprise advance through the Alps to appear on the Lombard plains had achieved its initial aim by early June, forcing Austrian C-in-C **Melas** to turn away from an invasion of Provence to face the threat to his communications. Napoleon had been relying on **Masséna's** troops besieged in **Genoa** to deny the port as an alternative Austrian supply line, and to form part of a pincer that would trap Melas as he moved east. News of the city's fall compelled him to try to provoke a battle before the Austrians were resupplied, and he manoeuvred his forward units into contact range during 7 and 8 June.

A detachment of 8,000 troops under **Lannes**, diverted en route to support **Murat's** westerly advance at Piacenza, found General Ott's 18,000 Austrians, up from Genoa, around Montebello. Though heavily outnumbered, Lannes launched an unauthorized attack on the morning of 9 June, holding the Austrians until **Victor's**

supporting division could reach the battlefield. Victor's subsequent flank attack inflicted heavy casualties on the surprised Austrians, who fell back in confusion towards Alessandria. Lannes's victory against the odds (for which he was belatedly honoured in 1808) shook Melas into a cautious concentration of his forces around Alessandria, and gave Napoleon his first real idea of the Austrian army's whereabouts, setting up a decisive confrontation at **Marengo** on 14 June.

Montenotte, Battle of

The first victory won by **Napoleon** as **Italian** front C-in-C in 1796, an attack on 12 April by 9,000 French troops against Montenotte, in the centre of scattered allied positions guarding **Piedmont** (*see* **Map 6**). A French offensive north from the Ligurian coast had been planned for 15 April, but was brought forward four days in response to allied C-in-C **Beaulieu's** poorly coordinated attack on 10 April. While Beaulieu's left wing became entangled in an unsuccessful attempt to storm French coastal positions around Voltri, Napoleon concentrated against Argenteau's 6,800 Austrians around Montenotte, then preparing a move on Savona. Early on 12 April, General La Harpe's French division reached Montenotte and launched an immediate frontal attack, while **Masséna** led a brigade through the hills to threaten the Austrian right flank. Argenteau recognized the danger to his flank too late, and Masséna's attack turned retreat into rout. French forces not only inflicted 2,500 casualties and captured 1,000 precious **muskets**, but drove a wedge between the main Austrian and Piedmontese armies in northern Italy. *See also* Second Battle of **Dego**.

Montereau, Battle of

Hard-earned victory for French forces defending Paris in 1814, fought on 18 February at Montereau, where the Yonne joins the Seine about 65km south-east of the capital (*see* **Map 26**).

Fresh from the serial triumphs of his **Six Days Campaign**, Napoleon turned south to halt **Schwarzenberg's** advance up the Seine at **Valjouan** on 17 February. By late that afternoon the whole of Schwarzenberg's army was retreating in three columns towards bridges over the Seine. Napoleon rushed two corps and the

Imperial Guard towards Montereau that evening, aiming to cross the river before the Prince of Württemberg's corps reached the town. He was let down by **Victor**, who ignored orders and halted his leading corps for the night northeast of Montereau, so that Württemberg's troops were established in strong positions north of the river when it arrived next morning.

A furious Napoleon replaced Victor with **Gérard**, who led a series of small-scale attacks until the arrival of additional **artillery** permitted a full-scale assault on allied positions at about three. Württemberg waited until a key ridge north of the town had been stormed before ordering a general withdrawal, which was reduced to flight as French **cavalry** charges swept into the town and captured both its bridges. Württemberg's forces lost 6,000 men (against about 2,500 French casualties) in escaping down the road to Bray, but evaded encirclement by **Macdonald**'s corps, which reached the town early on 19 February. Schwarzenberg's army was able to reconcentrate on Troyes, but failure to trap his enemy did not dissuade Napoleon from pursuit, or from once more rejecting allied peace terms. *See also* campaign for **France**.

Montgelas, Maximilian von (1759–1838)

Bavarian politician, a personal adviser to future Elector **Maximilian Joseph** from 1796 (when the latter was Duke of Zweibrücken), who became foreign minister of **Bavaria** in 1799 and was the country's central political figure for the next 18 years. As finance minister (1803–6 and 1809) and interior minister (1809) he sought to maintain Bavaria's independence and the political ascendancy of the ruling house while remaining closely allied to **Napoleon** and introducing limited socio-economic reforms on the French model. Unwilling to compromise royal authority by supporting a liberal constitution, he retired from high office in 1817.

Montmartre, Battle of

Name generally used to describe the last action of the 1814 campaign for **France**, a desperate and short-lived defence of Paris by French forces under Marshals **Marmont** and **Mortier** on 30–31 March. After driving French forces back on Paris

at **La-Fère-Champenoise** on 25 March, almost 150,000 allied troops converged at **Meaux** and advanced towards the capital along the Marne. Facing fewer than 25,000 demoralized French troops, and secure in the knowledge that **Napoleon** was stranded far to the east, they met no serious resistance until they were almost in the suburbs on 30 March.

A stand at Clichy by **Moncey**'s two militia divisions, and resistance by the two main corps around Romainville, could impose only a few hours' delay. Mortier's dwindling corps took up positions at Belleville, Marmont's at Montmartre, but the poor condition of the capital's defences, Napoleon's absence and the population's willingness to welcome the allies made prolonged resistance pointless. Marmont signed an armistice at two on the morning of 31 March, and was allowed to retire south of Paris while the allies entered the city.

They were greeted by an enthusiastic **Talleyrand** at the head of a provisional government that immediately declared Napoleon deposed. The emperor himself had set out from St Dizier on 28 March, and was at Essonnes on the Seine, 30km south of Paris, when he received news of the capital's surrender. Turning back to Fontainebleau, he attempted to raise an army for the continuation of hostilities, but was persuaded into his first **abdication** before it could be mobilized.

Montmirail, Battle of

The second of four French victories during the **Six Days Campaign** of February 1814. After destroying part of **Blücher**'s command at **Champaubert** on 10 February, and putting his 30,000 strike troops between its two wings, **Napoleon** elected to march his troops overnight through rain and mud to Montmirail, some 40km to the west, hoping to catch General **Sacken**'s Russian corps.

Recognizing that his army had been split in two, Blücher ordered **Yorck**'s advanced northern wing back to Montmirail that evening, but it was still a long way off when Sacken's 18,000 troops (and 90 guns) approached the town from the west next morning. In contact with forward French **cavalry** 10km west of Montmirail, Sacken ignored Yorck's suggestion that he move north to a rendezvous, and advanced into positions south of the road into town, around the village of Marchais.

Mud had delayed French deployment, and by mid-morning Napoleon could only call on about 6,800 infantry and 4,500 cavalry, although most were **Imperial Guard** veterans. Forced to detach a division against the approach of Yorck's 18,000 men from the north, he could only hold off repeated Russian attempts to break through the road east of Marchais.

Yorck's advance guards reached the northern fringes of the battle zone at about two, but were committed so slowly that Napoleon was free to launch an immediate attack against Sacken's left wing when **Mortier's** arrival brought his strength up to 20,000 men. Launched at about four, it overcame counter-attacks by Russian cavalry to rout Sacken's corps, which was pursued west until nightfall. Only the need to turn Mortier's reserves against Yorck, who soon retired out of range, enabled most of Sacken's command to escape north towards **Château-Thierry**.

The defeat cost Sacken about 4,000 casualties, and Napoleon about 2,000. Although by no means the decisive triumph immediately claimed by French **propaganda**, it shook Blücher's hitherto absolute faith in imminent allied victory, and he ordered a general withdrawal to Reims next day. *See* Battle of **Vauchamps**; Campaign for **France**; Map 26.

Montreal Offensive

The most ambitious **US Army** operation of the **Anglo-American War**, a two-pronged offensive by some 14,000 troops, easily the largest single force yet assembled by the independent **United States**, towards the Canadian town of Montreal in autumn 1813. Intended to exploit the confusion inflicted on General Prevost's British army at **Sackett's Harbor** in May, and to forestall its reorganization in Montreal, the operation envisaged a wide pincer movement. Overall commander General Wilkinson was to lead some 8,000 men up the St Lawrence from Lake Ontario, while General Hampton's column approached from the east via Lake Champlain (*see* **Map 27**). Hampton was frightened into a retreat to

Plattsburg and winter quarters by a British ruse around Chateauguay on 25 October, when a small force made enough noise in the woods to convince US troops that it was a large army, and Wilkinson retreated after defeat by a mere 800 British regulars at Chrysler's Farm on 11 November. The militia-based US armies fell apart during the winter, and the next American attack on Canada, at **Chippewa** in July 1814, was carried out by a far smaller force.

Moore, Sir John (1761–1809)

The most celebrated British soldier of the age after **Wellington**, Moore was the son of a well-known Scottish doctor and novelist, and was commissioned into the **British Army** at 15. He served in the American War of Independence, returning to sit as a Whig member of parliament from 1784, and purchased a regimental command in 1790. He led his troops during the occupation of **Corsica** four years later, and commanded a brigade during **Abercromby's** 1796 campaign in the **West Indies**, surviving a severe bout of fever.

Promoted major-general in 1798, he took part in suppression of that year's **Irish Rebellion**, and was shot through the head without suffering any permanent damage in **North Holland** (1799). He greatly enhanced a growing reputation as a field officer commanding a division at **Alexandria** in 1801, when he was again wounded and invalided home. After service in **Sicily** and Sweden during 1802, he returned to England, where he inaugurated a radical programme of infantry training.

By attempting to instil a sense of personal responsibility in every soldier, demanding rigid discipline in return for conscientious care and reward schemes, and concentrating on technical proficiency, Moore developed a force of light troops (later reincarnated as the Light Division) capable of holding its own against hitherto successful French **infantry tactics**. Although other British officers, notably **Craufurd**, were also engaged in important tactical reforms, Moore is generally regarded as the father of modern British infantry methods.

Promoted lieutenant-general in 1805, Moore led a division to aid **Sweden** in the 1808 **Russo-Swedish War**, but left after arguing with the king, and replaced **Dalrymple** as C-in-C of British forces in **Portugal** from August. After a period of acclimatization to **Peninsular War** conditions, he launched a raid into **Spain** in the late autumn, but was fatally wounded by a cannonball through the left shoulder in the process of extricating his army at **Corunna** on 16 January 1809.

Moreau, Jean Victor (1763–1813)

One of the most successful **French Army** generals to survive the **Revolutionary Wars**, Moreau was a lawyer's son, and studied law at Rennes before becoming a **National Guard** artillery captain in 1789. His unit was absorbed by the regular army in 1791, and he was a lieutenant-colonel in **Flanders** during the opening campaign against the **First Coalition**. Promoted brigadier-general in early 1794, and given a division under **Pichegru** in April, he developed a successful partnership with **Souham** at **Moescroen** and **Tourcoing**, and helped take **Nijmegen** in November.

Moreau replaced Pichegru in March 1795, and again in early 1796 as C-in-C on the southern sector of the **Rhine** front, where a bold autumn offensive from **Kehl** confirmed him as one of the army's rising stars. Compelled to retire by **Jourdan**'s failure further north, he completed a brilliant withdrawal to the Rhine at **Schliengen** in late October, and won a minor victory at **Diersheim** in April 1797 to end the war an established military hero.

Second-in-command on the **Italian** front when hostilities opened against the **Second Coalition**, he replaced **Schérer** as theatre commander in April 1799. Outnumbered by **Suvorov**'s Austro-Russian army, he was beaten at **Cassano** and driven back on Genoa before returning to the **Rhine** as Jourdan's replacement in the summer. He reorganized and revitalized a depressed army to beat **Kray** at **Höchstädt**, and though his efforts were overshadowed by **Napoleon**'s triumph at **Marengo**, his Rhine Army sealed **Austria**'s final defeat at **Hohenlinden** in December 1800.

Hitherto a staunch republican, and a supporter of the **Brumaire coup** in 1799, Moreau found his position ruthlessly undermined after he allowed himself to become a focus for opposition to Napoleon. Denied senior command, he was implicated in the **Cadoudal** conspiracy of early 1804 by police chief **Fouché**, and imprisoned on flimsy evidence. His sentence reduced to exile, he retired to the **United States**, but his military talents were not entirely forgotten in Europe. He returned at the request of Tsar **Alexander** in 1813, and served as a military adviser to Russian forces during the campaign in **Germany**, but was mortally wounded at **Dresden** in August.

Mortars

Short-barrelled, large-calibre **artillery** weapons that were a vital component of contemporary **siege warfare**. Anything up to 374mm calibre but seldom more than 1.5m long, mortars fired a heavy 'bomb' similar to the **common shell** used in howitzers, but weighted to land fuse-up so that it would always detonate. Angle of fire could be altered, but was usually left at 45 degrees, with variations in the propellant charge introduced to determine range (anything from 200m with a 0.5kg charge to about 2.5km with a 4kg charge). Capable of lobbing bombs to a great height, so that they could drop on targets almost vertically, mortars were immensely valuable weapons against besieged garrisons, but their great weight was a drawback. Mounted on large wooden platforms, because their recoil was too powerful for standard gun carriages, the bigger mortars could weigh up to about 2,000kg, and transport difficulties in any kind of rough terrain dictated the snail-like pace of contemporary **siege trains**. Smaller mortars, light enough to be carried by two strong men, were available and used, but did comparatively little damage and leaped into the air as fired. *See also* 'Bombs'.

Mortier, Adolphe Edouard Casimir Joseph (1768–1835)

One of **Napoleon**'s more mundane marshals, Mortier joined the Dunkirk **National Guard** in 1789, and was an elected captain from 1791. In **Flanders** during 1793–4, he fought at **Jemappes**, **Neerwinden** and **Fleurus**, before transferring to the **Rhine**, where he turned down promotion to brigadier-general in 1797. A brigade commander against the **Second Coalition** on the **Swiss** front, he was promoted divisional general in October 1799 after taking part in the second Battle of **Zurich**.

Entrusted with the occupation of **Hanover** in 1803, Mortier was one of the original **Marshalate** the following year, and commanded the **Imperial Guard** infantry before leading a reserve corps against the **Third Coalition** in 1805. His newly formed VIII Corps passed a severe test at **Dürrenstein**, and he replaced the wounded **Lannes** with V Corps in December. He led VIII Corps on the **Grande Armée's** northern flank against the **Fourth Coalition**. It took part at the sieges of **Stralsund** and **Danzig** in 1807, but also fought at **Heilsberg** and reached **Friedland** in time to spearhead the French left wing.

Ennobled as the Duke of Treviso in 1808, Mortier was transferred to **Spain** that autumn, fighting at **Somosierra** and **Saragossa** before joining **Soult's** corps in south-western Spain. Recalled from the **Peninsular** theatre in May 1811, he commanded the **Young Guard** for the **Russian campaign** of 1812, fighting at **Borodino** and serving as governor of **Moscow** before assuming temporary command of the Imperial Guard in early 1813. He was back with the Young Guard for the Battles of **Lützen**, **Bautzen**, **Dresden** and **Leipzig**, but switched to command of the 'Old Guard' during the defence of **France**. One of Napoleon's principal strike commanders during February 1814, Mortier fell back on Paris when his corps was cut off after the defeat at **Laon** in early March. Beaten at **La Fère-Champenoise**, he shared the final defence of the capital with **Marmont** at **Montmartre**.

Accepting royal service on Napoleon's **abdication**, Mortier rejoined the emperor during the **Hundred Days** of 1815, but was too ill to fight and went back to work for the king in July. Briefly out of favour for refusing to pass sentence on **Ney**, he became a successful postwar diplomat and politician. He was killed in a terrorist attack aimed at King Louis-Philippe, who had been at Neerwinden as General 'Egalité'.

Moscow, Occupation of (1812)

French forces occupied Moscow, Russia's second city and the centre of its religious culture, between 14 September and 19 October 1812.

After following the retreat of **Kutuzov's** Russian armies from the Battle of **Borodino** (7 September), advanced units of the central French army reached the city gates on 14 September, and Russian troops began pulling out of Moscow the same morning. Napoleon accepted Kutuzov's offer of the city's surrender in return for an unhindered withdrawal south towards Kolumna, and about 100,000 exhausted French survivors began entering Moscow that night. Napoleon arrived next day to take up residence in the Kremlin.

Most of Moscow's 300,000 citizens had fled on instructions from Russian military authorities, so that French attempts at pageant lacked an audience, and civil governor Count Rostopchin had ordered the city burned around the invader. Fires began on 15 September and eventually destroyed three-quarters of the city, leaving only the Kremlin quarter habitable by the time they abated two days later. Napoleon withdrew temporarily from the fires, and French troops embarked on a period of unrestrained looting, gorging themselves on the luxury goods that constituted most of Moscow's remaining supplies.

Choosing to regard the fires as the work of disorganized fanatics, Napoleon kept his troops quartered in Moscow while awaiting a peace offer from Tsar **Alexander**. None came. With the unanimous support of his advisers, Alexander ignored a personal letter from Napoleon in late September, and two French delegations (on 5 and 14 October) received similar treatment. Nothing was done to hasten Napoleon's departure from Moscow, because each passing week brought winter closer and strengthened a growing Russian manpower advantage.

Napoleon seems to have retreated into fantasy for a time, but the return of his second failed peace mission on 17 October finally convinced him that waiting was hopeless. He ordered a tactical withdrawal to Smolensk for 20 October, but departure plans were hastened by a surprise Russian attack around **Vinkovo** on 18 October, and the French army – reduced to 95,000 men and 500 guns, but augmented by thousands of wagonloads of loot – marched out of Moscow on the morning of 19 October. Marshal **Mortier** ignored orders to burn the rest of the city on departure. *See* **Russian Campaign**; **Map 23**.

Moss, Convention of

The agreement between **Sweden** and representatives of a Norwegian national assembly, signed on 14 August 1814, that ended Norway's attempt to decide its own future. Norway was a semi-autonomous province of **Denmark** until the Treaty of **Kiel** (January 1814) transferred it to Swedish control, but a Norwegian national assembly agreed a new liberal constitution and named Danish governor Prince Christian Frederick as king in May. The move provoked an immediate invasion by the **Swedish Army**, and Norwegian resistance had been reduced to defence of the fortress at Halden by the time the Convention was signed. Its terms required the Norwegians to demobilize and allow occupation pending union with Sweden. Christian Frederick was removed from executive control, which was to be exercised by his erstwhile ministers, and **Charles XIII** of Sweden (who became ruler of Norway in November) agreed to accept the new constitution.

Mount Tabor, Battle of *See* **Acre**, Siege of

Mouton, Georges (1770–1838)

A volunteer in 1792, Mouton fought the **First Coalition** at the **Rhine** and on the **Italian** front, and returned to Italy as an aide to **Joubert** in 1799, remaining in the theatre throughout the War of the **Second Coalition**. Promoted brigadier-general in 1805, he served with **Napoleon's** headquarters through the campaigns against the **Third** and **Fourth Coalitions** until severely wounded at **Friedland** in 1807. Given a divisional command later that year, he took part in the invasion of **Spain** in 1808 and played a major role in the French victory at **Medina del Río Seco**, but returned to France with Napoleon in January 1809.

Again with the emperor's headquarters during the campaign in **Germany** of 1809, he led a famous charge at **Landshut**, fought at **Eckmühl** and played an important part in the Battle of **Aspern–Essling**. He was ennobled as the Count of Lobau for leading the **Young Guard** attack on Essling, and afterwards was generally known by his title. He performed staff duties during the

1812 **Russian campaign**, again accompanying Napoleon back to France, and fought in Germany at **Lützen** and **Dresden**, where he was taken prisoner. Freed on Napoleon's **abdication**, he led a corps through the **Hundred Days** campaign, but was again captured at **Waterloo** and only returned home in 1818, eventually becoming a Marshal of France in 1831.

Murad Bey (1750–1801)

The **Mameluke** co-ruler of **Egypt** (with **Ibrahim Bey**) at the time of the French expedition to the **Middle East** in 1798, Murad led local forces at **Shubra Khit** and the **Pyramids**, but was driven into Upper Egypt after Ibrahim's forces withdrew into Syria. Though evading capture, he lost political influence while in hiding, and was a peripheral figure by the time he agreed a treaty with French commander **Kléber** in March 1801. Murad's new loyalties were never tested: he died of plague before reaching Cairo.

Murat, Joachim (1767–1815)

Of all the careers elevated in **Napoleon's** wake, none was more colourful and celebrated than that of Joachim Murat. The twelfth child of an innkeeper from Gascony, he died Europe's most famous **cavalry** commander and the deposed King of **Naples**, after a life crammed with spectacular triumphs and disasters.

Murat became a cavalry trooper to escape debts in 1787, and was commissioned in 1792. He fought in the initial campaigns against the **First Coalition** in **Flanders**, and was almost purged as an extremist after the **Thermidor coup** of summer 1794. Serving around Paris at the time of the 1795 **Vendémiaire coup**, he fetched the **artillery** with which Brigadier-General Bonaparte put it down, and was rewarded with appointment as a colonel on Napoleon's staff for the **Italian** campaign of 1796.

Promoted brigadier-general after delivering the **Cherasco** treaty with **Piedmont** to the **Directory** at the end of April, Murat led his **dragoons** with particular distinction at **Rivoli** in early 1797. He performed equally well in the **Middle East** the following year, earning battlefield promotion to divisional command at **Aboukir** in July 1799, and accompanying Napoleon back to France in August. Given command of the Consular Guard after the **Brumaire coup**, he completed his initiation to Napoleon's inner circle by marrying Caroline **Bonaparte** in early 1800.

Napoleon's cavalry commander through the **Italian campaign** of 1800, he occupied **Tuscany** in October, and remained poised to strike at Naples from central Italy until the War of the **Second Coalition** ended. Murat collected a string of honours before he next went to war, becoming one of the original **Marshalate**, a Grand Admiral and a Prince of the Empire (February 1805).

The campaign of 1805 against the **Third Coalition** demonstrated both Murat's strengths and weaknesses. In command of the advanced guard with **Lannes**, his vigour and offensive capabilities were important to the victories at **Ulm** and **Austerlitz**. On the other hand his impetuous seizure of **Vienna** reflected basic strategic failings, a feud with **Ney** over the action at **Albeck** hinted at excessive pride, and failure at **Hollabrünn** exposed the limitations of his intelligence. Redeeming himself after each error with prodigious feats of pursuit and endurance, he became Grand Duke of **Berg** and Cleves in March 1806.

Performing a similar operational role against the **Fourth Coalition**, Murat had a more consistent record during 1806–7, fighting at **Jena**, **Golymin**, **Heilsberg**, **Ionkovo** and **Eylau**, where a brilliant cavalry charge swelled his international fame. Otherwise in command of Napoleon's advance guard, he took the surrender of Prussian forces at **Prenzlau** and **Lübeck** in late 1806, was temporary C-in-C during the **Grande Armée's** march on **Warsaw**, and led the detachment to Königsberg in June 1807 that forced the Russians to fight at **Friedland**.

With Napoleon for the invasion of **Spain** in 1808, Murat was left in command at **Madrid**, and put down the city's rebellion in May before departing to replace Joseph **Bonaparte** as King of Naples on 15 July. Reaching his new kingdom on 6 September, Murat took his royal status seriously. Maintaining support in Naples by economic discrimination against outlying provinces, King Joachim employed his military talents to subdue Calabrian rebels and seize the British

outpost on **Capri**, but was never able to drive the British from **Sicily**.

He left his ambitious wife in control of Naples to join the **Russian campaign** in 1812, fighting in his usual combined role as cavalry commander and occasional temporary C-in-C. He spent much of the campaign's opening phases in exhausting and often fruitless pursuit of retreating Russian forces, but displayed all his old rashness at **Krasnoe** in August. After fighting at **Borodino**, he allowed the friendly behaviour of his many **Cossack** admirers to lull him into defeat at **Vinkovo** in October. In command of the last stages of the retreat from Russia, after Napoleon had returned to Paris, he left the front for Naples on 18 January 1813.

By that time Caroline had opened peace negotiations with the allies, and talks continued with Murat's consent. Announcing his dedication to Italian rather than Napoleonic interests after the French defeat at **Leipzig** in 1813, he brought Naples into the **Sixth Coalition** and launched an immediate invasion of French territories to the north, but his reluctance actually to fight during the **Italian campaign** of 1814 sealed failure to secure allied recognition of his throne at the Congress of **Vienna**.

Murat switched allegiance again on news of Napoleon's return from **Elba**. Declaring a War of 'Italian Independence', he launched a quixotic offensive against Austrian forces in Italy from March 1815, but it had collapsed by early May. Murat fled to France, anticipating arrest and execution in Naples, but Napoleon refused his services for the **Hundred Days** campaign, and he travelled back to Italy on news of **Waterloo**. He eventually returned with a small force to Calabria, where he was captured, tried on the spot and executed on 13 October.

Murray, George (1772–1846)

British staff officer, commissioned in 1789, who saw service as an infantry officer in **Flanders**, but subsequently filled administrative posts at **Quiberon Bay** (1796), **North Holland** (1799) and **Alexandria** (1801). After a spell as adjutant-general to British forces in the **West Indies**, he performed staff duties with the expedition to **Copenhagen** in 1807, **Moore's** 1808 mission to

Sweden and the **Corunna** campaign. From March 1809 until April 1814, with an interruption when he returned to Britain for a time in 1812, Murray served as quartermaster to British forces in the **Peninsular War**. Experienced, well organized, good at geography and comfortable with **Wellington**'s thought processes, he filled a role comparable with that played by **Berthier** during French **Grande Armée** operations. Promoted brigadier-general in June 1811, and major-general at the start of 1812, he was sent to organize British forces in the **Anglo-American War** from late 1814, and recalled too late to fight at **Waterloo**. He was chief of staff to allied forces occupying France from 1815 to 1818, and a long postwar career included a spell as minister for the colonies (1828–30).

Muskets

The infantryman's basic weapon throughout the period, the musket had changed little during the previous century, and most types shared a similar basic design. A standard 'muzzle-loader' consisted of a wooden butt, or stock, attached to a tubular iron barrel. A small quantity of gunpowder and a lead ball were inserted in the muzzle of the barrel and pushed to the far end. The powder was ignited through a small hole on the side of the barrel at the firer's end, the 'touch hole'. The most technologically complex element in muzzle-loader design was the 'flintlock' generally used to spark the powder: a trigger attached to the stock was connected to a spring-loaded hammer, or 'cock', on top of which two screws held a piece of flint; when the trigger was pulled, releasing the hammer, the flint struck a hinged steel plate, or 'frizzen', creating a spark and firing the gun. Musket balls generally weighed 20–30g, and were usually loaded in 'prepared' form, packaged with sufficient gunpowder in a twist of greased paper.

Training for musket use tended to concentrate overwhelmingly on loading drill, partly because actually firing the weapon required little skill, beyond firing from the right shoulder (to avoid eye burns through the touch hole), and coping with a powerful recoil. A ball could inflict appalling injuries on flesh and blood targets, and

could travel anywhere between 100 and 700m before losing lethal velocity (unless the musket was one of many produced with faulty barrels), but accuracy above 100m was rare, so that musket fire was generally best employed in mass volleys against whole armies. Five shots per minute was considered an exceptional performance by a unit in combat.

Though slow-firing, inaccurate and prone to damage, muskets used by contemporary armies were cheap, easy to mass-produce and extremely versatile. An experienced infantryman short of prepared cartridges could load powder and ball separately, or could replace the ball with a stone, uniform button or any other object of suitable dimensions. Even the flash emitted during discharge could set fire to an enemy's clothing at close quarters, although it could also ignite the surrounding countryside in dry conditions, as happened during several **Peninsular War** engagements.

All contemporary armies employed a wide variety of modifications on the basic musket pattern, but design differences were generally slight and had little impact on performance. An individual infantryman's skill apart, the most important factors governing both performance and frequency of use tended to be quality and quantity of production. The mass-produced French Charleville musket and the British Brown Bess (both generic terms covering a multitude of variants) were standard issue with their respective forces throughout the period, and **Austria**'s well-established arms factories produced high-quality weapons, including a few breech-loading muskets that proved too complex to produce in numbers. All three powers exported muskets to their less industrially developed allies, but the British became genuine mass suppliers in the modern sense, sending hundreds of thousands of Brown Bess derivatives to Prussia and Russia, overwhelmingly agricultural states unable to produce the weapons needed to supply expanding armies (and in Russia's case, incapable of manufacturing a reliable weapon). *See also* **Bayonets; Rifles; Infantry Tactics.**

N

Naples

Covering the whole of Italy south of the **Papal States**, the independent Kingdom of Naples had been ruled by the Spanish royal family since the sixteenth century, though it had passed under Austrian control for a time at the start of the eighteenth. Naples was politically united with the neighbouring island of **Sicily** from 1738, when Bourbon prince Charles (later Charles III of Spain) became ruler of the Kingdom of the Two Sicilies, and his young son took the thrones as **Ferdinand IV** (and Ferdinand III of Sicily) in 1759 (*see* **Map 1**).

Ferdinand was still in power at the start of the **Revolutionary Wars**, though policy was largely conducted by Queen Maria Carolina and her chief minister, English naval officer Sir John Acton. Their confirmed anti-republicanism was expressed in active membership of the **First Coalition** from 1793, and in concerted attempts to suppress mounting radicalism in Naples itself. French success in the **Italian campaigns** of 1796 induced Naples to make peace, but war broke out again in 1798, when the promptings of **Nelson** contributed to an extraordinary decision to invade central Italy in advance of any guarantees of **great power** support.

The disastrous **Neapolitan campaign** of 1798–9 confirmed the poor reputation of the **Neapolitan Army**, and left the kingdom open to a surge of popular republicanism as French armies advanced almost unopposed on the capital. The royal family fled to Sicily aboard Nelson's ship in December, leaving Naples in a state of nascent civil war between republican mobs and royalist *lazzarone* (Ferdinand was known as the *lazzaroni*, or yokel, king).

Invited to restore law and order by republican city notables, French forces under **Championnet** occupied Naples from 20 January 1799, and the kingdom became the Parthenopean Republic three days later. The new state never achieved financial or political stability, and faced an immediate royalist insurrection in the countryside, led and organized by Ferdinand's representative, Cardinal Ruffo.

Ruffo's Christian Army of the Holy Faith, a band of brigands and peasants equipped with Russian and Turkish help, moved on Naples from its base in Calabria, compelling French occupying troops to leave the city before Ferdinand returned to the mainland in July 1799. Naples remained at war with France until 1801, when the Treaty of **Florence** left Ferdinand free to exact full revenge on Neapolitan republicans.

Though technically allied to France, Ferdinand remained wary of **Napoleon**'s ambitions in Italy. Promised British military and economic aid, he provisionally agreed to join the **Third Coalition** against France in April 1805, prompting Napoleon to send Joseph **Bonaparte** and **Gouvion St Cyr** to occupy southern Italy with 20,000 troops. Neapolitan authorities signed an armistice with France on 4 February 1806, by which time Ferdinand had already fled to Sicily again, to be followed by his wife on 11 February. Joseph was crowned king in Naples on 30 March, and though a small British force under General

Stuart won a tactical victory at Maida in July, its rapid withdrawal left French forces free to reduce isolated royalist garrisons.

Joseph's regime was well intentioned and introduced some fiscal and social reforms, including the formal (if incomplete) abolition of feudalism in early August. Though he was more popular than Maria Carolina had ever been in Naples itself, the threat of restoration conspiracy was only extinguished by police chief Saliceti's anti-royalist terror campaign in the spring and early summer of 1807. Meanwhile brigandage remained rife in the provinces, declining only slightly in Calabria after the capture and execution of guerrilla leader Fra Diavolo in November 1806.

Joseph's reign laid the foundations of an efficient bureaucratic system, and of military reforms, but his relatively successful resistance to Napoleon's economic demands was the key to his government's stability. On his reluctant abdication to become King of Spain in July 1808, Napoleon's appointment of Murat as his successor was hedged with financial burdens that, along with enforcement of the Continental System, plunged the kingdom into economic crisis.

Murat became King Joachim on 1 August 1808, reaching Naples on 6 September. He opened his reign with the successful capture of Capri, and remained a popular figure throughout his reign, despite the imposition of draconian taxes on outlying provinces to spare the capital, his failure to mount a convincing attack on Sicily, the unpopularity of his army's enforced contribution to the Peninsular War, and his own deteriorating relations with Napoleon. Kept economically afloat by Joseph's largely intact bureaucracy, he was able to conduct successful police actions against carbonari and bandit activities, but 33,000 arrests in 1809 alone reflected epidemic lawlessness in a nation of only 5 million.

Murat allowed his ambitious wife Caroline Bonaparte to exercise considerable political control. She supervised the introduction of the Code Napoléon, effective from New Year's Day 1810, and acted as regent while he was absent for the 1812 Russian campaign. An incurable conspirator, whose prime concerns were dynastic, she initiated negotiations with the allies on her own

authority from late 1812. Murat was aware of these by the time he returned to Naples in early 1813, and announced his dedication to Italian rather than Napoleonic interests after the French defeat at Leipzig.

Subsequent negotiations with Habsburg diplomats brought Naples into the Sixth Coalition from January 1814, but Murat's reluctance to fight French forces during that year's brief Italian campaign confirmed allied mistrust, and he received no formal guarantees of his crown before Napoleon's return from Elba in March 1815. Hoping to exploit Austrian preoccupation with the restored French Empire, Murat launched a quixotic, self-proclaimed 'War of Italian Independence' and invaded northern Italy. His ill-prepared and poorly motivated army was routed at Tolentino in early May, and Austrian troops entered Naples on 23 May. Murat fled to France, eventually returning in October, when he landed on the Calabrian coast with a small force, but was captured and executed.

The death of his wife, whose machinations against the British in Sicily had ended with her exile, removed the only other serious obstacle to Ferdinand's restoration, which was subsequently confirmed by the Congress of Vienna. He quickly reversed the concessions forced upon him by British support for Sicilian liberals. Declaring the reunion of the 'Two Sicilies' in 1816, he presided over years of popular unrest that climaxed in an abortive revolution of 1820–1. Naples remained weak, divided and prey to frequent foreign military intervention on Ferdinand's death in 1825, and its socio-political condition deteriorated under his son Francis.

Napoleon I, Emperor *See* **Bonaparte,** Napoleon

Nassau

Independent duchy in northern Germany that was divided into three main portions, the lands of the Orange family and those of the two brothers heading the family's other main branch, Prince Frederick William of Nassau-Weilburg and Prince Charles William of Nassau-Usingen. The brothers ceded their territories west of the Rhine to France in 1801, accepting compensatory lands elsewhere, and shared the third sector after

William Frederick of **Orange** was stripped of his Nassau possessions for refusing to join the Confederation of the **Rhine** in 1806. Nassau-Usingen and Nassau-Weilburg each provided a regiment with the **French Army** until Nassau joined the allies after the Battle of **Leipzig** in 1813, and a fresh battalion was subsequently raised to fight with the allies, its two regiments playing a vital role at **Quatre Bras** in 1815. *See* **Map 1**.

National Convention

The elected legislative body that governed the republic of **France** from its proclamation on 22 September 1792, when it replaced the Legislative Assembly in name, until 27 October 1795, when it was it was officially superceded by The **Directory**.

National Guard (French)

The volunteer militia called into existence by the States-General at the start of the **French Revolution** in 1789, the National Guard formed the military arm of insurrection in Paris over the next three or four years, and remained the nation's principal home defence reserve until 1814. Enrolment in regional National Guard units was rendered obligatory for able-bodied males not in regular military service after the outbreak of war in 1792, a measure enacted whenever danger appeared to threaten the homeland and later extended to other regions under French control. Many units were absorbed into the regular **French Army** during the **Revolutionary Wars**, an expedient also used by **Napoleon** for the 1813 campaign in **Germany**, and the National Guard came into its own as a military force in early 1814, when it formed the backbone of a dwindling mobile army defending France.

Nations, Battle of the

Name sometimes used to describe the Battle of **Leipzig**.

Naval Warfare

In an age when ships had no rivals as a means of international communication or heavy haulage, European states maintained naval forces for a number of key tasks. Warships could act as protection for trading fleets, spearhead expansion or control **colonial** empires, defend home coasts in time of war, or menace hostile territory, navies and trade routes.

Though contemporary naval warfare was global in scope, foreshadowing the role of warships in twentieth-century world wars, its practical conduct depended on technology (and some systems) dating back to the Dark Ages. Wooden ships driven by wind power or oars were still at the whim of the elements, and getting ships to the right location, at the right time and in useful condition remained an enormous economic and logistic challenge.

Most European states were unable or unwilling to maintain big navies in efficient operational shape. Both **Prussia** and **Austria** virtually ignored naval development as a costly distraction from land warfare until well into the nineteenth century. **Sweden** and **Denmark** retained fairly powerful navies in 1792, but confined their interests to regional waters, and though **Russia** was emerging as a major maritime power in the Baltic and Black Seas, its navy was only just beginning to establish a strategic role by 1792. The **Ottoman Empire's** obsolete ships could hardly compete with modern European forces, and the navies of **Portugal**, **Naples** and **Venice** were decaying reminders of past glories.

The **Netherlands**, **Spain** and **France** had built global empires on the back of maritime success and retained important fleets at the start of the wars. The **Dutch Navy** was a small but efficient service before French conquest in 1795 signalled a rapid decline, but the large **Spanish** service had been crippled by state poverty, and the **French Navy**, though still the second most powerful in the world, was crumbling under the combined effects of financial neglect and revolution.

No navy in the world could begin to match the size and efficiency of the British **Royal Navy**. By far the richest nation on earth, and spared any major stake in European land warfare, **Great Britain** devoted enormous resources to protecting and expanding its position as the world's leading maritime trader. Its empire had been built on sea power, and only Britain could afford to pursue naval development as the heart of state strategy.

In an age when £200 per year made an Englishman fairly wealthy, about £100,000 bought a ship-of-the-line (or battleship) crammed with artillery, men and supplies. Its construction required time, large-scale dockyard facilities and a mass of (often imported) raw materials. Skill was also needed to produce the most complex machinery of the day, and many vessels laboured under severe design faults throughout their active careers.

Once in service, big ships needed regular supplies of everything from water and beer to preserved meats, tobacco and livestock, along with repair materials, gunpowder and an enormous weight of ammunition. They could be operated only by experts dependent on primitive navigational methods, could be virtually paralysed for weeks by contrary winds, and were in constant peril from the elements. As many big warships were wrecked, run aground or accidentally burned in wartime as were destroyed by any kind of hostile action, and any vessel left in harbour for too long would rot into uselessness, though the introduction of copper-bottomed keels since the mid-eighteenth century had slowed the process.

Though by no means built on standard lines, men-of-war fell into distinct classes. Ships-of-the-line were the largest warships afloat, ranging in size from old 50- or 64-gun vessels to massive three-deckers carrying between 100 and 130 guns. Used in fleets (of more than ten ships) or smaller groups to fight each other, to escort and support land forces overseas, and as the mainstays of blockades, they were also powerful individual weapons against coastal targets.

The eyes of battlefleets on patrol or blockade duty, and powerful detached weapons in their own right, fast frigates also performed as 'cruisers', policing coastlines and sea lanes as part of a constant campaign fought by all wartime navies for control of global trade routes. The bulk of this background war was conducted by light naval forces, with three-masted sloops or corvettes (10–24 guns) often the most powerful vessels operating in their sectors. Light forces and minor navies deployed a bewildering variety of smaller or converted ships, including cutters, brigs, gunboats, galleys and armed merchantmen, all engaged in operations against enemy light forces, merchant traffic, pirates or privateers.

Armour was not a factor in contemporary naval warfare, and most ships smaller than sloops were militarized by simply adding guns and naval personnel, but specialist craft in regular use included bombs, fireships, floating batteries, transports and shallow-draught gunships designed specifically for Baltic use by Swedish and Russian forces.

Naval weaponry was not particularly specialized, or subject to major innovation during the war years, universal lack of interest in Robert Fulton's 1810 proposals for underwater craft reflecting a general mistrust of costly experimentation. Marines and armed boarding parties used standard muskets, but seamen also carried cutlasses and anything else to hand, while pistols were popular with officers as back-up to their swords. Naval artillery was adapted from standard field and siege designs, with the biggest ships firing long-barrelled 24-pounders, and smaller vessels anything from 2-pounders up. The use of light, short-barrelled carronades aboard warships, particularly by the British, reflected a tendency for many ship-to-ship combats to end in close-quarters fighting.

Large warships needed hundreds of men, many of them skilled, and chronic crew shortages crippled many wartime navies, particularly as the expanding scale of land warfare came to dominate European priorities after 1805. Though press gangs could make up numbers with kidnapped seamen, accounting for perhaps a third of all Royal Navy recruitment, death and desertion rates were generally high, and most services were desperate for men most of the time.

Crew morale and health were important factors governing naval performance, and the British enjoyed a clear lead over rivals. Crowded ships were ideal breeding grounds for contagions beyond the scope of contemporary medicine, but British naval authorities understood the connections between fresh food and scurvy, which remained endemic in other navies. British ships also practised basic hygiene, in contrast to the French practice of storing bodies in the hold pending land burials.

Conditions aboard warships were appalling by modern standards. Men in all navies lived under harsh discipline, in cramped, unhealthy spaces and often on bad food. Routine procedures were dull, but unpleasant and dangerous in themselves, and the chances of surviving any shipwreck or battle wound were slim (especially since very few sailors could swim).

Broadly speaking, life for senior officers aboard British ships, with survivable rations, personal possessions on board, some degree of privacy and a fighting chance of prosperity through **prize money**, was about as good as it could be on active naval service. Other British naval personnel, including junior officers, non-commissioned (warrant) officers, gunners, skilled and unskilled ratings and **marines**, enjoyed many of the same benefits and could rely on eventually receiving pay. The same applied to a welter of auxiliary staff, including personal servants, carpenters, butchers, cooks, sail-makers and ship's boys, though no crew in any navy was safe from mal-treatment at sea by a rogue captain, who remained absolute master of his ship unless illegally overthrown.

All navies suffered small-scale mutinies in port and at sea as a matter of routine, and though the most notorious mutinies of the day occurred in British home fleets – at **Spithead**, the **Nore** and elsewhere in 1797 – they involved no refusal to fight, and bore the character of modern strikes over pay and conditions. Other navies were seldom in a position to suffer any strategic loss through inaction caused by their frequent mutinies, but French commanders during the **Revolutionary Wars** found their authority generally undermined by interference from on-board political commissars.

The irresolution of justifiably pessimistic commanders, combined with crew shortages and the ill effects of prolonged inactivity, spoiled the technical performance of well-designed French and Spanish ships. Generally outclassed by British manoeuvring and gunnery skills, they ran a greatly increased risk of damage at sea, and were frequently left dismasted and unmanageable by rough weather.

Dominated by the elements, the naval tactics of the early 1790s were fairly simple. When in contact with hostile forces, an attacker would aim to achieve a position downwind of the opponent, preventing any rapid escape, before moving into close contact as quickly as possible against the wind. The means of reaching this position in fleet strength had been enshrined as a tactical orthodoxy, designed to limit the possibility of either side suffering annihilation.

Hostile fleets would each form a line ahead. The two battle lines would either pass in opposite directions, in which case the engagement would be brief unless both opted to turn round and renew it, or one would overtake the other, in which case the battle would develop as a number of essentially separate duels between individual or small groups of ships. An attacking fleet's approach manoeuvres, concerned with presenting a small target, would give way to combat manoeuvres at the closest possible range as both parties attempted to bring broadsides to bear.

Unless a ship had already lost masts or been set ablaze by long-range fire, a close-range fight would generally be decided by gunnery technique, with faster rate of fire enabling one side (usually the British) to inflict greater attrition. Most ships surrendered before they were sunk, captains preferring inevitable defeat to almost certain death in the water, but if neither hauled down its flag, close-range combat was usually decided by boarding parties, crews scrambling between ships to undertake murderous skirmishes for local control.

Close-battle tactics were largely the domain of individual captains, but some standard differences between national services were discernible. French and Spanish warships tended to open fire at long range, aiming high to damage the rigging of an approaching opponent. British and Dutch crews tended to hold their fire until the last possible moment, seeking to cause maximum deck damage with a low-trajectory opening broadside, a method that took nerve and discipline but was generally more effective.

Close-combat tactics remained essentially unchanged throughout the 1793–1815 period, but approach tactics underwent a significant wartime transformation after 1796. Essentially the province of the Royal Navy, as the only force without a vested interest in avoiding big naval battles, fleet attacks were turned into bids for total victory by a new generation of commanders, including **Jervis**, **Duncan** and **Nelson**. Confident of their combat superiority, British fleets began launching attacks through enemy battle lines, approaching fast with the wind and risking destruction as they passed between hostile broadsides, before turning to destroy their confused victims. By concentrating their warships to isolate and outnumber particular sections of enemy battle lines, they won a series of crushing fleet victories in the 1797–1805 period.

Exorcizing any threat from hostile fleets was only part of the complex naval strategy conducted by the British **Pitt** government from 1793. Primarily directed to defeat France by blockade of its coasts and suffocation of its trade, British naval forces undertook a simultaneous campaign of colonial expansion, were concentrated to repel a possible invasion of **England**, policed a global trade network and performed an auxiliary role in various ill-fated European military adventures. Lack of strategic focus kept the Royal Navy at full stretch throughout the wars, even after any challenge from other fleets had faded, and contributed to its long-term difficulty in translating maritime supremacy into a direct threat to French continental hegemony.

The only naval force able to think in offensive terms, the Royal Navy spent the first half of 1793 mobilizing, after which it repeatedly proved its tactical dominance, but displayed the effects of peacetime complacency and made little strategic headway. Its blockades were ineffective, allowing French squadrons to attack trade routes and bring their own **convoys** safely into port, and its successes were marginal. Capture of the main French Mediterranean base at **Toulon** in summer 1793 was thrown away, and **Howe's** celebrated **First of June** victory over the French Atlantic Fleet in 1794 was both poorly exploited and a strategic defeat. Other opportunities to attack French fleets were missed at **Leghorn**, Ile de **Groix** and the **Hyères Islands**, while colonial successes and individual victories by British warships had little impact on the continental war.

The **First Coalition's** collapse in 1795–6 was a turning point in the naval war. As the Spanish and Dutch navies became French allies, the latter captured by land forces at **Texel**, French conquest of the Channel coast forced the British to mass ships for home defence, and **Napoleon's** successes on the **Italian** front drove them out of

their Mediterranean bases. Evacuation of the Mediterranean in December 1796 left the Royal Navy clearly on the defensive, but operational reforms were already in progress, and its opponents quickly proved themselves incapable of effective offensive action.

French attempts to support an invasion of **Ireland** at **Bantry Bay** failed miserably, and the Royal Navy's new tactical aggression inflicted crushing defeats on the Spanish at Cape **St Vincent** and the Dutch at **Camperdown** in 1797. French plans for a cross-Channel invasion were postponed indefinitely after a rehearsal at the **Saint Marcoufe Islands** in spring 1798, and when the Toulon fleet ventured out to support Napoleon's expedition to the **Middle East** it was virtually wiped out by Nelson at the **Nile** (1 August 1798). Nelson's victory ended French pretensions to Mediterranean control, hastened formation of the **Second Coalition** and announced a spectacular expansion of British responsibilities.

The Mediterranean was the principal theatre of naval conflict during the next three years of war. Russian and **Turkish** fleets entered the theatre to take the French **Ionian Islands**, and the Russians moved on to conduct coastal operations in the Adriatic. British Mediterranean forces under Jervis and **Keith** were kept at full stretch, blockading the French and Spanish coasts, establishing bases at **Minorca** and **Sicily** before taking **Malta** and **Alexandria**.

Despite improved efficiency, this breadth of commitment helped compromise British naval efforts to make a strategic difference on the continent, as the London government again tried to use the whip hand everywhere at once. The Mediterranean Fleet was too scattered to punish occasional Franco-Spanish sorties (like '**Bruix's Cruise'** in 1799) or intervene decisively at **Genoa** or any north **Italian** location. Other European resources were frittered away in marginal and often ill-prepared **amphibious** operations, including fruitless attacks on **Ostende**, **Belleisle**, **Tenerife**, **Ferrol** and **Cadiz**.

Blockade warfare was meanwhile becoming a global diplomatic issue. Belligerent navies routinely outraged neutral governments by stopping and searching their vessels for goods unilaterally declared contraband. French forces in the **West Indies** managed to provoke the **United States** into a regional war of small-scale naval skirmishes (1798–1800), but the British were inevitably the main enforcers of stop and search policy. As well as encouraging worldwide mistrust of Britain, seizures provided a cause for the **Armed Neutrality** League of northern states in 1800–1, put in its (strategically marginal) place by Nelson's brilliant tactical victory over the Danish fleet at **Copenhagen**.

Recognition that naval supremacy was not winning the war fuelled British readiness to agree the Peace of **Amiens** in 1801, returning almost all the Royal Navy's overseas conquests to their original owners. Few expected the peace to last, but French and Spanish forces had slipped further into decay by the time war broke out in 1803. The only substantial naval operation undertaken in peacetime, the French expedition to **Santo Domingo**, was a waste of scarce resources and experienced seamen.

The pattern of naval warfare already established was more sharply defined after 1803. British forces quickly re-established a firm hold over global sea lanes, and set about recapturing colonial outposts almost at leisure. By 1814, the Royal Navy had helped take most of the minor islands in the West Indies, controlled the **Indian Ocean**, and had secured possession of the South African **Cape Colony**, failing only in an over-ambitious attempt to break into Spanish **South America** at **Buenos Aires** (1806–7).

At the same time, increasingly efficient commercial blockades exerted a powerful, if slow-burning, influence on the French imperial economy, forcing development of European overland trade and contributing to an unsustainable drain on French satellite economies. Napoleon's retaliatory **Continental System**, a blanket ban on British trade imposed from 1806, was both unpopular and toothless, promoting a smuggling boom, provoking stricter British blockade regulations by new **Orders in Council**, and ultimately increasing the economic impact of Britain's naval strategy.

One reason behind the Continental System's failure was its almost complete lack of naval support on the high seas, where Nelson's last victory, at **Trafalgar** in October 1805, punished

Napoleon's one attempt to use his fleets as offensive weapons and ended any threat from French or Spanish fleets. Coming just as Napoleon was defeating the **Third Coalition**, Trafalgar set slowly tightening limits on his imperial ambitions and effectively guaranteed British imperial security, but still did not provide the Royal Navy with a way to win the war outright.

No more major naval battles were fought during the wars. Apart from attempts to catch French commerce raiders, like those at **Santo Domingo** (1806) and the **Basque Roads** (1809), routine operations enabled British merchant fleets to establish an overwhelming grip on postwar global trade. British warships elsewhere made an unsuccessful attempt at strategic intervention through the **Dardanelles** in February 1807, and finished off the Danish fleet with a pre-emptive strike on **Copenhagen** a few weeks later, provoking a six-year **Gunboat War** against Danish light forces. The closest any navy came to helping decide the principal land campaigns was in the **Peninsular** theatre, where Royal Navy control of the Iberian coastline enabled British ships to attack coastal positions at will, sustain **guerrilla** forces and provide forward supplies for **Wellington's** long offensives.

A small British squadron entered the Baltic during the **Russo-Swedish War** of 1808–9, when Russian forces confirmed their growing confidence with victories over Swedish light units at **Sandöström** and **Palvasund**. The Russian fleet in the Mediterranean remained in the theatre until late 1807, and its last action before leaving via Gibraltar was an impressive victory over the Turks off **Lemnos**. Probably the world's second most powerful by 1814, the Russian Navy maintained steady postwar development even after it was overtaken by a resurgent French service.

Despite its short-term strategic disappointments, the Royal Navy had extended its lead over the rest of the world's navies by 1815. No major power was able to challenge its supremacy until the twentieth century, but naval operations during the **Anglo-American War** (1812–15) provided a warning postscript to the eighteenth. Though unable to prevent British blockade from devastating American overseas trade, the tiny **US Navy** inflicted several embarrassing defeats on individual British warships and its light forces won a famous victory on **Lake Erie**, reminders that naval aptitude and enterprise were not confined to the British Isles. *See* **Maps 8, 18–20.**

Neapolitan Army

The mainland army of **Naples** was reputedly the most inept ground force in Europe in 1792. It sent detachments to aid allied forces at **Toulon** and on the **Italian** front during 1793–4, and opened the War of the **Second Coalition** with an invasion of French-controlled central Italy. The brief **Neapolitan campaign** that followed confirmed its reputation, and it was of little use when French forces conquered Naples again in 1805.

A new force was organized from scratch along **French Army** lines in 1806. Eight infantry and four **cavalry** regiments were in service by late 1809, and seven more had been cobbled together from disbanded units and deserters by June 1814. A **rifle** corps performed internal operations against **guerrillas**, and an élite Royal Guard of four infantry regiments accompanied the king on military operations.

Raised from a reluctant Neapolitan peasantry and southern Italy's criminal classes, the new army was hardly an improvement on its predecessor. Regularly sent overseas so that the burden of their payment would pass to the French treasury, Neapolitan troops were mostly committed to the **Peninsular War**, and regarded as a liability by **Napoleon**. They suffered a final embarrassment under **Murat's** independent command in May 1815, when they were comprehensively routed by Austrian forces at **Tolentino**.

Neapolitan Campaign (1798–9)

The opening campaign of the War of the **Second Coalition** on the European mainland, triggered by the **Neapolitan Army's** rash invasion of the **Papal States** in November 1798. Urged on by British admiral **Nelson**, staying in **Naples** after his victory at the **Nile**, the Neapolitan court took the extraordinary decision to fight alone against France for reasons that remain uncertain. King **Ferdinand** may have hoped to push the major powers into rapid action, but though Russian tsar **Paul** was keen to open offensive operations in Italy, the arrival of Austrian general **Mack** to take command of the Neapolitan Army on 6

October did not mean that **Austria** was ready for war.

French central Italian commander **Championnet** was alerted by Mack's appointment, and preparing an attack on Naples, but his forces were scattered. He had only 5,000 men around Rome when 40,000 Neapolitan troops moved north from Capua in five columns on 23 November. A portion of the attacking force reached the city's outskirts two days later, and preliminary attacks persuaded Championnet to withdraw north. King Ferdinand entered Rome in triumph on 29 November and invited exiled pope **Pius VI** to return.

Meanwhile Mack's extreme left- and right-hand columns, aiming at Terni and Magliano respectively, were halted by outlying French forces, and his own subsequent capture of Magliano ended in panic-stricken retreat as soon as **Macdonald's** 6,000 troops from the west coast appeared in the vicinity. French east coast forces under General Casabianca drove a fourth column back from Ascoli, and 5,000 troops ferried to the Tuscan city of Leghorn (Livorno) by the **Royal Navy** remained largely inert after taking the port.

Recognizing that his army's fragile morale was crumbling, and that lack of Austrian support would free French reinforcements from the north, Mack launched unsuccessful attacks into Umbria on 4 and 10 December before retreating from Rome on 13 December, preceded by an anxious monarch. Championnet stayed in Rome until late December, when news arrived that **Sérurier's** division was moving to his aid from **Piedmont**, and then led 23,000 troops (including 2,000 **cavalry**) south.

Mack drew up his remaining 25,000 troops on the frontier around Capua, their poor morale not improved by the royal family's flight to **Sicily** (23–26 December), and Macdonald's French vanguard approached forward Neapolitan positions on 30 December. Neapolitan troops had little fight left in them, so that bandits and lack of supplies were the main obstacles to subsequent French advance, but Capua itself was still holding out when panic-stricken authorities from Naples itself arranged an armistice on 10 January 1799. In return for a promise not to occupy the capital, the Neapolitans ceded frontier towns and agreed to pay an indemnity.

Riots erupted in Naples when French commissioners arrived to collect the first indemnity payment on 15 January, giving Neapolitan republicans a pretext for inviting Championnet to restore order (and persuading Mack to enter protective French custody). French columns under the younger **Kellermann** and **Duhesme** moved towards Naples from 20 January, brushing aside any volunteers who blocked their path. Aided by a few regular troops still at their posts (mostly Swiss and Albanian units), volunteers put up sterner resistance at the city gates, but Championnet took effective control of the city on 23 January.

French forces captured 20,000 men and 60 guns during their short offensive, and Championnet's public announcements of liberal intentions helped secure broad support from Neapolitans for the immediate creation of a republic, but the demands of an **Italian campaign** to the north prevented effective suppression of opposition in the countryside or any attempt to wrest Sicily from British protection. *See* **Map 9**.

Neapolitan Navy

The Kingdom of the Two Sicilies possessed ten old **ships-of-the-line**, six of 74 guns and four of 50, along with ten **frigates** and miscellaneous small craft, but it performed a largely decorative role during the **Revolutionary Wars** (although two of its 74-gunners took part in the occupation of **Toulon**). Partly destroyed when King **Ferdinand IV** left **Naples** for **Sicily** in 1798, it suffered further reduction on his second departure in 1806. Surviving vessels were divided between the Bourbon navy in **Sicily**, which was rendered superfluous by a powerful **Royal Navy** presence, and the French-controlled Neapolitan Navy, which was never remotely strong enough to challenge Britain's absolute control of southern Italian waters.

Neerwinden, Battle of

Major defeat suffered by French forces near the east Belgian village of Neerwinden, some 35km west of Liège, on 18 March 1793 (*see* **Map 2**). French C-in-C **Dumouriez** had suspended his invasion of the independent **Netherlands** and rushed south on 10 March to Louvain, where the remains of **Miranda**'s army were reassembling after its defeat at **Maastricht**. Still a popular French hero, Dumouriez was able to rally dispirited troops for an attack on Austrian forces approaching from the Meuse.

After winning a minor success to halt Archduke **Charles**'s Austrian advance guard south of Louvain, Dumouriez drew up his army on heights north-east of Tirlemont on 16 March, overlooking the route south between the Geete and the Meuse. Reinforced to around 45,000 men (most of them raw recruits), it was led by General Valence on the right, Louis-Philippe 'Egalité' in the centre and Miranda on the left. The 39,000 men of **Saxe-Coburg**'s main Austrian army arrived next day, and deployed in two lines under Ferrari and **Colloredo**, with **Clairfait** and Charles commanding reserve forces on the flanks. The two armies were separated by a small stream, the Little Geete.

A full-scale French attack opened at about nine on the morning of 18 March. A preliminary advance by Valence was driven back beyond Neerwinden by Clairfait's reserves, but the main French attack in the centre retook the village. Neerwinden became the focus of fierce fighting and changed hands three more times before French commanders paused to reorganize at around noon. While Dumouriez prepared his right and centre for a renewed assault on Neerwinden, Miranda attacked Charles in the north, but his *fédérés* were routed and chased back towards Tirlemont. Free to join the battle at Neerwinden, Charles reached the area in the early evening, forcing Dumouriez to retire beyond the Geete.

Though not decisive, the defeat cost the French army perhaps 4,000 losses (against about half as many Austrian) and shattered its fragile morale. When Austrian forces threatened to move further west next day, Dumouriez could only retreat to new positions in front of Louvain, and withdrew into the city when he was attacked on 23 March. Within a matter of days, the army's recall to France and his own defection had brought the French campaign on the Meuse to an end.

Nelson, Horatio (1758–1805)

Generally accepted as the greatest battle commander in the history of European **naval warfare**, Nelson was the son of a village clergyman in Norfolk, eastern England, and joined the **Royal Navy** as a boy of 12. Despite his lack of social or professional influence, his luminous talent and thirst for action brought rapid promotion. After service in the **West Indies**, the Arctic and the East Indies, he was commissioned lieutenant in 1777, and promoted captain two years later.

He commanded a **frigate** under Samuel **Hood** in America from 1780, and subsequently earned some notoriety in the West Indies, where he enforced the letter of much-abused laws restricting the trading activities of local merchants. Married to Frances Nisbet in 1787, he left the Caribbean later that year, living in Norfolk on half pay until the outbreak of war against France in 1793, when he was given command of the **ship-of-the-line** *Agamemnon* and attached to Hood's Mediterranean Fleet.

During the next three years, Nelson established himself as one of the fleet's most enterprising and aggressive captains. His ship played a major part in the **siege** and capture of **Corsica** in 1794, when he suffered injuries that left him blind in one eye (though some modern sources suggest he may have exaggerated the damage by way of augmenting his pension), and it was the only British vessel to emerge with much credit from **Hotham**'s missed opportunity at **Leghorn** the following March.

Nelson's aggression, cool under fire and ability to inspire others had impressed all his commanding officers, despite his somewhat manic appearance and undiplomatic enthusiasms, and he was given every opportunity to use his talents once the meritocrat **Jervis** became fleet C-in-C from 1795. Left behind in command of a vital observation squadron when the British abandoned the **Mediterranean** in late 1796, he returned to the fleet to play a crucial role in command of the *Captain* at **St Vincent** in February 1797.

His initiative at St Vincent earned Nelson a knighthood, promotion to rear-admiral and popular adulation in **Great Britain**. An ill-conceived raid on **Tenerife** in July 1797, though unsuccessful and evidence of a reckless streak that could sometimes cloud his judgment, was concluded with sufficient panache to enhance his reputation (though it cost him an arm). After he led a strike force to the **Middle East** in summer 1798, and annihilated the French fleet in a brilliant action at the **Nile**, his fame spread throughout Europe.

Wounded in the head at the Nile, Nelson recuperated in **Naples**, where he renewed an acquaintance made in 1793 with Emma **Hamilton**, and began an open, often scandalous affair that lasted for the rest of his life. His time in Naples marked the start of a controversial phase in his life, as he became enmeshed in the labyrinthine politics of the Neapolitan court. He considerably exceeded his authority, as well as overriding British strategic priorities, by committing local Royal Navy forces to the 1798 **Neapolitan campaign**, and his subsequent attempts to attack French positions on the Italian mainland diluted naval strength in the theatre at an important time.

Most commentators have attributed Nelson's behaviour to a combination of political naïveté, Hamilton's baleful influence and the after-effects of his head wound. On leave after establishing the British presence on **Sicily**, his performance during a tour of Europe's minor courts often suggested a man out of his depth, and though his popular image in Britain was never seriously tarnished, he was regarded as unstable by some senior naval officers by the time he was recalled to active service in early 1801.

Rejuvenated, promoted vice-admiral and hungry for action, Nelson was appointed second-in-command of the fleet sent to attack **Copenhagen**, answering his critics with another brilliant tactical triumph in early April. After taking command of the fleet and cruising the Baltic, he returned home to a peerage and a brief period of domestic tranquillity with Hamilton and their daughter, Horatia.

On the breakdown of the Anglo-French **Amiens** peace in 1803, Nelson took command of the Mediterranean Fleet, the posting he had always wanted. With his greatest friend, **Collingwood**, as second-in-command, Nelson forged the fleet into what he termed a 'band of brothers'. Building on the work of Jervis, he developed a close personal bond with his captains, ensuring that they were thoroughly informed about the fleet's tactical and strategic priorities. Though his characteristic determination to tempt French Mediterranean forces into battle allowed **Villeneuve**'s Combined Fleet to escape from the theatre in spring 1805, careful planning and his fleet's all-round efficiency paid off handsomely during the long pursuit that ended at **Trafalgar** in October.

Nelson's death at Trafalgar, along with the momentous scale of his victory, sealed his place as Britain's quintessential military hero, and his elaborate state funeral was marked by genuine popular grief. Though excitable, prone to vainglory and capable of folly on the grand scale, he also won real affection from the officers and men who served under him.

As a tactician, Nelson drew on the examples of **Howe**, Jervis, **Duncan** and others, but added new levels of pre-planning and an aggression born of his almost obsessive need to annihilate Britain's enemies. In combat, he possessed a unique ability to take bold, invariably successful, tactical or psychological action at times of crisis, and was always willing, as he did at Copenhagen, to disobey orders in ruthless pursuit of total victory.

Neresheim, Battle of

Rearguard action fought by the Austrian army of Archduke **Charles** on 11 August 1796 to prevent French interference with its withdrawal from the **Rhine** to the Danube. After pulling back from **Ettlingen** in mid-July, Charles established new headquarters at Nördlingen from 3 August, and his 55,000 troops took up positions on an extended line running north from the Danube. As **Moreau**'s French army approached the Austrian centre beyond Neresheim, and took control of roads leading to Nördlingen, Charles pulled in his flank forces to launch a counter-attack in six columns on the night of 10–11 August. Too complex, it lost cohesion in driving rain, and Moreau was able to move reserves to meet separate crises as they arose. Though driven back on their left, French forces held Neresheim in the centre, and rebuffed repeated Austrian attacks on their right around Eglingen. While Moreau prepared a counter-attack for the next morning, Charles withdrew his army behind the Danube overnight. *See* Battle of **Friedberg**; **Map 3**.

Netherlands, The

The northern European area generally known to contemporaries as the Netherlands, or Holland (after one of its provinces), had been divided along political, religious and racial lines since the region's revolt against Habsburg rule in the sixteenth century. Southern provinces and their Walloon Catholic populations were still under Habsburg rule, and generally known as the Austrian Netherlands up to 1789. The seven independent, Protestant provinces in the north had formed the federal republic of the United Provinces, originally under the rule of an elected *Stadholder*, although the Orange dynasty had enjoyed hereditary possession of the office since the mid-eighteenth century.

The **French Revolution** provided a powerful stimulus to nationalist agitation in the Austrian Netherlands. The Vonckist rebellion of 1789 temporarily ejected Austrian forces, and an independent 'United States of Belgium' was proclaimed, but its rapid collapse into factionalism helped Habsburg emperor **Leopold II** to regain control in November 1790. French armies found the Belgians willing allies in the overthrow of Austrian rule during the War of the **First Coalition**, and their invasion of **Belgium** in 1792 was the prelude to a long campaign in **Flanders** and on the Sambre, culminating in allied retreat after **Fleurus** in June 1794. Under French occupation from that summer, Belgium was formally annexed by France, along with the principality of Luxembourg, on 30 September 1795.

The annexed territories were administered as nine *départements* of metropolitan **France** for the rest of the war period, and subject to the same widespread social and legal reforms. The Walloon provinces were among the most industrially advanced regions in Europe and experienced rapid economic growth under French control, the city of Ghent becoming an important international textile centre, while the region's mining and iron-producing industries enjoyed substantial booms.

The northern United Provinces had been a

major European maritime power in the late seventeenth and early eighteenth centuries. Eclipsed by the rise of **Great Britain** and riven by chronic internal factionalism, it was in manifest decline by the 1790s. William Frederick of **Orange** maintained his increasingly tenuous hold on power through alliances concluded in 1788 with **Prussia** and Britain. Opposition leaders tended to look for support to France, and the pro-French Patriot Party provided aid to republican armies after the government joined the First Coalition in 1793.

French invasion of the United Provinces in late 1794 forced William to flee to Britain (where he died in April 1806), and placed the Patriots in power. Abolishing the federal constitution, they established the Batavian Republic in 1795 and agreed an alliance with France that ensured client status. Modelled along French lines, the new republic was an inherently unstable rehearsal of old internal divisions, experiencing three coups d'état during the first half of 1798 alone, while war against Britain wrecked its overseas trade and colonial empire. Frequent changes of government and constitution made little difference to the state's consequent economic problems, and political reorganization along something close to its original federal lines was eventually forced through under the eyes of French troops in October 1800.

The end of hostilities with Britain in 1801 revived the Dutch economy for a short time, but the collapse of the **Amiens** peace in 1803 brought renewed demands from France for military and financial contributions. The failure of the latest constitution to deliver these, along with the continued influx of British goods into Holland, prompted yet another change of regime in April 1805, when **Napoleon** appointed Rutger Schimmelpenninck as his viceroy (or Grand Pensionary) for the republic. Schimmelpenninck embarked on a programme of educational, political and administrative reforms that helped permanently undermine Holland's provincial structure, but resigned in June 1806 in protest at Napoleon's conversion of the state into a puppet monarchy for his brother, Louis **Bonaparte**.

Louis accepted the title King of Holland on 5 June 1806, and continued Schimmelpenninck's work, but increasing popularity with his Dutch subjects was balanced by deteriorating relations with his brother. His failure to enforce the closure of Dutch ports to British trade in line with the **Continental System**, in part a response to economic hardship suffered after a winter of severe lowland flooding, provoked a ban on Dutch imports to France from September 1808.

His dissatisfaction with Louis mounting, Napoleon appointed **Bernadotte** to command French forces against the British **Walcheren expedition** without consulting the king in autumn 1809, and French forces began occupying the kingdom from January 1810. Louis was forced to cede his southern provinces to France in March, but French occupation of the rest of the country followed. Louis's abdication on 1 July triggered Holland's formal annexation, and his replacement by French governor-general **Lebrun** on 13 July.

As well as arousing antipathy elsewhere in Europe, particularly in **Russia**, Napoleon's seizure of Holland was highly unpopular with the Dutch. Serious disturbances followed the introduction of **conscription** in February 1811, and revelation of Dutch losses after the **Russian campaign** of 1812. Demonstrations in favour of exiled *Stadholder* William VI took place all over Holland during the early stages of the 1813 campaign for **Germany**, and the approach of allied forces across the Dutch frontier prompted popular uprisings in Amsterdam on 15 November and in The Hague two days later.

William VI landed on the Dutch coast at Schlevinghen on 30 November, was proclaimed sovereign of the Netherlands on 2 December, and accepted the country's centralized, Napoleonic constitution the following March. Part of Belgium was left in French hands by the first Treaty of **Paris** in 1814, but the Treaty of London (14 June 1814) united Belgium and Holland under his control as King **William I** of the Netherlands. The 1815 Paris Treaty restored Belgium's 1789 frontiers, and William exchanged his lands in **Nassau** for the Duchy of Luxembourg, arrangements confirmed by the Congress of **Vienna**. Formally crowned in Brussels on 27 September 1815, William was never able to establish secure control over the persistently nationalist Walloons, and Belgium achieved independence in 1831 after a successful revolt in 1830. *See also* **Colonial Warfare; Dutch Army; Dutch Navy.**

New Orleans, Battle of

The last and most celebrated battle of the **Anglo-American War** (1812–15), fought outside the great Mississippi River port on 8 January 1815, two weeks after the war had been ended by the Treaty of **Ghent**. The defeat of **Napoleon** in Europe enabled the British government to transfer large-scale reinforcements to the American theatre during 1814. A force of 14,250 veteran troops was landed near New Orleans on 13 December, the final element in a triple offensive that included attacks on **Plattsburg** and **Washington** (*see* **Map 27**). Led by the experienced General **Pakenham**, it was halted some 10km from the city during the night of 23–24 December by US forces under General **Jackson**, after which the Americans retired to the settlement of Chalmette and both sides prepared for a repeat confrontation.

Jackson had rushed his force from Baton Rouge on news of the British landing. His 5,000 troops included only about 700 **US Army** regulars, along with regional state militia and a few unemployed local pirates. Launching repeated raids to slow down British preparations, Jackson supervised construction of wooden fortifications across the only open ground between the river's north bank and a dense swamp. When Pakenham eventually attacked the position on 8 January, Jackson's well-sited artillery decimated a frontal assault by 5,300 British troops. An immediate second attempt received similar treatment and the British fled for the coast, having lost more than 2,000 men (including Pakenham) in less than an hour.

Though strategically valueless in the light of the peace agreement, Jackson's unexpected victory provided a massive boost to US self-esteem, transforming the general into a national hero and helping establish the federal republic in the hearts and minds of a people accustomed to state autonomy. On the British side, the embarrassment of defeat merely confirmed the wisdom of ending a conflict that had never been necessary or popular.

Ney, Michel (1769–1815)

Distinguished by his red hair, fiery temper and combat bravery, Ney was fellow Gascon **Murat's** only serious rival as the most dashing of Napoleon's marshals. He joined the royal French **hussars** in 1787, and was an NCO in **Flanders** during the opening actions against the **First Coalition** in 1792. Commissioned in October of that year, and transferred to the **Rhine** in 1794, he first came to wider notice at **Altenkirchen** in June 1796. He was promoted brigadier-general after the victory at **Forcheim** in August, and presaged future glories with an exemplary rearguard action at **Amberg.**

Briefly an Austrian **prisoner of war** in 1797, he began the war against the **Second Coalition** under **Bernadotte** on the Rhine, achieving divisional rank in March 1800. Transferred to the **Swiss** front under **Masséna**, he was seriously wounded at **Frauenfeld** in May, and returned to the Rhine on his recovery, fighting at **Hohenlinden** in December. Given peacetime commands in **Switzerland**, and with the invasion force for **England**, he was appointed marshal in May 1804.

Ney led the **Grande Armée's** VI Corps against the **Third Coalition** in 1805. After the débâcle of **Albeck** in October, which triggered a lifelong feud with Murat, he redeemed himself with a brilliant performance at **Elchingen** a few days later, but missed the triumph at **Austerlitz** after leading his corps into the Tyrol to block Archduke **John's** Austrian army. He played a full part in victory over the **Fourth Coalition** from autumn 1806. Though rebuked for a premature attack at **Jena**, he led the siege of **Magdeburg** in its aftermath, and fought in all the major actions against the Russians in 1807, performing with great enterprise at **Friedland** in June.

Created Duke of Elchingen in June 1808, he joined the attempted conquest of **Spain** two months later, but suffered a temporary eclipse in the **Peninsular** theatre. Criticized by Napoleon for a leisurely performance at **Tudela** in November 1808, he took part in the failed pursuit of **Moore's** British force to **Corunna** in early 1809, and was Masséna's quarrelsome second in command at the **Torres Vedras** lines in autumn 1810. Dismissed from his post during the retreat from **Portugal** late that year, he saw no further action until 1812.

Ney's experiences during the **Russian campaign** restored his reputation, but eroded many of the qualities that made him a brilliant battlefield commander. He fought at the first Battle of **Krasnoe**, was wounded at **Smolensk**, and was in the thick of the action at **Borodino**, but his corps's greatest contribution was made during the retreat from **Moscow**. Taking over rearguard duties after the Battle of **Fiodoroivskoy** in early November, it was cut off from the main army after the second **Krasnoe** battle, but Ney led a few survivors across the Dnieper at **Gusinoe** to rejoin Napoleon, earning the emperor's praise as 'the bravest of the brave'. He lived up to the name during the last weeks of the year, performing wonders in appalling conditions to protect a shrinking army's retreat across the **Beresina**. Reputedly the last imperial soldier to leave Russia, he was honoured as Prince of the Moscowa in March 1813.

Like many French officers, Ney never fully recovered from the horrors of 1812. He played a prominent role in the 1813 campaign for **Germany**, but displayed signs of uncertainty at **Bautzen** in May, and blundered to defeat at **Dennewitz** in September. The defection of Baron **Jomini** deprived Ney of his principal strategic adviser from August, and exposed his own analytical limitations, but he retained Napoleon's trust and was given command of the **Young Guard** for the defence of **France**. Close by Napoleon's side throughout the campaign, he atoned for serious errors at **Craonne** with another vital rearguard success at **Laon**, but his morale had collapsed by late March. He led officers urging Napoleon to step down in early April, and headed the deputation sent to Paris with the offer of **abdication**, becoming royal cavalry C-in-C in its aftermath.

Ney announced his loyalty to the crown when Napoleon returned from **Elba** in spring 1815, and was sent to arrest him, but he and his troops defected amid emotional scenes at Auxerre on 14 March. His appointment to command the French left wing during the **Hundred Days** campaign was something of a disaster. He was outmanoeuvred and outwitted at **Quatre Bras**, his performance in operational control of the battlefield contributing to final defeat at **Waterloo**.

Ney's subsequent fate was a matter of intense controversy throughout contemporary Europe. Arrested for treason by the royal government on 3 August 1815, he could not be tried until sufficient senior officers had been found willing to judge one of the empire's most popular military figures. Eventually on trial from 4 to 6 December, he was shot next day.

Nice, Annexation of

The first significant action in the **Italian** theatre during the War of the **First Coalition**, a French invasion of Savoy (part of **Piedmont**) and the autonomous province of Nice (*see* **Map 9**). Both regions had long been considered ripe for annexation, and a French army had been gathering on the south-western frontier since spring 1792. Local French commander Montesquieu eventually sent Casabianca's division across the Savoyard frontier towards Mount Cenis on the night of 20–21 September, and Laroche advanced along the coast towards Nice. Outnumbered by about three to one, General Lazary's 8–10,000 Piedmontese withdrew into the mountains, and Montesquieu had established his headquarters at Chambéry by 23 September. Five days later, Admiral Truguet's **French Navy** squadron from Toulon landed 8,000 troops outside Nice in support of Laroche, and the town's 8,000-strong garrison retired into the hills to protect Turin. French forces advanced to occupy Montalbon and Villefranche, but halted short of the Alps, and Truguet took his nine **ships-of-the-line** to Genoa, where he forced the city to ally with republican France (*see* **Ligurian Republic**).

Nijmegen, Capture of

The Duke of **York's** last defeat before his departure from the **Flanders** front in late 1794, a failed attempt to hold the outpost fortress of Nijmegen, on the River Waal about 10km east of the Rhine (*see* **Map 2**). French sector commander **Pichegru** had halted the northern advance of his exhausted army in late October, pausing to complete the capture of outposts on the allied left. Venloo fell to **Moreau's** 7,000 troops on 26 October, and they moved to Nijmegen, where a preliminary attack failed next day. Unable to get across the

Waal to invest the town fully, Moreau brought up five divisions in a semicircle around its southern perimeter and set up a steady bombardment from 2 November. Able to reinforce the garrison at will from the north, York temporarily silenced French **artillery** with a sortie on the night of 3–4 November, but it was back in action within two days, and **Souham** took one of the outer forts on 7 November. York pulled out that night, and prepared to draw his entire army behind the Rhine, but 3,000 Dutch troops left behind were unwilling to be sacrificed and attempted to quit Nijmegen shortly afterwards, losing some 2,000 prisoners in the resulting chaos.

Nile, Battle of the

The destruction of the **French Navy**'s eastern Mediterranean fleet by Admiral **Nelson**'s slightly larger British fleet in Aboukir Bay, at the mouth of the Nile, on 1 August 1798 (*see* **Map 7**).

Nelson's 14 **ships-of-the-line** and seven **frigates** had been detailed to intercept French forces en route for **Egypt** in June, but had been forced to return to the British supply base at **Sicily** before **Napoleon**'s Army of Egypt reached its destination on 1 July. Admiral **Brueys**'s 13 ships-of-the-line and four frigates had been lying off the Egyptian coast ever since, protecting the rear of French forces fighting in the **Middle East**, and were waiting for the British when they returned at the end of the month.

Though slightly outnumbered, the French outgunned their attackers. Seeking to make use of this advantage, Brueys anchored his ships close to the coast, guns ready for firing out to sea, on the assumption that lack of space to landward would force British ships to break off their expected head-on charge and turn along his line of broadsides (*see* **Naval Warfare**).

He was wrong. With characteristic boldness, Nelson attacked as soon as he arrived, launching his fleet against the vanguard and centre of the French line in the late afternoon of 1 August. Two British ships (*Goliath* and *Zealous*) found room to get between Aboukir Island and the front of the line, enabling them to turn their guns on the virtually unprotected French inner flank, and several more of Nelson's captains subsequently forced their way through gaps between French ships. Heavy combat continued into the evening, but the relative inefficiency of French crews contributed to their difficulties and Brueys's fleet was steadily destroyed in crossfire. Brueys was among those killed when his 120-gun flagship, *l'Orient*, blew up at about ten that night.

Only four ships (two ships-of-the-line and two frigates) eventually escaped under **Villeneuve** to the new French base at **Malta**, and the defeat ended a brief period of French naval freedom in the **Mediterranean**. Nelson's victory catapulted him to international fame, helped spark a popular uprising in **Cairo** and condemned French land forces in Egypt to effective isolation from Europe. In a broader context, it bolstered the military confidence of other European **great powers**, and hastened the formation of the **Second Coalition** against France.

Nive, Battle of the

The third major operation undertaken by **Wellington**'s allied army during its invasion of south-western France in late 1813, an assault begun on 9 December that drove **Soult**'s defending French forces back from strong positions guarding the approaches to Bayonne (*see* **Peninsular War; Map 5**).

After his defeat at the **Nivelle** in November, Soult and some 60,000 troops had withdrawn to the strongly fortified city of Bayonne. The city was well protected from the west by a broad ocean channel, and Soult expected an allied attack to cut inland from the coast. He deployed most of his forces behind the River Nive, running south-east from the city and threatening the flank of any such move. Wellington, whose 72,000 troops enjoyed massive **cavalry** superiority over French horsemen, planned to attack Bayonne from the coast and from the east, an option that called for half his army to approach the city from positions beyond the Nive.

Operations began on 16 November, when allied forces seized a French bridgehead over the Nive around Cambo, at the extreme east of the line. Flooding forced Wellington to postpone any further advance until 9 December, when **Hill** and two divisions forded the Nive at Cambo and **Beresford**'s four crossed via **pontoons** near Ustaritz, 7km to the north-west. Both got across the river without meeting serious opposition, forcing Soult to pull back his line towards Bayonne, where a direct advance by **Hope**'s 30,000 troops had established a line inland from the coast some 10km from the city by nightfall.

Hope's scattered dispositions and relative isolation offered Soult the opportunity to counter-attack. Unnoticed by allied lookouts, he concentrated 50,000 troops south of Bayonne during the night and launched a surprise attack the following morning. **Clausel**'s four divisions drove **Alten**'s British Light Division, the link between Hope and Wellington, back to Arcangues, but their subsequent move east was halted by **Dalhousie**'s division, deployed by Wellington overnight as a precautionary measure. Hope's forces were meanwhile attacked by three divisions under **Reille**, and fell back some 5km before French troops on both sectors tired in mid-afternoon.

The day's fighting ended without a major breakthrough, and three German battalions echoed events elsewhere by deserting to the allies during the night. Wellington had transferred two British divisions back across the Nive by morning, and their appearance forced Soult to abandon a second attack near the coast after it had again surprised Hope's frontline force. A final French effort near the coast faltered after initial gains on 12 December, and Soult withdrew his army that night, taking up positions east of Bayonne. A sudden overnight rise in the river made rapid transfer of allied reinforcements to Hill impossible, and encouraged Soult to attack him around **St Pierre** next day. Both sides had suffered about 1,600 casualties between 9 and 12 December.

Nivelle, Battle of the

The second stage of **Wellington**'s advance into south-western France during the **Peninsular War**, an attack on 10 November 1813 against a French defensive line curving along the River Nivelle's west bank for some 30km from the Biscay coast (*see* **Map 5**).

French commander **Soult** had retired to the new line after defeats at **Irun** and **Vera** in early October had forced him back from the Pyrenees, and had partially fortified the position by the

time allied forces were ready to attack again. With only 63,000 troops at his disposal, and suffering serious supply shortages, Soult elected to construct his strongest fortifications along the 8km sector closest to the coast, which was held by **Reille**'s 23,000 men.

Wellington could call on 82,000 men, a quarter of them untried **Spanish Army** troops. Aiming to get behind Soult's coastal lines, he detailed 19,000 men under General **Hope** to pin Reille with a frontal attack, sent **Hill**'s 26,000 against **Drouet** in the south, and led **Beresford**'s 36,000 troops (with most of the army's **artillery**) against the hill strongpoint of La Petite Rhune in the centre.

The allied operation began at six on the morning of 10 November with a preliminary attack against La Petite Rhune by **Alten**'s Light Division, which took the position after two hours of hard fighting. The main allied assault then struck at the 'hinge' linking Clausel's sector with Drouet's, and seized the bridge over the Nivelle at Amotz at about eleven. Reille's forces were prevented from reinforcing the centre by Hope's attacks, and a counter-attack by **Foy**'s division on the extreme French left was driven back by Morillo's supporting Spanish brigade.

Allied forces had broken through in the centre by mid-afternoon, and were threatening to cut off Soult's coastal forces as his whole army retreated across the Nivelle. Needing time to reconcentrate his scattered divisions in muddy conditions, and concerned that a counter-attack might cut off his inland flank, Wellington made little attempt to trap Reille, and Soult was able to withdraw east to a new line along the River **Nive**, having lost 4,351 casualties and 70 guns. Wellington's army lost 2,450 men during the day.

Nore Mutiny

The last in a series of mutinies that rocked the British **Royal Navy** during the spring and early summer of 1797. Sailors in bases all around Britain had been encouraged to express their many grievances over pay and conditions by the April success of the **Spithead** mutineers, and the ships of the Thames Estuary base at the Nore, a subdivision of the North Sea Fleet, were taken over by their crews on 12 May.

Led by disgraced former officer Richard Parker, self-styled 'President of the Floating Republic', the mutiny quickly degenerated into violence, exacerbated by the refusal of naval authorities to discuss terms. Mutineers sent delegates to encourage action in the main North Sea base at Yarmouth on 24 May, and North Sea commander **Duncan** was abandoned by all but two of his ships on 29 May as he sailed to resume his **blockade** of the Dutch in Texel.

Navy minister Spencer put aside plans to meet such specific grievances as had been identified once it became clear that Parker's avowed revolutionary aims did not command unanimous support. The government resorted to cutting the mutineers' supply lines and conducting a vigorous **propaganda** campaign portraying the sailors as **Jacobin** traitors, and mutineers contributed to their own unpopularity with a series of revenge attacks on officers, and a demonstration seizure of all traffic entering or leaving the Thames on 2 June.

The rebellion began to crumble after the government repeated an offer to pardon all but the ringleaders on 6 June. Officers regained control of two ships (*Leopard* and *Repulse*) on 9 June, and all but two ships had returned to duty by 12 June. The mutiny ended with the overthrow of Parker's regime aboard the *Sandwich* on 15 June. Parker was executed on 30 June, and of 411 other ringleaders arrested, 300 were pardoned and 28 were executed.

North Holland, Invasion of (1799)

The Anglo-Russian invasion of the French-occupied **Netherlands** that formed the northern wing of the **Second Coalition**'s sprawling land offensive in 1799. The operation was instigated by a British government chronically short of resources for land warfare. With only one moderately small army available for offensive operations, it rejected calls for an attack in the **Mediterranean** and opted for the apparently safer expedient of an invasion across the Channel.

An attack on the Netherlands, ideally followed by an invasion of France via Lille, represented the best chance of receiving practical support from allied **Russia**. British strategists also entertained hopes of attracting support from **Prussia**, inflaming an anti-French rebellion in the Netherlands or seizing **Dutch Navy** warships under **blockade** in their home port of Helder.

Having secured the promise of 17,000 Russian troops for the operation, the British wavered over the precise choice of target before eventually ordering General **Abercromby**, in command of preliminary landings, to choose according to conditions on the spot. Abercromby sailed on 8 August, but bad weather kept his 18,000 troops off the Dutch coast for almost three weeks, wrecking any hope of surprise. Troops finally got ashore on 27 August, landing in North Holland for an attack towards Amsterdam.

Regional French commander **Brune** had concentrated most of his 20,000 troops to the southwest, preferring to protect the direct invasion route to France, and defence of North Holland had been left to Dutch generals Dumonceau and Daendels. The latter's failure to deploy his troops close to the beach in the face of British naval bombardment allowed Abercromby's force to get ashore despite a series of chaotic landings. Divisional general **Moore** followed up this initial success by seizing Helder on 28 August, enabling **Royal Navy** warships to enter the harbour two days later and capture seven Dutch **ships-of-the-line**, 18 **frigates**, many small craft and 6,000 sailors, whose virulent anti-French attitude proved exceptional.

Franco-Dutch defences were in disarray, and a rapid advance could probably have taken Amsterdam, but Abercromby's troops were tired after weeks at sea and desperately short of wheeled transport. He elected to wait for the Russians and overall C-in-C the Duke of **York**, taking up positions along the Zype Canal, a few kilometres south of Helder, where an attack by **Vandamme**'s 10,000 French troops (with support from Dutch militia) failed on 10 September.

The allied force around Helder had reached 48,000 men by mid-September, including the first 12,000 Russian troops under General Hermann. Still desperately short of wagons, food supplies and medical facilities, it failed to break through Brune's latest defensive positions some 10km south of the River Waal on 19 September in what is known as the Battle of **Bergen**. Two further attempts launched on 2 and 6 October fared no better with the help of 4,000 Russian reinforcements, after which allied commanders elected to withdraw.

Controversial at the time, the withdrawal is now generally accepted as necessary in view of worsening weather, morale, shortages, health and inter-allied relations. A local armistice was agreed on 10 October, with a subsequent convention allowing for peaceful evacuation of the invasion force by the end of November in exchange for 8,000 French **prisoners of war** from Britain. Apart from securing the valuable naval prize of the Dutch fleet, the expedition had achieved none of its aims and cost perhaps 9,000 casualties. *See* **Map 12**.

Norway

Although recognized as a sovereign kingdom since the late fourteenth century, Norway was ruled by the Danish monarch from 1449, but passed to the Swedish crown in 1815 and did not achieve full independence until 1905. *See also* **Denmark; Sweden**.

Novi, Battle of

Climax of a brief French summer offensive during the 1799 **Italian campaign**, a confrontation on 15 August between **Suvorov's** Austro-Russian army and **Joubert's** French forces advancing north between the Scrivia and Bormida rivers (*see* **Map 9**). Joubert had replaced **Moreau** as C-in-C of French forces penned against the Genoan coast in July. Ordered to reverse a string of allied victories, and reinforced to a total strength of about 47,000 men, he concentrated 38,000 troops for an advance north towards the Po valley from 9 August.

Joubert halted on 14 August, along a line east of the Scrivia centred on Novi, and prepared to meet Suvorov's approaching main body, thought to be about 43,000 strong. Unknown to Joubert, the fall of **Mantua** in late July had freed **Kray** and 20,000 allied reinforcements to move west, but Suvorov gave the French no time to withdraw in the face of changed odds, and attacked all along the line early on 15 August.

An unsophisticated set of frontal assaults made some progress against the French left, and Joubert was killed within an hour, but Moreau (not yet transferred to the **Rhine**) took over the defence with no loss of cohesion, and the allied attack had stalled by eleven. Suvorov ordered up his strategic reserve (**Melas**) and led two unsuccessful frontal assaults in the centre around Novi, while Kray's repeated efforts made no progress on the Austrian left. Melas arrived to threaten the French right wing at about five, after which fighting rose to a climax all along the front. While Melas drove towards Novi from the south, and Kray persisted with his ill-starred attacks to the north, Suvorov was able to bring up **artillery** and force his way into the town.

Moreau's attempted withdrawal was cut off by allied forces, and turned to rout as it was caught by **Bagration's** pursuing Russians. Only Watrin's division was able to retire from the battle in good order, and though allied forces lost some 7,000 killed and wounded during the day, slightly lower French casualties were offset by the loss of perhaps 5,000 prisoners, 40 guns and all strategic initiative. With both sides exhausted by the summer heat, Austrian pursuit was short-lived, allowing Moreau to fall back on **Genoa**.

O

Obidos, Skirmish at *See* Battle of **Rolica**

Ocaña, Battle of

The defeat that ended a Spanish offensive towards Madrid in autumn 1809. After **Welles-ley**'s victory at **Talavera** in July had prompted a French withdrawal on the capital, the Central **Junta** in Seville assembled an Army of the Centre under General Areziega for an advance north from Andalusia. Setting out in early November, Areziega's 50,000 troops had reached Aranjuez, on the Tagus about 50km south of Madrid, by 16 November (*see* **Map 22**). They then paused for rest, giving **Soult** time to concentrate a force of similar strength and advance on their positions. Areziega retreated as soon as French moves became apparent, but was caught by pursuing forces on 19 November, 20km to the south at Ocaña. The total dominance of French **cavalry** over Spanish, demonstrated every time they met during the **Peninsular War**, triggered mass panic among Areziega's infantry. The ensuing rout claimed 19,000 Spanish casualties, some 15,000 of them as prisoners, against 2,000 French losses, and left the whole of southern Spain temporarily undefended. *See also* Battle of **Alba des Tormes**.

O'Donnell, Joseph Henry (1769–1834)

One among several Spanish generals of Irish descent to lead formations during the **Peninsu-lar War**, O'Donnell fought **Suchet**'s forces in Catalonia during 1810, and commanded a division under **Wellington** during the campaigns of 1813–14. Best known for leading the siege of Pamplona, the last French garrison on Spanish soil by late 1813, he occupied a number of senior commands after the Bourbon restoration, but spent his last years in exile after accusations of treachery during the French invasion in 1822.

Old Guard

Name given to veteran formations within the élite arm of the Napoleonic **French Army** after 1809. *See* **Imperial Guard**.

Oldenburg

Small north German state ruled by the kings of **Denmark** until 1773, when it was ceded to the Russian royal family (*see* **Map 1**). William, second Duke of Oldenburg, was Tsar **Paul I**'s brother-in-law, and had come to power in 1785, but fled into exile when French imperial forces invaded Oldenburg in 1806. Restored the follow-ing year after agreeing to join the Confederation of the **Rhine**, the duke refused Napoleon's offer to exchange his territories for lands around Erfurt in 1810, and was punished by French seizure of the duchy in March, after which it was incorporated into **Hanover**. The seizure was a major source of friction between the tsar and France in the months leading up to Napoleon's invasion of 1812, and after the collapse of the French Empire **Alexander I** was primarily res-ponsible for ensuring that Oldenburg was increased in size by the addition of Birkenfeld and raised to the status of Grand Duchy.

Opelchenie

The Russian word for 'militia', used to describe reserve infantry forces raised from among the empire's untrained serf population to supplement **Russian Army** strength in times of national emergency. The first attempt to raise Opelchenie forces, in 1806, provoked fears of a peasant uprising among the landed aristocracy and the few active units were disbanded after the Peace of **Tilsit** in 1807. Such fears were forgotten in 1812, and the Opelchenie became a focus for patriotic resistance among the peasant classes, contributing more than 220,000 troops to imperial service by 1814. Grouped into 'cohorts' of three battalions (one usually equipped with **muskets**, the others with **pikes**), Opelchenie troops were used for secondary duties at the front, often as orderlies or manual labourers. They were unable to perform coherent manoeuvres, their only real combat value being as part of a massed **bayonet** charge, a role they seem to have performed with innate resolution.

Oporto, Battle of

The expulsion of French occupying forces from **Portugal**'s second city on 12 May 1809 by a British expeditionary force under General **Wellesley**, and the prelude to his first invasion of **Spain** that summer (*see* **Peninsular War**). Wellesley and 25,000 men arrived in Lisbon on 22 April to reinforce the 16,000 British troops already in Portugal. After a brief but intensive reorganization – during which he streamlined his army's command structure, added light infantry companies to each brigade as **skirmishers** and began reconstruction of the **Portuguese Army** – Wellesley led 16,000 British and 2,400 Portuguese troops (supported by 24 guns) north from Lisbon towards Oporto on 8 May (*see* **Map 22**).

About 20,000 French troops under **Soult** had moved into northern Portugal to occupy Oporto from 22 March. Convinced that any British attack would come by sea, and busy with arrangements to found his own kingdom in the region, Soult made no attempt either to evacuate or defend the broad Douro River that guarded overland approaches from the south. River crossings had been one of Wellesley's operational specialities in **India**, and he used requisitioned boats to send his troops across the undefended Douro in broad daylight on 12 May, surprising the city garrison and driving it

north into the hills before the end of the day.

Soult continued his retreat all the way to the frontier and beyond. Spared the restraint by cautious superiors that had diluted his 1808 victory at **Vimeiro**, Wellesley left a defensive garrison at Oporto and turned the rest of his force east in search of **Victor**'s isolated French army in western Spain (*see* Battle of **Talavera**).

Orange, William Frederick, Prince of (1772–1843)

The exiled *Stadholder* of the **Netherlands** after William V of **Orange** died in 1806, William Frederick was stripped of his lands in **Nassau** after failing to join the Confederation of the **Rhine**. He regained political control from 1813, when he became sovereign prince of the restored independent Netherlands, and was given the title King William I in 1815.

Orange, William V, Prince of (1748–1806)

Hereditary *Stadholder* of the independent **Netherlands** since his father's death in 1751, and effective ruler since 1766, William V had ended his country's long friendship with **Great Britain** during the American War of Independence (1775–83), and been forced to rely on Prussian support to preserve his offices against factional and radical pressure in 1787. Faced with invasion by France in late 1792, he had little choice but to join Britain and **Prussia** in the **First Coalition**, and commanded a Dutch corps during subsequent campaigns in **Flanders**. French conquest of the Netherlands forced him to flee to Britain the following year, and he gave fairly supine support to the Anglo-Russian invasion of **North Holland** in 1799, before sliding into apathetic acceptance of the Napoleonic regime.

Orange, William, Prince of (1792–1849)

The eldest son and heir of Dutch ruler William Frederick, Prince of **Orange**, he led I Corps with **Wellington**'s composite allied army during the **Hundred Days** campaign of 1815. He proved prone to unfortunate interventions at critical moments, notably when he led a premature and potentially disastrous counter-attack at **Quatre Bras** during the afternoon of 16 June. Wounded at **Waterloo**, he became the second king of post-war Holland when he succeeded his father in 1840.

Oranges, War of the

Name given to the brief conflict of May and June 1801 between **Spain** and **Portugal**. Provoked by French and Spanish plans to partition Portugal, it was triggered by a Franco-Spanish demand of January 1801 that Portuguese regent Prince **John** sever ties with **Great Britain**. John responded by declaring war on Spain in February, and **Godoy** commanded the **Spanish Army**'s invasion when it eventually got under way in mid-May. Peace was agreed almost as soon as Spanish operations began (and before promised French reinforcements arrived), and the war was ended by the Treaty of Badajoz on 7 June. Portugal agreed to cede the small frontier province of Olivenza to Spain, pay indemnities of 20 million francs to France, close its ports to British shipping and declare its neutrality.

Orders in Council (British)

A series of executive decrees issued by the British **Perceval** government in November and December 1807, a response to **Napoleon**'s introduction of the **Continental System** that introduced tightened regulations for neutral shipping seeking to trade with **France** or any of Britain's enemies. Orders in Council published on 11, 15 and 25 November, and on 18 December, required neutral shipping leaving or bound for hostile harbours to enter a British port, unload its cargo, pay customs duty and purchase a trading licence. Failure to do so left merchantmen, their cargoes and crew open to seizure at sea. Because the **Royal Navy** was powerful enough to make the orders at least partially effective, they created enormous diplomatic problems with neutral states, playing a significant part in driving both **Denmark** and the **United States** to war against Britain. *See also* **Blockade**.

Organic Articles

An appendix added by **Napoleon** to the **Concordat** agreement with the Roman Catholic Church of July 1801 before its publication the following April and without the knowledge of Rome. The articles fundamentally altered the proposed relationship between the French state and a restored Church, giving the secular government control over all religious seminary schools, the right to insist that teachers promote republican principles, and the right to reject any bulls, legates or other communications from the papacy. A new catechism was to be introduced for the whole of **France**, designed to announce the deity's approval of the Napoleonic regime. An outraged **Pius VII** attempted to secure revocation of the articles by remaining on good terms with Napoleon, but his failure sparked renewed hostility between Paris and Rome, culminating in the Pope's imprisonment from 1809.

Orthez, Battle of

The opening engagement of allied C-in-C **Wellington**'s final offensive during the **Peninsular War**, fought around the south-western French town of Orthez on 27 February 1814 (*see* **Map 5**). French commander **Soult** had lost some 10,000 troops and 35 guns to **Napoleon**'s campaign for **France** further north, leaving him with about 54,000 men to defend Bayonne. He had divided his forces in two, deploying about half along the River Joyeuse, to the east of allied positions on the **Nive**, and the rest along the Adour in front of the city.

Though Wellington could call on 88,000 troops, he had sent 25,000 Spanish troops home in his determination to cultivate the hearts and minds of local populations. This approach also entailed proper payment for requisitioned goods, and allied forces in 1814 generally enjoyed greater local support than their native opponents.

Planning to put himself between the two French forces, Wellington sent 13,000 troops under **Hill** east from the Nive on 14 February, and **Hope**'s 31,000 men opened a major diversion across the wide Adour Estuary west of Bayonne on 23 February, improvising a bridge to get 15,000 troops over the river by 26 February. The 36,000 French troops facing Hill meanwhile pulled back to the town of Orthez, 50km east of Bayonne, and Wellington arrived next day with his 31,000 reserves.

Soult was already thinking in terms of a withdrawal to Toulouse, where he might hope to find supplies and reinforcements, but his army was strongly placed on high ground to the north of Orthez. Wellington's first attack on the French position faltered short of the main French lines, but a second, more coordinated attack seized the heights by early afternoon, and Soult ordered a general withdrawal to the north-east after Hill had worked round to threaten French lines of retreat. Pursued for the rest of the day, French forces lost some 4,000 men and six guns at Orthez, against 2,146 allied casualties. *See* Battle of **Toulouse**.

Ostende Raid

British **amphibious** raid against the French-controlled port of Ostende of May 1798, intended to destroy its canal link with Bruges and prevent the concentration of transport vessels for a French invasion of **England**. A **Royal Navy** squadron under Commodore **Popham** (three **frigates**, along with **sloops, bombs** and **gunboats**) carried 1,200 troops under General Eyre Coote safely across the Channel from the south-eastern English port of Margate to land without opposition just outside Ostende in the small hours of 19 May. The guns of the town opened fire on British positions at daylight, and Coote was ready to re-embark after his troops had destroyed a canal sluice and several small craft, but rising winds prevented Popham's ships from reaching the shore. After failing to bluff garrison commander Muscar into surrender, Coote settled his troops for the night on the beach, where they were surrounded and captured by garrison forces next morning.

Ostermann-Tolstoi, Ivan, Count (1770–1837)

Able Russian field commander, the grandson of Tsar **Paul I**'s chancellor, he commanded a division against French forces at **Eylau** and **Friedland** in 1807, and was a corps commander at **Ostronovo** and **Borodino** in 1812. During the 1813 campaign for **Germany** he fought at **Bautzen** and commanded the allied rearguard during the actions around **Dresden**, leading 44,000 troops to victory over **Vandamme** at **Kulm** on 30 August.

Ostrach, Battle of

The first major action fought between French and Austrian forces on the **Rhine** front in 1799. General **Jourdan**'s 37,000 French troops had crossed the river on 1 March, and moved east

beyond the Black Forest towards twice as many Austrians, advancing from the Bavarian frontier under Archduke **Charles**. The two armies made preliminary contact in the region between the Danube and Lake Constance, and **Lefebvre**'s French advance guard took up positions on hills behind a small stream running through Ostrach. After a day of preparations, Charles launched a three-pronged attack on the morning of 21 March. It forced back **Gouvion St Cyr**'s division on the French left, and though **Souham**'s reserves helped Lefebvre hold the Ostrach, inflicting heavy casualties on two Austrian columns advancing up the heights, Jourdan ordered a retreat during the afternoon to maintain contact with St Cyr. After withdrawing in good order, French forces destroyed the bridge at Ostrach, preventing Charles from pursuit until the following day and enabling Jourdan to reorganize at the communications centre of **Stockach**. *See* **Map 4**.

Ostronovo, Battle of

Inconclusive engagement in western Russia between **Murat**'s French **cavalry** and advanced guards of **Barclay de Tolly**'s Russian First Army. Fought on 25 and 26 July 1812 around the town of Ostronovo, on the River Dvina, the action helped convince **Napoleon** that the Russian commander intended to give battle at **Vitebsk**, and he prepared an attack accordingly. *See also* **Russian Campaign**.

Ottoman Empire

Contemporary international references to Turkey or the Sublime Porte described the Ottoman Empire, a great swathe of the Middle East and south-eastern Europe ruled from Constantinople (Istanbul) by the Sultan of Turkey in his capacity as Khalif of the orthodox Muslim world (*see* **Map 1**). Executive control over the empire rested with the sultan's appointed Grand Vizier and cabinet, at the head of a mostly Turkish bureaucracy, although the governors of the empire's provinces enjoyed considerable autonomy in a socio-economic system that operated on medieval principles of personal allegiance and tribute.

The empire had lost territory and bureaucratic cohesion since its heyday in the fifteenth century. Ottoman government had been pushed out of north-west Africa by Spanish and French colonists, and had been losing ground for two centuries in south-east Europe, where Austrian and Russian expansion towards the Anatolian Turkish heartlands dominated the decades before 1790. The latest in a series of unsuccessful wars against **Russia, Austria** or both had opened in August 1787 with a surprise Turkish attempt to regain the Crimea, and ended with the empire's northern frontier rolled back to the Dniester by the Peace of Jassy in January 1792.

Serial military failure in the north, along with commercial penetration of **Egypt**, the Persian Gulf and the eastern Mediterranean by French and British merchants, encouraged an epidemic of provincial and ethnic separatism. Along with native Turks, and many smaller linguistic or religious groups, the sultan ruled large Arab, Syrian, Armenian, Kurdish, Greek, Slav and Circassian minorities. Popular and political movements for national independence were particularly strong among the Christian Greeks and Slavs, their ambitions encouraged by the proximity of European armies and the semi-independent status of many regional governors.

Selim III came to power in April 1789, and embarked on a programme of administrative reforms intended to modernize the empire's economy, administration and armed forces. His attempts to introduce European ideas into the **Turkish Army** provoked bitter conservative opposition from the **Janissaries**, the military caste that traditionally provided the empire's chief warriors, and efforts to bring the provinces under closer central control signalled an upsurge in disobedience among regional governors.

The Porte maintained its traditional friendship with **France** after the execution of **Louis XVI**, viewing republican ideas primarily as a potential antidote to Christian imperialism, but subsequent French expansionism caused alarm. **Napoleon**'s agents were already spreading anti-Ottoman **propaganda** throughout the Balkans when French annexation of the **Ionian Islands** in 1797 triggered a breakdown of diplomatic relations, an end to negotiations for military cooperation and the dismissal of French advisers in Constantinople.

Turkey became a partner in the **Second** Coalition against France in response to the French invasion of the **Middle East** in July 1798. French assumptions that the Ottoman government would not risk an attempt to defend distant Egypt had not taken into consideration the need to maintain vital food supplies from the province to Constantinople. As food prices doubled in the month after the French invasion, Selim III faced pressure to bolster his faltering regime by mounting a military response, and a Russian offer of naval support brought a declaration of **jihad** (holy war) against France in September.

The defeat of successive Turkish forces sent to challenge French occupation of Egypt, and their part in the region's gathering civil war, soon persuaded Constantinople that the war was more troublesome than valuable. The government signed a peace at **El Arish** in January 1800, but the British refused to allow Turkey to abandon the Coalition. With a powerful British fleet on his doorstep, the sultan had little choice but to remain at war until the Coalition collapsed, signing a preliminary peace with France in October 1801, and a formal agreement the following June.

The end of hostilities ushered in a brief period of economic respite, but internal strife raged unabated. Egypt subsided into a civil war that absorbed Turkish armies and resources sent to resolve it; Adrianople flared into rebellion against its provincial governor in 1804; and the violent revolt of the fundamental Wahhabi sect in the Arabian hinterlands defied suppression. Most seriously, chronic unrest in Serbia erupted into full-scale nationalist uprising under the leadership of **Kara Djordje** in early 1804; and the threat of separatist action spread to the provinces of modern Romania (Moldavia and Wallachia). Imperial punitive measures brought Russian troops across the Dniester in October 1806, and a Turkish declaration of war followed on 27 December. The British failed to force the sultan into peace by sending a fleet through the **Dardanelles**, and the **Russo-Turkish War** rumbled on indecisively until 1812.

Selim's bid for administrative modernization provoked inevitable opposition, and a mutiny among troops in Black Sea garrisons matured into a Janissary conspiracy at the centre during the first months of 1807. Despite efforts to appease reactionary opinion, Selim was deposed by a palace coup on 29 May, and his cousin took power as Mustapha IV. Mustapha oversaw an immediate return to traditional administrative methods, but a pro-reform movement gathered among troops under Bairakta Pasha during a temporary armistice with Russia (arranged at **Tilsit** in July 1807), and his forces had fought their way to Constantinople by July 1808. Mustapha was himself deposed on 28 July, and his brother became Sultan Mahmud II once the death of Selim at the hands of Janissaries had been confirmed. Mahmud appointed Bairakta as Grand Vizier, but his return to a policy of reform was interrupted by a Janissary uprising in November. Defeated only after heavy fighting around the sultan's palace, the rebels killed Bairakta and forced Mahmud to halt reforms pending the solution of pressing problems to the north.

The government's effective paralysis had enabled the Serbian independence movement to take firm hold by late 1808, and a national council elected Kara Djordje as hereditary monarch on 26 December. No serious attempt was made to regain control of Belgrade until the war with Russia was ended by the Peace of **Bucharest** in May 1812. A Turkish invasion had forced Djordje to flee the country for Austria (and then Russia) by September 1813, and the Turkish Army occupied the Serbian capital in October, but renewed rebellion flared from August 1815, and the government was forced to appoint rebel leader Milos Obrenovich as governor.

Ottoman Turkey was barely a factor in the diplomatic reorganization that followed the defeats of France in 1814–15, and the period of general European peace that followed made little difference to the Ottoman body politic's beleaguered condition. A Greek uprising of February 1821, which attracted interference from Russia, Austria and Britain, demonstrated that the impending collapse of Ottoman Turkey would remain a live issue warping European diplomacy through the nineteenth century.

Oudinot, Nicholas Charles (1767–1847)

A stoic and competent battle commander, Oudinot was a **cavalry** captain with five years'

military experience in 1789, and a lieutenant-colonel in 1792. He fought on the **Rhine** front throughout the War of the **First Coalition**, suffering the first of his 22 wounds at **Geisberg** in December 1793, and was a brigadier-general from the following June. He was wounded at **Trier** in August, again in October 1795 (after which he was an allied prisoner for three months) and received serious injuries during **Moreau's** retreat to the Rhine in September 1796.

With **Masséna's** command in the **Swiss** theatre from early 1799, he fought at **Frauenfeld** and both **Zurich** battles, achieving divisional rank in April. He sustained three more wounds before joining Masséna on the **Italian** front in early 1800, and survived the siege of **Genoa** to join **Brune's** easterly advance after **Marengo**. Under **Lannes** against the **Third Coalition** in 1805, he was badly hurt at **Hollabrünn**, but returned to action in February 1807 to lead his division at **Danzig** and (despite a broken leg) at **Friedland**.

Raised to the peerage in 1808, Oudinot fought at **Abenseberg** and **Aspern–Essling** in 1809 before taking corps command for the first time at **Wagram**, where his performance earned promotion to marshal on 12 July and a dukedom (of Reggio) the following year. His corps spearheaded the early French advance beyond **Vilna** during the 1812 **Russian campaign**, but he suffered another severe wound at the first Battle of **Polotsk** in August. Returning to the front for the second Polotsk battle in November, he shared rearguard duties with **Ney** at the **Beresina**, where he was wounded again and invalided home.

Given independent control of 120,000 troops for a drive on Berlin after a good performance at **Bautzen** in May 1813, he was returned to corps command after his advance collapsed at **Gross-Deeren** in late August, and fought under Ney at **Dennewitz** in September. After leading a **Young Guard** corps at **Leipzig**, he fought through the campaign for **France** of early 1814. Wounded again at **Brienne**, he fought at **Vauchamps**, **Valjouan**, **Montereau** and **Arcis-sur-Aube**, where he received his last wound. After urging the emperor's **abdication** in April, he became royal governor of Metz, and refused **Napoleon's** summons during the **Hundred Days** to become an active postwar servant of the monarchy.

Ouvrard, Gabriel-Julien (1770–1846)

French entrepreneur whose career exemplified the survival of hard-nosed contemporary capitalism through the political and ideological upheavals of post-revolutionary **France**. Ouvrard made a fortune by anticipating a press boom and investing in paper, but was put under house arrest in 1800 for failure to meet contracts for supplying the **French Navy**. Released in 1802, he became a successful grain importer, but was ruined again two years later when the failure of a scheme to run Spanish colonial treasure through the British **blockade** triggered a financial crisis in Paris. Imprisoned in 1810 as an agent of **Fouché's** secret efforts to make peace with the British, he was released in 1813 and won contracts to supply allied armies during the 1814 campaign. Similarly employed by the Napoleonic army of the **Hundred Days**, he became a successful financial adviser and military supplier to the postwar restoration government.

P

Paget, Edward (1775–1849)

English infantry officer, a younger brother of Henry **Paget**, who was commissioned into the **British Army**'s élite Life Guards at 16, and secured regimental command at 18, enjoying some success in **Flanders** during 1794–5. He witnessed the naval battle of Cape **St Vincent** in 1797, and became a full colonel the following year. Wounded at **Alexandria** in 1801, and promoted brigadier-general in October 1803, he reached divisional rank in early 1805. With **Mediterranean** garrisons from 1806 to 1808, he commanded **Moore**'s reserve in **Sweden** and led a brigade at **Corunna**. He returned to the **Peninsular War** with **Wellesley** later that year, losing an arm while leading the attack that took **Oporto**. Promoted lieutenant-general and knighted, his wound kept him out of action until autumn 1812, when he returned as **Wellington**'s second-in-command for the retreat from **Burgos**. Captured on 17 November, he played no further part in the wars, but was a postwar C-in-C in **India**.

Paget, Henry William, Earl of Uxbridge (1768–1854)

London-born **cavalry** officer and politician, a member of the British House of Commons from 1790 to 1810, and of the upper House of Lords on succeeding his father as Earl of Uxbridge in 1812. Paget raised his own infantry regiment for service in the **Flanders campaign** of 1794–5, and took part in the 1799 **North Holland** expedition. He headed **Moore**'s cavalry during the Spanish campaign of late 1808, winning minor

victories at **Sahagún** and **Benavente** before successfully screening Moore's retreat to **Corunna**. Paget was in command of **Wellington**'s cavalry at **Waterloo**, where he lost a leg, and ended a long postwar career as a field marshal in 1852.

Pajol, Claude Pierre (1772–1844)

French **cavalry** officer, a volunteer NCO in 1791 and commissioned in 1792, who fought on the **Rhine** during the **Revolutionary Wars**, and took part in all the **Grande Armée**'s eastern campaigns from 1805 to 1809. With **Davout**'s corps for the 1812 **Russian** invasion, he was given a divisional command in August, but was seriously wounded after **Borodino** and missed the rest of the campaign. Back in action at **Dresden** in 1813, but injured before the defeat at **Leipzig**, he returned to lead a scratch **National Guard** cavalry unit during the early stages of the battle for **France** until wounded at **Montereau** in February 1814. No crypto-royalist, Pajol led a cavalry division at **Ligny** and **Wavre** during the **Hundred Days** campaign, and retired rather than serve the restored monarchy. He rejoined the army after playing an active part in the 1830 revolution.

Pakenham, Edward (1778–1815)

British soldier, commissioned in 1794 and a lieutenant-colonel from 1799, who served in the **West Indies** (1801–3) and at **Copenhagen** (1807) before joining **Wellington**'s army in **Portugal** as a staff officer from 1809. He led a brigade at **Busaco** in 1810 and took over **Picton**'s division from April 1812, leading the successful frontal attack at **Salamanca** later that year. The brother of Wellington's wife, Pakenham was promoted major-general in 1812 and led the main assault on the second day at **Sorauren** in July 1813. He was appointed adjutant-general to the army in June 1813 (and was free to take up the post from August), performing the role reluctantly but effectively until the end of the **Peninsular War**, after which he crossed the Atlantic to take overall command of British forces fighting the **Anglo-American War**. He reached the **United States** in December 1814, in the midst of a poorly executed British attempt to capture **New Orleans**. Ordering his forces into a frontal attack on **Jackson**'s well-prepared defences, he was killed during its comprehensive failure on 8 January 1815.

Palafox y Melzi, José (1780–1847)

Aragonese soldier, who accompanied Prince **Ferdinand** to the **Bayonne** conference in April 1808 as a regular **Spanish Army** officer. When Ferdinand was removed to France in May Palafox escaped back to his province, where he and his brother Francisco raised rebel forces against the French invasion. As general of the Aragonese army during the early stages of the **Peninsular War**, his limited capacity for field command was exposed during the 1808 campaign at the Ebro that culminated in defeat at **Tudela**, but he won enduring fame for his leadership at the two sieges of **Saragossa**. Taken prisoner on the fall of Saragossa, he was held in France until 1814. On returning to Spain he was appointed captain-general of Aragon, and became Duke of Saragossa in 1836.

Palm, Johann (1766–1806)

Nuremberg bookseller arrested in April 1806 for publishing a pamphlet criticizing **Napoleon**, and subsequently executed. The arbitrary nature of the punishment triggered outrage in the German press, particularly in **Prussia**, where the incident helped convince King **Frederick William III** to declare war on France (*see* War of the **Fourth Coalition**).

Palvasund, Battle of

The second important naval action fought in the island clusters between south-west **Finland** and Aaland during the **Russo-Swedish War** of 1808–9. After their defeat at **Sandöström** in August 1808,

Swedish Navy light forces had attacked a part of the Russian shallows fleet in Grönvikssund and forced it to take shelter in the Palvasund channel. Swedish forces blockaded the passage with two lines of **sloops**, a total of 33 warships, but local Russian commander Admiral Mäsojidov opted to split his 87 small ships into one central and two flank divisions for a breakout attempt. His attack opened in fog at dawn on 18 September, and although the Russian left wing suffered almost immediate defeat, Mäsojidov pressed home attacks on the other flank, forcing the Swedes to withdraw by nine that morning. Though the Russians made several subsequent attempts to break through new Swedish positions in Grönvikssund, they made no progress before winter halted naval operations in the Baltic for several months. *See* **Map 18**.

Pamplona, Siege of

Guarding the main inland passes through the Pyrenees from Spain into France, the city of Pamplona was one of only two major French strongholds on Spanish soil following **Wellington**'s success at **Vitoria** in June 1813. Spanish general O'Donnell and 11,000 troops were detached to invest Pamplona, and had surrounded the city by 30 June. The French garrison, some 3,000 men under General Cassan, almost succeeded in breaking out on 27 July, when a sortie timed to coincide with **Soult**'s advance from the **Roncesvalles** Pass prompted O'Donnell to order a retreat, but the **siege** was restored on the arrival of another Spanish division under General d'España. Wellington's simultaneous arrival in the sector, and his defeat of Soult at **Sorauren**, sealed the garrison's fate, though the well-supplied city held out until 31 October before Cassan surrendered the last French foothold in Spain to d'España. *See* **Peninsular War**; Maps 5, 22.

Pancorbo, Battle of *See* **Espinosa**, Battle of

Papal States

The states and principalities ruled by the Papacy in place of secular government. Largely concentrated in central Italy, with Rome as their administrative and political capital, the Papal States included enclaves elsewhere in Europe, notably Avignon in southern France, and were a long-term by-product of the close association between the Holy See and many of medieval Italy's most powerful ruling families.

Encompassing a multitude of fiscal and bureaucratic systems, most of them unreformed since the Middle Ages, the States were in severe economic difficulties by the late eighteenth century. The Papal Army, comprising three line regiments, fortress garrisons and two (later three) companies of cavalry, had become a by-word for inefficiency and disorganization.

Pope **Pius VI** came out in opposition to the French Revolution at an early stage, but was powerless to prevent the loss of Avignon in 1791. Mounting mutual antagonism was exacerbated in February 1793 by the assassination of a French envoy in Rome, and the Papal Army fought a brief campaign against French forces during the **Italian campaign** of 1796, suffering defeat at Fort Urban on 23 June before signing a provisional peace.

The Pope continued to conspire with other regional leaders against French interests until **Napoleon's** brief invasion of central Italy in early 1797, and a defeat at the Senio on 5 February compelled the Papacy to sign the Peace of Tolentino (19 February), agreeing to drop compensation claims for the loss of Avignon, disband the army and pay an indemnity in return for the departure of occupying forces.

The growth of popular republicanism in Rome provided an excuse for the return of French forces to the city a year later. Following the death of French general Duphot during Roman street disturbances in December 1797 – for which Papal minister **Consalvi** was held responsible – an army under **Berthier** entered the city and sponsored proclamation of a Roman republic on 15 February 1798. While French troops (and generals) pillaged the city, Pius VI was imprisoned in Siena and later moved to Valence, where he died in August 1799.

Elected in Venice the following March, and able to return to Rome after the **Second Coalition's** successes in Italy, Pope **Pius VII** proved amenable to friendly relations with France, signing the **Concordat** agreement in July 1801 and travelling to Paris for Napoleon's imperial coronation in 1804. His subsequent unwillingness to annul the marriage of Joseph **Bonaparte** presaged a period of increasing tension, and Napoleon lost patience after Pius refused to join the **Continental System**, sending an army to occupy Rome in 1808 and taking control of the other Papal States next year. The Pope reacted by excommunicating the invaders, but was imprisoned in France and forced to renounce the decision.

The States were governed as an autonomous part of the French Empire, contributing a battalion of infantry to the imperial war effort, until May 1814, when Pius VII returned to Rome. The Congress of **Vienna** subsequently confirmed their 1792 territorial boundaries, and the restored pontiff allowed many French-inspired sociopolitical reforms to stand. *See* **Map 1**.

Paper Money *See* **War Finance**; **Bank Crisis**, British

Paris, Treaty of (1814)

The agreement, signed on 30 April 1814, between the victorious allies and the government of restored French king **Louis XVIII** that formally ended the War of the **Sixth Coalition**. The treaty imposed no financial indemnities on **France** and, largely thanks to the determined diplomacy of **Talleyrand**, allowed the restored kingdom to retain territories acquired before November 1792, including much of Germany west of the Rhine. French colonies in the **West Indies** were ruthlessly stripped by **Great Britain**, while **Spain** recovered its lost half of **Santo Domingo**, and France agreed to accept the solutions of the Congress of **Vienna**, scheduled for September 1814, to all other territorial questions thrown up by the war.

Paris, Treaty of (1815)

Agreement signed on 20 November 1815 between the government of French king **Louis XVIII** and the allies of the **Seventh Coalition**. In return for formally ending hostilities and withdrawing their forces from French soil, the allies revised the 1814 **Paris** Treaty to reduce **France** to its 1790 borders. *See* **Maps 1, 30**.

Parma and Piacenza

The small north Italian duchy of Parma and Piacenza had been a pawn of Europe's major royal families since the extinction of its ruling

Farnese dynasty in 1731. Ruled by Duke Ferdinand, a member of **Spain's** Bourbon dynasty, it was overrun by French forces during the **Italian campaign** of 1796. In return for an indemnity of 6 million lire (and some choice works of art) Ferdinand was allowed to retain his position until his death in 1802, when the duchy was annexed by **France** and administered as a separate province. Ferdinand's son was compensated with the Kingdom of Etruria (**Tuscany**) by the **Lunéville** Treaty of 1801. Parma was absorbed into **France** as the province of Taro from 1808, and its small army distributed among French formations. After **Napoleon's** abdication, the duchy formed the heart of the lands allocated to his second wife, **Marie-Louise** of Austria, by the Congress of **Vienna**, but reverted to Ferdinand's son (King Louis of Etruria) after a revolution in 1831. *See* **Map 1**.

Parole

The system by which captives are released on an oath of good behaviour was an important regulating factor in an age when the maintenance of **prisoners of war** presented major problems for any army in the field. Mass parole was generally arranged by field commanders in the process of negotiating local peace terms. It required a written promise from defeated commanders that they and their troops would refrain from taking further part in the war concerned for the duration or a specified period of time. The system's obvious weakness was its basis in trust. Though many signatories kept to the letter and spirit of their parole, flagrant violations were commonplace, as were more devious attempts to circumvent terms, whether by enrolling in an allied army or by fighting in actions designated as separate from the war proper (such as internal or **colonial** policing). Attempts were occasionally made to pre-empt such practices by branding or otherwise marking released prisoners, but they were rare and the geographical breadth of the wars rendered parole-breaking, like **desertion**, virtually unstoppable.

Parthenopean Republic *See* **Naples**

Paul I, Tsar (1754–1801)

The mentally unstable son of **Catherine II** ('the Great'), he became autocratic ruler of **Russia** on her death in 1796. His brief reign was characterized by unrest at court and an erratic foreign policy, the latter apparently driven by a powerful faith in his destiny as the arbiter of European affairs. Paul committed Russia to the **Second Coalition** in 1798, but withdrew from the alliance in late 1799 as part of a dramatic diplomatic volte-face. Adopting a sudden anti-British stance, he instigated the **Armed Neutrality** league of northern powers in active opposition to Britain's **blockade** tactics, and had opened negotiations for mutual cooperation with **Napoleon** by early 1801. Whatever his ultimate plans, Paul's diplomatic adventures were short-lived. In an obvious state of advancing dementia, he was assassinated on 24 March 1801. He may have been strangled by his son, **Alexander I**, who quickly restored relations with Britain.

Pellew, Edward (1757–1833)

The **Royal Navy's** first wartime hero, Pellew was born in Cornwall and went to sea at 13, achieving instant celebrity (and a knighthood) in June 1793, when his 36-gun *Nymph* defeated a French **frigate** in the first Anglo-French naval engagement of the **Revolutionary Wars**. He had enhanced his reputation by the destruction or capture of another five French frigates while on patrol duties for the Channel Fleet before late 1796, when he helped disperse the French **Bantry Bay** expedition. In January 1797 he achieved the unprecedented feat of defeating a **ship-of-the-line**, hounding the 74-gun *Droits de l'Homme* to destruction.

Pellew entered parliament after the **Amiens** peace, a conventional step for unemployed war heroes, but was recalled to service as a rear-admiral in 1804, commanding the Royal Navy's **Indian Ocean** forces. Promoted vice-admiral in 1809, and recalled to the North Sea Fleet in 1810, he subsequently served as second-in-command with the **Mediterranean** Fleet, and ended the wars as a full admiral. Ennobled as Lord Exmouth in 1816, he commanded the naval base at Plymouth until 1821.

Pembrokeshire Raid

French landing on mainland **Great Britain** in February 1797, intended as a raid on the west coast port of Bristol and undertaken by a scratch force of 1,400 troops, known as the Black Legion and largely recruited from prisons. Escorted by two **frigates**, and two smaller warships, the force landed on the north coast of Devon on 20 February. Re-embarked two days later on the approach of local **militia** forces, it crossed the Severn Estuary to land at Fishguard, on the Pembrokeshire coast of Wales. Commanded by American mercenary Colonel Tate, the French brigade had no **artillery** and few uniforms, but advanced into the countryside on 23 February, apparently hoping to attack Liverpool. On encountering 3,000 Welsh militiamen under Lord Cawdor that afternoon, Tate immediately opened surrender negotiations, and his men became prisoners next day.

The expedition's escort squadron, which had sailed as soon as the troops moved inland, was intercepted off Brest on 9 March by two **Royal Navy** frigates, which captured the 40-gun *Résistance* and a **corvette**. The raid's principal effect was to intensify British defensive awareness, but first reports of the landing did trigger the **Bank Crisis**, briefly threatening Britain's credit system.

Peninsular War

The prolonged struggle for control of the Iberian Peninsula between the forces of imperial **France** and those of **Spain**, **Portugal** and **Great Britain**. Triggered by French invasion in 1808, and subsequent Spanish rebellion, it ended with Anglo-Portuguese armies well established inside south-western France in April 1814.

In the aftermath of victory over the **Fourth Coalition** in 1807, control of the Iberian Peninsula appeared both practicable and desirable to **Napoleon**. The easy conquest of pro-British Portugal in autumn 1807 closed the biggest single loophole in his **Continental System**, but its enforcement by his Spanish allies remained notoriously lax, and they could not be trusted to cooperate efficiently with ambitious French **naval** strategies. Exploiting the **Spanish Army's** manifest weakness, and using the chaotic state of Spanish court politics as a pretext for intervention, French forces occupied border **fortresses** from mid-February 1808, and had taken Madrid by late March (*see* Invasions of **Portugal**, **Spain**).

Napoleon expected the Spanish people to react gratefully, or at least passively, to French restoration of law and order, but popular outrage at his virtual abduction of the Bourbon royal family to **Bayonne** in April, along with the behaviour of occupying forces in the capital, triggered the **Madrid Uprising** in early May. Though quickly put down, the revolt heralded an explosion of anti-French popular violence from late May, escalating as news spread of Crown Prince **Ferdinand's** deposition in favour of Joseph **Bonaparte**, proclaimed King of Spain on 6 June.

The pro-French governors of Badajoz, Cartagena and Cadiz were assassinated, and the provincial **juntas** of Valencia, Seville and the Asturias began raising armies. By 10 June, when the Seville junta took the vital step of appealing for aid (via Gibraltar) to Britain, the standard of rebellion had been raised in every province, and military governor **Murat** was fast losing control over the capital. With few other options for continental intervention, Britain responded in late June. An army under General **Wellesley** was sent to Portugal, and the **Royal Navy** successfully evacuated a Spanish corps in French service from its station in Gothenburg, as well as seizing French shipping in Cadiz.

Some 120,000 French troops were active in the Iberian Peninsula, including **Moncey's** 30,000 around Madrid, **Dupont's** 24,000 along the upper Tagus, **Bessières's** reserve army in old Castille and Aragon, **Duhesme's** 13,000 men near Barcelona, and **Junot's** 25,000-strong Army of Portugal. The 100,000 troops of the regular Spanish Army were not concentrated, although some 30,000 men were massed under **Blake** and **Cuesta** in Galicia and a similar number were commanded by **Castaños** in Andalusia. Despite rapid volunteer reinforcement, Spanish forces were in no condition to undertake a war.

Napoleon sought to end the rebellion quickly and cheaply with a series of simultaneous offensives towards important strategic points, but inexperienced French conscripts operating in extreme heat and difficult terrain proved unable to carry them out. Moncey was forced to abandon a drive on Valencia, though on his way back to Madrid he met and defeated a force of 17,000 Spanish rebels under General Cervellon. Dupont's force sacked Córdoba before withdrawing on Andujar, while Bessières was unable to reach Santander and forced to besiege **Saragossa**. By the time General **Savary** reached Madrid to take over command from Murat (bound for **Naples**) on 18 June, the French offensives had manifestly failed and rebel forces were expanding.

Recognizing at last that a major effort would be needed to pacify Spain, Napoleon issued orders in early July to secure French positions pending the arrival of large-scale reinforcements from eastern Europe. An unexpected victory over Spanish forces at **Medina del Río Seco** on 14 July effectively secured communications along the Madrid–Burgos–Bayonne road through Galicia, but Dupont's relatively isolated force in Andalusia met with disaster at **Bailén** (20 July), triggering a reversal of French fortunes. King Joseph's subsequent withdrawal from Madrid to the Ebro, and abandonment of Saragossa's first siege, reduced French occupation to Spain's north-eastern corner.

The proposed relocation of 100,000 troops to Spain would leave only 150,000 men to guard the rest of the French Empire, and Napoleon was unable to open operations until he had confirmed Tsar **Alexander** I's diplomatic support at the **Erfurt** summit of autumn 1808. King Joseph and **Jourdan** (who had replaced Savary) were meanwhile forbidden to undertake their planned offensive on Madrid, and instead ordered to protect the line of the Ebro.

Spanish forces fell to regional infighting in the aftermath of Bailén. A rebel Supreme Junta met in Madrid from late September but devoted itself largely to bickering among its 325 regional delegates. It failed to appoint an overall military commander, dealing instead with regional 'captains-general' who were often old-regime dignitaries deeply suspicious of the junta's constitutionalist tendencies. The British army meanwhile achieved little beyond Wellesley's impressive inaugural victory at **Vimeiro** (21 August), which was spoiled by the generous terms given to Junot at **Cintra** by new C-in-C **Dalrymple**. Beset by logistic and diplomatic problems under his more aggressive successor,

Moore, 30,000 British troops spent the autumn languishing in Lisbon.

About 250,000 Spanish troops were under arms by late October, backed by **guerrillas** springing up behind French lines, but most were scattered in garrisons, besieging Barcelona, inside Saragossa or en route for the front. At the Ebro itself some 31,000 Galicians and Asturians under Blake were to the north around Reynosa, Castaños led 34,000 men in positions around Logroño, General Galuzzo controlled about 13,000 men near Burgos, and the **Palafox** brothers led another 42,000 in the south-east, though only 25,000 were at the front.

The central junta planned to attack the 75,000 French troops already assembled with a wide pincer movement to cut French Pyrenean communications. The plan left only a thin screen in the centre around Burgos, employed no coordinating supreme commander, and diluted front-line strength by detaching a large force to Barcelona. It broke down at once. A preliminary French attack took Logroño on 25 October, prompting Castaños and Palafox to suspend attacking preparations further east. When ordered to resume the attack, they held their exposed forward positions but did not advance.

Napoleon's preparations for his own offensive were almost complete. He planned to draw the Spanish pincers into the mountains before smashing through the centre, cutting their lines of retreat and driving on Madrid. **Ney** and Moncey were deploying in the south-east, **Lefebvre** and **Victor** to the north-west, when an impulsive attack by Lefebvre at Pancorbo on 31 October frightened Blake's force back towards Reynosa. Napoleon prioritized its destruction, but Blake won a limited victory at **Valmaseda** (5 November) before resuming his retreat.

The French offensive was launched on 6–7 November, winning victories over Blake at **Espinosa** and in the centre at **Gamonal** (both 10 November). Moving his HQ to Burgos, Napoleon sent **Soult** to Reynosa and ordered Ney to begin operations on the opposite flank. Soult just missed Blake's force at Reynosa, and took the well-stocked port of Santander on 16 November. Ney began a move across the rear of Castaños and the Palafox brothers on 14 November, but arrived too late to cut off Spanish forces defeated by **Lannes** (Moncey's replacement) at **Tudela** on 23 November.

Though Napoleon's armies were already suffering from supply shortages, disciplinary problems and guerrilla attacks, Madrid lay at his mercy. He moved on the capital with 45,000 men from 28 November, flanking corps and Moncey's force, again besieging Saragossa, bringing his total strength to some 130,000 men.

Embroiled in another command debate after dismissing Generals Castaños, Blake and Belvedere, the Madrid junta could only raise 20,000 regular troops for the defence of Madrid (though it turned down Moore's offer of aid). With only 2,500 men left after forward defences were crushed at the **Somosierra** Pass on 30 November, the junta resorted to panic measures, arming 20,000 citizens, throwing up fortifications and siting artillery around the city. Napoleon's demands for surrender were refused throughout 2 and 3 December, but accepted next day after an artillery bombardment and a minor attack that took the commanding Retiro Heights. As the junta fled for Badajoz, French troops reoccupied a sullen, silent city.

Once established in Madrid, Napoleon embarked on a lightning programme of social, political and fiscal reforms, abolishing medieval anachronisms (including the Inquisition), instituting radical tax reforms and restricting Church powers. Though often overdue, and in themselves acceptable to many Spaniards, the reforms aroused opposition by the dictatorial manner of their application, and did nothing to enhance the absent Joseph's authority.

Ignoring any possible threat from Moore, Napoleon dispatched **Mortier** to bolster the siege of Saragossa, and **Gouvion St Cyr** to pacify Catalonia. Keeping strong forces around Madrid, and preparing drives against Seville and Lisbon respectively, he sent only Soult's 17,000 men north-east to police Leon (where **Romana** was reassembling the remains of Blake's army) and Old Castile.

Moore had in fact decided to undertake a limited offensive into north-east Spain as a means of disrupting French operations further west. Napoleon became aware of Moore's presence in the general area on 19 December, by which time General **Dumas**, quartermaster with Victor's corps, had ordered its three divisions to Soult's aid on his own initiative. Approving Dumas's actions, Napoleon abandoned plans for his westward offensive and rushed most of his army north to teach the British a lesson.

The first French troops left Madrid on 20 December, aiming at Moore's presumed location around Valladolid, and Soult's relatively isolated corps only became aware of Moore's presence when its advanced **cavalry** was routed at **Sahagún** on 21 December, but news that Napoleon had taken the bait was enough to send Moore's 30,000 men hurrying for Astorga in a bid to escape before they were crushed.

Though Ney's pursuing corps got through the Guadarramas mountains on 21 December, the rest of the French army was delayed by bad weather, giving the British a convincing head start in a race to reach naval bases at Corunna and Ferrol, some 300km from Sahagún. Despite the sufferings of relatively inexperienced troops in appalling weather, and a consequent loss of discipline, the British held their lead. A minor British victory at **Benavente** on 29 December, and Moore's safe arrival at Astorga the same day, convinced Napoleon that he could not be cut off, and the pursuit was scaled down.

Most of the French army was withdrawn to Madrid or sent to besiege Leon, and the chase was left to 36,000 men under Soult. Napoleon himself left Astorga for Valladolid on 6 January, and ten days later hastened to Paris to deal with signs of Austrian aggression and the **Talleyrand–Fouché** conspiracy. While Napoleon made arrangements to hand over command, Moore continued his retreat from Astorga, fighting off a belated attack by Soult at **Corunna** on 16 January before his army completed its evacuation two days later. Moore himself was killed in the battle, but his sortie into northern Spain had fatally disrupted Napoleon's Spanish strategy.

Napoleon never returned to Spain, and French Peninsular operations never recovered the coherence of 1808. His insistence that the war was as good as won with Moore's departure, and that mopping-up operations could be handled by subordinates under his direct, but long-range, command, has been viewed as one of his greatest strategic errors. Compounded by a stubborn refusal to change his mind over the next five years, or to contemplate a defensive posture in Spain, it led him to pour resources piecemeal into a conflict that could only be won by concerted efforts, and was hardly worth winning in strategic terms.

Napoleon was underestimating not only the depth of popular hostility in Spain, which could still field 135,000 native troops, but also British determination to fight. Though only 16,000 British troops remained in the peninsula, protecting Lisbon, the **Portland** government had already begun organizing reinforcements, which the Royal Navy could deliver to unconquered south-western Spain and Portugal at any time. Spanish resistance proved impervious to battle or territorial losses throughout the war, and a series of setbacks in early 1809 caused no serious damage to its roots. These included the fall of Saragossa (20 February), Soult's invasion of northern Portugal and occupation of Oporto (22 March), as well as reverses at Ciudad Real (27 March) and **Medellín** (28 March), before Wellesley returned to Lisbon with 25,000 British reinforcements on 22 April.

Given overall command of British operations for the first time, Wellesley spent two weeks reorganizing his army, and laying the foundations for a new **Portuguese Army**, then marched 18,500 troops north from 8 May. He drove Soult out of **Oporto** four days later before turning his strike force east, crossing the frontier (3 July) and pursuing Victor's isolated corps towards Madrid. He halted after defeating the French at **Talavera** over three days in late July, eventually returning to the frontier in the early autumn to escape supply problems and the threat from French armies to the north. Now ennobled as Lord **Wellington**, he prepared for the counter-invasion that seemed certain to follow.

French victory over the **Fifth Coalition** had brought peace elsewhere in mainland Europe by autumn 1809, leaving Napoleon free to concentrate a major army in Spain. Although distracted from leading the expedition himself, he persuaded a fatigued **Masséna** to take command, with **Berthier** as his chief of staff and the expulsion of British forces as his primary objective. By mid-October 80,000 French troops were across the Pyrenees en route for the Portuguese frontier, and a Spanish attempt to take the offensive was crushed at **Ocaña** on 19 November.

Though distracted by political upheavals in Britain, where Portland's ministry had been replaced by **Percival**'s less predictable cabinet, Wellington made use of the time available to organize a comprehensive plan of defence. Able to secure only 25,000 British troops from a government made cautious by recent failure at **Walcheren**, he devoted time, supplies and General **Beresford** to building up Portuguese strength, thus doubling his command by the following spring.

Rather than attempt to hold the long frontier, Wellington planned a campaign of tactical withdrawal, leading Masséna away from his supply bases and into the defensible highlands around Lisbon. Calling on the Portuguese to revive the national tradition of *ordanenza* (mass removal of supplies and resources into protected lands around the capital), Wellington established a series of virtually impregnable lines around the Torres Vedras hills, close enough to Lisbon to enable orderly evacuation if necessary.

Wellington withdrew into Portugal in late 1809, wintering at Beira and riding out a spate of criticism from London, where opponents of the Peninsular expedition presented his apparent inactivity as evidence of crisis. The bulk of Anglo-Portuguese forces remained near the frontier until Masséna's columns entered Portugal in June, when they retired west along the Coa and upper Mondego rivers.

Combat was restricted to rearguard skirmishes, apart from Wellington's well-orchestrated defensive victory at **Busaco** in September 1810. By the time Masséna reached the **Torres Vedras** lines in mid-October, defenders were established in prepared positions, and acute lack of food and supplies forced his dwindling army to withdraw five weeks later. Wellington followed cautiously, aware that he could only be dislodged from Portugal if he lost a major battle, and Masséna's starving force was able to reach the town of Santarem for the winter.

French strategy for the Peninsula in 1811

remained the same as that of 1810 – to find, engage and expel the British – but Wellington, his reputation cemented by the defeat of Masséna, was ready to take the offensive. Although ultimately aiming to cut the road between Madrid and France around Burgos, he was characteristically determined to protect his lines of retreat, and his primary targets were the fortresses of **Badajoz** and **Ciudad Rodrigo**, which guarded the two roads between Spain and Portugal.

The year opened with two defeats for Spanish forces (at Olivenza on 22 January and on the Gebora River on 19 February) and the failure of an Anglo-Spanish expedition to relieve **Cadiz**, where the Supreme Junta had been under siege since January 1810. The latter was mitigated by General **Graham**'s unlikely victory at nearby **Barrosa** on 5 March, and Masséna began a withdrawal from Santarem towards the Spanish frontier on the same day, signalling the start of Wellington's spring campaign.

British forward units had the better of relatively minor engagements with French rearguards as Wellington shepherded Masséna out of Portugal before turning west to follow his own agenda. Soult's 25,000 troops from Cadiz had captured Badajoz on 10 March, putting the French in control of both vital fortresses and leaving Wellington's 58,000 troops (without a **siege train**) poised between two enemy forces. While Wellington invested the frontier fortress of Almeida (which blocked the road to Ciudad Rodrigo) with 38,000 men, Beresford was sent to invest Badajoz with the remaining 20,000.

Wellington's textbook **siege** eventually took Almeida on 11 May, after beating Masséna's reinforced army at **Fuentes de Oñoro** (3–5 May), but Beresford was forced to abandon the siege at Badajoz and fight off Soult's army at **Albuera** on 16 May. Wellington concentrated for a renewed siege of Badajoz, but was forced to withdraw on 20 June after **Marmont** (Masséna's replacement) and Soult united to march on the town. Returning north to Ciudad Rodrigo, Wellington abandoned his investment of the fortress on 20 September, when word came of a new French relief operation. Though **Picton**'s division was almost trapped at **El Bodón** on 25 September,

the allied army made good its retreat into Portugal for the winter. Further east, **Suchet** won a series of autumn victories in late September and October against Blake's army in Aragon, and won the first success of 1812 by taking Valencia on 8 January.

Suchet's victory masked a fundamental shift in the Iberian balance of power at the start of 1812. Napoleon relaxed his long-range personal supervision of French operations to concentrate on the **Russian campaign**, leaving Joseph and chief of staff Jourdan with greater independence but fewer troops. The recall of 27,000 troops to France forced Marmont to transfer 10,000 men from western Spain, and Wellington exploited his opponent's weakness with a surprise winter attack on Ciudad Rodrigo, which was in his hands by 20 January. Wellington then swung his forces south to Badajoz, which fell to a costly assault on 6 April. In control of the two 'gateways to Portugal', he was now in position to attack into the heart of Spain.

Wellington chose to leave Soult entangled around Cadiz, watched by Hill's corps, and led 50,000 troops north towards Burgos from 13 June. He inflicted a shattering defeat on Marmont east of **Salamanca** on 22 July, compelling Soult's southern force to retreat from Cadiz in its wake (24 August) and opening the road to Madrid, which welcomed allied forces on 12 August. Wellington led 35,000 men north towards **Burgos** from 19 September, but was forced to withdraw on 21 October and lost 6,000 troops during an arduous retreat, abandoning Madrid on 30 October and finally reaching Ciudad Rodrigo on 20 November.

Despite its ultimate reversal, Wellington's foray into Spain had taken some 20,000 prisoners and cleared southern Spain of French forces. French failure in Russia had meanwhile forced a defensive policy on Napoleon's commanders in Spain, but though strategic reality suggested a withdrawal beyond the Pyrenees, the emperor ordered Joseph to take up defensive positions along the River Douro. Wellington spent the winter reorganizing his command chain, training reinforcements and attempting to organize Spanish forces, formally under his control as commander-in-chief since 2 October 1812.

French strength in the Peninsula still amounted to some 200,000 troops in spring 1813, most of them concentrated in the north beyond the Douro, and Wellington commanded about 106,000 effectives (including 25,000 Spanish regulars). Joseph focused his defence along the river between Zamorra and Valladolid, anticipating an allied offensive from the south, but Wellington planned a wide sweep to outflank the French northern wing. The problem of supplying an army so far from the British bases in Portugal, regarded as insuperable by French planners, was solved by using the Royal Navy to seize the northern port of Santander as a supply base.

Along with a welter of guerrilla attacks in northern Spain, two major diversionary operations were launched to mask Wellington's intentions: **Murray** and 18,000 men undertook a (fruitless) raid on **Tarragona**, and Hill led 30,000 troops in a feint towards Salamanca, an operation timed to coincide with the rest of the army's departure from Portugal on 22 May 1813. Hill's feint convinced Joseph, who abandoned Madrid on 27 May and withdrew towards the Douro, but Wellington's capture of Zamorra finally revealed the danger to the French right flank on 2 June.

French forces fell back on Burgos, but Wellington ignored the fortress and continued his outflanking manoeuvre, compelling Joseph to blow up the castle and pull further east from 12 June. Joseph eventually made a stand at the communications centre of **Vitoria**, where his army was resoundingly beaten on 22 June. Vitoria was one of Wellington's most brilliant performances, and his most important strategic success in Spain. Coinciding with the summer **armistice** in **Germany**, it was an important boost to allied morale, encouraged **Austria** to join the **Sixth Coalition**, and effectively ended French occupation.

Joseph retreated to the Pyrenean frontier, after which he returned to Paris, and Soult's Army of Andalusia pulled back from Valencia. Soult took overall command of the theatre when he reached Bayonne on 11 July, by which time only isolated garrisons at **Pamplona** and **San Sebastian** were still in French hands, and reorganized his forces into a single, 80,000-strong Army of Spain for a counter-offensive through the Pyrenean passes.

Wellington halted his advance at the northwest Pyrenees to rest his army, now down to 60,000 men, and prepare for the anticipated French counter-attack. Sending detachments to invest the two remaining garrisons, and block the three main routes through the mountains, he strung a thin cordon along the front line and backed it with a strong central reserve. Expecting Soult to attack along the coast to relieve San Sebastian, he grouped two-thirds of his strength in the northern sector.

Soult in fact advanced towards Pamplona with 61,000 troops, winning preliminary actions at the **Maya** and **Roncesvalles** passes on 25 July to move behind Wellington's lines of retreat from the San Sebastian area. Taken by surprise, Wellington rode south from San Sebastian to take command of the defence at **Sorauren**, where his decisive victory on 30 July brought the last major French offensive of the war to an end.

Soult's weakened army made one more attempt to dislodge the allies, launching attacks across the Bidassoa River at **Vera** and **San Marcial** on 31 August. Both failed, and the fall of San Sebastian on the same day marked the beginning of the war's final phase, with both sides spending September in preparation for a campaign inside south-western France.

As allied forces converged on Napoleon's armies around **Leipzig**, Wellington crossed the Bidassoa into France at both **Irun**, near the northern coast, and a little further inland at **Vera**. Moving towards Bayonne with greater confidence once Pamplona had surrendered on 31 October, Wellington broke through French positions at the **Nivelle** on 10 November, and those at the **Nive** on 12 December, fighting off a determined counter-attack by Soult at **St Pierre** next day. Despite sending 25,000 Spanish troops home to curtail their reprisal activities on French soil, Wellington had surrounded Bayonne by the end of the year.

Inside Spain, a year of liberation had triggered celebratory destruction of all things French, and an almost immediate resumption of political infighting. The Spanish Regency Council's refusal to ratify the **Valençay** treaty of 11 December between Napoleon and King Ferdinand foreshadowed a decade of strife between a reactionary crown and a wide-spectrum, relatively liberal opposition.

The last French troops in Spain, Suchet's forces in Catalonia, retired into France before Wellington launched his final offensive in mid-February 1814. The demands of Napoleon's campaign for **France**, in progress further north, had reduced Soult's command to about 55,000 troops, grouped in seven divisions. Masked by **Hope's** strong diversion, Wellington drove Soult back from **Orthez** on 27 February, but the diversion of allied troops to the **Bordeaux** rebellion and a rearguard action at **Tarbes** helped the dwindling French army reach Toulouse on 24 March.

News of Napoleon's **abdication** on 6 April had not reached **Toulouse** by the time Wellington attacked the city four days later. After heavy fighting, Soult abandoned Toulouse on 11 April and agreed to an armistice the following night. It is uncertain whether the last action of the war, a costly French sortie from besieged **Bayonne** on 14 April, was undertaken with or without knowledge of the ceasefire, but a war that had eventually claimed an estimated 300,000 French casualties came to a formal end when Soult capitulated on 17 April. *See* **Maps 5, 22.**

Percival, Spencer (1762–1812)

Minor aristocrat who was prime minister of **Great Britain** from 1809 until his death. Perceval trained as a lawyer and entered parliament in 1796, serving as solicitor-general (1801) and attorney-general (1802) in the **Addington** administration, and as Chancellor of the Exchequer (finance minister) from 1807 under **Portland**. Trusted by King **George III** for his anti-Catholic views, and with a well-deserved reputation for diligence, Perceval was appointed prime minister following Portland's death in September 1809. He was regarded as a stop-gap nonentity, but his pragmatism and the lack of any concerted opposition attempt to take power enabled his government to survive, though its policies betrayed no particular long-term purpose. His position as his own Chancellor invited blame for mounting tax burdens, and spontaneous

popular celebrations greeted news that he had been shot dead by deranged bankrupt John Bellingham in the lobby of the Commons on 11 May 1812. In an attempt to avert the **Anglo-American War**, Perceval had just agreed to revoke the 1806 **Orders in Council**, but his death delayed their actual revocation long enough to ensure that the new **Liverpool** administration faced an immediate crisis across the Atlantic.

Pérignon, Catherine Dominique (1754–1818)

Commissioned into the royal **French Army** in 1780, Pérignon was a colonel with the **National Guard** from 1789, but was more of a politician than a soldier. Given a division on the **Pyrenean** front in 1793, he fought at **Truillas** and **Le Boulon** before taking command of French forces west of Perpignan on the death of **Dugommier** in November 1794. He captured **Figueras** and **Rosas** before his replacement by **Schérer** in March 1795, when he was recalled and elected to the Council of **Five Hundred**. Ambassador to Madrid for two years from summer 1795, he returned to action in 1799 under **Moreau** and **Joubert** on the **Italian** front, but was wounded and captured at **Novi** in August. Released in 1800, he was one of four retired members of the original **Marshalate** in 1804, subsequently serving as military governor in **Parma** (1806–8) and **Naples** (1808–13). After an enthusiastic return to royal service in 1814, he was stripped of his imperial titles by **Napoleon** during the **Hundred Days**, but was reinstated and ennobled by the restored monarchy.

Perpignan, Battle of

The first major action of the Franco-Spanish **Pyrenean** campaign, fought in mid-July 1793 for the French frontier city of Perpignan. Spanish general Ricardos advanced towards the city through the southern Pyrenees from mid-April, but delayed a full-scale attack until his army had been strengthened with **artillery** and 8,000 reinforcements. French reinforcements under General Flers had reached the area when 12,000 Spaniards advanced from Ceret on 19 May, and they repelled a series of Spanish attacks against Perpignan's outer defences from 13 to 16 July. Ricardos launched 15,000 troops in five columns against the city from all directions on 17 July, but logistic preparations did not match the plan's complexity. All but one of the columns got lost on the approach, and a counter-attack against the flank of the few troops that did get through drove them into full retreat by the end of the day, minus 1,000 casualties. As the best French troops were transferred to other fronts, and the Spanish awaited reinforcement, the war in the southern Pyrenees lapsed into stalemate. *See* **Map 5**.

Perrée, Jean-Baptiste Emmanuel (1761–1800)

One of the most respected French naval officers of the **Revolutionary Wars**, Perrée began his career as a merchant seaman in 1773, but transferred to military service in 1792. As captain of the **frigate** *Prosperine*, he captured 63 ships (including a **Dutch Navy** 32-gunner) during a highly successful commerce raiding cruise in 1793, and undertook further raids over the next two years, earning national fame at a time when attacks on enemy trade were the **French Navy's** most useful contribution to the war effort.

Perrée's 38-gun *Minerve* and two other French frigates captured the British **ship-of-the-line** *Berwick* on 7 March 1795, but he was taken prisoner after another frigate action off Toulon on 24 June. Freed in 1797, he served under **Brueys** in the **Middle East** the following year, commanded the flotilla that accompanied French troops up the Nile, and took part in the Battle of **Shubra Khit**. He fought British forces under **Smith** while escorting **artillery** into Syria in 1799, but was again captured in June, when the British **Mediterranean** Fleet intercepted the five vessels he was leading back to France.

Exchanged and confirmed as rear-admiral, he was entrusted with running supplies into besieged **Malta**, where his flagship, the 74-gun *Généreux*, was intercepted by **Nelson** in the 80-gun *Foudroyant* on 18 February 1800. Perrée gave battle so that his smaller ships could escape, but was forced to surrender after a fierce engagement in which he was mortally wounded.

Perry, Oliver Hazard (1785–1819)

Born in Rhode Island, Perry was the most conspicuously successful **US Navy** commander of the **Anglo-American War** (1812–15). As commodore of the light warship flotilla on the Great Lakes, he gave valuable assistance to land forces before their defeat at **Stony Creek** in spring 1813, and defeated **Royal Navy** forces on **Lake Erie** in the autumn before ferrying troops to another failure at **Thames River**. Moved south to the Potomac in the later stages of the war, he died of yellow fever while on a mission to aid republican rebels in **South America**. His younger brother Matthew became one of the US Navy's most respected commanders in the mid-nineteenth century.

Phélypeaux, Antoine le Picard de (1768–99)

French aristocrat, a student alongside **Napoleon** at the Paris military academy in the early 1780s, who joined the royal **artillery** but became an émigré in 1791. He fought republican forces on the **Rhine** until 1795, when he re-entered France to stir up royalist rebellion and was arrested. He escaped from France in 1797, but returned to help free **Royal Navy** captain Sir Sidney **Smith**, a feat that earned him a commission as a **British Army** colonel. Accompanying Smith's squadron in the **Middle East** from 1798, Phélypeaux put his training to excellent use at **Acre** in 1799, organizing the town's defences to frustrate Napoleon's **siege**, but was a victim of the town's plague epidemic.

Pichegru, Jean-Charles (1761–1804)

French soldier from a peasant background, an elected lieutenant-colonel in 1792, who was promoted brigadier-general in 1793, and given divisional command later that year. After a brief spell commanding on the **Rhine**, he earned his greatest fame in **Flanders** as commander of the Army of the North from 1794, winning a series of victories against the Duke of **York's** allied forces and conquering the **Netherlands**. Back on the Rhine, in command of its northern sector, he achieved little with an autumn offensive around **Mannheim** in 1795, and was replaced by **Moreau** for the 1796 campaign. Elected to the Council of **Five Hundred**, Pichegru was its president during the **Fructidor coup** of 1797, and was deported to the distant colony of Guiana in its aftermath. He escaped in 1798 and travelled to Britain, where he became involved in the **Cadoudal** conspiracy against the **Consulate**. Arrested in Paris after its failure in 1804, he was found strangled in his prison cell on 5 April.

Picton, Thomas (1758–1815)

British infantry officer, commissioned in 1771, who was promoted at a conventional speed for those without influence, and was a major when he went to the **West Indies** in 1794. He remained in the Caribbean as governor of Trinidad (until 1803) and then of Tobago. A brigadier-general from 1801, he returned home to face charges of torturing a female prisoner and, though found guilty, was acquitted on appeal in 1806. Promoted major-general in 1808, he took part in the siege of Flushing during the 1809 **Walcheren expedition**, and commanded the 'Fighting' 3rd Division with **Wellington's** army in the **Peninsular War** from 1810. He fought at **Busaco**, **Torres Vedras**, **Fuentes de Oñoro** and **Ciudad Rodrigo** before he was seriously wounded leading the final capture of **Badajoz** in 1812. Knighted and promoted lieutenant-general, he returned to Spain to fight at **Vitoria** in 1813, and remained in the theatre until the end of the war the following year. He led a division during the **Hundred Days** campaign of 1815, was wounded at **Quatre Bras**, and died leading an important counter-attack at **Waterloo**.

Piedmont

North-west Italian state, including the major city of Turin and most of **Savoy**, that was ruled by the kings of **Sardinia**. Menaced by French invasion forces across the Alps, Piedmontese troops briefly invaded France in 1793 and fought with Austrian forces during the **Italian campaigns** until effectively conquered by **Napoleon** in May 1796, when King Victor Amadeus III signed the Peace of **Cherasco**. His son, Charles Emmanuel IV, sacrificed the last vestige of its independence when he abandoned Turin in late 1798, and a puppet Piedmontese Republic was established under French auspices in 1799. After retiring to Sardinia, Charles Emmanuel returned to the mainland in 1799, hoping to capitalize on the **Second Coalition's** early successes, but departed after French victory at **Marengo** in 1800. The republic was absorbed into **France** proper from

1802, after which Piedmontese troops fought as a small part of the **French Army**, and became part of an imperial north Italian province in 1809, but was restored to the Kingdom of Sardinia by the postwar Congress of **Vienna**. *See* **Maps 21, 30**.

Pikes

By no means every army was able to equip all its infantry forces with **muskets**, and the medieval pike, a simple wooden staff, was still the basic offensive weapon of many soldiers in irregular, volunteer militia or reserve formations who were unable to provide their own firearms. Manifestly useless against forces armed with guns, the pike was never a weapon of choice, though short ceremonial pikes were used as badges of office by senior NCOs in some major armies.

Pillnitz, Declaration of

Joint statement issued by the rulers of **Prussia** and **Austria** on 27 August 1791, after their meeting at the west German town of Pillnitz, inviting other European monarchs to join them in forcing the French revolutionary government to restore King **Louis XVI** to his rightful status. The declaration was less ideologically motivated than it appeared: Prussian king **Frederick William II** was bent on a war of territorial aggrandizement, and Habsburg emperor Leopold II was bluffing. The refusal of **Great Britain** to sign the declaration rendered it entirely cosmetic, and Leopold announced that its conditions had been fulfilled after the French king accepted a new constitution in September. Published in **France** alongside a polemic (if unofficial) émigré commentary, it fuelled the subsequent **Brissotin** campaign for a French war of national defence against an international conspiracy.

Pirna, Battle of

Important secondary action fought on 26 August 1813 near the town of Pirna, on the south bank of the River Elbe about 20km east of **Dresden**, which was then under attack by a large allied army under Austrian prince **Schwarzenberg**. Reports from the city persuaded **Napoleon** to scale down a planned offensive towards Pirna and Königstein in the rear of Schwarzenberg's advance and return to Dresden late on 25 August, but General **Vandamme** and 32,000 men (but no **artillery**) crossed the Elbe to drive Prince **Eugen's** 12,500 men out of Pirna the following evening. Allied commanders were forced to divert General **Ostermann's** 26,000 men to the sector, reducing the manpower available at Dresden but enabling the obstruction of Vandamme's advance across their rear lines at **Kulm** on 30 August. *See* Campaign for **Germany**; **Map 25.**

Pistols

Contemporary pistols were muzzle-loaded, one-shot devices, universally issued to **cavalry** and officers throughout the period but almost valueless as combat weapons. No easier to use than the **carbines** also carried by mounted troops, they were inaccurate at anything but very close range, when they were far less useful than the rider's **sabre**. They were standard weapons with **naval** officers, who carried them as close-combat weapons during boarding actions, and an important socio-political arbiter in élite European and American societies accustomed to settling disputes by duelling.

Pitt, John *See* **Chatham**, Earl of

Pitt, William (1759–1806)

The most important political figure in wartime **Great Britain**, Pitt was prime minister from 1783 to 1801, and again from 1804 until his death. Known as Pitt the Younger to distinguish him from his namesake father, the greatest British statesman of the mid-eighteenth century, he was the younger brother of John Pitt, who inherited the family title as Lord **Chatham**. Chancellor of the Exchequer (finance minister) at 23, he was appointed premier by King **George III** in defiance of a Whig majority in the House of Commons, subsequently displaying gifts for political and financial management that earned great popularity during a period of government stability and economic prosperity.

Pitt's view of government was essentially pragmatic, and he thought in imperial rather than European terms. Though supported by the king as a bastion of conservative values, he was open to more radical thinking and generally prepared to embrace political compromise (as well as intrigue) in the name of commercial expansion. As such he and his main cabinet lieutenants,

Grenville and **Dundas**, were not ideally equipped as war leaders, and his popularity gradually shrank during the **Revolutionary Wars**.

Historians echo contemporary criticism of Pitt for allowing Britain to drift into the **First Coalition** without clear aims in 1793, and for his subsequent dilution of the British war effort into a series of strategically irrelevant **colonial** conquests. Posterity regards his diplomatic success in forming the **Second Coalition** with greater sympathy than its abject military failure generated at the time, and his management of Britain's **war finance**, though possibly his greatest contribution to national welfare, involved tax changes that provoked opposition among the élite classes.

Like most British Tories, Pitt sympathized with Burke's horrified reaction to the **French Revolution**, but he viewed war in 1793 as an undesirable distraction from imperial development, an attitude only gradually transformed into hardened belligerence as French expansion menaced European markets and home security. By the turn of the century, when war-weariness and military disappointment had made peace with France an overwhelmingly popular option, Pitt was out of step with public and political opinion. His parliamentary position nevertheless remained virtually impregnable, most of the leading opposition figures having joined his government with **Portland** in 1794.

An austere figure, over-sensitive to criticism but utterly dedicated to his work, Pitt had many more political followers than close friends, and a lifetime of mounting debt testified to his lack of interest in personal wealth. By the end of 1800 he was exhausted and dispirited after 17 years in power, and relations with the king were close to breakdown. He resigned in February 1801, along with most of his leading followers, over George's refusal to permit **Catholic emancipation** in return for formal **Union** with **Ireland**, and passed three years recovering his self-esteem (though not his health) as leader-in-waiting and critic of the **Addington** government.

Capable of ruthless intrigue, and more interested in power than most of his rivals, Pitt joined forces with Whig opponents to engineer Addington's downfall and his own return to office in 1804, but lost the support of Grenville and others by reneging on an agreement to include his most inveterate foe, **Fox**, in the cabinet. Despite a reduced parliamentary base, Pitt recovered much popularity during his last months in power, his formation of the **Third Coalition** and a great victory at **Trafalgar** contrasting dramatically with Addington's relative inertia. Worn out at 47, Pitt died in January 1806, and his reputation was spared the backlash from French victory at **Austerlitz**. Instead it grew steadily during the last decade of war, nostalgia for his unifying qualities reflecting a leadership vacuum created by his death.

Pius VI, Pope (1717–99)

Born Giovanni Angelo Barschi in Cesena, Italy, he became a cardinal in 1773 and Pope two years later. An inveterate but largely ineffective antagonist of the **French Revolution** and its anticlerical policies, he helped orchestrate opposition to French control during the **Italian campaigns** of 1794–7, but was forced into a humiliating peace with France in February 1797 and imprisoned a year later after the French occupation of Rome. He was held first at Siena, and then moved to Valence in France, where he died in August 1799. *See also* **Papal States**.

Pius VII, Pope (1742–1823)

Born in Cesena, Luigi Barnaba Chiarimonti became a cardinal in 1785, and succeeded **Pius VI** as Pope in March 1800. Elected in Venice, he returned to Rome later that year, and the withdrawal of French troops from the **Papal States** opened the way for rapprochement with **Napoleon** by the **Concordat** agreement in July 1801. Subsequent modification of the agreement by the **Organic Articles** rekindled mutual tension, and though Pius travelled to Paris for Napoleon's imperial coronation in 1804, he failed to secure any relaxation of the articles. His subsequent refusal to annul the marriage of Joseph **Bonaparte** or join the **Continental System** contributed to Napoleon's decision to annex the Papal States, and excommunicating the invaders in June 1809 merely brought imprisonment. Held in Genoa and Savona, he was eventually taken to Fontainebleau, where he was compelled to sign a revised Concordat accepting the annexation. A prisoner until Napoleon's defeat in 1814,

when he returned to Rome, he was unable to persuade the Congress of **Vienna** to restore the enclave at Avignon. He subsequently retained some of the liberal social reforms introduced by the French regime, but used a restored Papal army to suppress **carbonari** activities.

Platov, Matvei Ivanovich (1751–1818)

Leader (hetman) of the Don **Cossacks**, and their senior **cavalry** commander, Platov was a veteran of **Suvorov's** campaigns against the **Ottoman Empire**, and led the advance guard of the **Russian Army** during the **Russian campaign** of 1812 and the subsequent campaigns in **Germany** and **France**. A well-known figure in Europe after he entered Paris at the head of his colourful light horsemen in 1814, his greatest successes came during the **Grande Armée's** desperate retreat from **Moscow**, although victories at **Inkovo** and **Vinkovo** demonstrated his ability to surprise more coherent formations.

Plattsburg, Battle of

The last major action along the Canadian frontier during the **Anglo-American War** of 1812–15 was the successful defence of Plattsburg, gateway to the upper Hudson River in the far northeastern US, against a large-scale British offensive via Lake Champlain in September 1814. General Prevost, the British governor of northern Canada, was able to lead no fewer than 14,000 **Peninsular War** veterans south down the shore of Lake Champlain, protected by a flotilla of light warships. Only 1,500 **US Army** regulars under General Macomb, backed by 3,000 local militia, were guarding the base at Plattsburg, protected from attack across the lake by a relatively powerful **US Navy** flotilla. Prevost launched simultaneous land and naval attacks on 11 September, and although British infantry forced the Americans out of well-prepared positions, the naval battle ended as an overwhelming American victory. Denied mastery of the lake, and facing bombardment if he stayed where he was, Prevost abandoned stores and equipment to speed his withdrawal across the frontier. *See* **Map 27**.

Poland

Once a powerful central European empire, the Kingdom of Poland had entered terminal decline by the second half of the eighteenth century.

Poised between the expansionist empires of **Austria**, **Prussia** and **Russia**, its internal politics riven by the disputes of their respective supporters, Poland was an elective monarchy, ruled by King Stanislaus Poniatowski (Stanislaus II) since 1864. A Russian nominee, Stanislaus was powerless to influence a quarter of the kingdom's partition by its three neighbours in 1772, or a new constitution imposed in 1775, which concentrated political power in the hands of a permanent council of nobles and restricted the army to 30,000 troops.

The Polish national diet overturned the constitution with Prussian encouragement in 1788, abolishing the council of nobles and expanding the army to 65,000 men. Amid fears that an elected successor to Stanislaus would herald further loss of territory, the diet granted the monarchy hereditary status in May 1791, after an alliance with Prussia in March had apparently guaranteed security against any aggressive Russian reaction.

Happy to give support to Polish exiles bent on restoration of the 1775 constitution, **Catherine II** exploited the outbreak of war in France to launch an invasion of Poland in spring 1792. Though Prussia failed to honour its alliance, the 46,000 troops of the Polish Army held out until July before the king and diet leader Kollontaj gave in to émigré demands (*see* **Russo-Polish War**). Amid mass resignations by disgusted Polish officers, Russian forces again entered the country from the east in early 1793, prompting a Prussian invasion from the west. The two empires settled any potential dispute by each seizing a large portion of territory when the Second Partition was agreed in September 1793, reducing independent Poland to a third of its original size.

Polish nationalism, long a force uniting popular and aristocratic ambitions, became a catalyst for uprising after the Second Partition, but the **Polish rebellion** of 1794 was crushed by Russian and Prussian forces in the autumn. A Third Partition terminated the country's independent existence in 1795, but did little to bring peace to the region, which remained a constant source of mutual suspicion between Russia, Austria and Prussia. Though rebel leader Kosciusko retired into

exile, large numbers of nationalist soldiers and politicians emigrated to continue the fight for renewed independence, most putting their faith in republican **France**, which was able to field **Polish forces** in the **Italian campaigns** from 1796.

Popular support for the basic ideals of the **French Revolution** had been stronger in Poland than perhaps anywhere else in Europe, and faith in basic French sympathy for the Polish cause extended to the Napoleonic regimes. **Napoleon** himself was happy to let his Polish supporters and soldiers believe he planned their future independence, but never saw Poland as anything more than a convenient source of manpower and a diplomatic bargaining chip.

When Napoleon moved to occupy the Prussian sector of Poland after his victories against the **Fourth Coalition** in late 1806, he was welcomed by the citizens and their aristocratic leaders as a potential saviour, recruiting 50,000 fresh troops and winning a devoted lover in Marie **Walewska** during his brief stay in Warsaw. The emperor went some small way to satisfying Polish ambitions by transforming the Prussian sector and its 2.5 million Poles into the Duchy of Warsaw by the Treaties of **Tilsit** (8 July 1807) and Dresden (22 July).

Though nominally independent, garrisoned by at least some Polish troops, and a member of the Confederation of the **Rhine**, the duchy was no more than a French imperial satellite. Ruled by Saxon king **Frederick Augustus** as grand duke, it was effectively governed by Napoleon's appointed French representative, though senior administrative posts were held by Poles. It was given a constitution modelled on the **Code Napoléon**, and serfdom was abolished, along with some of the aristocracy's feudal privileges. Though it regained territory lost to Austria by the Third Partition in 1809, the duchy was never large enough to be self-supporting.

Napoleon's guarantees of Austria's remaining Polish possessions had eroded support for France long before the 1812 **Russian campaign**, but Polish forces took part in the invasion, sustained by hints that Jérôme **Bonaparte** was about to become king of a restored Poland. By the time the Duchy of Warsaw disappeared with the French retreat from eastern Europe at the end of the year, Warsaw itself falling to Russian forces on 18 February 1813, some Polish nobles were prepared to believe that the tsar would champion national rights, and **Alexander I** was able to attend the Congress of **Vienna** in the guise of Poland's protector.

The shape of postwar Poland presented one of the most difficult problems facing the peace conference, but nationalists derived little satisfaction from the solution imposed in 1815, sometimes known as the Fourth Partition. Apart from a tiny independent republic based on Krakow, the country was again divided among the three eastern empires, and although the expanded Russian sector was disguised as an autonomous kingdom ('Congress Poland'), Tsar Alexander was its appointed king. Polish nationalism remained a powerful regional force, and fuelled large-scale national uprisings in 1830 and 1863, but the country did not recover independent status until the 1920s.

Polish Forces

The army of independent **Poland** broke the terms of the country's First Partition in 1772 by beginning expansion to a strength of 65,000 troops in 1791, and a frontline army of 46,000 men (14 regular regiments reinforced by volunteer militia) took the field during the following year's **Russo-Polish War**. Built around regular units that refused to be absorbed by Russian forces after the Second Partition of 1793, a revived army was at the heart of the **Polish rebellion** in 1794, and fought well until overwhelmed by superior numbers at **Maciejowice** and **Praga**.

Poland disappeared with a Third Partition in 1796, and surviving Polish units were absorbed into other imperial armies, but many officers and men emigrated into French service. Organized under **Dombrowski**, but officially in the service of the **Cisalpine Republic**, three Polish battalions fought in the **Italian campaign** of 1796–7, and had expanded by 1800 to comprise an 'Italian Legion' and a 'Danube Legion'. They were reorganized as the **French Army**'s first three foreign demi-brigades in 1801, but two were virtually wiped out by disease at **Santo Domingo** in 1803.

In October 1806 **Napoleon** charged Dombrowski with raising a new division of Poles for imperial service. Based around veterans of the Polish Legions, this became the core of the Duchy of **Warsaw**'s army, which fought with the French but also carried out garrison and frontier protection duties. The army expanded steadily up to 1812, ultimately providing 21 infantry regiments, 20 cavalry regiments and 104 field guns, and served in every major French theatre. Grouped as the **Grande Armée**'s VIII Corps under **Poniatowski** until his death at **Leipzig** in 1813, and then under Dombrowski, dwindling Polish forces remained loyal to Napoleon until his **abdication**, when most returned to home to retirement or service in the army of 'Congress Poland'. *See also* **Lances**.

Polish Rebellion (1794)

Full-scale nationalist uprising in **Poland** that was a reaction to the country's Second Partition in September 1793. Triggered by a mutiny of army units threatened with incorporation into Russian formations in early 1794, it brought former army commander Kosciusko back from Leipzig, where he led a group seeking French support for a republican uprising, to join rebel forces at Krakow in April. Nationalist forces drove the Russians out of most of eastern Poland, but Kosciusko's appointment as national dictator could not heal divisions within his advisory supreme council. After holding off attacks on Warsaw throughout the summer, rebels faced with a combined Russian and Prussian invasion suffered decisive defeats at **Maciejowice** (4 October) and **Praga** (5 November), after which the country was occupied and again partitioned.

Polotsk, First Battle of

One of the few major actions to take place during the opening phase of the 1812 **Russian campaign**, fought at the River Dvina around Polotsk on 17 and 18 August 1812. From mid-July, when Russian First Army commander **Barclay de Tolly** abandoned strong defences at Dünaburg and Drissa to move south-east towards a rendezvous with the Second Army, **Wittgenstein**'s northern wing had been engaged in an isolated contest with **Oudinot**'s corps in the region around Polotsk. An initial French advance had been reversed by early August, but Oudinot was reinforced from 16 August by **Gouvion St Cyr's** corps, bringing his strength up to about 35,000 men. Oudinot launched an attack against Wittgenstein's 28,000 troops on 17 August, but frontal assaults failed to break the Russian lines, and Oudinot was badly wounded during the evening. Gouvion St Cyr took command of a renewed attack next day, making skilful use of flank attacks to drive Wittgenstein back across the Dvina. Though hardly a decisive victory, and strategically almost irrelevant, the battle encouraged **Napoleon** to advance his main armies deeper into Russia and earned St Cyr his marshal's baton. *See* **Map 23**.

Polotsk, Second Battle of

Limited attack by French forces on the northern wing of the retreat from **Moscow** during the latter part of the 1812 **Russian campaign**. Despite its defeat at the first Battle of **Polotsk** in August, **Wittgenstein's** Russian corps had prevented the combined forces of **Oudinot** and **Gouvion St Cyr** from progressing further east during the autumn, and was reinforced to 35,000 men in pursuit of the French withdrawal from October. Recognizing that Oudinot might be forced back too quickly to stop Wittgenstein cutting off his own retreat at the Beresina, **Napoleon** reinforced the northern flank with **Victor's** corps, his principal tactical reserve, and on 7 November ordered it to drive Wittgenstein back beyond Polotsk. Victor concentrated more than 25,000 troops around the village of Smoliani and attacked on 14 November, forcing the Russians to retreat in disarray and inflicting an estimated 5,000 casualties on Wittgenstein's army. Though the setback prevented Wittgenstein from reaching the **Beresina** before the French armies, they were outpaced by Admiral **Tshitshagov's** army coming up from the south.

Poniatowski, Josef Anton (1763–1813)

A nephew of King Stanislaus II of **Poland**, but born in Vienna, Poniatowski followed his father into the **Austrian Army** in 1778, and was wounded in 1788 while serving against **Ottoman** forces in the Balkans. Accepting a commission as a general in the Polish Army, he commanded forces fighting the Russian invasion in 1792, and

campaigned against the Russians again during the rebellion of 1794. He retired after its defeat, first to Vienna and then to his eastern Polish estates, but was recalled to public life in 1806 by Prussian king **Frederick William III**, who appointed him governor of the Prussian province of Warsaw. A committed nationalist, he welcomed **Napoleon's** conquest of Prussian Poland during the War of the **Fourth Coalition**, and accepted command of the first **Polish** division to enter French imperial service early in 1807.

Poniatowski became one of the French emperor's most trusted field commanders, combining military duties with the war ministry of the Duchy of **Warsaw** from 1808. He led imperial forces in Galicia during the War of the **Fifth Coalition** in 1809, and commanded V Corps (made up of Polish and **Saxon** troops) for the invasion of **Russia** in 1812, playing a leading role in the Battles of **Smolensk** and **Borodino**. He returned to the task of building up Polish forces in Warsaw after being wounded at the **Beresina** in November, but returned to corps command in **Germany** from July 1813. He was promoted marshal during the Battle of **Leipzig**, but was among those drowned trying to swim the River Elster during the engagement's closing stages.

Pont-à-Chin, Battle of *See* Battle of **Tournai**

Pontooneers *See* **Engineers**

Pontoons

Portable bridges carried by armies for improvised river crossings, and manned by **engineers** or (in French service) specialist *pontonniers*. Contemporary pontoons consisted of a number of shallow boats, transported on wheeled vehicles, which were launched into a river with two-man crews and tied side by side at right angles to a taut line thrown between the banks. Wooden beams, or 'baulks', were then laid across the line of boats, and planks ('chesses') placed on top, held in position by gang-boards along the outer edges. A single pontoon bridge could not support more than about 2,500kg, forcing heavy traffic to travel slowly and at prolonged intervals, with cavalry dismounted and guns dismantled. By lashing together two or more bridges, their load-bearing could be increased, but crossing a wide, fast river remained a hazardous business, and large-scale loss of life was commonplace when pontoons were swept away

Popham, Home Riggs (1762–1820)

British naval officer who went to sea in 1778, but served with the East India Company from 1787 until the outbreak of war in 1792. He was a lieutenant with naval forces protecting the expedition to **Flanders** in 1793, and was promoted captain in 1794. In command of a squadron supporting the failed British raid on **Ostende** in May 1798, he performed a similar role during the next year's **North Holland** expedition, taking his gunboats up the Dutch canals to take part in the Battle of **Bergen**. Commodore in command of naval forces sent to reoccupy the **Cape Colony** in 1806, he suffered the first major setback to his career at **Buenos Aires** later that year. He was subsequently at **Copenhagen** in 1807, and returned to his specialist role during the **Peninsular War**, leading a raiding squadron off the northern Spanish coast. Perhaps his greatest contribution to Britain's wartime campaigns was the development of the improved ship-to-ship signalling system that bore his name, which was an invaluable boost to operational efficiency after its general introduction at the turn of the century. Eventually knighted and promoted rear-admiral in 1815, he held a command in the **West Indies** from 1817, retiring just before his death.

Portalis, Jean-Etienne-Marie (1746–1809)

Provençal lawyer, imprisoned in Paris during the **Terror**, who was a leading right-wing spokesman in the Council of **Ancients** after 1795, was exiled after the 1797 **Fructidor coup** and returned to favour after the **Brumaire coup**, becoming a member of the Council of State under the **Consulate** in 1800. Admired as particularly hardworking by contemporaries, he served as **Napoleon's** chief adviser on religious matters until his death, drafting both the **Concordat** and the **Organic Articles**, helping prepare the **Code Napoléon** and becoming Minister of Ecclesiastical Affairs in 1804.

Portland, William Cavendish Bentinck, Duke of (1738–1809)

Veteran British Whig politician, a cabinet minister for the first time in 1765 and prime minister in 1783, before switching political allegiance to serve as Home Secretary under **Pitt** (1794–1801). Portland became prime minister of **Great Britain** for the second time on the fall of **Grenville's** 'Ministry of All the Talents' in 1807, but functioned as little more than a figurehead, largely ignored by a squabbling cabinet. After a duel between war minister **Castlereagh** and foreign minister **Canning** in September 1809 had forced both men out of office, the elderly and ailing Portland resigned, and died shortly afterwards.

Portugal

Once a formidable maritime power, the Kingdom of Portugal had fallen behind the mainstream of European socio-industrial development by the late eighteenth century. Creation of wealth within an overwhelmingly rural, and largely feudal, economy depended on seaborne trade and exploitation of the country's colonies in **South America**, both protected by an alliance with **Great Britain** that dated back to the fourteenth century.

Queen Maria I held the throne from 1777 until 1816, but her second son **John** of Braganza took effective control of government after she went mad in 1788, and was formally named as Prince Regent in 1799. Married to the daughter of Spanish king **Charles IV**, and determined to stem any flow of republican ideas to Lisbon, John allied with **Spain** for an attack on **France** in March 1793, but was isolated by the Franco-Spanish Treaty of **Basle** in 1795.

Threatened by Franco-Spanish plans to partition the country, John appealed for help from Britain, and a British expeditionary force under General **Stuart** sustained Portugal's independence until 1798. An attempt to reach an agreement with Napoleon in 1799 foundered on the issue of Portuguese trading relations with Britain, which was using Lisbon as a **Royal Navy** base, and Portugal was forced to cede a small parcel of territory to Spain after a French-sponsored invasion, known as the War of the **Oranges**, in 1801.

Portugal announced its neutrality after the collapse of the **Amiens** peace in 1803, and paid a further indemnity to France later in the year, but John's relations with Britain remained good while those with **Napoleon** worsened steadily. Napoleon's principal grievances concerned Portugal's restoration of docking rights to the Royal Navy and John's refusal to enforce the **Continental System** against British trade. Following a hysterical **propaganda** campaign against the Braganzas, Napoleon invaded Portugal (with Spanish connivance) in autumn 1807, and French forces were in control of Lisbon from 30 November.

The royal family, government and fleet had fled for Brazil under Royal Navy escort three days before the French reached the capital, leaving the Bishop of Oporto in charge of a regency council to manage affairs in Europe. Prince John was still in South America when peace was signed with France and the Braganzas formally restored in May 1814, and the regency council meanwhile resisted all demands for liberal reform. A radical plot to overthrow the government was uncovered in 1817, and its leaders executed on the orders of the army's British C-in-C General **Beresford**, but an alliance of liberal and military leaders established a constitutional monarchy after a coup in August 1820, and John accepted the de facto revolution on his eventual return in 1821. *See* **Peninsular War**; **Map 22**.

Portugal, Invasion of (1807)

The virtually unopposed occupation of **Portugal** in autumn 1807 by a French army under General **Junot**. **Napoleon**'s decision to invade, made possible by the conclusion of east European peace at **Tilsit** in July 1807, reflected his irritation at Portugal's continued support for **Great Britain**. Portuguese regent Prince **John** had refused to join the **Continental System** against British trade, and Lisbon was being used as a **Royal Navy** base.

Diplomatic moves against the Portuguese monarchy preceded French military preparations for invasion, but only just. Napoleon issued his first ultimatum to Portugal on 19 July, demanding the closure of ports to British shipping by 1 September, but the creation of Junot's army was under way as early as 2 August, and Portuguese shipping was banned from French ports after 9 August.

While French troops moved towards the Pyrenees, and a new ultimatum demanded that Portugal declare war on Britain, Prince John found himself caught between irresistible powers on land and sea. In November, encouraged by news of British failure in **Buenos Aires**, he attempted to appease Napoleon by accepting virtually all his demands. It was not enough, and the emperor declared war over John's refusal to deliver British property in Portugal to French authorities.

Junot had begun moving his 25,000 men into allied Spain from Bayonne on 17 September, and the Treaty of **Fontainebleau** (27 October) sealed Spanish cooperation with the invasion. Ordered to occupy Lisbon by 1 December, capture the royal family and take the Portuguese fleet intact, Junot reached the central Portuguese border town of Alcántara by mid-November and entered the capital with a day to spare. Though it had met no significant military opposition, supply shortages, lack of shelter and garrison requirements had reduced Junot's force to about 2,000 frontline troops.

News that the Portuguese fleet had been evacuated to Brazil two days earlier, under Royal Navy protection and with the royal family on board, prompted Napoleon to open his administration of the country by imposing a fine of 100 million francs. Portugal was subsequently partitioned along the lines agreed at Fontainebleau. *See* **Peninsular War**; **Map 22**.

Portuguese Army

The land forces of **Portugal**, primarily a **naval** power in its heyday, were of negligible military value throughout the **Revolutionary Wars**. A few Portuguese units fought with **Spanish Army** forces during the **Pyrenean campaigns** of 1793–5, and British general **Stuart** trained a brigade for **Mediterranean** service while on secondment to the country in 1796–7. The army's principal action of the period, the War of the **Oranges** against **Spain** in 1801, ended in defeat within a month.

Disbanded after the unopposed French conquest of **Portugal** in 1807, the army was rebuilt under British auspices when the French were driven out. British general **Beresford** began the process of reconstruction as C-in-C, and a Portuguese marshal, from spring 1809. Using a relatively enlightened system of rewards and punishments to enforce rigid discipline, and replacing most of the army's existing officers with younger, more energetic men, he made himself very unpopular in Portugal but created a thoroughly effective fighting force of some 25,000 regular troops, backed by a local militia for home defence. Equipped by the British, and deployed alongside British regiments, they played a full part in all **Wellington's** campaigns over the next five years.

Portuguese Navy

Though a nation with a long seafaring history and a **colonial** empire, **Portugal** had allowed its navy to fall victim to poverty and political apathy by 1792. Hardly used during the War of the **First Coalition**, it underwent a degree of reform after Lisbon became an important **Royal Navy** base in 1796, and sent a squadron to aid the British blockade of **Malta** in 1799–1800. Though it performed adequately in the **Mediterranean**, it could be kept at sea for only a few months, and lack of efficient dockyard facilities meant that the navy's next (and last) major wartime operation was its wholesale evacuation to Brazil after the French invasion of **Portugal** in 1807.

Posen, Treaty of

Agreement signed on 11 December 1806 by **France**, **Prussia** and **Saxony**, elevating the latter to the status of an independent kingdom in return for membership of the Confederation of the **Rhine** and an undertaking to provide 20,000 troops for French imperial service. A postscript to Prussia's overwhelming defeat in the **Jena–Auerstädt campaign**, the treaty was essentially a Franco-Saxon alliance forced on an impotent Prussian government.

Poserna, Battle of

The most serious of several minor actions fought on 1 May 1813, at the start of the first French offensive in **Germany**. On the right wing of French forces advancing from the River Saale, two corps under **Ney** and **Marmont** were detailed to reach **Lützen** and guard the eastern flank of a drive on Leipzig. Ney's leading divisions met heavy resistance in the area between Poserna and Rippach, but eventually drove off General **Winzingerode's** Russian **cavalry** to

resume their advance east. French cavalry commander **Bessières** was among those killed during the action. *See* **Map 25**.

Potsdam, Treaty of

The secret agreement between Russian tsar **Alexander I** and Prussian king **Frederick William III**, signed in Frederick the Great's tomb at Potsdam on 3 November 1805, that effectively committed **Prussia** to joining the **Third Coalition** against **France**. Motivated partly by sentiment, partly by the warlike Queen **Louise**, partly by the hope that the Austro-Russian alliance was about to crush **Napoleon**, Frederick William promised to field 180,000 troops against France if his offer of mediation was rejected. Before Prussian terms were even transmitted to Napoleon, the Coalition collapsed at **Austerlitz**. Thoroughly informed of the Potsdam arrangements by his agents, and backed by a victorious army on Prussia's borders, Napoleon was able to impose the punitive Convention of **Vienna** on an embarrassed Prussian government.

Praga, Battle of

The final defeat of **Polish forces** by invading Russian and Prussian armies in 1794. The defence of its fortified positions at Praga, just across the River Vistula from Warsaw, had been the greatest success of that year's rebellion in **Poland**, but the defeat of General Kosciusko's rebel army at **Maciejowice** on 5 October exposed the defences to the combined columns of Generals **Suvorov** and Fersen.

About 25,000 troops reached the Praga defences, manned by a similar number of ill-equipped Polish troops, on 2 November. Recognizing that the approach of winter made a **siege** impracticable, Suvorov waited only until his heavy **artillery** had arrived before launching an all-out attack on the positions at dawn on 5 November. Defenders were quickly and completely overwhelmed, losing 9,000 men captured and at least 10,000 killed or wounded during a panic retreat across the Vistula. The disaster took place in full view of the city itself, which surrendered on 7 November, and the last rebel force in the field, Prince **Poniatowski's** small corps, was rounded up shortly afterwards.

Prairial, Insurrection of

The second, and more serious, rebellion by Parisian wage-earners and unemployed (sans-culottes) during spring 1795. After left-wing 'Hébertist' politicians had failed to bring down the government in early April, when the insurrection of **Germinal** had been quickly suppressed, another cut in the bread ration brought protestors back on to the streets, and the Assembly was occupied by thousands of angry citizens on 20 May. As in April, they were ejected after milling around the chamber for several hours without organizing a coherent programme, but crowds remained on the streets for the next three days, gathering support from the suburbs. Government promises to enact a programme of price limitation eventually persuaded rebels to go home on the evening of 24 May, and savage repression followed. General **Menou** and 20,000 regular troops were sent into the most radical localities to round up suspected **Jacobin** sympathizers. Six deputies from the Mountain and another 36 people were executed, dozens more were deported and thousands arrested, decapitating the sans-culottes as a political force at a stroke and marking their demise as a decisive factor in Parisian politics. See also **France**.

Prenzlau

Town in northern **Prussia** that was the scene of General **Hohenlohe**'s surrender to French forces on 28 October 1806. With his armies in disarray after defeats at **Jena** and **Auerstädt**, Prussian king **Frederick William III** had left the war zone for exile in Königsberg, leaving Hohenlohe the unenviable task of commanding the retreat. Unable to regroup at the Elbe, and thus forced to abandon Berlin, Hohenlohe attempted to reach the comparative safety of the Oder, but was never more than a few hours ahead of pursuing French corps under **Murat**, **Bernadotte** and **Lannes**. He was accompanied by only 10,000 men when Murat's advance guard caught up with him at Prenzlau. Although by no means outnumbered, he accepted Murat's claim that 100,000 French troops were in the area and surrendered without investigating its validity, leaving **Blücher**'s secondary force, withdrawing north-west towards **Lübeck**, as the last coherent Prussian army in the field. See **Fourth Coalition, War of the; Map 16**.

Press Gangs

The notorious alternative to **conscription** employed by the contemporary **Royal Navy**. Britain's navy, its most important military resource and always short of manpower, was entitled to kidnap any seaman who could not prove he was currently employed, and carry him under guard to compulsory service aboard a warship. Onshore seizures could take place only in coastal towns, albeit anywhere in the British Empire, but merchant ships or **privateers** could be stopped as they approached home ports, and stripped of any unwary, paid-off crewmen still on board.

Seizures were carried out by the Impress Service, which sent regular officers out to ports or coastal regions in Britain, either accompanied by small groups of sailors or given money to hire local muscle. Parties from individual warships in need of crew replenishment (most of them, most of the time) were also sent ashore as temporary gangs all over the world. The service was also responsible for recruiting volunteers, who were paid a bounty for joining up, and for rounding up existing crews recalled from leave.

Though disapproved of at all levels of society, and frequently obstructed by land authorities, 'the press' provoked no concerted protest in wartime **Great Britain**. This reflected a broad consensus that conscription was both undesirable and unworkable (because the navy needed trained men). The rule forbidding impressment of non-seamen was open to abuse, but captains usually returned relatively useless 'landsmen' rather than risk prosecution by local magistrates.

Pressburg, Treaty of (1805)

The agreement between **France** and **Austria** that removed the latter from the **Third Coalition** in December 1805. Habsburg emperor **Francis II** asked for an armistice on the morning after the decisive Battle of **Austerlitz**, and **Napoleon** exacted a high price despite **Talleyrand**'s advice to encourage future friendship by granting a mild peace. Apart from the payment of indemnities, Austria was required to give up all its possessions in Italy, the Vorarlberg, southern Germany and the Tyrol, which was ceded to the new Kingdom of **Bavaria**. Bavaria was also freed from all obligations to the **Holy Roman Empire**, along with Napoleon's other ally, **Württemberg**. The Pressburg agreement was ratified on 26 December 1805, completing the removal of Habsburg influence in southern Germany and Italy, but guaranteeing that Austria would renew hostilities whenever a favourable opportunity arose. *See also* Convention of **Vienna**.

Pressburg, Treaty of (1809) *See* Treaty of **Schönbrunn**

Prisoners of War

Many irregular or non-European forces treated prisoners in strictly expedient fashion, either using them as hostages, killing them or abandoning them, but rules and conventions governed capture of hostiles by major European regular armies. Although pirates, brigands and **guerrilla** fighters could be summarily executed when captured, regular (Christian) troops had to be housed and cared for at the expense of their captors, who could expect recompense only from a favourable and unusually well-observed peace treaty.

All the main European belligerents erected military prison camps, although existing gaols were also used, and coastal states often kept prisoners in offshore hulks that were generally even less sanitary than land-based institutions. Offshore islands might be turned into prison communities, but the need for large garrison forces rendered this particularly expensive.

Prisoners could be disposed of in one of three ways. They could be induced to change sides, usually to join labour battalions, a policy particularly favoured by French commanders but unlikely to provide reliable service and still expensive. They could also be released on **parole**, which was cheap but often abused, or they could be exchanged for an officer of similar rank (or a similar number of ordinary troops), a more mutually profitable device that often took time and trouble to arrange and seldom involved large numbers of men.

Privateers

Essentially licensed pirates, protected from punishment as criminals by *lettres de marque* giving them government authorization for their actions, privateers were fast raiding ships carrying sufficient armament to sink or capture enemy trading vessels. Small enough to operate from harbours inaccessible to warships, and able to maintain their small crews far from major bases, they were a constant menace to merchant shipping all over the world in wartime. Privateering was an important means by which those naval powers unable to challenge the **Royal Navy**'s fleet superiority could conduct commercial warfare against **Great Britain**. French privateers were particularly numerous and successful, posing a constant threat to British trade wherever it was unprotected by fast **sloops** or other small warships. Their attacks in the **Mediterranean**, the **West Indies**, the Far East and even British home waters kept large numbers of Royal Navy units engaged in offshore patrols through to 1814.

Prize Money

The system by which wartime naval officers and crews were rewarded for the capture of enemy vessels and their contents. Having taken a warship, merchantman or **privateer**, and sent it to a friendly port under a skeleton 'prize crew', a captain was entitled to sell both prize and cargo to agents of its own government. Most undamaged equipment and goods would be purchased, and the proceeds divided among the successful crew.

According to standard practice in the British **Royal Navy**, which took far more prizes than any other, an eighth of the money went to the admiral commanding the successful ship's fleet, a quarter went to the captain, an eighth was divided among the commissioned officers, an eighth among the warrant officers, an eighth among the petty officers and a quarter among the rest of the crew. Ships on detached duty paid no admiral's share, and when more than one vessel took part in a capture, or was even within sight, all were deemed to deserve an equal share. The actual amount paid varied enormously according to the size, status and contents of a captured ship.

Captains could become landed gentry overnight with one spectacular success, and admirals on lucrative stations (especially the pirate-infested **West Indies**) could expect to get rich. An ordinary rating with a **sloop**'s relatively small crew might make six months' wages from the capture of a well-stocked merchantman, but could also become relatively rich if lucky enough to be part of a depleted crew involved in a major capture. Under these circumstances, the system provided an incentive for aggression at sea, and aided recruitment, but sometimes encouraged captains to neglect more mundane duties in search of prizes.

Propaganda

In an age of burgeoning mass literacy but entrenched parochialism at all but the highest social levels, wartime propaganda by governments, pressure groups and individuals was both ubiquitous and simplistic. Writers, illustrators and orators could make wild and unsubstantiated claims on most exotic subjects in the certainty that most of their audience had no access to the truth.

Widespread access to printing technology and a voracious popular appetite for newspapers and pamphlets in the more developed parts of Europe combined to make the printed word the overwhelmingly dominant medium of contemporary propaganda. A politician in **Great Britain**, **France** or the **Netherlands** still needed a gift for public speaking if he hoped to court popularity, but a speech was directed at a small audience of urban critics, and a powerful figure would expect it to be published in full throughout the land.

Written propaganda was by no means confined to governments and political pressure groups. Though all rulers, factions and important politicians employed propagandists to transmit their chosen messages, they competed in an essentially free market for popular favour in those countries that did not exercise strict censorship.

Freedom of the press was not a feature of most autocratic or feudal European regimes, but effective suppression of opposition propaganda was extremely difficult in a relatively unregulated world. The most strenuous and successful efforts were made in the Napoleonic empire, but extensive use of secret police, imprisonment and execution barely stemmed the flow of seditious material outside the heartlands of France itself.

War-related material produced for mass or élite consumption at home tended to specialize in exaggeration of success, concealment of failure, hero worship and demonization. These methods were considered normal, and their claims about distant foreign matters were generally irrefutable, but they were not always employed. British prime minister **Pitt** joined the **First Coalition** in 1793 with barely a nod to public opinion, confining himself to a dry speech outlining treaty obligations concerning the Scheldt.

The Enlightenment is accepted as the golden age of cartoon and caricature drawing, and illustrations were important wartime propaganda vehicles, particularly popular in Britain, France, Germany and the Low Countries. Able to get a message across quickly to both literate and illiterate audiences, elaborately captioned cartoons were particularly useful for discrediting opponents as individuals, specializing in ghastly parodies of personal features and graphic portrayals of unlikely vices. Graphic art could also perform a more monumental propaganda role, as demonstrated in the clear messages conveyed by celebrated artists such as **David** and **Goya**, working for and against French interests respectively.

Europe's élite and upper middle classes were sufficiently small in number to form a relatively narrow cultural constituency, and generally had the leisure to indulge in long periods of reading. The impact of Burke's passionate attack on French radicalism is the most famous contemporary example of a successful book performing a continent-wide propaganda function in a very short time. Academic tracts or lectures could also penetrate literate opinion on a grand scale, and were an important factor promoting the wartime development of ethnic identity in **Prussia**, other parts of western Germany and the Napoleonic Kingdom of **Italy**.

The most dedicated propagandist of the age, and recognized as such by informed contemporaries, was **Napoleon**. From the start of his career as a senior military commander he was careful to ensure that all his successes were suitably exaggerated, and that credit was focused on the right man, habits that remained with him until his death.

Once in power, he developed an elaborate state mechanism to suppress opposition presses and demagogues, and brought an army of cartoonists, satirists, journalists, pamphleteers and political commentators into government service. The post-revolutionary French government made use of official organs to disseminate propaganda, but the **Directory**'s *Rédacteur* was still essentially a newspaper, while the content of Napoleon's *Moniteur* foreshadowed the work of twentieth-century totalitarian states.

Napoleon placed great faith in symbolism and pageant as propaganda devices. His empire was adorned with images of power and endurance that generally imitated classical Rome, from the **standards** carried by his battalions to great public works in Paris. His formal appearances, whether at a public troop inspection or an international summit, were carefully orchestrated showpieces of imperial grandeur. It is perhaps fitting that Napoleon, as its most commited exponent, was eventually wartime propaganda's most spectacular victim, becoming by far the most caricatured and reviled figure in Europe after 1797.

Provera, Johann (1740–1804)

Born in northern Italy, Provera fought for **Austria** against the **Ottoman Empire** from 1790 and was promoted divisional general two years later. He held a command in the Po valley during the **Italian campaigns** of 1793, and remained in the theatre until 1796, taking part in **Beaulieu's** ill-fated campaign against **Napoleon's** Army of Italy before his capture and repatriation during the **Ceva** campaign in April. Given a divisional command for d'**Alvintzi's** last attempt to recover northern Italy in early 1797, he was detailed to march directly on besieged **Mantua**, but forced to surrender outside the city on 16 January. He was then sent as Austrian adviser to the army of the **Papal States**, but was dismissed in late 1797 at the insistence of Neapolitan king Joseph **Bonaparte**.

Prussia

The largest and most powerful state in northern Germany, the Kingdom of Prussia had grown in size and international importance during the long reign of Frederick the Great (1713–86). An acknowledged **great power** by the 1770s, it contained an estimated 8.7 million people in 1795, including 2.5 million natives of partitioned **Poland**. About three-quarters of all Prussians were rural peasants, and Frederick had overseen dramatic improvements in agricultural techniques and output, attracting a steady stream of immigrants from other German states. Berlin was by far the largest city, with a population approaching 185,000 by 1800, but the west of the country was more socially and politically developed than the east, which was dominated by huge rural estates governed along medieval lines.

The Prussian king was an absolute ruler, governing by decree through appointed ministers, and the throne was a hereditary possession of the house of Hohenzollern. The Hohenzollerns' military tradition was reflected in a particularly close connection between crown and army. The king drew most of his closest political advisers from an officer corps dominated by the *Junkers* class of rural, land-owning nobles, whose influence was a barrier to any hint of political radicalism and a stimulus to military expansionism.

Frederick's successful military career encouraged an unfortunate combination of ambition and complacency in his successors. The much-admired **Prussian Army** (the original 'war machine') was several decades out of date by the 1790s, but its reputation precluded reform. Meanwhile the system of government remained firmly rooted in the Middle Ages, even though north-western Germany was a hotbed of advanced political thinking.

Frederick had fought expensive wars, but balanced the books and minimalized internal opposition by harsh taxation laws and stern political censorship. His nephew and successor **Frederick William II** was a self-determined man, bent on territorial expansion but prone to short-term reliance on a succession of favoured advisers. He sought popularity by reducing the royal tax burden in 1787, but reacted to liberal criticism by restricting press and religious freedoms the following year, and remained rigidly opposed to their extension until his death.

Though he presided over internal stability, even stagnation, Frederick William's foreign policy helped destabilize relations between the major European powers. Guided by an aggressively nationalist court faction, under the leadership of chief minister von Hertzberg, Prussia sought to exploit Austro-Russian tensions as a means of acquiring more Polish territories, and interfered with internal disputes in the **Netherlands**. Neither policy had borne much territorial fruit by the early 1790s, but both had contributed to shifts in great power diplomacy.

Prussian diplomacy since 1740 had been built around rivalry with **Austria** and **Russia**, centred on contests for pre-eminence in Germany and Poland. Relations with **France** through the later eighteenth century had been cordial, if more apathetic than friendly, but the pillar of Prussian diplomacy was friendship with **Great Britain**. Britain had been Prussia's ally for most of Frederick's reign, but British pressure had forced Prussia to accept Habsburg rule in the **Austrian Netherlands** and a peaceful settlement in Poland by 1791, and its commitment to the status quo showed no sign of wavering. With only Ansbach and Bayreuth (acquired as part of the 1791 settlement) to show for its expansion drive, a frustrated Prussian government reversed its diplomatic thrust, embarking on a new era of friendly relations with Russia and Austria.

Though Berlin had shown little initial animosity towards the **French Revolution**, giving scant comfort to royalist émigrés, Prussia's enthusiasm for an invasion, rooted in the ascendant war party's belief that it would generate rich territorial pickings, was a vital factor enabling formation of the **First Coalition** in 1792. The subsequent war's prolonged failure to deliver tangible gains prompted another switch of policy, and Prussia abandoned the Coalition in 1795, making peace with France by the Treaty of **Basle** and concentrating on preventing a Russian takeover in Poland. The volte-face severely damaged the kingdom's overseas prestige, and neutrality allowed the army to slip even further behind the times.

The king died in 1797, and **Frederick William III** began his reign by relaxing some of the regime's more autocratic legislation, but soon reacted against the liberal inclinations of the formidable Queen **Louise** and some of his advisers. Though less reliant on military advice than his predecessor, he was even less capable of final decisions, a weakness reflected most clearly in his long-term inability to settle on a consistent foreign policy.

Moderates among his courtiers, such as foreign minister von **Haugwitz**, favoured a period of peaceful consolidation aimed at strengthening Prussia's social and economic structure, but competed for royal favour with an expansionist party gathered around the fiercely nationalist queen (born in **Mecklenberg**) and the reformist chief minister, von **Hardenberg**. The king wavered, but his commitment to peaceful development survived Russian efforts to entice Prussia into the **Second Coalition** in 1798.

The Coalition's defeat forced Berlin to come to terms with **Napoleon**, and a treaty with France was signed on 23 May 1802, by which Prussia ceded its possessions along the west bank of the Rhine in return for chunks of central western Germany, including much of **Westphalia**. Pro-French influences generally dominated the centre of Prussian political life over the next three years in contrast to a growing intellectual, literary and popular nationalism, personified by writers such as **Gentz** and **Arndt**.

Natural opponents of French appeasement, nationalist elements found a powerful ally in the queen, and by 1804 their influence had begun to sway the king. Hardenberg retained his predominance through the year, supervising a renewed treaty with France in June, and was able to prevent a vacillating king from joining the **Third Coalition** of 1805, but the queen got the better of him once the war was under way. A technical violation of Prussian neutrality (by French forces passing through Ansbach en route to **Ulm**) sealed an alliance with Russia and Austria at **Potsdam** in November.

Coming at a time when French defeat seemed probable, the decision to fight was viewed elsewhere as an expression of cynical state greed, but Napoleon's victory at **Austerlitz** in December left Prussia facing a victorious French host on its southern borders. The government had little option but to accept whatever settlement Napoleon chose to impose, but the Convention of **Vienna** (finalized in February 1806) was widely viewed inside Prussia as a national disgrace, and helped kindle a mood of outraged patriotism over the next decade.

Outrage among élite elements of Prussian society served to reinforce the hawkish attitudes of the most vehemently anti-French faction at court. Hardenberg, who had been dismissed at Napoleon's insistence, began secret negotiations in February for a new military alliance with Russia, and the resignation of Haugwitz left the field clear for the war party. Prussia's lurch into war against France in August 1806 was a triumph for emotion and optimism over logic. Without a settled plan of campaign, or any hope of rapid allied support, Prussia relied on limited military reforms undertaken since the mid-1790s, and was overwhelmed in a matter of days during the subsequent **Jena–Auerstädt campaign** (*see* War of the **Fourth Coalition**).

Frederick William and the court were forced to take refuge first in Memel and then in Königsberg, where the king and a small army contingent under General Lestoq maintained the appearance of Prussian resistance under Tsar **Alexander's** protection. Though a preliminary peace with Napoleon, the Convention of Charlottenburg, was signed by Prussian envoys on 16 November, it was rejected by the king five days later, and Frederick William remained at war with France until the Battle of **Friedland** the following June brought Russia to the peace table.

A Franco-Prussian armistice was signed on 25 June 1807, and the king met Napoleon two days later to discuss final peace terms. As in 1805, the French emperor demanded the dismissal of Hardenberg and imposed heavy penalties on the hapless Prussian monarch. As signed at **Tilsit** on 9 July, the peace agreement forced Prussia to cede all its territory west of the Elbe and most of its Polish possessions. A subsidiary treaty, signed three days later at Königsberg, required Prussia to pay a large war indemnity to France, and to restrict its army to a maximum strength of 42,000 men.

The peace reduced Prussia's size by almost half, left the kingdom with only about 5 million subjects and plunged its finances into disarray (the Prussian national debt almost doubled in the four years after 1806), but was the catalyst for national revival. New chief minister **Stein** took office in October, armed with more comprehensive powers than his predecessors, and presided over a series of political, military and social reforms that both modernized the Prussian state system and encouraged the growth of patriotic, German nationalist sentiment.

On 8 October 1807, five days after Stein's nomination as chief minister, the royal Emancipation Edict gave three years' notice of the abolition of serfdom and the establishment of universal land tenure rights (for males), creating a free property market for the first time in Prussia. Further edicts during the next three years curtailed trade monopolies, gave an unprecedented degree of autonomy to town governments, and reorganized central government, creating a Council of State and new ministries for foreign affairs, home affairs, finance and war. Meanwhile **Scharnhorst** supervised the army's transformation into a modern, genuinely national force, and **Humboldt** was appointed to create a completely new education system from February 1809.

Stein's reforms chimed with an increasingly active nationalist movement among the Prussian academic and middle classes, emphasized by expressions of nationalist intent like the abortive **Schill** uprising of May 1809. A celebrated series of lectures by the philosopher **Fichte**, delivered in Berlin between December 1807 and the following March, recommended the assertion of 'German' values against the Napoleonic system, and the anti-French **Tugendbund** was founded to promote anti-French sentiment in April 1808, enjoying official support from June.

Pressure from Napoleon forced Frederick William into dismissing Stein in late 1808, and the Tugendbund was officially dissolved shortly after the court's belated return to Berlin in December 1809. Scharnhorst was dismissed in 1810 at Napoleon's insistence, but Frederick William responded by recalling Hardenberg in June 1810. Reverting to one-man government, Hardenberg took the new title of Chancellor in October and continued Stein's reforming work.

The death of Queen Louise in July 1810 reduced the king to the role of grief-stricken bystander as Hardenberg abolished feudal restrictions on industrial practice and remaining tax exemptions, introducing a series of new taxes in an attempt to stem a mushrooming national debt. An extension of the land tenure laws in September 1811 allowed peasants freehold ownership of land for the first time, completing the legal emancipation of most Prussians, and the citizen status of Prussian Jews was recognized in March 1812.

Through these changes, and the crescendo of patriotic tub-thumping that accompanied them, Frederick William remained an ally of France. Poverty and lingering military weakness kept Prussia strictly neutral during the 1809 War of the **Fifth Coalition**, and the king agreed to commit 20,000 troops to Napoleon's 1812 **Russian campaign**. The invasion's failure had already kindled an upsurge of nationalist enthusiasm by the time Prussian general **Yorck** neutralized his troops in Russia by the Convention of **Tauroggen** in December, and though Frederick William disowned the agreement, a sense of imminent war with France caused great excitement throughout Germany.

After retreating French forces occupied Berlin, and the king left the capital for Breslau on 22 January 1813, Prussian preparations for war gathered pace during February. Authorization for the formation of volunteer **Jäger** units was issued on 3 February, and a national volunteer reserve (**Landwehr**) was established six days later. Meanwhile Stein, now in the tsar's service, raised 20,000 troops in East Prussia for a 'war of liberation'. Prussia eventually formed an alliance with Russia at **Kalisch** on 26 February, and declared war against France on 13 March.

Frederick William played a very secondary role in strategic direction of the 1813–14 campaigns in **Germany** and **France**, but was carried along by the aggression of his Russian ally and his own military commanders, especially **Blücher**. Prussia's major contribution to the victories, and subsequent commitment to Napoleon's final defeat during the **Hundred Days** campaign of 1815, restored the kingdom's good name among European diplomats, and ensured that Prussia won back most of its lost territories at the Congress of **Vienna**. The settlement took Prussia's population above 10 million, and finally established the kingdom as the only credible rival to Austria as the standard-bearer of German nationalism.

The liberal reforms that had done much to foster the growth of national spirit in Prussia were abandoned as the kingdom drifted into postwar reaction as part of the **Holy Alliance** of conservative monarchs. Restrictions were imposed on independent political organizations, academic freedoms and the press, and popular movements demanding representative government suffered harsh repression in 1819 and 1830. Frederick William continued to devote funds to education, presided over the reconstruction of state finances and established a customs union throughout northern Germany, but none of these measures addressed the relative lack of political development that would haunt the Prussian monarchy into the twentieth century. See **Maps 1, 16, 30**.

Prussian Army

The emergence of **Prussia** as a **great power** during the eighteenth century was largely due to the efforts of an army honed under Frederick the Great into Europe's most efficient and reliable land force. It had won its greatest victories during the Seven Years War (1756–63), but its tactics and structure had hardly changed by the 1790s, and it had failed to keep pace with military developments elsewhere. It none the less enjoyed a very high reputation, particularly in Berlin.

The army that fought with the **First Coalition** from 1792 to 1795, and in **Poland** during 1794, comprised about 200,000 men. The basis of its renown was a superbly drilled and turned-out infantry arm, which consisted of 52 line regiments (rising to 57 by 1804) and 20 battalions of light infantry **fusiliers** (rising to 24), a total of about 130,000 officers and men. A combination of conscripts and mercenaries (mostly drawn from smaller German states), it was extremely well disciplined, but good order was maintained by a brutal regime that deliberately stifled initiative among the rank and file.

Prussian **cavalry** before 1806 consisted of 12 **dragoon** regiments (rising to 14 by 1803), 12 of **cuirassiers** and 12 of **hussars**, a total of 37–40,000 men. Throughout the 1790s, they were given their traditional combat role as packets of shock troops, but divisional organization and a cavalry brigade under central command were introduced shortly before the **Jena–Auerstädt** campaign, when inexperience of methods long familiar to their opponents left them too scattered to mass effectively in battle.

The army's **artillery** arm was recognizably out of date long before 1806, making little effort to absorb the lessons of the superior **Gribeauval** system used by the **French Army** since the 1770s. The four field artillery regiments amassed a total of 216 12-pounders and 72 howitzers in 1806, while a single 6-pounder gun was attached to each infantry battalion for close support. Twenty companies of horse artillery were each equipped with six relatively cumbersome 6-pounders, along with two medium howitzers. Reorganization was again attempted just before the 1806 campaign, with the formation of three new artillery brigades, each deploying 90 cannon and 30 howitzers.

In keeping with the precepts favoured by Frederick the Great, and aided by excellent educational facilities, the officers and senior NCOs who comprised the army's stock of trained **engineers** were of high quality. The army's **field train** was also well organized and supplied, but like the force as a whole it was slow-moving, designed for the snail-like operations of eighteenth-century positional warfare.

A largely aristocratic officer corps included a number of professional soldiers attracted to the king's service from other German states, but was primarily drawn from the semi-feudal East Prussian land-owning nobility, or Junkers. Aggressively confident in the army's excellence, close to the throne and deeply conservative in outlook, they were a powerful force against change. Resistance to new ideas was also encouraged by an ageing high command, generally relics of the Frederickan era and typified by the cautious, formal leadership of **Brunswick** during the opening campaigns at **Valmy** and on the **Rhine** in 1792–3.

At the very top, Frederick's careful pragmatism was not apparent in his successors. Both **Frederick William II** and **Frederick William III** saw themselves as soldier-kings, but neither evinced much interest in military realities or reform. Preoccupied with easy territorial gain, both pursued policies of limited military commitment that enabled the army to avoid serious defeat before

1806, but also masked the depth of its failings.

Prussian armies virtually ceased operations in the west after 1793, and Prussia quit the First Coalition altogether in spring 1795. The Prussian Army's next major operation – apart from a relatively easy success against the **Polish rebellion** in 1794, and the unopposed occupation of Hamburg during the **Armed Neutrality** of 1801 – was the short and disastrous campaign of 1806.

Though reorganization along divisional lines was under way by the time the army mobilized in the late summer 1806, it was by no means complete, and already rendered obsolete by **Napoleon**'s preference for the **corps system**. The army's guns and small arms, particularly its **muskets**, were still antiquated and inadequate, as were its rigidly linear **infantry tactics** and obsession with operational coherence above mobility. Most of the army's generals (and a significant proportion of regimental colonels) were over 60, and it was once more commanded by the elderly Brunswick.

Along with the king and his chief military adviser, the octogenarian Möllendorf, Brunswick was responsible for the fatal combination of aggression and indecision that passed for Prussian military strategy in 1806, and was among those killed during the rout that followed at **Jena** and **Auerstädt** in mid-October. The army had been all but destroyed by early November, leaving Napoleon in control of Berlin and opposed by a remnant of fewer than 20,000 troops around the new royal residence of Königsberg. With the defeat of his Russian **Fourth Coalition** allies in 1807, Frederick William could only accept a punitive peace at **Tilsit** that restricted the army to a maximum strength of 42,000 men and forced it to shed many of its more competent commanders.

From this low point in its fortunes, the Prussian Army enjoyed a slow but ultimately spectacular metamorphosis, as unavoidable recognition of the need for drastic reform coincided with a national upsurge in patriotic sentiment. Popular opposition to the tightening grip of French control over Germany was deliberately channelled into identification with martial virtues by a combination of academic and bureaucratic influences based in Berlin. In close concert with civilian ministers like **Stein** and **Hardenberg**, war minister **Scharnhorst** and his staff set in motion a process of reform that modernized the army's organization and restructured training systems to encourage an overt pride in national service.

Manpower restrictions were overcome by reducing the period of conscript service, enabling creation of a fully trained **Landwehr** reserve army, and the formation of volunteer **Freikorps** units among the middle classes was given strong, if clandestine, support. Both proved valuable adjuncts to frontline forces during the campaigns of 1813–14, and Major **Schill**'s unit was one of many Freikorps to perform a valuable **propaganda** function during the years of uneasy French alliance.

The reform group were not allowed to remain in office for long, such was the hold exercised by Napoleon over a terrified Frederick William, but missionary zeal for national reconstruction went beyond individuals. By 1810, when Scharnhorst was dismissed on Napoleon's instructions, political and military authority in Prussia were virtually indistinguishable, and his work continued through a network of unofficial channels. The same system found ways to employ many other officers, such as the notoriously aggressive **Blücher**, who had been removed from the army after Tilsit.

In need of allied troops to take part in the **Russian campaign**, Napoleon allowed Prussia to double the size of its army in 1812, but took a contingent of Prussian troops for the invasion in return. General **Yorck**'s 20,000-strong corps operated on the northern wing of the **Grande Armée** throughout the ensuing campaign, and took part in the siege of **Riga** under **Macdonald**. Retreating with the rest of the invading force at the end of the year, Yorck expressed the views of most of his countrymen by signing a unilateral neutrality agreement with Russian forces at **Tauroggen**. In the wake of Yorck's decision, anti-French activity throughout Germany snowballed, and even Frederick William could only delay Prussia's inevitable declaration of war on France until mid-February.

With Prussia a core member of the **Sixth Coalition**, the army played a major, and on the whole successful, part in the campaigns of 1813–14. Able to put some 60,000 men into the field at once, and more than 150,000 by autumn 1813, it was broadly divided into two main contingents during the campaign for **Germany**. While **Bülow**'s corps helped protect Berlin in the north of the theatre, senior field commander Blücher led the larger Army of Silesia to the east.

After taking part in all the major actions of the campaign, and winning particular credit with victories over Napoleon's subordinates at **Gross-Beeren** and the **Katzbach**, Prussian forces joined their allies at the climactic Battle of **Leipzig** in October. Again intermingled with allied formations during the 1814 campaign for **France**, Prussian forces operated in scattered corps through late January and February. Blücher's main body found its early advances on Paris from the east thwarted by a combination of his superiors' caution and Napoleon's hit-and-run operations, but joined up with corps under **Kleist** and **Winzingerode** to win an important victory at **Laon** in March.

The Prussian Army's reputation had been considerably revived when the War of the **Sixth Coalition** ended. Though still relatively ponderous, it was led by a rather younger senior command, and had become more flexible in its approach to both tactics and offensive **strategy**. Blücher was neither young nor able to modify his attacking style, but his partnership with pragmatic chief of staff **Gneisenau** (who assumed the position after Scharnhorst was mortally wounded at **Lützen** in 1813) was one of the period's most successful double acts.

The partnership was reunited for the **Hundred Days** campaign of 1815, when 120,000 Prussian troops formed the eastern half of the allied force in Flanders. When Blücher went missing after the initial defeat at **Ligny**, Gneisenau took command and prepared to retreat on his communications. Blücher's return to action, and his insistence on turning his army towards **Wellington**'s positions, was vital to allied victory at **Waterloo**.

The process of creating a genuinely national Prussian Army, begun by Scharnhorst, bore full fruit in the wars of the mid-nineteenth century, when the 'nation in arms' completed the political unification of Germany and again defeated France. The army's revived reputation as the finest force in Europe was then assumed by a German Army, overwhelmingly dominated by Prussian forces and methods, that confirmed its operational excellence in the world wars of the twentieth century.

Prussian Navy

In line with Frederick the Great's determination to devote all military resources to development of the **Prussian Army**, and despite its status as a North Sea and Baltic trading power, **Prussia** had no conventional navy during the 1792–1815 period. In part also a reflection of long-term friendship with **Great Britain**, the lack devalued Prussia's adherence to the anti-British **Armed Neutrality** campaign of 1800–1, and though a small force of coastguard vessels and **gunboats** was formed to provide some means of enforcing the **Continental System** from 1806, it did not enjoy full military status.

Public Safety, Committee of

An executive committee appointed from among its number by the French **National Convention** in April 1793, a response to the crisis that followed defeat at **Neerwinden** and the defection of **Dumouriez**. Originally comprising nine members, but later expanded to 12, it functioned as little more than a watchdog over the Convention's council of ministers until it was joined by **Robespierre** and his allies in July, after which it exploited wide judicial powers to become the effective government of **France**. As such it was the principal agency through which the **Terror** was conducted, and provided the framework of authority for **Carnot**'s successful reorganization of the **French Army**. Though the committee remained in being after Robespierre's fall in July 1794, its powers were spread among the Convention's other standing councils, and it ceased to exist after the **Vendémiaire** coup of October 1795.

Pultusk, Battle of

One of two indecisive engagements (the other was at **Golymin**) fought in the region north of Warsaw on 26 December 1806. Having conceded **Warsaw** without a fight in late November, advanced Russian forces in **Poland** had linked up with Marshal **Kamenskoi**'s main body, but still appeared bent on a rapid retreat north for the winter. Acting on this assumption, **Napoleon** attempted to bring the Russians to a major battle. Four corps in the Warsaw area marched against the presumed centre of the Russian position on the Narev River from mid-December, and two more advanced east from Thorn to cut off the supposed Russian line of retreat at Soldau and Mlava.

Russian forces had in fact reversed their retreat, advancing south beyond Pultusk towards the River Ukra, aiming to establish forward positions for the forthcoming spring campaign. The main French advance, hampered by appalling road conditions, met serious resistance at the Ukra and the Narev on 21 and 22 December, before Kamenskoi changed his mind, withdrawing most of his forces towards Streshegozin on Christmas Eve. Still seeking a decisive battle, Napoleon ordered **Davout** to march directly on Streshegozin, and **Augereau** to strike at the Russians' line of march. **Lannes**, with perhaps 20,000 troops, was sent to Pultusk, where he met **Bennigsen**'s 35,000 Russians on the morning of 26 December.

Despite wet and windy conditions, and a three to one disadvantage in **artillery**, outnumbered French troops attacked through thick mud, gaining a foothold in the town before Russian **artillery** strength drove them back. Before Bennigsen could exploit his advantage he was forced to turn his right wing (led by **Barclay de Tolly**) to meet one of Davout's divisions from the west, and inconclusive fighting continued until shortly after dusk, by which time the French were glad of a chance to reorganize. Though he had suffered some 8,000 casualties, against an estimated 5,000 Russian losses, Lannes expected to resume the battle the next day, but Bennigsen fulfilled his original instructions from Kamenskoi and withdrew up the banks of the Narev during the night.

Relative failure at Pultusk, and the similar result 20km north-west at Golymin, persuaded Napoleon that further offensive operations were impossible until the weather improved, and he ordered the army into winter quarters on 29 December. *See* War of the **Fourth Coalition**; **Map 17**.

Pyramids, Battle of the

Engagement near the town of Embabeh, some 50km north-west of Cairo, that was the first serious attempt by local forces to halt the French invasion of the **Middle East** in July 1798. After defeat at **Shubra Khit** on 13 July, regional governors **Murad Bey** and **Ibrahim Bey** assembled a much larger force either side of the Nile. Some 6,000 **Mameluke** horsemen and about 14,000 native Egyptian infantry were on the east bank, and on the west bank, directly in the path of the French advance, Murad commanded another 6,000 Mamelukes, 20,000 Egyptian infantry and a few better-trained **Turkish Army** units. An estimated 14,000 Arab horsemen lurking in the rear were not under his control.

French commander **Napoleon** could muster only 28,000 men, but they possessed modern firearms and unity of purpose, while largely untested Egyptian troops owed scant loyalty to the Ottoman regime, and rivalry between the regional governors prevented cooperation between their army's two wings.

As French forces edged towards Murad in **infantry squares**, inflicting heavy casualties on repeated Mameluke charges, Ibrahim retreated into Syria for Turkish reinforcement. Though Murad's horsemen kept charging until they collapsed, Napoleon drove his infantry forward during the pauses between assaults, supported by flank attacks from **Desaix's** division. Egyptian infantry and Arab cavalry played little active role, and by sunset the defenders had fled the field. The French suffered only 300 casualties, against some 2,000 Mameluke losses and perhaps 5,000 Egyptian.

The remnants of Murad's force retreated up the Nile, pursued by Desaix, until caught and dispersed at Sadiman in July. Napoleon then led the main body of his army into Cairo, while a battery of writers turned his easy, tactically unsophisticated victory into a major **propaganda** triumph, and came up with a grandiose title for a battle fought without a pyramid in sight. *See* **Map 7.**

Pyrenean Campaign (1793–5)

The ragged and indecisive frontier war between **France** and **Spain** that followed from the latter's adherence to the **First Coalition** in early 1793. Spanish preparations for war had been under way since mid-1792, but so slowly that their suspension after **Valmy** was almost imperceptible. Resumed once **Great Britain** (and its **subsidies**) entered the war in early 1793, they were substantially complete by the time the French government declared war against Spain on 7 March.

Though committed to an attack on France by the British alliance, the **Spanish Army** was in no condition to mount one, and could only muster some 35,000 ill-equipped troops for operations all along the Pyrenean frontier. The military resources of France were meanwhile stretched to the limit by campaigns in **Flanders** and on the **Rhine**, and an invasion force sent to Spain comprised only about 8,000 recruits under General Servan. Servan took up positions guarding the passes at the north-western end of the frontier, while a scattering of garrison forces and volunteer militia performed a similar task in the east.

The campaign opened with Spanish attacks at both ends of the line. Northern Spanish forces under General Caro won a series of minor spring successes, including the defeat of Servan at Sarre in mid-May and the capture of Château-Pignon by La **Romana** on 6 June. Meanwhile General Ricardos picked off small French garrisons holding approaches to Perpignan in the south, but paused for reinforcements from late April. Repulsed when he eventually attacked **Perpignan** in mid-July, and stopped by General Dagobert when he tried to outflank the city via Mont Louis, Ricardos pulled back after his advance guard was surprised by a French counter-attack on 17 September. Now commander of the sector as a whole, the veteran Dagobert failed in a bid to drive the Spanish back across the Pyrenees at **Truillas** on 22 September.

Under a new commander, General Daoût, and strengthened from war minister **Carnot's** growing manpower fund, French forces soon resumed the offensive, but attacks from Perpignan failed on 2 and 3 October, as did a night operation in mid-month. Another new French commander, General Thurreau, launched a strike against the frontier port of Rosas in late October, supported by a secondary attack against the Spanish left at Ceret, but both failed. Command passed to

Doppet, who failed again at Ceret on 26 November and fell back towards Perpignan after a Spanish counter-attack on 7 December. Required to contribute 15,000 of his troops to the recapture of rebel Toulon, Doppet's last failure on 19 December left some 8,000 French troops penned inside Perpignan.

In the west, Caro and 24,000 troops were defending the Bidassoa around San Marcial and the main passes through the mountains into France. Weak French forces launched attacks on the line at government insistence from late August, but were defeated with ease, after which the sector remained quiet while both sides built up strong fortified positions in the mountains around the frontier. Caro's 20,000 troops, outnumbered by 35,000 Frenchman, launched a general attack against the French fort line on 5 February 1794, but returned to the defensive after they were stopped by a counter-attack.

Command of about 30,000 Spanish troops in the south-east had passed to General de la Union, Ricardos having fallen ill (he died at Madrid in March), and Dugommier had taken over 35,000 French troops occupying a line south of Perpignan from Thiur to the coast. French forces opened offensive operations from 27 March, advancing to overrun Spanish positions at Le Boulon in late April, while Dagobert led an independent inland drive against the Spanish left wing.

Dugommier's forces, led by Augereau, Pérignon and Victor, shrugged off ineffectual Spanish counter-attacks on 19 May and took the port of Collioure after a siege on 29 May (storms having prevented a Spanish Navy relief operation). The last serious actions of the spring took place on the inland flank where a new advance by Doppet, Dagobert's successor, was forced back from Camprodón by a Spanish counter-attack on 18 June, and Cuesta's 4,000 men failed to get behind French lines near Belver. De la Union's attempt to save the besieged outpost of Bellegarde failed at St Laurent on 13 August, and the town surrendered on 17 September, by which time the Spanish commander was involved in secret (though fruitless) peace talks.

Fighting resumed on the north-western sector in late July, and new French C-in-C Muller won an important victory at San Marcial on 1 August, driving new Spanish commander Colomera back on Pamplona by mid-August. Moncey took over from Muller for the autumn campaign, and was reinforced to about 65,000 men for an advance south into Navarre from 15 October. After early successes, French attacks were thwarted by bad weather in the mountains, and Colomera clung to Pamplona for the winter.

A French offensive against 50,000 troops holding the Spanish line in the east had begun on 17 November, forcing defenders to abandon Figueras and retire on Gerona, a move that left the roads open into central Spain. Both Dugommier and de la Union were killed during the offensive, which left the French army in control of the roads into Spain.

The new year began with a French siege of Rosas, which was taken in early February, but new commander Schérer's offensives over the Fluvia failed in April and May. With Spanish general Urrutia's army reinforced to 35,000 men, and dug into strong positions along the river, the calm induced by rumours of peace was interrupted only by a major French foraging raid.

Moncey's army in the western Pyrenees, depleted by sickness and detachments to pacify La Vendée, was unable to mount an offensive until late June, when its attacks drove the two wings of the Spanish army (now commanded by Castelfranco) towards Bilbao and beyond Pamplona. Moncey had settled down to besiege Pamplona when news of the Treaty of Basle (signed on 22 July) ended fighting in the theatre. *See* **Map 5**.

Q

Quadrilateral, The

Contemporary name given to the area at the centre of Austrian imperial administration in Italy that was the key to military domination of the Lombard plains. Bordered to the east and west by the Adige and Mincio rivers, and by the Alps and the Po to the north and south, it guarded the main passes leading from Italy into **Austria**. The Quadrilateral was protected by four powerful **fortresses**: Peschiera and **Mantua** on the Mincio; **Verona** and Legnano on the Adige. Apart from Mantua, the administrative capital of the Austrian regime, they all belonged to the nominally independent republic of **Venice** in 1792. *See* **Italian Campaigns; Map 6.**

Quadruple Alliance

Agreement signed between **Great Britain, Austria, Prussia** and **Russia** on the same day as the second Treaty of **Paris**, 20 November 1815, by which the four self-proclaimed **great powers** of Europe agreed to attend regular congresses aimed at ensuring continental stability. The alliance formed the basis of the Congress System by which the peace of Europe was maintained over the next four decades, though **France** was effectively co-opted as fifth great power at the Aix-la-Chapelle congress of 1818. *See* Congress of **Vienna.**

Quatre Bras, Battle of

One of two battles fought in Belgium on 16 June 1815 that opened the **Hundred Days** campaign. Fighting centred on the town of Quatre Bras, a vital crossroads linking **Wellington's** allied army to the west with **Blücher's** Prussian force gathering for a confrontation with French forces at **Ligny** (*see* **Map 28**). Because Wellington had misinterpreted initial French moves into Belgium on 14–15 June, no provision was made to defend Quatre Bras, which lay in the path of **Ney's** advancing French left wing.

A single brigade of some 4,000 **Nassau** troops, part of the Prince of **Orange's** allied corps, had been ordered forward beyond Quatre Bras during the afternoon of 15 June, and was in position to block advanced French **cavalry** under **Lefebvre-Desnouëttes** later that day. Faced with opposition of unknown strength in gathering darkness, Ney postponed further action until morning, and a second allied brigade arrived to reinforce the position during the evening. Divisional commander General Perponcher subsequently continued to strengthen the position in tacit defiance of Wellington's initial orders to move west.

Primarily as a gesture to reassure shaky Belgian morale, Wellington and the Prince of Orange were guests at a ball given in Brussels by the Duchess of Richmond on the night of 15–16 June. News reached Wellington overnight that revealed his initial mistake, and fresh orders went out redirecting his forces towards their eastern flank and a rendezvous with Blücher. Most were too far away to provide immediate support, but Wellington led the 25,000 troops of his reserve from Brussels towards Quatre Bras at seven thirty next morning.

Ney had been personally briefed on the

importance of Quatre Bras by **Napoleon** at Charleroi during the night, but issued no attack instructions to his corps commanders before morning and eventually ordered **Reille**'s 22,000 troops forward at eleven. The first French attacks towards the town began just after two in the afternoon, by which time only 7,800 infantry, 50 cavalry and 16 guns were defending the position. Strung out along a 3km line across the road south to Charleroi, they faced another 20,000 troops of **Drouet**'s corps coming up in support.

Allied troops were holding good positions at the crossroads, on high ground fronted by wooded areas, a number of farm buildings and fields of high corn. Reille attacked with extraordinary caution, slowly clearing woodland south of the crossroads to take outlying strongpoints on the allied left and centre, but was forced to commit Jérôme **Bonaparte**'s reserve division against the right-wing outpost at Pierrepoint Farm before he could move against positions west of the crossroads.

Perponcher's beleaguered line was on the point of cracking when Wellington reached the scene at about three, followed by a Dutch–Belgian cavalry brigade from Nivelles and **Picton**'s 8,000 British troops. Allied cavalry launched an unsuccessful counter-attack, but further French advances were halted as more reinforcements arrived to bring Wellington's strength up to 21,000 men.

Ney could still expect to bring decisive numbers to bear if Drouet's corps reached the battlefield, but just after four he received orders from Napoleon assuming that Quatre Bras was taken and calling for a flank attack at Ligny. Suddenly aware that Quatre Bras was important, but misreading Napoleon's priorities, Ney ordered Drouet north to join the attack on the town. A second order redirected Drouet to Ligny, where his eventual arrival caused great confusion, but he was called back again when Ney found out, and by early evening his potentially decisive reserves had played no part in either battle.

Meanwhile a sustained French cavalry attack in the centre had been beaten back by four thirty. In a premature act of desperation, Ney sent a virtually unsupported brigade of **Kellermann**'s cavalry charging through British infantry to take

temporary possession of the crossroads. When it was forced to flee with heavy casualties, an enraged Ney abandoned tactical control over the battle and plunged into the fighting at the head of a renewed French infantry charge. It was reversed by a major allied counter-attack at six thirty, once final reinforcements had brought Wellington's strength up to 36,000 men and 70 guns. In the continued absence of Drouet, allied attacks had recaptured forward positions by the time fighting ended at about nine.

Allied forces lost about 4,800 men at Quatre Bras, against some 4,000 French casualties. Though Wellington had forced a draw against heavy odds, and Napoleon's victory at Ligny was less complete than he imagined, the day's fighting had left French forces poised for a large-scale attack on Wellington while Blücher's defeated army retreated eastward. *See also* Battle of **Waterloo**.

Queenston Heights, Battle of

The climax of the first major attempt by US forces to invade Canada during the **Anglo-American War**, fought in October 1812 near the town of Queenston on the US–Canadian Niagara frontier (*see* **Map 27**). A preliminary US attempt to seize those parts of southern Canada coveted by its northernmost states had barely got under way in July before it was driven back by Anglo-Canadian garrison forces. General van Rensaler led a much larger force of 900 regular **US Army** troops and almost 2,300 state militiamen up to the east bank of the Niagara River on 15 October, but after the regulars had made a rough boat crossing into Canadian territory, many militia refused to follow on the grounds that they had not agreed to serve abroad. Van Rensaler's depleted force met General Brock's frontier garrison, dug into high ground, later the same day. Though Brock was killed in the ensuing action, his 600 **British Army** regulars and 400 Canadian militia took 700 prisoners and inflicted another 250 casualties, ending the invasion.

Quesnoy, Siege of

One of two sieges that distracted the **First Coalition**'s offensive in **Flanders** beyond strategic usefulness in the autumn of 1793. About 100,000 allied troops had begun driving outnumbered

French forces back from the Belgian frontier from the second week in August, but the strategic differences that had plagued inter-allied relations came to a head on 10 August, when **York**'s half of the army marched north to besiege **Dunkirk**. Austrian C-in-C **Saxe-Coburg** sealed the offensive's failure by settling down to besiege the French garrison at Quesnoy as a prelude to taking on the garrison at Cambrai. The actual **siege** was brief, beginning on 28 August and ending with the garrison's surrender on 11 September. Belated French attempts at a relief operation from Cambrai were repulsed with about 3,000 losses, but the respite granted to hard-pressed republican forces gave both the **Terror** and **Carnot**'s military reforms time to take significant effect. *See* **Map 2**.

Quiberon Expedition

Ill-fated British attempt to aid royalist French rebels in La **Vendée** by landing an **émigré** army on the north-west coast of **France**, launched in summer 1795 after months of delay had seen the rebellion's partial suppression by republican forces under **Hoche**. A **Royal Navy** squadron based on three **ships-of-the-line** under Admiral Warren left Portsmouth in mid-June, carrying about 3,000 French royalist troops, 80 cannon and a supply of small arms for rebels expected to meet them in Brittany. After Alexander **Hood**'s Channel Fleet had prevented interference from **Villaret**'s warships off the Ile de **Groix**, Warren sailed into Quiberon Bay, Brittany, on 25 June (*see* **Map 18**).

Royalist troops landed two days later, chasing away 250 local militia and making contact with several thousand **Chouan** rebels under **Cadoudal**. Emigré commander the Comte d'Hervilly led perhaps 12,000 troops (including untrained local peasantry) north to take Penthiévre, the only **fortress** on the small Quiberon peninsula, on 30 June. Ignoring local leaders, Hervilly refused to advance further, allowing Hoche to advance and seal the neck of the peninsula.

While Hoche paused to gather reinforcements, Hervilly sent detachments by sea to get around the flanks of republican positions. The southern force surprised the far republican left on 11 July, and marched inland to attack some 3,000 troops holding fortified positions on 16 July, when it was routed (and Hervilly killed) by concealed artillery. The northern detachment, misinformed by local rebels, marched away from a planned rendezvous and was halfway to St Malo when it was dispersed by republican forces.

Though reinforced by a second émigré unit on 15 July, the force at Quiberon was already dissolving into command bickering when deserters helped republicans recapture the Penthiévre fort on the night of 20–21 July. Hoche followed up with an immediate attack on royalist field troops, catching them unprepared and driving them on to the beaches. Delayed by a gale, British **frigates** were eventually able to rescue some 3,500 troops, but Hoche captured about 6,000 rebels, along with supplies for 40,000 troops and six supply ships that subsequently blundered into the bay. Most of those rescued slipped back into France, but a few diehards and British **marines** occupied the offshore Ile Dieu, where they were joined by a third expeditionary division under **Artois**. Unable to make contact with royalists ashore, the garrison was withdrawn in the autumn.

R

Raab, Battle of

Subsidiary French victory on 14 June 1809 that prevented Archduke **John**'s Austrian army from reaching the Danube in time for the decisive battle at **Wagram**. It also established the reputation of Italian viceroy **Beauharnais** as a military commander.

Beauharnais had pursued John's larger force from Italy, defeating its right wing at **Sankt Michael** and driving the remainder into Hungary while he marched to join **Napoleon** near Vienna. Reinforced to a total strength of some 43,000 troops (including **Macdonald**'s observation corps in Hungary), he was sent to prevent John's remaining 35,000 men from reaching Vienna along the Raab River. Leading his strike force of about 24,000 men, Beauharnais caught up with the relatively slow Austrian columns near the town of Raab, just over 100km south-east of the capital.

Eugene launched his **cavalry** (under **Montbrun** and **Grouchy**) against the Austrian left shortly before noon on 14 June. It quickly overran forward positions, but was then switched against John's cavalry on the plain east of the river. A French infantry assault against the main infantry positions opened in mid-afternoon, and the Austrian left again fell back, but the centre held until about five, when the arrival of French reserves and news of a cavalry threat to his rear persuaded John to retreat. He withdrew north, leaving a strong garrison at Raab, and Beauharnais rejoined Napoleon after the **fortress** fell on 25 June, having inflicted about 5,000 losses and suffered some 3,000. *See* **Map 12**.

Radetzky, Joseph Wenzel, Count (1766–1858)

Bohemian-born **Austrian Army** officer, a veteran of campaigns against the **Ottoman Empire** in the 1780s, who fought on the **Flanders**, **Rhine** and **Italian** fronts during the **Revolutionary Wars**, and in the **Third Coalition** campaign of 1805. Promoted general after the Battle of **Aspern–Essling** in 1809, he commanded divisions throughout the campaigns for **Germany** and **France** in 1813–14, and eventually governed Austrian Italy for 26 years until his retirement in 1857.

Rapp, Jean (1771–1821)

One of **Napoleon**'s most trusted and durable personal aides, Rapp joined the old regime's cavalry arm in 1788, and was wounded several times against the **First Coalition** on the **Rhine**. An aide to **Desaix** during the **Middle East** campaign, and with his chief when he was killed at **Marengo** in June 1800, he was appointed to Napoleon's staff next day. Promoted brigadier-general in 1803, he was made a divisional general after leading a **cavalry** charge against the **Imperial Russian Guard** at **Austerlitz** in 1805. He fought at **Jena** in 1806, and was wounded at **Golymin**, becoming governor of **Danzig** after its capture in 1807. He played an important role at **Aspern–Essling** in 1809, and suffered several wounds at **Borodino** in 1812, returning to Danzig in 1813. Forced to surrender his isolated garrison in late 1813, he was imprisoned by the Russians until after the **abdication**, but rejoined Napoleon during the **Hundred Days** of 1815, commanding the small detachment at the Rhine that continued fighting until almost two weeks after **Waterloo**. In exile until 1817, he held minor court posts on his return.

Rastatt, Battle of

The second stage of **Moreau**'s French offensive across the **Rhine** north-east of Strasbourg in summer 1796. After defeating allied forces at the **Kinzig** on 28 June, Moreau reorganized his army into three corps for a drive into Germany. Austrian sector commander Latour meanwhile retired to the River Murg, on the edge of the Black Forest, concentrating about 18,000 men between Rastatt and Gernsbach by 4 July (*see* **Map 3**). Although 25,000 allied reinforcements were on their way south with Archduke **Charles**, Latour chose to accept battle rather than abandon strong positions. Moreau attacked the entire line on 5 July, driving back Latour's left at Gernsbach and then striking the centre around Kuppenheim, where defenders withdrew across the Murg after a three-hour fight. The French left wing made no progress around Rastatt, where defenders with strong **artillery** and **cavalry** support were protected by woods south of the town, but took the woods by evening, and Latour responded by retiring 20km to **Ettlingen** overnight. Both sides suffered an estimated 500 casualties during the day.

Ratan, Battle of

Failed attempt by Swedish forces to trap a Russian army advancing south on Stockholm during the latter stages of the **Russo-Swedish War** in 1809. Attacking Russian forces had crossed the frozen Gulf of Bothnia from Finland to reach the north-eastern Swedish port of Umeå when an armistice was signed in March 1809. By the time the truce broke down in May, the spring thaw had enabled the **Swedish Navy** to resume operations in the gulf. While **Swedish Army** forces distracted the Russians at Umeå with a frontal attack, a large Swedish fleet under Admiral von Puke put to sea on 15 August 1809 to attack them in the rear. Some 11,000 troops aboard 40 transports, escorted by three **ships-of-the-line**, five **frigates**, 40 **sloops**, six **galleys** and four **bombs**, reached the Swedish coast at Ratan late next day, and

troops were disembarked on 17 August. Shortly after getting ashore, Swedish forces were attacked by 9,000 Russian troops under General Kamenski, and thrown back with about 1,000 losses after an all-day battle. Disobeying Puke's orders, land forces withdrew to positions on a small peninsula south of Ratan, and barely held off attacks by inferior numbers until Kamenski eventually withdrew after two days to avoid Swedish units approaching overland. Puke's **marines** failed to cut off his withdrawal, and the front saw no further action before the war ended in mid-September. *See* **Map 18**.

Ratisbon, Battles for

The town of Ratisbon, a strategically important Danube crossing on the northern frontier of **Bavaria**, was the focus of early operations by both French and Austrian forces during the early stages of the War of the **Fifth Coalition** in April 1809.

The major Austrian offensive that opened on 9 April aimed pincers at Ratisbon from both sides of the Danube. Marshal **Davout**'s occupying III Corps began a cautious evacuation at the first sign of danger, but was ordered back into the town by temporary French C-in-C **Berthier**. Instructed to withdraw south once **Napoleon** reached the front, he moved out of Ratisbon on 18 April, leaving a garrison of only 2,000 men. Facing a direct attack by 23,000 Austrian troops, and another corps approaching from the south, the garrison surrendered without destroying the town bridge on 20 April.

Three days later, in the aftermath of French victory at **Eckmühl**, French forces pursuing Archduke **Charles**'s beaten army were severely delayed by 6,000 Austrian rearguards at Ratisbon. In the presence of Napoleon, who was slightly wounded in the foot by a spent musket ball, the Austrians repelled two full-scale assaults on the fortifications. A third attack, led from the front by Marshal **Lannes**, put the town in French hands before dark, but the capture cost 1,000 French casualties and left the bridge in Austrian hands. Combined with news that alternative bridges at Straubing had been destroyed, the delay persuaded Napoleon to call off the pursuit and turn his army towards Vienna. *See* **Map 12**.

Reichenbach, Convention of

The secret agreement, signed on 19 July 1813 and subsequently confirmed at **Teplitz**, by which Austrian emperor **Francis** agreed to join the **Sixth Coalition**, provided **Napoleon** refused to accept peace terms to be presented during the ongoing **armistice**. The terms included French concession of almost all territory east of the Rhine, and were designed to be unacceptable. Their inevitable rejection triggered **Austria's** declaration of war on 12 August. *See also* Campaign for **Germany**.

Reille, Honoré Charles Michel Joseph (1775–1860)

A volunteer with the **French Army** in 1791, Reille was commissioned the following year and fought at **Toulon** in 1793. Also active on the **Italian** front during the **Revolutionary Wars**, he was posted to **Naples** in 1802 and promoted brigadier-general the following year. He sailed with **Villeneuve's** ill-fated expedition in 1805, but was recalled shortly before **Trafalgar** to fight against the **Third Coalition**. Given divisional command at the end of 1806, after taking part in most of that year's battles against the **Fourth Coalition**, Reille served at **Friedland** (1807) as one of **Napoleon's** aides, and spent 1808 in the **Peninsular** theatre. Transferred east for the campaign against Austria of 1809, he fought at **Aspern–Essling** and **Wagram**, before becoming Napoleon's informant with **Bernadotte's** command in northern Germany. He returned to Spain in 1811, fighting at **Vitoria** in 1813, and led a corps under **Soult** during the final campaigns in the theatre. A corps commander during the **Hundred Days** of 1815, operating with **Ney's** left wing at **Quatre Bras** and **Waterloo**, he entered royal service in 1819 after a period in exile, enjoying a long and successful career as a military administrator.

Reims, Battle of

Small but stunning allied defeat during the latter stages of the 1814 campaign for **France**, a surprise strike on 13 March by **Napoleon's** main army against General St Priest's Russian corps occupying Reims. St Priest had been detailed to form the link between the two main allied armies menacing Paris, and his 14,500 men occupied Reims early on 12 March. Retreating south-west from

his defeat at **Laon** (9–10 March), and facing disaster on every other front, Napoleon marched his troops for the city that night.

Marmont's leading corps took St Priest completely by surprise the following afternoon, and he was killed as French attacks reached the city walls by nightfall. Russian forces attempted a counter-attack that night, but Napoleon's battlefield strength had grown to 25,000 men, and he responded by bringing up **artillery** to blast through the city's western gate. Defenders fled, pursued by French **cavalry**, and Napoleon occupied Reims for a total of 700 casualties. Shocked by the sudden loss of 6,000 troops, and aware that Napoleon had cut across their mutual communications, allied commanders **Blücher** and **Schwarzenberg** halted their respective advances, giving Napoleon an opportunity to rush his tiring troops to aid **Macdonald's** hard-pressed forces at the Seine. *See* **Map 26**.

Republican Calendar

The new system of dating, also known as the Revolutionary Calendar, adopted by the French **National Convention** on 5 October 1793. The Convention took its own proclamation of the French republic on 22 September 1792 as the first day of a new epoch in human affairs, and it was renamed Day One of the first month in Year I. The 30-day months taken from that date were named to describe natural phenomena, with an extra five or six days added gratuitously to the end of each year. Vendémiaire, the vintage month (from 22 September), was followed by Brumaire (foggy), Frimaire (frosty), Nivôse (snowy), Pluviôse (rainy), Ventôse (windy), Germinal (fertile), Floréal (floral), Prairial (the month of meadows), Messidor (harvest), Thermidor (heat) and Fructidor (fruit). The calendar was abolished by **Napoleon** during Nivôse, Year 15, which again became late December 1806.

Revolutionary Calendar *See* **Republican Calendar**

Revolutionary Wars

The name sometimes applied to the War of the **First Coalition**, or to the Wars of the First and **Second Coalition** together. The 'revolutionary' period is considered ended after 1801, by which time **Napoleon** was in full control of **France**.

Rey, Louis Emmanuel (1768–1846)

French officer, commissioned in 1792 and promoted brigadier-general in 1796, who served in the **Italian campaigns,** and as **Gouvion St Cyr's** chief of staff in the **Peninsular** theatre before becoming governor of **San Sebastian** in 1811. His conduct of its defence against an allied **siege** in 1813 at last earned promotion to divisional general in November, though he remained an allied prisoner until May 1814, re-emerging during the **Hundred Days** as governor of Valenciennes.

Reynier, Jean Louis Ebénézer (1771–1814)

French soldier who fought at **Jemappes** in 1792, and was promoted brigadier-general in 1795. Chief of staff with **Moreau** at the **Rhine** in 1796, and subsequently raised to divisional command, he took part in the **Middle East** expedition from 1798 and fought at the Battle of the **Pyramids.** Sent home in 1800 after a dispute with C-in-C **Menou,** he was exiled from France after killing General Destaing in a duel, but was eventually recalled to replace **Berthier** as war minister in 1808. Subsequently an active divisional commander against the **Fifth Coalition** in 1809, and in the **Peninsular War** from 1810 to 1811, he led VII Corps on the southern flank of the **Grande Armée** during the 1812 **Russian campaign.** His career reached its zenith during the campaign for **Germany** in 1813, when he led VII Corps at **Bautzen, Dresden, Gross-Beeren** and **Dennewitz,** where he was perhaps the only French commander to emerge with credit. He held off strong allied forces during the French withdrawal from **Leipzig** in October, but was taken prisoner. Released on exchange in February 1814, he died two weeks later.

Rheims, Battle of *See* **Reims,** Battle of

Rhine Campaign (1799–1800)

The struggle for control of south-western Germany between **France** and the **Second Coalition,** begun with a French offensive against Austrian forces across the Rhine in March 1799. Though **Austria** had agreed in principle to join **Russia** in an attack on republican France, Emperor **Francis II** was in no hurry to begin hostilities. After refusing to take part in the

Neapolitan campaign in November 1798, Vienna resisted demands for action from Tsar **Paul I** into the new year. By the late winter, Paul was threatening to withdraw the 60,000 troops he had moved into position for a proposed joint offensive across the Rhine, but the French **Directory** government cut through bickering by declaring war against Francis on 12 March.

Motivated by the need to distract an increasingly hostile public from its failings, and by misplaced confidence in a **French Army** that had undergone a marked decline since 1797, the Directory had been planning an offensive into Germany for months. An army with a nominal strength of 135,000 men had been assembled for the task, spearheaded by **Jourdan's** 37,000 troops along the river between Kehl and Hunningen, and **Masséna's** 45,000 in **Switzerland.** Otherwise **Bernadotte's** 48,000 men were threatening Mannheim further north, and **Brune's** 15,000 were guarding the **Netherlands.**

They faced a larger and better-equipped, but tactically fossilized, **Austrian Army.** In the north, Archduke **Charles** led 54,000 infantry and 27,000 **cavalry** along the River Lech, while Hotze commanded 27,500 men east of the Swiss border, and **Bellegarde's** 47,000 men guarded the Tyrol, with another 7,000 patrolling the mountains. The Austrians could also call on forces from the **Italian** theatre if necessary, and were expecting Russian reinforcements within weeks.

Crossing the Rhine on 1 March, well before the declaration of war, Bernadotte moved east after taking the surrender of Mannheim on 2 March. Jourdan advanced less cautiously to reach the Black Forest on 6 March, and then continued into the plains beyond without waiting for Masséna to move up on his southern flank. Charles responded by advancing from the Lech and launching a full-scale attack against French advanced positions at **Ostrach** on 21 March. It could not prevent Jourdan's orderly withdrawal beyond the vital road junction of **Stockach,** but a resumed French advance on the town was decisively beaten on 25 March. His army's morale faltering, and exposed to a flank attack by Hotze's forces in eastern Switzerland, Jourdan retreated towards the Black Forest next day.

Charles waited at Stockach for reinforcements, and sent them into the Alps from 3 April to protect his main positions against any flank attack. The move was enough to persuade General Ernould, who replaced Jourdan, to pull all his forces back behind the Rhine on 5–6 April, leaving only a few observation outposts on the east bank.

With the threat of isolation forcing Bernadotte's northern corps back across the river, the Directory could only adopt a defensive posture along the Rhine, placing the sector under Masséna's overall control. Charles, recognizing that Switzerland held the key to any sustainable eastward advance, made no attempt to attack the Rhine positions in force, contenting himself with minor operations to clear French outposts and establish bridgeheads across the river.

While campaigns in Switzerland and Italy dictated the course of the war during the summer, reduced forces on the Rhine front were largely restricted to outpost skirmishing, and a brief French offensive around **Mannheim** was abandoned when Charles returned to the theatre with reinforcements in mid-September. Under instructions to prepare a northward march in support of the Anglo-Russian **North Holland** expedition, Charles made no offensive move before allied retreat from the **Swiss** front instigated a winter of mutual reorganization.

Russian troops had quit western Europe by spring 1800, and Charles soon relinquished command along the Rhine to **Kray**, who could call on a total of about 140,000 men in the theatre. Ordered to undertake a secondary attack into eastern France in support of the main Austrian offensive in northern Italy, his advance was met by **Moreau's** invigorated Army of the Rhine and Switzerland, and was quickly pushed back on Ulm when he attempted to advance in May. Moreau attacked Kray at **Höchstädt** in June, and had driven him back to Munich by the time Napoleon's victory at **Marengo** brought the Austrians to the conference table. A truce on the Rhine front was agreed at Parsdorf on 28 July.

The breakdown of talks was followed by a resumption of French attacks from 28 November 1800. Moreau advanced south-east from Munich, and his defeat of Archduke **John's** Austrian army at **Hohenlinden** finally forced Vienna to seek a lasting peace, signed at **Lunéville** the following February. The peace recognized French conquests east of the Rhine, forcing a fundamental reorganization of the **Holy Roman Empire's** ramshackle political structure to compensate the larger German states for territorial losses, and signalling the disappearance of many small independent statelets. *See* **Maps 3,4**.

Rhine Campaigns (1792–7)

The region either side of the Rhine, south of the **Netherlands** and north of **Switzerland**, was a principal theatre of conflict between **France** and the allies of the **First Coalition** (*see* **Map 3**). The first major offensive in the theatre – planned after the alliance of **Austria**, **Prussia** and the states of the **Holy Roman Empire** in July 1792 – was launched across the Rhine the following month, when allied forces under the Duke of **Brunswick's** cautious control marched on Paris.

Confident of easy success against a **French Army** short of equipment, uniforms and discipline, Brunswick adopted orthodox eighteenth-century **cordon** tactics. Accompanied by King **Frederick William II**, the Prussian army crossed the Rhine around Koblenz on 1 August, proceeding along the Moselle to pass the French frontier on 19 August. Expecting France to self-destruct at any moment, Brunswick took time to reduce the powerful **fortresses** in his path. Longwy was invested on 20 August, and surrendered four days later, but allied armies paused before moving on to Verdun, which capitulated on 2 September.

With hostile forces also preparing to invade across the Rhine towards Strasbourg and from Belgium, Paris appeared doomed, but Brunswick's 80,000 men advanced so slowly that Generals **Dumouriez** and the elder **Kellermann** were able to unite between his advanced divisions and halt them at **Valmy** on 20 September. One of the greatest upsets in European military history, Valmy revitalized French popular morale and sent the allied invasion into reverse. Plagued by rain, mud, supply problems and dysentery, Brunswick's army pulled back into the Argonne from 30 September, establishing new positions on the frontier beyond Longwy by 21 October.

Successes at **Nice** in the south and **Lille** in the north had already eased French fears of immediate conquest, and a major victory at **Jemappes** in early November brought northern republican forces to the Dutch frontier. Meanwhile French Rhine sector commanders Kellermann and Custine devoted their energy to quarrelling until the latter was transferred to the Alps. Custine then moved up to Mainz, and took the prosperous city of Frankfurt by late October.

Brunswick advanced 50,000 Prussians to retake Frankfurt (with the help of local residents) on 2 December, and Custine's 30,000 men withdrew across the Rhine to Mainz for the winter. Meanwhile Kellermann's replacement on the Moselle, General Bournonville, was ordered into Luxembourg, where five attacks failed to dislodge **Hohenlohe**'s 10,000 Prussians from Trier between 6 and 15 December, when freezing conditions made further combat impossible.

The Coalition appeared militarily unstoppable by spring 1793: **Great Britain**, Spain, **Portugal** and **Naples** had joined as active members, and British **subsidies** had secured the passive adherence of Russia. On the eastern frontiers, a French invasion of the independent Netherlands was stopped at **Neerwinden**, and Brunswick defeated Custine on 28 March at **Bingen**. Absorbed in strategic differences and wrangles over indemnities, Brunswick made no effort to follow Custine's subsequent retreat to Worms, and settled down to besiege **Mainz**.

Mainz eventually fell on 22 July, just before a belated French relief operation got fully under way. With the reluctant approval of a new French government facing crisis in **Flanders** and rebellion at home, the 40,000 troops of the relieving Army of the Moselle could only withdraw west of the Saar (Sarre). Leaving 6,000 men around Trier, the Army of the Rhine drew south, detaching 10,000 men to patrol the Vosges mountains and deploying 15,000 as an advance guard around Bliescastel.

Brunswick's 100,000 troops east of the Rhine eventually advanced slowly from mid-August, and a victory at **Weissenburg** on 14 October drove the Bliescastel force south to the defence of Strasbourg. The allies then settled down for a winter of strategic disputes and small-scale sieges, but were counter-attacked by reorganized French forces from late November. The Army of the Moselle, advancing east from the Saar under **Hoche**, was unable to take Kaiserslautern on the allied right at the end of November, but helped new Army of the Rhine commander **Pichegru** win a minor triumph at the **Geisberg** (26 December) that sent the squabbling allies back over the Rhine.

The start of campaigning in 1794 saw Möllendorf in command of 60,000 Prussians (and **Saxons**), and the Duke of Saxe-Teschen controlling 35,000 Austrians in the theatre, but command changes brought no vigour to allied operations. Prussian preoccupation with **Poland** was such that only renewed British subsidies prevented Möllendorf from withdrawing his forces altogether, and he remained passive until May, when he crossed the Rhine to exploit the transfer north of **Jourdan**'s 15,000 French troops. Prussian forces took Kaiserslautern on 23 May, prompting a French withdrawal to Bliescastel and the River Queich, but made no attempt to exploit the success. By June both allied contingents in the theatre had effectively ceased operations, and Möllendorf's refusal to aid northern forces defeated by Jourdan at **Fleurus** provoked the suspension of British subsidies.

Suppression of the **Vendée** rebellion freed French reinforcements for the Rhine in June, and by the end of the month front commander Michaud could call on 115,000 troops ranged between the Saar and the Rhine. An offensive aimed at driving the allies east of the Rhine failed on 2 July, but an attack through the **Vosges** Mountains on 13 July split the allied wings, triggering their withdrawal to Mannheim and Worms.

Carnot had also strengthened Moreaux's Army of the Moselle to 24,000 men for a major assault on what was now an allied outpost at Trier, and some 5,000 Prussians abandoned the town on 9 August. Reinforced by **Lebrun**'s 11,000 men from the Ardennes, Moreaux was not counterattacked, but Mihaud was surprised by Hohenlohe's strike at his weakened lines in the Vosges on 17 September, and withdrew to Landstuhl and Spire. Once Mihaud's scattered left wing had reassembled at Pirmasens, the front fell relatively quiet for the rest of the year.

Prussia's withdrawal from the coalition by the Treaty of **Basle** in spring 1795 left about 170,000 Austrian troops along the Rhine, in two armies under **Clairfait** and **Würmser**, facing some 145,000 French troops under Pichegru and Jourdan. Neither side made any serious attempt at attack during the first half of the year, and apart from a successful siege of **Luxembourg**, the next major French offensive in the theatre began in September, opening a season of ultimately fruitless operations either side of the river around **Mannheim**. Both armies were exhausted by the time a mutually agreed local truce took effect on New Year's Day.

Clairfait resigned his command at the start of 1796, but the truce held through a spring dominated by **Napoleon**'s successes on the **Italian** front. New Austrian C-in-C Archduke **Charles** spent the season in painstaking repair of the Rhine army's morale and organization, and French plans for a new offensive by Jourdan and **Moreau** (who had replaced Pichegru) were delayed by shortages of ammunition, equipment and supplies.

Charles was almost ready to advance on the Rhine when he was obliged to detach Würmser and 30,000 troops to meet the crisis in Italy, and it was Jourdan who reopened operations in June, crossing the river to defeat the Austrian northern wing around **Altenkirchen** on 4 June, but suffering a minor defeat at **Ukerath** on 20 June as he retreated in the face of reinforcements.

Moreau's offensive against depleted Austrian forces on the upper Rhine soon compelled Charles to rush his 25,000 reinforcements south again. After a feint at Mannheim, Moreau suddenly swung south to cross the Rhine at **Kehl**, defeating Austrian general Latour at the **Kinzig** on 28 June and at **Rastatt** in early July. Charles reinforced Latour to fight a drawn battle at **Ettlingen** on 9 July, but his remaining forces in the far south retreated after defeat at **Haslach** on 14 July. Charles had by then decided to pull his entire army east to the Danube, abandoning **Württemberg**, **Baden** and a host of minor Rhineland principalities to French conquest. They all made their peace on French terms during the second half of July, and Charles crossed the Danube after the failure of his counter-attack

at **Neresheim** on 11 August. Meanwhile Jourdan profited by his absence to recross the Rhine and drive defenders back from **Forcheim** on 7 August.

With the rest of the Holy Roman Empire clamouring for a negotiated peace, Charles counterattacked. Marching the bulk of his army north, he caught and defeated Jourdan at **Amberg** on 24 August, and intercepted the subsequent French retreat at **Würzburg** on 3 September. Repeated Austrian attacks at the Lahn forced Jourdan's further withdrawal from 17 September, and his right wing began recrossing the Rhine at Neuwied and Bonn on 20 September.

Charles was in no position to exploit his success, because Moreau had defeated Latour's depleted force at **Friedberg** on 24 August, and then threatened Munich before news of Jourdan's retreat prompted a withdrawal from 10 September. While Charles tried to cut off his retreat, Moreau checked Latour's laborious pursuit at **Biberach** in early October, avoided a trap at **Emmendlingen**, and won a defensive victory at **Schliengen** to get safely over the Rhine at Hunningen by 26 October.

After an arduous and ultimately inconclusive campaign had left both armies incapable of further operations, a **Directory** anxious to reinforce Bonaparte's army in Italy offered Vienna an armistice. It was refused, and Charles spent the rest of the year besieging French bridgeheads at Kehl and Hunningen, which fell on 10 January and 5 February respectively.

The Austrian crisis in Italy obliged Charles to quit the front with 30,000 troops in early February 1797, leaving only some 80,000 men guarding the Rhine from Düsseldorf to Basle. They faced Moreau's 60,000 men in the south, and about 70,000 more under Hoche in the north, but both French armies delayed planned offensives until Napoleon's Italian campaign was almost over. Hoche caught Werneck's scattered northern forces in a pincer attack around **Altenkirchen** on 18 April, and Moreau routed Latour's attack at **Diersheim** two days later, but any prospect of significant strategic gain was ended by the Preliminaries of **Leoben**, word of which brought the Rhine campaign to an effective end on 22–23 April.

Rhine, Confederation of the

The coalition of German states and principalities organized by **Napoleon** in July 1806 to replace the politically redundant **Holy Roman Empire**. It initially comprised 16 signatories and eventually incorporated every German state except **Prussia** and **Austria**, including Jérôme **Bonaparte**'s satellite kingdom of **Westphalia**.

The Confederation entailed the absorption of most smaller German states by their larger neighbours, but Napoleon's dynastic, military and fiscal motives for control outweighed any ideological commitment to social change. The **Code Napoléon** was applied to the Confederation from summer 1807, but was seldom imposed in its entirety and is generally regarded as a failure in Germany. There were exceptions – **Bavaria** abolished feudal privileges and established enduring principles of fiscal and judicial equality – but the majority of rulers were unwilling to risk outraging local traditions or established privileges, and if anything the Confederation helped stabilize the position of feudal élites in Germany.

The Confederation's larger states gained a great deal of territory under Napoleonic protection, but were required to provide military and economic support for the French war effort, and alliance with France became increasingly unpopular throughout Germany. In an atmosphere of rising German nationalism, Napoleon faced the possibility of revolt in the Confederation states as early as 1809, and his disastrous **Russian** invasion of 1812 paved the way for mass defection to the allied cause during the campaign for **Germany** in 1813. Bavaria, **Saxony** and **Württemberg**, the three largest fully independent members, changed sides in October, and the Confederation ceased to exist once the French army retreated to the Rhine in November.

Most of the surviving German states were subsequently returned to prewar systems of government, but Napoleon's experiment did have important long-term effects. Most of the smaller German statelets disappeared for ever, and common antipathy towards French control was an important stimulus to future national unification. *See* **Map 21**.

Richery, Joseph de (1757–99)

One of many genuinely poor minor nobles in mid-eighteenth-century **France**, Richery went to sea as a merchant cabin boy before joining the **French Navy** in 1774. Remaining in the service after the **French Revolution**, he was stationed in the **Indian Ocean** at the start of the **Revolutionary Wars**, and was promoted captain in 1793. Recalled and dismissed during the anti-royalist reaction of 1794, he returned to command at Toulon in September 1795, and led that year's successful **convoy** attack off Cape **St Vincent**. Promoted rear-admiral in March 1796, he led seven **ships-of-the-line** and three **frigates** (along with ten **Spanish Navy** battleships) on a highly successful commerce raiding expedition to the British Newfoundland fisheries, reaching the Bay of Bulls on 4 September and sinking or seizing 80 ships. Returning to the Atlantic port of Rochefort in November, he spent the rest of his career under British **blockade**, apart from a brief breakout in December to join the ill-starred **Bantry Bay** expedition.

Ried, Treaty of

Settlement agreed between **Austria** and **Bavaria** on 6 October 1813 that sealed the latter's defection from **Napoleon** to the **Sixth Coalition**. Austria recognized its neighbour's status as an independent kingdom, and was promised the return of territories ceded to Bavaria under duress since 1805.

Rifles

A more sophisticated version of the **musket**, with the inside of the barrel rifled to put spin on the ball, the contemporary rifle was a highly accurate weapon over distances of several hundred metres. Rifles were well known in the eighteenth century, but had been developed for hunting rather than military use, and were not employed in great numbers by armies of the war period. Partly because contemporary **infantry tactics** called for a high rate of fire rather than accuracy, and partly because rifles were relatively slow and costly to produce, their use was largely restricted to specialist marksmen.

First developed in Germany, rifles were most common with **Austrian** and **Prussian** forces, and became an established part of British military culture during the **Peninsular War**, but were never fully accepted by the **French Army**, which issued rifles to light infantry officers (and some NCOs) but withdrew them in 1807. Though sometimes deployed in battalion strength with German and British forces, riflemen were more often attached to infantry units in small numbers. Usually picked as good marksmen, they operated primarily as **snipers** and **skirmishers**, needing to remain hidden whenever possible, and rifles were accordingly designed for loading in a horizontal position. Apart from a few specialist hunting weapons, wartime rifles differed in detail rather than performance, but the mass-produced British Baker Rifle was probably the most common of myriad types used. *See also* **Bayonets**.

Riga, Siege of

Now the capital of independent Latvia, the Baltic port of Riga was part of imperial **Russia**'s Courland province in 1812, and an important supply point for Russian forces defending the road between East Prussia and St Petersburg. Courland was the primary target for the French **Grande Armée**'s northernmost corps, some 30,000 troops under **Macdonald**, during the early stages of the **Russian campaign**, and by the end of July 1812 it had been occupied.

After taking Mitau without a fight and driving scattered Russian formations back into the fortress of Riga, Macdonald was expected to follow up with a rapid thrust in support of **Oudinot**'s corps further south, but instead detached a division east to take Dünaburg and deployed the majority of his force to besiege Riga (*see* **Map 23**). Macdonald's corps comprised General **Yorck**'s 17,000-strong **Prussian Army** contingent and a **Polish** division, along with a few **Bavarian** and **Westphalian** units, so that mistrust of his troops' aggressive intentions may have contributed to his caution, but his main problem was manpower shortage. Once 5,000 troops had been left to garrison the conquered province, and the Poles sent to Dünaburg, fewer than 10,000 men remained to mount the **siege** against 15,000 defending troops led by General Essen (with help from Prussian Colonel **Clausewitz**). Protected by strong fortifications, uninterrupted maritime supply lines and offshore naval support, the garrison faced little real pressure from French forces through the sum-

mer, and although Macdonald eventually concentrated some 27,000 men for the siege during the autumn, their attempts to storm the walls were repelled with relative ease.

After the failure of a final assault, and in the absence of orders from Napoleon, Macdonald abandoned the siege on 19 December and retreated on his own initiative towards Tilsit, but the withdrawal was hindered by the delaying tactics of Prussian formations. Never remotely enthusiastic allies, and subject to a steady fraternization campaign by Russian troops during the siege, Yorck's Prussians had fallen far behind when they allowed themselves to be surrounded and 'captured' by Russian forces on 30 December (*see* Convention of **Tauroggen**). Barely troubled by **Wittgenstein**'s leisurely pursuit, Macdonald and his loyal Poles reached Tilsit to find that **Murat** had led the main French army still further west, and were forced to continue their march to the Vistula, where they met with the remnant of the Grande Armée in mid-January 1813.

Rivoli, Battle of

The engagement, fought east of Lake Garda around the town of Rivoli on 14–15 January 1797, that ended the last Austrian attempt to relieve **Mantua** and recover control of northern Italy during the War of the **First Coalition**. After the defeat of its invasion in late 1796, and the subsequent breakdown of Austro-French peace negotiations, **Alvintzi**'s Austrian army around Bassano was reinforced to 45,000 men. French C-in-C **Napoleon** could call on almost 55,000 troops in the new year, backed by a re-equipped **artillery** arm, but almost half were stationed in garrisons or besieging Mantua. The rest of his army was deployed to guard the major routes north into Austria on either bank of Lake Garda, at Verona and on the lower Adige.

Alvintzi launched a new, three-pronged offensive from the north early in the new year. Sending 6,000 men against Verona, and **Provera**'s 9,000 towards Mantua via the lower Adige, he led some 28,000 troops against **Joubert**'s 10,000 on the upper Adige. Provera drove **Augereau**'s forward units back on Legnano from 8 January, and Napoleon heard the news on 11 November. Rushing to Verona to find the city under attack, he delayed any definite response until 13 November, when news of Alvintzi's movements confirmed the focus of Austrian operations. Leaving 3,000 men to hold Verona, Napoleon led the rest of his army north to join Joubert's defence at Rivoli.

Alvintzi was slowly preparing to advance on Rivoli in six coordinated columns and attack French positions from all directions. Napoleon reached the battle zone ahead of **Masséna**'s division in the small hours of 14 November, in time to organize defence of the plateau north of Rivoli and launch a dawn strike against Austrian forces gathering in front of it. Joubert's attack enjoyed early success against the Austrian left, but slowed after an Austrian attack forced Napoleon to commit reserves to the other end of the line. Joubert was then outflanked by Quasdanovich and his division, which took the village of San Marco by eleven o'clock.

As Masséna's troops came into line, Napoleon risked attack from the north by turning Joubert's entire force east to repel the threat, and then rushed it back to the plateau for an attack on the Austrian centre and right. Thoroughly outwitted but not quite beaten, Alvintzi kept his battered forces in position overnight, while Napoleon departed for Verona with Masséna's division. Joubert led French attacks at Rivoli next morning, driving the three Austrian columns to the north into full retreat towards La Corona. Cut off by pursuit forces under Vial and **Murat**, they suffered another 5,000 casualties making their escape back up the Adige, bringing total Austrian losses over the two days to 14,000 men, including 11,000 prisoners.

Robespierre, Maximilien de (1758–94)

The moving spirit behind the radical takeover of French republican government in 1793–4, and briefly effective dictator of **France**, Robespierre was born in the north-eastern French town of Arras and came to Paris as a deputy for the Third Estate in 1789. Attaching himself to the radical left, his passionate commitment to revolutionary ideals and theatrical oratory won mass popular acclaim. Strong on martyrdom and purification, he was a natural choice as the Assembly's public accuser in 1791.

He resigned the post in April 1792 in protest at a war he expected would lead to dictatorship, but was chief spokesman for the left-wing 'Mountain' in the **National Convention**, and the dominant figure in the **Jacobin** Club in 1793.

Mobilizing mass support against the moderate Girondins, he took control of the Legislature when they were driven from office in early June, and joined the Committee of **Public Safety** in July.

Using denunciation and arrest to secure the executions of Hébert, **Danton** and their supporters by April 1794, he wielded unchallenged power at the centre for the next three months, developing legislative mechanisms to intensify the **Terror** and increasing the pace of executions. Rapid loss of popularity was compounded by the grandiose introduction in May of a new 'rational' state religion, the Cult of the Supreme Being, and mounting political hostility came to a head in late July, when he was overthrown by the **Thermidor coup**. A genuine ideologue, he greeted his downfall as a necessary part of the revolutionary process and made no attempt to rouse the masses in his defence. He was executed on 28 July 1794, along with chief disciple St Just and 20 others.

Rockets *See* **Congreve Rockets**

Roer, Battle of the

French attack on 2 October 1794 against Austrian positions behind the River Roer, about 40km west of Bonn and Cologne. Austrian forces under **Clairfait** had withdrawn east to the Roer in late September, after being driven back from **Ayvaille** by French commander **Jourdan**'s opening attack of the autumn. Jourdan ignored war minister **Carnot**'s instruction to pause until the fall of Maastricht in his rear, and concentrated about 100,000 troops against the Roer early on 2 October. General **Championnet** took Aldenhoven in the centre, before joining **Lefebvre** for a successful attack on Linnich, but destruction of the nearby bridge prevented them from crossing the river that day. **Kléber**'s French left wing eventually silenced well-placed Austrian **artillery** on the far bank before his two divisions (**Ney** and **Bernadotte**) swam the river to take their immediate targets. On the French right, **Schérer** forced Latour's defenders to retreat across the river at about seven in the evening. While French forces spent the night building bridges, Clairfait ordered his army east across the Rhine, finally ending any pretence at Austrian defence of **Flanders** and the Low Countries. *See* **Map 2**.

Rolica, Battle of

The first set-piece engagement fought by British forces in the **Peninsular War**, a successful attack of 16 August 1808 by General **Wellesley**'s expeditionary force on a smaller French detachment sent to delay its advance towards Lisbon. It was a very minor triumph, but its importance was inflated by contemporary British **propaganda**, reflecting the paucity of the **British Army**'s achievements elsewhere.

Wellesley and 9,500 men had landed on 1 August at the mouth of the Mondego River, about 110km north of Lisbon, and were joined by 5,000 troops from Cadiz before moving south on 10 August. Regional French commander **Junot** responded by sending 4,400 troops under General Delaborde to pin the British down until reinforcements arrived.

The two forces met just north of Obidos on 15 August, when Wellesley's vanguard ran into Delaborde's main positions after an outpost skirmish at Acobaça. French troops withdrew south to a line in front of Rolica, where Wellesley launched a pincer attack next morning, but Delaborde pulled back to a ridge just beyond the village. A second pincer attack overran outnumbered French forces by late afternoon, but only after one column had advanced ahead of schedule, triggering an unplanned assault on the French centre. Delaborde withdrew, having lost about 600 men and inflicted 479 casualties, while Wellesley moved on towards a meeting with Junot at Vimeiro. *See* **Map 22**.

Roman Republic *See* **Papal States**

Romana, Pedro de la (1761–1811)

One of the younger and better Spanish generals of the period, Romana fought on the eastern sector of the **Pyrenean** front during the War of the **First Coalition**, and in 1807 was given command of the Spanish corps attached to **Bernadotte**'s French forces in northern Europe. In response to Spanish appeals for British aid against French invasion in summer 1808, the **Royal Navy** evacuated the corps from Gothenberg and pitched it into the **Peninsular War**, where it linked up with General **Blake**'s Army of Galicia. Romana eventually commanded the Army of Galicia's defeated remnant at León. Appointed to the Supreme Junta at Seville in 1809, Romana led a Spanish army operating in **Portugal** from 1810 until his death.

Roncevalles Pass, Battle of the

One of two battles fought for control of the north-west Pyrenean passes on 25 July 1813, and the last clear French success of the **Peninsular War**. After victory at **Vitoria** in June had brought his army to the Pyrenees, **Wellington** stretched his forces along an 80km front, and sent detachments to besiege **San Sebastian** and **Pamplona**. Recognizing the limits of allied resources, French C-in-C **Soult** launched attacks against both the **Maya** and Roncesvalles passes. Some 40,000 men, the majority of his strike force, accompanied Soult to Roncesvalles, held by 13,000 allied troops under General **Cole**.

French columns under **Reille** and **Clausel** advanced along plateaux either side of the best road through the pass from six in the morning on 25 July. Reille's wing bypassed a Spanish division on the western side and advanced about 6km to Linduz, where it was held by two allied brigades until halted completely by thick late-afternoon fog. On the eastern side, Clausel was held up for four hours by 2,000 men of General Byng's British brigade, but eventually forced them out of excellent defensive positions and back to Altobiscar before the fog set in. Cole's outnumbered troops still held good positions, but he ignored orders to hold them and withdrew towards Pamplona that evening. Pursued by Soult, he took up new positions on 27 July around **Sorauren**, where he was joined by Wellington for a stand next day. *See* **Map 5**.

Rosas, Siege of (1794–5)

Laborious French attack during the winter of 1794–5 on the east **Pyrenean** frontier port of Rosas, garrisoned by 4,000 troops and home to Admiral Gravina's 13 Spanish **ships-of-the-line**. French commander **Pérignon** moved on Rosas after his capture of **Figueras** in November 1794, but freezing conditions slowed **siege** operations and the town's outer defences only fell on 31 January. Offered no help by Spanish troops at the River Fluvia to the south, garrison and naval forces evacuated the town on the night of 2–3 February, just after French **artillery** had opened a first significant breach in the main walls. *See* **Map 5**.

Roskilde, Battle of

Action, also known as the Battle of Kjöge, fought on 29 August 1807 between British forces investing **Copenhagen** and General Castenkiold's much smaller **Danish Army** detachment. Lord **Cathcart's** 30,000 troops had been landed on the coast of **Denmark** in early August to enforce British seizure of the Danish fleet, and were primarily engaged in surrounding the city. While the **Royal Navy's** warships menaced Copenhagen harbour, **Wellesley's** British reserve division was sent in pursuit of Castenkiold's 5,000 troops, Denmark's only standing army at large. Caught near Roskilde, some 20km east of the capital, Castenkiold was forced to surrender after simultaneous British attacks from the front and rear. Won at little British cost, the action distinguished Wellesley's first European command as a success, and removed any danger of practical interference with British coercive measures. *See* **Map 18**.

Rothschild, Mayer Amschel

(1743–1812)

The founder of the great Jewish financial dynasty was established in Frankfurt, as principal banker to the Prince of **Hesse-Cassel**, at the start of the **Revolutionary Wars**. Exploiting the desperate need for loans facing all the main belligerents (and a large number of smaller states), Rothschild and his sons expanded their interests into Europe's major capitals as purveyors of **war finance**. Among many commissions, they arranged the transactions of British **subsidies** to European rulers, transferred funds to the **Peninsular** theatre on London's behalf, and controlled the borrowing policy of bankrupt **Denmark**.

Roundshot

The most basic and common type of **artillery** ammunition, a solid cast metal ball, of weight and size depending on the cannon, that was designed simply to smash through whatever it hit.

Roveredo, Battle of

The opening engagement of the **Italian campaign** in autumn 1796, fought on 4 September around Roveredo, in the foothills of the Tyrolean Alps some 50km south of Trent (*see* **Map 6**). Following instructions from the **Directory** government, **Napoleon** led 33,000 troops up the River Adige towards Trent from late August. His Austrian counterpart, **Würmser**, divided his army to meet the threat, leading 20,000 troops down the River Brenta to get across Napoleon's line of retreat, and leaving 25,000 men under General Davidovich to defend the road to Trent. Davidovich drew up 14,000 troops in positions between the village of Marco and the road junction at Roveredo, where they were attacked by **Masséna's** 10,000 men on 4 September. While a brigade threatened the Austrian flank, Masséna's frontal attack overwhelmed the position with relative ease, sustaining perhaps 200 casualties and taking 6,000 prisoners. Davidovich withdrew survivors into the mountains, and Trent was occupied by French forces next day. Leaving 10,000 troops to watch for any counter-attack from the Tyrol, Napoleon marched the rest of his army down the Brenta in pursuit of Würmser.

Royal Navy

The naval service of **Great Britain** was by far the most powerful and efficient in the late eighteenth-century world. It could call on a total of 175 **ships-of-the-line**, 146 **frigates** and 120 **sloops** in 1790, along with hundreds of smaller or specialist craft, and most of its ships were in fairly good condition. Its crews, a third of them **press gang** victims, were the healthiest, most competent and least discontented in Europe, while its officer corps reflected a long national tradition of seafaring excellence. Generally speaking, the navy displayed a level of *esprit de corps* rivalled only in the much smaller **Dutch Navy** (and later in the **US Navy**), and enjoyed significantly better dockyard facilities than its rivals.

As sword and shield of the expanding British Empire, the Royal Navy was required to perform an enormous variety of tasks on a global basis. Its main battle fleets were expected to protect vital trade routes from, and possessions in, the **Mediterranean**, the **West Indies** and the **Indian Ocean** (especially in **India** itself, though the East India Company maintained its own fleet of small trade-protection warships), as well as sustaining a worldwide web of smaller **colonial** outposts.

Closer to home, the Channel Fleet was charged with protecting Britain's vast coastline from interference or invasion, and stood ready to intervene in the Baltic should trade or vital raw materials supplies be threatened. British warships were also expected to blockade hostile coastlines or ports, function as the principal communications link throughout the empire, and provide support for any overseas military or diplomatic initiatives.

With crew requirements rising from 15,000 in 1792 to 120,000 by 1797, and peaking at 140,000 in 1812–13, the navy was always short of manpower, but suffered less in that respect than most other European forces. Unlike all of its rivals, it was also able to rely on sufficient funding to keep its fleets in good fighting condition. The cost of building and repairing ships, along with the business of maintaining food, water, spares, raw materials, ammunition and other necessities for several hundred men at sea for several months, was enormous by contemporary standards. Total navy budgets in 1792 were almost £4 million (comparable with the entire national budget of the **Netherlands**), and spiralled in wartime to hold steady at close to £25 million per year after 1805, about an eighth of national expenditure. Funds were supplied by an annual government grant subject to parliamentary consent.

Navy budgets occasioned no serious popular or political opposition in a nation that understood (sometimes even exaggerated) the importance of naval power to its safety and prosperity. The most successful war in Britain's history, the Seven Years War (1756–63), had been won by the navy, and its strategy of **blockade** tactics backed by colonial aggression was expected to triumph again in any future war. This confidence worked against any serious expansion of the **British Army**, generally regarded as a secondary force for use in colonial policing or home defence, and bred complacency. By early 1793, when Britain joined the **First Coalition** against France, thirty-year-old tactics and strategies had been enshrined as orthodoxy, and the expectation of painless victory ingrained in popular, professional and political attitudes.

Britain only had 25 ships-of-the-line ready for action in early 1793, but a temporary shortfall of crews and materials was not perceived as dangerous. Most of the other important navies were aligned against France, and the **French Navy's** post-revolutionary disorganization had rendered it incapable of any major offensive action. By the late autumn, a total of 84 battleships were in service, including 24 in the Channel, the same number in the Mediterranean, 12 in the West Indies and two dozen in reserve, putting the **Pitt** government in position to launch an offensive strategy.

Instead it tried to launch several strategies at once, asking the navy to blockade France, sweep up French colonies around the world, destroy French shipping and support a variety of military adventures, but not focusing resources on any one ambition. Extended beyond efficiency, and hidebound by its tactical traditions, the navy repeatedly proved its technical superiority over all-comers during the next five years, but failed to capitalize on early French weakness and isolation. From 1795, military decisions and alliances left it increasingly isolated and threatened all over Europe, until by late 1796 it found itself fighting a defensive war.

Victories in minor actions aside, the capture of **Toulon** by Admiral **Hood**'s growing Mediterranean Fleet in August 1793 was the navy's first great success, but failure to hold the port ultimately provided the French republic with a famous victory and left it with a serviceable fleet. The navy's lack of bases in the Mediterranean was addressed with the painstaking capture of **Corsica** in 1794, but lax blockades enabled the French fleet to continue an effective campaign against British **convoys**. The navy's greatest success in European waters, **Howe**'s acclaimed **First of June** victory over **Villaret**'s Brest Fleet in 1794, was a poorly exploited tactical triumph and a strategic defeat, enabling a vital French grain convoy to slip into port while it was taking place. Further afield, a fleet under **Jervis** enjoyed predictable early success in the West Indies, but its conquests were short-lived and its absence was keenly felt on European blockade stations. Meanwhile opportunities to inflict another defeat on French fleets in their home waters were missed at **Leghorn**, Ile de **Groix** and the **Hyères Islands** in 1795.

The failures of cautious men like **Hotham** and the **Hood** brothers hastened important front-line command changes, but soon came home to roost. French alliances with the **Netherlands** and **Spain** in July 1795 forced the Royal Navy to deploy a fleet against the Dutch in the North

Sea, and effectively doubled its Mediterranean and Atlantic commitments. Too stretched to offer more than limited assistance to allied ground forces during the following year's **Italian campaign**, the Mediterranean Fleet was forced to abandon Leghorn (Livorno), Elba and Corsica in the wake of **Napoleon's** spring conquests. With no other major bases east of Gibraltar, new commander Jervis could only withdraw from the theatre altogether in December.

Its fortunes hardly affected by the progress of another successful offensive in the West Indies, the navy was reduced to occasional Mediterranean forays from Gibraltar or Lisbon, and French fleets were able to continue their predatory raids against British convoys (*see* Action off St Vincent). Offensive potential was further stifled by the need to secure the Channel against French preparations for the invasion of **England**. For the first time in many decades, the navy found itself facing criticism at home from nervous opposition politicians and newspapers.

The illusion of facing a genuinely threatening combination of naval forces was short-lived. Failure at **Bantry Bay** re-emphasized the French Navy's offensive weakness, and **Pellew's** extraordinary destruction of the *Droits de l'Homme* suggested its competence was still declining. The reality behind any Dutch or Spanish naval challenge was exposed in 1797, Jervis demolishing the Spaniards at **St Vincent** in June, and **Duncan** disposing of the Dutch at **Camperdown** in October. Both victors displayed a determination to inflict total defeat on their opponents that reflected important changes in British naval attitudes and practice.

Command at sea was being carried out with a new vigour. Jervis had turned the Mediterranean Fleet into a formidable fighting force capable of enforcing effective blockades and winning decisive battles. Though mutinies by home fleets at **Spithead** and the **Nore** gave a startled British people a glimpse into the abyss of naval collapse in 1797, their overall effects were beneficial. Mutineers did not, as many feared, hoist flags of republican revolution, but issued a timely reminder of their indispensability in the process of winning concessions that enhanced service reliability.

Admiral **Nelson's** crushing defeat of French

forces at the **Nile** (1 August 1798) was Britain's most strategically important contribution to the **Second Coalition**. It re-established Britain's Mediterranean dominance at a stroke, but once more left the navy with too many responsibilities. By the start of 1799, overall strength had risen to 192 ships-of-the-line, 25 old 50-gunners no longer considered as line ships, 226 frigates and 345 sloops or similar vessels, yet Mediterranean forces were barely strong enough to handle a sudden torrent of extra duties.

Along with the usual blockades and trade protection tasks, its warships were needed in **Egypt**, **Malta**, the **Ionian Islands**, **Naples**, **Minorca** and along the eastern Mediterranean coasts. Although Jervis and his successor, **Keith**, managed to achieve all their basic objectives in the theatre, enforcing blockades with increasing severity and restricting the effects of French sorties like '**Bruix's Cruise**', they could not fulfil any strategic offensive role.

The story was broadly the same on other fronts. A series of ill-planned combined raids failed against **Ostende**, **Ferrol** and **Cadiz**, while other sideshow victories masked strategic failure. French naval forces aiding the 1798 **Irish Rebellion** were intercepted and defeated; Nelson confirmed his status as the navy's hero at **Copenhagen**; Admiral **Saumarez** won a small victory over Franco-Spanish units at **Algeciras**; and the accumulation of French, Spanish and Dutch colonies continued apace. Though all contributed to the steady erosion of morale among its enemies, the navy still was not winning the war, and the Anglo-French **Amiens** peace of 1801 found it still defending Britain's coastlines against possible invasion.

Though the navy was rapidly scaled down from 1802, and was far from ready when war resumed in 1803, its opponents had slipped deeper into decay, and the blockade system was reinstituted within days of war being declared on 16 May. With Jervis now installed as First Lord of the Admiralty, 40 new 74-gunners were put under construction, and naval **artillery** standardized. Both measures encouraged a steady widening of the gap between the British and other European services during a second decade of warfare that saw the Royal Navy assume total and unchallenged control of the world's sea lanes.

The new war began with a familiar reclamation of colonial prizes in the West Indies, but reached its naval climax quickly. The mass escape of French and Spanish fleets to the Caribbean in the early summer of 1805, in line with **Napoleon**'s determination to decoy the British away from defence of the Channel, culminated in their Combined Fleet's virtual annihilation by Nelson at **Trafalgar** on 21 October. Coming just before Napoleon's almost equally conclusive land victory over the **Third Coalition** at **Austerlitz**, Trafalgar ended any serious threat to the navy from hostile battlefleets for the rest of the century.

The navy had in effect won its war by the end of 1805, and fought no more great battles during the next decade. Having defined the limits of French imperial expansion, ended the threat of invasion, and established a slow but unbreakable stranglehold on the Napoleonic economy, naval strategists cast about for the best way to make use of supreme power.

The struggle with the French Navy, reduced to picking off its periodic attempts to use battleship squadrons as commerce raiders, brought minor victories at **Santo Domingo** and the **Basque Roads**, but was otherwise largely confined to trade warfare as British blockades competed with Napoleon's multinational **Continental System**.

Several attempts at strategic intervention elsewhere meanwhile brought little reward: part of **Collingwood**'s chronically over-extended Mediterranean Fleet forced a passage through the **Dardanelles** to Constantinople in spring 1807, but withdrew without achieving anything tangible; an improvement in combined operations with the army was discernible in the ruthless success of a punitive attack on **Copenhagen** in the summer; and the presence of a small fleet in the Baltic to aid **Sweden** during the **Russo-Swedish War** of 1808–9 made very little difference to the outcome. Only the navy's excellent, if unspectacular, work supporting military efforts in the **Peninsular War** (1808–14) made an important direct contribution to Napoleon's eventual defeat.

Small-scale conflicts formed a constant backdrop to the navy's strategic efforts up to 1815. Most sprang from its role as global trade policeman, and although hundreds of **privateers** and small warships were captured or destroyed, along with a respectable haul of merchant prizes, British ships were generally less successful against well-organized and motivated light forces. The remnants of the **Danish Navy** held their own throughout the **Gunboat War** of 1807–14, and British warships met their only conclusive defeats against US Navy frigates and light forces during the **Anglo-American War** of 1812–15.

American sea power was to develop a world role in the late nineteenth century, but the oceans belonged to the Royal Navy in 1815. It had grown stronger in relation to all its rivals and, with the benefit of a few minor reforms, its administrative machinery had orchestrated 22 years of global war without serious breakdown. As such, the British Navy was both the most successful armed force of the period (the **French Army** being its only real rival) and the defining institution of the age. *See* **Naval Warfare; Maps 18, 19.**

Ruffin, François Amable (1771–1811)

A volunteer with the revolutionary **French Army** in 1792, Ruffin began the War of the **First Coalition** as a captain on the **Flanders** front, achieving rapid promotion to battalion command before moving to the **Rhine** with **Jourdan**'s staff. He returned to the Rhine under **Ney** in 1799, serving through the campaign against the **Second Coalition** and fighting at **Hohenlinden** in 1800. A brigadier-general from February 1805, he was with **Oudinot**'s corps during the campaigns of 1805–7, fighting at **Austerlitz** and **Friedland**. Sent to the **Peninsular** theatre as a divisional general in 1808, he served under **Victor** at **Somosierra** and **Talavera**, but was wounded at **Barrosa** in spring 1811, and died in captivity a few weeks later.

Russia

The Russian Empire had been ruled by the head of the Romanov dynasty as tsar since 1613, and was a true autocracy, governed by the monarch without a formal cabinet, full-time ministers or any form of consultative body. The military successes of Peter the Great had helped establish the Romanovs among Europe's most secure rulers, and Russia had emerged from centuries of isolation into the orbit of western European diplomacy by the time he died in 1725.

The estimated 37.5 million people living in

'European Russia' west of the Urals by the late eighteenth century included Finns, Poles, Germans, Slavs, Caucasians and many smaller ethnic groups. Most were engaged in agricultural labour as serfs on private estates, or as 'state peasants' under slightly less restrictive terms on royal lands. The majority were Orthodox Christians, but displayed a semi-religious loyalty to the tsar as their 'little Father' under God.

Romanov supremacy was not seriously threatened by periodic peasant uprisings or palace coups during the early eighteenth century, and relative internal stability provided the platform for an expansionist drive during the reign of **Catherine** the Great, who took power in 1762. Catherine's principal targets were the declining frontier powers of **Sweden**, **Poland** and the **Ottoman Empire**, and her annexation of the Crimea in 1783 was an undisguised prelude to further expansion. Though her ambitions were threatened and resources stretched by simultaneous wars against Sweden and the Turks in the late 1780s, at a time of bad harvests and drought, alliance with **Austria** helped turn the tide in the south during 1789, and the eventual Russo-Turkish Peace of Jassy (January 1792) brought the imperial frontier up to the Dniester.

Territorial expansion fuelled Russia's rapid development from an almost landlocked, largely subsistence economy into a major European trading power. Russia's merchant fleet multiplied eightfold in the eight years after 1775 to become a major player in the Baltic markets, and had begun making its presence felt in both the Black Sea and the eastern **Mediterranean** by the 1780s. Pockets of industrial development had grown up for military purposes around the major cities, of which St Petersburg (220,000 people in 1800) and Moscow (250,000) were far and away the largest, but iron remained the only important non-agricultural export.

Russia's diplomatic position among the **great powers** of Europe in the early 1790s was dominated by direct territorial rivalries with Austria and **Prussia**. Potential disputes with **France** over their mutual ambitions in the eastern Mediterranean had been soothed by a Black Sea trade agreement in January 1787, and increasingly close relations reflected the slow breakdown of Anglo-Russian friendship. A major Baltic trade

rival, and a sponsor of increased Prussian influence in northern Germany, **Great Britain** treated Russia's territorial appetite as an affront to the balance of power it sought to preserve, and the **Pitt** government's failed attempt to force Catherine into a moderate peace with Turkey brought the two states close to war in spring 1791.

Once an armistice with Turkey had been agreed on her own terms, Catherine was free to reassert control over Poland, where a rebellion had installed a provisional independent government in May 1791. Outraged condemnation of the **French Revolution**, financial support for **émigrés**, and passive adherence to the **First Coalition** (finalized by British subsidies in March 1793) did not prevent an invasion of Poland as soon as hostilities were under way on the eastern French frontiers (*see* **Russo-Polish War**). Partly because years of frontier war had exhausted her finances, Catherine rejected repeated requests for military assistance against France, and concentrated on partitioning Poland until 1795.

Catherine began planning the conquest of Persia, Afghanistan and Turkey after a third partition had disposed of Poland, but French success in the **Italian campaigns** of 1796 persuaded her to maintain the balance of power by supporting Austria. Preparations were under way to send 64,000 troops to Italy when she died on 17 November 1796, but her successor, **Paul I**, immediately aborted **Suvorov**'s mission to Italy and ended **Russian Navy** cooperation with British **blockade** forces.

The mentally unstable Paul's refusal to translate vehement anti-French sentiment into action may have been a means of annoying his dead mother. Many of the practices and institutions employed by Catherine were abolished, the **Russian Army** was remodelled along deeply anachronistic lines, and some 12,000 military or bureaucratic officials were dismissed. A dramatic upsurge in internal unrest also argued against foreign adventure, with peasant risings affecting 32 Russian provinces from 1795 to 1798, as did a danger that any army sent abroad would be contaminated by radical ideology. Prussian neutrality from 1795 was a further restraining factor, as were a 215 million rouble national debt and a budget deficit of some 23 million roubles in 1796.

Paul's first important foreign initiative was an attempt to mediate a European peace in spring 1797, but it was pre-empted by the Preliminaries of **Leoben** in April 1797, and he finally abandoned his peacemaking efforts after the Austro-French Peace of **Campo Formio**. The treaty gave France control of the **Ionian Islands**, threatening Russian interests in the eastern Mediterranean, and Paul's immediate response was an alliance with the knights ruling **Malta** (29 November 1797). France was also believed to be planning aid for Polish nationalists, and the existence of **Polish forces** already in French service helped convince Paul by early 1798 that France had become a dangerous and greedy potential enemy on two fronts.

French preparations for the **Middle East** expedition were viewed in St Petersburg as the preamble to any one of several anti-Russian operations, prompting diplomatic overtures to Constantinople in April, and resumption of co-operation with the **Royal Navy** from 3 May. French seizure of Malta triggered mobilization of the Black Sea fleet pending a formal appeal for help from the Turkish government, and 11,000 troops were moved up to the Ottoman frontier at the Dniester. Turkish willingness to cooperate, and the news that **Napoleon** had landed in distant **Egypt**, encouraged plans for a joint offensive against the Ionian Islands, carried out from October 1798.

Paul played a major role in the formation of the **Second Coalition** against France, committing troops to the **Italian campaign**, the **Swiss** front and an Anglo-Russian invasion of **North Holland** in 1799. Although Suvorov's army won its opening actions, allied military fortunes declined rapidly after the summer. Disillusioned with the performance of his allies, and especially infuriated by British attempts to capture Malta, Paul withdrew from the Coalition in December 1799.

Paul now embarked on an anti-British crusade, organizing a second **Armed Neutrality** league of Baltic powers against British blockade, opening talks with Napoleon in January 1800, and ordering an army of 20,000 **Cossacks** from Orenburg into an invasion of **India** in early 1801. Devastated by bad weather en route, the Cossacks never reached the Indian frontier, and the Armed Neutrality league was already collapsing when Paul was assassinated by palace conspirators during the night of 23–24 March.

Heavily implicated in his father's murder, new tsar **Alexander** I began his reign by restoring many of Catherine's administrative practices and personnel. He experimented with liberal ideas early in his reign, undertaking a series of meetings with young advisers **Czartoryski**, Stroganov, Korchubey and Novosiltsov (otherwise known as the Unofficial Committee) aimed at formulating constitutional reforms, but making only limited practical progress. Something like a cabinet system of government was adopted from 8 September 1802, when eight ministries meeting in council replaced boards of appointed experts as the tsar's chief advisers, though their nominal responsibility to a senate of notables meant little in practice. A Free Labourers Law, passed on 20 February 1803, made provision for noble landlords to emancipate their serfs, but was not taken up with much enthusiasm and probably freed fewer than 50,000 labourers, most of them in the prosperous Baltic provinces.

Alexander's interest in internal reform was interrupted by the pressure of international affairs. Shah Fath Ali's active opposition to Russian annexation of Georgia (1800) prompted an invasion of Persia in 1804, beginning a war along the Caspian coast and in the Caucasus that lasted until the Treaty of Gulistan, signed on 12 October 1813, ceded all Transcaucasia to Russia on a permanent basis.

This minor diversion was dwarfed by another war against France, as Alexander's initial admiration for Napoleon turned to outraged disapproval and he joined the **Third Coalition** on 11 April 1805. His armies were defeated at **Austerlitz**, and again at **Friedland** when he fought in a **Fourth Coalition** with Prussia, and Alexander could only agree an alliance with Napoleon at **Tilsit** in 1807. Meanwhile forceful Ottoman repression of independence movements in Wallachia and Moldavia provoked Russian intervention in late 1806, opening the six-year **Russo-Turkish War** in the region.

Tilsit failed to resolve the basic issues undermining Franco-Russian relations, leaving room for rivalry in the Middle East (despite a token French attempt to mediate in the Russo-Turkish dispute in August 1807) and mutual suspicion along the new common frontier in Prussian Poland, now the French puppet Duchy of **Warsaw**. The treaty also tied Russia to Napoleon's **Continental System** of trade warfare against Britain, sowing the seeds of mutual exasperation in the future and having an immediately damaging effect on Baltic trade. The alliance did leave Alexander free to pursue outstanding territorial claims in the north, and the **Russo-Swedish War** of 1808–9 added Finland to his empire.

Peace with France also signalled a revival of attempts at limited social reform. Guided by the increasingly influential **Speranski** from 1809, Alexander began a process of legal codification and considered bureaucratic reforms aimed at establishing promotion on merit. Speranski's most ambitious project – a new constitution based around an appointed Council of State, an executive of ministers, an independent judiciary and (largely powerless) elected assemblies – aroused opposition from a powerful conservative faction at court, as did a series of parallel reforms of the army instigated from 1810 by war minister **Barclay de Tolly**. Though the Council of State was formally established from 1 January 1810, the tsar was driven into the arms of francophobe conservatives as the alliance with Napoleon began to crumble, dismissing Speranski and other reforming ministers on 17 March 1812.

The Franco-Russian alliance had been confirmed in autumn 1808 at **Erfurt**, but relations had reached breaking point by late 1811, and war seemed inevitable by April 1812, when Alexander set impossible preconditions for adherence to the Continental System. Alexander had secured his other frontiers with a Swedish alliance at **St Petersburg** (9 April) and the Peace of **Bucharest** with Turkey (28 May) by the time Napoleon's army's invaded Russia in June 1812, and negotiations with Britain matured into an alliance in July (*see* War of the **Sixth Coalition**).

The arduous and ultimately triumphant **Russian campaign** of 1812 took an enormous toll of the empire's economic resources, devastating prime agricultural lands in the west and wrecking a system of **war finances** hitherto based on taxation. Aware that the French armies could not sustain their long-range occupation indefinitely, the tsar never seriously considered offer-

ing Napoleon the peace terms he was expecting, and the invasion galvanized his subjects into a similarly stern response. The spontaneous formation of **guerrilla** units behind French lines was a manifestation of popular patriotism, devotion to the tsar and determination to expel the invader. Far from seeking political 'liberation' at the hands of Napoleon, Russian soldiers and civilians displayed the same blind loyalty throughout the campaign, whether under fire or occupation.

The process of driving the French from the empire, and subsequent Russian campaigns in **Germany** and **France** during 1813–14, assumed the characteristics of a personal crusade for the tsar. He was the most determined among allied leaders pressing for complete destruction of the Napoleonic order, and his aggression was underpinned by a growing commitment to religious mysticism, which in turn informed an increasingly conservative political outlook.

As part of a successful campaign to secure allied recognition of Russian control at the Congress of **Vienna**, Alexander was careful to treat conquered Poland with consideration, forbidding reprisals against Napoleonic collaborators and granting the province an experimental constitution in November 1815. Once established as Grand Duke of a semi-autonomous 'Congress Poland', Alexander sponsored the **Holy Alliance** of European monarchs, a declaration of conservative intent that couched royal responsibilities in religious terms, and formed a blueprint for the rest of his reign.

Controlling influence over postwar government policy passed to the veteran **Arakcheyev**, who presided over a decade of reaction, repressing political opposition among nobles and military officers demanding constitutional reform and the end of serfdom. Faced with the need to cut military expenditure after the peace, but also by a requirement to protect expanding frontiers, Arakcheyev developed the system of 'military colonies', settling troops in frontier territories as farmers or cottage manufacturers. Though its long-term socio-economic effects have provoked controversy ever since, the policy contributed to a recovery of both agriculture and trade by the early 1820s. *See* **Maps 1, 23, 30**.

Russian Army

Charged with protecting and extending the tsar's vast dominions, and involved in regular frontier conflicts with **Sweden**, **Poland** and the **Ottoman Empire**, the army of imperial **Russia** was the most consistently active land force in Europe at the start of the **Revolutionary Wars**. Able to draw on a population of almost 44 million by the turn of the century, it raised most of its recruits and conscripts from the sprawling class of rural serfs.

Service was for life until 1793, after which the term was reduced to 25 years, and **conscription** took the form of imperial levies imposed at the tsar's pleasure. Some years passed with no levy, but there were three in 1812, and the call-up might demand anything from one man in every 250 on the imperial tax rolls (producing about 50,000 recruits) to one man in 20.

Manpower reserves were extended in 1806–7, and on a larger scale in 1812, by formation of **Opelchenie** militia forces drawn from the unconscripted peasantry, and the French invasion of 1812 also brought uncounted irregulars under arms as partisan **guerrillas**. Regular Russian forces were particularly distinguished by the large numbers of **cavalry** they deployed. For the 1805 campaign some 50,000 mounted regulars were augmented by 77,000 enlisted **Cossack** light cavalry, and thousands more Cossack irregulars took part in the defensive campaign of 1812.

An illiterate army accustomed to poverty and obedience was cheap to feed and house, and ordinary soldiers displayed a deep religious faith, closely entwined with tsar and motherland, that contributed to a renowned capacity for endurance. Commanders often won great loyalty by spending a lifetime with one regiment, but the army of the 1790s employed what was by reputation the least competent officer corps among the **great powers**. Most junior officers came untrained and illiterate from the minor land-owning gentry, and senior command was largely restricted to the empire's bloated aristocracy, providing lifetime sinecures for high-born amateurs. Imperial expansion had brought an increasing number of relatively competent foreign officers into senior posts by the 1790s, but they were a divisive influence, generating mistrust among native Russians.

The army possessed no staff organization or overall guide to tactics before 1796. The largest permanent formation was the regiment, and large-scale manoeuvres were dogged by incoherence, while transport, commissary and **medical** services were primitive at best, non-existent at worst. Criminal profiteering among civilian suppliers was rampant even by contemporary standards.

The army's training and operational techniques had undergone some modernization under **Catherine II** in the early 1790s, and it performed well enough during the 1792 **Russo-Polish War**, but the accession of **Paul I** in 1796 brought a sudden return to the outdated **infantry tactics** of Frederick the Great. Reflecting the influence of Paul's favourite officer, General **Arakcheyev**, they were ignored by many individual commanders, and by **Suvorov** when he returned to senior command in the 1799 **Italian campaign**.

More positive reforms got under way once **Alexander I** replaced Paul in 1801. The peacetime infantry arm was steadily expanded, until by 1805 it comprised 77 line infantry regiments and 13 of élite **grenadiers** (a total of about 200,000 men), along with 28,000 **Jägers**. The practice of grouping peacetime forces regionally as 'Inspections' was ended from 1806, with reorganization into permanent brigades and 18 divisions (each of three brigades), rising to 25 by 1809.

The pace and depth of reform intensified after the **Tilsit** peace of 1807 – as demonstrated during the **Russo-Swedish War** of 1808–9 – and with the appointment of **Barclay de Tolly** as war minister in 1810. Though the army's support problems remained unresolved, and worsened when depot and supply troops became frontline reserves in 1812, some improvements were made to internal communications, standing defences and infantry weaponry, including the introduction of a more efficient **musket**. More thoroughgoing administrative changes established a **corps system** and a rudimentary central staff organization.

Though Barclay de Tolly displayed limitations as field commander, and Alexander's regular operational interference was seldom helpful, the army was more competently led at senior level after 1805. The veteran **Kutuzov** displayed much of Suvorov's doggedness, though not his aggression, and **Buxhowden** fought a highly effective campaign in the **Russo-Swedish War**. The loss of **Bagration** in 1812 deprived the army of an exceptional battle leader, but the inspirational **Platov** survived to lead his Cossacks into Paris.

On the eve of the 1812 **Russian campaign**, the regular army deployed a total of almost 400,000 men in 160 infantry regiments, 60 cavalry regiments and 124 artillery batteries, along with an expanded **Imperial Russian Guard** and another 30,000 enlisted Cossacks. The process of updating tactics had only begun in 1811, and rapid expansion reduced training to a very basic level, so that troops pursuing the French retreat from **Moscow** were generally capable of only the simplest manoeuvres.

By the time they reached the Polish border in late 1812, Russian armies were hardly in better condition than their opponents, but the empire's relatively stable **war finances** enabled the tsar to replenish battered forces before and during the 1813–14 campaigns for **Germany** and **France**. The Russian Army won no great victories of its own after 1812, and played no active part in the 1815 **Hundred Days** campaign, but its success in 1812 and subsequent durability confirmed its arrival as a permanent major factor in European great power calculations.

Russian Campaign (1812)

The mass invasion of **Russia** by French and allied armies in 1812. Begun by **Napoleon's** advance across the River Niemen at the head of more than 650,000 troops in late June, it ended with the completion of a disastrous retreat by about 93,000 survivors in late December.

War between **France** and Russia in 1812 was the culmination of a steady deterioration in relations between Napoleon and Tsar **Alexander I** since the Peace of **Tilsit** had ended hostilities between them in July 1807 (*see* War of the **Sixth Coalition**). The irretrievable breakdown of relations between the two states dates from 15 August 1811, when Napoleon launched a bitter public attack on the tsar during a speech in Paris. Alexander refused to be provoked at the time, but both sides had begun making diplomatic preparations for war by early 1812.

In late January 1812 Napoleon's German allies were warned to mobilize, and demands for troops were sent to both **Prussia** and **Austria**. Alexander

offered to address lapses in the **Continental System** in April, but set impossible conditions that merely infuriated Napoleon, and he soon turned to securing peace on his other frontiers. The Convention of **St Petersburg** between Russia and Sweden, signed on 9 April, guaranteed Crown Prince **Bernadotte's** benevolent neutrality in the event of war with France, and the Peace of **Bucharest** bought peace on the Turkish frontier in May (*see* **Russo-Turkish War**). Negotiations for an alliance with **Great Britain**, eventually signed in July, were also put in hand.

Alexander's military preparations centred on a series of **Russian Army** reforms carried out under minister of war **Barclay de Tolly** since 1810. Some improvements were made to internal communications, standing defences and infantry weaponry, notably the introduction of a more efficient **musket**, and more extensive administrative changes had produced an army of some 410,000 men by 1812. Organized into a **corps system**, with about 210,000 men making up the three main frontline armies, it boasted particularly impressive **artillery** support.

Practical French preparations for an attack on Russia had begun with a build-up of garrison strengths in Germany and **Poland** during 1810. Plans for attacking Britain and the Middle East were cancelled in 1811, and peace overtures (somewhat half-heartedly) directed to London. Standing armies of occupation in eastern Europe were meanwhile brought up to a strength of 200,000 men, and by late spring 1812 Napoleon could call on almost 450,000 men in three frontline armies, although the overall quality of a multinational **French Army** had declined since 1809.

The main French strike force was an army group of about 250,000 men under the emperor's personal command, including **Murat's** two cavalry corps, the **Imperial Guard** and three army corps under **Davout**, **Ney** and **Oudinot**. The other two main frontline armies – some 80,000 men under Eugène de **Beauharnais**, and more than 70,000 under Jérôme **Bonaparte** – were primarily intended to undertake diversionary attacks on the wings of the main advance. Two more detached corps guarded the extreme flanks – **Macdonald's** 32,500 men near the Baltic coast and **Schwarzenberg's** 34,000-strong Austrian contingent on the southern wing – and another 225,000 troops were in reserve or garrison formations. Imperial defence devolved upon frontier garrisons and about 80,000 conscripted **National Guard** troops.

Napoleon's forces, drawn up along the Vistula frontier of Poland, faced perhaps 218,000 troops defending western Russia by June 1812, divided into two main forces. About 127,000 men (including 19,000 cavalry and supported by 584 guns) were with Barclay de Tolly's First Army in the north, deployed along the east bank of the Niemen between Courland and southern Lithuania; the Second Army's 48,000 men (including about 11,000 cavalry) were moving slowly north with **Bagration** from positions south of the Pripet Marshes. A Third Army under General Tormazov, drawn from troops no longer needed on other frontiers, would eventually muster some 43,000 men, but was still being formed around Volhynia in early June. Some estimates put Second and Third Army strength at 65,000 and 80,000 men respectively.

The vast hinterland of western Russia is effectively divided for military purposes into two theatres, either side of the central Pripet Marshes. Much of the land suitable for large-scale military operations was in relatively barren condition, and the northern sector is subdivided by a series of great rivers, several of which formed ideal defensive barriers. A general shortage of good roads was compounded by an unfriendly climate, rendering dust a hindrance whenever mud was not.

Broadly aware of enemy dispositions by the late spring, Napoleon envisaged a direct thrust across the northern sector of the front, aiming to get between the two main Russian armies prior to destroying them one at a time, though his plans remained flexible and may have included an alternative scheme to attack towards St Petersburg. Russian battle plans were less well developed by mid-1812, and concerned primarily with defence, although whether a policy of permanent retreat was adopted in advance remains open to question. The First Army planned to pull back from the Niemen and unite with the Second further east, holding the line of the Rivers Dvina, Beresina and Dnieper while swinging an expanded Third Army moved

against the French rear. Construction of fortifications was begun around the main river crossings, but little was complete (and the two main armies were still far apart) by the time the French attack came.

Mobilized in February, Napoleon's forces were in position along the Vistula by 15 May, and the order to move into Russian Poland and East Prussia was issued on 26 May. Napoleon announced that French forces were responding to invitations from Polish nationalist groups, and the **Grande Armée** met no opposition en route for the Russian frontier. Napoleon's final diplomatic preparations, notably an assembly of his allies at Dresden and the dispatch for **propaganda** purposes of a plea for peace to St Petersburg, delayed the actual invasion until the night of 23 June. The main central army crossed into Russia over the next two days, meeting virtually no opposition and sighting only a few isolated **Cossack** patrols. Once Kovno was occupied without a fight it became clear that Barclay de Tolly was withdrawing north-east to the line of the Dvina around Drissa, and that Bagration was retiring north to catch up with the First Army.

Deciding that he could still get between the two armies, Napoleon ordered a drive on **Vilna**, where Barclay de Tolly was reported to be on 26 June, but transport problems delayed any attack on the city until 28 June, by which time the First Army had withdrawn east towards Sventsiani. Uncertain of the exact whereabouts of either main Russian force, Napoleon then divided his own army in two, sending a large detachment under Murat in pursuit of the First Army, while Davout led the remainder in search of Bagration, then being followed north by Schwarzenberg and **Reynier**. Napoleon himself waited with a small reserve at Vilna, but Davout and Jérôme contrived to let Bagration escape south-east from **Minsk** in early July.

Napoleon ordered Davout to prevent Bagration from linking up with Barclay de Tolly, while he concentrated in support of Murat's forces, currently restricted to observation of the First Army's strong positions around Dünaburg and Drissa. His plan to attack the positions and simultaneously threaten St Petersburg, again intended to force the Russians to battle, was frustrated when Barclay de Tolly suddenly abandoned the

Drissa fortifications during the night of 18 July.

Napoleon pushed east once he realized that the two Russian armies were planning to meet at Vitebsk. Bagration's defeat at **Mohilev** on 23 July prevented him from reaching the rendezvous, but after a clash between vanguards at **Ostronovo** (25–26 July) Barclay de Tolly again withdrew and French forces took **Vitebsk** unopposed on 28 July.

Extreme heat and hunger were already sapping French health and morale, and Napoleon's armies had suffered an estimated 100,000 losses by the time they reached Vitebsk, when the central advance paused for a week's rest. Other French forces remained busy: in the south, Reynier and Schwarzenberg were forced to combine against the new Russian Third Army around Brest-Litovsk; north of Vitebsk, Oudinot and **Gouvion St Cyr** were heavily engaged around **Polotsk**, where they won a largely cosmetic victory in mid-August; meanwhile Macdonald's forces even further north occupied Dünaburg and began a **siege** of **Riga**.

The two Russian armies finally met up at Smolensk on 4 August, but Napoleon's plans to surround them were pre-empted by a Russian counter-offensive. Anxious to provide some proof of offensive intent, and aware that the French were dangerously extended, Barclay de Tolly and Bagration moved west from Smolensk on 6 August at the head of almost 120,000 men, including 18,000 cavalry and supported by 650 guns. The advance was slow to develop, partly because of a breakdown in personal relations between the two commanders, and fizzled out after a minor victory at **Inkovo** on 8 August. By the time it was resumed, from 13 August, Napoleon was moving on Smolensk.

The planned encirclement of Russian positions at **Smolensk** was spoiled by a prolonged delay at **Krasnoe** on 14 October, and Napoleon's own sluggish performance, so that most of the Russians again escaped after two days' fighting (16–17 August). By this time the French army as a whole (excluding forces south of the Pripet Marshes) had shrunk to a fighting strength of about 156,000 men, strung out along an 800km front like a gigantic arrowhead pointed at Moscow. Food shortages were becoming critical, exacerbated by Russian destruction of everything

in the path of their retreat, while regular small-scale Cossack raids were eroding anyway fragile morale.

Napoleon rested his forces at Smolensk, and considered spending the winter there, but it was already short of supplies. Still hoping a major victory would end the campaign quickly, and aware of the propaganda implications of any more cautious approach, he issued orders for an advance towards Moscow on 24 August.

Napoleon was convinced that Russian commanders would accept a fight if Moscow were threatened, and that Alexander would sue for peace if it fell. He was right on the first count, wrong on the second. In an atmosphere of almost religious public support for the regime in its hour of peril, Alexander discarded the policy of retreat along with Barclay de Tolly, and appointed the veteran **Kutuzov** as overall commander on 29 August. Charged with destroying the invader, Kutuzov prepared to draw the French into battle on his terms.

The French moved on Moscow from 25 August in three columns, Napoleon leading in the centre, Beauharnais guarding the northern flank, and Prince **Poniatowski** now commanding the southern wing. Heavy rain slowed progress on the march, and Napoleon was on the point of ordering a return to Smolensk when the weather improved at the end of the month. On 5 September the French advance met most of Kutuzov's army in strong defensive positions around the village of **Borodino**, about 120km from Moscow, and the two forces fought an enormous pitched battle on 7 September (*see* **Map 24**). A clumsy struggle, and the most expensive of the war years in terms of casualties, Borodino left the battered French in possession of the field but without a decisive victory.

French forces followed the subsequent Russian retreat, fighting occasional actions with rear-guards but in no condition to force Kutuzov into another major battle. Napoleon was happy to accept a Russian offer to surrender **Moscow** in return for an unhindered withdrawal, and French forces occupied the city from 14 September, but it was a bleak triumph, solving none of the army's supply problems and failing to trigger a Russian peace offer. After a surprise Russian attack on Murat's screening cavalry around

Vinkovo on 18 October, Napoleon led his 95,000 survivors back towards Smolensk from 19 October.

Napoleon opted for a south-westerly retreat to Smolensk that would lead the army through fertile areas, but meant an inevitable clash with Kutuzov's forces around Kaluga, and he changed his mind after a hard-earned victory at **Malo-yaroslavets**, about 110km south-west of Moscow, on 24 October. The army was turned back towards Oshogivo and the route west from Borodino, a crucial decision that is quoted as evidence of his personal decline during the campaign.

Napoleon reached Viasma on 31 October, where news from other sectors revealed the extent of his army's exposure. To the south of the main army, Schwarzenburg's corps was retreating towards the Bug, offering little protection against an advance across Napoleon's path by 34,000 troops under Admiral **Tshitshagov**. In the north, **Wittgenstein**'s 30,000-strong Russian corps was pushing back Gouvion St Cyr's composite French command to threaten lines of retreat across the Beresina.

Despite his claims that Russian surrender was imminent, Napoleon's army was manifestly disintegrating. Its sprawling, dispirited columns stretched for 80km, with up to 30,000 stragglers stumbling along at the rear. Food shortages had accounted for almost all its horses, and effective strength was dwindling daily. Able to call on very few reinforcements, it was under constant attack by Kutuzov's vanguards, and suffered a morale-sapping defeat at **Fiodoroivskoy** on 3 November that virtually destroyed Davout's rearguard.

Napoleon issued orders on 7 November to **Victor**, now commanding forces on the French northern flank, to push the Russians back beyond **Polotsk** at all costs, and on 9 November the emperor reached Smolensk. The city's supplies might have kept the French army alive for two weeks, but starving troops consumed all the food in three days, while the first heavy snows of the winter killed off most surviving animals. With little choice but to continue the retreat towards supplies at Vitebsk and Minsk, Napoleon left Smolensk at the head of an estimated 41,500 men on 12 November.

The French rearguard, now under Ney, finally reached Smolensk next day, and departed west on 17 November, as Napoleon was launching a limited counter-attack at **Krasnoe**. Ney was given up for lost when the main army moved on to reach Orsha two days later, where it found the Dnieper bridges intact but learned of Minsk's capture, along with 2 million French rations. Its garrison had fled to Borisov on the Beresina, where Tshitshagov was heading to intercept the retreat, and Napoleon issued orders for his central and northern forces to abandon most of their equipment (including **pontoons**) for a rapid march to the town. The head of Napoleon's column was about 40km from Borisov by the evening of 21 November, when Ney and 900 survivors of III Corps rejoined headquarters, having crossed the Dnieper further north at **Gusinoe**.

News that the bridges at Borisov had fallen to a powerful attack by Tshitshagov on 21 November reached Napoleon next day at Bobr, prompting orders organizing every available officer into fighting units, including the élite **Escadrille Sacrée**. Oudinot's local victory at **Loshnitsa** on 23 November returned the town of Borisov to French control, but the Beresina bridges had been destroyed and Tshitshagov was in possession of the west bank.

Russian forces had been following a plan to draw all the French armies towards an encirclement around Borisov since late October. It had been proposed by the tsar's personal advisers, but was pursued with little vigour by Kutuzov, whose 50,000 troops were suffering almost as badly as Napoleon's, and who may have preferred to let winter destroy the French. Aided by the dilatory nature of Kutuzov's approach from the east, and by Tshitshagov's rash response to diversionary actions further south, Napoleon executed a carefully conceived plan for the **Beresina** crossing from 25 to 29 November, but lost another 20,000 troops in the process.

By the morning of 29 November, Napoleon's main body was across the river and free to march on Vilna. With Wittgenstein shadowing its northern flank, and Tshitshagov's army on its tail, it was exposed to frequent raids, along with lethal cold, for the remainder of the retreat into Poland. Though estimates of the number of survivors at this stage vary considerably, it was shrinking fast, and **Bavarian** forces under **Wrede** suffered a similar collapse moving back from

Gloubokoie towards a rendezvous east of Vilna.

Napoleon told senior commanders that he was leaving the army for Paris at Smorgoni on 5 December. The decision was not unexpected or opposed by his marshals, and his presence in Paris was manifestly needed to restore popular and political confidence in the empire. Putting Murat in temporary command of the retreat, he left Smorgoni at ten that evening, reached Warsaw (after narrowly avoiding capture by **guerrilla** forces) on 10 December and was in Paris eight days later.

Murat led the vanguard into Vilna on 8 December, and the last troops reached the city two days later. Its stores were undisturbed and plentiful, but breakdown of discipline prevented their efficient distribution and claimed more lives to the combined effects of alcohol and temperatures far below freezing. Worried about the Russians, Murat ignored orders to allow eight days' rest in Vilna, abandoning 20,000 wounded to move the first units out of the city on 9 December.

Cold was the real enemy now, rendering supply depots useless and their defence pointless. Most remaining wagons and guns, along with the army's treasure chest (containing 10 million francs), were abandoned on the icy slopes next day, and only 7,000 fit troops (along with perhaps 15,000 walking wounded) remained by the time the leading elements reached Kovno on 11 December.

The French rearguard eventually reached the Niemen border on 14 December and Ney, one of few French commanders (Beauharnais was another) to emerge from the campaign with an enhanced reputation, was reportedly the last man to leave Russian soil. Pursuing Russian forces, themselves reduced to 40,000 men by the conditions, halted at the frontier, granting the French uninterrupted passage to Königsberg.

A few French units were still in Russia. Marshal Macdonald's corps, occupying positions around Riga since August, only began withdrawing towards Tilsit on 19 December, and lost more than half its strength when Russian general Diebnitz cut off and surrounded General **Yorck**'s 17,000-strong Prussian column on 25 December. Five days later Yorck signed the Convention of **Tauroggen**, declaring his troops neutral and presaging the mass defection of Napoleon's German

allies. Macdonald brought the remains of his command into Königsberg on 3 January 1813.

In the south, Schwarzenberg and Reynier pursued General **Sacken**'s flank forces as far as Slonim, but turned their forces west on 14 December and reoccupied Bialystok en route for the frontier. Almost unchallenged, Reynier took his troops to Saxony and Schwarzenberg took his Austrians home, concluding an armistice of his own with the Russians after entering imperial territory.

Napoleon's calamitous invasion of Russia signalled the imminent collapse of his imperial system. It had cost about 570,000 troops, including 200,000 as prisoners, along with more than 1,000 guns and some 200,000 trained horses, and the French Empire never recovered from the over-extension of resources that it entailed. By early 1813 Napoleon's army, his reputation and his diplomatic bulwarks were all but shattered, and his enemies were closing in. He still faced the danger of revolt in Paris, the continuing drain of the **Peninsular War** and the threat of Britain's naval mastery, but within a few weeks he would be plunged into massive struggle for control of central Europe. *See* Campaign for **Germany, 1813**.

Russian Navy

The Russian Empire had little interest in **naval warfare** until the reign of Peter the Great, who moved the capital to St Petersburg partly as a means of encouraging interest in sea power. With ready access to a wealth of raw materials, the navy had amassed 67 **ships-of-the-line** and 36 **frigates** by 1790, along with some 700 smaller warcraft, many of them shallow-draught **sloops**.

As with other branches of government administration, supreme command of the navy rested with the tsar, who made most important decisions in person. Otherwise the senior naval official was the chairman of the Admiralty College at St Petersburg, but he could only advise the monarch. Although never given the same priority as the **Russian Army** in an era dominated by great land battles, the navy grew steadily in size and competence during the war period. Many of its senior officers either were British or had trained with British ships, and general standards of seamanship, gunnery, discipline and command were reasonably high.

The navy's home operational waters were in the Baltic and Black Seas, with a small squadron also patrolling the Caspian Sea. Both main theatres were well suited to **amphibious** operations, and it maintained strong **marine** forces, particularly in the Baltic, where it also deployed large numbers of small, shallow-draught gunships, aping **Swedish Navy** designs, and a variety of outdated **galleys**. The Baltic Fleet was based at Cronstadt, in the Gulf of Finland, with detachments operating from Balticsport (near Revel) and Danamünde (near Riga). After **Russia** captured the Crimea in the 1780s, the Black Sea Fleet was based on Sebastopol, while the Caspian squadron operated out of Astrakhan.

Although generally successful in its regional campaigns against **Sweden** and the **Ottoman Empire**, the navy seldom ventured out of its main hunting grounds until 1798, when a squadron was sent into the North Sea to assist the British **blockade** of the Dutch coast. A temporary peace with Constantinople also enabled part of the Black Sea Fleet to enter the **Mediterranean** under Admiral Ushakov in 1798. After joining the **Turkish Navy** in capturing the **Ionian Islands**, Ushakov escorted **Suvorov's** army to the **Italian** front in 1799 and helped besiege **Ancona**.

The fleet remained in the Adriatic after Russia left the **Second Coalition**, and was reinforced by five battleships under Admiral Seniavin in 1805, taking part in attempts to defend **Naples** before joining units already at Corfu to bring Russian Mediterranean strength up to 13 ships-of-the-line, nine frigates and 23 other warships. After aiding native Montenegrin forces resisting French conquest of **Illyria**, Seniavin and most of his fleet sailed to join the British **Dardanelles** expedition in February 1807, and lured the (now hostile) Turkish fleet to defeat at **Lemnos** later that year, but the Franco-Russian alliance agreed at **Tilsit** in July forced Russian warships to evacuate the theatre in December.

The other major campaign undertaken by the wartime Russian Navy was triggered by the **Russo-Swedish War** of 1808–9. By the end of 1808 its Baltic fleet comprised 13 ships-of-the-line, seven frigates and 12 other ships, but the campaign's only major warship action brought a minor defeat off Balticsport, where a 74-gunner was lost. The massed flotillas of shallows craft held off Swedish attacks at **Palvasund** in September 1808 and **Ratan** the following August, victories that were vital to the conquest of Finland in 1809.

The navy played a peripheral role in the **Russian campaign** and the subsequent struggles further west, although its sailors fought as ground troops in 1812–13 and warships again joined British forces blockading the North Sea coast. By 1815, with shipbuilding continuing to outstrip losses, it had become the second most powerful naval force in the world, though it remained far inferior to the Royal Navy and was soon overtaken by a resurgent postwar **French Navy**. *See* **Map 18**.

Russo-Polish War (1792)

Russian tsarina **Catherine** the Great's opportunistic invasion of **Poland**, launched in May 1792 while her main rivals for control of the region, **Austria** and **Prussia**, were distracted by the early actions of the War of the **First Coalition** against France. On the pretext of supporting exiled opponents of the Polish constitution, some 60,000 Russian troops crossed the frontier on 18 May. Weathering pinprick attacks by some of Prince **Poniatowski's** 46,000 Polish troops scattered around the country, General Rokovski's Russians drove defenders steadily back towards the River Bug in the south. Further north, in Lithuania, **Polish** forces suffered a major defeat near Vilna in mid-June that prompted a retreat to Warsaw. A successful attack by 17,000 Russians on Polish forward positions east of Warsaw on 18 July, persuaded King Stanislaus to accept the constitutional changes demanded by Russia's client exiles, but the ensuing truce left Poland defenceless when Russian and Prussian forces moved in to occupy and partition the country in 1793.

Russo-Swedish War (1808-9)

Peace with **France** at **Tilsit** in July 1807 freed **Russia** to resume its long-standing expansionist campaign against **Sweden**. Encouraged by Napoleon, who was anxious to bring Scandinavia into the **Continental System**, Russia invaded the undefended Swedish province of **Finland** in February 1808, and **Denmark** (also a French ally) declared war on Sweden the following month.

The war went badly for Sweden. A British support force that reached Gothenburg in May sailed home after an increasingly unstable king imprisoned C-in-C **Moore**, and Russian forces captured the key Finnish **fortress** of Sveaborg later that month. A Swedish invasion of Norway was held by the Danes, with support from **Bernadotte's** French Army of the North, and a series of defeats in the autumn forced abandonment of Finland in November.

At sea, Admiral Chanichov's **Russian Navy** battlefleet remained penned in its base at Cronstadt after an initial setback against **Swedish Navy** fleet units at Gothland in April 1808, and the loss of a **ship-of-the-line** to **Royal Navy** forces in the theatre in August. An Anglo-Swedish **blockade** of Cronstadt, commanded by British admiral **Saumarez**, was abandoned in the autumn.

Both Russia and Sweden possessed fleets of small warcraft designed for warfare in the Baltic. They clashed in August 1808 amid the cluster of small islands between Aaland and the Finnish coast, as 160 Russian vessels and **Buxhowden's** land forces sought to force shallows en route for Stockholm (*see* **Map 18**). Defeat at **Sandöströmm** on 2 August prompted Swedish retirement from the shallows, but a counter-attack on 30 August drove the Russians back on **Palvasund**, where they held off another Swedish attack on 18 September. Poorly deployed and concentrated, Swedish naval forces then fell back to reorganize.

Amid turmoil in Stockholm surrounding the coup that brought **Charles XIII** to power, Russian forces advanced across the frozen Bothnia Strait in three columns to threaten the capital from the north. Stockholm was temporarily saved by an armistice signed in late March 1809, but it was not ratified by the tsar. Russian advances resumed in May, virtually unopposed until a Swedish attack failed at **Ratan** in August,

and a move on Stockholm was imminent when Charles signed the punitive Treaty of Frederickshamm on 17 September, giving Russia formal possession of Finland and the Aaland islands. Peace with Denmark followed, neither side gaining by the Treaty of Jönköping (10 December), and Sweden agreed to join the Continental System in January 1810.

Russo-Turkish War (1806–12)

The **Ottoman Empire** and **Russia** had spent much of the later eighteenth century fighting over **Catherine** the Great's expansionist drive into the Crimea and the provinces of the Upper Danube (*see* **Map 1**). The Danube provinces of Bessarabia, Wallachia and Moldavia were governed by semi-autonomous local grandees, and moves towards independence, along with French diplomatic pressure, triggered their formal deposition by Sultan Selim III on 25 August 1806. The dispatch of **Turkish Army** forces to the region prompted Tsar **Alexander** to send an army under General Michelson into the principalities. Russian troops crossed the Dniester on 16 October 1806, and entered Bucharest eight days later, bringing a Turkish declaration of war on Russia on 27 December. The war was a desultory affair. Russian forces remained on the defensive until after the **Tilsit** peace of 1807 ended war against **Napoleon**, but were soon refocused on the **Russo-Swedish War**. Never able to field more than about 30,000 troops in the region, but facing Turkish forces paralysed by supply shortages and internal disruption, Russian armies took Bessarabia in 1809 before advancing into Moldavia and Wallachia, but deteriorating relations with France slowed further exploitation and triggered the generous peace agreed by theatre C-in-C **Tshitshagov** at **Bucharest** in May 1812.

S

Saalfeld, Battle of

A preamble to the Battles of **Jena** and **Auerstädt**, fought on 10 October 1806 between the French **Grande Armée**'s V Corps (**Lannes**) and the advance guard of the Prussian right wing, commanded by Prince Louis Ferdinand. Napoleon had sent his army north through the Thuringian Forest's three parallel roads from 8 October, planning to get behind the Prussian army gathering in Saxony, but had no accurate idea of Prussian dispositions beyond the woodlands.

Prince Louis was only at Saalfeld on 10 October because orders to rejoin **Hohenlohe**'s main body had been insufficiently clear. With Hohenlohe concentrating some miles to the northwest, and the Duke of **Brunswick**'s main Prussian army hovering around Erfurt, Louis's 8,000 men were outnumbered and isolated when Lannes's leading divisions launched an attack out of the forest. The Prussians fought hard for four hours, losing 4,000 men before finally collapsing when Prince Louis, regarded as a potentially brilliant soldier, was killed in action. Lannes suffered only 200 casualties. *See* **Jena–Auerstädt Campaign**; **Map 16**.

Sabres

The cut and thrust of military debate concerning the use of the sabre, the **cavalry** trooper's basic weapon, was a permanent feature of the war period. Argument centred on the correct use of the sabre as an attacking weapon, French authorities recommending the thrust, or stab, as most likely to inflict serious injury, while other armies preferred the slash, or cut, as less likely to leave a trooper exposed to counter-attack.

French heavy and medium cavalry units were all equipped with narrow, straight blades for executing the thrust. Because the weight of the blow was vital to the effectiveness of the cut against troops wearing **armour**, their counterparts in most allied armies were equipped with heavy, straight-bladed sabres, hatchet-shaped for the slash but completely unsuitable for thrusts. Most light cavalry used curved sabres, designed for the cut but versatile enough to be used as a thrusting weapon. *See also* **Cossacks**.

Sacile, Battle of

The principal action in Italy during the War of the **Fifth Coalition** in 1809. As the **Austrian Army**'s opening spring offensives got under way, some 37,000 French imperial troops under Eugéne de **Beauharnais**, viceroy in the puppet Kingdom of **Italy**, faced Archduke **John**'s 40,000 Austrian troops advancing through the Tyrol. Drawing up his army east of the River Piave, Beauharnais attacked the Austrians around Sacile, some 60km north of Venice, on 16 April (*see* **Map 9**). His frontal attack was held off by Austrian forces in good positions, and French forces withdrew after John launched a counter-move around their left flank. Both sides suffered about 2,000 casualties, and the front fell quiet as Beauharnais pulled his troops back beyond the Adige into the fortified **Quadrilateral** region. News of **Napoleon**'s early successes on the Danube brought John's offensive to a premature end a few days later, and Beauharnais followed his retirement into Austria. *See also* Battle of **Raab**.

Sacken, Dmitri Osten, Count (1790–1881)

Son of a Russian general, and one of the younger generation of commanders who emerged to lead the **Russian Army** during 1812–14, Sacken fought at **Eylau** in 1807 and led a division throughout the **Russian campaign** in 1812. Given corps command during the campaign for **Germany** in 1813, he led his forces through the battle for **France** the following year, and his prodigiously long military career ended with participation in the Crimean War more than 40 years later.

Sackett's Harbor, Battle of

Abortive attack in late May 1813 by a mixed force of British troops, Canadian militia and native warriors against the US arsenal on the eastern shore of Lake Ontario at Sackett's Harbor. Transported by British light naval forces, the attackers were landed near the arsenal on 28 May. Sackett's Harbor was defended by only 600 **US Army** regulars under General Jacob Brown, but they held off determined if unsophisticated attacks for two days before British commander General Prevost withdrew his exhausted army to **Montreal**, which became the target of a new American offensive in the autumn. *See also* **Anglo-American War, 1812–15.**

Sahagún, Action at

Minor engagement fought on 21 December 1808 along the road from Soldana to León, that was the only offensive action undertaken by General **Moore**'s British force during its brief **Peninsular War** sortie of late 1808. Following his occupation of Madrid in early December, **Napoleon** had made plans to advance further west, aware that Moore's army was somewhere in **Spain** but sure that it was retreating. Only **Soult**'s 17,000 troops were left to protect the north-eastern provinces of the country.

Moore and 15,000 infantry were in fact about four days from Madrid, waiting for **artillery** and **cavalry** to arrive at Salamanca, where they remained until 28 November. News of the French victory at **Tudela** convinced Moore to prepare a retreat, but he changed his mind after the delayed columns arrived and instead marched

east on Valladolid from 11 December, hoping to distract Napoleon from further conquest before escaping to the coast at Corunna.

Moore was under several illusions. He believed General **Romana**'s claim that he had 15,000 men at León ready to fight, that Napoleon had only 80,000 troops in Spain, and (until 11 December) that Madrid was still in Spanish hands. A captured courier revealed on 14 December that almost 200,000 French troops were in the theatre, but also that Soult's corps was isolated and marching for León from Soldana. Seeing an opportunity to surprise Soult en route, Moore turned his army north towards Sahagún on 15 December.

British strength rose above 30,000 with the belated arrival of **Baird**'s supporting column from Corunna before Moore learned on 20 December that Soult was still at Soldana, ruling out a major attack on his corps. Though British cavalry drove Soult's reconnaissance forces from the field at Sahagún next day, the success entailed loss of overall surprise, and Moore made no attempt to follow up. After two days' rest at Sahagún for two days, news of massed French movements north from Madrid sent British forces hastening towards Astorga and **Corunna** from 24 December. *See* **Map 22.**

St Amand, Battle of

The last French attempt to halt allied reconquest of **Flanders** in spring 1793, fought on 8 May around St Amand, some 15km south of Tournai (*see* **Map 2**). Defeat at **Neerwinden** in late March had forced French armies back to the Franco-Belgian frontier, where new theatre commander Dampierre had managed to deploy some 30,000 troops by late April. Pursuit was slowed by inter-allied strategic disputes, but **York**'s multinational force reached Tournai on 23 April to bring allied strength at the frontier up to about 45,000 men.

Urged on to the offensive by his government, Dampierre launched an attack against the whole allied line on 1 May. Intended to establish contact with troops isolated at Condé, it achieved only a minor success in the extreme south near St Amand, and suffered 2,000 casualties. Required to attack again, Dampierre concentrated against St Amand on 8 May, but found the sector reinforced and fell back when counter-attacked. French forces held off attacks in the woods south of St Amand next day, but retired to Lille overnight. Sticking rigidly to orthodox **cordon** tactics, allied C-in-C **Saxe-Coburg** let them go, opening sieges of Condé and Valenciennes to secure absolute control of the frontier. *See also* War of the **First Coalition**.

St Cyr *See* **Carra St Cyr**, Claude; **Gouvion St Cyr**, Laurent

St Dizier, Battle of

Napoleon's first offensive action after assuming direct command of forces defending **France** in late January 1814. Too weak to attempt a major confrontation with either of the allied armies advancing on Paris, he attempted to isolate and attack the southern wing of **Blücher**'s force to the east. Ordering **Marmont** to advance on Bar-le-Duc, between Blücher and General **Yorck**'s northern column, **Napoleon** led 34,000 men towards Blücher's reported position approaching St Dizier on the Marne. By the time Napoleon reached the front on 26 January, Blücher's 25,000 Prussians had taken the town and forced **Victor**'s corps back towards Vitry, and he reached the area too late to catch them in the process of crossing the river. Though St Dizier was recaptured after a fight with rearguards on 27 January, the bulk of Blücher's army was already en route for Brienne. Anxious to prevent its rendezvous with **Schwarzenberg**'s army to the south, Napoleon turned in pursuit. *See* Battle of **Brienne**; Map 26.

St Gotthard Pass, Actions in the
(1799)

The overture to Russian marshal **Suvorov**'s epic march from the **Italian** front to the **Rhine** via the **Swiss** front in autumn 1799. Transferred from north-west Italy to Switzerland after a summer shift in **Second Coalition** strategy, the 20,000 men of Suvorov's main column reached Taverna, at the opening of the St Gotthard Pass, on 15 September, but then wasted three days waiting in vain for Austrian transport vehicles before heading up the pass without **artillery**. General Lecourbe's 13,000 French troops, detached from **Masséna**'s army in Switzerland, held excellent defensive positions in the pass, and held off

Suvorov's repeated attacks with ease, but their flank was threatened by 6,000 Russians sent across the mountains further east, and they were forced to retreat down the River Reuss to Wasen.

Starving Russian troops entered Amstetten on 25 September, consumed everything they could find, and marched on to reach Altdorf next day, where the mountains and Lake Lucerne (patrolled by a French **gunboat** flotilla, and otherwise denuded of shipping) blocked any further advance. Discovering on 28 September that his allies had retreated and that he was effectively surrounded, Suvorov could only lead his men east through the mountains towards Austrian and Russian forces in the Rhine valley. About 5,000 exhausted survivors eventually met up with **Korsakov**'s Russian corps around Lake Constance in late October, and were then recalled to Russia. *See* **Map 4**.

St Hilaire, Louis Vincent Joseph le Blond (1766–1809)

French officer who received his commission with the army of the old regime in 1783, and who served on the **Italian** front against the **First Coalition**, commanding his first brigade in 1795. He fought at **Bassano** the following year, but was wounded in both legs shortly afterwards and invalided home. Promoted to divisional command in 1799, he was with the army preparing to invade **England** at St Omer from 1803, and led his division as part of **Soult**'s IV Corps against the **Third Coalition** in 1805. His division played a vital role at **Austerlitz**, taking part in the decisive assault on the Pratzen Heights, and he maintained a reputation as an aggressive, pugnacious commander through the campaigns against the **Fourth Coalition** in 1806–7, fighting at both **Jena** and **Eylau**. Ennobled by Napoleon in 1808, he led his division into Germany again in 1809, taking part in the Battle of **Eckmühl**, after which he was publicly promised a marshal's baton by the Emperor. Before the promotion was formalized, he died of wounds received on 22 May at **Aspern–Essling**.

St Laurent, Battle of

The last major offensive by **Spanish Army** forces during the **Pyrenean campaigns** of 1794, an unsuccessful attempt in August to relieve the frontier town of Bellegarde, blockaded by 35,000 French troops under General **Dugommier** since the early summer. Spanish eastern sector commander de la Union attacked French lines on 13 August, concentrating against **Augereau**'s right wing at St Laurent. The main attack by some 15,000 Spanish troops had been driven back in disorder by midday, and a secondary attack by 5,000 men near the coast met a similar fate. An attempted landing near Bagnols by **gunboats** of the **Spanish Navy** was turned back by a single French battalion. De la Union pulled his army back to its original starting lines during the afternoon, and Dugommier drew his forces closer around Bellegarde, which surrendered on 17 September, just before a second Spanish relief attempt came to rapid grief in the hills well short of the town.

St Lucia

The French Caribbean island of St Lucia, one of the Windward chain, was one of the most heavily contested theatres of conflict in the **West Indies** after 1793. Part of General Grey's British expeditionary force, escorted by warships under **Jervis**, attacked St Lucia in late March 1794, and preliminary assaults were enough to secure the island's surrender on 1 April. Incited by agents from French **Guadeloupe**, rebellion forced the British to abandon St Lucia on 19 June 1795, but some 3,000 troops under **Abercromby** landed on the island the following April, fighting their way across the island to take the surrender of 2,000 French and native troops on 26 May. Both sides suffered at least 500 casualties during the campaign. Though returned to France by the **Amiens** treaty in 1802, St Lucia was retaken with ease in June 1804, remaining in British hands up to and after the Congress of **Vienna**. *See* **Map 20**.

Saint Marcoufe Islands

A cluster of small islands just off the French coast west of Le Havre that was occupied by the **Royal Navy** in 1795, and was still occupied by 500 British seamen and **marines** in spring 1798, when it was attacked by French forces in a rehearsal for the planned invasion of **England**. A fleet of 33 flat-bottomed French transports, laden with troops, left Le Havre on 7 April. Sighted by three British **frigates**, the party was

forced to take shelter on the River Orne, above Caen, where it was reinforced by another 40 troopships and escorting **gunboats** before returning to sea in early May. Taking advantage of calm conditions that made pursuit difficult for British warships, 52 transports reached the islands on 6 May, but their attack was repulsed by the garrison. With British frigates unable to get within effective firing range, most of the French force escaped to Cherbourg, but plans for a second attempt on the islands were postponed pending a more favourable balance of naval power in the Channel. *See* **Map 8**.

St Michele, Battle of *See* Battle of **Ceva**; **Italian Campaign** (1794–7)

St Petersburg, Convention of (1812)

Alliance between **Russia** and **Sweden**, signed in Stockholm on 5 April 1812 and in St Petersburg four days later. The agreement was initiated by Swedish crown prince **Bernadotte**, whose adopted country's vital trade with **Great Britain** was being wrecked by the French **Continental System**. He sent an offer to Tsar **Alexander I** in February 1812, promising to attack northern Germany in the event of Franco-Russian war, and requesting Russian support for the conquest of Norway, then controlled by **Denmark**. In accepting the offer, with the proviso that Denmark would receive territorial compensation, the tsar secured western Russia's northern borders in anticipation of **Napoleon**'s attack along the central frontier. *See also* War of the **Sixth Coalition**.

St Pierre, Battle of

The last major action of the **Peninsular War** in 1813, fought in the aftermath of the Battle of the **Nive** on 13 December, when French commander **Soult** attacked **Hill**'s isolated allied detachment just east of Bayonne (*see* **Map 5**). Hill's 14,000 men had been cut off from the rest of **Wellington**'s allied army by a sudden flood of the Nive the previous night. They were occupying strong positions on three hills near the village of St Pierre d'Irube, some 5km from Bayonne, with the main road to the city running through the broadest of them in the centre.

Soult attacked the three positions with 33,000 men from eight a.m. on 13 December, at least four hours before Hill could expect allied reinforcements across the one serviceable Nive bridge. British forces held the southern hill, protected by heavily wooded approaches, but were driven off the northern hill, exposing the flank of the crucial central position. French attacks came close to breaking through in the centre, and Hill was still engaged in heavy fighting when Wellington reached the scene with the first of four reinforcement divisions at around noon.

Allied forces were ready to launch a counterattack two hours later, by which time Soult's demoralized troops were close to mutiny. Left under Hill's control, it drove French forces into full retreat within an hour. Having lost an estimated 3,000 casualties and inflicted 1,775, Soult withdrew into **Bayonne** itself.

St Vincent, Action off Cape (1795)

French naval victory that was typical, in all but scale, of the successes enjoyed by outnumbered republican forces against a superior but ill-managed **Royal Navy** before 1797. No match for the British in battle, the **French Navy**'s offensive efforts were primarily directed at allied commercial traffic, and its battlefleets functioned as hit-and-run raiders whenever they could slip past British **blockades**. French admiral **Richery** led six **ships-of-the-line** and three **frigates** west out of Toulon on 14 September 1795, evading the particularly lax blockade of British **Mediterranean** commander **Hotham**, who heard of the escape a week later but only left Leghorn (Livorno) in pursuit on 5 October. Richery fell upon a British **convoy** of 63 merchantmen, escorted by three ships-of-the-line, off Cape St Vincent on 7 October, forcing the battleship *Censeur* to surrender and capturing 31 merchant ships, a commercial disaster at least equivalent to the loss of several major warships. *See* **Map 8**.

St Vincent, Battle of Cape

Crushing victory by the British **Royal Navy**'s Mediterranean Fleet over a much larger **Spanish Navy** fleet on 14 February 1797. The collapse of the **First Coalition**, and consequent lack of bases, had compelled British naval forces to withdraw from the **Mediterranean** altogether in 1796. The fleet under **Jervis** was based on Lisbon, and its primary task was to prevent Spanish

forces joining planned French attempts to invade **England** or **Ireland**.

Spanish admiral Cordova left Cartagena with 27 **ships-of-the-line** and 12 **frigates** on 31 January, under orders to join the French fleet at Brest for a joint sweep into the English Channel. Jervis had taken station off Cape St Vincent, across the route of any force moving north from the Mediterranean, and was informed of the Spanish approach by **Nelson**, returning from a detached reconnaissance with two frigates on 13 February. Though he had only 15 ships-of-the-line, and was outgunned ship for ship, Jervis had honed his forces to a high pitch of fighting efficiency and accepted battle without hesitation.

The Spanish fleet was sighted at dawn on 14 February. Cordova's formation had split during overnight mist into two loosely grouped divisions, the smaller to the rear, and was in the process of attempting to reconcentrate. Exploiting a lucky wind change in his favour, Jervis ordered his ships into line at about eleven for a dash through the gap between them. Led by **Troubridge** in the 74-gun *Culloden*, the British line made contact with the larger (windward) Spanish division half an hour later, and the two fleets exchanged broadsides as the British sailed through in its wake.

Once beyond the 19 Spanish battleships to windward, the leading British vessels executed a full turn to resume their attack, while the leading Spanish ships sought to get across the rear of the British line and join the eight detached battleships to leeward. They were blocked by Nelson, aboard the 74-gun *Captain* three from the rear of the line, who pulled his ship out of position into the path of the Spaniards as they attempted to turn. This desperate but effective measure bought time for Troubridge and the returning vanguard ships to come up in support, and by early afternoon the battle was reaching a climax around Nelson's position.

The superior gunnery, discipline and condition of British ships proved decisive in a series of fierce mêlées, and they won a number of dramatic individual successes during the battle's later stages. Captain **Collingwood** in the 74-gun *Excellent* forced the surrender of two already damaged Spanish vessels, including the three-deck *Salvador del Mundo*; and Nelson led the boarding and seizure of two more Spanish battleships (*San Nicolas* and *San Josef*) from the decks of the crippled *Captain*. After surviving multiple attacks for several hours, Cordova's flagship (the 130-gun *Santísima Trinidad*) eventually hauled down its colours shortly before four, effectively ending the battle.

A rescue operation by some of the largely undamaged Spanish leeward division forced Jervis to close around his own damaged ships and release the *Santísima Trinidad*, before the Spanish ran for Cadiz at nightfall. Content with having thwarted any threat to British home waters, taken four major prizes and captured 5,000 prisoners (against 300 British losses), Jervis made no attempt at pursuit. A major boost to fragile British morale, and the end of Spanish pretensions to independent fleet activity, his victory earned Jervis the title of Earl St Vincent and transformed newly promoted Rear-Admiral Nelson into a British national hero. *See* **Map 18**.

St Vincent, Earl of *See* **Jervis**, John

Salamanca, Battle of

The most important engagement of the **Peninsular War** in 1812, fought on 22 July around a series of ridges some 6km south of Salamanca. After seizing **Ciudad Rodrigo** and **Badajoz** in early 1812, **Wellington** left screening forces on his flanks and led 51,000 troops north towards Salamanca from 13 June. **Marmont's** 49,000 troops took up positions east of the city, and the two armies spent most of July manoeuvring in search of an advantage.

The catalyst for battle was Marmont's attempt to move south and west from his position some 15km east of the city on 21 July. Aimed at cutting allied links with Portugal, the move was shadowed by British forces based on Salamanca itself, and both armies were still crossing the River Tormes in appalling weather conditions that night. Aware (unlike Marmont) that 13,000 French reinforcements were on their way, Wellington tracked French forces next day as they wheeled south-west to take the commanding hill of Greater Arapile, but kept his troops hidden behind ridges north of the position.

Wellington ordered a precautionary concentration just west of the hill shortly before noon, and Marmont mistook the pause in allied manoeuvres for an opportunity to lose his shadow. His leading division rushed forward to cut the road to Portugal, but was attacked and routed during the late afternoon by **Pakenham's** division, deployed to block just such a move. Three more British divisions then emerged from behind the ridge to attack the flanks of Marmont's advancing army.

Marmont had already been severely wounded and his deputy, General Bonnet, had been killed. Command devolved on General **Clausel**, who launched 12,000 men into a space between attacking divisions under **Leith** and **Cole**, but Wellington had already closed the gap with 5,500 reserves. After a 30-minute struggle, the charge collapsed and Clausel ordered a full-scale withdrawal.

The battle cost the French army about 13,000 men, half of them prisoners. The remainder escaped because General Ferrey's rearguard division was able to hold off allied attacks hindered by bush fires, and because Wellington halted pursuit in the mistaken belief that Spanish forces had blocked the route back across the Tormes at **Alba**. The defeat was still a massive blow to French control in Spain, forcing a full-scale imperial withdrawal beyond Madrid, and secured Wellington's reputation as an attacking general, though it suffered from an almost immediate backlash after failure at **Burgos**. *See* **Map 22**.

Saliceti, Antoine-Christophe (1757–1809)

Corsican politician, trained as a lawyer, who travelled to Paris in 1789 as a delegate to the States General, and was a **Jacobin** member of the **National Convention**. He was a political representative with the army besieging **Toulon**, where he met the young **Napoleon**, and was an important supporter of Bonaparte in a similar role on the **Italian** front in 1794. He survived the **Thermidor** coup, when he was responsible for both Napoleon's arrest and his subsequent release, and ostentatiously rallied former radicals to support of the **Brumaire coup** in 1799, for which he was rewarded with a series of minor diplomatic missions. He became Joseph **Bonaparte's** chief of police in **Naples** from 1806 (and war minister from 1807), organizing the suppression of royalists around the capital and authorizing ferocious reprisal attacks against provincial rebels. Saliceti retained his police post with reduced powers under **Murat**, and took part in the French seizure of the **Papal States** in 1809. He died suddenly on his return to Naples, but rumours of poisoning were not confirmed.

Sambre, Battles of the

A series of hard-fought and costly struggles during May and June 1794 for control of the River Sambre, at the southern end of an extended front line through **Flanders** and Belgium. The southern arm of a major French offensive begun in late April had been slow to get under way, but the combined forces of Generals Chardonnier and Desjardins, some 50,000 men, advanced north-east from 10 May towards Austrian positions on the Sambre below Charleroi (*see* **Map 2**).

Three divisions of reinforcements reached Austrian sector commander Kaunitz at around the same time, giving him about 30,000 troops, but they could not stop three French divisions capturing the south bank outpost at Thuin before crossing the river on 12 May. Kaunitz retreated towards Charleroi, but French attacks on his new positions collapsed in disarray next day, and Austrian **cavalry** reserves drove all three French divisions back across the Sambre by nightfall.

Ordered to make a second attempt towards Charleroi, French armies again got across the Sambre on 20 May, and held their ground against Austrian attacks the following day. Kaunitz renewed his attacks on 24 May, concentrated against a French right wing depleted by the detachment of **Kléber's** 15,000 men on an outflanking manoeuvre. Driven back on the river, French forces escaped relatively intact because Kléber doubled back to cover the army's retreat across the Sambre, a rearguard action that won **Bernadotte** great credit.

Having lost 8,000 men in the two attempts, Charbonnier and Desjardins were anxious to rest their demoralized troops and await **Jourdan's** arrival with 40,000 reinforcements from the **Rhine**, but were ordered into a third river crossing on 26 May. Fatigued attackers took only a single outpost before grinding to a halt, but

caught Austrian forces in the midst of redeployment, and new commander the Prince of **Orange** was induced to retire his left wing on Charleroi. After overwhelming forward defences on 29 May, French forces surrounded the town next day, but were counter-attacked from the north and west on 3 June, and driven back over the Sambre east of Charleroi with some 2,000 losses.

Jourdan arrived to take command of a newly constituted Army of the Sambre and Meuse next day, and a much larger French force resumed the investment of Charleroi from 12 June. A counter-attack four days later temporarily restored allied communications with the town, but resumption of the **siege** on 18 June convinced Austrian C-in-C **Saxe-Coburg** to call in all his forces against it (*see* Battle of **Fleurus**).

San Giuliano, Battle of

Minor success for **Moreau's** French forces on the **Italian** front in summer 1799, fought around the villages of San Giuliano and Cassina-Grossa, some 15km west of Alessandria (*see* **Map 9**). Pinned against the Ligurian coast by **Suvorov's** allied offensive in May, Moreau was obliged to advance east with his 14,000 troops in support of **Macdonald's** army marching north from Naples. While Suvorov concentrated to defeat Macdonald at the **Trebbia** (18–19 June), Moreau moved slowly towards **Bellegarde's** allied rearguard, and launched a two-pronged attack against 9,000 Austrian troops around San Giuliano on 21 June. Though Austrian **cavalry** eventually halted **Grouchy's** frontal attack, Moreau sent reserves against Bellegarde's flank during the afternoon and drove the Austrian line into retreat. Bellegarde suffered some 2,500 casualties, against about 1,000 French, but his retirement west to the Bormida threatened French forces with encirclement when Suvorov turned to his aid, prompting Moreau's hasty departure towards **Genoa** and a rendezvous with the remnants of Macdonald's force.

San Idelfonso, Convention of

Secret agreement signed by **France** and **Spain** on 7 October 1800 by which the Spanish government exchanged six **ships-of-the-line** and its vast North American colony of **Louisiana** for control of **Tuscany**, which passed to the heir of the Duke of **Parma**, son-in-law of King **Charles IV**. Confirmed by the Treaty of Aranjuez in March 1801, the San Idelfonso agreement constituted a very good bargain for France, which anyway annexed Tuscany in 1808.

San Marcial, Battle of (1794)

Key victory for French forces on the northwestern sector of the **Pyrenean** front in summer 1794. Exploiting a mounting superiority in men and **artillery**, French sector commander Muller launched an offensive against the centre of Spanish fortified lines on 24 July. While diversionary operations pinned Spanish forces at the coast and on the inland flank, French forces drove defenders beyond Elizondo by 27 July and moved up to Berra. New Spanish commander Colomera withdrew his army behind the Bidassoa around Irun and San Marcial, but Muller was already moving **Moncey** from Elizondo towards Irun, and General Frégeville moved on the main Spanish position at San Marcial from 31 July. Attacked from three sides on 1 August, the San Marcial garrison beat a rapid retreat to Oyarzan, abandoning 200 guns. French troops poured across the frontier, taking San Sebastian on 4 August and moving inland to take Tolosa five days later. Half Colomera's force retired on Pamplona, the remainder to Mondragón, but the French paused to reinforce the sector and did not attack again that autumn. *See* **Map 5**.

San Marcial, Battle of (1813)

Defensive victory by Spanish forces on 31 August 1813 that, along with the simultaneous British success at **Vera**, halted the last French incursion into Spain of the **Peninsular War**. After his July offensive had collapsed at **Sorauren**, French commander **Soult** still hoped to relieve the besieged northern Spanish port of **San Sebastian**, and prepared a two-pronged attack west across the River Bidassoa (*see* **Map 5**).

Delayed two hours by heavy mist, three divisions under **Reille** attacked across a ford at the monastery of San Marcial, some 10km inland, from eight in the morning on 31 August. Their initial attack on a ridge held by General Friere's three Spanish divisions had failed before strong **artillery** support was in position, and a second attempt at noon fared little better. French forces took a small area on the far left of the Spanish position, but Soult was unable to rally his troops to a third major attack and withdrew during the late afternoon. Friere's troops lost 1,679 men during the day, inflicting about 2,500 casualties.

San Sebastian, Siege of

The northern Spanish port of San Sebastian came under French control in 1808, and was one of two strongholds in Spain to remain in French hands after the Battle of **Vitoria** in June 1813. Unwilling to risk an immediate offensive across the Pyrenees, allied commander **Wellington** sent a relatively small Spanish force to invest French-held **Pamplona** and detached General **Graham** with 25,000 troops to take San Sebastian.

Graham's forces had placed the city, and General **Rey's** 6,000 garrison troops, under **siege** by 28 June, but it presented a formidable obstacle to attack. Situated on a spur of land between the Urmea River and the Bay of Biscay, it was protected from the sea by a castle just to the north, and the weaker land defences to the east could only be approached by crossing the river. An attack by this route was driven off with heavy losses on 25 July, after which news of **Soult's** successes at **Maya** and **Roncesvalles** forced Wellington to suspend offensive operations until after his victory at **Sorauren**.

A second major assault on the town's east wall took place on 31 August, by which time sufficient heavy **artillery** had arrived to make several breaches. Launched at low tide (about eleven in the morning), it again suffered severe casualties wading across the river, and had achieved nothing by twelve thirty, when Graham ordered his artillery to fire at defenders over the heads of attacking troops. An unusual and risky ploy, it paid off when a shell blew up the garrison's ammunition store. Allied troops broke into the town soon afterwards, and surviving defenders withdrew into the castle, where they eventually surrendered on 8 September. The siege cost 1,700 French casualties, not including prisoners, and 3,700 allied, most of them during the final attack, which was followed by a five-day looting spree that left the town in ruins and created serious friction between the British and Spanish governments. *See* **Peninsular War**; Maps 5, 22.

Sandöström, Battle of

Small but important naval encounter during the **Russo-Swedish War** of 1808–9, fought on 2 August 1808 in the Sandöström Sound, one of myriad shallow waterways among the islands littering the south-west coast of **Finland** (*see* **Map 18**). As **Buxhowden**'s Russian army sought to exploit early victories by pushing across the archipelago towards Stockholm, the **Swedish Navy**'s Army Fleet of small warships was charged with preventing the union of two similar Russian fleets through Sandöström. Though the Army Fleet outnumbered its Russian counterparts, and possessed better ships, commanding admiral Hjelmstjerna settled for stringing a line of 22 **sloops** across the passage and waiting to be attacked. When the attack came, he was not able to bring up reserves before the right of his defensive line collapsed, and Swedish forces withdrew. Hjelmstjerna's counter-attack on 30 August halted further Russian advances through the maze of narrow waterways, prompting Buxhowden's retirement to **Palvasund**.

Sankt Michael, Battle of

French victory over Austrian forces retreating from the Kingdom of **Italy** in May 1809, as the War of the **Fifth Coalition**'s decisive campaign got under way further north. Archduke **John**'s 65,000 Austrian troops had won an inconclusive victory at **Sacile** on 16 April, but had withdrawn north-east on news of French successes at **Abensberg** and **Eckmühl**. Italian viceroy **Beauharnais**, his smaller army still reorganizing behind the Adige, launched an energetic pursuit, advancing on Leoben to get between John and General **Jellacic**'s reinforcements approaching from the Tyrol. On 25 May, Beauharnais launched his entire force of some 30,000 troops against Jellacic's positions near the village of Sankt Michael, driving back outnumbered defenders and inflicting 3,000 casualties. The defeat persuaded John to pull east into Hungary, away from **Napoleon**'s army on the Danube. Leaving **Macdonald** and 15,000 troops to watch John, Beauharnais marched to join the emperor at the end of the month. *See* Battle of **Raab**; **Map 9**.

Santo Domingo

French colony in the **West Indies**, comprising the slightly smaller western side of the large Caribbean island of Hispaniola (*see* **Map 7**). Santo Domingo was a favourite haunt of French **privateers** from spring 1793, prompting a British raid from Barbados to take the south-western settlement of Cape Tiburon in February 1794. A stronger British attack took Port-au-Prince on 5 June, when a **Royal Navy** squadron of four **ships-of-the-line** and three **frigates** terrorized town authorities into surrendering.

An invasion across the frontier with Spanish Hispaniola had by then trapped French governor-general Lavaux in a coastal fort. Lavaux was able to use his government's unequivocal rejection of slavery to enlist the support of experienced native leader Toussaint **L'Ouverture**, who liberated the French on 25 June, and had taken several Spanish garrisons, as well as Cape Tiburon by December.

Spanish cession of Hispaniola to France by the Treaty of **Basle** in 1795 only deepened a condition of near anarchy on the island as a whole. Though British forces retained their foothold in Port-au-Prince, French occupation of the north-west was bolstered by a naval squadron and General Rochembeau's 1,200 troops from France on 12 May. They made little difference. European troops on both sides were quickly reduced to virtual uselessness by sickness.

With L'Ouverture establishing himself as an independent leader of native forces, British troops were evacuated from Santo Domingo in May 1798, and French regulars followed later in the year. L'Ouverture gradually cleared the island of Europeans to take full control of a united Haiti by 1801, ushering in a brief period of peace and trade-related local prosperity, before the Anglo-French **Amiens** peace freed **Napoleon** to send an army across the Atlantic.

General **Leclerc** and 20,000 troops sailed from Brest on 11 December 1801, reached Haiti in early February, and quickly overwhelmed local forces. L'Ouverture was deported to France, but Leclerc was among thousands of disease victims before the end of the year. Despite reinforcements from Napoleon, a renewed uprising in 1803 forced Rochembeau to quit the island for good in November, by which time 25,000 French troops had died there since 1796. Haiti formally declared its independence on 1 January 1804, when rebel leader Dessalins was proclaimed Emperor James I. Under almost permanent threat of reconquest over the next two decades, the regime had little choice but to reopen its ports to French privateers, which remained a menace to British commerce until 1814.

Santo Domingo, Battle of

The destruction of a French naval squadron in the harbour of Santo Domingo by **Royal Navy** forces under Admiral **Duckworth** on 6 February 1806. French admiral Leisségues and five **ships-of-the-line** had been part of a fleet that had escaped the British **blockade** of Brest in late 1805. Accompanied by 1,000 troops, they had begun attacking British merchant shipping and trading posts from the independent republic of Haiti, where Duckworth and seven ships-of-the-line surprised them on 6 February and launched an immediate attack. Though the anchored French ships fought well, the unequal struggle ended with three captured and two run aground. The defeat, and the failure of a second squadron under Willaumez later in the year, temporarily ended **French Navy** attempts to use fleet units that survived **Trafalgar** as commerce raiders in the **West Indies**. *See* Map 20.

Saorgio Offensive

The opening French offensive of the 1794 **Italian campaign**, a drive along the Ligurian coast of northern Italy that was the first major operation planned by **Napoleon**. About 45,000 Austrian and Piedmontese troops were holding strong positions in the mountains to the north of the French Army of Italy's coastal positions, and the **Royal Navy** was strangling its supply line through **Genoa**. His troops short on morale and food, but ordered to attack by the **Directory** government, French commander **Dumerbion** put his faith in the army's political representatives (**Saliceti** and Augustin Robespierre), who ensured wholesale adoption of artillery commander Bonaparte's plans for a spring offensive.

After a series of delays caused by heavy snow, a French advance began on 16 April 1794, led by 22,000 troops organized into two strike forces

and a tactical reserve under Napoleon's control. One wing drove east along the coast towards the Piedmontese **privateer** base at Oneglia, the other attacked into the mountains towards Ormea and the line of the River Tanaro, backed by a diversionary attack towards the main Piedmontese positions further west around Saorgio.

The mountain attack was led by **Masséna**'s two brigades, which reached Ormea without serious opposition before turning west to cut lines of retreat from Saorgio, forcing the garrison's surrender in the face of Dumerbion's remaining 21,000 men, advancing more slowly in their wake. The coastal attack swept beyond Oneglia to take Albenga and Loano, putting the important Col de l'Argentières, Tende and St Bernard passes under French control by the time operations were halted in early May. Napoleon's division of forces, and concern to undermine his opponent's line of retreat, became trademarks of French offensive warfare over the next two decades. *See* **Map 9**.

Sappers

Seventeenth-century English term for troops who dug narrow communicating trenches, or saps, during **siege** operations, it was used more generally to describe military **engineers** of all types by the late eighteenth-century.

Saragossa, Sieges of

The city of Saragossa, on the River Ebro in Aragon, was targeted by the first French offensive during the **Peninsular War**, launched in June 1808 as rebellion against French occupation flared all over **Spain** (*see* Map 22). Part of **Bessières**'s reserve corps attacked the city's weak southern defences on 15 June, but was stopped by the assembled citizenry and 1,500 rebel troops under José **Palafox**. Having suffered 700 casualties, French commander **Lefebvre-Desnouëttes** retired to begin **siege** operations.

After an attempt by Palafox to bring more Spanish troops into the city failed on 24 June, new French commander Verdier launched a full-scale attack with 8,000 troops on 4 July. Though the local height of Monte Toreno was taken, Saragossa's defences had been strengthened by mass construction of barricades, and the French lost another 500 men before falling back.

Verdier's next attack, on 4 August, established a position inside the city by nightfall, but Spanish reinforcements arrived next day and Verdier withdrew again. By the time Verdier abandoned the siege on 17 August, French losses totalled 3,500 men against an estimated 5,000 Spanish casualties.

After the Spanish defeat at **Tudela** in late November 1808, Palafox retired into Saragossa and began intensive preparations to meet a renewed siege, cramming the city with 35,000 troops and almost twice as many construction workers, but failing to amass sufficient provisions. French corps under **Moncey** and **Mortier**, a total of 45,000 men, began the second siege on 20 December, and **mined** their way through the outer defences over the next three weeks. New overall commander **Lannes** began a major infantry assault on the city on 16 January, and savage street fighting continued until 20 February, when hunger and disease forced defenders to capitulate. The success had cost 10,000 French casualties and none of the city's 54,000 defenders escaped.

Sardinia

Controlled since 1720 by the Savoyard rulers of **Piedmont**, the island kingdom of Sardinia committed troops to the **First Coalition** against France from 1792, but was otherwise one of the quietest corners of western Europe during the war years. King Victor Amadeus III signed the Peace of **Cherasco** with France shortly before his death in 1796, and his son Charles Emmanuel IV retired to Sardinia in December 1798, but moved to **Naples** after a failed attempt to recover Piedmont in 1799 and abdicated (for the second and last time) in 1802. His brother Victor Emmanuel I (ruled 1802–21) settled in the capital Cagliari, from 1806, and remained on the island until 1814, when the Congress of **Vienna** restored the kingdom's lands in Piedmont and Savoy. *See* **Map 1**.

Saumarez, James (1757–1836)

A Channel Islander, Saumarez began the **Revolutionary Wars** as a captain in the **Royal Navy**, serving in home waters and on **blockade** duty at Brest until his transfer to the **Mediterranean** in 1796. One of several gifted British naval commanders nurtured to brilliance under Mediterranean C-in-C **Jervis**, he took the surrender of the Spanish flagship at Cape **St Vincent**, and was **Nelson's** senior captain at the **Nile** in 1798, leading the bulk of the fleet back to Gibraltar in its aftermath and supplying anti-French rebels at **Malta** en route. As rear-admiral in command of a squadron at Gibraltar, Saumarez defeated a larger Franco-Spanish force at **Algeciras** in July 1801, thwarting a planned combined attack on the **West Indies** from Ferrol. He subsequently commanded squadrons in the Channel Islands (1803–7) and the Baltic (1808–13), reaching the rank of vice-admiral in 1807 and becoming a full admiral after the end of naval hostilities in 1814.

Savary, Anne Jean Marie René (1774–1833)

French soldier who joined the revolutionary army as a cavalryman in 1790 and was commissioned next year. After five years' service on the **Rhine** he took part in the 1798 **Middle East** expedition on the staff of **Desaix**, and was on **Napoleon's** staff after his chief was killed at **Marengo** in 1800. Promoted brigadier-general in 1803, Savary became a trusted hatchet man, helping expose the **Cadoudal** plot in 1804 and organizing the execution of the Duc d'**Enghein**. A divisional general from February 1805, he was at **Austerlitz**, **Jena** and **Friedland**, and was briefly envoy to St Petersburg after the Peace of **Tilsit**. Primarily responsible for duping the Spanish royal family into attending the **Bayonne** Conference in 1808, he was created Duke of Rovigo just afterwards.

Savary accompanied Napoleon to **Erfurt** and through the campaigns of 1808–9 before replacing **Fouché** as minister of police in 1810, a post he held until 1814. Though an apparently natural choice for the job, he lacked his predecessor's cunning or investigative skills, and was almost dismissed after being captured in bed during the 1812 **Malet Conspiracy**. He retired after the first **abdication**, but rejoined Napoleon during the **Hundred Days** and later tried to stow away aboard the ship taking the former emperor to exile on St Helena. Arrested by British authorities and sent to Malta, he eventually returned to France in 1819.

Savoy

Once an independent state, the Alpine province of Savoy had been divided in 1760, when the ruling kings of **Sardinia** had ceded the west of the region to the French monarchy, the rump being absorbed into **Piedmont**. An inevitable target for wartime French expansionism, Piedmontese Savoy was invaded in 1792, and eventually annexed to **France** in 1796. *See* **Italian Campaigns**, 1792–7; **Map 1**.

Saxe-Coburg, Frederick Josias, Prince of (1737–1815)

The younger son of a minor German grand duke, Saxe-Coburg began his military career during the Seven Years War and made his reputation commanding Austrian forces against the **Ottoman Empire** in 1788–90. Appointed to lead **First Coalition** forces assembled to defend the **Netherlands** in 1793, he enjoyed initial success at **Neerwinden** but displayed characteristic overcaution and inflexibility during the subsequent campaign in **Flanders**. By the time he resigned his command in August 1794, French forces were poised on the Dutch frontier, and he received no further military employment during two decades of quiet retirement.

Saxon Army

Apart from a small force that fought with the **First Coalition**, the Saxon Army was at peace until 1806, when it formed an autonomous branch of the **Prussian Army** during the **Jena–Auerstädt** campaign. The army's infantry strength in 1806 comprised about 19,000 men, organized as ten regiments of line infantry and one of élite Grenadier Guards, along with four heavy and five light **cavalry** regiments.

King **Frederick Augustus** was committed to providing 20,000 men for French imperial service from late 1806. Most fought in the 1809 War of the **Fifth Coalition** as IX Corps under **Bernadotte**, and their reputation suffered a major blow when it broke and fled at **Wagram** in July. The army was scaled down in 1810, when infantry strength was reduced to about 14,000 men and one heavy cavalry regiment disbanded, but some 15,000 Saxon infantry and almost 1,200 cavalry served with **Reynier's** VII Corps during the 1812 **Russian campaign**, and two regiments of heavy cavalry with **Grouchy** were prominent at **Borodino**.

The remains of the Saxon Army formed two divisions under Bernadotte for much of the 1813 campaign in **Germany**, but defected to the allies during the Battle of **Leipzig**. Survivors of the 1813 campaign formed the basis of a new force for allied service, which eventually contributed nine infantry regiments (four of them **Landwehr**) and three cavalry regiments to the campaigns of 1814–15.

Saxony

The north German Electorate of Saxony had emerged from turmoil surrounding its ruling family's election to the throne of **Poland** to pursue a cautious foreign policy under Elector **Frederick Augustus** III. Turning down the Polish crown in 1791, he generally avoided unnecessary entanglements abroad as he sought to improve the state's ramshackle economic condition. The **Saxon Army** fought on the **Rhine** with the **First Coalition**, discharging its obligations to the **Holy Roman Empire**, but Frederick Augustus agreed a mutual neutrality treaty with **France** in 1796.

The alliance broke down in 1806, when neighbouring **Prussia** effectively compelled Frederick Augustus to join the **Fourth Coalition**, but was quickly re-established after French victory at **Jena–Auerstädt**, and Saxony joined the Confederation by the **Rhine** by the Treaty of **Posen** (11 December 1806). Apart from the legal emancipation of its small Catholic population, the new kingdom was not subject to large-scale constitutional reform.

After committing troops to **Napoleon's** campaigns of 1809 and 1812, the Saxon government wavered long and hard before aiding France in the 1813 struggle for **Germany**. After intense negotiations it agreed to fulfil its obligations to the Confederation on 10 May, and subsequent good faith was encouraged by the presence of a powerful French garrison in the capital, **Dresden**. The king's refusal to renounce an increasingly unpopular alliance was undermined by the defection of Saxon troops at **Leipzig** in October, and he was imprisoned after French forces abandoned Dresden in November. Prussian plans to annex Saxony were thwarted by **Austria** and

Great Britain at the postwar Congress of Vienna, but a compromise settlement still left Berlin in control of more than half the country after 1815. *See* Maps 1, 21, 30.

Scharnhorst, Gerhard Johann David von (1755–1813)

German staff officer who joined his native Hanoverian Army in 1778, becoming an artillery instructor and an admired military theorist. He served under the Duke of York's command in Flanders in 1793–5, fighting at Hondschoote, and accepted an offer to enter Prussian service as a lieutenant-colonel (with a minor title) in 1801, becoming a teacher at the Berlin War Academy for officer training. On Brunswick's staff during the Jena–Auerstädt campaign of 1806, he transferred to Blücher's corps in its aftermath, and was among the Prussian remnant fighting alongside Russian forces in 1807. After Tilsit had reduced the Prussian Army to a skeleton force of 42,000 men, he was promoted major-general and given the task of reform as Director of the War Department.

Scharnhorst's period in office from 1808 to 1810, when pressure from Napoleon forced his dismissal, is celebrated as crucial to Prussia's subsequent military renaissance and to the development of popular German nationalism. In concert with reforming politicians such as Stein and Hardenberg, and aided by Gneisenau, he modernized the army's organization, sponsored the final rejection of outmoded infantry tactics, and created a national militia (Landwehr) that provided a constructive outlet for popular patriotism. Recalled to become Blücher's chief of staff in 1812, he took part in the opening stages of the 1813 campaign for Germany, but was fatally wounded during the Battle of Lützen in May, and died in Prague two months later.

Schérer, Barthelemy Louis Joseph (1747–1804)

Schérer had served Austria, France and the independent Netherlands during a 25-year military career by the time of his retirement as a junior officer in 1790, but re-enlisted for France in 1792. Posted to the Rhine front, he became a brigadier-general in September 1793, and commanded forces completing the sieges of allied fortresses in Flanders the following summer. He led the French right under Jourdan at the Roer in the autumn, before taking over from Dumerbion on the Italian front in November. Quickly transferred to take command of French forces on the eastern sector of the Pyrenean front, he led the successful siege of Rosas in spring 1795, but returned to the Italian theatre as C-in-C from 1 October. His bold winter offensive won success at Loano in late November, but refusal to accept the Directory government's orders for further attacks prompted his replacement by Napoleon the following March.

Returning to Paris, he was war minister from 1797 until returned to Italy as C-in-C in February 1799, but he resigned after the failure of his opening offensive at Verona and returned home to face corruption charges. They were dropped once Napoleon became First Consul, but he was not given another command.

Schiarino-Rizzino, Convention of

The armistice agreed between Austrian field marshal Bellegarde and French viceroy Beauharnais that closed the Italian campaign of 1814. Signed on 16 April, after news had reached the theatre of Napoleon's defeat and abdication, the Convention required Beauharnais to evacuate French troops, but allowed him to retain control of viceregal territories with the help of his Italian troops, and to negotiate with the victorious allies for the Kingdom of Italy's postwar survival.

Schill, Ferdinand Baptista von (1776–1809)

Saxon-born soldier and German nationalist, acclaimed as a patriotic martyr by nationalist agitators against French rule from 1809 to 1813. Schill fought at Jena as a junior officer with the Prussian Army, and subsequently organized a Freikorps of 1,000 men to carry out raids against French occupying forces in northern Germany. His unit was absorbed into regular Prussian forces after the Peace of Tilsit in 1807, and Schill was promoted major, but he marched his men across the frontier into Westphalia in May 1809 and proclaimed a nationalist uprising. Although it occupied border areas for a short time, Schill's relatively tiny force was driven back into Swedish Pomerania by Jérôme Bonaparte's army, and he was killed when it was defeated at Stralsund. *See* **Map 16.**

Schliengen, Battle of

The final engagement on the **Rhine** front in 1796, a last-ditch attempt by Austrian C-in-C Archduke **Charles** to prevent the escape across the river of **Moreau**'s battered French army, which had retreated from **Emmendlingen** to take up positions stretching some 15km east from Steinstatt to the hills around Kandern. Charles attacked all along the line on 23 October, and took Steinstatt in the morning, but initial gains in the centre could not be exploited, and the stronger French right had given ground only slowly by the time pouring rain turned to fog, ending fighting in the early evening. Moreau withdrew overnight, and completed a highly efficient retreat without further interference on 26 October, when the last of his forces crossed the Rhine at Hunningen. *See* **Map 4.**

Schönbrunn, Peace of *See* Convention of **Vienna** (1806)

Schönbrunn, Treaty of

The agreement (sometimes known as the second Treaty of Pressburg) between Emperors **Francis** and **Napoleon** that ended the War of the **Fifth Coalition** in 1809. An armistice was signed at **Znaim** on 12 July 1809, in the aftermath of Napoleon's victory at **Wagram**, but Francis proved reluctant to come to final terms and threatened to resume hostilities. Briefly encouraged by the British landing at **Walcheren**, all prospect of a renewed Austrian war effort had faded by the time the treaty was eventually signed on 14 October. **Austria** ceded the provinces of Frioul, Carniola and Carinthia, the city of Trieste and most of its territory in **Illyria** to France, while **Bavaria** received the Inn-Viertel provinces and Salzburg, Austrian **Poland** was brought into the Duchy of **Warsaw**, and **Russia** was given part of Galicia. Francis was charged a war indemnity of about 85 million francs, confirmed his adherence to the **Continental System**, recognized Joseph **Bonaparte** as King of **Spain**, and agreed to restrict the **Austrian Army** to 150,000 men. Napoleon considered these terms particularly moderate. *See* **Map 21.**

Schwarzenberg, Karl Philipp, Prince (1771–1820)

Viennese nobleman, commissioned into the **Austrian Army** in 1788, who led **cavalry** on the eastern French frontiers during the **Revolutionary Wars**, playing a prominent role at **Landrecies** in 1794, and was promoted brigadier-general in 1796. A divisional general from 1800, he commanded some of the few Austrian troops to escape encirclement at **Ulm** in 1805, and was appointed ambassador to St Petersburg in 1806. He remained in Russia until 1809, but was transferred to Paris after the Peace of **Schönbrunn** had re-established **Austria**'s alliance with **Napoleon**.

Given command of Austrian forces committed to Napoleon's 1812 **Russian invasion**, he led his corps on the right of the French advance, displaying characteristic caution in fulfilling a largely peripheral role south of the Pripet Marshes. When Austria joined the **Sixth Coalition** in August 1813, Schwarzenberg was given overall command of allied forces in **Germany**, and personal command of the main Army of Bohemia, but hardly exercised supreme authority. Travelling with the Austrian, Russian and Prussian monarchs, and frequently in dispute with allied generals, he found his deeply cautious strategies overruled during the campaign for **France**. Again in command of Austrian forces en route for France when fighting ended in 1815, he retired in 1817.

Sebastiani, Horace François (1772–1851)

French infantry officer, commissioned in 1789, who fought on the **Italian** front against the **First Coalition**, and played a minor role in the **Brumaire coup** of 1799 that brought **Napoleon** to power. He was a colonel with the Reserve Army at **Marengo** in 1800 before undertaking a diplomatic mission to the **Ottoman Empire** in 1801. Promoted brigadier-general on his return to France two years later, he took part in the capture of **Vienna** and the victory at **Austerlitz** in 1805, and received divisional rank in December. He was ambassador to Constantinople from 1806, and won international fame by organizing Turkish defences to repel the British **Dardanelles** expedition in 1807.

From August 1808 Sebastiani served in the **Peninsular War**, first under **Lefebvre**, but as a corps commander from February 1809. He fought at **Talavera** and **Ocaña** in 1809, and was ennobled in November, before accompanying **Soult** into south-western Spain the following year. Recalled in 1811, he led a cavalry division during the 1812 **Russian campaign** and took over **Montbrun**'s command after **Borodino**, but his forward units were surprised at **Vinkovo** in October. He retained a frontline role through the campaign for **Germany**, fighting at **Leipzig** and **Hanau**, and the 1814 defence of **France**, when he was with **Macdonald**'s corps.

Sebastiani held a command on the Rhine during the **Hundred Days** of 1815, and was subsequently exiled to Britain, but returned to pursue a political career as a left-wing deputy through the 1820s, and held a number of senior positions during the 1830s, including that of foreign minister (1830–2) and ambassador to London (1835–40).

Second Coalition, War of the

The struggle between republican **France** and the second combination of major European powers ranged against it, begun in late 1798 and ended by the Austro-French peace of February 1801. The peace that followed the eventual collapse of the **First Coalition** in 1797 had never seemed likely to last, partly because **Austria** was manifestly bent on reversing its defeats in the **Italian** theatre, but primarily because France remained at war with **Great Britain**. Anglo-French conflict was largely confined to **naval** and **colonial** warfare in 1797–8, but British strategic orthodoxy demanded a search for continental land allies, and the French **Directory** government was committed to channelling the nation's volatile energies into continental expansion or anti-British adventures.

Annexations had already expanded the French republic to its 'natural' frontiers at the Rhine, the Alps and the Pyrenees, and established buffer states in the **Netherlands** and northern Italy. The process of further expansion into Italy was begun in February 1798 with the occupation of the **Papal States**, and French forces took control of **Switzerland** in April. Upheavals in Italy did not tempt Austria into risking a premature resumption of hostilities, but were seen in **Russia** as part of an attempt to dominate the **Mediterranean**. The impression was encouraged by French occupation of the **Ionian Islands** and above all by **Napoleon**'s expedition to the **Middle East**.

Primarily aimed at disrupting British interests, Napoleon's move on **Egypt** caused intense alarm in St Petersburg and was a direct attack on the **Ottoman Empire**, paving the way for an alliance between all three. Russia mobilized troops on its south-western frontiers, agreed in August to send troops to encourage an Austrian invasion of Italy and sought an alliance with Constantinople. The **Royal Navy**'s destruction of French Mediterranean sea power at the **Nile** (1 August 1798) provided the final catalyst for concerted Russo-Turkish action in the form of a leisurely joint attack on the Ionian Islands from October.

In this context, the surprise invasion of the Papal States by **Naples** in November amounted to an invitation for united action against France. Local naval commander **Nelson** warped British Mediterranean policy to provide coastal support, and Russian tsar **Paul** concluded an alliance with the Neapolitan court before accepting British premier **Pitt**'s flattering invitation to take the lead in organizing a formal Second Coalition.

Prussia could not be persuaded to join, instead providing guarantees of benevolent neutrality to Russia and Austria, but British **subsidies** otherwise eased the Coalition's rapid formation. An Anglo-Russian alliance on 29 December was joined by the dispossessed Vatican, **Portugal** and several German states. Though Austria remained reluctant to make any firm commitment, its slow preparations for an invasion of Italy were already under way, and French aggression eventually forced **Francis II** into a formal alliance in June 1799.

Though it appeared formidable, the Coalition laboured under important weaknesses. Its major allies ignored Pitt's condition that they exchange pledges renouncing any separate peace, and its overall offensive plan ignored the importance of Switzerland as the key to any attack on France, depending instead on the coordinated success of separate forces attacking in Italy, southern Germany and the Netherlands.

Encouraged by relatively easy success in the **Neapolitan campaign**, which delivered southern Italy into French hands as the Parthenopean Republic by early 1799, the Directory was planning its own series of ambitious spring offensives. Attacks were ordered by **Macdonald** in Naples, **Schérer** in northern Italy, **Masséna** in Switzerland and **Jourdan** (with **Bernadotte**) east of the Rhine. Only **Brune**'s 25,000 men in the Netherlands were expected to remain on the defensive, charged with preventing an anticipated Anglo-Russian landing. All its forces were well below paper strength, with only some 50,000 reserves in the process of training, and the **French Army** was not the well-motivated attacking force it had been in 1796–7. Its offensives suffered accordingly.

On the **Rhine** front, Jourdan's advance beyond the Black Forest was reversed at **Stockach** in late March, after which the theatre remained relatively quiet until the late summer while Austrian C-in-C Archduke **Charles** transferred his attentions to Switzerland. Masséna's **Swiss** campaign got off to a good start, advancing through the Grisons, but he was forced back to maintain contact with the Jourdan's retreat, and eventually halted Charles's steady advance just west of **Zurich** in early June. Given overall command of the Rhine and Swiss fronts, and holding vital ground on the flank of any advance either side of the Alps, Masséna too went on to the defensive while the fate of French forces in Italy remained in doubt.

Schérer began his **Italian campaign** with a failed attempt to take **Verona** in late March, before Austrian forces could be reinforced by **Suvorov**'s Russian army from the eastern Mediterranean. Schérer's replacement by **Moreau** in mid-April, and Suvorov's arrival at about the same time, marked the opening of an allied offensive that swept outnumbered French forces back to the Genoese coastline, and crushed Macdonald's army from Naples at the **Trebbia**.

Though the threat to Moreau's rear posed by British control of the Mediterranean failed to materialize, reflecting the **British Army**'s funda-

mental weakness and the Royal Navy's over-extension, the inability of '**Bruix's Cruise**' to relieve forces stranded in Egypt emphasized the extent to which the **French Navy** was banished from its own backyard.

With further Russian reinforcements due, and republican armies already unable to cope with superior allied numbers, the French military position was critical by summer 1799. Beset by economic chaos, basic shortages and internal strife, the latter hardly soothed by its attempt to apply Jourdan's **Conscription** Law from late June, the government ordered August offensives at **Novi** in Italy and **Mannheim** on the Rhine, but their failure seemed to presage an allied invasion of France on one of the two fronts. France was saved by a seismic shift in allied strategic direction, inspired by Austria and effective from early September.

As the Coalition power with most direct interest in the Rhine and northern Italy, Austria had no desire to risk further loss of influence in Germany, or to see Russia established as a Mediterranean power. Habsburg chief minister **Thugut** had been alarmed by Suvorov's behaviour following his capture of Turin, when he had proclaimed the restoration of the monarchy in **Piedmont** on his own authority, and the **Aulic Council** reorganized its military priorities. Transferring Archduke Charles back from the Swiss front to the Rhine, it effectively forced new Russian reinforcements and Suvorov's army to hold the front at Zurich, where Masséna had been strengthened through the summer. Austrian forces under **Melas** were left to carry the fight into Provence from northern Italy, denied any hope of British military aid from the Mediterranean once the Coalition's northern strategy had belatedly focused on an Anglo-Russian invasion of **North Holland**.

Suvorov received orders to swing around towards Masséna's right flank on 27 August, but logistic problems and French resistance delayed his march into position long enough for Masséna to win a pivotal victory over depleted allied forces at **Zurich** in late September. Austrian and Russian armies were driven from Switzerland to the Rhine during October, and the Anglo-Russian expedition was forced to accept humiliating terms and evacuate North Holland after failing to pierce Brune's lines at **Bergen**.

These unexpected disasters helped alienate Tsar Paul from his Coalition partners, and Russia formally withdrew from its alliance obligations in December (*see* **Armed Neutrality**). Meanwhile Napoleon slipped into France from Egypt, where he had been effectively cut off from the world since August 1798, and took power in November's **Brumaire coup**.

The new French **Consulate** regime, with Napoleon as its effective head, came to power publicly committed to a period of peaceful reconstruction, but though negotiations with the Coalition opened during the winter break in campaigning, Britain and Austria rejected French claims in the Netherlands and Italy respectively. While talks dragged on, and allied obduracy became the lifeblood of French **propaganda** to a war-weary population, both sides prepared for a resumption of hostilities in the spring.

The main Austrian armies were massed on the Rhine, where **Kray** commanded some 140,000 troops, and in northern Italy, where Melas controlled more than 100,000 men. Napoleon meanwhile embarked on rapid reconstruction of the French Army, instituting the **corps** system throughout, raising additional manpower for both main theatres, and creating a central Reserve Army stationed around Dijon for rapid deployment on either front. By April 1800 the Reserve Army comprised some 53,000 men, half of them experienced troops, but it was never taken seriously by Austrian planners.

Most authorities agree that Napoleon's original intention was to launch a spring offensive into Germany, threatening Vienna. His position not yet secure, he could only ask Rhine C-in-C Moreau to concentrate in Switzerland for a bold strike against the rear of Kray's army. Moreau's insistence on a straightforward, and less risky, frontal attack forced Napoleon to plan a decisive blow in Italy from late March, but it was preempted by an Austrian offensive in Italy from 5 April, ultimately aimed at the French naval base of Toulon.

Initially successful, Melas lost the initiative by electing to await the fall of **Genoa** before attempting an invasion, giving Napoleon just time to march the Reserve Army through the **Great St Bernard Pass**, place himself across the Austrian rear, and win a narrow but decisive victory at **Marengo** on 14 June. Marengo triggered a full-scale Austrian withdrawal from the Po valley, and a secondary Austrian offensive on the Rhine was halted by Moreau, who had advanced to Munich by the time a truce was arranged at Parsdorf on 28 July.

His summer successes secured Napoleon's political position, and prompted a resumption of peace talks at Leoben, but did not end the war. Though Napoleon was anxious to deliver peace to the French people, Thugut and Emperor Francis did not regard Austrian armies as beaten, and negotiations dragged inconclusively through the summer until a renewed British subsidy persuaded Austria to end the period of truce.

Hostilities were resumed on 22 November 1800, and six days later a three-pronged French offensive was ordered by Napoleon, whose political responsibilities kept him in Paris. Supported by secondary advances from Brune in the Adige and Macdonald in the Alps, Moreau drove directly for Vienna, meeting and beating the main Austrian army at **Hohenlinden** on 3 December. Combined with minor successes by Brune, Macdonald and **Murat** (who reconquered the Papal States), Hohenlinden broke the last bond of the Second Coalition, and Francis II took Austria out of the war at **Lunéville** on 8 February 1801.

Although Portugal remained loyal to its ancient ally, and the Ottoman Empire was prevented from making peace with the French in the Middle East, Britain could expect no significant military assistance from either source. Facing increasing diplomatic isolation and the residual possibility of an invasion of **England**, a weary Pitt had resigned in February 1801. The new **Addington** administration reflected a national sense of resignation by opening negotiations towards an Anglo-French peace, and to the relief of all Europe a preliminary ceasefire was arranged at **Amiens** in October. *See* **Maps 4, 7–10**.

Semaphore

A system of relaying messages over long distances by using visible signals transmitted between exposed points. Much faster and more reliable than conventional means of overland communication – by courier, pony express, beacon flare or carrier pigeon – semaphore (or telegraph) was first introduced by the Frenchman Claude Chappé in 1792, when he installed 22 relay stations to carry messages between Paris and Lille.

The system was adopted the next year by French war minister **Carnot** for military communications to the eastern frontier, and was subsequently extended to cover communications between Paris and most important French cities, as well as between permanent stations and front-line locations during land campaigns. Beginning with the installation of the first permanent signal chain between London and Portsmouth in 1796, other countries gradually introduced similar, though less comprehensive, systems of long-range signalling. Signal codes varied both between and within national or military systems.

Though semaphore could transmit overland messages at speeds of up to 200kph, long messages slowed the system and were prone to become garbled in transit. Overall efficiency was entirely dependent on clear conditions, so that messages were often held up for days by bad weather, and semaphore was almost invariably useless amid the smoke and haze of a battlefield.

Septinsular Republic *See* Ionian Islands

Serbia *See* Ottoman Empire; Kara Djordje Petrovic

Seringapatam Campaign (1799)

The most important military action fought in contemporary **India**, a well-coordinated attack by Anglo-Indian forces in May 1799 to destroy the power of **Tipu Sahib**, ruler of the independent south-west Indian state of Mysore and the principal immediate threat to British imperial rule over the southern part of the subcontinent.

Anglo-Indian forces under Lord Cornwallis had besieged and taken Seringapatam in 1792, after Tipu had invaded neighbouring Travancore. The subsequent partition of Mysore, and Britain's imposition of an indemnity, had left the

imperial administration with a bitter and resourceful enemy, and Tipu had been a target for French aid and encouragement ever since.

News that Tipu had been corresponding with the French governor of Mauritius, with a view to coordinating a military uprising, reached London in the summer of 1798, prompting British war minister **Dundas** to send extra troops to the imperial governor in Calcutta. Earl Mornington, the erstwhile Richard **Wellesley**, had just taken up the governorship, and was determined to pursue British security in India through military aggression. Confident that Tipu would eventually provide provocation for armed intervention, he built up an army in Madras and arranged an alliance with Mysore's neighbour, the Nizam of Hyderabad.

News of **Nelson's** victory at the **Nile** reached British Indian authorities late in 1798, easing fears of a French invasion and freeing Mornington to bring the Mysore question to a head. Tipu's refusal to accept a British envoy, a reflection of his belief in **Napoleon's** imminent arrival with a French army, triggered the launch of a British invasion, and General Harris led 37,000 troops across the Madras frontier on 11 February 1799. They included 16,000 Hyderabad troops temporarily under the command of Colonel Wellesley, the governor-general's brother and future Duke of **Wellington**, who had been responsible for the expedition's much-admired logistic arrangements. Another British force, 6,000 troops under General **Stuart**, moved south on Mysore from Bombay at the same time.

Tipu's French-trained army mustered about 50,000 troops, and he made use of his interior lines of communication to launch a surprise attack on Stuart at Periapatam on 6 March. Though he forced the British into a rapid tactical withdrawal, Tipu was forced to turn for his eastern frontiers by the Madras contingents, and suffered a partial defeat when he took on their combined weight at Malavelly on 22 March. Retiring into the powerful fortress of Seringapatam, he prepared to wait out a British **siege**, confident that tropical conditions and long supply lines would force its collapse.

The only viable approach to the fortress was masked by a swift river, 300m across, and Harris waited until his supply situation had become critical before risking an assault on the walls beyond. The attack went in on 4 May, and was distinguished by a highly efficient river crossing before repeated charges broke through the walls. Tipu had massacred all his prisoners before the attack, and was among thousands of his army killed by vengeful Anglo-Indian troops. The fortress was securely in British hands by nightfall, and Mysore was subsequently partitioned between the British East India Company and Hyderabad, with a small rump state remaining under the rule of a British-sponsored princeling. Arthur Wellesley was stationed in Mysore as civil governor for another four years. *See* **Map 11**.

Sérurier, Jean Mathieu Philibert
(1742–1819)

Veteran French soldier, commissioned as a militiaman in 1755, he was a lieutenant-colonel at Perpignan in 1791, but was dismissed from the army as a crypto-royalist in 1792. Reinstated and posted to the **Italian** theatre, he was promoted brigadier-general in 1793 and was a divisional general from June 1795. He fought at the first Battle of **Loano** that year, and led his division through **Napoleon**'s successful 1796 campaign. He returned from illness to win the battle of **La Favorita** in January 1797, but again fell sick and only returned to Italy as governor of **Venice** in August. He held various Italian administrative posts until April 1799, when he was forced to surrender to **Suvorov**'s Russian army. Paroled and returned to Paris, he supported the **Brumaire coup** and was rewarded with a place in the Senate and appointment as an honorary marshal in 1804. An old-fashioned figure, out of place in nineteenth-century warfare, he never again held an active command.

Seventh Coalition, War of the

Name sometimes given to the **Hundred Days** campaign of 1815. The Seventh Coalition of European states against **France** was agreed at the Congress of **Vienna** on 13 March, when reports that **Napoleon** had returned to France were confirmed, and signed by **Great Britain**, **Russia**, **Austria** and **Prussia** on 25 March. Hostilities effectively ended after the successful defence of Paris by **Davout**'s forces on 30 June, more than a

week after Napoleon's abdication, but the Coalition was only formally ended by the Treaty of **Paris** on 20 November.

Ships-of-the-line

Also known as 'line-of-battle ships', and later simply called battleships, ships-of-the-line were those vessels deemed large and powerful enough to sail in the 'line of battle' that was the tactical basis of contemporary **naval warfare**. At the top of the range, the largest ships-of-the-line were floating castles with three gun decks, mounting between 100 and 130 cannon. Particularly favoured by the **Spanish** and **French** navies, but also used as flagships by the **Royal Navy**, these huge first-raters could produce a devastating broadside, but were cumbersome battle weapons, requiring highly skilled seamanship. The major navies based their battle lines on more handy 80- or 74-gun ships, two-deckers perhaps 50m long and requiring a crew of 6–700 men, ideally at least half of them skilled seamen.

Modern ships-of-the-line were immensely expensive to build and run, consuming a wealth of raw materials, some or all of which had to be imported by most naval powers. At the leading edge of late eighteenth-century technology, their construction and operation required levels of skill and precision that were sometimes beyond dockyards and crews: nobody knew, for example, why the British 80-gunner *Victory*, perhaps the most famous warship of the age, needed 38 tons of ballast in the hold to keep it upright.

Every navy also included smaller, older two-deckers in its battlefleets, the British because they needed so many fleets and other navies on cost grounds. Vessels mounting 60–70 guns (but usually 64) were not uncommon, and old 50-gunners remained in service with all battle lines at the start of the period, although the British withdrew them as soon as replacements could be built.

A floating battery of great power, a single battleship was a formidable strategic weapon in its own right, capable of dominating hostile coastlines, but ships-of-the-line were deep-keeled, relatively sluggish vessels, often at risk from inshore shallows. Foul weather, bad seamanship or accident claimed 37 ships-of-the-line between

1793 and 1815, compared with 43 (of 62 or more guns) destroyed by hostile action, and bold coastal attacks like **Nelson's** at the **Nile** and **Copenhagen** were beyond the daring of many commanders aware that they risked fragile symbols of national power.

Shrapnel

The first effective airburst **artillery** projectile, and the major contemporary development in the field of ammunition, the 'spherical case shot' was invented in 1794 by British artillery officer Henry Shrapnel (1761–1842) and soon came to be known after its inventor. The shrapnel shell comprised a metal casing, thinner than that of an ordinary exploding shell (which it resembled from the outside), and packed with large-bore **musket** balls or scraps of metal. A timed fuse permitted a delayed explosion, showering enemy troops with high-velocity, close-range fire.

Shrapnel was used exclusively by British forces during the Napoleonic period. First employed during **colonial** operations in Surinam during 1804, it accounted for 15 per cent of all British shell stocks (and half of all howitzer ammunition) a decade later. Also used in the warheads of **Congreve rockets**, shrapnel's main operational drawback was a tendency to explode in the barrel when too strong a charge was employed, but this was not a problem when use was confined to howitzers or **mortars**. Though an undoubted success, able to inflict personnel casualties on a far higher scale than any other projectile with equivalent range, shrapnel was initially treated with suspicion by some contemporary commanders, and even in 1813 it was dismissed as 'of trifling significance' by **Wellington**.

Shubra Khit, Battle of

The first major action of the **Middle East** campaign, fought near the French forward base at El Rahmaniya on 13 July 1798. The two wings of the French advance into Egypt, led by overall commander **Napoleon** and General **Desaix**, had united by the Nile at El Rahmaniya the previous day. **Murad Bey**, Ottoman co-governor of **Egypt**, brought up 10,000 **Mameluke** cavalry north of the settlement at Shubra Khit and prepared to attack.

Inexperienced in the development of European weaponry or tactics, Murad's élite horsemen made several charges, but Napoleon organized his five under-strength divisions into **infantry squares** and repelled them all. A parallel engagement between **gunboats** on the Nile ended when French **artillery** was switched to river targets and blew up an Egyptian munitions ship.

Stung by the loss of several hundred troops, Murad suddenly withdrew south to cooperate with co-ruler **Ibrahim Bey** in raising a much larger force, and Napoleon was able to march for Cairo the following morning. Though already suffering from poor preparation for desert conditions, French forces lost only 20 dead and 50 wounded during the battle. *See also* Battle of the **Pyramids**.

Sicilian Army

The Sicilian branch of the Bourbon dynasty's Kingdom of the Two Sicilies underwent separate military reorganization after the first French occupation of **Naples** in 1799. In anticipation of hostile invasion, the island's five regular infantry brigades and six **cavalry** regiments were augmented by militia battalions raised from the Sicilian provinces. Further reorganization under British auspices in 1808 halved the number of cavalry regiments and introduced 12 volunteer regiments for garrison and light infantry duties. A battalion of Albanian cavalry, one of the **Neapolitan Army's** foreign units that remained loyal to King **Ferdinand IV**, was disbanded under the terms of Sicily's 1812 constitution. Sicilian forces joined their British allies in repelling an invasion force from Naples at Messina in September 1810, and intervened briefly in the **Italian campaign** in 1814. Most units, including local volunteers, were incorporated into the reformed army of the 'Two Sicilies' after 1816. *See also* **Neapolitan Navy**.

Sicily

Island kingdom ruled by the Bourbon family in conjunction with **Naples** (as the Kingdom of the Two Sicilies) since 1738, when the future King Charles III of Spain became ruler of both. Charles's son, the 'yokel king' **Ferdinand IV**, ruled the two kingdoms from 1759, and his alliance with the **First Coalition** reinforced Sicily's strategic importance as a central **Mediterranean** naval base. Ferdinand fled to the Sicilian capital of Palermo during the French occupation of Naples in 1798–9, and returned after the second French invasion in February 1806. In between, the Franco-Neapolitan Treaty of Florence (28 March 1801) closed Sicily to **Royal Navy** shipping until Naples joined the **Third Coalition** in 1805.

The British government secured renewed tenure on Sicily with warships and garrison troops, repelling an ill-conceived invasion from **Murat**'s Naples in September 1810, but the island's strategic value was undermined by chronic political instability. Against a background of rising popular radicalism and nationalism, Ferdinand pursued a policy of repressive reaction, and was forced to hand over power to a regency government in 1809. British ambassador Bentinck arrived in July 1811 and embarked on a programme of reforms to rescue the monarchy, but was hindered by Queen Maria Carolina's suspicions of a British takeover bid until he forced her into exile in June 1813. Bentinck persuaded Ferdinand to reclaim the throne in 1812, supervised the introduction of a relatively liberal constitution and led an Anglo-Sicilian force on the mainland during the **Italian campaign** of 1814. Ferdinand returned to his reactionary ways when the British withdrew, ushering in an era of turbulent republican opposition to the monarchy by revoking the constitution shortly after Bentinck's departure in July 1814. *See also* **Carbonari**.

Sidmouth, Viscount *See* **Addington**, Henry

Siege Train

A specialist version, sometimes also known as a battery train, of the **field train** used by most fighting forces of the period. It travelled only as fast as its most cumbersome heavy **artillery** and **mortars**, but no **siege** facing powerful **fortress** walls could expect to succeed before it arrived. Usually operating against second-line targets, or protected by strong screening forces from attack near the front, siege trains crawling through rear areas became a favourite target of rebels and **guerrillas** operating behind the lines of occupying forces.

Siege Warfare

The reduction of **fortresses** and other static defensive positions had been a central feature of European warfare in the century before 1792, but the ensuing decades were a period of transition. During the mannered, dynastic wars of the earlier eighteenth century, the operations of relatively small armies tended to be dominated by the possession of important strongholds, and campaigns were often decided by the fall or relief of a single besieged fortress, with rulers accepting the regional control implied.

The **First Coalition**'s early offensives on the **Flanders** and **Rhine** fronts followed this orthodoxy, laying siege to every frontier fortress in their path, and were ultimately defeated by French mobility and aggression, triggering a shift in the pattern of contemporary warfare. Destruction or decisive defeat of armies became the basic aim of military **strategy**, and though some of the many sieges that took place before 1815 were of vital strategic importance, particularly during the 1796–1801 **Italian campaigns** and the **Peninsular War**, most were secondary operations in the context of wars determined by field engagements.

If their capture was no longer the index of military success, the strong fortress-cities that punctuated inland landscapes were generally major supply centres located at important road junctions or river crossings. Their large garrisons threatened the rear of any offensive that simply passed them by, and it was necessary at least to prevent their breakout, forcing attackers to undertake the costly and protracted distraction of a siege operation.

The techniques of contemporary siegecraft bore the stamp of Enlightenment rationalism. Detailed, precise and developed for wars in which little of importance took place elsewhere, they were concerned to remove any element of chance from the steady process of attacking operations. Since time was on the side of attackers, speed was not considered a priority unless troops were needed for another siege.

Imposing a local blockade to cut supply routes would eventually starve out any garrison, but slowly enough almost to guarantee a relief operation. Blockade was more usually the first step towards development of a full siege, which involved approaching, breaching and finally assaulting the fortifications in an attempt to capture the position outright.

The next stage in the attacking process was to surround the target with infantry trenches and **artillery** batteries. Once **engineers** had completed the first ring of trenches, known as 'parallels' because they ran roughly parallel with the fortress walls, and strongpoints beyond the fortress walls had been taken or isolated, the process of moving steadily closer to the walls began with construction of the first 'saps', trenches leading towards the fortress from the outer ring. A second ring of parallels would then be dug joining the inner tips of the saps, and the process repeated until the third or fourth ring was close enough to the walls for heavy artillery to blow a hole in a chosen sector. Once this had been achieved, a planned assault would concentrate on the breach created, ideally breaking into the fortified area and overwhelming the garrison.

Construction of the necessary trenches involved a great deal of earth-moving, which had to be handled manually by large numbers of infantry, and was likely to be interrupted by garrison raids, **sniper** attacks or bombardments from fortress artillery. These were also directed at siege guns, which anyway faced a difficult task with barely adequate technology. Only the biggest guns and **mortars** were capable of breaching thick fortress walls. Notoriously difficult to transport, they slowed the arrival of **siege trains**, and required an enormous supply of ammunition to create a useful breach.

If the gap eventually created was sufficiently large to convince both sides that an attack was viable, and no relief army was expected, garrison commanders usually sought surrender terms. If the situation was less clear-cut, the resulting battles were often exercises in carnage, especially if attacking troops were required to scale the walls by ladder (or 'escalade').

The storming of a small or well-defended breach in fortifications was regarded as a tactic of last resort by most commanders, and was usually accompanied by a number of diversionary attacks on other parts of the fortress, aimed at dissipating garrison resources. Even if successful, attackers committed to a fortress assault could expect to suffer severe casualties as the climax to months of arduous trench warfare, and the consequences of determined garrison defence often rebounded on civilian populations subject to destructive rampages by their embittered conquerors.

Sieyès, Emmanuel Joseph (1748–1836)

A central figure during the early phases of the **French Revolution**, the 'Abbé Sieyès' was a leader of those minor French clergy demanding political rights for the Third Estate in 1789. He proposed the transformation of the States-General into a National Assembly in June, helped draft the 'Declaration of the Rights of Man' and supervised the division of **France** into new political *départements*. Though a founding member of the **Jacobin** Club, he was left behind by the Revolution's radicalization, and gradually withdrew from the political limelight in the early 1790s. Elected to the Legislative Assembly, he survived the **Terror** by assiduous avoidance of controversy, and declined an offer to join the original **Directory** in late 1794. After performing diplomatic duties in the **Netherlands** during 1795, he gradually returned to the centre of affairs, serving a spell as president of the Council of **Five Hundred** and giving important support to the government during the 1797 **Fructidor** coup.

Ambassador to Berlin in 1798, Sieyès finally joined the Directory in spring 1799, and almost immediately began plotting its downfall. As principal organizer of the **Brumaire coup** in November 1799, he allied himself with **Napoleon** (after **Moreau** had turned him down and Joubert had been killed), but the association was brief. Sieyès was one of the original leaders of the **Consulate**, and wrote its first constitution, but was politically outmanoeuvred by Napoleon and accepted retirement after only a few weeks. Handsomely rewarded for his cooperation, and subsequently ennobled as a count of the empire, he was eventually exiled by the restored monarchy in 1815, returning to France only after the revolution of 1830.

'Six Days Campaign'

Name often given to the period of intense military activity in **France** from 10 to 14 February

1814, during which **Napoleon** inflicted four defeats on **Blücher's** allied army threatening Paris. Operating with a small force, never more than about 30,000 strong, Napoleon was able to translate imaginative tactics into action far more efficiently than had been possible with the gigantic hosts of 1812 and 1813. His troops covered almost 130km during the five days, despite heavy rain and thick mud, and inflicted 20,000 casualties at **Champaubert**, **Montmirail**, **Château-Thierry** and **Vauchamps** (*see* **Map 26**). Though these limited successes could not ultimately force a negotiated peace on the allies, the combination of rapid manoeuvre, tactical brilliance and endurance on the part of young French conscripts forced Blücher to suspend his advance up the Marne to Paris.

Sixth Coalition, War of the

The sixth, and ultimately successful, war fought by an alliance of major European nations against republican **France**. Brought into practical existence when French armies invaded **Russia** in June 1812, it ended with **Napoleon's** abdication in April 1814 and the subsequent Treaty of **Paris**.

Despite continued **naval warfare** against **Great Britain** and gradual escalation of the Peninsular War, the French Empire enjoyed a period of relative peace after the collapse of the **Fifth Coalition** in 1809, but a sharp decline in Franco-Russian relations already hinted at another major conflict. French alliance with Russia, created at **Tilsit** in 1807 and reaffirmed at **Erfurt** the following year, was always viewed as a short-term expedient by Napoleon; Tsar **Alexander's** initial fascination with the French emperor was soon eroded by a combination of francophobia at court and diplomatic friction over **Poland**.

Arguments over the **Continental System**, Napoleon's marriage to Habsburg duchess **Marie-Louise**, French seizure of lands belonging to the tsar's brother-in-law, the Duke of Oldenburg (February 1811), and **Bernadotte's** election as Crown Prince of **Sweden** (May 1811) all encouraged mutual suspicion, but relations became openly hostile from 15 August 1811, when Napoleon launched a scathing public attack on the tsar, accusing him of warmongering.

Despite his intrigues with senior Polish nobles, the tsar retained a preference for negotiated settlement almost to the last day of peace, and the impetus to war over the next few months came primarily from France. Once a period of peace had restored his empire's strength, Napoleon was free to equate its need for security with a desire to eliminate his last great continental rival, and was already making the necessary military arrangements.

Both sides began diplomatic preparations for war from early 1812. Napoleon's German allies, including **Prussia** and **Austria**, were sent demands for troops in January, and the tsar made peace with Sweden and the **Ottoman Empire**. Russian negotiations with **Great Britain** were also put in hand, and they matured into Anglo-Russian alliance in July, marking the official formation of the Sixth Coalition.

At war with Russia and Britain once he invaded the former on 24 June 1812, Napoleon marched an army of more than 600,000 men east to reach **Moscow** by the autumn. From that point his empire crumbled rapidly. His army was destroyed retreating from Russia, and rebuilt forces were driven back from Poland to the Rhine during 1813. Meanwhile British, Spanish and Portuguese forces were driving east across Spain, and were across the south-western frontiers of France by the time allied armies mounted a final invasion across the Rhine in late 1813.

With hardly any troops or economic resources left, Napoleon fought a brilliant but ultimately doomed campaign in eastern France through the first months of 1814, while Austrian forces moved into Italy and **Wellington** approached **Toulouse**. By the time he eventually abdicated on 6 April, his military, diplomatic and political isolation were complete. *See* **Russian Campaign**, 1812; Campaign for **Germany**, 1813; Campaign for **France**, 1813–14; **Peninsular War**; **Italian Campaign**, 1813–14; Congress of **Vienna**; **Maps 23–26**.

Skirmishers

Light infantry foot soldiers, considered a relatively unimportant adjunct to the art of European warfare for most of the eighteenth century, and generally used, as the name suggests, in minor actions away from the main field of battle. Their role was transformed in the republican **French Army**, which called its skirmishers *tirailleurs* and deployed them en masse in battle to disrupt enemy defensive formations in advance of a charge by line infantry. *See also* **Infantry Tactics**.

Sloops

Small, fast warships, designed to fire broadsides from a single gun deck, that were the workhorses of contemporary **naval warfare**. Though the term was technically restricted to three-masted warships, it was regularly applied to almost any sail-rigged vessel mounting between ten and 24 guns, including **corvettes**, cutters and brigantines, and the major navies employed them in their hundreds. Often the largest ships in service with minor navies, sloops seldom operated with major battlefleets, except as courier vessels. They were more usually attached to smaller squadrons for commerce protection and **colonial** duties, and were the mainstays of coastal patrol operations all over the world. The best sloops were fast enough to outrun any larger warship and powerful enough to overcome anything smaller, although they could seldom catch stripped-down **privateers**.

Smith, 'Sir' William Sidney (1764–1840)

One of the wartime **Royal Navy**'s most colourful and controversial commanders, Smith was the son of a naval officer, and enjoyed sufficient influence to become a captain at 19. Decorated while serving with the **Swedish Navy** in the late 1780s (hence his adopted title), he joined the **Turkish Navy** for a time before 1793, but purchased a ship at Smyrna when he heard that Britain was at war, sailing to join **Hood**'s fleet occupying **Toulon**.

Responsible for the destruction of ten French warships during the allied evacuation, and rewarded with a regular **frigate** command, he was captured in action against a French **privateer** in 1796, and held prisoner in France until his escape in May 1798. Given a **ship-of-the-line** on detached duty in the eastern **Mediterranean**, he won fame by helping to defeat **Napoleon** at **Acre** in 1799, but ruined his reputation by

assuming diplomatic powers and signing the unacceptable **El Arish** peace with French C-in-C **Kléber** in January 1800.

Though he was a rear-admiral under **Collingwood** in the Mediterranean from 1804, he was regarded as too reckless to be entrusted with control over a squadron and usually given detached duties. He did take part in the **Dardanelles** expedition of 1807, and his many individual exploits included the successful evacuation of the royal family during the French invasion of **Portugal** in 1808. Promoted vice-admiral in 1810, he was Mediterranean second-in-command two years later, and was at **Waterloo** in a private capacity in 1815. Talented but infamously boastful, and never popular among his peers, he became a full admiral in 1821 but never commanded a fleet.

Smolensk, Battle of

French attack of 16–18 August 1812 on the important Russian city of Smolensk, the climax of **Napoleon**'s attempts to force a decisive confrontation during the opening phase of the **Russian campaign**. After retreating east throughout July, the two Russian armies in the field had linked up on 4 August at Smolensk, on the River Dnieper about 450km west of Moscow (*see* **Map 23**). Despite Russian First Army commander **Barclay de Tolly**'s half-hearted counteroffensive north-west of the city, Napoleon led about 175,000 troops against Smolensk from 12 August. Deployed in a form of the **Bataillon Carré** introduced at **Jena** in 1806, they were launched across the Dnieper south of Smolensk in two columns, commanded by Napoleon himself and **Davout**. Once across the river, they were to turn east and strike at Smolensk from the south bank, seizing the city and severing communications with Moscow.

Carried out in great secrecy, the Dnieper crossing was completed on 14 August, but the advance on Smolensk itself was delayed by **Murat**'s failure to deal with Russian advance guards at **Krasnoe** later that day, and by Napoleon's decision to pause for regrouping on 15 August. Russian Second Army commander **Bagration** had time to move General Raevski's corps into the city, which was held by 20,000 men and 72 guns when French forces reached the outskirts early on 16 August. While Russian forces massed north of the Dnieper, and three French corps gathered around the suburbs to the south-east and south-west, Napoleon allowed only minor attacks that day, and they had made little impression on the city defences by nightfall.

To the surprise of Russian commanders expecting a French sweep east on to the Moscow road, Napoleon ordered all three of his corps to fight their way through the suburbs next day. Though **artillery** caused enormous damage to buildings in the city, French attacks could not dislodge well-positioned Russian defenders (now commanded by General **Doctorov**) from its solid fortifications. By the time attacks were called off at dusk, the two days' actions had cost about 10,000 French casualties and 12–14,000 Russian.

Still concerned that he might be cut off from Moscow, Barclay de Tolly took the decision, momentous in terms of Russian imperial prestige, to pull Doctorov's men out of Smolensk during the night of 17–18 August, and part of Ney's corps occupied the ruined city in the small hours. The rest of 18 August was characterized by mutual indecision. Barclay de Tolly and Bagration quarrelled, and the latter unilaterally withdrew his forces towards Moscow, leaving the crossroads east of Smolensk at Lubino virtually unguarded. Barclay de Tolly followed suit late in the evening, but Napoleon did nothing at all on 18 August, a bout of uncertainty that characterized his management of the campaign.

Napoleon sent **Junot**'s corps to occupy Lubino on 19 August, but it moved slowly and missed Barclay de Tolly. Having yet again occupied territory without bringing ultimate victory closer, and with his army now down to about 100,000 hungry and exhausted effectives, Napoleon took the fateful decision to advance still further east and seek a showdown around Moscow (*see* Battle of **Borodino**). *See* **Map 23**.

Smoliani, Battle of

Alternative name for the Second Battle of **Polotsk**, after the village at the centre of the action.

Snipers

Marksmen, usually armed with **rifles**, deployed by contemporary armies and navies to pick off selected enemy personnel. Sniping was a particular feature of **siege** operations during the period, but such was the range and accuracy of a rifle in skilled hands that many casualties were inflicted as forces manoeuvred into or out of battle positions. In contrast to the largely indiscriminate killing undertaken by modern snipers, Enlightenment sniping was focused on the assassination of notables (and conservation of ammunition), so that opportunities to attack ordinary soldiers were often ignored and a disproportionate number of victims were senior officers.

Sommagices Conference

Vital allied meeting held at the eastern French town of Sommagices on 24 March 1814, as the campaign for **France** approached its climax. After **Napoleon**'s defeat at **Arcis-sur-Aube** on 20–21 March, his plan for a sweep east to the Marne at St-Dizier was revealed to allied leaders by captured documents. Southern army commander **Schwarzenberg** was tempted to retreat, but decided on 22 March to move north towards a junction with **Blücher**'s army. Further captured messages soon revealed that Paris was in a state of panic, that its defences were incomplete, and that open opposition to Napoleon was rife, prompting the meeting at Sommagices, during which Russian tsar **Alexander** bullied a reluctant Schwarzenberg into a change of plan. While General **Winzingerode** led 10,000 men towards St-Dizier to disguise allied intentions, and Napoleon waited at the town for reinforcements, both main allied armies were sent directly up the Marne towards Paris, thus calling the French emperor's bluff and effectively deciding the campaign.

Somosierra, Battle of

The only serious attempt by **Spanish Army** forces to defend Madrid against French invasion in autumn 1808, a desperate stand by General San Juan's small army at the Somosierra Pass on 29–30 November 1808. It stood little chance of holding off 45,000 French veterans, and the battle is chiefly noted for **Napoleon**'s bizarre tactics.

The collapse of Spanish attempts to defend the Ebro had left only some 21,000 organized troops between Napoleon and Madrid, and he advanced his central strike force towards the capital from

Aranda on 28 November (*see* **Peninsular War**). General Eguia, the newly appointed commander at Madrid, split his forces to guard the two northern approach roads, sending 8,000 men under General Heredia north-west to the Guadarramas hills, and San Juan's 12,500 troops north to the Somosierra Pass.

Napoleon moved the main body of his army through Somosierra, sending only a cavalry screen to the Guadarramas, and reached its northern foothills at Buceguillas early on 29 November. San Juan had divided his already inadequate strength, keeping 9,000 men and six guns on a commanding plateau covering the pass, and advancing the rest to occupy the village of Sepulveda. An attack on the village by **Savary**'s troops failed that day, but the garrison fled for Segovia in the night and French troops moved on the main position from dawn.

French infantry could have worked round unoccupied hillsides either side of the Spanish position, but Napoleon opted for the quicker expedient of a frontal attack. Doubt surrounds the motives for his subsequent decision to order the position taken by a single, unsupported squadron of **Polish** light cavalry. The seven officers and 80 troopers duly mounted two charges into the mouths of the Spanish guns, suffering 60 casualties and failing just short of their target. Napoleon then returned to a more coordinated attack, ultimately scattering defenders with a more powerful **cavalry** charge. Spanish casualties probably numbered less than 1,000, but San Juan was hanged by his own men when he attempted to halt their flight and no coherent force opposed Napoleon's advance to Madrid's suburbs by the evening of 1 December. *See* **Map 22**.

Sorauren, Battles of

The climactic confrontation of Marshal **Soult**'s final **Peninsular War** offensive, fought in two stages on 28 and 30 July 1813 around the village of Sorauren, some 10km north-west of **Pamplona** (*see* **Maps 5, 22**). After breaking through the north-western Pyrenees on 25 July with victories at the **Maya** and **Roncesvalles** passes, Soult hoped to resupply at Pamplona and sweep behind **Wellington**'s allied army concentrated near the coastal frontier.

Wellington was in the north, supervising the siege of **San Sebastian**, when he received news on the evening of 26 July that Soult's 36,000 troops were approaching Pamplona. Completely surprised by the move, he rode south to take personal command at Sorauren, where General **Cole** had re-formed his lines after retreating from Roncesvalles.

Cole had deployed his 13,000 men along a steep ridge south-east of the village, facing 25,000 French troops just to the north. **Picton**'s 5,000 troops (and elements of O'Donnell's Spanish force besieging Pamplona) protected his right against attack from **Foy**'s 8,000 French. The commotion caused by Wellington's arrival on the morning of 27 July, accompanied only by his secretary, boosted allied morale and persuaded Soult to delay an attack in case allied reinforcements had arrived, and 6,000 British reinforcements had reached Cole's left wing when he eventually attacked at twelve thirty next day.

The new arrivals broke up a preliminary attack before Soult launched a full-scale frontal assault on the centre of the allied ridge. Wellington's efficient manipulation of reserves enabled him to repel possible breakthroughs on each flank, and French troops were repeatedly driven back from the crest of the ridge. Foy's attack on Picton to the south-east made no progress, and though a flank operation by 2,000 French troops on the far allied right drove Spanish troops from a small hill at the second attempt, it was ambushed by 400 British reserves and eventually driven back. The arrival of fresh allied divisions under **Hill** and **Dalhousie** prompted a French withdrawal to starting positions around Sorauren at about four.

Soult had lost some 4,000 men during the day, against 2,652 allied casualties, and was no nearer Pamplona, but spent 29 July planning a strike to the west that might still cut communications between Wellington and his northern forces. Three divisions under **Drouet** advanced west of Sorauren on 30 July, and drove Hill's forces back to Lizaso, but Soult was unable to extricate the rest of his army in time to avoid Wellington's attack on the same day, which routed 14,000 remaining French troops as they attempted to withdraw, inflicting another 3,500 casualties in the process.

Soult ordered a general retreat to the frontier later the same day, and had lost 13,000 men in six days by the time French forces were back through the northernmost Pyrenean pass at Vera (Maya and Roncesvalles having been retaken by the allies). Too weak to contemplate another offensive, apart from a minor strike at the Bidassoa in late August, he could only concentrate resources for the defence of France.

Souham, Joseph (1760–1837)

Souham began his military career as a regular with the royal **French Army**, and was an elected regimental commander of **fédérés** from August 1792. He made his name as part of **Pichegru's** Army of the North during the **Flanders campaign** against the **First Coalition** in 1793–4, beating **York** at **Dunkirk**, **Tournai**, **Tourcoing** and **Nijmegen**, and inflicting several defeats on Austrian forces. A close associate of **Moreau**, both in the north and on the **Rhine** from 1799, Souham was always mistrusted by **Napoleon**, and was imprisoned in 1804. He did not receive another command until 1807, after which he led divisions in Italy and the **Peninsular War**, holding off **Wellington** at **Burgos** in 1812. He was wounded at both **Lützen** and **Leipzig** in 1813, and was in Paris when it fell the following year. He rejoined the royal army on the restoration, was not accepted into Napoleon's service during the **Hundred Days**, and served the Bourbons for the next 15 years, becoming governor of Strasbourg after the 1830 revolution.

Soult, Nicolas Jean de Dieu (1760–1837)

One of an impressive pantheon of Gascon-born soldiers (including **Murat**, **Ney** and **Lannes**) who rose to international renown under **Napoleon**, Soult was a clerk's son, and joined the royal **French Army** as a private in 1775. A sergeant in 1791, he was commissioned in 1792 and a battalion commander when he first achieved public distinction in August 1793, winning a minor action on the **Rhine** during **Pichegru's** advance to the **Geisberg**. He fought at **Fleurus** under **Lefebvre** in June 1794, and was promoted brigadier-general in October. As part of **Jourdan's** army on the Rhine he fought at **Altenkirchen** and **Ukerath** in early summer 1796.

Back under Jourdan's command on the **Rhine** in 1799, he fought at **Ostrach** and **Stockach** before transferring to the **Swiss** front in April, where he led a division under **Masséna** and took part in both battles of **Zurich**. He followed Masséna to the **Italian** front, breaking a leg and becoming a **prisoner of war** during the siege of **Genoa**. After his exchange he helped put down anti-French uprisings in **Piedmont** and served with occupying forces in **Naples**.

By now established as one of Napoleon's most trusted military subordinates, and a formidable battle tactician, Soult was appointed to the **Marshalate** in 1804, and commanded IV Corps against the **Third Coalition** in late 1805. He made his international reputation leading the decisive charge at **Austerlitz**, and fought at **Jena**, **Eylau** and **Heilsberg** in 1806–7 but missed the victory at **Friedland**. A prime beneficiary of Napoleon's willingness to buy loyalty, he was a wealthy man before he became Duke of Dalmatia in 1808.

Soult accompanied Napoleon's invasion of **Spain** later that year, leading the final stages of the pursuit to **Corunna** and occupying **Portugal** in March 1809. Driven out of **Oporto** by **Wellesley's** Anglo-Portuguese force in May, he defeated Spanish forces at **Ocaña** during the summer and was Jourdan's successor as Joseph **Bonaparte's** chief of staff. Unhappy in the role, he left Madrid for south-western Spain in 1810, finding himself embroiled in a defensive campaign around **Badajoz** while mounting a major siege at **Cadiz**. Forced to retire north-west after **Marmont's** defeat at **Salamanca** in 1812, Soult retook Madrid and pursued Wellington's subsequent retreat from **Burgos**.

Temporarily seconded to **Germany** in 1813, he led the **Imperial Guard** until after the battle of **Bautzen**, when he returned to the **Peninsular War** as theatre C-in-C, charged with recovering an almost hopeless situation after the defeat at **Vitoria**. He fought an epic defensive campaign over the next ten months, retreating slowly into and beyond the Pyrenees until defeat at **Orthez** and a final confrontation at **Toulouse** in April (several days after Napoleon's **abdication**) persuaded him to surrender.

Not given a senior command by the restored

monarchy, Soult was quick to rejoin Napoleon during the **Hundred Days** of 1815, but was ill-employed as chief of staff to the army for the **Waterloo** campaign. He spent the next four years in exile east of the Rhine, was restored to the army lists in 1820 and subsequently capitalized on his position as the most celebrated of Napoleon's surviving marshals to pursue an extremely successful political career.

His brother Pierre (1770–1843) saw long-term service in Spain, was a divisional general from 1813 and took part in all the final actions beyond the Pyrenees, eventually retiring as a lieutenant-general in 1825.

South America

Apart from British Canada, the independent **United States** and Portuguese Brazil, almost the whole of mainland America was owned by **Spain** in 1792. Spanish **Louisiana** remained larger than the infant USA, and the vast territory of Mexico extended up the western seaboard to the Canadian frontier. All of central America was part of Mexico, while the colonies of New Argentina (modern Argentina, Paraguay, Uruguay and Bolivia) and New Granada (Colombia) dominated the south. In spite of Spain's fragile economic, political, and military condition, it had managed to sustain the flow of trade and bullion from south and central America throughout the eighteenth century, but imperial administrations on the continent were only loosely controlled from Madrid by the 1790s, and colonial development was limited to coastal settlements and a few inland trading depots.

Spain's declaration of war against **Great Britain** in October 1796 roused the predatory instincts of a British government easily distracted from European land wars by the prospect of **colonial** expansion. Various paper schemes for expeditions to South America were considered by war minister **Dundas** during the mid-1790s, encouraged by General **Miranda**, an ambitious native of Venezuela who had defected from the revolutionary **French Army**.

When British forces did eventually mount an (unauthorized) expedition to **Buenos Aires** in 1806–7, Argentina's successful resistance acted as a catalyst to an independence movement among the colonists, and internal chaos erupted once news of King **Ferdinand VII**'s deposition crossed the Atlantic. The royal governor and a replacement appointed by the rebel **junta** in Spain, Balthasar de Cisneros, were both overthrown, and a civil war was eventually ended when an independence party led by Generals Belgrano and San Martín proclaimed an independent republic (the 'United Provinces of the Río de la Plata') in 1816.

Separate rebel juntas were set up in Bogotá, Caracas and Santiago de Chile in 1810, becoming the focus for well-developed independence movements, and a major Mexican revolt broke out in September 1810. Venezuela declared itself independent on 5 July 1811, triggering more than a decade of war between royalists and nationalists that saw Simón **Bolívar** emerge as the acknowledged founder of a clutch of republics in the north, but fail in his bid to establish a continent-wide federation. Spain retained control of Mexico, and refused to recognize the loss of its southern empire until the 1840s, but was never remotely wealthy enough to win it back.

The arrival of the exiled Portuguese royal family to take up residence from 1808 warped a simultaneous move to independence in Brazil, but nationalists bullied King **John** into returning to Europe in 1821, and his son Pedro declared independence the following year. Portuguese forces sent to re-establish control in Brazil were defeated by defence forces organized with British help, and the support given to nationalists by Britain and the United States was economically inspired. Washington's recognition of South American republics in 1822 opened an era of US commercial infiltration, aided by the new **US Navy**, that would eventually supersede European influence on the continent. *See* **Map 19**.

Spain

The most powerful and prosperous European state of the sixteenth century, Spain was in manifest decline by the late eighteenth. Economically and socially backward compared to industrializing powers, it had languished under a succession of uninspired Bourbon monarchs, and was ruled by the particularly stupid and despotic **Charles IV** from 1788.

Charles ruled as an absolute monarch, summoning an assembly of notables (Cortes) only for ceremonial purposes, and the majority of his 10.5 million subjects (1797) were illiterate peasants under feudal obligation to an aristocracy backed by a powerful and fiercely orthodox Catholic Church. The rural economy generated insufficient tax or trade income to sustain the monarchy, which was heavily dependent on **colonial** revenue and resources. Spain had lost control of **Naples**, **Sicily**, **Milan**, Gibraltar and the **Netherlands** by 1713, but had since expanded its American empire, and protection of its generally ill-managed overseas possessions was the main preoccupation of Spanish foreign policy.

The nation's internal politics, plagued by disputes between provinces, collapsed into factionalism under Charles, a process that hastened the **Spanish Army**'s descent into a ramshackle collection of mutually antagonistic regional forces. The **Spanish Navy**, once the most powerful in the world, had meanwhile decayed beyond the capacity to challenge the British **Royal Navy** on anything approaching equal terms.

Military weakness had encouraged the survival of Spain's long-standing alliance with **France**, also ruled by the Bourbon family and equally hostile to British imperial expansion. Though strained and of little practical use to either party, the 'Family Compact' was essentially intact at the time of the **French Revolution**, but subsequent treatment of the French Church and monarchy shocked conservative opinion in Spain. Charles quickly introduced legislation to restrict the spread of radical ideas, and chief minister **Floridablanca** bombarded Paris with protests on behalf of **Louis XVI**, but awareness of Spain's economic and military weakness stopped him short of provoking war. His replacement from February 1792, the elderly Count Aranda, proclaimed Spanish neutrality and established diplomatic relations with the French National Assembly.

Imprisonment of the French royal family triggered Spanish agreement to join the **First Coalition** on 24 August, but French victory at **Valmy** moved the goalposts, and Aranda reaffirmed Spain's neutrality just before his replacement on 15 November by the queen's lover, Manuel **Godoy**. Facing French demands for recognition of the republic in return for continued peace, court attitudes hardened when Britain proposed an alliance in January 1793, and war became a popular issue after the French king's execution later that month, which provoked mass demonstrations in Madrid.

The French regime declared war on 7 March 1793, convinced that an invasion would trigger popular rebellion against the Bourbons. Backed by popular enthusiasm, and expecting a British naval **blockade** to end the war quickly, Madrid responded with an invasion of south-western France. Spanish forces soon lost their initial advantage on the **Pyrenean** front, and French armies were inside Spain when the war was ended by the Treaty of **Basle** in July 1795. An associated alliance with France entailed a declaration of war against Britain in October 1796, and an inert government's ability to maintain its colonies came to depend on French support, especially after the navy's defeat at **St Vincent** (February 1797).

Godoy remained a malevolent defining force in Spanish politics for the next decade. Detested by the aristocracy and the masses for his greed, incompetence and hold over court policy, he was the prime target of an opposition party centred on the relatively untainted figure of Crown Prince **Ferdinand**, whose feud with his father matured to reach treasonable proportions. With both sides looking to Paris for backing, the **Directory** government was able to force Godoy's replacement by the liberal reformer Savandra in March 1798, but he was reinstated at **Napoleon**'s insistence in 1800.

Napoleon had already taken **Louisiana** from Spain by the Treaty of **San Idelfonso** in October 1800, and subsequently pushed Godoy into the War of the **Oranges** against **Portugal** in 1801. Two years later he extracted a promise to enforce Portuguese neutrality, along with a monthly indemnity of 6 million francs, and pressure to join the fight against **Great Britain** brought a Spanish declaration of war on 12 December 1804. Almost exclusively **naval**, the Spanish war effort effectively ceased after defeat at **Trafalgar** in October 1805, and Godoy lost any influence when he was caught conspiring with Napoleon's enemies just before the **Jena–Auerstädt campaign** in 1806. Godoy remained pliable, allowing French forces invading **Portugal** to garrison Spain by the Treaty of **Fontainebleau** in October 1807, but his days were numbered.

Political chaos surrounding the royal family came to a head at the same time. Godoy had Ferdinand arrested for treason on 29 October, and appeals for mediation from both sides gave Napoleon an excuse to invade Spain in March 1808. Though his armies quickly occupied the capital, his enforced deposition of the Bourbons (and Godoy) at **Bayonne** proved disastrous, and the **Madrid Uprising** in May signalled the start of a national rebellion against French rule that was often beaten but never broken. Sustained by increasingly effective British support, and backed by **guerrillas** behind French lines, the rebellion was a genuine expression of popular commitment to crown and Church that defied French military might until the general peace of 1814 (*see* **Peninsular War**).

Those parts of Spain not under French occupation during the 1808–14 period were governed in the name of the Bourbon monarchy by regional councils of notables (**juntas**). A central junta was convened at Aranjuez in September 1808, and remained Spain's nominal governing body throughout the war. Meeting in Seville from November, but driven west by French armies, it was besieged in Cadiz for most of the war. Never able to rise above regional disputes, or the gulf between its traditionalist and liberal elements, it was broadly responsible for the strategic incoherence of the rebellion's military operations, but achieved some political reform. A new Cortes met near Cadiz from September 1810, its structure altered to include a majority of elected commoners, and a new constitution was passed on 19 March 1812, establishing a national code of law and freedom of the press. Religious freedom was still denied to non-Catholics, but the infamous Inquisition was abolished the following February.

Occupied Spain came under the nominal rule of King Joseph **Bonaparte**, and was subject to widespread fiscal, social, religious and legal reforms, many of them introduced by Napoleon during his brief stay in Madrid of 1808. Though often in line with the modernizing aims of liberal Spaniards, their effectiveness was limited by overriding opposition to imperial control. Joseph enjoyed little cooperation from his subjects, apart from a cross-section of pro-French intellectuals and merchants known as **Afrancesados**, and his effective authority was reduced from 1810, when Catalonia, Aragon, Biscay, Navarre, Burgos and Valladolid came under direct French military administration.

The expulsion of French forces in 1813–14 brought Ferdinand, a virtual prisoner in France since 1808, back to Spain on 24 March 1814. An undeserving object of popular adulation, he promptly renounced his approval of the 1812 constitution and mobilized military support to seize power in Madrid. The constitution was abolished on 4 May, and leading liberals arrested in Madrid on 10 May. The first of several rebellions took place under former guerrilla leader **Espoz y Mina** at Pamplona in September, and was put down with exemplary ferocity. Military coups were subsequently attempted in Corunna (September 1815), Catalonia (April 1817) and Cadiz (July 1819), before revolt against Ferdinand's repressive regime became generalized in 1820. Ferdinand was forced to accept the constitution in March 1820, and appointed a more liberal cabinet, but regular military uprisings continued until 1823, when the intervention of a French army restored absolute royal control. *See* **South America; Map 22.**

Spain, Invasion of (1808)

The attempted conquest of **Spain** by French forces in spring 1808. Spain was a French ally at the start of 1808, but a poor one, lax in its application of the **Continental System** against British trade, militarily inept and a reluctant participant in joint **naval** operations. Apart from the strategic benefits of conquest, **Napoleon** seems to have believed that Spanish **colonial** wealth could make an important contribution to French war expenses, but above all he thought the takeover of Spain would be easy.

The **Spanish Army** was clearly no match for

French forces, and its defensive capabilities had been undermined by the Treaty of **Fontaine-bleau** (October 1807), which had allowed French troops to garrison supply routes for the conquest of **Portugal**. Meanwhile the feud between Spanish king **Charles IV** and his son **Ferdinand** had seen the latter arrested for treason in October 1807, and national administration had degenerated into regional factionalism, offering an almost legitimate case for French intervention to restore law and order.

Both Charles and Ferdinand had already appealed to France for mediation, but a temporary reconciliation persuaded Napoleon to bide his time in late 1807. While garrison units in Spain were strengthened, and reinforcements were gathered on the border, the French press opened a loud **propaganda** campaign against Spanish chief minister **Godoy** in early 1808. French troops in Spain moved to occupy **fortresses** at the Pyrenean passes from 16 February, and had completed their seizure by the end of the month, helped by several ruses designed to effect bloodless takeover from their bemused 'allies'. With the passes open to reinforcements, a reserve army under **Bessières** brought French strength in Spain up to 118,000 men.

As French forces moved west, and Napoleon announced his friendly intentions, Charles hesitated in Madrid until mid-March before fleeing for Spain's South American colonies. He was halted on 17 March at Aranjuez, some 50km south of the capital, where rioting locals prevented his escape and frightened him into abdicating in favour of Ferdinand, who was widely regarded as an improvement. Charles subsequently retracted his abdication, but the crisis gave Napoleon an opportunity to summon both feuding parties (and Godoy) to a conference of 'reconciliation' just inside the French border at **Bayonne**.

Murat's advance guard reached Madrid on 24 March, without meeting concerted opposition. It was well received by a populace anticipating a return to lawful government, but the realities of military occupation soon provoked unrest. While Murat struggled with the complexities of Spanish politics, refusing to recognize Ferdinand

as king, military governor **Grouchy** was required to put down the first outbreak of popular rioting at the beginning of April. A month of relative calm followed, pending the outcome of the Bayonne summit, but its deposition of the Bourbons sparked the national uprising, beginning in **Madrid** at the start of May, that kept Napoleon's armies at war in the country until 1814. *See* **Peninsular War; Map 22**.

Spanden, Action at *See* Battle of **Heilsberg**

Spanish Army

The regular Spanish Army of the early 1790s reflected the poverty, administrative backwardness and social rigidity of **Spain**. Army pay and conditions were so poor that only the lowest classes of society could be induced to enlistment voluntarily, and the system of partial **conscription** (known as the *quinta* because it ostensibly called up one in five of the male population) was hopelessly undermined by evasions and exemptions.

Apart from a small Guard élite, infantry forces in the 1790s comprised 35 line and 12 light regiments, along with ten foreign mercenary regiments. Line regiments, each with a paper strength of about 2,200 men, were organized into eight regionally based brigades from 1806, and this remained the infantry arm's basic structure until 1814.

Regular **cavalry** comprised eight regiments of **dragoons**, two of **chasseurs** and two of **hussars**, about 7,500 troops in theory (plus a few Guard squadrons), but horses were never available for more than about half that number. Unreliable, undisciplined and ill-trained, the cavalry was perhaps the least admired of Spain's armed forces, and the many ad hoc regiments that sprang up after 1808 were of even less value to planned operations.

Spanish **artillery** was organized into four regionally based regiments, and earned a reputation for stubborn defence of its weapons, though many of its field guns were museum pieces. The **engineers** mustered about 2,200 officers and men by 1806, while supply and transport requirements for all arms depended entirely on local requisitioning in the absence of any organized **field train**.

From 1804 the regular army was backed by a large Provincial Militia, which provided four 'divisions' of two battalions each, along with 42 district battalions, and drew its officers from among local dignitaries. Spain's last lines of official military reserve were 114 companies of urban militia, spread around 20 towns and cities, and 42 companies of superannuated veterans in home defence units.

Regulations required a third of all Spanish regular officers to be drawn from the ranks, but all posts above captain were effectively restricted to members of the sprawling nobility, and officer training capacity was reduced to a single military college in the 1790s. At the top of the command chain, regional 'captains-general' were almost independent of overall strategic direction, inadequately provided by the crown until 1808 and by the central rebel **junta** thereafter. Often deeply conservative, old-regime figures, they wasted a great deal of energy on personal rivalries and disputes with political authorities. Commanders like **Cuesta** – almost caricatures of pride, incompetence and xenophobia – were more typical than reasonably competent generals like La **Romana** or **Blake**.

Poor standards of leadership, along with the lack of any standard drill code and shortage of modern equipment, were reflected in the army's wartime record. After beginning a mobilization that was expected to take ten months in August 1792, it stumbled to defeat by second-line French forces on the **Pyrenean** front (1793–5). As a French ally, it won a limited and largely bloodless victory against **Portugal** in the 1801 War of the **Oranges**, and its best troops (La Romana's division) served with French imperial forces in northern Europe until 1808, when British warships brought them home to fight with the rebellion.

Regular forces won a few morale-boosting victories during the **Peninsular War**, notably at **Bailén** in July 1808, but suffered a great many more defeats, yet their resistance was never decisively broken. French failure to coordinate the country's final conquest, the efforts of **guerrilla** forces behind enemy lines, the effectiveness of British military support and a gradual improvement in efficiency under British influence all contributed to the army's resilience, but its identification with genuine popular patriotism was the key to its survival, providing a supply of well-motivated volunteers to replace a stream of casualties and **deserters**.

The regime of Joseph **Bonaparte** made efforts to raise an army for French imperial service in Spain. Based around a Royal Guard of two battalions (expanded to two regiments in 1809) drawn from French units, it eventually comprised seven cavalry and seven infantry regiments, along with two light infantry battalions and a mercenary Irish regiment. Never up to strength, or entrusted with operations in politically sensitive areas, it played little significant part in the Peninsular War, although virtually the whole army, some 5,000 troops, was present at **Vitoria** in 1813.

Spanish Navy

Once a world-class sea power, **Spain** had allowed its large navy to fall into a state of obvious decay by the late eighteenth century. The navy was still large, possessing 74 **ships-of-the-line** in 1792, but even the 56 vessels considered fit for service had been ill-maintained to the point of uselessness. On the positive side, Spain could call on some of the most powerful warships afloat, notably the enormous 130-gun *Santísima Trinidad*, and a seafaring tradition that provided a steady supply of competent captains.

Shortage of funds, administrative laxity and corruption at every stage in the supply chain had left the navy's fleets desperately short of crews and equipment, and reduced dockyards to infamous levels of inefficiency. Though it could muster some 64,000 sailors, 20,000 auxiliaries and 16,000 marines in 1798, this was by no means enough, and numbers declined severely over the next decade.

The navy's prime function was the protection of Spain's far-flung overseas possessions, and of the sea lanes that carried colonial treasure to the monarchy's needy coffers. Its principal opponent was the larger and more efficient **Royal Navy**, performing a similar role in support of dynamic British trade expansion and generally more than a match for Spanish forces in small-scale **colonial** actions.

At the start of the **Revolutionary Wars** three main Spanish fleets were stationed in home waters, at Cartegena, Ferrol and Cadiz. Like their French counterparts, they were committed to an essentially defensive **naval** strategy, avoiding the lottery of large-scale confrontations with other major fleets. Spanish warships cooperated with the Royal Navy from 1793 to 1795, taking part in operations at **Toulon** and elsewhere in the western Mediterranean, and occasionally attempting to aid land forces on the **Pyrenean** front. They were allies of France against the British for most of the 1796–1808 period, suffering major defeats when caught by superior forces at **St Vincent** in 1797 and at **Trafalgar** in 1805. Effectively crippled after the latter disaster, the navy virtually ceased fleet operations, making little effort to escape a solid British **blockade** of Spanish ports, and its ships-of-the-line were allowed to rot in peace once alliance with the British had rendered any naval contribution to the **Peninsular War** superfluous.

Speranski, Mikhail Mikhailovich (1772–1839)

Russian statesman, the son of a rural priest, who was a professor of mathematics and physics in St Petersburg when appointed principal adviser to Tsar **Alexander I** in 1809. Charged with extensive constitutional and administrative reform, his initial proposals were based on the **Code Napoléon** and provoked immediate opposition from powerful vested interests at court. Though he established an advisory Council of State in 1810, and instituted a regular system of imperial budgets, he was able to achieve little else before the conservative backlash that accompanied worsening relations with France forced his dismissal in 1812. Partially restored to favour as governor of Siberia from 1816, he returned to St Petersburg from 1825 and played an important role as a legal reformer under Tsar Nicholas I.

Spithead Mutiny

The first of several major revolts by sailors of the British **Royal Navy** that threatened to paralyse **Great Britain**'s principal protection against invasion during the spring and summer of 1797. British seamen's principal grievances were pay-related, most particularly their failure to receive a wage rise in 150 years, but petitions posted at sea to the 'sailor's friend', retired admiral **Howe**, were dismissed as the work of a few troublemakers in early 1797. More petitions were delivered direct to the Admiralty and the parliamentary opposition when the fleet returned to Spithead, off the English south coast town of Portsmouth, in late March. Barely concealed preparations were then put in hand to take control of the fleet pending a response.

Channel Fleet commander Alexander **Hood** (Lord Bridport) gave the Admiralty advance warning of the proposed mutiny on 14 April, along with precise details of its timing, but received orders to put to sea. His announcement of the orders on 16 April, Easter Sunday, triggered the mutiny itself two days earlier than planned, and the fleet quickly passed under the direct control of two sailors' delegates from each ship. While the delegates drew up a detailed list of demands for improved pay and conditions, an offer of an immediate small pay rise was rejected on 18 April, but discipline was maintained and mutineers expressed willingness to fight any foreign invasion should the need arise. The mutiny ended on 24 April after Bridport and navy minister Spencer promised to address all grievances.

It erupted again on 5 May, when a man was killed amid violence on Admiral Colpoys's flagship. Reflecting fears that the government would renege on its pay arrangements, the second mutiny was ended on 15 May by the personal appeals of Howe and delegates from the original mutineers, along with rapid parliamentary assent to a new Sailors' Bill. As well as causing widespread public anxiety, the mutinies sparked further outbreaks at Plymouth and aboard the ships of **Duncan**'s fleet in the North Sea, as well as a much more violent revolt among disaffected sailors at the east coast base of the **Nore**.

Stadion, Johann Philipp von (1763–1824)

Minor German noble, born at Mainz, who was Austrian ambassador to London from 1790 until his resignation in late 1794. Reconciled with Habsburg foreign policy in 1801, he returned to office as ambassador to Berlin before moving to

St Petersburg, where he took part in negotiations for the formation of the **Third Coalition**. Appointed imperial foreign minister after the Austrian defeat at **Austerlitz**, he was chief adviser to Emperor **Francis** for the next three years, arguing for a war of revenge against France, and promoting educational reform to stimulate popular nationalism among the empire's German speakers. An opponent of the more cautious Archduke **Charles**, Stadion got his war in 1809 and resigned after Austrian defeat at **Wagram**. He re-emerged in 1813, negotiating the **Reichenbach** accord by which **Austria** agreed to join the **Sixth Coalition**, and played an important role in post-war economic reconstruction as **Metternich's** finance minister from 1814.

Staël, Anne Louise Germaine de (1766–1814)

French writer and socialite, the daughter of pre-revolutionary finance minister Jacques Necker, and an important critic of the Napoleonic regime. Born in Paris, she published her first work of romantic fiction in 1786, and established a salon that became a famous centre of political debate during the early phases of the **French Revolution**. Her initial support for change waned as its aims became more radical, and she left for Switzerland in 1792, spending only a brief spell in Paris during the next five years. When she was allowed back to Paris in 1797, her reopened salon was more than ever the centre of Parisian political and artistic life, and her personal fame mushroomed after publication of the novel *Delphine* in 1802. Her early admiration for **Napoleon** had by then turned to fierce criticism, and her association with potential rivals **Moreau** and **Bernadotte** helped persuade the First Consul to order her out of Paris in autumn 1803. Her home in Switzerland became a magnet for exiled critics of the Napoleonic regime, and for Napoleon's agents, before she made a triumphant return to Paris in 1814, when the restored monarchy returned 2 million francs it owed to her late father.

Standards (Military)

The use of individual flags, banners or emblems (generically known as 'colours') by military units had originally been conceived as a means of identification. It was maintained into the late eighteenth century largely as a matter of morale, although standards could act as rallying points during confused actions. All armies carried flags or pennants (for **cavalry** forces) decorated with distinctive national and unit insignia, and entrusted their protection in action to 'colour parties', usually consisting of a junior officer and several NCOs. The symbolic and **propaganda** value of such emblems was heightened by **Napoleon's** adoption of regimental and battalion 'Imperial Eagles' from 1804. A gilt-painted model of the bird, mounted on a **pike** and bearing the unit's identification, the eagle was an innovation despite its self-consciously classical style, but its psychological effect was reversed in case of loss, and losses prompted the decision to restrict the issue of eagles to the first (and best) battalion of each regiment from 1808.

Stein, Heinrich Friedrich Karl, Baron vom (1757–1831)

German administrator and politician, born in **Nassau**, who became one of the principal architects of social reform in **Prussia** after its defeats of 1806–7, and is seen as a founding father of German nationalism. Trained as a lawyer, he entered Prussian service in 1780 and directed the regional economy of Prussian-controlled **Westphalia** before becoming trade minister in 1804. He resigned in 1806, having failed to persuade King **Frederick William III** to adopt liberal reforms, but was recalled after the Treaty of **Tilsit** in 1807 and charged with reconstruction of Prussia's war-ravaged economy.

As chief minister, and finance minister in a four-man cabinet from 1808, he abolished the last remnants of Prussian serfdom and other restrictions preventing peasant land ownership, cancelled local customs barriers and abolished monopolies that interfered with commercial growth. He also gave important support to the **Prussian Army** reforms being carried out by **Scharnhorst** and **Gneisenau**, and his particularly strong backing for a policy of universal **conscription** reflected a desire to foster German national identity. His views have since been criticized as promoting dangerous myths of national destiny tied to military aggression, and they were anathema to **Napoleon**, who forced his dismissal from an obedient Prussian king in the same year.

Stein fled Prussia for **Austria** in January 1809, but moved to St Petersburg as a diplomatic adviser to Tsar **Alexander** in 1812. He played an important part in negotiations tying Prussia and Austria to the **Sixth Coalition**, and his unstinting hostility towards Napoleonic France chimed with Alexander's determination to win total victory in 1814. A strident voice demanding harsh peace terms at the Congress of **Vienna**, but out of sympathy with the reactionary attitudes intrinsic to the **Holy Alliance**, he retired to academic life shortly afterwards.

Stockach, Battle of

The engagement that ended French offensives on the **Rhine** during 1799, fought on 25 March around the south German town of Stockach (*see* **Map 4**). The initial advance of **Jourdan**'s 40,000 French troops from the Rhine had been halted by Austrian commander Archduke **Charles** at **Ostrach** on 21 March, and they had fallen back beyond the vital road junction at Stockach. Aware that he was outnumbered, but anxious to make contact with **Masséna**'s forces in Switzerland, Jourdan ordered his forces forward to reoccupy the town from dawn on 25 March.

Charles had sent Meerveldt's advance guard forward on a reconnaissance sortie from his positions just behind Stockach the same morning, anticipating a further French retreat to link up with Masséna on the south side of Lake Constance. Meerveldt advanced as far as Emmingen, but fell back when faced with a frontal attack by **Gouvion St Cyr**'s division and the sudden appearance of **Soult**'s French advance guard in his rear. Misinterpreting this opening success as a total victory, Jourdan ordered his whole force forward to cut off a presumed Austrian retreat, but Charles was able to send **cavalry** support to Meerveldt and organize strong **artillery** batteries on the heights in front of Stockach.

Soult's pursuit of Meerveldt was reversed by the arrival of Austrian reinforcements from Stockach, and a manoeuvre against the Austrian left flank by **Souham** and Ferino was ambushed by prepared artillery batteries just south of the town,

and driven into the hills for the night. St Cyr's division on the French left was recalled from its advance on Mosskirch while bridges over the river were still intact, and withdrew all the way to the Black Forest along the south bank of the Danube.

Otherwise the end of the day found both armies approximately where they had started, each diminished by some 5,000 casualties, but Jourdan knew he was exposed to encirclement by other Austrian armies in the theatre, and began pulling his entire force back into the Black Forest next day. The withdrawal brought his dismissal, and French forces on the Rhine maintained a purely defensive posture while the focus of the fighting switched to the **Swiss** and **Italian** fronts.

Stockholm, Treaty of

A postscript to the Russo-Swedish Convention of **St Petersburg**, the Stockholm agreement between **Great Britain** and **Sweden** confirmed the latter's military cooperation with the **Sixth Coalition**. Signed on 3 March 1813, it granted Sweden **subsidies** of £1 million, along with possession of Guadeloupe, on the condition that the Swedish government quash the island's slave trade.

Stony Creek, Battle of

British victory on 6 June 1813 that ended the third invasion of Canada by US forces during the **Anglo-American War** of 1812–15. The American offensive had begun with an attack on York (Toronto) by 1,600 troops under General Pike, who had captured and burned the town on 24 April. An **amphibious** attack by 4,000 troops under Colonel Winfield Scott, ferried across Lake Ontario by Commodore **Perry**'s light naval forces, forced General Vincent's 700 British troops to abandon Fort St George, and captured the fort on 27 May. Vincent retreated into Canada but turned at Stony Creek and surprised pursuing forces, which blundered into an ambush and were scattered. Generals Windler and Chandler, commanding the pursuit, retreated back to Fort St George, and US forces made no further incursions into Canada before a counterattack drove them back beyond the frontier at Fort Niagara, which fell to the British on 18 December. *See* **Map 27**.

Stralsund, Siege of

Subsidiary French operation aimed at opening up Swedish Pomerania to French conquest during the latter stages of the War of the **Fourth Coalition**. While **Napoleon**'s main army headed towards a major confrontation with Russian forces, Marshal **Mortier** and 13,000 men were sent to besiege Swedish general Essen's equally strong garrison at Stralsund. The **siege** opened on 30 January 1807, but Mortier was required to pull most of his troops back to Stettin in late March, and sorties destroyed most of the siege works before he returned to drive defenders back into the **fortress** by mid-April. Under pressure to rejoin Napoleon's army gathering for the Battle of **Friedland**, Mortier agreed an armistice with Essen on 19 April, and it remained in force when **Sweden** ceded Pomerania to France later in the year. *See* **Map 21**.

Strategy

The formulation and application by governments of policies designed to further national interests or, in military terms, the theory and practice of deploying armed forces as part of wider campaign plans. Distinguished from **grand tactics** aimed at securing immediate victory over an enemy army, the business of large-scale manoeuvre had become a science by the late eighteenth century, but the orthodox **cordon** system used by the **First Coalition**'s armies for both defensive and offensive campaigns was quickly exposed by improvised French **infantry tactics**. The mobility and aggression encouraged by French tactics on the **Flanders** and **Rhine** fronts were harnessed by **Napoleon** to develop successful alternative methods of strategic attack.

Broadly speaking, Napoleon employed two basic campaign strategies throughout his career. When in a position of strength, facing outnumbered or disorganized forces, he would rush the bulk of his army into positions in their rear that could only be ignored at enormous risk, hoping to envelop confused opponents as they turned to protect their communications. Partly reliant on the psychological effects of surprise and potential isolation, this method was first successful at **Ceva** and **Lodi** in 1796, and was employed

another two dozen times over the next 20 years. When Napoleon was faced by superior forces, he usually sought to divide his enemy, get between its segments and rely on a rapid transfer of reserves to defeat them in detail. His first offensive as a C-in-C, at **Saorgio** in April 1796, set the pattern for this strategy, and it was central to his planning for the campaigns of 1814 and 1815.

Napoleon did not have a monopoly on strategic success. **Wellington**'s basic **Peninsular** strategy was to lure French forces to their own destruction by advancing into positions that could not be ignored and defeating the attack that followed, either by careful defensive deployment or by withdrawing to break exhausted pursuers against prepared defences. Though arguably forced on generals by circumstances, the **Russian Army**'s strategy of permanent retreat succeeded in 1812, and **Sixth Coalition** strategy during the 1813–14 campaigns was another negative success, the **Trachenberg Plan** calling for retreat whenever Napoleon himself was on the battlefield and advances only against his less daunting subordinates.

Stuart, John (1759–1815)

American-born soldier, educated in London, who fought for the British in the American War of Independence, and took part in the **Flanders** campaign of 1793–5 before taking an appointment as military adviser to the **Portuguese Army**. Transferred to command British land forces in the **Mediterranean** during autumn 1798, he led the capture of **Minorca** in November but was never given sufficient reinforcements to undertake major operations in support of the **Second Coalition**. Stuart resigned his command the following year in protest at plans to cede **Malta** to **Russia**, but returned to the Mediterranean under **Abercromby** in 1801 and commanded a division at **Alexandria**. Returning to England on the Peace of **Amiens**, he was back in the Mediterranean to command British land forces based on **Sicily** from 1806. He was knighted for his limited but tactically significant victory over French forces on the Italian mainland at **Maida** that summer, and commanded the Anglo-Sicilian force that repulsed **Murat**'s invasion of Sicily in 1810, but resigned again later that year, this time in protest at the lack of material support from the **Liverpool** government.

Studienka, Battle of

The name sometimes given to the actions fought by French forces east and west of the **Beresina** to protect the river crossing in progress at Studienka on 27 and 28 November 1812. West of the river, **Oudinot** and **Ney** fought off attacks by Admiral **Tshitshagov's** Russian army; **Victor's** corps was gradually forced back to positions immediately east of the river by **Wittgenstein's** corps approaching from the north-east, but held out until ordered to withdraw across the Beresina that evening. *See* **Russian Campaign; Map 23.**

Subsidies

The financial and material contributions made by **Great Britain** to its allies as incentives to prosecute war against France were a constant feature of the 1793–1815 period. Weapons, uniforms and other supplies formed a significant portion of aid, but all Britain's allies received some financial support. Cash donations varied in size from sums of less than £100,000, which could buy the allegiance of small governments, to £2–3 million for the active support of a **great power**, usually paid in instalments in an attempt to ensure long-term commitment.

Prussia, **Russia** and **Austria** were the main beneficiaries of subsidies. They often negotiated successfully for increases during the course of campaigns, and successive British governments were willing to make new offers, but what appeared a mutually beneficial policy provoked inter-allied arguments that contributed to Britain's diplomatic isolation before 1812. Defeated allies (and French **propaganda**) complained that Britain was using its wealth to prolong a war that was increasing its commercial power, and were accused in return of repeated failure to fulfil commitments. Both were right. Britain's expenditure on subsidies represented a tiny fraction of its burgeoning wealth, while its allies, especially Prussia before 1795, frequently broke promises made for sums of money that were highly significant in terms of their much smaller economies.

Suchet, Louis Gabriel (1770–1826)

French soldier, who joined the **National Guard** of his native Lyon in 1791, and was a battalion commander by the time he met **Napoleon** during the siege of **Toulon** in 1793, an operation in which he distinguished himself by capturing British general O'Hara. He played a busy part in the **Italian campaigns** of 1794–7, suffering two wounds and ending the campaign as **Brune's** chief of staff in **Switzerland**. Promoted brigadier-general in March 1798, and to divisional command next year, he was chief of staff under **Joubert** and **Masséna** during the Italian campaign against the **Second Coalition**.

Governor of Padua and inspector-general of the army during the relative peace of 1801–5, Suchet returned to active service leading a division against the **Third Coalition**. At **Ulm**, **Höllabrun** and **Austerlitz** in 1805, he fought at **Jena** and **Pultusk** in 1806, ending the War of the **Fourth Coalition** as a provisional corps commander.

He was one of few French commanders to emerge with credit from the **Peninsular War**. With the invasion of **Spain** in 1808, he took part in both sieges of **Saragossa**, and subsequently won a series of minor victories in Aragon that pacified the region and earned his marshal's baton in June 1811. He was created Duc d'Albufera in January 1812, and took Valencia shortly afterwards, but was on the defensive against Anglo-Spanish armies from 1813 and finally withdrew into France in February 1814.

Suchet's record as an administrator was unique among French authorities in Spain. As military governor of Aragon, he maintained the region's traditional feudal structure and insisted that it be administered by native officials, irritating the imperial government but providing it with a better financial return than any other province. As governor of Catalonia from November 1813, he established a liberal regime that was genuinely popular with some Catalans, and suffered less disruption from **guerrillas** than any other occupying regime.

Suchet took service with the restored French monarchy in 1814, but rejoined Napoleon during the **Hundred Days** of 1815. Surprisingly excluded from frontline command, he instead led a small force guarding the Alps. Exiled after agreeing an armistice with Austrian forces in **Piedmont**, he came home to retirement in 1819.

Suvorov, Alexander Vasilievich (1729–1800)

Widely regarded in contemporary and modern **Russia** as the greatest general ever to serve the tsars, and popularly credited with never losing a battle, Suvorov enjoyed a formidable international reputation at the start of the **Revolutionary Wars** but had little recent experience of fighting in western Europe. A brigadier-general since 1763, he won a series of actions during subsequent wars against **Poland** (1768–72) and the **Ottoman Empire** (1773–4) before playing a leading part in the suppression of internal opposition to **Catherine** the Great.

Established as Catherine's most trusted commander, he was governor of the newly conquered Crimea from 1786, and resumed his role as scourge of the frontiers with a successful campaign against Ottoman forces around the upper Danube from 1787 to 1790, for which he was ennobled as Count Suvorov-Rimnisky. Promoted field marshal as reward for putting down the **Polish rebellion** of 1794, he was denied a senior command by Tsar **Paul I** after Catherine's death in 1796.

Russia's participation in the **Second Coalition** brought him back into action as the only Russian general with sufficient prestige to lead an expeditionary force to the **Italian** front. Taking command on the front in mid-April, he defeated French forces at **Cassano**, the **Trebbia** and **Novi**, ending the summer poised to invade southern France, an achievement for which he was honoured as Prince Italiiski by the tsar.

An unsophisticated man, who specialized in merciless reprisals against beaten foes, Suvorov was no great tactician or strategist. Most of his victories came through determined application of brute force, and he was a great believer in ferocious infantry charges. An indefatigably aggressive commander, his unshakeable personal bravery and brutal application of discipline won awed respect among the **Russian Army**'s peasant conscripts and **Cossacks**.

None of these qualities equipped him for diplomatic adventures, and his proclamation of a restored monarchy for **Piedmont** in summer 1799 was a serious mistake, outraging Vienna and triggering his transfer to the **Swiss** front. Delayed transferring through the **St Gotthard Pass**, he was compelled to follow retreating allied armies to the Rhine, undertaking an epic march in hostile Alpine conditions that wiped out most of his army. Recalled when Paul quit the Coalition at the end of the year, he was denied honours or recognition for his final campaign on his return to St Petersburg. A sick man, and apparently devastated by the loss of royal favour, he retired and died the following May.

Sweden

Though still the dominant force in Scandinavian affairs, the Kingdom of Sweden had been forced on to the defensive since its defeat by a combination of other regional powers during the Great Northern War of 1700–21. The subsequent rise of **Russia** as a Baltic power threatened to detach its eastern province of **Finland**, Prussian expansionism menaced the country's southern frontiers, and long-standing disputes with neighbouring **Denmark** centred on the possession of **Norway**.

As a potential source of pressure on Habsburg territories in northern Europe, Sweden had long maintained friendly relations with **France**, and the autocratic King Gustavus III was a committed opponent of the **French Revolution**. He was attempting to form an anti-French alliance when he was shot and mortally wounded at the Stockholm opera house in March 1792, the victim of an assassin in the pay of noble conspirators. His son was only 14, and though nominal power was in the hands of a regent (Duke Charles of Sudermania), practical control passed to the leader of the noble ministerial faction, Baron Reuterholm.

Reuterholm kept Sweden's practical involvement in the French war to a minimum, while moving towards rapprochement with Denmark and France against Russia. A defensive treaty was signed with Denmark in March 1794 and, after the failure of a Russian-sponsored coup, an alliance with France was signed in June 1795, but Franco-Swedish relations cooled after

Gustavus IV came of age in November 1796.

The king's main priorities were the re-establishment of royal autocracy, beginning with Reuterholm's dismissal and exile, and economic recovery, to which his introduction of general land enclosure laws in 1803 made a significant contribution. In line with most popular and political opinion, the need for peaceful prosperity kept Gustavus out of the **Second Coalition**, and though fear of diplomatic isolation induced Sweden to join the **Armed Neutrality** league in 1800–1, great pains were taken to avoid any actual conflict with **Great Britain**.

Equally hostile to liberal ideas and the ambitions of **Napoleon**, Gustavus spent a long sabbatical in **Baden** during 1803–5, sharing local outrage when the Duc d'**Enghein** was abducted in March 1804 and returning bent on war against France. Overruling ministerial preferences for neutrality, he joined the **Third Coalition** in April 1805, but it was defeated before his forces were in the field. Though Sweden escaped immediate punishment by Napoleon, its neutrality was fatally compromised, and Sweden became increasingly dependent on diplomatic support from Britain, especially after **Trafalgar**.

Gustavus bowed to British pressure and joined the **Fourth Coalition** in 1806, when a Swedish division reached **Lübeck** just in time to be captured by French forces mopping up after victories at **Jena** and **Auerstädt**. Though French commander **Bernadotte** earned great credit in Sweden for his courteous treatment of prisoners, renewed French attacks in Pomerania had driven Swedish forces into the **fortress** of **Stralsund** by spring 1807, and Gustavus had to cede the province to Napoleon as the price of peace.

The Franco-Russian alliance agreed at **Tilsit** in July 1807 freed the tsar to resume attacks on Sweden, and a failed Swedish attempt to retake Pomerania and Rügen in August reinforced French hostility. The **Russo-Swedish War** of 1808–9 detached Finland permanently from Stockholm, and after his quarrel with General **Moore** deprived the Swedes of British support, Gustavus was overthrown by a military coup on 11 March 1809.

Former regent Duke Charles was placed at the head of a provisional government, and a national assembly (Riksdag) called to prepare a parliamentary constitution in May. Having accepted its terms, the elderly and childless regent was proclaimed King **Charles XIII** on 5 June. As crown prince and heir, the Riksdag selected Prince Christian Augustus, the Danish viceroy in Norway and a potential guarantor of Scandinavian unity. Meanwhile the deteriorating military situation compelled Charles to sign the punitive Treaty of Frederickshamm on 17 September, and peace with Denmark followed on 10 December. Sweden agreed to join Napoleon's **Continental System** in January 1810.

Christian Augustus died in May 1810, and the Riksdag's election of Bernadotte as his replacement appeared to seal Franco-Swedish friendship. Effective regent from late October, Bernadotte declared war on Britain in November, but his sustained failure to enforce the Continental System infuriated Napoleon, who refused support for Swedish plans to occupy Norway in February 1811, and took the rest of Pomerania the following January. Bernadotte reached agreement for mutual support against Denmark and France with Russian tsar **Alexander I** at **St Petersburg** in April 1812, and Sweden's membership of the **Sixth Coalition** was sealed by British recognition of the pact at **Stockholm** in spring 1813.

Able to override domestic doubts, Bernadotte introduced **conscription** in late 1812 to provide soldiers for an expedition against France in 1813. Swedish forces landed in Stralsund in May 1813, but were not fully committed to the campaign for **Germany** until mid-July, after which they formed part of the allied northern wing until the peace of 1814. Bernadotte was rewarded with Norway, acquired from a bankrupt Denmark by the Treaty of **Kiel** in January 1814, and bullied into accepting Charles XIII as its king. Charles died in 1818, and was succeeded by Bernadotte as King Charles XIV, who presided over a period of peaceful internal stability, and whose family still occupy the Swedish throne at the end of the twentieth century. *See* **Maps 1, 30**.

Swedish Army

The Swedish Army of the late eighteenth century was based around a small regular force, augmented in time of war by volunteer reserves given 28 days' training every spring. This basic arrangement remained in place until late 1812, when **Bernadotte** introduced **conscription** to create an army for the 1813 campaign in **Germany**, calling up males between 21 and 25 for a five-year period of compulsory service. Until then, wartime strength amounted to eight **cavalry** and 14 line infantry regiments, along with ten **jäger** regiments and the three Guard regiments. A Guard regiment and one of the army's four **artillery** regiments were disbanded after the loss of Finland in 1809, and engineering troops were drawn as needed from line forces, though officers and NCOs were specially trained. The army also administered coastal naval forces for **amphibious** operations (*see* **Swedish Navy**). When Swedish forces landed in Germany in 1813, they recruited new formations from captured troops and occupied territories, including a regiment of French and German ex-prisoners and a **Landwehr** unit from Pomerania.

Sweden was neutral during the **Revolutionary Wars**, and the army saw no significant action after being mobilized in support of the **Third Coalition** in 1805. A division sent to northern Germany to support **Prussia** in 1806 was promptly captured by French forces at **Lübeck**, and the army fared badly against **Danish** and **Russian** forces during the **Russo-Swedish War** of 1808–9. Following Bernadotte's commitment to the **Sixth Coalition**, an enlarged conscript army of 30,000 troops reached northern Germany in May 1813, and was fully committed against French forces from July. Sweden's crippling poverty meant that many of its troops fought using captured equipment, but it won significant victories under Bernadotte's command at **Gross-Beeren** and **Dennewitz**, before joining other allied forces at **Leipzig**. Swedish forces played a peripheral role in the 1814 campaign for **France**, functioning as an occupation force in northern Germany and seizing the Danish province of Holstein.

Swedish Navy

The Kingdom of **Sweden** possessed two separate navies. The 'Army Fleet', manned by a combination of naval recruits and **Swedish Army** volunteer reserves, comprised two 'divisions' of small inshore and landing craft, stationed at Stockholm and Helsingfors (Helsinki). The 'High Seas Fleet' comprised 27 **ships-of-the-line** and 12 **frigates** in 1790, and was employed for conventional **naval warfare** in and around the Baltic. Though a match for **Russian Navy** forces in the theatre, it seldom ventured beyond home waters, and avoided battles with the practised certainty of a declining service lacking money or efficient dockyards.

Swedish naval forces were most actively engaged during the 1808–9 **Russo-Swedish War**. Stationed in **Finland**, the Army Fleet took part in regular **amphibious** operations, but was never properly concentrated, suffering heavy losses at **Sandöström**, **Palvasund** and **Ratan** before it was all but lost when the province was occupied in autumn 1809. High seas units, with 12 battleships and eight frigates ready for active service, cooperated with British admiral **Saumarez** to destroy the 74-gun *Vsevolod* in August 1808, and blockaded the Russian fleet in Balticsport (near Revel) for a time after further British reinforcements arrived, but undertook no other actions against major warships.

Swiss Campaign (1799)

Under the **Directory** government's control since 1798, **Switzerland** was in many ways the key to ultimate French victory over the **Second Coalition**. French occupying forces under **Masséna** controlled the Alpine passes linking France, Austria and Italy in early 1799, and were well placed to interrupt communications or attack the flank of allied armies on the **Rhine** and **Italian** fronts.

Both sides' offensive plans for 1799 largely ignored the importance of Switzerland. The opening French offensive on the Rhine in March was intended to coincide with an advance east by Masséna's 48,000 troops, but his advance into the Grisons and the Vorarlberg stalled after driving Austrian corps under Hötze and **Belle-garde** back as far as Feldkirch.

With all hope of an immediate offensive on the Rhine abandoned after Jourdan's defeat at **Stockach**, the government gave Masséna overall command of both armies, and he was reinforced to a total of about 100,000 troops for the defence of Switzerland. By mid-May, further French disasters in Italy had cut him off from **Moreau's** army to the south, and forced him to detach General Lecourbe into the mountains to guard against an attack from **Suvorov's** allied army in Turin.

Meanwhile Austrian forces were advancing from the Rhine to form a strike force of about 110,000 men under Archduke **Charles**. Distracted by an epidemic of local anti-French uprisings, Masséna withdrew his forces from the eastern Grisons region before attacking Charles on 26 May around **Frauenfeld**, and then pulled back to strong positions around **Zurich**. Repeated Austrian attacks against his left flank from 4 to 7 June forced him into a final withdrawal to powerful fortifications in the mountains east and west of Zurich.

Charles ceased offensive operations on 7 June and established fortified positions of his own, detaching 10,000 troops under Bellegarde to aid Suvorov's ongoing Italian campaign (*see* Battle of **San Giuliano**). The summer passed in occasional skirmishes on an otherwise quiet front. Charles waited for Russian reinforcements under **Korsakov**, and Masséna ignored repeated government orders to take the offensive, preferring cautious defence as long as the fate of Italy remained in doubt. The positions of the two armies, both about 75,000 strong, were largely unchanged by early August, putting severe pressure on food supplies in eastern Switzerland.

Masséna was eventually persuaded into an attack in support of **Joubert's** offensive towards Novi, massing strength on his right flank, where mountain specialist General Lecourbe led repeated attacks on Austrian positions from 14 to 17 August. Though forced to pull back his left wing, Charles received 25,000 Russian reinforcements at about the same time, and attempted to counter-attack across the River Aar north-west of Zurich on the night of 16–17 August. Unable to fix **pontoons** across the fast, stone-bedded river

that night, his forces were halted by sector commander **Ney** and 10,000 men in the morning, but the threat was enough to throw Masséna back on to the defensive.

The expected allied offensive never came. The sudden lurch in Coalition strategy that transferred Suvorov's Russians from Italy to Switzerland also moved Charles and 36,000 troops to the Rhine from 26 August, leaving the separated forces of Hötze and Korsakov (some 60,000 men in total) to hold the Swiss front while the necessary manoeuvres took place. Masséna seized his opportunity to attack the allied armies separately, but a plan to strike Korsakov in force on 30 August was spoiled by a sudden rise in the River Aar, though **Soult** and Lecourbe drove Hötze's 25,000 troops back into the Grisons.

Taking advantage of Suvorov's delays and tribulations as he struggled beyond the **St Gotthard Pass**, Masséna launched a second attempt to exploit the separation of Hötze and Korsakov, whose armies were still deployed either side of Lake Zurich, by attacking them simultaneously. His two-pronged offensive on 25–26 September, known as the Second Battle of **Zurich**, drove both allied armies back to the Rhine in some disarray, and was a turning point in the war. Suvorov, with no allies left to meet, could only struggle through the mountains to the Rhine, and French control of Switzerland was not seriously threatened during the remaining months of the war. Russian forces quit western Europe altogether during the winter, and the front was driven east beyond Munich by Moreau's combined Swiss and Rhineland command in response to an attempted Austrian advance the following spring. *See* **Map 4**.

Swiss Forces

Each of the 13 cantons that comprised **Switzerland** in 1792 provided its own army for national defence, and although expected to combine against any threat they shared no common equipment, uniform or organizational structure. Switzerland also provided troops for the prerevolutionary **French Army**, and its forces fought for **France** after the formation of the Helvetic Republic in 1803, providing a regiment of **chasseurs**, three of infantry and supporting

artillery. Once annexed by France, the provinces of Neuchâtel and Valois each provided an infantry battalion for French service. A small number of Swiss émigrés, mostly drawn from the fiercely anti-French canton of Berne, fought for the allies against France, and three Swiss regiments eventually served in the wartime **British Army**. Colonel de Mouron's unit, which had transferred from Dutch service after it was captured at **Ceylon** in 1795, was unique in rejecting other European exiles and remaining almost entirely Swiss throughout the period.

Switzerland

A fully independent state since 1649, Switzerland was a federation of 13 small republics, or cantons, with a population approaching 1.5 million in the late eighteenth century. With no pretensions to military prowess, it relied on internal stability and its imposing geographical defences to preserve its independence, along with very close ties to **France**.

A natural refuge for European republican exiles, Switzerland found its internal peace fatally undermined by the spread of French revolutionary ideas. A Helvetian Club of Paris was founded in 1790 to transmit revolutionary **propaganda** to the cantons, and helped trigger popular uprisings that culminated in the French annexation of Porrentuy province in 1791. Switzerland remained neutral during the War of the **First Coalition**, but remained a fertile breeding ground for radical ideology, and the country became a target for French expansionism after the Peace of **Campo Formio** in 1797.

French conquest of Switzerland was planned during a meeting between Swiss radical agitator Peter Ochs and French representatives, led by **Napoleon**, on 8 December 1797. Invited by local radicals to intervene in defence of an uprising in Vaud, a French army under **Brune** entered Switzerland in February 1798. Despite armed opposition from the small Bernese army, the cantons capitulated on 5 March.

Mulhouse had already been annexed by France on 28 January, and Geneva followed on 15 April, but the rest of Switzerland was transformed into the Helvetic Republic from late April. The new republic's 23 cantons were governed from Lucerne by a Directory on the French pattern, but its client status and the prime motivation behind French involvement were highlighted by a mutual alliance treaty signed on 2 August, guaranteeing French use of the Alpine passes for all time.

Loss of independence sparked widespread popular unrest, usually met by punitive French countermeasures, and civil disorder intensified when Austrian, Russian and French armies caused considerable economic damage during a prolonged **Swiss campaign** in 1799. Political centralization along French lines from January 1800 fuelled factional disputes among Swiss leaders, with Ochs heading a 'unitary' party in dispute with 'federalists' seeking to retain local freedoms. Napoleon brought both factions to Paris for a conference in December 1802, and his Act of Meditation, finalized the following February, heralded a more fundamental reorganization.

Now known as the Helvetic Confederation, or (for the first time) Switzerland, the new republic comprised 19 reconstituted cantons, each with control over its own finances, customs and education system, but covered by a common legal code. Napoleon named himself as the Confederation's protector, or Mediator, and concluded a full alliance with the new state in November 1803.

Technically neutral, Switzerland remained firmly under French control for the next decade, contributing troops to the imperial **French Army** and sacrificing territory in line with Napoleon's political or strategic requirements. Neuchâtel was occupied by French troops in 1806, and given as a principality to **Berthier**; the Alpine passes of the Valais (made an independent republic by Napoleon in 1802) became the French *département* of Simplon in July 1810; and imperial forces occupied Ticino from January 1811.

French defeat at **Leipzig** in 1813 prompted a Swiss declaration of neutrality on 15 November, but this was not backed by the withdrawal of Swiss troops from French service, and Austria invaded in December. Threatened with conquest, the diet abolished the 1803 constitution, heralding a prolonged dispute before a minority of cantons (headed by Berne) committed to the restoration of the pre-revolutionary system was overruled by a majority in favour of retaining the new, broader-based federal structure, a loose federation of 22 cantons (increased by the reincorporation of Neuchâtel, Geneva and the Valois). The new constitution was recognized by the Congress of **Vienna**, and Swiss neutrality placed under a general guarantee that finally ended the country's dependence on French support. *See* **Map 30**.

T

Tagliamento, Battle of the *See* Invasion of the **Frioul**

Talavera, Battle of

The first major British success in **Spain** during the **Peninsular War**, a defensive victory in late July 1809 against a much larger French force just east of the Portuguese frontier. Having advanced from Lisbon to drive **Soult**'s occupying army from **Oporto** on 12 May, General **Wellesley**'s 18,000 troops had entered Spain on 3 July and linked up with General **Cuesta**'s Estremaduran army. Joseph **Bonaparte**'s French armies in Spain were widely dispersed and operating under virtually independent commanders, and **Victor**'s force had advanced, unsupported, almost to the frontier.

Wellesley marched east along the Tagus in the hope of catching Victor in isolation, ignoring Cuesta's demands for an immediate attack and tracking the French withdrawal towards Madrid until it halted at the junction of the Tagus and the Alberche River. Victor took up position near the town of Talavera and awaited reinforcements. As allied forces approached, a further French withdrawal on 26 July enticed Cuesta's 20,000 Spaniards into an uncoordinated advance across the plains, but **Jourdan**'s army from Madrid (with King Joseph in attendance) had arrived to bring French strength up to 40,000 men, and the attack was routed.

Cuesta's forces were chased back beyond Talavera, where British and Portuguese troops were left to defend the shallow heights above the plain. Wellesley concentrated his forces north of Talavera, facing east, and Jourdan confidently launched piecemeal attacks as soon as infantry were in position. Well-disciplined defenders, aided by remnants of the Spanish force brought under Wellesley's personal command, held off frontal attacks during the night of 27–28 July, throughout the following day and into the morning of 29 July, when the arrival of **Craufurd**'s light **cavalry** prompted a French withdrawal.

A major **propaganda** triumph, earning Wellesley a peerage as Lord **Wellington**, Talavera proved something of an empty victory. Hopes of an advance on Madrid were undermined by the approach of armies under **Ney** and Soult from the north, and the Spanish inability to provide supplies forced the British to retire south-west towards the frontier from August. *See* **Map 22**.

Talleyrand–Fouché Plot

Political intrigue, aimed at warping the French imperial succession in the event of **Napoleon**'s death during his invasion of **Spain**, that was fomented in November 1808 between French arch-chancellor **Talleyrand**, police chief **Fouché** and the inevitable Caroline **Bonaparte**, arch-conspirator and Queen of **Naples**. The three reached a secret agreement that Caroline's husband, **Murat**, possessed the necessary popularity and political naïveté to make an ideal successor to the emperor, but their plans were revealed to Napoleon by Italian viceroy **Beauharnais**, who intercepted a message from Talleyrand to the Neapolitan king. Napoleon survived to return to

Paris in early 1809. Needing both Murat and Fouché for the imminent war against **Austria**, he exercised his wrath on Talleyrand, who accepted public disgrace with characteristic charm. Murat never expected to be fully forgiven for his part in the affair, and fears for his future encouraged later attempts to win popular support as a sponsor of Italian nationalism.

Talleyrand-Périgord, Charles Maurice de (1754–1838)

Paris-born statesman and diplomat, a supreme pragmatist whose colourful personal life, gift for survival and penetrating wit illuminated the heart of French politics for most of a long and turbulent career.

Heir to his family's titles until lamed by a fall in early childhood, Talleyrand was instead sent into the Church, becoming a very worldly young prelate, whose disdain for religious affairs was no obstacle to elevation as Bishop of Autun from spring 1789. Representing the diocese at the States-General later that year, he helped draw up the National Assembly's 'Declaration of the Rights of Man', and proposed its confiscation of Church property. President of the Assembly from February 1790, he finally abandoned the priesthood the following January, after his demonstrations of support for the Catholic faith had brought him into conflict with the revolutionary regime.

Talleyrand's diplomatic career began with a mission to London in early 1792, but he was unable to win guarantees of neutrality from the **Pitt** government. Threatened, like all nobles, by the **Jacobin** radicalization of French politics, he became an **émigré** from December 1792, spending time in Britain, the **United States**, the **Netherlands** and western Germany before returning to **France** in September 1795. His well-earned reputation for cynicism sat well with the **Directory** government's policy of playing radical and royalist extremists off against each other, and he formed political alliances with the equally unscrupulous **Barras** and **Fouché**, becoming foreign minister in July 1797. He was perhaps the most influential voice in the government during 1798, recognizing the need for an expansionist policy to defuse internal social and economic

crises. An early admirer of **Napoleon**, he also gave vital support to the **Middle East** expedition.

Talleyrand resigned in early 1799, preferring to conspire against a crumbling regime from without, but he remained close to Director **Sieyès** and was one of the principal organizers of the **Brumaire** coup that brought Napoleon to power in November. Returning to the foreign ministry from December 1799, he was Napoleon's chief political fixer and strategic adviser over the next few years, playing a central role in the establishment of the life consulate in 1802 and the empire two years later.

Though a genuine admirer of Napoleon's abilities and personality, Talleyrand was nobody's yes-man. A critic of actions against the Duc d'**Enghein** in 1804 – on political rather than moral grounds – he made consistent efforts to persuade Napoleon into the moderation that might promote long-term peace with defeated enemies. His failure, and a growing belief that Napoleon's limitless ambition was bound to end in disaster, gradually convinced him to make his own plans for European peace.

After playing an important role in organizing the Confederation of the **Rhine** in 1806, for which he was created Prince of Benevento, he began to distance himself from Napoleon from 1807. He resigned the foreign ministry that year, and was probably in contact with British authorities during the **Tilsit** negotiations. Though he remained an indispensable diplomatic and political executive, he kept Russian tsar **Alexander** informed of French state secrets during the **Erfurt** conference, and Napoleon's mistrust was confirmed by the **Talleyrand–Fouché** conspiracy of late 1808. Publicly humiliated in its aftermath, but retaining his ambiguous position among Napoleon's advisers, Talleyrand became the clandestine leader of a peace party in Paris once the emperor was committed to the 1812 **Russian campaign**.

Talleyrand opened direct negotiations with the allies from 1812, and led the delegation welcoming their armies into Paris in spring 1814. After negotiating the Treaty of **Paris** with the allies, he served the restored **Louis XVIII** as foreign minister, but remained in contact with the former emperor on **Elba**. He adopted a typically compromising position during the **Hundred Days** of 1815, leading the Senate's cautious acceptance of the Second Empire but helping orchestrate Napoleon's final removal after **Waterloo**.

Talleyrand's greatest diplomatic triumph came at the postwar Congress of **Vienna**, where his brilliant exploitation of allied strategic differences re-established France among the **great powers** of Europe and secured relatively moderate peace terms. Though he impressed his fellow delegates, who were instrumental in his brief elevation to prime minister, he was detested and mistrusted by the restored royal regime, and soon lost his offices, spending the next 15 years as a loud but relatively unimportant voice in the Senate. He enjoyed a last taste of power after 1830, when he played in leading role in the July revolution that overthrew the monarchy, and was a highly successful ambassador to London until his eventual retirement in 1834.

Tarbes, Battle of

The penultimate engagement of the **Peninsular War**, fought on 20 March 1814, an attempt by allied C-in-C **Wellington** to trap **Soult's** retreating French army before it could reach the relative security of Toulouse. Following his withdrawal from **Orthez** in late February, Soult made efforts to elude allied pursuit while Wellington paused to send a detachment in support of a royalist uprising in **Bordeaux**. By the time the allied advance resumed from around St Sever on 18 March, Soult had moved south-east towards the Pyrenees, and Wellington attempted to pin him against the mountains. He sent **Beresford's** corps ahead to cut the three available roads leading north from Soult's positions around Tarbes, but the southernmost was kept open by two French divisions after a fierce fight on the afternoon of 20 March. Casualties were light (80 French and 120 allied), but the action enabled Soult to evade Wellington's advance and retreat on **Toulouse**. *See* **Map 5**.

Tarragona, Siege of

One of two major diversionary operations launched by allied forces in the **Peninsular** theatre during the early summer of 1813, designed to mask the main thrust of **Wellington's** offensive in northern Spain. Before **Hill's** strong

detachment launched a feint at Salamanca and Madrid, **Murray** led 16,000 troops from Alicante to the Catalan port of Tarragona, with orders to attack the town and keep **Suchet's** regional army fully occupied. Landed by a **Royal Navy** squadron on 2 June at Salou Bay, some 10km south of Tarragona, Murray's force was joined by 8,000 **Spanish Army** troops under General Copons before opening a **siege** of General Bertoletti's 1,600-strong garrison.

Two French forces were in position to relieve the port, but only 6,000 troops had been sent to the town when Murray ordered his troops to re-embark on 11 June. Overruling the protests of naval commander Hallowell, and while Copons retreated inland, Murray got his force on board ships during the afternoon of 12 June, spiking the expedition's heavy **artillery** in the belief that a French attack was imminent. General Matthieu's relief column had in fact abandoned the attempt, and only returned to occupy Tarragona after the British had departed for Alicante. *See* **Map 22**.

Tarvis, Battle of

The main action during **Napoleon's** 1797 invasion of the Austrian **Frioul** region, and the last serious clash between French and Austrian forces on the **Italian** front during the War of the **First Coalition**. Some 32,000 troops had moved east across the Tagliamento on 16 March and moved up to the River Isonzo, while a detachment of 11,000 troops under General **Masséna** was ordered to take Tarvis on the northern flank. Austrian C-in-C Archduke **Charles** sent three divisions under General Lusignan to occupy a gorge dominating the town, but Masséna's fast-moving force got there first, and the Austrians were trapped once Napoleon's main body came up from the south-west. Most of Lusignan's troops escaped into the mountains, but about 5,000 men and 32 guns fell into French hands. Dissuaded from direct resistance, Charles retired towards the Rhine to ensure his army's long-term survival while Napoleon swept on to Klagenfurt and Leoben. *See* **Map 9**.

Tauroggen, Convention of

The agreement by which General **Yorck's** 17,000 Prussian troops attached to Marshal **Macdonald's**

French X Corps became neutrals during the last stages of the 1812 **Russian campaign**. Operating on the northern flank of the French invasion force, Yorck's troops were in the vicinity of **Riga** from August until Macdonald was ordered to follow the retreat of the main army in December. Harassed by pursuing Russian forces under General Diebitsch, himself a former Prussian officer, Yorck's column was isolated and surrounded on 25 December, and signed the Convention after five days of negotiations. Disowned by Prussian king **Frederick William III**, who remained a French ally for the time being, and dismissed as treachery by **Napoleon**, the agreement evoked a powerful response from nationalist elements in **Prussia** and neighbouring states, and sparked the broader movement for 'national liberation' during the 1813 campaign for **Germany**.

Tenerife, Attack on (1797)

Optimistic British assault on the main defences of the Spanish Canary Isles, carried out by about 1,000 sailors and **marines** on 24 July 1797. British **Mediterranean** C-in-C **Jervis** detached **Nelson** with four **ships-of-the-line** and four **frigates** from his **blockade** of Cadiz on 15 July, charged with taking the port of Santa Cruz and capturing a Spanish treasure fleet expected from Mexico. Arriving off Tenerife on 20 July, Nelson was prevented by contrary winds from approaching the harbour over the next two days, but brought 600 men ashore in longboats on the night of 24 July. Undetected until they were within a few hundred metres of the shore, but subjected to heavy fire as they landed, the force lost Nelson to a bullet in the arm (which was promptly amputated) before fighting its way into the town square. Out of ammunition, and cut off from the shore as 8,000 French and Spanish troops on the island were mobilized in its defence, the British party escaped capture because the local Spanish governor, threatened with the town's bombardment by British battleships, agreed to generous terms for its departure on 25 July. *See* **Map 19**.

Tengen, Battle of

One of the first actions during the War of the **Fifth Coalition**, a small but significant encounter between French and Austrian forces in the Danube theatre on 19 April 1809.

The Austrian offensive on the Danube, aimed towards Ratisbon, had opened on 9 April, and had caught French formations widely separated. By the time **Napoleon** reached the front on 17 April, Austrian commander Archduke **Charles** and at least 80,000 troops were threatening to cut off the two northern French corps of **Davout** and **Lefebvre**. Unaware of the size of Austrian forces facing them, Napoleon ordered Lefebvre's 20,000 Bavarians to hold off the advance, while Davout was instructed to join them with his 47,000 troops.

Davout duly moved his corps over the Danube from Ratisbon on 18 April, but ran into Charles's central army the next day around Kelheim and Albach. Confident in his numerical superiority, Charles prepared his attack too slowly. Prince Hohenzollern's westernmost corps did attack French forces around the village of Saal, but was repulsed by two French divisions. Davout's other two divisions (**St Hilaire** and Friant) fought a successful rearguard action at nearby Tengen, before following the rest of the corps to Abensberg.

Though they had only defeated a part of the Austrian advanced guard, both Lefebvre and Davout believed that they had put Charles's entire army to flight, and informed Napoleon accordingly. The mistake influenced Napoleon's decision to launch an offensive at **Abensberg** on 20 April, and he was understandably slow to provide reinforcements the following day, when Davout's forces were barely able to hold off a renewed Austrian advance. *See* **Map 12**.

Teplitz, Treaties of

Formal alliances signed with **Prussia** and **Russia** (9 September 1813), and with **Great Britain** (30 October 1813), by which **Austria** confirmed its adherence to the **Sixth Coalition**, sealed at **Reichenbach** in July. The first treaty included an agreement among the three empires to cooperate in deciding the postwar future of **Poland**.

Terror, The

Contemporary term for the ruthless socio-economic and political measures adopted by French leaders to ensure the Republic's survival during 1793–4. The mechanisms for centralized dictatorship had been established by the relatively moderate 'Girondin' government of 1792–3, which had created the Committees of **Public Safety** and General Security to protect it against subversion in Paris, and had sent 'representatives on mission' into the provinces to supervise the enactment of central government policies. After the government's overthrow by **Jacobin** elements in June 1793, provincial representatives and volunteer *armées révolutionnaires* came under strict control of the committees, which were themselves dominated by **Robespierre** and his allies.

The Terror was formally adopted as government policy in September. Over the next few months Paris was purged of political opponents, commodity speculators and other perceived enemies of state, culminating in the 'Grand Terror' of June and July 1794, when some 1,300 people were executed at the guillotine. The pattern was repeated in the provinces, where committed left-wing 'terrorists' such as **Fouché** and Tallien conducted merciless witchhunts and supervised the forced requisition of food, raw materials and money for the capital or the frontline armies. Military forces on the frontiers were subject to similar supervision and purged of many government opponents, while strong armies were assembled to put down royalist rebellions in the west and south with exemplary savagery.

Though it remains notorious as the blueprint for state terrorism by twentieth-century dictatorships, the Terror is generally credited with saving **France** at a time of grave national crisis. It enabled the Jacobin government to marshal resources against the simultaneous threats of invasion, economic collapse, civil war in the provinces and potential anarchy in Paris. Without ruthless dictatorial rule, war minister **Carnot** could not have carried through the military reforms that brought vital victories over **First Coalition** forces in spring 1794.

By reducing the immediate need for emergency measures, the Terror's success undermined support for its instigators. Popular revulsion against continued bloodletting and denial of civil rights had set in before the **Thermidor** coup that overthrew Robespierre in July 1794, and the Terror was quickly dismantled by the moderate liberal regime that took power in its aftermath.

Texel Island, Capture of (1795)

Bizarre victory by French **cavalry** forces over the **Dutch Navy** on 30 January 1795, at which time collapse of the **First Coalition**'s campaign in **Flanders** had left the independent **Netherlands** at the mercy of republican forces. In the grip of widespread popular republicanism, Amsterdam welcomed French commander **Pichegru** on 20 January, after which cavalry forces moved north, preceded by large numbers of loyalist Dutch refugees en route for the busy port of Helder (*see* **Map 2**). The main Dutch Navy base on Texel Island, separated from Helder by a narrow strip of salt water, housed 12 **ships-of-the-line** and numerous smaller craft, but the deepest winter frost in decades had trapped all shipping and frozen the channel to the mainland. A unit of French **dragoons** (with light **artillery** support) galloped across the ice on 30 January to surprise and capture the entire fleet, boosting French naval power at a stroke and striking a major strategic blow against **Great Britain**. The coup provided a base for prospective invasions of **England** over the next decade, and forced the **Royal Navy** to maintain a **blockade** of the Dutch fleet until its virtual annihilation at **Camperdown** in 1797. *See* Invasion of **North Holland**.

Thames River, Battle of

The major success of the US campaign along the Canadian border during the **Anglo-American War** of 1812–15, a victory over a combined British, Canadian and native force at Thames River, just east of Detroit, in October 1813. One of several key positions occupying the frontier lands linking the Great Lakes, Detroit had been in British hands since August 1812, but the **US Navy**'s victory on Lake **Erie** allowed Commodore **Perry** to transport 7,000 troops across the lake and menace the town in late September 1813. British garrison commander General Proctor promptly evacuated his 800 regular troops back into Canada, along with 1,000 native American allies under Chief Tecumseh, but Harrison set off in immediate pursuit after taking Detroit on 29 September. Proctor's outnumbered forces were caught at Thames River on 5 October, and forced to surrender when Tecumseh's death triggered the flight of their allies. Its immediate object achieved, Harrison's force retired on Detroit pending the outcome of the US Army's main autumn offensive against Montreal. *See* Map 27.

Thermidor Coup

The parliamentary seizure of power in France on 27 July 1794 that overthrew the brief dictatorship of Robespierre's Committee of Public Safety. Robespierre's regime had been in power since June 1793, and in unchallenged power since spring 1794, when the last of its direct political opponents had gone to the guillotine. It had quickly lost both political and popular support (almost the same thing in Paris at that stage) by establishing the mechanisms of the Terror in law, raising the pace of executions and imposing a new state religion that satisfied nobody. In late July, as St Just proposed his formal establishment as dictator and popular calls for his head mounted, the Convention turned against Robespierre. Snubbed in the chamber on 26 July, he was arrested and beaten on 27 July, given a token trial and executed next day, along with St Just and 20 other disciples. A moderate faction under Barras took over the main revolutionary committees, and a period of reconciliation followed. The laws supporting the Terror were repealed, and many of those associated with the Jacobin regime, including Carnot and Fouché, invited to serve in the new administration, although many more extreme Jacobins were exiled or imprisoned. *See also* Directory.

Thielmann, Johann Adolf, Freiherr von (1765–1824)

Born in Dresden, Thielmann commanded a Saxon cavalry brigade with the French Grande Armée during the 1812 Russian campaign, fighting at Borodino in September. His Saxon division garrisoned Torgau during the next year's campaign in Germany, but he led his troops in defecting to the allies on 12 May and subsequently fought against French forces in the theatre. Promoted to corps command in Blücher's Prussian army during the Hundred Days Campaign of 1815, he fought at Ligny on 16 June, and two days later his troops held off attacks by a larger French force at Wavre while the rest of the Prussian contingent marched to Waterloo.

Third Coalition, War of the

The war of 1805 between greater France and the third European coalition ranged against it since 1792, an alliance including Great Britain, Russia, Austria, Sweden, Naples and a number of minor German states.

The catalyst for European coalition was Britain's critical need for allies in 1805. Alone at war with France since the breakdown of the Amiens peace in May 1803, Britain faced the imminent prospect of invasion across the Channel, and found its naval blockade policy weakened by the strain of full-scale home defence (*see* Invasion of England). The return to power in 1804 of William Pitt, the moving spirit behind the Second Coalition of 1798–1801, brought renewed diplomatic efforts to rekindle continental opposition to French expansionism.

Pitt's approaches met a positive response from Russian tsar Alexander I, whose personal rapprochement with Napoleon had been fatally undermined by the French government's murder of royal exile the Duc d'Enghein in May 1804. After prolonged negotiations, Alexander signed a provisional alliance with Britain, Sweden and Naples at St Petersburg on 11 April 1805. Habsburg emperor Francis had signed a preliminary offensive alliance with Russia the previous November, and Austria formally joined the Coalition on 9 August, led to war by a hawkish court faction's misplaced confidence in Austrian Army reforms.

The new allies concocted a highly ambitious offensive scheme to achieve their stated aim of restoring Europe's 1789 boundaries. Austrian forces were to launch a secondary attack in Italy, hold off any French move into the Tyrol, and mount a major offensive into France from Bavaria. Some 200,000 Russian troops would march to join the Bavarian offensive, and a joint Anglo-Neapolitan expedition would provide a diversion in southern Italy. Another subsidiary attack was planned against the north German coast by Swedish and British expeditionary forces, but Britain's role was otherwise confined to naval warfare and the provision of fighting funds to the tune of £12.5 million.

Coalition land forces were being mobilized by August, and Napoleon (now Emperor of the

French) was forced to respond, though he had probably already decided that invasion of England was impossible, and may have welcomed the chance to redirect his highly trained army from the Channel coast. After a brief period of indecision, he gave orders for its rapid redeployment from Boulogne and other camps on 26 August.

Allied campaign strategy was already well known in European diplomatic circles, and to Napoleon, but the French emperor maintained strict and effective secrecy around his own plan to exploit the wide gaps between Coalition armies. Dispatching **Masséna** to command 50,000 troops in Italy, with orders to prevent Austrian commander Archduke **Charles** from crossing the Alps into Bavaria, he sent 20,000 more to protect Naples under **Gouvion St Cyr**, and left 30,000 in Boulogne under General **Brune**. The bulk of the renamed **Grande Armée** was sent into Germany, aiming to attack General **Mack**'s army in **Bavaria** before Russian support arrived.

French redeployment in Bavaria was carried out with extraordinary speed and precision, and the subsequent envelopment of Mack's army at **Ulm** (where it surrendered on 20 October) was a triumph of strategic planning and manoeuvre against an indecisive foe. But though it shattered Austrian confidence, Napoleon's victory still left him seriously exposed.

Three Russian armies, though delayed, were still approaching from the east (in staggered columns led by **Kutuzov**, **Buxhowden** and **Bennigsen**), and about 32,000 Austrian troops were still active in Germany. To the south, he was depending on Masséna's outnumbered forces to prevent perhaps 80,000 troops under Charles in Italy, and Archduke **John**'s 20,000 men in the Tyrol, from moving north to threaten his rear. On moving east from Ulm in late October to occupy friendly Munich, Napoleon's problems mounted with news of deepening economic crisis in France, **Nelson**'s crushing victory at **Trafalgar**, and **Prussia**'s provisional decision to join the Coalition.

Provoked in part by French violation of its neutrality during the march on Ulm, but largely the result of Tsar Alexander's personal diplo-macy, Prussian mobilization added weight to **Talleyrand**'s pleas for a merciful peace with Austria and rapid withdrawal. Napoleon ignored him, choosing instead to advance further east. Relying on allied lethargy to protect his far north, and on Masséna to keep the southern Austrian armies busy, he aimed to attack Kutuzov's advanced Russian force while it could still be taken in isolation.

Kutuzov took the prudent course, and retreated towards reinforcements as Napoleon marched his army from Munich for Vienna on 28 October. Forward units led by **Lannes** and **Murat** caught up with Kutuzov at **Amstetten**, 150km west of Vienna, on 5 November, but the Russians quickly broke off the engagement and resumed a north-easterly march. Meanwhile, Masséna and Charles fought an indecisive three-day engagement at **Caldiero** (29–31 October), delaying a planned Austrian withdrawal from Italy into Bavaria.

After weeks of hard marching, Kutuzov's numerical strength was down to some 40,000 men by early November, and he was intent on withdrawing beyond the Danube. He could not prevent General Merveldt's 10,000-strong Austrian remnant from departing towards Vienna on 1 November (though they were soon defeated by **Davout** at **Zell**), but he had no intention of risking his fatigued army in defence of the Austrian capital.

When messages to that effect fell into Murat's hands, he and Lannes ignored Napoleon's strategic priorities and rushed to Vienna, allowing Kutuzov to cross the Danube unhindered, and to double back for a surprise attack on General **Mortier**'s isolated advanced corps at **Dürrenstein** (11 November). Kutuzov then continued his withdrawal towards Buxhowden's second wave, while Murat soothed Napoleon's wrath by tricking his way past the **Vienna** defences. The emperor entered Vienna in triumph on 14 November, securing vital supplies of food, weapons and ammunition in the process.

Archduke Charles now hastened homeward from Italy, but Napoleon ordered Masséna to harry his rearguards and sent **Marmont** with an army to block his route to Vienna. The two French forces were able to push Charles and

John (still in the Tyrol) east towards Hungary, where they could play no part in Napoleon's coming confrontation with Austro-Russian forces north of Vienna.

The main bulk of the Grande Armée drove north-east in pursuit of Kutuzov, who was beset by supply problems and continued to avoid battle. Murat caught Russian rearguards near the town of **Hollabrünn** on 15 November, but was deceived by a reversal of his subterfuge at Vienna, and Kutuzov escaped north-east thanks to Prince **Bagration**'s determined covering action.

Murat reached the well-stocked city of Brno on 19 November, the same day that Kutuzov's ragged army met up with Buxhowden's fresh contingent at Olmütz, some 65km to the north-east. They were joined on 24 November by 10,000 élite troops of the **Imperial Russian Guard** and, with an Austro-Russian attack now a viable possibility, Tsar Alexander and Emperor Francis arrived to take personal command of their armies.

Nobody was more anxious for an allied attack than Napoleon. With the Prussians mobilizing and funds running short, he needed a quick and decisive victory. Over the next few days he concealed his numerical strength, hinted at peace negotiations and ostentatiously withdrew troops from forward positions, by way of persuading the allies to fight at a location of his own choosing. His efforts helped tilt a divided allied command into aggression, and the Austro-Russian armies attacked at **Austerlitz** on 2 December.

Diluted only by failure to pursue retreating Russian survivors, Austerlitz was perhaps Napoleon's greatest tactical victory, destroying the allied armies and sending shock waves all round Europe. Austrian emperor Francis sued for peace next day, and the Third Coalition promptly fell apart.

While some 25,000 Russians troops limped home, Austria ratified the punitive Peace of **Pressburg** on 26 December. Prussia hastened to adopt a neutral pose, though it was not spared punishment by the Convention of **Vienna** (ratified on 24 February 1806), and the Anglo-Swedish expedition to the Elbe was quickly abandoned. Pitt died at the start of 1806, and the new **Grenville** government immediately began putting out peace feelers, but Napoleon, back in Paris from 26 January, treated British approaches with ill-disguised contempt. They were abandoned after the death of Fox, and Britain had lost the taste for rapprochement by the time Prussia returned to war in the summer. *See* War of the **Fourth Coalition**; Map 12.

Thugut, Johann Amadeus, Baron (1736–1818)

The first in a series of civilian advisers to dominate the military policy of Habsburg emperor **Francis II**, Thugut was imperial foreign minister throughout the **Revolutionary Wars**, and exercised a powerful influence on the **Austrian Army** through the **Aulic Council**. Able to secure senior command appointments for otherwise mediocre supporters like **Bellegarde**, he was the driving force behind opposition at court to the cautious, reforming policies of Archduke **Charles**. Sticking rigidly to **Austria**'s prewar priorities through the 1790s, he reduced imperial commitment to the **First Coalition** from 1794 to concentrate more resources on expansion into **Poland**, and his insistence that **Suvorov**'s allied Russian army be moved away from imperial targets on the **Italian** front fatally warped the offensive strategy of the **Second Coalition** in 1799. Thugut's consistently unrealistic view of Austrian military strength, and willingness to take **subsidies**, lay behind his subsequent refusal to contemplate peace before it became unavoidable, and he was forced into retirement after the defeat at **Hohenlinden** in late 1800.

Tilsit, Treaties of

The agreements by which **Russia** and **Prussia** made peace with **Napoleon** in July 1807, bringing to an end the **Fourth Coalition** against France. Since its effective defeat in 1806, Prussia had depended on Russian support to remain at war, but the comprehensive French victory at **Friedland** (14 June 1807) quickly brought Tsar **Alexander I** to terms. When **Murat**'s French cavalry, advancing from Friedland, reached the River Niemen on 19 June they were met by Russian envoys requesting an armistice (*see* **Map 17**).

Napoleon met the tsar on a barge moored in the middle of the Niemen on 25 June, and the two emperors opened formal negotiations in the

French-occupied town of Tilsit the following day. Two weeks of discussions and ceremonial followed, during which the tsar was feted as an honoured guest while King **Frederick William III** of Prussia was treated to a series of indignities befitting his role as king of a conquered country.

An alliance between France and Russia was signed on 7 July and ratified two days later. In return for acceptance of French control in the **Ionian Islands** and the Dalmatian coast, Napoleon agreed not to obstruct Russian expansion into Finland, Asia or European Turkey, even though the sultan was then a French ally. This effective division of mainland Europe into eastern and western spheres of influence was completed by Alexander's agreement to future membership of the **Continental System** against British trade and his promise to commit naval forces against British **Mediterranean** interests. According to some contemporary sources, the emperors also made a joint decision to promote deposition of the Spanish and Portuguese royal families.

Despite personal attempts to inspire Napoleon's mercy by Queen **Louise**, Prussia paid a very high price for peace. All Prussian possessions west of the River Elbe were taken by the new Kingdom of **Westphalia**, Prussian-controlled sectors of **Poland** (except for the small province of Bialystok, given to Russia) became the Grand Duchy of **Warsaw**, and **Danzig** was declared a free city. The remaining provinces of Prussia were to be occupied by French forces pending payment in full of extortionate war indemnities. Frederick William was required to recognize all Napoleon's recently created kingdoms, and to join the Continental System. The Franco-Prussian alliance was signed on 9 July (and ratified three days later).

The treaties confirmed Napoleon's mastery of central and western Europe, and created an impression of lasting friendship with the tsar, leaving **Great Britain** isolated from a status quo that seemed to offer the prospect of long-term continental peace. In fact, apart from assuring the future hostility of Prussia, the treaties created conditions for Franco-Russian dispute in Poland, and disguised Napoleon's private determination to keep Russia out of Constantinople. The most substantial guarantee of peace to emerge from Tilsit was Alexander's new-found personal admiration for Napoleon, and that had faded by the time the two met again at **Erfurt** in 1808. *See* **Map 21.**

Tipu Sahib (1749–99)

Son and heir of Hyder Ali, the warlord sultan who seized control of Mysore (in southern **India**) in the mid-eighteenth century, and who fought a series of expansionist wars against local princes and British colonists before his death in 1782. Given military training by imported French advisers, Tipu fought the British in the early 1780s and again from 1789 until 1792, when British imperial forces captured the fortress of Seringapatam and compelled him to accept a punitive peace, stripping him of half his domains and taking two of his sons as hostages.

The sultan's ferocious hatred of British authority eventually attracted renewed French support in the late 1790s. Encouraged by the French colonial governor of Mauritius, and a letter from **Napoleon** advising him to expect the arrival of an 'invincible' army via the **Middle East**, Tipu prepared another offensive in 1798. He was pre-empted by the new British viceroy, Earl Mornington (Richard **Wellesley**), and killed along with thousands of his troops when **Seringapatam** fell in May 1799, his death marking Mysore's eclipse as an independent subcontinental power.

Tirailleurs

The French term for **skirmishers**.

Tolentino, Battle of

The final action of **Murat's** self-proclaimed 'War of **Italian Independence'** in 1815. Murat's **Neapolitan Army** was already retreating from minor Austrian attacks when General **Bianchi's** 11,000 troops got behind its withdrawal at Tolentino on 30 April. Murat pulled 15,000 men back beyond Ancona on the same day, leaving General Carascosa to hold the town and coming up against Bianchi on 2 May. A Neapolitan **cavalry** attack that day pushed Bianchi back to secondary positions, but Murat's hopes of a second-day success were ruined when attacks opened ahead of schedule and failed because no supporting reserves were ready. Neapolitan **artillery** managed to hold off Austrian counter-attacks until news that 20,000 Austrians were approaching the frontier further east prompted a general retreat. It rapidly degenerated into rout, and Murat himself reached **Naples** on 18 May to find the city under **Royal Navy** control.

Tolentino, **Treaty of** *See* **Papal States**

Tone, Wolfe (1763–98)

Dublin-born Irish nationalist, and a founder of the United Irishmen independence movement in the early 1790s, who worked for Catholic reform causes and produced anti-British **propaganda** until his flight under threat of arrest in 1795. After visiting the **United States** he reached Paris in February 1796, and began lobbying war minister **Carnot** for an expedition to aid Irish rebels. His enthusiasm and exaggerated representations of Irish republican sympathies earned an advisory command with the French expedition to **Bantry Bay** in late 1796, and he resumed his campaign after its failure. With the squadron intercepted en route for Ireland off **Lough Swilly** in October 1798, he was captured and sentenced to death in Dublin for treason, but killed himself in prison.

Torgau

Town and **fortress** on the River Elbe, in **Saxony**, that was the subject of operations illustrating the confused political situation throughout the Confederation of the **Rhine** during the 1813 campaign for **Germany**. Though nominally under French control in March 1813, the fortress was garrisoned by 6,000 **Saxon** troops under General **Thielmann**. Aware that King **Frederick Augustus** was anxious to remain neutral for as long as possible, Thielmann held off an allied **siege** from 10 March, but refused to allow **Ney's** relief corps to enter the fortress in early May. He relented on 11 May, after **Napoleon** had threatened the king with war, and was dismissed from command as his troops rejoined French formations. The fortress eventually fell to a second allied siege, begun on 4 October and successfully concluded at the end of the month. *See* **Map 25**.

Torres Vedras, Lines of

The powerful set of fortifications devised by **Wellington** for the defence of Lisbon against a French invasion of **Portugal** in 1810. The invasion was launched as retaliation for the Anglo-Portuguese sortie into Spain of 1809, and led by Marshal **Masséna**, who crossed the Pyrenees with 65,000 troops in October 1809. Given time to prepare his defence of Portugal, and aware that his relatively small army could not hope to hold the long frontier with Spain, Wellington chose to defend only the approaches to Lisbon, an option that had the advantages of practicability and security, in that his army could be evacuated from the port if necessary.

After studying the reports of French engineers with **Junot's** occupying army of 1808, and reconnoitring the ground in person, Wellington devised a series of three fortified lines north and west of Lisbon. Bound by the sea to the west and the River Tagus to the east, the lines were constructed by Lisbon militia and more than 5,000 Portuguese volunteers, with 150 British NCOs and 18 British **engineers**. Walls and other obstacles were built wherever a hill or defile presented an opportunity, but the completed lines were in fact a total of 152 separate, mutually supporting redoubts, each holding at least three guns and 200 men. The largest redoubt, one of seven major strongpoints around Monte Agraco, held 1,600 troops and 25 guns.

Wellington ordered lateral roads built across the fortified zone to facilitate rapid mass redeployment to any one of a dozen preordained points, and a sophisticated **semaphore** system between redoubts was manned by the **Royal Navy**, which also provided a flotilla of 14 **gunboats** to guard the Tagus. While his frontline army waited for Masséna at the frontier, Wellington manned the fortifications with 25,000 Portuguese and Spanish troops under his command, but he retired his whole army behind the lines after his defensive victory at **Busaco** in late September. Allied forces were fully in position by 10 October, and Masséna's vanguard's reached the first line around Monte Agraco on the same day.

Masséna's initial impression that the defences were impregnable was borne out by the failure of a probing attack against the Agraco sector on 14 October. Masséna immediately wrote to **Napoleon** explaining the futility of any major attack, and was even supported by **Ney**. French forces were able to linger in front of the lines for a month, in the forlorn hope that the allies might choose capitulation, before starvation forced a retreat north to Santarem during the night of 15–16 November.

Masséna's withdrawal is generally regarded as a turning point in the **Peninsular War**. His army suffered serious losses to hunger, disease, **desertion** and **guerrilla** attacks without achieving anything, and was eventually forced into Spain for supplies the following spring. On the allied side, Wellington's strategic foresight, organizational gifts and pragmatism had brought a major victory at little cost, and the continued existence of the lines made his army's future expulsion from Portugal virtually impossible. *See* **Map 22**.

Toulon, Siege of

The **French Navy's** most important **Mediterranean** base, the southern French city of Toulon was a centre of royalist rebellion in the years after 1789, and had joined **Lyon** and Marseilles in revolt against the regime by late July 1793. The recapture of Marseilles by republican forces on 25 August, and their subsequent advance towards Toulon, persuaded the city's royalist leaders to accept the protection of a **Royal Navy** fleet that had appeared off the coast two days earlier. Reinforced by 17 Spanish **ships-of-the-line** under Admiral Gravina on 27 August, British Mediterranean C-in-C **Hood** took the city's surrender next day.

Greeted as a potentially war-winning coup in Britain, the capture placed 31 French ships-of-the-line in allied hands and threatened to provide a focus for anti-republican rebellion all over **France**, but Hood's urgent requests for large-scale troop reinforcements went unanswered by a **Pitt** government preoccupied with the campaign in **Flanders**. Attacks by General Carteaux's 15,000 troops drawn from the **Pyrenean** front were repulsed during the autumn, but only about 8,000 fit British, **Neapolitan** and assorted allied troops were defending the city when British general O'Hara took command of ground forces on 22 October.

French forces around Toulon were built up during November, as was the influence of **Napoleon**, then an artillery major. With support from the besieging army's political officers (**Saliceti** and Augustin Robespierre), he proposed an offensive plan that aimed to capture the heights over the harbour as a base for pouring shot into the allied fleets. Carteaux's replacement by **Dugommier** ensured the plan's official acceptance by mid-November.

After waiting for reinforcements from General **Doppet**, bringing his strength above 25,000 men, Dugommier launched two divisions (Labarre and **Victor**) against the heights on 17 December. They suffered an estimated 3,000 casualties, but had captured several hill forts by the end of the day, and Hood could only retire from Toulon on 18 and 19 December, taking as many of the city's royalist sympathizers as could be crammed aboard his ships.

Though they managed to scuttle part of the French fleet (a task carried out by Sir Sidney **Smith**), the recapture of Toulon left allied forces with the difficult task of maintaining a **blockade** on the port, and was a major boost to republican morale. Napoleon was promoted brigadier-general, giving him the opportunity to make his mark in a senior capacity during the following year's **Italian campaign**. *See* **Map 8**.

Toulouse, Battle of

The last major action of the **Peninsular War**, fought on 10 April 1814 outside the southern French city of Toulouse, where Marshal **Soult's** 42,000 remaining troops had retired after their escape from encirclement at **Tarbes** in late March. Soult reached Toulouse on 24 March, and **Wellington's** 50,000 allied troops approached the city two days later, but the strength of its natural defences and the relative weakness of allied **artillery** delayed any attack.

Wellington needed to cross the Garonne to get at half of Soult's army deployed on the far side. The river proved too wide for allied **pontoons** on 27 March, and poor roads halted **Hill's** corps when it got across a little further south on 30 March. A third crossing attempt succeeded some 18km north of the city on 4 April, but floods swept away its bridge to delay an attack on the city until dawn on 10 April, Easter Sunday.

A complex operation, the attack suffered from

poor coordination during the morning. Its main thrust, by **Beresford** against the city's south-eastern defences, made only slow progress and suffered heavy casualties before defenders finally began withdrawing from the ridge at about five in the evening. Fighting ended within another hour, as Soult pulled back into the city itself, leaving Wellington's battered and scattered forces, which had suffered 4,500 casualties during the day, short of supplies and vulnerable to counter-attack.

Soult had lost 3,250 men and was in no mood to resume battle. He abandoned Toulouse during the night of 11–12 April, leading his army (minus 1,600 wounded and most of its artillery) to Carcassonne, and the allies occupied the city unopposed next day. Early that evening Wellington received word of allied victory and Napoleon's **abdication**, news that he hastened to convey to Soult. Though suspicious, the French commander agreed an armistice that, apart from a bizarre sortie by the French garrison of **Bayonne** on 14 April, brought the Peninsular War to an end. *See* **Map 5**.

Tourcoing, Battle of

Attack by **Pichegru**'s French Army of the North that ended the **First Coalition**'s offensive ambitions in **Flanders** during spring 1794. A French advance in north-west Flanders had been under way since late April, led by **Souham** and **Moreau**. Failures at **Moescroen** and **Courtrai** had left allied forces strung out along a 100km front from St Amand to Thielt by mid-May, but their leaders agreed an ambitious plan to concentrate scattered forces for a simultaneous advance across French rear lines to Tourcoing (*see* **Map 2**).

The hastily planned, six-pronged operation opened on 16 May, but only **York**'s multinational column was in position near the town two days later. Austrian delays and misunderstandings meanwhile allowed Souham and Moreau to use interior lines and amass 45,000 troops in front of Lille. They attacked York's 30,000 troops scattered around Tourcoing on the morning of 18 May, focusing early assaults against General Otto's advance guard. York's main body was marching to Otto's aid when it was caught in a

flank attack around Roubaix by 16,000 men under General Bonneau. York pulled back to Tournai, suffering 3,000 casualties in the process and receiving no support from Austrian commanders, who responded by returning to their starting places.

The battle, during which allied supreme commander **Francis II** was almost captured, did nothing for faltering inter-allied relations. While Pichegru organized a further advance on **Tournai**, Austrian and Prussian leaders were preparing to abandon war on the French eastern frontier to deal with the crisis in **Poland**.

Tournai, Battle of

Inconclusive action in **Flanders**, also known as the Battle of Pont-à-Chin, fought on 23 May 1794 between **Pichegru**'s French Army of the North and **York**'s allied corps around the town of Tournai (*see* **Map 2**). Allied defeat at **Tourcoing** on 18 May had left York's 30,000 British, German and Dutch troops isolated in the face of **Souham**'s 50,000-strong French northern wing.

Advancing early on 23 May against York's positions just west of the Scheldt, French forces pushed **Hanoverian** outposts back across the river on the allied right, but only **Macdonald**'s brigade enjoyed any success elsewhere. Making full use of new **infantry tactics** to swamp British defenders in clouds of **skirmishers**, it took the central stronghold at Pont-à-Chin, which changed hands five times as York brought up two divisions of reserves. All the French columns eventually withdrew to their starting places after a bloody day's fighting had cost each side an estimated 4,000 casualties, and Pichegru turned to besiege an isolated allied garrison at Ypres, where 6,000 allied troops surrendered on 17 June.

Trachenberg Plan

Tactical orthodoxy agreed by allied commanders on 15 August 1813, immediately after the breakdown of the **armistice** that had halted fighting in **Germany** for more than two months. Broadly speaking, it was decided to avoid any major confrontation with **Napoleon** himself, and that any one of the four main allied forces making contact with the emperor's command would withdraw while the others massed for battle with detachments led by subordinates. Intended to frustrate Napoleon and whittle away his strength, the plan reflected allied commanders' lack of confidence in any major offensive action and their respect for Napoleon's combat record. It also worked, cheating Napoleon of the opportunity to inflict a crushing defeat on the allies throughout the next ten months.

Trafalgar, Battle of

The most important naval engagement of the wars, a comprehensive defeat of combined French and Spanish fleets under **Villeneuve** by **Nelson's** British fleet off Cape Trafalgar on 21 October 1805. The battle itself ended a long campaign of naval manoeuvre on both sides of the Atlantic, set in train by **Napoleon's** determination to invade **England** in late 1804.

With allied French and Spanish fleets pinned in distant ports by **blockades**, and anyway no match for the British in combat, an invasion could not realistically hope to reach Britain as long as the **Royal Navy** barred its way. In an attempt to secure temporary local superiority, Napoleon conceived an elaborate decoy plan to distract the Royal Navy from home waters while his own fleets concentrated in the Channel as invasion escorts.

Neither the **French Navy** nor the **Spanish Navy** was in a fit condition for complex operations, but Napoleon had little interest in the technical realities of **naval warfare**. He ordered Atlantic Fleet commander **Ganteaume** to slip past the blockade of Brest, chase off the relatively small squadron blockading Spanish warships at Ferrol, and sail with his allies for the **West Indies**. Meanwhile Villeneuve's fleet was to escape blockaded Toulon, pick up Spanish warships from Cadiz and sail for a rendezvous at Martinique. Assuming that a large proportion of British naval strength would be sent in pursuit, both would hurry back to Europe, brushing aside anything still guarding the western approaches to enter the Channel.

Any outside chance of the fleets matching Napoleon's elaborate vision in practice quickly disappeared with Ganteaume's failure to escape Brest, but Villeneuve enjoyed an auspicious start. British **Mediterranean** C-in-C Nelson had maintained an open blockade on Toulon, in the hope

of enticing the French fleet out to destruction and to enable regular checks on Spanish ports. Villeneuve and the French fleet slipped out of Toulon during one of these checks in late March 1805 and collected reinforcements from Cadiz, gaining a three-week head start on Nelson, who searched for French forces around the eastern Mediterranean before receiving intelligence of their true movements. When the British Mediterranean Fleet reached the West Indies in early June, Villeneuve's Combined Fleet was just beginning its journey back to Europe.

In the light of Ganteaume's failure, Villeneuve's new instructions were to call at Ferrol and then Brest, driving off the blockade squadrons before taking the entire fleet into the Channel. He reached the eastern Atlantic still four days ahead of the faster British fleet, and Nelson turned south for Gibraltar, but his own turn to the north was spotted by a fast British courier vessel. Met some 150km off Cape Finisterre by Admiral Calder's 15 ships-of-the-line from the British blockade squadrons, Villeneuve took the Combined Fleet into shelter at Vigo after a partial engagement on 22 July.

Sickness, lack of specialist equipment, supply shortages and overcrowding with troops for the proposed invasion had eroded the fighting capacity of Villeneuve's already inefficient vessels, but he took advantage of British redeployment to sail for Ferrol. At Ferrol he received new and vague orders either to relieve Brest or to sail round the northern coast of Britain, pick up troops from bases in the **Netherlands**, and enter the Channel from the east. He also received permission to retire on Cadiz in the event of unforeseen dangerous circumstances, and took advantage of this escape clause at the first hint of British presence to the north.

Nelson had returned to England on leave when news of the Combined Fleet's return to Cadiz reached London in early September. He left Portsmouth aboard HMS *Victory* on 14 September, and took command of the blockading force off Cadiz two weeks later. Aware that the Combined Fleet was preparing for sea, he laid plans to attack it in two columns, aiming to isolate an outnumbered portion of the Franco-Spanish battle line before bringing the action to a mêlée that his superior ships could only win.

Villeneuve had no desire to challenge British technical superiority in a fight, but was given little choice. Napoleon had abandoned invasion plans in the face of the **Third Coalition**, and ordered Villeneuve to re-enter the Mediterranean with his entire force before landing his ground forces in southern Italy. The orders also insisted that his ships seek to engage the enemy, abandoning a policy of cautious flight that had become an embarrassment to the imperial name. Unfavourable reports from military officers with the fleet subsequently persuaded Napoleon to replace Villeneuve, who hurried to sea on rumours of his imminent demise.

The wind turned fair for the Franco-Spanish fleet to sail south-west, still bulging with troops, on 19 October. With Nelson having detached six ships-of-the-line for resupply at Gibraltar, the British fleet was outnumbered by 27 battleships to 33, but Villeneuve had no illusions about turning numerical superiority into victory. He expected to be attacked, was aware of Nelson's probable tactics, and approached certain defeat with a fatalistic pessimism.

Shadowed by British **frigates**, the Combined Fleet sailed south all through 19 and 20 October. Anxious not to frighten it back into port, Nelson kept his major warships out of visual range until the night of 20 October, when he brought his ships-of-the-line towards their prey. The two fleets were some 20km apart by dawn, when the British began to move round from the west towards the rear of the line of battle slowly being formed by Villeneuve.

Ahead of a light north-westerly wind (signalling the approach of an Atlantic storm), the British fleet manoeuvred into two loose columns: Nelson in the *Victory* led 11 battleships towards the Franco-Spanish vanguard; second-in-command **Collingwood**, aboard the *Royal Sovereign*, led 15 towards the rear of the Combined line. As they approached, the Combined Fleet attempted to turn towards Cadiz and run for home, but the clumsy manoeuvre achieved only confusion, leaving Villeneuve's line strung out in two ragged divisions when the British ships began to come within long cannon range shortly before noon.

The British approach made no concessions to formal battle tactics: the fastest ships in each of the columns, now about 2km apart, simply raced into action at top speed, with slower vessels following as best they could. Collingwood's flagship, far ahead of the rest of his column, broke through the Combined line at midday, passing behind Spanish admiral Alava's *Santa Ana*, leader of the 16 French and Spanish battleships of Villeneuve's ragged rear column. Although temporarily outnumbered, Collingwood was soon joined by other British ships, and the planned mêlée was soon under way .

Meanwhile Nelson, with *Victory* and *Temeraire* leading the way, struck at the rear half of Villeneuve's forward division, *Victory* passing just astern of the Spanish *Santísima Trinidad* and Villeneuve's flagship *Bucentaure*, before ramming the French *Redoutable*. The collision caused severe damage to both ships, and casualties mounted as crews fell to close-quarters fighting, but the British battleships following *Victory* moved into the gap created to inflict heavy punishment on the French and Spanish flagships. As the leading six Combined Fleet ships-of-the-line moved off unmolested, remaining vessels found themselves outgunned and outmanoeuvred in a chaos of gunfire, with regular arrivals of slower British ships steadily lengthening the odds against them.

At about one fifteen, a **sniper** aboard the *Redoutable* shot and mortally wounded Nelson, by which time the condition of hostile ships around *Victory* had degenerated almost beyond resistance. Nelson died shortly before the last of 18 Franco-Spanish ships to surrender hauled down its colours at around five in the evening. The remainder escaped, and although four ships from the unengaged vanguard made a brief attempt to intervene, they were chased off by the last two British ships to reach the scene.

Few of the British ships were in any condition for pursuit, and Collingwood could only organize his battered fleet and its prizes that night. The expected storm struck next day, and lasted for a week, so that the British were hard pressed to avoid losing several of their clumsy, dismasted battleships. One captured French ship escaped to Cadiz, and all but four of the other prizes were destroyed on the rocks, but Collingwood earned justified praise for preserving his own battered fleet from loss. Ships apart, the battle had been expensive for both sides, with the British suffering 1,314 casualties, and the Combined Fleet almost twice as many.

Trafalgar was the last great naval battle of the period, and marked a shift in the pattern of contemporary naval warfare. Victory secured long-term British dominance of the world's sea lanes against any potential combination of European navies, enabling the Royal Navy to concentrate on army support and trade protection duties. It also imposed permanent geographical and economic limits on French imperial expansion, putting into a global perspective Napoleon's confirmation as the master of European land warfare at **Austerlitz** a few weeks later. *See* **Maps 14, 18.**

Transpadane Republic *See* **Cisalpine Republic**

Trebbia, Battle of the

Important engagement between **Suvorov's** Austro-Russian army in northern Italy and **Macdonald's** French force from **Naples**, fought on 18–19 June 1799 along the River Trebbia running south of Piacenza (*see* **Map 9**). The opening phase of that year's **Italian campaign** had seen **Moreau's** French forces in the north penned against the west coast. Macdonald responded to **Directory** orders and marched north to Moreau's aid, reaching Lucca on 29 May, and taking 1,500 prisoners in capturing Modena on 12 June. Strengthened to 35,000 men by the addition of **Victor's** division from 14 June, Macdonald marched on Piacenza.

Suvorov responded by concentrating to support General Ott's 6,000 Austrians in the city, leaving **Bellegarde's** 10,000 men to watch Moreau. Victor's division drove Ott out of Piacenza on 16 June, but Suvorov sent **Melas** and **Bagration** to his aid next day, and French forces withdrew to positions on the Trebbia. By the morning of 18 June Macdonald had positioned his army, minus two divisions still coming up from the rear, with its back to the river, and Suvorov's 50,000 troops attacked all along the line at about ten.

The main attack was concentrated against the French left, where Macdonald had relied on mountainous terrain to compensate for manpower shortage. Fighting in the sector raged all afternoon, with both sides sending in reserves before Macdonald abandoned an increasingly unequal struggle, withdrawing his entire army across the river after dark. Confident that Moreau was moving to threaten Suvorov's rear, and reinforced by his two missing divisions, Macdonald launched a counter-attack all along the allied line the next morning, but Victor's frontal assault was halted after heavy fighting claimed 3,000 casualties on each side. A counter-attack by Melas and the Austrian reserve then routed two divisions to Victor's right, and the rest of the French force followed their flight towards Piacenza, suffering 10,000 casualties before it got back across the Trebbia.

With morale, ammunition and supplies low, and Moreau's whereabouts still unknown, Macdonald withdrew to the River Nura during the night. Suvorov sent two divisions to block Moreau and crossed the Trebbia in pursuit of Macdonald on 20 June, but the French had escaped through Parma to Reggio by the time he gave up on 22 June. The Russian commander then turned his attention to Moreau, who had just attacked Bellegarde's force at **San Giuliano**.

Trianon Decree

Regulations issued by **Napoleon** on 5 August 1810 that modified the **Continental System** of economic warfare against **Great Britain** established by the **Berlin** and **Milan decrees** of 1806–7. The decree in effect recognized the practical impossibility of enforcing the system, and the massive smuggling boom it had created in French-controlled ports, permitting entry of British colonial goods into Europe, though at very high tariffs, and the export of grain to Britain. The latter concession inadvertently saved Britain from the worst effects of a poor harvest, thus weakening the system at precisely the moment when it could have done most damage.

Trier, Battle of *See* **Rhine Campaign** (1792–6)

Trinidad, Capture of (1797)

Opening action of a British offensive against Spanish colonies in the **West Indies**, launched in 1797 on the orders of a **Pitt** government excited by opportunities for imperial expansion but naïve about the realities of **colonial** operations. By the time **Abercromby's** British army in the Caribbean received instructions to attack Trinidad, half its original 9,000 men had been killed by disease, and reinforcements had only brought his effective strength up to 4,000 men. Transported from the Windward Islands by a **Royal Navy** squadron, they reached Trinidad on 16 February, to find four Spanish **ships-of-the-line** and a **frigate** in the harbour. The Spanish burned their ships to avoid capture next day, destroying all but the 74-gun *San Danasco*, which was taken as a British prize. Troops were then landed, and the island's garrison surrendered almost immediately. Abercromby was ordered on to Puerto Rico, where 3,000 men landed on 17 June, but his weakening force suffered 225 casualties attempting to storm the island's strong **fortress**, before abandoning the operation at the end of the month.

Troubridge, Thomas (1758–1807)

British **Royal Navy** commander who made his name in the **Mediterranean** during the mid-1790s, when C-in-C Admiral **Jervis** regarded him as the most capable officer in a fleet that boasted **Nelson** and **Collingwood** among its captains. After leading the British line with distinction at Cape **St Vincent** in 1797, he fought under Nelson at the **Nile** and commanded squadrons off **Naples** and **Malta**, before returning to Britain and a senior Admiralty post on preliminary signature of the **Amiens** peace in 1801. Troubridge returned to action as a rear-admiral in 1804, but was lost at sea aboard the battleship *Blenheim* in the **Indian Ocean** three years later.

Truillas, Battle of

The defeat of General Dagobert's French army attacking south from Perpignan on 22 September by **Spanish Army** forces under General Ricardos, and the high point of Spanish success during the **Pyrenean campaign** of 1793–5. A French counter-attack on 17 September had forced Ricardos back from **Perpignan** to a line centred on Truillas. Newly appointed French commander Dagobert concentrated every available soldier in a bid to drive the Spanish back across the Pyrenees, and launched some 18,000 French

troops against the Spanish line on the morning of 22 September. After Spanish reserves had halted early French successes against his left wing, Ricardos switched them against Dagobert in front of Truillas, forcing a French withdrawal during the afternoon. Ricardos suffered only 1,500 losses during the engagement, and inflicted about four times as many on Dagobert's army, but French forces were by now receiving large-scale reinforcements from war minister **Carnot's** growing manpower reserve. *See* **Map 5**.

Tshitshagov, Pavel (1767–1849)

Russian general who, though generally known by his honorary rank of admiral, is not known to have held any naval command. He commanded Russian reinforcements sent to **North Holland** in 1799, and fought in the **Russo-Turkish War**, signing the Peace of **Bucharest** that ended the conflict in May 1812. In August he took operational command of Russian forces in Moldavia after **Kutuzov** became overall C-in-C. Forming the northern wing of the Third Army's double thrust against **Schwarzenberg's** corps on the extreme south of the French advance, his forces captured Minsk in mid-November, and played a major part in attempts to prevent the French **Beresina** crossing.

Tudela, Battle of

The third major defeat suffered by Spanish forces facing French invasion armies across the River Ebro in November 1808 (*see* **Peninsular War**). The collision of Spanish offensive manoeuvres with **Napoleon's** more incisive countermoves had brought French victories at **Espinosa** and **Gamonal**, and by mid-November the only obstacles to French control of Madrid were the south-eastern armies of Generals **Castaños** and **Palafox**. Due to advance on Pamplona and Caparrosa in late October, they switched to a defensive posture at the first sign of French offensive operations. They ignored the Supreme **Junta's** orders to resume the attack, and **Moncey's** corps on the French left had been instructed not to provoke their retreat, so that the sector saw little action until Napoleon was ready for his own attack.

French forces under **Ney** were ordered to move east from Longroño across the rear of Castaños on 18 November, and **Lannes** (who had arrived to replace Moncey) advanced frontally with 34,000 troops. Castaños, just recovered from illness, became aware of Ney's movements on 21 November, and reacted with a partial and inefficient withdrawal to the area around Tudela, though **Saragossa** offered greater security. His 31,000 Spanish troops were barely in position when Lannes attacked on the morning of 23 November.

French attacks quickly panicked poorly trained infantry, and Spanish failure to deploy **cavalry** at the height of the battle contributed to the loss of 26 guns and perhaps 5,000 casualties by evening. The remains of Castaños's army fled for the Cuenca Mountains, but might have been caught had Lannes directed his final attacks against the broken Spanish centre, or if Ney had reached a position to cut off the retreat before 26 November. Napoleon criticized Ney, but he had not been given sufficient time for the journey across difficult country. *See* **Map 22**.

Tugendbund

A loose network of German nationalists, literally the 'League of Virtue', founded in **Prussia** by young nobles, military officers and a clique of Königsberg literati in April 1808. Concerned with the elevation of German national life in general, its causes included religious revival and the fostering of patriotic spirit, as well as the ultimate destruction of French power east of the Rhine. Given support by reforming ministers **Stein** and **Scharnhorst**, but dissolved as a potential cause of friction with France by order of King **Frederick William** in December 1809, the league maintained a subterranean existence over the next five years, and provided inspiration for a flowering of similar organizations (*Deutsche Gesellschafte*) all over Germany in 1814.

Turkish Army

The land forces of the **Ottoman Empire** fell into two distinct main categories: the **Janissaries**, a class of élite warriors that numbered perhaps 100,000 men by the end of the eighteenth century; and an unquantifiable horde of untrained levies, called upon by regional authorities to fulfil medieval personal obligations at times of emergency. The empire also housed, though did

not necessarily control, a wide variety of regional or tribal forces, ranging from the fanatical Islamic fundamentalist Wahhabi of central Arabia and the **Mamelukes**, an autonomous Janissary offshoot in **Egypt**, to the personal armies of provincial warlords and bureaucrats.

Ottoman armies in the field were created for specific operations and were composites of Janissaries, peasant levies and local forces, the latter usually reliable only as long as their particular interests were served. Tribal or irregular formations were often mounted, but were largely untrained and did not fulfil the well-defined roles assigned to European **cavalry**, while the empire's few field **artillery** weapons were deployed with whoever happened to possess them. Command was conferred by social or administrative position, and many Ottoman officers had no formal training, although Janissaries were instructed within their regiments (or *ortas*) and the sultan frequently hired professional officers from European armies.

Selim III's attempt to establish a new regular army and organize it (through French advisers) along modern European lines failed in the face of uncompromising Janissary reaction, culminating in the palace coup of 1807. A counter-coup that brought the reformist Mahmud II to power later that year did not break the Janissary hold over Ottoman military life, and they remained a block to reform until their final dissolution after a failed uprising in 1826. Though the Turkish Army was still no match for the best European forces, its subsequent openness to new ideas and renewed status as the genuine instrument of government policy contributed substantially to the Ottoman Empire's survival into the twentieth century.

Turkish Navy

Like the **Turkish Army**, the navy of the **Ottoman Empire** was a combination of regular and irregular forces using a mixture of traditional and relatively modern equipment. In 1790 it comprised 30 **ships-of-the-line**, designed to imitate the major warships of European navies, along with 50 **frigates** and about 100 oar-drawn **galleys**. Smaller ships included large numbers of coastal craft, their design reflecting the traditional seafaring cultures of their particular region. Most of the major warships were crewed by recruits from the empire's Aegean provinces, and the navy's sailing skills were well regarded by contemporaries, but the poor condition of many ships and a complete innocence of contemporary **naval** theory greatly reduced their combat effectiveness against European forces.

Not subject to discernible strategic direction by the Ottoman government, naval forces were largely restricted to domestic duties around Constantinople or transporting troops around the empire. They were unable to prevent Russian dominance of the Black Sea throughout the period, but did cooperate with the **Russian Navy** in attacking the **Ionian Islands** in 1798. The navy's most active period came during the early stages of the **Russo-Turkish War** (1806–12). It could not prevent British **Mediterranean** forces from reaching Constantinople via the **Dardanelles** in 1807, and its major warships were lured to defeat by the Russians off **Lemnos** later that year. Mediterranean operations then effectively ceased, while light coastal forces maintained a continuous but largely unsuccessful campaign against Russian Black Sea commerce.

Turkey *See* **Ottoman Empire**

Tuscany

Central Italian grand duchy, owned by the Habsburg family since 1737, that was ruled by Grand Duke Ferdinand III, second son of Austrian emperor Leopold II, from 1792 (*see* **Map 1**). Technically neutral during the War of the **First Coalition**, Tuscany remained on friendly terms with the allies, allowing British warships to use its coast for **Mediterranean** operations. Napoleon's

successful **Italian campaign** of 1796 forced Tuscany into a pro-French neutrality, reinforced by another French pacification mission in early 1797, but jeopardized by a republican uprising that followed French occupation of Florence in 1799. Ferdinand fled into exile, and popular support for his restoration, backed by military aid from the **Papal States** and **Austria**, drove French forces out of Tuscany until the region was reoccupied in October and placed under **Murat**'s provisional governorship.

Tuscany was transformed into the Kingdom of Etruria by the Treaty of **Lunéville** in 1801, and the crown was given to the Bourbon Duke of **Parma**. On his death in 1803 it passed under the control of his mother, Queen Marie-Louise of **Spain**, as regent for her infant grandson, Charles Louis. Etruria became three French *départements* by the Franco-Spanish Treaty of **Fontainebleau** in 1808. Its small army was absorbed into imperial forces, and it remained under the military governorship until Eliza **Bonaparte** became grand duchess in March 1809.

The region remained relatively quiet until Napoleon's **abdication** in 1814, when Eliza was exiled and Murat's **Neapolitan** forces moved into Tuscany before handing it back to Austrian administration. Grand Duke Ferdinand was formally restored in September 1814, remaining in power (apart from a brief exile during the **Hundred Days**) until his death in 1824 and retaining many of the more liberal elements of French constitutional reform (*see* **Code Civil**).

Two Sicilies, Kingdom of the *See* **Naples**; **Sicily**

U

Uhlans

Light **cavalry**, armed with **lances**, in German or **Polish** service; the name derives from the Turkish *oghlan*, meaning 'child'.

Ukerath, Battle of

Minor action fought on the **Rhine** front east of Bonn on 20 June 1796, a postscript to the French victory at **Altenkirchen** and the Austrian left wing's subsequent withdrawal to the Lahn. As Austrian C-in-C Archduke **Charles** brought up reinforcements from south-east of Mainz, and French commander **Jourdan** concentrated 70,000 men on the north bank, the two armies faced each other along an 80km front at the Lahn by mid-June. The Austrians attacked first, General Werneck's right wing crossing the Lahn at Wetzlar to defeat **Lefebvre**'s division on 15 June. Werneck moved forward to Greifenstein next day, and the rest of the Austrian army crossed the Lahn further west, but Jourdan withdrew his centre and right across the river at Neuwied on the evening of 17 June. **Kléber**'s French left wing paused next day on the way back to Bonn at Ukerath, and **Kray**'s 14,000 pursuing Austrians defeated its rearguards south of the town on 19 June. Kléber's full-scale counterattack failed next morning, and the French fell back to the Rhine. *See* **Map 3**.

Ulm, Surrender of (1805)

The capitulation of Austrian forces under General **Mack** on 20 October 1805, after they had been first confused and then surrounded by the French **Grande Armée**'s rapid advance. The Bavarian town of Ulm, about 150km east of the Rhine, was the main forward supply base for a planned Austrian invasion of south-eastern France, intended as the important element of the **Third Coalition**'s ambitious offensive programme.

Beset by factional disputes at the highest level, the **Austrian Army** had been divided into three for the year's campaign. Large forces were earmarked for attacks into northern Italy, under Archduke **Charles**, and through Bavaria, under Mack and Archduke **Ferdinand** (as nominal C-in-C). They were to be linked by Archduke **John**'s small covering force in the Tyrol.

After a long period of wavering, Emperor **Francis** eventually accepted Mack's scheme to give the German operation priority, and to advance deep into **Bavaria** pending the arrival of 200,000 promised Russian reinforcements. The plan not only assumed that **Napoleon** would launch his main counter-offensive in Italy, but overlooked the difference between the western and Gregorian calendars in estimating the Russians' time of arrival.

The Austrian army moved out of its depots on 3 September. Elector **Maximilian** of Bavaria refused to be bullied into abandoning his alliance with Napoleon, and Austrian troops entered the country on 8 September, occupying Munich four days later. Mack was by then aware that French forces had already reached the Rhine but was certain that any attack would come through the Black Forest. Sure that new **infantry tactics** would give him the edge in any direct confrontation, he pushed further into Bavaria, overruling Ferdinand's objections by appealing directly to the emperor. The main Austrian force of some 50,000 men was hurried to positions facing west either side of Ulm, while a detachment of 12,000 under General Kienmayer was sent north to Ingolstadt and General **Jellacic**'s division (11,000 men) was called up from Archduke John's army to guard the southern flank.

Mack was entering a trap. Russian forces were still weeks from the front, and Napoleon had accurately anticipated all the Austrians' opening moves. Aware of the Coalition's overall offensive strategy, and disillusioned with his own plans for invasion of **England**, the French emperor recognized that some 400,000 allied troops could soon be in the field, but also that the main Austrian armies would be isolated during the first weeks of the war. His own army was in superb fighting condition, and he calculated that it could surprise Mack before allied reinforcements reached Bavaria.

Napoleon had guessed that Austrian forces would concentrate around their usual supply centre at Ulm, and planned to get behind them. On 26 August he issued orders for the general redeployment of his forces, sending **Masséna** to northern Italy and **Gouvion St Cyr** to Naples, but ordering the main bulk of his army (reinforced to about 210,000 men) to march on the Danube from the Channel coast.

Sending 40,000 troops (**Lannes**'s corps and **Murat**'s cavalry) through the Black Forest, under instructions to feign a full-scale invasion, he deployed **Augereau**'s corps as a rearguard along the Rhine. Five more corps and the **Imperial Guard** were ordered into Germany further north, picking up 25,000 **Bavarian Army** troops on the way, and the whole force was to reconvene on Mack's lines of retreat around Augsburg on the River Lech. Napoleon himself remained at Boulogne until 3 September, and then spent almost three weeks attempting to manage a government financial crisis before joining his army.

The Grande Armée's concentration in Bavaria was carried out with a speed and precision that astonished contemporaries. It owed much to brilliant administrative work, careful reconnaissance of planned routes and good weather in the early stages of the march, but the army's high pitch of training and motivation was an important factor, along with the advantages of its **corps system**, which enabled each component to travel self-sufficiently along a different road.

French forces were ordered across the Rhine on the night of 24–25 September, by which time **semaphore** had reported Mack's apparently inert presence around Ulm. When he did move, it was in the wrong direction. Hypnotized by the approach of Lannes and Murat, he edged westward to meet the expected threat in late September, and stayed there even after most of the French force had turned north to join the main advance. On 2 October, when the Grande Armée began a gigantic wheel south behind the Austrian positions, its movements were still a mystery to Mack.

Despite the onset of bad weather, French forces reached the Danube on 6 October, though **Bernadotte**'s northernmost corps had violated Prussian neutrality by cutting through the Ansbach region (helping push **Prussia** into belated Coalition membership). During the next 24 hours they occupied a 100km front either side of the Danube's junction with the Lech, directly blocking Mack's retreat to the east or north-east, and Napoleon prepared to meet either an immediate Austrian breakout attempt or an attack from the east by the Russians.

Though at last alerted to French positions, Mack made no attempt to disrupt them at this stage. Ignoring Ferdinand's demands for a withdrawal eastward, he merely directed his forces to close on Ulm, convincing himself that Napoleon was about to be crushed in an Austro-Russian pincer. Meanwhile Murat and Lannes virtually destroyed a forward Austrian unit at Wertingen on 8 October, taking 2,000 prisoners, and **Soult**'s corps made virtually unimpeded progress towards the Austrian supply depots at Landsberg. Though the French campaign suffered a setback at **Albeck** on 11 October, Austrian forces made no attempt to exploit the one clear breakout opportunity they were to be given.

Napoleon began making plans to advance directly on Ulm from 12 October, when Bernadotte reported that General **Kutuzov**'s forward Russian columns were still some 300km away, and combat along the Danube intensified from 14 October, when **Ney** managed to cross the river and defeat advanced Austrian forces at **Elchingen**. By the end of the day, large French forces were approaching Mack's main positions from both sides of the Danube and from the south, at which point Ferdinand took matters partly into his own hands, leading some 6,000 **cavalry** in an escape north to Heidenheim, where they joined Wrebeck's forces driven from Elchingen.

On 15 October Ney's corps stormed the Austrian defences at Michelsburg, and Napoleon gave orders for Ulm itself to be bombarded the next day. Mack finally recognized his plight and, with army morale in steep decline, applied for a temporary armistice in the hope that Kutuzov would arrive to bale him out. Knowing that the nearest Russians were still at least 150km away, Napoleon granted a ceasefire on 17 October, on the understanding that Mack would surrender if no help arrived within eight days.

Hastened by the surrender of Wrebeck and 8,000 men to Murat at Trochtelfingen on 19 October, and of 12,000 more at Neustadt next day, the dispirited Austrians surrendered Ulm five days ahead of schedule on 20 October. About 10,000 of the garrison escaped, but the remaining 25,000 infantry and 2,000 cavalry became prisoners. The last significant Austrian force in Bavaria, General Jellacic's division, was routed by Augereau's corps at the Iller near Kempten on 21 October.

The destruction of Mack's army shaped the war as a whole, giving Napoleon an opportunity to attack the Russian expeditionary force in isolation and shattering Austrian self-confidence. Though Archdukes John and Charles still remained in the field, Ulm served to make Charles even more cautious about risking the empire's last major army, which played no important part in the campaign that climaxed at **Austerlitz**. Held solely responsible for the débâcle, Mack was court-martialled and sentenced to death (later commuted to imprisonment), but basic flaws in the Austrian Army's planning and operational systems were ignored. Archduke Ferdinand, who eventually limped into Prague with some 2,000 survivors, was treated as a returning hero. *See* **Map 12**.

Union, Act of

The legislation that united **Great Britain** and **Ireland** as the United Kingdom, effective from 1 January 1801. The Act was promoted by the British **Pitt** government as a means of ending civil unrest in the colony, and forcing social reform on a narrow, self-interested colonial administration. It was passed by the Irish parliament only in return for important political concessions (including 100 seats in the London House of Commons), and sold to the oppressed southern Irish majority on Pitt's promise of **Catholic emancipation**, subsequently refused by King **George III**.

United Provinces *See* **Netherlands**, The

United States of America

The infant American republic had won its independence from **Great Britain** in the 1780s, and the first US president, George Washington, took office in 1789. The republic's semi-autonomous states, 16 in 1789, were governed by an elected federal administration, headed by the president (chosen every four years by indirect male suffrage through a college of states' electors) and his nominated cabinet, that directly controlled outlying territories occupied but not yet granted full statehood. The president's executive powers were (and are) subject to assent from two directly elected chambers of Congress, the lower House of Representatives and the smaller Senate.

A growing population approaching 6 million was concentrated along the north-east coastline, and the republic in 1790 covered only some 2.3 million square kilometres east of the Appalachian Mountains, but the westward migration that characterized the first half of the nineteenth century was already under way by the late 1780s. The federal government's prime concerns were pacification of indigenous peoples, regulation of continental expansion and maintenance of the fragile union between states.

The states were fundamentally opposed to any involvement in European power politics, but the competing empires of Britain, **France** and **Spain** still owned most of North America between them, and dominated the rich trading waters of the Caribbean, so that the US was required to conduct its diplomacy in the context of their mutual disputes. The immigrant US population was also largely European in character and outlook, and its political leaders were drawn from wealthy communities with well-established contacts among the European ruling classes.

The colonial American economy had been dominated by trade with Europe, and the well-developed, politically sophisticated New England states on the north-eastern seaboard were determined to secure independent American trade links with the rest of the world. This nascent economic imperialism was a source of great political controversy within the US, and embroiled the republic in the fall-out from European **naval warfare**, much of which took place along the main trade routes in the Caribbean and Atlantic. American maritime trade was directly threatened by the **blockade** tactics of major naval powers, and the **Royal Navy**'s aggressive attempts to halt US trade with Britain's enemies remained a source of mutual friction despite the **London** agreement of 1794.

Relations with European states remained peaceful through Washington's presidency, but the 1790–4 period saw a series of US military expeditions on the western frontier against native American tribes. Washington's retirement in 1797 and subsequent replacement by vice-president John Adams, who had been the main political force behind the creation of a **US Navy**, signalled a hardening of attitudes towards European interference with economic development. The government responded to French expansion in the **West Indies** by declaring war on France in late 1798. The conflict amounted to little more than a few skirmishes between light naval forces (*see Constellation*), and had little impact on internal US politics, but was not formally ended until 1800.

Congress moved to the republic's new capital city of Washington shortly before the presidential election of December 1800, when Adams and his Federalist Party, guardians of states' autonomy, were defeated by the centralist Democratic Republicans. Thomas Jefferson took office in March 1801, though only after a protracted round of political haggling (and 36 ballots) had resolved a tie with running mate Aaron Burr, a débâcle that prompted a constitutional

amendment in 1804 separating the elections for president and vice-president.

Jefferson's first four-year term of office was marked by a gathering secession movement in New England and increasing involvement in overseas affairs. The naval **Barbary War** in the **Mediterranean** (1801–5) won exemption from tributes to regional pirates, and the **Louisiana Purchase** from France (1802) more than doubled the republic's size once occupation was complete in spring 1804.

Expansion intensified fears among New Englanders that their autonomy and mercantile priorities would be permanently undermined by a majority of centralist, westward-looking new states. Vice-President Burr ran for the state governorship of New York on a separatist ticket in April 1804, but his heavy defeat was followed by a duel with his chief antagonist, Federalist leader Alexander Hamilton (who was killed), and the movement's temporary eclipse was completed by Jefferson's re-election in December.

Foreign policy during Jefferson's second term was dominated by deteriorating relations with Britain, the only real threat to maritime security after the Battle of **Trafalgar** in 1805. Royal Navy seizures of US cargoes and crews brought a formal protest from the Senate in February 1806, and retaliation in the form of a Non-Importation Act banning British goods from the US. Passed in April 1806, and in effect from 15 November, the Act was soon suspended pending negotiations in London, but an Anglo-American treaty to protect US shipping was greeted as a climbdown by American opinion, and Jefferson never presented it to the Senate for ratification.

The **Chesapeake** incident, a brief fight between US and British warships in June 1807, intensified mutual distrust and strengthened political arguments for complete abandonment of external trade in favour of internal growth. After a demand that the Royal Navy quit American waters was ignored, Jefferson signed the first Embargo Act on 22 December, banning US citizens from taking part in any maritime trade. Though it rekindled discontent in New England, it was strengthened in January and March 1808. Another Democratic Republican,

James Madison, began his presidency with a clampdown on embargo evasions, but protests triggered repeal of the Embargo Acts in March, and their replacement by a Non-Intercourse Act restricting the ban to British and French trade.

The Macon Bill of May 1810 restored trade with Britain and France, but a steady deterioration of diplomatic relations with London was accelerated by another minor naval battle in May 1811, when the **frigate** *President* killed nine men by firing on a British **sloop**. Demands that Britain rescind its **Orders in Council** were rejected in April 1812, and Congress overrode committed New England opposition to declare war on Britain in June.

No more than a series of loosely connected skirmishes by European standards, and barely a factor in the British national war effort during the period, the **Anglo-American War** of 1812–15 is generally viewed as a watershed in US history, establishing a sense of national, rather than state, identity in the hearts and minds of the US population. It was nevertheless fought against a backdrop of constant bickering among the states, raised in number to 18 since the addition of Ohio on 1 March 1803 and Louisiana (a fraction of the colonial territory, based on New Orleans and western Florida) on 4 June 1812.

North-eastern states remained firmly opposed to the war, some refusing to answer federal demands for men and resources, and the **Hartford Convention** of New England states was on the point of demanding curbs to the power of central government when peace negotiations (begun in August 1814, shortly before the British occupied and burned **Washington**) ended the war on 24 December 1814. News of the Treaty of **Ghent** reached the US in February 1815, rendering the efforts of the Hartford delegates irrelevant, and a commercial convention with Britain ended trade disputes in July, leaving the US free to expand both its territorial and its mercantile frontiers. *See* **Maps 19, 27.**

US Army

On the assumption that no national war effort would ever again be required, the **United States** had disbanded its army after the struggle for independence, relying on volunteer militia for regional defence. A regular army was re-established in the late 1780s, comprising only 840 men by 1789 and boasting 5,120 men, including four **cavalry** troops and four **artillery** companies, by December 1792. Intended only to provide garrisons for vulnerable frontier outposts, it was expected to form the core of a militia-based force in case of national emergency.

Reduced in size in 1796, but expanded by a recruitment drive offering land as reward for five years' service from 1808, the regular army had reached a strength of 35,600 men on the eve of the 1812 **Anglo-American War**, organized as 17 infantry, three artillery and two cavalry regiments. Few units approached their paper strength in practice, and although the West Point military academy was opened in 1802 (with the need to train **engineers** its priority), most officers were trained by their superiors at regimental level. Recruitment was never easy in a nation where militarism and restriction of constitutionally enshrined freedoms were fundamentally alien to much of the population, and expansion was made possible by reducing the enlistment period to 12 months and doubling the land reward to 320 acres.

Similar problems limited the value of militia forces for anything but defence of their own territories. Militia forces frequently operated under the dual control of local and federal administrations, and generally accepted orders from the former when they clashed. They were apt to fight, run or go home on their own authority, the inefficiency of their wartime deployment rivalling that of a **British Army** operating thousands of miles from home.

US Navy

Though the **United States** was ideologically committed to the rejection of war (against white Christians) as an instrument of state policy, a US Navy was formed in 1794 under pressure from east coast trading interests, led by Vice-President John Adams. Intended solely for the protection of maritime commerce, the navy possessed no **ships-of-the-line** during the next two decades, but was built around some of the finest smaller warships in the world, notably **frigates** like the 44-gun *President* or the 36-gun *Chesapeake*, which were immensely powerful for their size but retained the manoeuvrability of their European equivalents. American crews were well disciplined, efficient and better motivated than most of their contemporaries. Their reputation was improved by minor actions against French shipping during the war of 1798–1800, and by **Mediterranean** successes against the **Barbary** pirates (1801–5), but the navy's performance during the **Anglo-American War** of 1812–15 was particularly outstanding. Though unable seriously to disrupt a mounting British coastal **blockade**, it won a series of small victories over British frigates and light forces, most notably at **Lake Erie** in 1813. Though of limited strategic significance, they caused serious embarrassment to the hitherto invincible **Royal Navy** and were a mainstay of US wartime morale.

Ushant, Action off (1795)

Inconclusive engagement on 3 June 1795 near the island of Ushant, just off the coast of Brittany, that offered the **French Navy** a rare opportunity to inflict a significant battle defeat on its British counterpart (*see* **Map 18**). A **Royal Navy** squadron cruising off Ushant sighted a French wine convoy en route for Brest on 30 May, and gave chase. Led by Admiral Cornwallis in the 100-gun *Royal Sovereign*, with another four **ships-of-the-line** and three **frigates**, the squadron drove away Admiral Vence's six escorting warships and captured eight merchantmen. While Cornwallis resumed his cruise, a revenge mission was organized from Brest, and **Villaret** brought a fleet out of the port to rendezvous with Vence on 12 June. The combined French force, 12 ships-of-the-line and 11 frigates, sighted the British on 16 June, and came up within firing range next morning. By noon on 17 June the two fleets were fully engaged, but superior gunnery and discipline helped the heavily outnumbered British to hold their own. Though the British 74-gunner *Mars* was severely damaged, Cornwallis blocked attempts to finish it off, and the French fleet headed home empty-handed that evening.

Uxbridge, **Earl of** *See* **Paget**, Henry William

V

Valençay, Treaty of

Agreement signed on 11 December 1813 by emissaries of French emperor **Napoleon** and ex-King **Ferdinand** of **Spain** that made provision for the latter's restoration in return for an end to the **Peninsular War** and a trade agreement with France. Ferdinand had been a virtual prisoner in the south-western French city of Valençay since his enforced abdication at **Bayonne** in 1808, and Napoleon's sole motive for offering him freedom was the need to concentrate resources for the defence of **France**. This was well known to the Spanish regency government in Madrid, and it refused to ratify the treaty, but Napoleon eventually released Ferdinand in March 1814 in the (unfounded) hope that he would honour the agreement once he was back in power.

Valenciennes Offensive

The opening offensive of the War of the **First Coalition**, launched on 29 April 1792 by **French Army** forces on the Belgian frontier. General Rochambeau's columns advanced across the frontier into the **Austrian Netherlands** at Valenciennes and just east of Lille, while another army under **Lafayette** marched up the Sambre towards Namur.

Ill-equipped and ill-disciplined, many of them released from prison to take part, Rochambeau's (nominal) 50,000 men fled at the first sign of opposition from Austrian garrison forces. General **Beaulieu**'s division drove Biron's column back from Valenciennes, taking only 100 prisoners, and the 3,000 Austrians beyond Lille were enough to

reverse a secondary advance under General Dillon, who was murdered by his troops in the aftermath. The failures forced Lafayette to abandon his march on Namur, but Austrian forces made no attempt to exploit their victories.

Rochambeau was replaced by Lückner for a second French attempt that pushed into Belgium to take Courtrai on 18 June, but Lafayette's supporting advance was ambushed by the Duke of Saxe-Teschen's 12,000 men near Mauberge on 10 June. The invasion folded when local Austrian forces opened limited counter-attacks later that month. Lückner was forced to abandon Courtrai on 30 June, and ponderous Austrian advances forced French forces back to the frontier by mid-July. *See* **Map 2.**

Valjouan, Battle of

Successful French counter-attack on 17 February 1814 against forward units of **Schwarzenberg**'s allied army menacing Paris from the south-east (*see* Campaign for **France**). While **Napoleon** was engaged in the **Six Days Campaign** against **Blücher**'s army further north, Schwarzenberg had advanced his 150,000 troops north across the Seine. By 15 February the combined forces of **Oudinot**, **Victor** and **Macdonald** had retreated to a line around Guignes and Chalmes, only some 30km from Paris, but Schwarzenberg halted his advance to evaluate potential threats from French **guerrillas**, from **Augereau**'s (largely illusory) army forming around Lyon, and from Napoleon's reported approach. He was still debating a withdrawal when Napoleon and the

Imperial Guard reached Guignes on the afternoon of 16 February, after marching 75km in 36 hours.

Ordering General Maison in Belgium to prevent Bülow's army in the far north from joining the drive on Paris, Napoleon summoned every available man from the capital's garrison and launched 60,000 troops against Wrede's leading allied corps next morning. Schwarzenberg was just beginning a withdrawal towards Bray, but was too late to save Wrede. His forward cavalry was overrun by Grouchy and Gérard, who then drove his advance guard at Valjouan back beyond Nangis. Spreading his forces wider, Napoleon left Macdonald to complete the pursuit of Wrede, and sent Oudinot to intercept the retreat of Wittgenstein's corps at Nogent, while he hurried towards Montereau, determined to cross the Seine ahead of the retreating Austrians. *See* Map 26.

Valmaseda, Battle of

Minor victory for General Blake's Spanish rebel forces over Victor's French corps around the northern Spanish village of Valmaseda on 5 November 1808 (*see* Map 22). Retreating into the mountains after his defeat at Pancorbo on 31 October, but reinforced to a strength of 24,000 men by the arrival of General Romana, Blake suddenly turned to rescue a unit trapped by General La Vilette's leading French division. Spanish troops stormed the village and surrounded La Vilette's outnumbered force, but it fought its way to safety with only 300 casualties after forming a single infantry square, and the approach of Lefebvre's French corps soon compelled Blake to resume his retreat. *See also* Peninsular War.

Valmy, Battle of

The surprise victory by a French army of ill-equipped and virtually untrained volunteers over a highly disciplined Prussian army advancing on Paris. Fought on 20 September 1792, Valmy saved revolutionary France from almost certain conquest. Famously described by the writer Goethe (who was with the Prussians as an observer) as a watershed in the history of the world, it ended an era of mannered, dynastic wars, decided by rules of engagement and position.

The ponderous invasion of France by Brunswick's 100,000 men had eventually taken the fortress of Verdun on 2 September, and began advancing up the virtually undefended road to Paris next day. French C-in-C Dumouriez was moving his 30,000 troops from Sedan to link up with (the elder) Kellermann's 20,000 coming up from Metz, aiming to block the narrow roads through the Argonne Forest to Châlons. Snail-like Prussian progress gave the French time to unite in front of Brunswick's main body on 19 September, but some 34,000 Prussians under Clairfait and Kalkreuth had marched around the French southern flank and crossed the Aisne the previous day, so that Dumouriez was compelled to turn his army to face them.

Brunswick made no effort to come up behind Dumouriez, who kept his own forces back to guard the main road while Kellermann formed the centre of a crescent-shaped line around Valmy. Flanked by divisions under Stengel to his right and Chabot to his left, Kellermann took up positions on a small hill, and was attacked once clearing mist revealed his depositions to the Prussians next morning. A preliminary Prussian move in poor visibility took the outpost village of La Lune before mist delayed further action until about midday, when an artillery duel focused on Kellermann's hilltop divisions.

To the surprise of observers, the raw French fédérés held their ground under bombardment, and an hour later their musket fire helped repel a Prussian infantry advance, though signs of the line wavering prompted Dumouriez to send 4,000 reserves to Stengel's wing, where Clairfait's division mounted the most vigorous attack. After another prolonged bombardment, and in heavy rain, the Prussians attempted a second advance at about four, with equal lack of success. Brunswick made no further attempt at a breakthrough that day, and desultory firing finally ceased at about seven in the evening.

The battle, such as it was, claimed a total of 180 Prussian casualties and about 600 French, but failure to sweep its opponents aside amounted to an amazing defeat for an army regarded as Europe's finest, and had a disproportionately powerful effect on the morale of both sides. While despair turned to enthusiastic optimism in the hysterical atmosphere of Paris, Prussian confidence evaporated. Heavy rain helped dissuade Brunswick and King **Frederick William II** from any immediate resumption of attacks, while supply problems and dysentery weakened their army. Brunswick pulled back into the Argonne from 30 September and retreated all the way to the frontier, establishing new positions east of Longwy in the third week of October, at which point Dumouriez abandoned a faltering pursuit and returned to Paris to plan an invasion of Austrian **Belgium**. *See* **Map 3**.

Vandamme, Dominique Joseph René (1770–1830)

A vigorous, enterprising and consistently aggressive field commander, Vandamme first saw military service in 1790 as a volunteer in the **West Indies**, and returned to France to join the regular infantry in 1791. He formed his own **chasseur** company for service in **Flanders** on the outbreak of war in 1792, and was promoted brigadier-general after leading **Jourdan's** advance guard at **Hondschoote**. He fought at **Courtrai** the following May, and took part in the conquest of the **Netherlands** in January 1795, but was suspended for looting between June and September, when he was transferred to the army assembling for an invasion of **England**.

Vandamme was back in frontline action with **Moreau's** army on the **Rhine** in early 1797, and returned to the theatre for the opening campaigns against the **Second Coalition** in 1799, commanding a division under **Jourdan** at **Stockach**. After leading French reinforcements to **North Holland** that autumn, he returned to the Rhine for the 1800 campaign, but was again suspended for corruption in 1801. He returned to service in 1803 and fought under **Soult** against the **Third Coalition** in 1805. They quarrelled after **Austerlitz**, and he was given little opportunity to shine during the campaigns of 1806–7, seeing action only at **Magdeburg** and other second-line **sieges**.

After spells as regional governor in Boulogne and Lille, he played a full part in the 1809 Danube campaign, leading 12,000 **Württemberg** troops at **Abensberg**, and fighting at **Landshut** and **Eckmühl** under **Lefebvre**, before taking

command of VII Corps at **Wagram**, where he was wounded. A second period of administrative duty in northern France was followed by a corps command with **Jérôme Bonaparte's** southern wing of the **Grande Armée** for the 1812 **Russian campaign**, but he was once more dismissed for excessive looting in July.

His incurable plundering may have prevented Vandamme's elevation to the **Marshalate**, but Napoleon could hardly do without such a loyal and experienced fighter during the 1813 campaign for **Germany**. Given command of a large detached force for the first time during operations around **Dresden** in August, he won a preliminary victory at **Pirna** but was heavily defeated and taken prisoner at **Kulm**. Held in Russia until after Napoleon's **abdication** in 1814, he was exiled by the monarchy and returned to action during the **Hundred Days**, leading a corps under **Grouchy** at **Ligny** and **Wavre**. After a second period of exile, in the US and the Netherlands, he returned to France and retirement in 1819.

Vaubois, Charles Henri (1748–1839)

French **artillery** officer, who became a lieutenant-colonel of volunteer forces in 1791 after two decades' service with the royal army. Promoted brigadier-general while serving with the Army of the Alps in September 1793, he took part in the siege of **Lyon** before returning to the Alps, where he was given divisional command in 1796. Transferred that autumn to **Napoleon's** Army of Italy, he was at the siege of **Mantua** and fought at **Roveredo**, but was transferred to Corsica the following January. He joined the expedition to the **Middle East** from the island in May 1798, leaving it again at **Malta**, where he served as commandant until his surrender to **Royal Navy** forces in September 1800. He retired in 1801, but was recalled to service with the **National Guard** in 1809, and again in 1812.

Vauchamps, Battle of

The fourth defeat inflicted on **Sixth Coalition** forces during the **Six Days Campaign** in **France** of February 1814. After his incomplete victory over part of **Blücher's** command at **Château-Thierry** on 12 February, Napoleon was forced to rush south, where Schwarzenberg's resumed offensive had reached the Seine west of Montereau. **Marmont**'s corps was left to follow Blücher's apparent retreat on Reims, but Blücher had anticipated Napoleon's move and returned to the attack on 13 February. Facing about 22,000 men under Generals **Kleist** and Kapzevitch, Marmont slowly withdrew from Vertus to positions west of Vauchamps, buying time for Napoleon to lead the **Imperial Guard** back to the northern sector.

Grouchy's cavalry arrived in time to repel Blücher's frontal attack against the Vauchamps positions on the morning of 14 February, and **Zeiten**'s division on the allied right was severely mauled before Blücher achieved a limited disengagement. He withdrew altogether once the approach of the Guard brought French strength up to about 25,000 men, and though Grouchy managed to cut off the retreat beyond Champaubert, mud prevented French **artillery** from reaching the scene, and allied troops were eventually able to break through towards the relative safety of Châlons. By the end of the day, when Napoleon marched the Guard south towards a confrontation with Schwarzenberg at **Valjouan**, he had inflicted some 7,000 losses on Blücher and suffered only 600 casualties. *See* **Map 26**.

Vendée, La

The Atlantic region north and south of the River Loire was the most consistently royalist part of **France** throughout the period, and a constant thorn in the side of early republican governments. Alienated by the execution of the king and the government's enforced secularization of the clergy, the region's peasantry broke into armed uprising when confronted by attempts at **conscription** in mid-March 1793. A series of localized attacks by peasant mobs bearing the royal flag had taken over half a dozen towns by the end of the month, providing rebels with sufficient arms and supplies to extend their ambitions. Leaders began to emerge, notably minor noble Roche-Jacquelin, who captured an entire French division south of Saumur on 5 May.

The need to keep troops at the frontiers, and the wild nature of the Vendéan terrain, made it almost impossible to crush the rebellion in the short term, but its opportunistic successes were not backed by a coherent strategy and its fortunes fluctuated. The rebels took Saumur on 7 June, but were repulsed from Nantes by the garrison on 28–29 June. They suffered a defeat at the Loire on 15 July, but overwhelmed General Biron's division two days later and inflicted similar punishment on troops transferred from **Mainz** in September.

The best hope of expanding the rebellion lay in aid from **Great Britain**, which deployed sufficient naval power to intervene on the Atlantic coast. British plans to assist the rebels were delayed by troop shortages and the time taken to equip **Royal Navy** forces, so that a **French Navy** squadron blockading the coast from June met no serious opposition (apart from a mutiny aboard its ships) until early December.

In expectation of British aid, rebel columns undertook ragged sieges of St Malo and Grenville on the Brittany coast from late October, but returned south before the British arrived. Caught and defeated at Le Mans on 13 December they were annihilated north of Nantes on 22 December by government forces under **Kléber**. Meanwhile a belated expeditionary force of some 12,000 British, German and **émigré** troops arrived off the Brittany coast on 2 December, but found no rebels and sailed away.

The defeat by no means pacified the region. While the **Chouan** movement took hold in Brittany, small armies of royalists maintained a prototypical **guerrilla** campaign further south. Roche-Jacquelin was killed in March 1794, and his successor Stofflet led attempts to reorganize the struggle, but war minister **Carnot** agreed peace with rival rebel leader Charette at Nantes on 18 February 1795. Pursued by government forces, Stofflet signed a treaty on 20 April, but émigré influences and renewed hope of a British expedition brought the united rebels back into the field a month later. Joining up with Chouan leaders around Vannes, they suffered a final defeat to **Hoche**, with only **Cadoudal** and a few other well-connected leaders escaping abroad. Meanwhile an émigré and British force reached **Quiberon** Bay from late June, but withdrew after a costly and messy engagement.

La Vendée remained in a state of smouldering

civil war into early 1796, when the **Directory** regime gave Hoche sufficient resources to hunt down surviving leaders. Stofflet and Charette were captured and executed before Hoche wiped out the last major rebel band, 6,000 men in Brittany, during April. Local battles between royalists and republicans blighted western France until the restoration. **Bordeaux** rebelled with British aid in spring 1814, and the **Hundred Days** of 1815 brought renewed uprising to La Vendée, but it was efficiently suppressed by imperial troops under General Lamarque.

Vendémiaire Coup

Failed coup in Paris of 5 October 1795 (13 Vendémiaire by the **Republican calendar**) that was a turning point in the politics of republican **France** and in the career of **Napoleon**. After crushing a royalist rebellion in La **Vendée**, the unpopular **National Convention** government published its Constitution of the Year III in late September 1795, proposing to transfer most of its membership to a Legislative Assembly and place a **Directory** of Seven in control of executive power. It gave more moderate royalists, seeking a return to the constitutional monarchy of 1791, an opportunity to rouse the volatile mob of politically active Parisian citizens in defence of a threat to their electoral rights.

After Parisian local assemblies had rejected the constitution in angry meetings all over the city, perhaps 25,000 citizens and **National Guard** militia prepared to march on the Convention chamber at the Tuileries Palace on 5 October. With only 5,000 regular troops at hand, and their commander (**Menou**) having declared for the royalists, the Convention placed **Barras** in charge of its defence. Barras responded by summoning Napoleon, who had remained in Paris after his resignation from the army on 15 September, and who launched immediate countermeasures.

Sending a **cavalry** detachment under **Murat** to secure the city's **artillery** park, and deploying its guns in the streets leading to the Tuileries, he ordered several volleys of **grapeshot** fired into the crowd as it swept towards the palace. At point-blank range, they killed at least 200 people and wounded perhaps 400. The crowd fled,

enabling Napoleon's troops to restore order throughout the city by the end of the day.

Napoleon's brutal pragmatism, which he subsequently celebrated in understatement as a 'whiff of grapeshot', freed the government from the burden of mob sanction for the duration and dramatically reversed his own temporary decline in fortune. A grateful government appointed him second in command of the Army of the Interior on 10 October, made him a divisional general on 16 October, and gave him overall command of interior forces ten days later.

Venetian Navy

Once a great naval power, **Venice** still possessed 20 **ships-of-the-line**, ten **frigates** and 29 **sloops** by 1790, but they were all of obsolete design and most were in very poor condition. Much of the fleet was scrapped when Venice was partitioned between **France** and **Austria** by the 1797 **Campo Formio** treaty, but a few small craft were requisitioned to form the core of a new **Austrian Navy**, and the **French Navy** took possession of the four best battleships. They proved largely useless, functioning as floating batteries protecting Venice and the Adriatic coast, but saw some action against raids by British, Russian and Turkish warships from the **Mediterranean**.

Venice

A rich and powerful trading empire during the Middle Ages, Venice had declined dramatically by the late eighteenth century. Though still ruled by a doge from the heart of the ancient capital, its autonomy depended on the goodwill of **Austria**, the power in control of northern Italy until the mid-1790s. The government retained sufficient independence to remain technically neutral during the War of the **First Coalition**, but after much of the 1796–7 **Italian campaign** had been fought on Venetian territory the state was partitioned by the Treaty of **Campo Formio** (October 1797). Austrian forces ended more than a millennium of independent statehood by occupying the city of Venice early the following year. Control over former Venetian lands was regularly contested by French and Austrian armies over the next 16 years, but Austria was confirmed in possession after 1814, and Venice remained part of the Habsburg Empire until it was united with an independent Italy in the 1860s. *See* **Ionian Islands; Map 1**.

Vera, First Battle of

Minor but convoluted engagement fought over two days from 31 August 1813 that, along with defeat at **San Marcial**, ended **Soult's** last attempt to attack into Spain during the **Peninsular War**. The southern wing of a two-pronged advance west across the Bidassoa, the attack at Vera opened at dawn on 31 August, when General **Clausel** led four divisions across the river, intending to swing north towards besieged **San Sebastian**. The final allied assault against the port took place on the same day, and allied C-in-C **Wellington** had ordered **Dalhousie's** division to mount a diversionary attack just south of Vera.

The more immediate presence of the British Light Division blocking his path slowed Clausel during the morning, and he had made little progress by mid-afternoon when Soult called off the operation from St Marcial. The tidal river had meanwhile risen to trap some 10,000 French troops on the allied side, and it was morning before they found a crossing place at a narrow stone bridge near Vera. The 80 British riflemen holding the bridge were not reinforced, for which temporary Light Division commander General Skerrett was eventually sent home, but held off French charges through the afternoon of 1 September, inflicting 200 casualties before they were overwhelmed. The two-day action cost a total of 1,300 French casualties against 850 allied losses. *See* **Map 5**.

Vera, Second Battle of

Allied attack on 7 October 1813 against the strong central sector of Marshal **Soult's** line holding the north-western Pyrenees. Secondary to **Wellington's** main attack that day around **Irun**, the operation at Vera was carried out by General **Alten's** British Light Division, supported by two Spanish divisions. They were heavily outnumbered along the sector as a whole by **Reille's** 15,000 French troops, and their attack focused on strong fortifications around the dominant hill of La Grande Rhune just north-east of the town.

Covered by a diversion near Maya, the attackers fought their way up steep slopes to take another position to the west, and French forces retired from the whole sector with the loss of 1,300 casualties and all their **artillery**, leaving the garrison at La Grande Rhune to surrender next day. Allied forces lost 850 men at Vera, but the day's two victories carried the **Peninsular War** beyond the frontier and into the French **Nivelle** valley. *See* **Map 5**.

Verona, Battle of

The opening offensive of the **Italian campaign** in 1799, launched in late March by **Schérer's** French Army of Italy against Austrian positions east of the River Adige. Faced with the prospect of an Austro-Russian offensive against his scattered and outnumbered army, Schérer chose to attack before Russian reinforcements could arrive. Dividing some 25,000 frontline troops into two main contingents, Schérer moved towards the bank of Lake Garda on 26 March, while **Moreau** attacked the **fortress** city of Verona.

Austrian positions were centred on Padua (not, as Schérer believed, Rivoli), and the Adige from Verona to Legnano was guarded by five mutually supporting fortified camps on the west bank. Though attacking French forces took a number of these, and **Sérurier's** division captured Rivoli, no substantial French force was able to establish itself across the Adige during a day of fierce fighting all along the front.

During the night General **Kray**, commanding Austrian forces in the temporary absence of C-in-C **Melas**, began concentrating his forces to defend Verona, where Moreau had taken control of roads west of the river. Missing the chance to strike the weakened Austrian flank, Schérer stayed where he was in expectation of a counter-attack. By 30 March, when Sérurier's vanguard crossed the Adige at Polo to support Moreau, Kray's vastly superior numbers were in position to chase it back across the river, inflicting 5,000 casualties and forcing the whole of Schérer's line north of Verona back on to his centre. *See* Battle of **Magnano; Map 9**.

Victor, Claude Perrin (1764–1841)

Though he joined the pre-revolutionary **French Army** as a bandsman, Victor (born Claude-Victor Perrin) made his name as an aggressive combat officer, first coming to national attention under

Dugommier on the Pyrenean front in 1794. He led a division during the Italian campaign of 1799, taking part in defeats at Magnano, the Trebbia and Genola, but was more successful under Napoleon during the 1800 campaign, playing an important part at Montebello and commanding a corps at Marengo in June.

Chief of staff to Lannes before taking over I Corps from the wounded Bernadotte at Friedland in 1807, he was promoted marshal for his decisive contribution to the victory. Ennobled in 1808 as the Duc de Belluno in 1808 (the title was a pun on 'beau-soleil', a nickname derived from his sunny nature), he spent the next four years as a corps commander in the Peninsular War, suffering defeats at Valmaseda and Talavera before joining Soult's unsuccessful siege of Cadiz.

He rejoined Napoleon for the 1812 Russian campaign, playing an important role in the retreat across the Beresina in late November, and fought at Dresden and Leipzig in 1813, but gave a lacklustre performance during the following year's defence of France. Temporarily dismissed after the Battle of Montereau in February, Victor declared for a restored monarchy shortly before Napoleon's abdication, and remained loyal to Louis XVIII throughout the Hundred Days of 1815. He presided over the postwar commission judging those who had defected, and was war minister from 1821 to 1823.

Vienna, Capture of (1805)

The capital of Austria was occupied by French forces for the first time on 12 November 1805, when forward units of the Grande Armée entered and took control of the virtually undefended city. Vienna had been threatened with occupation since General Mack's capitulation at Ulm in October had left the empire without a major force available for home defence. Once it became clear that the only allied army in a position to defend the capital, General Kutuzov's 40,000 Russians, was retiring towards reinforcements north of the Danube, Napoleon ordered his army in pursuit, but Murat and Lannes broke off the chase to make a dash for Vienna (see Battles of Amstetten, Dürrenstein).

Napoleon's fury at their impulsive behaviour was moderated by the manner in which they took the city. Vienna's antiquated fortifications were badly in need of repair, and its garrison consisted of ill-led, outnumbered second-line troops. Evacuation of court, government and most of the richer citizens had eroded local morale, and Vienna had been declared an open city, but Murat and Lannes found the vital Danube bridge defended by garrison troops and charges placed for its destruction. Bluffing their way past astonished Austrian guards with loud announcements that an armistice had been agreed, the two marshals walked calmly across the bridge and seized the position before the local commander, the elderly (and subsequently disgraced) Count Auersperg, could decide on resistance.

Napoleon entered Vienna in triumph on 14 November. Prestige and pageant apart, the city provided a guaranteed Danube crossing for the rescheduled pursuit of Kutuzov, along with 2,000 artillery pieces, 100,000 muskets and plentiful ammunition for both. Vienna remained under French occupation until December, when it was restored to Habsburg control under the terms of the Treaty of Pressburg.

Vienna, Congress of

The international conference called by the victorious great powers of the Sixth Coalition to determine the internal boundaries of Europe in the wake of Napoleon's defeat in 1814. Summoned for September 1814, the congress got fully under way from 1 November and sat through 41 sessions until the signature of its Final Act on 9 June 1815, though its map-making work was temporarily halted in March to enable the hasty formation of the Seventh Coalition against France.

The congress proceeded from enforcement of the first Treaty of Paris and formal dissolution of the French Empire, but its essential task was to combine widespread dynastic restoration, distribution of territorial prizes to the victors and establishment of long-term security after 22 years of wars. Though representatives of all the smaller nations involved attended the congress – and many were employed on the various sub-committees dealing with damage claims, statistical records and minor diplomatic issues – the power of territorial distribution was restricted to representatives of **Great Britain**, **Russia**, **Austria** and **Prussia**.

These were led by **Castlereagh** and **Wellington** for Britain, Tsar **Alexander I** and chief adviser **Stein** for Russia, **Metternich** for Austria, and Prussian premier **Hardenberg**. Papal envoy Cardinal **Consalvi** took part in those debates relevant to Vatican interests, and Friedrich von **Gentz**, a Prussian in Austrian service, acted as congress secretary-general. French delegate **Talleyrand**, though not officially part of the decision-making process, was able to exploit disputes between the allies to gain acceptance as a voting member at the most important sessions, but could gain little for France in the face of determined hostility from Metternich and the tsar.

The congress was dominated by arguments over issues that had always divided the allies, with the future of **Poland** causing the most trouble. A Russian and Prussian proposal to annex Poland and **Saxony** respectively persuaded Britain and Austria to force compromise by signing an alliance with France in January 1815. Alexander eventually became ruler of a reduced, semi-autonomous 'Congress Poland', the rest going to Prussia and Austria, while Saxony lost just under half its territory to Prussia.

Settlement of the Polish and Saxon questions triggered compensatory territorial changes elsewhere. Berlin made up for failure in Saxony by taking Posen and Danzig from Poland, a large chunk of **Westphalia** and Swedish Pomerania, with **Sweden** gaining assent to its annexation of Norway in return. Austria meanwhile took Galicia, and gained the provinces of Dalmatia, Carniola and Salzburg, along with a new northern Italian kingdom of Lombardy-Venetia.

The congress recognized new authorities in the **Netherlands**, the free city of Krakow, and a loose German confederation of 39 surviving small states. Prewar ruling dynasties were restored in **Spain**, **Naples**, **Piedmont**, **Tuscany** and the small north Italian duchy of Modena, while **Switzerland** was returned to federal status and given a multilateral guarantee of neutrality. A number of general regulatory measures were also introduced, including the establishment of free navigation along the Rhine and Meuse rivers, and the formulation of a diplomatic code that held sway until 1914. Broader recommendations included a general condemnation of the slave trade, and an expression of support for the constitutional rights of Jews.

Britain's position was unique in that its ambitions were not centred on Europe. Foreign minister Castlereagh ensured that Britain retained most of its **colonial** conquests, and obtained a temporary protectorate over the **Ionian Islands**, but identified peaceful balance between the great continental powers, or the 'Concert of Europe', as the best means of ensuring global security. His pragmatic quest for lasting peace found an ally in Metternich, and the two are generally regarded as the moving spirits behind the final Vienna agreement. They were also the most influential advocates of 'Congress diplomacy', which ran to four more summit meetings over the next seven years and helped maintain a general European peace that lasted for an unprecedented four decades. *See* **Map 30**.

Vienna, Convention of (1806)

The preliminary treaty imposed on **Prussia** by **Napoleon** as punishment for its belated adherence to the ill-fated **Third Coalition** in 1805. Prussian envoy **Haugwitz** reached Napoleon at Brno with an ultimatum on 28 November, but was not granted an audience until 15 December, by which time defeat at **Austerlitz** had destroyed the Coalition. Fully aware of the envoy's original mission, Napoleon subjected Haugwitz to intense psychological pressure before securing his acceptance of a punitive mutual 'friendship' treaty.

The Convention required Prussia to cede Cleves to **Murat**, Neuchâtel to **Berthier**, Ansbach to **Bavaria** and Wesel to **France**. Prussia was to share in all economic measures taken by Napoleon against **Great Britain**, and the consolation of acquiring **Hanover** was tainted by the fact that it belonged to **George III** of England. In no position to argue, Frederick William made characteristic attempts to delay a decision before the Convention was formally ratified on 24 February 1806. The agreement ruined Haugwitz, made Prussia a laughing stock in European diplomatic circles, and ignited a mood of national outrage that encouraged a quick return to war (*see* War of the **Fourth Coalition**).

Villaret de Joyeuse, Louis Thomas (1748–1812)

One of relatively few former royal officers to remain with the post-revolutionary **French Navy**, Villaret was promoted captain in 1793 and attached to the Atlantic Fleet at Brest. He was a rear-admiral before the end of the year, as reward for successfully escorting an American food **convoy** through a lax British **blockade**. Though defeated by **Howe** at the Battle of the **First of June**, Villaret handled his forces with a sober competence that belied his inexperience, and fulfilled his primary mission by diverting attention from another vital food convoy. Hailed as a victor at home, and promoted vice-admiral, Villaret became increasingly depressed by the overall inefficiency of his fleet, and was relieved to be replaced by de Galles before the 1796 **Bantry Bay** expedition. He turned to politics as a member of the Council of **Five Hundred**, but was exiled as a suspected royalist after the **Fructidor coup** of September 1797. Returned to favour and command at Brest under the **Consulate** in 1800, he led the naval element of the **Santo Domingo** expedition in 1802. He remained in the **West Indies** as military commander of Martinique and St Lucia, becoming a count of the empire in 1808, until the islands were taken by the British in 1809. Shunned for his surrender, he lived in semi-retirement at Rouen until 1811, when he was recalled to imperial service as governor of **Venice**, where he died.

Villeneuve, Pierre Charles Jean Baptiste Silvestre de (1763–1806)

One of the more competent **French Navy** commanders to remain with the service through the revolutionary period, Villeneuve joined the old regime's navy in 1778. Promoted captain in February 1793, he was suspended shortly afterwards because he came from a minor noble family, but restored to favour and promoted rear-admiral in 1796. Unable to get his ships to sea in time to join the 1796 **Bantry Bay** expedition, he commanded a division of the French fleet annihilated at the **Nile** in 1798, escaping destruction with two **ships-of-the-line** and two **frigates**.

Villeneuve became a vice-admiral in May 1804, and commander of the Toulon fleet in December. As such he was central to the complex operations that led up to the climactic battle at **Trafalgar** in October 1805, when his fleet was virtually wiped out and he was taken prisoner. Though his hand had been forced by **Napoleon**, Villeneuve was officially and popularly blamed for the disaster, and committed suicide shortly after his return to France on **parole** in April 1806.

Vilna, Battle of

The first attempt by **Napoleon** to force battle during the **Russian campaign** of 1812. The spearhead of the French invasion had crossed the River Niemen into Russia by 25 June, and had occupied Kovno unopposed before Napoleon concluded that **Barclay de Tolly's** Russian First Army was already retiring north-east to strong defensive positions on the River Dvina. In the hope of catching it, Napoleon ordered his main advance to continue to Vilna. Jérôme **Bonaparte's** 55,000 men of the southern wing, based around Warsaw, were instructed to pin down Prince **Bagration's** smaller Second Army, then moving north towards a rendezvous with Barclay de Tolly.

French advance was delayed by transport problems, as vast supply convoys became bogged down in the rear, and Napoleon was compelled to halt his forward units while the flanking army of **Beauharnais** attempted to catch up. News on 26 July that Barclay de Tolly was still at Vilna, and that Beauharnais was at last across the Niemen, prompted the French emperor to risk extending his supply lines a little further, and **Murat** led 52,000 troops against the city on 28 June.

He was too late. Barclay de Tolly had already withdrawn across the River Vilia towards Sventsiani and the assault was met only by rearguard **artillery**, which retired after destroying anything useful to the invaders. Instructing Murat to pursue Barclay de Tolly, but to avoid a major battle in his absence, Napoleon halted at Vilna to turn the bulk of his strength against Bagration, who was reported approaching from the southwest. *See* Manoeuvre on **Minsk**; **Map 23**.

Vimeiro, Battle of

The **British Army's** first major battle of the **Peninsular War**, fought just north of Lisbon on

21 August 1808, when General **Wellesley**'s British expeditionary force, having won a minor engagement at **Rolica** on 16 August, was attacked by a smaller French army under **Junot**. The failure of initial French offensives against Spanish rebels, defeat at **Bailén** and Joseph **Bonaparte**'s subsequent retreat from Madrid had left Junot's 13,000-strong Army of Portugal as the only major force available to meet Wellesley's 15,000-strong army. Hoping to surprise the British at Vimeiro before they were fully established, Junot attacked on arrival, but skilfully deployed defenders held off four frontal charges, inflicting some 2,500 casualties and suffering about 700.

Heavily outnumbered and without supplies for a long retreat in hostile country, the French army retired on Lisbon, but British offensive operations were halted by Wellesley's cautious superiors, Burrard and **Dalrymple**. They negotiated the extremely lenient Convention of **Cintra**, allowing Junot home and sparking a controversy in Britain that briefly threatened to end Wellesley's active career.

British victory at Vimeiro cleared Portugal of French occupying forces, albeit temporarily, and helped undermine the myth of French invincibility, encouraging the Austrian court in particular towards renewed war against France. It also established Wellesley's credentials as a commander under European conditions, introduced the defensive tactics that were the key to many of his subsequent successes and reinforced his own conviction that **Napoleon** could be beaten. *See* Map 22.

Vinkovo, Battle of

Surprise attack by Russian forces on French advanced guards stationed south-west of **Moscow** on 18 October 1812. Lulled by weeks of fraternization with their erstwhile enemies, **Murat**'s screening forces were unprepared for the two-pronged attack around Vinkovo, some 50km from Moscow. While **cavalry** under General Denisov took on and defeated **Sebastiani**'s cavalry corps, General **Baggavout**'s infantry attacked Murat's central position, some 3km away. Briefly threatened with encirclement by the infantry attack, but not pressed by any Russian commitment of

reserves, Murat led a fighting withdrawal to Voronovo, where new positions had been established by the end of the day. Russian commander **Kutuzov** made no attempt to follow up his limited success, but it persuaded **Napoleon** to bring forward his planned retreat to Smolensk. *See* **Russian Campaign; Map 23**.

Vitebsk, Capture of

The unopposed seizure of Vitebsk, on the River Dvina, by French forces on 28 July 1812, and the anticlimactic conclusion to **Napoleon**'s third attempt to force a major battle during the **Russian campaign**, following failures at **Vilna** and **Minsk**. **Barclay de Tolly**'s Russian First Army had retreated to strong positions on the Dvina from Vilna, but moved south-east from 18 July, planning to join **Bagration**'s smaller Second Army for a stand at Vitebsk.

Davout's covering force to the south engaged and defeated Bagration at **Mohilev** on 23 July, preventing any immediate junction of the Russian armies, and the main French strike force began moving towards Vitebsk along the west bank of the Dvina next day. **Murat**'s advanced cavalry fought Russian forces at **Ostronovo** on each of the next two days, but Napoleon paused to complete his concentration on 27 July. Deprived of Bagration's aid, Barclay de Tolly changed his mind about a battle and withdrew from the town that day, so that the French attack found it undefended next morning. While Napoleon's central forces paused for rest, both Russian forces headed for a new rendezvous point at **Smolensk**, having suffered some 8,000 casualties at Mohilev and Ostronovo. *See* **Map 23**.

Vitoria, Battle of

Pivotal allied victory over French forces in the **Peninsular War**, a battle fought on 21 June 1813 for control of the north-eastern Spanish road junction of Vitoria (*see* **Map 22**). **Wellington**'s summer offensive had begun with a successful feint against the main French defences on the Douro, and the appearance of **Graham**'s 60,000 troops to his north in early June had surprised French C-in-C Joseph **Bonaparte** into a hasty retreat.

Supplied from a new forward base at Santander, Wellington's rapid flank march outpaced

Joseph's attempts to make a stand at Burgos (abandoned on 12 June) or the River Ebro, but 66,000 French troops reached the east bank of the River Zadorra around Vitoria ahead of the allied army on 19 June. Anxious to win time for the safe evacuation of baggage and equipment trains, Joseph and chief of staff **Jourdan** prepared to defend the position.

The final approach to Vitoria from the west crossed an open plain, some 12km wide, and Joseph deployed his 66,000 defenders in three lines along a narrow front across its southern half. General **Gazan**'s 35,000 men formed the front line about 8km from the town, holding the forward slopes of the plain's dominant hill; **Drouet**'s division held the main Madrid–Bayonne road some 2km to the east, and **Reille**'s division was on the road just west of Vitoria. The positions were strong against a frontal attack, but only if it came from the west. Hurried by news that **Clausel** was gathering French reinforcements in Pamplona, Wellington attacked the town from several directions at once on 21 June, after spending a day concentrating 79,000 men in the area (including 27,500 **Portuguese** and 7,000 **Spanish Army** troops).

Operations opened in steady rain at eight in the morning, when **Hill** attacked Gazan's line from the south. His troops struggled to take the Puebla Heights, but achieved their main aim of attracting reserves to the French left wing. Two divisions (**Dalhousie** and **Picton**) were ordered to work their way round mountains fringing the plain before striking against the French right, but were not in position by the time Graham's force had cut the Bayonne road in the French rear, and Wellington was ready to lead two divisions in a frontal assault.

About to launch his frontal attack anyway, Wellington was informed that a bridge over the Zadorra to the north of Gazan's line, at Tres Puentes, was intact and virtually unguarded. Displaying characteristic opportunism, he ordered a brigade of light infantry and regiment of **hussars** to seize the bridge, and prepared to push his central divisions across in support of Dalhousie. Picton, in position but intended as a reserve, then launched a successful attack on his own initiative just east of Tres Puentes, and all three British divisions tore into the northern flank of French forces still focused on the southern heights.

Gazan pulled back his forward positions at about three, at which point Dalhousie's division appeared east of Picton and took the village of St Marguerita, triggering abandonment of the first French line. Gazan attempted to re-form his forces alongside Drouet's, but an attack at their point of contact quickly forced a breakthrough. Steady pressure by Graham's corps had meanwhile forced Reille's third line to redeploy north of Vitoria itself, guarding the south bank of the Zadorra. Graham attacked the Zadorra bridges at around four, scattering defenders after a short but ferocious struggle, and Joseph ordered a general retreat an hour later.

Reille's troops recovered to attempt a rearguard action around the town, but were soon forced to join what became a rout as roads became jammed with fleeing troops, supply wagons, camp followers and the loot of several years' imperial occupation. Along with 2,000 stragglers, bringing total French losses for the day up to about 8,000, Joseph's army was forced to leave behind all but two of its 153 guns, more than 400 **caissons**, 100 supply wagons and an enormous amount of booty. Discovery of the latter contributed to a breakdown in allied discipline and enabled many French troops to escape. Unable to rouse or reorganize his tired army, which had lost 5,100 men during the day, Wellington made no serious attempt at pursuit through continuing heavy rain.

Vitoria was one Wellington's most impressive victories, organized at very short notice and distinguished by his control over complex manoeuvres around a very wide battle area. The defeat's scale effectively ended French hopes of re-establishing imperial control in Spain, forcing Joseph's army back to the Pyrenees and defence of its own frontiers. It was also a huge **propaganda** success for the allies, reversing the depression that had followed **Napoleon**'s German victories at **Lützen** and **Bautzen**. On the somewhat casual initiative of British regent Prince **George**, who was sent Jourdan's captured baton after the battle, the rank of field marshal was introduced to the **British Army** as a means of rewarding Wellington for these achievements.

Voronzov, Mikhail (1782–1856)

Russian soldier and diplomat, son of a minor St Petersburg nobleman, who fought in the **Russo-Turkish War** of 1806–12 and commanded a division during the 1812 **Russian campaign**. Elevated to corps command during the 1813 campaign in **Germany**, he fought with the allied Army of the North in the Netherlands during the opening phases of the following year's campaign in **France**, but marched south to join **Blücher** in time to play a leading role at the Battle of **Craonne** in March. A long and distinguished postwar career culminated in his appointment to command Russian forces in the Caucasus from 1844.

Vosges, Battle of the

French attack on allied positions in the Vosges Mountains that opened the autumn campaigning season on the **Rhine** in 1794. Reinforced to a total strength of about 115,000 men, French theatre commander Michaud faced perhaps 70,000 Prussian, Saxon and Austrian troops holding a line south-east from Kaiserslautern to Spire (*see* **Map 3**). With the **First Coalition** on life support from British **subsidies**, and no real prospect of allied aggression, Michaud launched an offensive all along the allied line on 2 July.

Only **Desaix** on the far French right made any progress, but his drive up the Rhine was halted by Prussian **cavalry**, and reversed with 1,000 losses after counter-attacks by **Blücher** and the Prince of Baden.

On war minister **Carnot's** orders, a second French offensive opened on 13 July. While **Gouvion St Cyr** resumed attacks against the allied right around Kaiserslautern, and Desaix was restricted to a demonstration bombardment, General Taponier's corps in the centre drove **Hohenlohe's** Prussians back through the gorges and ravines of the Vosges, taking Tripstadt and mountain strongholds further east. Unable to draw large-scale reinforcements from Kaiserslautern, and given almost no help by nearby Austrians, Hohenlohe pulled his entire force out of the mountains during the night.

The day's fighting cost the allies an estimated 3,000 casualties, 80 per cent of them Prussian, and isolated Kalkreuth's Prussians in the west from allied forces nearer the Rhine. The latter responded by retreating to the Rhine at Mannheim, maintaining only a small bridgehead east of the river, while Prussian C-in-C Möllendorf ordered Hohenlohe and Kalkreuth back to Worms on 16 July.

W

Wachau, **Battle of** *See* Battle of **Leipzig**

Wagram, Battle of

The climax to the War of the **Fifth Coalition**, a decisive confrontation between French and Austrian armies just north-east of Vienna on 5–6 July 1809. The battle followed from **Napoleon's** second attempt to get his army on to the north bank of the Danube, after the Austrian army of Archduke **Charles** had thwarted the first at **Aspern–Essling** in May.

Napoleon began calling up his outlying forces for a second crossing attempt within 36 hours of his setback at Aspern–Essling. He was strengthened by the arrival of **Beauharnais** from Italy (who kept Archduke **John's** approaching force at bay with a victory at **Raab** in mid-June) and **Marmont** from **Illyria**, so that about 160,000 French troops were around Vienna by the beginning of July. By pressing as many captured weapons as possible into service, French **artillery** strength was raised to some 500 guns.

As in May, Napoleon intended to use the island of Lobau as a staging post for the crossing, and it was transformed into a fortified camp. Several new bridges were built connecting it to the French-held bank, care being taken to protect them against both high water and interference from river missiles, and building materials for rapid construction of northern bridges were stockpiled on the island.

Charles made no attempt to exploit his relative strength immediately after Aspern–Essling, and instead pulled most of his troops back to covering positions further north. His army was bolstered by 60,000 militia troops and his artillery support was almost doubled, giving him more than 450 guns, but he remained more concerned with repelling future French attacks, and with hopes that Napoleon would ask for terms, than with any aggressive ambitions of his own. He was further distracted by the prospect of John's arrival, by hopes of an anti-French uprising in southern Germany, and by developments to the east, where **Poniatowski's** Polish forces were making inroads into Austrian-controlled Galicia.

When French forces began to mass on Lobau during the first two days of July, Charles anticipated a repeat of the earlier attempt to cross from the island's north-west corner, and moved up to defend the Aspern–Essling position in strength. French preparations were in fact a feint, disguising plans to cross from the eastern end of Lobau before sweeping on to the Austrian left flank.

As more and more troops poured on to Lobau, French diversionary operations – including an attack in the west against Stedlau on 2 July – persuaded Charles to change his mind. On 3 July leading formations were moved back to their original positions some 10km north of the Danube, on a line running from Gerasdorf through Wagram and east along the River Russbach.

Part of **Oudinot's** corps began the crossing operation at about nine in the evening of 4 July. In continuing storms, and distracted by a French bombardment of the Aspern–Essling position, advance guards were completely surprised by multiple crossings from the eastern corner of the island. Executed with barely a hitch and hardly a casualty, they continued through the night and eventually utilized ten pontoon bridges. By ten a.m. on 5 July more than 150,000 French troops were taking up their attack positions around a strong bridgehead east of Essling.

Charles had not been informed of major developments until after dawn, and three French corps were fanning out towards his main positions by the time he realized the seriousness of the situation. While **Davout** drove towards Glinzendorf on the French right, with Beauharnais's Army of Italy in support, Oudinot's corps approached Baumersdorf in the centre, supported by **Bernadotte**. **Masséna**'s left wing enjoyed the greatest success, sweeping west to take both Essling and Aspern by early evening.

With no sign of John approaching, Charles had effectively lost his numerical advantage. His forces were far less concentrated than Napoleon's, which occupied the central position between two Austrian wings and could outnumber either. Changing his original battle plan, Charles decided to concentrate against the weaker French left, where perhaps 65,000 Austrians faced Masséna's 27,000 men, but his troops were still gathering when a full-scale French attack on the Russbach position opened just after seven.

To exploit the Austrian centre's relative weakness, Napoleon had ordered Davout and Oudinot to attack the Russbach line, while Beauharnais and Bernadotte made a bid to break through the centre at Wagram and Masséna performed holding operations on the left. The attack failed. Oudinot was forced back with heavy losses around Baumersdorf, and Davout received his orders too late to make any effective contribution. The advance in the centre began well, but a counter-attack from **Bellegarde**'s troops and part of Hohenzollern's command halted Beauharnais, putting **Macdonald**'s division to flight. To their left Bernadotte was unable to storm Wagram, and he finished the night back at his starting position in Aderklaa.

Having made no significant gains, Napoleon spent the latter part of the night finalizing the deployment of his 36,000 reserves in preparation for a morning assault on the Russbach, to be followed by a flank attack towards Markgraf neusiedl by Davout on the right and by a massive drive through the centre at Wagram. Charles meanwhile reactivated an earlier plan to envelop the French centre, concentrating two corps for the main attack against Masséna and relying on John's arrival to close the pincer on the opposite flank.

The Austrian offensive opened first, with a preliminary attack just before dawn by Rosenburg's corps against the French right. Napoleon reinforced Davout from the reserve, and the Austrians were in retreat over the Russbach by six. Ordering Davout to resume preparations for his own attack, Napoleon discovered that Bernadotte had shortened his line during the night by withdrawing from the vital central position of Aderklaa on his own authority. Bernadotte was ordered to retake the village, but his **Saxon** troops fled under withering Austrian artillery fire during a counter-attack from Charles's reserve. Napoleon had dismissed Bernadotte from command by the time a second attack secured Aderklaa, and the main Austrian operation against Masséna had been under way for almost an hour.

Advancing just after eight, some 36,000 Austrian troops, under Kollowrath and Klenau, steamrollered the single French division in its path back to the Danube at the Mühlen salient, opposite Lobau's north-western corner. Only slow Austrian exploitation of the success, and the bold initiative of Beauharnais in sending Macdonald's troops to plug the gap, gave Napoleon sufficient breathing space to devise and execute counter-measures.

Masséna's other three divisions were pulled from the line and marched along the front to link Macdonald and the rest of the army. The gap in the centre was then filled by the rest of Beauharnais's command and an improvised battery of 112 guns. Macdonald halted Kollowrath's inner element of the advancing Austrian right at great cost, and Klenau's outer corps was slowed by the fire of artillery sited on Lobau. Masséna had reached his new position by noon, and the French left stabilized.

Davout was meanwhile making hard-won gains on the far right, holding off a heavy counter-attack to take Markgrafneusiedl before midday. Reactivating his original plan for the day, Napoleon then ordered an all-out attack on the Austrian centre. Oudinot's corps was sent against Wagram, and the vital task of breaking through towards Süssenbrünn to isolate the Austrian right wing was given to Macdonald's 8,000 remaining troops, supported by General **Lauriston's** massed artillery battery.

Macdonald's initial attack was beaten back, suffering 75 per cent casualties, and Napoleon was forced to commit almost his last reserves in support of a second assault, leaving only a skeleton force to guard against the possibility of Archduke John's belated arrival. As Macdonald finally broke through, and Davout made slow but steady progress in the east, Masséna advanced to retake Aspern by two, and the combined forces of Beauharnais, Oudinot and Marmont forced their way into Wagram.

Charles had been ordering a tactical withdrawal when the latest series of French attacks began, and could only retreat, though his intentions were by no means clear to the French amid the chaos of battle. Heavy fighting continued along the line throughout the afternoon, and eventually died down between eight and nine in the evening. John's 13,000 troops made a brief appearance to the east at about four, only to be driven off by the light cavalry force watching that flank.

During the night Charles extricated most of his army, largely untroubled by French forces still expecting to resume the battle next day. Pursuit of the beaten Austrians did not get under way until late next day, but Charles was eventually caught by Marmont and Masséna on 10 July at **Znaim**, and signed an armistice two days later.

Fought in blistering July heat, the French victory at Wagram was decisive, triggering the negotiating process that culminated in the Treaty of **Schönbrunn**. It was also very costly. Despite the claims of French **propaganda**, Napoleon lost at least 32,500 men killed or wounded (including 40 generals), and another 7,000 as prisoners. Official Austrian figures, undoubtedly conservative, admitted to more than 37,000 losses. *See* **Map 15**.

Walcheren Expedition

The belated contribution made by **Great Britain** to the **Fifth Coalition's** land campaign of 1809, an invasion of Walcheren, a large island off the Zeeland coast of the **Netherlands**, close to the border of greater **France** (*see* **Map 2**).

Most of the island belonged to Louis **Bonaparte's** Kingdom of Holland, but the town of Flushing and surrounding districts had been annexed by France in 1807, in an attempt to curb flagrant abuses of the **Continental System**. Walcheren had been considered as an alternative invasion site to **North Holland** in 1799, and attracted British planners as both a direct (albeit peripheral) attack on French territory, and an opportunity to reopen important trade links to Antwerp.

British preparations for the invasion, begun in April 1809, were not complete until late July, by which time news of **Austria's** defeat at **Wagram** had ended any hope of invading France, but British C-in-C Lord **Chatham** regarded the possible capture of Antwerp and destruction of French shipping on the Scheldt as sufficient incentive to go ahead with the operation. He arrived off Walcheren on 29 July with 40,000 troops, strong **artillery** support and a massive **Royal Navy** escort of 35 **ships-of-the-line**, 23 **frigates** and 16 other warships.

While Chatham got his men ashore and occupied the island, surrounding General Monnet's French garrison at Flushing, Franco-Dutch authorities made hasty attempts to strengthen pitifully inadequate defences. The demands of the Danube and **Peninsular** campaigns had left Louis with only about 7,000 fit troops, and they were ordered to hold the islands between Walcheren and the mainland while reinforcements were concentrated on Antwerp. They failed to do so, and Flushing fell on 15 August, but Chatham's offensive was already grinding to a halt under the twin burdens of disease (a debilitating plague known as Walcheren Fever) and his own lethargy.

By the time **Bernadotte** arrived in Antwerp to take command from Louis on 16 August, the city could call on four French **National Guard** divisions, a regular infantry division and a Dutch division sent from Germany. By the end of the month Bernadotte's strength was up to about

30,000 men, and French vessels on the Scheldt had arrived safely at Antwerp, blocking the river behind them. Meanwhile Chatham had lost more than 8,000 men to disease by the end of August, and was suffering another 500 losses per week, with predictable effects on morale.

Recognizing that an attack on Antwerp could no longer succeed, and personally determined to avoid contamination as sick lists mushroomed, Chatham withdrew with part of his force on 14 September, leaving General Eyre Coote and 15,000 troops to hold their positions. Despite a slight abatement of the fever, Coote was forced to withdraw forward units to Walcheren in October, and abandoned the island with his government's permission on Christmas Eve. A waste of time, men and money – costing an estimated £1 million and 17,000 casualties – the expedition reduced many of the **British Army**'s best formations to long-term uselessness, and its main strategic effect was to give **Napoleon** an excuse for hounding Louis into abdication.

Walewska, Countess Marie (1789–1817)

Young Polish noblewoman who caught the eye of **Napoleon** during his stay in **Warsaw** during January 1807. Encouraged by associates among the nobility, she responded positively to his advances in the hope that he would look favourably on claims for the restoration of **Poland**, and though destined to have no discernible effect on Napoleon's basically opportunist attitude to Polish nationalism, her self-sacrifice soon turned to enduring love. For a few years her sentiments were returned with enthusiasm. Walewska visited both Paris and Vienna, and became known popularly as 'the emperor's Polish wife', but was cast aside in late 1809 once Napoleon had decided on marriage to Habsburg archduchess **Marie-Louise**. This apparently devastating blow, coming when she was pregnant with Napoleon's illegitimate son (Alexandre, born in May 1810), did not shake her loyalty. She remained on friendly terms with Napoleon throughout the empire's last years, and paid him a final visit during his first exile on **Elba** in 1814.

War Finance

The cost of war had always been more than most treasuries could bear for long, reflecting the enormous expense of arming, feeding and paying field forces (especially navies), but the length and intensity of conflicts between 1792 and 1815 placed an unprecedented strain on the economies of belligerent states.

No government could pay war costs from its normal tax revenue, and few could sustain war for long on increased taxes alone. Loans could be obtained from private financiers (like the **Rothschild** family) in money markets all over Europe, especially in London, Amsterdam and the **Hanseatic** towns. Usually offered at high interest, loans could easily get out of control, and the more sustainable system of funding loans by drawing on future credit (in the form of national debt) was only fully developed in **Great Britain** and the **Netherlands**. Reliance on paper money was dangerous in the short term. Unless confidence in national prosperity was sufficiently high, popular and commercial refusal to accept paper substitutes at face value was commonplace, and their depreciation could fuel serious inflation.

No other regime experienced a financial collapse as spectacular as that suffered in post-revolutionary **France**, where the debasement of paper *assignats* triggered hyperinflation and complete collapse of the currency. France subsequently accounted for some 65 per cent of budget outlay in taxes, but this represented a severe drain on the economies and political stability of conquered territories. Dependence on tax and paper also reflected credit weakness during the 1790s, and **Napoleon**'s later mistrust of loans.

Austria paid for half of its war expenses out of taxes during the 1790s, and made up the rest by raising loans and introducing paper money. Lack of confidence in the new currency was reflected in galloping inflation, with the number of notes in circulation rising thirtyfold between 1795 and 1810. Indemnities and loss of territory triggered acute financial crisis after 1809, and the notes were replaced in February 1811 by new currency at the rate of five to one. Vienna subsequently printed paper money so fast that inflation and the cost of later campaigns left the state virtually bankrupt by 1815.

The autocratic rulers of **Russia** faced no social barriers to massive taxes, tripling vodka duty in the five years after 1806, and were able to cover most war expenditure with taxation until 1812, after which the government paid for its wars by printing more and more paper money. The number of roubles in circulation had multiplied sevenfold between 1790 and 1813, and paper notes had fallen to 20 per cent of their original value in the same period.

The finances of most other belligerent states suffered from military costs, reduction in trade revenues through commercial **blockade**, exploitation by French authorities or all three, but their economies were relatively tiny. **Prussia**, emerging as a major military power, and the small but wealthy Netherlands were run on annual government expenditure of about £5–7 million per annum, little more than an eighth that of France in 1813.

Great Britain's wartime financial position was unique. Its costs, dominated by expenditure on the massive **Royal Navy** but hardly affected by **subsidies** to allies, were running at about £200 million per annum by the later war years, but Britain ended the period far richer than it had been in 1792, when it was easily the wealthiest nation on earth. The keys to Britain's success were a well-developed credit system, a steady increase in its already massive share of world trade, a manufacturing boom uninterrupted by war and the astute financial management of prime minister **Pitt** in the 1790s.

During the first five years of war, Pitt relied on loans to make up shortfalls in revenues from import duties and assessed property taxes, both of which were rising fast. Recognition that the war was likely to last a long time, and the **bank crisis** of 1797 (which triggered a remarkably smooth transition to predominantly paper money), convinced Pitt to seek alternative sources of funds, and he had introduced the novelties of public subscription loans and **income tax** by 1799. Though both were successful, they provided less than 10 per cent of the government's needs, and with property tax revenues remaining stable through the early nineteenth century (probably a sign of increased evasion), an ongoing boom in trade revenues was the basis of Britain's financial good health in 1815.

War of 1812

Name commonly used in Britain, Canada and the US to describe the **Anglo-American War** of 1812–15.

Warfare *See* **Amphibious Warfare; Artillery (Land); Artillery (Naval); Cavalry; Colonial Warfare; Engineers; Grand Tactics; Infantry Tactics; Naval Warfare; Siege Warfare; Strategy**

Warsaw, Grand Duchy of

The puppet state created by **Napoleon** from the Prussian sector of partitioned Poland in July 1807, and governed as a virtual French satellite until occupied by Russian forces in early 1813. *See also* **Poland**.

Warsaw, Occupation of (1806)

On 11 November 1806, shortly after concluding the **Jena–Auerstädt campaign**, **Napoleon** ordered his army from **Prussia** into the part of **Poland** under Prussian administration (*see* **Map 17**). The move aimed to forestall the meeting of some 56,000 Russian troops west of the Vistula with 15,000 Prussians around the Polish city of Thorn, and to put French forces in position for a spring campaign in 1807. It also offered the chance to pose as liberator of a partitioned former nation that had displayed solid support for French causes since the 1790s.

Under the temporary command of **Murat**, whose **cavalry** formed the advance guard, four French corps took part in the march. They met no military resistance, but thousands of troops fell sick crossing barren plains along primitive roads made treacherous by mud and ice. By the time Murat's cavalry eventually reached Warsaw on 28 November, well in advance of the main force, the Russian army had withdrawn beyond the Vistula, and General Lestoq's Prussians abandoned Thorn on 3 December.

Napoleon eventually reached the Polish capital on 19 December, and stayed until 30 January. He and his officers received a very warm welcome from the city population, reflecting the (largely misplaced) hopes of national restoration entertained by many Polish nobles, and the emperor began a long association with Countess Marie **Walewska**.

Washington, Occupation of

The capital of the **United States** was captured by British forces on 25 August 1814 and occupied through the closing stages of the **Anglo-American War**. A force of 5,000 British veterans, transferred to America from the late **Peninsular War**, had landed some 65km away at Chesapeake Bay and overrun 6,500 state militia (supported by 400 **US Navy** personnel) at Bladensburg on 24 August. On entering Washington unopposed next day, British commander General Ross ordered the city's destruction, and most of its public buildings, including the Capitol and the White House, were burned.

The capture of a capital city might have ended, and would certainly have inhibited, resistance in many centralized European countries, but had very little impact on the political or military war effort of the United States, which was anyway close to reaching a peace agreement. Washington was a small city, purpose-designed as the seat of federal government, and had only housed the administration since 1800. It held no special place in the hearts and minds of citizens whose loyalties were still primarily focused on state rather than federation. Some radical opponents of the war in the pro-European northeastern states even expressed satisfaction at the demise of Washington as a symbol of federal power, and the occupation's main effect was to boost British morale.

Ross re-embarked his army on 12 September in an attempt to repeat his success further north against Baltimore, landing 25km from the city but meeting strong resistance from entrenched Maryland militia. Repeated British attacks failed to break through the defences, and Ross was killed in action before the operation was abandoned two days later. *See* **Map 27**.

Waterloo, Battle of

The climactic engagement of the **Hundred Days** campaign in 1815, and the last major battle of the Napoleonic Wars, fought on 18 June around the ridge of Mont-St-Jean, on the road to Brussels just south of Waterloo.

One of the two allied armies facing **Napoleon's** attack north across the Sambre, **Blücher's** four Prussian corps had been defeated at **Ligny** on 16 June and begun retreating on Liège. The other allied force, **Wellington's** composite British, Belgian, Dutch and German army, had fought an inconclusive battle against **Ney's** French right wing at **Quatre Bras** on the same day, and had withdrawn north up the road to Brussels next morning. Napoleon followed, determined to strike before the Prussians recovered to rejoin the fight, but was too slow to prevent Wellington's force taking good positions atop a ridge at Mont-St-Jean by nightfall. French forces halted just short of the position, and both sides passed the night in pouring rain.

Napoleon was certain of victory next day, and his main concern was that Wellington might escape before dawn. Presuming a Prussian retreat, he paid little attention to overnight reports from right-wing commander **Grouchy**, whose 33,000 troops were following the Prussians north towards their presumed destination of Wavre. Grouchy could have been ordered north-west to block any Prussian move towards Mont-St-Jean, but Napoleon sent him no instructions that night.

By dawn on 18 June it had stopped raining, though the ground at Mont-St-Jean remained soaking. The two sides occupied ridges some 1,500m apart, north and south of a shallow valley, each straddling the road to Brussels and each formed into a line some 5km across.

The French army, a total of almost 72,000 troops (including 15,750 **cavalry**) and 246 guns, was deployed to give an impression of strength, displaying virtually every available man to allied eyes. **Drouet's** corps stood east of the road, and **Reille's** formed the front line to the west, its positions bordered by the road south to Nivelles. Most of the French **cavalry** was drawn up just behind them, but two divisions of cavalry and **Mouton's** 10,000 troops occupied a central position a little further back. The **Imperial Guard**, under **Drouot**, formed the reserve to the rear.

Wellington's dispositions were considerably more complex, and heavily biased to his right because Prussian reinforcements were expected on the left. His line generally ran just north of the lateral road following the Mont-St-Jean crest, with the majority of troops hidden from French view (and **artillery** fire) on the reverse slopes of the crest. Most of **Hill's** corps was positioned west of the Nivelles road, and a division (**Chassé**) was protecting the village of Braine l'Alleud a couple of kilometres further west. On Hill's left, the Prince of **Orange** had crammed his corps between the two converging main roads, and **Picton's** reserve corps held the area just east of the Brussels road. A detached division and two cavalry brigades held the far left of the allied line, and **Paget's** heavy cavalry was behind the centre right.

In front of the line to the right, troops from **Nassau** and **Hanover** occupied the woods and château of Hougoumont, and detachments to its left were holding La Haie Sainte farm just west of the Brussels road. A sandpit on the other side of the highway, an exposed position a little further left, and the farms of Papelotte, Frischermont and La Haie completed the forward defences. In total, Wellington deployed just over 67,500 men (including 12,400 cavalry), supported by 156 guns.

Both sides could have been stronger: Wellington made no effort to recall 17,000 troops sent as a precaution against a (now improbable) French attack from the west; and Napoleon's eventual reply to Grouchy next morning merely instructed him to occupy Wavre. Napoleon also rejected suggestions from chief of staff **Soult** for precautions against Prussian intervention, and accepted Drouot's argument that the ground was too wet for artillery manoeuvres, postponing any major attack until one in the afternoon.

The latter decision was fatal, because **Bülow's** Prussian corps (30,000 men) had been marching west from Wavre since dawn, followed by a second corps under Pirch. Having insisted on marching to Wellington's aid despite opposition from chief of staff **Gneisenau**, who remained around Wavre with the other two Prussian corps (**Zeiten** and **Thielmann**), Blücher himself set out at about eleven to join forward units.

Napoleon's battle plan, issued at about the same time, envisaged a straightforward series of frontal attacks against the allied line, led by Drouet's corps on the French right, with Reille in support and the increasingly unreliable Ney in operational command. Preceded by no more than token diversionary operations, it aimed directly at the Mont-St-Jean position, and was probably intended to cut Wellington's line of retreat up the Brussels road as quickly as possible. Ignoring the need to deal thoroughly with allied forward outposts, the plan suffered disruptions from the start.

Jérôme **Bonaparte's** division of Reille's corps opened the first diversionary attack against the Hougoumont position at eleven thirty. After an hour of costly and unsuccessful infantry assaults on the château and surrounding buildings, Jérôme called up help from a second division (**Foy**) rather than simply deploying artillery, turning a small-scale diversion into a major action but attracting few allied reserves.

Napoleon's main assault against the centre left of the allied line opened at one o'clock with a bombardment by a massed battery of 84 guns, but it had little effect on troops hidden from view. As Drouet's corps was about to advance in its wake, the first reports reached Napoleon of Bülow's 30,000 men approaching from the east. Undaunted, he sent a (highly optimistic) summons to Grouchy and ordered Mouton to deploy east against Bülow, before authorizing Drouet's attack.

Drouet's advance was not preceded by the customary cavalry attack, and was conducted in battalion-wide columns, making formation of **infantry squares** difficult and offering a big artillery target. It also lacked reserve support, because Mouton had elected to wait for Bülow more than 2km south of the main battlefront. Though it took several allied outposts, it was halted by the detachment defending La Haie Sainte, and all three attacking divisions suffered serious casualties scrambling up the slope. Picton's 4,000 reserves arrived to bolster the allied line, and he was killed leading counter-attacks that held the French, before Paget's heavy cavalry charged into Drouet's infantry formations, inflicting heavy casualties and taking 3,000 prisoners in driving the rest back down the slope. British troopers set off in reckless pursuit, reaching the massed cannon across the valley, where they lost 2,500 casualties to a well-timed counter-attack by fresh French cavalry.

The ongoing struggle for Hougoumont apart, the battle abated for a time after three, enabling Wellington to reinforce La Haie Sainte, bring up more reserves and retake Papelotte at the eastern end of the line. At the same time Napoleon received news that Grouchy was out of support range, but spurned any opportunity to abandon the battle and ordered Ney into an all-out assault on La Haie Sainte. Ney's first attack was repulsed, but he mistook routine withdrawals of casualties and empty wagons for a general allied retreat, and ordered up a heavy cavalry brigade for a pursuit charge. Excited cavalry commanders rushed to join the charge, and by four o'clock 5,000 horsemen, including **Lefebvre-Desnouëttes's** light cavalry, were moving to attack the allied line west of La Haie Sainte.

Ney's cavalry charge, a tactical wild card based on a misconception, went in at a gentle trot because of the soft ground. Without infantry or horse artillery support, and forced to take a route that blocked French artillery, it could make little impact on allied infantry squares. Wellington ordered his gunners to abandon their weapons intact, taking shelter inside the squares at the last possible moment, and attackers could not spike the unattended guns before they were forced back down the slope by British cavalry. A renewed French charge was met by British artillery, its gunners back at their posts, and collapsed before it reached the squares on the crest.

As Ney's charge was opening, Bülow's corps was emerging from Paris Wood in the east to face an immediate attack from Mouton's 10,000 men. Outnumbered French troops were soon forced back on Plancenoit, and the village fell to a Prussian attack shortly after five. Napoleon sent a **Young Guard** division to support Mouton, who was ordered to link up with the right wing of Drouet's corps. He also ordered part of the reserve cavalry to Ney's assistance, but impetuous commanders again overreacted and the whole of the Guard cavalry rode forward to join a second series of ill-supported charges against the allied squares.

Allied infantry suffered heavy losses as Ney led eight charges, supported by only a single battery of horse artillery, and Wellington was forced to commit all his reserves, but his line had not broken when exhaustion forced French cavalry to retire. Some 6,000 French infantry had been available throughout the action but were ignored by

Ney until after the cavalry's failure. Belatedly ordered forward against the crest at about six, they suffered 2,500 casualties during a brief advance.

Napoleon had arrived at the sector, and supervised a coordinated operation by part of **Donzelot's** division, with cavalry and artillery support, that drove defenders out of La Haie Sainte and the sandpit just to its east. Ney was able to site artillery within 300m of the allied line and wreak havoc with Wellington's central formations, which began to waver. Perhaps influenced by Ney's earlier mistakes, Napoleon refused to commit reserves for another attempt on the crest, sending most of the Guard to reinforce Mouton in the east, where it quickly stabilized the French right behind the village of Plancenoit.

Meanwhile Ney's artillery decimated allied brigades beyond La Haie Sainte, but Wellington was able to hold his ground by transferring troops from the allied right wing. At the same time the approach of Zeiten's Prussian corps – the third to leave Wavre, at two that afternoon – was clearly visible to the north-east, moving to link Wellington's left and Bülow's right. Knowing time was short, Napoleon rushed nine battalions of the Guard to the centre as soon as possible, and ordered them forward at seven o'clock. Attempts to rally disorganized infantry by pretending that the approaching troops were Grouchy's backfired as the truth became clear, and the Guard attacked alone.

Wellington had completed the transfer of infantry and cavalry from the west of the line to stiffen the threatened sector, and had learned the time and probable direction of the French attack from a deserter. The Guard advanced in a single column up the Brussels road, detaching two battalions towards Hougoumont (still in allied hands) before veering left to attack the line west of the highway. The French column then split in two, though whether by design or because rear columns moved up too quickly remains unclear.

On the right, French grenadiers came up against élite British Guards occupying the crest just west of La Haie Sainte, and drove up to within 60m of the allied line before defenders rose up from hidden positions behind a low bank and poured fire into the advancing infantry. Napoleon's élite veterans could only fall back, and the French column of **chasseurs** on the left was similarly surprised by a British brigade hidden in a cornfield. When a single British regiment moved against its left flank, the entire column wheeled to face the threat, at which point Wellington launched all available infantry into a counter-attack. Costly for both sides, the brief struggle that followed ended with a disorderly French withdrawal.

As the sight of the hitherto invincible **Old Guard** in flight was absorbed by stunned French forces, and Prussian attacks at the east of the line came close to a breakthrough, Wellington ordered his 40,000 men forward from the top of the crest. Napoleon's army collapsed under the weight of the charge, most men fleeing in unstoppable panic towards Genappes. Guard units in the centre achieved an orderly fighting withdrawal over the next two hours, and Young Guard troops holding Plancenoit clung to their crumbling positions until nine.

Napoleon left the front at about eight to rally forces at Genappes, narrowly avoiding capture by Prussian cavalry in the process, but found chaos beyond reorganization and continued to Quatre Bras, where he hoped to find an intact reserve division. Allied pursuit was led by 4,000 relatively fresh Prussian cavalry under Gneisenau's personal command, but few of the chasing squadrons advanced beyond Genappes that night, and all contact with the French had been lost by the time Napoleon reached Quatre Bras next morning. Finding no reserves there, he travelled on to Philippeville, where he handed over reorganization duties to **Soult** and hastened to Paris.

Napoleon's army had suffered an estimated 25,000 casualties at Waterloo, and lost another 16,000 men in the immediate aftermath (half as prisoners, half as deserters), along with 220 guns. Wellington's army lost 15,000 men, and more than 7,000 of the 45,000 Prussian troops eventually involved in the battle were casualties.

Generally recognized as an epoch-making event, Waterloo has tended to dominate the modern reputations of the main protagonists. Blücher's role at Waterloo has merited straight-

forward admiration from most quarters, and his characteristic determination to aid allied forces made victory possible. Wellington has been criticized for several errors in the days leading up to the battle, and for his failure to concentrate all available troops at Mont-St-Jean, but his choice of battleground and performance during the engagement have attracted universal praise. His efficient deployment of reserves, the success of his various tactical ruses and above all the quality of his personal leadership throughout 18 June were crucial factors inspiring a hard-won victory.

Napoleon could (and later did) claim to have been let down by his senior commanders, but was ultimately responsible for their several failures. Better men could have been appointed, and the emperor could have exercised more effective control over his subordinates. Napoleon's multiple personal errors have been attributed by some historians to his decline through illness, but whatever their cause, occasional lethargy and consistent overconfidence were fundamental to his eventual defeat. *See* Battle of **Wavre; Maps 28, 29**.

Wattignies, Battle of

French victory on 15–16 October 1793 that finished off the **First Coalition's** feeble autumn offensive in **Flanders**. Divided and desultory, the allied advance had received warning of the **French Army's** new-found vigour at **Hondschoote** on 8 September, when **York's** wing was forced back from **Dunkirk**. French war minister **Carnot**, who had planned the victory, then gathered troops east of the frontier for a strike against **Saxe-Coburg's** static Austrian army.

Saxe-Coburg had deployed 20,000 men to besiege Mauberge, which was under heavy bombardment and down to half rations by mid-October, and another 100,000 allied troops were spread out either side of the Sambre. **Jourdan**, the latest general to risk leading the French Army of the North, concentrated about 40,000 ill-equipped **fédérés** around Guise for the relief of Mauberge, and advanced in five columns from 13 October. Coburg responded by moving most of his forces south-east of Mauberge to cover all possible approaches, positioning **Clairfait's** 19,000 troops on heights around Wattignies, about 10km from the town.

After skirmishes with allied outposts on 14 October, Jourdan's columns attacked Coburg's line the following morning. The French left and centre were thrown back to their starting positions with several thousand losses, but Jourdan's right had established good positions overlooking Wattignies by nightfall. Jourdan transferred 7,000 troops from his left wing to his right, and attacked Wattignies with 22,000 troops on the morning of 16 October. The attack overwhelmed Austrian positions and persuaded Coburg to raise the **siege** that night, having suffered perhaps 5,000 casualties. French forces suffered an estimated 7,000 casualties, and were unable to pursue Coburg's hasty retreat into Belgium.

Wavre, Battle of

Engagement between **Grouchy's** right wing of the French army in Belgium and the rearguard of **Blücher's** Prussian army, fought on 18 June 1815 around the Belgian town of Wavre, about 15km to the west of the simultaneous battle taking place at **Waterloo**. Grouchy had been detailed to pursue Blücher's retreating army north-east after its defeat at **Ligny** while **Napoleon** concentrated for an attack on **Wellington's** second allied army.

Grouchy's pursuit did not begin until midday on 17 June, and his 33,000-strong force (supported by 80 guns) had lost contact with the bulk of its quarry by nightfall. Acting on what reconnaissance he had, Grouchy ordered **Vandamme** and **Gérard** to follow the Prussians north, guessing that they were heading for Brussels via Wavre. The Prussian army had been at Wavre, but Blücher had decided against any further retreat, and instead began moving west towards Wellington's positions at Mont-St-Jean from dawn the next day, a possibility that neither Grouchy nor Napoleon took seriously. Ordered merely to keep up the pursuit by an overconfident Napoleon, Grouchy heard the opening salvos from Waterloo at eleven thirty on the morning of 18 June, but ignored them to continue his sluggish advance on Wavre.

Most of Blücher's army was already well on its way to the Waterloo battle by the time Grouchy's corps attacked Prussian positions on the River Dyle between Limale and Wavre that afternoon.

The single Prussian corps defending the positions, 17,000 men and 46 guns under **Thielmann**, held off Grouchy's straightforward frontal attacks, with particularly severe fighting taking place around the bridge at Limale. Grouchy eventually received a call for help from Napoleon at five, far too late to move that day, and he held his positions overnight. Renewed French attacks had just got under way next morning when news arrived of Napoleon's defeat at Waterloo, and Grouchy began an exemplary withdrawal that brought 25,000 troops safely back across the French border to Philippeville by 21 June. Both sides lost an estimated 2,500 men at Wavre. *See* **Hundred Days Campaign; Map 28**.

Weissenburg, Battle of

Ultimately fruitless allied victory on the **Rhine** front against French forces defending northern approaches to Alsace in October 1793. After his belated capture of **Mainz** in late July, allied C-in-C **Brunswick** waited until mid-August before advancing his 100,000 troops south against the French Army of the Rhine. Driven from forward positions at Bliescastel on to a ragged line of outposts between the Vosges Mountains and the river, Rhine Army commander Carlen's 25,000 troops slowed pursuit by repeated counterattacks, but Brunswick was ready to attack by early October. Austrian forces under **Würmser** overran the weaker left of the French position at Weissenburg on 14 October, and **Hohenlohe's** Prussians moved on Bitche, their combined attacks forcing Carlen to retreat on Strasbourg. Strasbourg was in turmoil, and might easily have fallen to a quick attack, but allied disputes over Austrian designs on the city encouraged Brunswick to halt for **sieges** of Fort Vauban, which capitulated on 14 November, and Bitche, which held out until relieved by French counter-attacks. *See* Battle of the **Geisberg; Map 3**.

Wellesley, Arthur

The name used by **Wellington** between 1798 and his ennoblement. Christened Arthur Wesley, he was a colonel on Indian service when his brother became Marquis of **Wellesley** in 1797, and himself used the elongated form after May 1798. Knighted in 1805, while still in India, he styled himself Sir Arthur Wellesley until autumn

1809, when he was created Viscount Wellington in honour of his victory at **Talavera**.

Wellesley, Richard Colley, Marquis of (1760–1842)

The Irish-born Wellesley, older brother of the Duke of **Wellington**, succeeded his father as Earl of Mornington (an Irish title) in 1781 and entered parliament in London three years later. Raised to the British peerage in 1797, and soon afterwards appointed governor-general of **India**, he was very much considered his family's rising star. He ruled India with conspicuous success until 1805, making ready use of aggressive diplomacy and military coercion to defeat **Tipu Sahib**'s Mysore army, disarm sporadic French attempts at disruption and effectively cement British control of the subcontinent. By the time he was recalled in 1805, he had doubled the territories and revenues of the British East India Company (which administered the civilian **colonial** economy). He returned to Britain with a reputation for arrogance and self-aggrandizement, and never fulfilled his anticipated role at the heart of British politics, though he was foreign minister under **Perceval** from 1809 to 1812, and gave some support to his brother's then controversial **Peninsular** campaign. Increasingly in his brother's shadow, he played little active role in central politics during the **Liverpool** years, but served as Lord Lieutenant of Ireland from 1821 to 1828.

Wellington, Arthur, Duke of (1769–1852)

Easily the most successful commander to lead troops against French forces during the Revolutionary or Napoleonic Wars, Wellington was born Arthur Wesley, fourth son of the relatively impoverished Anglo-Irish Earl of Mornington. He attended schools in Britain, the Austrian Netherlands and France before joining the **British Army** as a lieutenant in 1787, and served with a number of regiments before reaching the rank of captain in 1792. Meanwhile he gained political experience as a member of the Dublin parliament (1790–5) and aide to successive Lords-Lieutenant of Ireland.

Lent money by his older brother to buy a regimental colonelcy in 1793, Wesley commanded his unit in action during the latter stages of

York's campaign in **Flanders**, and saw combat for the first time at **Boxtel** in late 1794. Impressed by the ineptitude of British operations in Flanders, he studied military theory in some depth before his regiment was sent to **India** in 1797. At this stage his career was overshadowed by the successes of his brother Richard, who became Marquis of **Wellesley** that year (prompting Arthur to style his name Wellesley from May 1798), and viceroy of India soon afterwards. Given opportunities to shine by Richard, he soon established himself as one of the most efficient British officers on the subcontinent.

Wellesley led a largely native force during the **Seringapatam campaign** of 1799, when his organizational and staff work earned considerable praise, and subsequently proved a firm, incorruptible and occasionally obstinate governor of the region. Though illness prevented him from joining Indian forces sent to the **Middle East** during 1801, he saw plenty of action inside southern India over the next five years. Promoted major-general in 1802, he presided over the final subjugation of the Mahrattas in 1803, and learned much about the logistical and tactical requirements of warfare in difficult terrain.

By the time Wellesley followed his brother back to Britain in 1805, he was a highly experienced field commander, but found that **colonial** expertise was no substitute for seniority when it came to selection for European postings. Given charge of a home defence brigade guarding against French invasion of southern **England**, he found the leisure to marry Katherine Pakenham in 1805, a union that remained polite rather than passionate, and to become a British member of parliament from 1806.

Helped by his brother's prestige, Wellesley adapted quickly and successfully to London political life. He was appointed Secretary for Ireland with the **Portland** government in 1807, and his military career took a more interesting turn that summer, when he led a division during the raid on **Copenhagen**. A minor victory at **Roskilde** in late August earned him some renown at home, and his next appointment brought promotion to lieutenant-general in field command of the British expedition to **Portugal** of summer 1808.

Initial successes at **Rolica** and **Vimeiro** won him considerable fame, and demonstrated the defensive principles upon which many of his subsequent victories were founded, but were soured when General **Dalrymple** arrived to take overall command and negotiated the lenient **Cintra** convention with French general **Junot**. Recalled to face a court of enquiry into Cintra, which exonerated him, Wellesley returned to Portugal in independent command of British forces from April 1809.

Applying methods that would serve him well over the next five years, he immediately set in motion the training of **Portuguese** forces to augment his small army, and undertook a thorough overhaul of his own troops' logistic and field organization. At the same time, he conceived and prepared a precise plan to drive occupying French forces from the north of the country.

A brilliant victory over **Soult's** army at **Oporto** in May cleared Portugal of French troops, and his subsequent foray into **Spain** was crowned by a defensive victory at **Talavera** in July. Though the latter success had been forced on him by the ineptitude of his **Spanish Army** allies, and the approach of powerful French reinforcements compelled him to withdraw into Portugal for the winter, the new Lord Wellington ended 1809 as Britain's foremost field soldier.

British involvement in the **Peninsular War** remained controversial, and European opinion expected French countermeasures to drive Wellington's army from Lisbon during 1810. Displaying a characteristically independent and unflinching regard for the wider strategic implications of his actions, Wellington adopted a policy of tactical retreat in defence of Portugal, drawing **Masséna's** invading army on to pre-prepared and virtually impregnable fortifications around Lisbon. The campaign that ended with abject French retreat from the **Torres Vedras** lines was one of Wellington's finest achievements, immunizing Portugal from future conquest and providing a secure springboard for the invasion of Spain in 1811.

During the next three years Wellington was the scourge of French generals in Spain, combining his political, administrative and military skills to dominate the Peninsular theatre. He quickly learned to plan for the inefficiency of his Spanish allies, and relied more heavily on the Portuguese forces, trained by **Beresford**, that consistently provided about half of his army. Using his growing political influence at home to ensure the allocation of sufficient supplies, and refusing to expand his army beyond its means of support, he fashioned a highly effective fighting force, rendered virtually unbeatable by his precise, pragmatic tactical and strategic planning.

Wellington was sometimes dismissed by contemporary critics, particularly in France, as a purely defensive general, an assessment derived from his excellent use of terrain and the disciplined display of his troops during early victories, and reinforced by a similar performance during 1811. Determined not to repeat **Moore's** overextension of 1808, he resolved to capture the fortresses at **Badajoz** and **Ciudad Rodrigo**, guarding the roads from Portugal into Spain, before attempting any major offensive towards Madrid.

After being thwarted by superior French numbers, and forced back to the frontier by the end of the year, Wellington seized Ciudad Rodrigo with a surprise winter strike in early 1812 (for which was he was made an earl). Badajoz fell in the spring, and Wellington advanced into the heart of Spain, winning a major victory over **Marmont** at **Salamanca** in July and moving on to occupy Madrid in August

Though he broke his own rules by attempting an autumn siege of **Burgos** with insufficient force, and was compelled to make an arduous, inglorious retreat into Portugal by the year's end, the 1812 campaign cleared south-western Spain of French forces and confirmed Wellington's credentials as a field commander, proving his ability to fight offensive battles of manoeuvre as well as defensive battles of position. Made C-in-C of Spanish forces in October 1812, and showered with Spanish and Portuguese titles, he had also become a major European celebrity.

Though sometimes idiosyncratic, and always at ease among Britain's social élites, Wellington lacked the flamboyance associated with other great military figures of the age. Soberly dressed, often aloof and a generally stern advocate of the work ethic, he nevertheless won the respect and devotion of his officers, and was well served by subordinates such as **Graham, Hill, Craufurd** and **Pakenham**. He also earned genuine popularity with troops that were the best supplied and cared for in Europe, even if he always regarded ordinary soldiers as the 'scum of the earth', reflecting an élitist conservatism untroubled by contemporary radicalism.

After 1812, the fall in numbers and quality of French forces in Spain gave Wellington the initiative in the theatre, and he seized his opportunity in 1813, launching a meticulously planned thrust towards the Ebro that repeatedly outflanked Joseph **Bonaparte**'s forces and won a decisive victory at **Vitoria** in June. Perhaps Wellington's greatest single triumph, Vitoria brought him a dukedom and promotion to the new rank of field marshal. It also effectively ended French occupation of Spain. Though French forces were reorganized under **Soult**, and fought a dogged defensive campaign either side of the Pyrenean frontier, Wellington's victories at **Sorauren**, the **Bidassoa**, the **Nivelle** and the **Nive** had carried the fight into south-western France by early 1814.

By the time of **Napoleon**'s first **abdication** in April, Soult's dwindling army had been driven back to **Toulouse** and Wellington had made himself master of south-western France, again demonstrating his political skills by preventing Spanish reprisals and supervising prompt payment for all requisitioned supplies. With the outbreak of peace, he returned to Britain for the first time since 1809, and enjoyed a few weeks as the toast of London before accompanying **Castlereagh** to the Congress of **Vienna**, where he remained as one of the chief delegates until Napoleon's escape from **Elba** in spring 1815.

Appointed to command the multinational force that made up half of allied strength in Flanders during the **Hundred Days** campaign, he misread Napoleon's intentions when the French advance got under way in June. Deploying to protect routes to the coast, his forces lost contact with the Prussian army under **Blücher**, allowing Napoleon to get between the two allies. Fortunate that **Ney** was slow to attack the vital junction at **Quatre Bras**, Wellington reacted quickly once the truth became clear, and his retreat on **Waterloo** set up a first and last direct confrontation with Napoleon on 18 June. Though distinguished by his efficient exercise of direct command, the battle was not one of Wellington's most imaginative performances, and his victory owed much to the enterprise of Blücher and the errors of Napoleon.

After serving as military governor of occupied Paris, and at the later Vienna sessions, Wellington embarked on a long political career, beginning with his appointment as ordnance minister with the **Liverpool** government in 1818. He remained with the administration until 1827, leading a number of important diplomatic missions before resigning over the **Canning** government's entanglement in Greek affairs. Commander-in-chief of the army from 1827 until his death, he was prime minister from early 1828 until November 1830, and briefly in 1834, but his entrenched opposition to social reform and refusal to intervene in European disputes cost him political and popular esteem.

By 1841, when he returned to the cabinet as minister without portfolio, his popularity had been fully restored, but he remained a staunch opponent of socio-political reform up to and beyond his retirement from public life in 1846, and always inspired awed respect rather than the affection reserved for naval hero Horatio **Nelson**'s more fleeting talents.

West Indies, Campaigns in the

The inhabited islands of the Caribbean were an important staging post for trade with the Americas, a source of enormous contemporary wealth and the main forum for contemporary **colonial warfare**. Their ownership had been spread among the maritime empires of western Europe since the sixteenth century, and the four most interested parties were at war from early 1793, when **Great Britain**, **Spain** and the independent **Netherlands** entered the **First Coalition** against **France**.

British Caribbean authorities began preparing offensive operations from Barbados as soon as the news reached them during March, and operations in the theatre opened on 15 April with a minor attack on the French garrison of Tobago. General Grey's force from Britain reached the Caribbean in January 1794, escorted by a **Royal Navy** fleet under **Jervis** and charged with seizing as many French colonies as possible. It attacked Martinique from 20 March, and secured the island's surrender three days later, before moving on to take **St Lucia**, but its capture of **Guadeloupe** in April was reversed by a relief force from France in October.

British naval and troop detachments established a foothold at **Santo Domingo** (the French-controlled eastern half of Hispaniola) in June 1794, opening a long and turbulent struggle for control of the colony involving British, French and Spanish troops, as well as native forces led by local leader Toussaint **L'Ouverture**.

Expansion of French military resources allowed the dispatch of 3,000 extra troops to the Caribbean in November 1794, and they joined French forces on Guadeloupe in January 1795. Using agents to spread word of French anti-slavery policy, and supplying arms to prospective insurgents, Guadeloupe commander Hughes incited rebellion against British authorities all along the Windward chain to the south. Beginning in March, French-supported uprisings drove the British out of St Vincent, Grenada and St Lucia, but the offensive ended with the defeat of a small force sent by Hughes to Martinique, which was driven off by **Dalhousie**'s forces in December. A separate rising by the Maroon hill people of British Jamaica ended at the same time with their mass deportation to Nova Scotia (though some survivors were ultimately relocated to Sierra Leone).

Dutch colonies in the West Indies were available for British conquest after France conquered the Netherlands in 1795, and an expedition took the wealthy settlements at Demerara, Essequibo and Berbice in April 1796, but the major British operation in the theatre that spring was the recapture of the Windwards by a force under **Abercromby** that took St Lucia, St Vincent and Grenada by mid-June. More reinforcements from France reached Santo Domingo in May, as anarchy deepened with Spanish cession of the island's eastern side to France at **Basle**.

Spain declared war on Britain in October 1796, and a London government inevitably out of touch with local realities ordered Abercromby into a new offensive against Spanish colonies in

1797. Though more than half his original 9,000 men had died from yellow fever, Abercromby captured **Trinidad** in February, but was unable to overcome stronger defences at Puerto Rico in June.

Apart from the festering struggle for Santo Domingo, and permanent **naval** campaigns against targets of opportunity, the theatre remained relatively quiet after 1797. Although 3,000 Spanish troops launched unsuccessful attacks on British Honduras in August 1798, the moribund state of most European forces in the Caribbean was emphasized by that year's British and French withdrawal from Santo Domingo. Interference with its trade meanwhile brought the **United States** into a local war with France (1798–1800). It amounted to no more than a few naval skirmishes and was ultimately settled by diplomacy, but gave the infant **US Navy** its first taste of combat success (*see* USS *Constellation*).

Between 1799 and 1802, British forces completed the straightforward capture of Surinam (1799), Curaçao (1800), the Virgin Islands, St Bartholomew, St Martin and St Eustatius (all in 1801), but all the West Indian colonies except Trinidad were returned to their previous owners under the terms of the Anglo-French **Amiens** treaty. **Napoleon** used the brief period of peace to send a powerful force against the Santo Domingo rebels in 1802, but its eventual collapse to disease and the island's declaration of independence (as Haiti) in 1804 marked the effective end of French strategic interest in the West Indies.

The process of British accumulation started again with the resumption of war against France in 1803, and met little concerted opposition over the next decade. St Lucia and Tobago were retaken in June, Demerara and Barbice in September, and Surinam in May 1804. Though Curaçao held out against attack that year, it fell on 1 January 1807, and British forces subsequently picked off small island colonies almost at will, though they were denied serious reinforcements by the extent of government commitments elsewhere.

French and allied operations in the theatre after 1803 were largely restricted to attacks on British trade shipping. Though **Villeneuve**'s massive Combined Fleet caused alarm on reaching Martinique in summer 1805, it departed at once to a disaster at **Trafalgar** that reduced the danger of any major naval attack on the West Indies. Two squadrons of **French Navy** commerce raiders did reach the theatre in 1806, but the biggest British naval victory in the theatre at Santo Domingo Bay ensured that only two battleships got home (one led by Jérôme **Bonaparte**).

Otherwise the main threats to British peace in the region until 1815 were **privateers**, many of them operating out of Haiti, and occasional raids by the **US Navy**'s expertly handled warships during the **Anglo-American War**. There was no question of Britain repeating the generosity of Amiens after Napoleon's final defeat, and it retained all its French and Spanish Caribbean conquests at the postwar Congress of **Vienna**. *See* **Map 20**.

Westphalia

The German Duchy of Westphalia had achieved independence from **Saxony** in the twelfth century, and was ruled by archbishops of Cologne until 1803, when it was partitioned between **Prussia** and **Hesse-Darmstadt** as part of the **Holy Roman Empire**'s drastic reorganization (*see* **Map 1**). The Kingdom of Westphalia was a Napoleonic creation, bearing little territorial resemblance to its predecessor.

Proclaimed under the kingship of Jérôme **Bonaparte** in July 1807, as part of the **Tilsit** treaty, the new Westphalia comprised territories that had been under French military control since late 1806. Essentially a buffer state protecting France from Prussia, it included **Hesse-Cassel**, **Brunswick**, parts of Saxony, some Prussian territories, southern **Hanover** and a host of minor north German independencies, as well as the key Elbe fortress at **Magdeburg**. The kingdom's capital was at Cassel, and almost 2 million people inhabited its eight provinces.

Westphalia was formally established as a member of the Confederation of the **Rhine** from December 1807, when Jérôme and a committee of regional notables embarked on prolonged consultations over a new constitution with Arch-Chancellor **Cambacérès** and French foreign minister **Champagny**. They delayed the imposi-

tion of imperial obligations and the **Code Napoléon**, and helped establish the regime's enduring, if shallow, popularity. Ably assisted by Siméon and other German bureaucrats, Jérôme had abolished feudal law and medieval privilege from Westphalia by mid-1808, governing through his appointed council most of the time. He summoned a parliament (*Ständeversammlung*) to agree taxes in 1808 (twice) and 1810, but abandoned representative government when it forced changes to his tax programme.

Jérôme needed taxes. Napoleon had saddled Westphalia with a standing debt approaching 50 million francs, took another 7 million a year for himself and charged about 10 million a year for the upkeep of French troops. With only 34 million per year in revenue (1807), and unable to raise loans, Jérôme was forced to sell off state properties to find cash. Denied significant trade expansion by the **Continental System** and its landlocked status, and facing an across-the-board decline in industry relative to agriculture, the kingdom lurched deeper into debt every year.

Jérôme fulfilled all his economic and military obligations to France, keeping the **Westphalian Army** up to strength despite serious losses, and displaying a recognition of his subordinate role that probably saved him from deposition by Napoleon. Anti-Napoleonic elements made several attempts to depose him during the War of the **Fifth Coalition** in 1809. The Prussian-sponsored **Dörnberg** uprising was thwarted in April, an attempt to rouse former Prussian territories by the quixotic Major von **Schill** failed in May, and an invasion by the exiled Duke of **Brunswick** and his **Black Legion** was defeated by Westphalian forces in August.

Enlarged from January 1810 by the addition of more Hanoverian territory (much of which was annexed by France later that year), Westphalia effectively ceased to exist when allied forces drove Jérôme from Cassel in October 1813, though the king defended his capital until the last moment and departed only to save Napoleon from embarrassment. Its dissolution was confirmed by the Congress of **Vienna**, which rejected Hesse-Cassel's claims to the territories and authorized their absorption by Prussia. *See* **Map 21**.

Westphalian Forces

Recruited by **conscription** from 1807, with the addition of two regiments reconstituted from the forces of **Hesse-Cassel** and various small units drawn from other German states, the army of **Westphalia** was a component of French imperial forces and reached a maximum strength of some 20,000 men. Among the best of the forces recruited from the French imperial satellite territories, they suffered an estimated 11,000 casualties during the **Peninsular War**, and fought against the **Fifth Coalition** of 1809, when they operated in **Saxony** and against invading forces based around the Brunswickian **Black Legion**. They formed a corps with the French **Grande Armée** during the 1812 **Russian campaign**, led by Jérôme **Bonaparte** until his replacement in July, but only some 50 infantry and 60 **cavalry** were still under arms by the time they returned. Elite Westphalian forces comprised four Guard infantry and two Guard cavalry regiments. A Guard regiment of **hussars** was recruited from French veterans in 1813, but otherwise Jérôme ignored the strong advice of his brother and manned élite units with native troops.

Winter, Johann William de
(1750–1812)

Born at Texel in North Holland, de Winter joined the **Dutch Navy** at 12, and was a lieutenant when complicity in the anti-Orangist rising of 1787 forced his flight to France. He served with the revolutionary **French Army** under **Dumouriez** and **Pichegru** in 1792–3, but returned to his homeland as a rear-admiral after the **Netherlands** passed under French control. A vice-admiral in command of the Dutch fleet at the Texel from 1796, he became a British **prisoner of war** after its defeat at the Battle of **Camperdown** in October, but was exchanged next year. Noted for his courtesy and physical size, de Winter served as the Batavian Republic's ambassador to Paris from 1798 until 1802, and was created a Dutch marshal by King Louis **Bonaparte** in 1806, in which capacity he supervised land defences against the British **Walcheren expedition** in 1809. The absorption of the Netherlands into the French Empire prompted his return to Paris in 1810, and he died there two years later.

Winzingerode, Ferdinand, Baron
(1770–1818)

Originally commissioned into the **Austrian Army**, Winzingerode held minor commands during the **Revolutionary Wars** before transferring to Russian service as a soldier and diplomat. Sent to Berlin and Vienna to help negotiate the **Third Coalition** against France in 1805, he was taken prisoner at the Battle of **Austerlitz** but released shortly afterwards. He fell into disfavour with Tsar **Alexander** after his release when he openly opposed the Peace of **Tilsit** with **Napoleon**, but was recalled to command for the 1812 **Russian campaign**. Winzingerode was captured again in October, but escaped to lead a corps through the campaigns in **Germany** and **France**, and was with **Blücher's** victorious army when it entered Paris on 31 March 1814.

Wittgenstein, Ludwig, Prince of
(1769–1843)

One of a cadre of Prussian nobles traditionally employed in the service of the Russian tsars, Wittgenstein commanded a division at **Austerlitz** in 1805, led Russian forces during the **Russo-Swedish War** of 1808–9, and headed a corps on the northern flank during the early stages of the 1812 campaign. Defeated at **Polotsk** in August, he subsequently commanded the defence of St Petersburg. He led an army of reinforcements into **Germany** from early 1813, and took command of Russian forces in the theatre from **Kutuzov** in March, but argued with allied commanders and was superseded by **Barclay de Tolly** in May. He fought on through the campaigns of 1813–14 in a subordinate capacity, and eventually retired a field marshal in 1828.

Wrede, Carl Philipp, Baron von
(1767–1838)

The busiest senior **Bavarian Army** commander of the period, Wrede led a brigade against the French at **Hohenlinden** in 1800, but commanded a division fighting with French forces through the campaigns of 1805–7. He held the same position during the war of the **Fifth Coalition** in 1809, when his division was part of **Lefebvre's** corps and played an important role at the decisive battle of **Wagram**, where he was wounded. Bavarian Army units formed **Gouvion**

St Cyr's corps in 1812, and Wrede led a **cavalry division** in the **Russian campaign**, rising to command the redesignated Army of the Inn during the opening phase of the campaign for **Germany**. After leading negotiations for **Bavaria's** defection to the **Sixth Coalition**, he led a combined Austro-Bavarian force against the French at **Hanau** in October 1813, and fought through the campaign for **France**. Never far from the heart of Bavarian politics, he represented his country at the Congress of **Vienna**, and eventually became President of the Bavarian High Council in 1822.

Würmser, Dagobert Sigismond (1724–97)

Born in Strasbourg, Würmser began his military career with the French Army in the mid-1740s before transferring his services east of the Rhine and taking a commission in the **Austrian Army**. He commanded the siege of **Mainz** in 1793, and led the Army of the Upper Rhine two years later, before his transfer from the **Rhine** to the **Italian** front in June 1796. He was placed in control of 50,000 troops for the reconquest of Lombardy, but his pedestrian competence was no match for **Napoleon**. His first invasion was abandoned after defeat at **Castiglione**, and he joined besieged forces in **Mantua** after a second defeat at **Bassano**, dying shortly after his final surrender to French forces in February 1797.

Württemberg

The largely Protestant Grand Duchy of Württemberg occupied the region between the upper Rhine and upper Danube in southern Germany, and had suffered decades of internal unrest under the Catholic Duke Charles Eugene, who died in 1793. His successor Louis Eugene (1793–5) contributed troops to the **First Coalition's** campaigns on the **Rhine** as a member of the **Holy Roman Empire**, but French invasion forced Duke Frederick Eugene (1795–7) to withdraw in autumn 1796. His Protestant son, Duke Frederick II, joined the **Second Coalition** in 1799, but signed a bilateral treaty with **Napoleon** on 20 May 1802, after the state had again been overrun and ravaged by French forces. In return for his territories west of the Rhine, Frederick received nine former imperial towns further east (collectively styled 'New Württemberg').

Frederick took the title Elector in 1803, and provided troops for Napoleon's campaign against the **Third Coalition** by a new treaty signed on 8 October 1805. Rewarded with territorial gains by the Treaties of **Brno** and **Pressburg**, he became king of a united New and Old Württemberg in January 1806, and gained more land by joining the Confederation of the **Rhine** later that year. Relations with the French Empire were cemented by the engagement of Frederick's daughter to Jérôme **Bonaparte** in 1806, and their marriage in August 1807.

Provision of troops for the 1809 campaign against the **Fifth Coalition** generated further territorial gains, but weaknesses in the state's relationship with France surfaced after the Württemberg corps (about 14,000 men) was virtually wiped out during the 1812 **Russian campaign.** Frederick had ended experiments in constitutional government on becoming king and was never a particularly popular ruler. Facing a rising tide of discontent at French military and economic demands, and against a background of growing popular and élite German nationalism, he reluctantly committed troops for Napoleon's campaign in **Germany**, but the refusal of Württemberger **cavalry** to charge Prussian troops at **Leipzig** heralded his defection from the alliance with France on 18 October.

Frederick's troops fought with the allies for the remainder of the War of the **Sixth Coalition**, and in return the Congress of **Vienna** confirmed the territorial gains made since 1803. Internal unrest continued in peacetime, but abated after Frederick's death in 1816. His son, King William I, was more liberally inclined, and granted Württemberg a parliamentary constitution in September 1819. *See* **Maps 1, 21, 30.**

Würzburg, Battle of

The second major engagement of Archduke **Charles's** counter-offensive east of the **Rhine** in autumn 1796, fought on 3 September as **Jourdan's** northern French army retreated from its defeat at **Amberg**. Exhausted, short of supplies, and with Austrian forces hard on their heels, Jourdan's 40,000 troops paused for rest at Schweinfurt on 31 August, but found communications with reinforcements around Mainz cut next day, when the Austrian left wing under General Hotze occupied Würzburg to the south-west.

Under government pressure to end his demoralizing withdrawal, but with little idea of Austrian strength or positions, Jourdan chose to launch an attack on Würzburg. **Lefebvre**'s division was left as a rearguard at Schweinfurt, and **Bernadotte**'s vanguard led 30,000 troops from the town on 2 September. Charles had already reinforced Hotze's positions in the heavily wooded approaches from Schweinfurt, and deployed **Kray**'s corps on his far right to outflank the French advance, bringing his total strength up to about 44,000 men.

The battle opened early on 3 September with a blind **artillery** duel in thick morning fog, before Charles sent Kray forward against the flank of **Championnet**'s French left, forcing Jourdan to call up urgent reinforcements from Schweinfurt after his outnumbered cavalry reserve had been brushed aside. He was already too late. While Hotze drove back weakening attacks on the city, Charles sent Wartensleben's reserve against the French left in mid-afternoon, and Jourdan's routed troops fled north-west up the only open road towards Arnstein. Having lost 2,000 men, Jourdan was able to escape ponderous Austrian pursuit to reach Frankfurt on 6 September, when he was reinforced from Mainz before returning to the Rhine. *See* **Map 3**.

Y

Yorck, Johann David Ludwig (1759–1830)

Prussian officer, born in Potsdam, who entered military service in 1772, but sought more rapid advancement with the army of the **Netherlands** from 1781. Returning to Prussia in 1787, he fought in **Poland** during 1794 and was captured at **Lübeck** with **Blücher** in 1806. Promoted to divisional command in 1807, Yorck led the Prussian corps attached to the French forces during the 1812 **Russian campaign**. His signature of the **Tauroggen** agreement, neutralizing his troops during the final days of the campaign, made him famous in **Prussia** and fuelled an upsurge of anti-French sentiment throughout Germany. He played an active role in the campaigns of 1813–14, leading a corps at **Bautzen**, **Leipzig**, **Montmirail** and **Laon**, and was made Count of Wartenburg in recognition of his wartime services.

York, Frederick Augustus, Duke of (1763–1827)

The second son of British king **George III**, Frederick Augustus became Duke of York at 21. He received military training in **Hanover**, and strengthened his German connections by marrying the eldest daughter of Prussian king Frederick William II in 1791. In command of the Anglo-German force in **Flanders** from 1793 to 1795, his irresolute performance gave rise to the 'Grand Old Duke of York' rhyme that remains embedded in British folklore, but he was promoted field marshal (in the **Hanoverian Army**) after the expedition's withdrawal. He was named overall C-in-C of the **British Army** in 1798, and concern for allied prestige led to his appointment as C-in-C of the Anglo-Russian invasion of **North Holland** in 1799. He was not given another field command after its failure, but proved a much more effective administrator, displaying a valuable enthusiasm for reform. He helped officers such as **Moore** and **Craufurd** introduce new training methods, encouraged the foundation of Sandhurst military academy and moderated the army's draconian punishment system. He resigned over a corruption scandal involving his mistress in 1809, but was exonerated and reinstated as C-in-C in 1811, retaining the post for the remainder of the war period.

Young Guard

The name given to formations of the élite French troops drawn from the best of each year's **conscription** intake. *See also* **Imperial Guard**.

Z

Zeiten, Hans Ernst Karl, Graf von (1762–1841)

Prussian cavalry officer, given divisional command for the first time during the 1813 campaign for **Germany**, whose unit fought at **Leipzig** but was virtually wiped out by **Grouchy**'s cavalry at **Vauchamps** in February 1814, less than two weeks after reaching the theatre. Promoted lieutenant-general for the **Hundred Days** campaign of 1815, he commanded the **Prussian Army**'s I Corps at **Ligny** and **Waterloo**, replacing **Blücher** as Prussian C-in-C during the subsequent occupation of France.

Zell, Battle of

Subsidiary action during the War of the **Third Coalition**, also known as the Battle of Maria Zell, fought in the foothills of the Tyrolean Alps on 6 November 1805. While **Napoleon** was pursuing Coalition armies east of **Ulm**, French corps under **Marmont** and **Davout** were ordered to prevent interference from **Austrian Army** forces to the south, in northern Italy and the Alps. Davout's column entered the Alpine foothills in late October, plundering Austrian supply depots en route, and surprised General Merveldt's 10,000 men guarding the passes around the village of Zell. Attacked across the snow before he had time to organize proper defensive positions, Merveldt lost 8,000 men before managing to reassemble his routed corps in Hungary.

Znaim, Battle of

The action that concluded the War of the **Fifth Coalition**'s Danube campaign, and an epilogue to the Battle of **Wagram** (5–6 July 1809). Austrian commander Archduke **Charles** had retreated north-west from Wagram on 7 July, and had regrouped on the River Thaya around the town of Znaim by the time the first pursuing French forces, 10,000 men under **Marmont**, reached the area on 10 July. Against odds of four to one, Marmont launched his two divisions into an attack, hoping to keep the Austrians pinned down until the main French army could arrive. Although Marmont was in trouble by early evening, his men kept the battle going until **Masséna**'s corps arrived next morning, when French attacks against **Bellegarde**'s Austrian corps were resumed. Aware that overwhelming French forces were not far away, a dispirited Charles called for a ceasefire that evening, and negotiations for an armistice were opened on **Napoleon**'s arrival a few hours later. It was signed on 12 July, and Marmont received his marshal's baton the same day. *See* **Map 12**.

Zurich, First Battle of

The first major attempt by Austrian forces fighting the **Swiss campaign** of 1799 to break through **Masséna**'s defences around Zurich. French forces had withdrawn from advanced positions in eastern Switzerland after defeat at **Frauenfeld** in late May, and were concentrated for the defence of powerful fortifications in the mountains either side of Zurich, which was largely protected from frontal attack by thick woodland. Austrian commander Archduke **Charles** opted to attack the mountain position of Zurichberg on Masséna's right, but the first assault on 4 June was repulsed after heavy fighting had cost each side some 2,500 casualties. A second attack later in the day came closer to succeeding, and was only halted by Masséna himself at the head of a reserve detachment of **grenadiers**. Charles was planning a third attempt for late on 5 June, but Masséna had decided that his relatively small army could not hold its positions indefinitely, and abandoned 150 guns in retiring across the River Limmat to new positions overlooking Zurich from the west. These new obstacles were too much for the archduke, who ceased offensive operations on 7 June, by which time the French had suffered about 1,700 casualties and the Austrians twice as many. A period of relative calm settled over the front until mid-August, punctuated by local uprisings as starvation and banditry overcame the people of eastern **Switzerland**. *See* **Map 4**.

Zurich, Second Battle of

Successful attack by **Masséna's** French forces around Zurich on 25 and 26 September 1799 that turned the year's **Swiss campaign** decisively against the allies of the **Second Coalition**. Taking advantage of the allied decision to remove Archduke **Charles** and his army to the **Rhine**, and of Russian marshal **Suvorov's** delay in reaching the front through the **St Gotthard Pass**, Masséna divided his 50,000 troops for simultaneous attacks on the two allied armies still in Switzerland, which were separated by Lake Zurich.

Masséna attacked **Korsakov's** 25,000 Russians on the allied right with 39,000 troops on 25 September. A feint against Korsakov's right wing was followed by frontal attacks that drove his left into Zurich itself after Masséna committed reserves to **Mortier's** wing during the afternoon. Only the arrival of a division from Hötze's Austrian army saved the Russian centre on the dominant height of Zurichberg, but **Oudinot's** attackers were driven off the mountain just before dark, and Korsakov fought his way out of potential encirclement next morning. Intending to withdraw to the Rhine, he decided to risk taking the shorter route through Eglisau, exposing his army to merciless flank attacks as French forces swarmed into and beyond Zurich, and losing some 8,000 men and 100 guns before escaping.

On the southern sector of the Swiss front, 11,500 French troops under **Soult** advanced across the River Linth between Lakes Zurich and Wallerstatt before dawn on 26 September. Striking at a weak point held by only two battalions, French forces drove Hötze's Austrians steadily back to Kaltenbrun, and took the town by evening. Hötze was killed early in the day and his deputy, General Petrasch, ordered a general withdrawal, losing 1,800 men during a rearguard action at Senkenn before retiring all the way to the Rhine via Wallerstatt. A detached Austrian division under Jellacic, deployed to establish contact with Suvorov, was compelled to follow. *See* **Map 4**.

CHRONOLOGY OF THE WARS
1792-1815

1792

March
2 Habsburg emperor Leopold II dies.

April
19 First performance of *La Marseillaise* at Strasbourg • **Brunswick**'s invasion army crosses French frontier
20 France declares war on **Francis II** as King of Hungary
29 Initial French offensive fails at **Valenciennes**, Flanders

May
18 Russian forces invade **Poland**

June
18 Second French offensive in **Flanders** takes Courtrai
26 Austro-Prussian alliance establishes **First Coalition**
30 French forces retreat from Courtrai

July
24 Prussia declares war on France

August
1 First Coalition forces cross the Rhine
24 Spain provisionally joins the First Coalition

September
5 'September Massacres', France
20 French victory at **Valmy**, France • First French offensive opens on the **Italian** front

22 French republic proclaimed
25 Allied forces invest **Lille**
28 French forces occupy **Nice**, Piedmont

October
6 Allies withdraw from **Lille**

November
6 French victory at **Jemappes**, Low Countries
15 French forces occupy Brussels, Low Countries

December
2 French conquest of **Belgium** completed, Low Countries

1793

January
21 French king **Louis XVI** executed, Paris

February
1 France declares war on Britain and the Netherlands

March
6 Battle of **Maastricht**, Low Countries
7 France declares war on Spain
18 Allied victory at **Neerwinden**, Low Countries
27–28 Battle of **Bingen**, Rhine

April
5 **Dumouriez** defects to Austrian lines, Low Countries
6 Committee of **Public Safety** established, France

14 Allied siege of **Mainz** established, Rhine

15 British attack on Tobago opens war in the **West Indies**

May
8 Battle of **St Amand**, Low Countries

June
2 Radical **Jacobins** take control of French **National Convention**

5 British take Port-au-Prince, West Indies

July
17 Battle of **Perpignan**, Pyrenees

22 Allies take **Mainz**, Rhine

August
28 **Toulon** surrenders to the allies • Siege of **Quesnoy** begins, Low Countries

31 Siege of **Dunkirk** begins, Low Countries

September
8 Battle of **Hondschoote**, siege of Dunkirk lifted, Low Countries

11 **Quesnoy** falls to allied forces, Low Countries

22 Battle of **Truillas**, Pyrenees

October
5 **Republican Calendar** adopted, France

8 End of royalist rebellion in **Lyon**

14 Battle of **Weissenburg**, Rhine

15–16 Battle of **Wattignies**, Low Countries

December
19 Allied and royalist forces evacuate **Toulon**

26 Battle of the **Geisberg**, Rhine

1794

January
6 **Brunswick** resigns as allied Rhine C-in-C

April
1 British take **St Lucia**, West Indies

5 Death of **Danton**, France

16 French **Saorgio** offensive opens, Italy

20 British capture **Guadeloupe**, West Indies

26 Battle of **Landrecies**, Low Countries

29 Battle of **Moescroen**, Low Countries

29–30 Battle of **Le Boulon**, Pyrenees

May
11 Battle of **Courtrai**, Low Countries

18 Battle of **Tourcoing**, Low Countries

23 Battle of **Tournai**, Low Countries

June
1 Battle of the **First of June**, North Atlantic

4 French forces concentrated on the **Sambre**, Low Countries

6 New French offensive opens in Italy

26 French victory at **Fleurus**, Low Countries

July
13 Battle of the **Vosges**, Rhine

27 Coup of **Thermidor**, France

28 **Robespierre** executed, France

August
1 Battle of **San Marcial**, Pyrenees

6 **Napoleon** arrested, Italy

10 British forces take **Corsica**, Mediterranean

20 Napoleon released

25 French invasion of the Netherlands opens

September
14 Action at **Boxtel**, Low Countries

17 Battle of **Ayvaille**, Low Countries

21 First Battle of **Dego**, Italy

October
2 Battle of the **Roer**, Low Countries

5 Battle of **Maciejowice**, Poland

6 French complete recapture of **Guadeloupe**, West Indies

9 French forces occupy Cologne, Rhine

November
5 Battle of **Praga**, Poland

7 Warsaw surrenders to Russian and Prussian forces; end of **Polish rebellion**

12 Paris **Jacobin** Club closed down

17 Anglo-American **London Naval Agreement**

18 French take **Nijmegen**, Low Countries

26 Fall of **Figueras**, Pyrenees

December
2 Duke of **York** leaves **Flanders**

1795

January
17 Prince of **Orange** renounces offices, Netherlands

20 French forces occupy Amsterdam, Netherlands

30 French cavalry captures Dutch fleet at **Texel**, Netherlands

February
21 Law of religious tolerance promulgated by French National convention government

3 French forces take **Rosas**, Pyrenees

March
12 Naval action off **Leghorn** (Livorno), Mediterranean

25 British **Flanders** expedition sails home from Bremen

April
5 Franco-Prussian peace signed at **Basle**

25 French offensive opens at the **Fluvia**, Pyrenees

June
19 French retake **St Lucia**, West Indies

23 Naval action off Ile de **Groix**, France

27 French royalists land at **Quiberon Bay**, France

July
12 Franco-Spanish peace signed at **Basle**

13 Naval action off the **Hyères Islands**, Mediterranean

21 Royalists defeated at **Quiberon**, France

September
6 French **Mannheim** offensive begins, Rhine

14 British take Dutch **Cape Colony**

15 Napoleon resigns from the army

October
5 Napoleon puts down **Vendémiaire coup**, Paris

7 British convoy destroyed by French warships off Cape **St Vincent**

27 **Directory** takes power, France

November
23 Battle of **Loano**, Italy

1796

January
1 Austro-French armistice begins on the Rhine front

February
14 British forces take Dutch **Ceylon**

March
2 Napoleon given command of French forces in Italy

9 Napoleon marries **Joséphine**

April
11 Napoleon's first offensive opens, Italy

12 Battle of **Montenotte**, Italy

14–15 Second Battle of **Dego**, Italy

16–17 Battle of **Ceva**, Italy

21 French victory at **Mondovi**, Italy

28 Piedmont makes peace with France at **Cherasco**, Italy

May
8 Action at **Codogno**, Italy

10 Battle of **Lodi**, Italy

13 French troops occupy Milan, Italy

26 British recapture **St Lucia**, West Indies

30 Action at **Borghetto**, Italy; first siege of **Mantua** opens, Italy

June
4 First Battle of **Altenkirchen**, Rhine

19 Battle of **Ukerath**, Rhine

24 **Moreau** crosses the Rhine at **Kehl**

28 Battle of the **Kinzig**, Rhine • Milan citadel surrenders to French forces, Italy

July
5 Battle of **Rastatt**, Rhine

9 Battle of **Ettlingen**, Rhine

14 Battle of **Haslach**, Rhine

31 French abandon siege of Mantua, Italy

August
3–5 Battles of **Lonato** and **Castiglione**, Italy

7 Battle of **Forcheim**, Rhine

11 Battle of **Neresheim**, Rhine

17 Dutch fleet surrenders to British at Cape Colony

19 Franco-Spanish Treaty of **San Ideltonso**
24 Battle of **Friedberg**, Rhine • Battle of **Amberg**, Rhine • Siege of **Mantua** restored

September
3 Battle of **Würzburg**, Rhine
4 Battle of **Roveredo**, Italy
8 Battle of **Bassano**, Italy

October
2 Battle of **Biberach**, Rhine
8 Spain declares war on Britain
19 Battle of **Emmendlingen**, Rhine
23 Battle of **Schliengen**, Rhine
26 Last of Moreau's army recrosses the Rhine

November
2 French reoccupy **Corsica**, Mediterranean
12 Battle of **Caldiero**, Italy
15–17 Battle of **Arcola**, Italy
17 Tsarina **Catherine II** ('the Great') dies

December
22 French fleet arrives off **Bantry Bay**, Ireland

1797

January
3 Last French ships leave **Bantry Bay**, Ireland
13 French ship-of-the-line *Droits de l'Homme* sunk by British frigates
14–15 Battle of **Rivoli**, Italy

February
2 Fall of **Mantua**, Italy
14 Battle of Cape **St Vincent**, Atlantic
17 British capture **Trinidad**, West Indies
19 Peace between France and the **Papal States**
22 French troops land in **Pembrokeshire**, Wales
24 French troops surrender in **Pembrokeshire**, Wales
25–27 British **bank crisis**

March
10 French forces invade Austrian **Frioul** from Italy
17 Battle of **Tarvis**, Frioul

April
16 **Spithead** naval mutiny begins, Britain

17 Preliminary Austro-French peace signed at Leoben
18 Second Battle of **Altenkirchen**, Rhine
20 Battle of **Diersheim**, Rhine

May
12 **Nore** mutiny begins, Britain
15 End of **Spithead** mutiny, Britain

June
15 End of **Nore** mutiny, Britain
28 French forces occupy **Ionian Islands**, Mediterranean

July
9 **Cisalpine Republic** established, Italy
24–5 Failed British attack on **Tenerife**

September
3–4 **Fructidor coup**, Paris
27 Russo-Turkish forces arrive off **Ionian Islands**, Mediterranean

October
11 Naval battle of **Camperdown**, North Sea
17 Austro-French **Campo Formio** treaty signed, Italy

1798

March
3 Russo-Turkish forces complete capture of **Ionian Islands**, Mediterranean

April
12 Napoleon receives orders at Toulon to undertake **Middle East** expedition

May
6 French attack **Saint Marcoufe** islands, Brittany
19 **Floréal coup**, Paris • British raid on **Ostende**, Low Countries • **Middle East** expedition sails from Toulon
24 Start of **Irish rebellion** around Dublin

June
12 French forces take **Malta**

July
1 French forces land in Egypt
13 Battle of **Shubra Khit**, Middle East

21 Battle of the **Pyramids**, Egypt

22 French occupy Cairo

August

1 Naval battle of the **Nile**

22 French forces land at **Killala Bay**, Ireland

September

5 Mass **conscription** introduced, France

8 Surrender of French forces in Ireland

9 Sultan of Turkey declares **jihad** against France

October

12 Irish leader Wolfe **Tone** captured at sea, **Lough Swilly**

November

7 Russian tsar **Paul** elected head of the Maltese Order of St John

19 **Minorca** surrenders to British forces, Mediterranean

23 Naples invades central Italy

29 Neapolitan forces enter Rome

December

13 Neapolitan forces retreat from Rome

1799

January

1 First **income tax** introduced, Britain

23 Naples becomes the Parthenopean Republic

February

10 French forces leave Cairo for Syria, Middle East

11 British forces invade Mysore, India

March

12 France declares war on Austria

17 Siege of **Acre** opens, Middle East

21 Battle of **Ostrach**, Rhine

25 Austrian victory at **Stockach**, Rhine

26 French offensive opens at the Adige, Italy

30 Battle of **Verona**, Italy

April

5 Battle of **Magnano**, Italy

15 **Suvorov**'s Russian army reaches the Italian front

25 'Bruix's Cruise' escapes from Brest blockade, France

26 Battle of **Cassano**, Italy

29 Allies occupy Milan, Italy

May

4 British take **Seringapatam**, India

20 Napoleon ends siege of **Acre**, Middle East

26 Battle of **Frauenfeld**, Switzerland

June

4–7 First battle of **Zurich**, Switzerland

18–19 Battle of the **Trebbia**, Italy

21 Battle of **San Giuliano**, Italy

July

15 Turkish forces occupy **Aboukir**, Middle East

25 First French attacks on Aboukir, Middle East

August

2 French take Aboukir, Middle East

8 'Bruix's Cruise' returns to Brest

15 Allied victory at **Novi**, Italy

24 Napoleon leaves Egypt

26 French offensive around **Mannheim**, Rhine

27 British troops land in **North Holland**, Netherlands • Suvorov's Russian army ordered to quit Italy for Switzerland • Tsar Paul I issues invitations to **Armed Neutrality** league against Britain

30 British naval forces seize the Dutch fleet at Helder, Netherlands

September

18 French surrender Mannheim, Rhine

19 Battle of **Bergen**, Netherlands

25–26 Second Battle of **Zurich**, Switzerland

October

9 Napoleon reaches the French coast at Fréjus

10 Anglo-Russian forces agree to evacuate **North Holland**, Netherlands

16 Napoleon reaches Paris

November

4 Battle of **Genola**, Italy

9–10 **Brumaire coup** in Paris, **Consulate** takes power

December

25 Napoleon named as First Consul of France

1800

January
21 Convention of **El Arish** agreed, Middle East

March
14 Election of Pope **Pius VII**, Venice
20 Battle of **Heliopolis**, Middle East

April
20 Allied siege of **Genoa** begins, Italy

May
15 French Reserve Army enters **Great St Bernard Pass**, Italy

June
2 French Reserve Army occupies Milan, Italy
4 Fall of **Genoa**, Italy
9 Battle of **Montebello**, Italy
14 French victory at **Marengo**, Italy • General **Kléber** assassinated at Cairo, Middle East
15 Austrian forces agree to evacuate northern Italy
19 Battle of **Höchstädt**, Rhine

July
28 Austro-French truce on the Rhine front

August
18 British **Ferrol** raid, Spain

September
5 French forces on **Malta** surrender, Mediterranean

October
6 British raid on **Cadiz** abandoned, Spain
7 Spain cedes **Louisiana** to France

December
3 French victory at **Hohenlinden**, Rhine
16 Denmark and Sweden sign **Armed Neutrality** agreement with Russia
18 Prussia joins **Armed Neutrality** league
25 Austro-French armistice signed at Steyr

1801

January
1 Act of **Union** annexes Ireland to Britain
15 'Ganteaume's Cruise' escapes blockade of Brest, France

February
4 British **Pitt** cabinet resigns, **Addington** becomes premier
8 Austro-French Treaty of **Lunéville** signed

March
8 British forces land in Egypt, Middle East
20–21 Battle of **Alexandria**, Middle East
23 Tsar **Paul I** of Russia assassinated
28 Franco-Neapolitan **Florence** treaty signed

April
2 British naval victory at **Copenhagen**, Denmark

May
14 Pasha of Tripoli declares war on the United States

June
7 Treaty of Badajoz ends War of the **Oranges**, Portugal

July
13–14 Naval night battle of **Algeciras**, Mediterranean
15 Pope Pius VII and Napoleon sign first **Concordat** agreement

August
31 French Middle East forces surrender

October
1 Preliminary Anglo-French peace signed at **Amiens**

December
11 French army leaves France for **Santo Domingo**

1802

February
5 French force reaches **Santo Domingo**, West Indies

March
25 Final Anglo-French **Amiens** treaty signed

April
18 Concordat agreement published, including the **Organic Articles**

May
20 France and **Württemberg** sign alliance

August
2 Napoleon proclaimed Life Consul, France

October
15 French forces invade **Switzerland**

1803

May
2 US purchase of **Louisiana** agreed, Paris
18 Britain declares war on France

1804

January
1 **Santo Domingo** declares independence as Haiti, West Indies
14 Failure of **Cadoudal** plot against Napoleon, Paris

March
14 Duc d'**Enghein** abducted by French troops, Baden
21 **Code Civil** published, France • Duc d'**Enghein** executed for treason, France

May
18 Napoleon proclaimed Emperor, France
19 **Marshalate** established, France

December
2 Coronation of Emperor Napoleon I, France
12 Spain declares war on Britain

1805

March
22 Napoleon officially launches naval **Trafalgar** campaign

April
11 Provisional alliance between Russia, Britain, Sweden and Naples at St Petersburg
26 US marines land in Tripoli, **Barbary War** ends

May
26 Napoleon crowned King of **Italy**

August
9 Austria formally joins the **Third Coalition**
26 Napoleon orders the **Grande Armée** to quit the Channel coast for Bavaria

September
8 Austrian forces advance into Bavaria

October
11 Battle of **Albeck**, Bavaria
20 Austrian forces surrender at **Ulm**, Bavaria
21 **Nelson** killed during British naval victory at **Trafalgar**
31 Second Battle of **Caldiero**, northern Italy, ends after three days

November
3 Prussia signs **Potsdam** treaty with Russia
5 Battle of **Amstetten**, Bavaria
11 Battle of **Dürrenstein**, Bavaria
12 **Murat** takes **Vienna**
15 Battle of **Hollabrünn**, Bavaria

December
2 Allies routed at **Austerlitz**
3 Habsburg emperor **Francis** sues for peace
12 Baden and Württemberg sign **Brno** treaty with France
26 Austro-French Treaty of **Pressburg** ratified

1806

January
23 Death of **Pitt**, Britain
26 Napoleon returns to Paris from Vienna

February
6 Naval action off **Santo Domingo**, West Indies
24 Franco-Prussian Convention of **Vienna** ratified

March
30 Joseph Bonaparte crowned King of Naples

June
5 Louis Bonaparte proclaimed King of Holland

July
6 Battle of **Maida**, Naples
9 British forces occupy **Buenos Aires**
12 Napoleon abolishes the **Holy Roman Empire**
25 Confederation of the **Rhine** established

August
6 **Holy Roman Empire** ceases to exist
7 Prussian government makes secret decision for war against France

September
24 Napoleon leaves Paris to join the Grande Armée in Germany

October
7 Prussian war ultimatum reaches Napoleon
8 French troops enter Saxony
10 Battle of **Saalfeld**, Saxony
14 French victories at **Jena** and **Auerstädt**, Saxony
17 Battle of **Halle**, Prussia
20 Siege of **Magdeburg** opens, Prussia
27 Napoleon enters Berlin
28 Prussian troops surrender at **Prenzlau**

November
1 Napoleon announces **Berlin Decrees** against British trade
6 Blücher surrenders last Prussian field army near **Lübeck**
11 Fall of **Magdeburg**
28 First French troops reach **Warsaw**

December
11 France and Saxony sign Treaty of **Posen**
26 Battles of **Pultusk** and **Golymin**, Poland

1807

January
30 Siege of **Stralsund** opens, Pomerania

February
3 Battle of **Ionkovo**, Poland
7–8 Battle of **Eylau**, Poland

19 British warships enter the **Dardanelles**, Mediterranean

March
3 British ships quit the **Dardanelles**, Mediterranean
18 French siege of **Danzig** opens, Poland

April
19 **Stralsund** siege ended

May
27 Fall of **Danzig**, Poland

June
10–11 Battle of **Heilsberg**, Poland
14 French victory at **Friedland**, Poland
19 Battle of **Lemnos**, eastern Mediterranean • French troops reach the River Niemen, Poland
25 Napoleon and Tsar Alexander meet on the Niemen
27 British *Leopardstown* attacks USS *Chesapeake*, N. Atlantic

July
7 Franco-Russian peace signed at **Tilsit**
9 Franco-Prussian peace signed at **Tilsit**
19 French ultimatum to Portugal

September
2–5 British forces bombard **Copenhagen**

October
27 Franco-Spanish **Fontainebleau** treaty signed

November
11 First British **Orders in Council** issued
23 Napoleon announces first **Milan Decree** against British trade
30 French forces enter Lisbon, Portugal

December
17 Napoleon announces second **Milan Decree** against British trade
22 US Embargo Act forbids foreign trade

1808

February
16 French invasion of **Spain** begins

March

17 King **Charles IV** of Spain abdicates for the first time

24 French forces reach Madrid, Spain

April

16 **Bayonne** conference begins, France

May

2 **Madrid** uprising, Spain

June

6 Joseph **Bonaparte** proclaimed King of Spain

10 Spanish rebels appeal to Britain for aid

15 First siege of **Saragossa** opens, Spain

July

14 Battle of **Medina del Río Seco**, Spain

20 French defeat at **Bailén**, Spain • End of **Bayonne** conference, France

August

1 Murat proclaimed King of Naples • First British troops reach Portugal

2 Battle of **Sandöström**, Baltic

17 French abandon siege of Saragossa, Spain

16 Action at **Rolica**, Portugal

21 Battle of **Vimeiro**, Portugal

22 Convention of **Cintra**, Portugal

September

6 Murat arrives in Naples as king

18 Battle of **Palvasund**, Finland

27 Napoleon and Tsar **Alexander I** meet at **Erfurt**

October

14 **Erfurt** congress ends

25 Spanish Ebro offensive suspended, Spain

November

5 Battle of **Valmaseda**, Spain

6 French Ebro offensive opens, Spain

10 Battles of **Espinosa** and **Gamonal**, Spain

23 Battle of **Tudela**, Spain

29–30 Battle of **Somosierra**, Spain

December

20 Second siege of **Saragossa** opens, Spain

21 Battle of **Sahagún**, Spain

26 **Kara Djordje** proclaimed King of independent Serbia

29 Action at **Benavente**, Spain

1809

January

16 Battle of **Corunna**, Spain

18 Last British troops evacuated from **Corunna**

February

8 Austria secretly agrees to war against France

20 Fall of **Saragossa**, Spain

March

22 French forces take **Oporto**, Portugal

28 Battle of **Medellín**, Spain

April

11–12 Naval action in the **Basque Roads**, France

16 Battle of **Sacile**, Italy • Austrian Danube offensive crosses the Isar

17 Napoleon reaches the Danube front

18 Battle of **Tengen**, Danube

20 Battle of **Abensberg**, Danube

21 French forces take **Landshut**, Danube; Napoleon slightly wounded

22 French victory at **Eckmühl**, Danube • **Wellesley** takes command of British forces in Portugal

23 **Dörnberg** rising crushed, Westphalia • Action at **Ratisbon**, Danube

May

3 Battle of **Ebersberg**, Danube

12 Battle for **Oporto**, Portugal

13 Vienna surrenders to French forces

21–22 Battle of **Aspern–Essling**, Danube

June

14 Battle of **Raab**, Danube

July

5–6 French victory at **Wagram**, Danube

10 Battle of **Znaim**, Danube

12 Austro-French armistice on the Danube

27–29 Battle of **Talavera**, Spain

August

17 Battle of **Ratan**, Finland

September
17 Treaty of Frederickshamm ends **Russo-Swedish War**

October
14 Austro-French Treaty of **Schönbrunn** signed
18 Franco-Neapolitan capture of **Capri**, Mediterranean

November
19 Battle of **Ocaña**, Spain

December
15 Napoleon and **Joséphine** divorce

1810

February
5 French forces invest **Cadiz**
20 Tyrolean rebel leader **Hofer** executed, Bavaria

March
11 Napoleon marries **Marie-Louise** of Austria by proxy

April
2 Formal marriage of Napoleon in Paris

July
1 Louis **Bonaparte** abdicates as King of Holland
9 France annexes Holland

August
5 Napoleon's **Trianon Decree** modifies the **Continental System**

September
27 Battle of **Busaco**, Portugal

October
10 French forces reach the **Torres Vedras** lines, Portugal

November
16 French forces retreat from the **Torres Vedras** lines, Portugal

1811

January
26 French besiege **Badajoz**, Spain

March
2 US imposes trade sanctions against Britain
5 Battle of **Barrosa**, Spain
5 French forces quit Portugal
9 **Badajoz** falls, Spain
11 Napoleon's heir born

May
7 British besiege **Badajoz**, Spain
16 Battle of **Albuera**, Spain

June
20 French forces relieve **Badajoz**, Spain

July
5 Venezuela declares independence from Spain

August
15 Napoleon attacks Alexander I in Paris speech

September
25 Battle of **El Bodón**, Spain

1812

January
20 Wellington takes **Ciudad Rodrigo**, Spain

March
16 Wellington opens third siege of **Badajoz**
17 Alexander I dismisses reforming ministers

April
9 Russo-Swedish Convention of **St Petersburg**

May
28 Peace of **Bucharest** ends Russo-Turkish War

June
19 US declares war on Britain, start of **Anglo-American War**
23 First French troops cross **Russian** frontier
28 French forces occupy **Vilna**, Russia

July
8 French forces occupy **Minsk**, Russia

14 Jérôme **Bonaparte** quits his Grande Armée command

18 Russian forces abandon Drissa position

22 French defeat at **Salamanca**, Spain

23 Battle of **Mohilev**, Russia

25–26 Battle of **Ostronovo**, Russia

28 French forces take **Vitebsk**, Russia

August

4 Russian First and Second Armies meet at Smolensk

6 Russian offensive opens from Smolensk

8 Battle of **Inkovo**, Russia

12 Wellington takes Madrid, Spain

13 Russian offensive briefly resumed

14 First Battle of **Krasnoe**, Russia

15 British capture Fort Dearborn, US

16–18 Battle of **Smolensk**, Russia

17–18 First Battle of **Polotsk**, Russia

24 Napoleon orders advance on **Moscow**, Russia • French abandon siege of **Cadiz**, Spain

26 **Kutuzov** becomes Russian field C-in-C

September

7 Battle of **Borodino**, Russia

14 French forces occupy **Moscow**, Russia

19 Wellington besieges **Burgos**, Spain

October

2 Wellington becomes Spanish Army C-in-C

15 Battle of **Queenston Heights**, Canada

18 Battle of **Vinkovo**, Russia

19 French forces quit **Moscow**, start of retreat from Russia

21 Wellington retreats from **Burgos**, Spain

24 Battle of **Maloyaroslavets**, Russia

29 **Malet** and co-conspirators executed, France

30 Wellington abandons Madrid

November

3 Battle of **Fiodoroivskoy**, Russia

14 Second Battle of **Polotsk**, Russia

17 Second Battle of **Krasnoe**, Russia

20 Allied retreat from **Burgos** reaches Ciudad Rodrigo, Spain

21 **Ney's** corps rejoins French army after **Gusinoe** crossing, Russia

23 Battle of **Loshnitsa**, Russia

25–29 Remnant of the French army recrosses the **Beresina**

December

5 Napoleon quits the Grande Armée for Paris

8 Surviving French troops enter Vilna

14 Last Grande Armée units reach the Niemen border with Poland

18 Napoleon returns to Paris

19 **Macdonald** begins withdrawal from **Riga**

25 Yorck's Prussian corps surrounded west of Riga

28 Convention of **Tauroggen** secures neutrality of Prussian forces

1813

January

16 Russian forces resume westward advance across the Vistula, Poland

February

7 Russian forces occupy Warsaw

28 Prussia ratifies preliminary **Kalisch** agreement with Russia

March

3 Anglo-Swedish **Stockholm** treaty

6 Retreating French forces reach the Elbe

12 French forces abandon Hamburg, Germany

13 Prussia declares war on France

27 Allied forces occupy Dresden, Germany

April

3 Battle of **Möckern**, Germany

24 US forces capture York (Toronto), Canada

May

1 French offensive in **Germany** opens; action at **Poserna**

2 Battle of **Lützen**, Germany

8 French forces reoccupy Dresden, Germany

20–21 Battle of **Bautzen**, Germany

27 French abandon Madrid, Spain

28 French reoccupy Hamburg, Germany

28–30 Battle of **Sackett's Harbor**, US

June

1 French forces advance to Breslau, Germany

2 Allies besiege **Tarragona**, Spain

4 **Armistice** agreed in Germany

6 Battle of **Stony Creek**, Canada

12 Siege of Tarragona abandoned, Spain • French forces abandon Burgos, Spain

21 Allied victory at **Vitoria**, Spain

28 Siege of **San Sebastian** opens, Spain

30 Siege of **Pamplona** opens, Spain

July

7 Sweden joins the **Sixth Coalition**

11 **Soult** takes command of French forces at the Pyrenees, Spain

19 Austria signs **Reichenbach** agreement with the allies

25 French offensive opens at **Maya** and **Roncesvalles** passes, Spain

28–30 Battle of **Sorauren**, Spain

August

12 Austria declares war on France

13 Prussian advance ends German armistice three days early

23 Battle of **Gross-Beeren**, Germany

26 Battle of **Pirna**, Germany

26–27 Battle of **Dresden**, Germany

30 Battle of **Kulm**, Germany

31 Fall of **San Sebastian**, Spain • First Battle of **Vera**, Spain • Second Battle of **San Marcial**, Spain

September

6 Battle of **Dennewitz**, Germany

10 Battle of Lake **Erie**, Canada

24 French forces retire behind the Elbe, Germany

October

5 Battle of **Thames River**, US

6 Austro-Bavarian Treaty of **Ried**

7 Wellington crosses the **Bidassoa**, Spain

9 Battle of **Düben**, Germany

12 Russo-Persian peace signed at Gulistan

14 Battle of **Liebertwolkwitz**, Germany

16–18 Allied victory at **Leipzig**, Germany

18 Württemberg and Saxony join **Sixth Coalition**

30 Battle of **Hanau**, Germany

31 French surrender at **Pamplona**, Spain

November

11 US **Montreal** offensive ends, Canada • French garrison surrenders Dresden, Germany

10 Battle of the **Nivelle**, Pyrenees

24 Baden joins the **Sixth Coalition**

December

9–12 Battle of the **Nive**, Pyrenees

11 Treaty of **Valençay** between Napoleon and Ferdinand of Spain

13 Battle of **St Pierre**, Pyrenees

22 First allied troops cross the Rhine to invade **France**

1814

January

11 Murat's Naples joins the **Sixth Coalition**

14 **Denmark** signs peace with Coalition allies at **Kiel**

22 Prussian forces cross the Meuse, France

25 Napoleon leaves Paris for the front

27 Battle of **St Dizier**, France

29 Battle of **Brienne**, France

February

1 Battle of **La Rothière**, France

3 Peace talks open at Châtillon-sur-Seine

10 Battle of **Champaubert** opens **Six Days Campaign**, France

11 Battle of **Montmirail**, France

12 Battle of **Château-Thierry**, France

14 Battle of **Vauchamps**, France

17 Battle of **Valjouan**, France

18 Battle of **Montereau**, France

21 Napoleon makes new peace offer to Emperor Francis – it is rejected

25 Allied war council at **Bar-sur-Aube**, France

26 Allies besiege **Bayonne**, Pyrenees

27 Battle of **Orthez**, Pyrenees

27–28 Battle of **Meaux**, France

March

7 Battle of **Craonne**, France

9 Allied **Chaumont** agreement, France

9–10 Battle of **Laon**, France

12 Bordeaux rebels proclaim King **Louis XVIII**, France

13 Battle of **Reims**, France

20 Battle of **Tarbes**, Pyrenees • Battle of **Arcis-sur-Aube**, France

24 Allied war council at **Sommagices**, France • King **Ferdinand VII** returns to Spain

25 Battle of **La-Fère-Champenoise**, France

31 French forces surrender at **Montmartre** and Paris, France

April
6 Napoleon signs unconditional **abdication**

10 Battle of **Toulouse**, Pyrenees

14 Louis XVIII lands at Calais, France • Final action of Peninsular War at **Bayonne**, Pyrenees

16 Austro-Italian armistice of **Schiarino-Rizzino**, Italy • **Fontainebleau** treaty makes Napoleon ruler of Elba

17 Soult surrenders to Wellington, **Peninsular War** ends

26 Viceroy **Beauharnais** leaves Italy for exile • Bayonne garrison surrenders

28 Napoleon sails for **Elba**

30 Treaty of **Paris** ends War of the Sixth Coalition

May
27 Davout surrenders **Hamburg**, Germany

29 Former empress Joséphine dies

June
14 William of Orange proclaimed King of Belgium and Holland

July
5 Battle of **Chippewa**, Canada

25 Battle of **Lundy's Lane**, Canada

August
14 Convention of **Moss**, Norway

September
11 Battle of **Plattsburg**, US

November
1 Congress of **Vienna** opens

December
24 Treaty of **Ghent** ends Anglo-American War

1815

January
8 Battle of **New Orleans**, US

February
26 Napoleon leaves **Elba**

March
1 Napoleon reaches France

7 Napoleon welcomed into Grenoble

14 Ney rejoins Napoleon at Auxerre, France

15 Murat's Naples declares war on Austria

19 Royal government quits Paris

20 Napoleon enters Paris and takes power (start of the **Hundred Days**)

25 Seventh Coalition formed in Vienna

May
2–3 Neapolitan forces defeated at **Tolentino**, Italy

19 Murat flees Naples

June
9 Congress of **Vienna** closes

15 French forces advance across the Sambre, Low Countries

16 Battles of **Ligny** and **Quatre Bras**, Low Countries

18 Allied victory at **Waterloo** and Battle of **Wavre**, Low Countries

21 Napoleon returns to Paris

22 Napoleon abdicates

August
3 Ney arrested, France

September
26 Holy Alliance of conservative monarchs signed at Vienna

October
13 Murat executed in Calabria, Italy

December
7 Ney shot for treason

THE MAPS

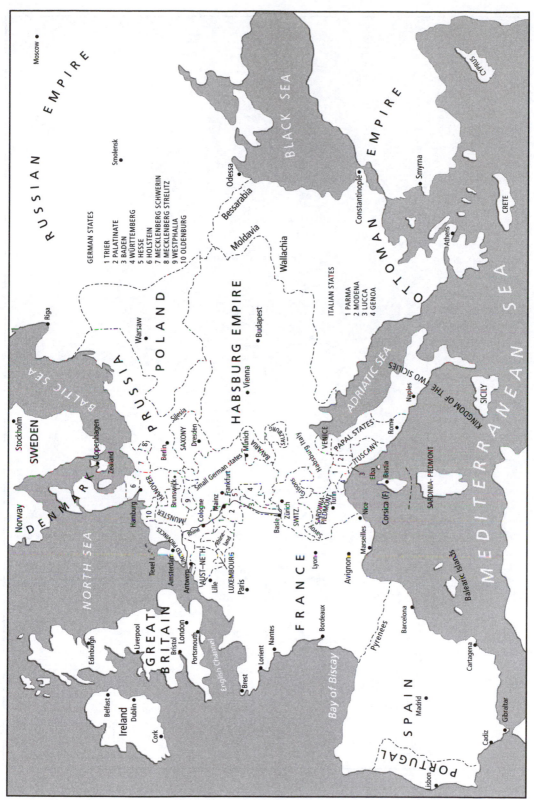

GERMAN STATES

1 TRIER
2 PALATINATE
3 BADEN
4 WÜRTTEMBERG
5 HESSE
6 HOLSTEIN
7 MECKLENBERG SCHWERIN
8 MECKLENBERG STRELITZ
9 WESTPHALIA
10 OLDENBURG

ITALIAN STATES

1 PARMA
2 MODENA
3 LUCCA
4 GENOA

RUSSIAN EMPIRE

Moscow

Smolensk

Riga

OTTOMAN EMPIRE

BLACK SEA

Odessa

Bessarabia

Moldavia

Wallachia

Constantinople

Smyrna

Athens

CRETE

CYPRUS

POLAND

Warsaw

HABSBURG EMPIRE

Budapest

Vienna

PRUSSIA

SWEDEN

Stockholm

BALTIC SEA

NORWAY

DENMARK

Copenhagen
Zealand

NORTH SEA

Berlin

SAXONY

Dresden

Silesia

Hamburg

HANOVER

MUNSTER

Brunswick

Frankfurt

Cologne

Mainz

Small German states

BAVARIA

Munich

SALZBURG

Habsburg Italy

VENICE

PAPAL STATES

Rome

TUSCANY

Elba

Bastia

Corsica (F)

SARDINIA-PIEDMONT

Turin

Nice

Naples

SICILY

KINGDOM OF THE TWO SICILIES

ADRIATIC SEA

MEDITERRANEAN SEA

Balearic Islands

UNITED PROVINCES

Texel I.

Amsterdam

Antwerp

AUST-NETH.

Lille

LUXEMBOURG

Paris

Rhine

Rhine-land

SWITZ.

Basle

Zürich

Geneva

Savoy

FRANCE

Lyon

Avignon

Marseilles

Bordeaux

Nantes

Lorient

Brest

English Channel

Bay of Biscay

Pyrenees

GREAT BRITAIN

Edinburgh

Liverpool

Bristol

London

Portsmouth

Ireland

Belfast

Dublin

Cork

SPAIN

Madrid

Barcelona

Cartagena

Cadiz

Gibraltar

PORTUGAL

Lisbon

Map 1: Europe, 1792

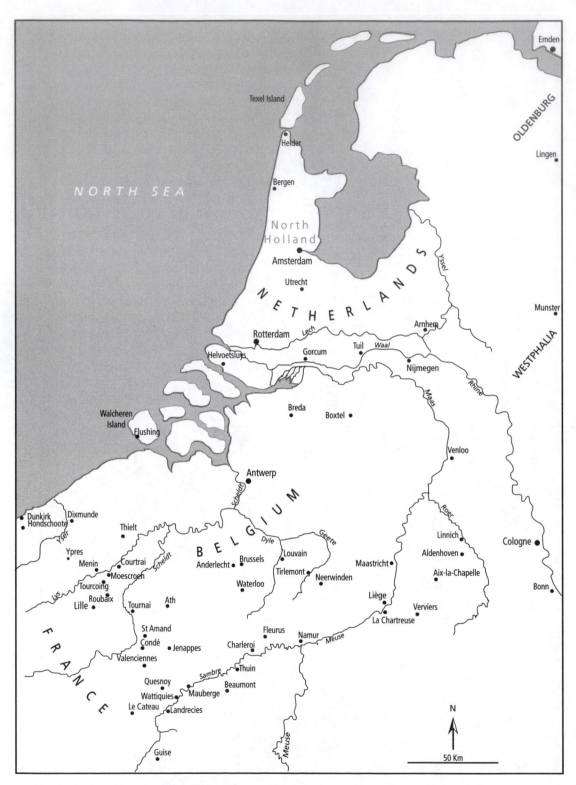

Map 2: The Low Countries, 1792–1814

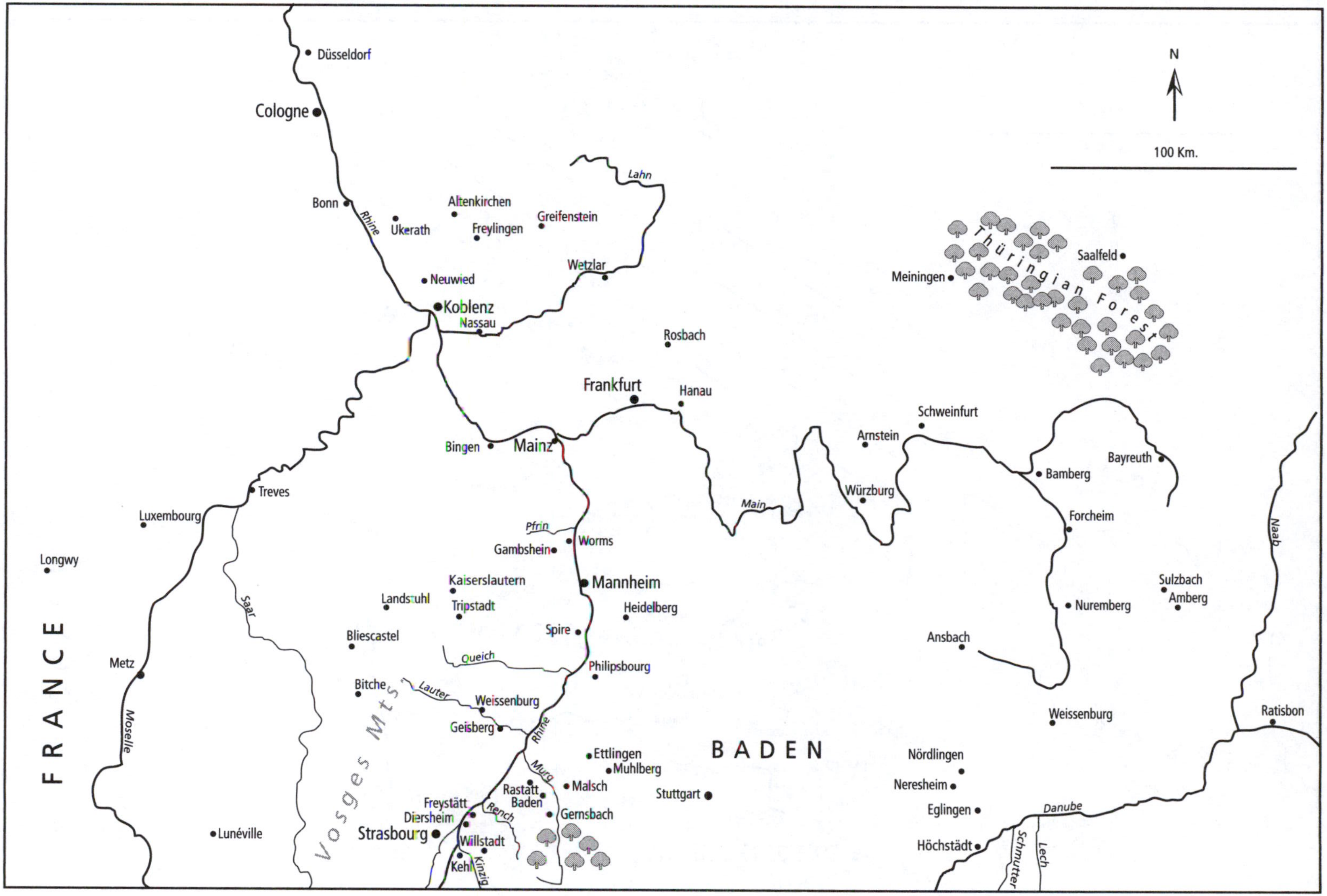

Map 3: Middle Rhine, 1792–1800

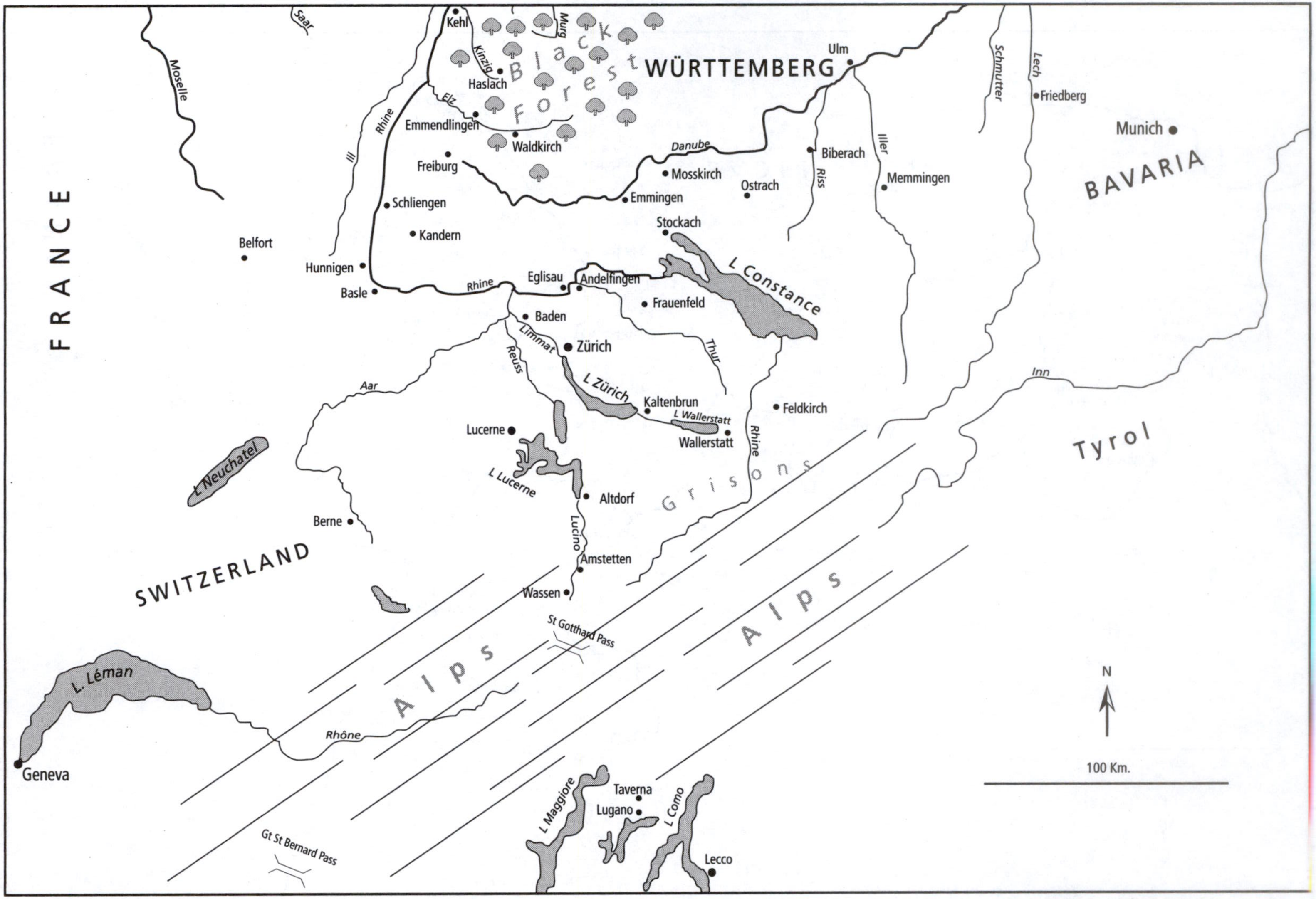

Map 4: Upper Rhine and Switzerland, 1792–1800

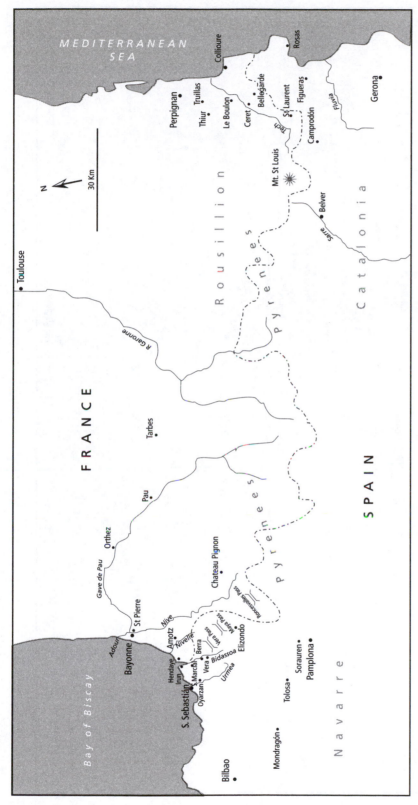

Map 5: Pyrenean Theatre, 1793–1814

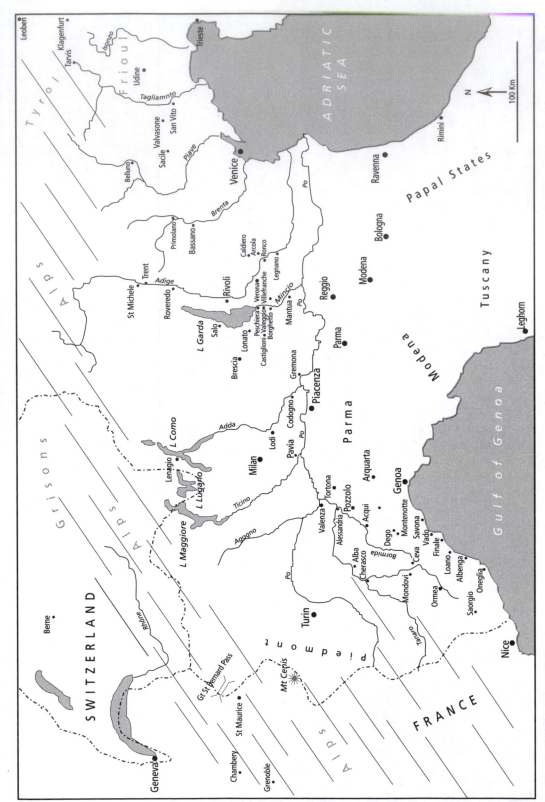

Map 6: Northern Italy, 1792–7

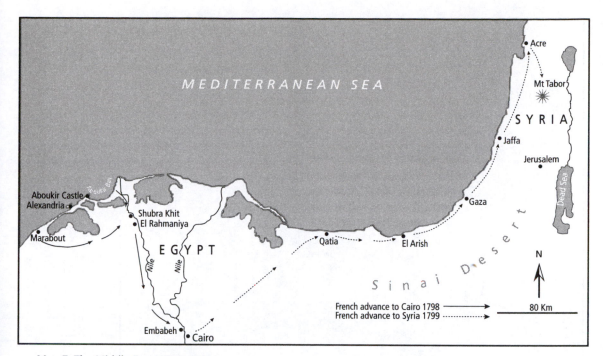

Map 7: The Middle East, 1799–1801

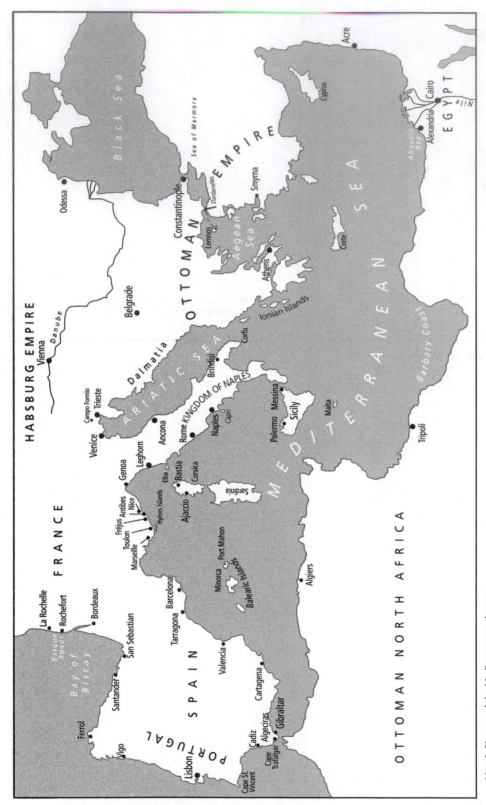

Map 8: Biscay and the Mediterranean theatres

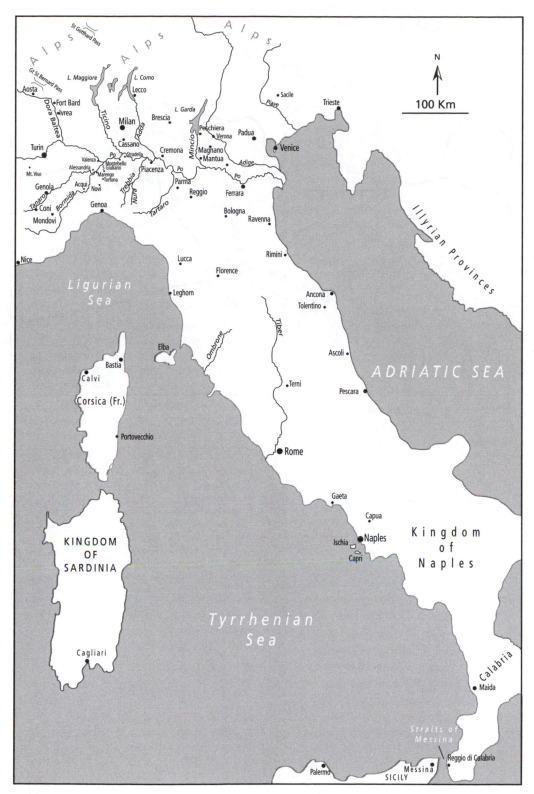

Map 9: Italy, 1798–1814

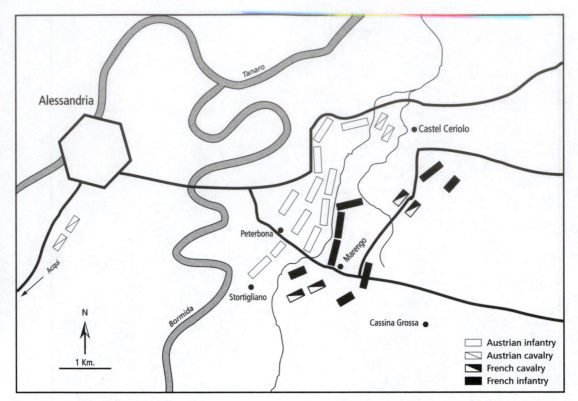

Map 10: Marengo, the opening phase

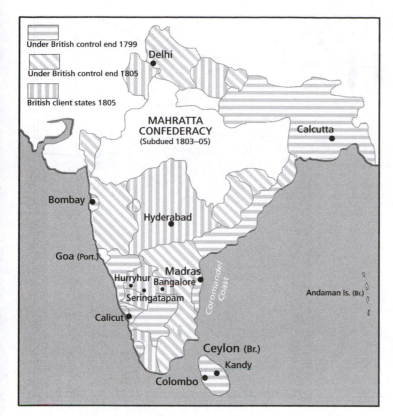

Map 11: India, 1799–1805

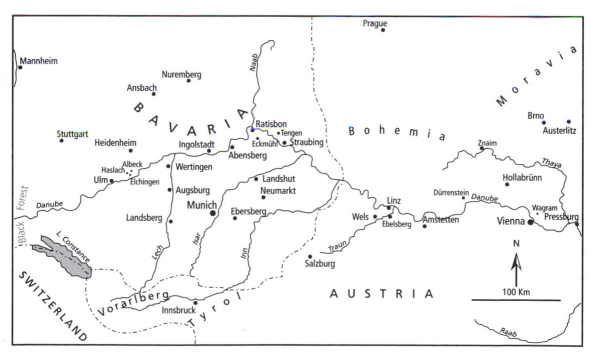

Map 12: Danube theatre, 1805–9

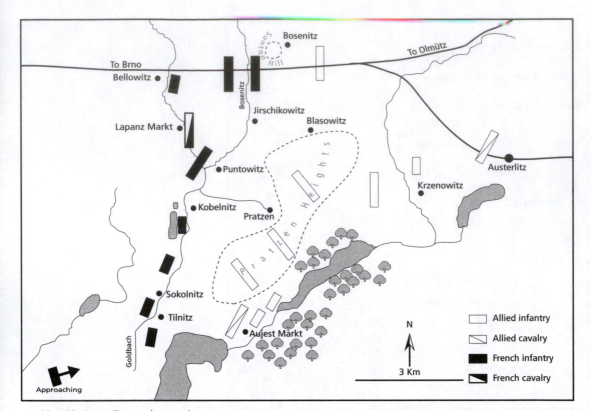

Map 13: Austerlitz, early morning

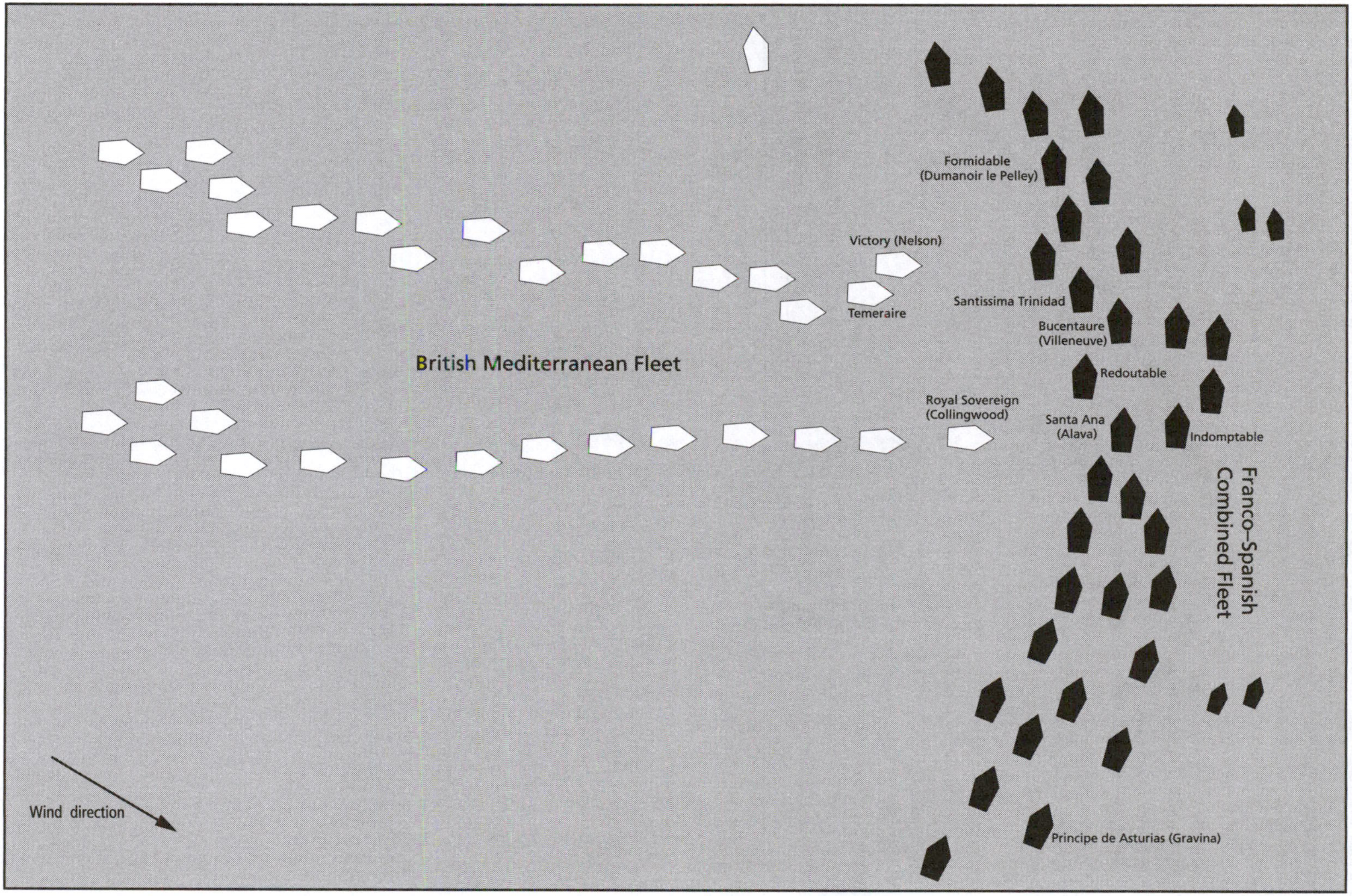

Map 14: Trafalgar, situation just before noon

Franco–Spanish Combined Fleet

Indomptable

Redoutable

Bucentaure (Villeneuve)

Santissima Trinidad

Formidable (Dumanoir le Pelley)

Santa Ana (Alava)

Principe de Asturias (Gravina)

Royal Sovereign (Collingwood)

Victory (Nelson)

Temeraire

British Mediterranean Fleet

Wind direction

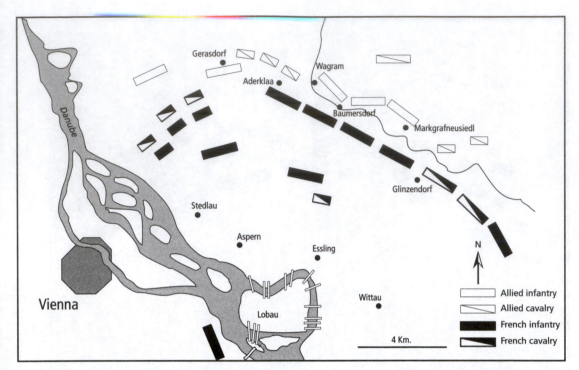

Map 15: Wagram, positions early on the first evening

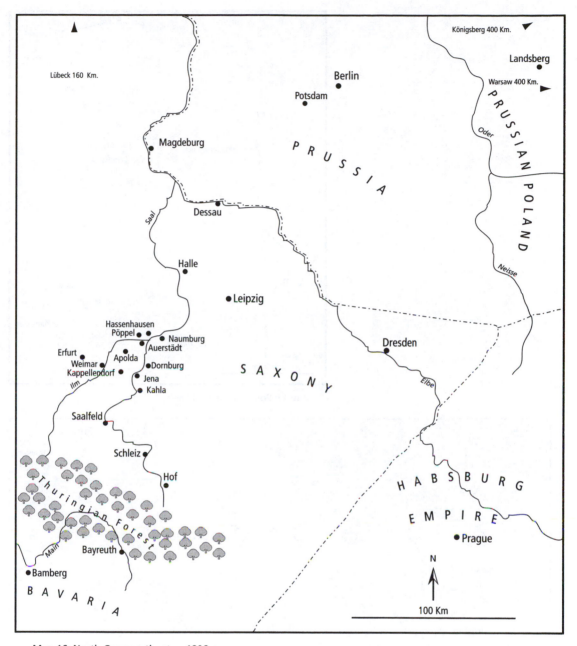

Map 16: North German theatre, 1806

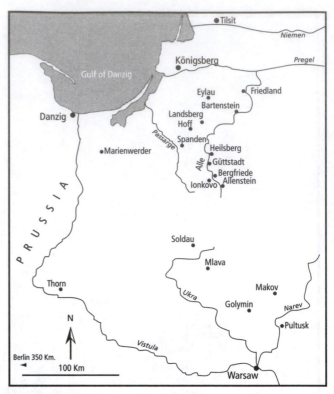

Map 17: Polish Theatre, 1806–7

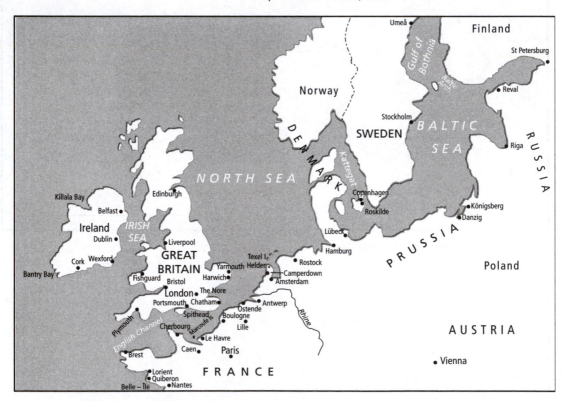

Map 18: Northern naval theatre, principal locations

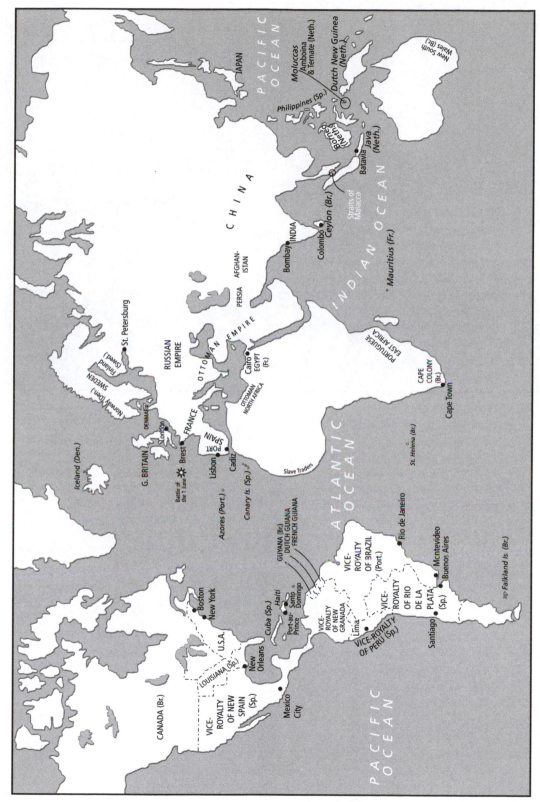

Map 19: World colonial, 1799

561

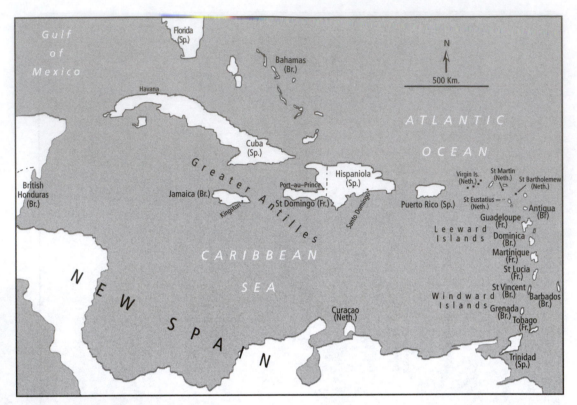

Map 20: The Caribbean, 1792

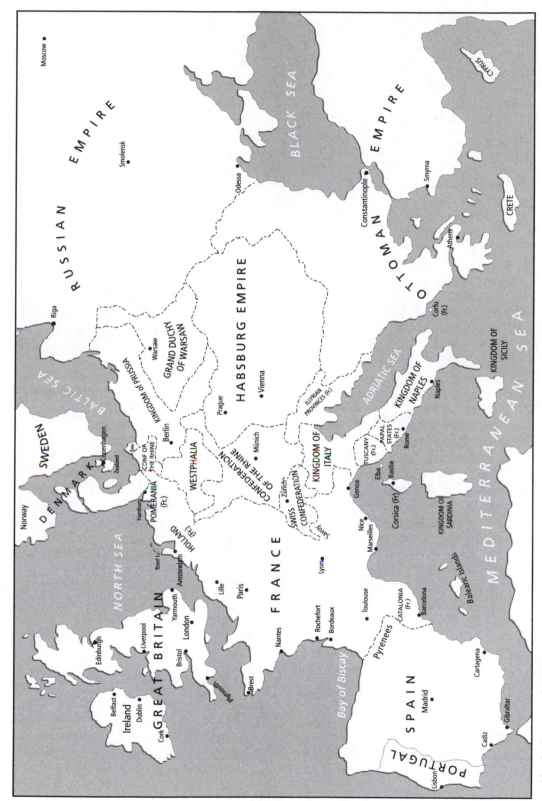

Map 21: Europe, early 1812

Map 22: Peninsular theatre, 1807-14

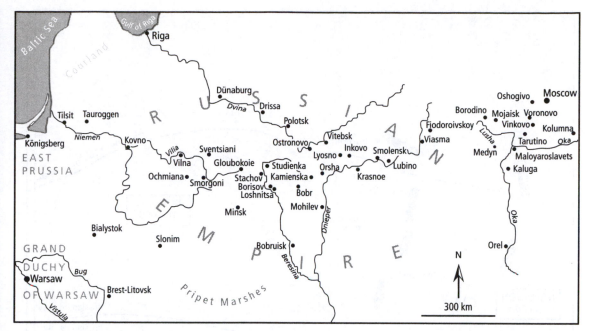

Map 23: Russian theatre, 1812

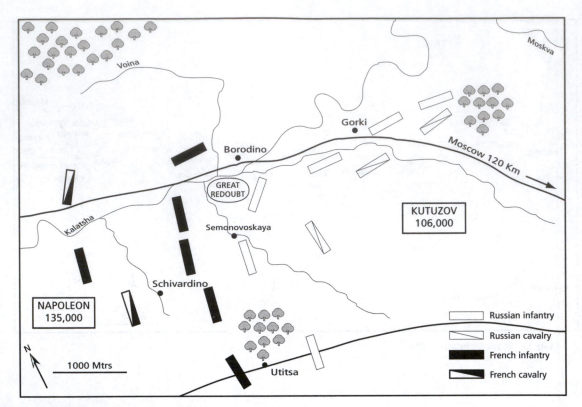

Map 24: Borodino, opening positions

566

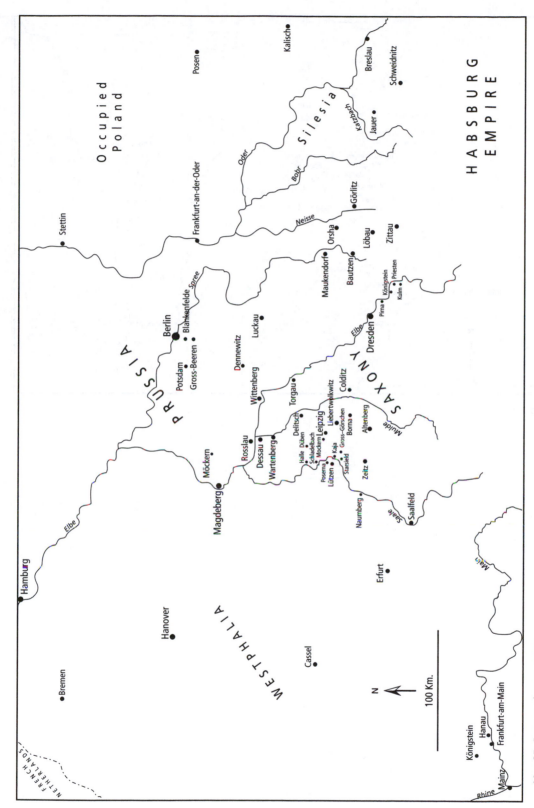

Map 25: German theatre, 1813

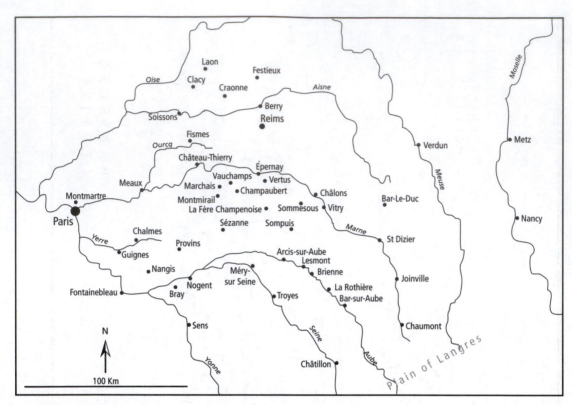

Map 26: Eastern France, 1814

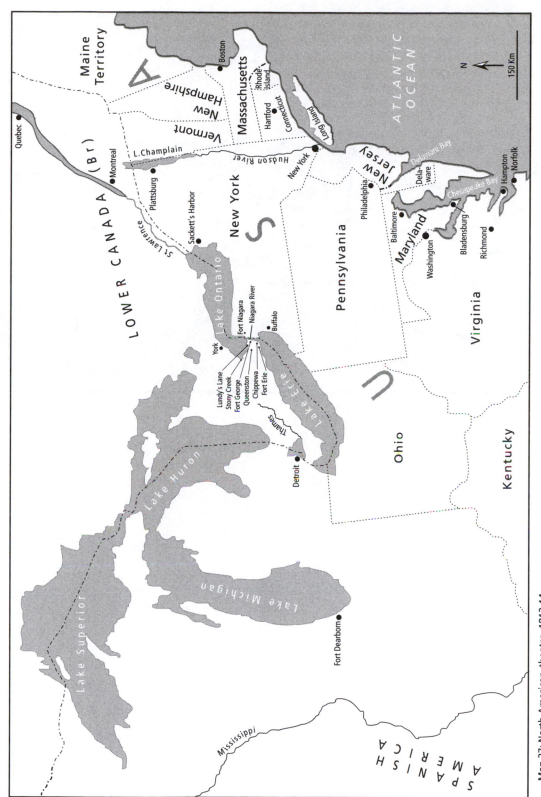

Map 27: North American theatre, 1812-14

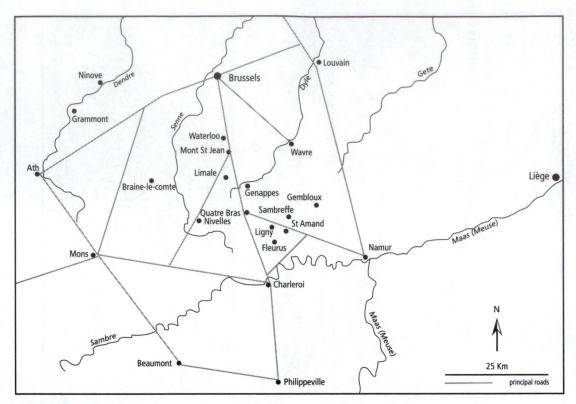

Map 28: Flanders, 1815

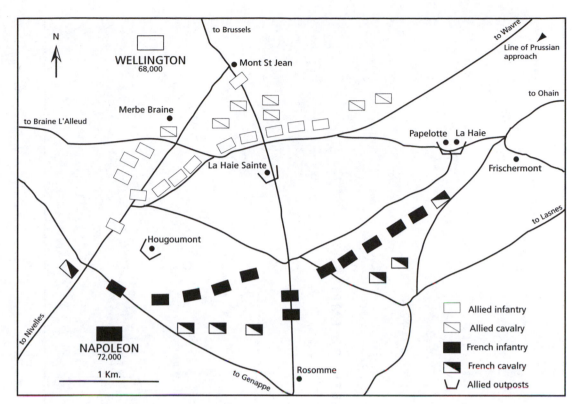

N

WELLINGTON
68,000

to Brussels

● Mont St Jean

to Wavre

Line of Prussian
approach

to Ohain

to Braine L'Alleud

Merbe Braine ●

Papelotte   La Haie

La Haie Sainte

Frischermont

to Lasnes

Hougoumont

NAPOLEON
72,000

to Nivelles

1 Km.

to Genappe

Rosomme
●

Allied infantry

Allied cavalry

French infantry

French cavalry

Allied outposts

Map 29: Waterloo, morning positions

Map 30: Europe, 1815